THE JUSTICES OF THE UNITED STATES SUPREME COURT 1789-1969

Their Lives and Major Opinions

VOLUME III

THE JUSTICES OF THE UNITED STATES SUPREME COURT 1789-1969

Their Lives and Major Opinions

LEON FRIEDMAN & FRED L. ISRAEL
EDITORS
with an Introduction by
LOUIS H. POLLAK
DEAN, YALE UNIVERSITY LAW SCHOOL

CHELSEA HOUSE PUBLISHERS in association with
R. R. BOWKER COMPANY, NEW YORK & LONDON
1969

Published by the R. R. Bowker Company (A XEROX COMPANY)
1180 Avenue of the Americas, New York, N.Y. 10036
in association with Chelsea House Publishers

Standard Book Number: 8352-0217-8/Library of Congress Catalog Card Number: 69:13699
Printed and bound in the United States of America

Table of Contents

VOLUME III

Edward Douglas White

☆ 1845–1921 ☆

APPOINTED BY GROVER CLEVELAND

ASSOCIATE JUSTICE: 1894–1911

APPOINTED BY WILLIAM HOWARD TAFT

CHIEF JUSTICE: 1911–1921

Edward Douglas White

by

JAMES F. WATTS, JR.

THE DEATH OF Chief Justice White of the Supreme Court in the spring of 1921 produced a crop of rich eulogies which compared the Louisianan favorably with the great legal statesmen in American history, with Marshall and Calhoun and Webster, and even with his own contemporary Oliver Wendell Holmes. For twenty-seven years this massive black-robed man had adorned the Court, first as an Associate Justice for sixteen years after his 1894 appointment by President Cleveland, and later as Chief Justice following President Taft's unusual decision in 1911 to advance a Chief Justice up from the ranks of the Court itself. During this extended period White participated in hundreds of important Court decisions, and also circulated in the highest reaches of Washington political society. Although he lacked that attention-getting spark which produces a national celebrity, his long tenure, his powerful position, and his arresting personality marked by kindness and dignity nevertheless served to establish Edward Douglas White as one of the capital's dominant figures. Accordingly, White's eulogists translated their regret into traditionally inflated praise.

The liberal *Nation* refused to join in this acclaim for the rather conservative White, and managed a more accurate prediction of the historic place of the late Chief Justice by claiming that

> *By reason of his striking personality and his lovable human traits, the late Chief Justice will for a while receive higher tributes to his judicial services than time is apt to confirm.* [The Nation, *June 1, 1921, CXII at 781*]

Ironically, while White's renown has diminished, as predicted, with the passage of years, his major influence on the nature of American civilization is consequently too little realized. While history does vaguely recall White as the progenitor of the "rule of reason," the major significance of this piece of judicial

JAMES F. WATTS, JR. is Assistant Professor of History at City College of New York and author of a forthcoming biography of Breckinridge Long.

license is not popularly understood. The "rule of reason," unofficially adopted after Chief Justice White's two 1911 majority opinions in cases involving the oil and tobacco trusts, permanently dulled the cutting edges of the Sherman Anti-Trust Act by bestowing upon a frequently conservative Supreme Court the subjective determination of the "reasonableness" of corporations engaged in restraint of trade. It continues even today to provide the ill-defined guidelines for the legal relationship between the federal government and the oligopolies which dominate American business.

The fundamental importance of this enduring relationship lies in the nature of our society, at the core of which is a highly developed industrial complex so pervasive in its social implications that the lives of virtually every American family are intimately affected. That the American civilization has developed in its unique form is due in large part to the effects of an economic pattern which has in turn been dependent upon the kind of industrial centralization and rationalization allowed by the "rule of reason." Certainly the vigorous application of the Sherman and Clayton Anti-Trust Acts would have produced quite different economic and social patterns.

The man most responsible for laying the foundations of this societal blueprint descended from an old and interesting American family. When a young Irish boy named James White came across the Atlantic sometime during the 1730's he unknowingly became the first of a family of successful American merchants, planters, politicians and jurists. Young White settled in the Philadelphia of Ben Franklin, and in time became such a highly successful merchant that he could afford the luxury of sending his son and namesake abroad to be educated.

The younger James White, born in 1749, lived a long and adventurous life during the exciting decades which surrounded the American war for independence. After taking a medical degree in Paris, White returned to Philadelphia to practice medicine as well as to dabble in revolutionary politics. By the 1780's, apparently dissatisfied with the predictability of his life in Philadelphia, the grandfather of the future Chief Justice began a series of adventures that would continue for nearly a quarter of a century. He first moved to Fayetteville, North Carolina, quickly "read" enough law to qualify for the state bar, and simultaneously developed political associations important enough to gain an appointment to the North Carolina delegation to the Annapolis Convention of 1786, where Alexander Hamilton's trenchant criticisms of the Articles of Confederation began the brief but violent struggle to write a new federal Constitution.

James White himself did not follow the controversy along to the Philadelphia Constitutional Convention the following summer. Instead, apparently more interested in individual involvement in the young nation's growing pains, he served for a time as the first United States Superintendent of Indian Affairs. Then he was on the move again, this time into Tennessee, where he established his political credentials once more by being named as Tennessee's territorial delegate to the United States Congress in 1794. Within another five years, however, the peripatetic physician-lawyer-politician again took the road westward, this time on beyond the nation's borders and into the roiling French frontier territory of Louisiana. In addition to the adventurous climate to which he always seemed to be attracted, White here found a favorable religious environment as well, since he had carried on the Roman Catholicism of his Irish immigrant father.

The year following President Jefferson's 1803 purchase of the trackless Louisiana Territory from the Emperor Napoleon, the future state of Louisiana was organized as a federal Territory of the United States, and the enterprising James White secured appointment as the first United States district judge in the Cajun country of southwest Louisiana. Here the erstwhile Philadelphia physician finally came to rest. He died in 1809, leaving some money and unlimited connections to his son, Edward Douglas White.

Edward White, who was born in 1794 during his father's Tennessee period, made good use of his inheritance. Only fifteen when his father died, the young man nonetheless sought to emulate him. Young White continued on in the law, first at the University of Nashville and later by "reading" in a private law office in Donaldsonville, Louisiana. His father's connections plus the son's own talents produced almost immediate success. In 1825, the thirty-one-year-old Edward White accepted the governor's appointment to the New Orleans City Court. Four years later, Judge White was elected to the first of his three consecutive terms in Congress. In 1835, Louisiana Whigs nominated and elected Congressman White as Louisiana's seventh governor. Prevented by state law from succeeding himself, Governor White was sent back to Congress for another two terms, before an 1842 defeat returned him permanently to his sugar plantation at Thibodaux.

During his continuous involvement in politics White had not neglected his own personal affairs. By November 3, 1845, the time of the arrival of his son and namesake, the future Chief Justice, the White family enjoyed a plantation home which commanded 1600 thriving acres of sugar beets. Two years later these resources constituted at least partial compensation for a family which included five children when the elder Edward D. White suddenly died.

Although his son inherited the advantages of comparative wealth and privilege, the years of his boyhood seem abruptly brief, clouded over as they were by the spectre of violent civil war. Ned White's formal education, nearly all of it Jesuit-directed, was unnaturally short, especially for a man of his later calling. In 1851 his remarried mother sent him off to a New Orleans convent school for five years. At age eleven, the boy traveled all the way to Emmitsburg, Maryland, for a year of prep school at Mt. St. Mary's, which was immediately followed by entrance into the Jesuit's Georgetown College in September of 1857.

The young boy from the sugar plantation did fairly well in school, although his academic performance fell safely short of honors. As the great war approached, however, White decided to join the general exodus of young southerners. He returned to Louisiana early in 1861 and for a brief period continued his studies under Jesuit tutelage. But the patriotic lures of wartime soon proved irresistible, and before the year of Fort Sumter spent itself, the sixteen-year-old Edward D. White had happily donned the Rebel gray.

The combination of his comparative youth plus an elevated educational and social background kept White from the front lines. For the most part he served as an *aide de camp* at various headquarters through the first eighteen months of the uneven struggle. In July of 1863, however, White was among the thousands of Rebel troops trapped by General Nathaniel Banks' siege of Port Hudson on the lower Mississippi. The outgunned southerners endured weeks of attack before finally surrendering a bloody and disease-ridden battlefield. For White and thousands of other captured Rebels, the war had ended. He straggled southward on foot in the bedraggled company of hundreds of defeated Rebs, finally arriving exhausted in Thibodaux.

As the weeks passed slowly into months and the brutal war ran its relentless course, White began to put his life in perspective, and to think of the future. While the battlefield and the frustration of bitter defeat had already taught the eighteen-year-old a great deal about "life," his truncated education had not allowed him to pursue anything definite. Now he was forced to consider the future, always capricious but now made even more complex and disturbing by the obliteration of the whole social order within which White and nearly all southerners felt so comfortable. By the time of Appomattox, the young sugar planter had plotted his future course.

Soon after the fighting stopped, Edward White entered the offices of a noted Louisiana lawyer named Edward Bermudez and began the traditional process of reading under the direction, more or less, of the master. Simultaneously, White enrolled for courses in the School of Law of the University of Louisiana, the Jesuit institution which later became Tulane University. Three years later, in 1868, White passed the Louisiana Bar and began his long and distinguished career.

As a young New Orleans-based lawyer, White's particular interest lay in rebuilding the old political structure. He identified himself totally with the Redeemers who struggled relentlessly to destroy the hated Republican carpetbagger administrations. He spoke out defiantly against the reconstructionists, praised Confederate loyalists, and once even took to the barricades during a particularly violent clash. The steady waning of federal zeal for Reconstruction enhanced the political fortunes of stalwarts like White, who easily got himself elected to the state senate in 1874.

Through the ensuing five years White furthered his political standing within a Democratic party which had regained control in Baton Rouge after the squalid Compromise of 1877 by which Louisiana Democrats joined with other southerners to provide Republican Rutherford B. Hayes with just enough votes to enter the White House, in return for a Republican pledge to withdraw support for the remaining Radical Republican state administrations, including Louisiana. Consequently, Louisiana Democrats headed by Governor Nicholls, political mentor of young Edward White, swept back into full control. Nicholls, an old friend of the first Edward White, rewarded his faithful lieutenant handsomely in 1878 by naming the thirty-three-year-old lawyer an associate justice of the Louisiana Supreme Court.

Yet even this apparently sacrosanct position was not beyond the never-to-be-underestimated exotic vagaries of Louisiana politics. A Democratic faction antagonistic to the Nicholls' wing roared into power in what amounted to a struggle over the infamous Louisiana Lottery, replaced the governor while his term had another year to run, and then inaugurated a new constitution which prohibited men of Edward White's tender years from holding high judicial office. This internecine political struggle produced the temporary victory of the pro-lottery men and forced such opponents of this redolent scheme as White back into private life.

Through most of the 1880's while he remained in a kind of political exile White interested himself in a number of significant civic projects. Perhaps the most important of these was the establishment of Tulane University in 1884, in which White served as a legal advisor and later as a member of the governing board.

These were also the years during which the enterprising young man from Thibodaux solidified his professional standing. He became associated with a succession of profitable and influential New Orleans law firms, and also held a succession of prestigious posts in the New Orleans Law Association.

As he neared forty, Edward D. White settled into an easy pattern of life, assured of status by his powerful legal and political connections, secured financially by healthy fees and the plantation down in Thibodaux, happy with the cosmopolitan delights of New Orleans and its French Quarter where he lived. White's ever expanding girth easily identified him as he passed from opulent dark brown clubs and crystal-chandeliered restaurants to the soaring Gothic Catholic Cathedral and the cool and quiet ivy of Tulane. He spoke French fluently, and dearly loved the rich variety of New Orleans culture. This pleasant and comfortable approach to middle age had very few obstructions.

One of the most formidable was a certain Miss Virginia Montgomery, an Alabama belle whom White doggedly pursued in the 1870's up to the moment that Miss Montgomery became Mrs. Kent. The disappointed suitor then resigned himself to the rigors of bachelorhood. But Mr. Kent unexpectedly passed on in the 1880's, and White once again took up the chase, only to be rebuffed once more. All of his persuasive powers could not convince the Widow Kent to become anything more than purely a "good friend," and this was how the relationship stood as White set out in 1888 to surmount yet another difficult obstacle, the return to political power.

Through the 1880's Louisiana politics was consumed by the corrupt lottery. In 1888 the anti-lottery forces of ex-Governor Nicholls reemerged to fight in the gubernatorial election against the rival faction headed by the aptly named Henry Clay Warmoth. Edward White eagerly joined in and managed the Nicholls' campaign throughout an exceptionally bitter struggle which swept the ex-governor back into power. The triumphant Nicholls subsequently prevailed upon his legislature for various patronage benefactions, among the most important of which was the appointment of Edward D. White to the United States Senate. On December 7, 1891, the new junior senator from Louisiana began his short but highly successful three year career in the Upper House.

Southern politicians since Calhoun have struggled unsuccessfully with the logically insoluble dilemma within which their understandable desire to attract federal largesse to their own state confronts the rigid strictures of the states' rights philosophy. The working guideline has generally held that while opposing the central government's "unconstitutional" regulation of economic relationships within the state, southerners simultaneously seek out as large a volume of unrestricted federal funds as possible.

Edward White's Senate career clearly illustrated this basic approach. He was considered a loyal Cleveland Democrat, and could be counted on to support the administration as frequently as the peculiarities of his own state's special interests would allow. This meant that White stoutly opposed even his own party's efforts to expand federal regulatory powers when Louisiana interests were involved. Such was the case in the summer of 1892 when the Senate locked in a debate over a bill which would empower the government to regulate and tax forms of speculation in various agricultural "options" and "futures," a speculative bidding system which frequently produced rampant graft. The nature of this bill, which suggested the kind of progressive regulatory legislation which would become popular ten years hence, stood a good chance of passage until influential southerners mounted a furious rhetorical assault. Senator White, widely respected and already far more influential in the Senate than his brief experience would suggest, rose to the floor on July 21 and started in. The huge Louisianan looked almost like a late nineteenth century caricature of a senator, with long and thick hair ringing his florid oval face, pacing slightly, nervously, gently swinging a wide expanse of vest-covered torso around the ornate chamber filled with prosperous-looking frock coated men. White was never a particularly distinguished orator, but in the two days during which he held the floor he at least made his position crystal clear in fighting this philosophically opprobrious piece of legislation. "Is it denied that these [options and futures] are valid contracts?" he asked. "Is it denied that they are contracts made under the State law and under protection of the State courts?" No senator rose to rebut the rhetorical questions, and the Louisianan proceeded with the familiar states' rights litany which Calhoun had expressed so brilliantly just two generations before:

> *. . . I ask Senators, mindful of their great oath to support the Constitution of the United States, where within the four walls of that Constitution can they find a pretext for this great usurpation of authority? If the theory which this bill propounds is true every vestige of State autonomy has been wiped off, and to-day, instead of having a government of limited and restrictive powers, each government moving by the force of constitutional gravity in its own orbit, we stand* [as] *the most unlimited and arbitrary government on the face of God's*

earth. [*Sister Marie Carolyn, Edward Douglas White, Chief Justice of the United States* (*Washington, D.C., 1943*) *29. Hereafter, Sister Marie Carolyn,* EDW.]

The force of the opposition generated by Senator White and a large number of like-minded men on Capitol Hill combined with a general political milieu in which *laissez faire* concepts of government still prevailed to defeat this modest attempt to cope with tainted speculation through an increase in the regulatory powers of the federal government.

At the same time that the Louisiana senator fought so strongly against government interference with business, especially the obnoxious idea of federal taxes, he staunchly supported high tariff walls to protect Louisiana sugar as well as the tradition of federal bounty payments to domestic sugar growers, of which he was one. Not only did White admit no philosophical inconsistency in seeking liberal federal subsidies at the public expense of much higher sugar prices, he also proved quite willing to simultaneously attack his own party.

President Cleveland staked much of his dwindling political capital on a thoroughgoing reform of a tariff schedule which mainly protected and enriched special interest groups. The reform measure, introduced late in 1893, sought to expand the duty-free list while substantially lowering the imposts on other goods. After surviving the House in fairly good shape, the bill introduced by Representative Wilson was pounced upon by a band of senators who ripped through its every section, building protective safeguards wherever interests were threatened, adding new duties for formerly free commodities, raising rates across the board.

No senator was busier in this furious battle than Louisiana's White, whose adroit logrolling skills served to protect sugar from the free-traders and reductionists. In the process, however, White had to endure the accompanying strains which the tariff battle placed on his relationship with the President.

For his part, Cleveland could do little. Even many Senate Democrats had turned openly on their floundering leader, whose popularity plummeted throughout the panicky winter of 1893 and into the violent and bloody summer of 1894.

One measure of Cleveland's political impotence during the tariff fight was his inability to place a man in a Supreme Court vacancy. When Justice Samuel Blatchford of New York had died in July of 1893, a half century of precedent demanded the appointment of another New Yorker; however, the even stronger tradition of senatorial courtesy prevented this, since Cleveland and the two New York senators fervently hated one another. Senior Senator David B. Hill, whose political fiefdom lay across upstate New York, had in the early 1880's served as Governor Grover Cleveland's lieutenant governor. A decade later, however, the ambitious Hill bitterly broke with Cleveland when the 1892 Democratic convention gave to the ex-President the opportunity to become the only man in American history to serve two non-consecutive terms in the White House. The cause of the Cleveland-Hill break was simple: Hill wanted the nomination for himself. Instead, he went to the Senate in 1892 as Cleveland reentered the White House, and the vendetta continued.

The question of Justice Blatchford's replacement provided Hill with an excellent opportunity for increasing Grover Cleveland's misery during the tariff fight. First the President nominated a New York lawyer named William Hornblower, but Hill and his downstate colleague Senator Murphy indicated their opposition in the Senate, which rejected Hornblower by thirty to twenty-four on January 15, 1894. Cleveland responded a month later with the name of another New York barrister, Wheeler Peckham, but once again the Senate bowed to the wishes of Hill and Murphy, forty-one to thirty-two on February 16.

The battered President was furious with the Senate, mostly for what it was doing to his tariff plans, but also because of the two slaps on the Court appointment. On February 15, 1894, he sent for Senator White, who arrived at 1600 Pennsylvania Avenue fully prepared for an angry squabble on the tariff, but who left with an appointment to the Supreme Court.

White's appointment came about for many reasons. Most immediately, the Senate could not prolong Cleveland's embarrassment by holding up the nomination of one of its own members; in fact, White won unanimous Senate confirmation the next day. In addition, Cleveland had high respect for the Louisianan's integrity. Despite their fundamental differences over the tariff, White had generally supported the administration, and believed in the sanctity of the gold standard quite as much as did the President himself. The Senator had also stood firmly behind Cleveland's controversial refusal to annex Hawaii, an anti-imperialist stand which also protected Louisiana sugar from the possibility of duty-free Hawaiian competition. Furthermore, given the mounting intra-party attacks on Cleveland's conservatism, the dispensation of this piece of important patronage to the South made good political sense.

President Cleveland was very mistaken if he had hoped that this appointment would immediately remove one of his strongest tariff opponents in the midst of the Wilson-Gorman tariff fight. For even after the Senate confirmed his nomination to the High Court, White refused to accept it. Through the remainder of February and into March he led the battle for sugar protection.

The Justice-elect was not oblivious to the criticism to which his equivocal role gave rise. He nonetheless had no second thoughts about the wisdom of his dubious decision to remain in the Senate for weeks after his confirmation to a position which he would—obviously—eventually accept. In several letters to prominent members of the Roman Catholic hierarchy, for example, the Senator managed to convey effectively the combined instincts of a shrewd politician, devoted statesman, and humble suppliant. On March 10, 1894, during the period in which he came under heaviest criticism, White explained to the prominent James Cardinal Gibbons of Baltimore:

> *At the time the appointment came to me, the people of our state were engaged in a great struggle to protect their material interests. All the threads of this struggle were in my hands and to release them, I felt, might lead to disaster.*

> *For these reasons, I determined, after much anxiety and solicitude, to await the action of the Senate Finance Committee. . . . The committee having made a report which is reasonably favorable, I felt that I might leave . . . ; hence I will accept the office and will enter upon the discharge of its duties on Monday next. . . . Its responsibilities are great and my qualifications are limited; but I trust Almighty God will give me the strength which I so much require to fill them creditably.* [*In Sister Marie Carolyn,* EDW, *39 n. 146.*]

The eventual success of White's cause mirrored the total victory of the protectionist forces. In the final version of the Wilson-Gorman Act, domestic sugar producers gained a stout forty percent *ad valorem* duty on all incoming raw sugar. After the weeks and months of haggling in corridors and clubs and committee rooms, the scarred act passed the Senate bearing the marks of 334 changes from the original House version. On the average, tariffs were raised to 41.3 percent, thereby totally obliterating the President's campaign promise of tariff reform. The bitter Cleveland, alluding to Democratic complicity, branded the act as "a piece of party perfidy," and, the veto at this point being merely an empty threat, allowed it to become law without his signature.

The passage of time healed over the political wounds of Cleveland's unsuccessful second term. The basic issues remained, but younger men rose to contest them; Cleveland himself went off to live out his years in the attractive tranquility of Princeton. One of the ex-President's most enduring legacies was his snap decision to elevate Senator White to the Supreme Court. Taken away from the brawling political wars just as Populist insurgency reached its crescendo, White now moved into the more dignified mode of life for which his tastes and genial temperament were particularly well suited.

In the spring of 1894 the newest Justice refurbished his spacious home on Rhode Island Avenue, a handsome nineteenth century red mansion. At the top of the winding center staircase, he filled a comfortable study with walls of yellow law books and with the two commanding likenesses of Marshall and Webster as well. For the next twenty-seven years White wrote decisions in all of his hundreds of cases in this room, usually dictating to a stenographer and later correcting the typescript. He became an indefatigable worker, to the extent that by the time he had completed working over a decision and dictating it, his amazingly retentive memory allowed him to repeat it verbatim without consulting his notes. In the years to come, White would on occasion become so involved while delivering an oral opinion that he would neglect his notes and recite his usually involuted and obscure reasoning from memory.

His life also soon benefited from another welcome change, as the elusive Widow Kent finally agreed to White's long-standing offer and became Mrs. White in November of 1894.

The Supreme Court which White entered was already involved in a period of significant judicial transition, as the revolutionary economic and social effects of industrialization had upset traditional patterns throughout American life. Increasingly large numbers of men and women abandoned the old ways of self-sufficiency for the siren song blared by the whistles of urban factories. While the ethos of individualism lingered on, in actuality most Americans were enveloped in an all embracing industrial matrix, within which they worked at the whim of an unknown, unseen corporate master, performing increasingly simplified tasks without having any personal relationship to a finished product. No longer did they control their own destinies. The individual, increasingly without any differentiating skill, became a replaceable object, to be used and discarded, to be worked as long as possible in frequently unsafe and unpalatable surroundings, and to be compensated on a scale determined solely by men who neither knew him nor showed any particular interest in his well-being.

The onset of this new urban industrial America, so different from the rural and largely agricultural land of generations past, demanded some new definitions of individual and property rights, especially as the roars of protest swelled. The multiplying ranks of Bryan's bucolic crusaders paralleled the increasing violence of workers' demonstrations, which periodically erupted from the time of the bloody railroad strikes of 1877 to the crushing Pullman affair of 1894. No longer able to cope as individuals with powerful new economic forces such as the railroads and banks and corporations which now shaped their lives, the protesters demanded collective action from state legislators and the federal government to redress their grievances. At the same time, conservatives looked increasingly to the courts to protect them from threats posed by radicals and reformers of all types. Accordingly, the next quarter-century became a period of significant constitutional reinterpretation, and Edward D. White participated in all of it.

In the broadest terms, the Court was called upon to define the constitutional limits of two sometimes overlapping judicial areas: the concept of substantive due process of law, and the boundaries within which the federal government would be allowed to implement various types of regulatory social legislation. Several types of cases were included in the latter determination including the issues which arose from the creation of federal regulatory power through legislation passed under the central government's commerce and taxation powers. In addition, the Court fully defined the scope of the power of the Interstate Commerce Commission, dealt hesitantly with the problem of constitutional guarantees for the inhabitants of America's New Empire and finally determined the future of the Sherman Anti-Trust Act. These complex issues which stemmed from the attempts of the federal government to impose widescale economic controls were frequently intermixed with the problems which the Court created for itself by the adoption of the concept of substantive due process of law.

From the writing of the Constitution down to the twentieth century, the concept of due process of law referred almost entirely to procedural questions, the courts ruling from time to time on questions pertaining to the protection by individuals of their life, liberty or property against arbitrary acts of the federal government. Originally confined to an inconspicuous sentence fragment of the

Fifth Amendment, which held that "no person shall . . . be deprived of life, liberty, or property without due process of law. . .," this clause again found its way into the Constitution with the ratification of the Fourteenth Amendment in 1868. This Radical Republican attempt to protect the civil liberties of the freedmen from encroachments by state governments was later invested with a fundamentally different construction by a succession of Supreme Court decisions of the 1890's. By defining a corporation as a legal "person," the Court sought to prevent both the Congress and the state legislatures from tampering with private property in the public interest, since a narrow definition of due process naturally would find all regulatory legislation in violation of some "person's" property rights. Thus the substantive element was added: the Court took upon itself the task of setting limits to the controls which various legislative bodies sought to impose upon private property. Since the Court assumed this responsibility at a time when public demands for a wide variety of regulatory legislation were greatly increasing—indeed, perhaps because of these demands—sharp battles over judicial interpretation became inevitable.

The erratic nature of Court decisions over the next twenty-five years involving both substantive due process and the growth of federal regulatory powers indicated the Court's continued inability to define the limits of government interference with private enterprise. The rampant subjectivism of these years created a situation whereby judicial decision-making became either a blatant function of a Justice's social philosophy or a totally pragmatic sequence in which cases were resolved on their own merits, one by one, almost without consciousness of legal logic or precedent.

Those few Justices who possessed sharply defined ideological predilections consistently delivered opinions based on little more than their own *a priori* assumptions. Rigid conservatives like Stephen Field and his nephew David J. Brewer automatically rejected progressive laws as assaults on capital. Later Justices Willis Van Devanter and James C. McReynolds were to slide into this same category. Somewhere on the opposing side of the spectrum near the turn of the century sat John Marshall Harlan, who usually stood out as a champion of the expansion of federal powers. After his death, Louis D. Brandeis arrived to become a vigorous advocate of national supremacy. In addition, the towering presence of Oliver Wendell Holmes strengthened the Court throughout these trying years, and although Holmes thoroughly objected to the practice of allowing personal feelings to influence judicial decisions, he nonetheless opposed the vagaries of the Court's subjectivism by serving as its self-appointed conscience on legal logic.

The great majority of men who sat on the Supreme Court with Edward D. White through his twenty-seven years, however, did not possess the ideological and philosophical certitude that governed a few of their colleagues. Most Justices were men with the healthiest regard for private property and capital, and many, especially the large number who came from small-town America, arrived at the Court lacking impressive credentials in legal scholarship. Some were geographical appointees, filling the seat reserved for the West like Joseph McKenna of California or for the South like Howell E. Jackson of Tennessee. Other appointments were mostly political, as Cleveland's appointment of White or Theodore Roosevelt's naming of William H. Moody. Still others reflected the purely personal wishes of the President, as with Taft's selection of Horace H. Lurton. Such varied criteria notwithstanding, several of these rather casually selected men proved to be quite competent jurists; yet often their own backgrounds plus the absence of guidelines during the early years of the twentieth century encouraged them to oscillate wildly in making the decisions which affected the new American industrial society.

The jagged pattern of Justice White's decisions in a few of the basic cases involving substantive due process is indicative of the Court's stunning ambivalence. The application of substantive due process to the attempts by various state legislatures to regulate maximum hours of daily labor produced the famous bakers' case, *Lochner* v. *New York,* 198 U.S. 45 (1905). Here, a Court split five to four ruled that a New York state law that limited bakers to an eight-hour workday was an unconstitutional interference with freedom of contract, and thus violated due process by not allowing bakers to work as long as they saw fit. White voted with the minority. Just three years later, a unanimous Court in *Muller* v. *Oregon,* 208 U.S. 412 (1908) upheld an Oregon law limiting women to an eight-hour workday. When the state of Oregon attempted a few years later to pass similar maximum hours legislation for men, however, the unanimity of the *Muller* case disappeared in a six to three split. In *Bunting* v. *Oregon,* 243 U.S. 426 (1917), moreover, Justice White fully reversed his earlier view. His minority vote in the *Lochner* case was based upon the right of states to limit contracts in the public interest. Later, in *Muller,* he and the rest of the Court had been dazzled by the sociological impact of the famous Brandeis Brief, and consequently agreed to consider the probable effects of law (or in this case, the lack of a law) as well as the question of its constitutionality. Yet in the *Bunting* case, White silently supported the minority view that denied to the Oregon legislature the right to pass maximum hours legislation.

White also reversed his once favorable attitude toward limiting the freedom of contract in the public interest in two cases involving "yellow-dog" contracts, by which prospective employees were forced as a condition of employment to pledge not to join unions. In *Adair* v. *United States,* 208 U.S. 161 (1908), White joined the six to two majority which invalidated a federal statute barring such contracts, on the grounds that it impaired workingmen's freedom of contract under the due process clause of the Fifth Amendment. When the Court used the same reasoning in striking down a Kansas anti–"yellow-dog" law, in *Coppage* v. *Kansas,* 236 U.S. 1 (1915), White once again joined the majority in defending freedom of contract. By the time of the *Coppage* decision of 1915 and the *Bunting* opinion of 1917, White no longer utilized the reasoning which guided his agreement with Justice Harlan's vigorous dissent in the *Lochner* case of 1906.

Judicial hairsplitting within the murky confines of substantive due process also affected White's decisions on other aspects of social legislation. In *New York Central Railroad Company* v. *White,* 243 U.S. 188 (1917), Justice White joined the unanimous Court in upholding the New York state Workmen's Compensation Act of 1914. Yet the same year, in *Mountain Timber Co.* v. *Washington,* 243 U.S. 219 (1917), when the Court upheld a Washington state workmen's compensation act by a five to four vote, White sided with the minority. The scant difference between the two state laws which caused White to adjudge the former as constitutional and the latter as unconstitutional turned on the Washington act's requirement that all employers must make contributions to the state compensation fund regardless of the propensity of accidents of their own company. The New York law, on the other hand, merely required employers to carry compensation insurance. In White's judgment, the Washington legislature had violated due process, while the New York legislature had not.

The judicial whimsy sometimes indicated by Justice White's erratic pattern in these basic substantive due process cases should not obscure the fact that White tended to vote conservatively, especially as he grew older. Yet by his significant deviations in supporting the extension of national regulatory power, White tarnished the states' rights, plantation southern stereotype which had been attached to him from the beginning of his public life. In the myriad of cases involving the rise and expansion of the regulatory power of the federal government, White's unpredictable record accurately reflected the ambiguity of the Court itself.

Since the Constitution reserves for the several states the power to legislate for the general good in cases involving health, morals, and general welfare, the proponents of federal regulation were forced to find more indirect methods of coping with the powerful new economic forces unleashed by industrialization. Primarily, the progressives utilized the constitutional power of Congress to regulate commerce as their chief means of social control, and, in a series of cases heard between 1903 and 1919, the Supreme Court generally sanctioned a variety of laws which made use of the commerce clause as well as the power to levy taxes to promote health, morals, and the general welfare.

As in the due process cases, Justice White's views on the proper scope of federal regulatory activities changed over the years. In *Champion* v. *Ames,* 188 U.S. 321 (1903), the first case involving the elasticized commerce clause, the Court upheld by five to four a federal law which prohibited use of the mails to ship lottery tickets across state lines. The purpose of the law was to discourage gambling, heretofore a province of the states, but Justice Harlan's majority opinion held that ". . . Congress may arbitrarily exclude from commerce among the states any article . . . which it may choose, no matter with what motive. . . ." (Alfred H. Kelly and Winfred A. Harbison, *The American Constitution: Its Origins and Development,* 3rd edition [New York, 1963] 587. Hereafter, Kelly and Harbison, *American Constitution.*) This strong claim for a virtual federal *carte blanche* over all aspects of interstate manufacturing and commerce split the Court, but Justice White supported Harlan's liberal nationalist interpretation.

White further indicated his acceptance of this philosophy in delivering the Court's majority opinion one year later in *McCray* v. *United States,* 195 U.S. 27(1904). In this six to three decision, White upheld the federal government's utilization of a second indirect means of imposing social controls, the use of taxation. His opinion sustained an act of Congress which, at the behest of the dairy industry, levied a high tax on artificially colored oleomargarine, while barely taxing naturally colored oleo at all. The motives of Congress, White held, were irrelevant for the Court's purposes, since the Congress obviously possessed the right to levy this particular tax if it saw fit.

The government, as emboldened by these permissive decisions as it was shocked by conditions involving public health and morals, soon utilized its commerce and tax powers to attack food adulteration, prostitution, child labor and the narcotics traffic. Each of the resulting laws was tested in the Supreme Court; of these Court tests, the first challenged the Pure Food and Drug Act of 1906 in *Hipolite Egg Company* v. *United States,* 220 U.S. 45 (1911). The Court unanimously stood behind Justice McKenna's opinion which upheld the act on the grounds that the federal government possessed vast comprehensive powers to regulate all forms of interstate commerce. Soon thereafter, in *Hoke* v. *United States,* 227 U.S. 308 (1913), the Court upheld the Mann Act of 1910 which relied on the commerce power to halt interstate prostitution. The pattern thus set by these decisions, in which Justice White concurred, apparently set no limits to the power of the federal government under the commerce clause.

Yet any expectation that these precedents would be extended as other commerce clause cases came before the Court underestimated the highly subjective nature of this judicial period, as White's role in two subsequent decisions clearly illustrated. In the hotly disputed case of *Hammer* v. *Dagenhart,* 247 U.S. 251 (1918), the Court ruled unconstitutional the Keating-Owen Child Labor Law of 1916 which had barred from interstate commerce all products which had been manufactured in any way by child labor. Justice Day's majority opinion for the five to four Court harkened back to the long discredited dictum of *United States* v. *E. C. Knight Company,* 156 U.S. 1 (1895) which had posited a clear distinction between "commerce" and "manufacturing," and thereby limited federal control to the former. Day also objected to Congress' motives in using the commerce clause for social control, as well as infringing on the regulatory province of state governments. Although each of these objections had already been dismissed by the previous commerce clause cases, Day nonetheless attracted the support of a majority which included White. As if to indicate his own repudiation of the commerce power, White himself led the attack on the government's attempt to control the narcotics traffic through the tax power. In *United States* v. *Doremus,* 249 U.S. 86 (1919), White's minority opinion in a five to four decision which barely upheld the Federal Narcotics Act was based on his opposition to "a mere attempt by Congress to exert a power not delegated; that is, the reserved police power of the states." (*United States* v. *Doremus, supra* at 95, cited in Kelly and Harbison, *American Constitution,* 597.) Absent altogether was White's claim in *McCray* v. *United States,* 195 U.S. 27 (1904), fifteen years before, that the Court should not concern itself with the motives behind the tax laws but solely with the constitutional right of the Congress to levy taxes.

Perhaps this violation of logic and repudiation of precedent was merely a function of White's advancing age. And perhaps the same explanation fits those of his colleagues whose voting patterns also reveal such marked deviations.

White and the Court proved to be far more consistent in a series of cases which restored to the Interstate Commerce Commission the powers which the Court of the 1890's had taken from it. In *Illinois Central Railroad Company* v. *Interstate Commerce Commission,* 206 U.S. 441 (1907), the Court had held that the factual data upon which the I.C.C. based a prosecution were to be accepted as *prima facie* evidence, thereby freeing the Commission from the expense and trouble of submitting to an investigation of its own investigation. Three years later, in *Interstate Commerce Commission* v. *Illinois Central Railroad Company,* 215 U.S. 452 (1910), White delivered the majority opinion as the Court stated that it recognized the validity of the commission's regulatory orders, thereby giving legal sanction both to the I.C.C. and, by extension at least, to the other federal regulatory commissions that were rapidly appearing. White objected, however, when the Court granted to the I.C.C., by six to three in *Interstate Commerce Commission* v. *Chicago, Rock Island, and Pacific Railway Company,* 218 U.S. 88 (1910), the virtual right to control rates on all interstate lines. But this was the trend of the Court's thinking, and three years later White joined with all of his colleagues in *United States* v. *Atchison, Topeka, and Santa Fe,* 234 U.S. 476 (1914), which settled once and for all the constitutionality of the delegation of rate-fixing powers by the Congress to the Interstate Commerce Commission.

Another example of a series of closely related cases in which the Court moved in one direction concerned the vexing problem of determing the constitutional rights of the various peoples swept into the American imperial net at the turn of the century. The so-called Insular Cases asked one basic question: does the Constitution follow the flag? After the strident cries of Anti-Imperialist Leaguers and expansionist jingoes had died away, the Supreme Court was left to answer the question. Eventually, the novel concept of Justice White prevailed in providing the answer.

In *DeLima* v. *Bidwell,* 182 U.S. 1 (1901), the Court upheld by five to four the contention of Puerto Rican sugar exporters that since Puerto Rico was no longer a "foreign country" the "foreign" import duties collected on their sugar in New York were illegal. A four-man minority, which included White, contended that some degree of protection for United States goods was entirely proper, especially since Puerto Rico was not fully a part of the United States. This basic idea of making a legal differentiation between the continental United States and its overseas area remained with White. In a companion case to *DeLima* v. *Bidwell, supra, Downes* v. *Bidwell,* 182 U.S. 244 (1901), the five to four majority shifted to the other side, this time supporting Justice Brown's opinion that the Constitution only followed the flag when Congress explicitly extended it; that the Congress had not done so; and that, therefore, the Foraker Act of 1900, which imposed duties on goods imported from Puerto Rico to the same extent as those imported from foreign countries, was valid despite the constitutional provisions against non-uniform duties throughout the United States. Of greater historical significance than Brown's tortured logic was White's concurring opinion, which introduced the idea of "incorporation."

White argued in *Downes* v. *Bidwell* (and in each of the succeeding Insular Cases over ten years) that the test of the applicability of constitutional guarantees in overseas possessions was the "incorporation" or lack thereof of a particular area, either by the Congress or by treaty. Since this ambiguous term rarely appeared in treaties or in congressional orders, the Court was left to its own devices in interpreting its meaning and applicability.

The utilization of the doctrine of "incorporation" quickly came. In the 1903 case of *Hawaii* v. *Mankichi,* 190 U.S. 197 (1903), where a manslaughter conviction based on the assent of only three-fourths of the jury clearly violated the Bill of Rights, the Court refused to reverse the decision. Justice Brown again held, as in *Downes* v. *Bidwell, supra,* that Congress had not extended the Constitution to Hawaii. Once again, Justice White's concurring opinion argued that Hawaii had not been "incorporated" into the United States. A year later, in *Dorr* v. *United States,* 195 U.S. 138 (1904), Brown's "extension" doctrine was replaced by the "incorporation" concept of White, as the Court here sanctioned constitutional irregularities in the Philippine Islands on the grounds that Congress had not seen fit to "incorporate" the Islands within the full protection of the Constitution. In 1905, in *Rassmussen* v. *United States,* 197 U.S. 516 (1905), the Court decided that Alaska had been "incorporated," and White's opinion reversed the conviction of a brothel-keeper who had been denied trial by a twelve-man jury. In this case White attempted to clarify his doctrine by claiming that Alaska's "incorporation" placed it in a legal area lying someplace between statehood and colony, whereas Puerto Rico and the Philippines remained merely possessions or dependencies.

Later cases sealed the triumph of "incorporation," as in *Dowdell* v. *United States,* 221 U.S. 325 (1911) and *Balzac* v. *Porto Rico,* 258 U.S. 298 (1922), which confirmed earlier judgments that neither the Philippines nor Puerto Rico had been "incorporated." Justice White, always the leading exponent of this doctrine, had thus answered the question "Does the Constitution follow the flag?" with the reply "Sometimes." The failure of the Court to define "incorporation" produced total judicial subjectivity which at times fostered the violation of the rights and privileges of foreign peoples who found themselves under United State control but who were protected by neither the letter nor the spirit of the

American Constitution. At least in the Insular Cases, however, the Court's subjectivism possessed the modest attribute of consistency.

The subjective nature of the Insular Case decisions thus fitted into the pattern of these two decades during which the pervasive impact of industrialization disturbed legal foundations along with the rest of American society. The purely judicial by-products of industrialization were extensive, as protesters and reformers gradually forced governments to act in new ways which disrupted existing property relationships, thus necessitating judicial reinterpretation. This new economy begat a new social order and a new politics, both at home and abroad. The Court, sometimes befuddled and usually inconsistent, consequently found itself veering to the right with substantive due process and to the left with the commerce clause. After 1900 it gave back to the Interstate Commerce Commission more than it had taken away in the 1890's. Yet the Court simultaneously refused to export the Bill of Rights to many of America's subject peoples.

The effects of these decisions naturally altered and guided the existing direction of the American civilization. However, decisions taken by the Court in 1911 on the nature and application of the Sherman Anti-Trust Act ultimately were to have a far greater historical significance: they were to shape the future course of American society. These fundamental decisions were largely the personal work of Edward D. White, who unexpectedly became Chief Justice in the last days of 1910.

By the middle of 1910 only White, Harlan and McKenna remained from the Court of the 1890's. The attrition rate among their colleagues had been particularly high during the Taft years, culminating in the deaths of Justices Peckham, Brewer and Chief Justice Fuller within a ten month period from October, 1909 to July, 1910. Speculation over Fuller's successor naturally covered several names, including the novel possibility of the promotion of one of the Associate Justices. In this category, the choice apparently lay between White and Charles Evans Hughes. Indeed, when Taft had appointed Hughes to the Court in April of 1910, the President had virtually promised to promote the distinguished looking New Yorker upon the expected death of Melville Fuller. Yet when Fuller died just a few weeks later, Taft hesitated. The summer months passed into late autumn and still the White House remained silent. (Alpheus T. Mason, *William Howard Taft: Chief Justice* 34–40 [1964]. Hereafter, Mason, *Taft.*)

The major reason for the President's lengthy delay seems, at least in hindsight, to be embarrassingly obvious. Because his administration was beset by numerous political and personal problems such as trouble with the Congress and with the press, difficulty with the LaFollette progressives, and unpleasantness due to the growing animus of Colonel Roosevelt, the beleaguered President knew by mid-term that his chances for re-election grew slimmer with each passing day. And, ironically enough for a successful politician, Taft never had felt comfortable in the White House or, indeed, in the whole political hubris. His own preferences were simple, and he made no particular secret of them: William Howard Taft wanted to be Chief Justice more than anything else in the world. "It seems strange," he lamented after Fuller's death, "that the one place in the government which I would have liked to fill myself I am forced to give to another." (Mason, *Taft,* 34.)

Thus if the fifty-three-year-old President appointed forty-eight-year-old Hughes as Chief Justice, his own hopes of someday sitting in the Court's center chair very likely would be shattered, given a Chief Justice's average incumbency of seventeen years as well as the relative youth and robust good health of Hughes. In contrast, Edward D. White, already sixty-five, supported a superabundance of girth only slightly inferior to the magnificent proportions of the President himself.

Early in December Taft somewhat sheepishly reached his decision, informing White of his intentions but cancelling at the last moment a similar meeting with the disappointed Hughes. While other considerations occurred to Taft in the making of White's appointment, they seem scarcely more elevated than the President's narrow concern for his own chances for the Chief Justiceship. Taft marked well White's Roman Catholicism. While incapable of personal bias himself, the President well understood religious voting patterns, and had convinced himself that "the Catholics" had elected him in 1908 and just possibly might do so again in 1912. This conviction allowed him to reverse the paranoid anti-Catholicism of those days by resolutely naming a Catholic to a position of such great power and influence.

As an additional motivating factor, Taft also realized the utility which the precedent of appointing a Chief Justice from the other party might possibly have in a Democratic future.

Almost immediately after taking control of the Court early in 1911, the new Chief Justice persuaded his colleagues to ignore strong precedent and to legally sanctify what one scholar has termed "the most curious *obiter dictum* ever indulged in by the Supreme Court of the United States," that is, the so-called "rule of reason." (Robert B. Dishman, "Mr. Justice White and the Rule of Reason, 13 *Review of Politics* 229–243 [1951].)

White's fight to apply his "rule of reason" to the Sherman Anti-Trust Act had a long and curious history. For over fifteen years he claimed legal justification for a selective rather than a comprehensive application of the act by arguing that the common law allowed "reasonable" restraint of trade. While the common law does differentiate, it sanctions restraint only when the restraint is an incidental or secondary effect rather than the primary purpose of an agreement specifically designed to stifle competition.

The Court had consistently and explicitly denied White's common law argument for "reasonableness," first in 1897 in *United States* v. *Trans-Missouri Freight Association,* 166 U.S. 290 (1897). The association, which was made up of eighteen previously competing railroads which had entered into rate and schedule agreements, defended itself against Sherman Act prosecution by arguing in part that their combination constituted "reasonable" restraint of trade, while the act prohibited only "unreasonable" restraints. The majority opinion in a five to four split denied that Congress intended this construction of the act or that the common law sustained it. But in his 10,000 word dissent, Justice White presented an ill-defined "rule of reason," to which he gave various meanings. He asked for "reasonable" moderation in interpreting the association's actions, suggested that the passage of the act itself might have been "unreasonable," and concluded with the contention that the Court's decision would produce "unreasonable" consequences for the American economy by severely limiting business expansion.

The next year, the Court once again split five to four in a very similar case, *United States* v. *Joint Traffic Association,* 171 U.S. 505 (1898). This association of thirty-one railroads had agreed on the usual procedures for settling rates and sharing profits, and had consequently been indicted under the Sherman Act. Nearly all of the arguments advanced in *Trans-Missouri* were again presented, with Justice White reiterating his views on the absence of "reason" in the majority's decision. As before, the majority concluded that the Sherman Act prohibited the intentional restraint of trade practiced by this association, and also that any different interpretation would repudiate the *Trans-Missouri* decision, which the Court had no intention of doing.

The majority opinion did include one minor qualification, which would in time be used by the corporations in presenting their case for "reason." In accordance with the common law, Justice Peckham declared that some contracts which had the effect of restraining trade might be held legal under the Sherman Act if the restraint occurred as a secondary consequence rather than as the primary purpose of the contract. This naturally did not apply in either the *Trans-Missouri* or the *Joint Traffic* cases.

The next milestone in the development of the "rule of reason" came six years later in the famous case of *Northern Securities Co.* v. *United States,* 193 U.S. 197 (1904). In the Court's five to four decision to dissolve this Hill-Harriman-Morgan holding company, the concept of "reason" played a significant part. Four of the majority—Justices Harlan, Day, Brown, and McKenna—cited previous decisions to deny altogether the applicability of any "rule of reason." Justice Brewer attached himself to the majority for the opposite reason, finding against Northern Securities because it was engaged in "unreasonable" restraint of trade. White himself, curiously enough, did not argue "reason" in this case; he voted with the minority on the grounds that the Sherman Act did not apply to this intra-state commercial transaction. Moreover, White aligned himself with the minority opinion of Holmes, which categorically affirmed both the *Trans-Missouri* and *Joint Traffic* decisions.

In view of the low state to which "reason" and its effect on the Sherman Act had fallen by 1904, its subsequent full triumph seven years later is rather remarkable. The occasion came about in 1911 as a result of the government's successful prosecution under the Sherman Act of the Standard Oil Company, the

Oil Trust. A federal district court had held Standard Oil in violation of the act and ruled that it must be dissolved into its component parts. Standard carried its appeal to Washington where a unanimous Supreme Court, speaking through Chief Justice White, upheld the district court's ruling. In so doing, however, seven of the eight Associate Justices agreed with their Chief's opinion that the basis upon which the Standard appeal was denied rested upon the Court's decision that the business practices of the Oil Trust constituted "unreasonable" restraint of trade, prohibited by the Sherman Act, rather than the kind of "reasonable" restraint which the Court implied would now be permissible under the act.

The Chief Justice followed several lines of reasoning in justifying this abrupt reversal of the existing interpretation of the Sherman Act. First he applied the test of the common law, and found that it embraced all aspects of restraint of trade, not merely the secondary or technical restraints alluded to in *Joint Traffic.* Logically extended, White argued, "reason" could and should be applied in all antitrust prosecutions under this construction of the common law. Secondly, he argued that newly emergent forms of economic structure demanded legal recognition, otherwise arrangements necessary to modern business would be prohibited, to the nation's detriment. To prevent this, White advanced a pragmatic application of the Sherman Act, arguing that

> . . . *in every case where it is claimed that an act or acts are in violation of the* [*Anti-Trust*] *statute the rule of reason, in the light of the principles of law and the public policy which the act embodies, must be applied.* [Standard Oil Co. *v.* United States, 221 U.S. 1, *66, in Dishman, "White and the Rule of Reason," 240.*]

In attempting to explain away the precedents which this new interpretation violated, White advanced conflicting arguments. At one point he suggested that no conflict in fact existed, that a correct understanding of the context of the previous rulings disclosed only judicial consistency. If such was not the case, the Chief Justice gratuitously added, then the former Court had erred in failing to apply the "rule of reason."

Two weeks later, White repeated most of the same arguments in the nearly parallel case of *United States* v. *American Tobacco Company,* 221 U.S. 106 (1911). Once again White led the Court in ordering the "reorganization" but not the dissolution of the Tobacco Trust, thus leaving the strong implication that the American Tobacco Company was considered by the Court to be engaged in "reasonable" restraint of trade, thereby also underscoring the doctrine recently established in the Oil Trust case.

The major factors which brought about the establishment of the "rule of reason" involved politics and personalities as much as strict judicial interpretation. Through most of these years the striking figure of Theodore Roosevelt dominated the stage, and Roosevelt's basic contentions about the proper structure of American business neatly dovetailed with those of Justice White. At the heart of what Roosevelt was later to call the New Nationalism rested the conviction that the size and power of any corporation was less important than its capacity for serving public as well as private interests. The monster corporation, the trust, the interlocked combine, might by their efficiency and ability to rationalize an industry, serve the public interest far more than would a plethora of small, inefficient companies which adhered strictly to the old American ideal of independent competition in the marketplace. In distinguishing between monster corporations, the Roosevelt approach would measure a "good" corporation in terms of its potential to improve the material quality of American life; a "bad" corporation, conversely, attempted to enrich itself through exploitation, regardless of possible pernicious social effects. While the "good" corporation might flourish under the government's watchful eye, such "bad" combinations as Northern Securities or the Beef Trust would be smashed through the Sherman Act.

As a result, the fact that businesses combined in a conscious effort to restrain trade mattered little to Roosevelt as long as the result of such combinations served public interests as well. This was Roosevelt's "rule of reason," and he consequently agreed with his friend White that a stern and comprehensive application of the sweeping provisions of the Sherman Act would be foolishly "unreasonable" at best and would be utterly destructive of economic growth at worst.

Yet all of Roosevelt's power and persuasiveness could never undo the Court's clear-cut judgment on the Sherman Act. While Roosevelt's Department of Justice might only prosecute "bad" corporations under the act, succeeding years might well see the Court applying the strict construction set down in *Trans-Missouri* and *Joint Traffic* to all kinds of business combinations.

Chief Justice White not only prevented this from happening, but also created the strange guidelines that continue to govern antitrust prosecutions. White had been a very junior member of the Court at the time of the *Trans-Missouri* and *Joint Traffic* decisions, but by 1911 he had come to dominate it. Only irascible old John Marshall Harlan of Kentucky and the silent, unpredictable Joseph McKenna remained from the 1897 Court, as White's accession to the Chief Justice's place paralleled a great transformation in the Court's personnel. In 1909 Horace Lurton had replaced Peckham, and in April, 1910 Hughes replaced Brewer. With White in Fuller's place, Willis Van Devanter, and Joseph Lamar arrived. With such a wholesale influx of new men, White's prestige and influence would naturally increase tremendously. He had served continuously since 1894 and now became the first Associate Justice in the nation's history to be successfully elevated to the Court's leadership. Moreover, his genial personality, commanding presence in Court, and easy familiarity with Washington's most powerful men all conspired to enhance his personal influence.

Furthermore, most of the Associate Justices were predisposed in one way or another to defer to the long cxperience of their new Chief. The recently appointed Lamar of Georgia and Van Devanter of Wyoming were small-town lawyers, as were two more legally experienced Justices, Lurton and William R.

Day. Their clientele had always included banks and railroads and utility companies, and none of the four had any serious doubts about the sanctity of private enterprise or the enduring notion that the business of America truly was business, as free and unfettered as possible. Hughes, the third appointee of 1910, generally managed to convey the "image" of progressivism, yet his liberalism in these early years naturally never approached the point of disrupting the basis of the American business system. The erratic Joseph McKenna might have opposed the Chief Justice's 1911 decisions, as he went off on liberal tangents from time to time. In the *Northern Securities* case, for example, he had fully supported the argument that the Sherman Act banned *"all* direct *restraints* imposed by any combination, conspiracy, or monopoly." (*Northern Securities Co.* v. *United States, supra* at 331, in Dishman, "White and the Rule of Reason," 237. Emphasis in the original.) Yet in 1911 this grizzled McKinley Republican, his stern features underscored by a gray arc of chinwhiskers, sat silently as the Chief Justice read his two opinions.

The remaining two members of the Court, Justices Holmes and Harlan, might have been expected to oppose the Chief Justice with vigor. The brilliant and sardonic New Englander had already written at some length on the Sherman Act in dissenting in *Northern Securities,* when he fully accepted the implications of the *Trans-Missouri* and *Joint Traffic* decisions. Then, in 1904, he had written, "I accept those decisions absolutely not only as binding upon me, but as decisions which I have no desire to criticize or abridge." (*Northern Securities Co.* v. *United States, supra,* at 405, in Dishman, "White and the Rule of Reason," 238.) But in his dissent Holmes also alluded to a distinction which he believed the common law to make in regard to monopoly: not all combinations in restraint of trade were illegal; only those agreements which violated the public interest were to be outlawed. Thus, even though Holmes had once admitted that the Sherman Act itself did not permit this very distinction, his understanding of the common law implications allowed him to align himself quietly with White's decisions.

Only the combative Harlan rose up against the Chief Justice. Such was the force of the old Kentuckian's dissent, however, that his minority of one constituted a great attacking force. Then in his seventy-eighth year and within weeks of death, the independent old man showed not a sign of weakness. Confident in his views after thirty-four years on the Court, he clamped down on his cud of tobacco and reminded the Court that he too had participated in the *Trans-Missouri* and *Joint Traffic* decisions, but he, moreover, clearly remembered the definitive nature of their conclusions. The redoubtable Harlan particularly resented the rhetorical legerdemain by which the Chief Justice attempted to deny any inconsistency between the earlier decisions and the 1911 cases. For Harlan, this verbal subterfuge "surprises me quite as much as would a statement that black was white or white was black." Going beyond this heavy-handed sarcasm, Harlan defended his departed colleagues of the majority in the earlier cases as being quite able to identify reason when they came upon it:

. . . they knew quite as well as others what the rules of reason require when a court seeks to ascertain the will of Congress as expressed in a statute. It is obvious from the opinions in the former cases that the majority did not grope about in darkness, but in discharging the solemn duty put on them they stood out in the full glare of the "light of reason" and felt and said time and again that the Court could not, consistently with the Constitution, and would not, usurp the functions of Congress by indulging in judicial legislation. . . . [United States *v.* American Tobacco Co., supra, *at 191–192, 198, in Dishman, "White and the Rule of Reason," 242.*]

While Harlan may have had the logic, it has been said, White had the votes. The Court's acceptance of the "rule of reason" had the immediate effect of severely circumscribing the Sherman Act, as in *United States* v. *Winslow,* 227 U.S. 202 (1913), when the Court found the Shoe Machinery Trust a "reasonable" monopoly. In 1920, a similar finding in the Steel Trust case of *United States* v. *United States Steel Corporation,* 251 U.S. 417 (1920), ushered in the age of kaleidoscopic corporate mergers which has continued on to very recent years when business is dominated by mammoth agglomerations. The Sherman Act is still brandished by the government from time to time to bring pressure on wayward oligopolies, but its original teeth have long since been extracted.

The "rule of reason" proved to be the only legacy of White's long years on the High Court. Its importance remains manifest in making explicable the paradox of a nation whose ethic deplores monopoly and prizes self-sufficiency yet promotes oligopoly and practices economic dependence.

In the years after this fundamental decision shaped the nation's economic future by encouraging industrial combination, the Court moved on to other considerations. The rush of cases involving progressive legislation slowed during the war years. Then the Court made several significant decisions, such as in the famous Espionage Act case of *Schenck* v. *United States,* 249 U.S. 47 (1919), when Justice Holmes enunciated his famous "clear and present danger" dictum, and *Abrams* v. *United States,* 250 U.S. 616 (1919), which upheld the stifling Sedition Act.

In these and the many other wartime cases, Chief Justice White voted unreservedly to grant to the federal government virtually whatever it asked for. The aging Chief Justice's fervent patriotism even transcended the judicial conservatism of his later years, as in the 1917 case of *Wilson* v. *New,* 243 U.S. 332 (1917), when White led a five to four majority in upholding the Adamson Eight-Hour Act, which mandated railroad workers' hours and wages, on the grounds of national emergency.

Not long after the war's end the ravages of time took hold. By 1920, when the Chief Justice reached seventy-five, cataracts made reading more difficult, although he did manage to keep up with his work as well as with the diamond exploits of his hero, Ty Cobb.

His last few months on the bench were marred by an unseemly campaign on the part of William Howard Taft to force White's resignation. With the

Harding landslide of 1920 came a resurgence of Taft's old ambitions to occupy the Court's center chair. Now the conditions he foresaw in appointing White in 1910 had come to pass. The ex-President also felt that White was under some obligation to resign in his favor, although White never confirmed any such understanding. With a Republican again in the White House (and a most tractable one at that) the determined Taft refused to allow sensitivity or decorum to interfere with his consuming ambition.

Although Taft's ambitions for the Chief Justice's place were widely known throughout his years at the Yale Law School, the persistent ex-President left nothing to chance. Shortly after Senator Harding's election, Taft joined the long procession to Marion, Ohio and there made his desires unmistakably clear to the beseiged President-elect. Harding's receptivity buoyed Taft's spirits to the extent that his efforts were then concentrated on finding ways of encouraging White's resignation.

Late in 1920 Taft received encouragement from one observation "that the Chief Justice looked very feeble and it seemed . . . that he might soon retire." (Mason, *Taft,* 79.) But the old man hung on through the winter and into the spring of 1921. Moreover, he acknowledged all of the rumors about Taft's accession by sharply proclaiming his determination to remain, adding testily that he knew of no vacancies on the Court open to the ex-President. In March, the undaunted Taft decided to make an on-the-spot investigation for himself, and went to Washington to see the Chief Justice. There the disappointed heir-apparent heard White report that only a cataract condition prevented him from enjoying excellent health. The crestfallen Taft even went on to consult with White's personal physician, but left Washington with the crushing impression that the Chief Justice had no intention of stepping down, and that the approach of his own sixty-fourth birthday signalled the beginning of the end of his own most cherished desire. (See Mason, *Taft,* 76–87.)

Yet the next Chief Justice's wait proved to be much shorter than he anticipated. On May 13 an ambulance rushed the suddenly stricken White to a Washington hospital. The next day he rallied for a time, but then gradually drifted away to death on May 19. Two days later, the President led all of official Washington to St. Matthews Church for the requiem mass. Later, as the great-grandson of an immigrant Irish merchant was buried in Oak Hill Cemetery, the editorial tributes began to spread across the nation.

The fame and significance of Chief Justice White has naturally receded sharply with the passage of time, but perhaps undeservedly so, given his major legacy as well as his general philosophical approach. The Rule of Reason is an excellent example of traditional American unwillingness to allow precedents, fixed principles or set philosophical or ideological systems to interfere with material progress. By forcing through his Rule, White substantially contributed to changing the direction of the society's development. In so doing, he unconsciously employed the kind of pragmatism which has always been the essence of American problem-solving.

SELECTED BIBLIOGRAPHY

The most detailed study of Justice White is the uncritical work by Sister Marie Carolyn Klinkhamer, *Edward Douglas White, Chief Justice of the United States* (Washington, D.C., 1943). See also the same author's "The Legal Philosophy of Edward Douglas White," 35 *University of Detroit Law Journal* 174 (1957). Some additional information is in Lewis C. Cassidy's effusive "An Evaluation of Chief Justice White," 10 *Mississippi Law Journal* 136 (1938). Very valuable is Robert B. Dishman, "Mr. Justice White and the Rule of Reason," 13 *The Review of Politics* 229 (1951). His personal papers have not survived.

Edward Douglas White

REPRESENTATIVE OPINIONS

STANDARD OIL OF N.J. v. UNITED STATES, 221 U.S. 1 (1911)

This most significant case was resolved in a highly ironical fashion: the United States Government successfully prosecuted the Oil Trust under the Sherman Anti-Trust Act, but in so doing produced a legal benchmark which would henceforth effectively prevent the destruction of trusts *per se*. In this case, a federal district court had held that Standard Oil was in violation of the Sherman Act and therefore must be divided into its component parts. Standard Oil took its appeal to the Supreme Court, which upheld the district court ruling in a unanimous opinion delivered by the Chief Justice. In his argument, however, White based the Court's decision on the premise that Standard's business practices had been "unreasonable" in terms of the Sherman Act. This dictum left the clear implication that "reasonable" restraint of trade was not prohibited by the antitrust laws, a clear signal to the other giant corporations. Henceforth, federal indictments under the Sherman Act would be successfully countered by the corporations under this "rule of reason" as expounded by Edward Douglas White in 1911.

MR. CHIEF JUSTICE WHITE delivered the opinion of the court.

The Standard Oil Company of New Jersey and 33 other corporations, John D. Rockefeller, William Rockefeller and five other individual defendants prosecute this appeal to reverse a decree of the court below. Such decree was entered upon a bill filed by the United States under authority of § 4, of the act of July 2, 1890, c. 647, p. 209, known as the Anti-trust Act, and had for its object the enforcement of the provisions of that act. The record is inordinately voluminous, consisting of twenty-three volumes of printed matter, aggregating about twelve thousand pages, containing a vast amount of confusing and conflicting testimony relating to innumerable, complex and varied business transactions, extending over a period of nearly forty years. In an effort to pave the way to reach the subjects which we are called upon to consider, we propose at the outset, following the order of the bill, to give the merest possible outline of its contents, to summarize the answer, to indicate the course of the trial, and point out briefly the decision below rendered.

The bill and exhibits, covering one hundred and seventy pages of the printed record, were filed on November 15, 1906. Corporations known as Standard Oil Company of New Jersey, Standard Oil Company of California, Standard Oil Company of Indiana, Standard Oil Company of Iowa, Standard Oil Company of Kansas, Standard Oil Company of Kentucky, Standard Oil Company of Nebraska, Standard Oil Company of New York, Standard Oil Company of Ohio and sixty-two other corporations and partnerships, as also seven individuals were named as defendants. The bill was divided into thirty numbered sections, and sought relief upon the theory that the various defendants were engaged in conspiring "to restrain the trade and commerce in petroleum, commonly called 'crude oil,' in refined oil, and in the other products of petroleum, among the several States and Territories of the United States and the District of Columbia and with foreign nations, and to monopolize the said commerce." The conspiracy was alleged to have been formed in or about the year 1870 by three of the individual defendants, viz.: John D. Rockefeller, William Rockefeller and Henry M. Flagler. The detailed averments concerning the alleged conspiracy were arranged with reference to three periods, the first from 1870 to 1882, the second from 1882 to 1899, and the third from 1899 to the time of the filing of the bill.

The general charge concerning the period from 1870 to 1882 was as follows:

"That during said first period the said individual defendants, in connection with the Standard Oil Company of Ohio, purchased and obtained interests through stock ownership and otherwise in, and entered into agreements with, various persons, firms, corporations, and limited partnerships engaged in purchasing, shipping, refining, and selling petroleum and its products among the various States for the purpose of fixing the price of crude and refined oil and the products thereof, limiting the production thereof, and controlling the transportation therein, and thereby restraining trade and commerce among the several States, and monopolizing the said commerce."

To establish this charge it was averred that John D. and William Rockefeller and several other named individuals, who, prior to 1870, composed three separate partnerships engaged in the business of refining crude oil and shipping its products in interstate commerce, organized in the year 1870, a corporation known as the Standard Oil Company of Ohio and transferred to that company the business of the said partnerships, the members thereof becoming, in proportion to their prior ownership, stockholders in the corporation. It was averred that the other individual defendants soon afterwards became participants in the illegal combination and either transferred property to the corporation or to individuals to be held for the benefit of all parties in interest in proportion to their respective interests in the combination; that is, in proportion to their stock ownership in the Standard Oil Company of Ohio. By the means thus stated, it was charged that by the year 1872, the combination had acquired substantially all but three or four of the thirty-five or forty oil refineries located in Cleveland, Ohio. By reason of the power thus obtained and in further execution of the intent and purpose to restrain trade and to monopolize the commerce, interstate as well as intrastate, in petroleum and its products, the bill alleged that the combination and its members obtained large preferential rates and rebates in many and devious ways over their competitors from various railroad companies, and that by means of the advantage thus obtained many, if not virtually all, competitors were forced either to become members of the combination or were driven out of business; and thus, it was alleged, during the period in question the following results were brought about: *a.* That the combination, in addition to the refineries in Cleveland which it had acquired as previously stated, and which it had either dismantled to limit production or continued to operate, also from time to time acquired a large number of refineries of crude petroleum, situated in New York, Pennsylvania, Ohio and elsewhere. The properties thus acquired, like those previously obtained, although belonging to and being held for the benefit of the combination, were ostensibly divergently controlled, some of them being put in the name of the Standard Oil Company of Ohio, some in the name of corporations or limited partnerships affiliated therewith, or some being left in the name of the original owners who had become stockholders in the Standard Oil Company of Ohio and thus members of the alleged illegal combination. *b.* That the combination had obtained control of the pipe lines available for transporting oil from the oil fields to the refineries in Cleveland, Pittsburgh, Titusville, Philadelphia, New York and New Jersey. *c.* That the combination during the period named had obtained a complete mastery over the oil industry, controlling 90 per cent of the business of producing, shipping, refining and selling petroleum and its products, and thus was able to fix the price of crude and refined petroleum and to restrain and monopolize all interstate commerce in those products.

The averments bearing upon the second period (1882 to 1899) had relation to the claim:

"That during the said second period of conspiracy the defendants entered into a contract and trust agreement, by which various independent firms, corporations, limited partnerships and individuals engaged in purchasing, transporting, refining, shipping and selling oil and the products thereof among the various States turned over the management of their said business, corporations and limited partnerships to nine trustees, composed chiefly of certain individuals defendant herein, which said trust agreement was in restraint of trade and commerce and in violation of law, as hereinafter more particularly alleged."

The trust agreement thus referred to was set out in the bill. It was made in January, 1882. By its terms the stock of forty corporations, including the Standard Oil Company of Ohio, and a large quantity of various properties which had been previously acquired by the alleged combination and which was held in diverse forms, as we have previously indicated, for the benefit of the members of the combination, was vested in the trustees and their successors, "to be held for all parties in interest jointly." In the body of the trust agreement was contained a list of the various individuals and corporations and limited partnerships whose stockholders and members, or a portion thereof, became parties to the agreement. This list is in the margin.[1]

[1] *1st. All the stockholders and members of the following corporations and limited partnerships, to wit:*

Acme Oil Company, New York.
Acme Oil Company, Pennsylvania.
Atlantic Refining Company of Philadelphia.
Bush & Co. (Limited).
Camden Consolidated Oil Company.
Elizabethport Acid Works.
Imperial Refining Company (Limited).
Charles Pratt & Co.
Paine, Ablett & Co.
Standard Oil Company, Ohio.
Standard Oil Company, Pittsburgh.
Smith's Ferry Oil Transportation Company.
Solar Oil Company (Limited).
Sone & Fleming Manufacturing Company (Limited).

Also all the stockholders and members of such other corporations and limited partnerships as may hereafter join in this agreement at the request of the trustees herein provided for.

2d. The following individuals, to wit:

W. C. Andrews, John D. Archbold, Lide K. Arter, J. A. Bostwick, Benjamin Brewster, D. Bushnell, Thomas C. Bushnell, J. N. Camden, Henry L. Davis, H. M. Flagler, Mrs. H. M. Flagler, John Huntington, H. A. Hutchins, Charles F. G. Heye, A. B. Jennings, Charles Lockhart, A. M. McGregor, William H. Macy, William H. Macy, Jr., estate of Josiah Macy, William H. Macy, Jr., executor; O. H. Payne, A. J. Pouch, John D. Rockefeller, William Rockefeller, Henry H. Rogers, W. P. Thompson, J. J. Vandergrift, William T. Wardwell, W. G. Warden, Joseph L. Warden, Warden, Frew & Co., Louise C. Wheaton, H. M. Hanna, and George W. Chapin, D. M. Harkness, D. M. Harkness, trustee, S. V. Harkness, O. H. Payne, trustee; Charles Pratt, Horace A. Pratt, C. M. Pratt, Julia H. York, George H. Vilas, M. R. Keith, trustees, George F. Chester.

Also all such individuals as may hereafter join in the agreement at the request of the trustees herein provided for.

The agreement made provision for the method of controlling and managing the property by the trustees, for the formation of additional manufacturing, etc., corporations in various States, and the trust, unless terminated by a mode specified, was to continue "during the lives of the survivors and survivor of the trustees named in the agreement and for twenty-one years thereafter." The agreement provided for the issue of Standard Oil Trust certificates to represent the interest arising under the trust in the properties affected by the trust, which of course in view of the provisions of the agreement and the subject to which it related caused the interest in the certificates to be coincident with and the exact representative of the interest in the combination, that is, in the Standard Oil Company of Ohio. Soon afterwards it was alleged the trustees organized the Standard Oil Company of New Jersey and the Standard Oil Company of New York, the former having a capital stock of $3,000,000 and the latter a capital stock of $5,000,000, subsequently increased to $10,000,000 and $15,000,000 respectively. The bill alleged "that pursuant to said trust agreement the said trustees caused to be transferred to themselves the stocks of all corporations and limited partnerships named in said trust agreement, and caused various of the individuals and copartnerships, who owned apparently independent refineries and other properties employed in the business of refining and transporting and selling oil in and among said various States and Territories of the United States as aforesaid, to transfer their property situated in said several States to the respective Standard Oil Companies of said States of New York, New Jersey, Pennsylvania and Ohio, and other corporations organized or acquired by said trustees from time to time. . . ." For the stocks and property so acquired the trustees issued trust certificates. It was alleged that in 1888 the trustees "unlawfully controlled the stock and ownership of various corporations and limited partnerships

---

3d. A portion of the stockholders and members of the following corporations and limited partnerships, to wit:

American Lubricating Oil Company.
Baltimore United Oil Company.
Beacon Oil Company.
Bush & Denslow Manufacturing Company.
Central Refining Co. of Pittsburg.
Chesebrough Manufacturing Company.
Chess Carley Company.
Consolidated Tank Line Company.
Inland Oil Company.
Keystone Refining Company.
Maverick Oil Company.
National Transit Company.
Portland Kerosene Oil Company.
Producers' Consolidated Land and Petroleum Company.
Signal Oil Works (Limited).
Thompson & Bedford Company (Limited).
Devoe Manufacturing Company.
Eclipse Lubricating Oil Company (Limited).
Empire Refining Company (Limited).
Franklin Pipe Company (Limited).
Galena Oil Works (Limited).
Galena Farm Oil Company (Limited).
Germania Mining Company.
Vacuum Oil Company.
H. C. Van Tine & Company (Limited).
Waters-Pierce Oil Company.

Also stockholders and members (not being all thereof) of other corporations and limited partnerships who may hereafter join in this agreement at the request of the trustees herein provided for."

engaged in such purchase and transportation, refining, selling, and shipping of oil," as per a list which is excerpted in the margin.[1]

The bill charged that during the second period quo warranto proceedings were commenced against the Standard Oil Company of Ohio, which resulted in the entry by the Supreme Court of Ohio, on March 2, 1892, of a decree adjudging the trust agreement to be void, not only because the Standard Oil

[1] *List of Corporations the Stocks of Which Were Wholly or Partially Held by the Trustees of Standard Oil Trust,*

	Capital Stock.	S. O. trust ownership.
New York State:		
Acme Oil Company, manufacturers of petroleum products.	$300,00	Entire.
Atlas Refining Company, manufacturers of petroleum products.	200,000	Do.
American Wick Manufacturing Company, manufacturers of lamp wicks.	25,000	Do.
Bush & Denslow Manufacturing Company, manufacturers of petroleum products.	300,000	50 per cent.
Chesebrough Manufacturing Company, manufacturers of petroleum.	500,000	2,661–5,000
Central Refining Company (Limited), manufacturers of petroleum products.	200,000	1–67.2 per ct.
Devoe Manufacturing Company, packers, manufacturers of petroleum.	300,000	Entire.
Empire Refining Company (Limited), manufacturers of petroleum products.	100,000	80 per cent.
Oswego Manufacturing Company, manufacturers of wood cases.	100,000	Entire.
Pratt Manufacturing Company, manufacturers of petroleum products.	500,000	Do.
Standard Oil Company of New York, manufacturers of petroleum products.	5,000,000	Do.
Sone & Fleming Manufacturing Company (Limited), manufacturers of petroleum products.	250,000	Do.
Thompson & Bedford Company (Limited), manufacturers of petroleum products.	250,000	80 per cent.
Vacuum Oil Company, manufacturers of petroleum products.	25,000	75 per cent.
New Jersey:		
Eagle Oil Company, manufacturers of petroleum products.	350,000	Entire.
McKirgan Oil Company, jobbers of petroleum products.	75,000	Do.
Standard Oil Company of New Jersey, manufacturers of petroleum products.	3,000,000	Do.
Pennsylvania:		
Acme Oil Company, manufacturers of petroleum products.	300,000	Do.
Atlantic Refining Company, manufacturers of petroleum products.	400,000	Do.
Galena Oil Works (Limited), manufacturers of petroleum products.	150,000	86¼ per cent.
Imperial Refining Company (Limited), manufacturers of petroleum products.	300,000	Entire.
Producers' Consolidated Land and Petroleum Company, producers of crude oil.	1,000,000	65/132 per cent.
National Transit Company, transporters of crude oil.	25,455,200	94 per cent.
Standard Oil Company, manufacturers of petroleum products.	400,000	Entire.
Signal Oil Works (Limited), manufacturers of petroleum products.	100,000	38¾ per cent.

Company of Ohio was a party to the same, but also because the agreement in and of itself was in restraint of trade and amounted to the creation of an unlawful monopoly. It was alleged that shortly after this decision, seemingly for the purpose of complying therewith, voluntary proceedings were had apparently to dissolve the trust, but that these proceedings were a subterfuge and a sham because they simply amounted to a transfer of the stock held by the trust in 64 of the companies which it controlled to some of the remaining 20 companies, it having controlled before the decree 84 in all, thereby, while seemingly in part giving up its dominion, yet in reality preserving the same by means of the control of the companies as to which it had retained complete authority. It was charged that especially was this the case, as the stock in the companies selected for transfer was virtually owned by the nine trustees or the members of their immediate families or associates. The bill further alleged that in 1897 the Attorney-General of Ohio instituted contempt proceedings in the quo warranto case based upon the claim that the trust had not been dissolved as required by the decree in that case. About the same time also proceedings in quo warranto were commenced to forfeit the charter of a pipe line known as the Buckeye Pipe Line Company, an Ohio corporation, whose stock, it was alleged, was owned by the members of the combination, on the ground of its connection with the trust which had been held to be illegal.

The result of these proceedings, the bill charged, caused a resort to the alleged wrongful acts asserted to have been committed during the third period, as follows:

"That during the third period of said conspiracy and in pursuance thereof the said individual defendants operated through the Standard Oil Company of New Jersey, as a holding corporation, which corporation obtained and acquired the majority of the stocks of the various corporations engaged in purchasing, transporting, refining, shipping, and selling oil into and among the various States and Territories of the United States and the District of Columbia and with foreign nations, and thereby managed

	Capital Stock.	S. O. trust ownership.
Ohio:		
Consolidated Tank-Line Company, jobbers of petroleum products.	1,000,000	57 per cent.
Inland Oil Company, jobbers of petroleum products.	50,000	50 per cent.
Standard Oil Company, manufacturers of petroleum products.	3,500,000	Entire.
Solar Refining Company, manufacturers of petroleum products.	500,000	Do.
Kentucky:		
Standard Oil Company, jobbers of petroleum products.	600,000	Do.
Maryland:		
Baltimore United Oil Company, manufacturers of petroleum products.	600,000	5,059–6,000
West Virginia:		
Camden Consolidated Oil Company, manufacturers of petroleum products.	200,000	51 per cent.
Minnesota:		
Standard Oil Company, jobbers of petroleum products.	100,000	Entire.
Missouri:		
Waters-Pierce Oil Company, jobbers of petroleum products.	400,000	50 per cent.
Massachusetts:		
Beacon Oil Company, jobbers of petroleum products.	100,000	Entire.
Maverick Oil Company, jobbers of petroleum products.	100,000	Do.
Maine:		
Portland Kerosene Oil Company, jobbers of petroleum products.	200,000	Do.
Iowa:		
Standard Oil Company, jobbers of petroleum products.	600,000	60 per cent.
Continental Oil Company, jobbers of petroleum products.	300,000	62½ per cent.

and controlled the same, in violation of the laws of the United States, as hereinafter more particularly alleged."

It was alleged that in or about the month of January, 1899, the individual defendants caused the charter of the Standard Oil Company of New Jersey to be amended; "so that the business and objects of said company were stated as follows, to wit: 'To do all kinds of mining, manufacturing, and trading business; transporting goods and merchandise by land or water in any manner; to buy, sell, lease, and improve land; build houses, structures, vessels, cars, wharves, docks, and piers; to lay and operate pipe lines; to erect lines for conducting electricity; to enter into and carry out contracts of every kind pertaining to its business; to acquire, use, sell, and grant licenses under patent rights; to purchase or otherwise acquire, hold, sell, assign, and transfer shares of capital stock and bonds or other evidences of indebtedness of corporations, and to exercise all the privileges of ownership, including voting upon the stock so held; to carry on its business and have offices and agencies therefor in all parts of the world, and to hold, purchase, mortgage, and convey real estate and personal property outside the State of New Jersey.' "

The capital stock of the company—which since March 19, 1892, had been $10,000,000—was increased to $110,000,000; and the individual defendants, as theretofore, continued to be a majority of the board of directors.

Without going into detail it suffices to say that it was alleged in the bill that shortly after these proceedings the trust came to an end, the stock of the various corporations which had been controlled by it being transferred by its holders to the Standard Oil Company of New Jersey, which corporation issued therefor certificates of its common stock to the amount of $97,250,000. The bill contained allegations referring to the development of new oil fields, for example, in California, southeastern Kansas, northern Indian Territory, and northern Oklahoma, and made reference to the building or otherwise acquiring by the combination of refineries and pipe lines in the new fields for the purpose of restraining and monopolizing the interstate trade in petroleum and its products.

Reiterating in substance the averments that both the Standard Oil Trust from 1882 to 1899 and the Standard Oil Company of New Jersey since 1899 had monopolized and restrained interstate commerce in petroleum and its products, the bill at great length additionally set forth various means by which during the second and third periods, in addition to the effect occasioned by the combination of alleged previously independent concerns, the monopoly and restraint complained of was continued. Without attempting to follow the elaborate averments on these subjects spread over fifty-seven pages of the printed record, it suffices to say that such averments may properly be grouped under the following heads: Rebates, preferences and other discriminatory practises in favor of the combination by railroad companies; restraint and monopolization by control of pipe lines, and unfair practises against competing pipe lines; contracts with competitors in restraint of trade; unfair methods of competition, such as local price cutting at the points where necessary to suppress competition; espionage of the business of competitors, the operation of bogus independent companies, and payment of rebates on oil, with the like intent; the division of the United States into districts and the limiting of the operations of the various subsidiary corporations as to such districts so that competition in the sale of petroleum products between such corporations had been entirely eliminated and destroyed; and finally reference was made to what was alleged to be the "enormous and unreasonable profits" earned by the Standard Oil Trust and the Standard Oil Company as a result of the alleged monopoly; which presumably was averred as a means of reflexly inferring the scope and power acquired by the alleged combination.

Coming to the prayer of the bill, it suffices to say that in general terms the substantial relief asked was, first, that the combination in restraint of interstate trade and commerce and which had monopolized the same, as alleged in the bill, be found to have existence and that the parties thereto be perpetually enjoined from doing any further act to give effect to it; second, that the transfer of the stocks of the various corporations to the Standard Oil Company of New Jersey, as alleged in the bill, be held to be in violation of the first and second sections of the Anti-trust Act, and that the Standard Oil Company of New Jersey be enjoined and restrained from in any manner continuing to exert control over the subsidiary corporations by means of ownership of said stock or otherwise; third, that specific relief by injunction be awarded against further violation of the statute by any of the acts specifically complained of in the bill. There was also a prayer for general relief.

Of the numerous defendants named in the bill, the Waters-Pierce Oil Company was the only resident of the district in which the suit was commenced and the only defendant served with process therein. Contemporaneous with the filing of the bill the court made an order, under § 5 of the Anti-trust Act, for the service of process upon all the other defendants, wherever they could be found. Thereafter the various defendants unsuccessfully moved to vacate the order for service on non-resident defendants or filed pleas to the jurisdiction. Joint exceptions were likewise unsuccessfully filed, upon the ground of impertinence, to many of the averments of the bill of complaint, particularly those which related to acts alleged to have been done by the combination prior to the passage of the Anti-trust Act and prior to the year 1899.

Certain of the defendants filed separate answers, and a joint answer was filed on behalf of the Standard Oil Company of New Jersey and numerous of the other defendants. The scope of the answers will be adequately indicated by quoting a summary on the subject made in the brief for the appellants.

"It is sufficient to say that, whilst admitting many of the alleged acquisitions of property, the formation of the so-called trust of 1882, its dissolution in 1892, and the acquisition by the Standard Oil Company of New Jersey of the stocks of the various corporations in 1899, they deny all the allegations respecting combinations or conspiracies to restrain or monopolize the oil trade; and particularly that the so-called trust of 1882, or the acquisition of the shares of the defendant companies by the Standard Oil Company of New Jersey in 1899, was a combination of *independent or competing* concerns or corporations. The averments of the petition respecting the means adopted to monopolize the oil trade are traversed either by a denial of the acts alleged or of their purpose, intent or effect."

On June 24, 1907, the cause being at issue, a special examiner was appointed to take the evidence, and his report was filed March 22, 1909. It was heard on April 5 to 10, 1909, under the expediting act of February 11, 1903, before a Circuit Court consisting of four judges.

The court decided in favor of the United States. In the opinion delivered, all the multitude of acts of wrongdoing charged in the bill were put aside, in so far as they were alleged to have been committed prior to the passage of the Anti-trust Act, "except as evidence of their (the defendants') purpose, of their continuing conduct and of its effect." (173 Fed. Rep. 177.)

By the decree which was entered it was adjudged that the combining of the stocks of various companies in the hands of the Standard Oil Company of New Jersey in 1899 constituted a combination in restraint of trade and also an attempt to monopolize and a monopolization under § 2 of the Anti-trust Act. The decree was against seven individual defendants, the Standard Oil Company of New Jersey, thirty-six domestic companies and one foreign company which the Standard Oil Company of New Jersey controls by stock ownership; these 38 corporate defendants being held to be parties to the combination found to exist.[1]

The bill was dismissed as to all other corporate defendants, 33 in number, it being adjudged by § 3 of the decree that they "have not been proved to be engaged in the operation or carrying out of the combination."[2]

The Standard Oil Company of New Jersey was enjoined from voting the stocks or exerting any control over the said 37 subsidiary companies, and the subsidiary companies were enjoined from paying any dividends as to the Standard Oil Company or permitting it to exercise any control over them by virtue of the stock ownership or power acquired by means of the combination. The individuals and corporations were also enjoined from entering into or carrying into effect any like combination which

[1] *Counsel for appellants says: "Of the 38 (37) corporate defendants named in section 2 of the decree and as to which the judgment of the court applies, four have not appealed, to wit: Corsicana Refining Co., Manhattan Oil Co., Security Oil Co., Waters-Pierce Oil Co., and one, the Standard Oil Co. of Iowa, has been liquidated and no longer exists."*

[2] *Of the dismissed defendants 16 were natural gas companies and 10 were companies which were liquidated and ceased to exist before the filing of the petition. The other dismissed defendants, 7 in number, were: Florence Oil Refining Co., United Oil Co., Tidewater Oil Co., Tide Water Pipe Co. (L't'd), Platt & Washburn Refining Co., Franklin Pipe Co. and Pennsylvania Oil Co.*

would evade the decree. Further, the individual defendants, the Standard Oil Company, and the 37 subsidiary corporations were enjoined from engaging or continuing in interstate commerce in petroleum or its products during the continuance of the illegal combination.

At the outset a question of jurisdiction requires consideration, and we shall, also, as a preliminary, dispose of another question, to the end that our attention may be completely concentrated upon the merits of the controversy when we come to consider them.

First. We are of opinion that in consequence of the presence within the district of the Waters-Pierce Oil Company, the court, under the authority of § 5 of the Anti-trust Act, rightly took jurisdiction over the cause and properly ordered notice to be served upon the non-resident defendants.

Second. The overruling of the exceptions taken to so much of the bill as counted upon facts occurring prior to the passage of the Anti-trust Act,—whatever may be the view as an original question of the duty to restrict the controversy to a much narrower area than that propounded by the bill,—we think by no possibility in the present stage of the case can the action of the court be treated as prejudicial error justifying reversal. We say this because the court, as we shall do, gave no weight to the testimony adduced under the averments complained of except in so far as it tended to throw light upon the acts done after the passage of the Anti-trust Act and the results of which it was charged were being participated in and enjoyed by the alleged combination at the time of the filing of the bill.

We are thus brought face to face with the merits of the controversy.

Both as to the law and as to the facts the opposing contentions pressed in the argument are numerous and in all their aspects are so irreconcilable that it is difficult to reduce them to some fundamental generalization, which by being disposed of would decide them all. For instance, as to the law. While both sides agree that the determination of the controversy rests upon the correct construction and application of the first and second sections of the Anti-trust Act, yet the views as to the meaning of the act are as wide apart as the poles, since there is no real point of agreement on any view of the act. And this also is the case as to the scope and effect of authorities relied upon, even although in some instances one and the same authority is asserted to be controlling.

So also is it as to the facts. Thus, on the one hand, with relentless pertinacity and minuteness of analysis, it is insisted that the facts establish that the assailed combination took its birth in a purpose to unlawfully acquire wealth by oppressing the public and destroying the just rights of others, and that its entire career exemplifies an inexorable carrying out of such wrongful intents, since, it is asserted, the pathway of the combination from the beginning to the time of the filing of the bill is marked with constant proofs of wrong inflicted upon the public and is strewn with the wrecks resulting from crushing out, without regard to law, the individual rights of others. Indeed, so conclusive, it is urged, is the proof on these subjects that it is asserted that the existence of the principal corporate defendant—the Standard Oil Company of New Jersey—with the vast accumulation of property which it owns or controls, because of its infinite potency for harm and the dangerous example which its continued existence affords, is an open and enduring menace to all freedom of trade and is a byword and reproach to modern economic methods. On the other hand, in a powerful analysis of the facts, it is insisted that they demonstrate that the origin and development of the vast business which the defendants control was but the result of lawful competitive methods, guided by economic genius of the highest order, sustained by courage, by a keen insight into commercial situations, resulting in the acquisition of great wealth, but at the same time serving to stimulate and increase production, to widely extend the distribution of the products of petroleum at a cost largely below that which would have otherwise prevailed, thus proving to be at one and the same time a benefaction to the general public as well as of enormous advantage to individuals. It is not denied that in the enrmous volume of proof contained in the record in the period of almost a lifetime to which that proof is addressed, there may be found acts of wrongdoing, but the insistence is that they were rather the exception than the rule, and in most cases were either the result of too great individual zeal in the keen rivalries of business or of the methods and habits of dealing which, even if wrong, were commonly practised at the time. And to discover and state the truth concerning these contentions both arguments call for the analysis and weighing, as we have said at the outset, of a jungle of conflicting testimony covering a period of forty years, a duty difficult to rightly perform and, even if satisfactorily accomplished, almost impossible to state with any reasonable regard to brevity.

Duly appreciating the situation just stated, it is certain that only one point of concord between the parties is discernible, which is, that the controversy in every aspect is controlled by a correct conception of the meaning of the first and second sections of the Anti-trust Act. We shall therefore—departing from what otherwise would be the natural order of analysis—make this one point of harmony the initial basis of our examination of the contentions, relying upon the conception that by doing so some harmonious resonance may result adequate to dominate and control the discord with which the case abounds. That is to say, we shall first come to consider the meaning of the first and second sections of the Anti-trust Act by the text, and after discerning what by that process appears to be its true meaning we shall proceed to consider the respective contentions of the parties concerning the act, the strength or weakness of those contentions, as well as the accuracy of the meaning of the act as deduced from the text in the light of the prior decisions of this court concerning it. When we have done this we shall then approach the facts. Following this course we shall make our investigation under four separate headings: First. The text of the first and second sections of the act originally considered and its meaning in the light of the common law and the law of this country at the time of its adoption. Second. The contentions of the parties concerning the act, and the scope and effect of the decisions of this court upon which they rely. Third. The application of the statute to facts, and, Fourth. The remedy, if any, to be afforded as the result of such application.

First. The text of the act and its meaning.

We quote the text of the first and second sections of the act, as follows:

"Section 1. Every contract, combination in the form of trust or otherwise, or conspiracy, in restraint of trade or commerce, among the several States, or with foreign nations, is hereby declared to be illegal. Every person who shall make any such contract, or engage in any such combination or conspiracy, shall be deemed guilty of a misdemeanor, and, on conviction thereof, shall be punished by fine not exceeding five thousand dollars, or by imprisonment not exceeding one year, or by both said punishments, in the discretion of the court.

"Sec. 2. Every person who shall monopolize, or attempt to monopolize, or combine or conspire with any other person or persons, to monopolize any part of the trade or commerce among the several States, or with foreign nations, shall be deemed guilty of a misdemeanor, and, on conviction thereof, shall be punished by fine not exceeding five thousand dollars, or by imprisonment not exceeding one year, or by both said punishments, in the discretion of the court."

The debates show that doubt as to whether there was a common law of the United States which governed the subject in the absence of legislation was among the influences leading to the passage of the act. They conclusively show, however, that the main cause which led to the legislation was the thought that it was required by the economic condition of the times, that is, the vast accumulation of wealth in the hands of corporations and individuals, the enormous development of corporate organization, the facility for combination which such organizations afforded, the fact that the facility was being used, and that combinations known as trusts were being multiplied, and the widespread impression that their power had been and would be exerted to oppress individuals and injure the public generally. Although debates may not be used as a means for interpreting a statute (*United States* v. *Trans-Missouri Freight Association,* 166 U.S. 318, and cases cited) that rule in the nature of things is not violated by resorting to debates as a means of ascertaining the environment at the time of the enactment of a particular law, that is, the history of the period when it was adopted.

There can be no doubt that the sole subject with which the first section deals is restraint of trade as therein contemplated, and that the attempt to monopolize and monopolization is the subject with which the second section is concerned. It is certain that those terms, at least in their rudimentary meaning, took their origin in the common law, and were also familiar in the law of this country prior to and at the time of the adoption of the act in question.

We shall endeavor then, first to seek their meaning, not by indulging in an elaborate and learned analysis of the English law and of the law of this country, but by making a very brief reference to the elementary and indisputable conceptions of both the English and American law on the subject prior to the passage of the Anti-trust Act.

a. It is certain that at a very remote period the words "contract in restraint of trade" in England came to refer to some voluntary restraint put by contract by an individual on his right to carry on his trade or calling. Originally all such contracts were considered to be illegal, because it was deemed they were injurious to the public as well as to the individuals who made them. In the interest of the freedom of individuals to contract this doctrine was modified so that it was only when a restraint by contract was so general as to be coterminous with the kingdom that it was treated as void. That is to say, if the restraint was partial in its operation and was otherwise reasonable the contract was held to be valid:

b. Monopolies were defined by Lord Coke as follows:

" 'A monopoly is an institution, or allowance by the king by his grant, commission, or otherwise to any person or persons, bodies politic or corporate, of or for the sole buying, selling, making, working, or using of anything, whereby any person or persons, bodies politic or corporate, are sought to be restrained of any freedom or liberty that they had before, or hindered in their lawful trade.' (3 Inst. 181, c. 85.)"

Hawkins thus defined them:

" 'A monopoly is an allowance by the king to a particular person or persons of the sole buying, selling, making, working, or using of anything whereby the subject in general is restrained from the freedom of manufacturing or trading which he had before.' (Hawk. P. C. bk. 1, c. 29.)"

The frequent granting of monopolies and the struggle which led to a denial of the power to create them, that is to say, to the establishment that they were incompatible with the English constitution is known to all and need not be reviewed. The evils which led to the public outcry against monopolies and to the final denial of the power to make them may be thus summarily stated: 1. The power which the monopoly gave to the one who enjoyed it to fix the price and thereby injure the public; 2. The power which it engendered of enabling a limitation on production; and, 3. The danger of deterioration in quality of the monopolized article which it was deemed was the inevitable resultant of the monopolistic control over its production and sale. As monopoly as thus conceived embraced only a consequence arising from an exertion of sovereign power, no express restrictions or prohibitions obtained against the creation by an individual of a monopoly as such. But as it was considered, at least so far as the necessaries of life were concerned, that individuals by the abuse of their right to contract might be able to usurp the power arbitrarily to enhance prices, one of the wrongs arising from monopoly, it came to be that laws were passed relating to offenses such as forestalling, regrating and engrossing by which prohibitions were placed upon the power of individuals to deal under such circumstances and conditions as, according to the conception of the times, created a presumption that the dealings were not simply the honest exertion of one's right to contract for his own benefit unaccompanied by a wrongful motive to injure others, but were the consequence of a contract or course of dealing of such a character as to give rise to the presumption of an intent to injure others through the means, for instance, of a monopolistic increase of prices. This is illustrated by the definition of engrossing found in the statute, 5 and 6 Edw. VI, ch. 14, as follows:

"Whatsoever person or persons . . . shall engross or get into his or their hands by buying, contracting, or promise-taking, other than by demise, grant, or lease of land, or tithe, any corn growing in the fields, or any other corn or grain, butter, cheese, fish, or other dead victual, whatsoever, within the realm of England, to the intent to sell the same again, shall be accepted, reputed, and taken an unlawful engrosser or engrossers."

As by the statutes providing against engrossing the quantity engrossed was not required to be the whole or a proximate part of the whole of an article, it is clear that there was a wide difference between monopoly and engrossing, etc. But as the principal wrong which it was deemed would result from monopoly, that is, an enhancement of the price, was the same wrong to which it was thought the prohibited engrossment would give rise, it came to pass that monopoly and engrossing were regarded as virtually one and the same thing. In other words, the prohibited act of engrossing because of its inevitable accomplishment of one of the evils deemed to be engendered by monopoly, came to be referred to as being a monopoly or constituting an attempt to monopolize. Thus

Pollexfen, in his argument in *East India Company* v. *Sandys,* Skin. 165, 169, said:

"By common law, he said that trade is free, and for that cited 3 Inst. 81; F. B. 65; 1 Roll. 4; that the common law is as much against 'monopoly' as 'engrossing;' and that they differ only, that a 'monopoly' is by patent from the king, the other is by the act of the subject between party and party; but that the mischiefs are the same from both, and there is the same law against both. Moore, 673; 11 Rep. 84. The sole trade of anything is 'engrossing' *ex rei natura,* for whosoever hath the sole trade of buying and selling hath 'engrossed' that trade; and whosoever hath the sole trade to any country, hath the sole trade of buying and selling the produce of that country, at his own price, which is an 'engrossing.'"

And by operation of the mental process which led to considering as a monopoly acts which although they did not constitute a monopoly were thought to produce some of its baneful effects, so also because of the impediment or burden to the due course of trade which they produced, such acts came to be referred to as in restraint of trade. This is shown by my Lord Coke's definition of monopoly as being "an institution or allowance . . . whereby any person or persons, bodies politic or corporate, are sought to be restrained of any freedom or liberty that they had before or hindered in their lawful trade." It is illustrated also by the definition whch Hawkins gives of monopoly wherein it is said that the effect of monopoly is to restrain the citizen "from the freedom of manufacturing or trading which he had before." And see especially the opinion of Parker, C. J., in *Mitchel* v. *Reynolds* (1711), 1 P. Williams, 181, where a classification is made of monopoly which brings it generically within the description of restraint of trade.

Generalizing these considerations, the situation is this: 1. That by the common law monopolies were unlawful because of their restriction upon individual freedom of contract and their injury to the public. 2. That as to necessaries of life the freedom of the individual to deal was restricted where the nature and character of the dealing was such as to engender the presumption of intent to bring about at least one of the injuries which it was deemed would result from monopoly, that is an undue enhancement of price. 3. That to protect the freedom of contract of the individual not only in his own interest, but principally in the interest of the common weal, a contract of an individual by which he put an unreasonable restraint upon himself as to carrying on his trade or business was void. And that at common law the evils consequent upon engrossing, etc., caused those things to be treated as coming within monopoly and sometimes to be called monopoly and the same considerations caused monopoly because of its operation and effect, to be brought within and spoken of generally as impeding the due course of or being in restraint of trade.

From the development of more accurate economic conceptions and the changes in conditions of society it came to be recognized that the acts prohibited by the engrossing, forestalling, etc., statutes did not have the harmful tendency which they were presumed to have when the legislation concerning them was enacted, and therefore did not justify the presumption which had previously been deduced from them, but, on the contrary, such acts tended to fructify and develop trade. See the statutes of 12th George III, ch. 71, enacted in 1772, and statute of 7 and 8 Victoria, ch. 24, enacted in 1844, repealing the prohibitions against engrossing, forestalling, etc., upon the express ground that the prohibited acts had come to be considered as favorable to the development of and not in restraint of trade. It is remarkable that nowhere at common law can there be found a prohibition against the creation of monopoly by an individual. This would seem to manifest, either consciously or intuitively, a profound conception as to the inevitable operation of economic forces and the equipoise or balance in favor of the protection of the rights of individuals which resulted. That is to say, as it was deemed that monopoly in the concrete could only arise from an act of sovereign power, and, such sovereign power being restrained, prohibitions as to individuals were directed, not against the creation of monopoly, but were only applied to such acts in relation to particular subjects as to which it was deemed, if not restrained, some of the consequences of monopoly might result. After all, this was but an instinctive recognition of the truisms that the course of trade could not be made free by obstructing it, and that an individual's right to trade could not be protected by destroying such right.

From the review just made it clearly results that outside of the restrictions resulting from the want of power in an individual to voluntarily and unreasonably restrain his right to carry on his trade or business and outside of the want of right to restrain the free course of trade by contracts or acts which implied a wrongful purpose, freedom to contract and to abstain from contracting and to exercise every reasonable right incident thereto became the rule in the English law. The scope and effect of this freedom to trade and contract is clearly shown by the decision in *Mogul Steamship Co.* v. *McGregor* (1892), A. C. 25. While it is true that the decision of the House of Lords in the case in question was announced shortly after the passage of the Anti-trust Act, it serves reflexly to show the exact state of the law in England at the time the Anti-trust statute was enacted.

In this country also the acts from which it was deemed there resulted a part if not all of the injurious consequences ascribed to monopoly, came to be referred to as a monopoly itself. In other words, here as had been the case in England, practical common sense caused attention to be concentrated not upon the theoretically correct name to be given to the condition or acts which gave rise to a harmful result, but to the result itself and to the remedying of the evils which it produced. The statement just made is illustrated by an early statute of the Province of Massachusetts, that is, chap. 31 of the laws of 1778–1779, by which monopoly and forestalling were expressly treated as one and the same thing.

It is also true that while the principles concerning contracts in restraint of trade, that is, voluntary restraint put by a person on his right to pursue his calling, hence only operating subjectively, came generally to be recognized in accordance with the English rule, it came moreover to pass that contracts or acts which it was considered had a monopolistic tendency, especially those which were thought to unduly diminish competition and hence to enhance prices—in other words, to monopolize—came also in a generic sense to be spoken of and treated as they had been in England, as restricting the due course of trade, and therefore as being in restraint of trade. The dread of monopoly as an emanation of governmental power, while it passed at an early date out of mind in this country, as a result of the structure of our Government, did not serve to assuage the fear as to the evil consequences which might arise from the acts of individuals producing or tending to produce the consequences of monopoly. It resulted that treating such acts as we have said as amounting to monopoly, sometimes constitutional restrictions, again legislative enactments or judicial decisions, served to enforce and illustrate the purpose to prevent the occurrence of the evils recognized in the mother country as consequent upon monopoly, by providing against contracts or acts of individuals or combinations of individuals or corporations deemed to be conducive to such results. To refer to the constitutional or legislative provisions on the subject or many judicial decisions which illustrate it would unnecessarily prolong this opinion. We append in the margin a note to treatises, &c., wherein are contained references to constitutional and statutory provisions and to numerous decisions, etc., relating to the subject.[1]

It will be found that as modern conditions arose the trend of legislation and judicial decision came more and more to adapt the recognized restrictions to new manifestations of conduct or of dealing which it was thought justified the inference of intent to do the wrongs which it had been the purpose to prevent from the beginning. The evolution is clearly pointed out in *National Cotton Oil Co.* v. *Texas,* 197 U.S. 115, and *Shawnee Compress Co.* v. *Anderson,* 209 U.S. 423; and, indeed, will be found to be illustrated in various aspects by the decisions of this court which have been concerned with the enforcement of the act we are now considering.

Without going into detail and but very briefly surveying the whole field, it may be with accuracy said that the dread of enhancement of prices and of other wrongs which it was thought would flow from the undue limitation on competitive conditions caused by contracts or other acts of individuals or corporations, led, as a matter of public policy, to the prohibition or treating as illegal all contracts or acts which were unreasonably restrictive of competitive conditions, either from the nature or character of the contract or act or where the surrounding circumstances were such as to justify the conclusion that they had not been entered into or performed with the legitimate purpose of reasonably forwarding personal interest and developing trade, but on the contrary were of such a character as to give

[1] *Puddy's Beach on Private Corporations, vol. 2, pp. 1403,* et seq., *chapter on Trusts and Monopolies; Cooke on Trade and Labor Combinations, App. II, pp. 194–195; Am.* N *Eng. Ency. Law, 2d ed., article "Monopolies and Trusts," pp. 844,* et seq.

rise to the inference or presumption that they had been entered into or done with the intent to do wrong to the general public and to limit the right of individuals, thus restraining the free flow of commerce and tending to bring about the evils, such as enhancement of prices, which were considered to be against public policy. It is equally true to say that the survey of the legislation in this country on this subject from the beginning will show, depending as it did upon the economic conceptions which obtained at the time when the legislation was adopted or judicial decision was rendered, that contracts or acts were at one time deemed to be of such a character as to justify the inference of wrongful intent which were at another period thought not to be of that character. But this again, as we have seen, simply followed the line of development of the law of England.

Let us consider the language of the first and second sections, guided by the principle that where words are employed in a statute which had at the time a well-known meaning at common law or in the law of this country they are presumed to have been used in that sense unless the context compels to the contrary.[1]

As to the first section, the words to be interpreted are: "Every contract, combination in the form of trust or otherwise, or conspiracy in restraint of trade or commerce . . . is hereby declared to be illegal." As there is no room for dispute that the statute was intended to formulate a rule for the regulation of interstate and foreign commerce, the question is what was the rule which it adopted?

In view of the common law and the law in this country as to restraint of trade, which we have reviewed, and the illuminating effect which that history must have under the rule to which we have referred, we think it results:

a. That the context manifests that the statute was drawn in the light of the existing practical conception of the law of restraint of trade, because it groups as within that class, not only contracts which were in restraint of trade in the subjective sense, but all contracts or acts which theoretically were attempts to monopolize, yet which in practice had come to be considered as in restraint of trade in a broad sense.

b. That in view of the many new forms of contracts and combinations which were being evolved from existing economic conditions, it was deemed essential by an all-embracing enumeration to make sure that no form of contract or combination by which an undue restraint of interstate or foreign commerce was brought about could save such restraint from condemnation. The statute under this view evidenced the intent not to restrain the right to make and enforce contracts, whether resulting from combination or otherwise, which did not unduly restrain interstate or foreign commerce, but to protect that commerce from being restrained by methods, whether old or new, which would constitute an interference that is an undue restraint.

c. And as the contracts or acts embraced in the provision were not expressly defined, since the enumeration addressed itself simply to classes of acts, those classes being broad enough to embrace every conceivable contract or combination which could be made concerning trade or commerce or the subjects of such commerce, and thus caused any act done by any of the enumerated methods anywhere in the whole field of human activity to be illegal if in restraint of trade, it inevitably follows that the provision necessarily called for the exercise of judgment which required that some standard should be resorted to for the purpose of determining whether the prohibitions contained in the statute had or had not in any given case been violated. Thus not specifying but indubitably contemplating and requiring a standard, it follows that it was intended that the standard of reason which had been applied at the common law and in this country in dealing with subjects of the character embraced by the statute, was intended to be the measure used for the purpose of determining whether in a given case a particular act had or had not brought about the wrong against which the statute provided.

And a consideration of the text of the second section serves to establish that it was intended to supplement the first and to make sure that by no possible guise could the public policy embodied in the first section be frustrated or evaded. The prohibitions of the second embrace "Every person who shall monopolize, or attempt to monopolize, or combine or conspire with any other person or persons, to monopolize any part of the

[1] Swearingen *v.* United States, *161 U.S. 446;* United States *v.* Wong Kim Ark, *169 U.S. 649;* Keck *v.* United States, *172 U.S. 446;* Kepner *v.* United States, *195 U.S. 100, 126.*

trade or commerce among the several states, or with foreign nations, . . ." By reference to the terms of § 8 it is certain that the word person clearly implies a corporation as well as an individual.

The commerce referred to by the words "any part" construed in the light of the manifest purpose of the statute has both a geographical and a distributive significance, that is it includes any portion of the United States and any one of the classes of things forming a part of interstate or foreign commerce.

Undoubtedly, the words "to monopolize" and "monopolize" as used in the section reach every act bringing about the prohibited results. The ambiguity, if any, is involved in determining what is intended by monopolize. But this ambiguity is readily dispelled in the light of the previous history of the law of restraint of trade to which we have referred and the indication which it gives of the practical evolution by which monopoly and the acts which produce the same result as monopoly, that is, an undue restraint of the course of trade, all came to be spoken of as, and to be indeed synonymous with, restraint of trade. In other words, having by the first section forbidden all means of monopolizing trade, that is, unduly restraining it by means of every contract, combination, etc., the second section seeks, if possible, to make the prohibitions of the act all the more complete and perfect by embracing all attempts to reach the end prohibited by the first section, that is, restraints of trade, by any attempt to monopolize, or monopolization thereof, even although the acts by which such results are attempted to be brought about or are brought about be not embraced within the general enumeration of the first section. And, of course, when the second section is thus harmonized with and made as it was intended to be the complement of the first, it becomes obvious that the criteria to be resorted to in any given case for the purpose of ascertaining whether violations of the section have been committed, is the rule of reason guided by the established law and by the plain duty to enforce the prohibitions of the act and thus the public policy which its restrictions were obviously enacted to subserve. And it is worthy of observation, as we have previously remarked concerning the common law, that although the statute by the comprehensiveness of the enumerations embodied in both the first and second sections makes it certain that its purpose was to prevent undue restraints of every kind or nature, nevertheless by the omission of any direct prohibition against monopoly in the concrete it indicates a consciousness that the freedom of the individual right to contract when not unduly or improperly exercised was the most efficient means for the prevention of monopoly, since the operation of the centrifugal and centripetal forces resulting from the right to freely contract was the means by which monopoly would be inevitably prevented if no extraneous or sovereign power imposed it and no right to make unlawful contracts having a monopolistic tendency were permitted. In other words that freedom to contract was the essence of freedom from undue restraint on the right to contract.

Clear as it seems to us is the meaning of the provisions of the statute in the light of the review which we have made, nevertheless before definitively applying that meaning it behooves us to consider the contentions urged on one side or the other concerning the meaning of the statute, which, if maintained, would give to it, in some aspects a much wider and in every view at least a somewhat different significance. And to do this brings us to the second question which, at the outset, we have stated it was our purpose to consider and dispose of.

Second. The contentions of the parties as to the meaning of the statute and the decisions of this court relied upon concerning those contentions.

In substance, the propositions urged by the Government are reducible to this: That the language of the statute embraces every contract, combination, etc., in restraint of trade, and hence its text leaves no room for the exercise of judgment, but simply imposes the plain duty of applying its prohibitions to every case within its literal language. The error involved lies in assuming the matter to be decided. This is true because as the acts which may come under the classes stated in the first section and the restraint of trade to which that section applies are not specifically enumerated or defined, it is obvious that judgment must in every case be called into play in order to determine whether a particular act is embraced within the statutory classes, and whether if the act is within such classes its nature or effect causes it to be a restraint of trade within the intendment of the act. To hold to the contrary would require the conclusion either that every contract, act or combination of any kind or nature, whether it operated a restraint on trade or not, was within the statute, and thus the statute would be destructive of all right to contract or agree or combine in any respect whatever as to subjects embraced in interstate trade or commerce, or if this conclusion were not reached, then the contention would require it to be held that as the statute did not define the things to which it related and excluded resort to the only means by which the acts to which it relates could be ascertained—the light of reason—the enforcement of the statute was impossible because of its uncertainty. The merely generic enumeration which the statute makes of the acts to which it refers and the absence of any definition of restraint of trade as used in the statute leaves room for but one conclusion, which is, that it was expressly designed not to unduly limit the application of the act by precise definition, but while clearly fixing a standard, that is, by defining the ulterior boundaries which could not be transgressed with impunity, to leave it to be determined by the light of reason, guided by the principles of law and the duty to apply and enforce the public policy embodied in the statute, in every given case whether any particular act or contract was within the contemplation of the statute.

But, it is said, persuasive as these views may be, they may not be here applied, because the previous decisions of this court have given to the statute a meaning which expressly excludes the construction which must result from the reasoning stated. The cases are *United States* v. *Freight Association,* 166 U.S. 290, and *United States* v. *Joint Traffic Association,* 171 U.S. 505. Both the cases involved the legality of combinations or associations of railroads engaged in interstate commerce for the purpose of controlling the conduct of the parties to the association or combination in many particulars. The association or combination was assailed in each case as being in violation of the statute. It was held that they were. It is undoubted that in the opinion in each case general language was made use of, which, when separated from its context, would justify the conclusion that it was decided that reason could not be resorted to for the purpose of determining whether the acts complained of were within the statute. It is, however, also true that the nature and character of the contract or agreement in each case was fully referred to and suggestions as to their unreasonableness pointed out in order to indicate that they were within the prohibitions of the statute. As the cases cannot by any possible conception be treated as authoritative without the certitude that reason was resorted to for the purpose of deciding them, it follows as a matter of course that it must have been held by the light of reason, since the conclusion could not have been otherwise reached, that the assailed contracts or agreements were within the general enumeration of the statute, and that their operation and effect brought about the restraint of trade which the statute prohibited. This being inevitable, the deduction can in reason only be this: That in the cases relied upon it having been found that the acts complained of were within the statute and operated to produce the injuries which the statute forbade, that resort to reason was not permissible in order to allow that to be done which the statute prohibited. This being true, the rulings in the cases relied upon when rightly appreciated were therefore this and nothing more: That as considering the contracts or agreements, their necessary effect and the character of the parties by whom they were made, they were clearly restraints of trade within the purview of the statute, they could not be taken out of that category by indulging in general reasoning as to the expediency or non-expediency of having made the contracts or the wisdom or want of wisdom of the statute which prohibited their being made. That is to say, the cases but decided that the nature and character of the contracts, creating as they did a conclusive presumption which brought them within the statute, such result was not to be disregarded by the substitution of a judicial appreciation of what the law ought to be for the plain judicial duty of enforcing the law as it was made.

But aside from reasoning it is true to say that the cases relied upon do not when rightly construed sustain the doctrine contended for is established by all of the numerous decisions of this court which have applied and enforced the Anti-trust Act, since they all in the very nature of things rest upon the premise that reason was the guide by which the provisions of the act were in every case interpreted. Indeed intermediate the decision of the two cases, that is, after the decision in the *Freight Association Case* and before the decision in the *Joint Traffic Case,* the case of *Hopkins* v. *United States,* 171 U.S. 578, was decided, the opinion being delivered by Mr. Justice Peckham, who wrote both the opinions in the *Freight Association* and the *Joint Traffic Cases*. And, referring in the *Hopkins Case* to the broad claim made as to the rule of interpretation announced in the *Freight Association Case,* it was said (p. 592): "To treat as condemned by the act all agreements under which, as a result, the cost of conducting an interstate commercial business may be increased would enlarge the application of the act far beyond the fair meaning of the language used. There must be some direct and immediate effect upon interstate commerce in order to come within the act." And in the *Joint Traffic Case* this statement was expressly reiterated and approved and illustrated by example; like limitation on the general language used in *Freight Association* and *Joint Traffic Cases* is also the clear result of *Bement* v. *National Harrow Co.,* 186 U.S. 70, 92, and especially of *Cincinnati Packet Co.* v. *Bay,* 200 U.S. 179.

If the criterion by which it is to be determined in all cases whether every contract, combination, etc., is a restraint of trade within the intendment of the law, is the direct or indirect effect of the acts involved, then of course the rule of reason becomes the guide, and the construction which we have given the statute, instead of being refuted by the cases relied upon, is by those cases demonstrated to be correct. This is true, because as the construction which we have deduced from the history of the act and the analysis of its text is simply that in every case where it is claimed that an act or acts are in violation of the statute the rule of reason, in the light of the principles of law and the public policy which the act embodies, must be applied. From this it follows, since that rule and the result of the test as to direct or indirect, in their ultimate aspect, come to one and the same thing, that the difference between the two is therefore only that which obtains between things which do not differ at all.

If it be true that there is this identity of result between the rule intended to be applied in the *Freight Association Case,* that is, the rule of direct and indirect, and the rule of reason which under the statute as we construe it should be here applied, it may be asked how was it that in the opinion in the *Freight Association Case* much consideration was given to the subject of whether the agreement or combination which was involved in that case could be taken out of the prohibitions of the statute upon the theory of its reasonableness. The question is pertinent and must be fully and frankly met, for if it be now deemed that the *Freight Association Case* was mistakenly decided or too broadly stated, the doctrine which it announced should be either expressly overruled or limited.

The confusion which gives rise to the question results from failing to distinguish between the want of power to take a case which by its terms or the circumstances which surrounded it, considering among such circumstances the character of the parties, is plainly within the statute, out of the operation of the statute by resort to reason in effect to establish that the contract ought not to be treated as within the statute, and the duty in every case where it becomes necessary from the nature and character of the parties to decide whether it was within the statute to pass upon that question by the light of reason. This distinction, we think, serves to point out what in its ultimate conception was the thought underlying the reference to the rule of reason made in the *Freight Association Case,* especially when such reference is interpreted by the context of the opinion and in the light of the subsequent opinion in the *Hopkins Case* and in *Cincinnati Packet Company* v. *Bay,* 200 U.S.. 179.

And in order not in the slightest degree to be wanting in frankness, we say that in so far, however, as by separating the general language used in the opinions in the *Freight Association* and *Joint Traffic cases* from the context and the subject and parties with which the cases were concerned, it may be conceived that the language referred to conflicts with the construction which we give the statute, they are necessarily now limited and qualified. We see no possible escape from this conclusion if we are to adhere to the many cases decided in this court in which the Anti-trust Law has been applied and enforced and if the duty to apply and enforce that law in the future is to continue to exist. The first is true, because the construction which we now give the statute does not in the slightest degree conflict with a single previous case decided concerning the Anti-trust Law aside from the contention as to the *Freight Association* and *Joint Traffic cases,* and because every one of those cases applied the rule of reason for the purpose of determining whether the subject before the court was within the statute. The second is also true, since, as we have already pointed out, unaided by the light of reason it is impossible to understand how the statute may in the future be enforced and the public policy which it establishes be made efficacious.

So far as the objections of the defendants are concerned they are all embraced under two headings:—

a. That the act, even if the averments of the bill be true, cannot be constitutionally applied, because to do so would extend the power of Congress to subjects *dehors* the reach of its authority to regulate commerce, by enabling that body to deal with mere questions of production of commodities within the States. But all the structure upon which this argument proceeds is based upon the decision in *United States* v. *E. C. Knight Co.,* 156 U.S. 1. The view, however, which the argument takes of that case and the arguments based upon that view have been so repeatedly pressed upon this court in connection with the interpretation and enforcement of the Anti-trust Act, and have been so necessarily and expressly decided to be unsound as to cause the contentions to be plainly foreclosed and to require no express notice. *United States* v. *Northern Securities Co.,* 193 U.S. 197, 334; *Loewe* v. *Lawlor,* 208 U.S. 274; *Swift & Co.* v. *United States,* 196 U.S. 375; *Montague* v. *Lowry,* 193 U.S. 38; *Shawnee Compress Co.* v. *Anderson,* 209 U.S. 423.

b. Many arguments are pressed in various forms of statement which in substance amount to contending that the statute cannot be applied under the facts of this case without impairing rights of property and destroying the freedom of contract or trade, which is essentially necessary to the well-being of society and which it is insisted is protected by the constitutional guaranty of due process of law. But the ultimate foundation of all these arguments is the assumption that reason may not be resorted to in interpreting and applying the statute, and therefore that the statute unreasonably restricts the right to contract and unreasonably operates upon the right to acquire and hold property. As the premise is demonstrated to be unsound by the construction we have given the statute, of course the propositions which rest upon that premise need not be further noticed.

So far as the arguments proceed upon the conception that in view of the generality of the statute it is not susceptible of being enforced by the courts because it cannot be carried out without a judicial exertion of legislative power, they are clearly unsound. The statute certainly generically enumerates the character of acts which it prohibits and the wrong which it was intended to prevent. The propositions therefore but insist that, consistently with the fundamental principles of due process of law, it never can be left to the judiciary to decide whether in a given case particular acts come within a generic statutory provision. But to reduce the propositions, however, to this their final meaning makes it clear that in substance they deny the existence of essential legislative authority and challenge the right of the judiciary to perform duties which that department of the government has exerted from the beginning. This is so clear as to require no elaboration. Yet, let us demonstrate that which needs no demonstration, by a few obvious examples. Take for instance the familiar cases where the judiciary is called upon to determine whether a particular act or acts are within a given prohibition, depending upon wrongful intent. Take questions of fraud. Consider the power which must be exercised in every case where the courts are called upon to determine whether particular acts are invalid which are, abstractly speaking, in and of themselves valid, but which are asserted to be invalid because of their direct effect upon interstate commerce.

We come then to the third proposition requiring consideration, viz:

Third. The facts and the application of the statute to them.

Beyond dispute the proofs establish substantially as alleged in the bill the following facts:

1. The creation of the Standard Oil Company of Ohio;

2. The organization of the Standard Oil Trust of 1882, and also a previous one of 1879, not referred to in the bill, and the proceedings in the Supreme Court of Ohio, culminating in a decree based upon the finding that the company was unlawfully a party to that trust; the transfer by the trustees of stocks in certain of the companies; the contempt proceedings; and, finally, the increase of the capital of the Standard Oil Company of New Jersey and the acquisition by that company of the shares of the stock of the other corporations in exchange for its certificates.

The vast amount of property and the possibilities of far-reaching control which resulted from the facts last stated are shown by the statement which we have previously annexed concerning the parties to the trust agreement of 1882, and the corporations whose stock was held by the trustees under the trust and which came therefore to be held by the New Jersey corporation. But these statements do not with accuracy convey an appreciation of the situation as it existed at the time of the entry of the decree below, since during the more than ten years which elapsed between the acquiring by the New Jersey corporation of the stock and other property which was formerly held by the trustees under the trust agreement, the situation of course had somewhat changed, a change which when analyzed in the light of the proof, we think, establishes that the result of enlarging the capital stock of the New Jersey company and giving it the vast power to which we have referred produced its normal consequence, that is, it gave to the corporation, despite enormous dividends and despite the dropping out of certain corporations enumerated in the decree of the court below, an enlarged and more perfect sway and control over the trade and commerce in petroleum and its products. The ultimate situation referred to will be made manifest by an examination of § § 2 and 4 of the decree below, which are excerpted in the margin.[1]

Giving to the facts just stated, the

---

[1] SECTION 2. *That the defendants John D. Rockefeller, William Rockefeller, Henry H. Rogers, Henry M. Flagler, John D. Archbold, Oliver H. Payne, and Charles M. Pratt, hereafter called the seven individual defendants, united with the Standard Oil Company and other defendants to form and effectuate this combination, and since its formation have been and still are engaged in carrying it into effect and continuing it; that the defendants Anglo-American Oil Company (Limited), Atlantic Refining Company, Buckeye Pipe Line Company, Borne-Scrymser Company, Chesebrough Manufacturing Company, Consolidated, Cumberland Pipe Line Company, Colonial Oil Company, Continental Oil Company, Crescent Pipe Line Company, Henry C. Folger, Jr., and Calvin N. Payne, a copartnership doing business under the firm name and style of Corsicana Refining Company, Eureka Pipe Line Company, Galena Signal Oil Company, Indiana Pipe Line Company, Manhattan Oil Company, National Transit Company, New York Transit Company, Northern Pipe Line Company, Ohio Oil Company, Prairie Oil and Gas Company, Security Oil Company, Solar Refining Company, Southern Pipe Line Company, South Penn Oil Company, Southwest Pennsylvania Pipe Lines Company, Standard Oil Company, of California, Standard Oil Company, of Indiana, Standard Oil Company, of Iowa, Standard Oil Company, of Kansas, Standard Oil Company, of Kentucky, Standard Oil Company, of Nebraska, Standard Oil Company, of New York, Standard Oil Company, of Ohio, Swan and Finch Company, Union Tank Line Company, Vacuum Oil Company, Washington Oil Company, Waters-Pierce Oil Company, have entered into and became parties to this combination and are either actively operating or aiding in the operation of it; that by means of this combination the defendants named in this section have combined and conspired to monopolize, have monopolized, and are continuing to monopolize a substantial part of the commerce among the states, in the territories and with foreign nations, in violation of section 2 of the anti-trust act.*

* * * * *

SECTION 4. *That in the formation and execution of the combination or conspiracy the Standard Company has issued its stock to the amount of more than $90,000,000 in exchange for the stocks of other corporations which it holds, and it now owns and controls all of the capital stock of many corporations, a majority of the stock or controlling interests in some corporations and stock in other corporations as follows:*

Name of company.	Total capital stock.	Owned by Standard Oil Company.
Anglo-American Oil Company, Limited	£1,000,000	£999,740
Atlantic Refining Company	$5,000,000	$5,000,000
Borne-Scrymser Company	200,000	199,700
Buckeye Pipe Line Company	10,000,000	9,999,700
Chesebrough Manufacturing Company, Consolidated	500,000	277,700
Colonial Oil Company	250,000	249,300
Continental Oil Company	300,000	300,000

weight which it was deemed they were entitled to, in the light afforded by the proof of other cognate facts and circumstances, the court below held that the acts and dealings established by the proof operated to destroy the "potentiality of competition" which otherwise would have existed to such an extent as to cause the transfers of stock which were made to the New Jersey corporation and the control which resulted over

Name of company.	Total capital stock.	Owned by Standard Oil Company.
Crescent Pipe Line Company	3,000,000	3,000,000
Eureka Pipe Line Company	5,000,000	4,999,400
Galena-Signal Oil Company	10,000,000	7,079,500
Indiana Pipe Line Company	1,000,000	999,700
Lawrence Natural Gas Company	450,000	450,000
Mahoning Gas Fuel Company	150,000	149,900
Mountain State Gas Company	500,000	500,000
National Transit Company	25,455,200	25,451,650
New York Transit Company	5,000,000	5,000,000
Northern Pipe Line Company	4,000,000	4,000,000
Northwestern Ohio Natural Gas Company	2,775,250	1,649,450
Ohio Oil Company	10,000,000	9,999,850
People's Natural Gas Company	1,000,000	1,000,000
Pittsburg Natural Gas Company	310,000	310,000
Solar Refining Company	500,000	499,400
Southern Pipe Line Company	10,000,000	10,000,000
South Penn Oil Company	2,500,000	2,500,000
Southwest Pennsylvania Pipe Lines	3,500,000	3,500,000
Standard Oil Company (of California)	17,000,000	16,999,500
Standard Oil Company (of Indiana)	1,000,000	999,000
Standard Oil Company (of Iowa)	1,000,000	1,000,000
Standard Oil Company (of Kansas)	1,000,000	999,300
Standard Oil Company (of Kentucky)	1,000,000	997,200
Standard Oil Company (of Nebraska)	600,000	599,500
Standard Oil Company (of New York)	15,000,000	15,000,000
Standard Oil Company (of Ohio)	3,500,000	3,499,400
Swan and Finch Company	100,000	100,000
Union Tank Line Company	3,500,000	3,499,400
Vacuum Oil Company	2,500,000	2,500,000
Washington Oil Company	100,000	71,480
Waters-Pierce Oil Company	400,000	274,700

That the defendant National Transit Company, which is owned and controlled by the Standard Oil Company as aforesaid, owns and controls the amounts of the capital stocks of the following-named corporations and limited partnerships stated opposite each, respectively, as follows:

Name of company.	Total capital stock.	Owned by National Transit Company.
Connecting Gas Company	$825,000	$412,000
Cumberland Pipe Line Company	1,000,000	998,500
East Ohio Gas Company	6,000,000	5,999,500
Franklin Pipe Company, Limited	50,000	19,500
Prairie Oil and Gas Company	10,000,000	9,999,500

That the Standard Company has also acquired the control by the ownership of its stock or otherwise of the Security Oil Company, a corporation created under the laws of

the many and various subsidiary corporations to be a combination or conspiracy in restraint of trade in violation of the first section of the act, but also to be an attempt to monopolize and a monopolization bringing about a perennial violation of the second section.

We see no cause to doubt the correctness of these conclusions, considering the subject from every aspect, that is, both in view of the facts established by the record and the necessary operation and effect of the law as we have construed it upon the inferences deducible from the facts, for the following reasons:

a. Because the unification of power and control over petroleum and its products which was the inevitable result of the combining in the New Jersey corporation by the increase of its stock and the transfer to it of the stocks of so many other corporations, aggregating so vast a capital, gives rise, in and of itself, in the absence of countervailing circumstances, to say the least, to the *prima facie* presumption of intent and purpose to maintain the dominancy over the oil industry, not as a result of normal methods of industrial development, but by new means of combination which were resorted to in order that greater power might be added than would otherwise have arisen had normal methods been followed, the whole with the purpose of excluding others from the trade and thus centralizing in the combination a perpetual control of the movements of petroleum and its products in the channels of interstate commerce.

b. Because the *prima facie* presumption of intent to restrain trade, to monopolize and to bring about monopolization resulting from the act of expanding the stock of the New Jersey corporation and vesting it with such vast control of the oil industry, is made conclusive by considering, *1,* the conduct of the persons or corporations who were mainly instrumental in bringing about the extension of power in the New Jersey corporation before the consummation of that result and prior to the formation of the trust agreements of 1879 and 1882; *2,* by considering the proof as to what was done under those agreements and the acts which immediately preceded the vesting of power in the New Jersey corporation as well as by weighing the modes in which the power vested in that corporation has been exerted and the results which have arisen from it.

Recurring to the acts done by the individuals or corporations who were mainly instrumental in bringing about the expansion of the New Jersey corporation during the period prior to the formation of the trust agreements of 1879 and 1882, including those agreements, not for the purpose of weighing the substantial merit of the numerous charges of wrongdoing made during such period, but solely as an aid for discovering intent and purpose, we think no disinterested mind can survey the period in question without being irresistibly driven to the conclusion that the very genius for commercial development and organization which it would seem was manifested from the beginning soon begot an intent and purpose to exclude others which was frequently manifested by acts and dealings wholly inconsistent with the theory that they were made with the single conception of

---

Texas, which owns a refinery at Beaumont in that State, and the Manhattan Oil Company, a corporation, which owns a pipe line situated in the States of Indiana and Ohio; that the Standard Company, and the corporations and partnerships named in Section 2, are engaged in the various branches of the business of producing purchasing and transporting petroleum in the principal oil-producing districts of the United States, in New York, Pennsylvania, West Virginia, Tennessee, Kentucky, Ohio, Indiana, Illinois, Kansas, Oklahoma, Louisiana, Texas, Colorado and California, in shipping and transporting the oil through pipe lines owned or controlled by these companies from the various oil-producing districts into and through other states, in refining the petroleum and manufacturing it into various products, in shipping the petroleum and the products thereof into the states and territories of the United States, the District of Columbia and to foreign nations, in shipping the petroleum and its products in tank cars owned or controlled by the subsidiary companies into various states and territories of the United States and into the District of Columbia, and in selling the petroleum and its products in various places in the states and territories of the United States, in the District of Columbia and in foreign countries; that the Standard Company controls the subsidiary companies and directs the management thereof so that none of the subsidiary companies competes with any other of those companies or with the Standard Company, but their trade is all managed as that of a single person.

advancing the development of business power by usual methods, but which on the contrary necessarily involved the intent to drive others from the field and to exclude them from their right to trade and thus accomplish the mastery which was the end in view. And, considering the period from the date of the trust agreements of 1879 and 1882, up to the time of the expansion of the New Jersey corporation, the gradual extension of the power over the commerce in oil which ensued, the decision of the Supreme Court of Ohio, the tardiness or reluctance in conforming to the commands of that decision, the method first adopted and that which finally culminated in the plan of the New Jersey corporation, all additionally serve to make manifest the continued existence of the intent which we have previously indicated and which among other things impelled the expansion of the New Jersey corporation. The exercise of the power which resulted from that organization fortifies the foregoing conclusions, since the development which came, the acquisition here and there which ensued of every efficient means by which competition could have been asserted, the slow but resistless methods which followed by which means of transportation were absorbed and brought under control, the system of marketing which was adopted by which the country was divided into districts and the trade in each district in oil was turned over to a designated corporation within the combination and all others were excluded, all lead the mind up to a conviction of a purpose and intent which we think is so certain as practically to cause the subject not to be within the domain of reasonable contention.

The inference that no attempt to monopolize could have been intended, and that no monopolization resulted from the acts complained of, since it is established that a very small percentage of the crude oil produced was controlled by the combination, is unwarranted. As substantial power over the crude product was the inevitable result of the absolute control which existed over the refined product, the monopolization of the one carried with it the power to control the other, and if the inferences which this situation suggests were developed, which we deem it unnecessary to do, they might well serve to add additional cogency to the presumption of intent to monopolize which we have found arises from the unquestioned proof on other subjects.

We are thus brought to the last subject which we are called upon to consider, viz:

Fourth. The remedy to be administered.

It may be conceded that ordinarily where it was found that acts had been done in violation of the statute, adequate measure of relief would result from restraining the doing of such acts in the future. *Swift* v. *United States,* 196 U.S. 375. But in a case like this, where the condition which has been brought about in violation of the statute, in and of itself, is not only a continued attempt to monopolize, but also a monopolization, the duty to enforce the statute requires the application of broader and more controlling remedies. As penalties which are not authorized by law may not be inflicted by judicial authority, it follows that to meet the situation with which we are confronted the application of remedies twofold in character becomes essential: 1st. To forbid the doing in the future of acts like those which we have found to have been done in the past which would be violative of the statute. 2d. The exertion of such measure of relief as will effectually dissolve the combination found to exist in violation of the statute, and thus neutralize the extension and continually operating force which the possession of the power unlawfully obtained has brought and will continue to bring about.

In applying remedies for this purpose, however, the fact must not be overlooked that injury to the public by the prevention of an undue restraint on, or the monopolization of trade or commerce is the foundation upon which the prohibitions of the statute rest, and moreover that one of the fundamental purposes of the statute is to protect, not to destroy, rights of property.

Let us then, as a means of accurately determining what relief we are to afford, first come to consider what relief was afforded by the court below, in order to fix how far it is necessary to take from or add to that relief, to the end that the prohibitions of the statute may have complete and operative force.

The court below by virtue of § § 1, 2, and 4 of its decree, which we have in part previously excerpted in the margin, adjudged that the New Jersey corporation in so far as it held the stock of the various corporations, recited in § § 2 and 4 of the decree, or controlled the same was a combination in violation of the first section of the act, and an attempt to monopolize or a monopolization contrary to the second section of the act. It commanded the dissolution of the combination, and therefore in effect, directed the transfer by the New Jersey corporation back to the stockholders of the various subsidiary corporations entitled to the same of the stock which had been turned over to the New Jersey company in exchange for its stock. To make this command effective § 5 of the decree forbade the New Jersey corporation from in any form or manner exercising any ownership or exerting any power directly or indirectly in virtue of its apparent title to the stocks of the subsidiary corporations, and prohibited those subsidiary corporations from paying any dividends to the New Jersey corporation or doing any act which would recognize further power in that company, except to the extent that it was necessary to enable that company to transfer the stock. So far as the owners of the stock of the subsidiary corporations and the corporations themselves were concerned after the stock had been transferred, § 6 of the decree enjoined them from in any way conspiring or combining to violate the act or to monopolize or attempt to monopolize in virtue of their ownership of the stock transferred to them, and prohibited all agreements between the subsidiary corporations or other stockholders in the future, tending to produce or bring about further violations of the act.

By § 7, pending the accomplishment of the dissolution of the combination by the transfer cf stock and until it was consummated, the defendants named in § 2, constituting all the corporations to which we have referred, were enjoined from engaging in or carrying on interstate commerce. And by § 9, among other things a delay of thirty days was granted for the carrying into effect of the direction of the decree.

So far as the decree held that the ownership of the stock of the New Jersey corporation constituted a combination in violation of the first section and an attempt to create a monopoly or to monopolize under the second section and commanded the dissolution of the combination, the decree was clearly appropriate. And this also is true of § 5 of the decree which restrained both the New Jersey corporation and the subsidiary corporations from doing anything which would recognize or give effect to further ownership in the New Jersey corporation of the stocks which were ordered to be retransferred.

But the contention is that, in so far as the relief by way of injunction which was awarded by § 6 against the stockholders of the subsidiary corporations or the subsidiary corporations themselves after the transfer of stock by the New Jersey corporation was completed in conformity to the decree, the relief awarded was too broad: *a.* Because it was not sufficiently specific and tended to cause those who were within the embrace of the order to cease to be under the protection of the law of the land and required them to thereafter conduct their business under the jeopardy of punishments for contempt for violating a general injunction. *New Haven R. R.* v. *Interstate Commerce Commission,* 200 U.S. 404. Besides it is said that the restraint imposed by § 6—even putting out of view the consideration just stated—was moreover calculated to do injury to the public and it may be in and of itself to produce the very restraint on the due course of trade which it was intended to prevent. We say this since it does not necessarily follow because an illegal restraint of trade or an attempt to monopolize or a monopolization resulted from the combination and the transfer of the stocks of the subsidiary corporations to the New Jersey corporation that a like restraint or attempt to monopolize or monopolization would necessarily arise from agreements between one or more of the subsidiary corporations after the transfer of the stock by the New Jersey corporation. For illustration, take the pipe lines. By the effect of the transfer of the stock the pipe lines would come under the control of various corporations instead of being subjected to a uniform control. If various corporations owning the lines determined in the public interests to so combine as to make a continuous line, such agreement or combination would not be repugnant to the act, and yet it might be restrained by the decree. As another example, take the Union Tank Line Company, one of the subsidiary corporations, the owner practically of all the tank cars in use by the combination. If no possibility existed of agreements for the distribution of these cars among the subsidiary corporations, the most serious detriment to the public interest might result. Conceding the merit, abstractly considered, of these contentions they are irrelevant. We so think, since we construe the sixth paragraph of the decree, not as depriving the stockholders or the corporations, after the dissolution of the combination, of the power to make normal and lawful contracts or agreements, but as restraining them from, by any device whatever, recreating directly or indirectly the illegal combination which the decree dissolved. In other words we construe the sixth paragraph of the decree, not as depriving the stockholders or corporations of the right to live under the law of the land, but as compelling obedience to that law. As therefore the sixth paragraph as thus construed is not amenable to the criticism directed against it and cannot produce the harmful results which the arguments suggest it was obviously right. We think that in view of the magnitude of the interests involved and their complexity that the delay of thirty days allowed for executing the decree was too short and should be extended so as to embrace a period of at least six months. So also, in view of the possible serious injury to result to the public from an absolute cessation of interstate commerce in petroleum and its products by such vast agencies as are embraced in the combination, a result which might arise from that portion of the decree which enjoined carrying on of interstate commerce not only by the New Jersey corporation but by all the subsidiary companies until the dissolution of the combination by the transfer of the stocks in accordance with the decree, the injunction provided for in § 7 thereof should not have been awarded.

Our conclusion is that the decree below was right and should be affirmed, except as to the minor matters concerning which we have indicated the decree should be modified. Our order will therefore be one of affirmance with directions, however, to modify the decree in accordance with this opinion. The court below to retain jurisdiction to the extent necessary to compel compliance in every respect with its decree.

And it is so ordered.

Rufus Peckham

☆ 1838–1909 ☆

APPOINTED BY

GROVER CLEVELAND

YEARS ON COURT

1896–1909

Rufus Peckham

by

RICHARD SKOLNIK

IN THE DECADES after the Civil War, corporate America, re-enacting the epic struggle of the pioneer, subdued the American continent and began tapping its wealth. By the last years of the nineteenth century, with the battle largely over, big business turned to the more delicate task of achieving stability and protecting its investments. There was to be no peaceful enjoyment of gains, no passive acceptance of the new power structure. Too ruthless in its methods, too successful in its enterprises, and too indifferent to its critics, corporate America was assailed by those very large groups whom it had once exploited or ignored. Farmers, laborers, small businessmen, reformers, all increasingly organized and articulate, demanded that something be done to remedy the gross inequities resulting from the years of business domination. The big businessman, sensitive, insecure, and easily frightened, construed these demands to be part of a monstrous conspiracy to subvert all that he had so painstakingly constructed. Fierce in his resistance, he would demonstrate that those qualities of inventiveness, boldness, and moral blindness with which he had created his economic empire could serve equally well in defense of it. The legal process, deceptively calm, aloof, and seemingly impartial, had always proven to be a valuable first line of defense. Accordingly, this resourceful antagonist, this most pragmatic of men, once more prepared to invoke the abstractions of the law to protect him against the realities of the situation.

But to use the law for these purposes required a virtual legal revolution and to stage a revolution within a traditionally minded institution was no easy matter. It involved neither bold upheavals nor emotional appeals but rather consisted of new definitions, subtle distinctions, and the careful creation of twilight zones. To work such a transformation became the job of a determined band of corporate lawyers and the Supreme Court emerged as the principal

RICHARD SKOLNIK is Assistant Professor of History at City College of New York.

agency committed to ratifying these new legal arrangements. Accordingly, the Court refitted such old workhorses as "due process of law" and the doctrine of reasonableness and created such fresh concepts as "liberty of contract" and emerged with a modern arsenal of weapons well suited for its struggle with Populists, Trust Busters, labor organizers, and Mugwump reformers. By insisting upon the right to pass on the reasonableness and appropriateness of legislative enactments, the Supreme Court made clear that it was prepared to use these weapons, notwithstanding the fact that this involved intrusion upon the political scene and limitations upon the freedom of action of local officials. This judicial offensive carried the day and, though Bryanism sent a scare across corporate America in 1896, the real threat already had been met and subdued by the action of the judiciary. By emasculating the Sherman Act, striking down the income tax, supporting the business community in the Debs case, and restricting the scope of the police powers, the Court made it clear that it would not preside over the dissolution of the business empire in America.

Rufus Peckham rose to the Court in 1896 after the judicial revolution had taken place and the foundations of the new legal conservatism had already been laid. A primary task for the Court now was not further innovation but stabilization and formalization. The new doctrines required explicit definition and extensive application. This task of conservation well suited the temperament of Peckham and it is as a stolid defender of the received wisdom that he performed his most notable services for the Court. Peckham welcomed the applications of substantive due process and the expanded definitions of liberty of contract. He rarely sympathized with the state's use of its police powers and seemed unwilling to acknowledge the difficulties raised by judicial subjectivity and interventionism. Though occasionally outspoken in his beliefs, Peckham did not emerge as a commanding figure on the Court. Lacking a creative legal mind, he was not identified with any significant departures in legal interpretation. Yet during the years of his service, he would not be without influence. Besides writing a number of important majority opinions, his presence on the Court helped fashion its contemporary image as a safe, solid bulwark against social disorder and experimentation.

Peckham's life and earlier career yield a number of clues useful to the analyst of his judicial behavior. The Peckham family early sank its roots into the American soil. Peckham could trace his American ancestors back to seventeenth-century New York and could take pride in the fact that his family was among the oldest in the state. In the nineteenth century the Peckham family, settled in Albany, seemed entirely representative of that backbone of American society—the solid respectable Protestant stock living in comfortable but not notably wealthy circumstances.

Considerable evidence exists to suggest that the greatest influence on Rufus Peckham, Jr. was his father. The careers of the two men followed remarkably similar paths. Both were lawyers who had spent a good portion of their lives in public office. Both knew the serenity of the judicial chamber and the turbulence of the political arena. The elder Peckham had been district attorney of Albany County while in his twenties and later served on the New York Supreme Court and Court of Appeals. In between he managed a term in Congress as a Democrat in 1852. His son subsequently became a very youthful District Attorney of Albany County, member of the Supreme Court and Court of Appeals and an active and influential Democratic politician. Peckham, Jr. first joined his father's law firm, Peckham and Tremain, and subsequently associated for a time with the latter's son in the new partnership of Peckham and Tremain. Both father and son were to die while still serving on the bench.

In physical appearance there was little to distinguish the two. Lawyers who had pleaded before both were astounded by the resemblance. One observer confessed that "the example of heredity in the matter has long been a topic of bar comment." This outward congruity seemed to be merely a reflection of a more profound similarity in demeanor, character, and attitude. The elder Peckham typified the sturdy, pugnacious, independent, hard-working, inner-directed man of the nineteenth century. A resolution passed by the New York State Bar Association referred to him as "generous and manly, imbred with a lofty sense of honor and a dignity of personal character that provoked no undue familiarity." A contemporary remarked that he was neither a learned lawyer nor a patient student but a man with "an imperious will" and "strong passions and prejudices." Peckham, Sr. seemed to him to love "principle rather than precedent" and to reflect "more than he studied." Finally he noted that Peckham "drove for the goal of justice without much regard for what might be crushed under his wheels." These traits of the father seem largely to have been passed on to the son. The younger Peckham, while more urbane, cultured, and less rough hewn, still retained the father's dignified aloofness, inflexibility, passionate prejudices, and decidedly subjective approach to the law. This tendency to emulate the father was probably intensified when the latter was lost at sea in a ship collision while on vacation from his position on the New York Court of Appeals. If Peckham on the United States Supreme Court would one day seem unresponsive to the needs of a rapidly changing society it may be that, still influenced by his father, what he saw was a different and older America.

Lest Peckham be labelled an atavistic relic, it must not be forgotten that he operated successfully in an area that ordinarily required a firm grasp of existing realities. Peckham, prominent in Albany County politics, was closely affiliated with the upstate wing of the Democratic party in New York. An active partisan, he was an effective spokesman for the upstate Democrats; his dignified appearance and oratorical powers were often decisive factors at Democratic state conventions. A strong Tilden supporter at the national Democratic convention in 1876 and an intimate of such upstate leaders as Daniel Manning, Daniel Lamont, and Grover Cleveland, Peckham was often called upon to guide delicate political maneuvers. Perhaps the most urgent task of these up-staters was not defeating the Republicans, but preventing New York City's Tammany Democrats from gaining control of the party machinery in the state. To this end they encouraged and sought to ally with all manner of Democratic splinter groups in New York City. Peckham as an up-stater and avid party man participated in the campaign against Tammany, his hostility intensified no doubt by the fact that his brother, the eminent lawyer, Wheeler Peckham, had been among those associated with the prosecution of the Tweed Ring. Peckham demanded the extirpation of Tammany Hall. It "must go down," he thought, "before the Democrats can live." He led a successful move in the Democratic state convention of 1881 to prevent the seating of the Tammany delegation. Two years earlier, at another convention, Peckham had helped thwart Tammany efforts to block the renomination of the Democratic incumbent for governor. On the former occasion Peckham had warned against yielding to Tammany demands because there was nothing that could "be compared to the tyranny of a minority." In light of Peckham's later career, this warning was not without its touch of irony.

Peckham's personal friendship with such upstate leaders as Cleveland and Manning suggests that he probably shared their views on political and social matters. More important, these connections enabled him to secure a number of important judicial nominations from the Democratic party. When Governor Grover Cleveland invited Peckham to the executive mansion to join the long election night vigil in 1884, it seemed evident that a Cleveland presidential victory would one day rebound to the benefit of Rufus Peckham.

Peckham's influence within the Democratic party was also a function of his standing within the city of Albany. Born in that city in 1837, the son of a prominent father, Peckham gained recognition there as an effective official and as a successful lawyer. Among his many clients was the Albany and Susquehanna Railroad which he defended in its battle against the Erie Railroad led at the time by Jim Fiske and Jay Gould. Peckham also attracted considerable attention for his vigorous efforts as District Attorney for Albany County from 1869 to 1872, and as a special assistant to the state Attorney General in a series of criminal prosecutions. Some time after this, Peckham served as corporation counsel for the city of Albany. Beyond doubt, Peckham, married to the daughter of a wealthy New York City merchant, a trustee of many local banks, president of the Albany hospital and the Albany County Democratic Committee, stood as a leading citizen of his community.

His labors for the Democratic party and his reputation as a keen lawyer and able public official began to yield sizable dividends for Peckham in the 1880's. Defeated in his attempt to gain the Democratic nomination for the New York Court of Appeals in 1882, Peckham won election to the Supreme Court in 1883 and three years later was elected to the New York Court of Appeals, the highest tribunal in the state. This latter nomination and election in 1886 occasioned considerable discussion. It appeared to have been engineered by the Cleveland administration as part of its efforts to retain control over the state Democratic party. While observers were unanimous in praising Peckham's ability and personal character, doubts were expressed about the propriety of the nomination and the wisdom of electing so keen a Democratic partisan to the sensitive position on the state's highest court.

Peckham's political prowess served him well during the 1886 campaign. When threatened Tammany defections jeopardized his chances for election, Peckham sent his law partner to New York City to obtain the support of Henry George and his Single Tax followers, who were then contesting the mayoralty. A bargain was reached, and history must record one of its more intriguing ironies, in that Peckham's advancement, which was ultimately to lead to the Supreme Court, received a considerable boost from the forces of Henry George. Though Peckham donned the mantle of judicial neutrality he maintained a lively interest in, and retained some influence over, political affairs. From time to time he even received attention as a possible candidate for high elective office. From 1886, however, to his elevation to the Supreme Court of the United States some ten years later, the major interest of Peckham would be his service as a justice on New York's highest court.

The New York Court of Appeals, one of the most eminent and influential judicial bodies in the nation, had, since the days of Chancellor Kent, displayed a distinctly conservative outlook. This was evident in its early and continuous use of the due process clause to protect vested rights and in the frequency with which it overturned legislative enactments. More striking, however, was its apparent willingness to accept the new definitions of due process and individual liberties emerging among certain dissenting Justices on the United States Supreme Court in the 1870's and '80's. Peckham's tenure on the Court probably served to reinforce his original predisposition in favor of such interpretations. By the time he reached the Supreme Court, these ideas would be well formulated in his mind and ready for widespread application.

Most of Peckham's decisions on the New York Court of Appeals, as well as the New York Supreme Court, contained few surprises. In straightforward, unadorned prose he expressed legal views which would raise few eyebrows within court circles. In decisions on employer liability, *Hickey* v. *Jaffe,* 105 N.Y. 26 (1887), foreign corporations, *Demarest* v. *Flack,* 128 N.Y. 205 (1891), and municipal taxation, *Association for Colored Orphans* v. *Mayor,* 104 N.Y. 581 (1887), Peckham was content to rely upon well-established legal precepts. Despite this fact, a number of his decisions gained wide attention because the issues and the parties involved had generated considerable public interest.

One such case, *People* v. *O'Brien,* 46 Hun. 525 (1886), was decided by Peckham in 1886 just before he left the Supreme Court. The case grew out of the exposed corruption of a score of New York City aldermen, a scandal second only to the notorious Tweed episode. In 1884, a group of schemers, by bribing members of the New York City Board of Aldermen had succeeded in obtaining a franchise for the Broadway Surface Railroad Company which they controlled. This group had no intention of operating surface transportation facilities. It had in fact quickly leased its lines to two other companies. On the basis of their franchise, however, the plotters had been able to sell bonds, the proceeds of which they pocketed. When these machinations were uncovered, a grand jury indicted the aldermen, some of whom fled the country, and a state legislative act dissolved the corporation. Legal questions arose concerning the validity of the leases the Broadway Company had signed with the two transportation companies and the status of the franchise the now dissolved company had obtained, albeit illegally. Peckham in his decision adopted an interesting view of corporate eschatology, ruling in effect that corporations might be dissolved by the legislature but their privileges lingered on. Public policy respecting franchises, he thought, was "to keep them alive in perpetuity notwithstanding the insolvency or death of the corporate owner." The franchise therefore still belonged to the now defunct company, and its bondholders could exercise claims against it. Peckham also upheld the validity of the traffic arrangements entered into by the company. Peckham's decision was criticized by those who saw it as favorable to the original schemers, but with the validation of bondholder claims, the recognition of the traffic agreements, and the indictment of the bribe takers general satisfaction prevailed.

Another publicized case developed when New York City took action after an intensive examination of its tenement houses had revealed the indescribably wretched conditions of these structures, in *Health Dept.* v. *Rector,* 145 N.Y. 32 (1895). The city obtained legislation at Albany permitting the Board of Health to direct the owners of substandard tenements to install adequate water supply facilities. The disclosure that the venerable Trinity Church owned considerable amounts of deteriorated tenement properties caused a sensation, though hardly comparable to that resulting from the fact that the church was unwilling to comply with Board of Health directives and undertook to challenge the constitutionality of the legislation. Peckham speaking for the majority found little difficulty in upholding the statute as a legitimate attempt to deal with a health matter and therefore well within the scope of the state's police powers.

In a number of less publicized cases, Peckham displayed a capacity for vigorous thought and expression. He won much praise for his lively dissent in an 1891 ballot case, *People* v. *Board of Canvassers,* 129 N.Y. 395. He protested the fact that over a thousand votes had been thrown out in Onondaga County after the state election because they had been cast with improper ballots inadvertently distributed by an official election agent. Because the votes came from predominantly Republican districts, Peckham's nonpartisan attitude was universally applauded—a revealing commentary on prevailing expectations of judicial neutrality. Peckham thought the disfranchisement under the circumstances "unnecessary" and "unreasonable" and saw it as a "burlesque on the Ballot Act and its construction." In this instance, Peckham indicated that procedural exactitude must yield to insure substantive justice.

In the unusual case of *Schuyler* v. *Curtis,* 147 N.Y. 434 (1895), a nephew of Miss Mary Hamilton Schuyler, then deceased fourteen years, sued to enjoin the erection of a statue to his aunt by the Woman's Memorial Fund. The plaintiff claimed that the right of privacy had been invaded without consent and that Miss

Schuyler, a sensitive and shy woman, and never a public figure, would not have approved of such a memorial. The primary reason for the suit, however, appeared to be that the fund planned to display the Schuyler statue alongside one of Susan B. Anthony, and that Miss Schuyler allegedly would have been, and her relatives would be, scandalized by this apparent association. Peckham admitted that the rights of privacy constituted a somewhat ill-defined area and he therefore found it useful to employ as a criteria for judgment the "sensitivities of the reasonable man." It seemed clear to him, however, that whatever rights Miss Schuyler once enjoyed died with her, a curious view of the extinction of personal rights when set alongside Peckham's attitudes toward the life of corporate privilege expressed in *People* v. *O'Brien.* Furthermore the "reasonable man," he thought, would not find such a well-intentioned memorial offensive. "Feelings that are thus easily and unnaturally injured and distressed are much too sensitive," he observed, "to be recognized by our purely earthly tribunal." Although "many of us may, and probably do, totally disagree with those advanced ideas of Miss Anthony," Peckham conceded that the suffragette possessed "ennobling qualities." He concluded that the plaintiff's case was "fanciful" and refused to grant the injunction. It is of some interest to note that Judge Gray in his dissent spoke of the sacred right of privacy and construed this right as "a form of property." Peckham's "reasonable man" was unwilling to go this far.

The most significant of Peckham's decisions, historically speaking, were those in which he outlined certain ideas and attitudes which were soon to be associated with the new judicial conservatism. One component of this new outlook was the willingness of the bench to intrude into the political arena and decide on the efficacy and appropriateness of public policy decisions. In the tenement house case Peckham had indicated that it was for the courts to judge the reasonableness of the new regulations concerning water taps. Judicial interventionism assumed a new dimension when Peckham dissented from the majority in *Talcott* v. *City of Buffalo,* 125 N.Y. 280 (1891). The question before the Court was whether or not a taxpayer could act to restrain a governing body in a city from official action within its power and discretion without proving the existence of fraud, collusion, corruption, or bad faith. The majority thought that under the circumstances the citizen was powerless to act, but Peckham believed otherwise. He observed that the courts could be used to enjoin action that involved patent waste of the property or funds of the public. The existence of frequent elections as a restraining force on public officials failed to impress Peckham. "Experience has shown," noted Peckham, that they have "the very slightest deterrent effect." Only the courts could provide an effective and immediate corrective against official wrongdoing, so Peckham believed, and he therefore welcomed the extension of judicial authority into this sphere as an "exceedingly healthful" practice. The judicial writ might one day replace the reform campaign.

People v. *Gillson,* 109 N.Y. 389 (1888), provided Peckham with an opportunity to further elaborate upon his judicial conservatism. Here Peckham struck down a state law prohibiting the inclusion of a gift or reward with the sale of food. He could not accept this as a legitimate exercise of state authority but classified it as that kind of law "which has been so frequent of late, a kind which is meant to protect some class in the community against the fair, free, and full competition of some other class . . ." More important, Peckham proved receptive to the new definitions of individual liberty with their *laissez faire* implications, first advanced by Supreme Court Justices Field and Bradley and generally followed by Peckham's predecessors on the New York Court of Appeals. The term "liberty," Peckham contended, was "not dwarfed into mere freedom from physical restraint" but was "deemed to embrace the right of man to be free in the enjoyment of the faculties with which he has been endowed by the Creator, subject only to such restraints as are necessary for the common welfare." In this instance the attempt to prevent certain merchandising techniques involved an arbitrary interference with individual liberty without the redeeming factor of a direct relationship to the state's police powers. Peckham, of course, thought it was for the courts, not the legislature, to determine what were valid enactments under the police powers, a view prominently identified with the new judicial conservatism.

Although it is generally thought that Peckham's conservatism found its most trenchant expression in *Lochner* v. *New York,* 198 U.S. 45 (1905), an examination of *People* v. *Budd,* 117 N.Y. 1 (1889), reveals a far more developed and skillfully sustained conservative statement. It is this case rather than the Lochner decision that merited Holmes' grand rebuke. In *People* v. *Budd* Peckham dissented from the majority view which upheld the state's authority in fixing maximum charges for grain elevators. In doing so, he advanced in bold, unrestrained fashion virtually the complete conservative litany, along with some unusual variations. Peckham met the issue squarely. He simply rejected the common law doctrine of "affected with a public interest" developed in England by Lord Chief Justice Hale and accepted by the Supreme Court in *Munn* v. *Illinois,* 94 U.S. 113 (1877). In an extraordinary discussion of judicial relativism Peckham conceded that the doctrine may at one time have had a certain validity or at least could "be pardoned on account of ignorance, sparseness of population, difficulties of communication and rural and unsettled habits of life." Moreover, Lord Hale could not be held entirely responsible for his rather indiscreet creation because he wrote "when views of governmental interference with the private concerns of individuals were carried to the greatest extent" and therefore "he was naturally and necessarily affected by the atmosphere of the times in which he lived." Peckham, although admitting that "all men, however great and however honest, are almost necessarily affected by the general belief of their times," experienced little difficulty in declaring flatly that his own views on the matter represented the highest level of enlightenment. Continued adherence to the old ideas of paternal government, he proclaimed, would "wholly ignore the later and as I firmly believe the more correct ideas which an increase of civilization and a fuller knowledge of the fundamental laws of political economy, and a truer conception of the proper functions of government have given us at the present day." In short, government regulation of property by rate fixing was an anachronism whose success could not be "other than of the most ephemeral nature" due to its basic departure from "the general laws of trade" and the inevitable operations of supply and demand.

Peckham believed that even if the doctrine had a certain relevance it could not be extended to apply to grain elevators. There was nothing uniquely public about these facilities; they enjoyed no special privileges and could not be used without the consent of their owners. Heavy use by the public and the offering of goods to the public did not justify placing them "at the mercy of the public in respect to charges and prices." Because anyone could enter this business Peckham would not classify it as a monopoly nor subject it to public regulation.

Peckham warned against the continued acceptance of such principles by the courts. In the classic though somewhat stylized fashion of the conservatives, Peckham invoked a procession of horribles to point out that few areas of human endeavor would be free from public regulation were the criteria for such intervention simply the fact of heavy use by the public or the application of public good and general welfare considerations. Moreover, "to uphold legislation of this character is to provide the most frequent opportunity for arraying class against class," thus introducing a new "competition for the possession of the government so that legislative aid may be given to the class in possession thereof in its contests with rival classes or interests in all sections and corners of the industrial world." To avert this, Peckham begged the Court not to "strain after holding such species of legislation constitutional. It is so plain an effort to interfere with what seems to me the most sacred rights of property and the individual's liberty of contract that no special intendment in its favor should be indulged in . . ." The constitutional clauses preventing the denial of life, liberty, or property without due process of law must have "a large and liberal interpretation." In a passionate peroration Peckham hurled his final bolts of vilification. "The legislation under consideration is not only vicious in its nature, communistic in its tendency and in my belief wholly ineffective to permanently obtain the results aimed at, but illegal." The Peckham of *Lochner* v. *New York* surely needs no introduction after *People* v. *Budd.*

Peckham's appointment to the Supreme Court climaxed a prolonged struggle between President Cleveland and Senator Hill of New York, both competing for control over the Democratic party in New York State. It began in 1894 when Cleveland nominated William B. Hornblower, a prominent New York City lawyer, to the Supreme Court. Senator Hill then announced his opposition to the candidate and prepared to invoke senatorial courtesy. Hill's objections arose from Hornblower's participation in the celebrated Maynard episode. Isaac Maynard had become the target of severe criticism when, as deputy attorney general of New York State in 1893, it was alleged that he had tampered with certain election returns so as to assure Democratic control of the state senate. Suspicions of his complicity seemed to be confirmed when he received an interim appointment to the New York Court of Appeals by the then Governor Hill, seemingly as a reward for his services. The New York Bar Association, outraged by the incident, appointed an investigating committee which uncovered Maynard's wrongdoing. The association subsequently led a successful campaign to prevent the election of Maynard to a full term on the Court. Hornblower had been involved in the anti-Maynard campaign and had thus incurred the enmity of Hill. Although President Cleveland recognized that he could not obtain the confirmation of Hornblower, he was determined not to yield to Hill. As evidence of the President's combativeness he next announced the nomination of Wheeler H. Peckham, the brother of Rufus. Wheeler H. Peckham had simply been president of the New York Bar Association at the time it had moved against Maynard. Once more Hill met this direct challenge by calling upon his colleagues to respect senatorial courtesy. The President, defeated in his confrontation with Hill, passed over the legal talent of New York and selected Senator Edward White of Louisiana, a nomination quickly confirmed.

With the death of Justice Jackson in 1895, Cleveland appeared ready to renew his struggle with Hill. He approached Hornblower once more, but this time the New York lawyer declined to accept the nomination. Frederic Coudert, another leading member of the New York Bar, turned down a similar offer. By this time, Cleveland, eager to appoint a New Yorker to the bench, was prepared to yield to Hill. Hill had, during the Hornblower affair, indicated his approval of Rufus Peckham, and Cleveland, in a tactful letter to the New York senator, now inquired to determine whether he was still acceptable. Hill offered no objection even though Peckham had often been aligned against him in Democratic party affairs. Peckham received the official nomination in December of 1895, and gained confirmation easily in that same month. His nomination occasioned few comments. All agreed that he was a respectable and able man and that his elevation to the Supreme Court would assure its continued adherence to sound principles.

Peckham was probably not surprised by his appointment to the Court. His friend Grover Cleveland had often predicted, "We'll get you down to Washington yet, Rufus." Peckham did not appear especially jubilant over the nomination. He had always found more enjoyment sitting upon the lower trial courts than appearing in the more rarified and scholastic environments of the appellate courts. That Peckham was something less than exultant may be seen in his comment to a friend, shortly after the nomination: "If I have got to be put away on the shelf I suppose I might as well be on the top shelf." Once arriving in Washington, however, Peckham, with the devotion of the Puritan following a calling, threw himself into his work. He was rarely seen in Washington society, accepted few invitations to public affairs, and made no public addresses. He was, however, not entirely enveloped by the impersonality of his judicial robes. For example, in 1896 he was advising President Cleveland to avoid any commitment respecting a third term and in 1907 he received attention as a possible gubernatorial nominee in New York. The rest of Peckham's life, however, would be spent on the Supreme Court and, judging from his physical appearance at least, few could question his right to be there. His strong clear features, Roman nose, chiseled chin, unusually long wavy hair and full bushy mustache, both turning silvery gray, combined to create a figure of distinction.

Peckham's years on the Supreme Court coincided with the rise of the Progressive Movement with its penchant for legislative activism. Even before Peckham arrived, the Court had already made clear in the *Pollock* and *Knight* cases, 158 U.S. 601 (1895) and 156 U.S. 1 (1895), its resistance to what it considered to be dangerous social experiments and its intention to scrutinize carefully legislative enactments involving threats to private property and individual liberties. Peckham, therefore, joined a court whose views in many ways resembled his own. Consequently, he found little difficulty in siding with the majority in most instances. His dissenting opinions, moreover, rarely broke new legal ground but rather reflected older doctrines and attitudes vitalized on occasion by the fervor with which he expressed them.

It is probably in Peckham's treatment of that most extraordinary of judicial creations, liberty of contract, that his philosophy becomes most sharply etched. Peckham, while on the New York Court of Appeals, had already accepted the rather exuberant and spacious definitions of liberty originally found in the dissenting opinions of Supreme Court Justices Bradley and Field. Once on the Supreme Court, Peckham helped convert these views into majority opinions and added them to the arsenal of legal weapons available for the protection of business enterprise. In *Allgeyer* v. *Louisiana,* 165 U.S. 578 (1897), the shift was accomplished. The case involved a challenge to a Louisiana law which prohibited individuals or brokers from contracting for fire and marine insurance with foreign companies that had failed to comply with state regulations. The Court had previously upheld similar legislation as valid exercises of state authority. Peckham, however, viewed the matter differently. He could have interpreted the law as involving undue interference with interstate commerce and declared it void on that account. Instead he chose to see it as an infringement upon the liberty of the individual and thus provided himself with an opportunity to expatiate upon the full meaning of liberty. It included, he thought, more than freedom from mere physical restraint but embraced "the right of the citizen to be free in the enjoyment of all his faculties; to be free to use them in all lawful ways; to live and work where he will; to earn his livelihood by any lawful calling; to pursue any livelihood or avocation; and for that purpose to enter into all contracts which may be proper, necessary and essential to his carrying out to a successful conclusion the purposes above mentioned." Peckham moved boldly here, acting as if the above definition of liberty had been long established by the Court, whereas in fact its status until then had been doubtful. Peckham persuaded the Court that the right to pursue a trade also entailed the "right to make all proper contracts in relation thereto" and thus artfully laid the basis for the further immunity of business from legislative control. The extent of the state's police powers received little attention from Peckham here. He was content to announce that the scope of such powers "must be left for determination to each case as it arises." This view obviously sanctioned continued judicial activism, a situation congenial to Peckham's way of thinking.

In *Holden* v. *Hardy,* 169 U.S. 366 (1898), Peckham dissented from the majority ruling which upheld a Utah statute prohibiting the employment of workingmen in mines, smelters, or oil refineries for more than eight hours in any one day, except in emergencies. The Court shared Peckham's concern for the right of liberty of contract as set forth in the *Allgeyer* case, but it felt that this right must at times yield to the intervention of the state in the legitimate exercise of its police powers. Although Peckham offered no explanation for his dissent, it was apparent that he was unwilling to accept infringements upon what he considered to be the sacred right to liberty of contract. In 1905, in *Jacobson* v. *Massachusetts,* 197 U.S. 11, the Court was asked to rule on the validity of a state law requiring compulsory vaccination. It found little difficulty in accepting this limitation on the individual's liberty particularly because the sensitive matter of business regulation was not involved and the element of health protection was so clearly paramount. Peckham again refused to concur with the majority, but once more, in the absence of a dissenting opinion, his reasons for doing so are not known. It may be that because liberty, in the original sense of physical restraint, was involved, Peckham was willing to accept the view of Jacobson that the law was "hostile to the inherent rights of every free man to care for his own body and health in such a way as to him seems best."

Recognizing Peckham's attachment to the idea of liberty of contract and his presumptions against state regulation, his decision in *Lochner* v. *New York,* 198 U.S. 45 (1905), was scarcely surprising. Nevertheless it created a storm of controversy and for many it seemed to epitomize the existing temper of the Court. His decision is generally cited as representing the high water mark of the Court's tendency toward abstraction, intervention, and patronization and suspicion of state legislative bodies. Peckham's rhetoric, logic, and conclusions in this case have been endlessly scrutinized by scores of legal scholars seeking to expose the weaknesses and prejudices in the judicial thinking of the day.

In *Lochner* the Court prepared to rule on the constitutionality of a New York State statute limiting bakery employees to a ten-hour workday or a sixty-hour work week. The law had already been upheld by the New York Supreme Court and Court of Appeals but only by the narrowest of margins. Peckham, who had disapproved of a somewhat similar exercise of state regulation in *Holden* v. *Hardy,* found no reason to change his mind here. With him as umpire the police powers were normally at a distinct disadvantage in their battles with liberty of contract. It appeared that Peckham, in the minority in *Holden* v. *Hardy* and *Jacobson* v. *Massachusetts,* was emboldened by the fact that he was now speaking for the majority. His decision was thus strong, opinionated, and reminiscent of the emotional intensity he had displayed in *People* v. *Budd.*

Peckham began by conceding the existence of the "somewhat vaguely termed police powers, the exact description and limits of which have not been attempted by the courts." In previous decisions the Court had imposed, he thought, a liberal construction on the extent of the police powers and had, in this way, approved their application in many dubious cases. Peckham feared that were this trend to continue the police powers would become a "mere pretext" and might ultimately be employed to support the supreme sovereignty of the state. That the limits "of the police power [have] been reached and passed in this case," seemed self-evident to Peckham.

The police powers could not be invoked in support of the legislation, Peckham insisted, because it was not at all clear that a distinct health problem existed within the bakeries. Nor could the state, he added, have intended it as a labor law because "there is no contention that bakers as a class are not equal in intelligence and capacity to men in other trades or manual occupations." They could "in no sense" be considered "wards of the state." Such personal observations conflicted directly with Peckham's assurances that it was "not a question of substituting the judgment of the Court for that of the legislature." Indeed, Peckham was quite prepared to offer a number of judgments as to the healthfulness of bakeries. He indicated an awareness of certain statistics on the matter but said only that they tended to support his position. Peckham began by arbitrarily limiting his discussion to questions involving the health of bakery employees only. Considerations of the public's health were not deemed relevant. There had been some suggestion that a link existed between shorter hours and cleaner bread but Peckham considered the connection to be too tenuous and shadowy to be recognized by the Court. Casting aside all doubts Peckham proclaimed that "clean and wholesome bread does not depend upon whether the baker works but ten hours per day or sixty hours a week."

Peckham thought the law had incorrectly implied that the bakery environment was singularly unwholesome. To his view there was "no fair doubt that the trade of baker in and of itself is not an unhealthy one to that degree which would authorize the legislature to interfere with the right of labor." Moreover, the health of the bakers had already been ensured by the state through a host of sanitary regulations enforced on such premises. Were the statute at issue accepted, the people would soon be at "the mercy of legislative majorities," Peckham warned. If "some small amount of unhealthfulness" proved sufficient "to warrant legislative interference with liberty" there would be no end to the "meddlesome interference with the rights of the individual . . ." Peckham, disturbed that legislative intervention "seems to be on the increase," indulged in his gift for evil prophecy and predicted with sweeping sarcasm that upholding the regulation of bakers' hours would lead to similar legislation respecting lawyers, professional men, athletes, artisans, and "urban workers working where the sun penetrates but a short time." He concluded somewhat ominously by observing that the Court was not oblivious to the real motives behind such laws. He did not elaborate but it appeared that once more he had detected some powerful interest group attempting to bend the state to its will. Peckham apparently believed that by striking down such legislation the Court might convince these interests that their tactics were futile, thus protecting the state from the clash of contending forces and classes. Peckham might even have believed that through such decisions as *Lochner* he was promoting social harmony.

Peckham's majority in this case was a narrow one. Four Justices demurred, with Justices Harlan and Holmes writing the dissenting opinions. Harlan disputed Peckham's position of presumptive guilt and contended instead that the Court should be predisposed in favor of legislative enactments especially when in the present instance there was a "substantial relation between the means employed by the state and the end sought to be accomplished by the legislation." Harlan recognized that the question of health was not one of abstract opinion or prejudice and referred to existing statistical data and health studies which cast doubts on the salubrity of bakeries. Holmes, in a pithy and spirited dissent, called for judicial tolerance and forbearance and reminded his brethren that the Constitution was "made for people of fundamentally differing views." Rather than interpreting the statute as the result of special interest group pressure, Holmes viewed it more tolerantly and broadly as "a first installment of a general regulation of the hours of work."

These arguments may have impressed Peckham because three years afterward he retreated from his defense of liberty of contract and joined a unanimous Court in upholding an Oregon statute prohibiting the employment of women in mechanical establishments, factories, and laundries for more than ten hours in any one day, in *Muller* v. *Oregon,* 208 U.S. 412 (1908). He did not provide the Court with an explanation for his views. Whether he was influenced by the Brandeis Brief, mellowed by old age, or convinced that the weaknesses and differences of women merited special treatment, is difficult to determine. Judging from his opposition to the woman's rights movement the latter explanation may have been the deciding factor. Thus with few exceptions Peckham stood as the stalwart champion of the liberty of contract, regarding it not as a recent creation of the judges but as an eternal verity.

Peckham also rendered a number of notable opinions related to the enforcement of the Sherman Act of 1890 which had declared illegal every contract combination or trust acting in restraint of trade. The Supreme Court's decision in *United States* v. *E. C. Knight Co.,* 156 U.S. 1 (1895), had severely curtailed the effectiveness of the law by erecting a distinction between production and commerce and limiting the operation of the law to matters involving the latter. Peckham's decisions halted the attrition of the 1890 law and to some degree restored its vigor. Peckham generally sympathized with efforts to halt the spread of monopoly, recognizing that failure to do so would result in the destruction of the small businessman and an end to the effective operation of the laws of competition. In *United States* v. *Trans-Missouri Freight Association,* 166 U.S. 290 (1897), these ideas appear most cogently. Arguing against the contention that combinations often reduced prices, Peckham maintained that the real price of such reductions would be "dearly paid for by the ruin of small dealers and worthy men" engaged in the same line of business. In a ringing and prescient declaration Peckham warned against the displacement of the rugged, individual entrepreneur by the submissive organization man. "It is not for the real prosperity of any country that such changes should occur which result in transferring an independent business man, the head of his establishment, small though it might be, into a mere servant or agent of a corporation for selling the commodities which he once manufactured or dealt in, having no voice in shaping the business policy of the company and bound to obey orders issued by others."

The case itself involved a government suit against eighteen railroads charged with creating an association in order to fix rates. Spokesmen for the railroads contended that the Sherman Act intended to reach only those who were engaged in the manufacture or sale of the articles of commerce and did not apply to the agents of commerce. Peckham rejected this view and maintained that the "railroad companies are instruments of commerce and their business is commerce itself." The railroads insisted furthermore that what was prohibited was merely unreasonable restraints of trade. Peckham, however, refused "to read into the act by way of judicial legislation an exception that is not placed there by the lawmaking branch of the government." Peckham warned that to accept the idea of reasonableness would plunge all involved into a thicket of subjectivity and confusion because there was "an infinite variety of facts entering into the question of what is a reasonable rate." The Supreme Court would later accept the idea of reasonableness and find itself entangled in the morass of technical details that Peckham had envisioned. Finally Peckham disputed the railroad companies' contentions that theirs was an industry where competition no longer served a useful function and that they therefore were entitled to special consideration. Peckham noted that there was "no guaranty of financial health to be found in entering agreements for the maintenance of rates . . ." Peckham had held his ground on all fronts. He did so again in *United States* v. *Joint Traffic Association,* 171 U.S. 505 (1898), a similar case involving a combination of railroads to fix rates. Here the defendants insisted that preventing the combination involved infringement upon their rights to liberty of contract. Peckham, normally sensitive to such pleas, remained unmoved. The liberty of contract claimed, he replied, was not relevant because the contract was an improper one and there was surely no freedom to enter into illegal contracts.

Peckham, in *Addyston Pipe and Steel Company* v. *United States,* 175 U.S. 211 (1899), moved some distance toward recapturing the ground lost by the immunity given to manufacturers in the *Knight* case. In this instance six corporations engaged in the manufacture, sale, and transportation of iron pipe were accused of violating the Sherman Act because of collusive bidding on contracts to sell and deliver the pipe to out-of-state customers. Peckham in upholding the government denied that a total monopoly was necessary as proof of restraint of trade. Higher prices by themselves, he asserted, served to lessen the amount of trade. Peckham distinguished this case from *Knight* by noting that the bids specifically involved selling and delivery rather than manufacturing and that there was therefore a direct and immediate affect upon interstate commerce.

Peckham here rejuvenated the Sherman Act but hardly nursed it back to full strength. He still recognized its inapplicability where sales were an incident to and not the direct result of manufacture and he also accepted the distinction between the direct and indirect affect on interstate commerce. Thus in an earlier decision, *Hopkins* v. *United States,* 171 U.S. 578 (1898), he declared that the Kansas City Live Stock Exchange was not engaged directly in interstate commerce even though its members bought and sold cattle outside the state and sent agents through many states soliciting business. Those who expedited and channeled the stream of commerce were not, however, directly affecting it, ruled Peckham. He thus sustained but did not materially strengthen the Sherman Act.

Peckham's attitude toward judicial procedures in criminal cases merits some attention in view of his previous experience as a prosecutor in Albany and the general sensitivity toward substantive as well as procedural due process among conservatives. In a number of cases, especially *Stevenson* v. *United States,* 162 U.S. 313 (1896) and *Mills* v. *United States,* 164 U.S. 645 (1897), Peckham ordered retrials after uncovering improper procedures in the trial court that he believed had exerted a substantive affect on the ultimate decisions. In the latter case, involving a rape conviction, Peckham warned that such a charge was "easy to be made and hard to be defended against" and therefore "great caution is required . . . in order that the natural indignation of men . . . may not be misdirected." In most instances, however, Peckham displayed the prosecutor's mentality. When, in *Sandy White* v. *United States,* 164 U.S. 100 (1896) and *Crain* v. *United States,* 162 U.S. 625 (1896), attempts were made to overturn lower court convictions because of errors in the trial record, Peckham refused to accept such arguments. The errors, he asserted, involved the "merest technicality" and had no bearing on the outcome of the decision. In the *Crain* case, Peckham, in a manner recalling *People* v. *Budd,* engaged in a display of relativistic chest thumping by comparing his own enlightened age with earlier and more primitive periods. In the latter, procedural matters and technical questions "stood between the criminal and the enforcement of a most severe, if not cruel penalty." But, insisted Peckham, "these times have passed and the reasons for the strict and slavish adherance to mere form have passed with them."

Peckham's cavalier attitude toward procedural matters in criminal cases emerged most vividly in *Maxwell* v. *Dow,* 176 U.S. 581 (1900). Peckham upheld a criminal conviction in Utah despite the absence of a grand jury indictment and the presence of only an eight-member trial jury. Such procedures would have been disallowed had they occurred within the federal court system, but the states were not bound by the requirements contained within the federal Bill of Rights, argued Peckham. The Fourteenth Amendment could not be used as a bridge to transfer federal safeguards into the state's judicial processes. Suggesting the existence of a duel citizenship, Peckham offered the view that "the Fourteenth Amendment does not profess to secure to all persons in the U.S. the benefit of the same laws and the same remedies." Procedural diversity therefore was to be tolerated, even respected. "It is emphatically the case of the people by their organic laws providing for their own affairs and we are of the opinion that they are much better judges of what they ought to have in these respects than anyone else can be. It is a case of self protection and the people can be trusted to look out and care for themselves."

The almost embarrassing contradictions of Peckham's conservative thinking can hardly be overlooked. In the defense of property rights he virtually ransacked the procedural process to uncover the slightest irregularities which might disrupt the due processes of law. In criminal cases, however, proper procedure assumed the form of mere window dressing. When the states attempted in their own fashion to regulate economic activities he was apt to raise the cry of meddlesome interference. When on the other hand the states introduced varying and less stringent procedural standards in criminal cases, this experimentation was praised as intelligent accommodation to local circumstances. Consistency here seemed to exist only in Peckham's persistent subjectivity. When legislation accorded with his social philosophy, legal obstacles would not be strewn in its path. When he thought state enactments unwise, meddlesome, or unduly experimental, they were likely to be blocked by judicial construction. But such conclusions are perhaps too simple and incomplete. Many cases were borderline affairs and in those Peckham's decisions could not be predicted. Two cases, *Fallbrook Irrigation District* v. *Bradley,* 164 U.S. 112 (1896) and *Willcox* v. *Consolidated Gas Company,* 212 U.S. 19 (1909), may be used to illustrate this point.

The *Fallbrook* case involved a California statute permitting the creation of local irrigation districts which were authorized to exercise the power of eminent domain and to assess all landowners in the district to support irrigation projects, whether they be willing or unwilling participants and whether they benefited directly or not. Peckham, after observing that the requirements of procedural due process had been met, upheld the law because the property that had been taken was destined for public use and public benefits in the form of increased productivity of California soils would accrue. The determination of public use could not be decided by a remote authority. "The people of California," Peckham asserted, "and the members of her legislature must in the nature of things be more familiar with the facts and circumstances which surround the subject . . . than anyone who is a stranger to her soil." To the argument that many who were taxed would not benefit at all while others would gain disproportionately, Peckham replied that it was "not essential that the entire community or even any considerable portion thereof should directly enjoy or participate in an improvement in order to constitute a public use." Over the dissenting views of Justices Fuller and Field, Peckham though not distinguishing clearly between public use and public purpose concluded that "in such cases the absolute right of each individual owner of land must yield to a certain extent . . . for what is declared upon the whole to be for the public benefit." These words do not appear to be those of an unregenerate conservative.

In *Willcox* v. *Consolidated Gas Company, supra,* the New York company categorized the rate scale, imposed by the State's Public Service Commission but not yet in effect, as confiscatory and asked the Supreme Court to overturn it. Peckham was unwilling to accept the company's evaluation without more conclusive evidence. "The case must be a clear one," he stated, "before the courts ought to be asked to interfere with state legislation upon the subject of rates," and the case was anything but clear since the rates had not yet gone into effect. In the absence of a practical demonstration of the consequences of these lower rates there was little reason to accept them as inherently confiscatory, given the ample evidence that reduced rates frequently led to increased consumption and higher profits. Perkham noted that, given the diversity of conditions across the nation and the peculiar nature of different businesses, there was "no particular rate of compensation which must in all cases and in all parts of the country be regarded as sufficient for capital invested in business enterprise." In the present case, with the gas company in a virtually monopolistic position Peckham ruled that a six per cent return on capital investment seemed fair. He struck down, however, lower court rulings which he thought had unduly inflated the value of the company's property. "Good will," for example, could not be added to the value of the property because of the company's monopolistic position. Peckham's decision thus upheld the existing Public Service Commission's rates and deferred court action until some future time when a plaintiff might offer more substantial proof of their confiscatory character. Once more, while Peckham emerges as alert to the rights of property and sensitive to the various conditions affecting profit margins, he does not stand as the zealous guardian of inflexible abstractions.

The age of Supreme Court Justices assures the nation that the Court will reflect the views of men whose education and experience derive from an earlier generation. This is all quite deliberate and calculated to provide a court whose opinion will reflect a mature wisdom. Difficulties arise, however, when a society which has undergone abnormally rapid changes finds its organic law interpreted by men of another and very different era. The case of Peckham is most instructive here. Peckham was clearly a man of the nineteenth century, primarily of small town and rural America, a man not caught up by the dynamism of the late nineteenth century, somewhat insulated by his many years on the bench and inclined toward the past because of an identification with his father. He absorbed the values and expectations of his own age and environment and there is little evidence that he ever seriously questioned them. But he came to the Court in an era in which American society was struggling to cope with and adjust to widespread cleavages and dislocations, the outcome of years of rapid changes and general indifference to their consequences. The problem would not be solved by stubbornly clinging to older views or devising legal constructions which discouraged experimentation and thwarted local efforts. In all fairness, Peckham in certain of his decisions and *obiter dicta* recognized that conditions had changed and that the law would have to follow suit. Yet while he took some tentative steps toward understanding the twentieth century, they were not large enough so that Rufus Peckham, Sr. would not have recognized his son.

In 1909 Peckham died while still serving on the bench. Aside from the sincere regrets expressed by his colleagues and the praise forthcoming from his former associates, there was notably scant coverage of his passing. It appeared that America, caught up within the ferment of the Progressive spirit and hopeful about the future, no longer cared to recognize those who had suspected change and had looked to the past exclusively for guidance.

SELECTED BIBLIOGRAPHY

Reliable materials on the life and career of Peckham can be found only in bits and snatches and then not too easily. No book or essay has yet appeared on him. In Allan Nevins, *Grover Cleveland* (New York, 1932) and Louis Boudin, *Government by Judiciary* (New York, 1932) there are some items of interest. Of the small number of periodical and newspaper pieces published during his lifetime few provide much useful information. Perhaps the most valuable is A. Oakey Hall, 8 *Green Bag* (1896). In addition, 13 *Law Notes* 168 (1895) and 55 *Albany Law Journal* 287 (1895) provide some biographical material. Furthermore, during Peckham's tenure on the Supreme Court *The Review of Reviews, Harpers Weekly, The Outlook,* and *Current Literature* occasionally carried small items about Peckham. *The New York Tribune* paid some attention to Peckham's political activities in New York State. The issues of September 13, 1879, September 30, October 1, 2, and December 25, 1886 detail some of these activities. At his death, tributes were paid to him by friends and members of the legal profession. These may be found in the *Proceedings of the New York State Bar Association* (1910) and 215 U.S. v–xiii (1909). His opinions therefore remain the greatest source of information about this somewhat obscure Justice.

Rufus Peckham

REPRESENTATIVE OPINIONS

ALLGEYER v. LOUISIANA 165 U.S. 578 (1897)

The case represented a major expression by the Court of the relatively new doctrine of freedom of contract, one which until then had been employed only by those in dissent. The case thus represented the coming of age and acceptance of this doctrine. In dispute was a Louisiana statute which levied a fine on those persons using marine insurance companies that had failed to qualify under state law. Just two years before in *Hooper* v. *California* the Court had upheld the powers of the state to exclude foreign fire and marine insurance companies if they failed to comply with state laws. This time Justice Peckham, speaking for the majority, ruled otherwise. Peckham chose not to nullify the law on the basis of state interference with interstate commerce but rather interpreted it as an interference with the individual's liberty of contract. This liberty according to Peckham embraced "not only the right of the citizen to be free from . . . mere physical restraint," but included the right to enter into all contracts for a wide variety of lawful purposes especially in relation to his calling. In this case the police powers remained in the background, Peckham noting that their extent "must be left for determining to each case as it arises." Nevertheless, Allgeyer, by establishing and giving broad definition to the freedom of contract, represented a major triumph for the *laissez faire* principle.

MR. JUSTICE PECKHAM, after stating the case, delivered the opinion of the court.

There is no doubt of the power of the State to prohibit foreign insurance companies from doing business within its limits. The State can impose such conditions as it pleases upon the doing of any business by those companies within its borders, and unless the conditions be complied with the prohibition may be absolute. The cases upon this subject are cited in the opinion of the court in *Hooper* v. *California,* 155 U.S. 648.

A conditional prohibition in regard to foreign insurance companies doing business within the State of Louisiana is to be found in article 236 of the constitution of that State, which reads as follows: "No foreign corporation shall do any business in this State without having one or more known places of business, and an authorized agent or agents in the State, upon whom process may be served."

It is not claimed in this suit that the Atlantic Mutual Insurance Company has violated this provision of the constitution by doing business within the State.

In the *State of Louisiana* v. *Williams,* 46 La. Ann. 922, the Supreme Court of that State held that an open policy of marine insurance, similar in all respects to the one herein described, and made by a foreign insurance company, not doing business within the State and having no agent therein, must be considered as made at the domicile of the company issuing the open policy, and that where in such case the insurance company had no agent in Louisiana it could not be considered as doing an insurance business within the State.

The learned counsel for the State also admits in his brief the fact that the contract (*i.e.* the open policy) was entered into at New York City.

In the course of the opinion delivered in this case by the Supreme Court of Louisiana that court said:

"The open policy in this case is conceded to be a New York contract; hence the special insurance effected on the cotton complained of here was a New York contract.

"The question presented here is the simple proposition whether under the act a party while in the State can insure property in Louisiana in a foreign insurance company, which has not complied with the laws of the State, under an open policy—the special contract of insurance—and the open policy being contracts made and entered into beyond the limits of the State.

* * * * *

"We are not dealing with the contract. If it be legal in New York, it is valid elsewhere. We are concerned only with the fact of its having been entered into by a citizen of Louisiana while within her limits affecting property within her territorial limits. It is the act of the party, and not the contract, which we are to consider. The defendants who made the contract did so while they were in the State, and it had reference to property located within the State. Such a contract is in violation of the laws of the State, and the defendants who made it were within the jurisdiction of the State, and must be necessarily subject to its penalties, unless there is some inhibition in the Federal or state constitution, or that it violates one of those inalienable rights relating to persons and property that are inherent, although not expressed, in the organic law. It does not forbid the carrying on by the insurance company of its legalized business within the State. It is a means of preventing its doing so without subscribing to certain conditions which are recognized as legitimate and proper. It does not destroy the constitutional right of the citizens of New York to do business within the State of Louisiana or of the citizens of Louisiana from insuring property. It says to the citizens of New York engaged in insurance business that they must, like its own citizens, pay a license and have an authorized agent in the State as prerequisite to their doing said business within its State, and says to its own citizens: You shall not make a contract while in the State with any foreign insurance company which has not complied with the laws. You shall not in this manner contravene the public policy of the State in aiding and assisting in the violation of the laws of the State. The sovereignty of the State would be a mockery if it had not the power to compel its citizens to respect its laws.

* * * * *

"The defendants while in the State undoubtedly insured their property located in the State in a foreign insurance company under an open policy. The instant the letter or communication was mailed or telegraphed the property was insured. The act of insurance was done within the State and the offence denounced by the statute was complete.

* * * * *

"There is in the statute an apparent interference with the liberty of defendants in restricting their rights to place insurance on property of their own whenever and in what company they desired; but in exercising this liberty they would interfere with the policy of the State that forbids insurance companies which have not complied with the laws of the State from doing business within its limits. Individual liberty of action must give way to the greater right of the collective people in the assertion of well-defined policy, designed and intended for the general welfare."

The general contract contained in the open policy, as well as the special insurance upon each shipment of goods of which notice is given to the insurance company, being contracts made in New York and valid there, the State of Louisiana claims notwithstanding such facts that the defendants have violated the act of 1894, by doing an act in that State to effect for themselves insurance on their property then in that State in a marine insurance company which had not complied in all respects with the laws of that State, and that such violation consisted in the act of mailing a letter or sending a telegram to the insurance company in New York describing the cotton upon which the defendants desired the insurance under the open marine policy to attach. It is claimed on the part of the State that its legislature had the power to provide that such an act should be illegal and to subject the offender to the penalties provided in the statute. It is said by the Supreme Court that the validity of such a statute has been decided in principle in this court in the case of *Hooper* v. *California,* 155 U.S. 648.

We think the distinction between that case and the one at bar is plain and material. The State of California made it a misdemeanor for a person in that State to procure insurance for a resident of the State from an insurance company not incorporated under its laws, and which had not filed a bond required by those laws relative to insurance. Hooper was a resident of San Francisco and was the agent of the firm of Johnson & Higgins, who were insurance brokers residing and having their principal place of business in the city of New York, but having also a place of business in the city and county of San Francisco, of which the defendant had charge as their employé and agent. In response to a request from a Mr. Mott, a resident of the State of California, the defendant Hooper procured through his principals, Johnson & Higgins, an insurance upon the steamer Alliance, belonging to said Mott, in the China Mutual Insurance Company, which was a company not then and there incorporated under the laws of California, and not having itself or by its agent filed the bond required by those laws relating to insurance. The policy was delivered by the defendant Hooper to Mott, the insured, at San Francisco, who thereupon paid Hooper, as agent of Johnson & Higgins, the premium for the insurance. The case states that "all the verbal acts of Mott, the insured, and also of the defendant and all his acts as agent in procuring said insurance, were done in the city and county of San Francisco." The court held that the whole transaction amounted to procuring insurance within the State of California by Hooper, residing there and for a resident in the State, from an insurance company not incorporated under its laws and which had not filed the bond required by the laws of the State relative to insurance; that Hooper, the defendant, acted as the agent of his principals in New York City, who were average adjusters and brokers there, and who had a place of business in San Francisco, and that Hooper, as such broker, having applied for the insurance to his principals in New York City, received the policy from them for delivery in San Francisco, and the premium was there paid.

Upon the question as to the place where the contract was made, Mr. Justice White, speaking for the court said: "It is claimed, however, that, irrespective of this [commerce] clause, the conviction here was illegal, first, because the statute is by its terms invalid, in that it undertakes to forbid the procurement of a contract outside of the State; and, secondly, because the evidence shows that the contract was in fact entered into without the territory of California. The language of the statute is not fairly open to this construction. It punishes 'every person who in this State procures or agrees to procure for a resident of this State any insurance,' etc. The words 'who in this State' cannot be read out of the law in order to nullify it under the Constitution."

In the case before us the contract was made beyond the territory of the State of Louisiana, and the only thing that the facts show was done within that State was the mailing of a letter of notification, as above mentioned, which was done after the principal contract had been made.

The distinction between a contract made within and that made without the State is again referred to by Mr. Justice White in the same case as follows: "It is said that the right of a citizen to contract for insurance for himself is guaranteed by the Fourteenth Amendment, and that, therefore, he cannot be deprived by the State of the capacity to so contract through an agent. The Fourteenth Amendment, however, does not guarantee the citizen *the right to make within his State, either directly or indirectly, a contract, the making whereof is constitutionally forbidden by the State. The proposition that, because a citizen might make such a contract for himself beyond the confines of his State, therefore he might authorize an agent to violate in his behalf the laws of his*

State, within her own limits, involves a clear non sequitur, and ignores the vital distinction between acts done within and acts done beyond a State's jurisdiction."

We do not intend to throw any doubt upon or in the least to shake the authority of the *Hooper case,* but the facts of that case and the principle therein decided are totally different from the case before us. In this case the only act which it is claimed was a violation of the statute in question consisted in sending the letter through the mail notifying the company of the property to be covered by the policy already delivered. We have then a contract which it is conceded was made outside and beyond the limits of the jurisdiction of the State of Louisiana, being made and to be performed within the State of New York, where the premiums were to be paid and losses, if any, adjusted. The letter of notification did not constitute a contract made or entered into within the State of Louisiana. It was but the performance of an act rendered necessary by the provisions of the contract already made between the parties outside of the State. It was a mere notification that the contract already in existence would attach to that particular property. In any event, the contract was made in New York, outside of the jurisdiction of Louisiana, even though the policy was not to attach to the particular property until the notification was sent.

It is natural that the state court should have remarked that there is in this "statute an apparent interference with the liberty of defendants in restricting their rights to place insurance on property of their own whenever and in what company they desired." Such interference is not only apparent, but it is real, and we do not think that it is justified for the purpose of upholding what the State says is its policy with regard to foreign insurance companies which had not complied with the laws of the State for doing business within its limits. In this case the company did no business within the State, and the contracts were not therein made.

The Supreme Court of Louisiana says that the act of writing within that State, the letter of notification, was an act therein done to effect an insurance on property then in the State, in a marine insurance company which had not complied with its laws, and such act was, therefore, prohibited by the statute. As so construed we think the statute is a violation of the Fourteenth Amendment of the Federal Constitution, in that it deprives the defendants of their liberty without due process of law. The statute which forbids such act does not become due process of law, because it is inconsistent with the provisions of the Constitution of the Union. The liberty mentioned in that amendment means not only the right of the citizen to be free from the mere physical restraint of his person, as by incarceration, but the term is deemed to embrace the right of the citizen to be free in the enjoyment of all his faculties; to be free to use them in all lawful ways; to live and work where he will; to earn his livelihood by any lawful calling; to pursue any livelihood or avocation, and for that purpose to enter into all contracts which may be proper, necessary and essential to his carrying out to a successful conclusion the purposes above mentioned.

It was said by Mr. Justice Bradley, in *Butchers' Union Company* v. *Crescent City Company,* 111 U.S. 746, 762, in the course of his concurring opinion in that case, that "The right to follow any of the common occupations of life is an inalienable right. It was formulated as such under the phrase 'pursuit of happiness' in the Declaration of Independence, which commenced with the fundamental proposition that 'all men are created equal, that they are endowed by their Creator with certain inalienable rights; that among these are life, liberty and the pursuit of happiness.' This right is a large ingredient in the civil liberty of the citizen." Again, on page 764, the learned justice said: "I hold that the liberty of pursuit—the right to follow any of the ordinary callings of life—is one of the privileges of a citizen of the United States." And again, on page 765: "But if it does not abridge the privileges and immunities of a citizen of the United States to prohibit him from pursuing his chosen calling, and giving to others the exclusive right of pursuing it, it certainly does deprive him (to a certain extent) of his liberty; for it takes from him the freedom of adopting and following the pursuit which he prefers; which, as already intimated, is a material part of the liberty of the citizen." It is true that these remarks were made in regard to questions of monopoly, but they well describe the rights which are covered by the word "liberty" as contained in the Fourteenth Amendment.

Again, in *Powell* v. *Pennsylvania,* 127 U.S. 678, 684, Mr. Justice Harlan, in stating the opinion of the court, said: "The main proposition advanced by the defendant is that his enjoyment upon terms of equality with all others in similar circumstances of the privilege of pursuing an ordinary calling or trade, and of acquiring, holding and selling property, is an essential part of his rights of liberty and property, as guaranteed by the Fourteenth Amendment. The court assents to this general proposition as embodying a sound principle of constitutional law." It was there held, however, that the legislation under consideration in that case did not violate any of the constitutional rights of the plaintiff in error.

The foregoing extracts have been made for the purpose of showing what general definitions have been given in regard to the meaning of the word "liberty" as used in the amendment, but we do not intend to hold that in no such case can the State exercise its police power. When and how far such power may be legitimately exercised with regard to these subjects must be left for determination to each case as it arises.

Has not a citizen of a State, under the provisions of the Federal Constitution above mentioned, a right to contract outside of the State for insurance on his property—a right of which state legislation cannot deprive him? We are not alluding to acts done within the State by an insurance company or its agents doing business therein, which are in violation of the state statutes. Such acts come within the principle of the *Hooper case* (*supra*), and would be controlled by it. When we speak of the liberty to contract for insurance or to do an act to effectuate such a contract already existing, we refer to and have in mind the facts of this case, where the contract was made outside the State, and as such was a valid and proper contract. The act done within the limits of the State under the circumstances of this case and for the purpose therein mentioned, we hold a proper act, one which the defendants were at liberty to perform and which the state legislature had no right to prevent, at least with reference to the Federal Constitution. To deprive the citizen of such a right as herein described without due process of law is illegal. Such a statute as this in question is not due process of law, because it prohibits an act which under the Federal Constitution the defendants had a right to perform. This does not interfere in any way with the acknowledged right of the State to enact such legislation in the legitimate exercise of its police or other powers as to it may seem proper. In the exercise of such right, however, care must be taken not to infringe upon those other rights of the citizen which are protected by the Federal Constitution.

In the privilege of pursuing an ordinary calling or trade and of acquiring, holding and selling property must be embraced the right to make all proper contracts in relation thereto, and although it may be conceded that this right to contract in relation to persons or property or to do business within the jurisdiction of the State may be regulated and sometimes prohibited when the contracts or business conflict with the policy of the State as contained in its statutes, yet the power does not and cannot extend to prohibiting a citizen from making contracts of the nature involved in this case outside of the limits and jurisdiction of the State, and which are also to be performed outside of such jurisdiction; nor can the State legally prohibit its citizens from doing such an act as writing this letter of notification, even though the property which is the subject of the insurance may at the time when such insurance attaches be within the limits of the State. The mere fact that a citizen may be within the limits of a particular State does not prevent his making a contract outside its limits while he himself remains within it. *Milliken* v. *Pratt,* 125 Mass. 374; *Tilden* v. *Blair,* 21 Wall. 241. The contract in this case was thus made. It was a valid contract, made outside of the State, to be performed outside of the State, although the subject was property temporarily within the State. As the contract was valid in the place where made and where it was to be performed, the party to the contract upon whom is devolved the right or duty to send the notification in order that the insurance provided for by the contract may attach to the property specified in the shipment mentioned in the notice, must have the liberty to do that act and to give that notification within the limits of the State, any prohibition of the state statute to the contrary notwithstanding. The giving of the notice is a mere collateral matter; it is not the contract itself, but is an act performed pursuant to a valid contract which the State had no right or jurisdiction to prevent its citizens from making outside the limits of the State.

The Atlantic Mutual Insurance Company of New York has done no business of insurance within the State of Louisiana and has not subjected itself to any provisions of the statute in question. It had the right to enter into a contract in New York with citizens of Louisiana for the purpose of insuring the property of its citizens, even if that property were in the State of Louisiana, and correlatively the citizens of Louisiana had the right without the State of entering into contract with an insurance company for the same purpose. Any act of the state legislature which should prevent the entering into such a contract, or the mailing within the State of Louisiana of such a notification as is mentioned in this case, is an improper and illegal interference with the conduct of the citizen, although residing in Louisiana, in his right to contract and to carry out the terms of a contract validly entered into outside and beyond the jurisdiction of the State.

In such a case as the facts here present the policy of the State in forbidding insurance companies which had not complied with the laws of the State from doing business within its limits cannot be so carried out as to prevent the citizen from writing such a letter of notification as was written by the plaintiffs in error in the State of Louisiana, when it is written pursuant to a valid contract made outside the State and with reference to a company which is not doing business within its limits.

For these reasons we think the statute in question, No. 66 of the Laws of Louisiana of 1894, was a violation of the Federal Constitution, and afforded no justification for the judgment awarded by that court against the plaintiffs in error. That judgment must, therefore, be

Reversed, and the case remanded to the Supreme Court of Louisiana for further proceedings not inconsistent with this opinion.

LOCHNER v. NEW YORK 198 U.S. 45 (1905)

This case is invariably cited by those formerly critical of the Supreme Court's tendency toward abstractions and indifference to certain pressing social and economic problems. In it, Justice Peckham, speaking fo a sharply divided court (5–4), struck down a New York State law limiting the hours of labor in bakeshops to sixty hours in one week or ten hours in any one day. Although it was assumed the statute would be upheld on the basis of the state's police powers, Peckham, while acknowledging the application of these powers for certain legislation of this sort, felt that the present law could not be sustained on that basis. Rather, in this instance, the liberty guaranteed by the Fourteenth Amendment, the right of free contract, took precedence. Peckham saw no reason why the baking trade merited special attention by the state, and wondered aloud where state intervention might end were the law before the Court sustained. The dissent of Justice Harlan cited existing studies which indicated the detrimental effects of bakeshop labor and concluded that the state's police powers were broad enough to regulate such conditions. Justice Holmes, in a famous dissent, delivered a grand rebuke to Peckham and the majority for their invocation of abstract economic theories, and called for judicial tolerance since the Court was "made for people of fundamentally differing views."

Mr. Justice Peckham, after making the foregoing statement of the facts, delivered the opinion of the court.

The indictment, it will be seen, charges that the plaintiff in error violated the one hundred and tenth section of article 8, chapter 415, of the Laws of 1897, known as the labor law of the State of New York, in that he wrongfully and unlawfully required and permitted an employé working for him to work more than sixty hours in one week. There is nothing in any of the opinions delivered in this case, either in the Supreme Court or the Court of Appeals of the State, which construes the section, in using the word "required" as referring to any physical force being used to obtain the labor of an employé. It is assumed that the word means nothing more than the requirement arising from voluntary contract for such labor in excess of the number of hours specified in the statute. There is no pretense in any of the opinions that the statute was intended to meet a case of involuntary labor in any form. All the opinions assume that there is no real distinction, so far as this question is concerned, between the words "required" and "permitted." The mandate of the statute that "no employé shall be required or permitted to work," is the substantial equivalent of an enactment that "no employé shall contract or agree to work," more than ten hours per day, and as there is no provision for special emergencies the statute is mandatory in all cases. It is not an act merely fixing the number of hours which shall constitute a legal day's work, but an absolute prohibition upon the employer, permitting, under any circumstances, more than ten hours work to be done in his establishment. The employé may desire to earn the extra money, which would arise from his working more than the prescribed time, but this statute forbids the employer from permitting the employé to earn it.

The statute necessarily interferes with the right of contract between the employer and employé, concerning the number of hours in which the latter may labor in the bakery of the employer. The general right to make a contract in relation to his business is part of the liberty of the individual protected by the Fourteenth Amendment of the Federal Constitution. *Allgeyer* v. *Louisiana,* 165 U.S. 578. Under that provision no State can deprive any person of life, liberty or property without due process of law. The right to purchase or to sell labor is part of the liberty protected by this amendment, unless there are circumstances which exclude the right. There are, however, certain powers, existing in the sovereignty of each State in the Union, somewhat vaguely termed police powers, the exact description and limitation of which have not been attempted by the courts. Those powers, broadly stated and without, at present, any attempt at a more specific limitation, relate to the safety, health, morals and general welfare of the public. Both property and liberty are held on such reasonable conditions as may be imposed by the governing power of the State in the exercise of those powers, and with such conditions the Fourteenth Amendment was not designed to interfere. *Mugler* v. *Kansas,* 123 U.S. 623; *In re Kemmler,* 136 U.S. 436; *Crowley* v. *Christensen,* 137 U.S. 86; *In re Converse,* 137 U.S. 624.

The State, therefore, has power to prevent the individual from making certain kinds of contracts, and in regard to them the Federal Constitution offers no protection. If the contract be one which the State, in the legitimate exercise of its police power, has the right to prohibit, it is not prevented from prohibiting it by the Fourteenth Amendment. Contracts in violation of a statute, either of the Federal or state government, or a contract to let one's property for immoral purposes, or to do any other unlawful act, could obtain no protection from the Federal Constitution, as coming under the liberty of person or of free contract. Therefore, when the State, by its legislature, in the assumed exercise of its police powers, has passed an act which seriously limits the right to labor or the right of contract in regard to their means of livelihood between persons who are *sui juris* (both employer and employé), it becomes of great importance to determine which shall prevail—the right of the individual to labor for such time as he may choose, or the right of the State to prevent the individual from laboring or from entering into any contract to labor, beyond a certain time prescribed by the State.

This court has recognized the existence and upheld the exercise of the police powers of the States in many cases which might fairly be considered as border ones, and it has, in the course of its determination of questions regarding the asserted invalidity of such statutes, on the ground of their violation of the rights secured by the Federal Constitution, been guided by rules of a very liberal nature, the application of which has resulted, in numerous instances, in upholding the validity of state statutes thus assailed. Among the later cases where the state law has been upheld by this court is that of *Holden* v. *Hardy,* 169 U.S. 366. A provision in the act of the legislature of Utah was there under consideration, the act limiting the employment of workmen in all underground mines or workings, to eight hours per day, "except in cases of emergency, where life or property is in imminent danger." It also limited the hours of labor in smelting and other institutions for the reduction or refining of ores or metals to eight hours per day, except in like cases of emergency. The act was held to be a valid exercise of the police powers of the State. A review of many of the cases on the subject, decided by this and other courts, is given in the opinion. It was held that the kind of employment, mining, smelting, etc., and the character of the employés in such kinds of labor, were such as to make it reasonable and proper for the State to interfere to prevent the employés from being constrained by the rules laid down by the proprietors in regard to labor. The following citation from the observations of the Supreme Court of Utah in that case was made by the judge writing the opinion of this court, and approved: "The law in question is confined to the protection of that class of people engaged in labor in underground mines, and in smelters and other works wherein ores are reduced and refined. This law applies only to the classes subjected by their employment to the peculiar conditions and effects attending underground mining and work in smelters, and other works for the reduction and refining of ores. Therefore it is not necessary to discuss or decide whether the legislature can fix the hours of labor in other employments."

It will be observed that, even with regard to that class of labor, the Utah statute provided for cases of emergency wherein the provisions of the statute would not apply. The statute now before this court has no emergency clause in it, and, if the statute is valid, there are no circumstances and no emergencies under which the slightest violation of the provisions of the act would be innocent. There is nothing in *Holden* v. *Hardy* which covers the case now before us. Nor does *Atkin* v. *Kansas,* 191 U.S. 207, touch the case at bar. The *Atkin case* was decided upon the right of the State to control its municipal corporations and to prescribe the conditions upon which it will permit work of a public character to be done for a municipality. *Knoxville Iron Co.* v. *Harbison,* 183 U.S. 13, is equally far from an authority for this legislation. The employés in that case were held to be at a disadvantage with the employer in matters of wages, they being miners and coal workers, and the act simply provided for the cashing of coal orders when presented by the miner to the employer.

The latest case decided by this court, involving the police power, is that of *Jacobson* v. *Massachusetts,* decided at this term and reported in 197 U.S. 11. It related to compulsory vaccination, and the law was held valid as a proper exercise of the police powers with reference to the public health. It was stated in the opinion that it was a case "of an adult who, for aught that appears, was himself in perfect health and a fit subject for vaccination, and yet, while remaining in the community, refused to obey the statute and the regulation adopted in execution of its provisions for the protection of the public health and the public safety, confessedly endangered by the presence of a dangerous disease." That case is also far from covering the one now before the court.

Petit v. *Minnesota,* 177 U.S. 164, was upheld as a proper exercise of the police power relating to the observance of Sunday, and the case held that the legislature had the right to declare that, as matter of law, keeping barber shops open on Sunday was not a work of necessity or charity.

It must, of course, be conceded that there is a limit to the valid exercise of the police power by the State. There is no dispute concerning this general proposition. Otherwise the Fourteenth Amendment would have no efficacy and the legislatures of the States would have unbounded power, and it would be enough to say that any piece of legislation was enacted to conserve the morals, the health or the safety of the people; such legislation would be valid, no matter how absolutely without foundation the claim might be. The claim of the police power would be a mere pretext—become another and delusive name for the supreme sovereignty of the State to be exercised free from constitutional restraint. This is not contended for. In every case that comes before this court, therefore, where legislation of this character is concerned and where the protection of the Federal Constitution is sought, the question necessarily arises: Is this a fair, reasonable and appropriate exercise of the police power of the State, or is it an unreasonable, unnecessary and arbitrary interference with the right of the individual to his personal liberty or to enter into those contracts in relation to labor which may seem to him appropriate or necessary for the support of himself and his family? Of course the liberty of contract relating to labor includes both parties to it. The one has as much right to purchase as the other to sell labor.

This is not a question of substituting the judgment of the court for that of the legislature. If the act be within the power of the State it is valid, although the judgment of the court might be totally opposed to the enactment of such a law. But the question would still remain: Is it within the police power of the State? and that question must be answered by the court.

The question whether this act is valid as a labor law, pure and simple, may be dismissed in a few words. There is no reasonable ground for interfering with the liberty of person or the right of free contract, by determining the hours of labor, in the occupation of a baker. There is no contention that bakers as a class are not equal in intelligence and capacity to men in other trades or manual occupations, or that they are not able to assert their rights and care for themselves without the protecting arm of the State, interfering with their independence of judgment and of action. They are in no sense wards of the State. Viewed in the light of a purely labor law, with no reference whatever to the question of health, we think that a law like the one before us involves neither the safety, the morals nor the welfare of the public, and that the interest of the public is not in the slightest degree affected by such an act. The law must be upheld, if at all, as a law pertaining to the health of the individual engaged in the occupation of a baker. It does not affect any other portion of the public than those who are engaged in that occupation. Clean and wholesome bread does not depend upon whether the baker works but ten hours per day or only sixty hours a week. The limitation of the hours of labor does not come within the police power on that ground.

It is a question of which of two powers or rights shall prevail—the power of the State to legislate or the right of the individual to liberty of person and freedom of contract. The mere assertion that the subject relates though but in a remote degree to the public health does not necessarily render the enactment valid. The act must have a more direct relation, as a means to an end, and the end itself must be appropriate and legitimate, before an act can be held to be valid which interferes with the general right of an individual to be free in his person and in his power to contract in relation to his own labor.

This case has caused much diversity of opinion in the state courts. In the Supreme Court two of the five judges composing the Appellate Division dissented from the judgment affirming the validity of the act. In the Court of Appeals three of the seven judges also dissented from the judgment upholding the statute. Although found in what is called a labor law of the State, the Court of Appeals has upheld the act as one relating to the public health—in other words, as a health law. One of the judges of the Court of Appeals, in upholding the law, stated that, in his opinion, the regulation in question could not be sustained unless they were able to say, from common knowledge, that working in a bakery and candy factory was an unhealthy employment. The judge held that, while the evidence was not uniform, it still led him to the conclusion that the occupation of a baker or confectioner was unhealthy and tended to result in diseases of the respiratory organs. Three of the judges dissented from that view, and they thought the occupation of a baker was not to such an extent unhealthy as to warrant the interference of the legislature with the liberty of the individual.

We think the limit of the police power has been reached and passed in this case. There is, in our judgment, no reasonable foundation for holding this to be necessary or appropriate as a health law to safeguard the public health or the health of the individuals who are following the trade of a baker. If this statute be valid, and if, therefore, a proper case is made out in which to deny the right of an individual, *sui juris,* as employer or employé, to make contracts for the labor of the latter under the protection of the provisions of the Federal Constitution, there would seem to be no length to which legislation of this nature might not go. The case differs widely, as we have already stated, from the expressions of this court in regard to laws of this nature, as stated in *Holden* v. *Hardy* and *Jacobson* v. *Massachusetts, supra.*

We think that there can be no fair doubt that the trade of a baker, in and of itself, is not an unhealthy one to that degree which would authorize the legislature to interfere with the right to labor, and with the right of free contract on the part of the individual, either as employer or employé. In looking through statistics regarding all trades and occupations, it may be true that the trade of a baker does not appear to be as healthy as some other trades, and is also vastly more healthy than still others. To the common understanding the trade of a baker has never been regarded as an unhealthy one. Very likely physicians would not recommend the exercise of that or of any other trade as a remedy for ill health. Some occupations are more healthy than others, but we think there are none which might not come under the power of the legislature to supervise and control the hours of working therein, if the mere fact that the occupation is not absolutely and perfectly healthy is to confer that right upon the legislative department of the Government. It might be safely affirmed that almost all occupations more or less affect the health. There must be more than the mere fact of the possible existence of some small amount of unhealthiness to warrant legislative interference with liberty. It is unfortunately true that labor, even in any department, may possibly carry with it the seeds of unhealthiness. But are we all, on that account, at the mercy of legislative majorities? A printer, a tinsmith, a locksmith, a carpenter, a cabinetmaker, a dry goods clerk, a bank's, a lawyer's or a physician's clerk, or a clerk in almost any kind of business, would all come under the power of the legislature, on this assumption. No trade, no occupation, no mode of earning one's living, could escape this all-pervading power, and the acts of the legislature in limiting the hours of labor in all employments would be valid, although such limitation might seriously cripple the ability of the laborer to support himself and his family. In our large cities there are many buildings into which the sun penetrates for but a short time in each day, and these buildings are occupied by people carrying on the business of bankers, brokers, lawyers, real estate, and many other kinds of business, aided by many clerks, messengers, and other employés. Upon the assumption of the validity of this act under review, it is not possible to say that an act, prohibiting lawyers' or bank clerks, or others, from contracting to labor for their employers more than eight hours a day, would be invalid. It might be said that it is unhealthy to work more than that number of hours in an apartment lighted by artificial light during the working hours of the day; that the occupation of the bank clerk, the lawyer's clerk, the real estate clerk, or the broker's clerk in such offices is therefore unhealthy, and the legislature in its paternal wisdom must, therefore, have the right to legislate on the subject of and to limit the hours for such labor, and if it exercises that power and its validity be questioned, it is sufficient to say, it has reference to the public health; it has reference to the health of the employés condemned to labor day after day in buildings where the sun never shines; it is a health law, and therefore it is valid, and cannot be questioned by the courts.

It is also urged, pursuing the same line of argument, that it is to the interest of the State that its population should be strong and robust, and therefore any legislation which may be said to tend to make people healthy must be valid as health laws, enacted under the police power. If this be a valid argument and a justification for this kind of legislation, it follows that the protection of the Federal Constitution from undue interference with liberty of person and freedom of contract is visionary, wherever the law is sought to be justified as a valid exercise of the police power. Scarcely any law but might find shelter under such assumptions, and conduct, properly so called, as well as contract, would come under the restrictive sway of the legislature. Not only the hours of employés, but the hours of employers, could be regulated, and doctors, lawyers, scientists, all professional men, as well as athletes and artisans, could be forbidden to fatigue their brains and bodies by prolonged hours of exercise, lest the fighting strength of the State be impaired. We mention these extreme cases because the contention is extreme. We do not believe in the soundness of the views which uphold this law. On the contrary, we think that such a law as this, although passed in the assumed exercise of the police power, and as relating to the public health, or the health of the employés named, is not within that power, and is invalid. The act is not, within any fair meaning of the term, a health law, but is an illegal interference with the rights of individuals, both employers and employés, to make contracts regarding labor upon such terms as they may think best, or which they may agree upon with the other parties to such contracts. Statutes of the nature of that under review, limiting the hours in which grown and intelligent men may labor to earn their living, are mere meddlesome interferences with the rights of the individual, and they are not saved from condemnation by the claim that they are passed in the exercise of the police power and upon the subject of the health of the individual whose rights are interfered with, unless there be some fair ground, reasonable in and of itself, to say that there is material danger to the public health or to the health of the employés, if the hours of labor are not curtailed. If this be not clearly the case the individuals, whose rights are thus made the subject of legislative interference, are under the protection of the Federal Constitution regarding their liberty of contract as well as of person; and the legislature of the State has no power to limit their right as proposed in this statute. All that it could properly do has been done by it with regard to the conduct of bakeries, as provided for in the other sections of the act, above set forth. These several sections provide for the inspection of the premises where the bakery is carried on, with regard to furnishing proper wash-rooms and water-closets, apart from the bakeroom, also with regard to providing proper drainage, plumbing and painting; the sections, in addition, provide for the height of the ceiling, the cementing or tiling of floors, where necessary in the opinion of the factory inspector, and for other things of that nature; alterations are also provided for and are to be made where necessary in the opinion of the inspector, in order to comply with the provisions of the statute. These various sections may be wise and valid regulations, and they certainly go to the full extent of providing for the cleanliness and the healthiness, so far as possible, of the quarters in which bakeries are to be conducted. Adding to all these requirements, a prohibition to enter into any contract of labor in a bakery for more than a certain number of hours a week, is, in our judgment, so wholly beside the matter of a proper, reasonable and fair provision, as to run counter to that liberty of person and of free contract provided for in the Federal Constitution.

It was further urged on the argument that restricting the hours of labor in the case of bakers was valid because it tended to cleanliness on the part of the workers, as a man was more apt to be cleanly when not overworked, and if cleanly then his "output" was also more likely to be so. What has already been said applies with equal force to this contention. We do not admit the reasoning to be sufficient to justify the claimed right of such interference. The State in that case would assume the position of a supervisor, or *pater familias,* over every act of the individual, and its right of governmental interference with his hours of labor, his hours of exercise, the character thereof, and the extent to which it shall be carried would be recognized and upheld. In our judgment it is not possible in fact to discover the connection between the number of hours a baker may work in the bakery and the healthful quality of the bread made by the workman. The connection, if any exists, is too shadowy and thin to build any argument for the interference of the legislature. If the man works ten hours a day it is all right, but if ten and a half or eleven his health is in danger and his bread may be unhealthful, and, therefore, he shall not be permitted to do it. This, we think, is unreasonable and entirely arbitrary. When assertions such as we have adverted to become necessary in order to give, if possible, a plausible foundation for the contention that the law is a "health law," it gives rise to at least a suspicion that there was some other motive dominating the legislature than the purpose to subserve the public health or welfare.

This interference on the part of the legislatures of the several States with the ordinary trades and occupations of the people seems to be on the increase. In the Supreme Court of New York, in the case of *People* v. *Beattie,* Appellate Division, First Department, decided in 1904, 89 N.Y. Supp. 193, a statute regulating the trade of horseshoeing, and requiring the person practicing such trade to be examined and to obtain a certificate from a board of examiners and file the same with the clerk of the county wherein the person proposes to practice such trade, was held invalid, as an arbitrary interference with personal liberty and private property without due process of law. The attempt was made, unsuccessfully, to justify it as a health law.

The same kind of a statute was held invalid (*In re Aubry*) by the Supreme Court of Washington in December, 1904. 78 Pac. Rep. 900. The court held that the act deprived citizens of their liberty and property without due process of law and denied to them the equal protection of the laws. It also held that the trade of a horseshoer is not a subject of regulation under the police power of the State, as a business concerning and directly affecting the health, welfare or comfort of its inhabitants; and that therefore a law which provided for the examination and registration of horseshoers in certain cities was unconstitutional, as an illegitimate exercise of the police power.

The Supreme Court of Illinois in *Bessette* v. *People,* 193 Illinois, 334, also held that a law of the same nature, providing for the regulation and licensing of horseshoers, was unconstitutional as an illegal interference with the liberty of the individual in adopting and pursuing such calling as he may choose, subject only to the restraint necessary to secure the common welfare. See also *Godcharles* v. *Wigeman,* 113 Pa. St. 431, 437; *Low* v. *Rees Printing Co.,* 41 Nebraska, 127, 145. In these cases the courts upheld the right of free contract and the right to purchase and sell labor upon such terms as the parties may agree to.

It is impossible for us to shut our eyes to the fact that many of the laws of this character, while passed under what is claimed to be the police power for the purpose of protecting the public health or welfare, are, in reality, passed from other motives. We are justified in saying so when, from the character of the law and the subject upon which it legislates, it is apparent that the public health or welfare bears but the most remote relation to the law. The purpose of a statute must be determined from the natural and legal effect of the language employed; and whether it is or is not repugnant to the Constitution of the United States must be determined from the natural effect of such statutes when put into operation, and not from their proclaimed purpose. *Minnesota* v. *Barber,* 136 U.S. 313; *Brimmer* v. *Rebman,* 138 U.S. 78. The court looks beyond the mere letter of the law in such cases. *Yick Wo* v. *Hopkins,* 118 U.S. 356.

It is manifest to us that the limitation of the hours of labor as provided for in this section of the statute under which the indictment was found, and the plaintiff in error convicted, has no such direct relation to and no such substantial effect upon the health of the employé, as to justify us in regarding the section as really a health law. It seems to us that the real object and purpose were simply to regulate the hours of labor between the master and his employés (all being men, *sui juris*), in a private business, not dangerous in any degree to morals or in any real and substantial degree, to the health of the employés. Under such circumstances the freedom of master and employé to contract with each other in relation to their employment, and in defining the same, cannot be prohibited or interfered with, without violating the Federal Constitution.

The judgment of the Court of Appeals of New York as well as that of the Supreme Court and of the County Court of Oneida County must be reversed and the case remanded to the County Court for further proceedings not inconsistent with this opinion.

Reversed.

Joseph McKenna

☆ 1843–1926 ☆

APPOINTED BY

WILLIAM McKINLEY

YEARS ON COURT

1898–1925

Joseph McKenna

by

JAMES F. WATTS, JR.

TWENTIETH CENTURY IMMIGRATION restrictions and perhaps the numbing effects of a homogenous mass culture have successfully obscured from most Americans the exciting promise which attracted millions of nineteenth century immigrants to these shores. The legendary gold-paved streets of the New World glittered in the imaginations of the oppressed and hungry, of men seeking adventure and men covetous of the main chance. Through the years from Jackson to Lincoln the northern and western Europeans poured out from Scandinavia and Germany and the Low Countries, from France and the British Isles, driven by persecution and deprivation, attracted by the splendid dreams of freedom and opportunity.

No more enduring immigrant lifeline has existed than that forged by the millions of Irish who have steadily transplanted themselves to the United States from the early nineteenth century to the present moment. Incited to leave in massive numbers by religious persecution, the evils of English absentee ownership embedded in a feudal economic system, and the terrible potato famine which unbelievably caused the death from starvation and disease of over one million men, women, and children during the late 1840's, the Irish arrived in America's northeastern port cities by the hundreds of thousands.

One of this faceless multitude of Irishmen was a young baker named John McKenna, who survived the harsh passage and landed in Philadelphia in 1842. Settling into the Irish quarter in the southwestern section of the city, McKenna opened a small bakery, and then found and almost immediately married Mary Ann Johnson, who had come across a few years earlier. The next year, on August 10, 1843, they proudly watched as their first child, Joseph, was christened in the St. Philip Neri Roman Catholic Church. (See Brother Matthew

JAMES F. WATTS, JR. is Assistant Professor of History at City College of New York and author of a forthcoming biography of Breckinridge Long.

McDevitt's published Catholic University of American doctoral dissertation, Joseph McKenna, *Associate Justice of the United States* [Washington, D.C., 1946]. Hereafter cited as McDevitt, *McKenna.*)

Young John McKenna quickly learned that many of the promises of the New World were not to be achieved automatically. His family increased almost yearly, but the income derived from his bakery scarcely provided for much more than food and shelter. Besides enduring an economic insecurity different only in kind from that of the Old World, the McKennas also faced the vicious threats of the early Know-Nothing movement, which grew to menacing proportions in the Philadelphia of the late 1840's. Bloody fistfights produced riots and then small arms fire in the vicinity of the McKenna home in 1844, and the constant harassment of Catholics steadily became an increasing burden for a struggling young immigrant like McKenna, now insecurely settled in a new land and charged with demanding economic responsibilities.

Despite his financial difficulties, the seriousness of which is suggested by the fact that McKenna moved his bakery every few months in attempts to survive, he never despaired, never lost hope in the American Dream. Because McKenna was determined that his children should enjoy the benefits which had been denied to him by time and circumstance, he managed to pay the tuition which admitted his eight-year-old son Joseph to the "college" which undaunted Philadelphia Catholics opened in 1851. For the following four years the McKenna boy attended this school, which later became formally organized as St. Joseph's College. All this time, however, his father kept himself alert to the possibilities of seizing some opportunity to escape from the frustrating and threatening treadmill of Philadelphia's Irish ghetto.

Eventual success began with the stories that filtered eastward from the Pacific coast in the 1850's, tales of extravagant opportunities and almost automatic success which greatly excited John McKenna. A brand new land, away from old city streets with their economic frustrations and religious discrimination lay waiting in California, with its Catholic heritage and its golden image.

The major obstacle to the emigration of the McKenna family to California naturally concerned money. The swiftest and safest route to California was the steamship route from New York to Panama, then overland by railroad across the isthmus and on by ship up the coast. Yet the stiff one-way fare of approximately $150 per head foreclosed this possibility to lower-class people like the McKennas.

Suddenly, in the mid-1850's, a rate war broke out between the competing Panama steamship companies, with fares dropping radically. John McKenna immediately pulled up his shallow Philadelphia roots, hurried his family to New York, and boarded the first available ship. All survived the difficult weeks in third-class "accommodations" and, early in 1855 the McKennas and other veteran immigrants sailed through the Golden Gate, penniless but delighted.

John McKenna soon settled the family in the infant inland port town of Benicia, at the southern end of the Napa Valley below Vallejo, about forty nautical miles inland from the Golden Gate. Here McKenna began his short and happy reign of prosperity, as his ubiquitous bakery now thrived in this frontier town, at least to the extent that he could make some modestly profitable real estate investments. The proud Irishman could also take delight in the fact that his children were properly dressed as they marched off to Sunday Mass, or as they attended the local schools, which was a luxury that not so many others could afford.

For three or four years John McKenna enjoyed a few of life's fruits, before the classic outlines of Irish tragedy appeared. Suddenly stricken in 1858, he died almost immediately, leaving a widow and six children. Fifteen-year-old Joseph now became the man of the family. Even after this shock, the terrible specter of sudden and heartbreaking disaster refused to leave, as the two youngest children soon joined their father in the graveyard on the hill.

The steeling experiences of the next few years permanently influenced Joseph McKenna's long life. By necessity, he acquired the habits of self-discipline and perseverence, of respect for authority and determination to achieve as much security as the capricious nature of the world would allow. Before and after school he worked, hard and faithfully, on any number of jobs. He toiled diligently if unspectacularly in school, realizing that education promised success in this new land of varied opportunities.

In the 1860's the excesses of the Civil War hardly touched far-off California, although passions certainly ran high and verbal explosions were frequent. For his part, McKenna, now in his twenties and charged with steady family responsibility, let the War pass him by. He had decided to spend all of his time ingesting from an assortment of law books as much random information as the modest requirements to pass the California Bar examination demanded. Very quickly thereafter, in the same April week of 1865 in which General Lee presented his sword to General Grant, Joseph McKenna satisfactorily answered some questions and thereby gained admission to the California Bar.

McKenna's eventual triumph over various forms of adversity through strict adherence to the Puritan code suggests the stereotypical American success story, and in a sense the image is accurate. Yet the road to American success has always exacted some toll, and belief in God, country, and doing the day's work never adequately explains success in the United States, and certainly not in the case of the shrewd and ambitious young lawyer from Benicia.

Although he rarely engaged in private practice McKenna used his ostensible legal qualifications over the decades as stepping-stones toward political success. Since the Republican party had swept to victories on all political fronts throughout the nation, including California, McKenna decided that his family's steady allegiance to the Democrats did not comport with political realities as he found them.

The California Republican party had profited from the strong and powerful leadership of Leland Stanford, the pioneer railroad builder who became the state's first Republican governor in 1861. Early in the 1860's McKenna had attached himself to this potent new political machine and, in this free-wheeling society, six months after his admission to the bar, the twenty-two-year-old McKenna was elected District Attorney of Solano County.

During his two two-year terms as district attorney, McKenna handled himself well, gaining in composure and confidence what he lacked in experience. He developed a competent courtroom manner through the handling of hundreds of often bizarre cases. More important, McKenna made and solidified dozens of significant Republican political contacts around the county. By 1869, when he decided not to stand for a third term, McKenna was well-known throughout the area in the most prominent legal and political circles.

Upon leaving office McKenna married Miss Amanda Bornemann of San Francisco, and the young couple began their fifty-five year marriage by making their home in Suisan City, a town fifteen miles to the north of Benicia, where for the next five years McKenna practiced law. He also spent a good deal of time in cultivating his political future, for in 1875 the local Republican organization nominated and elected him to represent the Solano County district in the State Assembly.

Just one year later this bright young man attempted to take another step up the political ladder when he received the party's nomination for Congress from California's Third District. McKenna and his opponent, incumbent Congressman John King Luttrell, made futile attempts to cover the 46,000 square miles of a constituency which meandered over three mountain ranges and into dozens of secluded valleys which sheltered countless isolated settlements. In this typically excessive American political campaign neither candidate allowed concern for accuracy to interfere with partisan rhetoric. In the end, although McKenna impressed his political mentors by making a strong race, he lost by about 1000 votes out of the more than 38,000 cast.

The ambitious young politician, who thoroughly enjoyed the rough and tumble of backwoods campaigning, had no intention of taking this defeat seriously. He merely returned home and began plotting strategy for the 1878 campaign, when he again secured the Republican nomination for what proved to be an unusually stormy campaign. Congressman Luttrell had decided to retire and McKenna's Democratic opponent, C. P. Berry, was as anxious to go to Washington as any novice politician.

Consequently the two men ranged through their vast district hurling insults at each other while simultaneously attempting to introduce as many embarrassing issues as possible. Both supported conservation and irrigation, but accused their opponent of favoring the special interests. The question of state aid for parochial schools raised some particularly sensitive problems for a Catholic like McKenna, but he quickly solved them by announcing that he was against any form of state aid. The exclusion of all Chinese immigrants became a popular rallying point for politicians of all stripes, and McKenna and Berry both attempted to outdo one another in their Oriental xenophobia. Tariffs and a new state constitution and the corruption in Sacramento all received due attention.

The failure of the legislature to regulate the railroads made McKenna particularly vulnerable due to his ties with Leland Stanford. McKenna countered by waving the Bloody Shirt, but Berry slyly alluded to the dangers inherent in electing a Catholic congressman. Both men were naturally drawn into discussions of national politics, with McKenna pointedly defending the tenure of General Grant against its Democratic vilifiers to the extent that on one occasion McKenna suggested that perhaps the quite familiar degree of corruption under the Republicans might be more desirable than the unknown excesses which would surely accompany the election of the Democrats.

Election day came and went with no decision possible. Day after day the votes were counted and re-counted, the tide swinging now one way, now the other. After seventeen days of the worst possible kind of agony for a politician, the electoral board certified the victory of C. P. Berry over Joseph McKenna by 189 votes out of about 40,000 cast.

Though stung by the disappointment of two consecutive defeats McKenna had long since learned to tolerate adversity by persevering that much harder. He remained just as determined to enter Congress, but now decided to await more promising conditions. For the next few years he kept his political fences in good repair and by 1883, when California Republicans were able to gerrymander a new Third District, McKenna was again ready for the race. Though saddled with the unenviable reputation of a two-time loser, McKenna fought all the harder since he realized that the party's nomination was now tantamount to victory. Others had the same realization, and in a bitter convention fight in the summer of 1884 McKenna only narrowly emerged as the candidate. After this struggle, the November election proved to be anti-climactic, and Joseph McKenna went off to Washington to join the Forty-ninth Congress when it convened early in 1885.

Soon after McKenna took his seat he began to display those characteristics which automatically established him as a faithful and trustworthy party man. For the folks at home, he introduced bills of personal privilege for Leland Stanford, pork barrel legislation for the Benicia Arsenal, and the extension of California railroad land grants. He opposed appropriations for the wretched survivors of Chinese miners murdered in a race riot, supported dairy farmers against the threat of oleomargarine, opposed repeal of the Silver Purchase Act and secured almost $400,000 for improving harbor and port facilities in the Bay area. All this, plus assiduous fence-mending, provided Congressman McKenna with an excess of political ammunition to use against the Democrats in the election of 1886, when he was returned for a second term.

McKenna's efforts in behalf of his constituency continued in his second congressional term. He staunchly defended all protected industries against the horrors of free trade, and the railroad systems against any form of regulation. Toward the latter end, McKenna joined in the minority vote against the creation of the commission proposed under the Interstate Commerce Act of 1887. In addition, the California congressman strongly supported the allocation of $3,-

000,000 to Stanford's Central Pacific for military transportation services despite the fact that this line was indebted to the government to the extent of $70,000,-000 at the time. The energetic McKenna introduced for the nativist clique a bill which would require each Chinese worker to carry an identification card, without which he would be subject either to deportation or to five years imprisonment. For the California wine merchants, McKenna submitted various amendments to the famous McKinley Tariff of 1890, each of which was specifically aimed at the restriction of foreign spirits. Finally, he managed to secure the usual pork barrel appropriations for his district, this time in the amount of about $500,000.

The local success of McKenna's political format was indicated by his continuing success at the polls. In 1888 he emerged with a comfortable 5,300 vote plurality and two years later, in the election of 1890, the Democrats of the Third District indicated their sense of futility by naming as Congressman McKenna's opponent an unknown man who had for years served as a lawyer for the Southern Pacific and for other large business combinations. This attempt to balance the scales of influence naturally failed, and McKenna returned to Washington for a fourth term.

In the course of the normal legislative logrolling which permitted McKenna to serve his clients so well he naturally built up a complex set of political relationships, making friends among powerful men, doing favors in return for others, and gradually piling up a stack of political due-bills. Much of McKenna's political power originated from the powerful House Ways and Means Committee, where he sat as the only member from a state west of the Rockies. The Chairman of Ways and Means, and one of McKenna's closest friends in Washington, was the handsome and well-regarded Republican politico, William McKinley of Ohio, who soon came to regard McKenna as a valuable and trusted ally in the committee's manifold political machinations. Even after McKinley left Washington in 1892 to return home as Ohio's governor, the two men continued their amiable relationship. In addition to McKinley, McKenna also indebted himself to a number of other influential Republicans, to the extent that his chances of benefiting from a high federal appointment grew stronger the longer the Republicans maintained their power.

In 1892 President Benjamin Harrison, faced with a vacancy in the far-western Ninth Circuit Court of Appeals, heeded the advice of Leland Stanford, who had come to Washington as United States senator in 1885, and announced the appointment of Congressman Joseph McKenna to this judicial post. The nomination immediately provoked a roar of protest from California, with charges that McKenna's appointment represented nothing more than a political payoff to Senator Stanford. Furthermore, the charges went on, McKenna's legal parochialism hardly qualified him for such a demanding position; he had practiced law only sporadically, and then only in and around Solano County; he had made few appearances in the federal courts, or before the California Supreme Court. Congressman McKenna, his critics charged, had always been little more than an ambitious party politician, and did not deserve to ascend to the federal bench.

As usual, party regularity prevailed and, after the storm had played itself out, the nomination was approved. In March of 1892 McKenna took the judicial chair he was to occupy for four years amid the continuing rumors that the Republicans had decided that McKenna would eventually replace the aging Justice Stephen J. Field of California on the Supreme Court.

To the circuit court came numerous cases affecting many of the special interests for which Congressman McKenna had toiled so hard. In matters affecting Stanford's Southern Pacific, for instance, McKenna naturally was particularly vulnerable; yet, despite angry protests, he nonetheless wrote some opinions highly favorable to the railroad. In one, *Southern Pacific Railway Co.* v. *Oakland,* 58 Fed. 50 (9th Cir., 1893), Judge McKenna granted to the Southern Pacific an injunction which prevented officials of the city of Oakland from appropriating a ferry pier from which another line in competition with Southern Pacific proposed to run a ship across the Bay. In a much more basic decision, *Southern Pacific Co.* v. *Board of Railroad Commissioners,* 78 Fed. 236 (9th Cir., 1896), which he handed down in 1896, Judge McKenna ruled against the California state legislature's attempts to regulate railroad passenger and freight rates, largely on his personal opinion that the rate schedule proposed by the legislature was too harsh. Despite these and a few other controversial opinions, all in all the bulk of McKenna's work on the Court of Appeals concerned the mundane rather than the exciting, and he spent his four years on the Ninth Circuit bench in relative obscurity. Charges that were made from time to time suggesting McKenna's laziness and indecision probably reflected his lack of legal expertise rather than the personal shortcomings and political motives which his opponents were always so anxious to find.

The smashing victory of his good friend Major McKinley in 1896 immediately returned attention to Joseph McKenna. The President-elect, in searching about for ways to repay old political debts and at the same time to balance his appointments geographically, naturally turned to McKenna. The papers filled with rumors of a Cabinet appointment for the Californian, with most of them sending McKenna to the Interior Department in deference to California's western "image." Ironically, neither McKinley nor McKenna would ever make this choice due to the fears of stirring up massive resentment by the appointment of a Roman Catholic as administrator of the federal Indian schools, an issue which somehow incited great fears in those days. Rather than invite trouble McKinley summoned McKenna to the front porch in Canton and easily disposed of political debts and western geographical representation by making his friend the next Attorney General of the United States.

At the news of this appointment the old rumors cropped up once more: McKenna would stay at the Department of Justice only for as long as it took to coax the eighty-one-year-old Justice Field into retirement. Actually, McKenna's tenure at the Justice Department proved to be even shorter than the prognosticators of the political press had forecast. McKinley had named his Attorney General–designate in January, McKenna took control in March, and in December, when Justice Field finally submitted his resignation, the President formally announced his intention of naming the Attorney General as Field's successor.

The predictable rash of opposition to this appointment quickly appeared. San Francisco newspapers cited McKenna's long association with the railroads and other west coast special interests. One Republican senator, quoted anonymously by *The New York Times,* charged that McKenna's appointment

> *. . . is the weakest nomination for the Supreme Court that has been offered to the Senate in many years, certainly the weakest in my recollection.* [The New York Times, *December 17, 1897, in McDevitt,* McKenna, *104.*]

A less reticent senator, the Populist William V. Allen of Nebraska, took the floor of the Upper House for several hours to denounce McKenna's nomination, reading in the process a number of anti-McKenna resolutions from the West Coast.

At length, however, both the Judiciary Committee and the Senate as a whole confirmed the nomination, and in January of 1898 Joseph McKenna joined the Supreme Court. His most ardent detractors would surely have increased the level of their dissent had they been able to foresee that Justice McKenna would spend twenty-seven years on the Court, and in the process deliver hundreds of opinions.

Of the nearly one hundred men who have served on the Supreme Court through the nation's history only about fifteen have survived terms as long as that of Joseph McKenna. He joined the Court early in 1898 as the rising Spanish-American crisis excited rural and largely insular America. Twenty-seven years later, in a radically different society, the eighty-two-year-old McKenna finally retired after having participated in many decisions which affected the direction of the society.

Although he had happily welcomed the President's nomination, McKenna knew he was not well prepared to assume the responsibilities of the Supreme Court. Shortly before his installation, the Justice-elect from California spent some time in New York at the Columbia University Law School in a feeble attempt to ready himself. Many years later, after McKenna's retirement, a veteran librarian at the Court recalled that upon taking up his duties McKenna felt overwhelmed by what was expected of him. As even his uncritical biographer writes,

> *In his early years on the bench he was frequently irritable, nervous and rather unhappy because he was not familiar with the law nor able to construct an opinion that would adequately express the convictions of his colleagues.* [*McDevitt,* McKenna, *202.*]

As one consequence of this insecurity, many of McKenna's early opinions were bewilderingly prolix, studded with countless references to established precedents. While the passage of time did allow McKenna to develop more confidence in his own judgment, the Justice never did develop any consistent legal philosophy. His mind uncluttered by the complex dicta of legal scholarship, McKenna tended to decide each case individually as it came before the Court, mostly on the basis of the application of "common sense." The net result of this erratic empiricism is a series of frequently conflicting opinions and votes in such sensitive areas as substantive due process of law, in which the social philosophy of the Justices usually governed their opinions.

By investing due process of law with substantive rather than merely procedural content through the late nineteenth century, the Court permitted the introduction of subjective considerations which permitted the Justices to decide whether or not legislative acts unreasonably threatened property rights. McKenna's interpretations of due process varied widely. For example, shortly after joining the Court, McKenna delivered a highly controversial opinion in *Magoun* v. *Illinois Trust and Savings Bank,* 170 U.S. 283 (1898), which upheld an inheritance tax statute of the Illinois state legislature, largely on the sweeping grounds that since the state created inheritance rights it logically possessed the power of abolishing those rights. Justice David J. Brewer, perhaps the most conservative member of the Court at the time, vigorously dissented, rejecting McKenna's entire line of reasoning, and insisting on the fundamental relationship between the rights of inheritance and the natural law in which these rights were founded. In subsequent cases involving inheritance cases, McKenna moved away from his original contention in the *Magoun* case. By 1906, when he delivered opinions in *Cahen* v. *Brewster,* 203 U.S. 543 (1906) and *Board of Education of the Kentucky Annual Conference of the Methodist Episcopal Church* v. *Illinois,* 203 U.S. 553 (1906), both of which involved inheritance tax laws, McKenna simply argued that the state possessed the right to regulate inheritances under the facts of the cases.

A further indication of McKenna's lack of judicial consistency involved the question of state regulation of corporations whose primary function affected what was loosely termed "the public interest." The concept that such businesses were subject to public regulation had been set in the famous *Munn* v. *Illinois* decision of 1877, 94 U.S. 113, but the broadest statement of the areas in which police power might be applied in the public interest came with Justice McKenna's decision in the case of *German Alliance Insurance Company* v. *Lewis,* 233 U.S. 389 (1914), when McKenna held that only a "broad and definite public interest" had to be involved to allow for public regulation. Six months later, when Justice Holmes applied this criterion and thereby upheld an Interstate Commerce Commission directive ordering a private oil line to carry the oil of competitors at a fixed rate in *The Pipe Line Cases,* 234 U.S. 548 (1913), McKenna dissented on the grounds that property rights were natural rights and not subject to the caprices of the kind of open-ended legislation suggested by his own opinion in the *German Alliance* case. Years later, in 1921, Holmes again used the precedent set by the *German Alliance* case in both *Block* v. *Hirsh,* 256 U.S. 135 (1921) and *Brown Holding Company* v. *Feldman,* 256 U.S. 170 (1921), but in each case McKenna strongly dissented.

McKenna nevertheless did not by any means categorically oppose increases in federal regulatory powers. In fact, perhaps the area in which the Justice displayed the most consistency was his advocacy of strong Federal police powers under the commerce clause. Since the federal government possessed no constitutional authority for legislating to protect public health, social welfare and morals, the proponents of increased federal police power were forced to find alternative ways for the federal authorities to cope with the effects of the industrial revolution, which nationalized markets and created conditions which were no longer susceptible to the regulatory capabilities of the several states. By using the commerce clause, the Congress sought to police the manufacture and shipping of all products which crossed a state line.

The reaction of members of the Supreme Court to this broadly based federal attempt to increase its police powers over all aspects of economic life thus depended to a considerable extent upon their individual definitions of the term "commerce." For example, Justice William R. Day, who sat with McKenna on the High Court for nearly two decades, clung tenaciously to an extremely narrow definition of the meaning of "commerce." For Day, the term meant transportation and only transportation, and consequently he opposed federal efforts to use the commerce power broadly. In the celebrated case of *Hammer* v. *Dagenhart,* 247 U.S. 251 (1918), Day wrote a majority opinion for an intensely divided five to four Court which nullified the Keating-Owen Child Labor Act. The issue in conflict was the right of the federal government to attack child labor through the commerce clause, which for Justice Day constituted tampering with manufacturing, which was not commerce. Justice McKenna, on the other hand, dissented, since he believed that the very broad interpretation of the police powers inherent in the commerce clause clearly sanctioned both the act and its intent under the government's commerce power.

The consistency of McKenna's broad interpretation of the commerce clause began as early as 1903 in the case of *Champion* v. *Ames,* 188 U.S. 321 (1903), when McKenna joined the majority in a five to four decision that upheld a federal law which used the commerce clause to prohibit the dissemination of lottery tickets through the mails. This case had originally established the notion of federal "police power," and was followed by a number of similar cases in which the government used the commerce clause to legislate in the public interest. In *Hipolite Egg Company* v. *United States,* 220 U.S. 45 (1911), for example, Justice McKenna spoke for a unanimous Court in upholding the constitutionality of the Pure Food and Drug Act. Although Congress could not directly prevent the processing of adulterated foods, the *Hipolite* decision confirmed its ability to prevent the transportation by interstate carriers of such foods. Shortly after this decision, McKenna again read a unanimous commerce clause opinion, this time sustaining the government's attempts to control prostitution through an application of the commerce clause, *Hoke* v. *United States,* 227 U.S. 308 (1913). The Mann Act, the issue in the *Hoke* case, sought to prohibit the interstate transportation of women for immoral purposes.

A somewhat related area in which McKenna also displayed some consistency concerned federal prosecutions of monopolies under the Sherman Anti-Trust Act. By the turn of the century the Sherman Act had been rendered impotent by a series of Court decisions of the 1890's, especially the 1895 decision in *United States* v. *E. C. Knight Company,* 156 U.S. 1 (1895), which denied the act's applicability to the Sugar Trust by making a distinction between manufacturing, which Congress had no power to regulate, and commerce, which the federal government could control.

The eventual fate of the Sherman Act was decided in four Supreme Court decisions in which Justice McKenna participated between 1904 and 1920. In the first, the landmark *Northern Securities Company* v. *United States,* 193 U.S. 197 (1904), the Sherman Act received new life when a Court split five to four decided for the government that any kind of stock transactions which constituted illegal combinations in restraint of trade came within the purview of the Sherman Act. The judgment, in which McKenna fully concurred, made no distinction between "good" and "bad" trusts, nor did it concern itself with the question of whether or not the Northern Securities scheme, a Hill-Harriman-Morgan holding company set up to settle a railroad war, was a "reasonable" business endeavor, although Justice Holmes' dissent did refer to this concept which was to prove so important seven years later.

In 1911 Chief Justice White wrote two opinions which permanently interwove the so-called rule of reason into the American constitutional fabric. In both *Standard Oil Company of New Jersey et al.* v. *United States,* 221 U.S. 1 (1911), and *United States* v. *American Tobacco Company,* 221 U.S. 106 (1911), the Court concluded that the intent of the Sherman Act was to destroy "unreasonable" monopolies. Both Standard Oil and American Tobacco lost these suits, but quickly reorganized their corporate structures, became "reasonable" monopolies, and resumed domination within their respective industrial spheres. The concept of the "rule of reason" had long appealed to Justice McKenna, and he concurred with the Chief Justice in both cases.

A few years later, in 1920, McKenna clearly indicated the extent of his acceptance of the "rule of reason" in the case of *United States* v. *United States Steel Corporation,* 251 U.S. 417 (1920), where he wrote the majority opinion for the Court's four to three decision in favor of the steel monopoly. McKenna tacitly admitted to the awesome economic power of United States Steel, even to its potential ability to restrain interstate commerce, to stifle trade, even its intent to monopolize the steel industry. But he nevertheless contended that the mere existence of the power to dominate an industry was not prohibited by the Sherman Act and, in the absence of some overt action to the contrary, the assumption could be made that the corporation was behaving "reasonably."

While McKenna and the majority of the Court were unwilling even to allow the establishment of Northern Securities in 1904, by 1920 McKenna's majority opinion held that the unconcealed monopolistic tendencies of United States Steel were "reasonable." Thus the Sherman Act, spawned in an age which firmly believed in competition among economic units, was gradually emasculated by the acceptance of the few huge rationalized combinations which came to control so much of American life.

Much more effective than the Sherman Act in the federal government's modest efforts to exercise its police power over corporations was the revived Interstate Commerce Commission. Two pieces of progressive legislation passed during the administrations of Theodore Roosevelt served to rescue the commission from the uselessness to which a series of enfeebling Court decisions during the 1890's had relegated it. In 1903 the Elkins Act attacked the system of rebates, and in 1906 the Hepburn Act allowed the commission to set railroad shipping rates whenever the complaints of shippers against the carriers proved to be valid.

The efficacy of the I.C.C.'s new powers largely depended upon the reaction of the Supreme Court, in the sense that the Court would decide whether or not to uphold the constitutionality of these relatively far-reaching new federal powers. Within a seven-year period the Court delivered four opinions which determined the future effectiveness both of the Interstate Commerce Commission in particular and of federal regulatory bureaus in general. In each of these decisions Justice McKenna, who had once voted against the establishment of the I.C.C., strongly supported the expansion of its powers.

McKenna read the decision in the first of these cases, *Illinois Central Railroad Company* v. *Interstate Commerce Commission,* 206 U.S. 441 (1907). Speaking for a Court which divided seven to one, McKenna laid down the dictum that all matters of fact found by the I.C.C. were not to be questioned but were to be accepted as accurate unless clear and unmistakable error was committed. This apparently innocuous decision had the effect of releasing the commission from the time-consuming and expensive necessity of establishing the absolute validity of the data upon which it rested its decisions. In 1910, Justice McKenna concurred with Justice White's opinion in *Interstate Commerce Commission* v. *Illinois Central Railroad Company,* 215 U.S. 452 (1910). This highly technical opinion, delivered for a Court which split five to one on the issue, explicitly stated that the federal courts did not intend to interfere with the purely administrative tasks of setting rates. This decision established the credibility of the orders and directives of federal commissions such as the Interstate Commerce Commission. In the same year, the Court spoke through McKenna's opinion in the case of *Interstate Commerce Commission* v. *Chicago, Rock Island, and Pacific Railway Company,* 218 U.S. 88 (1910) to reaffirm this decision. McKenna, speaking for a five to three majority, confirmed the validity of an I.C.C. directive by which the railroad was ordered to substitute an entirely new rate schedule.

Naturally the railroads, which had become accustomed through the *laissez-faire* years to operating under no restraints, strongly opposed this steady accretion of power by a federal agency which increasingly interfered with "normal" business practices. Thus in the 1914 *Intermountain Rate Cases, Atchison, Topeka, and Santa Fe,* 234 U.S. 476 (1914), the railroad attacked the right of the commission to exercise the power to fix rates on the grounds that rate-fixing was purely a congressional power. By this time, however, the Court had no qualms about the constitutionality of congressional delegation of power to federal regulatory boards and consequently rejected the railroad's contention unanimously, thereby clearing the way for the I.C.C. and other subsequently established federal agencies to regulate various aspects of business, commerce and labor. In each of these decisions, Justice McKenna played a significant part in the revival of the Interstate Commerce Commission, and in a larger sense, in the meaningful expansion of the police powers of the federal government.

McKenna's record was not nearly as consistent, however, in the most significant of the cases involving labor questions in which he participated. In 1908 Justice McKenna strongly dissented in *Adair* v. *United States,* 208 U.S. 161 (1908), when the Court by a six to two vote ruled unconstitutional a federal law banning yellow-dog contracts. McKenna's dissent held that under the commerce clause the government could modify conditions of labor since the relationship between employees and interstate carriers directly impinged upon commerce. More significant than this broad concept of the commerce power, to which McKenna held with some consistency, was his willingness to sanction the loss of the individual's liberty to enter freely into contractual relationships when that loss served the greater good of promoting the infinitely more effective collective contractual relationship afforded by a trade union.

Despite this broadly cast dissent, McKenna reversed himself completely in *Coppage* v. *Kansas,* 236 U.S. 1 (1915), another significant yellow-dog contract case just seven years later. The Kansas state legislature had passed a comprehensive bill which not only outlawed yellow-dog contracts, but went on to prescribe stiff criminal penalties for transgressors. The Court, in a five to four split, ruled that the legislation was unconstitutional since it interfered with the freedom of an individual worker to enter into any form of contractual relationship with his employer. This reasoning was consistent with the thinking of the majority in the *Adair* case, but Justice McKenna reversed himself. In the *Adair* case McKenna had approved of trade union collectivism transcending the unfettered rights of the individual in certain contractual arrangements. In the *Coppage* case, conversely, McKenna argued that the comprehensive nature of the law, applying as it did to all private enterprise rather than merely those which could be defined as serving the public interest, interfered too basically with individual contractual freedoms. Two years later, in *Mountain Timber Company* v. *Washington,* 243 U.S. 219 (1917), McKenna again refused to sanction legislative involvement in labor relations. Here in a five to four decision in which the Court approved a Washington state law that forced employers to make contributions to a state welfare fund, McKenna silently dissented.

McKenna's decisions again fit no particular pattern in the broad area of judicial interpretation opened up by the passage of social legislation aimed at alleviating the evils of industrial working conditions. In 1905 he joined with the more conservative members of the Court in the famous case of *Lochner* v. *New*

York, 198 U.S. 45 (1905), when a five to four decision threw out a New York law limiting the labor of bakery employees to ten hours a day. Three years later, in the even more famous case of *Muller* v. *Oregon,* 208 U.S. 412 (1908), the dazzling performance of attorney Louis Brandeis mesmerized McKenna along with the rest of his colleagues, who unanimously sustained an Oregon law limiting women to ten hours of work per day. Brandeis' presentation of compelling documentation proving that the failure to control the hours of labor would impose great hardship on the women involved, greatly impressed McKenna, and in succeeding decisions involving hours of labor, he tended to uphold progressive legislation. In *Wilson* v. *New,* 243 U.S. 332 (1917), McKenna joined a five to four majority sanctioning the constitutionality of the Adamson Eight-Hour Act of 1916, which limited the daily labor on railroads operating in interstate commerce to eight hours. The same year, in *Bunting* v. *Oregon,* 243 U.S. 426 (1917), McKenna wrote the majority opinion in a five to three vote which upheld the constitutionality of a law which limited daily working hours for men to ten, as *Muller* v. *Oregon, supra,* had done for Oregon women nine years previously. These later decisions of McKenna stood in sharp contrast with his vote in the *Lochner* case of 1905, when he and the majority of his colleagues struck down New York state's attempts to limit the daily working hours of its bakers.

But in 1923 McKenna came full circle, back to the *Lochner* case. He silently acquiesced in *Adkins* v. *Children's Hospital,* 261 U.S. 525 (1923), as the Court voted five to three to invalidate a Congressional Act of 1918 which authorized the fixing of minimum wages for women in the District of Columbia. McKenna in this case aligned himself with his rigidly anti-progressive colleagues, the Justices Sutherland, Van Devanter, McReynolds and Butler.

Yet in another area of judicial interpretation involving labor relations, McKenna generally upheld congressional attempts to make the railroads liable for injuries sustained by their employees while on the job. In 1908 the Court rejected such federal legislation in the *First Federal Employers' Liability Cases,* 207 U.S. 463 (1908), on a five to four vote, with McKenna in the minority. Four years later, after Congress had rectified some of the ambiguous language objected to by some members of the majority in the original version of the law, the case was resubmitted as *Second Federal Employers' Liability Cases,* 223 U.S. 1 (1912), with the Court upholding the law by a six to nothing vote in a decision in which McKenna did not participate. The Californian did indicate his continued support for the intent of this legislation however, by delivering a number of opinions which held railroads liable for injuries suffered by their employees. In the 1920 case of *Erie Railroad Company* v. *Collins,* 253 U.S. 77 (1920) and *Erie Railroad Company* v. *Szary,* 253 U.S. 86 (1920), McKenna's majority opinions benefited two railroad shops workers who had been injured through the negligence of others.

Despite this favorable reaction to cases involving employer liability, one of McKenna's strongest dissents came when he objected to a major effort to broaden the concept of the compensation rights of workingmen injured on the job. In *Arizona Employers' Liability Cases,* 250 U.S. 400 (1919), McKenna's dissenting opinion was couched in such extreme absolutist terms that it drew wide criticism. The Arizona law in question, which the Court upheld, made employers liable for all employees' injuries irrespective of any negligence on the part of the employer. Although McKenna had voted in the past to permit compensatory damages where no negligence was involved, he now adhered strictly to the old common law dictum of "no liability without fault." By ignoring the complexities of the new economic relationship fostered by industrialism, and also by conveniently overlooking other well-established aspects of the law which meted out penalties without considering "fault," McKenna wrote:

> *It seems to be of the very foundation of right—of the essence of liberty as it is of morals—to be free from liability if one is free from fault. It has heretofore been the sense of the law and the sense of the world, pervading the regulations of both, that there can be no punishment where there is no blame; and yet the court now by its decision erects the denial of these postulates of conduct into a principle of law and governmental policy. In other words, it is said to be a benefit to government to put the exact discharge of duty under the menace of penalty and invert the conceptions of mankind of the relation of right and wrong action. . . . Consider what the employer does: he invests his money in productive enterprise—mining, smelting, manufacturing, railroading—he engages employees at their request and pays them the wages they demand, he takes all of the risks of the adventure. Now there is put upon him an immeasurable element that may make disaster inevitable. . . . It must be seen . . . that the difference between the position of employer and employee, simply considering the latter as economically weaker, is not a justification for the violation of the rights of the former, and that individual rights cannot be made to yield to philanthropy. . . .*

Although the quilted pattern of McKenna's legal decisions largely defies logical analysis, the involvement of the United States in the First World War did persuade the Justice to make a number of decisions in which the rights and privileges of individuals were unvaryingly abandoned to the supposed needs of the nation. These decisions were prompted by the conflict between the Bill of Rights and two pieces of wartime legislation, the Espionage Act of 1917 and the Sedition Act of 1918. Basic provisions of these emergency laws included proscriptions against any encouragement of insubordination, obstruction of military recruiting or enlistment procedures, or general and largely unspecified interference with the prosecution of the war. In addition, the Sedition Act clamped such a restrictive ban on "seditious" materials that during one period the mails were closed to *The New York Times.*

In the series of cases which resulted from this legislation, Justice McKenna joined most of his colleagues in upholding the right of the government to limit constitutional rights during wartime. McKenna fully subscribed to the notable opinion delivered by Justice Holmes for the unanimous Court in *Schenck* v. *United States,* 249 U.S. 47 (1919), in which the Espionage Act received the

Court's sanction. Holmes' opinion denied the absolute nature of free speech by using the now-famous piece of imagery: "Free speech would not protect a man in falsely shouting 'Fire!' in a theatre, and causing a panic." Holmes went on to introduce the ostensibly simple dictum of "clear and present danger," which could circumscribe the rights guaranteed by the First Amendment.

No one on the Court supported the logical extenuations of this line of reasoning more strongly than did Justice McKenna. The mere fact that the nation was at war seemed to him to present a "clear and present danger," and any individual or collective actions which interfered with the successful prosecution of the war, McKenna believed, were *prima facie* acknowledgment of guilt under the open-ended terms of the Espionage and Sedition Acts.

In *Abrams* v. *United States,* 250 U.S. 616 (1919), McKenna concurred in the majority opinion by which Abrams was convicted under the Sedition Act of printing and circulating a pamphlet critical of the war, of capitalism, and of the allied intervention in Siberia. The same year, McKenna also participated in the Court's decision which jailed Eugene Debs for making a speech against militarism, *Debs* v. *United States,* 249 U.S. 211 (1919). In *Pierce* v. *United States,* 252 U.S. 239 (1920), McKenna fully subscribed to Justice Pitney's majority opinion which upheld the conviction under the Espionage Act of a socialist pamphleteer in spite of the fact that no evidence was adduced to show any kind of relationship between the circulation of the pamphlet and the provisions of the act.

The fact that many cases did not reach the Court until after the war had ended had no effect on McKenna's undeviatingly rigid view. In *Gilbert* v. *State of Minnesota,* 254 U.S. 325 (1920), the Court upheld the conviction of a man who had made an anti-war speech in violation of a state statute. In delivering the majority opinion, Justice McKenna claimed that the speech not only violated the Minnesota law, but also, in a much larger sense, threatened the welfare of the whole nation. McKenna denied the applicability of the First Amendment to the case by stating that "for the purposes of this case [we] may concede . . . that the asserted freedom [of speech] is natural and inherent, but it is not absolute, it is subject to restriction and limitation." The terms of "restriction and limitation," McKenna went on, were suggested by the *Schenck* case with its restrictions on speech and its enunciation of the "clear and present danger" concept. As McKenna wrote,

> *The Nation was at war with Germany, armies were recruiting, and the speech was the discouragement of that—its purpose was necessarily the discouragement of that. It was not an advocacy of policies or a censure of actions that a citizen had the right to make. The war was flagrant; it had been declared by the power constituted by the Constitution to declare it. . . . This was known to Gilbert . . . and every word that he uttered in denunciation of the war was false, was deliberate misrepresentation of the motives which impelled it, and the objects for which it was prosecuted. He could have had no purpose other than that of which he was charged. It would be a travesty on the constitutional privilege he invokes to assign him its protection.*

The vigor of McKenna's several opinions in the civil liberties cases that came out of the war belied the enfeebling effects of old age. In the early 1920's, as he neared his eightieth birthday, the ramrod-straight old man's mental alertness declined steadily. By 1922, when McKenna became the Court's senior member, his colleagues had realized that McKenna frequently missed the entire point of a case. On several occasions he was asked to redo his opinions, and then, embarrassingly for all concerned, to redo them again. Chief Justice Taft revealed the extreme nature of the situation when he wrote to his brother of McKenna that

> *I don't know what course to take with respect to him, or what cases to assign to him. I had to take back a case from him last Saturday because he would not write it in accordance with the vote of the Court. . . .* [*In McDevitt,* McKenna, *228.*]

In November of 1924 Taft called all of the other Associate Justices to his home and secured their agreement to a plan whereby the Court would not make decisions in cases in which McKenna's vote would be crucial. At the same time, Taft increased his efforts to persuade the stubborn old man to retire. (Alpheus T. Mason, *William Howard Taft: Chief Justice* [New York, 1964], 206 ff.; McDevitt, *McKenna,* 228–229.)

Finally, when Mrs. McKenna died in 1924, something went out of the aged Justice and he yielded to the rather overt desires of his colleagues. On January 25, 1925, his clear eyes glistening, the old Irishman left his seat permanently after twenty-seven years. For almost two years afterward McKenna lived quietly on in Washington, occasionally seeing one of an ever dwindling number of old friends, frequently taking motor rides into the countryside. On November 21, 1926, with his four children at his bedside, Joseph McKenna slept into death.

His life proved to be a vindication of an immigrant father's faith in the American Dream. In addition to living according to those virtues of hard work and determination which sustained so many transplanted Europeans, Joseph McKenna also mastered the art of American political success. As a faithful and trustworthy party regular, he served well the constituency upon which his political career depended. Simultaneously, he developed something of a national power base which was built upon his influence in the House of Representatives, numerous personal relationships, and an inflexible reputation for regularity. Just rewards naturally came through a Cabinet post and the later appointment to the High Court.

McKenna's accession to the Court marked a fundamental change in the nature of his career. For the first time he had no constituency, no responsibility to provide varying kinds of political service. Recognizing the very different demands which this major position of responsibility entailed as well as his own legal limitations, McKenna worked terribly hard to compensate for scholarly inadequacies. In addition, he refused to allow his reflex conservatism to dictate judicial opinions but instead displayed such a surprising degree of flexibility that his decisions sometimes tended to be almost erratic.

In many ways he supported the basic political changes which came with the

Progressive Era, and many of his decisions involving due process, the commerce clause and assorted elements of the embryonic federal police power are surprising in the light of his earlier steadfast adherence to conservative principles. As he grew older, his progressive opinions became fewer and fewer, and he tended to rely once again on the dogmatic precepts of an earlier time.

As in so many other instances, however, McKenna's adaptability and dogged determination to vindicate the trust placed in him compensated for the haphazard way in which American public men come to positions of great influence.

SELECTED BIBLIOGRAPHY

Although a few of McKenna's letters survive in various collections there are no McKenna manuscripts. The only formal study of his life is the uncritical biography by Brother Matthew McDevitt, *Joseph McKenna, Associate Justice of the United States* (Washington, D.C., 1946). McKenna received frequent but sparse mention in the press throughout his long career. See, for example, the San Francisco press coverage of his Supreme Court nomination in *The Examiner,* December 3 through December 6, 1897, and the *San Francisco Chronicle,* December 5, 1897, and January 22, 1898. For later mention, see 44 *Munsey's Magazine* 739 (1911). *The New York Times* also contains occasional accounts of McKenna's activities over the years; see February 25, 1913, January 16, 1917, both on the White Slave Act. His resignation from the Court is fulsomely covered in *The New York Times* of January 6, 1925, as was his death on November 22, 1926. Although other sources are sparse, for random insights consult Margaret Leech, *In the Days of McKinley* (New York, 1959), and Alpheus Mason, *William Howard Taft: Chief Justice* (New York, 1964).

Joseph McKenna

REPRESENTATIVE OPINIONS

HIPOLITE EGG CO. v. UNITED STATES, 220 U.S. 45 (1911)

This case centered upon the right of the federal government to exercise sweeping police powers under the commerce clause, a right which has been vigorously though unsuccessfully opposed since the enactment of regulatory legislation at the beginning of the twentieth century. The Pure Food and Drug Act of 1906 provided the legal basis for the federal government's seizure of a number of cases of preserved eggs from the Hipolite Egg Company. The Court's unanimous opinion, as presented by Justice McKenna, constituted a total affirmation of the government's right to prevent the interstate transfer of adulterated products. McKenna's decision passed over the constitutional question of congressional intent by ignoring the charge that in the Pure Food and Drug Act the Congress was in reality interposing itself through the commerce power in the traditional prerogatives of state and local governments to oversee food production. McKenna restricted his remarks to the question of interstate trade, and found that the Constitution allowed the federal government complete powers to regulate all aspects of it, including the seizure of the adulterated eggs.

MR. JUSTICE MCKENNA delivered the opinion of the court.

The case is here on a question of jurisdiction certified by the District Court.

On March 11, 1909, the United States instituted libel proceedings under § 10 of the act of Congress of June 30, 1906, c. 3915, 34 Stat. 768, against fifty cans of preserved whole eggs, which had been prepared by the Hipolite Egg Company of St. Louis, Missouri.

The eggs, before the shipment alleged in the libel, were stored in a warehouse in St. Louis for about five months, during which time they were the property of Thomas & Clark, an Illinois corporation engaged in the bakery business at Peoria, Ill.

Thomas & Clark procured the shipment of the eggs to themselves at Peoria, and upon the receipt of them placed the shipment in their storeroom in their bakery factory along with other bakery supplies.

The eggs were intended for baking purposes, and were not intended for sale in the original, unbroken packages or otherwise, and were not so sold. The Hipolite Egg Company appeared as claimant of the eggs, intervened, filed an answer, and defended the case, but did not enter into a stipulation to pay costs.

Upon the close of libellant's evidence, and again at the close of the case, counsel for the Egg Company moved the court to dismiss the libel on the ground that it appeared from the evidence that the court, as a Federal court, had no jurisdiction to proceed against or confiscate the eggs, because they were not shipped in interstate commerce for sale within the meaning of § 10 of the Food and Drug Act, and for the further reason that the evidence showed that the shipment had passed out of interstate commerce before the seizure of the eggs, because it appeared that they had been delivered to Thomas & Clark and were not intended to be sold by them in the original packages or otherwise.

The motions were overruled and the court proceeded to hear and determine the cause and entered a decree finding the eggs adulterated, and confiscating them. Costs were assessed against the Egg Company.

The decree was excepted to on the ground that the court was without jurisdiction *in rem* over the subject matter, and on the further ground that the court was without jurisdiction to enter judgment *in personam* against the Egg Company for costs.

The jurisdiction of the District Court being challenged, the case comes here directly.

Section 2 of the Food and Drug Act prohibits the introduction into any State or Territory from any other State or Territory of any article of food or drugs which is adulterated, and makes it a misdemeanor for any person to ship or deliver for shipment such adulterated article, or who shall receive such shipment, or, having received it, shall deliver it in original unbroken packages for pay or otherwise.

In giving a remedy § 10 provides that if "any article of food that is adulterated and is being transported from one State . . . to another for sale, or, having been transported, remains unloaded, unsold, or in original unbroken packages, . . . shall be liable to be proceeded against in any district court of the United States within the district where the same is found, and seized for confiscation by a process of libel for condemnation. . . . The proceeding of such libel cases shall conform, as near as may be, to the proceedings in admiralty . . . and all such proceedings shall be at the suit of and in the name of the United States."

The shipment to Thomas & Clark consisted of 130 separate cans, each can corked and sealed with wax. The eggs were intended to be used for baking purposes. The only can sold was that sold to the inspector for the purpose of having the eggs analyzed. They contained approximately two per cent of boric acid, which the court found was a deleterious ingredient, and adjudged that they were adulterated within the meaning of the Food and Drugs Act of June 30, 1906, c. 3915, 34 Stat. 771.

The Egg Company, whilst not contending that the shipment of the eggs was not a violation of § 2 of the act, and a misdemeanor within its terms, and not denying the power of Congress to enact it, presents three contentions: (1) Section 10 of the Food and Drugs Act does not apply to an article of food which has not been shipped for sale, but which has been shipped solely for use as a raw material in the manufacture of some other product. (2) A United States District Court has no jurisdiction to proceed *in rem* under § 10 against goods that have passed out of interstate commerce before the proceeding *in rem* was commenced. (3) The court had no jurisdiction to enter a personal judgment against the Egg Company for costs.

It may be said at the outset of these contentions that they insist that the remedies provided by the statute are not coextensive with its prohibitions, and hence that it has virtually defined the wrong and provided no adequate means of punishing the wrong when committed. Premising this much, we proceed to their consideration in the order in which they have been presented. The following cases are cited to sustain the first contention: *United States* v. *Sixty-five Casks of Liquid Extracts,* 170 Fed. Rep. 449, affirmed by the Circuit Court of Appeals in *United States* v. *Knowlton Danderine Company,* 175 Fed. Rep. 1022, and *United States* v. *Forty-six Packages and Boxes of Sugar,* in the District Court for the Southern District of Ohio, not yet reported.

The articles involved in the first case were charged with having been misbranded and consisted of drugs in casks, which were shipped from Detroit, Michigan, to Wheeling, West Virginia, there to be received by the Knowlton Danderine Company in bulk in carload lots and manufactured into danderine, of which no sale was to be made until the casks should be emptied and the contents placed in properly marked bottles.

It was contended that the articles, not having been shipped in the casks for the purpose of sale thus in bulk, but shipped to the owner from one State to another for the purpose of being bottled into small packages suitable for sale, and when so bottled to be labeled in compliance with the requirements of the act, were not transported for sale, and were therefore not subject to libel under § 10 of the act.

The contention submitted to the court the construction of the statute. The court, however, based its decision upon the want of power in Congress to prohibit one from manufacturing a product in a State and removing it to another State "for the purpose of personal use and not sale, or for use in connection with the manufacture of other articles, to be legally branded when so manufactured;" and concluded independently, or as construing the statute, that the danderine company, being the owner of the property, shipped it to itself and did not come within any of the prohibitions of the statute. The case was affirmed by the Circuit Court of Appeals, 175 Fed. Rep. 1022. The court, however, expressed no opinion as to the power of Congress. It decided that the facts did not exhibit a case within the purpose of the statute, saying: "No attempt to evade the law, either directly or indirectly or by subterfuges, has been shown, it appearing that the manufacturer had simply transferred from one point to another the product he was manufacturing for the purpose of completing the preparation of the same for the market. Under the circumstances disclosed in this case, having in mind the object of the Congress in enacting the law involved, we do not think the liquid extracts proceeded against should be forfeited. In reaching this conclusion we do not find it necessary to consider other questions discussed by counsel and referred to in the opinion of the court."

In *United States* v. *Forty-six Packages and Boxes of Sugar* the court construed the statute as applying only to transportation for the purpose of sale. To explain its view the court said: "Following the words 'having been transported' is an ellipse, an omission of words necessary to the complete construction of the sentence. These words are found in the preceding part of the section and, when supplied, the clause under which this libel is filed reads and means, 'any article of food, drug or liquor that is adulterated or misbranded within the meaning of this act, having been transported from one State to another *for sale* [italics ours], remains unloaded, unsold, or in original, unbroken packages, . . . shall be liable,' " etc. And the court was of opinion that this view was in accord with the other two cases which we have cited. This may be disputed. It may well be considered that there is no analogy between an article in the hands of its owner or moved from one place to another by him, to be used in the manufacture of articles subject to the statute and to be branded in compliance with it, and an adulterated article *itself* the subject of sale and intended to be used as adulterated in contravention of the purpose of the statute.

A legal analogy might be insisted upon if cakes and cookies, which are the compounds of eggs and flour which the record presents, could be branded to apprise of their ingredients like compounds of alcohol. The object of the law is to keep adulterated articles out of the channels of interstate commerce, or, if they enter such commerce, to condemn them while being transported or when they have reached their destination, provided they remain unloaded, unsold or in original unbroken packages. These situations are clearly separate, and we cannot unite or qualify them by the purpose of the owner to be a sale. It, indeed, may be asked in what manner a sale? The question suggests that we might accept the condition, and yet the instances of this record be within the statute. All articles, compound or single, not intended for consumption by the producer, are designed for sale, and, because they are, it is the concern of the law to have them pure.

It is, however, insisted that "the proceeding *in personam* authorized by the law was intended to, and no doubt is, capable of giving full force and effect to the law"; and, further, that a producer in a State is not interested in an article shipped from another State which is not intended to be sold or offered for consumption until it is manufactured into something else. The argument is peculiar. It is certainly to the interest of a producer or consumer that the article which he receives, no matter whence it come, shall be pure, and the law seeks to secure that interest, not only through personal penalties but through the condemnation of the article if impure. There is nothing inconsistent in the remedies, nor are they dependent. *The Three Friends,* 166 U.S. 1, 49.

The first contention of the Egg Company is, therefore, untenable.

2. Under this contention it is said that "the jurisdiction of the food and drugs act in question can go no farther than the power given to Congress under which it was enacted," and that the District Court, therefore, "had no jurisdiction *in rem* because at the time of the seizure the eggs had passed into the general mass of property in the State and out of the field covered by interstate commerce."

To support the contention, *Waring* v. *The Mayor,* 8 Wall. 110, is cited. That case involved the legality of a tax imposed by an ordinance of the city of Mobile upon merchants and traders of the city equal to one-half of one per cent on the gross amount of their sales, whether the merchandise was sold at public or private sale. Waring was fined for non-payment of the tax, and he brought suit to restrain the collection of the fine, alleging that he was exempt from the tax on the ground that the sales made by him were of merchandise in the original packages, as imported from a foreign country, and which was purchased by him, in entire cargoes, of the consignees of the importing vessels before their arrival, or while the vessels were in the lower harbor of the port. He obtained a decree in the trial court which was reversed by the Supreme Court of the State of Alabama. A writ of error was sued out from this court and the decree was affirmed, on the ground that Waring was not the shipper or consignee of the imported merchandise, nor the first vendor of it, and it was the settled law of the court "that merchandise in the original packages once sold by the importer is taxable as other property," citing *Brown* v. *Maryland,* 12 Wheat. 443; *Almy* v. *California,* 24 How. 173; *Pervear* v. *Commonwealth,* 5 Wall. 479. This also was said:

"When the importer sells the imported articles, or otherwise mixes them with the general property of the State by breaking up the packages, the state of things changes, as was said by this court in the leading case, as the tax then finds the articles already incorporated with the mass of property by the act of the importer. Importers selling the imported articles in the original packages are shielded from any such state tax, but the privilege of exemption is not extended to the purchaser, as the merchandise, by the sale and delivery, loses its distinctive character as an import."

This case is clear as far as it goes, but the facts are not the same as those in the case at bar.

In the case at bar there was no sale of the articles after they were committed to interstate commerce, nor were the original packages broken. Indeed, it might be insisted that we need go no farther than that case for the rule of decision in this. It affirms the doctrine of original packages which was expressed and illustrated in previous cases and has been expressed and illustrated in subsequent ones. It is too firmly fixed to need or even to justify further discussion, and we shall not stop to affirm or deny its application to the special contention of the Egg Company. We prefer to decide the case on another ground which is sustained by well-known principles.

The statute declares that it is one "for preventing . . . the transportation of adulterated . . . foods . . . and for regulating traffic therein;" and, as we have seen, § 2 makes the shipper of them criminal and § 10 subjects them to confiscation, and, in some cases, to destruction, so careful is the statute to prevent a defeat of its purpose. In other words, transportation in interstate commerce is forbidden to them, and, in a sense, they are made culpable as well as their shipper. It is clearly the purpose of the statute that they shall not be stealthily put into interstate commerce and be stealthily taken out again upon arriving at their destination and be given asylum in the mass of property of the State. Certainly not, when they are yet in the condition in which they were transported to the State, or, to use the words of the statute, while they remain "in the original, unbroken packages." In that condition they carry their own identification as contraband of law. Whether they might be pursued beyond the original package we are not called upon to say. That far the statute pursues them, and, we think, legally pursues them, and to demonstrate this but little discussion is necessary.

The statute rests, of course, upon the power of Congress to regulate interstate commerce, and, defining that power, we have said that no trade can be carried on between the States to which it does not extend, and have further said that it is complete in itself, subject to no limitations except those found in the Constitution. We are dealing, it must be remembered, with illicit articles—articles which the law seeks to keep out of commerce, because they are debased by adulteration, and which law punishes them (if we may so express ourselves) and the shipper of them. There is no denial that such is the purpose of the law, and the only limitation of the power to execute such purpose which is urged is that the articles must be apprehended in transit or before they have become a part of the general mass of property of the State. In other words, the contention attempts to apply to articles of illegitimate commerce the rule which marks the line between the exercise of Federal power and state power over articles of legitimate commerce. The contention misses the question in the case. There is here no conflict of national and state jurisdictions over property legally articles of trade. The question here is whether articles which are outlaws of commerce may be seized wherever found, and it certainly will not be contended that they are outside of the jurisdiction of the National Government when they are within the borders of a State. The question in the case, therefore is, What power has Congress over such articles? Can they escape the consequences of their illegal transportation by being mingled at the place of destination with other property? To give them such immunity would defeat, in many cases, the provision for their confiscation, and their confiscation or destruction is the especial concern of the law. The power to do so is certainly appropriate to the right to bar them from interstate commerce, and completes its purpose, which is not to prevent merely the physical movement of adulterated articles, but the use of them, or rather to prevent trade in them between the States by denying to them the facilities of interstate commerce. And appropriate means to that end, which we have seen is legitimate, are the seizure and condemnation of the articles at their point of destination in the original, unbroken packages. The selection of such means is certainly within that breadth of discretion which we have said Congress possesses in the execution of the powers conferred upon it by the Constitution. *McCulloch* v. *Maryland,* 4 Wheat. 316; *Lottery Case,* 188 U.S. 321, 355.

3. Had the court jurisdiction to adjudge costs against the Egg Company? This is contended, and in support of the contention the claimant assimilates this proceeding to one in admiralty. In consequence, it may be supposed of the provisions of § 10 of the Food and Drugs Act that the proceedings "shall conform, as near as may be, to the proceedings in admiralty," and *The Monte A,* 12 Fed. Rep. 331, and *The Alida,* 12 Fed. Rep. 343, are cited as deciding that in a proceeding *in rem* the court has no jurisdiction to assess the costs *in personam* against the claimant, who simply files an answer, but who does not enter into a stipulation to pay the costs of the proceeding. Too broad a deduction is made from these cases. They undoubtedly decide that a process *in rem* and *in personam* cannot be joined in admiralty in the same libel, but it was not held that this was because of a want of jurisdictional power in the court. Such view was disclaimed in *The Monte A,* and to show that the framing of a libel against the owner *in personam* and against the vessel *in rem* was not jurisdictional, the court said that a breach of a contract of affreightment could have been so framed "long before the adoption of the Supreme Court rules in admiralty."

It is stated in Benedict's Admiralty, § 204, that "the distinction between proceedings *in rem* and *in personam* has no proper relation to the question of jurisdiction." It may be, as stated in § 359 of the same work, that "in a suit *in rem,* unless some one intervenes, the power and process of the court is confined to the thing itself and does not reach either the person or property of the owner." If, however, the owner comes in, or an intervenor does, his appearance is voluntary. He becomes an actor and subjects himself to costs, and this even if his ownership be averred in the libel. Waple Proceedings In Rem, page 100, § 73; *United States* v. *422 Casks of Wine,* 1 Pet. 547.

And such seems to be the necessary effect of Admiralty Rules 26[1] and 34.[1] It is provided (Rule 34) that if a third person intervene, for his own interest, he is required to give a stipulation with sureties to abide the final decree rendered in the original or appellate court. It is in effect conceded that if such a stipulation be given, a judgment for costs can be rendered. But, upon what theory? The concession confounds the relation between the stipulation and the judgment, and makes the security for the payment of the judgment the source of jurisdiction to render it—jurisdiction according to the contention, which the court does not have as a Federal court.

Even, therefore, upon the supposition that the principles of the admiralty law are to apply to the proceedings under § 10, we think the court had jurisdiction to render a

[1] *For these Rules in full see 210 U.S. 552, 554.*

judgment for costs against the Egg Company.

So far out discussion has been in deference to the contention of the Egg Company, but it is disputable if the certificate presents a question of jurisdiction as to costs. The District Court gets its jurisdiction of the cause from § 10 of the Food and Drugs Act, and whether the libel may be *in rem* and *in personam,* or whether a personal judgment for costs can be rendered, may be said to be simply a question of the construction of the section, and not one which involves the jurisdiction of the court. In other words, the rulings of the court may be error only, not in excess of its power. It certainly had jurisdiction of the person of the Egg Company.

UNITED STATES v. UNITED STATES STEEL CORPORATION, 251 U.S. 417 (1920)

The disposition of this case indicates the final triumph of the "rule of reason" over the Sherman Anti-Trust Act. First formally recognized in the two 1911 anti-trust prosecutions of the Standard Oil Company and the American Tobacco Company, the notion of reasonableness held that not all combinations in restraint of trade were illegal, as the Sherman Act ostensibly held, but only those that were unreasonable in terms of the public interest. From this point on, as the Court took onto itself the responsibility for differentiating the reasonable from the unreasonable, the giant corporations came to court prepared with arguments testifying to their service in the public interest. Thus in 1920, when the government sought to apply the Sherman Act against the Steel Trust as it had against the Oil and Tobacco Trusts in 1911, United States Steel did not defend its monopolistic powers, or its ability to restrain trade. Justice McKenna's majority opinion in the Court's four to three decision overrode all economic and institutional objections and emphasized the absence in the Sherman Act of specific proscriptions against the mere existence of monopoly power. Despite its awesome potential, McKenna judged that since United States Steel had not employed this power against the public interest, it had acted reasonably, and he thereby dismissed the government's case and, in effect, also dismissed much of the Sherman Act as well.

MR. JUSTICE MCKENNA delivered the opinion of the court.

Suit against the Steel Corporation and certain other companies which it directs and controls by reason of the ownership of their stock, it and they being separately and collectively charged as violators of the Sherman Anti-Trust Act.

It is prayed that it and they be dissolved because engaged in illegal restraint of trade and the exercise of monopoly.

Special charges of illegality and monopoly are made and special redresses and remedies are prayed, among others, that there be a prohibition of stock ownership and exercise of rights under such ownership, and that there shall be such orders and distribution of the stock and other properties as shall be in accordance with equity and good conscience and "shall effectuate the purpose of the Anti-Trust Act." General relief is also prayed.

The Steel Corporation is a holding company only; the other companies are the operating ones, manufacturers in the iron and steel industry, twelve in number. There are, besides, other corporations and individuals more or less connected with the activities of the other defendants that are alleged to be instruments or accomplices in their activities and offendings; and that these activities and offendings (speaking in general terms) extend from 1901 to 1911, when the bill was filed, and have illustrative periods of significant and demonstrated illegality.

Issue is taken upon all these charges, and we see at a glance what detail of circumstances may be demanded, and we may find ourselves puzzled to compress them into an opinion that will not be of fatiguing prolixity.

The case was heard in the District Court by four judges. They agreed that the bill should be dismissed; they disagreed as to the reasons for it. 223 Fed. Rep. 55. One opinion (written by Judge Buffington and concurred in by Judge McPherson) expressed the view that the Steel Corporation was not formed with the intention or purpose to monopolize or restrain trade, and did not have the motive or effect "to prejudice the public interest by unduly restricting competition or unduly obstructing the course of trade." The corporation, in the view of the opinion, was an evolution, a natural consummation of the tendencies of the industry on account of changing conditions, practically a compulsion from "the metallurgical method of making steel and the physical method of handling it," this method, and the conditions consequent upon it, tending to combinations of capital and energies rather than diffusion in independent action. And the concentration of powers (we are still representing the opinion) was only such as was deemed necessary, and immediately manifested itself in improved methods and products and in an increase of domestic and foreign trade. Indeed an important purpose of the organization of the corporation was the building up of the export trade in steel and iron which at that time was sporadic, the mere dumping of the products upon foreign markets.

Not monopoly, therefore, was the purpose of the organization of the corporation but concentration of efforts with resultant economies and benefits.

The tendency of the industry and the purpose of the corporation in yielding to it were expressed in comprehensive condensation by the word "integration," which signifies continuity in the processes of the industry from ore mines to the finished product.

All considerations deemed pertinent were expressed and their influence was attempted to be assigned and, while conceding that the Steel Corporation, after its formation in times of financial disturbance, entered into informal agreements or understandings with its competitors to maintain prices, they terminated with their occasions, and, as they had ceased to exist, the court was not justified in dissolving the corporation.

The other opinion (by Judge Woolley and concurred in by Judge Hunt, 223 Fed. Rep. 161) was in some particulars, in antithesis to Judge Buffington's. The view was expressed that neither the Steel Corporation nor the preceding combinations, which were in a sense its antetypes, had the justification of industrial conditions, nor were they or it impelled by the necessity for integration, or compelled to unite in comprehensive enterprise because such had become a condition of success under the new order of things. On the contrary, that the organizers of the corporation and the preceding companies had illegal purpose from the very beginning, and the corporation became "a combination of combinations, by which, directly or indirectly, approximately 180 independent concerns were brought under one business control," which, measured by the amount of production, extended to 80% or 90% of the entire output of the country, and that its purpose was to secure great profits which were thought possible in the light of the history of its constituent combinations, and to accomplish permanently what those combinations had demonstrated could be accomplished temporarily, and thereby monopolize and restrain trade.[1]

[1] *As bearing upon the power obtained and what the Corporation did we give other citations from Judge Woolley's opinion as follows:*

"The ore reserves acquired by the corporation at and subsequent to its organization, the relation which such reserves bear to ore bodies then existing and subsequently discovered, and their bearing upon the question of monopoly of raw materials, are matters which have been discussed in the preceding opinion, and with the reasoning as well as with the conclusion that the corporation has not a monopoly of the raw materials of the steel industry, I am in entire accord."

"Further inquiring whether the corporation inherently possesses monopolistic power attention is next given to its proportion of the manufacture and sale of finished iron and steel products of the industry. Upon this subject there is a great volume of testimony, a detailed consideration of which in an opinion would be quite inexcusable. As a last analysis of this testimony, it is sufficient to say it shows that, large as was the corporation, and substantial as was its proportion of the business of the industry, the corporation was not able in the first ten years of its

The organizers, however (we are still representing the opinion), underestimated the opposing conditions and at the very beginning the Corporation instead of relying upon its own power sought and obtained the assistance and the coöperation of its competitors (the independent companies). In other words the view was expressed that the testimony did "not show that the corporation in and of itself ever possessed or exerted sufficient power when acting alone to control prices of the products of the industry." Its power was efficient only when in coöperation with its competitors, and hence it concerted with them in the expedients of pools, associations, trade meetings, and finally in a system of dinners inaugurated in 1907 by the president of the company, E. H. Gary, and called "the Gary Dinners." The dinners were congregations of producers and "were nothing but trade meetings," successors of the other means of associated action and control through such action. They were instituted first in "stress of panic," but, their potency being demonstrated, they were afterwards called to control prices "in periods of industrial calm." "They were pools without penalties" and more efficient in stabilizing prices. But it was the further declaration that "when joint action was either refused or withdrawn the Corporation's prices were controlled by competition."

The Corporation, it was said, did not at any time abuse the power or ascendency it possessed. It resorted to none of the brutalities or tyrannies that the cases illustrate of other combinations. It did not secure freight rebates; it did not increase its profits by reducing the wages of its employees—whatever it did was not at the expense of labor; it did not increase its profits by lowering the quality of its products, nor create an artificial scarcity of them; it did not oppress or coerce its competitors—its competition, though vigorous, was fair; it did not undersell its competitors in some localities by reducing its prices there below those maintained elsewhere, or require its customers to enter into contracts limiting their purchases or restricting them in resale prices; it did not obtain customers by secret rebates or departures from its published prices; there was no evidence that it attempted to crush its competitors or drive them out of the market, nor did it take customers from its competitors by unfair means, and in its competition it seemed to make no difference between large and small competitors. Indeed it is said in many ways and illustrated that "instead of relying upon its own power to fix and maintain prices, the corporation, at its very beginning sought and obtained the assistance of others." It combined its power with that of its competitors. It did not have power in and of itself, and the control it exerted was only in and by association with its competitors. Its offense, therefore, such as it was, was not different from theirs and was distinguished from theirs "only in the leadership it assumed in promulgating and perfecting the policy." This leadership it gave up, and it had ceased to offend against the law before this suit was brought. It was hence concluded that it should be distinguished from its organizers and that their intent and unsuccessful attempt should not be attributed to it, that it "in and of itself is not now and has never been a monopoly or a combination in restraint of trade," and a decree of dissolution should not be entered against it.

This summary of the opinions, given necessarily in paraphrase, does not adequately represent their ability and strength,

---

history to maintain its position in the increase of trade. During that period, its proportion of the domestic business decreased from 50.1 per cent. to 40.9 per cent. and its increase of business during that period was but 40.6 per cent. of its original volume. Its increase of business, measured by percentage, was exceeded by eight of its competitors, whose increase of business, likewise measured by percentage, ranged from 63 to 3779. This disparity in the increase of production indicates that the power of the corporation is not commensurate with its size, and that the size and the consequent power of the corporation are not sufficient competitors.

"From the vast amount of testimony, it is conclusively shown that the Steel Corporation did not attempt to exert a power, if such it possessed, to oppress and destroy its competitors, and it is likewise disclosed by the history of the industry subsequent to the organization of the corporation that if it had made such an attempt it would have failed. It is also shown by the testimony that, acting independently and relying alone upon its power and wealth, great as they were, the corporation has never been able to dominate the steel industry by controlling the supply of raw materials, restraining production of finished products, or enhancing and maintaining the prices of either."

but it has value as indicating the contentions of the parties, and the ultimate propositions to which the contentions are addressed. The opinions indicate that the evidence admits of different deductions as to the genesis of the Corporation and the purpose of its organizers, but only of a single deduction as to the power it attained and could exercise. Both opinions were clear and confident that the power of the Corporation never did and does not now reach to monopoly, and their review of the evidence, and our independent examination of it, enable us to elect between their respective estimates of it, and we concur in the main with that of Judges Woolley and Hunt. And we add no comment except, it may be, that they underestimated the influence of the tendency and movement to integration, the appreciation of the necessity or value of the continuity of manufacture from the ore to the finished product. And there was such a tendency; and though it cannot be asserted it had become a necessity, it had certainly become a facility of industrial progress. There was, therefore, much to urge it and give incentive to conduct that could accomplish it. From the nature and properties of the industry, the processes of production were something more than the stage and setting of the human activities. They determined to an extent those activities, furnished their motives, and gave test of their quality—not, of course, that the activities could get any immunity from size, or resources, or energies, whether exerted in integrated plants or diversified ones.

The contentions of the case, therefore, must be judged by the requirements of the law, not by accidental or adventitious circumstances. But what are such circumstances? We have seen that it was the view of the District Court that size was such a circumstance and had no accusing or excusing influence. The contention of the Government is to the contrary. Its assertion is that the size of the Corporation being the result of a "combination of powerful and able competitors" had become "substantially dominant" in the industry and illegal. And that this was determined. The companies combined, is the further assertion, had already reached a high degree of efficiency, and in their independence were factors in production and competition, but ceased to be such when brought under the regulating control of the Corporation, which by uniting them offended the law; and that the organizers of the Corporation "had in mind the specific purposes of the restraint of trade and the enormous profits resulting from that restraint."

It is the contention of the Corporation opposing those of the Government and denying the illegal purposes charged against it, that the industry demanded qualities and an enterprise that lesser industries do not demand and must have a corresponding latitude and facility. Indeed, it is insisted that the industry had practically, (to quote the words of Judge Buffington, he quoting those of a witness,) "reached the limit, or very nearly so, at which economies from a metallurgical or mechanical standpoint could be made effective," and "that instead, as was then the practice, of having one mill to make 10 or 20 or 50 products, the greatest economy would result from having one mill make one product, and make that product continuously." In other words, that there was a necessity for integration, and rescue from the old conditions—from their improvidence and waste of effort; and that, in redress of the conditions, the Corporation was formed, its purpose and effect being "salvage not monopoly," to quote the words of counsel. It was, is the insistence, the conception of ability, "a vision of a great business which should embrace all lines of steel and all processes of manufacture from the ore to the finished product and which by reason of the economies thus to be effected and the diversity of products it would be able to offer, could successfully compete in all the markets of the world." It is urged further that to the discernment of that great possibility was added a courage that dared attempt its accomplishment, and the conception and the courage made the formation of the Corporation notable but did not make it illegal.

We state the contentions, we do not have to discuss them, or review the arguments advanced for their acceptance or repulsion. That is done in the opinions of the district judges, and we may well despair to supplement the force of their representation of the conditions antecedent to the formation of the Corporation and in what respect and extent its formation changed them. Of course in that representation and its details there is guidance to decision, but they must be rightly estimated to judge of what they persuade. Our present purpose is not retrospect for itself, however instructive, but practical decision upon existing conditions, that we may not by their disturbance produce, or even risk, consequences of a concern that cannot now be computed. In other words, our consideration should be of not what the Corporation had power to do or did, but what it has now power to do and is doing, and what judgment shall be now pronounced—whether its dissolution, as the Government prays, or the dismissal of the suit, as the Corporation insists?

The alternatives are perplexing—involve conflicting considerations, which, regarded in isolation, have diverse tendencies. We have seen that the judges of the District Court unanimously concurred in the view that the Corporation did not achieve monopoly, and such is our deduction, and it is against monopoly that the statute is directed, not against an expectation of it, but against its realization, and it is certain that it was not realized. The opposing conditions were underestimated. The power attained was much greater than that possessed by any one competitor—it was not greater than that possessed by all of them. [Monopoly, therefore, was not achieved, and competitors had to be persuaded by pools, associations, trade meetings, and through the social form of dinners, all of them, it may be, violations of the law, but transient in their purpose and effect. They were scattered through the years from 1901(the year of the formation of the Corporation), until 1911, but, after instances of success and failure, were abandoned nine months before this suit was brought.] There is no evidence that the abandonment was in prophecy of or dread of suit; and the illegal practices have not been resumed, nor is there any evidence of an intention to resume them, and certainly no "dangerous probability" of their resumption, the test for which *Swift & Co.* v. *United States,* 196 U.S. 375, 396, is cited. It is our conclusion, therefore, as it was that of the judges below, that the practices were abandoned from a conviction of their futility, from the operation of forces that were not understood or were underestimated, and the case is not peculiar. And we may say in passing that the Government cannot fear their resumption for it did not avail itself of the offer of the District Court to retain jurisdiction of the cause in order that if illegal acts should be attempted they could be restrained.

What then can now be urged against the Corporation? Can comparisons in other regards be made with its competitors and by such comparisons guilty or innocent existence be assigned it? It is greater in size and productive power than any of its competitors, equal or nearly equal to them all, but its power over prices was not and is not commensurate with its power to produce.

It is true there is some testimony tending to show that the Corporation had such power, but there was also testimony and a course of action tending strongly to the contrary. The conflict was by the judges of the District Court unanimously resolved against the existence of that power, and in doing so they but gave effect to the greater weight of the evidence. It is certain that no such power was exerted. On the contrary, the only attempt at a fixation of prices was, as already said, through an appeal to and confederation with competitors, and the record shows besides that when competition occurred it was not in pretence, and the Corporation declined in productive powers —the competitors growing either against or in consequence of the competition. If against the competition we have an instance of movement against what the Government insists was an irresistible force; if in consequence of competition, we have an illustration of the adage that "competition is the life of trade" and is not easily repressed. The power of monopoly in the Corporation under either illustration is an untenable accusation.

We may pause here for a moment to notice illustrations of the Government of the purpose of the Corporation, instancing its acquisition after its formation of control over the Shelby Steel Tube Company, the Union Steel Company and, subsequently, the Tennessee Company. There is dispute over the reasons for these acquisitions which we shall not detail. There is, however, an important circumstance in connection with that of the Tennessee Company which is worthy to be noted. It was submitted to President Roosevelt and he gave it his approval. His approval, of course, did not make it legal, but it gives assurance of its legality, and we know from his earnestness in the public welfare he would have approved of nothing that had even a tendency to its detriment. And he testified he was not deceived and that he believed that "the Tennessee Coal and Iron people had a property which was almost worthless in their hands, nearly worthless to them, nearly worthless to the communities in which it was situated, and entirely worthless to any financial institution that had the securities the minute that any panic came, and that the only way to give value to it was to put it in the hands of people whose possession of it would be a guarantee that there was value to it." Such being the emergency it seems like an extreme accusation to say that the Corporation which relieved it, and, perhaps, rescued the company and the communities dependent upon it from disaster, was urged by unworthy motives. Did illegality attach afterwards and how? And what was the Corporation to do with the property? Let it decay in desuetude or develop its capabilities and resources? In the development, of course, there would be profit to the Corporation, but there would be profit as well to the world. For this reason President Roosevelt sanctioned the purchase, and it would seem a distempered view of purchase and result to regard them as violations of law.

From this digression we return to the consideration of the conduct of the Corporation towards its competitors. Besides the circumstances which we have mentioned there are others of probative strength. The company's officers and, as well, its competitors and customers, testified that its competition was genuine, direct and vigorous, and was reflected in prices and production. No practical witness was produced by the Government in opposition. Its contention is based on the size and asserted dominance of the Corporation—alleged power for evil, not the exertion of the power in evil. Or as counsel put it, "a combination may be illegal because of its purpose; it may be illegal because it acquires a dominating power, not as a result of normal growth and development, but as a result of a combination of competitors." Such composition and its resulting power constitute, in the view of the Government, the offence against the law, and yet it is admitted "no competitor came forward and said he had to accept the Steel Corporation's prices." But this absence of complaint counsel urge against the Corporation. Competitors, it is said, followed the Corporation's prices because they made money by the imitation. Indeed the imitation is urged as an evidence of the Corporation's power. "Universal imitation," counsel assert, is "an evidence of power." In this concord of action, the contention is, there is the sinister dominance of the Corporation—"its extensive control of the industry is such that the others [independent companies] follow." Counsel, however, admit that there was "occasionally" some competition, but reject the suggestion that it extended practically to a war between the Corporation and the independents. Counsel say, "They [the Corporation is made a plural] called a few—they called 200 witnesses out of some forty thousand customers, and they expect with that customer evidence to overcome the whole train of price movement shown since the Corporation was formed." And "movement of prices" counsel explained "as shown by the published prices . . . they were the ones that the competitors were maintaining all during the interval."

It would seem that "200 witnesses" would be fairly representative. Besides the balance of the "forty thousand customers" was open to the Government to draw upon. Not having done so, is it not permissible to infer that none would testify to the existence of the influence that the Government asserts? At any rate, not one was called, but instead the opinion of an editor of a trade journal is adduced, and that of an author and teacher of economics whose philosophical deductions had, perhaps, fortifications from experience as Deputy Commissioner of Corporations and as an employee in the Bureau of Corporations. His deduction was that when prices are constant through a definite period an artificial influence is indicated; if they vary during such a period it is a consequence of competitive conditions. It has become an aphorism that there is danger of deception in generalities, and in a case of this importance we should have something surer for judgment than speculation, something more than a deduction equivocal of itself even though the facts it rests on or asserts were not contradicted. If the phenomena of production and prices were as easily resolved as the witness implied, much discussion and much literature have been wasted, and some of the problems that are now distracting the world would be given composing solution. Of course competition affects prices but it is only one among other influences and does not more than they, register itself in definite and legible effect.

We magnify the testimony by its consideration. Against it competitors, dealers and customers of the Corporation testify in multitude that no adventitous interference was employed to either fix or maintain prices and that they were constant or varied according to natural conditions. Can this testimony be minimized or dismissed by inferring that, as intimated, it is an evidence of power not of weakness; and power exerted not only to suppress competition but to compel testimony, is the necessary inference, shading into perjury to deny its exertion? The situation is indeed singular, and we may wonder at it, wonder that the despotism of the Corporation, so baneful to the world in the representation of the Government, did not produce protesting victims.

But there are other paradoxes. The Government does not hesitate to present contradictions, though only one can be true, such being we were told in our school books the "principle of contradiction." In one competitors (the independents) are represented as oppressed by the superior power of the Corporation; in the other they are represented as ascending to opulence by imitating that power's prices which they could not do if at disadvantage from the other conditions of competition; and yet confederated action is not asserted. If it were this suit would take on another cast. The competitors would cease to be the victims of the Corporation and would become its accomplices. And there is no other alternative. The suggestion that lurks in the Government's contention that the acceptance of the Corporation's prices is the submission of impotence to irresistible power is, in view of the testimony of the competitors, untenable. They, as we have seen, deny restraint in any measure or illegal influence of any kind. The Government, therefore, is reduced to the assertion that the size of the Corporation, the power it may have, not the exertion of the power, is an abhorrence to the law, or as the Government says, "the combination embodied in the Corporation unduly restrains competition by its *necessary effect,* [the italics are the emphasis of the Government] and therefore is unlawful regardless of purpose." "A wrongful purpose," the Government adds, is "matter of aggravation." The illegality is statical, purpose or movement of any kind only its emphasis. To assent to that, to what extremes should we be led? Competition consists of business activities and ability—they make its life; but there may be fatalities in it. Are the activities to be encouraged when militant, and suppressed or regulated when triumphant because of the dominance attained? To such paternalism the Government's contention, which regards power rather than its use the determining consideration, seems to conduct. Certainly conducts we may say, for it is the inevitable logic of the Government's contention that competition must not only be free, but that it must not be pressed to the ascendency of a competitor, for in ascendency there is the menace of monopoly.

We have pointed out that there are several of the Government's contentions which are difficult to represent or measure, and, the one we are now considering, that is the power is "unlawful regardless of purpose," is another of them. It seems to us that it has for its ultimate principle and justification that strength in any producer or seller is a menace to the public interest and illegal because there is potency in it for mischief. The regression is extreme, but short of it the Government cannot stop. The fallacy it conveys is manifest.

The Corporation was formed in 1901, no act of aggression upon its competitors is charged against it, it confederated with them at times in offence against the law, but abandoned that before this suit was brought, and since 1911 no act in violation of law can be established against it except its existence be such an act. This is urged, as we have seen, and that the interest of the public is involved, and that such interest is paramount to corporation or competitors. Granted—though it is difficult to see how there can be restraint of trade when there is no restraint of competitors in the trade nor complaints by customers—how can it be worked out of the situation and through what proposition of law? Of course it calls for nothing other than a right application of the law and to repeat what we have said above, shall we declare the law to be that size is an offence even though it minds its own business because what it does is imitated? The Corporation is undoubtedly of impressive size and it takes an effort of resolution not to be affected by it or to exaggerate its influence. But we must adhere to the law and the law does not make mere size an offence or the existence of unexerted power an offence. It, we repeat, requires overt acts and trusts to its prohibition of them and its power to repress or punish them. It does not compel competition nor require all that is possible.

Admitting, however, that there is pertinent strength in the propositions of the Government, and in connection with them, we recall the distinction we made in the *Standard Oil Case* (221 U.S. 1, 77) between acts done in violation of the statute and a condition brought about which "in and of itself, is not only a continued attempt to monopolize, but also a monopolization." In such case, we declared, "the duty to enforce the statute" required "the application of broader and more controlling" remedies than in the other. And the remedies applied conformed to the declaration; there was prohibition of future acts and there was dissolution of "the combination found to exist in violation of the statute" in order to "neutralize the extension and continually operating force which the possession of the power unlawfully obtained" had "brought" and would "continue to bring about."

Are the case and its precepts applicable here? The Steel Corporation by its formation united under one control competing companies and thus, it is urged, a condition was brought about in violation of the statute, and therefore illegal and became a "continually operating force" with the "possession of power unlawfully obtained."

But there are countervailing considerations. We have seen whatever there was of wrong intent could not be executed, whatever there was of evil effect, was discontinued before this suit was brought; and this, we think, determines the decree. We say this in full realization of the requirements of the law. It is clear in its denunciation of monopolies and equally clear in its direction that the courts of the Nation shall prevent and restrain them (its language is "to prevent and restrain violations of" the act), but the command is necessarily submissive to the conditions which may exist and the usual powers of a court of equity to adapt its remedies to those conditions. In other words, it is not expected to enforce abstractions and do injury thereby, it may be, to the purpose of the law. It is this flexibility of discretion—indeed essential function—that makes its value in our jurisprudence—value in this case as in others. We do not mean to say that the law is not its own measure and that it can be disregarded, but only that the appropriate relief in each instance is remitted to a court of equity to determine, not, and let us be explicit in this, to advance a policy contrary to that of the law, but in submission to the law and its policy, and in execution of both. And it is certainly a matter for consideration that there was no legal attack on the Corporation until 1911, ten years after its formation and the commencement of its career. We do not, however, speak of the delay simply as to its time—that there is estoppel in it because of its time—but on account of what was done during that time—the many millions of dollars spent, the development made, and the enterprises undertaken, the investments by the public that have been invited and are not to be ignored. And what of the foreign trade that has been developed and exists? The Government, with some inconsistency, it seems to us, would remove this from the decree of dissolution. Indeed, it is pointed out that under congressional legislation in the Webb Act the foreign trade of the Corporation is reserved to it. And further, it is said, that the Corporation has constructed a company called the Products Company which can be "very easily preserved as a medium through which the steel business might reach the balance of the world," and that in the decree of "dissolution that could be provided." This is supplemented by the suggestion that not only the Steel Corporation, "but other steel makers of the country, could function through an instrumentality created under the Webb Act." [C. 50, § 2, 40 Stat. 516.]

The propositions and suggestions do not commend themselves. We do not see how the Steel Corporation can be such a beneficial instrumentality in the trade of the world and its beneficence be preserved, and yet be such an evil instrumentality in the trade of the United States that it must be destroyed. And by whom and how shall all the adjustments of preservation or destruction be made? How can the Corporation be sustained and its power of control over its subsidiary companies be retained and exercised in the foreign trade and given up in the domestic trade? The Government presents no solution of the problem. Counsel realize the difficulty and seem to think that its solution or its evasion is in the suggestion that the Steel Corporation and "other steel makers could function through an instrumentality created under the Webb Act." But we are confronted with the necessity of immediate judicial action under existing laws, not action under conceptions which may never be capable of legal execution. We must now decide and we see no guide to decision in the propositions of the Government.

The Government, however, tentatively presents a proposition which has some tangibility. It submits that certain of the subsidiary companies are so mechanically equipped and so officially directed as to be released and remitted to independent action and individual interests and the competition to which such interests prompt, without any disturbance to business. The companies are enumerated. They are the Carnegie Steel Company (a combination of the old Carnegie Company, the National Steel Company, and the American Steel Company), the Federal Steel Company, the Tennessee Company and the Union Steel Company (a combination of the Union Steel Company of

Donora, Pa., Sharon Steel Company of Sharon, Pa., and Sharon Tin Plate Company). They are fully integrated, it is said, possess their own supplies, facilities of transportation and distribution. They are subject only to the Steel Corporation is, in effect, the declaration, in nothing but its control of their prices. We may say parenthetically that they are defendants in the suit and charged as offenders, and we have the strange circumstance of violators of the law being urged to be used as expedients of the law.

But let us see what guide to a procedure of dissolution of the Corporation and the dispersion as well of its subsidiary companies, for they are asserted to be illegal combinations, is prayed. And the fact must not be overlooked or underestimated. The prayer of the Government calls for not only a disruption of present conditions but the restoration of the conditions of twenty years ago, if not literally, substantially. Is there guidance to this in the *Standard Oil Case* and the *Tobacco Case* [221 U.S. 1, 106]? As an element in determining the answer we shall have to compare the cases with that at bar, but this can only be done in a general way. And the law necessarily must be kept in mind. No other comment of it is necessary. It has received so much exposition that it and all it prescribes and proscribes should be considered as a consciously directing presence.

The Standard Oil Company had its origin in 1882 and through successive forms of combinations and agencies it progressed in illegal power to the day of the decree, even attempting to circumvent by one of its forms the decision of a court against it. And its methods in using its power was of the kind that Judge Woolley described as "brutal," and of which practices, he said, the Steel Corporation was absolutely guiltless. We have enumerated them and this reference to them is enough. And of the practices this court said no disinterested mind could doubt that the purpose was "to drive others from the field and to exclude them from their right to trade and thus accomplish the mastery which was the end in view." It was further said that what was done and the final culmination "in the plan of the New Jersey corporation" made "manifest the continued existence of the intent . . . and . . . impelled the expansion of the New Jersey corporation." It was to this corporation, which represented the power and purpose of all that preceded, that the suit was addressed and the decree of the court was to apply. What we have quoted contrasts that case with this. The contrast is further emphasized by pointing out how in the case of the New Jersey corporation the original wrong was reflected in and manifested by the acts which followed the organization, as described by the court. It said: "The exercise of the power which resulted from that organization fortifies the foregoing conclusions [as to monopoly, etc.], since the development which came, the acquisition here and there which ensued of every efficient means by which competition could have been asserted, the slow but resistless methods which followed by which means of transportation were absorbed and brought under control, the system of marketing which was adopted by which the country was divided into districts and the trade in each district in oil was turned over to a designated corporation within the combination and all others were excluded, all lead the mind up to a conviction of a purpose and intent which we think is so certain as practically to cause the subject not to be within the domain of reasonable contention."

The *Tobacco Case* has the same bad distinctions as the *Standard Oil Case*. The illegality in which it was formed (there were two American Tobacco Companies, but we use the name as designating the new company as representing the combinations of the suit) continued, indeed progressed in intensity and defiance to the moment of decree. And it is the intimation of the opinion if not its direct assertion that the formation of the company (the word "combination" is used) was preceded by the intimidation of a trade war "inspired by one or more of the minds which brought about and became parties to that combination." In other words the purpose of the combination was signalled to competitors and the choice presented to them was submission or ruin, to become parties to the illegal enterprise or be driven "out of the business." This was the purpose and the achievement, and the processes by which achieved this court enumerated to be the formation of new companies, taking stock in others to obscure the result actually attained, but always to monopolize and retain power in the hands of the few and mastery of the trade; putting control in the hands of seemingly independent corporations as barriers to the entry of others into the trade; the expenditure of millions upon millions in buying out plants not to utilize them but to close them; by constantly recurring stipulations by which numbers of persons, whether manufacturers, stockholders or employees, were required to bind themselves, generally for long periods, not to compete in the future. In the *Tobacco Case,* therefore, as in the *Standard Oil Case,* the court had to deal with a persistent and systematic lawbreaker masquerading under legal forms, and which not only had to be stripped of its disguises but arrested in its illegality. A decree of dissolution was the manifest instrumentality and inevitable. We think it would be a work of sheer supererogation to point out that a decree in that case or in the *Standard Oil Case* furnishes no example for a decree in this.

In conclusion we are unable to see that the public interest will be served by yielding to the contention of the Government respecting the dissolution of the company or the separation from it of some of its subsidiaries; and we do see in a contrary conclusion a risk of injury to the public interest, including a material disturbance of, and, it may be serious detriment to, the foreign trade. And in submission to the policy of the law and its fortifying prohibitions the public interest is of paramount regard.

We think, therefore, that the decree of the District Court should be affirmed.

So ordered.

Oliver Wendell Holmes

☆ 1841–1935 ☆

APPOINTED BY

THEODORE ROOSEVELT

YEARS ON COURT

1902–1932

Oliver Wendell Holmes

by

PAUL A. FREUND

OLIVER WENDELL HOLMES, JR., was born in Boston, March 8, 1841. His lineage was authentically Bostonian. His father was the celebrated physician and man of letters; his mother, Amelia Lee Jackson, was the daughter of a justice of the supreme judicial court of Massachusetts; Olivers and Wendells were to be found in ample number honorably inscribed in the memorial book of King's Chapel Burying Ground. As a boy Holmes attended E. S. Dixwell's private Latin School and then, as a matter of course, Harvard College, from which he was graduated, as class poet, in 1861.

Meanwhile, on the outbreak of the Civil War, Holmes had volunteered, and after graduation was commissioned a second lieutenant in the Twentieth Massachusetts regiment, part of the Army of the Potomac. He served for three years, the term of his enlistment, was wounded three times—at Ball's Bluff, at Antietam, and at Fredericksburg—and was mustered out as a captain in July, 1864. The bare recital of this wartime service hardly suggests its cardinal place in Holmes' spiritual development. Not only did it remain for him a supreme experience of man's capacity for selfless action and quiet heroism amid squalor and boredom and slaughter. More than that, it served to fix and deepen a native skepticism; for he found that among the bravest and noblest of his comrades were men who doubted the cause for which they were risking and giving their lives. Not certitude, he concluded, but courage in the face of the unknown and unknowable, was the mark of human grace. On a deeper level, it has been suggested, the loss of some of his dearest companions in battle was an experience so shattering to the young soldier that he was never emotionally prepared thereafter to make an unreserved commitment of the spirit, but only of the will. However that may be, it is surely true that his skepticism was saved from aridity by a romantic faith in striving, and from hollowness by a strong puritan sense of

PAUL A. FREUND is Carl M. Loeb University Professor at Harvard University. Among his many books are The Supreme Court of the United States *and* On Law and Justice.

obligation. The result was a philosophy strikingly like that of the later existentialists, which can be seen, to take one example, in a response to a tribute from the Boston bar on his fifty-ninth birthday:

> *The rule of joy and the law of duty seem to me all one. I confess that altruistic and cynically selfish talk seem to me about equally unreal. With all humility, I think "Whatsoever thy hand findeth to do, do it with thy might," infinitely more important than the vain attempt to love one's neighbor as one's self. If you want to hit a bird on the wing, you must have all your will in a focus, you must not be thinking about yourself, and, equally, you must not be thinking about your neighbor; you must be living in your eye on that bird. Every achievement is a bird on the wing."*

When Holmes returned from military service he entered Harvard Law School, was graduated in 1866, and was admitted to the bar in 1867. He was an assiduous practitioner, becoming in time a partner in the firm of Shattuck, Holmes, and Munroe. But although the practice of law absorbed his days—he liked to "think under fire"—his philosophical and scholarly appetite demanded other fare as well. He became one of the group known as the "Metaphysical Club," meeting at each other's homes to hear and discuss papers by one of their number. The group was made up of such heterodox minds as Charles S. Peirce, William James, Chauncey Wright, Nicholas St. John Green, and, of course, Holmes himself. Their common bent was to reduce pretentious philosophic ideas to the more manageable "If . . . then" form; indeed the name of the club must have had an ironic turn, save as its members might delight, in Holmes' favorite phrase, to "twist the tail of the cosmos." Whether the relation of the members to Holmes was one of influence or affinity—there must have been a good measure of the latter even to support the former—the skepticism of Holmes toward spacious generalities and specious theorems was reinforced in the circle of these friends, and it is hardly fanciful to suggest that his persistent conception of law, as simply a prediction of what judges will in fact decide in a given set of circumstances, took shape in the essentially logical-positivist atmosphere of the Metaphysical Club. The same can be said of his related repudiation of natural law and his designation of fundamental values as only his "can't helps." In his well-known essay "The Path of the Law," an address prepared for law students in 1897, he advised those who would understand law to wash in cynical acid such morally charged terms as right, duty, and malice, and instead to think of law as a "bad man" would, asking only what would be done to him if he pursued this course or that. "If . . . then" was the clue to understanding, though Holmes did not literally use the formula. At the age of ninety-one he was unrepentant. Writing to his friend Sir Frederick Pollock, he showed that the logical positivist in him might even outlive the puritan: "I am being happily idle, and persuading myself that ninety-one has outlived duty. I can imagine a book on the law, getting rid of all talk of duties and rights—beginning with the definition of law in the lawyer's sense as a statement of the circumstances in which the public force will be brought to bear upon a man through the Courts, and expounding rights as a hypostasis of a prophecy—in short, systematizing some of my old chestnuts. But I don't mean to do it."

During the years of practice Holmes turned from philosophical to historical-legal investigations. From 1870 to 1873 he served as editor of the American Law Review and as editor of the twelfth edition of Kent's *Commentaries on American Law,* undertaking to systematize great areas of doctrine in many fields of law. Then came an invitation to deliver a set of lectures at the Lowell Institute in Boston—an opportunity which set him to work feverishly on the essays that were published in 1881 as *The Common Law.* Believing as he did that to prove oneself a scholar it was necessary to publish a book before the age of forty, he managed to meet his deadline with a few weeks to spare.

The work was quickly recognized on both sides of the Atlantic as a seminal and important study, reflecting exceptional learning in the Germanic and medieval English sources and even more uncommon power and originality in arguing his organizing ideas. Probably the best-known passage in the book is the opening statement: "The life of the law has not been logic; it has been experience. The felt necessities of the time, the prevalent moral and political theories, intuitions of public policy, avowed or unconscious, even the prejudices which judges share with their fellow-men, have had a good deal more to do than the syllogism in determining the rules by which men should be governed. . . . The substance of the law at any given time pretty nearly corresponds, so far as it goes, with what is then understood to be convenient; but its form and machinery, and the degree to which it is able to work out desired results, depend very much upon its past." As Holmes' biographer, the late Mark DeWolfe Howe, has pointed out, this passage seems not so much a forecast of the body of the lectures as a thrust directed against the dominant thinking of Dean Langdell of the Harvard Law School, who, having recently introduced the case method of instruction, was employing it to teach law as a system of logically coherent theorems to be judged in terms of inner consistency and not at all on the score of practical convenience or utility.

The salient contribution of Holmes' book was, as Professor Howe shows, of a different order. Holmes was concerned to repudiate the Kantian and Hegelian metaphysic of law which stressed the primacy of the will and the unfolding of the idea of individual self-assertion, and to substitute a thesis more in harmony with the emerging scientific view of natural phenomena. Holmes argued that external or objective standards, not the subjective criterion of the will, are the measure of legal relations, whether in the formation of contracts, civil liability for injuries, or criminal responsibility. The objective standards are determinable in light of the expectations of the reasonable man, as society frames them in a given time and place. Blameworthiness in law is thus less a matter of inner moral defect than of failure to measure up to the calculus embodied in community standards, whether one is judging the liability of a medieval owner of trespassing cattle or of a railway engineer charged with negligence. It was a turn in basic legal thinking not unlike the movement away from idealism in metaphysics and the categorical imperative in morals toward pragmatism and utilitarianism. Along with this leitmotif Holmes sounded many incidental themes deriving from his searching historical studies: the subordination of Roman law to Germanic institutions as formative sources of English law; the accidental origins of much "form and machinery" in our law; the emancipating effect of historical understanding, leaving us freer than we may have supposed to depart from accepted doctrine which turns out not to be of the essence of a principle but only an anachronism. For Holmes history was a liberating discipline; when you get the dragon of doctrine out of his cave and into the light, he was fond of saying, you can measure its fangs and claws and ordinary mortals are emboldened to tame it or dispatch it.

Whatever Dean Langdell may have thought of the opening propositions in *The Common Law,* the work established Holmes' place in the scholarly world, and President Eliot invited him to become a professor of law at Harvard. A chair was endowed, largely through the good offices of Louis D. Brandeis, fifteen years Holmes' junior, with the understanding that Holmes would be its first occupant, and in the spring of 1882 he accepted the appointment. It was understood expressly that he would be free nevertheless to accept a judicial appointment. The stipulation became pertinent in very short order. After taking up his teaching duties in the fall of 1882, which included classes in jurisprudence, torts, agency, and suretyship, he was tendered an appointment to the Supreme Judicial Court by Governor Long. "It was a stroke of lightning," Holmes said, "which changed the whole course of my life." He accepted at once, perhaps sensing that an academic life would not fully satisfy his need to think under fire. Much later he wrote to Felix Frankfurter, who was himself pondering the move into teaching, "Academic life is but half life—it is withdrawal from the fight in order to utter smart things that cost you nothing except the thinking them from a cloister. My wife thinks I unconsciously began to grow sober with an inarticulate sense of limitation in the few months of my stay at Cambridge."

Holmes had married in 1872. His wife, Fanny Bowdich Dixwell, was the daughter of his old schoolmaster, and a woman of great talent and spirit whom he had courted for a number of years with the envious approbation of William James and other friends. There were no children of the marriage. Their early years together were the period of Holmes' absorption in his editorial tasks and the writing of the Lowell lectures, while carrying on a regular legal practice. They were years of virtual isolation from society, borne with composure while he was proving himself against the deadline of his fortieth year.

For almost twenty years, from January 3, 1883, Holmes served on the Massachusetts Supreme Judicial Court and wrote nearly 1,300 opinions. From August 5, 1899, he occupied the chief justiceship of the court. Some of his opinions there, notably in the field of labor law, were disturbing to the orthodoxy of the profession. In one of the most influential of these opinions, dissenting from a decree that enjoined peaceful picketing, he viewed the organization of labor, which was then only painfully emerging from the legal status of a criminal conspiracy, as a natural counterpoise to the corporate aggregation of capital: "If the policy on which our law is founded is too narrowly expressed in the term free competition, we may substitute free struggle for life. . . . One of the eternal conflicts out of which life is made up is that between the effort of every man to get the most he can for his services, and that of society, disguised under the name of capital, to get his services for the least possible return. Combination on one side is patent and powerful. Combination on the other is the necessary and desirable counterpart, if the battle is to be carried on in a fair and equal way." *Vegelahn* v. *Guntner,* 167 Mass. 92, 108 (1896). He became something of a hero to the political progressives, but this kind of appreciation repelled him: his business as a judge was to maintain neutrality, not to dispense favors, and the one should not be mistaken for the other. He had at least his normal share of human vanity, but undiscriminating praise, like approval from the uninitiate, could be no better than insulting. Later in life he was heard to say of student comment in law reviews, "I don't mind when the lads say I was wrong; it is when they say 'Mr. Justice Holmes was correct' that I find them insufferable."

By appointment of President Theodore Roosevelt, Holmes became an Associate Justice of the Supreme Court on December 8, 1902, and served in that capacity for more than twenty-nine years, during the Chief Justiceships of Fuller, White, Taft, and Hughes. It was a period in American constitutional development when a majority of the Court was disposed to view critically new forms of social legislation, to equate the unfamiliar with the unconstitutional. Against this nay-saying spirit Holmes continually protested, finding strength in his Marshallian conception of a Constitution, his skepticism, and the liberation from parochialism wrought by a grandly synoptic view of legal history. After 1916 he was joined and reinforced by Mr. Justice Brandeis. Although they generally concurred on constitutional issues they characteristically took different routes and employed different styles of argumentation. Holmes was content, in magisterial detachment, to let the popular lawmakers have their way, however misguided he felt were their efforts to regulate the asperities of the competitive system; there was no constitutional prohibition against legislatures making fools of themselves. Brandeis, while subscribing fully to the process of trial and error in the social as well as the physical sciences, was essentially a moralist and teacher, and would strike a didactic note in explaining the social context of challenged legislation, its remedial purposes, and the expert counsel that had entered into its formulation. Where Holmes' opinions, elevated, terse, and aphoristic, pierced the mind, Brandeis', richly textured and weightily structured, were meant to overwhelm. Holmes deplored the use of footnotes in judicial opinions; he had to endure thousands of them at the hand of his ally. When a changed outlook on the Court came to predominate, after Holmes' times, the shift was made easier by the record of his memorable dissents in cases that had struck down regulation of hours of labor, price control, and federal limitations on child labor. *Lochner* v. *New York,* 198 U.S. 45 (1905); *Tyson & Brothers* v. *Banton,* 273 U.S. 418 (1927); *Hammer* v. *Dagenhart,* 247 U.S. 251 (1918).

Legislative restrictions on freedom of speech fared differently in Holmes' philosophy. His skepticism, which led him to look with constitutional tolerance on dubious social and economic measures, impelled him to keep free from restraint the very springs of the experimental process, namely the dissemination of novel, unpopular, and even shocking ideas, under the guarantee of the First Amendment. Even here tolerance and immunity were not unlimited. Utterances that constituted a "clear and present danger" of some evil which the legislature had power to prevent could constitutionally be penalized. This test of proximity and degree was one he took over from the law of crimes, where it did service to differentiate mere preparation to commit an offense from an actual attempt at its commission. Thus in wartime an appeal directed specifically at registrants under the draft to resist military service could be punished, *Schenck* v. *United States,* 249 U.S. 47 (1919); but, in his view, a more diffuse appeal, through leaflets scattered from a loft building in the garment district of New York, fell on the protected side of the constitutional line, *Abrams* v. *United States,* 250 U.S. 616 (1919), dissent. The latter opinion so outraged Dean John H. Wigmore, the great scholar in the law of evidence and the proud holder of a colonelcy in the Judge Advocate General's Division, that he published a slashing critique entitled "Freedom of Speech and Freedom of Thuggery in Wartime." This cut close to the nerve, never far from the surface, of the old soldier. "Doubtless," Holmes said, "Dean Wigmore knows much more about law than I do. But I think I know a little more about war than he does."

Holmes came slowly to embrace the idea that the liberty of speech, press, and assembly guaranteed against congressional abridgment by the First Amendment was encompassed in the more general concept of "liberty" guaranteed in the Fourteenth Amendment against deprivation by the states. Nevertheless Holmes suggested that somewhat more latitude might be open to the states in this regard than to Congress—a position which was later endorsed successively by Justices Jackson and Harlan, but not by a majority of the Court.

The controversies over the scope of the First Amendment in Holmes' day centered mainly on what is traditionally called subversive libel; there the clear and present danger test has its most unforced applicability. How he would have responded to the more varied and subtle issues of a later day cannot be surmised with any assurance—questions of political defamation, street demonstrations, obscenity, political association, and refusal to disclose. A slight hint that he might have supported the authority of government more frequently than would some of his successors may be found in a case where he and Brandeis took opposed positions. In *Meyer* v. *Nebraska,* 262 U.S. 390 (1923), the Court struck down a law that forbade the teaching of modern foreign languages in the elementary grades. While Brandeis concurred, Holmes wrote a dissent suggesting that a public purpose to promote the use of English among the children of immigrants was enough to warrant the restriction on teaching and learning. But any projections of judgment into a period of different problems and a different climate of ideas is bound to be hazardous and unrewarding.

Certain of Holmes' philosophic positions have come under attack in late years. In law a predictive definition suffers with special severity from the limitations that attach to any dogma of radical empiricism. A merely predictive view is not likely to produce overarching concepts, like relativity in physics or privacy in law; it is not of much help to a judge who is himself obliged to shape the law; the "bad man" will miss the mark unless he is able to understand how his behavior will be regarded by a "good man" in the process of developing the law; a reduction of ends to personal "can't helps" is really an invitation to further analysis, to determine whether through comparative investigation and more rigorous criteria of utility and coherence those ends can either be validated more impersonally or else subjected to revision. In fairness, however, it must be said that Holmes was writing in a polemic context; he was concerned to combat the complacent moralism that characterized jurisprudential thought, and his rhetoric was designed to shock.

Other critics have levelled a more bitter charge, that Holmes' glorification of struggle and survival, his definition of truth as the power of the thought to get itself accepted in the competition of the market, belong to the politics of totalitarianism. But such critics are surely lacking in humor no less than in perception, for no one could associate a totalitarian outlook with Holmes' dedication to the preservation of the free market in ideas and the even-handed administration of justice.

Holmes' jaunty, challenging spirit was matched by his physical endowment. Tall, spare, fair-skinned, straight-backed until very old age, his strongly aquiline features were set off by cavalryman's moustachios and crested by an abundance of silvery hair. He cut, as the phrase goes, a very dashing figure.

On January 12, 1932, Holmes resigned from the bench. A visit from Chief Justice Hughes, with the approval of Justice Brandeis and other colleagues, was the occasion for suggesting that the time had come, and Holmes at once wrote out a letter to President Roosevelt. He spent his three remaining years living as before (his wife had died in 1929), the winters in Washington, the summers in Beverly Farms, Massachusetts. He died at his house in Washington on March 6, 1935, two days before his ninety-fourth birthday, and was buried in Arlington National Cemetery. By his will, after some specific bequests, he left the residue of his estate, about a quarter of a million dollars, to the United States of America. A joint committee recommended, and the Congress approved, the utilization of this fund to memorialize him through the preparation of a history of the Supreme Court, the publication of a selection of his opinions, and the support of an annual lectureship.

Others who have served on the Court have been preeminent for sagacity, knowledge of affairs, or prowess in unraveling the complexities of litigation. Holmes' distinction—and it is a supreme one—rests on breadth of intellect, an elegantly sparkling pen (forty specimens are included in the fourteenth edition of Bartlett's *Familiar Quotations*), and insights that have been vindicated by time and absorbed into the living philosophy of the Constitution.

The opinions reproduced here can serve to give only a glimpse of his mind's large range, but they do provide a savor of its quality. The *Abrams* case evoked perhaps his best-known and most deeply felt celebration of freedom for the thought that is despised. Though its grounding in the relativity of truth is offensive to natural-law thinkers, it is in practical consequence not very different from the rationale of toleration held by more orthodox believers, namely that although truth is ultimately sure and impregnable, the historical condition of man confines him to the apprehension of limited, partial, fragmentary aspects of truth, and the corrective process calls for open confrontation, lest the process of revelation through historical time be prematurely closed.

The *Tyson* and *Truax* cases illustrate Holmes' basic outlook on the role of judges toward legislative interventions in the field of commerce and industry. For the *nolumus* of the dominant majority on his Court he would substitute his judicial *nihil obstat.* When asked the first principle of judging, he was likely to say that he tried to remember he was not God.

SELECTED BIBLIOGRAPHY

Among the many writings on Justice Holmes are: Felix Frankfurter, "Oliver Wendell Holmes," in *Dictionary of American Biography,* Supplement One, reprinted in Frankfurter, *Mr. Justice Holmes and the Supreme Court* (2d ed., Cambridge, 1961); Mark DeWolfe Howe, *Justice Oliver Wendell Holmes,* vol. I, *The Shaping Years,* 1841–1870, vol. II, *The Proving Years,* 1870–1882 (Cambridge, 1957–1962); Francis Biddle, *Justice Holmes, Natural Law and the Supreme Court* (New York, 1961); Catherine D. Bowen, *Yankee from Olympus* (Boston, 1944); Felix Frankfurter, ed., *Mr. Justice Holmes* (New York, 1931); Samuel J. Konefsky, *The Legacy of Holmes and Brandeis* (New York, 1956); Max Lerner, *The Mind and Faith of Justice Holmes* (New York, 1948); James Willard Hurst, *Justice Holmes on Legal History* (New York, 1964); E. J. Bander, ed., *Justice Holmes Ex Cathedra: Wisdom and Humor of and about Justice Oliver Wendell Holmes* (Charlottesville, 1966).

The following are collections of the writings of Holmes: *Collected Legal Papers* (New York, 1920); *The Common Law* (Boston, 1881; new ed. by Howe, 1963); the following are also edited by Howe: *The Occasional Speeches of Justice Oliver Wendell Holmes* (Cambridge, 1962); *Holmes-Pollock Letters* (Cambridge, 1941); *Holmes-Laski Letters* (Cambridge, 1953); and *Touched with Fire: Civil War Letters and Diary of Oliver Wendell Holmes, Jr.* (Cambridge, 1946). See also *The Einstein Letters: Correspondence of Mr. Justice Holmes and Lewis Einstein, 1903–1905* (New York, 1964); A. Lief, ed., *Representative Opinions of Mr. Justice Holmes* (New York, 1931); H. C. Shriver, ed., *The Judicial Opinions of Oliver Weldell Holmes* [in the Supreme Judicial Court of Massachusetts] (Buffalo, 1940).

Oliver Wendell Holmes

REPRESENTATIVE OPINIONS

ABRAMS v. UNITED STATES, 250 U.S. 616 (1919)

This case was an outgrowth of the ill-starred American military intervention in Russia (with whom we were not at war) in 1918, ordered by President Wilson, an act so at odds with Wilson's normal character and judgment that, as Justice Brandeis later suggested, it may have marked the onset of the President's final cerebral illness. Abrams and four others were convicted, and he was sentenced to twenty years' imprisonment for preparing and disseminating leaflets urging munitions workers not to produce weapons that could be used against their brothers in Russia no less than against the German enemy. The defendants were Russian-born aliens, workers in the garment industry in New York. Their trial was presided over by Federal Judge Clayton of Alabama, sitting by designation during the summer in the Southern District of New York. He excluded as irrelevant testimony offered on behalf of the defendants by expert witnesses that our intervention actually weakened our war effort against the Central Powers. The pertinence of this from the defendants' standpoint rested on the charge against them; the statute, enacted in 1918, punished conspiracies to advocate curtailment of production of things necessary for the prosecution of the war, "with intent . . . to cripple or hinder the United States in the prosecution of the war."

The Supreme Court upheld the convictions on direct appeal from the district court, in an opinion by Justice Clarke, with a dissenting opinion by Justice Holmes, in which Justice Brandeis joined. The Court had no power to modify the sentences as such; review was limited to the validity of the convictions. Holmes attacked the convictions both on statutory grounds—that the evidence did not make out the requisite specific intent—and on the basis of the guarantee of freedom of speech in the First Amendment.

Two years after the Supreme Court decision, in November, 1921, President Harding ordered the defendants released on condition that they return to Russia at their own expense. The case is discussed at length, with excerpts from the trial record, in Zechariah Chafee, *Free Speech in the United States,* c. III (Cambridge, 1941).

MR. JUSTICE HOLMES dissenting.

This indictment is founded wholly upon the publication of two leaflets which I shall describe in a moment. The first count charges a conspiracy pending the war with Germany to publish abusive language about the form of government of the United States, laying the preparation and publishing of the first leaflet as overt acts. The second count charges a conspiracy pending the war to publish language intended to bring the form of government into contempt, laying the preparation and publishing of the two leaflets as overt acts. The third count alleges a conspiracy to encourage resistance to the United States in the same war and to attempt to effectuate the purpose by publishing the same leaflets. The fourth count lays a conspiracy to incite curtailment of production of things necessary to the prosecution of the war and to attempt to accomplish it by publishing the second leaflet to which I have referred.

The first of these leaflets says that the President's cowardly silence about the intervention in Russia reveals the hypocrisy of the plutocratic gang in Washington. It intimates that "German militarism combined with allied capitalism to crush the Russian revolution"—goes on that the tyrants of the world fight each other until they see a common enemy—working class enlightenment, when they combine to crush it; and that now militarism and capitalism combined, though not openly, to crush the Russian revolution. It says that there is only one enemy of the workers of the world and that is capitalism; that it is a crime for workers of America, &c., to fight the workers' republic of Russia, and ends "Awake! Awake, you Workers of the World! Revolutionists." A note adds "It is absurd to call us pro-German. We hate and despise German militarism more than do you hypocritical tyrants. We have more reasons for denouncing German militarism than has the coward of the White House."

The other leaflet, headed "Workers—Wake Up," with abusive language says that America together with the Allies will march for Russia to help the Czecko-Slovaks in their struggle against the Bolsheviki, and that this time the hypocrites shall not fool the Russian emigrants and friends of Russia in America. It tells the Russian emigrants that they now must spit in the face of the false military propaganda by which their sympathy and help to the prosecution of the war have been called forth and says that with the money they have lent or are going to lend "they will make bullets not only for the Germans but also for the Workers Soviets of Russia," and further, "Workers in the ammunition factories, you are producing bullets, bayonets, cannon, to murder not only the Germans, but also your dearest, best, who are in Russia and are fighting for freedom." It then appeals to the same Russian emigrants at some length not to consent to the "inquisitionary expedition to Russia," and says that the destruction of the Russian revolution is "the politics of the march to Russia." The leaflet winds up by saying "Workers, our reply to this barbaric intervention has to be a general strike!," and after a few words on the spirit of revolution, exhortations not to be afraid, and some usual tall talk ends "Woe unto those who will be in the way of progress. Let solidarity live! The Rebels."

No argument seems to me necessary to show that these pronunciamentos in no way attack the form of government of the United States, or that they do not support either of the first two counts. What little I have to say about the third count may be postponed until I have considered the fourth. With regard to that it seems too plain to be denied that the suggestion to workers in the ammunition factories that they are producing bullets to murder their dearest, and the further advocacy of a general strike, both in the second leaflet, do urge curtailment of production of things necessary to the prosecution of the war within the meaning of the Act of May 16, 1918, c. 75, 40 Stat. 553, amending § 3 of the earlier Act of 1917. But to make the conduct criminal that statute requires that it should be "with intent by such curtailment to cripple or hinder the United States in the prosecution of the war." It seems to me that no such intent is proved.

I am aware of course that the word intent as vaguely used in ordinary legal discussion means no more than knowledge at the time of the act that the consequences said to be intended will ensue. Even less than that will satisfy the general principle of civil and criminal liability. A man may have to pay damages, may be sent to prison, at common law might be hanged, if at the time of his act he knew facts from which common experience showed that the consequences would follow, whether he individually could foresee them or not. But, when words are used exactly, a deed is not done with intent to produce a consequence unless that consequence is the aim of the deed. It may be obvious, and obvious to the actor, that the consequence will follow, and he may be liable for it even if he regrets it, but he does not do the act with intent to produce it unless the aim to produce it is the proximate motive of the specific act, although there may be some deeper motive behind.

It seems to me that this statute must be taken to use its words in a strict and accurate sense. They would be absurd in any other. A patriot might think that we were wasting money on aeroplanes, or making more cannon of a certain kind than we needed, and might advocate curtailment with success, yet even if it turned out that the curtailment hindered and was thought by other minds to have been obviously likely to hinder the United States in the prosecution of the war, no one would hold such conduct a crime. I admit that my illustration does not answer all that might be said but it is enough to show what I think and to let me pass to a more important aspect of the case. I refer to the First Amendment to the Constitution that Congress shall make no law abridging the freedom of speech.

I never have seen any reason to doubt that the questions of law that alone were before this Court in the cases of *Schenck, Frohwerk* and *Debs,* 249 U.S. 47, 204, 211, were rightly decided. I do not doubt for a moment that by the same reasoning that would justify punishing persuasion to murder, the United States constitutionally may punish speech that produces or is intended to produce a clear and imminent danger that it will bring about forthwith certain substantive evils that the United States constitutionally may seek to prevent. The power undoubtedly is greater in time of war than in time of peace because war opens dangers that do not exist at other times.

But as against dangers peculiar to war, as against others, the principle of the right to free speech is always the same. It is only the present danger of immediate evil or an intent to bring it about that warrants Congress in setting a limit to the expression of opinion where private rights are not concerned. Congress certainly cannot forbid all effort to change the mind of the country. Now nobody can suppose that the surreptitious publishing of a silly leaflet by an unknown man, without more, would present any immediate danger that its opinions would hinder the success of the government arms or have any appreciable tendency to do so. Publishing those opinions for the very purpose of obstructing however, might indicate a greater danger and at any rate would have the quality of an attempt. So I assume that the second leaflet if published for the purposes alleged in the fourth count might be punishable. But it seems pretty clear to me that nothing less than that would bring these papers within the scope of this law. An actual intent in the sense that I have explained is necessary to constitute an attempt, where a further act of the same individual is required to complete the substantive crime, for reasons given in *Swift & Co.* v. *United States,* 196 U.S. 375, 396. It is necessary where the success of the attempt depends upon others because if that intent is not present the actor's aim may be accomplished without bringing about the evils sought to be checked. An intent to prevent interference with the revolution in Russia might have been satisfied without any hindrance to carrying on the war in which we were engaged.

I do not see how anyone can find the intent required by the statute in any of the defendants' words. The second leaflet is the only one that affords even a foundation for the charge, and there, without invoking the hatred of German militarism expressed in the former one, it is evident from the beginning to the end that the only object of the paper is to help Russia and stop American intervention there against the popular government—not to impede the United States in the war that it was carrying on. To say that two phrases taken literally might import a suggestion of conduct that would have interference with the war as an indirect and probably undesired effect seems to me by no means enough to show an attempt to produce that effect.

I return for a moment to the third

count. That charges an intent to provoke resistance to the United States in its war with Germany. Taking the clause in the statute that deals with that in connection with the other elaborate provisions of the act, I think that resistance to the United States means some forcible act of opposition to some proceeding of the United States in pursuance of the war. I think the intent must be the specific intent that I have described and for the reasons that I have given I think that no such intent was proved or existed in fact. I also think that there is no hint at resistance to the United States as I construe the phrase.

In this case sentences of twenty years imprisonment have been imposed for the publishing of two leaflets that I believe the defendants had as much right to publish as the Government has to publish the Constitution of the United States now vainly invoked by them. Even if I am technically wrong and enough can be squeezed from these poor and puny anonymities to turn the color of legal litmus paper; I will add, even if what I think the necessary intent were shown; the most nominal punishment seems to me all that possibly could be inflicted, unless the defendants are to be made to suffer not for what the indictment alleges but for the creed that they avow—a creed that I believe to be the creed of ignorance and immaturity when honestly held, as I see no reason to doubt that it was held here, but which, although made the subject of examination at the trial, no one has a right even to consider in dealing with the charges before the Court.

Persecution for the expression of opinions seems to me perfectly logical. If you have no doubt of your premises or your power and want a certain result with all your heart you naturally express your wishes in law and sweep away all opposition. To allow opposition by speech seems to indicate that you think the speech impotent, as when a man says that he has squared the circle, or that you do not care whole-heartedly for the result, or that you doubt either your power or your premises. But when men have realized that time has upset many fighting faiths, they may come to believe even more than they believe the very foundations of their own conduct that the ultimate good desired is better reached by free trade in ideas—that the best test of truth is the power of the thought to get itself accepted in the competition of the market, and that truth is the only ground upon which their wishes safely can be carried out. That at any rate is the theory of our Constitution. It is an experiment, as all life is an experiment. Every year if not every day we have to wager our salvation upon some prophecy based upon imperfect knowledge. While that experiment is part of our system I think that we should be eternally vigilant against attempts to check the expression of opinions that we loathe and believe to be fraught with death, unless they so imminently threaten immediate interference with the lawful and pressing purposes of the law that an immediate check is required to save the country. I wholly disagree with the argument of the Government that the First Amendment left the common law as to seditious libel in force. History seems to me against the notion. I had conceived that the United States through many years had shown its repentance for the Sedition Act of 1798, by repaying fines that it imposed. Only the emergency that makes it immediately dangerous to leave the correction of evil counsels to time warrants making any exception to the sweeping command, "Congress shall make no law . . . abridging the freedom of speech." Of course I am speaking only of expressions of opinion and exhortations, which were all that were uttered here, but I regret that I cannot put into more impressive words my belief that in their conviction upon this indictment the defendants were deprived of their rights under the Constitution of the United States.

TRUAX v. CORRIGAN, 257 U.S. 312 (1921)

The appellants, owners of a restaurant in Bisbee, Arizona, sued to enjoin their striking employees from continuing to picket and promote a boycott of the business. The defense was based on a statute of Arizona which forbade the courts of the state to issue injunctions in labor disputes, except where necessary to prevent irreparable injury to property or property rights and there was no adequate remedy at law. The trial court upheld this statutory defense and dismissed the suit; the supreme court of Arizona affirmed. On appeal to the United States Supreme Court, the case was argued in April, 1920; more than a year later, in June, 1921, after the death of Chief Justice White, it was set down for reargument; it was reargued in October, 1921, and decided December 19, 1921, in an opinion by White's successor, Chief Justice Taft. The Court reversed the decree below, holding that the Arizona law was an invalid deprivation of property without due process of law and a denial of equal protection of the laws in selecting labor disputes for immunity from the process of injunction. Justices Holmes, Brandeis, Pitney, and Clarke dissented. The dissent of Brandeis was one of his most massive opinions, occupying twenty-three pages, documented with fifty-one footnotes, tracing the development of labor law in England, the British Dominions, and the United States, and setting forth the serious dissatisfactions attending the injunctive process and the numerous limitations on its use in other fields as well as in labor controversies. Justice Holmes chose a more magisterial and summary tone, deprecating the shackles placed upon the legislatures in the name of the Constitution but his opinion derived in fact from parochial views of property and governmental authority held by judges.

The decision was invoked by opponents of the federal anti-labor injunction law of 1932, the Norris–La Guardia Act, but as it turned out, the dissenting opinions foreshadowed a more hospitable constitutional outlook toward legislative intervention of this kind.

MR. JUSTICE HOLMES, dissenting.

The dangers of a delusive exactness in the application of the Fourteenth Amendment have been adverted to before now. *Louisville & Nashville R. R. Co.* v. *Barber Asphalt Paving Co.,* 197 U.S. 430, 434. Delusive exactness is a source of fallacy throughout the law. By calling a business "property" you make it seem like land, and lead up to the conclusion that a statute cannot substantially cut down the advantages of ownership existing before the statute was passed. An established business no doubt may have pecuniary value and commonly is protected by law against various unjustified injuries. But you cannot give it definiteness of contour by calling it a thing. It is a course of conduct and like other conduct is subject to substantial modification according to time and circumstances both in itself and in regard to what shall justify doing it a harm. I cannot understand the notion that it would be unconstitutional to authorize boycotts and the like in aid of the employees' or the employers' interest by statute when the same result has been reached constitutionally without statute by Courts with whom I agree. See *The Hamilton,* 207 U.S. 398, 404. In this case it does not even appear that the business was not created under the laws as they now are. *Denny* v. *Bennett,* 128 U.S. 489.

I think further that the selection of the class of employers and employees for special treatment, dealing with both sides alike, is beyond criticism on principles often asserted by this Court. And especially I think that without legalizing the conduct complained of the extraordinary relief by injunction may be denied to the class. Legislation may begin where an evil begins. If, as many intelligent people believe, there is more danger that the injunction will be abused in labor cases than elsewhere I can feel no doubt of the power of the legislature to deny it in such cases. I refer to two decisions in which I have stated what I understand to be the law sanctioned by many other decisions. *Carroll* v. *Greenwich Insurance Co.,* 199 U.S. 401, 411. *Quong Wing* v. *Kirkendall,* 223 U.S. 59.

In a matter like this I dislike to turn attention to anything but the fundamental question of the merits, but *Connolly* v.

Union Sewer Pipe Co., 184 U.S. 540, raises at least a doubt in my mind of another sort. The exception and the rule as to granting injunctions are both part of the same code, enacted at the same time. If the exception fails, according to the *Connolly Case* the statute is bad as a whole. It is true that here the exception came in later than the rule, but after they had been amalgamated in a single act I cannot know that the later legislature would have kept the rule if the exception could not be allowed. If labor had the ascendancy that the exception seems to indicate, I think that probably it would have declined to allow injunctions in any case if that was the only way of reaching its end. But this is a matter upon which the State Court has the last word, and if it takes this view its decision must prevail. I need not press further the difficulty of requiring a State Court to issue an injunction that it never has been empowered to issue by the quasi-sovereign that created the Court.

I must add one general consideration. There is nothing that I more deprecate than the use of the Fourteenth Amendment beyond the absolute compulsion of its words to prevent the making of social experiments that an important part of the community desires, in the insulated chambers afforded by the several States, even though the experiments may seem futile or even noxious to me and to those whose judgment I most respect. I agree with the more elaborate expositions of my brothers Pitney and Brandeis and in their conclusion that the judgment should be affirmed.

TYSON & BROTHER v. BANTON, 273 U.S. 418 (1927)

The New York legislature in 1922 enacted a law regulating the maximum prices at which brokers could sell theatre tickets; the charge was not to exceed fifty cents plus the regular price printed on the ticket. Appellants, who were ticket brokers, sued in the Southern District of New York to enjoin the enforcement of the law against them, on the ground that it constituted a deprivation of property without due process of law, in violation of the Fourteenth Amendment. A three-judge court ruled against the brokers, and an appeal to the Supreme Court followed. That Court reversed, in an opinion by Justice Sutherland, with Justices Holmes, Brandeis, Stone, and Sanford dissenting. The majority declared that control over prices was a valid legislative measure only when the business was one "affected with a public interest," like common carriers, banks, and insurance companies, and that theatres were not within that category. Justice Stone's dissent undertook to show the abuses that marked the ticket-broker business, leading to excessive charges akin to those associated with monopolies, against which our laws had traditionally operated. Justice Holmes' dissent took broader philosophical ground, puncturing the judicial clichés that had set constitutional barriers to the public control of business profits.

The decision in this case was discredited, and the view of Justice Holmes adopted, in *Olsen* v. *Nebraska,* 313 U.S. 236 (1941), which sustained a law limiting the fees charged by employment agencies.

MR. JUSTICE HOLMES, dissenting.

We fear to grant power and are unwilling to recognize it when it exists. The States very generally have stripped jury trials of one of their most important characteristics by forbidding the judges to advise the jury upon the facts (*Graham* v. *United States,* 231 U.S. 474, 480), and when legislatures are held to be authorized to do anything considerably affecting public welfare it is covered by apologetic phrases like the police power, or the statement that the business concerned has been dedicated to a public use. The former expression is convenient, to be sure, to conciliate the mind to something that needs explanation: the fact that the constitutional requirement of compensation when property is taken cannot be pressed to its grammatical extreme; that property rights may be taken for public purposes without pay if you do not take too much; that some play must be allowed to the joints if the machine is to work. But police power often is used in a wide sense to cover and, as I said, to apologize for the general power of the legislature to make a part of the community uncomfortable by a change.

I do not believe in such apologies. I think the proper course is to recognize that a state legislature can do whatever it sees fit to do unless it is restrained by some express prohibition in the Constitution of the United States or of the State, and that Courts should be careful not to extend such prohibitions beyond their obvious meaning by reading into them conceptions of public policy that the particular Court may happen to entertain. Coming down to the case before us I think, as I intimated in *Adkins* v. *Children's Hospital,* 261 U.S. 525, 569, that the notion that a business is clothed with a public interest and has been devoted to the public use is little more than a fiction intended to beautify what is disagreeable to the sufferers. The truth seems to me to be that, subject to compensation when compensation is due, the legislature may forbid or restrict any business when it has a sufficient force of public opinion behind it. Lotteries were thought useful adjuncts of the State a century or so ago; now they are believed to be immoral and they have been stopped. Wine has been thought good for man from the time of the Apostles until recent years. But when public opinion changed it did not need the Eighteenth Amendment, notwithstanding the Fourteenth, to enable a State to say that the business should end. *Mugler* v. *Kansas,* 123 U.S. 623. What has happened to lotteries and wine might happen to theatres in some moral storm of the future, not because theatres were devoted to a public use, but because people had come to think that way.

But if we are to yield to fashionable conventions, it seems to me that theatres are as much devoted to public use as anything well can be. We have not that respect for art that is one of the glories of France. But to many people the superfluous is the necessary, and it seems to me that Government does not go beyond its sphere in attempting to make life livable for them. I am far from saying that I think this particular law a wise and rational provision. That is not my affair. But if the people of the State of New York speaking by their authorized voice say that they want it, I see nothing in the Constitution of the United States to prevent their having their will.

William R. Day

☆ 1849–1923 ☆

APPOINTED BY

THEODORE ROOSEVELT

YEARS ON COURT

1903–1922

William R. Day

by

JAMES F. WATTS, JR.

ANY BRIEF STUDY of the public life of William R. Day reveals a great deal about the nature of the society in which his days were spent. As a young man Day unobtrusively participated in the wide-open scramble of post–Civil War Ohio Republican politics from which his close friend William McKinley emerged so well. Later on, Day, as a small-town corporation lawyer, achieved wealth, status and security as a result of the unprecedented effect of new economic forces on Main Street. During the war with Spain, William R. Day was the parochial country lawyer who unexpectedly became Secretary of State just as the United States emerged as a great power. Still later, as a Supreme Court Justice, Day's instinctive nineteenth century *laissez faire* liberalism clashed head-on with the collective response forced by an industrial revolution that transformed most of the solutions of the past into empty shibboleths. Throughout his life Day brought with him the values most celebrated in the American Dream: deep ancestral roots, the Puritan value system, small-town respectability, the common touch, and the ability to perform adequately any task set before him. This self-effacing little man from Ohio fit the pattern perfectly, and while he obviously enjoyed the warmth of celebrity once he had experienced it, William Rufus Day spent little time in promoting himself. Like so many things in American life, his success was unplanned.

Justice Day was born on April 17, 1849, the direct descendant of prominent jurists. His mother, Emily Spaulding Day, never knew her grandfather, Chief Justice Zephania Swift of Connecticut, because one of his law clerks, Rufus Spaulding, had married the Justice's daughter and taken her away from New England to settle in the Western Reserve lands of Ohio which Connecticut had "reserved" for her own settlers when she abandoned her western land claims in 1786. Rufus Spaulding himself eventually became an Ohio Supreme Court

JAMES F. WATTS, JR. is Assistant Professor of History at City College of New York and author of a forthcoming biography of Breckinridge Long.

Justice and watched another young law clerk marry his own daughter. This young man, Luther Day, had also come to the Western Reserve from New England, and his marriage to Emily Spaulding produced a son, William Rufus Day, in 1849.

By mid-century Luther and Emily Day were comfortably settled about thirty miles southeast of Cleveland in the small town of Ravenna, seat of Portage County. William Day's first sixteen years were spent in the tranquil and easy-paced country surroundings of Ravenna, with its four whitewashed Protestant churches, varied stores and shops that hummed with comfortable excitement on Saturday nights, a school, two newspapers, and over a thousand inhabitants, most of whom could trace their roots to very similar towns in New England. Only the coming of the Civil War disrupted Ravenna's predictable rhythm. Free-soil sentiment ran deep, and nowhere more so than in young Day's own family. Both his father and his grandfather Rufus had sworn allegiance to the Democratic party almost since its inception, but in the disruptive days of the 1850's Luther Day and Rufus Spaulding broke away, repelled by Democratic equivocation on the slavery issue generally, and by the passage of the Fugitive Slave Act of 1850 in particular. The elder Day and his father-in-law found their political alternative in the anti-slavery Republican party, which elected Spaulding to Congress in 1862 and propelled Luther Day up the judicial ladder until he became Chief Justice of the Ohio Supreme Court in 1874. As young William Day absorbed the values of small town America he simultaneously adopted the political habits which guided his lifelong Republicanism.

The young man's formal education was typically abrupt in the traditional American desire to get on with life. At the age of sixteen he graduated from the local school and in September of 1866 left home, travelling to Ann Arbor to join the Class of 1870 at the University of Michigan. After four rather uneventful years, Day brought his bachelor's degree back with him to Ravenna, where he spent the next year reading in a local judge's law office. In 1871 he again returned to Ann Arbor, this time spending a year in the Michigan Law School. In the spring of 1872 the young man decided that the time had come to strike out on his own. Rather than returning to the protective confines of Ravenna, Day settled twenty-five miles farther south in the city of Canton. This random decision determined much of the nature of William Day's future life.

Day spent twenty-five years in Canton as a trial lawyer and partner in the city's leading law firm, Lynch and Day. These formative years also included his marriage, a rapid rise to prominence in Stark County legal and political affairs, the melding into the power structure of the city and, perhaps most importantly in the light of later events, the development of a particularly intimate friendship with another young Canton lawyer, William McKinley.

Soon after arriving in Canton in the spring of 1872 Day was admitted to the Ohio Bar and immediately entered into a law partnership with a slightly older man named William S. Lynch. Lynch had been born and raised in Canton and could provide the kind of local contacts that allowed the firm of Lynch and

Day to prosper. While Day concentrated on criminal law and built for himself something of a local reputation as a shrewd trial lawyer, Lynch turned his considerable talents to the more lucrative practice of corporate law. By the end of the Seventies, Lynch sat on several corporate boards, and Lynch and Day represented the considerable local interests of literally dozens of large and small corporations, including banks, railroads, utility companies and mines.

William Lynch also provided his younger partner with *entré* into Canton social and political circles. Before Day's arrival Lynch had been associated with a prominent Canton lawyer and businessman named Louis Schaefer, whose daughter Day met soon after settling in town. Three summers later, in August of 1875, Mary Elizabeth Schaefer began her thirty-seven year marriage to William Day.

In addition to serving as an inadvertent cupid, William Lynch's other activities bore directly on his partner's future. In the two consecutive elections of 1869 and 1871 Lynch had run unsuccessfully for prosecuting attorney of Stark County. Both times he was defeated by another Canton attorney, former Civil War hero Major William McKinley, Jr. In the intimate and self-contained world of small town politics, Day was naturally thrown into contact with his partner's political rival. Day and McKinley had both married daughters of old Canton families and out of their common interests in the law and politics and through the friendship of their wives, the two men soon became the closest of friends. Long after McKinley's steadily rising political career took him away from the politics of Canton and Stark County, he continued to rely on his friend Day for various kinds of assistance and advice.

Throughout the future President's progression from his first election to Congress in 1877 to the governor's chair in Columbus fifteen years later and on to the White House in 1896, Day remained a contented spectator, absolutely satisfied with the predictable but fulfilling life of a small-town lawyer and man of affairs. His wife bore four sons, thereby creating a mellow family atmosphere as well as reason for keeping busy in courtrooms and corporation offices. Day settled easily into the daily routines of small town life, providing for his growing family, actively participating in local political and social affairs, still occasionally taking the field in a polite game of baseball, a sport he enjoyed throughout his long life wherever he was. He escorted his wife and their brood to the Methodist Church, and sometimes played a random round of golf. Most townsmen recognized him as the son of the Chief Justice of the Ohio Supreme Court, and many predicted that he had a significant career of his own to make.

Yet Willian Day's ambitions operated within modest limits. The Seventies gave way to the Eighties and Day passed through his thirties, absolutely content with the life that revolved around a fairly prosperous law practice, a growing family, a close friendship with Congressman McKinley and a comfortable status position within Canton's middle-class establishment. In the quarter of a century that separated the foundation of Lynch and Day from 1896, when President McKinley summoned William Day to Washington, Day managed to preserve his basic pattern of life with only two minor interruptions. In 1886 both political parties drafted him for the position of judge of the Court of Common Pleas. Although he was flattered by this recognition of his political and legal status, Day nevertheless remained reluctant to interrupt a well-established pattern of existence; he served as Common Pleas judge for less than six months before resigning on the grounds that the position did not pay enough for him to meet his family responsibilities. Three years later, when President Benjamin Harrison nominated him for a United States District Court judgeship, Day accepted once more, yet even after the Senate had confirmed the appointment, he failed to fill the position. This time he suffered some form of physical breakdown, and resigned from the court without ever having joined it. About the only significant effect of these two temporary interruptions in the Canton lawyer's Main Street involvement was the permanent addition of the title of "Judge" to his name, an identifying mark which he bore for the remainder of his life.

Judge Day's lifelong concern with his health was natural considering his sparse physical proportions, for he was a wisp of a man who stood perhaps five and one-half feet tall and whose weight surely never approached 150 pounds. Even in his mid-thirties he kept close watch over what he considered to be his frail disposition, frequently taking vacations to revitalize a sagging constitution. Ironically, the older he became the heavier were his responsibilities. Not until he had almost reached fifty did he begin the very demanding federal service which was to continue unabated for over twenty-five additional years.

During this period Day became even more involved in the political and personal fortunes of William McKinley. While he never pushed himself to the center of the major's often disputatious political circle, Day always remained just outside, available whenever any of McKinley's various problems transcended the ken of the ambitious Ohio politicos. Perhaps the most vexatious affair in McKinley's career occurred shortly after his 1892 inauguration as Ohio's Chief Executive when a personal friend for whom the trusting major had endorsed a large pile of bank notes suddenly went into bankruptcy. Overnight the governor, whose immediate family assets were substantially less than $100,000, found himself stuck with a debt of over $130,000. Judge Day's aid was immediately enlisted. Joining with influential Republicans Myron T. Herrick, a Cleveland banker, and newspaper man H. H. Kohlstaat, an intimate of Cleveland industrialist Mark Hanna, Day moved quietly but swiftly in making the contacts that resulted in raising the sum of the governor's indebtedness, thus saving him from financial and personal embarrassment.

Once he had survived this threat to his political future, McKinley rapidly swept on to his party's leadership and to violent rhetorical combat with the Populist–Democrat legions of William Jennings Bryan. In the presidential race of 1896 the Ohio governor surrounded himself with a familiar circle of home-grown advisors, men like the redoubtable Marcus Alonzo Hanna, Congressman Bellamy Storer, senatorial candidate Joseph Foraker, the Cincinnati boss, and, naturally, Judge William Rufus Day. The taciturn Canton lawyer remained as close as was necessary to his now illustrious fellow townsman throughout an especially exciting campaign which miraculously transformed the prosaic Ohio town into the political hub of the nation. Every day packed trains disgorged excited visitors into the flag-bedecked streets that led to the comfortable Victorian home on East Market Street where McKinley and assorted associates went forth to greet the exuberant delegations. For his part, Judge Day instinctively recoiled from the incessant hoopla and, while he made himself available to suit the candidate's needs, felt far more comfortable sitting in the quiet of his own front porch a few blocks away.

Internecine political warfare broke out immediately after McKinley's sweeping victory over Bryan brought Ohio Republicans near to the enticing places of power left unvisited since the days of Hayes and Garfield. Quarrels erupted on all sides of the amiable President-elect. Foraker of Cincinnati, who was swept into the Senate on McKinley's coattails, stoutly resisted the vigorous efforts of Clevelander Hanna to join him in the Millionaire's Club as Ohio's other Senator. McKinley held firm for Hanna, although the new President did capitulate elsewhere when Foraker opposed the appointment of McKinley's friend Bellamy Storer as First Assistant Secretary of State and the President instead dispatched the disappointed Storer as Minister to Belgium. Hanna could not be as cavalierly dismissed, for the Cleveland industrial baron had not only contributed heavy financial support to the campaign but he and McKinley had also developed an exceptionally intense personal friendship. Since Hanna's only desire was the United States Senate, McKinley acquiesced in sponsoring an odious political shuffle in which John Sherman, the once distinguished but now enfeebled senior senator resigned his seat to accept the portfolio of the State Department. After months of wrangling, the blatant deal materialized, with the Ohio legislature appointing Hanna to join his enemy Foraker in the Senate, and with the politically scarred McKinley stuck with an assertive but totally incompetant Secretary of State.

As these and other political battles raged through the winter months of 1896 and into the spring of 1897, Judge Day quietly awaited the pleasure of the President-elect. Although rumors frequently placed the Canton lawyer in such congenial posts as Attorney General or Solicitor General, McKinley apparently decided to withhold the decision on placing his old and trusted friend until he discovered just where Day was most needed.

In the interim, McKinley decided in February of 1897 to send Day on a fact-finding tour of Cuba in an attempt to discover the extent of chaos on that unfortunate island in anticipation, perhaps, of later Executive action. Before the Judge could leave, however, political wrangling back in Ohio forced cancellation of the trip.

Perhaps McKinley's most pressing problem involved the filling of high posts in the State Department. Secretary Sherman's manifest incompetence persuaded McKinley—as noted above—to try to name as First Assistant Secretary of State his friend Bellamy Storer. But Senator Foraker had immediately vetoed Storer's appointment, for reasons entirely involved with Ohio Republican politics, and Storer went to Belgium instead. The only positive factor in Foraker's nasty vendetta was the final resolution of Judge Day's place in the administration.

On April 23, 1897, the White House announced the appointment of William R. Day as First Assistant Secretary of State. Critics immediately expressed surprise over the appointment to such a sensitive post of a man who possessed absolutely no diplomatic training, but they failed to appreciate that the President desperately needed at the State Department a man upon whose judgment he could totally rely. Secretary of State Sherman's incompetence dictated the appointment of his First Assistant Secretary of State.

As Day quietly moved into the incredibly ornate Army-Navy-State Building next to the White House, he entered into an anomalous institutional situation as well. Secretary Sherman's powers had declined to the extent that his mind could no longer disentangle even its antithetical impulses. At one point in 1898 Sherman simultaneously favored intervention in Cuba and the avoidance of war, anti-imperialism and protection of commercial advantages, and a limited naval power with broader functions for the Navy. Most of the diplomatic corps realized the nature of the unfortunate situation and merely treated the old man courteously while conducting their business as best they could with his First Assistant Secretary, whose normal reticence had deepened even further in this rather uncomfortable situation. Day did benefit from the President's full support and confidence, naturally, as well as from the assistance of the able Second Assistant Secretary, Alvee A. Adee, an utterly indispensable career official who spent more than forty years mastering the nuances and minutiae of diplomatic detail. Since Adee was stone deaf, the observation of one diplomat about McKinley's State Department soon reverberated along Embassy Row: "The head of the Department knows nothing; the First Assistant says nothing; the Second Assistant hears nothing." (Margaret Leech, *In the Days of McKinley* [New York, 1959], 152–153.)

The many limitations of his position seemed to affect Judge Day not at all. Because of his unselfish devotion to McKinley and to the nation's service, Day had accepted without complaint when the President called upon him to leave the contentment of Canton and the security provided by a $15,000 law practice for a subordinate position in far-off Washington that paid $4,500 and subjected a small-town lawyer to such unfamiliar pressures. Yet Day's native intelligence and steady tough-minded persistence, belied as they were by his silent demeanor, served to carry him through a troublesome two-year period during which his own immediate superior posed almost as much of a problem as did foreign potentates.

Judge Day's term as First Assistant Secretary lasted from April of 1897 until April of 1898. During this period the proud Sherman's irascibility grew apace with his diplomatic gaucherie. Though he could sometimes sense the general disparagement of his feeble diplomatic efforts, the Secretary unwittingly provided his critics with more ammunition. Among other things, Sherman unequivocally assured the Japanese Minister early in the summer of 1897 that the United States had absolutely no intention of annexing the Hawaiian Islands, just as the Department finished its work on the annexation treaty. Sherman knew nothing of it, of course, nor did Judge Day feel that prudence would allow for informing the often garrulous Secretary, since Sherman frequently gave out indiscreet statements to the press. In one such incident, in the summer of 1897, Sherman held an open-ended interview for reporters who represented such anti-McKinley newspapers as the *New York World.* In his free-wheeling comments the Secretary of State managed to insult both the British and the Japanese, and to predict the loss of Cuba by Spain. By the end of 1897, therefore, Day and others felt that merely leaving Secretary Sherman alone in public might do damage to American diplomacy, especially considering the heightening Cuban crisis.

American concern with Spanish Cuba had waxed and waned through most of the nineteenth century. At times sincere paternalistic humanitarianism had suggested active American intervention, at other times commercial venality had argued for the protection afforded by Spanish political "stability." But always before 1898 Spain's promises of reform and cruel repression of Cuban rebels had controlled chaos on the island and cooled American passions as well.

In 1895 an especially determined native insurrection had broken out, and by the end of 1897 many of the Spanish-American pressures that had been building up through the years seemed ready to cause a rupture if either nation desired war. Spain surely did not, for she could gain nothing but could easily lose the last valuable parts of her once proud empire. But the government in Washington seemed unable to formulate a steady policy, and was buffeted in various directions by such social phenomena as New York's yellow press war between William Randolph Hearst's *Journal* and Joseph Pulitizer's *World,* both of which gleefully fed upon the vicious Cuban struggle to increase their circulations, and in doing so frequently suggested an equation between McKinley's reluctance to intervene and his lack of manhood. Business interests, with $50,000,000 at stake, were ambivalent, some fearful of an increased destruction of property through American involvement, others raising concerned voices in unison with both sincere and demagogic politicians who appealed to American humanitarianism, virility and patriotism. The well-financed nationalist groups in New York, known as the Cuban Junta, urged intervention for their own reasons. Big Navy men like Assistant Navy Secretary Theodore Roosevelt and his circle of Large Policy advocates craved action of any sort, while the Anti-imperialist Leaguers like William Jennings Bryan and Mark Twain fulminated against it. As millions of Americans felt a curious swelling excitement, in Washington Major McKinley and his advisors pondered.

As the crisis quickened in January of 1898 Day spent most of his time in shuffling between the State Department and the White House, conferring almost daily with Spanish Minister Don Enrique Dupey de Lome and with the President. In his negotiations with the Spaniard the *de facto* Secretary of State clearly reflected his desire for some form of peaceful solution, pressing Dupey de Lome for assurances of meaningful reforms in Cuba while remaining unaffected by the war fever which was attacking Washington. The more intense war sentiment became, the harder the quiet little man struggled to promote some compromise that would satisfy the increasingly strident American jingoes. On January 24 Day secured Dupey de Lome's assent for a "good will" visit to Havana by the U.S.S. *Maine,* a flag-showing gesture which might decrease domestic bellicosity to some degree.

Ten days later the administration's shaky attempts to avert war began to collapse. Agents of the Cuban Junta had stolen a letter written by Sr. Dupey de Lome in which the Spanish Minister referred to President McKinley in the most unflattering terms. To receive the full propaganda benefits the Junta turned over the highly indiscreet letter to Hearst's *Journal* and when it appeared in blatant splendor in the editions of February 8, the nation was predictably rocked by fervent indignation.

On the following morning a Junta-affiliated New York lawyer named John J. McCook appeared in Judge Day's office. The wealthy McCook, who knew both Day and McKinley quite well, had strong Republican ties and spent most of his time working as a lobbyist for large American business interests in Cuba and for the Junta as well. Now he proudly presented the Dupey de Lome letter to the glum little man behind the large desk and left Judge Day with the problem of doing something immediately to prevent a diplomatic rupture.

Day then took the highly unusual step of going in person to the Spanish Legation. He confronted Sr. Dupey de Lome with the telltale letter, received confirmation of its validity, and accepted the harried diplomat's suggestion that he leave the country immediately.

A week later, on February 15, as the yellow press continued to make capital of the de Lome affair, the *Maine* exploded in Havana harbor. The shocking loss of over 250 American lives inflamed the country as had nothing before. The cries for war intensified: war, immediately and totally, a war of revenge, a war for humanity, for justice, for liberty.

Although the administration refused to be stampeded, attempts to avert war gradually yielded to patriotic passions. McKinley and Day, pressed hard by an increasingly bellicose Congress, steadily increased their demands on the Spanish. By the end of March Spain was in effect simply being asked to abandon its sovereignty in Cuba. This hardening line pleased such exponents of war as Theodore Roosevelt, who wrote to Elihu Root on April 5:

> *Thank heaven this morning it looks as if the administration has made up its mind to lead the movement instead of resisting it, with the effect of shattering the party and humiliating the nation. Judge Day, who . . . has been advocating peace under almost any conditions, has just told me that he has given up, and that the President seems to be making up his mind to the same effect.* [2 The Letters of Theodore Roosevelt, *ed. by E. E. Morison* (*Cambridge, Mass., 1951–1954*) *813*].

When the President sent his war message to Capitol Hill on April 11 he unloosened a chain of events the implications of which could scarcely have been foreseen. The "splendid little war" ran its course in about ten weeks, but still managed to produce such enduring political and patriotic legacies as Colonel Roosevelt and Admiral Dewey, the first modern American military heroes. More importantly, this relatively minor military adventure allowed this giant nation to exert its newly developed industrialized power in an international conflict, and consequently projected the United States as a great power for the first time. By December 10, when Day presided over the signing of the Treaty of Paris which officially ended the war, the United States had acquired a far-flung empire that stretched from the Caribbean to the South China Sea.

Judge Day served as a rather unenthusiastic participant throughout this hectic period. One of McKinley's first acts upon the outbreak of war had been to secure the resignation of John Sherman and to designate the reluctant Day as his successor. During the next few weeks Day spent much of his time quietly arguing against the kind of expansionist sentiment that increased so sharply after Dewey's triumph of May 1. In the subsequent dilemma over the disposition of the Philippines, Secretary Day carefully expressed his anti-annexationist views, which he continued to hold despite the pressures exerted on him by such powerful expansionists as Senator Henry Cabot Lodge and Captain Alfred Thayer Mahan. While Day favored some form of retention of the port facilities of Manila, he strongly opposed outright annexation of the Philippines *in toto*. The Judge argued on the philosophical basis of the American commitment to self-government as well as on the less exalted grounds of his aversion to assuming responsibility for "eight or nine millions of absolutely ignorant and many degraded people." (Ernest May, *Imperial Democracy: The Emergence of America as a Great Power* [New York, 1961] 250. See also Julius Pratt, *Expansionists of 1898* [Baltimore, 1951] 327.)

As usual, however, Day eventually deferred to McKinley's wishes. He resigned from the State Department in August in order to head the American delegation to the Peace Conference that met in Paris from October to December. There Day's opposition to outright annexation gradually weakened, and when the President finally secured "Divine Guidance" and decided upon annexation, his friend went ahead and negotiated the treaty which codified United States hegemony over Cuba and outright acquisition of Puerto Rico and Guam and, in return for $20,000,000, the seven thousand islands of the Philippines.

Before leaving for Paris, Judge Day strongly reiterated his desire to retire from public life and return to Canton. The President, while sympathetic to his friend's desires, was nonetheless determined to keep the Judge in public life and, as usual, McKinley once again prevailed. Thus in February of 1899 Day agreed to accept the presidential appointment to the bench of the United States Court of Appeals for the Sixth Circuit.

The Sixth Circuit Court enjoyed a great deal of prestige not only within its jurisdictional boundaries of Tennessee, Kentucky, Ohio and Michigan, but also in national legal circles. Its bench had produced a score of distinguished jurists, and when Judge Day arrived in Cincinnati in 1899 to join the court his presiding judge was William Howard Taft and one of his closest associates Horace H. Lurton of Tennessee, whom President Taft would place on the United States Supreme Court in 1909. In addition to the circuit court's legal prominence, its Cincinnati headquarters allowed Judge Day to spend much of his time in Canton.

Day thoroughly enjoyed his four years on the Sixth Circuit bench. He felt comfortable in the presence of the massive Taft, and especially so with the amiable Horace Lurton. The pleasant upper-middle-class life provided by the Cincinnati bench and bar and the closeness of Canton furnished an altogether comfortable style of life.

Soon after the century's turn, however, a rapid series of events shattered Day's tranquillity once more. Late in the drowsy summer of 1901 the nation was rocked by the shooting of the President in Buffalo. Nowhere did the hideous event strike harder than in Canton, where Judge Day received the shocking news and immediately set off for Buffalo. Then followed the unspeakable grief of the death of the beloved friend of so many days and so many ways. Life went on but would never be quite the same for Day, who never forgot: each year on McKinley's birthday his faithful old friend would appear at the Supreme Court wearing a carnation and carrying eight others for his colleagues.

After the burial Judge Day returned to his bench in Cincinnati. There the new presiding judge was Lurton, the genial Tennessean, since President Theodore Roosevelt had sent Taft away to the Philippine Islands as the first United States Civil Governor.

The ambitious Taft had made no secret of his desire to sit on the Supreme Court, and within a year the resignation of Justice George Shiras, Jr., gave to the new President his first opportunity to gratify the desires of his highly respected Ohio friend. Shiras announced his resignation in October of 1902, and Roosevelt immediately offered the seat to Taft, who wanted it badly but could not escape the sense of responsibility which he felt to the novel position which he had occupied for such a short time. Roosevelt refused to accept Taft's reasoning and made a second offer. Taft's determination bent, and he replied with a qualified acceptance that again emphasized the desirability of leaving him in Manila. The President received this equivocal response along with reports of popular pro-Taft demonstrations in Manila, and decided to leave the vascillating Taft where he was. (Alpheus T. Mason, *William Howard Taft: Chief Justice* [New York, 1964] 21–24.)

Even before dispatching his second appeal Roosevelt had decided that his alternate choice for the Court would be another highly respected Ohio man who had recently been associated with Taft, a man whose strong McKinley connections would do the President no harm in securing the Party's nomination in 1904. In January of 1903 Roosevelt travelled to Canton to commemorate McKinley's birthday and after being introduced to the crowds by Judge Day, responded to the introduction by thanking his old friend "Mr. Justice Day," the newest member of the Supreme Court of the United States.

Within the brief period of six years the modest and retiring country lawyer had moved from Lynch and Day of Canton to the Supreme Court in Washington. Probably this appointment alone could have persuaded him to give up the more ordered life of the Sixth Circuit bench. In any event, that spring he moved to the Capitol once more, into a fine home in the Columbia Heights section that came equipped with a spacious upstairs study, where Day did all of his legal work, as well as a billiard room on the top floor, where the wizened and solemn little man took most of his active recreation. Although he occasionally strolled around a golf course, the Judge's enthusiasm for sports remained focused on baseball, and he rode out to the ball park to cheer on the Washington Nationals whenever possible. Each fall's World Series would find Supreme Court pages scurrying around Mr. Justice Day's seat with the latest scores as they came over the news ticker.

Throughout William Rufus Day's nineteen years on the Supreme Court he remained one of the Court's most active members. Except for 1911, when his wife's death took him away for three months, and 1915, when a protracted illness felled him, Day participated in the vast majority of the Court's hundreds of decisions.

At about the time that Day joined the Court in 1903 issues began rapidly to appear which divided the "liberals" who were willing to sanction an increase in federal police powers from the "conservatives" who sharply opposed any increase in the regulatory functions of the central government. The conservative coalition could always count on Chief Justice Melville W. Fuller and Associate Justices Rufus W. Peckham and David J. Brewer. Usually, they would be joined by Justices Edward D. White and Henry B. Brown. The liberal members of the Court in 1903 included Justices John Marshall Harlan and Oliver Wendell Holmes and, usually, Joseph McKenna. By no means were these men always so arranged on decisions, however. Consistency did not appeal to most of them, and such distinctions as have been made only apply to the very general proposition of judicial willingness to sanction an expansion of the federal government's regulatory powers, usually under the commerce clause.

As the years went on and death and retirement took their toll, succeeding Presidents managed to appoint to the Court men whose legal approach differed from the conservatives who dominated its opinions in the late nineteenth and early twentieth centuries. During Day's tenure, moderate liberals such as William H. Moody, Horace H. Lurton, John H. Clarke and Charles Evans Hughes, in addition to Louis Brandeis, served on the Court. Their opinions were frequently countered, however, by the basically conservative approach taken by Willis Van Devanter, James C. McReynolds, Mahlon Pitney, William Howard Taft and Joseph McKenna, whose earlier erratic liberalism gave way in later years.

Throughout his nearly two decades, however, Justice William R. Day's position in this ideological lineup remained equivocal because of the curiously ambivalent legal philosophy which he brought with him to the bench. Day always held tightly to the concept of separate levels of government, each with its specific functions to perform. This inflexible construction of a dual federalism made Day always chary of the indiscriminate expansion of federal powers, notwithstanding the fact that he endorsed fully the police powers of the federal government when applied to antitrust cases. In most other areas, however, he clearly favored the utilization of state governments to promote whatever change seemed desirable to the people most involved. Perhaps his lifelong faith in the efficacy of state and local governments grew out of his small town experiences, which had been so satisfactory. Certainly he had developed a great deal of respect for the state courts from the example of his father and grandfather, both of whom had held such high state judicial appointments.

The basis of most of Day's legal philosophy stemmed from his narrow interpretation of the constitutional rights of the federal government to regulate commerce. Early twentieth century Congresses, possessing no general power to regulate in the interest of health, morals and public welfare, increasingly enforced regulation and control over business through their powers to regulate commerce and to tax. Day rejected this assumption of federal police power not because his social philosophy was opposed to progressive reform, but because of a crabbed and anachronistic definition of the meaning of commerce itself. Apparently, Day took this definition from the most famous decision of one of his early colleagues. In 1895 Chief Justice Fuller's majority opinion in *United States* v. *E. C. Knight Company,* 156 U.S. 1 (1895), had prevented the application of the Sherman Act against the Sugar Trust on the grounds that although the trust did indeed monopolize the manufacturing of sugar, the Sherman Act only permitted litigation against commerce, not manufacturing. As Fuller wrote:

> *Commerce succeeds to manufacture and is not a part of it. The power to regulate commerce is the power to prescribe the rule by which commerce shall be governed, and is a power independent of the power to suppress monopoly. . . . The fact that an article is manufactured for export to another state does not of itself make it an article of interstate commerce.*

Day's literal acceptance of this tortuous line of reasoning emerged in a number of cases. In *Delaware, Lackawanna and Western Railroad Company* v. *Yurkonis,* 238 U.S. 439 (1915), for example, Day applied Fuller's dictum by arguing that even if products were made or extracted for the sole and explicit purpose of interstate shipment, their manufacture or extraction could not be considered under the commerce clause, which had no relevance to goods prior to their shipment across interstate lines.

The most significant example of Day's concept of the commerce clause came in the Court's highly controversial 1918 decision which invalidated the Keating-Owen Child Labor Act of 1916. This excellent example of progressive legislation had outlawed the interstate shipment of products made by child labor; by taking such action the Wilson Administration had thus attempted to use the commerce clause to abolish child labor by severely limiting the marketability of child-made goods. But the Court, in a sharp five to four split in this case of *Hammer* v. *Dagenhart,* 247 U.S. 251 (1918), spoke through Justice Day in striking down the Act. Day's reasoning here was entirely consistent with his narrow view of the commerce clause. Once again he cited his unshakable belief that the processes of commerce must be distinguished from those of manufacturing, with commerce itself subject to regulation only when state boundaries were crossed, but with the regulation of such internal components of the manufacturing process as the conditions of labor being reserved in their entirety to the police power of the several states. (For an extended discussion of this and other aspects of Day's legal philosophy, see Joseph E. McLean, "William Rufus Day: Supreme Court Justice from Ohio," LXIV, no. 3 *The Johns Hopkins University Studies in Historical and Political Science,* 68–164 [Baltimore, 1946]. Hereafter cited as McLean, *Day.*)

This opinion clearly exposed Day's reasoning. The Keating-Owen Act, he argued, "does not regulate transportation among the states, but aims to standardize the ages at which children may be employed in mining and manufacturing within the states." As far as transportation *per se* was concerned, Day held that

> *. . . before transportation begins, the labor of their* [*the goods*] *production is over, and the mere fact that they were intended for interstate commerce transportation does not make their production subject to federal control under the commerce power.* [*McLean,* Day, *77.*]

While the specter of child labor naturally repelled the decent little man from Ohio, the restrictive legalism of his approach refused to allow the federal government to destroy it. Manufacturing involved the production of goods, commerce involved their transportation, and while federal authority applied to the latter when goods crossed state lines, only the states themselves could approach the former.

This legalistic distinction between commerce and transportation permitted Day to support congressional legislation aimed at regulating carriers in such cases as *Atchison, Topeka and Santa Fe Railway Company* v. *Robinson,* 233 U.S. 173 (1914). In addition, he wrote the majority opinion in the case of *Armour Packing Company* v. *United States,* 209 U.S. 56 (1908) which upheld the power of Congress to penalize shippers who managed to secure shipping rates below published levels.

Furthermore, Day strongly supported federal regulation of interstate transportation by upholding the investigatory powers of the Interstate Commerce Commission. In his dissent in *Harriman* v. *Interstate Commerce Commission,* 211 U.S. 407 (1908), in which the Court had limited the commission's subpoena prerogatives, Day noted that:

> [*W*]*hile it may be extremely inconvenient to compel the attendance of witnesses and the production of the papers, etc., throughout a domain so large as ours, that consideration does not detract from the power of Congress over the subject matter.* [*McLean,* Day, *73–74, n. 24.*]

Day did grant the applicability of the commerce clause in cases that involved the interstate transportation of impure or otherwise harmful products, as in *Pittsburgh Melting Company* v. *Totten,* 248 U.S. 1 (1918). He took the same view in *Caminetti* v. *United States,* 242 U.S. 470 (1917), where he wrote the Court's opinion upholding the right of Congress to prohibit passage of certain items in interstate commerce if such commerce endangered the public health. He also used this line of reasoning in *Hoke* v. *United States,* 227 U.S. 308 (1913) which sustained the Mann White Slavery Act.

Despite these modest concessions to the commerce clause, Judge Day consistently drew a clear line between state and federal police powers. In *Sligh* v. *Kirkwood,* 237 U.S. 52 (1915), Day's opinion upheld a state law which prohibited the shipment or commercial disposal of unripened citrus fruits. While this law, in Day's judgment, constituted a proper use of the police power of a state, the Justice carefully noted that it dealt with matters that "are not the legitimate subject of trade or commerce, now within the protection of the commerce clause of the Constitution." This distinction between state and federal police powers flowed easily from Day's reliance on a literal interpretation of the Tenth Amendment, the keystone to his belief in dual federalism.

While Justice Day was reluctant to accept the gradually increasing scope of the federal government's power to control and regulate aspects of the nation's economic and social life, he showed no reluctance to endorse the police powers of the several states. Indeed Day's adherence to the Tenth Amendment had little relationship to its later utilization by states' rights advocates to dam up the rising progressive tides.

In a series of cases involving the rights of the several states to promote and protect public health, safety and morals, Day consistently supported the extension of the police power of the various states. In *Lochner* v. *New York,* 198 U.S. 45 (1905), Day joined in the dissent when the Court voted five to four that a New York State statute which limited employment in bakeries to ten hours a day was unconstitutional. Four years later, in 1909, Day presented the opinion of the Court in *McLean* v. *Arkansas,* 211 U.S. 539 (1909), in which a state law promoting safer working conditions in mines was upheld. In 1913 Day wrote the Court's opinion in a very similar case, *Barrett* v. *Indiana,* 229 U.S. 26 (1913), which again sustained a state law affecting working conditions of miners. When the Court interrupted its moderately progressive drift regarding labor legislation in a rather startling 1915 decision in the case of *Coppage* v. *Kansas,* 236 U.S. 1 (1915), a decision which declared unconstitutional the Kansas law against yellow-dog contracts, Day wrote a crackling dissent. In his argument, with which Justice Hughes concurred, Day clearly championed progressivism on the state level by holding that

> . . . *nothing is better settled by the repeated decisions of this Court than that the right of contract is not absolute and unyielding, but is subject to limitation and restraint in the interests of the public health, safety, and welfare, and such limitations may be declared in the legislation of the State.* [*McLean,* Day, *120.*]

Several additional examples of Justice Day's espousal of state and local police power may be cited. In *Missouri Pacific Railway Company* v. *Omaha,* 235 U.S. 121 (1914), Day spoke for a unanimous Court in upholding an Omaha city ordinance that required the railroad to construct a viaduct at its own expense as a public safety measure. Another local statute was upheld by Day's decision for the Court in *New Orleans Gaslight Company* v. *Drainage Commission,* 197 U.S. 453 (1905) when the local gas company was ordered to incur the expense of moving its lines as a public health measure. Years later, in 1921, Day spoke for the Court in upholding a state's right to regulate the use of drugs within its borders in *Minnesota ex rel. Whipple* v. *Martinson,* 256 U.S. 41 (1921). A large number of additional cases illustrates the same disposition on Day's part, that is, wide latitude for state police powers to regulate within several broadly defined areas.

This general trend toward progressive legislation on both state and federal levels posed a major obstacle to the continued development of business combinations and at the same time stiffened the opposition of constitutional conservatives to the ever expanding regulatory powers of government. The Supreme Court, for its part, heard an increasing number of cases that involved the controversial concept of substantive due process of law. Simply put, this basic juridical shift introduced the subjective judicial determination of the reasonableness of state and federal regulatory legislation. The proper limits of the legitimate exercise of police power now became a judicial rather than simply a legislative question, and frequently the Court's acceptance or rejection of a piece of legislation hinged on the social philosophy of the Justices who made the decision.

In 1911 Chief Justice White delivered two opinions which employed this "rule of reason" as a weapon against the Sherman Act. In *Standard Oil Company of New Jersey et al.* v. *United States,* 221 U.S. 1 (1911) and in *United States* v. *American Tobacco Company,* 221 U.S. 106 (1911), the Court prevented the federal government from taking the "unreasonable" action of dissolving these two giant trusts. They were allowed to reorganize, and to continue their industrial dominance.

Although Justice Day silently concurred in both decisions, he consistently rejected the implications of the "rule of reason," as his legal philosophy and perhaps his personal inclinations led him to favor a vigorous use of the federal police power against the great financial and industrial combinations. Both the Sherman Act and later the Clayton Act fell clearly within Day's definition of the commerce powers of the federal government. He indicated this soon after his appointment, in the celebrated Northern Securities Case of 1904, *Northern Securities Co.* v. *United States,* 193 U.S. 197 (1904), when the Court struck down one of J. P. Morgan's patented holding companies by the vote of five to four, with the newly arrived William R. Day's vote making the difference.

In a number of succeeding cases involving antitrust proceedings, Day rejected corporate pleas of reasonable combination. In *United States* v. *Union*

Pacific Railway Company, 226 U.S. 61 (1912), Day upheld the Sherman Act and struck down consolidation of two competing railroad systems. Similar decisions followed in *Eastern States Retail Lumber Dealers Association* v. *United States,* 234 U.S. 600 (1914) and in *United States* v. *Southern Pacific Company,* 259 U.S. 214 (1922).

Judge Day's most forthright defense of the Sherman Act occurred in 1920 when a badly divided Court in *United States* v. *United States Steel Corporation,* 251 U.S. 417 (1920), ruled by a four to three vote that United States Steel's dominance of the steel industry did not constitute a violation of the Sherman Act. Speaking for Justices Pitney and Clarke, Day read a blistering dissent which frontally attacked all giant combinations, and even assailed the notion that huge rationalized industries were either inevitable or desirable. He accused United States Steel of open violation and defiance of the law, and strongly implied that his own colleagues should revert to a strict and literal adherence to the intent of the Sherman Act. That United States Steel did not totally control the industry was not the salient point for Day: Judge Gary and his Board of Directors did possess the power to stifle competition at the time of the suit, and unless the monopolistic tendencies of this corporation were reversed, Day fully believed, the implications for monopolistic control were inevitable.

This loud dissent, which called upon the federal government to do no less than reverse the basic results of the American industrial revolution, contrasted vividly with Day's refusal to sanction the use of federal power to undo the blatant evils of child labor in the *Hammer* v. *Dagenhart, supra,* case. Perhaps the common denominator in these seemingly antithetical tendencies toward federal power was Day's distrust of power per se. Major concentrations of economic power, like United States Steel, stood in clear violation of federal law and, additionally, stifled the impulses of individualism and competitiveness which Day held so highly. Consequently, the Judge had no qualms about employing federal power to the limits of the law to break up monopoly, encourage competition, and destroy unhealthy power concentrations. On the other hand, the power of the federal government was also a potentially dangerous development, as it seemed to gradually erode the historic prerogatives of the inferior governments and tended to encroach upon the lives of individual citizens.

William Day's cosmology, shaped in rural, pre-industrial America, carried a strong dose of nineteenth century liberalism well into the urban, industrialized twentieth century. To his credit, Day, in recognizing many of these vast social changes, adjusted his legal philosophy and became a moderate liberal in terms of favoring the extension of federal powers. Except for his stubborn reliance on Melville Fuller's odd definition of commerce, Justice Day generally cast his vote on the side of the twentieth century.

Day grew old on the High Bench. When Roosevelt appointed him in 1903 the fragile Judge was already fifty-four. Ironically, this frail, crockery-like figure of a man survived the younger and violently vigorous Rough Rider, and most of the rest of his peers as well. But the years did bring basic changes. Mrs. Day had died in 1911, and their son Rufus moved to Washington to live with his father and serve as legal secretary. There were still the annual summer trips to the Day cottage on Mackinac Island, but side visits to Canton became less frequent, and the press of work kept the Justice inside more and more. After nearly twenty years, the preparation of a heavy load of cases lost most of its appeal and, in October of 1922, Judge Day decided to retire from the Court.

Even then, optimistic at seventy-three, Day willingly accepted President Harding's commission to serve as an umpire on the Mixed Claims Commission established by the United States and German governments to adjudicate claims left over from the war. But the low-keyed activities of the Claims Commission still managed to tax Judge Day's endurance, and in May of 1923 he resigned, thus leaving the public service for the first time in over twenty-five years.

Early that summer, the Judge and his eldest son, William L. Day, opened their Mackinac camp as usual. Here the now enfeebled little man enjoyed a few more days of sun and bass fishing until death came on July 9. A fittingly simple and quiet burial followed in Canton, with a few dignitaries from high places once more incongruously present on Main Street for a time. Then the predictable drift of a small town summer returned and things were about the same as they had always been.

SELECTED BIBLIOGRAPHY

The only formal biographical study of Judge Day is Joseph E. McLean, *William Rufus Day: Supreme Court Justice from Ohio* (Baltimore, 1946), which provides a thin account of Day's life and times but is valuable for its treatment of his judicial career. Some details on Day's early life are provided by 32 *National Cyclopaedia of American Biography* 22 (1945). A truncated version of Day's life is Lester B. Shippee and Royal B. Way, "William Rufus Day," in *The American Secretaries of State and their Diplomacy,* Samuel Flagg Bemis, ed. (New York, 1958 edition), IX, 27–112. For additional data on Day's diplomatic interlude see Julius W. Pratt, *Expansionists of 1898* (Baltimore, 1936), especially 327 ff.; and Walter LaFeber, *The New Empire* (Ithaca, 1963), 334–398. Margaret Leech, *In the Days of McKinley* (New York, 1959) reveals the closeness of the relationship between the two Canton friends.

William R. Day

REPRESENTATIVE OPINIONS

HAMMER v. DAGENHART, 247 U.S. 251 (1918)

The Supreme Court's decision in this controversial case came through a five to four vote, with Justice Day presenting the majority opinion by which the Court declared that the Keating-Owen Child Labor Act of 1916 was unconstitutional. In passing this legislation the Congress had attempted to use the commerce clause to outlaw child labor. The Keating-Owen Act prohibited the interstate shipment of any goods which had been manufactured with the assistance of any form of child labor. But Justice Day refused to bend before the grave social issue presented. Instead, he based his decision on the long discredited dictum which had been laid down in 1895 by Chief Justice Fuller in *United States* v. *E. C. Knight Co.,* 156 U.S. 1 that "Commerce succeeds to manufacture and is not part of it." By accepting this premise, Day could conclude that while the federal government could regulate commerce, it had no constitutional powers under the commerce clause to regulate manufacturing.

MR. JUSTICE DAY delivered the opinion of the court.

A bill was filed in the United States District Court for the Western District of North Carolina by a father in his own behalf and as next friend of his two minor sons, one under the age of fourteen years and the other between the ages of fourteen and sixteen years, employees in a cotton mill at Charlotte, North Carolina, to enjoin the enforcement of the act of Congress intended to prevent interstate commerce in the products of child labor. Act of Sept. 1, 1916, c. 432, 39 Stat. 675.

The District Court held the act unconstitutional and entered a decree enjoining its enforcement. This appeal brings the case here. The first section of the act is in the margin.[1]

[1] *That no producer, manufacturer, or dealer shall ship or deliver for shipment in interstate or foreign commerce any article or commodity the product of any mine or quarry, situated in the United States, in which within thirty days prior to the time of the removal of such product therefrom children under the age of sixteen years have been employed or permitted to work, or any*

Other sections of the act contain provisions for its enforcement and prescribe penalties for its violation.

The attack upon the act rests upon three propositions: First: It is not a regulation of interstate and foreign commerce; Second: It contravenes the Tenth Amendment to the Constitution; Third: It conflicts with the Fifth Amendment to the Constitution.

The controlling question for decision is: Is it within the authority of Congress in regulating commerce among the States to prohibit the transportation in interstate commerce of manufactured goods, the product of a factory in which, within thirty days prior to their removal therefrom, children under the age of fourteen have been employed or permitted to work, or children between the ages of fourteen and sixteen years have been employed or permitted to work more than eight hours in any day, or more than six days in any week, or after the hour of seven o'clock P.M. or before the hour of 6 o'clock A.M.?

The power essential to the passage of this act, the Government contends, is found in the commerce clause of the Constitution which authorizes Congress to regulate commerce with foreign nations and among the States.

In *Gibbons* v. *Ogden,* 9 Wheat. 1, Chief Justice Marshall, speaking for this court, and defining the extent and nature of the commerce power, said, "It is the power to regulate; that is, to prescribe the rule by which commerce is to be governed." In other words, the power is one to control the means by which commerce is carried on, which is directly the contrary of the assumed right to forbid commerce from moving and thus destroy it as to particular commodities. But it is insisted that adjudged cases in this court establish the doctrine that the power to regulate given to Congress incidentally includes the authority to prohibit the movement of ordinary commodities and therefore that the subject is not open for discussion. The cases demonstrate the contrary. They rest upon the character of the particular subjects dealt with and the fact that the scope of governmental authority, state or national, possessed over them is such that the authority to prohibit is as to them but the exertion of the power to regulate.

The first of these cases is *Champion* v. *Ames,* 188 U.S. 321, the so-called *Lottery Case,* in which it was held that Congress might pass a law having the effect to keep the channels of commerce free from use in the transportation of tickets used in the promotion of lottery schemes. In *Hipolite Egg Co.* v. *United States,* 220 U.S. 45, this court sustained the power of Congress to pass the Pure Food and Drug Act which prohibited the introduction into the States by means of interstate commerce of impure foods and drugs. In *Hoke* v. *United States,* 227 U.S. 308, this court sustained the constitutionality of the so-called "White Slave Traffic Act" whereby the transportation of a woman in interstate commerce for the purpose of prostitution was forbidden. In that case we said, having reference to the authority of Congress, under the regulatory power, to protect the channels of interstate commerce:

"If the facility of interstate transportation can be taken away from the demoralization of lotteries, the debasement of obscene literature, the contagion of diseased cattle or persons, the impurity of food and drugs, the like facility can be taken away from the systematic enticement to and the enslavement in prostitution and debauchery of women, and, more insistently, of girls."

In *Caminetti* v. *United States,* 242 U.S. 470, we held that Congress might prohibit the transportation of women in interstate commerce for the purposes of debauchery and kindred purposes. In *Clark Distilling Co.* v. *Western Maryland Ry. Co.,* 242 U.S. 311, the power of Congress over the transportation of intoxicating liquors was sustained. In the course of the opinion it was said:

"The power conferred is to regulate, and the very terms of the grant would seem to repel the contention that only prohibition of movement in interstate commerce was embraced. And the cogency of this is mani-

article or commodity the product of any mill, cannery, workshop, factory, or manufacturing establishment, situated in the United States, in which within thirty days prior to the removal of such product therefrom children under the age of fourteen years have been employed or permitted to work, or children between the ages of fourteen years and sixteen years have been employed or permitted to work more than eight hours in any day, or more than six days in any week, or after the hour of seven o'clock postmeridian, or before the hours of six o'clock antemeridian.

fest since if the doctrine were applied to those manifold and important subjects of interstate commerce as to which Congress from the beginning has regulated, not prohibited, the existence of government under the Constitution would be no longer possible."

And, concluding the discussion which sustained the authority of the Government to prohibit the transportation of liquor in interstate commerce, the court said:

". . . the exceptional nature of the subject here regulated is the basis upon which the exceptional power exerted must rest and affords no ground for any fear that such power may be constitutionally extended to things which it may not, consistently with the guarantees of the Constitution, embrace."

In each of these instances the use of interstate transportation was necessary to the accomplishment of harmful results. In other words, although the power over interstate transportation was to regulate, that could only be accomplished by prohibiting the use of the facilities of interstate commerce to effect the evil intended.

This element is wanting in the present case. The thing intended to be accomplished by this statute is the denial of the facilities of interstate commerce to those manufacturers in the States who employ children within the prohibited ages. The act in its effect does not regulate transportation among the States, but aims to standardize the ages at which children may be employed in mining and manufacturing within the States. The goods shipped are of themselves harmless. The act permits them to be freely shipped after thirty days from the time of their removal from the factory. When offered for shipment, and before transportation begins, the labor of their production is over, and the mere fact that they were intended for interstate commerce transportation does not make their production subject to federal control under the commerce power.

Commerce "consists of intercourse and traffic . . . and includes the transportation of persons and property, as well as the purchase, sale and exchange of commodities." The making of goods and the mining of coal are not commerce, nor does the fact that these things are to be afterwards shipped or used in interstate commerce, make their production a part thereof. *Delaware, Lackawanna & Western R. R. Co.* v. *Yurkonis,* 238 U.S. 439.

Over interstate transportation, or its incidents, the regulatory power of Congress is ample, but the production of articles, intended for interstate commerce, is a matter of local regulation.

"When the commerce begins is determined, not by the character of the commodity, nor by the intention of the owner to transfer it to another state for sale, nor by his preparation of it for transportation, but by its actual delivery to a common carrier for transportation, or the actual commencement of its transfer to another state." (Mr. Justice Jackson in *In re Green,* 52 Fed. Rep. 113.) This principle has been recognized often in this court. *Coe* v. *Errol,* 116 U.S. 517; *Bacon* v. *Illinois,* 227 U.S. 504, and cases cited. If it were otherwise, all manufacture intended for interstate shipment would be brought under federal control to the practical exclusion of the authority of the States, a result certainly not contemplated by the framers of the Constitution when they vested in Congress the authority to regulate commerce among the States. *Kidd* v. *Pearson,* 128 U.S. 1, 21.

It is further contended that the authority of Congress may be exerted to control interstate commerce in the shipment of child-made goods because of the effect of the circulation of such goods in other States where the evil of this class of labor has been recognized by local legislation, and the right to thus employ child labor has been more rigorously restrained than in the State of production. In other words, that the unfair competition, thus engendered, may be controlled by closing the channels of interstate commerce to manufacturers in those States where the local laws do not meet what Congress deems to be the more just standard of other States.

There is no power vested in Congress to require the States to exercise their police power so as to prevent possible unfair competition. Many causes may coöperate to give one State, by reason of local laws or conditions, an economic advantage over others. The Commerce Clause was not intended to give to Congress a general authority to equalize such conditions. In some of the States laws have been passed fixing minimum wages for women, in others the local law regulates the hours of labor of women in various employments. Business done in such States may be at an economic disadvantage when compared with States which have no such regulations; surely, this fact does not give Congress the power to deny transportation in interstate commerce to those who carry on business where the hours of labor and the rate of compensation for women have not been fixed by a standard in use in other States and approved by Congress.

The grant of power to Congress over the subject of interstate commerce was to enable it to regulate such commerce, and not to give it authority to control the States in their exercise of the police power over local trade and manufacture.

The grant of authority over a purely federal matter was not intended to destroy the local power always existing and carefully reserved to the States in the Tenth Amendment to the Constitution.

Police regulations relating to the internal trade and affairs of the States have been uniformly recognized as within such control. "This," said this court in *United States* v. *Dewitt,* 9 Wall. 41, 45, "has been so frequently declared by this court, results so obviously from the terms of the Constitution, and has been so fully explained and supported on former occasions, that we think it unnecessary to enter again upon the discussion." See *Keller* v. *United States,* 213 U.S. 138, 144, 145, 146. Cooley's Constitutional Limitations, 7th ed., p. 11.

In the judgment which established the broad power of Congress over interstate commerce, Chief Justice Marshall said (9 Wheat. 203): "They [inspection laws] act upon the subject before it becomes an article of foreign commerce, or of commerce among the states, and prepare it for that purpose. They form a portion of that immense mass of legislation, which embraces everything within the territory of a state, not surrendered to the general government; all which can be most advantageously exercised by the states themselves. Inspection laws, quarantine laws, health laws of every description, as well as laws for regulating the internal commerce of a state, and those which respect turnpike-roads, ferries, &c., are component parts of this mass."

And in *Dartmouth College* v. *Woodward,* 4 Wheat. 518, 629, the same great judge said:

"That the framers of the constitution did not intend to restrain the states in the regulation of their civil institutions, adopted for internal government, and that the instrument they have given us is not to be so construed may be admitted."

That there should be limitations upon the right to employ children in mines and factories in the interest of their own and the public welfare, all will admit. That such employment is generally deemed to require regulation is shown by the fact that the brief of counsel states that every State in the Union has a law upon the subject, limiting the right to thus employ children. In North Carolina, the State wherein is located the factory in which the employment was had in the present case, no child under twelve years of age is permitted to work.

It may be desirable that such laws be uniform, but our Federal Government is one of enumerated powers; "this principle," declared Chief Justice Marshall in *McCulloch* v. *Maryland,* 4 Wheat. 316, "is universally admitted."

A statute must be judged by its natural and reasonable effect. *Collins* v. *New Hampshire,* 171 U.S. 30, 33, 34. The control by Congress over interstate commerce cannot authorize the exercise of authority not entrusted to it by the Constitution. *Pipe Line Cases,* 234 U.S. 548, 560. The maintenance of the authority of the States over matters purely local is as essential to the preservation of our institutions as is the conservation of the supremacy of the federal power in all matters entrusted to the Nation by the Federal Constitution.

In interpreting the Constitution it must never be forgotten that the Nation is made up of States to which are entrusted the powers of local government. And to them and to the people the powers not expressly delegated to the National Government are reserved. *Lane County* v. *Oregon,* 7 Wall. 71, 76. The power of the States to regulate their purely internal affairs by such laws as seem wise to the local authority is inherent and has never been surrendered to the general government. *New York* v. *Miln,* 11 Pet. 102, 139; *Slaughter House Cases,* 16 Wall. 36, 63; *Kidd* v. *Pearson, supra.* To sustain this statute would not be in our judgment a recognition of the lawful exertion of congressional authority over interstate commerce, but would sanction an invasion by the federal power of the control of a matter purely local in its character, and over which no authority has been delegated to Congress in conferring the power to regulate commerce among the States.

We have neither authority nor disposition to question the motives of Congress in enacting this legislation. The purposes intended must be attained consistently with constitutional limitations and not by an invasion of the powers of the States. This court has no more important function than that which devolves upon it the obligation to preserve inviolate the constitutional limitations upon the exercise of authority, federal and state, to the end that each may continue to discharge, harmoniously with the other, the duties entrusted to it by the Constitution.

In our view the necessary effect of this act is, by means of a prohibition against the movement in interstate commerce of ordinary commercial commodities, to regulate the hours of labor of children in factories and mines within the States, a purely state authority. Thus the act in a twofold sense is repugnant to the Constitution. It not only transcends the authority delegated to Congress over commerce but also exerts a power as to a purely local matter to which the federal authority does not extend. The far reaching result of upholding the act cannot be more plainly indicated than by pointing out that if Congress can thus regulate matters entrusted to local authority by prohibition of the movement of commodities in interstate commerce, all freedom of commerce will be at an end, and the power of the States over local matters may be eliminated, and thus our system of government be practically destroyed.

For these reasons we hold that this law exceeds the constitutional authority of Congress. It follows that the decree of the District Court must be

Affirmed.

UNITED STATES v. UNITED STATES STEEL CORPORATION, 251 U.S. 417 (1920)

In this case the majority of the Supreme Court agreed with the application of the "rule of reason" to the Steel Trust. By a four to three vote the Court concluded that the antitrust laws were not intended to destroy monopolies per se, but only those combinations which violated the public interest by their unreasonable behavior. Justice Day's vigorous minority opinion derided this construction. He reminded his colleagues that the original intent of the Sherman Act was to destroy monopolies like United States Steel. He emphasized the awesome actual and potential economic power of the Steel Trust, and called for its dismemberment. Implicit in Day's argument was his long time opposition to centralized economic power and his willingness to use the federal government as the instrument for its dismantling.

MR. JUSTICE DAY dissenting.

This record seems to me to leave no fair room for a doubt that the defendants, the United States Steel Corporation and the several subsidiary corporations which make up that organization, were formed in violation of the Sherman Act. I am unable to accept the conclusion which directs a dismissal of the bill instead of following the well-settled practice, sanctioned by previous decisions of this court, requiring the dissolution of combinations made in direct violation of the law.

It appears to be thoroughly established that the formation of the corporations, here under consideration, constituted combinations between competitors, in violation of law, and intended to remove competition and to directly restrain trade. I agree with the conclusions of Judges Woolley and Hunt, expressed in the court below (223 Fed. Rep. 161, *et seq.*), that the combinations were not submissions to business conditions but were designed to control them for illegal purposes, regardless of other consequences, and "were made upon a scale that was huge and in a manner that was wild," and "properties were assembled and combined with less regard to their importance as integral parts of an integrated whole than to the advantages expected from the elimination of the competition which theretofore existed between them." Those judges found that the constituent companies of the United States Steel Corporation, nine in number, were themselves combinations of steel manufacturers, and the effect of the organization of these combinations was to give a control over the industry at least equal to that theretofore possessed by the constituent companies and their subsidiaries; that the Steel Corporation was a combination of combinations by which directly or indirectly 180 independent concerns were brought under one control, and in the language of Judge Woolley (p. 167):

"Without referring to the great mass of figures which bears upon this aspect of the case, it is clear to me that combinations were created by acquiring competing producing concerns at figures not based upon their physical or their business values, as independent and separate producers, but upon their values in combination; that is, upon their values as manufacturing plants and business concerns with competition eliminated. In many instances, capital stock was issued for amounts vastly in excess of the values of the properties purchased, thereby capitalizing the anticipated fruits of combination. The control acquired over the branches of the industry to which the combinations particularly related, measured by the amount of production, extended in some instances from 80 per cent. to 95 per cent. of the entire output of the country, resulting in the immediate increase in prices, in some cases double and in others treble what they were before, yielding large dividends upon greatly inflated capital.

"The immediate, as well as the normal effect of such combinations, was in all instances a complete elimination of competition between the concerns absorbed, and a corresponding restraint of trade."

The enormous overcapitalization of companies and the appropriation of $100,000,000 in stock to promotion expenses were represented in the stock issues of the new organizations thus formed, and were the basis upon which large dividends have been declared from the profits of the business. This record shows that the power obtained by the corporation brought under its control large competing companies which were of themselves illegal combinations, and succeeded to their power; that some of the organizers of the Steel Corporation were parties to the preceding combinations, participated in their illegality, and by uniting them under a common direction intended to augment and perpetuate their power. It is the irresistible conclusion from these premises that great profits to be derived from unified control were the object of these organizations.

The contention must be rejected that the combination was an inevitable evolution of industrial tendencies compelling union of endeavor. Nothing could add to the vivid accuracy with which Judge Woolley, speaking for himself and Judge Hunt, has stated the illegality of the organization, and its purpose to combine in one great corporation the previous combinations by a direct violation of the purposes and terms of the Sherman Act.

For many years, as the record discloses, this unlawful organization exerted its power to control and maintain prices by pools, associations, trade meetings, and as the result of discussion and agreements at the so-called "Gary Dinners," where the assembled trade opponents secured coöperation and joint action through the machinery of special committees of competing concerns, and by prudent prevision took into account the possibility of defection, and the means of controlling and perpetuating that industrial harmony which arose from the control and maintenance of prices.

It inevitably follows that the corporation violated the law in its formation and by its immediate practices. The power, thus obtained from the combination of resources almost unlimited in the aggregation of competing organizations, had within its control the domination of the trade, and the ability to fix prices and restrain the free flow of commerce upon a scale heretofore unapproached in the history of corporate organization in this country.

These facts established, as it seems to me they are by the record, it follows that, if the Sherman Act is to be given efficacy, there must be a decree undoing so far as is possible that which has been achieved in open, notorious, and continued violation of its provisions.

I agree that the act offers no objection to the mere size of a corporation, nor to the continued exertion of its lawful power, when that size and power have been obtained by lawful means and developed by natural growth, although its resources, capital and strength may give to such corporation a dominating place in the business and industry with which it is concerned. It is entitled to maintain its size and the power that legitimately goes with it, provided no law has been transgressed in obtaining it. But I understand the reiterated decisions of this court construing the Sherman Act to hold that this power may not legally be derived from conspiracies, combinations, or contracts in restraint of trade. To permit this would be to practically annul the Sherman

Law by judicial decree. This principle has been so often declared by the decisions that it is only necessary to refer to some of them. It is the scope of such combinations, and their power to suppress and stifle competition and create or tend to create monopolies, which, as we have declared so often as to make its reiteration monotonous, it was the purpose of the Sherman Act to condemn, including all combinations and conspiracies to restrain the free and natural flow of trade in the channels of interstate commerce. *Pearsall* v. *Great Northern Ry. Co.*, 161 U.S. 646, 676, 677; *Trans-Missouri Freight Assn. Case*, 166 U.S. 290, 324; *Northern Securities Case*, 193 U.S. 197; *Addyston Pipe Co.* v. *United States*, 175 U.S. 211, 238; *Harriman* v. *Northern Securities Co.*, 197 U.S. 244, 291; *Union Pacific Case*, 226 U.S. 61, 88. While it was not the purpose of the act to condemn normal and usual contracts to lawfully expand business and further legitimate trade, it did intend to effectively reach and control all conspiracies and combinations or contracts of whatever form which unduly restrain competition and unduly obstruct the natural course of trade, or which from their nature, or effect, have proved effectual to restrain interstate commerce. *Standard Oil Co.* v. *United States*, 221 U.S. 1; *United States* v. *American Tobacco Co.*, 221 U.S. 106; *United States* v. *Reading Co.*, 226 U.S. 324; *Straus* v. *American Publishers' Assn.*, 231 U.S. 222; *Eastern States Retail Lumber Dealers' Assn.* v. *United States*, 234 U.S. 600.

This statute has been in force for nearly thirty years. It has been frequently before this court for consideration, and the nature and character of the relief to be granted against combinations found guilty of violations of it have been the subject of much consideration. Its interpretation has become a part of the law itself, and, if changes are to be made now in its construction or operation, it seems to me that the exertion of such authority rests with Congress and not with the courts.

The fourth section is intended to give to courts of equity of the United States the power to effectively control and restrain violations of the act. In none of the cases which have been before the courts was the character of the relief to be granted, where organizations were found to be within the condemnation of the act, more thoroughly considered than in the *Standard Oil* and *Tobacco Company Cases*, reported in 221 U.S. In the former case, considering the measure of relief to be granted in the case of a combination, certainly not more obnoxious to the Sherman Act than the court now finds the one under consideration to be, this court declared that it must be two-fold in character (221 U.S. 78): "1st. To forbid the doing in the future of acts like those which we have found to have been done in the past which would be violative of the statute. 2d. The exertion of such measure of relief as will effectually dissolve the combination found to exist in violation of the statute, and thus neutralize the extension and continually operating force which the possession of the power unlawfully obtained has brought and will continue to bring about."

In the *American Tobacco Company Case* the nature of the relief to be granted was again given consideration, and it was there concluded that the only effectual remedy was to dissolve the combination and the companies comprising it, and for that purpose the cause was remanded to the District Court to hear the parties and determine a method of dissolution and of recreating from the elements composing it "a new condition which shall be honestly in harmony with and not repugnant to the law." In that case the corporations dissolved had long been in existence, and the offending companies were organized years before the suit was brought and before the decree of dissolution was finally made. Such facts were considered no valid objection to the dissolution of these powerful organizations as the only effective means of enforcing the purposes of the Sherman Anti-Trust Act. These cases have been frequently followed in this court, and in the lower federal courts, in determining the nature of the relief to be granted, and I see no occasion to depart from them now.

As I understand the conclusions of the court, affirming the decree directing dismissal of the bill, they amount to this: that these combinations, both the holding company and the subsidiaries which comprise it, although organized in plain violation and bold defiance of the provisions of the act, nevertheless are immune from a decree effectually ending the combinations and putting it out of their power to attain the unlawful purposes sought, because of some reasons of public policy requiring such conclusion. I know of no public policy which sanctions a violation of the law, nor of any inconvenience to trade, domestic or foreign, which should have the effect of placing combinations, which have been able thus to organize one of the greatest industries of the country in defiance of law, in an impregnable position above the control of the law forbidding such combinations. Such a conclusion does violence to the policy which the law was intended to enforce, runs counter to the decisions of the court, and necessarily results in a practical nullification of the act itself.

There is no mistaking the terms of the act as they have hitherto been interpreted by this court. It was not intended to merely suppress unfair practices, but, as its history and terms amply show, it was intended to make it criminal to form combinations or engage in conspiracies or contracts in restraint of interstate trade. The remedy by injunction, at the instance of the Attorney General, was given for the purpose of enabling the courts, as the statute states, to prohibit such conspiracies, combinations and contracts, and this court interpreting its provisions has held that the proper enforcement of the act requires decrees to end combinations by dissolving them and restoring as far as possible the competitive conditions which the combinations have destroyed. I am unable to see force in the suggestion that public policy, or the assumed disastrous effect upon foreign trade of dissolving the unlawful combination, is sufficient to entitle it to immunity from the enforcement of the statute.

Nor can I yield assent to the proposition that this combination has not acquired a dominant position in the trade which enables it to control prices and production when it sees fit to exert its power. Its total assets on December 31, 1913, were in excess of $1,800,000,000; its outstanding capital stock was $868,583,600; its surplus $151,798,428. Its cash on hand ordinarily was $75,000,000; this sum alone exceeded the total capitalization of any of its competitors, and with a single exception, the total capitalization and surplus of any one of them. That such an organization thus fortified and equipped could if it saw fit dominate the trade and control competition would seem to be a business proposition too plain to require extended argument to support it. Its resources, strength and comprehensive ownership of the means of production enable it to adopt measures to do again as it has done in the past, that is, to effectually dominate and control the steel business of the country. From the earliest decisions of this court it has been declared that it was the effective power of such organizations to control and restrain competition and the freedom of trade that Congress intended to limit and control. That the exercise of the power may be withheld, or exerted with forbearing benevolence, does not place such combinations beyond the authority of the statute which was intended to prohibit their formation, and when formed to deprive them of the power unlawfully attained.

It is said that a complete monopolization of the steel business was never attained by the offending combinations. To insist upon such result would be beyond the requirements of the statute and in most cases practicably impossible. As we said in dealing with the Packers' combination in *Swift & Co.* v. *United States,* 196 U.S. 375, 396: "Where acts are not sufficient in themselves to produce a result which the law seeks to prevent—for instance, the monopoly—but require further acts in addition to the mere forces of nature to bring that result to pass, an intent to bring it to pass is necessary in order to produce a dangerous probability that it will happen. *Commonwealth* v. *Peaslee,* 177 Massachusetts, 267, 272. But when that intent and the consequent dangerous probability exist, this statute [Sherman Act], like many others and like the common law in some cases, directs itself against that dangerous probability as well as against the completed result."

It is affirmed that to grant the Government's request for a remand to the District Court for a decree of dissolution would not result in a change in the conditions of the steel trade. Such is not the theory of the Sherman Act. That act was framed in the belief that attempted or accomplished monopolization, or combinations which suppress free competition, were hurtful to the public interest, and that a restoration of competitive conditions would benefit the public. We have here a combination in control of one-half of the steel business of the country. If the plan were followed, as in the *American Tobacco Case,* of remanding the case to the District Court, a decree might be framed restoring competitive conditions as far as practicable. See *United States* v. *American Tobacco Co.,* 191 Feb. Rep. 371. In that case the subject of reconstruction so as to restore such conditions was elaborated and carefully considered. In my judgment the principles there laid down if followed now would make a very material difference in the steel industry. Instead of one dominating corporation, with scattered competitors, there would be competitive conditions throughout the whole trade which would carry into effect the policy of the law.

It seems to me that if this act is to be given effect, the bill, under the findings of fact made by the court, should not be dismissed, and the cause should be remanded to the District Court, where a plan of effective and final dissolution of the corporations should be enforced by a decree framed for that purpose.

MR. JUSTICE PITNEY and MR. JUSTICE CLARKE concur in this dissent.

William Moody

☆ 1853–1917 ☆

APPOINTED BY

THEODORE ROOSEVELT

YEARS ON COURT

1906–1910

William Moody

by

JAMES F. WATTS, JR.

AMONG THE MOST capricious of Clio's tricks is her ability to obscure totally men who in their time managed to nudge the direction of the course of events. Through misinterpretation or lack of evidence or just simple neglect, an army of men lie interred in the past, their lives forgotten, their impact on history unrecorded. Perhaps most of them deserve a silent obscurity; but for others this is not the case, as a study of their lives adds, at the least, depth and texture to our understanding of their times. Such a man was William Henry Moody, powerful and significant during an important era, totally forgotten today. A Massachusetts Republican political leader, congressman, twice a cabinet officer, Associate Justice of the Supreme Court, and personal confidant of two Presidents—all within one five-year period—Moody's briefly burning star illuminates some important aspects of Theodore Roosevelt's America.

William Moody was born two days before the Christmas of 1853 in the family's 200-year-old homestead outside of Newbury, Massachusetts, the eldest of two children born to Henry Lord Moody and the former Melissa Emerson. Henry and Melissa's son, and a few years later their daughter, were born into a family whose roots went as deeply into the soil of northeastern Massachusetts as any other Essex County family. The first William Moody had arrived from England fourteen years after the Mayflower and in 1635 was among the original settlers of Newbury, where the Moodys lived and died as ministers, sailors, and farmers through the seven generations which separated the pioneers from the child born on Henry Moody's farm in 1853. Through the decades the family tree bore such revered Massachusetts names as Sewall and Drummer and Emerson.

In addition to his lineage, the future Justice's pure New England heritage

JAMES F. WATTS, JR. is Assistant Professor of History at City College of New York and author of a forthcoming biography of Breckinridge Long.

was also shaped by the environment of Newbury and Essex County. From his ancestors Moody inherited the strong New England sense of justice, a feeling for proper conduct, a clear sense of right and wrong. His capacity for hard work grew out of the stern soil of his father's farm, land which yielded only reluctantly to the efforts of man. At the time that Moody was born the town of Newbury no longer dominated the northeastern corner of the state, the region where the Merrimac River approaches the Atlantic. Bustling Newburyport, located three miles to the north on the Merrimac's southern bank near the juncture of the river and the ocean, had split from the older settlement in 1764 and a century later had become the principal port of Essex County. It was to the family plot in the Newburyport cemetery that William Moody's body was brought to rest in 1917 after he, like his ancestors before him, had finished his life where it began.

Perhaps Moody's greatest pleasure through his sixty-four years of life was found in the rocky rolling hills of northeastern Massachusetts which swept down to meet the icy Atlantic. As a boy on his father's farm near Newbury he roamed over the pastures and into the uplands, through the climax forests to the sea. Fifty years later he would return from Washington as one of the most powerful men in the United States to seek refreshment and peace in the open spaces of his home country. Through adolescence and the years at Harvard, as a famous trial lawyer and later as congressman, Secretary of the Navy, Attorney General and Supreme Court Justice, William Moody travelled the land on foot and on horseback, seeking and finding the aesthetic release which is apparently so necessary for sensitive men of responsibility.

Sometime during these early days around Newbury, Moody also developed another lifelong penchant; he became, in the term of one of his friends a "baseball crank." Wherever he found himself, whatever his responsibilities, Moody always found time for baseball. Even in his late thirties, an advanced baseball age for any man, the block-chested Moody would hook on catcher's paraphernalia and squat behind the plate directing his home town team. In the 1890's he would serve as president of the New England Baseball League, and a decade further on would witness the trust-busting Attorney General of the United States vigorously cheering on Walter Johnson and the Washington Nationals or stopping for an hour at a sand-lot game. This vestige lingered from the childhood of a boy who was, according to one stern report, "not over-addicted to study nor passionately fond of books." Young Moody pursued the more congenial activities of boyhood, playing ball and roaming the spaces, as his family moved about Essex County in the 1850's and 1860's. From Newbury Henry Moody moved southward to other farmlands, first locating near Salem, later moving a few miles northwest to Danvers. Young Bill attended schools along the way and performed well enough to be admitted to Phillips Academy in Andover, where his Harvard preparation featured the captaining of the baseball team, presidency of the Philomathean Society, and a short suspension for some now-hidden prank. Both the young man and his schoolmasters endured, however, and in 1872 the nineteen-year-old Moody was graduated and sent on to Harvard.

An extended line of Moodys from various branches of the family had preceeded William H. of the class of 1876. This young man's eventual emergence as the outstanding member of this group was not foreshadowed by his early years in Cambridge, however, for the measure of William Moody's early success came more from a .300 batting average than anything else. Catcher Moody captained the freshman team with a good deal of distinction, even if Theodore Roosevelt's later remarks to a group of Harvard athletes misrepresented the diamond skills of his Attorney General: "Moody was a great athlete at Harvard and played on the nine. But if he had been satisfied with that, do you suppose he would now be Attorney General of the United States? No, indeed; nothing disgusts me more than to see the way many college athletes drop out of sight after leaving college."

Moody, according to his class historian, only slowly warmed to academic life; his gradually developed intellectual interests fully emerged during the second half of his undergraduate career. In his last two years at Harvard much of his time was spent doing private tutoring and reading literature and history; his 1876 A.B. was *cum laude,* with honors in history and a ranking of third in the class. Years later the mature Moody won acknowledgment as a man of fine literary tastes who knew his Kipling, Balzac, Stevenson and Thackeray.

Immediately after graduation came a curiously brief encounter with Harvard Law School. Moody entered in September of 1876 and promptly left four months later. He apparently objected to the school rather than to the law, for he soon moved into Boston and attached himself as a law clerk and reader in the offices of the famous Richard Henry Dana, whose 1840 publication of *Two Years Before the Mast* had guaranteed for him a permanent place in American letters. Dana's literary inclinations were always secondary to his involvement in the law, however, and during the eighteen months which young Moody spent reading in his offices Dana was thoroughly embroiled in the pungent political atmosphere of the Great Barbecue. In 1876 General Grant had nominated Dana as United States Ambassador to the Court of St. James, but the politically inept President had done so without consulting with the chief potentates of the Republican party, and as a consequence, the Senate refused to consent to the appointment. A year later, as Moody became attached to the firm, Dana was serving as senior United States counsel in the vexatious fisheries conflict with Canada. By 1878, when Dana embarked on the world tour during which he unexpectedly died of pneumonia in Rome, Moody felt that the eighteen months spent in the great man's law offices had sufficiently prepared him for the oral examination which was then the only requirement for entrance to the Massachusetts bar.

An almost heroic legend surrounds William Moody's bar examination in 1878. Upon appearing before this board of august legal scholars young Moody was informed that it would be impossible to examine him since the eighteen months which he had spent in preparing for the examination was only half as long as the period which the bar traditionally required. The brash young man refused to be put off, according to all available reports, and insisted that he be heard. The Bar Commission relenting, Moody proceeded to perform so brilliantly that the committee immediately pronounced him the best prepared student in the history of the bar. At the time of Moody's appointment to the Supreme Court in 1906 one political writer, in looking back over the years, concluded that Moody's bar examination of 1878 had become the standard of excellence for the Massachusetts bar.

Soon after this success Moody left Boston as a qualified attorney and headed straight for Essex County to make his career. He purchased a large old yellow and white colonial home in the old Merrimac River town of Haverhill, about twenty miles east of his birthplace. Here he lived with his unmarried sister for the rest of his life. Haverhill lay astride the river nearly equidistant from Newburyport on the ocean and the booming industrial centers of Lawrence and Lowell to the southwest. The young Moody settled into the practice of law at a time when all of New England was enjoying the great industrial boom of the Gilded Age. Essex County's swelling and diversified economy spread southward from the industrial river towns on the New Hampshire border to the expanding suburbs of Boston, with chemical and paper and textile mills, the burgeoning shoe industry, the fishing fleets of Gloucester and the yacht squadrons of Marblehead, the proliferating interests of General Electric and the United Shoe Machinery Company, summer resorts on the North Shore and lumbering up-country. Moody's Haverhill law practice began rather inauspiciously amidst this boom, however, as one report indicated that his fees for the first month amounted to $6.85. This picture quickly changed as the smart and ambitious young lawyer entered into a succession of partnerships which involved him in the always lucrative practice of corporation law. Various clients through the 1880's included electric utilities, gas, telephone and paper interests, and a consolidation of the anarchic electric railway system which involved more than thirty eastern Massachusetts and Rhode Island lines. Within the decade of the '80's, Moody gradually identified himself as one of the foremost lawyers in the region.

During the same period the aspiring young man also established his credentials as a dedicated participant in civic affairs. Naturally enough, he became president of the Haverhill Baseball Club. For three years he served on the school board, and from 1888 until 1890 acted as city solicitor. The personal respect and professional esteem which William Moody attracted during these years made his formal entry into regional political life almost inevitable. Moody's political persuasion, as the phrase once went, was Republican, as suited a solidly Republican area of a solidly Republican state. But the Haverhill lawyer's brand of Republicanism was of the new progressive type which appeared more and more frequently on the local and state levels as the last decade of the nineteenth century wore on. Moody's political philosophy blended elements of stern Puritan morality with a growing awareness that the wrenching economic changes occasioned by America's industrial revolution demanded that political institutions assume new dimensions to guarantee honesty and equal economic opportunity for all men.

In 1890 William Moody took the first step toward the national prominence he would achieve a decade later. His activities in the courtroom had favorably impressed a number of influential members of the bar. Other men, particularly in Republican political circles, had also been attracted by Moody's professional competence and personal substance. Thus the appointment of Moody in 1890 to fill the important and politically sensitive position of District Attorney for the Eastern District of Massachusetts came as no real surprise. During his five years in the post Moody took full advantage of the opportunities which it afforded for bright young men with political ambitions. Always the master of fact and detail, Moody's prosecutions covered cases with great public appeal, especially the trial of a number of Lawrence aldermen for taking graft in return for granting liquor franchises. This type of indictment always brought out the fighter in Moody. He could not tolerate dishonesty among public officials and truly delighted in taking them into full public view in the courtroom. In this particular case, Moody brushed aside threats and bullying and succeded in landing five of the aldermen in jail.

Much more noteworthy was District Attorney Moody's participation in one of the most bizarre and sensational criminal cases in the state's history, that of Lizzie Borden, the thirty-two-year-old Fall River spinster who allegedly butchered her father and stepmother in 1892. Although this case lay outside of Moody's Eastern District, the Attorney General personally selected him as one of the state's two prosecutors, an unenviable task since the defendant attracted such popular emotional support during the nationally publicized trial in New Bedford. Convinced of Lizzie's guilt and unaffected by public hostility, Moody joined District Attorney Hosea M. Knowlton in an unsparing prosecution. Their cross-examinations and charges to the jury were reported verbatim across the country and, according to one observer, revealed Moody's "singularly accurate and concise diction," his "clear, forceful, and convincing analysis." In this kind of situation Moody just naturally attracted attention to himself by the aggressive carriage of his stocky and muscular appearance, his combative style, the snap and directness of his questions, the clarity and logic of his arguments. While the case ended predictably with Lizzie's acquittal, Moody nonetheless won great respect for his performance under difficult circumstances from influential men throughout the state. His lack of success in the celebrated Fall River hatchet murders in no way impeded the forty-year-old district attorney's political career. Indeed by 1895 his reputation was fixed as one of the brightest young men in Republican circles.

In October of 1895, Police Commissioner Theodore Roosevelt of New York City journeyed to Boston to address a Republican Club dinner and to acquaint himself with some of the younger protégés of Senator Henry Cabot Lodge. A few days later, Roosevelt reported back in glowing terms to Lodge of the men whom he had met, especially "that very good young fellow Moody.

. . ." Here was the beginning of an extremely close personal and political relationship which would exist between the future President and the man who would in time serve him so well in several significant capacities.

Moody's rise up the ladder to power and influence began scarcely a month after his first dinner meeting with Roosevelt with the special election called to fill the vacancy in Massachusetts' Sixth Congressional District caused by the sudden death of Congressman William Cogswell. The Sixth District included Essex County and, according to one contemporary political reporter, the Haverhill lawyer had become so popular by the time of Cogswell's death that the Republicans considered no other candidate for the special election of November, 1895. Moody won easily and thereby began an electoral career of impressive dimensions: in each of his four congressional campaigns he was returned with approximately seventy percent of the vote, and would generally limit his campaign expenditures to a modest amount of postage.

Although Moody's departure for Washington in late 1895 marked the end of his official connection with Massachusetts state politics, he nonetheless carefully preserved his political base. The congressman presided over the writing of the party platform at the state convention in 1896, and served as convention chairman two years later. Widely sought after as a stump speaker, Moody devoted large amounts of time and energy to the fortunes of scores of local and state party candidates throughout the dozen or so years of his national prominence. Despite this continued involvement in state political life, 1895 marked a decisive turning point in Moody's career: henceforth his major role would be played upon the national stage.

In November of 1895, when William Moody took his seat in the Fifty-fourth Congress, he began a tenure of six and one-half years during which his importance in the lower House increased steadily. By the time he resigned from the Fifty-seventh Congress on April 30, 1902, to become Theodore Roosevelt's Secretary of the Navy, Moody had become one of the House's most respected and influential members.

Moody's rise to prominence was more calculated than meteoric. As a freshman congressman he did not attempt to make himself immediately conspicuous but rather set out in his own cautious and thorough manner to learn the intricate workings of the legislative system and to study carefully the men with whom he would work. Consequently, he spent almost an entire summer mastering the rules of the House, after which he was never surpassed in parliamentary dispute.

The Massachusetts congressman made his first major impact in the House while he was serving on the House committee which substantiated election results and which thus passed on the eligibility of members to assume their seats. To this committee came a bitter dispute from the Sixteenth Illinois Congressional District, where the Democratic candidate had apparently achieved victory over his Republican opponent by about forty votes. The Republican-dominated Elections Committee refused to accept this verdict, however, and reported to the

House floor a majority decision which called for the seating of the Republican. Congressman Moody, his sense of propriety offended by the apparent breach of ethics, not only became the only Republican to vote with the Democratic minority in committee, but he also took the minority report out onto the floor and led a battle which resulted in the probably unprecedented action of a partisan House rebuffing the majority of a committee of the same political complexion. When a later recount in Illinois officially reversed the election results, Moody was as willing to support the Republican candidate as he had been to oppose him under different circumstances.

A clear indication of the respect and admiration which Moody quickly accumulated came at the beginning of his second term with his appointment to the all-important Appropriations Committee, where his work became especially valuable due to his absolute mastery of detail and intimate knowledge of every item in every appropriation. The party leadership fell into the habit of relying upon Moody to answer questions on matters of appropriations from the floor, and the Massachusetts congressman was able to perform flawlessly. In time Moody's abilities were recognized to the extent that by the turn of the century he had become one of the most noticeable of the young Republicans.

With the tumultuous accession of Theodore Roosevelt to the presidency in 1901, Congressman Moody's star could only rise. By this time Moody's influence was so apparent that when the powerful Speaker-to-be "Uncle Joe" Cannon stood in the way of Roosevelt's plans for a bountiful naval appropriation, the President instinctively turned to Moody. In writing to Senator Lodge on November 11, 1901, about means of overcoming Cannon's opposition, Roosevelt revealed that he counted heavily on Moody. "He is naturally with us," the President wrote, "and he has more influence with Cannon than anyone and if he backs the Naval Committee they will win easily."

The easy relationship between President and congressman had ripened and matured through the preceeding few years. The men had a great deal in common, and even bore such a striking physical resemblance to each other that on Moody's daily horseback rides in Washington's Rock Creek Park he was frequently mistaken for the President. They were both exponents of vigor and the strenuous life and, like the man who became his political mentor, Moody was apparently tireless, in Washington or in Massachusetts, in town or in the countryside, now hiking and riding, now holding forth in conversations marked by a snapping direct style, striding up and down, puffing constantly on a cigar. With each passing day of Roosevelt's Presidency the nearly inevitable addition of William Moody to the administration came ever closer, and when the new President began, after a decent interval, to replace some McKinley appointees Moody was among his first selections.

On May 1, 1902, less than eight months after Roosevelt assumed office, William Moody became Secretary of the Navy, a post he was to hold until his appointment as Attorney General two years later. At age forty-nine, Moody became the youngest member of the Cabinet, which was as much a reflection on the aged Cabinet which Roosevelt inherited from McKinley as it was an indication of Moody's youth.

This appointment originated from an agreeable combination of the new Secretary's obvious qualifications for a major administrative post and definite political exigencies which probably dictated the move. The President, concerned about the possible inferiority of the American Navy during a period of worldwide naval expansion, had obviously been impressed by Moody's style and abilities. In addition, Senator Lodge eagerly sponsored his Massachusetts Republican colleague for the job for purely political reasons. The aging incumbent Navy Secretary was John D. Long, under whom Roosevelt had served so restlessly during the hectic days immediately preceeding the Spanish-American War. Not only was Long no friend of Roosevelt's blustering Large Policy for American expansionism, he was also a political enemy of Lodge's as well. Although both men were Massachusetts Republicans, Long had successfully cut Lodge off from most Navy Department patronage. By easing Long out, the President succeeded in substituting a man who was both willing and able to implement the Large Policy, and was in addition a close friend of one of the most powerful men in the Senate. As the *pièce de résistance,* Moody's resignation from the House provided a vacancy in the Sixth Massachusetts Congressional District which would be most conveniently filled by Augustus P. Gardner who happened to be Senator Lodge's son-in-law.

These political intricacies notwithstanding, Moody's elevation held more significance for the Navy than for Massachusetts politics. His indisputable influence in the Congress resulted in an expansive appropriation of over $65,000,000 during the Secretary's brief two-year tenure. More importantly, Moody aided materially in plotting entirely new directions for American naval power. Naturally Roosevelt himself played the major role in directing the expansion and the many innovations which he felt were absolutely essential if the United States was to play the great power role which he so desired. Yet the relationship between Roosevelt and Moody was such that what might have been intolerable interference worked out rather as amicable partnership. During the summer of 1902, for instance, the two men worked together very closely in planning and carrying out the well-publicized squadron maneuvers which constituted a clear break with past American naval strategy which emphasized the movement and activity of single ships.

As the months went on and the President's suggestions flooded Moody's desk, the Secretary crisply and efficiently implemented a bewildering assortment of reforms. Why not grant advances in pay and rank for sharpshooters, Roosevelt asked. What about shooting competitions between ships? Even matters of Naval personnel detained the President: "It seems to me that both Captains Bradford and O'Neil should go to sea as soon as possible, . . ." he informed the Secretary. Gun sights should be improved. Prizes should be awarded for target shooting. In one characteristic note written in April of 1904, Roosevelt fired a barrage of questions:

What steps have you taken to secure good marksmanship among our cruisers? And are the battleships on the Asiatic Station doing as well as the battleships elsewhere in marksmanship? It is the cruisers that would have to do most against torpedo boats, and I am particularly anxious to know how they are doing with guns of six-inch calibre or less. [4 The Letters of Theodore Roosevelt, *ed. E. E. Morison (Cambridge, 1951–1954) 776. Hereafter cited as* Letters of T. R.]

Although Secretary Moody came to the Department with no technical knowledge of naval matters, his quick intelligence and instinctive feel for the post were soon evident. Always ready with answers for the naval buff in the White House, Moody also offered a number of significant administrative and strategic suggestions of his own. He abolished much of the Department's bureaucratic tangle through a decentralization process which diffused authority to the point where only the most significant matters came to his desk. As Moody wrote, in true Rooseveltian fashion: "Too much routine work overwhelms a man and unfits him for creative and active work. I believe in men."

Moody's contributions to the strategic aspects of naval power were manifested in a number of ways. While still in the House, Moody had supported Roosevelt's undisguised determination to make the United States predominant in the Western hemisphere. A few months before the President's successful "revolution" in Panama had secured the vital canal route, Congressman Moody, working with the President and realizing with him the strategic juxtaposition of eastern Cuba to Panama, fought for the establishment of a powerful United States Navy base on Guantanamo Bay. In the fall of 1901 Moody led a band of doubting congressmen to Cuba to inspect the Guantanamo site, an excursion which smoothed the way for the inclusion in the Platt Amendment of 1902 the demand for a ninety-nine year lease on Guantanamo which is still in effect. In general, Moody fully supported the aggressive and ambitious "Big Stick" policy which Roosevelt pursued throughout Latin America. On the other side of the globe, Secretary Moody took primary responsibility for the creation of the still powerful American naval base at Subic Bay in the Philippine Islands. Other Moody reforms included his successful battle for congressional approval to double the size of the midshipman corps at Annapolis. In addition, Moody established the first joint Army-Navy Board for purposes of military coordination.

Theodore Roosevelt expressed satisfaction with Moody's performance in his characteristically excessive fashion. "Until Moody took hold of the navy," Moody's successor was informed by the President, "there had never been any real attempt to develop the system needed for securing such efficiency in a great modern navy." To Senator Lodge the President trumpeted that "one of the best turns you ever did me was when you got me to appoint Moody in the Cabinet. . . . What a trump he is!" Even such a demanding taskmaster as Roosevelt freely admitted that Moody "has run the Navy Department as it must be run. . . . In my judgment, we have never had as good a Secretary of the Navy as Moody."

The personal compatibility of the two men grew apace during these years. Moody accompanied the President on most of Roosevelt's frenetic two-month tour of the West in April and May of 1903. Out they went through the bad lands of Dakota, on to Yosemite and Yellowstone and the Grand Canyon, making speeches, reuniting with Rough Riders everywhere, camping out after an ox roast over a roaring fire, riding in a Little Missouri roundup, on to St. Louis to open the fabled World's Fair and ride on the trolley car, down the Santa Fe trail with characters named Lippy Slim, Hell-Roarin' Bill Jones and Calamity Joe. Throughout the tour Roosevelt vividly described his adventures in a series of letters addressed to various friends and associates. From the West Coast on May 22 the President reported on the state of the political climate to Senator Lodge, and added the sentiment that "Moody has been a real comfort. I have grown to like and respect him more and more. He is one of the strong men in public life and a first class fellow to boot."

Theodore Roosevelt's totally favorable estimate insured Moody's political future. His next step upward came in June of 1904 with the death of Senator Matthew S. Quay, the crusty old Republican boss of Pennsylvania. When the Pennsylvania legislature appointed Attorney General Philander Knox to succeed Quay, the President acted immediately to fill the vacancy in his Cabinet: "Probably Knox will go at once," he informed War Secretary Elihu Root on June 14. "In that case I shall appoint Moody to succeed him." It came to pass, and on July 1, 1904, William Moody began another brief two-year stint in an exceptionally demanding office, for the Department of Justice continued to be a focal point for controversy during this the most vigorous period of Roosevelt's antitrust activities.

Despite the pressing nature of his new duties Moody kept his political fences in good repair. Stump speaking and highly charged political rhetoric flowed naturally from high administration officers in those days, and Moody certainly did his share throughout the national, state and local campaigns of 1904, 1905 and 1906. In between, in the tranquil moments that he snatched at home in Haverhill, the neighbors still came to the Attorney General's handsome yellow and white colonial house for advice. The local butcher who sold meat across the New Hampshire line and did not understand the new Meat Inspection Act had it explained to him by the Attorney General of the United States. In like fashion, a grizzled sea captain came to discuss a twenty-year-old seizure claim against the British. "Bill Moody," it was said in town, "is a big man." In more pragmatic terms, as Roosevelt wrote to Lodge on October 20, 1906, ". . . Moody has more influence than any other man in that district."

Moody's importance to the President assumed major proportions during these years. In Roosevelt's campaign for election in 1904, Moody joined William Howard Taft, Philander Knox, and Elihu Root as the President's closest political confidants. After the successful campaign, Roosevelt fell into the habit of consulting Moody on nearly all matters, regardless of their relevance to the Justice Department. As a consequence, the Attorney General confidently expressed himself on unions, conservation, tariffs, arbitration treaties and a great variety of legislative proposals.

Moody played one of his most important roles as presidential advisor in the successful fight in 1906 to enact the Hepburn Act. This legislation, designed to give the Interstate Commerce Commission the power to judge "reasonable" railroad rates, was of vital importance in resurrecting the commission after a series of Supreme Court decisions in the 1890's had rendered it moribund. Throughout the first six months of 1906, Moody worked constantly at Roosevelt's side, drafting amendments and using his influence on Capitol Hill as a furious battle raged with conservative senators who wished the bill to provide the courts with great latitude in reviewing I.C.C. decisions. Roosevelt and Moody favored a much narrower span of judicial review, but relented, and the final compromise, which became law as the Hepburn Act in June of 1906, left the question of the latitude of judicial review purposely vague. In subsequent years Supreme Court decisions (many during Moody's own tenure on the Court) did allow the I.C.C. to exercise broad regulatory powers, and the commission thus became one of the Progressive Era's major instruments of reform.

During Moody's tenure the Justice Department became the focal point in Roosevelt's well-publicized attempts at prosecuting evildoers. To this task the Attorney General brought his characteristic vigor and aggressiveness. He inaugurated the practice of dispatching Justice Department agents to participate in all cases throughout the country which involved the general welfare. In addition, he personally argued more cases than any of his predecessors. Wherever applicable, he employed criminal rather than civil law, especially in antitrust prosecutions.

In general, trusts and the railroads constituted the administration's major legal problems. The difficulties of coping with them in an adequate fashion were increased tremendously by the conservative cast of the federal judiciary, especially the Supreme Court, whose narrow constitutional interpretation denied that the federal government could possess any rights to legislate for the general good in matters of health and welfare, these rights being reserved for the several states.

Thus the Roosevelt Administration found it necessary to push modest reform measures which the courts would, it was hoped, approve. Such was the case with the Elkins Act of 1903, an amendment to the Interstate Commerce Act which authorized the I.C.C. to outlaw rebates. Under Moody's direct supervision, suits charging railroad rate discrimination were brought in half a dozen states. In Milwaukee, for example, the Justice Department proved that the Milwaukee Refrigerator Transit Company was in fact the private railroad of the Pabst Brewing Company, which received a twelve percent rebate on all its shipping. In New York City, the Attorney General secured indictments against all the major trunk lines, and later successfully proved that they competed with each other in granting rebates to the American Sugar Refining Company, the

Sugar Trust. In his two and one-half years in office, Moody obtained about fifty indictments under the Elkins Act, with resultant fines of perhaps $1,000,000.

Attacking the trusts proved to be far more complex. For one thing, the political credo of Theodore Roosevelt's New Nationalism made a distinction between "good" trusts and "bad" trusts. When Roosevelt's Department of Justice went out hunting the trusts, consequently, it sought only one species of giant combination. In addition, a series of Supreme Court decisions in the 1890's had virtually emasculated the Sherman Anti-Trust Act, leaving the determination of the act's applicability to a conservative Court whose decisions most frequently depended upon the social philosophy of extremely property-conscious Justices. The difficulties of effective antitrust prosecution were further deepened by the tremendous financial and political power of the giant corporations. In addition, the old liberal agrarian tradition of *laissez faire* government certainly expired very slowly. Despite these very different kinds of limitation, Moody utilized the Sherman Act as if it were in reality a vigorous reform tool. In so doing, he accumulated an impressive assortment of indictments, convictions, and fines—but accomplished relatively little in lessening restraint of trade.

Nearly the entire assemblage of monopolistic interests met Moody's opposition. Among them, at one time or another, were monopolies in tobacco, oil, lumber, fertilizer, elevators, groceries, paper, meat and drugs. One contemporary journalist claimed that Moody "pursued wrongdoers from the scenes of their defiant or secret misdeeds, in the phosphate fields of Florida to the mining camps of Alaska, from the oil wells of Ohio to the lumber yards of the Hawaiian Islands."

In his most famous case, Moody went to Chicago and personally prosecuted the Beef Trust, *Swift and Company* v. *United States,* 196 U.S. 375 (1905). The government had obtained an injunction against the trust by arguing that a combination of corporations and individuals, after purchasing livestock and converting it to fresh meat, sold products in interstate commerce in such a manner as to suppress competition both in livestock and in fresh meats. When the trust appealed the injunction in 1904, Moody argued and won a perpetual injunction; the unabashed meat packers merely ignored it. This rebuke of the law infuriated the volatile Attorney General. He instigated a grand jury investigation in Chicago which indicted all the major packers, and then took a train from Washington and arrived on the scene to prosecute them personally. The packers immediately pleaded their immunity from prosecution by arguing that they had voluntarily divulged to the government confidential information regarding their profits and business methods, and since this was the information upon which Moody had built his case, the defendants faced self-incrimination. Moody obliterated this seemingly plausible defense in a blistering six-hour address to the Court in which he heaped ridicule and sarcasm upon the unbowed heads of Messrs. Armour and Swift. The excitable prosecutor directly attacked the defendants' claims of self-incrimination by developing the concept of a metaphorical "immunity bath," wherein monopolists could visit the spa at Washington to cleanse themselves, avoiding punishment by voluntarily confessing their sins. "Instead of running away from a subpoena they will run toward the government agent and serve a confession on him," Moody sarcastically charged. Washington would become a great resort where all of the greatest of the lawbreakers would at intervals gather to obtain immunity. "I see Mr. Swift and Mr. Armour en route to Washington," thundered the Attorney General to the jury, "and meeting there other magnates who have been washed in this immunity bath."

As a result of Moody's victory in this case, which was probably the Roosevelt administration's second most notable antitrust accomplishment after the trail blazing *Northern Securities* case of 1902, *Minnesota* v. *Northern Securities Company,* 184 U.S. 199 (1902), the Supreme Court first formulated the so-called stream of commerce doctrine which held corporations chartered in one state to be responsible for all of their interstate commercial activities. And, although the meat packers were upheld in their pleas of immunity from criminal conviction, the vigor of Moody's prosecution, which received nation wide recognition, quickly resulted in congressional legislation which barred "immunity baths."

No attempt should be made, however, to overemphasize Moody's success. The Beef Trust quickly reorganized, and retained its monopolistic power. Standard Oil, prosecuted by Moody in 1906 and later "dissolved," has never lost its real control over the American petroleum industry. Similarly, the staying power of other giant combinations clearly indicates the relative modesty of the Square Deal's antitrust campaigns to rid the economy of "bad" trusts. Moody operated within this limited sphere, and thus his successes must be judged within the rather restricted objectives of the New Nationalism rather than on the basis of the kind of full antitrust commitment of a Robert LaFollette or of Woodrow Wilson's New Freedom theories.

Like the President's, Moody's moderate progressivism stemmed more from a sense of indignation at blatant lawlessness than from any desire to disrupt American capitalism. Capable of instant indignation, Moody quickly pounced upon such obvious legal travesties as the southern "peonage" system, which held large numbers of laborers (mostly Negroes) in legal bondage for debt; in 1905, after listening to Attorney General Moody's arguments, the Supreme Court declared this nefarious system to be unconstitutional, (*Clyatt* v. *United States* 197 U.S. 207 [1905].) Another vivid illustration of Moody's instinctive reaction to knavery occurred in January of 1905 when the Justice Department discovered that loopholes in the District of Columbia laws of incorporation were permitting gross abuses. On one day in January Moody informed Roosevelt that a single individual had secured the incorporation of no less than thirty-eight different corporations, all with the same set of trustees, and with an aggregate capital of $43,000,000. Roosevelt reacted in a predictably outraged manner: Moody was ordered to draft immediately legislation which the President could send to Congress within the week; on January 30 a bill reached Congress; one week later, with the Attorney General in attendance, the President signed the bill and the loophole was closed.

William Moody's thoughtful receptivity to the basic changes which industrialization produced in all aspects of American life can be detailed on other levels as well. In discussing the emergence of trade unionism in 1904 with the famous journalist Jacob Riis, Moody took a decidedly "advanced" position, one which delighted the progressive Riis. As Moody put it,

> *I don't agree with labor in all its demands. I think that it is unreasonable in some of them, or some of its representatives are. But in the main line it is eternally right, and it is only by owning it and helping it to its rights that we can successfully choke off the exorbitant demands.* [*Jacob Riis,* Theodore Roosevelt: The Citizen (*New York, 1904*) *376–377.*]

The facility with which Moody stated his philosophy on trade unionism suggests the ease with which he wore many hats in the administration. In these busy years he served as political advisor to the President on an infinite variety of domestic and foreign matters, participated as both intriguer and stump speaker in Massachusetts Republican politics, vigorously followed the strenuous life wherever his fortunes took him, busted trusts and prowled as the public's watchdog. Yet in spite of his position as "one of the dominant figures in our national life," to quote one contemporary reporter, Moody frequently longed for the peaceful solitude of Essex County. After spending much of the summer of 1906 in the welcome surroundings of Haverhill, Moody was reluctant to return to his hectic public life and, without warning, informed the President of his desire to retire. "Lord how I hate to have you go!" replied the master of Sagamore Hill on August 28 in a letter which also carried a request that Moody defer his announcement until after the November elections.

These intentions of 1906 did not, of course, materialize. Before the end of the year he had assumed his position on the Supreme Court, where he remained until felled by a crippling illness in 1908. Although Moody's tenure on the Court officially terminated on November 20, 1910, actually he was unable to discharge his responsibilities for nearly two years prior to that date. His brief moment on the High Court obviously prevented Moody from emerging as a major judicial figure; moreover, a relative scarcity of data nearly precludes any detailed analysis of his legal philosophy. In general terms, however, Mr. Justice Moody vindicated President Roosevelt's abiding faith in him. As Roosevelt informed William Allen White on November 30, 1908, "Moody is entirely our kind of judge. If they were all like him we would have no trouble." In shocking contrast, according to the President, stood Moody's colleague, the conservative Justice David J. Brewer, who was simply characterized as "unfit."

Roosevelt's preoccupation with the qualifications of his Supreme Court nominees represented more than the normal presidential interest in appointing men of merit who would, hopefully, reflect a congenial legal philosophy. At the outset of Roosevelt's presidency the political nature of Chief Justice Melville W. Fuller's Court was decidedly conservative. The Chief Justice and six of his colleagues, Justices Brewer, Rufus W. Peckham, Edward D. White, Horace Gray, George Shiras, Jr., and Henry B. Brown, defended property rights as stoutly as had any other panel of the Court throughout the late nineteenth century. Only Justices Joseph McKenna and John Marshall Harlan could be classified as liberal nationalists who generally supported the expansion of federal powers through a loose Hamiltonian interpretation of the Constitution. Roosevelt's determination to change the political complexion of the Court rested upon a clear definition of any candidate's basic legal approach. "I want on the bench a follower of Hamilton and Marshall and not a follower of Jefferson and Calhoun," he informed Senator Lodge just prior to Moody's appointment in 1906, "and what is more I do not want any man who from frivolity, or disinclination to think, or ignorance, or indifference to popular moods, goes wrong on great questions." By 1906 the ravages of age and health had permitted the President to replace two staunch conservatives, Justices Gray and Shiras, with the liberal nationalists Oliver Wendell Holmes and William R. Day. Thus the vacancy created by the retirement of Justice Brown in 1906 offered to Roosevelt the possibility of making an appointment which would tip the balance in favor of a theoretically "liberal" Court.

Initially, Roosevelt had not intended to name Moody as Brown's replacement. His first choice had been Horace H. Lurton, a Tennessee Democrat and former Confederate soldier who also happened to be an intimate friend of both William Howard Taft and Associate Justice Day. Not only did Taft and Day push hard for Lurton's appointment, they also convinced the President of the Tennesseean's "soundness" on race questions, regulation of corporations, and labor. Roosevelt, furthermore, appreciated fully the political implications inherent in the appointment of a man who identified himself as a "Cleveland Democrat," for the President expected such a "non-partisan" appointment to redound to his own benefit.

Eventually, the intensity of partisan opposition to Lurton combined with the President's own desire to keep Moody in public life to alter Roosevelt's plan. Senator Lodge and William Moody himself vehemently opposed the Lurton appointment. "I knew how strongly Moody felt about Lurton," Roosevelt wrote to Lodge on September 4, 1906, "[but] I did not know how you felt. I think you both are entirely in error." Lodge brushed aside Roosevelt's arguments in a return letter dated six days later: "I am glad that Lurton holds all the opinions that you say he does and that you are so familiar with his views . . . but I do not see why Republicans cannot be found who hold those opinions as well as Democrats." For Lodge, there was but one candidate for the Court, and that was Moody. As the Senator informed the President, "Nothing would give me greater pleasure than to see him on the bench."

Despite Senator Lodge's eager sponsorship, the appointment of Moody carried with it a number of political disadvantages. There was the traditional matter of geographical representation, for example, since Oliver Wendell Holmes already "represented" Massachusetts. Much more compelling, however, was the widespread notion that the combative Attorney General was "too radical." A few months previously, in fact, Moody had almost singlehandedly caused the stock market to dip seventy-two points in one week when he announced his intention of prosecuting Standard Oil. His known sympathies with Roosevelt's social and political philosophy, his exuberance in seeking out and prosecuting various trusts, and the general suspicion that the President desired to obtain judicial sanction for his political views by appointing compliant judges—all of these factors had to be disregarded in deciding on Moody's appointment. Within a few weeks, Roosevelt had disregarded all of them, and on December 17, 1906, William Henry Moody became the sixtieth man in the history of the Republic to sit on the Supreme Court.

Within a scant five-year period the bright young man from Essex County, had occupied positions of considerable importance in each of the three branches of the federal government. At the age of fifty-three, the youngest man on the Court, Moody had reached the pinnacle of his career in the prime of life, and years of notable achievement seemed to stretch out ahead.

Justice Moody never enjoyed the opportunity of exercising completely his considerable judicial talents. During the period of his tenure the Court disposed of over 4,500 cases, yet Moody participated in only about 1,000 of them, or less than twenty percent. He spoke for the Court in sixty-seven cases, including five dissents; concurred in 939; and dissented himself in thirteen. Nearly all of his activity was confined to the Court's 1907 and 1908 terms, for he was absent from the bench throughout most of 1909 and all of 1910 as an acute case of rheumatism seized and gradually crippled him.

Moody's legal philosophy, as far as it can be systematized, can best be described as a moderate liberal nationalism. He essentially agreed with the Hamilton-Marshall interpretation of the Constitution which emphasized the implied powers that the federal government might assume to deal with the great variety of new problems of twentieth century America.

One representative example of Moody's legal philosophy may be found in the dissent which he wrote in the *First Employers' Liability Case,* 207 U.S. 463 (1908). This case splintered the Court, which based its five to four decision holding the Federal Employers' Liability Act of 1906 unconstitutional on four bases. The terms of the act had made every common carrier engaged in interstate commerce liable for all injuries and deaths sustained by employees while on the job. Justice Edward D. White's majority opinion attacked the comprehensive implications of the act. White agreed that Congress could constitutionally legislate on the liability of interstate carriers. He objected, however, to the vagueness of the act which, he felt, would permit unconstitutional federal tampering with carriers and their employees who were engaged solely in intrastate commerce. White's fears of federal tampering with the police powers of the several states were fully accepted by Justice Day. The most conservative men on the Court, Chief Justice Fuller and Justices Peckham and Brewer, also aligned themselves with the White opinion, despite the fact that in their opinion, Congress possessed no rights whatsoever to regulate any form of employer liability. Justice Moody led the dissenters. Arguing also in behalf of John Marshall Harlan and Joseph

McKenna, Moody first admitted the plausibility of White's argument, but went on to argue that a totally different interpretation made more sense to him. Since Congress obviously possessed the constitutional power to regulate interstate commerce, Moody held, Congress logically might also regulate the relationship between employer and employee in matters concerning interstate commerce. Moody also agreed with the remaining dissenter, Justice Holmes, who simply held that a different reading of the statute allowed for its constitutionality. The distinction between majority and minority in this case lay between Justice White's jealous defense of states' rights through a strict interpretation, and Justice Moody's willingness to expand to a moderate degree the powers of the central government through a loose interpretation of constitutional prerogatives.

In a similar but more limited case, *St. Louis, Iron Mountain and Southern Railway Company* v. *Taylor,* 210 U.S. 281 (1908), Moody spoke for the Court in declaring constitutional the Safety Appliance Act of 1905. This piece of progressive legislation increased the liability of employers in certain cases for failing to provide safe materiel and conditions for their employees.

Moody's concurrence in a large number of relatively obscure opinions further indicates the liberal nationalist bent of his legal philosophy. He assented in a series of cases the net effect of which was to increase the regulatory authority of state governments. In *Waters-Pierce Oil Co.* v. *Texas,* 212 U.S. 86 (1909), the state was upheld in imposing fines of over $1,500,000 on a Texas branch of Standard Oil. Moody also agreed in upholding a New York State statute fixing maximum allowable utility rates in the case of *Willcox* v. *Consolidated Gas Co.,* 212 U.S. 19 (1909). In *Hudson County Water Co.* v. *McCarter,* 209 U.S. 349 (1908), Moody agreed with a New Jersey law that prohibited the transportation of water across state lines. Finally, in the case of *Asbell* v. *Kansas,* 209 U.S. 251 (1908), Moody endorsed a Kansas statute requiring the prior inspection of all livestock entering the state. In each of these cases as well as in a number of others, Justice Moody consistently supported the expansion of the police powers of state legislatures.

Simultaneously, Moody's voting pattern in a number of cases involving the police powers of the federal government also indicated his liberal nationalism. His dissent in the *First Employers' Liability Case, supra,* and concurrence in *St. Louis, Iron Mountain and Southern Railway Co.* v. *Taylor, supra,* clearly indicated his willingness to expand federal authority into areas where it was not specifically barred. In the case of *Continental Wall Paper Co.* v. *Voight,* 212 U.S. 227 (1909), Moody concurred in the Court's opinion that corporations entering into illegal combinations have no constitutional rights in seeking recovery for goods sold on credit to a constituent company. In *Williamson* v. *United States,* 207 U.S. 425 (1908), he upheld the right of the Congress to bar any member convicted of subornation of perjury. Moody also agreed that the owner of a book's copyright could not restrict retail sales by arbitrarily setting a price and prohibiting cheaper sales, *Bobbs-Merrill Co.* v. *Ruth Macy,* 210 U.S. 339 (1908).

Moody's espousal of liberal nationalism had its limits, however, and in a significant number of cases he adopted a very cautious approach regarding the proper limits of legislative police power. In *Ex parte Young,* 209 U.S. 123 (1908), for example, Moody aided in striking down a progressive Minnesota law regulating railroad rates which, in the Court's judgment, provided for such severe penalties for its violation that interested parties were prevented from testing its constitutionality. Moody again spoke in behalf of scrupulous impartiality rather than reform zeal in *Londoner* v. *Denver,* 210 U.S. 373 (1908). Here the Court held unconstitutional a Denver city law by which street assessments were set by the city council without the granting of a full hearing to the assessed property owners. The Court, speaking through Justice Moody, demanded that due notice and an opportunity for a hearing for property owners be made prerequisites for the assessment of taxes. As Moody stated, "a hearing, in its very essence, demands that he who is entitled to it shall have the right to support his allegations by argument, however brief; and if need be, by proof, however informal." Furthermore, Moody, who had so vigorously used the Sherman Anti-Trust Act against corporations while Attorney General, now agreed as the Court employed the act against trade unions. In *Loewe* v. *Lawlor,* 208 U.S. 274 (1908), Moody thus concurred as the Court held that the Sherman Act applied to labor boycotts against manufacturers most of whose goods were sold in interstate commerce.

Moody's display of judicious caution in the aforementioned cases coincided with the development on the Court of an increasing subjectivism by which the Justices' decisions were increasingly made on the subjective basis of what each man considered to be reasonable. Perhaps the best example of this form of judicial interpretation during Moody's tenure on the bench came in the case of *Willcox* v. *Consolidated Gas Co., supra,* when the Court decided that a return of six percent on investment constituted a "reasonable" profit for this New York City gas company. Mr. Justice Moody concurred.

Yet another level of Moody's moderation concerned those rights which were clearly reserved for the states. While he only infrequently agreed with his conservative colleagues, White, Brewer, Peckham and Chief Justice Fuller on matters of states' rights, Moody did from time to time recognize this interpretation. In *Tilt* v. *Kelsey,* 207 U.S. 43 (1907), for example, Moody spoke for the Court in declaring the sovereign authority of the individual states with respect to the settlement of the succession of property upon death. Even in his dissent in the *First Employers' Liability Case, supra,* in 1908, in fact, Moody had acknowledged the supremacy of the several states in regulating intrastate commerce.

Ironically, considering Moody's general acceptance of loose construction and his own political predilections, probably his most publicized decision while on the Court was based upon a very narrow interpretation of individual rights. In *Twining* v. *New Jersey,* 211 U.S. 78 (1908), the defendant, in the process of being convicted of a statutory crime, had refused to testify in his own behalf. The

New Jersey trial court had instructed the jury that they might draw from Twining's actions an unfavorable inference. Although the Court's instruction to the jury conformed perfectly to New Jersey law, the defendant appealed to the Supreme Court charging a violation of the Fourteenth Amendment, alleging a violation of the privileges of a United States citizen and also the deprivation of liberty without due process. In refusing this appeal, Moody spoke for the Court in words strongly suggestive of the doctrine of judicial restraint which later became synonymous with Justices Holmes and Felix Frankfurter. Moody, in refusing to deal with the substance of the appeal, stated sharply that "if the people of New Jersey are not content with the law as declared in repeated decisions of their courts, the remedy is in their own hands."

The foregoing analysis of Mr. Justice Moody's legal philosophy should, once again, be tinged with careful qualifiers. So short was Moody's time on the bench, and so limited were the number of issues upon which he passed, that the systematization which has emerged here must be considered at best embryonic. By identifying these indications of Moody's juridical approach, a tentative outline of his legal philosophy is possible.

In general, Moody's legal approach was careful and cautious but distinctly progressive in a liberal nationalist sense. His Puritan heritage produced the kind of integrity which insisted upon absolute impartiality before courts of law, and where he felt that progressive legislation had circumscribed due process for propertied interests, as in *Ex parte Young, supra,* and *Londoner* v. *Denver, supra,* his concern for fair play obliged him to hold these two reform attempts unconstitutional. Moody also gave indications of his opposition to judge-made law, which is significant since the Court was in the midst of a period where the social and economic philosophies of individual Justices frequently determined the acceptability of legislation. While Moody occasionally accepted this reasoning, as in *Willcox* v. *Consolidated Gas Co., supra,* he appears to have believed strongly that legislation should be left to the legislatures and most forcefully expressed this point of view in *Twining* v. *New Jersey, supra.* Only where compelling reasons of public health, welfare, or morals impinged, as in the famed 1908 case of *Muller* v. *Oregon,* 208 U.S. 412 (1908), was Moody convinced by the arguments of sociological jurisprudence.

Perhaps the anchor of Moody's liberal nationalism rests in those areas of uncharted jurisdiction between state and federal authority. Where lines of jurisdiction were not clearly drawn, Moody consistently supported the steady extension of federal police power. While still Attorney General, Moody had strongly supported this principle in *Kansas* v. *Colorado,* 206 U.S. 46 (1907), which involved the irrigation from the Arkansas River of arid land within the boundaries of the two states. Moody pressed for comprehensive federal rights in controlling the whole Arkansas River irrigation system, arguing that there existed a gap of sovereignty, each state being restricted to its own territory. Although the Court unanimously rejected the Attorney General's contention, Moody held fast to the idea. Years later, in 1910, while himself a member of the

Court, Moody drafted a memorandum based on the gap of sovereignty concept for ex-President Roosevelt. Roosevelt, who had the natural ability of making all issues more controversial than they sometimes were, used Moody's material in a well-publicized speech in Denver on August 29, 1910, in which he excoriated the Supreme Court's decisions in the *Knight* and *Lochner* cases, *United States* v. *E. C. Knight Co.,* 156 U.S. 1 (1895); *Lochner* v. *New York,* 198 U.S. 45 (1905). Each of these cases, both Roosevelt and Moody believed, had created neutral ground in which neither state nor federal authority could function, thereby providing a vacuum for lawlessness, a haven where expert legal talent could lead men of great wealth. Roosevelt's position in this speech resulted directly from Moody's thinking on the matter. As the former President assured Lodge on September 12, 1910:

> *My point was to show by the use of these two decisions, which decisions were given me by Moody when he called my attention to the point as one which he would like to make, that the Courts not only sometimes erred in deciding against the National Government, but sometimes erred against states' rights, and thereby created a neutral ground in which no governmental body had any power.* [6 Letters of T. R. *123*.]

Moody's advice for Roosevelt's Denver speech indicated the continuation of the close relationship between the two men during these years. In an earlier controversial address, in September of 1907, while Roosevelt was still in the White House, a St. Louis audience heard the President call for federal regulation of all industrial corporations engaged in interstate business. Here again, Moody had provided the constitutional basis for Roosevelt's remarks, and in his letter of September 21 to the Justice the President referred to it as "*your* speech" (original emphasis). In November of 1908, as Roosevelt prepared his last State of the Union Message, he elicited suggestions from his friend Moody. During the same year Moody, along with the United States Navy's illustrious Alfred Thayer Mahan, served as co-chairman of a committee which drafted a plan calling for a total restructuring of the Navy which was later approved by President Taft.

Thus life in the nation's capitol seemed to go on as usual for William Moody. He worked hard and remained at the center of the government's activities. He enjoyed his friends and managed to catch a baseball game now and then. He exercised frequently on foot, horseback, and bicycle and in his mid-fifties he even took up golf.

William Moody's affliction came slowly at first, then with violent suddenness. Acute rheumatism expanded through his body, gradually disabling his muscles and joints, depleting his strength, sapping his energy, withering his powerful physique. Treated unsuccessfully first in Washington and later at a clinic in New York, by 1909 Moody had come home to Essex County for the last time. In October of that year both President Taft and Senator Lodge travelled to Haverhill for what must have been very difficult visits. Both men had known Moody intimately through the years when he lived each day with such gusto. And now, as Lodge wrote to Roosevelt, their friend would never again get out of bed and seemed but a shell of his former self after losing seventy-five pounds.

By this time there remained no question of Moody's ever returning to any form of active life. Shortly thereafter the Congress passed a bill conferring upon him special retirement benefits, and on November 10, 1910, William Henry Moody's public career came to an official end with his formal retirement from the Supreme Court. Theodore Roosevelt commemorated the occasion in a eulogistic *Outlook* article in which he characterized Moody's retirement as "a tragedy [from] the private and a real calamity from the public standpoint." Had Moody been able to remain on the Court, Roosevelt assured his readers, "he would have rendered such service as hardly any other man now in public life can hope to render." To Lodge the former President wrote of Moody: "How I wish he were Chief Justice!"

William Moody lived on as a semi-invalid for another seven years. Denied the use of his limbs and unable even to hold a pen or book, with the constant aid of his sister he was able to retain some of his lifelong interests. "I read a great deal about public affairs," his 1916 letter to his Harvard classmates noted, "all the decisions of the Supreme Court as they are delivered, much history, biography, and other literature. Or rather, all these things are read to me, for I can neither read nor write myself."

Death arrived silently in Haverhill one hour past midnight on the warm summer's night of July 1–2, 1917. Excitement had been running through the town for the last twenty-four hours with the news that Pershing's American Expeditionary Force had landed in France. The landing, the war, the America of Woodrow Wilson—all were indicative of the degrees to which the United States had changed since Moody's time of power. Not only did the Democrats control Washington, but events and the passage of time had even reduced Theodore Roosevelt to a carping caricature of his former self. Now, with Moody's death, Haverhill paused for a moment to pay respects to an old and honored friend. On July 6 services were held in the parlor of the venerable family home. Former President Taft and his wife stood near the casket, along with Chief Justice Edward D. White and Oliver Wendell Holmes. Eight Navy petty officers from Portsmouth fired their salutes and later accompanied the body to the family plot at Newburyport. After sixty-four years life had come full circle for William Henry Moody in the late afternoon of that mellow summer's day in Essex County. And history began its inexorable process of hiding away the vitality of the past.

SELECTED BIBLIOGRAPHY

The life of William Moody merits a biography, for which sufficient archival and secondary sources are available. The Moody manuscripts at the Library of Congress consist of sixteen volumes, and there is also a small Moody collection housed in the Haverhill Historical Society. Much of the material for this essay came from the two very valuable printed collections of Theodore Roosevelt's letters: Elting Morison, ed., *The Letters of Theodore Roosevelt,* 8 vols. (Cambridge, 1951–54); and *Selections from the Correspondence of Theodore Roosevelt and Henry Cabot Lodge, 1884–1918,* 2 vols. (New York, 1925). On Moody's early life, see *Representative Men of Massachusetts, 1890–1900* (Everett, Mass., 1898), 154–156; 14 *National Cyclopaedia of American Biography* 21 (New York, 1910). Moody was constantly in the popular press; see especially "Men We are Watching," 66 *Independent* 1564 (1906); L. A. Coolidge, "The New Secretary of the Navy," 54 *Independent* 744 (1902); Isaac F. Marcosson, "Attorney General Moody and His Work," 13 *World's Work* 8140 (1906). On his brief Court career, see 21 *Green Bag* 263 (1909); and 14 *Law Notes* 106 (1910), a harsh review of Moody's public career. On his melancholy later years, see 26 *Harvard Graduates' Magazine* 39 (1917–1918) and *The New York Times,* July 5, 6, 1917.

William Moody

REPRESENTATIVE OPINIONS

ST. LOUIS AND IRON MOUNTAIN RAILWAY v. TAYLOR, 210 U.S. 281 (1908)

This case decided the constitutionality of a typical progressive law, the Safety Appliance Act of 1905. In broadest focus, this act increased the liability of employers who failed to provide certain safety equipment. Justice Moody's opinion for a unanimous Court upheld the Safety Appliance Act's constitutionality, and in addition indicated Moody's liberal nationalism. To the defendant's charge that the act constituted an illegal delegation of legislative powers to the Interstate Commerce Commission, Moody flatly stated that "this is clearly a federal question," and not subject to interpretation. He later added that "jurisdiction so clearly warranted by the Constitution and so explicitly conferred by the act of Congress needs no justification." Only by congressional action in regulating all aspects of interstate commerce, Moody argued, "can a uniform construction of the statute laws of the United States be secured, so that they shall have the same meaning and effect in all the States of the Union," 210 U.S. at 293.

MR. JUSTICE MOODY delivered the opinion of the court.

The defendant in error, as administratrix of George W. Taylor, brought, in the Circuit Court of the State of Arkansas, this action at law against the plaintiff in error, a corporation owning and operating a railroad. Damages were sought, for the benefit of Taylor's widow and next of kin, on account of his injury and death in the course of his employment as brakeman in the service of the railroad. It was alleged in the complaint that Taylor, while attempting, in the discharge of his duty, to couple two cars was caught between them and killed. The right to recover for the death was based solely on the failure of the defendant to equip the two cars which were to be coupled with such draw bars as were required by the act of Congress known as the Safety Appliance Law. Act of March 2, 1893, c. 196, 27 Stat. 531. The defendant's answer denied that the cars were improperly equipped with draw bars, and alleged that Taylor's death was the result of his own negligence. At a trial before a jury upon the issues made by the pleadings there was a verdict for the plaintiff, which was affirmed in a majority opinion by the Supreme Court of the State. The judgment of that court is brought here for reexamination by writ of error. The writ sets forth many assignments of error, but of them four only were relied upon in argument here, and they alone need be stated and considered. It is not, and cannot be, disputed that the questions raised by the errors assigned were seasonably and properly made in the court below, so as to give this court jurisdiction to consider them; so no time need be spent on that. But the defendant in error insists that the questions themselves, though properly here in form, are not Federal questions; that is to say, not questions which we by law are authorized to consider on a writ of error to a state court. For that reason it is contended that the writ should be dismissed. That contention we will consider with each question as it is discussed.

The accident by which the plaintiff's intestate lost his life occurred in the Indian Territory, where, contrary to the doctrine of the common law, a right of action for death exists. The cause of action arose under the laws of the Territory, and was enforced in the courts of Arkansas. The plaintiff in error contends that of such a cause, triable as it was in the courts of the Territory created by Congress, the courts of Arkansas have no jurisdiction. This contention does not present a Federal question. Each State may, subject to the restrictions of the Federal Constitution, determine the limits of the jurisdiction of its courts, the character of the controversies which shall be heard in them, and specifically how far it will, having jurisdiction of the parties, entertain in its courts transitory actions where the cause of action has arisen outside its borders. *Chambers* v. *Baltimore & Ohio R. R.,* 207 U.S. 142. We have, therefore, no authority to review the decision of the state court, so far as it holds that there was jurisdiction to hear and determine this case. On that question the decision of that court is final.

The next question presented requires an examination of the act of Congress, upon which the plaintiff below rested her right to recover. Section 5 of the Safety Appliance Law is as follows, 27 Stat. 531:

"Within ninety days from the passage of this act the American Railway Association is authorized hereby to designate to the Interstate Commerce Commission the standard height of draw bars for freight cars, measured perpendicular from the level of the tops of the rails to the centers of the draw bars, for each of the several gauges of railroads in use in the United States, and shall fix a maximum variation from such standard height to be allowed between the draw bars of empty and loaded cars. Upon their determination being certified to the Interstate Commerce Commission, said Commission shall at once give notice of the standard fixed upon to all common carriers, owners or lessees engaged in interstate commerce in the United States by such means as the Commission may deem proper. But should said association fail to determine a standard as above provided, it shall be the duty of the Interstate Commerce Commission to do so before July first, eighteen hundred and ninety-four, and immediately to give notice thereof as aforesaid. And after July first, eighteen hundred and ninety-five, no cars, either loaded or unloaded, shall be used in interstate traffic which do not comply with the standard above provided for."

The action taken in compliance with this law by the American Railway Association, which was duly certified to and promulgated by the Interstate Commerce Commission, was contained in the following resolution, June 6, 1893—Int. Com. Comm. Rep. for 1893, pp. 74, 263:

"Resolved, that the standard height of draw bars for freight cars, measured perpendicular from the level of the tops of the rails to the centers of the draw bars, for standard guage railroads in the United States, shall be thirty-four and one-half inches, and the maximum variation from such standard heights to be allowed between the draw bars of empty and loaded cars shall be three inches.

"Resolved, that the standard height of draw bars for freight cars, measured perpendicular from the level of the tops of the rails to the centers of the draw bars, for the narrow gauge railroads in the United States, shall be twenty-six inches, and the maximum variation from such standard height to be allowed between the draw bars of empty and loaded cars shall be three inches."

It is contended that there is here an unconstitutional delegation of legislative power to the Railway Association and to the Interstate Commerce Commission. This is clearly a Federal question. Briefly stated, the statute enacted that after a date named only cars with draw bars of uniform height should be used in interstate commerce, and that the standard should be fixed by the

Association and declared by the Commission. Nothing need be said upon this question except that it was settled adversely to the contention of the plaintiff in error in *Buttfield* v. *Stranahan*, 192 U.S. 470, a case which in principle is completely in point. And see *Union Bridge Co.* v. *United States*, 204 U.S. 364, where the cases were reviewed.

Before proceeding with the consideration of the third assignment of error, which arises out of the charge, it will be necessary to set forth the course of the trial and the state of the evidence when the cause came to be submitted to the jury. This is done, not for the purpose of retrying questions of fact, which we may not do, but first to see whether the question raised was of a Federal nature, and second, to see whether error was committed in the decision of it. Taylor was a brakeman on a freight train, which had stopped at a station for the purpose of leaving there two cars which were in the middle of the train. When this was done the train was left in two parts, the engine and several cars attached making one section and the caboose with several cars attached making the other. The caboose and its cars remained stationary, and the cars attached to the engine were "kicked" back to make the coupling. One of the cars to be coupled had an automatic coupler and the other an old-fashioned link and pin coupler. That part of the law which requires automatic couplers on all cars was not then in force. In attempting to make the coupling Taylor went between the cars and was killed. The cars were "kicked" with such force that the impact considerably injured those immediately in contact and derailed one of them. One of the cars to be coupled (that with the automatic coupler) was fully and the other lightly loaded. The testimony on both sides tended to show that there was some difference in the height of the draw bars of these two cars, as they rested on the tracks in their loaded condition, but there was no testimony as to the height of the draw bars if the cars were unloaded, except that, as originally made some years before, they were both of standard height. But as to the extent of the difference in the height of the draw bars, as the cars were being used at the time of the accident, there was a conflict in the testimony. One witness called by the plaintiff testified that the automatic coupler appeared to be about four inches lower than the link and pin coupler. Although another, called also by the plaintiff, testified that the automatic coupler was one to three inches higher than the other. That the automatic coupler was the lower is shown by the marks left upon it by the contact, which indicated that it had been overriden by the link and pin coupler, and was testified to by a witness who made up the train at its starting point. Two witnesses called by the defendant testified to actual measurements made soon after the accident, which showed that the center of the draw bar of the automatic coupler was thirty-two and one-half inches from the top of the rail, and that of the link and pin coupler thirty-three and one-half inches from the top of the rail. The evidence therefore, in its aspect most favorable to the plaintiff, tended to show that the fully loaded car was equipped with an automatic coupler, which at the time was four inches lower than the link and pin coupler of the lightly loaded car. On the other hand, the evidence in its aspect most favorable to the defendant tended to show that the automatic draw bar of the loaded car was exactly one inch lower than the link and pin draw bar. It was the duty of the jury to pass upon this conflicting evidence, and it was the duty of the presiding judge to instruct the jury clearly as to the duty imposed upon the defendant by the act of Congress. Before passing to the consideration of the charge to the jury we will for ourselves determine the meaning of that act. We think that it requires that the center of the draw bars of freight cars used on standard gauge railroads shall be, when the cars are empty, thirty-four and one-half inches above the level of the tops of the rails; that it permits, when a car is partly or fully loaded, a variation in the height downward, in no case to exceed three inches; that it does not require that the variation shall be in proportion to the load, nor that a fully loaded car shall exhaust the full three inches of the maximum permissible variation and bring its draw bars down to the height of thirty-one and one-half inches above the rails. If a car, when unloaded, has its draw bars thirty-four and one-half inches above the rails, and, in any stage of loading, does not lower its draw bars more than three inches, it complies with the requirements of the law. If, when unloaded, its draw bars are of greater or less height than the standard prescribed by the law, or if, when wholly or partially loaded, its draw bars are lowered more than the maximum variation permitted, the car does not comply with the requirements of the law. On this aspect of the case the presiding judge gave certain instructions and refused certain instructions, both under the exception of the defendant. The jury were instructed, the italics being ours:

"I. The act of Congress fixes the standard height of loaded cars engaged in interstate commerce on standard gauge railroads at thirty-one and one-half inches, and unloaded cars at thirty-four and one-half inches measured perpendicularly from the level of the face of the rails to the centers of the draw bars, and this variation of three inches in height is intended to allow for the difference in height caused by loading the car to the full capacity, or by loading it partially, or by its being carried in the train when it is empty. Now, the law required that the two cars between which Taylor lost his life should be when unloaded of the equal and uniform height from the level of the face of the rails to the center of the draw bars of thirty-four and one-half inches, *and when loaded to the full capacity should be of the uniform height of thirty-one and one-half inches. Now, if the plaintiff by a preponderance of the evidence shows a violation of this duty on part of defendant, then this is negligence,* and if the proof by a preponderance also shows that this caused or contributed to the death of Taylor, then you should find for the plaintiff, unless it appears by a preponderance of the evidence that Taylor was wanting in ordinary care for his own safety, and that this want of care on Taylor's part for his own safety caused or contributed to the injury and death sued for, in which latter case you should find for the defendant.

"II. *If there was the difference between the height of the center of the draw bars in the two cars in question, as indicated in the first instruction,* then the question arises whether this difference caused or contributed to the injury and death of Taylor sued for. On that point if such difference existed, and but for its existence the injury and death of Taylor would not have happened, then such difference is said in law to be an efficient proximate cause of Taylor's injury and death, although it may be true that other causes may have coöperated with this one in producing the injury and death of Taylor, and but for these other coöperating causes the injury and death of Taylor would not have ensued. But if such difference in height of the center of the draw bars as aforesaid actually existed, yet if the injury and death of Taylor would have ensued just the same as it did without the existence of such difference in height of the center of the draw bars, then such difference in the height of the center of the draw bars is not in law an efficient proximate cause of the injury and death of Taylor."

The clear intendment of these instructions was that the law required that the draw bars of a fully loaded car should be of the height of thirty-one and one-half inches, and that if either of the cars varied from this requirement the defendant had failed in the performance of its duty. We find nothing in the remainder of the charge which qualifies this instruction, and we think it was erroneous. We should be reluctant to insist upon mere academic accuracy of instructions to a jury. But how vitally this error affected the defendant is demonstrated by the fact that its own evidence showed that the draw bar of the fully loaded car was thirty-two and one-half inches in height. Under these instructions the plaintiff was permitted to recover on proof of this fact alone. From such proof a verdict for the plaintiff would logically follow. The error of the charge was emphasized by the refusal to instruct the jury, as requested by the defendant, "that when one car is fully loaded and another car in the same train is only partially loaded, the law allows a variation of full three inches between the center of the draw bars of such cars, without regard to the amount of weight in the partially loaded car." This request, taken in connection with the instruction that the draw bars of unloaded cars should be of the height prescribed by the act, expressed the true rule, and should have been given. On the other hand, a request for instructions, which was as follows, "The court charges you that the act of Congress allows a variation in height of three inches between the centers of the draw bars of all cars used in interstate commerce, regardless of whether they are loaded or empty, the measurement of such height to be made perpendicularly from the top of the rail to the center of the draw bar shank or draft line," contained an erroneous expression of the law, and was correctly refused. It is based upon the theory that the height of the draw bars of unloaded cars may vary three inches, while the act, as we have said, requires that the height of the draw bars of unloaded cars shall be uniform.

But we have not the power to correct mere errors in the trials in state courts, although affirmed by the highest state courts. This court is not a general court of appeals, with the general right to review the decisions of state courts. We may only inquire whether there has been error committed in the decision of those Federal questions which are set forth in § 709 of the Revised Statutes, and it is strenuously urged that the error in this part of the case was not in the decision of any such Federal question. That position we proceed to examine.

The judicial power of the United States extends "to all cases, in law and equity, arising under this Constitution, the laws of the United States, and treaties made, or which shall be made, under their authority." Article III, § 2, Constitution. The case at bar, where the right of action was based solely upon an act of Congress, assuredly was a case "arising under . . . the laws of the United States." It was settled, once for all time, in *Cohens* v. *Virginia,* 6 Wheat. 264, that the appellate jurisdiction, authorized by the Constitution to be exercised by this court, warrants it in reviewing the judgments of state courts so far as they pass upon a law of the United States. It was said in that case (p. 416): "They [the words of the Constitution] give to the Supreme Court appellate jurisdiction in all cases arising under the Constitution, laws, and treaties of the United States. The words are broad enough to comprehend all cases of this description, in whatever court they may be decided;" and it was further said (p. 379): "A case in law or equity consists of the right of the one party, as well as of the other, and may truly be said to arise under the Constitution or a law of the United States, whenever its correct decision depends on the construction of either." But the appellante jurisdiction of this court must be exercised "with such exceptions and under such regulations as the Congress shall make." Article III, § 4, Constitution. Congress has regulated and limited the appellante jurisdiction of this court over the state courts by § 709 of the Revised Statutes, and our jurisdiction in this respect extends only to the cases there enumerated, even though a wider jurisdiction might be permitted by the constitutional grant of power. *Murdock* v. *Memphis,* 20 Wall. 590, 620. The words of that section material here are those authorizing this court to reëxamine the judgments of the state courts "where any title, right, privilege, or immunity is claimed under . . . any statute of . . . the United States, and the decision is against the title, right, privilege, or immunity specially set up or claimed under such . . . statute." There can be no doubt that the claim made here was specifically set up, claimed, and denied in the state courts. The question, therefore, precisely stated, is whether it was a claim of a right or immunity under a statute of the United States. Recent decisions of this court remove all doubt from the answer to this question. *McCormick* v. *Market Bank,* 165 U.S. 538; *California Bank* v. *Kennedy,* 167 U.S. 362; *San José Land and Water Co.* v. *San José Ranch Co.,* 189 U.S. 177; *Nutt* v. *Knut,* 200 U.S. 12; *Rector* v. *City Deposit Bank,* 200 U.S. 405; *Illinois Central Railroad* v. *McKendree,* 203 U.S. 514; *Eau Claire National Bank* v. *Jackman,* 204 U.S. 522; *Hammond* v. *Whittredge,* 204 U.S. 538. The principles to be derived from the cases are these: Where a party to litigation in a state court insists, by way of objection to or requests for instructions, upon a construction of a statute of the United States which will lead, or, on possible findings of fact from the evidence may lead, to a judgment in his favor, and his claim in this respect, being duly set up, is denied by the highest court of the State, then the question thus raised may be reviewed in this court. The plain reason is that in all such cases he has claimed in the state court a right or immunity under a law of the United States and it has been denied to him. Jurisdiction so clearly warranted by the Constitution and so explicitly conferred by the act of Congress needs no justification. But it may not be out of place to say that in no other manner can a uniform construction of the statute laws of the United States be secured, so that they shall have the same meaning and effect in all the States of the Union.

It is clear that these principles govern the case at bar. The defendant, now plaintiff in error, objected to an erroneous construction of the Safety Appliance Act, which warranted on the evidence of a judgment against it, and insisted upon a correct construction of the act, which warranted on the evidence a judgment in its favor. The denials of its claims were decisions of Federal questions reviewable here.

The plaintiff in error raises another question, which, for the reasons already given, we think is of a Federal nature. The evidence showed that draw bars which, as originally constructed, are of standard height, are lowered by the natural effect of proper use; that, in addition to the correction of this tendency by general repair, devices called shims, which are metallic wedges of different thickness, are employed to raise the lowered draw bar to the legal standard; and that in the caboose of this train the railroad furnished a sufficient supply of these shims, which it was the duty of the conductor or brakeman to use as occasion demanded. On this state of the evidence the defendant was refused instructions, in substance, that if the defendant furnished cars which were constructed with draw bars of a standard height, and furnished shims to competent inspectors and trainmen and used reasonable care to keep the draw bars at a reasonable height, it had complied with its statutory duty, and, if the lowering of the draw bar resulted from the failure to use the shims, that was the negligence of a fellow servant, for which the defendant was not responsible. In deciding the questions thus raised, upon which the courts have differed (*St. Louis & S. F. Ry.* v. *Delk,* 158 Fed. Rep. 931), we need not enter into the wilderness of cases upon the common law duty of the employer to use reasonable care to furnish his employé reasonably safe tools, machinery and appliances, or consider when and how far that duty may be performed by delegating it to suitable persons for whose default the employer is not responsible. In the case before us the liability of the defendant does not grow out of the common law duty of master to servant. The Congress, not satisfied with the common law duty and its resulting liability, has prescribed and defined the duty by statute. We have nothing to do but to ascertain and declare the meaning of a few simple words in which the duty is described. It is enacted that "no cars, either loaded or unloaded, shall be used in interstate traffic which do not comply with the standard." There is no escape from the meaning of these words. Explanation cannot clarify them, and ought not to be employed to confuse them or lessen their significance. The obvious purpose of the legislature was to supplant the qualified duty of the common law with an absolute duty deemed by it more just. If the railroad does, in point of fact, use cars which do not comply with the standard, it violates the plain prohibitions of the law, and there arises from that violation the liability to make compensation to one who is injured by it. It is urged that this is a harsh construction. To this we reply that, if it be the true construction, its harshness is no concern of the courts. They have no responsibility for the justice or wisdom of legislation, and no duty except to enforce the law as it is written, unless it is clearly beyond the constitutional power of the lawmaking body. It is said that the liability under the statute, as thus construed, imposes so great a hardship upon the railroads that it ought not to be supposed that Congress intended it. Certainly the statute ought not to be given an absurd or utterly unreasonable interpretation leading to hardship and injustice, if any other interpretation is reasonably possible. But this argument is a dangerous one, and never should be heeded where the hardship would be occasional and exceptional. It would be better, it was once said by Lord Eldon, to look hardship in the face than break down the rules of law. But when applied to the case at bar the argument of hardship is plausible only when the attention is directed to the material interest of the employer to the exclusion of the interests of the employé and of the public. Where an injury happens through the absence of a safe draw bar there must be hardship. Such an injury must be an irreparable misfortune to some one. If it must be borne entirely by him who suffers it, that is a hardship to him. If its burden is transferred, as far as it is capable of transfer, to the employer, it is a hardship to him. It is quite conceivable that Congress, contemplating the inevitable hardship of such injuries, and hoping to diminish the economic loss to the community resulting from them, should deem it wise to impose their burdens upon those who could measurably control their causes, instead of upon those who are in the main helpless in that regard. Such a policy would be intelligible, and, to say the least, not so unreasonable as to require us to doubt that it was intended, and to seek some unnatural interpretation of common words. We see no error in this part of the case. But for the reasons before given the judgment must be

Reversed.

FIRST EMPLOYERS' LIABILITY CASE, 207 U.S. 463 (1908)

In 1906 the Congress passed the Employers' Liability Act, a piece of progressive legislation which made every common carrier engaged in interstate commerce liable for all injuries and deaths sustained by employees while on the job. A case testing this act came to the Supreme Court two years later and produced widely divergent opinions in a five to four decision which declared the act to be unconstitutional on technical as well as substantive grounds. Justice Moody's dissenting opinion, with which three of his colleagues associated themselves, emphasized that the powers of Congress to regulate all interstate commerce extended to the relationship between all employers and employees who were involved in that commerce. This opinion reflected Moody's willingness to interpret the Constitution broadly in relation to congressional regulatory powers.

MR. JUSTICE MOODY, dissenting.

I am unable to agree in the judgment of the court. Under ordinary circumstances, where the judgment rests exclusively, as it does here, upon a mere interpretation of the words of a law, which may be readily changed by the lawmaking branches of the Government, if they be so minded, a difference of opinion may well be left without expression. But where the judgment is a judicial condemnation of an act of a coördinate branch of our Government it is so grave a step that no member of the court can escape his own responsibility, or be justified in suppressing his own views, if unhappily they have not found expression in those of his associates. Moved by this consideration, and solicitous to maintain what seem to me the lawful powers of the Nation, I have no doubt of my duty to disclose fully the opinions which, to my regret, differ in some respects from those of some of my brethren.

The only question which these cases present is the constitutionality of the Employers' Liability Act, which, briefly stated, provides a remedy for the injury or death of the employés of territorial, interstate and foreign common carriers, caused by the negligence of the carrier. The defendants were both interstate carriers, and these actions were brought to recover for the deaths of their employés who, at the time, were engaged in interstate transportation. The judgment of the court does not deny that it is within the power of the Congress to provide a remedy for the injury or death of employés engaged in the conduct of territorial, interstate and foreign commerce. It rests upon the ground that this statute is unconstitutional, because it seeks to do more than that, and regulates the liability of employers while engaged in intrastate commerce or in manufacture. At the threshold I may say that I agree that the Congress has not the power directly to regulate the purely internal commerce of the States, and that I understand that to be the opinion of every member of the court.

The constitutionality of the act was attacked in the arguments before us upon three grounds. First, because it seeks to control by provisions so inseparable that they are incapable of resolution into their several parts, not only the territorial, foreign and interstate business of carriers, but also their intrastate business, which, by the Constitution, is reserved for the government of the States. Second, because, if the act should be interpreted as not intruding upon the domain of the States by directly regulating commerce exclusively within the States, yet, that legislation fixing the obligation of employers engaged in interstate and foreign commerce to their employés in such commerce, for injuries suffered by the latter in the course of the employment, is not the regulation of commerce, and, therefore, is not within any power conferred by the Constitution upon Congress. Third, because, even if the act is concerned with a subject which is within the power of Congress, yet the specific changes made by it in the common law rules governing the relations of employer and employé exceed the legislative power or violate the constitutional prohibitions which restrict that power.

I am of opinion that the act is not open to any of the constitutional objections urged against it, and shall consider all of the objections in the order in which I have stated them.

In the consideration of the scope of the statute for the purpose of determining whether it seeks to control that part of commerce which is beyond the power of Congress and subject only to the government of the States, it is to be observed that the opening words of Congress are in recognition of the limitation of its authority and of the constitutional distinction between commerce among the States and with foreign nations on the one hand and commerce within the States on the other hand. The commands of the law are addressed only to "common carriers engaged in trade and commerce" in the Territories, with foreign nations, and among the States, and with respect to carriers engaged in commerce within the States the law is impressively silent. The expression and enumeration of the parts of commerce which are clearly within the control of Congress is equivalent to an exclusion of the part which is not within its control. In the careful selection of the language of this law the legislators may well have had in mind the words of Chief Justice Marshall which have received the constant approval of this court. He said (in *Gibbons* v. *Ogden,* 9 Wheat. 1, 194, 195):

"The subject to which the power is next applied is to 'commerce among the several States.' . . . Commerce among the States cannot stop at the external boundary line of each State, but may be introduced into the interior.

"It is not intended to say that these words comprehend that commerce, which is completely internal, which is carried on between man and man in a State, or between different parts of the same State, and which does not extend to or affect other States. Such a power would be inconvenient, and is certainly unnecessary.

"Comprehensive as the word 'among' is, it may very properly be restricted to that commerce which concerns more States than one. The phrase is not one which would probably have been selected to indicate the completely interior traffic of a State, because it is not an apt phrase for that purpose; and the enumeration of the particular classes of commerce to which the power was to be extended would not have been made had the intention been to extend the power to every description. The enumeration presupposes something not enumerated; and that something, if we regard the language or the subject of the sentence, must be the exclusively internal commerce of a State. The genius and character of the whole Government seem to be, that its action is to be applied to all the external concerns of the Nation, and to those internal concerns which affect the States generally; but not to those which are completely within a particular State, which do not affect other States, and with which it is not necessary to interfere, for the purpose of executing some of the general powers of the Government. The completely internal commerce of a State then, may be considered as reserved to the State itself."

These words of the Chief Justice have been regarded as delimiting accurately the constitutional boundaries of the respective powers over commerce of the Nation and the States. They have been frequently repeated, and, though differences have arisen in their application to the complicated affairs of mankind, never doubted, and universally approved. It is not easy to believe that Congress intended to dispute their authority. The reasoning which was thought worthy for the interpretation of the Constitution will not be misapplied if it be employed in the interpretation of a law passed in pursuance of the powers conferred by the Constitution. Why should it not be said of the law as it was said of the Constitution, that "the enumeration of the particular classes of commerce to which the power was to be extended, would not have been made had the intention been to extend the power to every description. The enumeration presupposes something not enumerated; and that something, if we regard the language, . . . must be the exclusively internal commerce of the State." From the enumeration of territorial, interstate, and foreign commerce, and the omission of the internal commerce of the State, is it not clear that the commerce which is exclusively internal to the State, and does not affect any other character of commerce, was intended to be outside the purview of the law? Does not a proper respect for the acts of Congress and the strong presumption that it will not exceed its powers, so frequently declared by this court, require us to believe that when the kinds of commerce within its undoubted control are carefully enumerated all the words of the law, however general, are to be referred solely to that commerce and no other?

If carriers were separated by a clear line of division, so that one class were engaged exclusively in interstate and foreign commerce, and the other class were engaged exclusively in commerce within the States, it would not, of course, occur to any mind that this act had any reference whatever to the state carriers. But there is no such hard and fast line of division. Carriers often, and where they are railroads, usually are, as a matter of fact, engaged both in interstate and foreign commerce over which Congress has the control, and intrastate commerce over which the States have the control. Applying the law under consideration to the conditions as they actually exist, it is said that its words are so general and sweeping as to comprehend within its benefits not only the employés of the interstate carrier engaged in the business of interstate carriage, but also the employés of the same carrier engaged in the business of intrastate carriage which it may and usually does conduct. Counsel illustrated their argument by suggesting that if a carrier doing an interstate business on the Pacific slope also conducted a local trolley line wholly along the Atlantic seaboard within a single State, an employé on the local trolley line would, by the terms of this act, be entitled to its benefits. If such be the necessary interpretation of the statute plainly it exceeds the power of Congress, for Congress certainly has no right to regulate the purely internal commerce of a State. Nor can the statute be saved by rejecting that part of it which is unconstitutional because its provisions are single and incapable of separation. The vicious part, if such exist, is so intermingled with that which is good that it cannot be eliminated without destroying the whole structure.

Which interpretation, then, should be adopted? That which regards the law as prescribing the liability of the carrier only to those employés who are engaged in the work of interstate and foreign commerce, or that which extends the benefits of the law also to those employés engaged in work which has no relation whatever to such commerce. In answering this question it must not be forgotten that, if the latter interpretation be adopted, in the opinion of the whole court the act is beyond the constitutional power of Congress. That is a consideration of vast importance, because the court has never exercised the mighty power of declaring the acts of a coördinate branch of the Government void except where there is no possible and sensible construction of the act which is consistent with the fundamental organic law. The presumption that other branches of the Government will restrain themselves within the scope of their authority, and the respect which is due to them and their acts, admits of no other attitude from this court. This is more than a canon of interpretation, it is a rule of conduct resting upon considerations of public policy, and, in the exercise of the delicate function of condemning the acts of coördinate and equal branches of the Government, under the same obligation to respect the Constitution as ourselves, has been observed from the beginning. I regard the rule as so vital and fundamental in this and all other parts of the case that I select almost at random some expressions of it by different justices of this court. When the power to declare an act of Congress void was still undecided, Mr. Justice Chase said in *Hylton* v. *United States,* 3 Dall. 171, p. 175: "If the court have such power, I am free to declare that I will never exercise it, but in a very clear case." Mr. Justice Strong said in *The Legal Tender Cases,* 12 Wall. 457, p. 531: "It is incumbent, therefore, upon those who affirm the unconstitutionality of an act of Congress to show clearly that it is in violation of the provisions of the Constitution. It is not sufficient for them that they succeed in raising a doubt." In *The Trade-Mark Cases,* 100 U.S. 82, Mr. Justice Miller said, p. 96: "When this court is called on in the course of the administration of the law to consider whether an act of Congress, or any other department of the Government, is within the constitutional authority of that department, a due respect for a coördinate branch of the Government requires that we shall decide that it has transcended its powers only when that is so plain that we cannot avoid the duty." In *Nicol* v. *Ames,* 173 U.S. 509, Mr. Justice Peckham said, p. 514: "It is always an exceedingly grave and delicate duty to decide upon the constitutionality of an act of the Congress of the United States. The presumption, as has frequently been said, is in favor of the validity of the act, and it is only when the question is free from any reasonable doubt that the court should hold an act of the lawmaking power of the Nation to be in violation of that fundamental instrument upon which all the powers of the Government rest." Mr. Justice White in *Buttfield* v. *Stranahan,* 192 U.S. 470, said, p. 492: "In examining the statute in order to determine its constitutionality we must be guided by the well-settled rule that every intendment is in favor of its validity. It must be presumed to be constitutional, unless its repugnancy to the Constitution clearly appears." Mr. Chief Justice Waite in *The Sinking Fund Cases,* 99 U.S. 700, said, p. 718: "It is our duty, when required in the regular course of judicial proceedings, to declare an act of Congress void if not within the legislative power of the United States; but this declaration should never be made except in a clear case. Every possible presumption is in favor of the validity of a statute, and this continues until the contrary is shown beyond a rational doubt. One branch of the Government cannot encroach upon the domain of another without danger. The safety of our institutions depends in no small degree on a strict observance of this salutary rule." Mr. Justice Story, in *United States* v. *Coombs,* 12 Pet. 72, said, p. 76: "If the section admits of two interpretations, one of which brings it within and the other presses it beyond the constitutional authority of Congress, it will become our duty to adopt the former construction; because a presumption never ought to be indulged, that Congress meant to exercise or usurp any unconstitutional authority, unless that conclusion is forced upon the court by language altogether unambiguous."

Citations of this character might be multiplied, but to no good purpose. There is no doubt that the rule exists, there is no doubt that it is wise, and promotes the mutual respect between the different branches of the Government which is so essential to the welfare of all, and that it requires us, if it is within our power, to give to the words of the statute before us a meaning which will confine its provisions to subjects within the control of Congress. If two interpretations are possible our plain duty is to adopt that which sustains the statute as a lawful exercise of authority and not that which condemns it as a usurpation.

The argument which supports a construction of the statute which would include within its provisions intrastate commerce is readily stated. It is said that "every common carrier" engaged in territorial, foreign, or interstate trade is made "liable to any of its employés . . . for all damages which may result from the negligence of any of its officers, agents, or employés, or by reason of any defect" in its instrumentalities, and that, as there is no qualification of or exception to the generality of the language descriptive of the employés or instrumentalities, it must be deemed to include those engaged and used solely in intrastate commerce, and even in manufacture, as well as those engaged and used in other commerce. But I venture to think that this argument rests upon too narrow ground. It contemplates merely the words of the statute; it shuts out the light which the Constitution sheds upon them; it overlooks the significance of the enumeration of the kinds of commerce clearly within the National control and the omission of the commerce beyond that control—an enumeration and omission which characterizes, colors and restrains every word of the statute—and it neglects the presumptions in favor of the validity of the law and of the obedience of Congress to the commands of the Constitution, which cannot with propriety be disregarded by this court. Taking into account these missing aids to construction, it becomes quite easy, quite reasonable, and, in my opinion, quite necessary, to construe the act as conferring its benefits only upon employés engaged in some fashion in the commerce which is enumerated in it and is undoubtedly under the control of Congress. Even without these guides for discovering the intent of Congress, which the uniform practice of the court compels us to use, it is natural to suppose that, when territorial, interstate, and foreign carriers only are mentioned and every such carrier is declared to be liable "to any of its employés," only its employés in such commerce are intended. With those guides the conclusion appears to me irresistible, for they show that if the words, "any of its employés," in the context where they are used, are capable of meaning all of the employés upon any kind of work, yet their generality should be restrained so as to include only those who are subject to the power of the lawmaking body. The case of *McCullough* v. *Virginia,* 172 U.S. 102, is precisely in point here. An act of the General Assembly of the State of Virginia provided for refunding the state debt by the issue of coupon bonds for two-thirds of the total amount of that debt. It was enacted that the coupons should "be receivable at and after maturity for all taxes, debts, dues, and demands due the State." There was at the time of the passage of the refunding act a provision of the constitution of Virginia requiring all school taxes to be paid in cash, and it had been held by this court that the constitutional provision disabled the Virginia legislature from providing that the coupons should be receivable for such taxes. *McGahey* v. *Virginia,* 135 U.S. 662. The argument was then made that as the statute providing for the receivability of the coupons for "all taxes, debts, dues, and demands due the State" was in part beyond the constitutional power of the legislature, the contract evidenced by that statute was entirely void. The court, speaking by Mr. Justice Brewer, answered this argument by saying, 172 U.S. 112: "It ignores the difference between the statute and the contract, and confuses the two entirely distinct matters of construction and validity. The statute precedes the contract. Its scope and meaning must be determined before any question will arise as to the validity of the contract which it authorizes. It is elementary law that every statute is to be read in the light of the Constitution. However broad and general its language, it cannot be interpreted as extending beyond those matters which it was within the constitutional power of the legislature to reach. It is the same rule which obtains in the interpretation of any private contract between individuals. That, whatever may be its words, is always to be construed in the light of the statute; of the law then in force; of the circumstances and conditions of parties. So, although general language was introduced into the statute of 1871, it is not to be read as reaching to matters in respect to which the legislature had no constitutional power, but only as to those matters within its control. And if there were, as it seems there were, certain special taxes and dues which under the existing provisions of the state constitution could not be affected by legislative action, the statute is to be read as though it in terms excluded them from its operation." The language quoted was not *obiter*. The case turned upon the construction of the statute and reversed the construction by the highest court of the State of its own statute, as well as its judgment, that the statute thus construed was inconsistent with the state constitution, because "all taxes" included taxes beyond the power of the legislature. I am unable to reconcile the judgment in that case with the conclusion which is reached by the court in this. The reasoning which, in that case, led the court to construe a statute providing that the coupons should be receivable for "all taxes" to mean only for such taxes as the legislature had the constitutional power to declare payable in such a manner, is equally potent to lead the court, in the case at bar, to construe a statute providing for the liability of the interstate and foreign carrier to "any of its employés" to mean only to any of its employés for whom Congress has the constitutional power to make such a provision. In that case there were taxes within the legislative control, and taxes without the legislative control of the Virginia assembly; in this case there are employés within the legislative control and employés without the legislative control of Congress; in that case the statute provided for "all taxes;" in this case the statute provides for "any employés;" in that case, examining the statute "in the light of the Constitution," this court declared that "however broad and general its language, it cannot be interpreted as extending beyond those matters which it is within the constitutional power of the legislature to reach," and if it appears that there were taxes beyond the control of the legislature, that the statute should be read "as though it in terms excluded them from its operation;" I am unable to imagine any reason why, examining the statute in this case with the aid of the same light, the court should not make the same declaration of its meaning. Moreover, it should be remembered that a circumstance leading in the same direction is present in the case at bar which was absent in that case, for, to repeat what has already been said, here the general words are used in a context which suggests, if it does not require, the less extended meaning.

It should be observed that the *McCullough case* was simply a case of construction. The court made no judicial amendment of the statute or exception from its provisions of any subject which came within them according to their proper meaning, ascertained with the aid of the light of the constitutional limits of the legislative power. Mr. Justice Brewer pointed out the distinction between the construction of the statute and its validity, saying: "The statute precedes the contract. Its scope and meaning must be determined before any question will arise as to the validity of the contract which it authorizes." Thus the case is distinguished from some others, much relied upon in the argument, which establish the proposition, that a single statutory provision is void if it is expressed in general words so used as to manifest clearly the intention to include within those words subjects beyond the constitutional power of the lawmaking body. The courts have no power to read into such a provision an exception for the purpose of saving that which is left from condemnation. A law which cannot endure the test of the Constitution without judical amendment must perish. *United States* v. *Reese,* 92 U.S. 214; *The Trade-Mark Cases,* 100 U.S. 82; *United States* v. *Harris,* 106 U.S. 629; *Baldwin* v. *Franks,* 120 U.S. 678; *United States* v. *Ju Toy,* 198 U.S. 253. See *Illinois &c Railroad* v. *McKendree,* 203 U.S. 514. But the rule derived from these cases is by no means decisive of the inquiry whether this statute must be construed as seeking to accomplish objects beyond the power of Congress. It can be made decisive only by begging the very question to be determined, and, in the words of Mr. Justice Brewer, confusing "the two entirely distinct matters of construction and validity." It merely expresses the judicial duty which arises after the question of construction is determined. A critical examination of the cases shows that in each of them, in the opinion of the court, the language of the statute admitted of no possible interpretation, except that Congress intended to deal, by a single and inseparable provision, with subjects without as well as subjects within its control. As was said in one of them, *United States* v. *Reese,* 92 U.S. 214, 220, there was "no room for construction unless it be as to the effect of the Constitution." It would be unprofitable to dwell upon all these decisions, and I content myself with the analysis of one, and that the one deemed by counsel who rely upon it as the most important and conclusive. In *The Trade-Mark Cases* it appeared that in an act entitled "An Act to Revise, Consolidate, and Amend the Statutes Relating to Patents and Copyrights," provision was made for the registration of trade-marks in the Patent Office. Some years later an act was passed providing for the punishment by fine and imprisonment of any person making fraudulent use of or counterfeiting trade-marks thus registered. The cases were indictments under this later act, and the question for decision was its constitutionality. The act was supported first upon the ground that it was authorized by that part of the Constitution which confers upon Congress the authority "to promote the progress of science and useful arts, by securing for limited times to authors and inventors the exclusive right to their respective rights and discoveries." The court, after saying, 100 U.S. 93, "that it is a reasonable inference that this part of the statute also was in the opinion of Congress an exercise of the power found in that clause of the Constitution," and that "it was mainly if not wholly to this clause that the advocates of the law looked for its support," held that this clause was not a sufficient source of authority for the act. The act was supported, second, upon the ground that the commerce clause of the Constitution supplied the requisite authority to Congress. But there was not a word in the act from which it could be inferred that Congress intended to exercise the power conferred by the commerce clause. The court, by Mr. Justice Miller, after pointing out that commerce within a State was beyond the control of Congress, said, p. 96: "When, therefore, Congress undertakes to enact a law, which can only be valid as a regulation of commerce, it is reasonable to expect to find on the face of the law, or from its essential nature, that it is a regulation of commerce with foreign nations, among the several States, or with the Indian tribes." Words could not be more happily chosen than these, to describe what the statute in the case at bar is on its face and from its essential nature. The justice then proceeds to say: "If it is not so limited it is in excess of the power of Congress. If its main purpose be to establish a regulation applicable to all trade, to commerce at all points, especially if it is apparent that it is designed to govern the commerce wholly between citizens of the same State, it is obviously the exercise of a power not confided to Congress." No words could be more happily chosen than these, to describe exactly what the statute in the case at bar is not. The court then taking the view, upon which there cannot be two opinions, that the act intended to establish a universal system of trade-mark legislation applicable to all commerce, held the statute void, saying, p. 98: "It is not within the judicial province to give to the words used by Congress a narrower meaning than that they are manifestly intended to bear, in order that crimes may be punished which are not described in language within the constitutional power of that body." The reasoning relied upon in this case to overthrow the statute, if applied to the statute before us, tends to support it.

I do not wish to be understood as saying that the group of cases I am now discussing does not furnish instances where the court has declined to limit the meaning of words in order to save the act. I only say, that in these cases it could not be done without violating the obvious intent of Congress as ascertained by the necessary meaning of the language it employed; in other words, that in these cases only one interpretation was possible and there was "no room for construction." They cannot be understood as deciding that general words may not, in view of the context where they are found, and, with the aid of the light of the Constitution, be restrained in their meaning, with the purpose and effect of giving them such a construction that the act may be sustained as a legitimate exercise of the legislative power. If they should be so understood they would be in flat conflict with the *McCullough case,* and with the spirit of the interpretation that prevailed in *United States* v. *Palmer,* 3 Wheat. 610, and *Church of the Holy Trinity* v. *United States,* 143 U.S. 457. In the former case it was held that an act which punished certain offenses committed by "any person or persons" upon the high seas should not be construed as including persons who might commit such offenses on board a vessel belonging to the subjects of a foreign state; Marshall, C. J., saying, p. 631: "The words of the section are in terms of unlimited extent. The words 'any person or persons' are broad enough to comprehend every human being. But general words must not only be limited to cases within the jurisdiction of the State, but also to those objects to which the legislature intended to apply them." In the latter case it was held that an act that forbade all persons from assisting the migration into the United States of "any alien or aliens, any foreigner or foreigners," under contract "to perform labor or services of any kind," did not include a minister of religion, though such a person was within the letter of the statute. These cases show that we may with propriety give to the words "any of its employés" the narrower meaning, and, because such meaning saves the act from condemnation, it is, I believe, our imperative duty to adopt it. No words need to be read into the act. It is required only that the words already there shall be applied to that commerce which Congress referred to, namely, territorial, foreign and interstate. Thus read, the whole statute is saved and no part of it is destroyed.

The natural meaning of the words of the statute considered together, each word receiving significance from those with which it is allied, the respect which is due to Congress, the belief which I hold that it would not intentionally overstep the clearly defined limits of its authority, and the principles of construction heretofore acted upon by this court, lead my mind to the settled conviction that the statute can be interpreted, and ought to be interpreted, as affording the remedy therein prescribed only to the employés of foreign, interstate and territorial carriers, who are themselves engaged in some capacity in such commerce in some of its manifold aspects. If this meaning be attributed to the words of the law, it is apparent that in the opinion of a majority of the court the law, in its main features at least, would be constitutional.

Entertaining these views of the meaning of the statute, I am compelled to go further and consider the other objections to it. I agree entirely with all that was said in the opinion of Mr. Justice White in support of the power of the Congress to enact a law of this general character, but, as I think that the judgments in these cases ought to be reversed, I cannot escape dealing with specific objections to the statute which he has not deemed it necessary to discuss. I think it better, therefore, to deal with all the questions that are necessarily raised in these cases.

I come now to the question whether the statute, thus construed, is in the execution of any power conferred by the Constitution upon the Congress. It is apparent that there is no such power unless it be found in that clause of the Constitution which authorizes Congress "to regulate commerce with foreign nations and among the several States and with the Indian tribes." It hardly needs to be said that the inability of the National Government, created by the Articles of Confederation, to deal effectively with commerce was one of the efficient causes of the call for the constitutional convention. No doubt the most urgent need of that time was a central government with powers adequate to control foreign commerce, but interstate commerce was not overlooked, though its principal importance then consisted in its relation to foreign commerce. [Federalist, No. 42, by Mr. Madison.] No one could then have foreseen the extent of the interstate commerce of our times, for no one could foretell the employment of the forces of steam and electricity which have so wonderfully aided its development. But the statesmen of that time, confident of the future and hopeful that they might devise a government which would endure, must have understood that the commerce which concerned more than one State, from its essential nature, was in part outside the territorial jurisdiction of any State, could not be governed efficiently by a single State, and, if left outside of the National control, would be subject to woeful embarrassment by the conflicting regulations of the several States into which it entered. It appears in the reports of the debates that these dangers were appreciated by the members of the convention, so far as they threatened that part of the commerce among the States which was conducted by water transportation, then the only part of such commerce of sufficient importance to attract public attention. But fortunately the spirit of the nation builder and not of the codemaker inspired and dominated the convention. Its members were not content to frame a system of laws sufficient for the present moment, which might in a few years become unsuited to or inadequate for the needs of the people. They undertook rather the task of devising a scheme of government and of allotting the powers usually exercised by governments between the existing States and the prospective Nation. Whenever such a power came under consideration its nature was examined, and it was then placed in the hands of that governmental agency which it was supposed could exercise it most advantageously. This very power furnishes a signal illustration of the method pursued. The convention did not determine how interstate commerce should be regulated but rather who should regulate it, and left, with certain limitations, the necessity, extent and nature of the regulation to the contemporaneous knowledge, wisdom and discretion of the body in whom the power was vested. We may well believe that, contemplating the subject with the enlarged vision of those who are building for a future unknown or dimly discerned, and seeing clearly that interstate like foreign commerce was, in the words of the resolutions with which Randolph opened the deliberations of the convention, a matter "to which the separate States are incompetent, or in whicn the harmony of the United States may be interrupted by the exercise of individual legislation," the convention was constrained to associate the two together in every draft of the Constitution proposed, and place them with the Indian trade, under the control of the National legislature. Madison's Journal, Scott's edition, pp. 67, 161, 164, 185, 362, 453, 654, 656, 704, 753.

The different kinds of commerce described have the common qualities that they are more extensive than the jurisdiction of a single State and liable to injury from conflicting state laws, and thereby are all alike distinguished from the purely internal commerce of the States. There is nothing in the words of the grant that permits the belief that the power is not coextensive over foreign, interstate, and Indian trade, or is anything less than the whole power which any government may properly exercise over either, though it may well be that the restrictive parts of the Constitution, its prohibitions and reservations, may operate differently on different kinds of commerce, or even on different aspects of the same kind of commerce.

It is said that Congress has never before enacted legislation of this nature for the government of interstate commerce on land, though it has for the government of such commerce upon the water and for the government of foreign commerce; that on the contrary the relations affected have been controlled by the undoubted power of the States to govern men and things within their respective dominions; and that this omission of Congress is of controlling significance. The fundamental fallacy of this argument is that it misunderstands the nature of the Constitution, undervalues its usefulness, and forgets that its unchanging provisions are adaptable to the infinite variety of the changing conditions of our National life. Surely there is no statute of limitations which bars Congress from the exercise of any of its granted powers, nor any authority, save that of the people whom it represents, which may with propriety challenge the wisdom of its choice of the time when remedies shall first be applied to what it deems wrong. It cannot be doubted that the exercise of a power for the first time may be called upon to justify itself. The fact that it is for the first time is a circumstance to be considered. But in this case it is a circumstance whose significance disappears in the light of history. Henry Adams, a writer of high authority, in the first chapter of his History of the United States, has drawn a vivid picture of the conditions of our National life at the beginning of the nineteenth century. The center of population was near Baltimore. The interior was almost impenetrable except by the waterways and two wagon roads from Philadelphia to Pittsburg and from the Potomac to the Monongahela. The scattered settlements of what was then the Western country were severed from the seaboard settlements by mountain ranges, and there was little connection between the two almost independent peoples. There was scarcely a possibility of trade between the States except along the seacoast and over the dangerous and uncertain rivers. "The experience of mankind," says the author, p. 7, "proved trade to be dependent on water communications, and as yet Americans did not dream that the experience of mankind was useless to them." We need not look beyond these conditions for an explanation why Congress, though it early and vigorously exercised its power of legislation over foreign commerce and interstate commerce by water, left it unused in respect to interstate commerce on the land. As population multiplied, bringing the isolated settlements nearer to each other, wealth increased, creating a wider demand for commodities, and roads and bridges came to be better and more numerous, doubtless overland commerce was somewhat stimulated. But the iron restrictions which nature had placed upon land transportation remained constant until they were unloosed by the operation of the steam railroad. The system of steam transportation began modestly by the construction of short lines, often wholly within a single State. These lines were lengthened by extensions and consolidations, until at the present time the States of the Union are all bound together by a network of interstate railroads. Their operation, aided by the quick and cheap transmission of the mails, and the communication of intelligence by electricity, has transformed the commerce of the country. Interstate commerce by land, once so slight as to be unworthy of the attention of the National legislature, has come to be the most important part of all trade, and it is not too much to say that the daily needs of the factory and the household are no longer dependent upon the resources of the locality, but are largely supplied by the products of other States.

It was not reasonably to be expected that a phenomenon so contrary to the experience of mankind, so vast, so rapidly developing and changing, as the growth of land commerce among the States, would speedily be appreciated in all its aspects, or would at once call forth the exercise of all the unused power vested in Congress by the commerce clause of the Constitution. Such a phenomenon demands study and experience. The habit of our people, accentuated by our system of representative government, is not so much in legislation to anticipate problems as it is to deal with them after experience has shown them to exist. So Congress has exercised its power sparingly, step by step, and has acted only when experience seemed to it to require action. A description of its action in this respect was given in *In re Debs,* 158 U.S. 564, where it was said, p. 579: "Congress has exercised the power granted in respect to interstate commerce in a variety of legislative acts. Passing by for the present all that legislation in respect to commerce by water, and considering only that which bears upon railroad interstate transportation (for this is the specific matter involved in this case), these acts may be noticed: First. That of June 15, 1866, c. 124. 14 Stat. 66, carried into the Revised Statutes as § 5258, which provides: 'Whereas the Constitution of the United States confers upon Congress, in express terms, the power to regulate commerce among the several States, to establish post roads, and to raise and support armies: Therefore, *Be it enacted by the Senate and House of Representatives of the United States of America in Congress assembled,* That every railroad company in the United States whose road is operated by steam, its successors and assigns, be, and is hereby, authorized to carry upon and over its road, boats, bridges, and ferries all passengers, troops, government supplies, mails, freight, and property on their way from any State to another State, and to receive compensation therefor, and to connect with roads of other States so as to form continuous lines for the transportation of the same to the place of destination.' Second. That of March 3, 1873, c. 252, 17 Stat. 584 (rev. Stat. §§ 4386 to 4389), which regulates the transportation of live stock over interstate railroads. Third. That of May 29, 1884, c. 60, § 6, 23 Stat. 31, 32, prohibiting interstate transportation by railroads of livestock affected with any contagious or infectious disease. Fourth. That of February 4, 1887, c. 104, 24 Stat. 379, with its amendments of March 2, 1889, c. 382, 25 Stat. 855, and February 10, 1891, c. 128, 26 Stat. 743, known as the 'Interstate Commerce Act,' by which a commission was created with large powers of regulation and control of interstate commerce by railroads, and the sixteenth section of which act gives to the courts of the United States power to enforce the orders of the commission. Fifth. That of October 1, 1888, c. 1063, 25 Stat. 501, providing for arbitration between railroad interstate companies and their employés; and, Sixth, the act of March 2, 1893, c. 196, 27 Stat. 531, requiring the use of automatic couplers on interstate trains, and empowering the Interstate Commerce Commission to enforce its provisions."

Since this decision other laws more fully regulating interstate commerce on land have been enacted, which need not here be stated. They show a constantly increasing tendency to exercise more fully and vigorously the power conferred by the commerce clause. It is well to notice, however, that Congress has assumed the duty of promoting the safety of public travel by enacting the Safety Appliance Law; an act to require reports of casualties to employés or passengers (31 Stat. 1446); a resolution directing the Interstate Commerce Commission to investigate and report on the necessity for block signals (34 Stat. 838); an act limiting the hours of service of employés, and the act under consideration. These acts, all relating to interstate transportation, demonstrate the belief of Congress that the safety of interstate travel is a matter of National concern, and its deliberate purpose to increase that safety by laws which it deems conducive to that end. I think, therefore, that we may consider whether this act finds authority in the commerce clause of the Constitution without embarrassment from any inferences which may be drawn from the inaction of Congress.

It is settled beyond the necessity of citing cases that the transportation of persons and property is commerce, in other words, that the business of carriers is commerce. Where, therefore, the business is foreign or interstate, Congress, it has frequently been decided, has the paramount, if not the sole, power to legislate for its direct control. An obstruction of such commerce by unlawful violence may be made punishable under the laws of the United States, suppressed by the armies of the United States, or, at the instance of the United States, enjoined in its courts. *In re Debs, ubi sup.* It is difficult to conceive how legislation may effectively control the business if it cannot regulate the conduct of those engaged in the business, while engaged in the business, in every act which is performed in the conduct of the business. The business of transportation is not an abstraction. It is the labor of men employed with the aid of instrumentalities, animal and mechanical, in carrying men and things from place to place. In every form of transportation, from the simplest to the most complex, whether the man carries the burden on his back, or drives an animal which carries it, or a locomotive which draws a car which carries it, the one and only constant factor is the labor of mankind. I am quite unable to understand the contention made at the bar that the power of Congress is to regulate commerce among the States and not to regulate persons engaged in commerce among the States, for in the case of transportation at least the labor of those engaged in it is commerce itself. How poor and meagre the power would be if, whenever it was exercised, the legislator must pause to consider whether the action proposed regulated commerce or merely regulated the conduct of persons engaged in commerce. The contention derives some plausibility from its vagueness. Of course the power to regulate commerce does not authorize Congress to control the general conduct of persons engaged therein, but, unless it is an idle and useless power, it authorizes Congress to control the conduct of persons engaged in commerce in respect to everything which directly concerns commerce, for that is commerce itself. It would seem, therefore, that when persons are employed in interstate or foreign commerce, as the employment is an essential part of that commerce, its terms and conditions, and the rights and duties which grow out of it, are under the control of Congress subject only to the limits on the exercise of that control prescribed in the Constitution. This has been the view always expressed or implied by this court. In his concurring opinion in *Gibbons* v. *Ogden,* 9 Wheat. 1, Mr. Justice Johnson said, p. 229: "Commerce, in its simplest signification, means an exchange of goods; but in the advancement of society, labor, transportation, intelligence, care and various mediums of exchange become commodities and enter into commerce; the subject, the vehicle, the agent, and their various operations, become the objects of commercial regulations." In *Cooley* v. *Board of Wardens,* 12 How. 299, the court in holding, *inter alia,* that a regulation of pilots is a regulation of commerce within the meaning of the commerce clause said (p. 316, by Justice Curtis) of the power: "It extends to the persons who conduct it, as well as to the instruments used." In the opinion of the court, delivered by Mr. Justice Field, in *Sherlock* v. *Alling,* 93 U.S. 99, it was said, p. 103: "It is true that the commercial power conferred by the Constitution is one without limitation. It authorizes legislation with respect to all the subjects of foreign and interstate commerce, the persons engaged in it and the instruments by which it is carried on." In delivering the opinion of the court in *Smith* v. *Alabama,* 124 U.S. 465, where a state statute requiring interstate locomotive engineers to obtain a license after a qualifying examination, and imposing a penalty for operating without such license, was sustained, Mr. Justice Matthews said, p. 479: "It would, indeed, be competent for Congress to legislate upon its subject matter and to prescribe the qualifications of locomotive engineers for employment by carriers engaged in foreign or interstate commerce." In sustaining a similar state statute, directed against color blindness, Mr. Justice Field said in *Nashville &c. Railway* v. *Alabama,* 128 U.S. 96, 99: "It is conceded that the power of Congress to regulate interstate commerce is plenary; that, as incident to it, Congress may legislate as to the qualifications, duties, and liabilities of employés and others on railway trains engaged in that commerce; and that such legislation will supersede any state action on the subject. But until such legislation is had, it is clearly within the competency of the State to provide against accidents on the train." In *Chicago &c. Railway* v. *Solan,* 169 U.S. 133, a state statute forbidding a contract limiting liability for injury was sustained, the court, by Mr. Justice Gray, saying, p. 137: "The rules prescribed for the construction of railroads, and for their management and operation, designed to protect persons and property, otherwise endangered by their use, are strictly within the scope of the local law. They are not, in themselves, regulations of interstate commerce, though they control, in some degree, the conduct and liability of those engaged in such commerce. So long as Congress has not legislated upon the particular subject, they are rather to be regarded as legislation in aid of such commerce, and as a rightful exercise of the police power of the State to regulate the relative rights and duties of all persons and corporations within its limits." This statement was assumed to be true in *Pennsylvania Railroad* v. *Hughes,* 191 U.S. 477, and *Martin* v. *Pittsburg &c. Railroad,* 203 U.S. 284. The case of *Peirce* V. *Van Dusen,* 78 Fed. Rep. 693, was decided by the Court of Appeals of the Sixth Circuit by Mr. Justice Harlan and Judges Taft and Lurton. The opinion was delivered by Mr. Justice Harlan. After sustaining a state statute, which modified the common law rules with respect to the liability for injuries of a carrier to its employés, he said of it: "The Ohio statute is not applicable alone to railroad corporations of Ohio, engaged in the domestic commerce of this State. It is equally applicable to railroad corporations doing business in Ohio, and engaged in commerce among the States, although the statute, in its operation, may affect in some degree a subject over which Congress can exert full power. The States may do many things affecting commerce with foreign nations and among the several States until Congress covers the subject by National legislation. . . . Undoubtedly the whole subject of the liability of interstate railroad companies for the negligence of those in their service may be covered by National legislation enacted by Congress under its power to regulate commerce among the States."

We may not trust implicitly to the accuracy of statements gathered from opinions where the precise question was not for decision. But where, as in these quotations, the statements were an essential part of the course of reasoning deemed appropriate for the disposition of the cases, where the same thought clothed in different words has been expressed at intervals from early times to the present day, and where no decision or judicial utterance has been found in opposition to them, they are entitled to profound respect, and furnish cogent evidence of what the law has always been supposed to be by the members of this court. They cannot be regarded lightly, and if we follow them they lead us to the conclusion that the national power to regulate commerce is broad enough to regulate the employment, duties, obligations, liabilities and conduct of all persons engaged in commerce with respect to all which is comprehended in that commerce. Upon what principle except this could this court have twice enforced the Safety Appliance Act, undisturbed by a doubt of its constitutionality? *Johnson* v. *Railroad,* 196 U.S. 1; *Schlemmer* v. *Railroad,* 205 U.S. 1. That act (27 Stat. 531) compelled interstate railroads to equip all their trains with power brakes operated from the engine, and all their cars with automatic couplers, grab-irons, and hand holds, by enacting that the use of engines and cars not thus equipped should be unlawful. There was no express provision that an employé injured by the failure of a railroad to comply with the law should be entitled to damages, but without doubt the liability of the railroad is implied. The common law rule governing the liability was materially changed by § 8, which abolished in part the doctrine of the assumption of risk by providing that the employé should "not be deemed to have assumed the risk" of the unlawful conditions, though he knew of them and continued in his employment. This section was enforced in most emphatic manner in the *Schlemmer case,* where Mr. Justice Holmes said, 205 U.S. 11: "An early, if not the earliest, application of the phrase 'assumption of risk' was the establishment of the exception to the liability of a master for the negligence of his servant when the person injured was a fellow-servant of the injured man." If the statute now before us is beyond the constitutional power of Congress, surely the Safety Appliance Act is also void, for there can be no distinction in principle between them. If Congress can create a liability to an injured employé for the existence of conditions in certain mechanisms which he uses, by declaring those conditions unlawful, it may create the same liability for negligence of the agents and imperfections in the instruments used in the carrier's work; if it may change the common law rule of the assumption of the risk of imperfect appliances, it may change the rule of the assumption of the risk of a careless fellow servant. I can conceive of no principle of constitutional law which enables us to say that the commerce clause authorizes Congress to fix upon the carrier a liability for an insufficient brake but not for a defective rail, for the absence of automatic couplers, but not for the negligent order which brings trains into collision, for an insecure grab-iron, but not for a heedless switchman. If Congress has the right to control the liability in any way it may control it in every way, subject, as all powers are subject, to the express prohibitions of the Constitution. Unless the cases on the safety appliance acts are deemed to have been inadvertently decided, they seem to be conclusive of this branch of the case. This seems to have been feared by counsel for one of the defendants, who in his brief said "that the giving of a right of recovery to an injured employé is a proper and necessary method for making effective the Safety Appliance Act . . . we do not admit."

But if we put aside the authority of precedents, and examine the nature and extent of the grant to Congress of power over commerce in the light of the settled principles of interpretation fit to be applied to the exposition of a constitution, we shall arrive at the same result. One main purpose and effect of the Constitution was to devise a scheme of efficient government. In order to accomplish this all the powers usually exercised by governments were distributed between the States and the Nation, except those deemed unfit or unsafe to be entrusted to either and withheld from both. In the allotment of powers to the Nation they were enumerated rather than defined. In the enumeration words of the largest import were employed, comprehending within their meaning grand divisions of the powers of government. The nature of the Constitution, said Chief Justice Marshall (*McCulloch* v. *Maryland,* 4 Wheat. 316, p. 407), "requires that only its great outlines should be marked, its important objects designated, and the minor ingredients which compose those objects be deduced from the nature of the objects themselves." The wide extent of the powers granted to Congress is expressed in a few simply worded provisions, all of which might be printed on a single page of its book of annual laws. Counsel have argued that the power to regulate commerce does not include the power to regulate the conduct of persons engaged in that commerce in respect of that commerce. This is what Mr. Justice Miller (110 U.S. 658) described as "the old argument often heard, often repeated, and in this court never assented to, that when a question of the power of Congress arises the advocate of the power must be able to place his finger on words which expressly grant it." Suppose that method of reasoning had been applied to the power "to establish post offices and post roads," under which Congress governs the postal system of the country as fully and freely in every detail as it is governed by any other nation. It could be said to Congress, you cannot carry the mail, you cannot issue money orders, you cannot determine what shall be excluded from the mail, you cannot regulate the conduct of those who are employed in the mail service, you cannot exempt them from militia duty, you cannot punish their theft or embezzlement, you cannot punish him who breaks and enters the post office or mail car—all these powers are reserved to the States. You can only establish post offices and post roads, and when that is done your power is exhausted. Yet Congress has done all these things and no one now doubts its power to do them, because the grant of power is of the whole governmental power over the subject. So, too, the power to regulate interstate and foreign commerce is the whole power which any government can exercise over that subject, it "is vested in Congress as absolutely as it would be in a single government having in its constitution the same restrictions on the exercise of the power as are found in the Constitution of the United States." Marshall, C. J., in *Gibbons* v. *Ogden, ubi sup.,* 197; *The Lottery Case,* 188 U.S. 321. We are brought then directly to the inquiry whether a power so extensive is a sufficient warrant for the enactment of the statute before us.

By what has been called the auxiliary power Congress may "make all laws which shall be necessary and proper for carrying into execution" its granted powers. It is settled that this provision authorizes the enactment of laws which, in the exercise of a wide discretion, Congress deems adapted to secure a legitimate end and calculated to effect any of the objects entrusted to it, and the exercise of that discretion, unless it violates some prohibition of the Constitution or is used as a pretext to accomplish some object not entrusted to the National Government, cannot be reviewed by the judicial branch of the Government without trespassing upon a domain which is peculiarly and exclusively the province of the legislative branch. If the statute under consideration be brought to the test of these principles there can be no doubt of its validity.

It cannot be denied that in that part of commerce which consists in transportation, the safety of those who are concerned in it as passengers or employés is of the first importance. As was said by Mr. Justice Gray, in *Chicago &c. Railway Co.* v. *Solan,* 169 U.S. 133, 135, "the fundamental principle on which the law of common carriers was established was the securing of the utmost care and diligence in the performance of their public duties." The Government having the relations which the National Government has to interstate commerce, pronounced by the court in the *Debs Case,* 158 U.S. 564, 578, to be "those of direct supervision, control, and management," which neglects to do what it is fitting for a government to do to insure the safety of public travel, fails in the performance of its highest duty. The lengthening list of casualties to employés and passengers on our railroads has arrested the public attention and created public alarm. Ought Congress alone to be indifferent? Or have we so weak a system of government that the only part of it which is clothed with direct authority over the commerce in which the casualties happen is powerless? What does the "direct supervision, control, and management" amount to if it does not include the power to pass any laws really calculated to lessen the great dangers of public travel? Congress, recognizing its responsibility and believing in its power, has enacted the group of laws to which reference has been made. Of one (the Safety Appliance Act) the Chief Justice said, in the *Johnson Case,* 196 U.S. 17, what is true of all: "The primary object of the act was to promote the public welfare by securing the safety of employés and travellers." That act, like this, in terms simply safeguarded the employé, but his safety cannot be separated from the safety of the traveller; both may be affected by the same act of negligence and the same defect in appliances, and suffer injury in the same disaster. Any law which promotes the safety of either promotes the safety of both. Much of the law of common carriers, whether created by decisions of the courts or by acts of legislatures, has been upon or influenced by the theory that the nature of the liabilities imposed upon the carriers directly affects the care, diligence and safety with which they conduct their business. For instance, one consideration which has influenced the courts in the judicial development of the fellow-servant doctrine is, that, by imposing upon the employé the risk of the carelessness of the men with whom he works, a greater degree of care and therefore of safety would result. The truth of this theory has been often disputed (see *Chicago &c. Railroad* v. *Ross,* 112 U.S. 377), and it is almost universally disregarded in modern legislation. It is of no importance here whether it is right or wrong. The only significance is that the greater or less liability in damages is generally regarded as having some relation to the safety of operation. It follows that if Congress, in the exercise of its plenary power over interstate and foreign transportation, deems that the safety of that transportation would be increased by enacting that those employed in it shall have a different remedy for injuries sustained by its negligent conduct than that furnished by the laws of the States, this court cannot, without overstepping the boundary which separates the judicial from the legislative field, declare the enactment void.

The power of Congress to enact the law under consideration, which seems so clearly to result from a just interpretation of the commerce clause, might not have been disputed but for the fact that up to this time the subject has been left to be dealt with by the States. If a doubt ever existed that the States could lawfully deal with the subject under the general legislative authority to govern their territory, which was undisturbed by the Constitution, that doubt was dispelled by the decision in *Sherlock* v. *Alling, ubi sup.,* 93 U.S. 99, and it is now agreed that the State may, in the absence of action by Congress, fix and determine the liability of all carriers while operating within the State, to those whom they employ for the injuries which are suffered in the course of the employment. But such authority in the State is not inconsistent with a like authority in the Nation. Where, as in the case of our dual government, the same territories and the same individuals are subject to two governments, each supreme within its sphere, both governments by virtue of distinct powers may legislate for the same ends. The exercise of the rightful authority of the Nation and the State, though it proceeds from different governmental powers, may reach and control the same subject. This result arises from the different relations to the community the subject may sustain; a drove of cattle may be at once interstate freight and the vehicle by which infectious disease may be brought within the borders of a State; a bridge may at the same time interrupt the navigation of the river and serve as a continuation of the highways of the State; a man, while the agent through which the transaction of interstate commerce is conducted, is at the same time one of the population, permanent or transient, of a State and subject to its general laws. There is no conflict in powers, though there may be conflict in legislation, referable to different powers. In such a case under our system the law of the State enacted by virtue of its undoubted powers must yield to the national law enacted in pursuance of the powers conferred by the Constitution. There is no necessity in this case to disturb the troublesome question when, if ever, even where Congress is silent, the States may exercise any direct power over interstate and foreign commerce. For the power hitherto exercised by the States over this particular subject has never been deemed to be a regulation of commerce, but rather an exercise of their authority to regulate generally the relations of men to each other, which may indirectly affect such commerce. "If a State," said Chief Justice Marshall (in *Gibbons* v. *Ogden, ubi sup.*, 204), "in passing laws on subjects acknowledged to be within its control, and, with a view to those subjects, shall adopt a measure of the same character with one which Congress may adopt, it does not derive its authority from the particular power which has been granted, but from some other, which remains with the State and may be executed by the same means. All experience shows that the same measure or measures, scarcely distinguishable from each other, may flow from distinct powers; but this does not prove that the powers themselves are identical." That the States may by their laws fix the relative rights, duties, obligations and liabilities of all persons or corporations within their territorial jurisdictions, and thus control in that respect those who are engaged in interstate and foreign commerce; that such laws do not proceed from any power to regulate such commerce, though incidentally and directly they do regulate it, but are to be referred to their general power over persons and things within their territories, and that all such laws, so far as they affect such commerce, must yield to the superior authority of the laws of Congress, is, I think, conclusively shown by the following cases: *Sherlock* v. *Alling,* 93 U.S. 99; *Smith* v. *Alabama,* 124 U.S. 465; *Nashville &c. Railway Co.* v. *Alabama,* 128 U.S. 96; *Hennington* v. *Georgia,* 163 U.S. 299; *New York &c. Railroad* v. *New York,* 165 U.S. 628; *Chicago &c. Railroad Co.* v. *Solan,* 169 U.S. 133; *Pennsylvania Railroad* v. *Hughes,* 191 U.S. 477; *Martin* v. *Pittsburg &c. Railroad,* 203 U.S. 284; *Peirce* v. *Van Dusen,* 78 Fed. Rep. 693. Upon principle and authority it, in my opinion, is clear that Congress had constitutional power over the subject with which it dealt in the statute before us.

There remains to be considered the objection that the specific provisions of the act exceed the legislative power over the subject. The powers of Congress are not only confined to those which may be inferred from the Constitution, but are also restrained by the express limits upon their exercise which are contained in that instrument. They are delegated and enumerated and then limited. Even when Congress enters upon a field in which it rightfully exercises the supreme governmental power, it is not supreme in the fullest sense. It does not enjoy complete sovereignty like that, for instance, of the British Parliament. All its legislation must obey the express commands of those parts of the Constitution which mark a limit beyond which legislation cannot go. The only limit upon the authority of Congress relevant to the discussion of this branch of the case is that which forbids Congress from depriving any person of his life, liberty or property without due process of law. Amendment VI. It is contended that, although the law deals with a subject under the control of Congress, it deals with it in such a manner as to violate that prohibition, and is therefore void. Before considering the contention it is desirable to state clearly the substantial provisions of the act. The remedy afforded by it is more generous to the employé than that given by the common law in several respects. The common law recognized no recovery of damages for death resulting from negligence; by the statute damages are recoverable for death as well as for injury. The common law allowed no recovery against the employer for the neglect of a fellow-servant engaged in a common employment; by the statute the employer is held responsible for the negligence of any of its officers, agents or employés, even though the guilty person is a fellow-servant of him who is injured or killed. The common law denied to one who by his negligence had contributed to his own injury the right to a remedy for the neglect of another which had been a concurring cause; by the statute the negligent sufferer may recover if his negligence be slight, and that of the employer gross in comparison, though the contributing negligence must be taken into account in reduction of the damages. The common law, as adjudged by this court, permitted the employé to enter into a contract renouncing his right to damages in case he incurred injuries in the course of his employment; the statute forbids such a contract. Thus four doctrines of the common law restrictive of the employés' rights are supplanted by others more favorable to him.

There can be no doubt of the right of a legislative body, having jurisdiction over the subject, to modify the first three of these rules of the common law in the manner in which this act of Congress does it. They are simply rules of law, unprotected by the Constitution from change, and like all other such rules must yield to the superior authority of a statute. They have so generally been modified by statute that it may well be doubted if they exist in their integrity in any jurisdiction. The common law rules have taken form through the decisions of courts, whose judges in announcing them were controlled by their views of what justice and sound public policy demanded. This is nowhere more clearly stated than by Chief Justice Shaw in *Farwell* v. *Boston & Worcester Railroad,* 4 Met. 49, the leading American case establishing the doctrine that one cannot recover against the master for the negligence of a fellow-servant, where he said: "In considering the rights and obligations arising out of particular relations, it is competent for courts of justice to regard considerations of policy and general convenience, and to draw from them such rules as will, in their practical application, best promote the safety and security of all parties concerned." But the economic opinions of judges and their views of the requirements of justice and public policy, even when crystallized into well-settled doctrines of law, have no constitutional sanctity. They are binding upon succeeding judges, but while they may influence they cannot control legislators. Legislators have their own economic theories, their own views of justice and public policy, and their views when embodied in a written law must prevail. Whenever the legislative power to change any of these rules of the common law has been drawn in question in this court it has been sustained. Various state statutes allowing a remedy against a railroad employer for the negligence of a fellow-servant have been held to be within the legislative power. *Missouri Pacific Railway Company* v. *Mackey,* 127 U.S. 205; *Minneapolis &c. Railway Company* v. *Herrick,* 127 U.S. 210; *Chicago, Kansas & Western Railroad Company* v. *Pontius,* 157 U.S. 209; *Tullis* v. *Lake Erie & Western Railroad,* 175 U.S. 348. State statutes, allowing a recovery for death, were sustained in *Steamboat Company* v. *Chase,* 16 Wall. 522, and *Sherlock* v. *Alling,* 93 U.S. 99, though the statute was attacked in the first case only on the ground that it intruded upon the admiralty jurisdiction exclusively vested in the courts of the United States, and in the second case because it interfered with interstate commerce, whose regulation was vested exclusively in Congress. Statutes of this kind have been in force in the States and doubtless in the Territories for many years, many cases have been tried under them, and in no case has it ever been claimed that anything in the Constitution removes them from the legislative power. The same observation may be made, though not so emphatically of statutes modifying the common law rule denying a recovery to one contributing to the injury by his own neglect. It is interesting to note that this court, acting upon the same reasons which doubtless influenced Congress in the enactment of this part of the statute, established a rule in principle the same, to govern the recovery in admiralty of damages by a person injured on a ship (*The Max Morris,* 137 U.S. 1, 14), holding that it promoted "the more equal distribution of justice, the dictates of humanity, the safety of life and limb and the public good." It is enough to say here that the decisions of the court in the safety appliance cases, supporting a statute changing the analogous common law doctrine of assumption of risk, are in principle conclusive that the whole subject of contributory negligence is under the control of the legislative power, in this respect unrestrained by any constitutional provision. But it is earnestly urged upon us that the statute under consideration, applying to all interstate common carriers and all their employés in that business, without distinguishing between that part of the business and employment which is dangerous and hazardous and that part which is not, and confined solely to the business of common carriage and its employers, is a deprivation of the employer's property without due process of law, in violation of the Fifth Amendment of the Constitution. The manner in which due process of law is said to be denied is by the denial of the equal protection of the laws by imposing unusual burdens upon a class of persons arbitrarily and capriciously selected. In support of this position cases from state courts interpreting state constitutions and cases from this court interpreting the restriction upon state action imposed by the Fourteenth Amendment, are indiscriminately cited. They furnish little aid.

It is not necessary in this case to determine how far, if at all, the requirement from the States of the equal protection of the laws made by the Fourteenth Amendment is included in the requirement from the Nation of due process of law made by the Fifth Amendment to the Constitution. It is enough to say that this statute complies with both. It is rather startling to hear that in enacting laws applicable to common carriers alone Congress has made a capricious and arbitrary classification. From time immemorial the common law has set apart those engaged in that business as a peculiar class, to be governed in many respects by laws peculiar to themselves. In separating carriers from those engaged in other interstate and foreign commerce, Congress has but followed the ancient classification of the common law, based upon reasons so obvious that they need no statement. Whether the law should be made to apply to all carriers or to carriers by railroad alone, or whether the employés should be classified according to the degree of danger which surrounds their employment, is a matter of legislative discretion with which we have no right to meddle. See *Union Pacific Railway Co.* v. *Mackey, ubi sup.*

I have confined my observations up to this point of the first three changes in the common law made by the statute. The fourth change, that forbidding the employé to make a contract releasing his employer from the consequences of his negligence, is open to a possible objection not common to the others. It is asserted that this part of the act violates the right of free contract which in some cases this court has protected against the exercise of the legislative power. Without intimating any opinion on that subject, it is enough to say that that part of the statute is separable from and independent of the remainder, and may stand or fall by itself, and that no question concerning it is raised in these cases. I see nothing in the provision that "all questions of negligence or contributory negligence shall be for the jury" which affects the right of jury trial guaranteed by the Seventh Amendment. Such questions always have been for the jury, and I cannot see that this enactment makes any change whatever.

I am of opinion, therefore, that the act should be sustained as a legitimate exercise of the authority of Congress, and that orders in these cases should be made accordingly.

Horace H. Lurton

☆ 1844–1914 ☆

APPOINTED BY

WILLIAM HOWARD TAFT

YEARS ON COURT

1910–1914

Horace H. Lurton

by

JAMES F. WATTS, JR.

HORACE HARMON LURTON'S accession to the Supreme Court came as a final reward for judicial services rendered over a thirty-five-year period. Patiently, almost step-by-step, the genial Tennessean ascended the state and federal judicial structures, always performing his duties scrupulously, always engendering trust in his integrity, never breaking new legal ground, never embracing controversy or encouraging turmoil. "He is said to have never had an enemy," wrote a colleague. "His friends were limited only by his acquaintanceship. . . ."

Lurton conceived of himself as a professional lawyer above everything else. Throughout fifty of his seventy years the study of the law comprised the man's avocation as well as his vocation. His deeply conservative nature conceived of the law as the basic instrument which held together a society constantly buffeted by winds of change. Although his legal philosophy was not the bleakly reactionary dogma of so many of his judicial contemporaries, Lurton always preserved a healthy respect for the status quo, and the bulk of his decisions consisted of complex ratiocinations justifying existing relationships, especially those involving property. Lurton held a strong faith in the belief that social stability could best be preserved by applying the solutions of the past to the problems of the present. Thus continuity, which he accounted a positive good, would be achieved through an even application of the law as derived from fixed principles and proven precedents. As the Tennessee jurist applied this philosophy through the years he acquired a favorable reputation for being a steady and predictable arbiter. "He did not attempt to render startling or sensational decisions," wrote one admiring observer, "but the just, steady-going judgments called for by justice and the enacted law."

In retrospect, the judgments made of Lurton by his contemporaries seem

JAMES F. WATTS, JR. is Assistant Professor of History at City College of New York and author of a forthcoming biography of Breckinridge Long.

at best to damn him with faint praise. Probably the best example is a memorial resolution adopted by the United States Court of Appeals for the Sixth Circuit soon after Justice Lurton's death on July 12, 1914. The resolution stated that "the quality of his mind was not striking or brilliant," and a few sentences later, in characterizing "men of Judge Lurton's type," freely admitted that "their achievements are not spectacular. . . ." In those days, before rhetoric had undergone the dilutive process of verbal inflation, this honest evaluation of Justice Lurton by some of his closest friends and associates conveys the commendable characteristics of honesty and accuracy. Accordingly, the resolution balanced Lurton's modest intellectual powers with the claim that "the solidity of his talent was unquestionable." In this manner, the admission of the unspectacular nature of Lurton's achievements was nicely harmonized with an endorsement of the type of stability characterized by Lurton and those like him; men who, according to the resolution:

> *. . . contribute an indispensable element of strength and solidity to our Supreme Court, and supply the foundation for that distinction which demands as a precedent condition sane and efficient performance of its severe routine tasks.* [*Memorial adopted by the United States Circuit Court of Appeals, at Cincinnati, Ohio, October 6, 1914, in 59* Ohio Law Bulletin, *389–393* (*1914*).]

Beyond this rather clearly defined sense of Lurton's *solidité,* an additional element of the man's nature had some significance. In effect, Judge Lurton became over the years of his service on the Tennessee Supreme Court and later on the United States Court of Appeals a kindly father figure in ermine robes, a courteous southern gentleman in whose court lawyers enjoyed to the fullest the practice of their profession. Lurton's appearance suggested the reincarnation of an ancient lawgiver: his large square face featured a classically high forehead rising above a thick unbroken line of grey-flecked eyebrows, beneath which were sunk a pair of gravely vacant eyes. The suggestion of classicism was completely shattered, however, somewhere between his ample nose and strong chin line by a massive walrus mustache, which covered both lips and effectively dominated his whole appearance. Peering down from his bench to the Court below, this rather striking figure was nonetheless able to convey a sense of gentleness and decorum to put his courtroom at ease. As some of his colleagues later reconstructed Lurton's judicial demeanor:

> *Cutting words were never on his lips. There were no scenes when he presided, and lawyers rejoiced in the evenness of his temper and the fairness of treatment which was accorded* [*to them*] *as a right.* [*12* Ohio Law Reporter *236* (*1914*).]

Lurton's pleasantly commanding presence on the bench developed naturally over a period of nearly forty years. His appointment in 1875 to a Tennessee chancery court began a succession of judicial involvements which included service on the Tennessee Supreme Court from 1886 until 1893 and on the United States Court of Appeals for the Sixth Circuit from 1893 until December of 1909, when his four and one-half year tenure on the United States Supreme Court commenced.

While the American environment was enduring the Great Barbecue, with all of its manifold excesses and excitements, Horace Lurton settled into the much more ordered world of bench and bar in rural Tennessee. Small town life certainly agreed with him, and his life was an expression of its value system. He lived most of his life in Clarksville, an old Cumberland River town of about 15,000 located about forty miles upriver northwest of Nashville. Lurton's English ancestors had originally settled in Virginia sometime in the eighteenth century, with elements of the family gradually moving westward in the great trans-Appalachian migration of the early nineteenth century. Horace Lurton's February 26, 1844, birth occurred in a Kentucky which was still dominated by Henry Clay, in the town of Newport, which faces Cincinnati across the Ohio River. Sometime during the 1850's Dr. Lycurgus Leonidas Lurton took his wife Sarah Ann and boy Horace southwesterly across the breadth of Kentucky and over the border into Tennessee to Clarksville. There Lurton's father practiced medicine for nearly twenty years before he abruptly changed the pattern of his life in 1870, when he was ordained a minister in the Protestant Episcopal Church. Young Horace grew up in Clarksville and attended the local schools until 1859 when, at the age of sixteen, he left home and travelled all the way to Chicago, where he was enrolled in the now extinct Douglas University. This trip to Chicago marked the beginning of Lurton's involvement in the world of affairs. The years soon to come found him in Cincinnati or Nashville or Washington, and yet his real home always remained Clarksville. There in the 'seventies and the 'eighties Judge Lurton became a pillar of the middle-class establishment: a full partner in the town's major law firm, president of the largest bank, a college trustee, a church vestryman.

This snug and somewhat mechanical world into which Horace Lurton fitted so comfortably contrasted sharply with the exciting tempo of his adventurous boyhood. Perhaps the prosaic nature of Lurton's later life can be explained at least in part by the fact that before he had yet reached his twenty-first birthday he had already experienced the kind of excitement and adventure which come to few men.

When the shots hit Fort Sumter, Horace Lurton immediately gave up his studies in Chicago. His sentiments were entirely southern and he thought of nothing but finding some way of joining the Confederate forces. Anxious as he was to get into the fight, Lurton's first responsibility lay in seeing that his parents, who were then with him, were returned to the comparative safety of Clarksville. The three Lurtons thus set out from Chicago on the long and possibly dangerous overland route through hundreds of miles of violent and emotionally split Illinois and Indiana and Kentucky. When they had safely reached southwestern Kentucky, within easy range of the Tennessee frontier, the young Lurton could wait no longer. Sending his parents on the extra few miles to Clarksville, Horace Lurton remained on in the Kentucky town of Bowling Green and joined up with the Fifth Tennessee Infantry Regiment.

The Fifth Tennessee (later the Thirty-Fifth) gave to the young volunteer the kind of action for which he craved, and Lurton responded. By the end of 1861, the eighteen-year-old boy had become a sergeant-major and a hardened campaign veteran. A lung infection, and perhaps a case of battle fatigue as well, soon intervened, however, and in February, 1862, Lurton returned to Clarksville with a medical discharge and orders to take a complete rest. The young man's "rest" lasted less than three weeks. When Sergeant Lurton arrived in Clarksville he learned of General Grant's move up the Cumberland a few miles to the west. He immediately reenlisted in the Second Kentucky Infantry and moved out to meet the combined land and sea forces of Grant and Admiral A. H. Foote as they approached the twin Confederate river strongholds of Forts Henry and Donnelson, the capture of which would open the river road to Nashville. Fort Henry fell quickly on February 6, but Grant met with fierce resistance a week later at Fort Donnelson from a large Confederate force that included Horace Lurton's Second Kentucky Infantry. For three days, from February 13 until the early morning hours of the 16th, the two armies raged at each other until the aggressiveness of Grant prevailed: Donnelson fell, the approach to Nashville lay open, and Grant hurried on to Shiloh. This major victory at Fort Donnelson brought with it a large cache of arms as well as some 12,000 rebel prisoners, among them Sgt. Horace Lurton.

As Grant drove on southward, Lurton and his comrades were marched far to the north to the prison at Camp Chase, in Columbus, Ohio. But Lurton escaped a few weeks later by taking advantage of Camp Chase's notoriously lax security provisions. Free in the countryside once more, Lurton and his friends immediately joined up with the swashbuckling guerilla band of General John Hunt Morgan.

For over a year Lurton rode with Morgan's irregular cavalry through a succession of daring raids. Throughout the entire month of July, 1862, for instance, Morgan and his men wreaked havoc with Union communications lines in Kentucky. Day after day, as James G. Randall has written, Morgan's lightning raids

> *. . . struck the line of the Louisville and Nashville* [*Railroad*] *in Kentucky, surprising small Union detachments, cutting railway tracks, wrecking bridges, capturing or destroying military stores, interrupting telegraph communications, intercepting Union dispatches, conveying false messages over the wire to the enemy, terrorizing small villages, and creating general havoc and confusion along the widely stretched Federal lines.* [*James G. Randall and David Donald,* The Civil War and Reconstruction, *(2d ed.; 1961) 406–7.*]

A month later, in August, Lurton's adventures with the Raiders brought him almost home to Clarksville, as Morgan's cavalry conducted a series of raids near Nashville which routed a substantially larger Union force under General R. W. Johnson. The skill of Morgan's horsemen and their hit-and-run tactics kept them in the field throughout 1862; not until the summer of 1863 did they finally meet their perhaps inevitable undoing. As the great mid-year campaign of Vicksburg and Gettysburg unfolded, Morgan's 2,500 irregulars began their famous and daring "Ohio raid," through central Kentucky into southern Indiana, on eastward to the outskirts of Cincinnati by mid-July, then along the upper Ohio. Hitting and running, and living off the land, they stole horses and supplies as they went, disrupting Union communications, plundering, killing. Finally surrounded on the upper Ohio at the end of July, most of Morgan's men were captured and imprisoned. Although Morgan himself escaped in November to ride for another year before being killed, the end of his effective guerilla activity came in July of 1863 with the imprisonment of most of his men in such major northern camps as the one on Johnson's Island in Lake Erie just north of Sandusky, Ohio, where Horace Lurton spent most of the rest of the war.

During this arduous eighteen-month prison stretch Lurton's troublesome lung condition again appeared, with his condition gradually deteriorating to the extent that his family feared for his life. The chart at the foot of the twenty-one-year-old veteran's bed was inscribed with the dread word "tuberculosis." Early in 1865 the thoroughly alarmed Sarah Ann Lurton, after seeing her son on Johnson Island, decided on the kind of drastic action which maternal instincts often dictate: she boarded a wartime train, and after riding for several days through "enemy" territory, arrived in Washington. Through some form of providence, or luck, she found a uniquely compassionate official who would disregard the passions of war and listen to the anguish of a southern mother's fears for her Confederate son's life. The story soon spread and reached the ears of the President himself. On February 23, 1865, Lincoln listened as Mrs. Lurton said, "Mr. President, my boy is doomed to death unless I can get him back to Tennessee. I want to take him home." According to the account often retold by Judge Lurton in later years, Lincoln replied: "I will parole him on sick leave." Sarah Ann Lurton objected, "But then it will be too late. I want to take him home with me." The President then reached for a pen and scribbled out the message, "Let the boy go home with his mother." As a consequence of this magnanimous act, the war ended for Horace Lurton two months before it did for those of his comrades who fought on until Appomattox in April. By the terms of President Lincoln's amnesty, Lurton had agreed not to rejoin his regiment, and he gladly returned to Clarksville. Throughout that nervous southern spring and summer, as the unpredictable Reconstruction began, young Lurton lived quietly, regaining his health and planning for the future.

Ironically enough, after such a full wartime commitment, during which he repeatedly risked his life for a cause the correctness of which he never questioned, Horace Lurton, at the age of twenty-one, had finished with politics. For the rest of his life, although always identifying himself as a Democrat, Lurton never again became involved in partisan affairs. For, sometime during the war, he had decided to immerse himself totally in the study of the law, and his new career began as soon as the guns fell silent.

The war's outbreak had interrupted his studies in Chicago and now he not only decided against returning there, but also decided against the continuation of formal undergraduate education altogether. Thus, in the late summer of 1865, Lurton again left his home town and travelled down to Nashville and then on eastward the few miles to Lebanon, the small town which contained the famous Cumberland University Law School. Writing of his own days as a Cumberland law student twenty-five years after Lurton's time, Cordell Hull boasted of the excellence of the faculty and of the quality of the student body, and termed Cumberland "a famous institution which had turned out many senators and congressmen—in fact, one of the greatest second-category law schools in the country." (Cordell Hull, 1 *Memoirs* 26–27).

Lurton spent two years of hard study at Cumberland, and soon after his graduation in June of 1867 he marked another important milestone by marrying Mary Francis Owen, daughter of a Lebanon physician. Their forty-four-year-long marriage was eventually to produce three sons and two daughters, as well as a lifetime of the closest personal relationship. Immediately after the ceremony the young couple returned to Clarksville where Lurton joined in a law partnership with Gustavus A. Henry. Soon thereafter, Lurton accepted an invitation to become a partner in the Clarksville law firm headed by James A. Bailey, a powerful Democratic politician who succeeded in 1875 to the unexpired Senate term of Andrew Johnson.

Young Lurton's early association with Senator Bailey during the 'seventies indicated a recognition of his potential by the most influential legal circles of the area, men who were attracted by Lurton's lifelong approach to the law: no matter how insignificant the case, Lurton doggedly searched out its implications, studied the precedents, and stinted no effort in behalf of every client.

As his reputation developed during the early 1870's the young Clarksville lawyer's ascendancy in Tennessee legal circles became mostly a matter of time. Lurton's first major opportunity came in July of 1875 when a Clarksville friend, Chancellor Charles G. Smith, decided to resign his position as presiding judge of the Sixth Chancery Division of Tennessee. Acting on the advice of local political leaders and bar officials, Governor James G. Porter decided to fill the post on an interim basis with the appointment of the thirty-one-year-old Horace Lurton, who thus became the youngest chancellor in Tennessee history. One year later, at the conclusion of the interim term, Lurton's peers on the bench voted unanimously to recommend his continuation in office, and he thus remained on this court of equity for an additional two years.

In 1878, as his first full term on the bench drew to a close, two basic problems forced Lurton to submit his resignation: with Senator Bailey in Washington and Horace Lurton spending most of his time in the chancellery court, the law firm was suffering badly. In addition, Lurton found it increasingly difficult to provide for an ever increasing family on the modest salary of the chancellery. Thus in 1878 Horace Lurton resigned from the court and joined in yet another legal partnership, this time with ex-Chancellor Smith.

With a solid professional reputation already established, Lurton in the next few years managed to attain financial and social prestige as well. He became president of the Farmers' and Merchants' National Bank in the late 'seventies, at about the same time that the Trinity Episcopal Church appointed him as a vestryman, a position which he held for the remainder of his life. In 1882, by which time his prominence had spread beyond Clarksville, Lurton was elected a trustee of the University of the South.

By the mid-1880's Horace Lurton had developed the kind of background that is usually essential for public men with ambition: family roots in the area, an admirable war record, proven professional competence, and solid middle-class respectability. Consequently, in 1886, when the two seats on the Tennessee Supreme Court designation for the north-central area came up for election, Lurton could make his move. He threw himself into the contest against two much more experienced jurists, one an incumbent Justice on the high court, the other a veteran lawyer with broad experience and solid political connections. Lurton conducted a vigorous stump campaign, travelling widely and calling on friends and associates throughout the area for aid and advice. His reputation and the confidence which he seemed to inspire, plus the added factor of his vigor and relative youth, were important factors in his success against significant odds. By running second, Horace Lurton became at age forty-two an Associate Justice of the Tennessee Supreme Court, where he remained until called to a higher court in 1893.

During the seven years which Lurton spent on the Tennessee Supreme Court several significant aspects of his basic approach to jurisprudence clearly emerged: gentleness, for example. Always a patient man in the years after his rather inflammatory youth, Lurton's kindness and courtesy pervaded the courtroom. Frequently he even took aside the losing lawyer in a case and attempted to convince him of the justice of the verdict. Furthermore, among his peers on the high court Lurton also assumed a commanding position. Always patient in listening to the diverse opinions of others, Lurton nonetheless possessed the transcendent ability of reconciling opposing arguments in such a way that his own point of view prevailed. On those occasions when Lurton saw fit to eschew compromise and take a strong view of his own, he was still nearly always able to bring the court along with him, and consequently only on rare occasions was he forced to file a dissent. Lurton's leadership became so strong so quickly that one contemporary report claimed: "In the opinion of the profession generally, Judge Lurton took the lead of the bench after his accession to it, and he maintained it so long as he was on the bench." Predictably enough, when the position of Chief Justice fell vacant in January, 1893, his colleagues voted unanimously for Horace H. Lurton, who then began what is perhaps one of the briefest tenures as a chief justice in all the history of the American legal system.

As President Grover Cleveland began his second term in 1893 one of his first official responsibilities involved filling the Supreme Court vacancy created by the death of the Mississippian Lucius Quintus Cincinnatus Lamar. Predictably, Cleveland selected another southerner, Howell Jackson, a Tennessean who conveniently possessed both strong Democratic political ties and lengthy judicial experience. Jackson had served in the Tennessee legislature and also, from 1881 until 1886, as a United States senator; by the time he replaced the departed Justice Lamar in 1893, Judge Jackson had for seven years been on the bench of the United States Court of Appeals for the Sixth Circuit, which met in Cincinnati.

In replacing Judge Jackson on the Court of Appeals the President preserved the identical political and regional composition by selecting Horace Lurton. For both men possessed a uniquely similar background, separated only by an age difference of about a decade. Each had served in the Confederate Army, graduated from the Cumberland University Law School (Jackson in 1856, Lurton eleven years later), served in high judicial office, considered themselves loyal Democrats, and possessed solid reputations in their communities. As a consequence of these fortuitous parallels, Lurton possessed the perfect qualifications for replacing Jackson in this very significant position.

Upon receiving the President's nomination, Horace Lurton immediately submitted his resignation as Chief Justice of the Tennessee Supreme Court, and travelled into Ohio once more, although this time his objectives there were much different than during his earlier visits with General Morgan. When he arrived in Cincinnati in 1893 Lurton had just passed his forty-ninth birthday. Hidden from him was the realization that he would spend the prime of his life on this Court of Appeals, for he remained there until 1910 when, nearing the age of sixty-six, he accepted President Taft's call to the United States Supreme Court.

At the time of Lurton's appointment, the United States Court of Appeals for the Sixth Circuit was dominated by its presiding judge, William Howard Taft, who had joined the court the previous year. Taft was only thirty-six in 1893, with a term as United States Solicitor General already behind him, and his years of power and responsibility still lying a few years ahead. In 1899, six years after Lurton joined this court, another Ohio Republican, William Rufus Day, came onto the Sixth Circuit bench. Day, a very close friend of President McKinley, had served as Secretary of State through most of 1898 during the height of the crisis with Spain; in 1903, he would begin a nineteen-year term on the United States Supreme Court. Lurton befriended both the massive Taft and the diminutive Day, and the solid friendship forged among the three men endured not only through their years together on the bench but also after the century's turn as well. Political differences never obstructed the relationship between the Tennessee Democrat and the two Ohio Republicans: partisan feelings were completely dissolved by the personal congeniality of the three men as well as by the innate juridical conservatism which they shared.

Judge Horace Lurton's rather consistent espousal of established property relationships developed as much from his belief in the proper mechanics of legal application as from political or ideological commitments. Throughout his long tenure on the court of appeals Lurton consistently revealed himself as a judicial technician. He would carefully listen to every case with infinite patience, scrupulously identify the basic issue, and then meticulously search back through the maze of legal history until he uncovered the correct precedent which provided a solution. One of Judge Lurton's closest friends, Ohio Governor Judson Harmon, once emphasized this ability of Lurton "to grasp essential facts and apply the right principles to them." Lurton's steady faith in the soundness of solving even the most vexing legal questions by the steady application of the fixed, tried and true principles of the past naturally produced his abhorrence for "judge-made" law. Deeply reverential toward the spirit of the separation of powers, Lurton opposed any blurring whatsoever of constitutional functions: legislatures subjectively determined what the law should be, the judiciary objectively determined what it was. As Lurton himself wrote a few years later: "The function of the judge does not include any alteration, modification or amendment of any authoritative enactment of the legislative body . . . a judge may not explain it away if he happens to think it a bad or unwise law."

Ironically, Lurton's consistent application of fixed principles to new situations in itself provided for the type of judicial intervention against which he claimed to stand so vigorously. The Judge found no inconsistency in preaching absolute judicial restraint while simultaneously utilizing inherent judicial powers of obstruction to delay the implementation of social legislation. Lurton clearly recognized the ability of the courts to frustrate popular social legislation, for he wrote in 1911:

> *To override constitutional methods spells revolution and tends to the destruction of a government of law. To yield to the clamor of a temporary majority upon the pretense that otherwise popular government is prevented is but to overthrow the barriers which the people themselves, under great deliberation, have erected against their own impulsive majorities. These impediments to hasty action are intended not only as bulwarks for the defense of minorities, but as defences against hotfooted action by temporary majorities in supposed exigencies.* [*193* North American Review *20 (1911)*.]

Lurton's ingrained conservatism thus found its roots in his dependence for legal wisdom upon fixed precedents frozen into the past. Many of the legal problems of his own time, however, resulted from unprecedented situations deriving from the industrial revolution, and consequently he found himself philosophically unable to participate in legal trailblazing.

Basically, Lurton shared this general conservative approach with the majority of his colleagues on the Sixth Circuit Court of Appeals, including Taft and Day. The philosophical cast of this court assumed some special significance during the period, moreover. According to one observer, Lurton and his colleagues "constituted easily the ablest of the contemporary Circuit Courts of Appeals, and their judgments and opinions were legal tender everywhere."

Lurton's stature among his colleagues and with the legal profession in general was enhanced by those qualities of his personality and demeanor which had so favorably impressed his Tennessee associates. Commentators on the affairs of the court rarely failed to mention Judge Lurton's ptaience and courtesy on the bench, no matter how trying the situation. In the sanctity of the judicial chambers, moreover, Lurton continued to practice the arts of compromise, displaying the greatest respect for differing opinions, frankly stating his own views, and always attempting to reconcile diverse positions. This he frequently accomplished, and with such a minimum of friction and acrimony that in the process he endeared himself to his colleagues. "In enumerating his judicial qualifications," Governor Harmon once wrote of this gentle hulk of a man, "the purity of his private character and his consistent but unobtrusive piety must not be omitted."

Throughout the 1890's and into the new century, for sixteen of the best years of his life, Horace Lurton lent his benign presence to the court of appeals in Cincinnati. With mixed feelings he watched his two Ohio colleagues—his very close friends Day and Taft—profit from the Republican salad days of McKinleyism. Day succeeded the senile John Sherman of Ohio as Secretary of State, serving throughout the hectic year of 1898, and in 1903 began a tenure on the Supreme Court of nearly twenty years. Taft left the court of appeals in 1900 and began his own even swifter ascent in Republican affairs, from Governor General of the Philippines to Secretary of War and presidential factotum to President of the United States, all within a decade.

Lurton remained behind in Cincinnati, seemingly settled for life. In 1900, as Taft left for the Philippines, the Court unanimously selected the fifty-six-year-old Tennessean to replace him as presiding judge. Thus Lurton settled even deeper into the comfortable world bounded by Cincinnati and Nashville legal circles, by the responsibilities of the Sixth Circuit Court and by the Law School at Vanderbilt University, where he served as a part-time professor from 1898 until 1905, and as Dean from 1905 until 1910. As the years unfolded and the Judge gradually passed beyond middle age, his future rule appeared to be quite predictable. His judicial responsibilities were clearly defined; in addition, the nation's strongly Republican political complexion militated against any major appointive post for a man like Lurton, who proudly styled himself as a "Cleveland Democrat."

Yet a variety of factors did intervene to disrupt the relative tranquility and predictability of Judge Lurton's life. Men like Taft and Day, even as they accumulated power and influence under Theodore Roosevelt, did not forget the deep impression which Horace Lurton had made upon them: integrity, courtesy, the congeniality of his gracious personality, the confidence which his safe and sane legal philosophy engendered. When Justice Henry B. Brown retired from the Supreme Court in 1906, therefore, Taft and Day immediately launched an all-out campaign to secure the appointment of their friend, the Cleveland Democrat from Tennessee.

President Theodore Roosevelt had his own well-developed ideas about nominees to the Court. He had inherited a decidedly conservative Court, seven of whose members defended property rights in the inflexible nineteenth century manner which quickly became an anathema to the modest progressivism of the Square Deal. "I want on the bench a follower of Hamilton and Marshall and not a follower of Jefferson and Calhoun," Roosevelt informed Lodge in 1906, "and what is more I do not want any man who from frivolity, or disinclination to think, or ignorance, or indifference to popular moods, goes wrong on great questions." By 1906 Roosevelt had managed to shift the Court's balance by the appointments of Day and Oliver Wendell Holmes, both of whom generally favored the broad liberal nationalist approach that the President found congenial. Thus the appointment of Henry Brown's replacement might, theoretically at least, tip the balance in favor of the "liberal" group of Day and Holmes and Justices John Marshall Harlan and Joseph McKenna. Although the legal philosophy of Horace Lurton seemed scarcely suited to Theodore Roosevelt's stated criteria, Taft and Day nonetheless convinced the President that their friend was the right man for the job.

Roosevelt apparently based his tentative decision to appoint Lurton to the High Court on a number of factors. As he wrote to Lodge on September 4, 1906, "Taft and Day, his two former associates, are very desirous of having him on." Furthermore, Lurton's two influential Republican friends were able to convince the President that Lurton was "right" on all the important issues. As Roosevelt described the convictions of the cautious and conservative Tennessee Democrat to the partisan Republican Senator from Massachusetts:

> *He is right on the Negro question; he is right on the power of the Federal Government; he is right on the insular business; he is right about corporations; and he is right about labor. On every question that would come before the bench he has so far shown himself to be in much closer touch with the policies in which you and I believe than even* [*Justice Edward D.*] *White, because he has been right about corporations, where White has been wrong. . . .*

In addition to this favorable impression of Lurton's judicial qualifications, Roosevelt also related to Lodge the political advantages inherent in making this particular appointment. By naming an ex-Confederate soldier and Tennessee Democrat, the President wrote, "I have shown . . . that I pay heed only to the real needs of the Court. . . ." Thus Roosevelt would justify filling the next Court vacancy with William H. Moody of Massachusetts, his Attorney General and close personal friend on the same grounds, that is, selecting the man best qualified for the position regardless of party and geography. The chief factor preventing the immediate appointment of Moody, in the President's eyes at least, was the fact that Massachusetts already had representation on the Court in the person of Oliver Wendell Holmes. "I have not definitely made up my mind," Roosevelt admitted to Lodge on September 4, "but the above represents my present intention."

Roosevelt's arguments failed totally to convince Henry Cabot Lodge. Despite the wishes of War Secretary Taft and Mr. Justice Day, the powerful Republican Senator had opposed Lurton's appointment from the start; he now increased his opposition. "I am glad that Lurton holds all the opinions that you say he does, and that you are so familiar with his views," wrote Lodge to the President on September 10 with perhaps just a trace of sarcasm, "but I do not see why Republicans cannot be found who hold these opinions as well as Democrats." Lodge went on to criticize the narrow legal views of southern Democrats, alluded to the fact that the Sixth Circuit Court of Appeals had already been tapped to fill three or four Supreme Court vacancies in recent years, and closed with a plea for the appointment of Attorney General Moody. The popular and extremely capable Moody, who possessed impeccable Republican credentials, had just privately informed Roosevelt and Lodge of his desire to return to private life, and both men were extremely anxious to dissuade him. As a consequence of these considerations, the President changed his mind: Moody received the Supreme Court appointment and Horace Lurton remained on the court of appeals until summoned to the Supreme Court three years later by another Republican President, William Howard Taft. (The Roosevelt-Lodge exchange cited above is found in *Selections from the Correspondence of Theodore Roosevelt and Henry Cabot Lodge, 1884–1918* 2 vols. [New York and London, 1925] 228–230.)

No additional Supreme Court openings occurred during the balance of Roosevelt's tenure in the White House, and Lurton, a bit disappointed, remained at his post in Cincinnati. Soon after Taft took office in the spring of 1909, however, no fewer than five seats on the Court were vacated in rapid order. Justice Rufus W. Peckham passed away in 1909, and within the next twelve months Chief Justice Melville W. Fuller and Justice David J. Brewer both died and Justice William H. Moody, crippled by rheumatism, resigned. In 1911, the seventy-eight-year-old John Marshall Harlan, on the bench since 1877, also died Consequently, President Taft had the rare opportunity of remolding the Court within a very brief period to fit his own specifications.

Throughout his life, Taft's major preoccupation had been with the American judicial system, and especially with the Supreme Court, to which he aspired for so many years prior to his 1920 appointment as Chief Justice. When Justice Peckham died in 1909, therefore, President Taft very carefully considered this his first appointment to the High Bench. In December, he named Judge Horace H. Lurton.

Making Lurton's appointment was not as easy for the President as it might have been, the enduring personal relationship between the two men notwithstanding. Many voices were raised contesting Taft's thoroughly favorable assessment of Lurton's judicial impartiality, for example. Seconding Samuel Gompers' assessment of Lurton as a "narrow conservative" were several Nashville lawyers, who took exception to Lurton's alleged favoritism toward corporations, especially railroads. As one of them, John J. Ventrees, wrote,

> *In these days judges are apt to be classified under two heads: those who place the emphasis upon property rights and those who place the emphasis on personal rights. To the former class belongs Judge Lurton.* [*48* Current Literature *272 (1910)*.]

Others objected to Lurton on the basis of his advanced age, sixty-six. Taft himself, upon taking office, had privately complained about the "near senility" of several of the older men on an aged Court; yet here he was contemplating the appointment of a man who would be the oldest ever to ascend to the Court. His own Attorney General, George Wickersham, frankly objected to the Lurton nomination on just this basis, and pointed out that sentiment in Washington legal circles and on the Court itself was running against Taft's favorite because of his advanced age.

Naturally, Lurton closely followed this controversy, responding to the critics in his usual benign manner: "I have seen some newspaper criticism of some judgments [of mine]," he admitted, mildly adding, "I can only stand upon the general judgment of my work and upon the integrity of my purpose. If I have not made mistakes I would have been immaculate." (7 *Ohio Law Reporter* 524 [1909].)

This mild December storm left the President very distressed. Suggestions that he overlook Lurton "tore at my heart strings," he wrote on December 6, adding that "there was nothing that I had so much at heart in my whole administration as Lurton's appointment." (Henry F. Pringle, 1 *The Life and Times of William Howard Taft* 531. For Taft's general assessment of the Court, see pp. 529–537.) After hesitating for a fortnight, the President made his decision, and on December 13 sent Judge Lurton's name to the Senate for confirmation. At the same time he wired his old friend:

> *It is just the truth to tell you that the only pleasure of my administration, as I have contemplated it in the past, has been to commission you a justice of the Supreme Court. . . . [Pringle, I* Taft *531.]*

Lurton was handed the President's wire during a Court meeting. He immediately instructed a page to inform his wife, but gave his associates no intimation of the news until the recess. After receiving the warm congratulations of his colleagues, the proud Justice-designate said:

> *I have felt that if the President, who knows me better than any one else, should conclude that I could better serve the country on the Supreme Bench during the remainder of my judicial career, I would regard it as the greatest honor which could come to me. Now that he has indicated his confidence, I tremble at the responsibility. [7* Ohio Law Reporter *523 (1909).]*

Within a few days Lurton had concluded the Court's affairs and returned to Tennessee to receive the plaudits of his many friends and associates. The morning after an impressive black-tie dinner in Nashville on the evening of December 23, the Lurton family boarded a train for Washington which followed a route that had been carefully selected by Judge Lurton. He had politely declined the invitation of several friends to stop over in Cincinnati, since he attached great symbolic significance to his journey northward. As he later wrote:

> *I felt that in appointing me, President Taft, aside from the manifestations of his friendship, had a kindly heart for the South; that he wished to draw the South to him with cords of affection. So, being all a Southerner myself, I determined to go to Washington through the South—every foot of the way.* [48 Current Literature *272 (1910).]*

Almost as soon as the family was settled in their Washington hotel they received as their first caller the President of the United States. Delighted with the prospect of close companionship once more, the ponderous Taft, swathed in a massive greatcoat, affectionately greeted the ruddy and robust Lurton, whose spryness belied his years, even though he had recently taken on a good deal of weight himself. After reliving some of the past and ranging over more topical problems, Lurton assured the President of his eagerness to take his place on the Court. A few days later, Horace Harmon Lurton, almost sixty-six years of age, was sworn in as the sixty-first Supreme Court Justice in the nation's history, with the twin distinctions of being the oldest man ever appointed to the High Court and also the only "ex-convict" in its history.

Lurton began hearing cases in the Supreme Court's 1910 term, during a period in which the Court was attempting—with some difficulty—to reconcile the conflicting demands for social and economic justice with the profit-making prerogatives of corporate enterprises. In a succession of decisions, Lurton joined with most of his new colleagues in sanctioning a modest increase in the police powers of the federal government while simultaneously protecting property rights to the extent that corporate power and monopolistic control gained rather than lost strength.

The Court's general willingness to sanction the growth of federal police power was perhaps most evident in a series of decisions which ostensibly upheld the Sherman Anti-Trust Act. In the two celebrated cases of 1911, Lurton participated in the unanimous decisions which forced the oil and tobacco trusts to reorganize (*Standard Oil* v. *United States,* 221 U.S. 1 [1911]; *United States* v. *American Tobacco Co.,* 221 U.S. 106 [1911]). The effect of these Court verdicts was much more apparent than real. While the Court upheld in both instances the government's contention that the trusts had violated the Sherman Act, Chief Justice Edward D. White's two opinions introduced the concept of "reasonable" monopolies. As a direct consequence, various trusts (including oil and tobacco) immediately reorganized their corporate structures, built up rhetorical defenses as "reasonable" combinations and, in effect, opened the way for the unprecedented and unopposed development of corporate combinations during the 1920's. The Sherman Act was emasculated as effectively by the White Court as it had been by the ultra-conservative Fuller Court during the 1890's.

While the Court during Lurton's brief tenure refused to use the Sherman Act effectively against the giant corporations, many of the Justices did employ the act vigorously when lesser combinations were involved. In 1912, for example, Justice Lurton delivered the unanimous Court's sharp and direct opinion in *United States* v. *Terminal Railroad Association of St. Louis,* 224 U.S. 383 (1912), a dispute involving a group of thirty-eight individuals and corporations who had gained control of all feasible means of railroad access to St. Louis. The Court found the Terminal Association to be in clear violation of the Sherman Act's provisions against rate discrimination and, by the terms of Lurton's brisk opinion, this local monopoly was ordered to be immediately dissolved.

Horace Lurton's willingness to flow with the tide of the Court's moderate liberal nationalism was manifested in several other instances. He concurred in a number of decisions which had the effect of modestly augmenting the government's regulatory powers. In *Second Employers' Liability Cases,* 223 U.S. 1 (1912), the unanimous Court sanctioned the right of Congress to regulate all phases of the relationship between interstate transportation carriers and their employees. In *Hipolite Egg Co.* v. *United States,* 220 U.S. 45 (1911), Lurton joined the unanimous Court in sustaining a broad interpretation of the Pure Food and Drug Act. Two years later, in *Hoke* v. *United States,* 227 U.S. 308 (1913), Lurton assented to Justice Joseph McKenna's strong endorsement of the constitutionality of the Mann Act, on the basis of the use of the commerce power to promote the general welfare.

The Supreme Court also confirmed the expanding powers of the Interstate Commerce Commission, which had been markedly strengthened by the passage of the Hepburn Act in 1906, in a series of later decisions in which Justice Lurton concurred. Among the more significant cases was *Interstate Commerce Commission* v. *Chicago, Rock Island and Pacific Railway Co.,* 218 U.S. 88 (1910), a four to three decision in which Justice Lurton's vote aided in resolving the issue in favor of the I.C.C. In 1913, in *Minnesota Rate Cases,* 230 U.S. 352 (1913), Lurton joined the unanimous Court in further strengthening the commission's hand.

By his decisions in these and in several other cases Horace Lurton established a fairly consistent voting pattern. He generally drifted along with the substantial majority of the Court, finding precedents that allowed him to support the slightly expanded powers assumed by the government during the Progressive Era.

And in antitrust cases, he consistently voted with a majority that upheld the Sherman Act (especially in issues involving lesser corporations) while at the same time rendering it powerless to deal with corporate giants by sanctioning the concept of "reasonable" monopolies.

One of Lurton's most significant decisions clearly revealed his approach to the antitrust question. In 1911, the A. B. Dick Company, a large Chicago manufacturer of duplicating machines, brought suit against one of its retailers who had refused to abide with company restrictions whereby an A. B. Dick office machine could be operated only with stencils and ink that was provided to retailers by the company. The case eventually came before the Supreme Court as *Henry* v. *A. B. Dick Co.,* 224 U.S. 1 (1912), where it was decided by a four to three margin, with Justice Lurton writing the majority opinion.

In formulating his thirty-eight page argument Lurton, after citing literally dozens of legal precedents, cast his argument on the narrow basis of the retailer's conscious violation of the restrictions placed upon the use of the machine by the A. B. Dick Company. The defendants had argued, in part:

> *The license restriction* [*imposed by the Company*] *is void because unreasonable and tending to create an unlawful, permanent monopoly in the patentee in something which is not protected in his patent.* [*224 U.S. at 6.*]

Lurton fully disagreed on two counts. For one thing, argued the Justice, the company had created the market in the first place by the creation and marketing of a new invention. "Had he kept his invention to himself," Lurton contended,

> *. . . no ink could have been sold by others for use upon machines embodying that invention. By selling it subject to the restriction he [the Company] took nothing from others and in no wise restricted their legitimate market. [224 U.S. at 32.]*

By the use of Justice Lurton's logic, therefore, certain monopolies could freely set whatever restrictions they so desired on the distribution and retailing of products which they alone controlled. In the words of this Lurton decision, ". . . if the right of use be confined by specific restriction, the use not permitted is necessarily reserved to the patentee." [224 U.S. at 24.]

In many other respects, Lurton continued to be a convinced traditionalist. Early in 1911, after nearly a year on the Court, Lurton published an extensive and candid account of his judicial philosophy in an article entitled "A Government of Law or a Government of Men?" 193 *North American Review* 9–25 (1911). The author quickly revealed the rhetorical nature of the title by equating "a government of men" with "despotism." He revealed himself as feeling very uncomfortable with increasing public demands for ameliorative legislation, demands which darkly suggested the rise of mob rule and demagogues playing on the ignorant masses of immigrants who were washing up on America's shores in such great numbers. In addition, the Justice scored judicial interpretations aimed at rectifying social ills, the increasingly popular theory of sociological jurisprudence. In Lurton's opinion, this "judge-made law" struck at the foundations of the American constitutional system. As he wrote:

> *The contention that the obligation of a Constitution is to be disregarded if it stands in the way of that which is deemed of public advantage, or that a valid law, under the Constitution, is to be interpreted or modified so as to accomplish that which the executive administering it, or a Court called upon to enforce it, shall deem to the public advantage, is destructive of the whole theory upon which our American Commonwealths have been founded. . . . It is a substitution of a government of men for a government of law. It is against this that I warn.* [Loc. cit., *12*.]

Since the activities of the Court consumed most of his time, Justice Lurton's activities in Washington were quite limited. He and his wife did not particularly enjoy Washington social life and, except for informal dinner parties with the Tafts and other close friends, they kept to themselves, retiring and rising early in the natural rhythm of the aging.

Lurton did agree to serve with Chief Justice White and Associate Justice Willis Van Devanter on a presidential committee charged with revising federal equity rules. The subject apparently fascinated Lurton, as he spent many months on the project, even visiting England in the summer of 1911 to study and confer with experts there on the subject. In testimony to his devoted work, the 1913 publication of *New Federal Equity Rules* was dedicated to the Tennessean.

Late in the 1913 term, his third on the Court, illness struck and Lurton was forced off the bench for several weeks, occasioning rumors of his impending retirement. The seventy-year-old Justice showed no such inclination, however. After a Florida vacation with his family, Lurton returned to Washington in April of 1914 and immediately resumed his place on the bench. He fully participated in deliberations until the term ended in June. On the first of July, the Lurtons arrived in Atlantic City for another period of total relaxation. The ocean air seemed to have restorative effects, as the aging Justice enjoyed spending the long days sitting and strolling the boardwalk. After returning from his nightly walk on July 11 in excellent spirits, Lurton retired about 9 P.M., only to be awakened in great pain four hours later. His wife immediately summoned a physician, but the cardiac damage had been severe. The death watch continued over four difficult hours before the end came at 5 A.M. on the twelfth of July, 1914, seventy years after birth.

Expressions of sympathy followed the funeral train on its southward journey to Clarksville. Celebrated jurists and country lawyers wired condolences, eulogies appeared in newspapers throughout the land, and Chief Justice Edward D. White arrived for Horace Lurton's funeral. All activity ceased in Clarksville on the afternoon of July 15. Thousands flooded the grounds of the Episcopal Church and Greenwood Cemetery to pay last respects to the then-famous man who had first arrived in town sixty years before as the gawky son of an itinerant physician-preacher. Horace Lurton had lived the American Dream, worked hard, played by the established rules, practiced moderation, done his best, achieved success, and satisfied most of his peers.

SELECTED BIBLIOGRAPHY

A three hundred item collection of Justice Lurton's correspondence is in the Manuscripts Division of the Library of Congress. The following materials provide various kinds of information about the Justice. On Lurton's early life in Tennessee see 8 *National Cyclopaedia of American Biography* 235 (1924); 5 *Green Bag* 231 (1893); 4 *Tennessee Historical Quarterly* 186 (1945). For Lurton's version of his mother's encounter with President Lincoln, see 107 *Outlook* 684 (1914). Various insights may be gained through reactions to his Supreme Court appointment, for which consult 22 *Green Bag* 1 (1910); 48 *Current Literature* 271 (1910); 12 *Ohio Law Reporter* 523 (1909); and 94 *Outlook* 2 (1910), which probably was written by Theodore Roosevelt and is so laudatory that it might constitute a partial repayment for Roosevelt's failure to appoint Lurton in 1906. Obituary notices provide additional information: see 59 *Ohio Law Bulletin* 389 (1914); 12 *Ohio Law Reporter* 233 (1914); and *The New York Times,* July 13; 14, 1914.

Horace H. Lurton

REPRESENTATIVE OPINIONS

HENRY v. A. B. DICK CO., 224 U.S. 1 (1912)

The complainant, the A. B. Dick Company, had sold to Henry, a New York City merchant, a duplicating machine which performed a patented stenciling process. The Dick Company made the stipulation that the process be used only with such unpatented A. B. Dick products as stencils and ink. When Henry sold to his customers another type of ink for use with the Dick stencil process, complainant sued, charging infringement of two letters patent. The defendant argued that the company's restrictions were "unreasonable and tending to create an unlawful, permanent monopoly in the patentee in something which is not protected in his patent" (224 U.S. at 6). Justice Lurton disagreed with the defendant in the majority opinion which he wrote for a Court that was divided by four to three. Lurton argued that the patentee had created the market with this invention, and that his restrictions in no way circumscribed the legitimate markets of others. He further held that a purchaser's property rights to a patented article, when "confined by specific restriction," were absolutely limited by those restrictions (224 U.S. at 24). By Lurton's decision, the A. B. Dick Company, which held a monopoly on the stencil-duplicating process, was freed to set whatever restrictions it so desired.

MR. JUSTICE LURTON delivered the opinion of the court.

This cause comes to this court upon a certificate under the sixth section of the Court of Appeals Act of March 31, 1891.

The facts and the questions certified, omitting the terms of the injunction awarded by the Circuit Court, are these:

"This action was brought by the complainant, an Illinois corporation, for the infringement of two letters patent, owned by the complainant, covering a stencil-duplicating machine known as the 'Rotary Mimeograph.' The defendants are doing business as co-partners in the City of New York. The complainants sold to one Christina B. Skou, of New York, a Rotary Mimeograph embodying the invention described and claimed in said patents under license which was attached to said machine, as follows:

"LICENSE RESTRICTION.

"This machine is sold by the A. B. Dick Co. with the license restriction that it may be used only with the stencil paper, ink and other supplies made by A. B. Dick Company, Chicago, U. S. A.

"The defendant, Sidney Henry, sold to Miss Skou a can of ink suitable for use upon said mimeograph with knowledge of the said license agreement and with the expectation that it would be used in connection with said mimeograph. The ink sold to Miss Skou was not covered by the claims of said patent."

"QUESTION CERTIFIED.

"Upon the facts above set forth the question concerning which this court desires the instruction of the Supreme Court is:

"Did the acts of the defendants constitute contributory infringement of the complainant's patents?"

There could have been no contributory infringement by the defendants, unless the use of Miss Skou's machine with ink not made by the complainants would have been a direct infringement. It is not denied that she accepted the machine with notice of the conditions under which the patentee consented to its use. Nor is it denied that thereby she agreed not to use the machine otherwise. What defendants say is that this agreement was collateral, and that its validity depended upon principles of general law, and that if valid the only remedy is such as is afforded by general principles of law. Therefore, they say that the suit is not one arising under the patent law, and one not cognizable in a Federal court, unless diversity of citizenship exists.

But before coming to the question whether this is a suit of which the Circuit Court had jurisdiction as a suit arising under the patent law, it may be well to notice an argument against jurisdiction based upon the suggestion that if a breach of such a license restriction will support a suit for infringement, direful results will follow. Chief among the results suggested are, an encroachment upon the authority of the state courts and an extension of the jurisdiction of the Federal courts. And to swell the grievance it is said that if it be held that a breach of such a restriction will support a suit for infringement, parties will be deprived of the right to have the validity and import of the license restriction determined by the general law, and be compelled to have their rights determined by the patent law.

We are unable to assent to these suggestions. We do not prescribe the jurisdiction of courts, Federal or state, but only give effect to it as fixed by law. If a bill asserts a right under the patent law to sell a patented machine subject to restrictions as to its use, and alleges a use in violation of the restrictions as an infringement of the patent, it presents a question of the extent of the patentee's privilege, which, if determined one way, brings the prohibited use within the provisions of the patent law, or, if determined the other way, brings into operation only principles of general law. Obviously, a suit for infringement, which must turn upon the scope of the monopoly or privilege secured to a patentee, presents a case arising under the patent law. The jurisdiction of the Circuit Court over such cases has, for more than a century, been *exclusive,* by the express terms of the statute, although, for the most part, its jurisdiction over other kinds of suits arising under the Constitution and laws of the United States is only concurrent with that of the state courts.

The suggestion, therefore, that we should refrain from ruling that a patentee may sell a patented machine subject to restrictions as to its use, and may predicate infringement upon a use in violation of the restrictions lest such a ruling may draw to the Federal courts cases which otherwise would not come to them, cannot be sustained without placing our decision upon considerations which are quite apart from the law. This, of course, we may not do. In determining questions of jurisdiction, this court has never shirked the responsibility of maintaining the lines of separation defined in the Constitution and the laws made in pursuance thereof, but, on the contrary, has been ever watchful to maintain those lines as obligatory alike upon all courts and all suitors.

We come, then, to the question, whether a suit for infringement is here presented.

That the license agreement constitutes a contract not to use the machine in a prohibited manner, is plain. That defendants might be sued upon the broken contract, or for its enforcement or for the forfeiture of the license, is likewise plain. But if by the use of the machine in a prohibited way Miss Skou infringed the patent, then she is also liable to an action under the patent law for infringement. Now that is primarily what the bill alleged, and this suit is one brought to restrain the defendants as aiders and abettors to her proposed infringing use.

That the patentee may waive the tort and sue upon the broken contract, or in assumpsit, is elementary. Robinson on Patents, § § 1225, 1250, and notes; *Steam Stone Cutter Co.* v. *Sheldons,* 15 Fed. Rep. 608; *Pope Mfg. Co.* v. *Owsley,* 27 Fed. Rep. 100; *Button Fastener Cases,* 77 Fed. Rep. 288, 291; *Wilson* v. *Sandford,* 10 How. 99. But if the patentee elect to waive the tort and sue upon the convenants or for a breach of contract, the suit would not be one dependent upon or arising out of the patent law, and a Federal court would have no jurisdiction unless diversity of citizenship existed. Robinson on Patents, § 1250; *Magic Ruffle Co.* v. *Elm City Co.,* 13 Blatchf. 151; *Goodyear* v. *Union India Rubber Co.,* 4 Blatchf. 63; *Goodyear* v. *Congress Rubber Co.,* 3 Blatchf. 449. This would be so although the damages for a breach would be measured by the loss resulting from the infringement. *Magic Ruffle Co.* v. *Elm City Co.,* 13 Blatchf. 151. After such a recovery in assumpsit, no further damages for the infringement can be claimed. *Steam Stone Cutter Co.* v. *Sheldons,* 15 Fed. Rep. 608.

The remedy which the complainant seeks may often determine whether the suit is one arising under the patent law and cognizable only in a court of the United States, or one upon a contract between the patentee and his assigns or licensees, and, therefore, cognizable only in a state court, unless there be diversity of citizenship. Thus, a bill to enforce a contract concerning the title to a patent, or an interest therein, or to declare a forfeiture of an assignment of an interest in a patent, or even a license to make, sell or use the patented thing, or an action to recover damages for a breach of a contract relating to a patent or a license thereunder, would not, because of the character of remedy or relief sought, be a suit cognizable in a United States court, although the facts stated might have justified a suit for infringement in a United States court, if the complainant had elected that remedy. To sustain the contention that a breach of the implied agreement not to use the machine in question except in a particular way might have supported a suit to forfeit the license, or an action for damages upon the broken contract, counsel have cited and commented at great length upon the cases of *Wilson* v. *Sandford,* 10 How. 99; *Dale Tile Mfg. Co.* v. *Hyatt,* 125 U.S. 46; *Albright* v. *Teas,* 106 U.S. 613; *Hartell* v. *Tilghman,* 99 U.S. 547; *Pratt* v. *Paris Gaslight & Coke Co.,* 168 U.S. 255; *Keeler* v. *Standard Folding Bed Co.,* 157 U.S. 659, and *Bement* v. *National Harrow Co.,* 186 U.S. 70; but an examination of these cases will disclose that while in some of them a suit for infringement might have been brought, the complainants had in fact brought suits to set aside or enforce contracts relating to patents, or licenses under patents. They were, therefore, not "Patent cases," but cases determinable upon principles of general law. In *Excelsior Wooden Pipe Co.* v. *Pacific Bridge Co.,* 185 U.S. 282; Mr. Justice Brown reviews the cases and shows so plainly why they were not patent cases that we shall only refer to that opinion.

To support their contention that the only remedy for a violation of the license under which Miss Skou acquired her machine is one in the state courts, counsel quote a paragraph from the same opinion in these words: "Now, it may be freely conceded that if the licensee had failed to observe any one of the three conditions of the license, the licensor would have been obliged to resort to the state courts, either to recover the royalties or to procure a revocation of the license. Such suit would not involve any question under the patent law." But the three conditions of the license there referred to were: First, to pay royalties; second, that the transferee would not transfer or assign the license without consent of the licensor; third, that the failure to use the license in the manufacture of pipe should operate to revoke it. It is evident that the licensee would not have infringed the patent by either failing to pay royalties, by assigning the license, or by neglecting to use his privilege. The licensor would clearly have been compelled to rely wholly upon his contract, as such, in any suit for the violation of any of the conditions named.

The test of jurisdiction is this: Does the complainant "set up some right, title or interest under the patent laws of the United States, or make it appear that some right or privilege will be defeated by one construction, or sustained by another, of those laws?" *Excelsior Wooden Pipe Co.* v. *Pacific Bridge Co.,* 185 U.S. 282; *Pratt* v. *Paris Gaslight & Coke Co.,* 168 U.S. 255, 259; *White* v. *Rankin,* 144 U.S. 628.

The bill alleges that the complainant's patent has been infringed by the breach of the conditions upon which the patented machine was sold. The remedy it seeks is an injunction against indirect infringement by the defendants. The facts stated upon the face of the bill may be insufficient to show an infringement of the patent; but the right to treat the conduct of the defendants as an indirect infringement is a right which the complainant sets up as arising under the patent law. One construction of the scope of the grant will sustain the rights asserted, if the facts be as alleged, and another will defeat those rights.

Whether a patentee may lawfully impose such restrictions, and whether their violation constitutes an infringement, are obviously questions arising under the patent law. In *Littlefield* v. *Perry,* 21 Wall. 205, 222, this court said: "An action which raises a question of infringement is an action arising 'under the law,' and one who has the right to sue for the infringement may sue in the Circuit Court. Such a suit may involve the construction of a contract as well as the patent, but that will not oust the court of its jurisdiction. If the patent is involved it carries with it the whole case."

Although the complainant might have sued upon the broken contract, or brought a bill to declare a forfeiture of the licensee's rights for breach of the implied convenant to operate it only in connection with materials supplied by it, it has elected to sue for infringement. To quote from Judge Shipman's opinion in *Magic Ruffle Co.* v. *Elm City Co.,* 13 Blatchf. 151, "It was competent for the complainants to take either one of the two remedies. . . . They could bring a bill alleging an injury to their exclusive rights under the laws of the United States, or, as the residence of the parties gave this court jurisdiction, could bring a proper suit, setting up a breach of the contract as the gravamen of their action."

That a patentee may effectually restrict the time, place or manner of using a patented machine, so that a prohibited use will constitute an infringement of the patent, is fully conceded. Thus, in the printed brief counsel for defendants say: "Aside from such special contracts, an agreement that the article shall be used only in a certain manner, can be made only by way of lease of the article, terminating the lease upon condition broken, or by way of conditional sale, by breach of which the title reverts to the seller." In either such case, counsel say, "a use of the article in violation of the condition may terminate the lease or sale of the article (which) would become the property of the patentee again, and a use thereof by the lessee or purchaser may constitute a violation of the patent, for which an infringement may lie. . . . He cannot make a sale with the condition attached that the article shall be used or disposed of in a certain manner, leaving the title, however, in the purchaser in case of a breach of the condition."

The books abound in cases upholding the right of a patentee owner of a machine to license another to use it subject to any qualification in respect of time, place, manner or purpose of use which the licensee agrees to accept. Any use in excess of the license would obviously be an infringing use and the license would be no defense. Robinson on Patents, §§ 915, 916 and notes. This is so elementary we shall not stop to cite cases.

The contention is not that a patentee may not permit the use of a patented thing with such qualifications as he sees fit to impose, and that a prohibited use will be an infringing one, but that he can only keep the article within the control of the patent by retaining the title. To put the contention in another form—it is, that any transfer of the patentee's property right in a patented machine carries with it the right to use the entire invention so long as the identity of the machine is preserved, irrespective of any restrictions placed by the patentee upon the use of the article and accepted by the buyer. It is said that by such a sale the patentee "disposes of all his rights under his patent, and thereby removes the article from the operation of the patent law." If he attempts to sell the machine for specified uses only and prohibit all others, the restriction is disposed of as constituting a collateral agreement such as any vendor of personal property might impose, and enforceable, if valid at all, only as a collateral contract.

The issue is a plain one. If it be sound, it concludes the case, and our response should be a negative one, since the violation of a mere collateral contract, which is not also an infringement of the patent would not be a case arising under the patent law. But is it true that where a patentee sells his patented machine for a specific and limited use, he does not thereby reserve to himself, as patentee, the exclusive right to all unpermitted uses which may be made of his invention as embodied in the machine sold? Obviously, this is a question arising under the patent law. By a sale of a patented article subject to no conditions the purchaser undeniably acquires the right to use the article for all the purposes of the patent so long as it endures. He may use it where, when, and how he pleases, and may dispose of the same unlimited right to another. This has long been the settled doctrine of this and all patent courts. *Mitchell* v. *Hawley,* 16 Wall. 544; *Livingston* v. *Woodworth,* 14 How. 546, 550; *Adams* v. *Burks,* 17 Wall. 453, 456; *Folding Bed Case* (*Keeler* v. *Standard Folding Bed Co.*), 157 U.S. 659, 666. By such an unconditional sale of the thing patented it is said to be "no longer within the limits of the monopoly. It passes outside of it, and is no longer under the protection of the act of Congress."

In the cases cited above, as well as in the leading case of *Bloomer* v. *McQuewan,* 14 How. 539, the statement that a purchaser of a patented machine has an unlimited right to use it for all the purposes of the invention, so long as the identity of the machine is preserved, was made of one who bought unconditionally, that is, subject to no specified limitation upon his right of use. The question of the effect of limitations upon the right of use arose, however, in *Mitchell* v. *Hawley,* and there we find the distinction was deemed material and the effect declared.

In that case one Taylor was the patentee, under a grant for a term of fourteen years, for a machine for felting hats. By what Mr. Justice Clifford calls "a conveyance of license, subject to certain restrictions or limitations," one Bayley was given the "exclusive right to make and use and to license to others the right to use the said machines in the States of Massachusetts and New Hampshire, during the remainder of the original term of said letters-patent," subject to a stipulation that "the licensee shall not in any way, or form, dispose of, sell, or grant any license to use the said machines beyond the expiration of the original term." There was also a provision that if the term of the patent should be extended Bayley should have the right to control the same in those two States, upon paying a reasonable compensation, etc.

Bayley, as such licensee, made and sold four machines to the appellant Mitchell, with the right to use them for felting hats in the town of Haverhill, Massachusetts, "under Taylor's patent bearing date May 3, 1864." Before the patent expired it was extended for the further term of seven years, the benefits of which extension for the said two States were assigned to the appellee Hawley. Hawley then filed his bill to restrain Mitchell from using the four identical machines which had been sold to him by Bayley. From a decree restraining their further use Mitchell appealed. Mr. Justice Clifford, before stating the facts upon which the judgment must rest as to the right of Mitchell as the purchaser of the machines to continue their use after the expiration of the original term of Taylor's patent, and after directing attention to what he termed "the well-grounded distinction between the grant of the right to make and vend the patented machine and the grant of the right to use it," which, he says, "was first satisfactorily pointed out by the late Chief Justice Taney, with his accustomed clearness and precision," says (p. 548):

"Purchasers of the exclusive privilege of making or vending the patented machine hold the whole or a portion of the franchise which the patent secures, depending upon the nature of the conveyance, and of course the interest which the purchaser acquires terminates at the time limited for its continuance by the law which created the franchise, unless it is expressly stipulated to the contrary. But the purchaser of the implement or machine for the purpose of using it in the ordinary pursuits of life stands on different grounds, as he does not acquire any right to construct another machine either for his own use or to be vended to another for any purpose. Complete title to the implement or machine purchased becomes vested in the vendee by the sale and purchase, but he acquires no portion of the franchise, as the machine, when it rightfully passes from the patentee to the purchaser, ceases to be within the limits of the monopoly."

In the succeeding paragraph he, in effect, limits what was above said to unconditional sales of such patented machines by adding this:

"Patented implements or machines sold to be used in the ordinary pursuits of life become the private individual property of the purchasers, and are no longer specifically protected by the patent laws of the State where the implements or machines are owned and used. Sales of the kind may be made by the patentee with or without conditions, as in other cases, but where the sale is absolute, and without any conditions, the rule is well settled that the purchaser may continue to use the implement or machine purchased until it is worn out, or he may repair it or improve upon it as he pleases, in same manner as if dealing with property of any other kind."

The force and bearing of this opinion cannot be escaped by suggesting that the court was referring to mere common-law contractual conditions, for the suit was to restrain infringement by the use of four machines which had been sold, *not leased*.

That the bill was one alleging and seeking to enjoin further use as an infringement of the patent is shown by the statement that "they," referring to the purchaser Mitchell and those associated with him, "appeared to the suits and filed an answer setting up as a defense to the charge of infringement that they are by law authorized to continue the use of the four machines just the same under the extended letters-patent as they had the right to do under the original patent, when the purchase was made by those under whom they claim, which is the only question in the case."

The question argued, as shown by the brief, as set out in the report, was there, as here, that by a sale of the machines "they were taken out of the reach of the patent law altogether, and that as long as the machines themselves lasted, the owner could use them." For the patentee it was urged that "the right to make and use and to license others to use was expressly limited by apt words, showing clearly an intent that it should not survive the original term of the patent." This latter was the argument which prevailed. Mr. Justice Clifford, after referring to the principle of law that one cannot convey a better title or right than he has, said (p. 550), touching the restriction imposed by Bayley on the machines sold by him to Mitchell: "The form of the license which he gave to the purchasers shows conclusively that he understood that he was not empowered to give a license which should extend beyond that limitation." Later, referring to this sale with license to use, the learned Justice says (p. 551): "The terms of the license which the seller gave to the purchasers were sufficient to put them upon inquiry, and it is quite obvious that the means of knowledge were at hand, and that if they had made the least inquiry they would have ascertained that their grantor could not give them any title to use the machine beyond the period of fourteen years from the date of the original letters-patent, as he was only a licensee and never had any power to sell a machine so as to withdraw it indefinitely from the operation of the franchise secured by the patent."

The distinction between the sale of a machine free from specific restrictions upon the right of use and a sale subject to such limitations becomes the more evident, in view of the fact that but for the license to use only for the remainder of the original patent term the purchaser would have acquired the right to continue the use during an extended term of the same patent. This was the express holding in the two prior cases of *Wilson* v. *Rousseau,* 4 How. 646, and *Bloomer* v. *McQuewan,* 14 How. 539, where the unlimited right of use by an unconditional purchaser was laid down in the strongest terms, and which cases are now relied upon by counsel in this case as equally applicable to a sale subject to a restricted use.

It is obvious that if Taylor, the patentee, could authorize Bayley to make and sell the patented machines, subject to the restriction that he should not sell for use beyond the terms of the original patent, and that a purchaser of the machines so made and sold by Bayley, with notice, would infringe the extended patent by a use after the original term had expired, it is because the exclusive right of the patentee embraces the right to make and sell patented machines subject to restrictions upon the right of use, which, if not observed, will support an action for infringement.

An absolute and unconditional sale operates to pass the patented thing outside the boundaries of the patent, because such a sale implies that the patentee consents that the purchaser may use the machines so long as its identity is preserved. This implication arises, first, because a sale without reservation, of a machine whose value consists in its use, for a consideration, carries with it the presumption that the right to use the particular machine is to pass with it. The rule and its reason is thus stated in Robinson on Patents, § 824: "The sale must furthermore be unconditional. Not only may the patentee impose conditions limiting the use of the patented article, upon his grantees and express licensees, but any person having the right to sell may at the time of sale restrict the use of his vendee within specific boundaries of time or place or method, and these will then become the measure of the implied license arising from the sale."

The argument for the defendants ignores the distinction between the property right in the materials composing a patented machine, and the right to use for the purpose and in the manner pointed out by the patent. The latter may be and often is the greater element of value, and the buyer may desire it only to apply to some or all of the uses included in the invention. But the two things are separable rights. If sold unreservedly the right to the entire use of the invention passes, because that is the implied intent; but this right to use is nothing more nor less than an unrestricted license presumed from an unconditional sale. A license is not an assignment of any interest in the patent. It is a mere permission granted by the patentee. It may be a license to make, sell and use, or it may be limited to any one of these separable rights. If it be a license to use, it operates only as a right to use without being liable as an infringer. If a licensee be sued, he can escape liability to the patentee for the use of his invention by showing that the use is within his license. But if his use be one prohibited by the license, the latter is of no avail as a defense. As a license passes no interest in the monopoly, it has been described as a mere waiver of the right to sue by the patentee. Robinson on Patents, § § 806, 808.

We repeat. The property right to a patented machine may pass to a purchaser with no right of use, or with only the right to use in a specified way, or at a specified place, or for a specified purpose. The unlimited right of exclusive use which is possessed by and guaranteed to the patentee will be granted if the sale be unconditional. But if the right of use be confined by specific restriction, the use not permitted is necessarily reserved to the patentee. If that reserved control of use of the machine be violated, the patent is thereby invaded. This right to sever ownership and use is deducible from the nature of a patent monopoly and is recognized in the cases.

In *Sawin* v. *Guild,* 1 Gall. 485, Mr. Justice Story, a. far back as 1813, recognized the distinction by holding that a sale of patented machines under an execution against the patentee did not render the sheriff liable under a statute which made any person liable who should sell a patented device without consent of the patentee, because the sheriff had merely sold the materials and had not undertaken to pass any right of use. But in *Wilder* v. *Kent,* 15 Fed. Rep. 217, it was held that under such an execution sale there passed whatever right of use the debtor had if the sale was unconditional.

Judge Lowell, in *Porter Needle Co.* v. *National Needle Co.,* 17 Fed. Rep. 536, after saying that an absolute and unqualified sale of a patented machine carried with it the right of use, said: "But the mere value of a patented machine is often, as is proved to be in this case, insignificant in comparison with the value of its use; and the courts have permitted a severance of ownership and right of use, if the patentee has chosen to dissever them and if his intent is not doubtful."

It is plain from the power of the patentee to subdivide his exclusive right of use that when he makes and sells a patented device that the extent of the license to use which is carried by the sale must depend upon whether any restriction was placed upon the use and brought home to the person acquiring the article.

That here the patentee did not intend to sell the machine made by it subject to an unrestricted use is of course undeniable from the words upon the machine, viz.:

"LICENSE RESTRICTION."

"This machine is sold by the A. B. Dick Co., with the license restriction that it may be used only with the stencil, paper, ink and other supplies made by A. B. Dick Co."

The meaning and purpose of this restriction was that while the property in the machine was to pass to the purchaser, the right to use the invention was restricted to use with other articles required in its practical operation, supplied by the patentee. It was stated at the bar, and appears fully in the opinion of Judge Ray (149 Fed. Rep. 424), who decided the case in the Circuit Court, that the patentee sold its machines at cost, or less, and depended upon the profit realized from the sale of other non-patented articles adapted to be used with the machine, and that it had put out many thousands of such machines under the same license restriction. Such a sale, while transferring the property right in the machine, carries with it only the right to use it for practicing the invention according to the terms of the license. To no other or greater extent does the patentee consent to the use of the machine. When the purchaser is sued for infringement by using the device, he may defend by pleading, not the general and unlimited license which is carried by an unconditional sale, but the limited license indicated by the metal tablet annexed to the machine. If the use is not one permitted, it is plainly an infringing use.

If, then, we assume that the violation of restrictions upon the use of a machine made and sold by the patentee may be treated as infringement, we come to the question of the kind of limitation which may be lawfully imposed upon a purchaser.

To begin with, the purchaser must have notice that he buys with only a qualified right of use. He has a right to assume, in the absence of knowledge, that the seller passes an unconditional title to the machine, with no limitations upon the use. Where, then, is the line between a lawful and an unlawful qualification upon the use? This is a question of statutory construction. But with what eye shall we read a meaning into it? It is a statute creating and protecting a monopoly. It is a true monopoly, one having its origin in the ultimate authority, the Constitution. Shall we deal with the statute creating and guaranteeing the exclusive right which is granted to the inventor with the narrow scrutiny proper when a statutory right is asserted to uphold a claim which is lacking in those moral elements which appeal to the normal man? Or shall we approach it as a monopoly granted to subserve a broad public policy, by which large ends are to be attained, and, therefore, to be construed so as to give effect to a wise and beneficial purpose? That we must neither transcend the statute, nor cut down its clear meaning, is plain. In *Bement* v. *National Harrow Co.,* 186 U.S. 70, 89, 90, 91 and 92, this court quoted with approval the language of Chief Justice Marshall in *Grant* v. *Raymond,* 6 Pet. 218, 241. Concerning the favorable view which the law takes as to the protection extended to the exclusive right, the court, through Chief Justice Marshall, said:

"It is the reward stipulated for the advantages derived by the public for the exertions of the individual, and is intended as a stimulus to those exertions. The laws which are passed to give effect to this purpose ought, we think, to be construed in the spirit in which they have been made; and to execute the contract fairly on the part of the United States, where the full benefit has been actually received, if this can be done without transcending the intention of the statute, or countenancing acts which are fraudulent or may prove mischievous. The public yields nothing which it has not agreed to yield; it receives all which it has contracted to receive. The full benefit of the discovery, after its enjoyment by the discoverer for fourteen years, is preserved, and for his exclusive enjoyment of it during that time the public faith is pledged."

If the patent be for a machine, the monopoly extends to the right of making, selling and using, and these are separable and substantial rights. In *Bloomer* v. *McQuewan,* 14 How. 539, 547, it is said that the grant is of "the right to exclude every one from making, using or vending the thing without the permission of the owner." In *Bement* v. *National Harrow Co.,* 186 U.S. 70, 90, there was involved the legality of certain contracts between patentees of and dealers in patented harrows. The purpose and effect of the combination and of the contracts between the parties was to fix and keep up the prices at which licensees might sell the patented harrows. It was claimed that the combination and contracts were obnoxious to the Sherman Act; but, upon the other side, it was said that as the contracts concerned only the sale of patented articles that act did not apply. The character of the monopoly granted under the patent act was therefore involved. Touching the right of the patentee to exclude all others from the use of his invention, the court quoted with approval what was said in the *Button Fastener Cases,* 77 Fed. Rep. 288, as follows:

"If he sees fit, he may reserve to himself the exclusive use of his invention or discovery. If he will neither use his device nor permit others to use it, he has but suppressed his own. That the grant is made upon the reasonable expectation that he will either put his invention to practical use or permit others to avail themselves of it upon reasonable terms, is doubtless true. This expectation is based alone upon the supposition that the patentee's interest will induce him to use, or let others use, his invention. The public has retained no other security to enforce such expectations. A suppression can endure but for the life of the patent, and the disclosure he has made will enable all to enjoy the fruit of his genius. His title is exclusive, and so clearly within the constitutional provisions in respect of private property that he is neither bound to use his discovery himself nor permit others to use it."

In the *Paper Bag Patent Case,* 210 U.S. 405, this right to exclude others from all use of the invention was held to be so comprehensive that a patentee was allowed to restrain, by injunction, one who was infringing his patent, although he had, during a long term of years, neither used his invention himself, nor allowed others to use it.

That there are limitations upon the right of vending and using a patented machine may be conceded. Thus, if the thing patented belong to a class of things which on account of their inherent danger to the public safety or health cannot be sold or used because prohibited by an exertion of the police power of a State, they will not be immune to such a law because patented. Upon this ground a patent for "an improved burning oil," was held not to take the article without the operation of a state statute forbidding the sale of oil which was unsafe for illuminating purposes. *Patterson* v. *Kentucky,* 97 U.S. 501. And so in the *Bement Case,* the court said of this exclusive grant of privilege (p. 90):

"It is true that in certain circumstances the sale of articles manufactured under letters patent may be prevented when the use of such article may be subject, within the several States, to the control which they may respectively impose in the legitimate exercise of their powers over their purely domestic affairs, whether of internal commerce or of police regulation."

In that case the question was not one of infringement, but one arising in a suit to enforce certain contracts directly restraining commerce in patented articles which were claimed to violate the Sherman law, although the agreements covered only patented articles. The court, after referring to the exceptions to the patentee's monopoly resulting from conflict with the police power of the State, said (p. 91):

"Notwithstanding these exceptions, the general rule is absolute freedom in the use or sale of rights under the patent laws of the United States. The very object of these laws is monopoly, and the rule is, with few exceptions, that any conditions which are not in their very nature illegal with regard to this kind of property, imposed by the patentee and agreed to by the licensee for the right to manufacture or use or sell the article, will be upheld by the courts. The fact that the conditions in the contracts keep up the monopoly or fix prices does not render them illegal."

Now, if this was a suit to recover damages upon the contract not to use the machine except in connection with other articles proper in its use made by the patentee, the only possible defense would be that the agreement was one contrary to public policy in that it affected freedom in the sale of such articles to the user of such machines. But that was the nature of the defense made to the suit to enforce the agreements under consideration in the *Bement Case.* The court in that case found that the contracts did include interstate commerce within their provisions and restrained interstate trade, but with reference to the Sherman Act said (p. 92):

"But that statute clearly does not refer to that kind of a restraint of interstate commerce which may arise from reasonable and legal conditions imposed upon the assignee or licensee of a patent by the owner thereof, restricting the terms upon which the article may be used and the price to be demanded therefor. Such a construction of the act we have no doubt was never contemplated by its framers."

As to whether the restrictions upon sales imposed by the agreements were "legal and reasonable conditions," the court said (p. 93):

"The provision in regard to the price at which the licensee would sell the article manufactured under the license was also an appropriate and reasonable condition. It tended to keep up the price of the implements manufactured and sold, but that was only recognizing the nature of the property dealt in, and providing for its value so far as possible. This the parties were legally entitled to do. The owner of a patented article can, of course, charge such price as he may choose, and the owner of a patent may assign it or sell the right to manufacture and sell the article patented upon the condition that the assignee shall charge a certain amount for such article."

If the stipulation in an agreement between patentees and dealers in patented articles, which, among other things, fixed a price below which the patented articles should not be sold, would be a reasonable and valid condition, it must follow that any other reasonable stipulation, not inherently violative of some substantive law, imposed by a patentee as part of a sale of a patented machine, would be equally valid and enforceable. It must also follow, that if the stipulation be one which qualifies the right of use in a machine sold subject thereto, so that a breach would give rise to a right of action upon the contract, it would be at the same time an act of infringement, giving to the patentee his choice of remedies.

But it has been very earnestly said that a condition restricting the buyer to use it only in connection with ink made by the patentee is one of a character which gives to a patentee the power to extend his monopoly so as to cause it to embrace any subject, not within the patent, which he chooses to require that the invention shall be used in connection with. Of course the argument does not mean that the effect of such a condition is to cause things to become patented which were not so without the requirement. The stencil, the paper and the ink made by the patentee will continue to be unpatented. Anyone will be as free to make, sell and use like articles as they would be without this restriction, save in one particular—namely, they may not be sold to a user of one of the patentee's machines with intent that they shall be used in violation of the license. To that extent competition in the sale of such articles, for use with the machine, will be affected; for sale to such users for infringing purposes will constitute contributory infringement. But the same consequence results from the sale of any article to one who proposes to associate it with other articles to infringe a patent, when such purpose is known to the seller. But could it be said that the doctrine of contributory infringement operates to extend the monopoly of the patent over subjects not within it because one subjects himself to the penalties of the law when he sells unpatented things for an infringing use? If a patentee says, "I may suppress my patent if I will. I may make and have made devices under my patent, but I will neither sell nor permit anyone to use the patented things," he is within his right, and none can complain. But if he says, "I will sell with the right to use only with other things proper for using with the machines, and I will sell at the actual cost of the machines to me, provided you will agree to use only such articles as are made by me in connection therewith," if he chooses to take his profit in this way, instead of taking it by a higher price for the machines, has he exceeded his exclusive right to make, sell and use his patented machines? The market for the sale of such articles to the users of his machine, which, by such a condition, he takes to himself, was a market which he alone created by the making and selling of a new invention. Had he kept his invention to himself, no ink could have been sold by others for use upon machines embodying that invention. By selling it subject to the restriction he took nothing from others and in no wise restricted their legitimate market.

A like objection has been made against injunctions restraining the sale for infringing purposes of a single element in a patent combination. It was said that to enjoin such sales, although the thing sold was intended to be used with other elements to complete an infringing combination, was to extend the scope of the patent so as to give to the patentee the same advantage as if the element had been claimed alone. But in *Davis Electrical Co.* v. *Edison Co.,* 60 Fed. Rep. 276, 280, Judge Putnam answered this, saying:

"Neither in such instances, nor in the case at bar, is the course of the law to be turned aside because the practical result may be to give a patentee for the time being more than the patent office contemplated, nor is the patentee to be deprived of his just rights because under some circumstances he gets incidental advantages beyond what he expressly bargained for. We do not in terms give the patentee the benefit of a claim for the filament alone, nor prohibit its use in some other combination than that set out in the second claim, if some ingenious way of making such other combination is ever discovered."

In *Thomson-Houston Co.* v. *Kelsey Co.,* 72 Fed. Rep. 1016, the language was adopted by Judge Townsend.

Neither can we see that the liability of the defendants for aiding and abetting an infringing use by Miss Skou would be different whether she had made her machine in open defiance of the rights of the patentee or had bought it under conditions limiting her right of use. If she had made it, she would have been liable to an action for infringement for making; and if she used it, she would become liable for such infringing use. But if the defendants knew of the patent and that she had unlawfully made the patented article, and then sold her ink or other supplies without which she could not operate the machine, *with the intent and purpose that she should use the infringing article by means of the ink supplied by them,* they would assist in her infringing use.

"Contributory infringement," says Judge Townsend in *Thomson-Houston Co.* v. *Kelsey Co.,* 72 Fed. Rep. 1016, 1017, "has been well defined as the intentional aiding of one person by another in the unlawful making or selling or using of the patented invention." To the same effect are *Wallace* v. *Holmes,* 29 Fed. Cases, 74, 79; *Risdon Iron & Locomotive Works* v. *Trent,* 92 Fed. Rep. 375; *Thomson-Houston Co.* v. *Ohio Brass Works,* 80 Fed. Rep. 712; *American Graphophone Co.* v. *Hawthorne,* 92 Fed. Rep. 516.

In the *Risdon Case,* a member of the firm which made the plans for the construction of certain mining machinery to be made in the owner's shop, and then superintended its erection at the mine, was held to be guilty of infringement, though he neither personally made nor used the machines which were found to be an infringement of valid patents. In *American Graphophone Co.* v. *Hawthorne,* one who sold a machine with knowledge that it was to be used to produce an infringing article was held to be liable as an infringer.

For the purpose of testing the consequence of a ruling which will support the lawfulness of a sale of a patented machine for use only in connection with supplies necessary for its operation bought from the patentee, many fanciful suggestions of conditions which might be imposed by a patentee have been pressed upon us. Thus it is said that a patentee of a coffee pot might sell on condition that it be used only with coffee bought from him, or, if the article be a circular saw, that it might be sold on condition that it be used only in sawing logs procured from him. These and other illustrations are used to indicate that this method of marketing a patented article may be carried to such an extent as to inconvenience the public and involve innocent people in unwitting infringements. But these illustrations all fail of their purpose, because the public is always free to take or refuse the patented article on the terms imposed. If they be too onerous or not in keeping with the benefits, the patented article will not find a market. The public, by permitting the invention to go unused, loses nothing which it had before, and when the patent expires will be free to use the invention without compensation or restriction. This was pointed out in the *Paper Bag Case,* where the inventor would neither use himself nor allow others to use, and yet was held entitled to restrain infringement, because he had the exclusive right to keep all others from using during the life of the patent. This larger right embraces the lesser of permitting others to use upon such terms as the patentee chooses to prescribe. It must not be forgotten that we are dealing with a constitutional and statutory monopoly. An attack upon the rights under a patent because it secures a monopoly to make, to sell and to use, is an attack upon the whole patent system. We are not at liberty to say that the Constitution has unwisely provided for granting a monopolistic right to inventors, or that Congress has unwisely failed to impose limitations upon the inventor's exclusive right of use. And if it be that the ingenuity of patentees in devising ways in which to reap the benefit of their discoveries requires to be restrained, Congress alone has the power to determine what restraints shall be imposed. As the law now stands it contains none, and the duty which rests upon this and upon every other court is to expound the law as it is written. Arguments based upon suggestions of public policy not recognized in the patent laws are not relevant. The field to which we are invited by such arguments is legislative, not judicial. The decisions of this court, as we have construed them, do not so limit the privilege of the patentee, and we could not so restrict a patent grant without overruling the long line of judicial decisions from Circuit Courts and Circuit Courts of Appeal, heretofore cited, thus inflicting disastrous results upon individuals who have made large investments in reliance upon them.

The conclusion we reach is that there is no difference, in principle, between a sale subject to specific restrictions as to the time, place or purpose of use and restrictions requiring a use only with other things necessary to the use of the patented article purchased from the patentee. If the violation of the one kind is an infringement, the other is also. That a violation of any such restriction annexed to a sale by one with notice constitutes an infringing use has been decided by a great majority of the Circuit Courts and Circuit Courts of Appeal, and has come to be a well-recognized principle in the patent law, in accordance with which vast transactions in respect to patented articles have been conducted. But it is now said that the numerous decisions by the lower courts have been erroneous in respect to the proper construction of the limit of the monopoly conferred by a patent, and that they should now be overruled. To these courts has been committed the duty of interpreting and administering the patent law. There is no power in this court to review their judgments, except upon a writ of certiorari, or to direct their decisions, save through a certified interrogatory for direction upon a question of law. This power to review by certiorari is one which has been seldom exercised in patent cases. A line of decisions, which has come to be something like a rule of property, under which large businesses have been conducted, should at least not be overruled except upon reasons so clear as to make any other construction of the patent law inadmissible.

The earliest of the reported cases in which the precise question here presented arose were cases arising in suits for the infringement of a patent upon an iron band connected by a buckle, intended for binding cotton bales. The band and this buckle were of iron. The buckle was so adjusted as that the band could be removed from the bale only by cutting. Upon the buckle were stamped the words: "Licensed to use only once." When cut from the bale the band and buckle were sold to persons, who used the buckles either upon a new band, or one repaired, and these bands were sold to planters to be used again in baling cotton. The question arose in a number of cases as to whether such second use of the buckles by one with notice, was an infringing use. In *American Cotton Tie Co.* v. *Simmons,* 3 Ban. & A. 320, Judge Shepley dismissed the bill. The case, upon appeal to this court, was reversed, upon the ground that that which had been done after the first use was a reconstruction, and not a repair, and was, therefore, an infringement. 106 U.S. 89. The court did not pass upon the question whether a second use of the buckles would be an infringing use. Another case arising under the same patent was that of *American Cotton Tie Supply Co.* v. *Bullard,* 4 Ban. & A. 520, decided by Judge Blatchford, who gave the question great consideration. "It is manifest," says Judge Blatchford, "that the owner of the patents intended, by the stamps upon the buckles and the imprints on the billheads, to grant a restricted license for the use of the ties and the buckles, and that the intended restriction was to a use of them once only, as baling ties. The words, 'licensed to use once only,' stamped on each buckle, were a notice to everyone who handled it that there was attached to it a restriction in the shape of a license, and of a license merely to use, and of a license to use only once. This was a lawful restriction." Concerning the question of the effect of this restriction upon subsequent buyers of the cotton with its bands and buckles, the court said: "It is difficult to see how, in view of the facts of the case, the owners of these patents can properly be said to have sold the buckles for the purpose of allowing them to be used in the ordinary pursuits of life and to pass into the markets of the country as an ordinary article of commerce. . . . The original license is fairly a license to have the buckle and the band confined a bale until the consumer needs to confine the bale no longer, and a license for no longer time. There is no purchase of buckle and band by a purchaser of the baled cotton, except as he purchases them confining the cotton and to confine it until it reaches the consumer, and such purchase of buckle and band is, in effect, only a purchase of them subject to such original license. It is quite as reasonable to say that the purchaser of the cotton buys subject to such license as it is to say that the licensor, having imposed the restricted license, permits it to be instantly destroyed. The former view is consistent with the original intention, and the latter view is inconsistent with it."

As indicating the trend of judicial opinion that such license restrictions annexed to patented articles, when sold, constitute licenses under the patent, and that their violation by persons having notice constitutes an infringement of the patent, we here set out in the margin a number of the reported cases.[1]

[1] Dickerson *v.* Matheson, *57 Fed. Rep. 524, Second Circuit Court of Appeals;* Heaton-Penin. Co. *v.* Eureka Specialty Co., *77 Fed. Rep. 288, Sixth Circuit Court of Appeals;* Tubular Rivet Co. *v.* O'Brien, *93 Fed. Rep. 200;* Cortelyou *v.* Lowe, *111 Fed. Rep. 1005, Second Circuit Court of Appeals;* Edison Phonograph Co. *v.* Kaufmann, *105 Fed. Rep. 960;* Edison Phonograph Co. *v.* Pike, *116 Fed. Rep. 863;* Victor Talking Machine Co. *v.* The Fair, *123 Fed. Rep. 424, Seventh Circuit Court of Appeals;* National Phonograph Co. *v.* Schlegel, *128 Fed. Rep. 733;* The Fair *v.* Dover Mfg. Co., *166 Fed. Rep. 117;* Æolian Co. *v.* Juelg Co., *155 Fed. Rep. 119, Second Circuit Court of Appeals;* A. B. Dick Co. *v.* Milwaukee Co., *168 Fed. Rep. 930, Seventh Circuit Court of Appeals;* Crown Cork & Seal Co. *v.* Brooklyn Co., *172 Fed. Rep. 225;* Rupp *v.* Elliott, *131 Fed. Rep. 730, Sixth Circuit Court of Appeals;* Commercial Co. *v.* Autolux Co., *181 Fed. Rep. 387;* Boesch *v.* Graff, *133 U.S. 697, where articles made in Germany under a German patent, and imported to this country, were held to infringe a United States patent for the same article; and* Dickerson *v.* Tinling, *84 Fed. Rep. 192, where it was held that one purchasing a patented article in Germany from the owners of a United States patent, having marked on it a condition that it should not be imported into the United States, was held guilty of infringement by bringing it into the United States.*

See also Curtiss on Patents, §§ 218–218a; Walker on Patents, §§ 300, 301, 302; Wilson *v.* Sherman, *1 Blatchf. 536.*

It would lengthen this opinion unreasonably to make quotations from these opinions to show either the grounds upon which they go or their applicability. Some of them concern sales subject to a restriction upon the price upon resale, and others relate to a requirement that the article sold shall be used only in connection with certain other things to be bought from the patentee. We deem it well, however, to refer to the opinion of the Circuit Court of Appeals of the Eighth Circuit, delivered by Judge (now Mr. Justice) Van Devanter in *National Phonograph Co.* v. *Schlegel,* cited above, because it draws so clearly the distinction between a conditional and an unconditional sale of a patented article. Speaking for the court, Judge Van Devanter said (128 Fed. Rep. 733, 735):

"An unconditional or unrestricted sale by the patentee, or by a licensee authorized to make such sale, of an article embodying the patented invention or discovery, passes the article without the limits of the monopoly, and authorizes the buyer to use or sell it without restriction; but to the extent that the sale is subject to any restriction upon the use or future sale the article has not been released from the monopoly, but is within its limits, and, as against all who have notice of the restriction, is subject to the control of whoever retains the monopoly. This results from the fact that the monopoly is a substantial property right conferred by law as an inducement or stimulus to useful invention and discovery, and that it rests with the owner to say what part of this property he will reserve to himself and what part he will transfer to others, and upon what terms he will make the transfer."

There is no collision between the rule against restrictions upon the alienation or use of chattels not made under the protection of a patent and the right of the patentee through his control over his invention. The distinction is pointed out by Mr. Justice Hughes in *Dr. Miles Medical Co.* v. *Park & Sons Co.,* 220 U.S. 373, 401.

The English patent law, like our own, grants to the patentee the exclusive right to make, to sell and to use. The decisions of the English courts upon the subject are, therefore, worthy of examination, and weight should be attached not only because of the respect due by reason of the similarity of statutes, but because many English patentees take out American patents and the converse. The English opinions which we shall refer to have to do with the sale of patented articles with restrictions upon the use.

The cases of *Incandescent Gaslight Co.* v. *Cantelo,* 12 Patent Law Reports, 262, decided in 1895, and *Incandescent Gaslight Co.* v. *Brogden,* 16 Patent Law Reports, 179, decided in 1899, were actions for the infringement of the Welsbach mantle patent for incandescent gas lighting. The mantles were sold subject to a license restriction, printed on the box containing them, that they should be used in connection with burners or apparatus sold or supplied by the patentee. In the *Cantelo Case* Mr. Justice Wills said (p. 264):

"The sale of a patented article carries with it the right to use it in any way that the purchaser chooses to use it, unless he knows of restrictions. Of course, if he knows of restrictions, and they are brought to his mind at the time of the sale, he is bound by them. He is bound by them on this principle: The Patentee has the sole right of using and selling the articles, and he may prevent anybody from dealing with them at all. Inasmuch as he has the right to prevent people from using them, or dealing in them at all, he has the right to do the lesser thing, that is to say, to impose his own conditions. It does not matter how unreasonable or how absurd the conditions are. It does not matter what they are if he says at the time when the purchaser proposes to buy, or the person to take a license, 'Mind, I only give you this license on this condition,' and the purchaser is free to take it or leave it as he likes. If he takes it, he must be bound by the condition. It seems to be common sense, and not to depend upon any patent law, or any other particular law."

Upon the evidence it was held that Cantelo not having bought direct, he did not have actual knowledge of the restriction, and he was given judgment for costs upon that defense.

In the subsequent case against Brogden, the complainants were given an injunction against future infringement, and an accounting for damages for past infringement, upon the second point in the claim, namely, that the defendant had sold, being a dealer, with notice of the restriction, for use upon a burner not made or supplied by the patentee. As to the effect of the sale subject to the license restriction as to the use, Lord Justice Kennedy said: "A patentee has a right, nor merely by sale without reserve, to give an unlimited right to the purchaser to use, and thereby to make a grant from which he cannot derogate, but may attach to it conditions, and if these conditions are broken then there is no license, because the licensee is bound up with the observance of the conditions."

In *British Mutoscope and Biograph Company* v. *Homer,* 17 Times Law Reports, 213, decided in 1901, it was held that the purchaser of a mutoscope under a rent distress warrant obtained no greater right to the use of the patented machine than that which pertained to the execution debtor, and that if the debtor had no right other than a strictly personal right to use, the purchaser obtained no right to the use. Mr. Justice Farwell, who delivered the opinion, cited and quoted with approval from the case of the *Incandescent Gaslight Co.* v. *Brogden,* 16 Patent Law Reports, 179, where it was said that a purchaser who buys with knowledge of the conditions under which his vendor is authorized to use a patented invention is bound by such conditions, and that such conditions are not contractual, but are incident to and a limitation of the grant of the licensee to use, so that if the conditions are broken there is no grant at all.

In *McGruther* v. *Pitcher,* 20 Times Law Reports, 652, it is held that the purchaser of an article made under a patent and sold originally subject to restrictions as to place or method of use is not bound by such restrictions unless he buys with notice of them, as such restrictions do not run with the goods and are obligatory only upon those persons who take the article with knowledge of the conditions.

In the very late case of the *National Phonograph Co.* v. *Menck,* decided in 1911 by the Judicial Committee of the Privy Council, and reported in 27 Times Law Reports, 239, the cases were cited and reviewed. Referring to the distinction between the principles applicable to sales of unpatented and patented articles, Lord Shaw, in delivering the opinion of the court said (p. 241): "To begin with, the general principle . . . applicable to ordinary goods bought and sold, is not here in question. The owner may use and dispose of these as he sees fit. He may have made a certain contract with the person from whom he bought, and to such a contract he must answer. Simply, however, in his capacity as owner, he is not bound by any restrictions in regard to the use or sale of the goods, and it is out of the question to suggest that restrictive conditions run with the goods. . . ." Referring to former cases, he proceeds: "All that is affirmed is that the general doctrine of absolute freedom of disposal of chattels of an ordinary kind is, in the case of patented chattels, subject to the restriction that the person purchasing them, and in the knowledge of the conditions attached by the patentee, which knowledge is clearly brought home to himself at the time of sale, shall be bound by that knowledge and accept the situation of ownership subject to the limitations. These limitations are merely the respect paid and the effect given to those conditions of transfer of the patented article which the law, laid down by statute, gave the original patentee a power to impose. Whether the law on this head should be changed and the power of sale *sub modo* should be withdrawn or limited is not a question for a court. It may be added that where a patented article has been acquired by sale, much, if not all, may be implied as to the consent of the licensee to an undisturbed and unrestricted use thereof. In short, such a sale negatives in the ordinary case the imposition of conditions and the bringing home to the knowledge of the owner of the patented goods that restrictions are laid upon him." Lord Shaw then referred to the case of the *Incandescent Light Co.* v. *Cantelo,* cited above, saying that, "The judgment in that case by Mr. Justice Wills forms undoubtedly a leading authority in the law of England." The passage above set out is then quoted in full.

The precise question here involved has never been decided by this court. It was raised in the *Cotton Tie Case,* 106 U.S. 89, but was passed by and the case decided upon the single ground that the defendants had infringed by a reconstruction of the bands after they had been cut. It was again presented in *Cortelyou* v. *Johnson,* 207 U.S. 196, 199, but was not decided, because it did not appear that the defendants, charged as contributory infringers as in the present case, had notice of the restriction upon the use of the patented machine.

In *Bobbs-Merrill Co.* v. *Straus,* 210. U.S. 339, 345, it was urged that the analogy between the right of one under the copyright statute to fix the price at which a copyrighted book might be sold by retailers by a mere notice accompanying the book, and the right of one selling a patented article subject to a condition that it should not be sold at less than a prescribed minimum price, was such as to entitle the owner of the copyright to treat a sale contrary to the notice as an infringing sale. But this court declined to consider the rule applicable to restrictive licenses accompanying the sale of a patented article, saying: "If we were to follow the course taken in the argument, and discuss the rights of a patentee, under letters patent, and then, by analogy, apply the conclusions to copyrights, we might greatly embarrass the consideration of a case under letters patent, when one of that character shall be presented to this court.

"We may say in passing, disclaiming any intention to indicate our views as to what would be the rights of parties in circumstances similar to the present case under the patent laws, that there are differences between the patent and copyright statutes in the extent of the protection granted by them. This was recognized by Judge Lurton, who wrote a leading case on the subject in the Federal courts (*The Button Fastener Case,* 77 Fed. Rep. 288), for he said in the subsequent case of *Park & Sons* v. *Hartman,* 153 Fed. Rep. 24:

" 'There are such wide differences between the right of multiplying and vending copies of a production protected by the copyright statute and the rights secured to an inventor under the patent statutes, that the cases which relate to the one subject are not altogether controlling as to the other.' "

Touching the question there involved, the court said (p. 350):

"The precise question, therefore, in this case is, does the sole right to vend (named in § 4952) secure to the owner of the copyright the right, after the sale of the book to a purchaser, to restrict future sales of the book at retail, to the right to sell it at a certain price per copy, because of a notice in the book that a sale at a different price will be treated as an infringement, which notice has been brought home to one undertaking to sell for less than the named sum? We do not think the statute can be given such a construction, and it is to be remembered that this is purely a question of statutory construction. There is no claim in this case of contract limitation, nor license agreement controlling the subsequent sales of the book.

"In our view the copyright statutes, while protecting the owner of the copyright in his right to multiply and sell his production, do not create the right to impose, by notice, such as is disclosed in this case, a limitation at which the book shall be sold at retail by future purchasers, with whom there is no privity of contract. This conclusion is reached in view of the language of the statute, read in the light of its main purpose to secure the right of multiplying copies of the work, a right which is the special creation of the statute. True, the statute also secures, to make this right of multiplication effectual, the sole right to vend copies of the book, the production of the author's thought and conception. The owner of the copyright in this case did sell copies of the book in quantities and at a price satisfactory to it. It has exercised the right to vend. What the complainant contends for embraces not only the right to sell the copies, but to qualify the title of a future purchaser by the reservation of the right to have the remedies of the statute against an infringer because of the printed notice of its purpose so to do unless the purchaser sells at a price fixed in the notice. To add to the right of exclusive sale the authority to control all future retail sales, by a notice that such sales must be made at a fixed sum, would give a right not included in the terms of the statute, and, in our view, extend its operation, by construction, beyond its meaning, when interpreted with a view to ascertaining the legislative intent in its enactment."

Though the Constitution gives to Congress power to promote "Science and Useful Arts," by securing for a limited time to writers and inventors "the exclusive right to their respective writings and discoveries," the legislation for this purpose had to be adapted to the difference between a "discovery" and a "writing." To secure to the author an exclusive right to his "writings" Congress provided that he should have "the sole liberty of printing, reprinting, publishing, completing, copying, executing, finishing and vending the same." Revised Statutes, § 4952. This is, in short, the sole right to multiply and vend copies of his production. While there are resemblances between the right of the author to "vend" his copyrighted production, and of the patentee to "vend" the patented thing, the inherent difference between the production of an author, be it a book, music or a picture, and that of an inventor, be it a machine, a process or an article, is so manifest that the exclusive right of one to multiply and sell was declared sufficient to give him that exclusive right to his writings proposed by the Constitution. To the inventor, by § 4884, Revised Statutes, there is granted "the exclusive right to make, *use* and vend the invention or discovery." This grant, as defined in *Bloomer* v. *McQuewan,* 14 How. 539, 549, "consists altogether in the right to exclude every one from making, *using* or vending the thing patented." Thus, there are several substantive rights, and each is the subject of subdivision, so that one person may be permitted to make, but neither to sell nor use the patented thing. To another may be conveyed the right to sell, but within a limited area, or for a particular use, while to another the patentee may grant only the right to make and use, or to use only for specific purposes. *Adams* v. *Burks,* 17 Wall. 453; *Mitchell* v. *Hawley,* 16 Wall. 544; *Rubber Co.* v. *Goodyear,* 9 Wall. 788, 799. Thus, in the case last cited the license was "to use the said Goodyear's gum-elastic composition for coating cloth for the purpose of japanning, marbling, and variegate japanning, at his own establishment, but not to be disposed of to others for that purpose without the consent of the said Charles Goodyear, . . . the right and license hereby conferred being limited to the United States, and not extending to any foreign country, and not being intended to convey any right to make any contract with the government of the United States." Of this license, this court said (p. 799):

"It authorizes Chaffee to use it himself. It gave him no right to authorize others to use it in conjunction with himself, or otherwise, without the consent of Goodyear, which is not shown, and not to be presumed. It was to be used at his own establishment, and not at one occupied by himself and others. Looking at the terms of the instrument, and the testimony in the record, we are satisfied that its true meaning and purpose were to authorize the licensee to make and sell India-rubber cloth, to be used in the place, and for the purposes, of patent or japanned leather. In our judgment it conveyed authority to this extent and nothing more."

The licensees were held to have infringed the license by uses not permitted.

We have already pointed out that in the *Bement Case,* 186 U.S. 91, it was said in respect of the power of a patentee that, in the sale of rights under a patent, "with few exceptions any conditions which are not in their nature illegal with regard to this kind of property, imposed by the patentee and agreed to by the licensee, for the right to manufacture, *or use, or sell the article* will be upheld by the courts." (Italics ours.) The question, as was said in reference to the copyright, is one of statutory construction. The kinds of property rights sought to be guaranteed and the terms of the two statutes are so different that very different constructions have been placed upon them. There is no collision whatever between the decision in the *Bobbs-Merrill Case* and the present opinion. Each rests upon a construction of the applicable statute, and the special facts of the cases.

The *Paper Roll Case* (*Morgan Envelope Co.* v. *Albany Paper Co.*), 152 U.S. 425, has been relied upon by the defendants. We do not question that case, nor anything it decides. But it has no application to the question here presented. This is manifest when that case is attentively examined. First, because here the ink and other supplies used in the operation of the complainant's rotary mimeograph patent were not made elements of the patent, as in the *Paper Roll Case;* and second, the toilet paper fixture in the *Paper Roll Case* was not sold with the license restriction that it was not to be used except in connection with paper supplied by the patentee. There was some evidence of a practice to sell the fixture only to those who used the patentee's paper; but this was far from proof of a specific license annexed to the sale of the fixtures that they were sold only to be used with paper supplied by the patentee. One who bought subject to no such restriction acquired the right to use the fixture with any paper. The opinion in that case is considered and analyzed in all of its aspects in the *Button Fastener Case,* 77 Fed. Rep. 288, 298–9.

We come then to the question as to whether "the acts of the defendants constitute contributory infringement of the complainants' patent."

The facts upon which our answer must be made are somewhat meagre. It has been urged that we should make a negative reply to the interrogatory as certified, because the intent to have the ink sold to the licensee used in an infringing way is not sufficiently made out. Undoubtedly a bare supposition that by a sale of an article which though adapted to an infringing use is also adapted to other and lawful uses, is not enough to make the seller a contributory infringer. Such a rule would block the wheels of commerce. There must be an intent and purpose that the article sold will be so used. Such a presumption arises when the article so sold is only adapted to an infringing use. *Rupp & Wittgenfeld Co.* v. *Elliott,* 131 Fed. Rep. 730. It may also be inferred where its most conspicuous use is one which will coöperate in an infringement when sale to such user is invoked by advertisement.

Kalem Co. v. *Harper Brothers,* decided at this term, 222 U.S. 55.

These defendants are, in the facts certified, stated to have made a direct sale to the user of the patented article, with knowledge that under the license from the patentee she could not use the ink, sold by them directly to her, in connection with the licensed machine, without infringement of the monopoly of the patent. It is not open to them to say that it might be used in a non-infringing way, for the certified fact is that they made the sale, "with the expectation that it would be used in connection with said mimeograph." The fair interpretation of the facts stated is that the sale was with the purpose and intent that it would be so used.

So understanding the import of the question in connection with the facts certified, *we must answer the question certified affirmatively.*

UNITED STATES v. TERMINAL R.R. ASSOCIATION, 224 U.S. 383 (1912)

The Terminal Railroad Association of St. Louis, comprised of thirty-eight corporate and individual members, had gained control over what Justice Lurton described as "every feasible means of railroad access to St. Louis. . . ." (224 U.S. at 393) The association, which supposedly acted merely as an impartial agent of every railroad line, was indicted by the federal government for favoring certain individuals and corporations and discriminating against others. Under the Sherman Act, the government charged the association with combination in restraint of trade; Justice Lurton delivered for a unanimous Court an opinion which fully sustained the government's charges, and the association was dissolved.

MR. JUSTICE LURTON delivered the opinion of the court.

The United States filed this bill to enforce the provisions of the Sherman Act of July 2, 1890, c. 647, 26 Stat. 209, against thirty-eight corporate and individual defendants named in the margin,[1] as a combination in restraint of interstate commerce and as a monopoly forbidden by that law. The cause was heard by the four Circuit Judges, who, being equally divided in judgment, dismissed the bill, without filing an opinion. From this decree the United States has appealed.

The principal defendant is the Terminal Railroad Association of St. Louis, hereinafter designated as the Terminal Company. It is a corporation of the State of Missouri, and was organized under an agreement made in 1889 between Mr. Jay Gould and a number of the defendant railroad companies for the express purpose of acquiring the properties of several independent terminal

[1] *The Terminal Railroad Association of St. Louis; The St. Louis Merchants' Bridge Terminal Railway Company; The Wiggins Ferry Company; The St. Louis Bridge Company; The St. Louis Merchants' Bridge Company; The Missouri, Kansas & Texas Railway Company; The St. Louis & San Francisco Railway Company; The Chicago & Alton Railway Company; The Baltimore & Ohio Southwestern Railroad Company; The Illinois Central Railroad Company; The St. Louis, Iron Mountain & Southern Railway Company; The Chicago, Burlington & Quincy Railway Company; The St. Louis, Vandalia & Terre Haute Railroad Company; The Wabash Railroad Company; The Cleveland, Cincinnati, Chicago & St. Louis Railway Company; The Louisville & Nashville Railroad Company; The Southern Railway Company; The Chicago, Rock Island & Pacific Railway Company; The Missouri Pacific Railway Company; The Central Trust Company of New York; A. A. Allen, S. M. Felton, A. J. Davidson, W. M. Green, J. T. Harahan, C. S. Clarke, H. Miller, Benjamin McKean, Joseph Ramsey, George E. Evans, C. E. Schaff, T. C. Powell, J. F. Stevens, A. G. Cochran, W. S. McChesney, Julius Walsh, V. W. Fisher and S. D. Webster.*

companies at St. Louis with a view to combining and operating them as a unitary system.

The terminal properties first acquired and combined into one system by the Terminal Company comprised the following: The Union Railway & Transit Company of St. Louis and East St. Louis; The Terminal Railroad of St. Louis and East St. Louis; The Union Depot Company of St. Louis; The St. Louis Bridge Company, and the Tunnel Railroad of St. Louis. These properties included the great union station, the only existing railroad bridge—the Eads or St. Louis Bridge—and every connecting or terminal company by means of which that bridge could be used by railroads terminating on either side of the river. For a time this combination was operated in competition with the terminal system of the Wiggins Ferry Company, and upon the completion of the Merchants' Bridge, in competition with it, and a system of terminals which were organized in connection with it. The Wiggins Ferry Company had for many years operated car transfer boats by means of which cars were transferred between St. Louis and East St. Louis.

Upon each side of the river it owned extensive railway terminal facilities, with which connection was maintained with the many railroads terminating on the west and east sides of the river, which gave such roads connection with each other, as well as access to many of the industrial and business districts on each side. In 1890 a third terminal system was opened up by the completion of a second railroad bridge over the Mississippi River at St. Louis, known as the Merchants' Bridge. This was a railroad toll bridge, open to every railroad upon equal terms. That it might forever maintain the potentiality of competition as a railroad bridge, the act of Congress authorizing its construction provided that no stockholders in any other railway bridge company should become a stockholder therein. But as this was a mere bridge company, it was essential that railroad companies desiring to use it should have railway connections with it on each side of the river. For this purpose two or more railway companies were organized and lines of railway were constructed connecting each end of the Merchants' Bridge with various railroad systems terminating on either side of the river. The Merchants' Bridge and its allied terminals were thereby able to afford many, if not all, of the railroads coming into St. Louis, access to the business districts on both sides of the river, and connection with each other.

Thus, for a time, there existed three independent methods by which connection was maintained between railroads terminating on either side of the river at St. Louis: First, the original Wiggins Ferry Company, and its railway terminal connections; second, The Eads Railroad Bridge and the several terminal companies by means of which railroads terminating at St. Louis were able to use that bridge and connect with one another, constituting the system controlled by the Terminal Company, and, third, The Merchants' Bridge and terminal facilities owned and operated by companies in connection therewith.

This resulted in some cases in an unnecessary duplication of facilities, but it at least gave to carriers and shippers some choice, a condition which, if it does not lead to competition in charges, does insure competition in service. Important as were the considerations mentioned, their independence of one another served to keep open the means for the entrance of new lines to the city, and was an obstacle to united opposition from existing lines. The importance of this will be more clearly seen when we come to consider the topographical conditions of the situation.

That the promoters of the Terminal Company designed to obtain the control of every feasible means of railroad access to St. Louis, or means of connecting the lines of railway entering on opposite sides of the river, is manifested by the declarations of the original agreement, as well as by the successive steps which followed. Thus, the proviso in the act of Congress authorizing the construction of the Merchants' Bridge, which forbade the ownership of its stock by any other bridge company or stockholder in any such company, was eliminated by an act of Congress, and shortly thereafter the Terminal Company obtained stock control of the Merchants' Bridge Company, and of its related terminal companies, and likewise a lease.

The Wiggins Ferry Company owned the river front on the Illinois shore opposite St. Louis for a distance of several miles. It had on that side and on its own property, switching yards and other terminal facilities. From these yards extended lines of rails which connected with its car transfer boats and with the termini of railroads on the Illinois side. On the St. Louis side of the river it had like facilities by which it was in connection with railway lines terminating on that side. That company was, consequently, able to interchange traffic between the systems on opposite sides of the river and to serve many industries. In 1892 the Rock Island Railroad Company endeavored to obtain an independent entrance to the city. For this purpose it sought to acquire the facilities owned by the Wiggins Ferry Company by securing a control of its capital stock. This was not deemed desirable by the railroad companies which jointly owned the Terminal Company's facilities, and to prevent this acquisition effort was made to secure control of the stock. The competition was fierce and the market price of the shares pushed to an abnormal price. The final result being in doubt, an agreement was reached by which the Rock Island Company was admitted to joint ownership with the other proprietary companies in all of the terminal properties which were operated by the Terminal Company or which should be acquired by it. The shares in the Ferry Company bought by the Rock Island were transferred to the Terminal Company at cost and were paid for by that company. These shares, united with those which had been acquired by the Terminal Company, enabled the latter to absorb the properties of the Ferry Company, and thus the three independent terminal systems were combined into a single system.

We come, then, to the question upon which the case must turn: Has the unification of substantially every terminal facility by which the traffic of St. Louis is served resulted in a combination which is in restraint of trade within the meaning and purpose of the Anti-trust Act?

It is not contended that the unification of the terminal facilities of a great city where many railroad systems center is, under all circumstances and conditions, a combination in restraint of trade or commerce. Whether it is a facility in aid of interstate commerce or an unreasonable restraint forbidden by the act of Congress, as construed and applied by this court in the cases of *The Standard Oil Company* v. *The United States,* 221 U.S. 1, and *The United States* v. *American Tobacco Company,* 221 U.S. 106, will depend upon the intent to be inferred from the extent of the control thereby secured over instrumentalities which such commerce is under compulsion to use, the method by which such control has been brought about and the manner in which that control has been exerted.

The consequence to interstate commerce of this combination cannot be appreciated without a consideration of natural conditions greatly affecting the railroad situation at St. Louis. Though twenty-four lines of railway converge at St. Louis, not one of them passes through. About one-half of these lines have their termini on the Illinois side of the river. The others, coming from the west and north, have their termini either in the city or on its northern edge. To the river the city owes its origin, and for a century and more its river commerce was predominant. It is now the great obstacle to connection between the termini of lines on opposite sides of the river and any entry into the city by eastern lines. The cost of construction and maintenance of railroad bridges over so great a river makes it impracticable for every road desiring to enter or pass through the city to have its own bridge. The obvious solution is the maintenance of toll bridges open to the use of any and all lines upon identical terms. And so the commercial interests of St. Louis sought to solve the question, the system of car ferry transfer being inadequate to the growing demands of an ever-increasing population. The first bridge, called the Eads Bridge, was, and is, a toll bridge. Any carrier may use it on equal terms. But to use it there must be access over rails connecting the bridge and the railway. On the St. Louis side the bridge terminates at the foot of the great hills upon which the city is built; on the Illinois side it ends in the low and wide valley of the Mississippi. This condition resulted in the organization of independent companies which undertook to connect the bridge on each side with the various railroad termini. On the Missouri side it was necessary to tunnel the hills, that the valley of Mill Creek might be reached, where the roads from the west had their termini. Thus, though the bridge might be used by all upon equal terms, it was accessible only by means of the several terminal companies operating lines connecting it with the railroad termini.

This brought about a condition which led to the construction of the second bridge, the Merchants' Bridge. This, too, was, and is, a toll bridge, and may be used by all upon equal terms. To prevent its control by the Eads Bridge Company, it was carefully provided that no stockholder in any other bridge company should own its shares. But this Merchants' Bridge, like the Eads Bridge, had no rail connections with any of the existing railroad systems, and these facilities, as in the case of the Eads Bridge, were supplied by a number of independent railway companies who undertook to fill in the gaps between the bridge ends and the termini of railroads on both sides of the river. It must be also observed that these terminal companies were in many instances so supplied with switch connections as not only to connect with the bridge, but also served to connect such roads with each other and with the industries along their lines. Now, it is evident that these lines connecting railroad termini with the railroad bridges dominated the situation. They stood, as it were, just outside the gateway, and none could enter, though the gate stood open, who did not comply with their terms. The topographical situation making access to the city difficult does not end with the river. The city lies upon a group of great hills which hug the river closely and rapidly recede to the west. These hills are penetrated on the west by the narrow valley of Mill Creek, which crosses the city about its center. Railways coming from the west use this valley, but its facilities are very restricted and now quite occupied. North of the city the hills drop back from the river gradually, and there exists a valley formed by the Mississippi and Missouri rivers. Railroads coming from the north on the west side of the river come by this valley. As we have stated before, the valley of the Mississippi at St. Louis is on the Illinois side of the river. Railroads coming from the east, northeast and southeast have their termini in that valley. As a consequence, there have grown up numerous cities and towns of some consequence as manufacturing places, the chief of which is East St. Louis.

The result of the geographical and topographical situation is that it is, as a practical matter, impossible for any railroad company to pass through, or even enter St. Louis, so as to be within reach of its industries or commerce, without using the facilities entirely controlled by the Terminal Company. The averment of the bill that the railroad companies, here defendants, being the sole stockholders of the Terminal Company, as we shall later see, compel all other railroad companies converging at St. Louis to use the facilities owned and operated by the Terminal Company, is, therefore, borne out by the facts of the situation. Nor is this effect denied, for the learned counsel representing the proprietary companies, as well as the Terminal Company, say in their filed brief: "There indeed is compulsion, but it is inherent in the situation. The other companies use the terminal properties because it is not possible to acquire adequate facilities for themselves. The cost to any one company is prohibitive." Obviously, this was not true before the consolidation of the systems of the Wiggins Ferry Company and the Merchants' Bridge Company with the system theretofore controlled by the Terminal Company. That the non-proprietary companies might have been compelled to use the instrumentalities of one or the other of the three systems then available, and that the advantages secured might not have been so great as those offered by the unified system now operated by the Terminal Company, must be admitted. But that there existed before the three terminal systems were combined a considerable measure of competition for the business of the other companies, and a larger power of competition, is undeniable. That the fourteen proprietary companies did not then have the power they now have to exclude either existing roads not in the combination, or new companies, from acquiring an independent entrance into the city, is also indisputable. The independent existence of these three terminal systems was, therefore, a menace to complete domination as keeping open the way for greater competition. Only by their absorption or some equivalent arrangement was it possible to exclude from independent entrance the Rock Island Company, or any other company which might desire its own terminals. To close the door to competition large sums were expended to acquire stock control. For this purpose the obligations of the absorbed companies were assumed and new funds obtained by mortgages upon the unified system.

The physical conditions which compel the use of the combined system by every road which desires to cross the river, either to serve the commerce of the city or to connect with lines separated by the river, is the factor which gives greatest color to the unlawfulness of the combination as now controlled and operated. If the Terminal Company was in law and fact the agent of all, the mere unification which has occurred would take on quite a different aspect. It becomes, therefore, of the utmost importance to know the character and purpose of the corporation which has combined all of the terminal instrumentalities upon which the commerce of a great city and gateway between the East and West must depend. The fact that the Terminal Company is not an independent corporation at all is of the utmost significance. There are twenty-four railroads converging at St. Louis. The relation of the Terminal Company is not one of impartiality to each of them. It was organized in 1889, at the instance of six of these railroad companies, for the purpose of acquiring all existing terminal instrumentalities for the benefit of the combination, and such other companies as they might thereafter admit to joint ownership by unanimous consent, and upon a consideration to be agreed upon. From time to time other companies came to an agreement with the original proprietors until, at the time this bill was filed, the properties unified were held for the joint use of the fourteen companies made defendants. In the contract of 1889, above referred to, the purpose of acquiring the first terminals combined, is declared to be, "that said properties may be held in perpetuity as a unit and developed and improved in the interest of the proprietary companies, for the purpose of furnishing adequate terminal facilities in St. Louis and East St. Louis." This purpose was carried out by the conveyance to "each of the proprietary companies . . . forever a right of joint use with each other and such other companies as may be admitted as proprietary lines to joint use thereof, of all said terminal properties . . . now held or that may be hereafter acquired in St. Louis and East St. Louis, . . . it being understood that the right herein granted to each proprietary company is not transferable to any extent whatever, but is to remain as an appurtenant to the railroad now owned by each proprietary company."

That these facilities were not to be acquired for the benefit of any railroad company which might desire a joint use thereof was made plain by a provision in the contract referred to which stipulated that other railroad companies not named therein as proprietary companies might only be admitted "to joint use of said terminal system on unanimous consent, but not otherwise, of the directors of the first party, and on payment of such a consideration as they may determine, and on signing this agreement," etc. Inasmuch as the directors of the Terminal Company consisted of one representative of each of the proprietary companies, selected by itself, it is plain that each of said companies had and still has a veto upon any joint use or control of terminals by any non-proprietary company.

By that and the supplemental agreement of December, 1902, the Ferry Company and the Merchants' Bridge Company having then been absorbed, the proprietary companies prescribed that the charges of the company shall be so adjusted as to produce no more revenue than shall equal the fixed charges, operating and maintenance expenses. Deficiencies for those purposes the proprietary companies guarantee to make good, though such payments are to be reimbursed by an increase in charges, if necessary.

We fail to find in either of the contracts referred to any provision abrogating the requirement of unanimous consent to the admission of other companies to the ownership of the Terminal Company, though counsel say that no such company will now find itself excluded from joint use or ownership upon application. That other companies are permitted to use the facilities of the Terminal Company upon paying the same charges paid by the proprietary companies seems to be conceded. But there is no provision by which any such privilege is accorded.

By still another clause in the agreement the proprietary companies obligate themselves to forever use the facilities of the Terminal Company for all business destined to cross the river. This would seem to guarantee against any competitive system, since the companies to the agreement now control about one-third of the railroad mileage of the United States.

In acquiring these properties the Terminal Company has assumed mortgage and stock dividend obligations of the constituent companies aggregating about twenty-five million dollars. It has executed its own mortgage upon all of its property to secure an issue of fifty million dollars of bonds, of which twenty million dollars worth have been sold, and the proceeds used in construction or in paying for the properties acquired. It has thus about forty-five million dollars of mortgage or fixed charges or liabilities. The company has an authorized capital stock of fifty million dollars. Of this about twenty-eight million dollars has been issued in equal proportions, to the several owning railroad companies. No dividends have ever been paid, and the company disclaims any purpose to pay dividends. We fail to find any obligation by which they may be prevented from paying dividends upon the stock held by the proprietary companies, or that in its treasury, if ever issued. Undoubtedly, the major part of this revenue arises from the business done by the proprietary companies through the Terminal Company, but that coming from other companies is, however, a large contribution. That no direct profit is derived by the owning companies from the operation of the terminals, may be true. But it is not clear that the proprietary companies do not make an indirect profit through ownership of obligations of the absorbed companies.

That through their ownership and exclusive control they are in possession of advantages in respect to the enormous traffic which must use the St. Louis gateway, is undeniable. That the proprietary companies have not availed themselves of the full measure of their power to impede free competition of outside companies, may be true. Aside from their power under all of the conditions to exclude independent entrance to the city by any outside company, their control has resulted in certain methods which are not consistent with freedom of competition. To these acts we shall refer later.

We are not unmindful of the essential difference between terminal systems properly so described and railroad transportation companies. The first are but instrumentalities which assist the latter in the transfer of traffic between different lines, and in the collection and distribution of traffic. They are a modern evolution in the doing of railroad business, and are of the greatest public utility. They, under proper conditions, do not restrain, but promote commerce.

The argument that the combination of the instrumentalities operated by the Terminal Company with those of the Merchants' Bridge Company was a combination of two competing lines of railroad, such as was condemned in *Northern Securities Company* v. *United States,* 193 U.S. 197, is not well founded. This combination if properly regarded as of parallel and competing lines would have been obnoxious to the seventeenth section of the constitution of Missouri. For the purpose of enforcing this Missouri prohibition, the State instituted a proceeding to dissolve the combination of the properties of the Merchants' Bridge Terminal Railroad Company with the Terminal Railroad Association of St. Louis, upon the ground that the railroads operated by those companies were parallel and competing lines of railroad. Relief was denied. The Missouri court held that the merger of mere railway terminals used to facilitate the public convenience by the transfer of cars from one line of railway to another, and instrumentalities for the distribution or gathering of traffic, freight or passenger, among scattered industries, or to different business centers of a great city, were not properly railroad companies within the reasonable meaning of the statutes forbidding combinations between competing or parallel lines of railroad. Referring to the legitimate use of terminal companies, the Missouri court said:

"A more effectual means of keeping competition up to the highest point between parallel or competing lines could not be devised. The destruction of the system would result in compelling the shipper to employ the railroad with which he has switch connection, or else cart his product to a distant part of the city, at a cost possibly as great as the railroad tariff.

"St. Louis is a city of great magnitude in the extent of its area, its population, and its manufacturing and other business. A very large number of trunk line railroads converge in this city. In the brief of one of the well-informed counsel in this case it is said that St. Louis is one of the largest railroad centers in the world. Suppose it were required of every railroad company to effect its entrance to this city as best it could and establish its own terminal facilities, we would have a large number of passenger stations, freight depots and switch yards scattered all over the vast area and innumerable vehicles employed in hauling passengers and freight to and from those stations and depots. Or suppose it became necessary in the exigency of commerce that all incoming trains should reach a common focus, but every railroad company provide its own track; then not only would the expense of obtaining the necessary rights of way be so enormous as to amount to the exclusion of all but a few of the strongest roads, but, if it could be accomplished, the city would be cut to pieces with the many lines of railroad intersecting it in every direction, and thus the greatest agency of commerce would become the greatest burden." 182 Missouri, 284, 299.

Among the cases in which the public utility of such companies has been recognized are: *Bridwell* v. *Gate City Terminal Co.* (Georgia), 10 L. R. A. (N. S.) 909; *Indianapolis Union Railroad Company* v. *Cooper,* 6 Ind. App. 202; *State ex rel.* v. *Martin,* 51 Kansas, 462; *Mayor* v. *Norwich E. W. Railroad Co.,* 109 Massachusetts, 103; *Union Depot Company* v. *Morton,* 83 Michigan, 265; *State* v. *St. Paul Union Depot*

Co., 42 Minnesota, 142; *Ryan* v. *Terminal Co.*, 102 Tennessee, 111, 124.

While, therefore, the mere combining of several independent terminal systems into one may not operate as a restraint upon the interstate commerce which must use them, yet there may be conditions which will bring such a combination under the prohibition of the Sherman Act. The one in question, counsel say, is not antagonistic to but in harmony with the Anti-trust Act, "because it expands competition by extending equal conveniences and advantages to all shippers located upon each of the three systems for all traffic to and from St. Louis; expedites and economizes the service." It is justified, they argue by "(1) the physical or topographical conditions peculiar to the locality; by (2) its commercial, industrial and railroad development and history; by (3) public opinion expressed legislatively and judicially, and (4) by the judgment of experienced railroad engineers and managers." From which consideration the same counsel say that the issue presented by this record is, "whether the common control or ownership of all the terminal facilities (mechanical devices for the exchange, receipt and distribution of traffic) of a large commercial and manufacturing center by all of the railroad companies, and for the benefit of all upon equal terms and facilities, without discrimination, is condemned by the Sherman act."

Let us analyze the proposition included in the issue, as stated by counsel, quoted above: Counsel assume that the combined terminals have come under a "common control or ownership." But this is not the case. That the instrumentalities so combined are not jointly owned or managed by all of the companies compelled to use them is a significant fact which must be taken into account for the purpose of determining whether there has been a violation of the Anti-trust Act. The control and ownership is that of the fourteen roads which are defendants. The railroad systems and the coal roads converging at St. Louis, which are not associated with the proprietary companies are under compulsion to use the terminal system, and yet have no voice in its control.

It cannot be controverted that, in ordinary circumstances, a number of independent companies might combine for the purpose of controlling or acquiring terminals for their common but exclusive use. In such cases other companies might be admitted upon terms or excluded altogether. If such terms were too onerous, there would ordinarily remain the right and power to construct their own terminals. But the situation at St. Louis is most extraordinary, and we base our conclusion in this case, in a large measure, upon that fact. The "physical or topographical condition peculiar to the locality," which is advanced as a prime justification for a unified system of terminals, constitutes a most obvious reason why such a unified system is an obstacle, a hindrance and a restriction upon interstate commerce, unless it is the impartial agent of all who, owing to conditions, are under such compulsion, as here exists, to use its facilities. The witness upon whom the defendants chiefly rely to uphold the advantages of the unified system which has been constructed, Mr. Albert L. Perkins, gives this as his unqualified judgment. He was and is an experienced railroad engineer and manager and is the railway expert of the Municipal Bridge and Terminal Board, a commission appointed under a city ordinance, headed by the mayor, to study and report legislation needed to relieve the terminal conditions of St. Louis. From his study of the local situation he expresses the opinion that the terminals of railway lines in any large city should be unified as far as possible, and that such unification may be of the greatest public utility and of immeasureable advantage to commerce, state and interstate. Neither does he find in the conditions at St. Louis any insurmountable objection to such unification. The witness, however, points out that such a terminal company should be the agent of every company, and, furthermore, that its service should not be for profit or gain. In short, that every railroad using the service should be a joint owner and equally interested in the control and management. This, he thinks, will serve the greatest possible economy, and will give the most efficient service without discrimination. When thus jointly owned and controlled, whether through the medium of a mere holding or operating company, such as the Terminal Company is, or by other means, the facilities would belong to each relatively to its own business and delivery would be made by each company over its own tracks to connecting lines or places of destination in the city. The charge for the haul thus lengthened would then be properly absorbed by the through rate, leaving nothing to be added to that to be charged the shipper or consignee but switching and storage charges proper.

The terminal properties in question are

not so controlled and managed, in view of the inherent local conditions, as to escape condemnation as a restraint upon commerce. They are not under a common control and ownership. Nor can this be brought about unless the prohibition against the admission of other companies to such control is stricken out and provision made for the admission of any company to an equal control and management upon an equal basis with the present proprietary companies.

There are certain practices of this Terminal Company which operate to the disadvantage of the commerce which must cross the river at St. Louis, and of non-proprietary railroad lines compelled to use its facilities. One of them grows out of the fact that the Terminal Company is a terminal company and something more. It does not confine itself to supplying and operating mere facilities for the interchange of traffic between railroads and to assistance in the collecting and distributing of traffic for the carrier companies. It, as well as several of the absorbed terminal companies, were organized under ordinary railroad charters. If the combination which has occurred is to escape condemnation as a combination of parallel and competing railroad companies, it is because of the essential difference between railroad and terminal companies proper—differences pointed out by the Missouri Supreme Court in the case heretofore referred to. Indeed, the defense to this proceeding is based upon the insistence that the Terminal Company is solely engaged in operating terminal facilities, defined in the briefs, "as mechanical devices for the exchange, receipt and distribution of traffic." This Terminal Company, in addition to its schedule for terminal charges proper, such as switching, warehousing, etc., files its rate-sheets for the transportation of every class of merchandise from the termini of the railroads on the Illinois side of the river to destinations across the river over its lines. These rates are applied to all traffic destined to cross the river, with certain exceptions to which we shall later refer, which originates within an irregular area of which St. Louis is the center, and having a diameter of from one to two hundred miles. This arbitrary operates to cast a burden upon short hauls, which has led to much complaint, as being both discriminatory and extortionate. An exception is made as to traffic originating within so much of this area as constitutes what is called "Green Line Territory," or which is destined to points within "Green Line Territory." This seems to be based upon competitive conditions caused by the great toll railway bridge at Memphis, Tennessee, the bridge toll being treated by lines using the bridge as a part of the through rate.

Another exception to the rule imposing this arbitrary is that it does not apply to traffic which originates in East St. Louis, whether it is destined to cross the river or not. The reason for this exemption, where such traffic does cross the river, is not apparent. Possibly, it may be said that it is because the traffic of St. Louis and East St. Louis should be treated as arising in the same commercial area. But this reason does not seem to apply to the traffic originating in St. Louis, which is bound east, though that of East St. Louis is altogether free from this arbitrary charge. The effect of this arbitrary discrimination is obviously injurious to the commerce and manufacturers of St. Louis, and is among the chief causes of complaint against the Terminal Company. Mr. Perkins, to whom we have before referred as a capable and impartial expert, says of the consequence of this curious exception out of the one hundred mile area rule, that "the effect of these charges was, of course, to put the man doing business in St. Louis at a disadvantage to that extent with the man doing business at East St. Louis on his eastern business." Again he says, that the practical operation was to give East St. Louis a distinct advantage in the manufacturing lines. Another practice which marks this Terminal Company as a transportation company which interposed itself between railroads having their termini on opposite sides of the river, and between the city itself and the roads terminating on the east side of the river, is that all traffic destined to cross the river at St. Louis, whether bound east or west, or destined for the city if coming from the east, is billed only to East St. Louis, and there rebilled to destination.

The practice of rebilling and of making a distinct hauling charge is an evident survival of the methods which existed when the eastern lines had no termini in St. Louis. They then billed to East St. Louis, and there turned the traffic over to one of the existing terminal companies, who made their own specific charges for the haul to places of delivery within the city. The practice has been continued after the reason for it has disappeared. The effect of this practice of rebilling at East St. Louis and of imposing this arbitrary upon traffic originating within one hundred miles of the city, destined to cross the river, seems to have been also applied to the large coal traffic between the Illinois coal mines, upon which the city is largely dependent.

We come now to the remedy. In determining what this should be we, as said by this court in *Standard Oil Company* v. *United States,* 221 U.S. 1, 78, must not overlook the fact that in applying a remedy "that injury to the public by the prevention of an undue restraint on, or the monopolization of trade or commerce is the foundation upon which the prohibitions of the statute rest, and moreover that one of the fundamental purposes of the statute is to protect, not to destroy, rights of property." If, as we have already said, the combination of two or more mere terminal companies into a single system does not violate the prohibition of the statute against contracts and combinations in restraint of interstate commerce, it is because such a combination may be of the greatest public utility. But when, as here, the inherent conditions are such as to prohibit any other reasonable means of entering the city, the combination of every such facility under the exclusive ownership and control of less than all of the companies under compulsion to use them violates both the first and second sections of the act, in that it constitutes a contract or combination in restraint of commerce among the States and an attempt to monopolize commerce among the States which must pass through the gateway at St. Louis.

The Government has urged a dissolution of the combination between the Terminal Company, the Merchants' Bridge Terminal Company and the Wiggins Ferry Company. That remedy may be necessary unless one equally adequate can be applied.

But the illegal restraint upon commerce among the States which we here find to exist consists in the possession acquired by the proprietary companies through the means and with the object we have stated of dominating commerce among the States carried on by other railroads entering or seeking to enter the city of St. Louis and by which such railroads are compelled either to desist from carrying on interstate commerce or to do so upon the terms imposed by the proprietary companies. This control and possession constitutes such a grip upon the commerce of St. Louis and commerce which must cross the river there, whether coming from the east or west as to be both an illegal restraint and an attempt to monopolize.

The power resulting from the combination even before completed by the acquisition of the Wiggins Ferry Company and its related terminals was exhibited when the Rock Island sought an independent entrance.

Some of its abuses are shown by the imposition of the arbitrary hauling charge imposed upon the artificially limited trade districts described. It is shown also by the maintenance of the system of billing traffic destined to cross the river at St. Louis, either east or west, or to St. Louis, if from points on the east side of the river, a practice so galling and universal as to practically "eliminate St. Louis from the railroad map," to quote the graphic, if extravagant, language of counsel for the United States, as respects the great traffic subject to the regulation.

Plainly the combination which has occurred would not be an illegal restraint under the terms of the statute if it were what is claimed for it, a proper terminal association acting as the impartial agent of every line which is under compulsion to use its instrumentalities. If, as we have pointed out, the violation of the statute, in view of the inherent physical conditions, grows out of administrative conditions which may be eliminated and the obvious advantages of unification preserved, such a modification of the agreement between the Terminal Company and the proprietary companies as shall constitute the former the *bona fide* agent and servant of every railroad line which shall use its facilities, and an inhibition of certain methods of administration to which we have referred, will amply vindicate the wise purpose of the statute, and will preserve to the public a system of great public advantage.

These considerations lead to a reversal of the decree dismissing the bill. This is accordingly adjudged and the case is remanded to the District Court, with directions that a decree be there entered directing the parties to submit to the court, within ninety days after receipt of mandate, a plan for the reorganization of the contract between the fourteen defendant railroad companies and the Terminal Company, which we have pointed out as bringing the combination within the inhibition of the statute.

First. By providing for the admission of any existing or future railroad to joint ownership and control of the combined terminal properties, upon such just and reasonable terms as shall place such applying company upon a plane of equality in respect of benefits and burdens with the present proprietary companies.

Second. Such plan of reorganization must also provide definitely for the use of the terminal facilities by any other railroad not electing to become a joint owner, upon such just and reasonable terms and regulations as will, in respect of use, character and cost of service, place every such company upon as nearly an equal plane as may be with respect to expenses and charges as that occupied by the proprietary companies.

Third. By eliminating from the present agreement between the Terminal Company and the proprietary companies any provision which restricts any such company to the use of the facilities of the Terminal Company.

Fourth. By providing for the complete abolition of the existing practice of billing to East St. Louis, or other junction points, and then rebilling traffic destined to St. Louis, or to points beyond.

Fifth. By providing for the abolition of any special or so-called arbitrary charge for the use of the terminal facilities in respect of traffic originating within the so-called one hundred mile area, that is not equally and in like manner applied in respect of all other traffic of a like character originating outside of that area.

Sixth. By providing that any disagreement between any company applying to become a joint owner or user as herein provided for and the Terminal or proprietary companies which shall arise after a final decree in this cause, may be submitted to the District Court, upon a petition filed in this cause, subject to review by appeal in the usual manner.

Seventh. To avoid any possible misapprehension, the decree should also contain a provision that nothing therein shall be taken to affect in any wise or at any time the power of the Interstate Commerce Commission over the rates to be charged by the Terminal Company, or the mode of billing traffic passing over its lines, or the establishing of joint through rates or routes over its lines, or any other power conferred by law upon such Commission.

Upon failure of the parties to come to an agreement which is in substantial accord with this opinion and decree, the court will, after hearing the parties upon a plan for the dissolution of the combination between the Terminal Company, the Wiggins Ferry Company, the Merchants' Bridge Company, and the several terminal companies related to the Ferry and Merchants' Bridge Company, make such order and decree for the complete disjoinder of the three stystems, and their future operation as independent systems, as may be necessary, enjoining the defendants, singly and collectively from any exercise of control or dominion over either of the said terminal systems, or their related constituent companies, through lease, purchase or stock control, and enjoining the defendants from voting any share in any of said companies or receiving dividends, directly or indirectly, or from any future combination of the said systems in evasion of such decree or any part thereof.

Reversed and remanded accordingly.

Charles Evans Hughes

☆ 1862–1948 ☆

APPOINTED BY WILLIAM HOWARD TAFT

ASSOCIATE JUSTICE: 1910–1916

APPOINTED BY HERBERT HOOVER

CHIEF JUSTICE: 1930–1948

Charles Evans Hughes

by

SAMUEL HENDEL

THE PUBLIC CAREER of Charles Evans Hughes began shortly after the turn of the century and ended just before Pearl Harbor. It was a career which in point of diversity of experience, personal distinction, and importance to America few men have ever rivaled. Most noteworthy was his service as governor of New York State, Associate Justice of the United States Supreme Court, candidate for the Presidency of the United States, recognized leader of the American bar, Secretary of State, and Chief Justice of the United States.

Paradoxically, in the course of this career Mr. Hughes has been extolled as a great liberal concerned with the preservation and extension of public rights against special privilege and denounced as an arch conservative who, in the phrase of Alpheus T. Mason, "proved himself a particularly fertile source of restrictive interpretation, an imaginative adapter of old dogma to serve as a sword against the rising popular demand for effective government." To some, including his official biographer, Merlo J. Pusey, he was extraordinarily open-minded, balanced, and objective while to others he was "one of the most politically calculating of men," who displayed a narrowness of understanding and an arid self-righteousness.

The Court, Justice Oliver Wendell Holmes asserted, responds to "the felt necessities of the time." And, "truth," wrote Francis Bacon, "is the daughter of time." Measured against these standards, how has the career of Charles Evans Hughes—and particularly his doctrines as a Justice of the Supreme Court and then as Chief Justice of the United States—withstood the test of time?

Charles Evans Hughes was born in Glens Falls, New York, on April 11, 1862. His father was a Baptist preacher and his mother had been a school

SAMUEL HENDEL, Professor of Political Science at City College of New York, is the author of Charles Evans Hughes and the Supreme Court.

teacher. The only child of the marriage, he was brought up in a household infused with intense religious zeal and moral fervor. As Hughes wrote in later life, "It was the fondest hope of my parents that I should enter the ministry and I was early 'dedicated' . . . I was constantly warned of the necessity of subduing evil inclinations, lest they 'grow with my growth and strengthen with my strength.'"

From a very early pre-school age his education, building on his natural precocity, was received at the hands of his father and mother at home. When he was sent to school at age six—an experience he found boring and confining—after three weeks he begged to be allowed to resume his studies at home. In support of his request he submitted "Charles E. Hughes' Plan of Study" in which he listed each subject to be studied and the time to be devoted to it. His request was granted. Before he was eight he was studying Greek. When Charles was not quite twelve his family moved to New York City where his father had accepted a position as secretary of the American Bible Union and Charles was enrolled in a public grammar school. It was here that he wrote a theme on "Happiness and Its Constituents" in which he solemnly warned that "whenever we turn aside from following Duty's beckoning finger, that moment happiness ceases"; and another on "Light Reading and Its Consequences," about which he declared that it "will not educate our moral sense, but will blind, pervert and weaken it."

At fourteen he was admitted to Madison College (now Colgate University) to prepare for the ministry. In September, 1878 (at age sixteen) he transferred to Brown University in Providence, a larger college with a Baptist tradition but with a more liberal atmosphere. Here he displayed an interest in some of the lighter diversions; attending theatre, playing poker (with matchsticks not money), smoking, and becoming an ardent baseball fan. At the same time he vigorously pursued his studies with sufficient distinction to earn admittance to Phi Beta Kappa at the end of his junior year. In November, 1880 he was elected as one of the editors of the Brunonian, the student newspaper. The next month he wrote his mother, "I feel no call to the ministry," and in March, 1881 added, "The more I think of the future, the more I incline toward the legal profession." At the age of nineteen, the youngest member in a class of forty-three, he was graduated with third highest honors.

Lacking financial means to enter law school immediately, he accepted a salary of $200 for the school year (with room and board) to teach Greek, Latin, and mathematics at the Delaware Academy at Delhi, New York. Many of his afternoons and evenings were spent reading law in the office of William M. Gleason, a Columbia Law School graduate.

Having persuaded his father to help, he entered Columbia Law School in the fall of 1882 and was graduated with highest honors in 1884. His outstanding record won him $500 a year for three years in return for part-time tutoring at the law school and a connection with the prominent law firm of Chamberlin, Carter and Hornblower. (He was later to learn that his mark on the bar examination had been 99½.) Within a few years he became a partner in a reorganized firm. On December 5, 1888, he married Antoinette Carter, the daughter of one of the partners. It was during the summer of 1890 that Hughes, having grown a beard as a matter of convenience, decided to keep it permanently; and it remained a characteristic mark of the man.

Despite an active and financially successful legal practice, in 1891, at age twenty-nine, partly because of ill health and partly because of the drudgery of phases of the practice of law, he decided to accept a full professorship at Cornell University Law School. Although he was extremely happy in his teaching, two years later he was persuaded to return to his law firm in New York but continued for some years as a special lecturer both at Cornell and New York Law Schools. Increasingly in the ensuing years he became a lawyer's lawyer, handling tough and complicated cases and gaining wide recognition for his legal talents.

Hughes entered public life at the age of forty-three in 1905 when, at the suggestion of Henry W. Taft, the younger brother of William Howard Taft, he was designated as counsel to the Stevens Committee, a joint New York State legislative committee set up to investigate gas and electric rates. He plunged into the investigation with great energy and phenomenal ability to master complex and technical data. He exposed the fact that the Consolidated Gas Company was charging rates based upon a valuation which included heavily watered stock and that the City of New York was paying for electric service at rates three times as high as those charged private consumers. His work led to substantial reductions in utility rates both for private consumers and the City of New York. His report called for the creation of a public service commission to regulate rates, investigate complaints, and otherwise enforce provisions of the law.

When later that same year (following in the wake of scandals) a legislative committee embarked upon an investigation of the insurance companies, it naturally sought Hughes as counsel. Again revealing a remarkable grasp of the intricacies of insurance and high finance, Hughes, over a period of three and one-half months and in fifty-seven public hearings, subjected the leaders of the insurance and financial world, including George W. Perkins and E. H. Harriman, to thorough and merciless examination. He revealed that part of the profits of underwriting syndicates found their way into the pockets of insurance executives; that inflated salaries, improper personal expenses, and nepotism were commonplace; that the business of insurance was overly concentrated; and that the insurance companies had contributed to campaign funds and carried on secret lobbying to influence legislation. This probe, although limited to New York, had nation-wide implications and impact, and led, over the course of years, to important reforms.

In 1906, partly through the influence of President Theodore Roosevelt, Mr. Hughes was nominated by acclamation as the Republican party candidate for governor of New York State to oppose William Randolph Hearst. In accepting the nomination, he defined "decent government" as "the supreme issue of this campaign." Mr. Hughes won by a margin of 57,897 votes and was the only Republican statewide candidate elected. His earlier exposures of corrupt business practices did not militate against his receiving generous Wall Street support.

In 1908 Hughes was reelected and served until October 10, 1910, when he was sworn in as an Associate Justice of the United States Supreme Court.

As governor he placed great emphasis on integrity and efficiency in government. Accordingly, he supported legislation to curb the use of corporate funds for political purposes, favored extension of the civil service, the direct primary, and the short ballot.

Additionally, Governor Hughes sought a proper balance between individual freedom and community interest which might require restrictions "to prevent the liberty of some from accomplishing the enthraldom of all." But such restrictions on individual freedom, he emphasized, must be adopted not out of sentiment but only when warranted by the facts. Accordingly, he sponsored an investigation which led to the enactment of New York's workmen's compensation law, urged passage of an anti-child labor law, and the setting up of public service commissions to regulate utility rates. On the other hand, he vetoed bills to reduce railroad rates because they were enacted without prior fact-finding investigations which would permit fair conclusions.

Another important principle enunciated by Governor Hughes was concern for an appropriate division of national and state power with proper regard for the essential bases and prerogatives of state power. This regard, he stated, led him to oppose New York State ratification of the income tax amendment; an amendment which, as he viewed it, was so broadly phrased as to permit federal taxation of state securities and hence impose burdens on its borrowing power.

Of special importance, in light of his later tasks, was Governor Hughes' unqualified defense of the authority of the Supreme Court as the final arbiter of all *constitutional* questions. He recognized that there were debatable differences of opinion with regard to the appropriate spheres of federal and state authority but he added, "We secure our peace and confidence by loyal acceptance of the decisions of our umpires."

Finally, based upon his special experience, he vigorously supported the establishment of public service commissions with adequate powers of regulation and vested with authority to make final determinations of fact if supported by evidence. It was in discussing this issue that Governor Hughes made what is perhaps the most frequently if partially quoted of his statements: "We are under a Constitution, but the Constitution is what the judges say it is, and the judiciary is the safeguard of our liberty and of our property under the Constitution."

On April 25, 1910, Hughes was nominated to the Supreme Court by President William Howard Taft. Members of Congress, the Supreme Court, and the conservative and liberal press, with few exceptions, acclaimed the nomination. Typically, the *World,* a liberal organ, commented that "Mr. Taft could not have made a better or a more popular selection." Among the few dissenters was William Jennings Bryan, who insisted that "no one who will examine his record can doubt that he is in close sympathy with the exploiting corporations."

Justice Hughes took his oath of office on October 10, 1910, and served for almost six years, resigning on June 10, 1916. Despite occasional criticism of his decisions, his work fulfilled the nearly universal acclaim that had greeted his designation.

The six years he served as Associate Justice (in marked contrast with the eleven years, from 1930 to 1941, in which he was Chief Justice) were not characterized by many far-reaching innovations or reversals nor by sharp and fundamental conflicts within the Court. It was a period of clarification, application, and extension of established doctrine to the exigencies of governing a vast, growing and complex industrial civilization. In this period Hughes wrote 151 opinions for the Court and dissented in only thirty-two cases. In only nine instances was there any dissent from his decisions and in only three did more than one Justice dissent.

Under our system, generally speaking, federal authority derives from delegations of power in the Constitution, such as to declare war or regulate commerce, while the states have residual sovereign authority, sometimes called general police power, such as to enact legislation in the interests of the health, safety, and welfare of their inhabitants. The central task of the Court, throughout its history, has been to reconcile those powers, federal, and state, with prohibitions *expressed* in the Constitution or, in the case of the states, with those *implied* from the nature of certain delegations to the federal government. Among the more important limitations on the power of the states with which Justice Hughes found himself concerned during his tenure as Associate Justice are those imposed by the involuntary servitude, due process, equal protection, and contract clauses of the Constitution.

With respect to the prohibition against involuntary servitude, it was Justice Hughes who spoke for the Court in *Bailey* v. *Alabama,* 219 U.S. 219 (1911), against strong dissents by Justices Holmes and Lurton, in striking down a statute which made failure to perform a labor contract without just cause and without refunding money paid *prima facie* evidence of intent to defraud, and punishable as a crime. Under the statute, while the presumption could be negated by evidence, the employee-defendant was not permitted to testify that he had not intended to defraud. Justice Hughes regarded the law simply as an inadmissible means of compelling an employee-debtor to work off his debt. The claim that it was within the province of the state to set up presumptions of and punish fraud was dismissed as an indirect attempt to transgress the constitutional prohibition against involuntary servitude. Such laws, he said, "furnish the readiest means of compulsion," peculiarly effective "against the poor and ignorant, its most likely victims." There was no more important concern, added Hughes, "than to safeguard the freedom of labor upon which alone can enduring prosperity be based."

In dissent, Justice Holmes argued that even on the assumption that the statute made a mere refusal to work according to contract a crime, it did not violate the Thirteenth Amendment. The Amendment, he said, did not outlaw contracts for labor nor deprive the state of the right to declare the breach of such contracts, without excuse, criminal. Furthermore, he maintained, involuntary servitude as a punishment for crime was expressly excepted from the prohibition of the amendment, and added, "If the contract is one that ought not to be made, prohibit it. But if it is a perfectly fair and proper contract, I can see no reason why the State should not throw its weight on the side of performance." Breach of a legal contract "without excuse is wrong conduct, even if the contract is for labor."

On the basic issues of this case not only was Justice Hughes' position more humanitarian than that of Holmes, it was also grounded in greater realism. In asserting that he could see no reason why the state should not throw its "weight on the side of performance," Justice Holmes failed adequately to recognize the distinction between ordinary civil penalty and criminal punishment for breach of contract. Viewed in terms of practical consequences, to place in the hands of the employer the powerful threat of criminal prosecution would render the laborer's service in a real sense involuntary servitude. This is particularly so because while the law set up a presumption of fraud, it did not permit the laborer to testify that he had not intended to defraud. Under the circumstances, as Hughes tellingly pointed out, "plainly the object of the statute was to hit cases which were destitute of such inferences, and to provide that the mere breach of the contract and the mere failure to pay the debt might do duty in their absence."

In *Miller* v. *Wilson,* 236 U.S. 373 (1915), Justice Hughes spoke for a unanimous court in holding a California law constitutional which forbade employment of women in selected establishments for more than eight hours a day against the claims that, as applied to a chambermaid in a hotel, it was a deprivation of liberty (of contract) without due process of law and a denial of equal protection of the laws. The liberty of contract guaranteed by the Constitution, said Hughes, is freedom from arbitrary restraint not immunity against measures to safeguard the public interest.

Hughes was able to speak for only a bare majority of the Court, however, when in *McCabe* v. *Atchison, Topeka & Santa Fe Railroad,* 235 U.S. 151 (1914), he found a state law which authorized *intrastate* carriers to provide sleeping cars and dining cars for white persons only a denial of equal protection of the laws. This was another occasion when Hughes' position proved more sensitive to the demands of equality than Holmes. In replying to a letter from Holmes, Hughes rejected the idea that it was consistent with equal protection to compel Negroes who sought sleepers to sit up all night until the railroad could make a "black sleeping car" pay. This, he characterized in his note, as "a bald, wholly unjustified discrimination against a passenger solely on account of race." In his formal opinion, while Hughes accepted the then established principle that a state might require "separate" accommodations for the white and black races, it did not follow, he reasoned, that it could deny "equal accommodations." He dismissed as "without merit" the argument that the lack of substantial Negro demand for special accommodations justified the law. Holmes concurred only in the result.

In another case, *Truax* v. *Raich,* 239 U.S. 33 (1915), Hughes spoke for all but one Justice of the Court in ruling that an Arizona statute which strictly limited the percentage of aliens who might be employed was unconstitutional not only as a denial of equal protection of the laws but also as in conflict with exclusive federal power to admit or exclude aliens, for "they cannot live where they cannot work."

Article I, Section 10 of the Constitution forbids a state to pass any "law impairing the obligation of contracts." This clause, as historically construed by the Supreme Court, imposed limitations on the legislative power of states not only to impair contracts between private persons but also with respect to their own contracts. The limitations of the contract clause posed special difficulties in the control of public utilities upon whom state authorities had bestowed great benefits and privileges, often with reckless abandon, little or no financial return and little or no reserved power of control. The chief constitutional argument on which utilities relied in seeking to thwart or limit attempted state control or regulation was that such action constituted impairment of their contracts. While, during Justice Hughes' tenure, none of the established principles was repudiated by the Court, there was considerable controversy over how the contract-grants to public utilities were to be construed in regard to general privileges conferred, rate regulation and tax immunity, that is, whether they were to be construed liberally in favor of the grantee or narrowly in favor of the state.

It may be said that no Justice in this period was prepared to go further in limiting the scope of the privileges granted and in extending the scope of the power reserved by the state than Justice Hughes. A few typical cases only can be mentioned. In *Grand Trunk Western R.R.* v. *South Bend,* 227 U.S. 544 (1913), Justice Hughes (and only one other) dissented from the decision of the Supreme Court that denied to a city power to repeal so much of a grant to a railway company to lay a double track as had not been availed of between 1861 and 1901. Again, Justice Hughes dissented when the Supreme Court in *Owensboro* v. *Cumberland Telephone & Telegraph,* 230 U.S. 58 (1913), denied to a city, which in 1889 had authorized a telephone company to place telephone poles and wires on its streets, power to require compensation for such grant in 1909.

In still another case, *Southern Pacific Co.* v. *Campbell,* 230 U.S. 537 (1913), Hughes held for the Court that although a common carrier had been authorized to collect such tolls "as it may prescribe" this provision did not "detract from the power of the State through its legislature, or the agency lawfully constituted thereby, to prescribe reasonable rates to be observed by the carrier."

The most important decisions of Justice Hughes in this term of service were undoubtedly in relation to the grant of power to the federal government to regulate interstate commerce. In several significant decisions Hughes spoke for the Court in a broad interpretation of the scope of federal interstate power. Typically, in *Baltimore & Ohio R.R.* v. *Interstate Commerce Commission,* 221 U.S. 612 (1911), Hughes upheld the power of Congress to regulate hours of labor of railway employees engaged in interstate commerce. He reasoned that hours of labor had "direct relation to the efficiency of the human agencies upon which protection to life and property necessarily depends" and that it was within the competence of Congress to seek to reduce the dangers to the employees themselves.

By all odds, however, the most significant and far-reaching of all Justice Hughes' decisions during his six years of service were in two epochal cases, the *Minnesota Rate Cases,* 230 U.S. 352 (1913), and in the Shreveport Case, *Houston, East & West Texas Railway Co.* v. *United States,* 234 U.S. 342 (1914). In these cases, the issue at stake was no less than whether federal power over purely intrastate commerce was to be deemed sufficient to bring order and uniformity out of the chaos and diversity of competing national and state regulation of railroad facilities—whether the Court would frustrate or encourage the establishment of a truly integrated national railway system. Specifically, the form in which the issue was raised was whether the federal interstate commerce power might be utilized to control purely *intrastate* railroad rates which were lower than *interstate* rates covering the same territory and, as a practical consequence, therefore negatively affected *interstate* carriers.

In the first of these cases which had been argued before the Court for four days and in which twenty-one states had intervened, Justice Hughes in a closely reasoned opinion delivered more than a year later (with the concurrence of the entire Court except for Justice McKenna who agreed only with the result) affirmed that the power of Congress to regulate interstate commerce is supreme and plenary and insisted that "the full control by Congress of the subjects committed to its regulation is not to be denied or thwarted by the commingling of interstate and intrastate operations." While he did not negate state action in this case, he nonetheless made it unmistakably clear that Congress had the authority, if it wished to exercise it, to subject the purely intrastate railroad traffic of a state which had become interwoven with the interstate railroad traffic of the nation to its control.

In the later of the two cases, the Shreveport Case, again fiercely argued and decided after months of delay, the Court faced the issue squarely and upheld an order of the federal Interstate Commerce Commission requiring railroad carriers to adjust and increase purely *intrastate* rates to conform with those fixed for *interstate* transportation. Speaking for all but two dissenting Justices, Hughes made reference to the "complete and paramount" character of the interstate commerce power of Congress. Its purpose, he said, was to make impossible the evils which had overwhelmed the Confederation. It had not left interstate trade to be destroyed or impeded by the rivalries of local governments. He categorically insisted that "Congress in the exercise of its paramount power may prevent the common instrumentality of interstate and intrastate commercial intercourse from being used in their intrastate operations to the injury of interstate commerce."

The far-reaching consequences of these decisions on the development of constitutional law can hardly be exaggerated. Apart from their tremendous importance in recognizing federal authority to mold an integrated system of transportation without regard to state boundaries which had little reality in the actual conduct of commerce, the decisions contributed greatly to fostering a recognition that conflicts between national and state power, in general, had to be resolved in terms of practical effects rather than loyalty to abstract conceptions of dual sovereignty. That, in any event, ultimately proved to be the primary basis upon which considerable power over the processes of local production (as distinguished from transportation) was accorded to the federal government, in a decision written many years later by Chief Justice Hughes, sustaining the constitutionality of the National Labor Relations Act in *National Labor Relations Board* v. *Jones & Laughlin Steel Corp.*, 301 U.S. 1 (1937).

With a record such as this, Justice Hughes, in terms of the general if somewhat indefinite criteria that have identified some Justices as liberals, clearly qualifies as one of the outstanding liberal members of the Court during his initial period of service; a view echoed by so vigorous a liberal as Fred Rodell who characterized these as "six stunningly liberal years."

On June 7, 1916, Hughes was nominated by the Republican party as its candidate for the Presidency of the United States to oppose the disciple of the New Freedom, Woodrow Wilson. As a very friendly biographer, Dexter Perkins, points out, Hughes' campaign "was mostly negative in character, critical rather than constructive, rarely elevated in tone, and rarely convincing as to future courses of action."

Hughes criticized the administration for its vacillating, inconsistent and humiliating policies in dealing with Mexico and Germany, and for neglecting preparedness, which made him appear as a supporter of a war policy against Wilson who, after all, had "kept America out of war." In search of a domestic issue, Hughes promised to meet the competition of "an energized" post-war Europe with a higher protective tariff. The performance was entirely lackluster. Nonetheless the result was close and Hughes retired on the night of November 6 mistakenly believing he was President-elect.

With his defeat, Hughes returned to practice law in New York City as the senior member of the firm of Hughes, Rounds, Schurman and Dwight. In the years that followed, until his designation as Secretary of State in 1921, the Hughes firm represented some of the leading corporations in the country and Hughes personally appeared in many cases before his former colleagues on the Supreme Court.

In the aftermath of the war, the hatred of socialists who had opposed the war and the continuing fear of socialism often led to indiscriminate attacks upon radicals or their sympathizers. Typical was the sudden action of the New York State legislature, early in 1920, in denying seats to five duly elected Socialist assemblymen as alleged members of a subversive party adhering to the revolutionary forces of Soviet Russia and pledged to the forcible overthrow of American government. Hughes reacted promptly. He wrote to the Speaker of the Assembly with the demand that if the charge is one of plotting revolution, then the evidence should be put before proper authorities and swift action taken. But he considered it a most serious mistake to deny Socialists, unconvicted of crime, the right to vote for their own candidates or to be seated if elected. The appeal was to no avail.

On the very day Warren G. Harding assumed the office of President of the United States, March 4, 1921, he named Charles Evans Hughes as his Secretary of State. Harding had little knowledge of foreign affairs and gave Hughes an unusually free hand in most matters in the conduct of his office. In his years at this post, from 1921 to 1925, he concerned himself with fostering and safeguarding American public and private interests abroad, attempting to build good relations with foreign countries (Soviet Russia excluded) and laying the foundations for peace.

Hughes, who had supported the League of Nations, made no attempt to press the issue in face of Harding's unequivocal opposition but was, however, instrumental in gaining Harding's support for American adherence to the World Court. In 1923 Hughes undertook to redefine the Monroe Doctrine in more palatable terms and, in general, made several noteworthy efforts to improve relations with Latin America. On the other hand, he refused to agree to recognition of the Soviet state pending "convincing evidence" of a restoration of "private property, the sanctity of contracts and the rights of free labor." He characterized Russia as "a gigantic economic vacuum."

By far the outstanding accomplishment of Mr. Hughes as Secretary of State was his successful stewardship of the Washington Disarmament Conference which opened its first plenary session in November, 1921, with Mr. Hughes as chairman and head of the American delegation. He astounded the delegates by his insistence upon immediate disarmament and his presentation of very concrete proposals for its effectuation down to the naming of specific vessels to be scrapped. His proposals for a ten-year holiday in the construction of capital ships and for the scrapping of specific battleships with a final ratio of 5–5–3–1.-75–1.75 for the United States, Great Britain, Japan, France and Italy were finally accepted with some compromises that were largely in deference to Japanese and French security claims. Also, under the driving leadership of Hughes, a nine-power treaty was concluded by the terms of which the signatories bound themselves to respect the "sovereignty, the independence, and the territorial and administrative integrity of China," and to recognize the Open Door principle. Senate approval was obtained for the mass of treaties growing out of the conference.

In March, 1925, Hughes resigned as Secretary of State and returned to the practice of law in order to "recoup his fortune." In the ensuing years until his designation as Chief Justice, Hughes engaged in a law practice of international scope and was the acknowledged leader of the American bar. He took several opportunities, however, to render important public service, most notably as a Judge of the Permanent Court of International Justice from 1928 to 1930.

The nearly universal acclaim that had greeted Hughes' designation as an Associate Justice was conspicuously lacking when on February 3, 1930 President Herbert Hoover nominated him to succeed William Howard Taft (who had resigned that very day) to be Chief Justice of the United States.

Numerous charges were brought against him in the bitter debate over confirmation but the fundamental one was stated by Senator George Norris, a Republican progressive, who headed the Committee on the Judiciary which had favorably reported the nomination over his opposition. "No man in public life," said Senator Norris, "so exemplifies the influence of powerful combinations in the political and financial world as does Mr. Hughes." Association with men of great wealth, and his own great fortune, were bound to have their effect, conscious or unconscious, on Hughes and he should not, therefore, "be called upon to sit in final judgment in contests between organized wealth and the ordinary citizen." His defenders argued that his "magnificent career" in every way "peculiarly qualified" him for the position. It was true that his extraordinary ability had naturally attracted to him as clients great business interests and that, as an advocate, he was compelled to present their side of cases with all his talent. But it did not follow that his state of mind was so affected that he could not thereafter sit as an impartial judge. In the final vote, the proponents mustered fifty-two yeas to twenty-six nays.

Charles Evans Hughes ascended the bench as Chief Justice of the United States on February 24, 1930 in the midst of the most serious and steadily worsening economic crisis in American history; a crisis which was to put the Court, the institution of judicial review, and the leadership of its Chief Justice to the severest test.

"He took his seat at the center of the Court," Justice Felix Frankfurter later wrote, "with a mastery, I suspect, unparalleled in the history of the Court, a mastery that derived from his experience as diversified, as intense, as extensive, as any man ever brought to a seat on the Court, combined with a very powerful and acute mind that could mobilize these vast resources in the conduct of the business of the Court."

Although the Chief Justice will ordinarily seek to distribute cases so that each Justice will have a fair share of the work with regard to significance and past experience as well as burden, he nevertheless retains considerable range of choice. In this process Hughes assumed a heavy share of the burden for himself, and in the years of his service which terminated with his retirement on July 1, 1941, wrote the opinion of the Court in 283 cases and dissented in twenty-three cases. As Chief Justice, Hughes did in fact write the opinion of the Court, or the dissenting opinion, in many leading cases—not without some twinge of unhappiness on the part of other Justices, as Alpheus T. Mason makes clear in his *Harlan Fiske Stone: Pillar of the Law*. However that may be, the tenure of Hughes as Chief Justice is unquestionably a record of opinions which in importance up to that time was excelled only by those of Chief Justice Marshall.

The attempt to analyze even a significant number of the prevailing opinions and dissents of Chief Justice Hughes would make this study unacceptably prolix. Attention will be given therefore only to some of his more important opinions and positions in two broad areas, those concerned with civil liberties and civil rights and those involving important economic issues.

In 1931, in *Stromberg* v. *California,* 283 U.S. 359, Hughes spoke for the Court in declaring a statute unconstitutional which made display of a red flag a criminal offense since in his view it might serve to proscribe peaceful and orderly opposition to government. He took the occasion to say that:

> *The maintenance of the opportunity for free political discussion to the end that government may be responsive to the will of the people and that changes may be obtained by lawful means, an opportunity essential to the security of the Republic, is a fundamental principle of our constitutional system.*

That same year, in *United States* v. *Macintosh,* 283 U.S. 605 (1931), Hughes dissented against the Court's decision to deny citizenship to one who would not commit himself in advance to bear arms. His dissent, to be sure, turned on the question of congressional intention but his own sympathies were made patent when he wrote: "There is abundant room for enforcing the requisite authority of law . . . without demanding that either citizens or applicants for citizenship shall assume by oath an obligation to regard allegiance to God as subordinate to civil power."

Within a week, the Chief Justice read another opinion in a civil liberties case, *Near* v. *Minnesota,* 283 U.S. 697 (1931); this time, however, he spoke for a (narrow) majority in striking down a statute which permitted abatement of a "Malicious, scandalous and defamatory newspaper, magazine or other periodical." The statute had been applied to a Minnesota newspaper which in nine articles had charged that a Jewish gangster was in control of gambling, bootlegging and racketeering in Minneapolis and that local police officials were guilty of illicit relations with gangsters and participation in graft.

The object of the statute, said Hughes, was not redress as under libel laws, but suppression and censorship. "The fact," he added, "that the liberty of the press may be abused by miscreant purveyors of scandal does not make any the less necessary the immunity of the press from previous restraints in dealing with official misconduct." The decision had far-reaching implications, not only in discouraging similar statutes but precisely because Hughes' pronouncement came in defense of a particularly odious publication.

In 1937, in two decisions affecting Communists, he gave broad scope to constitutional protection of freedoms. In the first, *DeJonge* v. *Oregon,* 299 U.S. 353 (1937), he upset a conviction which rested upon a statute making it a crime to *assist* in the conduct of a meeting called by any organization advocating criminal syndicalism or sabotage, and affirmed:

> *The greater the importance of safeguarding the community from incitements to the overthrow of our institutions by force and violence, the more imperative is the need to preserve inviolate the constitutional rights of free speech, free press and free assembly in order to maintain the opportunity for free political discussion, to the end that government may be responsive to the will of the people and that changes, if desired, may be obtained by peaceful means. Therein*

lies the security of the Republic, the very foundation of constitutional government.

(This libertarian declaration is one of the most frequently quoted of Hughes' statements. It appears, for example, in the 1967 decision of the Supreme Court in *Keyishian* v. *Board of Regents,* 385 U.S. 589, in which the Court upset its own precedent and declared unconstitutional provisions of a New York State law designed to prevent employment of subversives in the state school system.)

In the other case, *Herndon* v. *Lowry,* 301 U.S. 242 (1937), he joined in the majority opinion of Mr. Justice Roberts (against four dissents) to invalidate a Georgia statute which was applied to a Negro Communist charged with attempting to incite insurrection on the basis of his enrolling activities and possession of a booklet urging "Self-Determination for the Black Belt."

In general, he aligned himself with those members of the Court who sought to uphold legislation designed to protect the organizing activities of labor and to upset legislation designed to restrict those activities. In 1937, in *Senn* v. *Tile Layers Union,* 301 U.S. 468, he stood with a narrow majority of the Court which upheld a state law prohibiting the use of injunctions against peaceful picketing; and the following year, in *Lauf* v. *Shinner & Co.,* 303 U.S. 323 (1938), and *New Negro Alliance Co.* v. *Sanitary Grocery Co.,* 303 U.S. 552 (1938), he voted to sustain the general scope and validity of the procedural requirements of the Norris-LaGuardia Act regulating and limiting the issuance of injunctions in labor disputes. In 1939, in *Hague* v. *CIO,* 307 U.S. 496 (1939), he joined a majority of the Court in invalidating a Jersey City ordinance prohibiting assemblies on public streets without official permit. In 1940, in *Thornhill* v. *Alabama,* 310 U.S. 88, and *Carlson* v. *California,* 310 U.S. 106, he concurred in decisions which brought the right of peaceful picketing and the display of signs within the scope of "liberty" under the due process clause. Only in two important cases did he take a restrictive position. In 1941 he agreed with the majority opinion of Mr. Justice Frankfurter in *Milk Wagon Drivers Union* v. *Meadowmoor Dairies,* 312 U.S. 287, that peaceful picketing may be enjoined when enmeshed with violent conduct; and later joined in support of Mr. Justice Roberts' dissenting view, in *AFL* v. *Swing,* 312 U.S. 321 (1941), that picketing might be legally enjoined when part of an attempt to "organize" a business in which none of the employees was or wished to become a member of the union.

In the civil rights field, in *Missouri ex rel. Gaines* v. *Canada,* 305 U.S. 337 (1938), he spoke for the Court in ruling that the refusal of a state to furnish a Negro facilities for legal education available to whites within its borders constituted a denial of equal protection of the laws. Nor, he ruled, may the absence of sufficient demand by Negroes for legal education serve to excuse the discrimination. Whether particular facilities shall be provided may be conditioned on demand, but, if facilities are provided, substantial equality of treatment cannot be refused. The right to equal protection of the laws is not based on race. It is "a personal one."

Subsequently, in *Lane* v. *Wilson,* 307 U.S. 268 (1939), Hughes joined in a

Frankfurter opinion which invalidated an Oklahoma statute designed to restrict the Negro's right to vote by requiring registration within twelve days of all who had not voted in 1914 (when Negroes were barred by "grandfather" clauses from voting) with perpetual disenfranchisement for failure to so register.

This record thoroughly justifies the comment of then Attorney General Robert Jackson, on the occasion of Hughes' retirement from the bench, that "in the numerous cases dealing with civil liberties he has been a consistent and forthright champion of the American freedoms."

With respect to the critical economic questions that came before the Court, the year 1934 brought several decisions that aroused hope that the Roosevelt New Deal program would stand up well under constitutional challenge. Two decisions in particular, although relating to state legislation, enunciated principles that seemed encouraging.

In *Home Building & Loan Ass'n* v. *Blaisdell,* 290 U.S. 398 (1934), the constitutionality of the Minnesota Mortgage Moratorium Act was sustained by the margin of a single vote in a decision written by the Chief Justice. Although there was some ambiguity in Hughes' opinion, nonetheless it was couched in such sweeping terms as to suggest that constitutional prohibitions would have to yield to emergency conditions. Specifically, for example, in the face of a specific constitutional prohibition against legislation impairing the obligation of contract, he stated that "While emergency does not create power, emergency may furnish the occasion for the exercise of power"; and further that the State "continues to possess authority to safeguard vital interests of its people" even if it "has the result of modifying or abrogating contracts already in effect." In terms seldom spoken by a Supreme Court Justice, he affirmed that, "the policy of protecting contracts against impairment presupposes the maintenance of a government by virtue of which contractual relations are worthwhile,—a government which retains adequate authority to secure the peace and good order of society."

The last statement was doubtless made with reference to the violence and lawlessness evoked by widespread foreclosures of farm properties before the passage of the Minnesota statute. Whatever its inspiration, however, if it means what it seems to say, it announces a doctrine of stark and startling simplicity and importance. For it suggests that limitations of the Constitution may be put aside provided only that to enforce them would bring such a degree of violence and lawlessness as to place in jeopardy the authority of government to maintain peace and good order.

The second encouraging decision for proponents of the New Deal came in *Nebbia* v. *New York,* 291 U.S. 502 (1934), again decided by a slim majority in which the Chief Justice joined. In that case in fact, although not acknowledgedly, the Court reversed earlier precedent and sustained the validity of a New York statute fixing maximum and minimum prices for the sale of milk. In so doing it discarded the concept of "affected with a public interest" as a principle of limitation and made reasonableness the criterion of constitutionality against due process attack. No wonder that the distinguished constitutional law scholar, Edward S. Corwin, then spoke of "the inherent ability of governmental power under the Constitution to expand to meet new necessities."

It soon became apparent that such optimism was not warranted. On May 27, 1935 (the famed "Black Monday"), in *Louisville Joint Stock Land Bank* v. *Radford,* 295 U.S. 555, a unanimous Court, per Justice Brandeis, invalidated the national Frazier-Lemke Act for the relief of farm mortgage debtors. In essence, ruled the Court, the test of constitutionality in regard to mortgage relief legislation, whether national or state, was whether substantive rights were being impaired. *Blaisdell* was distinguished on the ground that, in that case, relief was limited to an emergency period while here relief was granted for a fixed period which might extend beyond the true emergency.

In a further attempt to aid agriculture, Congress, in 1933, enacted the Agricultural Adjustment Act, which the President later wrote had been designed "to help the farmers protect themselves by cooperative action against the accumulation of farm surpluses which had brought about disastrous farm prices and left agriculture practically prostrate throughout the country." The act had been predicated upon the taxing power of the United States and, although it actually produced millions of dollars in revenue, it was held, in effect, in *United States* v. *Butler,* 297 U.S. 1 (1936), not to levy a tax at all, but to constitute an expropriation of money from one group for the benefit of another and an invasion of the reserved powers of the states. Five members of the Court, including Chief Justice Hughes, concurred in the prevailing opinion of Mr. Justice Roberts. Justice Stone, joined in dissent by Justices Brandeis and Cardozo, charged the majority with a "tortured construction of the Constitution."

The nation-wide depression dried up tax sources and among the principal victims were municipalities. On May 24, 1934, acting under its bankruptcy power, Congress authorized municipal corporations, unable to pay their debts, to resort to federal bankruptcy courts for readjustment of their obligations. These courts were authorized to scale down debts with the consent of creditors holding 66⅔ per cent of the indebtedness despite the opposition of the balance of the creditors.

In May, 1936, in *Ashton* v. *Cameron County District,* 298 U.S. 513, the Supreme Court, by a vote of five to four, with Justice McReynolds as spokesman for the majority, invalidated the act as in excess of granted federal bankruptcy power and as in derogation of the sovereign power of the state to control its own fiscal affairs. In this connection, the Court took pains to assert that "neither consent nor submission by the states can enlarge the powers of Congress; none can exist except those which are granted."

Justice Cardozo, with the concurrence of three members of the Court, including the Chief Justice, voiced dissent. The legislation, he thought, constituted an appropriate exercise of federal bankruptcy power. Emphasizing the permissive nature of the act, he pointed out that it could not be invoked unless authorized by the state and he could not see, therefore, how it could be said to invade the sovereign power of the state.

Few issues brought before the Supreme Court in its entire history were as pregnant with importance to the economy of the nation as those relating to the action of Congress, taken on June 5, 1933, abrogating gold clause provisions in contracts, public and private. The action of Congress was the product of crisis conditions which had affected the entire world.

With regard to this legislation, three decisions were delivered by Chief Justice Hughes on February 18, 1935, in each of which, by the slim margin of a single vote, recovery was denied, although any other result would have had the most appalling effect upon the economy of the nation after almost two years of operation under the legislation.

In the first case, *Norman* v. *Baltimore & Ohio R.R.*, 294 U.S. 240 (1935), Chief Justice Hughes, speaking for the Court, sustained the validity of the gold clause resolution as applied to *private* contracts and to those made by *states* or their political subdivisions as within the authority granted by the Constitution to Congress to establish a national monetary system and over the subjects of revenue, finance, and currency.

The second case, *Nortz* v. *United States,* 294 U.S. 317 (1935), was disposed of in a brief opinion on highly technical grounds. The issue in *Perry* v. *United States,* 294 U.S. 330 (1935), was no less than whether holders of United States government obligations (running into billions of dollars) were entitled to insist that the United States honor its promise to pay in gold coin at the value at the time of issuance (or the equivalent value in current dollars). Chief Justice Hughes, while holding that the obligation of the United States was binding on its moral conscience and beyond its power of repudiation, nevertheless held the obligation unenforceable because the actual individual loss could not be fairly determined.

It is a permissible conclusion to draw from the opinion of the Chief Justice that, although he was not prepared to permit a recovery that would wreak havoc upon the economy, he was determined to deliver a lecture to the New Deal on what he regarded as its cavalier manner of repudiating obligations. Justice Cardozo, who concurred in the result, felt impelled to quarrel with that part of the opinion which went beyond the needs of the case and appeared to set up some indefinable obligation.

A single dissenting opinion was delivered by Justice McReynolds, with the concurrence of Justices Van Devanter, Sutherland and Butler, in the three gold clause cases. He characterized the actions of the government as "repudiation and spoliation of citizens by their sovereign," denied that such power was ever delegated to the federal government and said that "loss of reputation for honorable dealing will bring us unending humiliation; the impending legal and moral chaos is appalling." In his oral opinion Justice McReynolds had gone even further and at one point exclaimed, "This is Nero at his worst. The Constitution is gone." This language proved too vitriolic for the formal record and was excised.

With few significant exceptions, the Supreme Court, beginning with Marshall's famed decision in *Gibbons* v. *Ogden,* 9 Wheat. 1 (1824), had given a "plenary" interpretation to the interstate commerce power of Congress. While Congress had recourse to many of its delegated powers in seeking to regulate the economy in the midst of economic crisis, none was more important than the interstate commerce power.

It was on this power that President Roosevelt relied in a message to Congress on May 17, 1933, requesting passage of the National Industrial Recovery Act which he said would provide "the machinery necessary for a great co-operative movement throughout all industry in order to obtain wide reemployment, to shorten the working week, to pay a decent wage for the shorter week, and to prevent unfair competition and disastrous overproduction." In signing the bill, he commented that "history probably will record the National Industrial Recovery Act as the most important and far-reaching legislation ever enacted by the American Congress."

In *Schechter Poultry Corp.* v. *United States,* 295 U.S. 495 (1935), the Court unanimously invalidated the act under which codes had been established regulating minimum wages, maximum hours, collective bargaining, and unfair methods of competition. In the circumstances of this case in which the plaintiffs made few purchases and no sales outside the state, Chief Justice Hughes found the transactions regulated not to be "in" interstate commerce and only "indirectly" affecting such commerce. The distinction, the Chief Justice insisted, was "a fundamental one, essential to the maintenance of our constitutional system." Otherwise, there would be virtually "no limit to the federal power and for all practical purposes we should have a completely centralized government."

In May of 1936, the Court struck another blow at the New Deal program, this time by invalidating the Bituminous Coal Conservation Act of 1935. The legislation was the result of chronic ailments afflicting the coal industry involving cutthroat competition, price cutting and wage cutting, a breakdown of collective bargaining, heavy losses for operators, and violent and disorderly strikes which had led to bloodshed and martial law. The act imposed a tax with rebate provisions for those producers who submitted to its other provisions which established procedures for fixing minimum and maximum prices, gave employees the right to organize and bargain collectively with employers, and made certain provisions for fixing maximum hours and minimum wages.

The act was invalidated in *Carter* v. *Carter Coal Co.,* 298 U.S. 238 (1936), on several grounds but most significantly, in the majority opinion of Justice Sutherland, as an improper exercise of taxing power and in excess of the interstate commerce power of Congress as to certain of its inseparable provisions.

In a "separate opinion" Chief Justice Hughes agreed that the so-called tax was in reality a penalty; that the constitutional power of the federal government to impose the penalty must rest, if at all, upon the commerce clause; "that production—in this case mining—which precedes commerce, is not itself commerce; and that the power to regulate commerce among the several States is not a power to regulate industry within the State." In his view, the wage and hour section of the act went "beyond any proper measure of protection of interstate commerce and attempts a broad regulation of industry within the state." (Chief Justice Hughes did not, however, agree with the majority of the Court on the invalidity of the price-fixing provisions of the act.)

In February, 1937, in the wake of his stunning reelection in November, 1936, Franklin D. Roosevelt suddenly placed before Congress and the nation a plan to enlarge the Supreme Court; a plan which he said had been provoked by a series of Court decisions which "have cast doubts on the ability of the elected Congress to protect us against catastrophe." And "what was worse," he later wrote, "the language and temper of the decisions indicated little hope for the future" at a time when major New Deal legislation including the Social Security Act and the National Labor Relations Act were yet to come before the Court. There ensued a bitter and protracted struggle within Congress and the nation.

While the struggle was raging and still unresolved, the Supreme Court handed down a series of decisions reflecting a more tolerant view of the authority of national and state governments to cope with the exigencies and expectations of a modern society. On March 29, 1937, the Court, in *Wright* v. *Mountain Trust Bank,* 300 U.S. 440, unanimously sustained a revised version of the Frazier-Lemke Act for the relief of farm mortgagors and, more important, by a narrow majority, upheld a minimum wage for women law enacted by the state of Washington. The second of these cases, *West Coast Hotel* v. *Parrish,* 300 U.S. 379 (1937), is of special importance because it clearly and unequivocally affirmed that states would not be hobbled by the Court in attempting through social legislation to promote the health and welfare of their people.

The basis of attack upon the legislation, the Chief Justice pointed out, was that it was a deprivation of freedom of contract barred by the due process clause of the Fourteenth Amendment. "What is this freedom?" he inquired, and said,

> *The Constitution does not speak of freedom of contract. It speaks of liberty and prohibits the deprivation of liberty without due process of law. In prohibiting that deprivation the Constitution does not recognize an absolute and uncontrollable liberty. Liberty in each of its phases has its history and connotation. But the liberty safeguarded is liberty in a social organization which requires the protection of law against the evils which menace the health, safety, morals and welfare of the people. Liberty under the Constitution is thus necessarily subject to the restraints of due process, and regulation which is reasonable in relation to its subject and is adopted in the interests of the community is due process.*

The argument, he said, that adult employees should be deemed competent to make their own contracts had not been accepted by the Court when the parties had not stood upon an equality of bargaining power or where the public health demanded that a party to the contract be protected against himself. This, he said, was "peculiarly applicable" in relation to women in whose protection the state has a special interest since they were peculiarly subject to the overreaching of employers and their health was of concern to the community to prevent deterioration of the race.

The Court proceeded to repudiate, unequivocally, its own contrary precedent established in 1918 and to overturn (despite an inept attempt at rationalization) another established only nine months earlier (before Roosevelt's court proposal had been submitted). This result was achieved when Justice Roberts reversed his position to join in the new majority opinion.

Parenthetically, it is interesting to observe that while the Court experienced such great difficulty in sustaining minimum wages for *women* who presented, as Hughes suggested, a special case against freedom of contract under due process attack, and did so finally only after a lapse of nearly twenty years and by the narrowest of margins, the Court in 1941, when its composition had drastically changed, found it not at all troublesome to uphold minimum wages for *men, above* the subsistence level, as consistent with due process, by *unanimous* vote, in *United States* v. *Darby,* 312, U.S. 100 (1941).

One of the most fundamental decisions of the Supreme Court in its entire history (and probably one of the two most important decisions written by Hughes in his long dual career on the bench) was handed down the next month, on April 12, 1937, to be precise, in *National Labor Relations Board* v. *Jones & Laughlin Steel Corp.,* 301 U.S. 1, declaring valid the National Labor Relations Act of 1935, popularly known as the Wagner Act.

Before reaching the question of the relation of the act to the interstate commerce power of Congress, the Court was concerned with whether the basic rights given protection could withstand due process challenge. The right of employees to choose their own representatives and bargain collectively free from coercion by the employer, said the Chief Justice, "is a fundamental right" correlative with the right of the employer to organize its own business. "Discrimination and coercion to prevent the free exercise of the right of employees to self-organization and representation is a proper subject for condemnation by competent legislative authority." Restraints for the purposes of preventing an unjust interference with the right of employees to organize, to secure the redress of grievances, and to promote agreements with employers cannot be considered arbitrary or capricious. "The theory of the Act is that free opportunity for negotiation with accredited representatives of employees is likely to promote industrial peace and bring about the adjustments and agreements which the Act in itself does not attempt to compel."

The recognition of the right of self-organization and collective bargaining as a "fundamental right" and its protection as the appropriate concern of legislative power constituted a significant departure by the Court from a merely negative, Hobbesian conception of liberty as simply "an absence of law" upon which reliance had been placed by the Court in many earlier decisions in striking down social legislation. "Liberty" was now conceived of as a balance of rights and liberties with the Court, of course, retaining its ultimate right to determine the imbalance. There was at least the tacit recognition that the denial of the liberty of the employer to hire and fire at will must be weighed against the liberty of his employees to organize and bargain collectively.

The legislation having met the test of due process, the inquiry remained whether and the extent to which the rights given protection might be affirmatively encompassed within the delegated power of Congress to regulate interstate commerce.

Hughes then found that the act by its own terms purported to "reach only what may be deemed to burden or obstruct" interstate commerce, and turned to consider, specifically, whether the industrial relations and activities, in the manufacturing department of the corporation, affected such commerce "in such a close and intimate fashion as to be subject to federal control." In this connection, Hughes said that "giving full weight" to the employer's contention with respect to a break in the continuity of the stream of commerce (materials flowing in from many states, being transformed, and then moving out to all parts of the nation), "the fact remains that the stoppage of those operations would have a most serious effect upon interstate commerce. In view of [the corporation's] far-flung activities, it is idle to say that the effect would be indirect and remote." The corporation's enterprise, he added, "presents in a most striking way the close and intimate relation which a manufacturing industry may have to interstate commerce."

The four dissenting Justices, McReynolds, Van Devanter, Sutherland, and Butler, met the contention that the act validly regulated interstate commerce because, in the absence of rights of self-organization and collective bargaining, strikes would be engendered which would reduce the volume of goods moving in interstate commerce, with the rejoinder that "a more remote and indirect interference with interstate commerce or a more definite invasion of the powers reserved to the states is difficult, if not impossible, to imagine." Manufacturing, they insisted, was not "commerce" and relied upon principles "established" in the *Schechter* and *Carter* cases to the effect that the power of Congress under the commerce clause did not extend to relations btween employers and their employees engaged in manufacture.

Whether or not there is a legitimate basis for distinguishing the legislation and factual situations in the *Schechter* and *Carter* cases from the present one, the breadth of the Court's decision in the *Jones & Laughlin* case was of monumental significance. It rendered untenable the view that the reserved power of the states, or production and the labor relations being local, by *their very nature* limited the sphere of delegated federal power. It contributed to the growing recognition that with the rise of large-scale industry, as Professor Edward S. Corwin has written, "while production and commerce are distinguishable for some purposes, they are not distinguishable when it comes to regulating them; that, in short, the issue is between *national* regulation and *no* regulation—not between national and state regulation." Finally, it struck still another blow at the *laissez-faire* conception of liberty under due process which for so long had held dominance in the Court.

Only six weeks later, the Supreme Court in *Steward Machine Co.* v. *Davis,* 301 U.S. 548 (1937), per Justice Cardozo, by vote of five against the four rock-ribbed conservatives, upheld the unemployment insurance features of the social security law and the same day, in *Helvering* v. *Davis,* 301 U.S. 619 (1937), only two Justices dissented from the position of Justice Cardozo sustaining the old age tax and benefit provisions of the social security law.

While other factors were undoubtedly of considerable importance there can be no doubt that the minimum wage for women, Wagner Act and social security decisions of the Supreme Court contributed significantly to the defeat of President Roosevelt's plan to enlarge the Court. Singularly perspicacious was the opinion expressed by Robert Jackson: "In politics the black-robed reactionary Justices had won over the master liberal politician of our day. In law the President defeated the recalcitrant Justices in their own Court."

On June 2, 1941, Chief Justice Hughes, then seventy-nine years of age, wrote President Roosevelt that "considerations of health and age make it necessary that I should be relieved of the duties which I have been discharging with increasing difficulty." For this reason, said the Chief Justice, he availed himself of the opportunity of retiring effective "on and after July 1, 1941." Thus ended a period of more than eleven years of service by Charles Evans Hughes as Chief Justice of the United States. On August 17, 1948, at the age of eight-six, Charles Evans Hughes died.

It is a simple truism that our institutions are subjected to little, if any, critical analyses or attack in periods of relative prosperity and stability. The great significance of the decade of the 1930's, during which Mr. Hughes presided over the deliberations of the Supreme Court, is that it put to the severest test, in the crucible of a devastating economic crisis, the capacity of men and the value of institutions. In a very real sense, it posed the question of the survival-value of democracy itself. "One may search in vain," wrote Harlan F. Stone, Mr. Hughes' successor as Chief Justice, "for a period in the history of the Supreme Court in which the burden resting on the Chief Justice has been so heavy or when his task has been more beset with difficulties."

It may justly, I believe, be regarded as a tribute to the Chief Justice that he presided over a Court, sometimes rent with bitter differences, with great fidelity and skill. "To see him preside," wrote Justice Frankfurter in 1953, "was like witnessing Toscanini lead an orchestra."

It also appears evident from an examination of his record that Hughes had a deep devotion to the Bill of Rights. He led in the progressive incorporation of the basic civil liberties into the protection of due process under the Fourteenth Amendment and gave these liberties broad scope and meaning. He denounced the doctrine of guilt by association, sought to reconcile the demands of conscience and authority and affirmed that the safety of the Republic lay in responsiveness to the people and in their opportunity for the airing of grievances. To that much discriminated against segment of our population, the Negro, he sought generally to assure fair criminal procedures, the right to vote and equality of access to facilities of the state.

In respect to legislation affecting important economic interests in a period of economic crisis his position was more ambivalent. His essentially conservative cast of mind, based upon a lifetime of interest and experience, led him on occasion to array himself with the conservative members of the Court in resistance to change. But he was not unaware of the need to expand federal and state power to cope with the problems of modern society and he had little patience with the stubbornness characteristic of the conservatives who were apparently determined to stand by the foundation even if the edifice were to fall. When the pressure for innovation became great, and the risks to the nation and to the Court itself apparent, reluctantly at first, but increasingly he went along with change. Having sedulously sought to protect the precedents of the Court, sometimes at the risk of offending logic, he witnessed and often participated in the shattering of one precedent after another. He stood thus at the end as a kind of heroic and, in a sense, tragic figure, torn between the old and the new, seeking at first to stem the tide but then relentlessly caught up and moving with it.

SELECTED BIBLIOGRAPHY

The principal papers of Charles Evans Hughes, carefully organized and supplemented by Hughes' own biographical notes and by memoranda prepared by his secretary, Henry C. Beerits, are on deposit in the Library of Congress. Other of Hughes' papers, essays, lectures, and speeches, chronologically listed, consist of the following: *Addresses and Papers of Charles Evans Hughes, 1906–1908* (New York, 1908); *Public Papers of Charles Evans Hughes, Governor, 1907–1910,* 4 vols. (Albany, 1908–1910); *Conditions of Progress in Democratic Government* (New Haven, 1910); *Addresses and Papers of Charles Evans Hughes, 1906–1916* (New York, 1916); *Foreign Relations* (Chicago, 1924); *The Pathway of Peace* (New York, 1925); *Our Relations to the Nations of the Western Hemisphere* (Princeton, 1928); *The Supreme Court of the United States* (New York, 1928); *Pan-American Peace Plans* (New Haven, 1929); *The Permanent Court of International Justice* (New York, 1930). There are two published biographies of Hughes concerned to describe his entire career, namely, Merlo Pusey's full, semi-authorized *Charles Evans Hughes,* 2 vols. (New York, 1951); and Dexter Perkins, *Charles Evans Hughes and American Democratic Statesmanship* (Boston, 1956). Specialized full-length studies of Hughes include: William L. Ransom, *Charles E. Hughes* (New York, 1916), which deals with his work as an Associate Justice; Samuel Hendel, *Charles Evans Hughes and the Supreme Court* (New York, 1951), which focuses on Hughes' career both as an Associate Justice and as Chief Justice of the United States; Betty Glad, *Charles Evans Hughes and the Illusions of Innocence* (Urbana, 1966), which describes his diplomatic career; and Robert F. Wesser, *Charles Evans Hughes: Politics and Reform in New York, 1905–1910* (Ithaca, 1967), the title of which is fully explanatory. Literature dealing with the varied aspects of Hughes' long and distinguished careers is immense. A good point of departure is to consult the very useful bibliographical notes in the Perkins, Glad, and Wesser books, *supra.* Other references on Hughes' judicial career are: F. D. G. Ribble, "The Constitutional Doctrines of Chief Justice Hughes," 41 *Columbia Law Review* 1190 (1941); Chapter Three of Alpheus T. Mason, *The Supreme Court from Taft to Warren* (Baton Rouge, 1958); Samuel Hendel, "The 'Liberalism' of Chief Justice Hughes," 10 *Vanderbilt Law Review* 259 (1959); and Paul A. Freund, "Charles Evans Hughes: Chief Justice," 81 *Harvard Law Review* 4 (1967).

Charles Evans Hughes

REPRESENTATIVE OPINIONS

NATIONAL LABOR RELATIONS BOARD v. JONES & LAUGHLIN STEEL CORP., 301 U.S. 1 (1937)

In this, one of the most important decisions of the Supreme Court in its entire history, Chief Justice Hughes, speaking for a narrow majority, sustained the constitutional validity of the National Labor Relations Act of 1935 (the Wagner Act), which granted employees the right to organize and to bargain collectively with employers, whose activities made the denial of such right a burden upon or an obstruction to interstate commerce. Regarding the contention that the act was an unconstitutional denial of the authority of employers to hire and fire at will and hence a deprivation of due process of law, the Court held that the right of employees to organize and bargain collectively was a "fundamental" one which might appropriately be protected by law in order to promote industrial peace. The Court further ruled that the act was within the specifically delegated power of Congress to regulate interstate commerce. Chief Justice Hughes made short shrift of the argument that manufacturing was by its very nature local and not commerce in any form and pointed out that, in practical terms, a strike in the corporation's enterprises "would have a most serious effect upon interstate commerce." The monumental nature of this decision lay in the broad and unprecedented scope it was prepared to accord to the delegated powers of Congress as a basis for social legislation.

MR. CHIEF JUSTICE HUGHES delivered the opinion of the Court.

In a proceeding under the National Labor Relations Act of 1935,[1] the National Labor Relations Board found that the respondent, Jones & Laughlin Steel Corporation, had violated the Act by engaging in unfair labor practices affecting commerce. The proceeding was instituted by the Beaver Valley Lodge No. 200, affiliated with the Amalgamated Association of Iron, Steel and Tin Workers of America, a labor organiza-

[1] *Act of July 5, 1935, 49 Stat. 449, 29 U.S.C. 151.*

tion. The unfair labor practices charged were that the corporation was discriminating against members of the union with regard to hire and tenure of employment, and was coercing and intimidating its employees in order to interfere with their self-organization. The discriminatory and coercive action alleged was the discharge of certain employees.

The National Labor Relations Board, sustaining the charge, ordered the corporation to cease and desist from such discrimination and coercion, to offer reinstatement to ten of the employees named, to make good their losses in pay, and to post for thirty days notices that the corporation would not discharge or discriminate against members, or those desiring to become members, of the labor union. As the corporation failed to comply, the Board petitioned the Circuit Court of Appeals to enforce the order. The court denied the petition, holding that the order lay beyond the range of federal power. 83 F. (2d) 998. We granted certiorari.

The scheme of the National Labor Relations Act—which is too long to be quoted in full—may be briefly stated. The first section sets forth findings with respect to the injury to commerce resulting from the denial by employers of the right of employees to organize and from the refusal of employers to accept the procedure of collective bargaining. There follows a declaration that it is the policy of the United States to eliminate these causes of obstruction to the free flow of commerce.[2] The Act then defines the terms it uses, including the terms "commerce" and "affecting commerce." § 2. It creates the National Labor Relations Board and prescribes its organization. §§ 3–6. It sets forth the right of employees to self-organization and to bargain collectively through representatives of their own choosing. § 7. It defines "unfair labor practices." § 8. It lays down rules as to the representation of employees for the purpose of collective bargaining. § 9. The Board is empowered to prevent the described unfair labor practices affecting commerce and the Act prescribes the procedure to that end. The Board is authorized to petition designated courts to secure the enforcement of its orders. The findings of the Board as to the facts, if supported by evidence, are to be conclusive. If

[2] *This section is as follows:*

"Section 1. The denial by employers of the right of employees to organize and the refusal by employers to accept the procedure of collective bargaining lead to strikes and other forms of industrial strife or unrest, which have the intent or the necessary effect of burdening or obstructing commerce by (a) impairing the efficiency, safety, or operation of the instrumentalities of commerce; (b) occurring in the current of commerce; (c) materially affecting, restraining, or controlling the flow of raw materials or manufactured or processed goods from or into the channels of commerce, or the prices of such materials or goods in commerce; or (d) causing diminution of employment and wages in such volume as substantially to impair or disrupt the market for goods flowing from or into the channels of commerce.

"The inequality of bargaining power between employees who do not possess full freedom of association or actual liberty of contract, and employers who are organized in the corporate or other forms of ownership association substantially burdens and affects the flow of commerce, and tends to aggravate recurrent business depressions, by depressing wage rates and the purchasing power of wage earners in industry and by preventing the stabilization of competitive wage rates and working conditions within and between industries.

"Experience has proved that protection by law of the right of employees to organize and bargain collectively safeguards commerce from injury, impairment, or interruption, and promotes the flow of commerce by removing certain recognized sources of industrial strife and unrest, by encouraging practices fundamental to the friendly adjustment of industrial disputes arising out of differences as to wages, hours, or other working conditions, and by restoring equality of bargaining power between employers and employees.

"It is hereby declared to be the policy of the United States to eliminate the causes of certain substantial obstructions to the free flow of commerce and to mitigate and eliminate these obstructions when they have occurred by encouraging the practice and procedure of collective bargaining and by protecting the exercise by workers of full freedom of association, self-organization, and designation of representatives of their own choosing, for the purpose of negotiating the terms and conditions of their employment or other manual aid or protection."

either party on application to the court shows that additional evidence is material and that there were reasonable grounds for the failure to adduce such evidence in the hearings before the Board, the court may order the additional evidence to be taken. Any person aggrieved by a final order of the Board may obtain a review in the designated courts with the same procedure as in the case of an application by the Board for the enforcement of its order. § 10. The Board has broad powers of investigation. § 11. Interference with members of the Board or its agents in the performance of their duties is punishable by fine and imprisonment. § 12. Nothing in the Act is to be construed to interfere with the right to strike. § 13. There is a separability clause to the effect that if any provision of the Act or its application to any person or circumstances shall be held invalid, the remainder of the Act or its application to other persons or circumstances shall not be affected. § 15. The particular provisions which are involved in the instant case will be considered more in detail in the course of the discussion.

The procedure in the instant case followed the statute. The labor union filed with the Board its verified charge. The Board thereupon issued its complaint against the respondent alleging that its action in discharging the employees in question constituted unfair labor practices affecting commerce within the meaning of § 8, subdivisions (1) and (3), and § 2, subdivisions (6) and (7) of the Act. Respondent, appearing specially for the purpose of objecting to the jurisdiction of the Board, filed its answer. Respondent admitted the discharges, but alleged that they were made because of inefficiency or violation of rules or for other good reasons and were not ascribable to union membership or activities. As an affirmative defense respondent challenged the constitutional validity of the statute and its applicability in the instant case. Notice of hearing was given and respondent appeared by counsel. The Board first took up the issue of jurisdiction and evidence was presented by both the Board and the respondent. Respondent then moved to dismiss the complaint for lack of jurisdiction; and, on denial of that motion, respondent in accordance with its special appearance withdrew from further participation in the hearing. The Board received evidence upon the merits and at its close made its findings and order.

Contesting the ruling of the Board, the respondent argues (1) that the Act is in reality a regulation of labor relations and not of interstate commerce; (2) that the Act can have no application to the respondent's relations with its production employees because they are not subject to regulation by the federal government; and (3) that the provisions of the Act violate § 2 of Article III and the Fifth and Seventh Amendments of the Constitution of the United States.

The facts as to the nature and scope of the business of the Jones & Laughlin Steel Corporation have been found by the Labor Board and, so far as they are essential to the determination of this controversy, they are not in dispute. The Labor Board has found: The corporation is organized under the laws of Pennsylvania and has its principal office at Pittsburgh. It is engaged in the business of manufacturing iron and steel in plants situated in Pittsburgh and nearby Aliquippa, Pennsylvania. It manufactures and distributes a widely diversified line of steel and pig iron, being the fourth largest producer of steel in the United States. With its subsidiaries—nineteen in number—it is a completely integrated enterprise, owning and operating ore, coal and limestone properties, lake and river transportation facilities and terminal railroads located at its manufacturing plants. It owns or controls mines in Michigan and Minnesota. It operates four ore steamships on the Great Lakes, used in the transportation of ore to its factories. It owns coal mines in Pennsylvania. It operates towboats and steam barges used in carrying coal to its factories. It owns limestone properties in various places in Pennsylvania and West Virginia. It owns the Monongahela connecting railroad which connects the plants of the Pittsburgh works and forms an interconnection with the Pennsylvania, New York Central and Baltimore and Ohio Railroad systems. It owns the Aliquippa and Southern Railroad Company which connects the Aliquippa works with the Pittsburgh and Lake Erie, part of the New York Central system. Much of its product is shipped to its warehouses in Chicago, Detroit, Cincinnati and Memphis,—to the last two places by means of its own barges and transportation equipment. In Long Island City, New York, and in New Orleans it operates structural steel fabricating shops in connection with the warehousing of semi-finished materials sent from its works. Through one of its wholly-owned subsidiaries it owns, leases and operates stores, warehouses and yards for the distribution of equipment and supplies for drilling and operating oil and gas wells and for pipe lines, refineries and pumping stations. It has sales offices in twenty cities in the United States and a wholly-owned subsidiary which is devoted exclusively to distributing its product in Canada. Approximately 75 per cent. of its product is shipped out of Pennsylvania.

Summarizing these operations, the Labor Board concluded that the works in Pittsburgh and Aliquippa "might be likened to the heart of a self-contained, highly integrated body. They draw in the raw materials from Michigan, Minnesota, West Virginia, Pennsylvania in part through arteries and by means controlled by the respondent; they transform the materials and then pump them out to all parts of the nation through the vast mechanism which the respondent has elaborated."

To carry on the activities of the entire steel industry, 33,000 men mine ore, 44,000 men mine coal, 4,000 men quarry limestone, 16,000 men manufacture coke, 343,000 men manufacture steel, and 83,000 men transport its product. Respondent has about 10,000 employees in its Aliquippa plant, which is located in a community of about 30,000 persons.

Respondent points to evidence that the Aliquippa plant, in which the discharged men were employed, contains complete facilities for the production of finished and semi-finished iron and steel products from raw materials; that its works consist primarily of a by-product coke plant for the production of coke; blast furnaces for the production of pig iron; open hearth furnaces and Bessemer converters for the production of steel; blooming mills for the reduction of steel ingots into smaller shapes; and a number of finishing mills such as structural mills, rod mills, wire mills and the like. In addition there are other buildings, structures and equipment, storage yards, docks and an intra-plant storage system. Respondent's operations at these works are carried on in two distinct stages, the first being the conversion of raw materials into pig iron and the second being the manufacture of semi-finished and finished iron and steel products; and in both cases the operations result in substantially changing the character, utility and value of the materials wrought upon, which is apparent from the nature and extent of the processes to which they are subjected and which respondent fully describes. Respondent also directs attention to the fact that the iron ore which is procured from mines in Minnesota and Michigan and transported to respondent's plant is stored in stock piles for future use, the amount of ore in storage varying with the season but usually being enough to maintain operations from nine to ten months; that the coal which is procured from the mines of a subsidiary located in Pennsylvania and taken to the plant at Aliquippa is there, like ore, stored for future use, approximately two to three months' supply of coal being always on hand; and that the limestone which is obtained in Pennsylvania and West Virginia is also stored in amounts usually adequate to run the blast furnaces for a few weeks. Various details of operation, transportation, and distribution are also mentioned which for the present purpose it is not necessary to detail.

Practically all the factual evidence in the case, except that which dealt with the nature of respondent's business, concerned its relations with the employees in the Aliquippa plant whose discharge was the subject of the complaint. These employees were active leaders in the labor union. Several were officers and others were leaders of particular groups. Two of the employees were motor inspectors; one was a tractor driver; three were crane operators; one was a washer in the coke plant; and three were laborers. Three other employees were mentioned in the complaint but it was withdrawn as to one of them and no evidence was heard on the action taken with respect to the other two.

While respondent criticises the evidence and the attitude of the Board, which is described as being hostile toward employers and particularly toward those who insisted upon their constitutional rights, respondent did not take advantage of its opportunity to present evidence to refute that which was offered to show discrimination and coercion. In this situation, the record presents no ground for setting aside the order of the Board so far as the facts pertaining to the circumstances and purpose of the discharge of the employees are concerned. Upon that point it is sufficient to say that the evidence supports the findings of the Board that respondent discharged these men "because of their union activity and for the purpose of discouraging membership in the union." We turn to the questions of law which respondent urges in contesting the validity and application of the Act.

First. The scope of the Act.—The Act is challenged in its entirety as an attempt to regulate all industry, thus invading the reserved powers of the States over their local concerns. It is asserted that the references in the Act to interstate and foreign commerce are colorable at best; that the Act is not a true regulation of such commerce or of matters which directly affect it but on the contrary has the fundamental object of placing under the compulsory supervision of the federal government all industrial labor relations within the nation. The argument seeks support in the broad words of the preamble (section one[3]) and in the sweep of the provisions of the Act, and it is further insisted that its legislative history shows an essential universal purpose in the light of which its scope cannot be limited by either construction or by the application of the separability clause.

If this conception of terms, intent and consequent inseparability were sound, the Act would necessarily fall by reason of the limitation upon the federal power which inheres in the constitutional grant, as well as because of the explicit reservation of the Tenth Amendment. *Schechter Corp.* v. *United States,* 295 U.S. 495, 549, 550, 554. The authority of the federal government may not be pushed to such an extreme as to destroy the distinction, which the commerce clause itself establishes, between commerce "among the several States" and the internal concerns of a State. That distinction between what is national and what is local in the activities of commerce is vital to the maintenance of our federal system. *Id.*

But we are not at liberty to deny effect to specific provisions, which Congress has constitutional power to enact, by superimposing upon them inferences from general legislative declarations of an ambiguous character, even if found in the same statute. The cardinal principle of statutory construction is to save and not to destroy. We have repeatedly held that as between two possible interpretations of a statute, by one of which it would be unconstitutional and by the other valid, our plain duty is to adopt that which will save the act. Even to avoid a serious doubt the rule is the same. *Federal Trade Comm'n* v. *American Tobacco Co.,* 264 U.S. 298, 307; *Panama R. Co.* v. *Johnson,* 264 U.S. 375, 390; *Missouri Pacific R. Co.* v. *Boone,* 270 U.S. 466, 472; *Blodgett* v. *Holden,* 275 U.S. 142, 148; *Richmond Screw Anchor Co.* v. *United States,* 275 U.S. 331, 346.

We think it clear that the National Labor Relations Act may be construed so as to operate within the sphere of constitutional authority. The jurisdiction conferred upon the Board, and invoked in this instance, is found in § 10 (a), which provides:

"SEC. 10 (a). The Board is empowered, as hereinafter provided, to prevent any person from engaging in any unfair labor practice (listed in section 8) affecting commerce."

The critical words of this provision, prescribing the limits of the Board's authority in dealing with the labor practices, are "affecting commerce." The Act specifically defines the "commerce" to which it refers (§ 2 (6)):

"The term 'commerce' means trade, traffic, commerce, transportation, or communication among the several States, or between the District of Columbia or any Territory of the United States and any State or other Territory, or between any foreign country and any State, Territory, or the District of Columbia, or within the District of Columbia or any Territory, or between points in the same State but through any other State or any Territory or the District of Columbia or any foreign country."

There can be no question that the commerce thus contemplated by the Act (aside from that within a Territory or the District of Columbia) is interstate and foreign commerce in the constitutional sense. The Act also defines the term "affecting commerce" (§ 2 (7)):

"The term 'affecting commerce' means in commerce, or burdening or obstructing commerce or the free flow of commerce, or having led or tending to lead to a labor dispute burdening or obstructing commerce or the free flow of commerce."

This definition is one of exclusion as well as inclusion. The grant of authority to the Board does not purport to extend to the relationship between all industrial employees and employers. Its terms do not impose collective bargaining upon all industry regardless of effects upon interstate or foreign commerce. It purports to reach only what may be deemed to burden or obstruct that commerce and, thus qualified, it must be construed as contemplating the exercise of control within constitutional bounds. It is a familiar principle that acts which directly burden or obstruct interstate or foreign commerce, or its free flow, are within the reach of the congressional power. Acts having that effect are not rendered immune because they grow out of labor disputes. See

[3] *See Note 2,* supra, *p. 23.*

Texas & N. O. R. Co. v. *Railway Clerks,* 281 U.S. 548, 570; *Schechter Corp.* v *United States, supra,* pp. 544, 545; *Virginian Railway* v. *System Federation, No. 40,* 300 U.S. 515. It is the effect upon commerce, not the source of the injury, which is the criterion. *Second Employers' Liability Cases,* 223 U.S. 1, 51. Whether or not particular action does affect commerce in such a close and intimate fashion as to be subject to federal control, and hence to lie within the authority conferred upon the Board, is left by the statute to be determined as individual cases arise. We are thus to inquire whether in the instant case the constitutional boundary has been passed.

Second. The unfair labor practices in question.—The unfair labor practices found by the Board are those defined in § 8, subdivisions (1) and (3). These provide:

Sec. 8. It shall be an unfair labor practice for an employer—

"(1) To interfere with, restrain, or coerce employees in the exercise of the rights guaranteed in section 7."

"(3) By discrimination in regard to hire or tenure of employment or any term or condition of employment to encourage or discourage membership in any labor organization: . . ."[4]

Section 8, subdivision (1), refers to § 7, which is as follows:

"Sec. 7. Employees shall have the right to self-organization, to form, join, or assist labor organizations, to bargain collectively through representatives of their own choosing, and to engage in concerted activities, for the purpose of collective bargaining or other mutual aid or protection."

Thus, in its present application, the statute goes no further than to safeguard the right of employees to self-organization and to select representatives of their own choosing for collective bargaining or other mutual protection without restraint or coercion by their employer.

That is a fundamental right. Employees have as clear a right to organize and select their representatives for lawful purposes as the respondent has to organize its business and select its own officers and agents. Discrimination and coercion to prevent the free exercise of the right of employees to self-organization and representation is a proper subject for condemnation by competent legislative authority. Long ago we stated the reason for labor organizations. We said that they were organized out of the necessities of the situation; that a single employee was helpless in dealing with an employer; that he was dependent ordinarily on his daily wage for the maintenance of himself and family; that if the employer refused to pay him the wages that he thought fair, he was nevertheless unable to leave the employ and resist arbitrary and unfair treatment; that union was essential to give laborers opportunity to deal on an equality with their employer. *American Steel Foundries* v. *Tri-City Central Trades Council,* 257 U.S. 184, 209. We reiterated these views when we had under consideration the Railway Labor Act of 1926. Fully recognizing the legality of collective action on the part of employees in order to safeguard their proper interests, we said that Congress was not required to ignore this right but could safeguard it. Congress could seek to make appropriate collective action of employees an instrument of peace rather than of strife. We said that such collective action would be a mockery if representation were made futile by interference with freedom of choice. Hence the prohibition by Congress of interference with the selection of representatives for the purpose of negotiation and conference between employers and employees, "instead of being an invasion of the constitutional right of either, was based on the recognition of the rights of both." *Texas & N. O. R. Co.* v. *Railway Clerks, supra.* We have reasserted the same principle in sustaining the application of the Railway Labor Act as amended in 1934. *Virginian Railway Co.* v. *System Federation, No. 40, supra.*

Third. The application of the Act to employees engaged in production.—The principle involved.—Respondent says that whatever may be said of employees engaged

[4] *What is quoted above is followed by this proviso—not here involved*—"Provided, *That nothing in this Act, or in the National Industrial Recovery Act (U.S.C., Supp. VII, title 15, secs. 701–712), as amended from time to time, or in any code or agreement approved or prescribed thereunder, or in any other statute of the United States, shall preclude an employer from making an agreement with a labor organization (not established, maintained, or assisted by any action defined in this Act as an unfair labor practice) to require as a condition of employment membership therein, if such labor organization is the representative of the employees as provided in section 9 (a), in the appropriate collective bargaining unit covered by such agreement when made.*"

in interstate commerce, the industrial relations and activities in the manufacturing department of respondent's enterprise are not subject to federal regulation. The argument rests upon the proposition that manufacturing in itself is not commerce. *Kidd* v. *Pearson,* 128 U.S. 1, 20, 21; *United Mine Workers* v. *Coronado Coal Co.,* 259 U.S. 344, 407, 408; *Oliver Iron Co.* v. *Lord,* 262 U.S. 172, 178; *United Leather Workers* v. *Herkert & Meisel Trunk Co.,* 265 U.S. 457, 465; *Industrial Association* v. *United States,* 268 U.S. 64, 82; *Coronado Coal Co.* v. *United Mine Workers,* 268 U.S. 295, 310; *Schechter Corp.* v. *United States, supra,* p. 547; *Carter* v. *Carter Coal Co.,* 298 U.S. 238, 304, 317, 327.

The Government distinguishes these cases. The various parts of respondent's enterprise are described as interdependent and as thus involving "a great movement of iron ore, coal and limestone along well-defined paths to the steel mills, thence through them, and thence in the form of steel products into the consuming centers of the country—a definite and well-understood course of business." It is urged that these activities constitute a "stream" or "flow" of commerce, of which the Aliquippa manufacturing plant is the focal point, and that industrial strife at that point would cripple the entire movement. Reference is made to our decision sustaining the Packers and Stockyards Act.[5] *Stafford* v. *Wallace,* 258 U.S. 495. The Court found that the stockyards were but a "throat" through which the current of commerce flowed and the transactions which there occurred could not be separated from that movement. Hence the sales at the stockyards were not regarded as merely local transactions, for while they created "a local change of title" they did not "stop the flow," but merely changed the private interests in the subject of the current. Distinguishing the cases which upheld the power of the State to impose a non-discriminatory tax upon property which the owner intended to transport to another State, but which was not in actual transit and was held within the State subject to the disposition of the owner, the Court remarked: "The question, it should be observed, is not with respect to the extent of the power of Congress to regulate interstate commerce, but whether a particular exercise of state power in view of its nature and operation must be deemed to be in conflict with this paramount authority." *Id.,* p. 526. See *Minnesota* v. *Blasius,* 290 U.S. 1, 8. Applying the doctrine of *Stafford* v. *Wallace, supra,* the Court sustained the Grain Futures Act of 1922[6] with respect to transactions on the Chicago Board of Trade, although these transactions were "not in and of themselves interstate commerce." Congress had found that they had become "a constantly recurring burden and obstruction to that commerce." *Chicago Board of Trade* v. *Olsen,* 262 U.S. 1, 32; compare *Hill* v. *Wallace,* 259 U.S. 44, 69. See, also, *Tagg Bros. & Moorhead* v. *United States,* 280 U.S. 420.

Respondent contends that the instant case presents material distinctions. Respondent says that the Aliquippa plant is extensive in size and represents a large investment in buildings, machinery and equipment. The raw materials which are brought to the plant are delayed for long periods and, after being subjected to manufacturing processes, "are changed substantially as to character, utility and value." The finished products which emerge "are to a large extent manufactured without reference to pre-existing orders and contracts and are entirely different from the raw materials which enter at the other end." Hence respondent argues that "If importation and exportation in interstate commerce do not singly transfer purely local activities into the field of congressional regulation, it should follow that their combination would not alter the local situation." *Arkadelphia Milling Co.* v. *St. Louis Southwestern Ry. Co.,* 249 U.S. 134, 151; *Oliver Iron Co.* v. *Lord, supra.*

We do not find it necessary to determine whether these features of defendant's business dispose of the asserted analogy to the "stream of commerce" cases. The instances in which that metaphor has been used are but particular, and not exclusive, illustrations of the protective power which the Government invokes in support of the present Act. The congressional authority to protect interstate commerce from burdens and obstructions is not limited to transactions which can be deemed to be an essential part of a "flow" of interstate or foreign commerce. Burdens and obstructions may be due to injurious action springing from other sources. The fundamental principle is that the power to regulate commerce is the power to enact "all appropriate legislation" for "its protection and advancement" (*The*

[5] *42 Stat. 159.*

[6] *42 Stat. 998.*

Daniel Ball, 10 Wall. 557, 564); to adopt measures "to promote its growth and insure its safety" (*Mobile County* v. *Kimball,* 102 U.S. 691, 696, 697); "to foster, protect, control and restrain." *Second Employers' Liability Cases, supra,* p. 47. See *Texas & N. O. R. Co.* v. *Railway Clerks, supra.* That power is plenary and may be exerted to protect interstate commerce "no matter what the source of the dangers which threaten it." *Second Employers' Liability Cases,* p. 51; *Schechter Corp.* v. *United States, supra.* Although activities may be intrastate in character when separately considered, if they have such a close and substantial relation to interstate commerce that their control is essential or appropriate to protect that commerce from burdens and obstructions, Congress cannot be denied the power to exercise that control. *Schechter Corp.* v. *United States, supra.* Undoubtedly the scope of this power must be considered in the light of our dual system of government and may not be extended so as to embrace effects upon interstate commerce so indirect and remote that to embrace them, in view of our complex society, would effectually obliterate the distinction between what is national and what is local and create a completely centralized government. *Id.* The question is necessarily one of degree. As the Court said in *Chicago Board of Trade* v. *Olsen, supra,* p. 37, repeating what had been said in *Stafford* v. *Wallace, supra:* "Whatever amounts to more or less constant practice, and threatens to obstruct or unduly to burden the freedom of interstate commerce is within the regulatory power of Congress under the commerce clause and it is primarily for Congress to consider and decide the fact of the danger and meet it."

That intrastate activities, by reason of close and intimate relation to interstate commerce, may fall within federal control is demonstrated in the case of carriers who are engaged in both interstate and intrastate transportation. There federal control has been found essential to secure the freedom of interstate traffic from interference or unjust discrimination and to promote the efficiency of the interstate service. *Shreveport Case,* 234 U.S. 342, 351, 352; *Wisconsin Railroad Comm'n* v. *Chicago, B. & Q. R. Co.,* 257 U.S. 563, 588. It is manifest that intrastate rates deal *primarily* with a local activity. But in rate-making they bear such a close relation to interstate rates that effective control of the one must embrace some control over the other. *Id.* Under the Transportation Act, 1920,[7] Congress went so far as to authorize the Interstate Commerce Commission to establish a state-wide level of intrastate rates in order to prevent an unjust discrimination against interstate commerce. *Wisconsin Railroad Comm'n* v. *Chicago, B. & Q. R. Co., supra; Florida* v. *United States,* 282 U.S. 194, 210, 211. Other illustrations are found in the broad requirements of the Safety Appliance Act and the Hours of Service Act. *Southern Railway Co.* v. *United States,* 222 U.S. 20; *Baltimore & Ohio R. Co.* v. *Interstate Commerce Comm'n,* 221 U.S. 612. It is said that this exercise of federal power has relation to the maintenance of adequate instrumentalities of interstate commerce. But the agency is not superior to the commerce which uses it. The protective power extends to the former because it exists as to the latter.

The close and intimate effect which brings the subject within the reach of federal power may be due to activities in relation to productive industry although the industry when separately viewed is local. This has been abundantly illustrated in the application of the federal Anti-Trust Act. In the *Standard Oil* and *American Tobacco* cases, 221 U.S. 1, 106, that statute was applied to combinations of employers engaged in productive industry. Counsel for the offending corporations strongly urged that the Sherman Act had no application because the acts complained of were not acts of interstate or foreign commerce, nor direct and immediate in their effect on interstate or foreign commerce, but primarily affected manufacturing and not commerce. 221 U.S. pp. 5, 125. Counsel relied upon the decision in *United States* v. *Knight Co.,* 156 U.S. 1. The Court stated their contention as follows: "That the act, even if the averments of the bill be true, cannot be constitutionally applied, because to do so would extend the power of Congress to subjects *dehors* the reach of its authority to regulate commerce, by enabling that body to deal with mere questions of production of commodities within the States." And the Court summarily dismissed the contention in these words: "But all the structure upon which this argument proceeds is based upon the decision in *United States* v. *E. C. Knight Co.,* 156 U.S. 1. The view, however, which the argument takes of that case and the arguments based upon that view have been so repeatedly

[7] *§§ 416, 422, 41 Stat. 484, 488; Interstate Commerce Act, § 13 (4).*

pressed upon this court in connection with the interpretation and enforcement of the Anti-trust Act, and have been so necessarily and expressly decided to be unsound as to cause the contentions to be plainly foreclosed and to require no express notice" (citing cases). 221 U.S. pp. 68, 69.

Upon the same principle, the Anti-Trust Act has been applied to the conduct of employees engaged in production. *Loewe* v. *Lawlor,* 208 U.S. 274; *Coronado Coal Co.* v. *United Mine Workers, supra; Bedford Cut Stone Co.* v. *Stone Cutters' Assn.,* 274 U.S. 37. See, also, *Local 167* v. *United States,* 291 U.S. 293, 397; *Schechter Corp.* v. *United States, supra.* The decisions dealing with the question of that application illustrate both the principle and its limitation. Thus, in the first *Coronado* case, the Court held that mining was not interstate commerce, that the power of Congress did not extend to its regulation as such, and that it had not been shown that the activities there involved—a local strike—brought them within the provisions of the Anti-Trust Act, notwithstanding the broad terms of that statute. A similar conclusion was reached in *United Leather Workers* v. *Herkert & Meisel Trunk Co., supra, Industrial Association* v. *United States, supra,* and *Levering & Garrigues Co.* v. *Morrin,* 289 U.S. 103, 107. But in the first *Coronado* case the Court also said that "if Congress deems certain recurring practices, though not really part of interstate commerce, likely to obstruct, restrain or burden it, it has the power to subject them to national supervision and restraint." 259 U.S. p. 408. And in the second *Coronado* case the Court ruled that while the mere reduction in the supply of an article to be shipped in interstate commerce by the illegal or tortious prevention of its manufacture or production is ordinarily an indirect and remote obstruction to that commerce, nevertheless when the "intent of those unlawfully preventing the manufacture or production is shown to be to restrain or control the supply entering and moving in interstate commerce, or the price of it in interstate markets, their action is a direct violation of the Anti-Trust Act." 268 U.S. p. 310. And the existence of that intent may be a necessary inference from proof of the direct and substantial effect produced by the employees' conduct. *Industrial Association* v. *United States,* 268 U.S. p. 81. What was absent from the evidence in the first *Coronado* case appeared in the second and the Act was accordingly applied to the mining employees.

It is thus apparent that the fact that the employees here concerned were engaged in production is not determinative. The question remains as to the effect upon interstate commerce of the labor practice involved. In the *Schechter* case, *supra,* we found that the effect there was so remote as to be beyond the federal power. To find "immediacy or directness" there was to find it "almost everywhere," a result inconsistent with the maintenance of our federal system. In the *Carter* case, *supra,* the Court was of the opinion that the provisions of the statute relating to production were invalid upon several grounds,—that there was improper delegation of legislative power, and that the requirements not only went beyond any sustainable measure of protection of interstate commerce but were also inconsistent with due process. These cases are not controlling here.

Fourth. Effects of the unfair labor practice in respondent's enterprise.—Giving full weight to respondent's contention with respect to a break in the complete continuity of the "stream of commerce" by reason of respondent's manufacturing operations, the fact remains that the stoppage of those operations by industrial strife would have a most serious effect upon interstate commerce. In view of respondent's far-flung activities, it is idle to say that the effect would be indirect or remote. It is obvious that it would be immediate and might be catastrophic. We are asked to shut our eyes to the plainest facts of our national life and to deal with the question of direct and indirect effects in an intellectual vacuum. Because there may be but indirect and remote effects upon interstate commerce in connection with a host of local enterprises throughout the country, it does not follow that other industrial activities do not have such a close and intimate relation to interstate commerce as to make the presence of industrial strife a matter of the most urgent national concern. When industries organize themselves on a national scale, making their relation to interstate commerce the dominant factor in their activities, how can it be maintained that their industrial labor relations constitute a forbidden field into which Congress may not enter when it is necessary to protect interstate commerce from the paralyzing consequences of industrial war? We have often said that interstate commerce itself is a practical conception. It is equally true that interferences with that commerce must be appraised by a judgment that does not ignore actual experience.

Experience has abundantly demonstrated that the recognition of the right of employees to self-organization and to have representatives of their own choosing for the purpose of collective bargaining is often an essential condition of industrial peace. Refusal to confer and negotiate has been one of the most prolific causes of strife. This is such an outstanding fact in the history of labor disturbances that it is a proper subject of judicial notice and requires no citation of instances. The opinion in the case of *Virginian Railway Co.* v. *System Federation, No. 40, supra,* points out that, in the case of carriers, experience has shown that before the amendment, of 1934, of the Railway Labor Act "when there was no dispute as to the organizations authorized to represent the employees and when there was a willingness of the employer to meet such representative for a discussion of their grievances, amicable adjustment of differences had generally followed and strikes had been avoided." That, on the other hand, "a prolific source of dispute had been the maintenance by the railroad of company unions and the denial by railway management of the authority of representatives chosen by their employees." The opinion in that case also points to the large measure of success of the labor policy embodied in the Railway Labor Act. But with respect to the appropriateness of the recognition of self-organization and representation in the promotion of peace, the question is not essentially different in the case of employees in industries of such a character that interstate commerce is put in jeopardy from the case of employees of transportation companies. And of what avail is it to protect the facility of transporation, if interstate commerce is throttled with respect to the commodities to be transported!

These questions have frequently engaged the attention of Congress and have been the subject of many inquiries.[8] The steel industry is one of the great basic industries of the United States, with ramifying activities affecting interstate commerce at every point. The Government aptly refers to the steel strike of 1919–1920 with its far-reaching consequences.[9] The fact that there appears to have been no major disturbance in that industry in the more recent period did not dispose of the possibilities of future and like dangers to interstate commerce which Congress was entitled to foresee and to exercise its protective power to forestall. It is not necessary again to detail the facts as to respondent's enterprise. Instead of being beyond the pale, we think that it presents in a most striking way the close and intimate relation which a manufacturing industry may have to interstate commerce and we have no doubt that Congress had constitutional authority to safeguard the right of respondent's employees to self-organization and freedom in the choice of representatives for collective bargaining.

Fifth. The means which the Act employs.—Questions under the due process clause and other constitutional restrictions.—Respondent asserts its right to conduct its business in an orderly manner without being subjected to arbitrary restraints. What we have said points to the fallacy in the argument. Employees have their correlative right to organize for the purpose of securing the redress of grievances and to promote agreements with employers relating to rates of pay and conditions of work. *Texas & N. O. R. Co.* v. *Railway Clerks, supra; Virginian Railway Co.* v. *System Federation, No. 40.* Restraint for the purpose of preventing an unjust interference with that right cannot be considered arbitrary or capricious. The provision of § 9 (a)[10] that representatives, for the purpose

[8] *See, for example, Final Report of the Industrial Commission (1902), vol. 19, p. 844; Report of the Anthracite Coal Strike Commission (1902), Sen. Doc. No. 6, 58th Cong., spec. sess.; Final Report of Commission on Industrial Relations (1916, Sen. Doc. No. 415, 64th Cong., 1st sess., vol. I; National War Labor Board, Principles and Rules of Procedure (1919), p. 4; Bureau of Labor Statistics, Bulletin No. 287 (1921), pp. 52–64; History of the Shipbuilding Labor Adjustment Board, U.S. Bureau of Labor Statistics, Bulletin No. 283.*

[9] *See Investigating Strike in Steel Industries, Sen. Rep. No. 289, 66th Cong., 1st sess.*

[10] *The provision is as follows:* "SEC. 9 (*a*) *Representatives designated or selected for the purposes of collective bargaining by the majority of the employees in a unit appropriate for such purposes, shall be the exclusive representatives of all the employees in such unit for the purposes of collective bargaining in respect to rates of pay, wages, hours of employment, or other conditions of employment:* Provided, *That any*

of collective bargaining, of the majority of the employees in an appropriate unit shall be the exclusive representatives of all the employees in that unit, imposes upon the respondent only the duty of conferring and negotiating with the authorized representatives of its employees for the purpose of settling a labor dispute. This provision has its analogue in § 2, Ninth, of the Railway Labor Act which was under consideration in *Virginian Railway Co.* v. *System Federation, No. 40, supra.* The decree which we affirmed in that case required the Railway Company to treat with the representative chosen by the employees and also to refrain from entering into collective labor agreements with anyone other than their true representative as ascertained in accordance with the provisions of the Act. We said that the obligation to treat with the true representative was exclusive and hence imposed the negative duty to treat with no other. We also pointed out that, as conceded by the Government,[11] the injunction against the Company's entering into any contract concerning rules, rates of pay and working conditions except with a chosen representative was "designed only to prevent collective bargaining with anyone purporting to represent employees" other than the representative they had selected. It was taken "to prohibit the negotiation of labor contracts generally applicable to employees" in the described unit with any other representative than the one so chosen, "but not as precluding such individual contracts" as the Company might "elect to make directly with individual employees." We think this construction also applies to § 9 (a) of the National Labor Relations Act.

The Act does not compel agreements between employers and employees. It does not compel any agreement whatever. It does not prevent the employer "from refusing to make a collective contract and hiring individuals on whatever terms" the employer "may by unilateral action determine."[12] The Act expressly provides in § 9 (a) that any individual employee or a group of employees shall have the right at any time to present grievances to their employer. The theory of the Act is that free opportunity for negotiation with accredited representatives of employees is likely to promote industrial peace and may bring about the adjustments and agreements which the Act in itself does not attempt to compel. As we said in *Texas & N. O. R. Co.* v. *Railway Clerks, supra,* and repeated in *Virginian Railway Co.* v. *System Federation, No. 40, supra,* the cases of *Adair* v. *United States,* 208 U.S. 161, and *Coppage* v. *Kansas,* 236 U.S. 1, are inapplicable to legislation of this character. The Act does not interfere with the normal exercise of the right of the employer to select its employees or to discharge them. The employer may not, under cover of that right, intimidate or coerce its employees with respect to their self-organization and representation, and, on the other hand, the Board is not entitled to make its authority a pretext for interference with the right of discharge when that right is exercised for other reasons than such intimidation and coercion. The true purpose is the subject of investigation with full opportunity to show the facts. It would seem that when employers freely recognize the right of their employees to their own organizations and their unrestricted right of representation there will be much less occasion for controversy in respect to the free and appropriate exercise of the right of selection and discharge.

The Act has been criticised as one-sided in its application; that it subjects the employer to supervision and restraint and leaves untouched the abuses for which employees may be responsible; that it fails to provide a more comprehensive plan—with better assurances of fairness to both sides and with increased chances of success in bringing about, if not compelling, equitable solutions of industrial disputes affecting interstate commerce. But we are dealing with the power of Congress, not with a particular policy or with the extent to which policy should go. We have frequently said that the legislative authority, exerted within its proper field, need not embrace all the evils within its reach. The Constitution does not forbid "cautious advance, step by step," in dealing with the evils which are exhibited in activities within the range of legislative power. *Carroll* v. *Greenwich Insurance Co.,* 199 U.S. 401, 411; *Keokee Coke Co.* v. *Taylor,* 234 U.S. 224, 227; *Miller* v. *Wilson,* 236 U.S. 373, 384; *Sproles* v. *Binford,* 286 U.S. 374, 396. The question in such cases is whether the legislature, in

---

individual employee or a group of employees shall have the right at any time to present grievances to their employer."

[11] *See* Virginian Railway Co. *v.* System Federation, No. 40, *300 U.S. 515.*

[12] *See Note 11.*

what it does prescribe, has gone beyond constitutional limits.

The procedural provisions of the Act are assailed. But these provisions, as we construe them, do not offend against the constitutional requirements governing the creation and action of administrative bodies. See *Interstate Commerce Comm'n* v. *Louisville & Nashville R. Co.,* 227 U.S. 88, 91. The Act establishes standards to which the Board must conform. There must be complaint, notice and hearing. The Board must receive evidence and make findings. The findings as to the facts are to be conclusive, but only if supported by evidence. The order of the Board is subject to review by the designated court, and only when sustained by the court may the order be enforced. Upon that review all questions of the jurisdiction of the Board and the regularity of its proceedings, all questions of constitutional right or statutory authority, are open to examination by the court. We construe the procedural provisions as affording adequate opportunity to secure judicial protection against arbitrary action in accordance with the well-settled rules applicable to administrative agencies set up by Congress to aid in the enforcement of valid legislation. It is not necessary to repeat these rules which have frequently been declared. None of them appears to have been transgressed in the instant case. Respondent was notified and heard. It had opportunity to meet the charge of unfair labor practices upon the merits, and by withdrawing from the hearing it declined to avail itself of that opportunity. The facts found by the Board support its order and the evidence supports the findings. Respondent has no just ground for complaint on this score.

The order of the Board required the reinstatement of the employees who were found to have been discharged because of their "union activity" and for the purpose of "discouraging membership in the union." That requirement was authorized by the Act. § 10 (c). In *Texas & N. O. R. Co.* v. *Railway Clerks, supra,* a similar order for restoration to service was made by the court in contempt proceedings for the violation of an injunction issued by the court to restrain an interference with the right of employees as guaranteed by the Railway Labor Act of 1926. The requirement of restoration to service, of employees discharged in violation of the provisions of that Act, was thus a sanction imposed in the enforcement of a judicial decree. We do not doubt that Congress could impose a like sanction for the enforcement of its valid regulation. The fact that in the one case it was a judicial sanction, and in the other a legislative one, is not an essential difference in determining its propriety.

Respondent complains that the Board not only ordered reinstatement but directed the payment of wages for the time lost by the discharge, less amounts earned by the employee during that period. This part of the order was also authorized by the Act. § 10 (c). It is argued that the requirement is equivalent to a money judgment and hence contravenes the Seventh Amendment with respect to trial by jury. The Seventh Amendment provides that "In suits at common law, where the value in controversy shall exceed twenty dollars, the right of trial by jury shall be preserved." The Amendment thus preserves the right which existed under the common law when the Amendment was adopted. *Shields* v. *Thomas,* 18 How. 253, 262; *In re Wood,* 210 U.S. 246, 258; *Dimick* v. *Schiedt,* 293 U.S. 474, 476; *Baltimore & Carolina Line* v. *Redman,* 295 U.S. 654, 657. Thus it has no application to cases where recovery of money damages is an incident to equitable relief even though damages might have been recovered in an action at law. *Clark* v. *Wooster,* 119 U.S. 322, 325; *Pease* v. *Rathbun-Jones Engineering Co.,* 243 U.S. 273, 279. It does not apply where the proceeding is not in the nature of a suit at common law. *Guthrie National Bank* v. *Guthrie,* 173 U.S. 528, 537.

The instant case is not a suit at common law or in the nature of such a suit. The proceeding is one unknown to the common law. It is a statutory proceeding. Reinstatement of the employee and payment for time lost are requirements imposed for violation of the statute and are remedies appropriate to its enforcement. The contention under the Seventh Amendment is without merit.

Our conclusion is that the order of the Board was within its competency and that the Act is valid as here applied. The judgment of the Circuit Court of Appeals is reversed and the cause is remanded for further proceedings in conformity with this opinion.

Reversed

WEST COAST HOTEL v. PARRISH, 300 U.S. 379 (1937)

In this case, the Supreme Court by five to four vote in a decision by Chief Justice Hughes, in the midst of the "Court-packing" controversy, dramatically reversed a precedent established in 1918 and reaffirmed only nine months earlier, and clearly and unequivocally affirmed that the states would have broad latitude to legislate in the interests of the health, safety, and welfare of their inhabitants. In the specific case, Chief Justice Hughes ruled that a law fixing minimum wages for women, which conflicted with contracts for lower wages entered into between employer and employees, was a constitutional exercise of the police power of the state and did not constitute a deprivation of freedom of contract barred by the due process clause of the Fourteenth Amendment.

MR. CHIEF JUSTICE HUGHES delivered the opinion of the Court.

This case presents the question of the constitutional validity of the minimum wage law of the State of Washington.

The Act, entitled "Minimum Wages for Women," authorizes the fixing of minimum wages for women and minors. Laws of 1913 (Washington) chap. 174; Remington's Rev. Stat. (1932), §§ 7623 *et seq.* It provides:

"SECTION 1. The welfare of the State of Washington demands that women and minors be protected from conditions of labor which have a pernicious effect on their health and morals. The State of Washington, therefore, exercising herein its police and sovereign power declares that inadequate wages and unsanitary conditions of labor exert such pernicious effect.

"SEC. 2. It shall be unlawful to employ women or minors in any industry or occupation within the State of Washington under conditions of labor detrimental to their health or morals; and it shall be unlawful to employ women workers in any industry within the State of Washington at wages which are not adequate for their maintenance.

"SEC. 3. There is hereby created a commission to be known as the 'Industrial Welfare Commission' for the State of Washington, to establish such standards of wages and conditions of labor for women and minors employed within the State of Washington, as shall be held hereunder to be reasonable and not detrimental to health and morals, and which shall be sufficient for the decent maintenance of women."

Further provisions required the Commission to ascertain the wages and conditions of labor of women and minors within the State. Public hearings were to be held. If after investigation the Commission found that in any occupation, trade or industry the wages paid to women were "inadequate to supply them necessary cost of living and to maintain the workers in health," the Commission was empowered to call a conference of representatives of employers and employees together with disinterested persons representing the public. The conference was to recommend to the Commission, on its request, an estimate of a minimum wage adequate for the purpose above stated, and on the approval of such a recommendation it became the duty of the Commission to issue an obligatory order fixing minimum wages. Any such order might be reopened and the question reconsidered with the aid of the former conference or a new one. Special licenses were authorized for the employment of women who were "physically defective or crippled by age or otherwise" and also for apprentices, at less than the prescribed minimum wage.

By a later Act the Industrial Welfare Commission was abolished and its duties were assigned to the Industrial Welfare Committee consisting of the Director of Labor and Industries, the Supervisor of Industrial Insurance, the Supervisor of Industrial Relations, the Industrial Statistician and the Supervisor of Women in Industry. Laws of 1921 (Washington) c. 7; Remington's Rev. Stat. (1932), § § 10840, 10893.

The appellant conducts a hotel. The appellee Elsie Parrish was employed as a chambermaid and (with her husband) brought this suit to recover the difference between the wages paid her and the minimum wage fixed pursuant to the state law. The minimum wage was $14.50 per week of 48 hours. The appellant challenged the act as repugnant to the due process clause of the Fourteenth Amendment of the Constitution of the United States. The Supreme Court of the State, reversing the trial court, sustained the statute and directed judgment for the plaintiffs. *Parrish* v. *West Coast Hotel Co.,* 185 Wash. 581; 55 P. (2d) 1083. The case is here on appeal.

The appellant relies upon the decision of this Court in *Adkins* v. *Children's Hospital,* 261 U.S. 525, which held invalid the District of Columbia Minimum Wage Act, which was attacked under the due process clause of the Fifth Amendment. On the argument at bar, counsel for the appellees attempted to distinguish the *Adkins* case upon the ground that the appellee was employed in a hotel and that the business of an innkeeper was affected with a public interest. That effort at distinction is obviously futile, as it appears that in one of the cases ruled by the *Adkins* opinion the employee was a woman employed as an elevator operator in a hotel. *Adkins* v. *Lyons,* 261 U.S. 525, at p. 542.

The recent case of *Morehead* v. *New York ex. rel. Tipaldo,* 298 U.S. 587, came here on certiorari to the New York court, which had held the New York minimum wage act for women to be invalid. A minority of this Court thought that the New York statute was distinguishable in a material feature from that involved in the *Adkins* case, and that for that and other reasons the New York statute should be sustained. But the Court of Appeals of New York had said that it found no material difference between the two statutes, and this Court held that the "meaning of the statute" as fixed by the decision of the state court "must be accepted here as if the meaning had been specifically expressed in the enactment." *Id.,* p. 609. That view led to the affirmance by this Court of the judgment in the *Morehead* case, as the Court considered that the only question before it was whether the *Adkins* case was distinguishable and that reconsideration of that decision had not been sought. Upon that point the Court said: "The petition for the writ sought review upon the ground that this case [Morehead] is distinguishable from that one [Adkins]. No application has been made for reconsideration of the constitutional question there decided. The validity of the principles upon which that decision rests is not challenged. This court confines itself to the ground upon which the writ was asked or granted . . . Here the review granted was no broader than that sought by the petitioner . . . He is not entitled and does not ask to be heard upon the question whether the *Adkins* case should be overruled. He maintains that it may be distinguished on the ground that the statutes are vitally dissimilar." *Id.,* pp. 604, 605.

We think that the question which was not deemed to be open in the *Morehead* case is open and is necessarily presented here. The Supreme Court of Washington has upheld the minimum wage statute of that State. It has decided that the statute is a reasonable exercise of the police power of the State. In reaching that conclusion the state court has invoked principles long established by this Court in the application of the Fourteenth Amendment. The state court has refused to regard the decision in the *Adkins* case as determinative and has pointed to our decisions both before and since that case as justifying its position. We are of the opinion that this ruling of the state court demands on our part a reëxamination of the *Adkins* case. The importance of the question, in which many States having similar laws are concerned, the close division by which the decision in the *Adkins* case was reached, and the economic conditions which have supervened, and in the light of which the reasonableness of the exercise of the protective power of the State must be considered, make it not only appropriate, but we think imperative, that in deciding the present case the subject should receive fresh consideration.

The history of the litigation of this question may be briefly stated. The minimum wage statute of Washington was enacted over twenty-three years ago. Prior to the decision in the instant case it had twice been held valid by the Supreme Court of the State. *Larsen* v. *Rice,* 100 Wash. 642; 171 Pac. 1037; *Spokane Hotel Co.* v. *Younger,* 113 Wash. 359; 194 Pac. 595. The Washington statute is essentially the same as that enacted in Oregon in the same year. Laws of 1913 (Oregon) chap. 62. The validity of the latter act was sustained by the Supreme

Court of Oregon in *Stettler* v. *O'Hara,* 69 Ore. 519; 139 Pac. 743, and *Simpson* v. *O'Hara,* 70 Ore. 261; 141 Pac. 158. These cases, after reargument, were affirmed here by an equally divided court, in 1917. 243 U.S. 629. The law of Oregon thus continued in effect. The District of Columbia Minimum Wage Law (40 Stat. 960) was enacted in 1918. The statute was sustained by the Supreme Court of the District in the *Adkins* case. Upon appeal the Court of Appeals of the District first affirmed that ruling but on rehearing reversed it and the case came before this Court in 1923. The judgment of the Court of Appeals holding the Act invalid was affirmed, but with Chief Justice Taft, Mr. Justice Holmes and Mr. Justice Sanford dissenting, and Mr. Justice Brandeis taking no part. The dissenting opinions took the ground that the decision was at variance with the principles which this Court had frequently announced and applied. In 1925 and 1927, the similar minimum wage statutes of Arizona and Arkansas were held invalid upon the authority of the *Adkins* case. The Justices who had dissented in that case bowed to the ruling and Mr. Justice Brandeis dissented. *Murphy* v. *Sardell,* 269 U.S. 530; *Donham* v. *West-Nelson Co.,* 273 U.S. 657. The question did not come before us again until the last term in the *Morehead* case, as already noted. In that case, briefs supporting the New York statute were submitted by the States of Ohio, Connecticut, Illinois, Massachusetts, New Hampshire, New Jersey and Rhode Island. 298 U.S., p. 604, *note.* Throughout this entire period the Washington statute now under consideration has been in force.

The principle which must control our decision is not in doubt. The constitutional provision invoked is the due process clause of the Fourteenth Amendment governing the States, as the due process clause invoked in the *Adkins* case governed Congress. In each case the violation alleged by those attacking minimum wage regulation for women is deprivation of freedom of contract. What is this freedom? The Constitution does not speak of freedom of contract. It speaks of liberty and prohibits the deprivation of liberty without due process of law. In prohibiting that deprivation the Constitution does not recognize an absolute and uncontrollable liberty. Liberty in each of its phases has its history and connotation. But the liberty safeguarded is liberty in a social organization which requires the protection of law against the evils which menace the health, safety, morals and welfare of the people. Liberty under the Constitution is thus necessarily subject to the restraints of due process, and regulation which is reasonable in relation to its subject and is adopted in the interests of the community is due process.

This essential limitation of liberty in general governs freedom of contract in particular. More than twenty-five years ago we set forth the applicable principle in these words, after referring to the cases where the liberty guaranteed by the Fourteenth Amendment had been broadly described:[1]

"But it was recognized in the cases cited, as in many others, that freedom of contract is a qualified and not an absolute right. There is no absolute freedom to do as one wills or to contract as one chooses. The guaranty of liberty does not withdraw from legislative supervision that wide department of activity which consists of the making of contracts, or deny to government the power to provide restrictive safeguards. Liberty implies the absence of arbitrary restraint, not immunity from reasonable regulations and prohibitions imposed in the interests of the community." *Chicago, B. & Q. R. Co.* v. *McGuire,* 219 U.S. 549, 567.

This power under the Constitution to restrict freedom of contract has had many illustrations.[2] That it may be exercised in

[1] Allgeyer *v.* Louisiana, *165 U.S. 578;* Lochner *v.* New York, *198 U.S. 45;* Adair *v.* United States, *208 U.S. 161.*

[2] Munn *v.* Illinois, *94 U.S. 113;* Railroad Commission Cases, *116 U.S. 307;* Willcox *v.* Consolidated Gas Co., *212 U.S. 19;* Atkin *v.* Kansas, *191 U.S. 207;* Mugler *v.* Kansas, *123 U.S. 623;* Crowley *v.* Christensen, *137 U.S. 86;* Gundling *v.* Chicago, *177 U.S. 183;* Booth *v.* Illinois, *184 U.S. 425;* Schmidinger *v.* Chicago, *226 U.S. 578;* Armour & Co. *v.* North Dakota, *240 U.S. 510;* National Fire Insurance Co. *v.* Wanberg, *260 U.S. 71;* Radice *v.* New York, *264 U.S. 292;* Yeiser *v.* Dysart, *267 U.S. 540;* Liberty Warehouse Co. *v.* Burley Tobacco Growers' Assn., *276 U.S. 71, 97;* Highland *v.* Russell Car Co., *279 U.S. 253, 261;* O'Gorman & Young *v.* Hartford Insurance Co., *282 U.S. 249, 251;* Hardware Dealers Insurance Co. *v.* Glidden Co., *284 U.S. 151, 157;* Packer Corp. *v.* Utah, *285 U.S. 95, 111;* Stephenson *v.* Binford, *287 U.S. 251, 274;* Hartford Accident Co. *v.* Nelson Mfg. Co., *291 U.S. 352, 360;* Petersen Baking Co. *v.* Bryan, *290 U.S. 570;* Nebbia *v.* New York, *291 U.S. 502, 527–529.*

the public interest with respect to contracts between employer and employee is undeniable. Thus statutes have been sustained limiting employment in underground mines and smelters to eight hours a day (*Holden* v. *Hardy,* 169 U.S. 366); in requiring redemption in cash of store orders or other evidences of indebtedness issued in the payment of wages (*Knoxville Iron Co.* v. *Harbison,* 183 U.S. 13); in forbidding the payment of seamen's wages in advance (*Patterson* v. *Bark Eudora,* 190 U.S. 169); in making it unlawful to contract to pay miners employed at quantity rates upon the basis of screened coal instead of the weight of the coal as originally produced in the mine (*McLean* v. *Arkansas,* 211 U.S. 539); in prohibiting contracts limiting liability for injuries to employees (*Chicago, B. & Q. R. Co.* v. *McGuire, supra*); in limiting hours of work of employees in manufacturing establishments (*Bunting* v. *Oregon,* 243 U.S. 426); and in maintaining workmen's compensation laws (*New York Central R. Co.* v. *White,* 243 U.S. 188; *Mountain Timber Co.* v. *Washington,* 243 U.S. 219). In dealing with the relation of employer and employed, the legislature has necessarily a wide field of discretion in order that there may be suitable protection of health and safety, and that peace and good order may be promoted through regulations designed to insure wholesome conditions of work and freedom from oppression. *Chicago, B. & Q. R. Co.* v. *McGuire, supra,* p. 570.

The point that has been strongly stressed that adult employees should be deemed competent to make their own contracts was decisively met nearly forty years ago in *Holden* v. *Hardy, supra,* where we pointed out the inequality in the footing of the parties. We said (*Id.,* 397):

"The legislature has also recognized the fact, which the experience of legislators in many States has corroborated, that the proprietors of these establishments and their operatives do not stand upon an equality, and that their interests are, to a certain extent, conflicting. The former naturally desire to obtain as much labor as possible from their employees, while the latter are often induced by the fear of discharge to conform to regulations which their judgment, fairly exercised, would pronounce to be detrimental to their health or strength. In other words, the proprietors lay down the rules and the laborers are practically constrained to obey them. In such cases self-interest is often an unsafe guide, and the legislature may properly interpose its authority."

And we added that the fact "that both parties are of full age and competent to contract does not necessarily deprive the State of the power to interfere where the parties do not stand upon an equality, or where the public health demands that one party to the contract shall be protected against himself." "The State still retains an interest in his welfare, however reckless he may be. The whole is no greater than the sum of all the parts, and when the individual health, safety and welfare are sacrificed or neglected, the State must suffer."

It is manifest that this established principle is peculiarly applicable in relation to the employment of women in whose protection the State has a special interest. That phase of the subject received elaborate consideration in *Muller* v. *Oregon* (1908), 208 U.S. 412, where the constitutional authority of the State to limit the working hours of women was sustained. We emphasized the consideration that "woman's physical structure and the performance of maternal functions place her at a disadvantage in the struggle for subsistence" and that her physical well being "becomes an object of public interest and care in order to preserve the strength and vigor of the race." We emphasized the need of protecting women against oppression despite her possession of contractual rights. We said that "though limitations upon personal and contractual rights may be removed by legislation, there is that in her disposition and habits of life which will operate against a full assertion of those rights. She will still be where some legislation to protect her seems necessary to secure a real equality of right." Hence she was "properly placed in a class by herself, and legislation designed for her protection may be sustained even when like legislation is not necessary for men and could not be sustained." We concluded that the limitations which the statute there in question "placed upon her contractual powers, upon her right to agree with her employer as to the time she shall labor" were "not imposed solely for her benefit, but also largely for the benefit of all." Again, in *Quong Wing* v. *Kirkendall,* 223 U.S. 59, 63, in referring to a differentiation with respect to the employment of women, we said that the Fourteenth Amendment did not interfere with state power by creating a "fictitious equality." We referred to recognized classifications on the basis of sex with regard to hours of work and in other matters, and we observed that the particular points at which that difference shall be enforced by legislation were largely in the power of the State. In later rulings this Court sustained the regulation of hours of work of women employees in *Riley* v. *Massachusetts,* 232 U.S. 671 (factories), *Miller* v. *Wilson,* 236 U.S. 373 (hotels), and *Bosley* v. *McLaughlin,* 236 U.S. 385 (hospitals).

This array of precedents and the principles they applied were thought by the dissenting Justices in the *Adkins* case to demand that the minimum wage statute be sustained. The validity of the distinction made by the Court between a minimum wage and a maximum of hours in limiting liberty of contract was especially challenged. 261 U.S., p. 564. That challenge persists and is without any satisfactory answer. As Chief Justice Taft observed: "In absolute freedom of contract the one term is as important as the other, for both enter equally into the consideration given and received, a restriction as to the one is not greater in essence than the other and is of the same kind. One is the multiplier and the other the multiplicand." And Mr. Justice Holmes, while recognizing that "the distinctions of the law are distinctions of degree," could "perceive no difference in the kind or degree of interference with liberty, the only matter with which we have any concern, between the one case and the other. The bargain is equally affected whichever half you regulate." *Id.,* p. 569.

One of the points which was pressed by the Court in supporting its ruling in the *Adkins* case was that the standard set up by the District of Columbia Act did not take appropriate account of the value of the services rendered. In the *Morehead* case, the minority thought that the New York statute had met that point in its definition of a "fair wage" and that it accordingly presented a distinguishable feature which the Court could recognize within the limits which the *Morehead* petition for certiorari was deemed to present. The Court, however, did not take that view and the New York Act was held to be essentially the same as that for the District of Columbia. The statute now before us is like the latter, but we are unable to conclude that in its minimum wage requirement the State has passed beyond the boundary of its broad protective power.

The minimum wage to be paid under the Washington statute is fixed after full consideration by representatives of employers, employees and the public. It may be assumed that the minimum wage is fixed in consideration of the services that are performed in the particular occupations under normal conditions. Provision is made for special licenses at less wages in the case of women who are incapable of full service. The statement of Mr. Justice Holmes in the *Adkins* case is pertinent: "This statute does not compel anybody to pay anything. It simply forbids employment at rates below those fixed as the minimum requirement of health and right living. It is safe to assume that women will not be employed at even the lowest wages allowed unless they earn them, or unless the employer's business can sustain the burden. In short the law in its character and operation is like hundreds of so-called police laws that have been upheld." 261 U.S., p. 570. And Chief Justice Taft forcibly pointed out the consideration which is basic in a statute of this character: "Legislatures which adopt a requirement of maximum hours or minimum wages may be presumed to believe that when sweating employers are prevented from paying unduly low wages by positive law they will continue their business, abating that part of their profits, which were wrung from the necessities of their employees, and will concede the better terms required by the law; and that while in individual cases hardship may result, the restriction will enure to the benefit of the general class of employees in whose interest the law is passed and so to that of the community at large." *Id.,* p. 563.

We think that the views thus expressed are sound and that the decision in the *Adkins* case was a departure from the true application of the principles governing the regulation by the State of the relation of employer and employed. Those principles have been reënforced by our subsequent decisions. Thus in *Radice* v. *New York,* 264 U.S. 292, we sustained the New York statute which restricted the employment of women in restaurants at night. In *O'Gorman & Young* v. *Hartford Fire Insurance Co.,* 282 U.S. 251, which upheld an act regulating the commissions of insurance agents, we pointed to the presumption of the constitutionality of a statute dealing with a subject within the scope of the police power and to the absence of any factual foundation of record for deciding that the limits of power had been transcended. In *Nebbia* v. *New York,* 291 U.S. 502, dealing with the New York statute providing for minimum prices for milk, the general subject of the regulation of the use of private property and of the making of private contracts received an exhaustive examination and we again declared that if such laws "have a reasonable relation to a proper legislative purpose, and are neither arbitrary nor discriminatory, the requirements of due process are satisfied"; that "with the wisdom of the policy adopted, with the adequacy or practicability of the law enacted to forward it, the courts are both incompetent and unauthorized to deal"; that "times without number we have said that the legislature is primarily the judge of the necessity of such an enactment, that every possible presumption is in favor of its validity, and that though the court may hold views inconsistent with the wisdom of the law, it may not be annulled unless palpably in excess of legislative power." *Id.*, pp. 537, 538.

With full recognition of the earnestness and vigor which characterize the prevailing opinion in the *Adkins* case, we find it impossible to reconcile that ruling with these well-considered declarations. What can be closer to the public interest than the health of women and their protection from unscrupulous and overreaching employers? And if the protection of women is a legitimate end of the exercise of state power, how can it be said that the requirement of the payment of a minimum wage fairly fixed in order to meet the very necessities of existence is not an admissible means to that end? The legislature of the State was clearly entitled to consider the situation of women in employment, the fact that they are in the class receiving the least pay, that their bargaining power is relatively weak, and that they are the ready victims of those who would take advantage of their necessitous circumstances. The legislature was entitled to adopt measures to reduce the evils of the "sweating system," the exploiting of workers at wages so low as to be insufficient to meet the bare cost of living, thus making their very helplessness the occasion of a most injurious competition. The legislature had the right to consider that its minimum wage requirements would be an important aid in carrying out its policy of protection. The adoption of similar requirements by many States evidences a deepseated conviction both as to the presence of the evil and as to the means adapted to check it. Legislative response to that conviction cannot be regarded as arbitrary or capricious, and that is all we have to decide. Even if the wisdom of the policy be regarded as debatable and its effects uncertain, still the legislature is entitled to its judgment.

There is an additional and compelling consideration which recent economic experience has brought into a strong light. The exploitation of a class of workers who are in an unequal position with respect to bargaining power and are thus relatively defenceless against the denial of a living wage is not only detrimental to their health and well being but casts a direct burden for their support upon the community. What these workers lose in wages the taxpayers are called upon to pay. The bare cost of living must be met. We may take judicial notice of the unparalleled demands for relief which arose during the recent period of depression and still continue to an alarming extent despite the degree of economic recovery which has been achieved. It is unnecessary to cite official statistics to establish what is of common knowledge through the length and breadth of the land. While in the instant case no factual brief has been presented, there is no reason to doubt that the State of Washington has encountered the same social problem that is present elsewhere. The community is not bound to provide what is in effect a subsidy for unconscionable employers. The community may direct its law-making power to correct the abuse which springs from their selfish disregard of the public interest. The argument that the legislation in question constitutes an arbitrary discrimination, because it does not extend to men, is unavailing. This Court has frequently held that the legislative authority, acting within its proper field, is not bound to extend its regulation to all cases which it might possibly reach. The legislature "is free to recognize degrees of harm and it may confine its restrictions to those classes of cases where the need is deemed to be clearest." If "the law presumably hits the evil where it is most felt, it is not to be overthrown because there are other instances to which it might have been applied." There is no "doctrinaire requirement" that the legislation should be couched in all embracing terms. *Carroll* v. *Greenwich Insurance Co.,* 199 U.S. 401, 411; *Patsone* v. *Pennsylvania,* 232 U.S. 138, 144; *Keokee Coke Co.* v. *Taylor,* 234 U.S. 224, 227; *Sproles* v. *Binford,* 286 U.S. 374, 396; *Semler* v. *Oregon Board,* 294 U.S. 608, 610, 611. This familiar principle has repeatedly been applied to legislation which singles out women, and particular classes of women, in the exercise of the State's protective power. *Miller* v. *Wilson, supra,* p. 384; *Bosley* v. *McLaughlin, supra,* pp. 394, 395; *Radice* v. *New York, supra,* pp. 295–298. Their relative need in the presence of the evil, no less than the existence of the evil itself, is a matter for the legislative judgment.

Our conclusion is that the case of *Adkins* v. *Children's Hospital, supra,* should be, and it is, overruled. The judgment of the Supreme Court of the State of Washington is

Affirmed.

BAILEY v. ALABAMA, 219 U.S. 219 (1911)

This case posed sharply the issue (to come before the Court again and again) whether the Civil War amendments, in this instance the Thirteenth barring "involuntary servitude," were to be broadly construed to protect the freedom (and equality) of the Negro or more narrowly to permit ingenious forms of evasion or circumvention by state legislation. Under the statute in question, failure to perform a contract to labor, for which money had been paid in advance, without just cause and without repayment, constituted *prima facie* evidence of fraud punishable as a crime. Mr. Justice Hughes, speaking for a majority of the Court, concluded that the statute, peculiarly effective "against the poor and ignorant," was essentially designed to enable employers by threat of criminal prosecution to compel laborers to work off their debts and, therefore, in light of practical realities, imposed a form of involuntary servitude.

MR. JUSTICE HUGHES delivered the opinion of the court.

This is a writ of error to review a judgment of the Supreme Court of the State of Alabama, affirming a judgment of conviction in the Montgomery City Court. The statute, upon which the conviction was based, is assailed as in violation of the Fourteenth Amendment of the Constitution of the United States upon the ground that it deprived the plaintiff in error of his liberty without due process of law and denied him the equal protection of the laws, and also of the Thirteenth Amendment and of the act of Congress providing for the enforcement of that Amendment, in that the effect of the statute is to enforce involuntary servitude by compelling personal service in liquidation of a debt.

The statute in question is § 4730 of the Code of Alabama of 1896, as amended in 1903 and 1907. The section of the Code as it stood before the amendments provided that any person who with intent to injure or defraud his employer entered into a written contract for service and thereby obtained from his employer money or other personal property, and with like intent and without just cause, and without refunding the money or paying for the property refused to perform the service, should be punished as if he had stolen it. In 1903 (Gen. Acts, Ala., 1903, p. 345) the section was amended so as to make the refusal or failure to perform the service, or to refund the money or pay for the property, without just cause, *prima facie* evidence of the intent to injure or defraud. This amendment was enlarged by that of 1907. Gen. Acts, Ala., 1907, p. 636. The section, thus amended, reads as follows:

"Any person, who with intent to injure or defraud his employer, enters into a contract in writing for the performance of any act of service, and thereby obtains money or other personal property from such employer, and with like intent, and without just cause, and without refunding such money, or paying for such property, refuses or fails to perform such act or service, must on conviction be punished by a fine in double the damage suffered by the injured party, but not more than $300, one-half of said fine to go to the county and one-half to the party injured; and any person, who with intent to injure or defraud his landlord, enters into any contract in writing for the rent of land, and thereby obtains any money or other personal property from such landlord, and with like intent, without just cause, and without refunding such money, or paying for such property, refuses or fails to cultivate such land, or to comply with his contract relative thereto, must on conviction be punished by fine in double the damage suffered by the injured party, but not more than $300, one-half of said fine to go to the county and one-half to the party injured. And the refusal or failure of any person, who enters into such contract, to perform such act or service or to cultivate such land, or refund such money, or pay for such property without just cause shall be prima facie evidence of the intent to injure his employer or landlord or defraud him. That all laws and parts of laws in conflict with the provisions hereof be and the same are hereby repealed."

There is also a rule of evidence enforced by the courts of Alabama which must be regarded as having the same effect as if read into the statute itself, that the accused, for the purpose of rebutting the statutory presumption, shall not be allowed to testify "as to his uncommunicated motives, purpose or intention." *Bailey* v. *The State,* 161 Alabama, 77, 78.

Bailey, the plaintiff in error, was committed for detention on the charge of obtaining fifteen dollars under a contract in writing with intent to injure or defraud his employer. He sued out a writ of *habeas corpus* challenging the validity of the statute. His discharge was refused and the Supreme Court of the State affirmed the order, holding the statute to be constitutional. 158 Alabama, 18. On writ of error from this court it was held that the case was brought here prematurely, and the questions now presented were expressly reserved. *Bailey* v. *Alabama,* 211 U.S. 452.

Having failed to obtain his release on *habeas corpus,* Bailey was indicted on the following charge:

"The Grand Jury of said County charge, that before the finding of this indictment Alonzo Bailey with intent to injure or defraud his employer The Riverside Company, a corporation, entered into a written contract to perform labor or services for The Riverside Company, a corporation and obtained thereby the sum of Fifteen Dollars from the said The Riverside Company, and afterwards with like intent, and without just cause, failed or refused to perform such labor or services or to refund such money against the peace and dignity of the State of Alabama."

Motion to quash and a demurrer to the indictment were overruled. Upon the trial the following facts appeared: On December 26, 1907, Bailey entered into a written contract with the Riverside Company, which provided:

"That I, Lonzo Bailey for and in consideration of the sum of Fifteen Dollars in money, this day in hand paid to me by said The Riverside Co., the receipt whereof, I do hereby acknowledge, I, the said Lonzo Bailey do hereby consent, contract and agree to work and labor for the said Riverside Co. as a farm hand on their Scotts Bend Place in Montgomery County, Alabama, from the 30 day of Dec. 1907, to the 30 day of Dec. 1908, at and for the sum of $12.00 per month.

"And the said Lonzo Bailey agrees to render respectful and faithful service to the said The Riverside Co. and to perform diligently and actively all work pertaining to such employment, in accordance with the instructions of the said The Riverside Co., or ag't.

"And the said The Riverside Co. in consideration of the agreement above mentioned of the said Lonzo Bailey hereby employs the said Lonzo Bailey as such farm hand for the time above set out, and agrees to pay the said Lonzo Bailey the sum of $10.75 per month."

The manager of the employing company testified that at the time of entering into this contract there were present only the witness and Bailey and that the latter then obtained from the company the sum of fifteen dollars; that Bailey worked under the contract throughout the month of January and for three or four days in February, 1908, and then, "without just cause and without refunding the money, ceased to work for said Riverside Company, and has not since that time performed any service for said Company in accordance with or under said contract, and has refused and failed to perform any further service thereunder, and has, without just cause, refused and failed to refund said fifteen dollars." He also testified, in response to a question from the attorney for the defendant and against the objection of the State, that Bailey was a negro. No other evidence was introduced.

The court, after defining the crime in the language of the statute, charged the jury, in accordance with its terms, as follows:

"And the refusal of any person who enters into such contract to perform such act or service, or refund such money, or pay for such property, without just cause, shall be prima facie evidence of the intent to injure his employer, or to defraud him."

Bailey excepted to these instructions, and requested the court to instruct the jury that the statute, and the provision creating the presumption, were invalid, and further that "the refusal or failure of the defendant to perform the service alleged in the indictment, or to refund the money obtained from The Riverside Co. under the contract between it and the defendant, without cause, does not of itself make out a prima facie case of the defendant's intent to injure or defraud said Riverside Company."

The court refused these instructions and Bailey took exception.

The jury found the accused guilty, fixed the damages sustained by the injured party at fifteen dollars, and assessed a fine of thirty dollars. Thereupon Bailey was sentenced by the court to pay the fine of thirty dollars and the costs, and in default thereof to hard labor "for twenty days in lieu of said fine and one hundred and sixteen days on account of said costs."

On appeal to the Supreme Court of the State the constitutionality of the statute was again upheld and the judgment affirmed. 161 Alabama, 75.

We at once dismiss from consideration the fact that the plaintiff in error is a black man. While the action of a State through its officers charged with the administration of a law, fair in appearance, may be of such a character as to constitute a denial of the equal protection of the laws (*Yick Wo* v. *Hopkins,* 118 U.S. 356, 373), such a conclusion is here neither required nor justified. The statute, on its face, makes no racial discrimination, and the record fails to show its existence in fact. No question of a sectional character is presented, and we may view the legislation in the same manner as if it had been enacted in New York or in Idaho. Opportunities for coercion and oppression, in varying circumstances, exist in all parts of the Union, and the citizens of all the States are interested in the maintenance of the constitutional guarantees, the consideration of which is here involved.

Prior to the amendment of the year 1903, enlarged in 1907, the statute did not make the mere breach of the contract, under which the employé had obtained from his employer money which was not refunded or property which was not paid for, a crime. The essential ingredient of the offense was the intent of the accused to injure or defraud. To justify conviction, it was necessary that this intent should be established by competent evidence, aided only by such inferences as might logically be derived from the facts proved, and should not be the subject of mere surmise or arbitrary assumption.

This was the construction which the Supreme Court of Alabama placed upon the statute, as it then stood, in *Ex parte Riley,* 94 Alabama, 82. In that case the court said (pp. 83, 84):

"The ingredients of this statutory offense are: (1) a contract in writing by the accused for the performance of any act or service; (2) an intent on the part of the accused, when he entered into the contract, to injure or defraud his employer; (3) the obtaining by the accused of money or other personal property from such employer by means of such contract entered into with such intent; and (4) the refusal by the accused, with like intent, and without just cause, and without refunding such money, or paying for such property, to perform such act or service. This statute by no means provides that a person who has entered into a written contract for the performance of services, under which he has obtained money or other personal property, is punishable as if he had stolen such money or other personal property, upon his refusal to perform the contract, without refunding the money or paying for the property. A mere breach of a contract is not by the statute made a crime. The criminal feature of the transaction is wanting unless the accused entered into the contract with intent to injure or defraud his employer, and unless his refusal to perform was with like intent and without just cause. That there was an intent to injure or defraud the employer, both when the contract was entered into and when the accused refused performance, are facts which must be shown by the evidence. As the intent is the design, purpose, resolve or determination in the mind of the accused, it can rarely be proved by direct evidence, but must be ascertained by means of inferences from the facts and circumstances developed by the proof. *Carlisle* v. *The State,* 76 Alabama, 75; *Mack* v. *The State,* 63 Alabama, 136. In the absence, however, of evidence from which such inferences may be drawn, the jury are not justified in indulging in mere unsupported conjectures, speculations or suspicions as to intentions which were not disclosed by any visible or tangible act, expression or circumstance.—*Green* v. *The State,* 68 Alabama, 539." See also *Dor-*

sey v. *The State,* 111 Alabama, 40; *McIntosh* v. *The State,* 117 Alabama, 128.

We pass then to the consideration of the amendment, through the operation of which under the charge of the trial court this conviction was obtained. No longer was it necessary for the prosecution to comply with the rule of the *Riley case* (*supra*) in order to establish the intent to injure or defraud which, as the court said, constituted the gist of the offense. It was "the difficulty in proving the intent, made patent by that decision" which "suggested the amendment of 1903." *Bailey* v. *The State,* 158 Alabama, p. 25. By this amendment it was provided, in substance, that the refusal or failure to perform the service contracted for, or to refund the money obtained, without just cause, should be *prima facie* evidence of the intent to injure or defraud.

But the refusal or failure to perform the service, without just cause, constitutes the breach of the contract. The justice of the grounds of refusal or failure must, of course, be determined by the contractual obligation assumed. Whatever the reason for leaving the service, if, judged by the terms of the contract, it is insufficient in law, it is not "just cause." The money received and repayable, nothing more being shown, constitutes a mere debt. The asserted difficulty of proving the intent to injure or defraud is thus made the occasion for dispensing with such proof, so far as the *prima facie* case is concerned. And the mere breach of a contract for personal service, coupled with the mere failure to pay a debt which was to be liquidated in the course of such service, is made sufficient to warrant a conviction.

It is no answer to say that the jury must find, and here found, that a fraudulent intent existed. The jury by their verdict cannot add to the facts before them. If nothing be shown but a mere breach of a contract of service and a mere failure to pay a debt, the jury have nothing else to go upon, and the evidence becomes nothing more because of their finding. Had it not been for this statutory presumption, supplied by the amendment, no one would be heard to say that Bailey could have been convicted.

Prima facie evidence is sufficient evidence to outweigh the presumption of innocence and if not met by opposing evidence to support a verdict of guilty. "It is such as, in judgment of law, is sufficient to establish the fact; and, if not rebutted, remains sufficient for the purpose." *Kelly* v. *Jackson,* 6 Pet. 632.

We are not impressed with the argument that the Supreme Court of Alabama has construed the amendment to mean that the jury is not controlled by the presumption, if unrebutted, and still may find the accused not guilty. That court, in its opinion, said: "Again, it must be borne in mind that the rule of evidence fixed by the statute does not make it the duty of the jury to convict on the evidence referred to in the enactment, if unrebutted, whether satisfied thereby of the guilt of the accused beyond a reasonable doubt or not. On the contrary, with such evidence before them, the jury are still left free to find the accused guilty or not guilty, according as they may be satisfied of his guilt or not, by the whole evidence." 161 Alabama, 78.

But the controlling construction of the statute is the affirmance of this judgment of conviction. It is not sufficient to declare that the statute does not make it the *duty* of the jury to convict, where there is no other evidence but the breach of the contract and the failure to pay the debt. The point is that, in such a case, the statute *authorizes* the jury to convict. It is not enough to say that the jury may not accept that evidence as alone sufficient; for the jury may accept it, and they have the express warrant of the statute to accept it as a basis for their verdict. And it is in this light that the validity of the statute must be determined.

It is urged that the time and circumstances of the departure from service may be such as to raise not only an inference, but a strong inference, of fraudulent intent. There was no need to create a statutory presumption and it was not created for such a case. Where circumstances are shown permitting a fair inference of fraudulent purpose, the case falls within the rule of *Ex parte Riley* (*supra*) which governed prosecutions under the statute before the amendment was made. The "difficulty," which admittedly the amendment was intended to surmount, did not exist where natural inferences sufficed. Plainly the object of the statute was to hit cases which were destitute of such inferences, and to provide that the mere breach of the contract and the mere failure to pay the debt might do duty in their absence.

While in considering the natural operation and effect of the statute, as amended, we are not limited to the particular facts of the case at the bar, they present an illuminating illustration. We may briefly restate them. Bailey made a contract to work for a year at $12 a month. He received $15 and he was to work this out, being entitled monthly only to $10.75 of his wages. No one was present when he made the contract but himself and the manager of the employing company. There is not a particle of evidence of any circumstance indicating that he made the contract or received the money with any intent to injure or defraud his employer. On the contrary, he actually worked for upwards of a month. His motive in leaving does not appear, the only showing being that it was without legal excuse and that he did not repay the money received. For this he is sentenced to a fine of $30 and to imprisonment at hard labor in default of the payment of the fine and costs for 136 days. Was not the case the same in effect as if the statute had made it a criminal act to leave the service without just cause and without liquidating the debt? To say that he has been found guilty of an intent to injure or defraud his employer, and not merely for breaking his contract and not paying his debt, is a distinction without a difference to Bailey.

Consider the situation of the accused under this statutory presumption. If at the outset nothing took place but the making of the contract and the receipt of the money, he could show nothing else. If there was no legal justification for his leaving his employment, he could show none. If he had not paid the debt there was nothing to be said as to that. The law of the State did not permit him to testify that he did not intend to injure or defraud. Unless he were fortunate enough to be able to command evidence of circumstances affirmatively showing good faith, he was helpless. He stood, stripped by the statute of the presumption of innocence, and exposed to conviction for fraud upon evidence only of breach of contract and failure to pay.

It is said that we may assume that a fair jury would convict only where the circumstances sufficiently indicated a fraudulent intent. Why should this be assumed in the face of the statute and upon this record? In the present case the jury did convict, although there is an absence of evidence sufficient to establish fraud under the familiar rule that fraud will not be presumed, and the obvious explanation of the verdict is that the trial court in accordance with the statute charged the jury that refusal to perform the service, or to repay the money, without just cause, constituted *prima facie* evidence of the commission of the offense which the statute defined. That is, the jury were told in effect that the evidence, under the statutory rule, was sufficient, and hence they treated it as such. There is no basis for an assumption that the jury would have acted differently if Bailey had worked for three months, or six months, or nine months, if in fact his debt had not been paid. The normal assumption is that the jury will follow the statute and, acting in accordance with the authority it confers, will accept as sufficient what the statute expressly so describes.

It may further be observed that under the statute there is no punishment for the alleged fraud if the service is performed or the money refunded. If the service is rendered in liquidation of the debt there is no punishment, and if it is not rendered and the money is not refunded that fact alone is sufficient for conviction. By a statute passed by the legislature of Alabama in 1901 it was made a misdemeanor for any person, who had made a written contract to labor for or serve another for any given time, to leave the service before the expiration of the contract and without the consent of the employer, and to make a second contract of similar nature with another person without giving the second employer notice of the existence of the first contract. This was held unconstitutional upon the ground that it interfered with freedom of contract. *Toney* v. *The State,* 141 Alabama, 120. But, judging it by its necessary operation and obvious effect, the fundamental purpose plainly was to compel, under the sanction of the criminal law, the enforcement of the contract for personal service, and the same purpose, tested by like criteria, breathes despite its different phraseology through the amendments of 1903 and 1907 of the statute here in question.

We cannot escape the conclusion that, although the statute in terms is to punish fraud, still its natural and inevitable effect is to expose to conviction for crime those who simply fail or refuse to perform contracts for personal service in liquidation of a debt, and judging its purpose by its effect that it seeks in this way to provide the means of compulsion through which performance of such service may be secured. The question is whether such a statute is constitutional.

This court has frequently recognized the general power of every legislature to prescribe the evidence which shall be received, and the effect of the evidence in the courts of its own government. *Fong Yue Ting* v. *United States,* 149 U.S. 698, 749. In the exercise of this power numerous statutes have been enacted providing that proof of one fact shall be *prima facie* evidence of the main fact in issue; and where the inference is not purely arbitrary and there is a rational relation between the two facts, and the accused is not deprived of a proper opportunity to submit all the facts bearing upon the issue, it has been held that such statutes do not violate the requirements of due process of law. *Adams* v. *New York,* 192 U.S. 585; *Mobile, Jackson & Kansas City Railroad Co.* v. *Turnipseed,* decided December 19, 1910, *ante,* p. 35.

The latest expression upon this point is found in the case last cited, where the court, by Mr. Justice Lurton, said: "That a legislative presumption of one fact from evidence of another may not constitute a denial of due process of law or a denial of the equal protection of the law it is only essential that there shall be some rational connection between the fact proved and the ultimate fact presumed, and that the inference of one fact from proof of another shall not be so unreasonable as to be a purely arbitrary mandate. So, also, it must not, under guise of regulating the presentation of evidence, operate to preclude the party from the right to present his defense to the main fact thus presumed. If a legislative provision not unreasonable in itself prescribing a rule of evidence, in either criminal or civil cases, does not shut out from the party affected a reasonable opportunity to submit to the jury in his defense all of the facts bearing upon the issue, there is no ground for holding that due process of law has been denied him."

In this class of cases where the entire subject-matter of the legislation is otherwise within state control, the question has been whether the prescribed rule of evidence interferes with the guaranteed equality before the law or violates those fundamental rights and immutable principles of justice which are embraced within the conception of due process of law. But where the conduct or fact, the existence of which is made the basis of the statutory presumption, itself falls within the scope of a provision of the Federal Constitution, a further question arises. It is apparent that a constitutional prohibition cannot be transgressed indirectly by the creation of a statutory presumption any more than it can be violated by direct enactment. The power to create presumptions is not a means of escape from constitutional restrictions. And the State may not in this way interfere with matters withdrawn from its authority by the Federal Constitution or subject an accused to conviction for conduct which it is powerless to proscribe.

In the present case it is urged that the statute as amended, through the operation of the presumption for which it provides, violates the Thirteenth Amendment of the Constitution of the United States and the act of Congress passed for its enforcement.

The Thirteenth Amendment provides:

"SECTION 1. Neither slavery nor involuntary servitude, except as a punishment for crime whereof the party shall have been duly convicted, shall exist within the United States, or any place subject to their jurisdiction.

"SECTION 2. Congress shall have power to enforce this article by appropriate legislation."

Pursuant to the authority thus conferred, Congress passed the act of March 2, 1867, c. 187, 14 Stat. 546, the provisions of which are now found in §§ 1990 and 5526 of the Revised Statutes, as follows:

"SEC. 1990. The holding of any person to service or labor under the system known as peonage is abolished and forever prohibited in the Territory of New Mexico, or in any other Territory or State of the United States; and all acts, laws, resolutions, orders, regulations, or usages of the Territory of New Mexico, or of any other Territory or State, which have heretofore established, maintained, or enforced, or by virtue of which any attempt shall hereafter be made to establish, maintain, or enforce, directly or indirectly, the voluntary or involuntary service or labor of any persons as peons, in liquidation of any debt or obligation, or otherwise, are declared null and void."

"SEC. 5526. Every person who holds, arrests, returns, or causes to be held, arrested, or returned, or in any manner aids in the arrest or return of any person to a condition of peonage, shall be punished by a fine of not less than one thousand nor more than five thousand dollars, or by imprisonment not less than one year nor more than five years, or by both."

The language of the Thirteenth Amendment was not new. It reproduced the historic words of the ordinance of 1787 for the government of the Northwest Territory and gave them unrestricted application within the United States and all places subject to their jurisdiction. While the immediate concern was with African slavery, the Amendment was not limited to that. It was a charter of universal civil freedom for all persons, of whatever race, color or estate, under the flag.

The words involuntary servitude have a "larger meaning than slavery." "It was very well understood that in the form of apprenticeship for long terms, as it had been practiced in the West India Islands, on the abolition of slavery by the English government, or by reducing the slaves to the condition of serfs attached to the plantation, the purpose of the article might have been evaded, if only the word slavery had been used." *Slaughter House Cases,* 16 Wall. p. 69. The plain intention was to abolish slavery of whatever name and form and all its badges and incidents; to render impossible any state of bondage; to make labor free, by prohibiting that control by which the personal service of one man is disposed of or coerced for another's benefit which is the essence of involuntary servitude.

While the Amendment was self-executing, so far as its terms were applicable to any existing condition, Congress was authorized to secure its complete enforcement by appropriate legislation. As was said in the *Civil Rights cases:* "By its own unaided force and effect it abolished slavery, and established universal freedom. Still, legislation may be necessary and proper to meet all the various cases and circumstances to be affected by it, and to prescribe proper modes of redress for its violation in letter or spirit. And such legislation may be primary and direct in its character; for the Amendment is not a mere prohibition of state laws establishing or upholding slavery, but an absolute declaration that slavery or involuntary servitude shall not exist in any part of the United States." 109 U.S. 20.

The act of March 2, 1867 (Rev. Stat., §§ 1990, 5526, *supra*), was a valid exercise of this express authority. *Clyatt* v. *United States,* 197 U.S. 207. It declared that all laws of any State, by virtue of which any attempt should be made "to establish, maintain, or enforce, directly or indirectly, the voluntary or involuntary service or labor of any persons as peons, in liquidation of any debt or obligation, or otherwise," should be null and void.

Peonage is a term descriptive of a condition which has existed in Spanish America, and especially in Mexico. The essence of the thing is compulsory service in payment of a debt. A peon is one who is compelled to work for his creditor until his debt is paid. And in this explicit and comprehensive enactment, Congress was not concerned with mere names or manner of description, or with a particular place or section of the country. It was concerned with a fact, wherever it might exist; with a condition, however named and wherever it might be established, maintained or enforced.

The fact that the debtor contracted to perform the labor which is sought to be compelled does not withdraw the attempted enforcement from the condemnation of the statute. The full intent of the constitutional provision could be defeated with obvious facility if, through the guise of contracts under which advances had been made, debtors could be held to compulsory service. It is the compulsion of the service that the statute inhibits, for when that occurs the condition of servitude is created, which would be not less involuntary because of the original agreement to work out the indebtedness. The contract exposes the debtor to liability for the loss due to the breach, but not to enforced labor. This has been so clearly stated by this court in the case of *Clyatt, supra,* that discussion is unnecessary. The court there said:

"The constitutionality and scope of sections 1990 and 5526 present the first questions for our consideration. They prohibit peonage. What is peonage? It may be defined as a status or condition of compulsory service, based upon the indebtedness of the peon to the master. The basal fact is indebtedness. As said by Judge Benedict, delivering the opinion in *Jaremillo* v. *Romero,* 1 N. Mex. 190, 194: 'One fact existed universally; all were indebted to their masters. This was the cord by which they seemed bound to their masters' service.' Upon this is based a condition of compulsory service. Peonage is sometimes classified as voluntary or involuntary, but this implies simply a difference in the mode of origin, but none in the character of the servitude. The one exists where the debtor voluntarily contracts to enter the service of his creditor. The other is forced upon the debtor by some provision of law. But peonage, however created, is compulsory service, involuntary servitude. The peon can release himself therefrom, it is true, by the payment of the debt, but otherwise the service is enforced. A clear distinction exists between peonage and the voluntary performance of labor or rendering of services in payment of a debt. In the latter case the debtor, though contracting to pay his indebtedness by labor or service, and subject like any other contractor to an action for damages for breach of that contract, can elect at any time to break it, and no law or force compels performance or a continuance of the service. We need not stop to consider any possible limits or exceptional cases, such as the service of a sailor, *Robertson* v. *Baldwin,* 165 U.S. 275, or the obligations of a child to its parents, or of an apprentice to his master, or the power of the legislature to make unlawful and punish criminally an abandonment by an employé of his post of labor in any extreme cases. That which is contemplated by the statute is compulsory service to secure the payment of a debt." 197 U.S. pp. 215, 216.

The act of Congress, nullifying all state laws by which it should be attempted to enforce the "service or labor of any persons as peons, in liquidation of any debt or obligation, or otherwise," necessarily embraces all legislation which seeks to compel the service or labor by making it a crime to refuse or fail to perform it. Such laws would furnish the readiest means of compulsion. The Thirteenth Amendment prohibits involuntary servitude except as punishment for crime. But the exception, allowing full latitude for the enforcement of penal laws, does not destroy the prohibition. It does not permit slavery or involuntary servitude to be established or maintained through the operation of the criminal law by making it a crime to refuse to submit to the one or to render the service which would constitute the other. The State may impose involuntary servitude as a punishment for crime, but it may not compel one man to labor for another in payment of a debt, by punishimg him as a criminal if he does not perform the service or pay the debt.

If the statute in this case had authorized the employing company to seize the debtor and hold him to the service until he paid the fifteen dollars, or had furnished the equivalent in labor, its invalidity would not be questioned. It would be equally clear that the State could not authorize its constabulary to prevent the servant from escaping and to force him to work out his debt. But the State could not avail itself of the sanction of the criminal law to supply the compulsion any more than it could use or authorize the use of physical force. "In contemplation of the law the compulsion to such service by the fear of punishment under a criminal statute is more powerful than any guard which the employer could station." *Ex parte Hollman* (S. Car.), 60 S. E. Rep. 24.

What the State may not do directly it may not do indirectly. If it cannot punish the servant as a criminal for the mere failure or refusal to serve without paying his debt, it is not permitted to accomplish the same result by creating a statutory presumption which upon proof of no other fact exposes him to conviction and punishment. Without imputing any actual motive to oppress, we must consider the natural operation of the statute here in question (*Henderson* v. *Mayor,* 92 U.S. p. 268), and it is apparent that it furnishes a convenient instrument for the coercion which the Constitution and the act of Congress forbid; an instrument of compulsion peculiarly effective as against the poor and the ignorant, its most likely victims. There is no more important concern than to safeguard the freedom of labor upon which alone can enduring prosperity be based. The provisions designed to secure it would soon become a barren form if it were possible to establish a statutory presumption of this sort and to hold over the heads of laborers the threat of punishment for crime, under the name of fraud but merely upon evidence of failure to work out their debts. The act of Congress deprives of effect all legislative measures of any State through which directly or indirectly the prohibited thing, to wit, compulsory service to secure the payment of a debt may be established or maintained; and we conclude that § 4730, as amended, of the Code of Alabama, in so far as it makes the refusal or failure to perform the act or service, without refunding the money or paying for the property received, *prima facie* evidence of the commission of the crime which the section defines, is in conflict with the Thirteenth Amendment and the legislation authorized by that Amendment, and is therefore invalid.

In this view it is unnecessary to consider the contentions which have been made under the Fourteenth Amendment. As the case was given to the jury under instructions which authorized a verdict in accordance with the statutory presumption, and the opposing instructions requested by the accused were refused, the judgment must be reversed.

Reversed and cause remanded for further proceedings not inconsistent with this opinion.

Willis Van Devanter

☆ 1859–1941 ☆

APPOINTED BY

WILLIAM H. TAFT

YEARS ON COURT

1911–1937

Willis Van Devanter

by

DAVID BURNER

WILLIS VAN DEVANTER was born in Marion, Indiana, on April 17, 1859. His great-grandfather had been a gunpowder manufacturer in the American Revolution and his grandfather a captain in the War of 1812; his father Isaac, a lawyer and abolitionist, would be a provost marshal of his Indiana congressional district during the Civil War. Isaac had moved West to Indiana in 1850, and soon after married a local girl, Violetta Spencer. The couple had eight children, of whom Willis was first. He attended the Marion public schools and then went to Indiana Asbury University (later DePauw). He was graduated from this institution with an almost perfect record in history, mathematics, Greek, Latin, and deportment. The illness of Willis' father forced the son to go to work in 1878 after two distinguished years at college. The next year, however, he entered the University of Cincinnati Law School, where he served as librarian and worked with the arrangements committee for commencement ceremonies. Cincinnati was a school of the old style: daily lectures by the six-man faculty, including Deans Rufus King and Jacob Cox, precluded any classroom use of the case system. Only seniors were required to participate in a weekly moot court. Van Devanter worked well under the routine curriculum; upon graduating in 1881 he stood second in a class of sixty-five.

After earning his law degree Willis returned to Marion for three years to practice with his father's firm of Lacey and Van Devanter. In this period, during which he married Dellice Burhans of Michigan, he worked as assistant prosecuting attorney for the twenty-eighth Indiana judicial district. When Van Devanter's father retired, Willis moved with John Lacey to the booming cattle town of Cheyenne, Wyoming, where Lacey had been appointed chief justice of the

DAVID BURNER is Associate Professor of History at the State University of New York, Stony Brook. He is the author of The Politics of Provincialism: The Democratic Party in transition, 1918–1932.

Wyoming territorial supreme court. The twenty-five-year-old Van Devanter, who could have earned a comfortable living in Indiana, preferred the raw and boisterous frontier life and the opportunities it offered him. His quick action, according to a biography of his early years, showed "how much store he placed on the presence of a friend in power." Van Devanter was always good at making important "connections." When he arrived in Cheyenne in July, 1884, it was still a quiet town of nine thousand people. In the surrounding territory could be found cattle-rustlers, horse thieves, contentious cattle barons, and Indians quarreling with white settlers over public lands. As the wilderness disappeared, the need grew for able lawyers to handle increasingly complex disputes on land rights. Cheyenne served his ambitions; it was the capital of the territory, and the cattle business had brought one major railroad to the city and promised more. Van Devanter traveled the territory in stage coaches, bought the back files of Wyoming newspapers, and read avidly such texts as Thomas Cooley's *Constitutional Limitations*. He practiced alone, occasionally with horse thieves as clients, until 1887 when he and Charles N. Potter, an influential Republican, established a firm that soon boasted the Burlington Railroad as a client.

Van Devanter's career in Cheyenne coincided with an important chapter in Wyoming politics. The territory had been organized in 1868 under the auspices of the Union Pacific Railroad. In the 1870's Wyoming suffered a depression; after a period of prosperity in the early eighties as easterners invested in cattle, a new crash occurred in mid-decade. The sporadic course of the economy had its part in keeping territorial politics unsettled. In 1885 Van Devanter offered his support to the territorial governor, Francis E. Warren. Soon to be one of the new state's senators, Warren was a self-made man; a railroad hand after leaving the Union army, then a hardware store owner, he had made his fortune as owner of the Warren Land and Livestock Company. In time, Van Devanter became Warren's right-hand man, and Warren, along with Joseph M. Carey, controlled the Wyoming Republican party. Warren built his political machine for two reasons: to enrich himself and to further the development of Wyoming. In Warren's mind, and at times in fact, these two aims were identical. An effective political adviser, Van Devanter also became an important political figure; for not having to decide policy, he was able to progress in his own ambitions. Loyal and disciplined, he was, in Warren's words, "peculiarly apt and discreet." He also possessed necessary legal knowledge of land policy, irrigation, and government appropriations, which were of legislative concern. In 1892, when Warren ran unsuccessfully for reelection to the Senate, Van Devanter nevertheless excelled as chairman of the Republican state campaign. His methods were sometimes unorthodox. Since the fifteen to twenty thousand voters were spread out across the large state, he paid subsidies to newspapers and concentrated on using the written word to reach the voters, though he also traveled about the state by horseback and buckboard in his party's interests. He seems to have played a dubious role in the Johnson County war, a cattlemen's raid on alleged cattle thieves. In exchange for a character reference, he accepted political support from a Cheyenne gambler who had recently shot his wife's lover. The attitude on unlawful strikes that he would demonstrate during the 1930's as a Supreme Court Justice was foreshadowed in 1893, when through his efforts striking Idaho workers heading into Wyoming in a borrowed locomotive were promptly tossed into jail. In an election eve speech in 1894 he said, "Let one man who has received more and better wages this year than two years ago, let him stand up."

Van Devanter made a creditable record in public service. In 1886, at the age of twenty-seven, he worked on a commission to revise and compile the territorial statutes of Wyoming. He served as chairman of the resolutions committee at the territorial convention of that year. In 1887 and 1888 he was city attorney of Cheyenne, where he helped wage a vigorous campaign against prostitutes. In 1888 he was elected a member of the territorial legislature and was chairman of the judiciary committee. Finally, thanks to Warren's support, in 1889 President Harrison appointed him Chief Justice of the Territorial Supreme Court, although he was only thirty years old. This position was no sinecure; Van Devanter earned only three thousand dollars a year, traveled over the vast state, and spent much of his time on dull local cases. Of a dozen appeals in civil cases he had decided, none was overthrown. After Wyoming became a state in 1890, Van Devanter returned to private practice, which he found more lucrative and interesting. The firm of Lacey and Van Devanter handled Union Pacific Railroad business, including efforts to prevent injured workers from obtaining compensation. In a noteworthy case for the railroad, Van Devanter argued unsuccessfully before the Supreme Court that Wyoming statehood took precedence over various treaties guaranteeing land to Indians in *Ward* v. *Race Horse,* 163 U.S. 504 (1896). Here he helped channel the violence of young pioneers into legal action and at the same time heightened his professional reputation. He was kept quite busy by the Union Pacific. The railroad had been under investigation for many years by Senate and House committees as well as by the Federal Land Office. The charges of criminal activities included fraudulent land surveys of much of Wyoming and of a large portion of Montana, appropriations of coal lands of great value and of land along streams under the Desert Land Act thereby excluding actual settlers. In these years he continued to work for Warren and exerted pressures on the legislature in his behalf.

As the fortunes of the Republican party improved in the mid-1890's, Van Devanter hoped for national office. In the nineties he served as chairman of the Republican State Committee, attended as a delegate the national convention of 1896, and was chosen a member of the Republican National Committee. In 1897 he sought to become Solicitor General under President McKinley; upon failure, he set his sights on being an assistant attorney general entrusted with the preparation and conduct of important Supreme Court cases. But he was forced to accept a less important position with the same title in the Interior Department. He moved to Washington in 1897 and specialized there in legal matters involving public lands and Indian affairs. He came to have a quick appreciation of Indian rights and later as a Justice continued to have at least some special feeling for minority groups. Van Devanter aided in bringing those legal affairs up to date, and he also found time to lecture on equity jurisprudence at Columbian (now George Washington) University. By 1903 he had built a reputation sufficient to cause President Theodore Roosevelt to appoint him to the Eighth Circuit Court of Appeals.

Van Devanter's seven years as eighth circuit judge constituted a rehearsal for the kind of work he would do on the Supreme Court. Repeatedly he found himself dealing with jurisdictional disputes, various railroad cases, land claims, questions of negligence, and dozens of like issues that required careful reconstruction of events and invoking of applicable precedent. Van Devanter's circuit court service came at the height of the Progressive Era, but his decisions rarely reflected the social consciousness of the period. In *Portland Gold Mining Co.* v. *Duke,* 164 Fed. 180 (8th Cir. 1908), for instance, he reversed a decision favoring a worker injured through no fault of his own, but as a result of the company's failure to maintain reasonable safety procedures for the operation of machinery. Van Devanter would not question the morality of what he called the "settled rule that, as between Master and servant, the duty of so using a reasonably safe place, of so operating reasonably safe machinery, and of so conforming to an established and reasonably safe method of work, that injury will not be inflicted negligently, is the duty of those to whom the work is intrusted, and is no positive duty of the master."

In December, 1910, President Taft, after promoting Edward White to the Chief Justiceship, nominated Van Devanter for the post he had long dreamed of holding: Associate Justice of the Supreme Court; ex-Senator Warren and Senator Philander C. Knox, former attorney for the Carnegie Steel Company, had been major campaigners for their former protégé. Despite the opposition of progressives such as William Jennings Bryan, who referred to him as "the judge that held that two railroads running parallel to each other for two thousand miles were not competing lines, one of the roads being that of the Union Pacific!" and A. A. Johnson, former president of the University of Wyoming, the political, railroad, and judicial interests of the nominee stood him in good stead, and he was quickly confirmed.

Van Devanter was never a leading figure on the Court. He was quiet and rarely appeared in public. He eschewed controversy and accepted as his own provinces the areas of public lands, admiralty law, water rights, Indian controversies, and corporation law. His skill in deciding jurisdictional disputes caused him to be chosen to draft the Jurisdictional Act of 1925. He shone in conference as a student of procedure, a tireless worker, and a diplomatic critic of his colleagues' opinions. Justice Brandeis was especially appreciative of the knowledgeable suggestions made by his colleague; in a particularly difficult case Brandeis called in "Van Devanter, master of formulas that decided cases without creating precedents." Van Devanter's skill in negotiation owed much to his experience under Senator Warren. In comparison with most of his colleagues he wrote few opinions; in twenty-six years on the Court he delivered the majority view in only 346 cases. In his first decade on the Court, Van Devanter dealt mostly with conflicting land claims under the federal homestead laws and with Indians who appealed for settlement of their rights. His work was careful and learned, but owing to its dullness went unappreciated by most people.

Van Devanter's social views were not sharply focused until his final years on the Court—though he at first tended to progressivism, notably with regard to the commerce clause. In *Kieran* v. *Portland,* 223 U.S. 157 (1911), he upheld the Employees Liability Act of 1908 that applied to workers engaged in interstate commerce at the time of injury. Congress had corrected the constitutional deficiency in the original liability statute which the Supreme Court had voided in *Employers Liability Cases,* 207 U.S. 463 (1908), by the enactment of a new law. The Federal Employers' Liability Act of April 22, 1908, was so drafted as to apply only to carrier liability for the injuries of employees actually engaged in interstate commerce. True to its implied promise in the First Employers' Liability Cases, the court found no difficulty in holding the revised statute constitutional. Van Devanter's opinion in the Second Employers' Liability Cases, 223 U.S. 1 (1912), was a persuasive brief for the right of Congress to regulate virtually every phase of carrier employee relationships. Commerce, said Van Devanter, is an act. "It is performed by men, and with the help of things." These men and things are "the instruments and agents" of commerce. Therefore they can be regulated by commerce. Speaking for a unanimous Court, the New Deal critic of a later day wrote: "Congress, of course, can do anything . . . [with discretion] . . . to save the act of interstate commerce from prevention or intervention or interruption, or to make that act more secure, more reliable or more efficient." Earlier laws had been declared invalid on the ground that, in their sweeping inclusiveness, they had invaded intrastate commerce. Van Devanter's decision was persuasive for the right of Congress to regulate virtually every phase of carrier employee relationships. In a later case, *United States* v. *Simpson,* 252 U.S. 465 (1920), Van Devanter ruled that to be in interstate commerce, the movement of goods does not have to be accomplished by common carrier.

In *Southern Railway Company* v. *United States,* 222 U.S. 20 (1911), testing the constitutionality of the Safety Appliance Act of 1893 which outlawed the interstate use of railroad cars without automatic couplers, Van Devanter upheld the conviction of a company carrying interstate freight on an interstate line, even though no border was crossed. "Commerce," he wrote, "comprehends more than the mere exchange of goods. It embraces commercial intercourse in all its branches. . . ." The clause therefore extended legitimately to every instrument and agent by which such commerce is carried on. To be constitutional, however, a law based on the interstate commerce clause has to have "a real or substantial relation to some part of such commerce."

In opinions such as these, Van Devanter was perhaps reflecting not simply a desire to broaden the regulatory power of Congress, but a particular conception of commerce itself, as inherently national in scope. For in *Schaffer* v. *Farmers'*

Grain Company, 268 U.S. 189 (1925), he decided for limitation of state regulatory power. North Dakota had enacted a number of procedures protecting the seller at grain elevators. Since ninety per cent of the wheat bought by these elevators was shipped to other states, the North Dakota laws were an interference with interstate commerce, Van Devanter said for the Court. He again argued for a national scope of commerce in *Mayor of Vidalia* v. *McNeely,* 274 U.S. 676 (1931). The Justice ruled that local authority could not abridge operation of ferries traversing boundary waters.

One significant progressive decision written by Van Devanter in his early years concerned the income tax and its application to the salaries of federal judges, *Evans* v. *Gore,* 253 U.S. 245 (1920). The tax itself was valid, he held, since its enactment by constitutional amendment reflected the wishes of the people themselves. With this reasoning Van Devanter responded to various assertions that the amending power was in some way limited. Seven years is not an unduly lengthy time for passage of a constitutional amendment; and a congressional vote on an amendment is legal even though only two-thirds of those present have approved it, so long as a quorum exists. Since, however, the Constitution provides that compensation of judges must not be reduced during their term in office, the income tax could not be applied to those who were holding office at the time the amendment became law. Like the clause giving judges tenure during good behavior, the salary stipulation was intended to maintain a judiciary independent of public pressures.

A resolute dry, Van Devanter in 1920 wrote the decision upholding the Eighteenth Amendment in *Rhode Island* v. *Palmer,* 253 U.S. 350. In this, as in other prohibition cases, he avoided substantive discussion of the amendment's constitutionality. Neither did Van Devanter's decisions for the Court majority analyze the procedural arguments presented against the amendment; rather, he simply declared, "That amendment, by lawful proposal and ratification, has become a part of the Constitution." Van Devanter generally interpreted the regulation provisions broadly. Later in the decade he voted in favor of letting the government restrict the prescribing of liquor by physicians, *Lambert* v. *Yellowly,* 272 U.S. 581 (1926). But in 1929, named to a commission to investigate the sinking of a Canadian rum runner by the United States Coast Guard, he ruled in favor of the Canadians, awarding them $25,000 and demanding an apology from the American government.

In 1926 Van Devanter wrote one of his most important decisions. The case of *McGrain* v. *Daugherty,* 273 U.S. 135 (1927), challenged the right of the Senate to subpoena witnesses; the brother of the corrupt United States Attorney General had brought suit charging that the Senate had exceeded its power in bringing him into custody for ignoring two subpoenas. The purpose of congressional investigations, reasoned Van Devanter, is to enact legislation efficiently and neither house is invested with general power to compel disclosures of private affairs; but while the investigatory power of Congress is delimited, that power is equal to that of regular courts unless definite proof can be shown that the investigation's purpose is not to legislate. Van Devanter's conclusion resulted from a long historical survey of the legislative power to summon witnesses, including an investigation of practice in the British Parliament and in colonial legislatures. The Court upheld the subpoena in the case at hand.

While more libertarian than Justice Butler, Van Devanter showed no ardent interest in protecting civil liberties. He voted with the minority in upholding the notorious Minnesota "press gag" law in *Near* v. *Minnesota,* 283 U.S. 697 (1931). The all-white Texas primary law declared invalid in *Nixon* v. *Condon,* 286 U.S. 73 (1932), also received his approbation; a political party, to Van Devanter, was a private agency not within the purview of the Fourteenth Amendment. If it were, any such privately organized group would be subject to government control. Finally, one of his last dissents was in *Herndon* v. *Lowry,* 301 U.S. 242 (1937), where he voted to sustain the conviction of a Negro organizer for the Communist party under a Georgia insurrection law.

Most of Van Devanter's work continued to be in highly technical areas that bored other members of the Court. The Justices often called upon him to resolve the many tangled jurisdictional disputes which faced the Court. Van Devanter differentiated between constitutional and legislative courts and, although believing the latter independent, insisted the right of appeal to the Supreme Court remain unabridged. In *Eastern Cherokees* v. *United States,* 225 U.S. 582 (1912), he ruled inferior courts could not, when dealing with remanded cases, reopen issues previously settled by the Supreme Court. Van Devanter assumed a moderate position on the exercise of the Court's appellate jurisdiction over the state courts. He argued that a distinct federal question must exist before the Court could consider a particular case. Van Devanter, however, made no attempt to establish a broad, theoretical jurisdictional framework, preferring instead to deal with specific issues in specific cases. In *United States* v. *Quiver,* 241 U.S. 602 (1916), he held that tribal customs rather than state criminal laws apply to Indians under congressional regulation. In *Pennsylvania* v. *West Virginia,* 262 U.S. 553 (1923), he decided that the West Virginia legislature could not peremptorily halt piping of natural gas into Pennsylvania. In *Southwestern Telegraph Company* v. *Danahev,* 248 U.S. 590 (1918), he declared that the Supreme Court would not dispute the ruling of the highest state court on a state constitution, unless a right granted or secured by the United States Constitution was infringed.

Cases involving due process brought forth some of Van Devanter's most careful thinking. He concurred with the trend toward a broad interpretation of permissible congressional action compatible with due process, writing in the Second Employers' Liability Cases that the clause "admits of the exercise of a wide discretion in classifying according to general, rather than minute, distinctions." In consideration of a Mississippi tax case he wrote that a tax affords due process if it is enacted under a state statute in a manner neither unreasonably discriminatory nor arbitrary, will be used for a public purpose, and can be appealed by the taxpayer. Due process, he held, prevents a railroad from being required to operate its business at a loss, for this is a deprivation of property. This limitation on due process, however, cannot be extended to release a railroad from its obligation as a public utility to provide certain services in themselves unprofitable. In *Bryant* v. *Zimmerman et al.*, 278 U.S. 63 (1928), Van Devanter found that the Ku Klux Klan could be required to supply information on its rules, regulations and members (the Klan, by its activities, was an "enemy to the weal of our national commonwealth") even though other fraternal orders escaped the statute books.

But if the cases upon which Van Devanter sat during most of his tenure were such as to afford him a balanced posture between conservative and progressive points of view, he was the most intractable of the reactionary Justices of the 1930's. He voted against the NRA, the AAA—he rejected his own AAA benefit checks—the gold clauses, the first Frazier-Lemke Act, the Guffey Law, and all of the Wagner Act cases except the bus lawsuit. But he wrote only twenty-two opinions in the thirties, most of which concerned Indian rights, admiralty law, and jurisdictional disputes; none was outspoken, nor were most of his dissents especially articulate. Van Devanter was not feeble in the thirties but had always suffered from "pen paralysis." Justice Stone, though he admired Van Devanter for many traits, described him as the commander-in-chief of judicial reaction. Again, his influence was in discussion with his brother Justices; he has been called the foremost intellectual among the conservatives, and he managed to stay on friendly terms even with the liberal Justice Brandeis. According to friends he had decided in 1932 to retire—he had been able to write only one or two decisions each year; but the alleged rashness of President Roosevelt kept him on the bench. He had lost the energy that forty years before had sent him hunting grizzly bears with Buffalo Bill in Wyoming's Big Horn Mountains. In June, 1937, Van Devanter resigned at the age of seventy-eight, taking advantage of a new law permitting Justices to retire at full pay, and moved to New York, where he presided in the United States District Court. His long hours in the court probably hastened his death, which came on February 8, 1941.

To men like Reed Powell, Van Devanter was simply an "old dodo." But most or all of his colleagues thought otherwise. One tribute to Van Devanter had been written by the often critical Chief Justice Taft some twelve years before. The circumstance was that of Van Devanter's possible resignation from the Court to head the commission that would consider and report on the Eighteenth Amendment, but the sentiments were expressed privately and no doubt sincerely to William H. Taft. "The truth is," wrote the Chief Justice, "that Van Devanter has been very modest, and nobody knows the extent to which the whole Court are indebted to him for keeping the main line in reference to the condition of the law and their own decisions as well as the statutes." Van Devanter was "a very remarkable man," as well as a great influence on the Court, in Taft's opinion. Justice Stone also admired Taft's appointee, praising his craftsmanship and command of the intricacies of judicial procedure. In a eulogy Stone spoke of Van Devanter's opinions as "models of judicial exposition, never discursive, redundant, or sprinkled with irrelevant citations." Opinions such as his bolstered public confidence in the "thoroughness, integrity, and disinterestedness" of the Court.

SELECTED BIBLIOGRAPHY

A careful study of Van Devanter's early career has been written by Lewis L. Gould: "Willis Van Devanter in Wyoming Politics, 1884–1897," Unpublished doctoral dissertation (Yale University, 1966). Another doctoral dissertation on the Justice is James O'Brien Howard, "Constitutional Doctrines of Mr. Justice Van Devanter" (State University of Iowa, 1937). Eulogistic remarks are contained in *Proceedings in Memory of Mr. Justice Van Devanter,* 316 U.S. v–xlii (1941).

Willis Van Devanter

REPRESENTATIVE OPINIONS

RHODE ISLAND v. PALMER, 253 U.S. 350 (1920)

A prohibitionist himself, Van Devanter, in 1920, wrote this decision upholding the Eighteenth Amendment. To the Justice it appeared that adequate fulfillment of the amendment process virtually precluded any challenge to the amendment's constitutionality.

MR. JUSTICE VAN DEVANTER announced the conclusions of the court.

Power to amend the Constitution was reserved by Article V, which reads:

"The Congress, whenever two thirds of both Houses shall deem it necessary, shall propose Amendments to this Constitution, or, on the Application of the Legislatures of two thirds of the several States, shall call a Convention for proposing Amendments, which, in either Case, shall be valid to all Intents and Purposes, as Part of this Constitution, when ratified by the Legislatures of three fourths of the several States, or by Conventions in three fourths thereof, as the one or the other Mode of Ratification may be proposed by the Congress; Provided that no Amendment which may be made prior to the Year One thousand eight hundred and eight shall in any Manner affect the first and fourth Clauses in the Ninth Section of the first Article; and that no State, without its Consent, shall be deprived of its equal Suffrage in the Senate."

The text of the Eighteenth Amendment, proposed by Congress in 1917 and proclaimed as ratified in 1919, 40 Stat. 1050, 1941, is as follows:

"Section 1. After one year from the ratification of this article the manufacture, sale, or transportation of intoxicating liquors within, the importation thereof into, or the exportation thereof from the United States and all territory subject to the jurisdiction thereof for beverage purposes is hereby prohibited.

"Sec. 2. The Congress and the several States shall have concurrent power to enforce this article by appropriate legislation."

We here are concerned with seven cases involving the validity of that Amendment and of certain general features of the National Prohibition Law, known as the Volstead Act, c. 83, 41 Stat. 305, which was adopted to enforce the Amendment. The relief sought in each case is an injunction against the execution of that act. Two of the cases—Nos. 29 and 30, Original,—were brought in this court, and the others in district courts. Nos. 696, 752, 788 and 837 are here on appeals from decrees refusing injunctions, and No. 794 from a decree granting an injunction. The cases have been elaborately argued at the bar and in printed briefs; and the arguments have been attentively considered, with the result that we reach and announce the following conclusions on the questions involved:

1. The adoption by both houses of Congress, each by a two-thirds vote, of a joint resolution proposing an amendment to the Constitution sufficiently shows that the proposal was deemed necessary by all who voted for it. An express declaration that they regarded it as necessary is not essential. None of the resolutions whereby prior amendments were proposed contained such a declaration.

2. The two-thirds vote in each house which is required in proposing an amendment is a vote of two-thirds of the members present—assuming the presence of a quorum—and not a vote of two-thirds of the entire membership, present and absent. *Missouri Pacific Ry. Co.* v. *Kansas,* 248 U.S. 276.

3. The referendum provisions of state constitutions and statutes cannot be applied, consistently with the Constitution of the United States, in the ratification or rejection of amendments to it. *Hawke* v. *Smith, ante,* 221.

4. The prohibition of the manufacture, sale, transportation, importation and exportation of intoxicating liquors for beverage purposes, as embodied in the Eighteenth Amendment, is within the power to amend reserved by Article V of the Constitution.

5. That Amendment, by lawful proposal and ratification, has become a part of the Constitution, and must be respected and given effect the same as other provisions of that instrument.

6. The first section of the Amendment—the one embodying the prohibition—is operative throughout the entire territorial limits of the United States, binds all legislative bodies, courts, public officers and individuals within those limits, and of its own force invalidates every legislative act—whether by Congress, by a state legislature, or by a territorial assembly—which authorizes or sanctions what the section prohibits.

7. The second section of the Amendment—the one declaring "The Congress and the several States shall have concurrent power to enforce this article by appropriate legislation"—does not enable Congress or the several States to defeat or thwart the prohibition, but only to enforce it by appropriate means.

8. The words "concurrent power" in that section do not mean joint power, or require that legislation thereunder by Congress, to be effective, shall be approved or sanctioned by the several States or any of them; nor do they mean that the power to enforce is divided between Congress and the several States along the lines which separate or distinguish foreign and interstate commerce from intrastate affairs.

9. The power confided to Congress by that section, while not exclusive, is territorially coextensive with the prohibition of the first section, embraces manufacture and other intrastate transactions as well as importation, exportation and interstate traffic, and is in no wise dependent on or affected by action or inaction on the part of the several States or any of them.

10. That power may be exerted against the disposal for beverage purposes of liquors manufactured before the Amendment became effective just as it may be against subsequent manufacture for those purposes. In either case it is a constitutional mandate or prohibition that is being enforced.

11. While reccgnizing that there are limits beyond which Congress cannot go in treating beverages as within its power of enforcement, we think those limits are not transcended by the provision of the Volstead Act (Title II, § 1), wherein liquors containing as much as one-half of one per cent. of alcohol by volume and fit for use for beverage purposes are treated as within that power. *Jacob Ruppert* v. *Caffey,* 251 U.S. 264.

Giving effect to these conclusions, we dispose of the cases as follows:

In Nos. 29 and 30, Original, the bills are dismissed.

In No. 794 the decree is reversed.

In Nos. 696, 752, 788 and 837 the decrees are affirmed.

McGRAIN v. DAUGHERTY, 273 U.S. 135 (1927)

Mally S. Daugherty, the brother of Harding's Attorney General, Harry Daugherty, was subpoenaed to appear before a Senate committee in connection with their investigation into the Teapot Dome scandal. He refused to do so or to produce records of the bank of which he was president. The Sargeant of Arms of the Senate thereupon served a warrant on Daugherty which he challenged by a writ of *habeas corpus*. The Supreme Court then had to decide whether Congress could compel witnesses to appear before it and punish those who refused to do so. Van Devanter supported this power as a necessary and essential auxiliary to their legislative function.

MR. JUSTICE VAN DEVANTER delivered the opinion of the court.

This is an appeal from the final order in a proceeding in *habeas corpus* discharging a recusant witness held in custody under process of attachment issued from the United States Senate in the course of an investigation which it was making of the administration of the Department of Justice. A full statement of the case is necessary.

The Department of Justice is one of the great executive departments established by congressional enactment and has charge, among other things, of the initiation and prosecution of all suits, civil and criminal, which may be brought in the right and name of the United States to compel obedience or punish disobedience to its laws, to recover property obtained from it by unlawful or fraudulent means, or to safeguard its rights in other respects; and also of the assertion and protection of its interests when it or its officers are sued by others. The Attorney General is the head of the department, and its functions are all to be exercised under his supervision and direction.[1]

Harry M. Daugherty became the Attorney General March 5, 1921, and held that office until March 28, 1924, when he resigned. Late in that period various charges of misfeasance and nonfeasance in the Department of Justice after he became its supervising head were brought to the attention of the Senate by individual senators and made the basis of an insistent demand that the department be investigated to the end that the practices and deficiencies which, according to the charges, were operating to prevent or impair its right administration might be definitely ascertained and that appropriate and effective measures might be taken to remedy or eliminate the evil. The Senate regarded the charges as grave and requiring legislative attention and action. Accordingly it formulated, passed and invited the House of Representatives to pass (and that body did pass) two measures taking important litigation then in immediate contemplation out of the control of the Department of Justice and placing the same in charge of special counsel to be appointed by the President[2]; and also adopted a resolution authorizing and directing a select committee of five senators—

"to investigate circumstances and facts, and report the same to the Senate, concerning the alleged failure of Harry M. Daugherty, Attorney General of the United States, to prosecute properly violators of the Sherman Anti-trust Act and the Clayton Act against monopolies and unlawful restraint of trade; the alleged neglect and failure of the said Harry M. Daugherty, Attorney General of the United States, to arrest and prosecute Albert B. Fall, Harry F. Sinclair, E. L.

[1] *Rev. Stats. secs. 346, 350, 359, 360, 361, 362, 367; Judicial Code, secs. 185, 212; c. 382, secs. 3, 5, 25 Stat. 858, 859; c. 647, sec. 4, 26 Stat. 209; c. 3935, 34 Stat. 816; c. 323, sec. 15, 38 Stat. 736;* United States *v.* San Jacinto Tin Co., *125 U.S. 273, 278;* Kern River Co. *v.* United States, *257 U.S. 147, 155;* Ponzi *v.* Fessenden, *258 U.S. 254, 262.*

[2] *Cong. Rec. 68th Cong., 1st Sess., pp. 1520, 1521, 1728; c. 16, 43 Stat. 5; Cong. Rec. 68th Cong., 1st Sess., pp. 1591, 1974; c. 39, 43 Stat. 15; c. 42, 43 Stat. 16.*

Doheny, C. R. Forbes, and their co-conspirators in defrauding the Government, as well as the alleged neglect and failure of the said Attorney General to arrest and prosecute many others for violations of Federal statutes, and his alleged failure to prosecute properly, efficiently, and promptly, and to defend, all manner of civil and criminal actions wherein the Government of the United States is interested as a party plaintiff or defendant. And said committee is further directed to inquire into, investigate and report to the Senate the activities of the said Harry M. Daugherty, Attorney General, and any of his assistants in the Department of Justice which would in any manner tend to impair their efficiency or influence as representatives of the Government of the United States."

The resolution also authorized the committee to send for books and papers, to subpoena witnesses, to administer oaths, and to sit at such times and places as it might deem advisable.[3]

In the course of the investigation the committee issued and caused to be duly served on Mally S. Daugherty—who was a brother of Harry M. Daugherty and president of the Midland National Bank of Washington Court House, Ohio,—a subpoena commanding him to appear before the committee for the purpose of giving testimony bearing on the subject under investigation, and to bring with him the "deposit ledgers of the Midland National Bank since November 1, 1920; also note files and transcript of owners of every safety vault; also records of income drafts; also records of any individual account or accounts showing withdrawals of amounts of $25,000 or over during above period." The witness failed to appear.

A little later in the course of the investigation the committee issued and caused to be duly served on the same witness another subpoena commanding him to appear before it for the purpose of giving testimony relating to the subject under consideration—nothing being said in this subpoena about bringing records, books or papers. The witness again failed to appear; and no excuse was offered by him for either failure.

The committee then made a report to the Senate stating that the subpoenas had been issued, that according to the officer's returns—copies of which accompanied the report—the witness was personally served; and that he had failed and refused to appear.[4] After a reading of the report, the Senate adopted a resolution reciting these facts and proceeding as follows:[5]

"Whereas the appearance and testimony of the said M. S. Daugherty is material and necessary in order that the committee may properly execute the functions imposed upon it and may obtain information necessary as a basis for such legislative and other action as the Senate may deem necessary and proper: Therefore be it

"Resolved, That the President of the Senate pro tempore issue his warrant commanding the Sergeant at Arms or his deputy to take into custody the body of the said M. S. Daugherty wherever found, and to bring the said M. S. Daugherty before the bar of the Senate, then and there to answer such questions pertinent to the matter under inquiry as the Senate may order the President of the Senate pro tempore to propound; and to keep the said M. S. Daugherty in custody to await the further order of the Senate."

It will be observed from the terms of the resolution that the warrant was to be issued in furtherance of the effort to obtain the personal testimony of the witness and, like the second subpoena, was not intended to exact from him the production of the various records, books and papers named in the first subpoena.

The warrant was issued agreeably to the resolution and was addressed simply to the Sergeant at Arms. That officer on receiving the warrant endorsed thereon a direction that it be executed by John J. McGrain, already his deputy, and delivered it to him for execution.

The deputy, proceeding under the warrant, took the witness into custody at Cincinnati, Ohio, with the purpose of bringing him before the bar of the Senate as commanded; whereupon the witness petitioned the federal district court in Cincinnati for a writ of *habeas corpus*. The writ was granted and the deputy made due return setting forth the warrant and the cause of the detention. After a hearing the court held the attachment and detention unlawful and dis-

[3] *For the full resolution and two amendments adopted shortly thereafter see Cong. Rec., 68th Cong., 1st Sess., pp. 3299, 3409–3410, 3548, 4126.*

[4] *Senate Report No. 475, 68th Cong., 1st Sess.*

[5] *Cong. Rec., 68th Cong., 1st Sess., pp. 7215–7217.*

charged the witness, the decision being put on the ground that the Senate in directing the investigation and in ordering the attachment exceeded its powers under the Constitution, 299 Fed. 620. The deputy prayed and was allowed a direct appeal to this Court under § 238 of the Judicial Code as then existing.

We have given the case earnest and prolonged consideration because the principal questions involved are of unusual importance and delicacy. They are (a) whether the Senate—or the House of Representatives, both being on the same plane in this regard—has power, through its own process, to compel a private individual to appear before it or one of its committees and give testimony needed to enable it efficiently to exercise a legislative function belonging to it under the Constitution, and (b) whether it sufficiently appears that the process was being employed in this instance to obtain testimony for that purpose.

Other questions are presented which in regular course should be taken up first.

The witness challenges the authority of the deputy to execute the warrant on two grounds—that there was no provision of law for a deputy, and that, even if there were such a provision, a deputy could not execute the warrant because it was addressed simply to the Sergeant at Arms. We are of opinion that neither ground is tenable.

The Senate adopted in 1889 and has retained ever since a standing order declaring that the Sergeant at Arms may appoint deputies "to serve process or perform other duties" in his stead, that they shall be "officers of the Senate," and that acts done and returns made by them "shall have like effect and be of the same validity as if performed or made by the Sergeant at Arms in person."[6] In actual practice the Senate has given full effect to the order; and Congress has sanctioned the practice under it by recognizing the deputies—sometimes called assistants—as officers of the Senate, by fixing their compensation and by making appropriations to pay them.[7] Thus there was ample provision of law for a deputy.

The fact that the warrant was addressed simply to the Sergeant at Arms is not of special significance. His authority was not to be tested by the warrant alone. Other criteria were to be considered. The standing order and the resolution under which the warrant was issued plainly contemplated that he was to be free to execute the warrant in person or to direct a deputy to execute it. They expressed the intention of the Senate; and the words of the warrant were to be taken, as they well could be, in a sense which would give effect to that intention. Thus understood, the warrant admissibly could be executed by a deputy if the Sergeant at Arms so directed, which he did.

The case of *Sanborn* v. *Carleton,* 15 Gray 399, on which the witness relies, related to a warrant issued to the Sergeant at Arms in 1860, which he deputed another to execute. At that time there was no standing rule or statute permitting him to act through a deputy; nor was there anything in the resolution under which the warrant was issued indicative of a purpose to permit him to do so. All that was decided was that in the absence of a permissive provision, in the warrant or elsewhere, he could not commit its execution to another. The provision which was absent in that case and deemed essential is present in this.

The witness points to the provision in the Fourth Amendment to the Constitution declaring "no warrants shall issue but upon probable cause supported by oath or affirmation" and contends that the warrant was void because the report of the committee on which it was based was unsworn. We think the contention overlooks the relation of the committee to the Senate and to the matters reported, and puts aside the accepted interpretation of the constitutional provision.

The committee was a part of the Senate, and its members were acting under their oath of office as senators. The matters reported pertained to their proceedings and were within their own knowledge. They had issued the subpoenas, had received and examined the officer's returns thereon (copies of which accompanied the report), and knew the witness had not obeyed either subpoena or offered any excuse for his failure to do so.

The constitutional provision was not intended to establish a new principle but to affirm and preserve a cherished rule of the common law designed to prevent the issue of groundless warrants. In legislative practice committee reports are regarded as made under the sanction of the oath of office of its

[6] *Senate Journal 47, 51–1 Dec. 17, 1889; Senate Rules and Manual, 68th Cong., p. 114.*

[7] *41 Stat. 632, 1253; 42 Stat. 424, 1266; 43 Stat. 33, 580, 1288.*

members; and where the matters reported are within the committee's knowledge and constitute probable cause for an attachment such reports are acted on and given effect without requiring that they be supported by further oath or affirmation. This is not a new practice but one which has come down from an early period. It was well recognized before the constitutional provision was adopted, has been followed ever since, and appears never to have been challenged until now. Thus it amounts to a practical interpretation, long continued, of both the original common law rule and the affirming constitutional provision, and should be given effect accordingly.[8]

The principle underlying the legislative practice has also been recognized and applied in judicial proceedings. This is illustrated by the settled rulings that courts in dealing with contempts committed in their presence may order commitments without other proof than their own knowledge of the occurrence,[9] and that they may issue attachments, based on their own knowledge of the default, where intended witnesses or jurors fail to appear in obedience to process shown by the officer's return to have been duly served.[10] A further illustration is found in the rulings that grand jurors, acting under the sanction of their oaths as such, may find and return indictments based solely on their own knowledge of the particular offenses, and that warrants may be issued on such indictments without further oath or affirmation;[11] and still another is found in the practice which recognizes that where grand jurors, under their oath as such, report to the court that a witness brought before them has refused to testify, the court may act on that report, although otherwise unsworn, and order the witness brought before it by attachment.[12]

We think the legislative practice, fortified as it is by the judicial practice, shows that the report of the committee—which was based on the committee's own knowledge and made under the sanction of the oath of office of its members—was sufficiently supported by oath to satisfy the constitutional requirement.

The witness also points to the provision in the warrant and in the resolution under which it was issued requiring that he be "brought before the bar of the Senate, then and there" to give testimony "pertinent to the subject under inquiry," and contends that an essential prerequisite to such an attachment was wanting, because he neither had been subpoenaed to appear and testify before the Senate nor had refused to do so. The argument in support of the contention proceeds on the assumption that the warrant of attachment "is to be treated precisely the same as if no subpoena had been issued by the committee, and the same as if the witness had not refused to testify before the committee." In our opinion the contention and the assumption are both untenable. The committee was acting for the Senate and under its authorization; and therefore the subpoenas which the committee issued and the witness refused to obey are to be treated as if issued by the Senate. The warrant was issued as an auxiliary process to compel him to give the testimony sought by the subpoenas; and its nature in this respect is not affected by the direction that his testimony be given at the bar of the Senate instead of before the committee. If the Senate deemed it proper, in view of his contumacy, to give that direction it was at liberty to do so.

The witness sets up an interlocutory injunction granted by a state court at Washington Court House, Ohio, in a suit brought by the Midland National Bank against two members of the investigating committee, and contends that the attachment was in violation of that injunction and therefore unlawful. The contention is plainly ill-founded The injunction was granted the same day the second subpoena was served, but whether earlier or later in the day does not appear. All that the record discloses about the in-

[8] Prigg *v.* Pennsylvania, *16 Pet. 539, 620–621;* The Laura, *114 U.S. 411, 416;* McPherson *v.* Blacker, *146 U.S. 1, 35–36;* Ex parte Grossman, *267 U.S. 87, 118;* Myers *v.* United States, *272 U.S. 52.*

[9] Ex parte Terry, *128 U.S. 289, 307,* et seq.; Holcomb *v.* Cornish, *8 Conn. 375; Blackst. Com. 286.*

[10] Robbins *v.* Gorham, *25 N.Y. 588;* Wilson *v.* State, *57 Ind. 71.*

[11] Hale *v.* Henkel, *201 U.S. 43, 60–62;* Regina *v.* Russell, *2 Car. & Mar. 247;* Commonwealth *v.* Hayden, *163 Mass. 453, 455; Decision of Mr. Justice Catron reported in Wharton's Cr. Pl. & Pr., 8th ed., pp. 224–226.*

[12] *See* Hale *v.* Henkel, supra; Blair *v.* United States, *250 U.S. 273;* Nelson *v.* United States, *201 U.S. 92, 95; Equity Rule 52, 226 U.S. Appendix, 15;* Heard *v.* Pierce, *8 Cush. 338.*

junction is comprised in the paragraph copied in the margin from the witness's petition for *habeas corpus.*[13] But it is apparent from what is disclosed that the injunction did not purport to place any restraint on the witness, nor to restrain the committee from demanding that he appear and testify personally to what he knew respecting the subject under investigation; and also that what the injunction did purport to restrain has no bearing on the power of the Senate to enforce that demand by attachment.

In approaching the principal questions, which remain to be considered, two observations are in order. One is that we are not now concerned with the direction in the first subpoena that the witness produce various records, books and papers of the Midland National Bank. That direction was not repeated in the second subpoena; and is not sought to be enforced by the attachment. This was recognized by the court below, 299 Fed. 623, and is conceded by counsel for the appellant. The other is that we are not now concerned with the right of the Senate to propound or the duty of the witness to answer specific questions, for as yet no questions have been propounded to him. He is asserting—and is standing on his assertion—that the Senate is without power to interrogate him, even if the questions propounded be pertinent and otherwise legitimate—which for present purposes must be assumed.

The first of the principal questions—the one which the witness particularly presses on our attention—is, as before shown, whether the Senate—or the House of Representatives, both being on the same plane in this regard—has power, through its own process, to compel a private individual to appear before it or one of its committees and give testimony needed to enable it efficiently to exercise a legislative function belonging to it under the Constitution.

The Constitution provides for a Congress consisting of a Senate and House of Representatives and invests it with "all legislative powers" granted to the United States, and with power "to make all laws which shall be necessary and proper" for carrying into execution these powers and "all other powers" vested by the Constitution in the United States or in any department or officer thereof. Art. I, secs. 1, 8. Other provisions show that, while bills can become laws only after being considered and passed by both houses of Congress, each house is to be distinct from the other, to have its own officers and rules, and to exercise its legislative function independently.[14] Art. I, secs. 2, 3, 5, 7. But there is no provision expressly investing either house with power to make investigations and exact testimony to the end that it may exercise its legislative function advisedly and effectively. So the question arises whether this power is so far incidental to the legislative function as to be implied.

In actual legislative practice power to secure needed information by such means has long been treated as an attribute of the power to legislate. It was so regarded in the British Parliament and in the Colonial legislatures before the American Revolution; and a like view has prevailed and been carried into effect in both houses of Congress and in most of the state legislatures.[15]

This power was both asserted and exerted by the House of Representatives in 1792, when it appointed a select committee

[13] *"On the 11th day o April, 1924, in an action in the Court of Common Pleas of said Fayette County, Ohio, in which said The Midland National Bank was plaintiff and said B. K. Wheeler and Smith W. Brookhart were defendants, upon the petition of said bank said court granted a temporary restraining order enjoining and restraining said defendants and their agents, servants, and employees from entering into said banking room and from taking, examining, or investigating any of the books, accounts, records, promissory notes, securities, letters, correspondence, papers, or any other property of said bank or of its depositors, borrowers, or customers in said banking room and from in any manner molesting and interfering with the business and affairs of said bank, its officers, agents, servants, and the business of its depositors, borrowers and customers with said bank until the further order of said court. The said defendants were duly served with process and said action and duly served with copies of said temporary restraining order on said 11th Day of April, 1924, and said injunction has not been modified by said court and no further order has been made in said case by said court, and said injunction is in full force and effect."*

[14] *Story Const., secs. 545,* et seq.; *1 Kent's Com., p. 222.*

[15] *May's Parliamentary Practice, 2d ed., pp. 80, 295, 299; Cushing's Legislative Practice, secs. 634, 1901–1903; 3 Hinds' Precedents, secs. 1722, 1725, 1727, 1813–1820; Cooley's Constitutional Limitations, 6th ed., p. 161.*

to inquire into the St. Clair expedition and authorized the committee to send for necessary persons, papers and records. Mr. Madison, who had taken an important part in framing the Constitution only five years before, and four of his associates in that work, were members of the House of Representatives at the time, and all voted for the inquiry. 3 Cong. Ann. 494. Other exertions of the power by the House of Representatives, as also by the Senate, are shown in the citations already made. Among those by the Senate, the inquiry ordered in 1859 respecting the raid by John Brown and his adherents on the armory and arsenal of the United States at Harper's Ferry is of special significance. The resolution directing the inquiry authorized the committee to send for persons and papers, to inquire into the facts pertaining to the raid and the means by which it was organized and supported, and to report what legislation, if any, was necessary to preserve the peace of the country and protect the public property. The resolution was briefly discussed and adopted without opposition. Cong. Globe, 36th Cong., 1st Sess., pp. 141, 152. Later on the committee reported that Thaddeus Hyatt, although subpoenaed to appear as a witness, had refused to do so; whereupon the Senate ordered that he be attached and brought before it to answer for his refusal. When he was brought in he answered by challenging the power of the Senate to direct the inquiry and exact testimony to aid it in exercising its legislative function. The question of power thus presented was thoroughly discussed by several senators—Mr. Sumner of Massachusetts taking the lead in denying the power and Mr. Fessenden of Maine in supporting it. Sectional and party lines were put aside and the question was debated and determined with special regard to principle and precedent. The vote was taken on a resolution pronouncing the witness's answer insufficient and directing that he be committed until he should signify that he was ready and willing to testify. The resolution was adopted—44 senators voting for it and 10 against. Cong. Globe, 36th Cong., 1st Sess., pp. 1100–1109, 3006–3007. The arguments advanced in support of the power are fairly reflected by the following excerpts from the debate:

Mr. Fessenden of Maine. "Where will you stop? Stop, I say, just at that point where we have gone far enough to accomplish the purposes for which we were created; and these purposes are defined in the Constitution. What are they? The great purpose is legislation. There are some other things, but I speak of legislation as the principal purpose. Now, what do we propose to do here? We propose to legislate upon a given state of facts, perhaps, or under a given necessity. Well, sir, proposing to legislate, we want information. We have it not ourselves. It is not to be presumed that we know everything; and if any body does presume it, it is a very great mistake, as we know by experience. We want information on certain subjects. How are we to get it? The Senator says, ask for it. I am ready to ask for it; but suppose the person whom we ask will not give it to us: what then? Have we not power to compel him to come before us? Is this power, which has been exercised by Parliament, and by all legislative bodies down to the present day without dispute—the power to inquire into subjects upon which they are disposed to legislate—lost to us? Are we not in the possession of it? Are we deprived of it simply because we hold our power here under a Constitution which defines what our duties are, and what we are called upon to do?

"Congress have appointed committees after committees, time after time, to make inquiries on subjects of legislation. Had we not power to do it? Nobody questioned our authority to do it. We have given them authority to send for persons and papers during the recess. Nobody questioned our authority. We appoint committees during the session, with power to send for persons and papers. Have we not that authority, if necessary to legislation?

* * * * *

"Sir, with regard to myself, all I have to inquire into is: is this a legitimate and proper object, committed to me under the Constitution; and then, as to the mode of accomplishing it, I am ready to use judiciously, calmly, moderately, all the power which I believe is necessary and inherent, in order to do that which I am appointed to do; and, I take it, I violate no rights, either of the people generally or of the individual, by that course."

Mr. Crittenden of Kentucky. "I come now to a question where the coöperation of the two branches is not necessary. There are some things that the Senate may do. How? According to a mode of its own. Are we to ask the other branch of the Legislature to concede by law to us the power of making such an inquiry as we are now making? Has not each branch the right to make what inquiries and investigation it thinks proper to make for its own action? Undoubtedly. You say we must have a law for it. Can we have a law? Is it not, from the very nature of the case, incidental to you as a Senate, if you, as a Senate, have the power of instituting an inquiry and of proceeding with that inquiry? I have endeavored to show that we have that power. We have a right, in consequence of it, a necessary incidental power, to summon witnesses, if witnesses are necessary. Do we require the concurrence of the other House to that? It is a power of our own. If you have a right to do the thing of your own motion, you must have all powers that are necessary to do it.

"The means of carrying into effect by law all the granted powers, is given where legislation is applicable and necessary; but there are subordinate matters, not amounting to laws; there are inquiries of the one House or the other House, which each House has a right to conduct; which each has, from the beginning, exercised the power to conduct; and each has, from the beginning, summoned witnesses. This has been the practice of the Government from the beginning; and if we have a right to summon the witness, all the rest follows as a matter of course."

The deliberate solution of the question on that occasion has been accepted and followed on other occasions by both houses of Congress, and never has been rejected or questioned by either.

The state courts quite generally have held that the power to legislate carries with it by necessary implication ample authority to obtain information needed in the rightful exercise of that power, and to employ compulsory process for the purpose.

In *Burnham* v. *Morrisey,* 14 Gray 226, 239, the Supreme Judicial Court of Massachusetts, in sustaining an exertion of this power by one branch of the legislature of that Commonwealth, said:

"The house of representatives has many duties to perform, which necessarily require it to receive evidence and examine witnesses. . . . It has often occasion to acquire certain knowledge of facts, in order to the proper performance of legislative duties. We therefore think it clear that it has the constitutional right to take evidence, to summon witnesses, and to compel them to appear and testify. This power to summon and examine witnesses it may exercise by means of committees."

In *Wilckens* v. *Willet,* 1 Keyes 521, 525, a case which presented the question whether the House of Representatives of the United States possesses this power, the Court of Appeals of New York said:

"That the power exists there admits of no doubt whatever. It is a necessary incident to the sovereign power of making laws; and its exercise is often indispensable to the great end of enlightened, judicious and wholesome legislation."

In *People* v. *Keeler,* 99 N.Y. 463, 482, 483, where the validity of a statute of New York recognizing and giving effect to this power was drawn in question, the Court of Appeals approvingly quoted what it had said in *Wilckens* v. *Willet,* and added:

"It is difficult to conceive any constitutional objection which can be raised to the provision authorizing legislative committees to take testimony and to summon witnesses. In many cases it may be indispensable to intelligent and effectual legislation to ascertain the facts which are claimed to give rise to the necessity for such legislation, and the remedy required, and, irrespective of the question whether in the absence of a statute to that effect either house would have the power to imprison a recusant witness, I cannot yield to the claim that a statute authorizing it to enforce its process in that manner is in excess of the legislative power. To await the slow process of indictment and prosecution for a misdemeanor, might prove quite ineffectual, and necessary legislation might be obstructed, and perhaps defeated, if the legislative body had no other and more summary means of enforcing its right to obtain the required information. That the power may be abused, is no ground for denying its existence. It is a limited power, and should be kept within its proper bounds; and, when these are exceeded, a jurisdictional question is presented which is cognizable in the courts." . . . "Throughout this Union the practice of legislative bodies, and in this State, the statutes existing at the time the present Constitution was adopted, and whose validity has never before been questioned by our courts, afford strong arguments in favor of the recognition of the right of either house to compel the attendance of witnesses for legislative purposes, as one which has been generally conceded to be an appropriate adjunct to the power of legislation, and one which, to say the least, the State legislature has constitutional authority to regulate and enforce by statute."

Other decisions by state courts recognizing and sustaining the legislative practice are found in *Falvey* v. *Massing,* 7 Wis. 630, 635–638; *State* v. *Frear,* 138 Wis. 173; *Ex parte Parker,* 74 S.C. 466, 470; *Sullivan* v. *Hill,* 73 W. Va. 49, 53; *Lowe* v. *Summers,* 69 Mo. App. 637, 649–650. An instructive decision on the question is also found in *Ex parte Dansereau* (1875), 19 L. C. Jur. 210, where the legislative assembly of the Province of Quebec was held to possess this power as a necessary incident of its power to legislate.

We have referred to the practice of the two houses of Congress; and we now shall notice some significant congressional enactments. May 3, 1798, c. 36, 1 Stat. 554, Congress provided that oaths or affirmations might be administered to witnesses by the President of the Senate, the Speaker of the House of Representatives, the chairman of a committee of the whole, or the chairman of a select committee, "in any case under their examination." February 8, 1817, c. 10, 3 Stat. 345, it enlarged that provision so as to include the chairman of a standing committee. January 24, 1857, c. 19, 11 Stat. 155, it passed "An Act more effectually to enforce the attendance of witnesses on the summons of either house of Congress, and to compel them to discover testimony." This act provided, first, that any person summoned as a witness to give testimony or produce papers in any matter under inquiry before either house of Congress, or any committee of either house, who should wilfully make default, or, if appearing, should refuse to answer any question pertinent to the inquiry, should, in addition to the pains and penalties then existing,[16] be deemed guilty of a misdemeanor and be subject to indictment and punishment as there prescribed; and secondly, that no person should be excused from giving evidence in such an inquiry on the ground that it might tend to incriminate or disgrace him, nor be held to answer criminally, or be subjected to any penalty or forfeiture, for any fact or act as to which he was required to testify, excepting that he might be subjected to prosecution for perjury committed while so testifying. January 24, 1862, c. 11, 12 Stat. 333, Congress modified the immunity provision in particulars not material here. These enactments are now embodied in §§ 101–104 and 859 of Revised Statutes. They show very plainly that Congress intended thereby (a) to recognize the power of either house to institute inquiries and exact evidence touching subjects within its jurisdiction and on which it was disposed to act;[17] (b) to recognize that such inquiries may be conducted through committees; (c) to subject defaulting and contumacious witnesses to indictment and punishment in the courts, and thereby to enable either house to exert the power of inquiry "more effectually";[18] and (d) to open the way for obtaining evidence in such an inquiry, which otherwise could not be obtained, by exempting witnesses required to give evidence therein from criminal and penal prosecutions in respect of matters disclosed by their evidence.

Four decisions of this Court are cited and more or less relied on, and we now turn to them.

The first decision was in *Anderson* v. *Dunn,* 6 Wheat. 204. The question there was whether, under the Constitution, the House of Representatives has power to attach and punish a person other than a member for contempt of its authority—in fact, an attempt to bribe one of its members. The Court regarded the power as essential to the effective exertion of other powers expressly granted, and therefore as implied. The argument advanced to the contrary was that as the Constitution expressly grants to each house power to punish or expel its own

16 *The reference is to the power of the particular house to deal with the contempt.* In re Chapman, *166 U.S. 661, 671–672.*

17 *In construing section 1 of the Act of 1857 as reproduced in section 102 of the Revised Statutes, this Court said in* In re Chapman, *166 U.S. 661, 667:*

"It is true that the reference is to 'any' matter under inquiry, and so on, and it is suggested that this is fatally defective because too broad and unlimited in its extent; but nothing is better settled than that statutes should receive a sensible construction, such as will effectuate the legislative intention, and, if possible, so as to avoid an unjust or an absurd conclusion, Lau Ow Bew *v.* United States, *144 U.S. 47, 59; and we think that the word 'any,' as used in these sections, refers to matters within the jurisdiction of the two Houses of Congress, before them for consideration and proper for their action; to questions pertinent thereto; and to facts or papers bearing thereon."*

18 *This Court has said of the act of 1857 that "it was necessary and proper for carrying into execution the powers vested in Congress and in each house thereof."* In re Chapman, *166 U.S. 661, 671.*

members and says nothing about punishing others, the implication or inference, if any, is that power to punish one who is not a member is neither given nor intended. The Court answered this by saying:

(p. 225) "There is not in the whole of that admirable instrument, a grant of powers which does not draw after it others, not expressed, but vital to their exercise; not substantive and independent, indeed, but auxiliary and subordinate."

(p. 233) "This argument proves too much; for its direct application would lead to annihilation of almost every power of Congress. To enforce its laws upon any subject without the sanction of punishment is obviously impossible. Yet there is an express grant of power to punish in one class of cases and one only, and all the punishing power exercised by Congress in any cases, except those which relate to piracy and offenses against the laws of nations, is derived from implication. Nor did the idea ever occur to any one, that the express grant in one class of cases repelled the assumption of the punishing power in any other. The truth is, that the exercise of the powers given over their own members, was of such a delicate nature, that a constitutional provision became necessary to assert or communicate it. Constituted, as that body is, of the delegates of confederated States, some such provision was necessary to guard against their mutual jealousy, since every proceeding against a representative would indirectly affect the honour or interests of the state which sent him."

The next decision was in *Kilbourn* v. *Thompson,* 103 U.S. 168. The question there was whether the House of Representatives had exceeded its power in directing one of its committees to make a particular investigation. The decision was that it had. The principles announced and applied in the case are—that neither house of Congress possesses a "general power of making inquiry into the private affairs of the citizen"; that the power actually possessed is limited to inquiries relating to matters of which the particular house "has jurisdiction" and in respect of which it rightfully may take other action; that if the inquiry relates to "a matter wherein relief or redress could be had only by a judicial proceeding" it is not within the range of this power, but must be left to the courts, conformably to the constitutional separation of governmental powers; and that for the purpose of determining the essential character of the inquiry recourse may be had to the resolution or order under which it is made. The court examined the resolution which was the basis of the particular inquiry, and ascertained therefrom that the inquiry related to a private real-estate pool or partnership in the District of Columbia. Jay Cooke & Co. had had an interest in the pool, but had become bankrupts, and their estate was in course of administration in a federal bankruptcy court in Pennsylvania. The United States was one of their creditors. The trustee in the bankruptcy proceeding had effected a settlement of the bankrupts' interest in the pool, and of course his action was subject to examination and approval or disapproval by the bankruptcy court. Some of the creditors, including the United States, were dissatisfied with the settlement. In these circumstances, disclosed in the preamble, the resolution directed the committee "to inquire into the matter and history of said real-estate pool and the character of said settlement, with the amount of property involved in which Jay Cooke & Co. were interested, and the amount paid or to be paid in said settlement, with power to send for persons and papers and report to the House." The Court pointed out that the resolution contained no suggestion of contemplated legislation; that the matter was one in respect to which no valid legislation could be had; that the bankrupts' estate and the trustee's settlement were still pending in the bankruptcy court; and that the United States and other creditors were free to press their claims in that proceeding. And on these grounds the Court held that in undertaking the investigation "the House of Representatives not only exceeded the limit of its own authority, but assumed power which could only be properly exercised by another branch of the government, because it was in its nature clearly judicial."

The case has been cited at times, and is cited to us now, as strongly intimating, if not holding, that neither house of Congress has power to make inquiries and exact evidence in aid of contemplated legislation. There are expressions in the opinion which, separately considered, might bear such an interpretation; but that this was not intended is shown by the immediately succeeding statement (p. 189) that "This latter proposition is one which we do not propose to decide in the present case because we are able to decide the case without passing upon the existence or non-existence of such a power in aid of the legislative function."

Next in order is *In re Chapman,* 166 U.S. 661. The inquiry there in question was conducted under a resolution of the Senate and related to charges, published in the press, that senators were yielding to corrupt influences in considering a tariff bill then before the Senate and were speculating in stocks the value of which would be affected by pending amendments to the bill. Chapman appeared before the committee in response to a subpoena, but refused to answer questions pertinent to the inquiry, and was indicated and convicted under the act of 1857 for his refusal. The Court sustained the constitutional validity of the act of 1857, and, after referring to the constitutional provision empowering either house to punish its members for disorderly behavior and by a vote of two-thirds to expel a member, held that the inquiry related to the integrity and fidelity of senators in the discharge of their duties, and therefore to a matter "within the range of the constitutional powers of the Senate" and in respect of which it could compel witnesses to appear and testify. In overruling an objection that the inquiry was without any defined or admissible purpose, in that the preamble and resolution made no reference to any contemplated expulsion, censure, or other action by the Senate, the Court held that they adequately disclosed a subject-matter of which the Senate had jurisdiction, that it was not essential that the Senate declare in advance what it meditated doing, and that the assumption could not be indulged that the Senate was making the inquiry without a legitimate object.

The case is relied on here as fully sustaining the power of either house to conduct investigations and exact testimony from witnesses for legislative purposes. In the course of the opinion (p. 671) it is said that disclosures by witnesses may be compelled constitutionally "to enable the respective bodies to discharge their legitimate functions, and that it was to effect this that the act of 1857 was passed"; and also "We grant that Congress could not divest itself, or either of its houses, of the essential and inherent power to punish for contempt, in cases to which the power of either house properly extended; but, because Congress, by the act of 1857, sought to aid each of the houses in the discharge of its constitutional functions, it does not follow that any delegation of the power in each to punish for contempt was involved." The terms "legitimate functions" and "constitutional functions" are broad and might well be regarded as including the legislative function, but as the case in hand did not call for any expression respecting that function, it hardly can be said that these terms were purposely used as including it.

The latest case is *Marshall* v. *Gordon,* 243 U.S. 521. The question there was whether the House of Representatives exceeded its power in punishing, as for a contempt of its authority, a person—not a member—who had written, published and sent to the chairman of one of its committees an ill-tempered and irritating letter respecting the action and purposes of the committee. Power to make inquiries and obtain evidence by compulsory process was not involved. The Court recognized distinctly that the House of Representatives has implied power to punish a person not a member for contempt, as was ruled in *Anderson* v. *Dunn, supra,* but held that its action in this instance was without constitutional justification. The decision was put on the ground that the letter, while offensive and vexatious, was not calculated or likely to affect the House in any of its proceedings or in the exercise of any of its functions—in short, that the act which was punished as a contempt was not of such a character as to bring it within the rule that an express power draws after it others which are necessary and appropriate to give effect to it.

While these cases are not decisive of the question we are considering, they definitely settle two propositions which we recognize as entirely sound and having a bearing on its solution: One, that the two houses of Congress, in their separate relations, possess not only such powers as are expressly granted to them by the Constitution, but such auxiliary powers as are necessary and appropriate to make the express powers effective; and, the other, that neither house is invested with "general" power to inquire into private affairs and compel disclosures, but only with such limited power of inquiry as is shown to exist when the rule of constitutional interpretation just stated is rightly applied. The latter proposition has further support in *Harriman* v. *Interstate Commerce Commission,* 211 U.S. 407, 417–419, and *Federal Trade Commission* v. *American Tobacco Company,* 264 U.S. 298, 305–306.

With this review of the legislative practice, congressional enactments and court decisions, we proceed to a statement of our conclusions on the question.

We are of opinion that the power of inquiry—with process to enforce it—is an essential and appropriate auxiliary to the legislative function. It was so regarded and employed in American legislatures before the Constitution was framed and ratified. Both houses of Congress took this view of it early in their history—the House of Representatives with the approving votes of Mr. Madison and other members whose service in the convention which framed the Constitution gives special significance to their action—and both houses have employed the power accordingly up to the present time. The acts of 1798 and 1857, judged by their comprehensive terms, were intended to recognize the existence of this power in both houses and to enable them to employ it "more effectually" than before. So, when their practice in the matter is appraised according to the circumstances in which it was begun and to those in which it has been continued, it falls nothing short of a practical construction, long continued, of the constitutional provisions respecting their powers, and therefore should be taken as fixing the meaning of those provisions, if otherwise doubtful.[19]

We are further of opinion that the provisions are not of doubtful meaning, but, as was held by this Court in the cases we have reviewed, are intended to be effectively exercised, and therefore to carry with them such auxiliary powers as are necessary and appropriate to that end. While the power to exact information in aid of the legislative function was not involved in those cases, the rule of interpretation applied there is applicable here. A legislative body cannot legislate wisely or effectively in the absence of information respecting the conditions which the legislation is intended to affect or change; and where the legislative body does not itself possess the requisite information—which not infrequently is true—recourse must be had to others who do possess it. Experience has taught that mere requests for such information often are unavailing, and also that information which is volunteered is not always accurate or complete; so some means of compulsion are essential to obtain what is needed. All this was true before and when the Constitution was framed and adopted. In that period the power of inquiry—with enforcing process—was regarded and employed as a necessary and appropriate attribute of the power to legislate—indeed, was treated as inhering in it. Thus there is ample warrant for thinking, as we do, that the constitutional provisions which commit the legislative function to the two houses are intended to include this attribute to the end that the function may be effectively exercised.

The contention is earnestly made on behalf of the witness that this power of inquiry, if sustained, may be abusively and oppressively exerted. If this be so, it affords no ground for denying the power. The same contention might be directed against the power to legislate, and of course would be unavailing. We must assume, for present purposes, that neither house will be disposed to exert the power beyond its proper bounds, or without due regard to the rights of witnesses. But if, contrary to this assumption, controlling limitations or restrictions are disregarded, the decisions in *Kilbourn* v. *Thompson* and *Marshall* v. *Gordon* point to admissible measures of relief. And it is a necessary deduction from the decisions in *Kilbourn* v. *Thompson* and *In re Chapman* that a witness rightfully may refuse to answer where the bounds of the power are exceeded or the questions are not pertinent to the matter under inquiry.

We come now to the question whether it sufficiently appears that the purpose for which the witness's testimony was sought was to obtain information in aid of the legislative function. The court below answered the question in the negative and put its decision largely on this ground, as is shown by the following excerpts from its opinion (299 Fed. 638, 639, 640):

"It will be noted that in the second resolution the Senate has expressly avowed that the investigation is in aid of other action than legislation. Its purpose is to 'obtain information necessary as a basis for such legislative and other action as the Senate may deem necessary and proper.' This indicates that the Senate is contemplating the taking of action other than legislative, as the outcome of the investigation, at least the possibility of so doing. The extreme personal cast of the original resolutions; the spirit of hostility towards the then Attorney General which they breathe; that it was not avowed that legislative action was had in view until after the action of the Senate had been challenged; and that the avowal then was coupled with an avowal that other action was had in view—are calculated to create

[19] Stuart *v*. Laird, *1 Cranch 299, 309;* Martin *v*. Hunter's Lessee, *1 Wheat. 304, 351;* Ames *v*. Kansas, *111 U.S. 449, 469;* Knowlton *v*. Moore, *178 U.S. 41, 56, 92;* Fairbanks *v*. United States, *181 U.S. 283, 306,* et seq.

the impression that the idea of legislative action being in contemplation was an afterthought.

"That the Senate has in contemplation the possibility of taking action other than legislation as an outcome of the investigation, as thus expressly avowed, would seem of itself to invalidate the entire proceeding. But, whether so or not, the Senate's action is invalid and absolutely void, in that, in ordering and conducting the investigation, it is exercising the judicial function, and power to exercise that function, in such a case as we have here, has not been conferred upon it expressly or by fair implication. What it is proposing to do is to determine the guilt of the Attorney General of the shortcomings and wrongdoings set forth in the resolutions. It is 'to hear, adjudge, and condemn.' In so doing it is exercising the judicial function.

"What the Senate is engaged in doing is not investigating the Attorney General's office; it is investigating the former Attorney General. What it has done is to put him on trial before it. In so doing it is exercising the judicial function. This it has no power to do."

We are of opinion that the court's ruling on this question was wrong, and that it sufficiently appears, when the proceedings are rightly interpreted, that the object of the investigation and of the effort to secure the witness's testimony was to obtain information for legislative purposes.

It is quite true that the resolution directing the investigation does not in terms avow that it is intended to be in aid of legislation; but it does show that the subject to be investigated was the administration of the Department of Justice—whether its functions were being properly discharged or were being neglected or misdirected, and particularly whether the Attorney General and his assistants were performing or neglecting their duties in respect of the institution and prosecution of proceedings to punish crimes and enforce appropriate remedies against the wrongdoers—specific instances of alleged neglect being recited. Plainly the subject was one of which legislation could be had and would be materially aided by the information which the investigation was calculated to elicit. This becomes manifest when it is reflected that the functions of the Department of Justice, the powers and duties of the Attorney General and the duties of his assistants, are all subject to regulation by congressional legislation, and that the department is maintained and its activities are carried on under such appropriations as in the judgment of Congress are needed from year to year.

The only legitimate object the Senate could have in ordering the investigation was to aid it in legislating; and we think the subject-matter was such that the presumption should be indulged that this was the real object. An express avowal of the object would have been better; but in view of the particular subject-matter was not indispensable. In the *Chapman* case, where the resolution contained no avowal, this Court pointed out that it plainly related to a subject-matter of which the Senate had jurisdiction, and said "We cannot assume on this record that the action of the Senate was without a legitimate object"; and also that "it was certainly not necessary that the resolutions should declare in advance what the Senate meditated doing when the investigation was concluded." (166 U.S. 669–670.) In *People* v. *Keeler*, 99 N.Y. 463, where the Court of Appeals of New York sustained an investigation ordered by the Senate of that state where the resolution contained no avowal, but disclosed that it definitely related to the administration of a public office the duties of which were subject to legislative regulation, the court said (pp. 485, 487): "Where public institutions under the control of the State are ordered to be investigated it is generally with the view of some legislative action respecting them, and the same may be said in respect of public officers." And again: "We are bound to presume that the action of the legislative body was with a legitimate object if it is capable of being so construed, and we have no right to assume that the contrary was intended."

While we rest our conclusion respecting the object of the investigation on the grounds just stated, it is well to observe that this view of what was intended is not new, but was shown in the debate on the resolution.[20]

[20] *Senator George said: "It is not a trial now that is proposed, and there has been no trial proposed save the civil and criminal actions to be instituted and prosecuted by counsel employed under the resolution giving to the President the power to employ counsel. We are not to try the Attorney General. He is not to go upon trial. Shall we say the legislative branch of the Government shall stickle and halt and hesitate because a man's public reputation, his public character, may suffer because of that legislative action? Has*

Of course, our concern is with the substance of the resolution and not with any nice questions of propriety respecting its direct reference to the then Attorney General by name. The resolution, like the charges which prompted its adoption, related to the activities of the department while he was its supervising officer; and the reference to him by name served to designate the period to which the investigation was directed.

We think the resolution and proceedings give no warrant for thinking the Senate was attempting or intending to try the Attorney General at its bar or before its committee for any crime or wrongdoing. Nor do we think it a valid objection to the investigation that it might possibly disclose crime or wrongdoing on his part.

The second resolution—the one directing that the witness be attached—declares that his testimony is sought with the purpose of obtaining "information necessary as a basis for such legislative and other action as the Senate may deem necessary and proper." This avowal of contemplated legislation is in accord with what we think is the right interpretation of the earlier resolution directing the investigation. The suggested possibility of "other action" if deemed "necessary or proper" is of course open to criticism in that there is no other action in the matter which would be within the power of the Senate. But we do not assent to the view that this indefinite and untenable suggestion invalidates the entire proceeding. The right view in our opinion is that it takes nothing from the lawful object avowed in the same resolution and rightly inferable from the earlier one. It is not as if an inadmissible or unlawful object were affirmatively and definitely avowed.

We conclude that the investigation was ordered for a legitimate object; that the witness wrongfully refused to appear and testify before the committee and was lawfully attached; that the Senate is entitled to have him give testimony pertinent to the inquiry, either at its bar or before the committee; and that the district court erred in discharging him from custody under the attachment.

Another question has arisen which should be noticed. It is whether the case has become moot. The investigation was ordered and the committee appointed during the Sixty-eighth Congress. That Congress expired March 4, 1925. The resolution ordering the investigation in terms limited the committee's authority to the period of the Sixty-eighth Congress; but this apparently was changed by a later and amendatory resolution authorizing the committee to sit at such times and places as it might deem advisable or necessary.[21] It is said in Jefferson's Manual:[22] "Neither House can continue any portion of itself in any parliamentary function beyond the end of the session without the consent of the other two branches. When done, it is by a bill constituting them commissioners for the particular purpose." But the context shows that the reference is to the two houses of Parliament when adjourned by prorogation or dissolution by the King. The rule may be the same with the House of Representatives whose members are all elected for the period of a single Congress; but it cannot well be the same with the Senate, which is a continuing body whose members are elected for a term of six years and so divided into classes that the seats of one-third only become vacant at the end of each Congress, two-thirds always continuing into the next Congress, save as vacancies may occur through death or resignation.

Mr. Hinds in his collection of precedents says: "The Senate, as a continuing body, may continue its committees through the recess following the expiration of a

not the Senate power to appoint a committee to investigate any department of the Government, any department supported by the Senate in part by appropriations made by the Congress? If the Senate has the right to investigate the department, is the Senate to hesitate, is the Senate to refuse to do its duty merely because the public character or the public reputation of some one who is investigated may be thereby smirched, to use the term that has been used so often in the debate? . . . It is sufficient for me to know that there are grounds upon which I may justly base my vote for the resolution; and I am willing to leave it to the agent created by the Senate to proceed with the investigation fearlessly upon principle, not for the purpose of trying but for the purpose of ascertaining facts which the Senate is entitled to have within its possession in order that it may properly function as a legislative body." Cong. Rec., 68th Cong., 1st Sess., pp. 3397, 3398.

[21] *Cong. Rec., 68th Cong., 1st Sess., p. 4126.*
[22] *Senate Rules and Manual, 1925, p. 303.*

Congress";[23] and, after quoting the above statement from Jefferson's Manual, he says: "The Senate, however, being a continuing body, gives authority to its committees during the recess after the expiration of a Congress."[24] So far as we are advised the select committee having this investigation in charge has neither made a final report nor been discharged; nor has it been continued by an affirmative order. Apparently its activities have been suspended pending the decision of this case. But, be this as it may, it is certain that the committee may be continued or revived now by motion to that effect, and, if continued or revived, will have all its original powers.[25] This being so, and the Senate being a continuing body, the case cannot be said to have become moot in the ordinary sense. The situation is measurably like that in *Southern Pacific Terminal Co.* v. *Interstate Commerce Commission,* 219 U.S. 498, 514–516, where it was held that a suit to enjoin the enforcement of an order of the Interstate Commerce Commission did not become moot through the expiration of the order where it was capable of repetition by the commission and was a matter of public interest. Our judgment may yet be carried into effect and the investigation proceeded with from the point at which it apparently was interrupted by reason of the *habeas corpus* proceedings. In these circumstances we think a judgment should be rendered as was done in the case cited.

What has been said requires that the final order in the district court discharging the witness from custody be reversed.

Final order reversed.

[23] *Vol. 4, sec. 4544.*
[24] *Vol. 4, sec. 4545.*
[25] *Hinds' Precedents, Vol. 4, secs. 4396, 4400, 4404, 4405.*

Joseph Rucker Lamar

☆ 1857–1916 ☆

APPOINTED BY

WILLIAM HOWARD TAFT

YEARS ON COURT

1911–1916

Joseph Rucker Lamar

by

LEONARD DINNERSTEIN

Praised in his own generation yet forgotten by the next, Joseph Rucker Lamar possessed both the virtues and limitations of the Progressive Era's conservative lawyers. Contemporaries lauded him as worthy, able, and of unquestionable integrity. Although Lamar had no doubt earned these accolades, he lacked originality, and an abiding loyalty to a patrician background limited his understanding of a changing society's needs and prevented him from assuming a place in the forefront of American jurists.

In appearance, Joseph Lamar epitomized the Supreme Court Justice. Standing six feet tall, the erect and angular Georgian had well-proportioned and clear cut features: a large Roman nose, a high, broad forehead, and silvery gray hair. With a voice "singularly resonant, full-toned, and bell-like in quality," he would later be ranked by Associate Justice Charles Evans Hughes as the Court's "star performer" in rendering judgments from the bench. Lamar's great charm and conspicuous probity made him a genial colleague. "We all loved him," Associate Justice Oliver Wendell Holmes said, and there seem to have been no dissenting opinions. Thomas Gregory, President Woodrow Wilson's Attorney General, would later eulogize the Georgian for his most dominant characteristic of "a peculiarly winning courtesy, a kindly consideration for all with whom he came in contact." He was, in truth, "an old-fashioned southern gentleman, of charming manner, and of that type in which the South takes most pride."

In the five years that he served on the United States Supreme Court, 1911–1916, Lamar supported moderate state and federal regulation of private economic activities, favored an enlarged use of federal administrative powers, and advocated judicial intervention to protect personal liberty. He based some of his opinions, however, on narrow and traditional concepts about "liberty of contract," businesses "affected with a public interest" and the relationship of boycotts

LEONARD DINNERSTEIN is Assistant Professor of History at the Fairleigh Dickinson University and recently published The Leo Frank Case.

to the First Amendment guarantee of freedom of speech. Although Lamar wrote some decisions of importance, they failed to capture either popular or scholarly imaginations. Neither an originator nor an enunciator of novel constitutional interpretations, he was well suited to sit on the High Bench during a relatively quiescent period in Supreme Court history. Since his death historians have ignored him and he has been relegated, by default, to a place among the Court's forgotten men.

John Schmidhauser has written in *The Supreme Court: Its Politics, Personalities and Procedures* that there has been "a virtual monopolization of Supreme Court appointments by the socially privileged segment of the population dubbed 'old Americans.' " Joseph Rucker Lamar is a perfect example of this observation. Of patrician origin, affluent economic circumstances, and a socially prominent family, the Georgian jurist had an easy road to travel in life. His path was well defined by his forbears and his training was predicated upon the anticipation that he would naturally assume a role of leadership in society. Lamar's life accomplishment was to realize these expectations, but our quickly changing industrial society does not grant lasting fame to those whose major achievements lie in the reaffirmation of conventional concepts and standards.

Descended from two of Georgia's most distinguished families—the Ruckers and the Lamars—Joseph Rucker Lamar was born on October 14, 1857, at the plantation home of his maternal grandfather, Joseph Rucker, in Ruckersville, Elbert County, Georgia. On his father's side he traced his ancestry to Thomas Lamar, a French Huguenot, who had settled in Maryland during the 1670's. Four of Thomas Lamar's grandsons moved to South Carolina, and their descendants dispersed throughout the South. They included Mirabeau Lamar, poet and president of the Republic of Texas (1838 to 1841), and Lucius Quintus Cincinnatus Lamar, Associate Justice of the United States Supreme Court (1888 to 1893). The Ruckers also had had a distinguished heritage. They settled in Virginia and Georgia sometime before the 1730's. Joseph Rucker, of Scotch-Irish descent, had been a pioneer banker, merchant, planter and man of affairs. In 1790 he founded Ruckersville, a community later known for its lush rice and tobacco plantations. His youngest daughter, Mary, married James S. Lamar at the family estate on June 19, 1856. Sixteen months later she was delivered of their first son, Joseph Rucker. Two other children, Philip and Mary, were born before Mary Rucker Lamar died on January 27, 1864. In December, 1865, James Lamar remarried and moved his children from their grandfather's home to Augusta.

In Augusta the Lamar boys attended the renowned and academically demanding Richmond Academy. There they became friendly with Thomas Woodrow Wilson, a schoolmate and neighbor. The Lamars and Wilsons, in fact, had much in common. Dr. Joseph Wilson was the pastor of the leading Presbyterian Church in the city while James Lamar presided over the First Christian Church. The parsonages stood side by side and the sons of the two ministers played baseball together and belonged to the same debating society. In 1870 the

Wilsons moved to South Carolina. Joseph Lamar did not meet Woodrow Wilson again until 1913, in Washington, when each one had reached the pinnacle of his career. Both had obviously benefited from their rigorous childhood training which did much to prepare them for their preeminent roles in later life.

After leaving the Richmond Academy in Augusta, Lamar attended the Martin Institute in Jackson County, Georgia, and the Penn Lucy Academy in Baltimore. In 1874 he entered the University of Georgia in Athens. A serious illness forced him to leave the school after his second year, but he later resumed his studies and received his baccalaureate degree in 1877, from Bethany College in West Virginia, his father's alma mater. After graduation he studied law at Washington and Lee University but left before receiving a degree to serve as clerk for the prominent Augusta attorney, Henry Clay Foster. This practical experience helped him pass the Georgia bar examination which in those days consisted of a judge asking prospective lawyers a series of questions in the courtroom. In April, 1878, six months before reaching his twenty-second birthday, Joseph Rucker Lamar qualified to practice law in Georgia. So far his life had been exactly what tradition had dictated and his future would be more of the same. The following January 30 he married Clarinda Huntington Pendleton, daughter of the President of Bethany College. The union, which lasted until the Justice's death in 1916, produced three children: Philip Rucker, born in 1880; William Pendleton, born in 1882; and Mary, born—and deceased—in 1885.

After his marriage, Lamar taught Latin for a year at Bethany College, but when Henry Clay Foster offered the young attorney a partnership, in 1880, he quickly accepted. The two practiced together until the senior partner's death in 1890. Between 1886 and 1889 Lamar was the elected representative of Richmond County (which included the city of Augusta) in the lower house of Georgia's state legislature. Particularly concerned with law reform, he authored the Eminent Domain and Assignment Acts, legislation which led to more economical and expeditious administration of justice in the state.

Before the nineteenth century had ended, Lamar ranked among the most prominent attorneys in Georgia. Recognition of his superior legal talent came in 1893 when Governor J. M. Terrell and the justices of the state Supreme Court unanimously chose him as one of the commissioners to rewrite the state's law codes. Lamar was largely responsible for the revised Civil Code adopted in 1895, and this achievement stands as a monument to his public service. In 1898 the state Supreme Court again honored him with an appointment to the board examining prospective bar applicants. With the exception of the two years that he served on Georgia's Supreme Court, Lamar retained this post until elevated to the United States Supreme Court by President Taft. From 1905 to 1910 he served as the board's chairman.

Fame also came to the Augusta attorney because of his writings on the state's legal history. He had a strong feeling for Georgia's heritage and traditions and he always found time for scholarly pursuits. He traveled to London and with the skill and commitment of a dedicated historian examined the voluminous data on Georgia's legal institutions in colonial times; he also searched through the colonial documents of Richmond, Wilkes, and Chatham Counties (Georgia), and he claimed to have been one of two men who had ever investigated the Colonial Records of Georgia "page by page." These explorations in depth led to the unearthing of considerable new material which he utilized in providing fresh insights into many of the legal developments of Georgia. In "The Bench and Bar of Georgia during the Eighteenth Century," he demonstrated how the early Georgians "were the first law reformers and the first to endeavor to get rid of the encumbering technicalities of the English procedure." Lamar also pointed out in this essay how indebted members of the Georgian bar were to the earliest practitioners in the colony for "the simplicity of our practice and the advantages of our procedure." In "Georgia's Contribution to Law Reform," Lamar showed that between 1799 and 1818 the state pioneered in the codification of the common law. And in "A Century's Progress in Law" he discussed how the judiciary had waxed in American popular feeling between 1800 and 1900 and how the law had helped to elevate and exalt the individual. Other essays also won him acclaim; some were delivered, by request, before the bar associations of Alabama and Tennessee. Included among his other notable articles are "Work and Position of the American Court," "A History of the Organization of the Supreme Court," "Life of Judge Nisbet," "Georgia's Law Books," and "A Sketch of Howell Cobb." All of his works were characterized by careful research and presentation. They have also added immeasurably to the legal history of Georgia. Some of his analyses, in fact, have been deemed "the best in their field" by A. B. Saye in *A Constitutional History of Georgia.*

One of the leading citizens in Augusta, and widely known in legal circles throughout the state, Lamar was frequently called upon to deliver important addresses. For the most part, he uttered the conventional platitudes more eloquently than his peers. One of these speeches, however, won him a reputation as a social philosopher. It was delivered on Confederate Memorial Day, April 26, 1902, at the Confederate Memorial Cemetery in Athens, Georgia. Although in his stated topic, "The Private Soldier of the Confederacy," he eulogized the heroic deeds and the patriotic fervor of the southern man-in-the-ranks, he also took the occasion to speak out on the current treatment of the Negro. Lamar deplored the fact that after the end of the Civil War "the Negro [had] been given not only freedom but license." He insisted that the Negro could "only be elevated by education,—not the mere education of books, but the education that comes from contact with the superior mind." Imploring the southern farmer to tutor his Negro tenant, Lamar observed: "If we would direct his labor, it will be the betterment of all concerned." Although the Augusta attorney did not say anything that most leading southerners were not in agreement with, the subject was important because knowledgeable men throughout the nation were concerned with how the Negro could be productively integrated into American society. The speech, in fact, so impressed Albert Shaw, editor of the prominent

Review of Reviews, that he reprinted the talk and gave it wide circulation throughout the nation.

Lamar's legal talents had already been heralded in Georgia and therefore when a vacancy occurred on the state supreme court few observers failed to acclaim Governor J. S. Terrell's selection of the Augusta attorney to fill the position. Mrs. Lamar later wrote that a seat on the state's high bench had been one of her husband's cherished ambitions. He accepted the appointment on December 31, 1902, and took his seat two weeks later; he won popular approval when he successfully ran for reelection in 1904.

While on the Georgia supreme court (1903–1905), Lamar's decisions impressed his colleagues for their terse expressions and convincing reasoning. In some of his more notable rulings he enjoined Georgia from taxing a private college, upheld the state's police powers in regulating public health, morals, and safety, and refused to enforce an oral promise to change an employee's wage made after a written contract had been signed.

In the case of *Linton* v. *Lucy Cobb Institute,* 117 Georgia 678 (1903), the state of Georgia had attempted to collect taxes from the private college because it charged tuition. The state contended that only free schools should be tax exempt and that those charging fees were, in fact, deriving an income from the buildings used for teaching purposes. Lamar ruled that the college charged its students merely to pay a portion of the education costs and not with the intent of deriving a profit. The ruling precluded any further taxation of private schools in Georgia.

Lamar, in a decision foreshadowing the dominant judicial trend and his own positions taken while on the United States Supreme Court, upheld Georgia's right to regulate the sale of cotton seed on the ground that the state has the right of "preserving the public health, the public morals, or the public safety." (See *Bazemore* v. *The State,* 121 Georgia 619 [1905].) The law in question prohibited the sale of cotton seed except under certain conditions, stipulated by statute, because it was a product which could easily be stolen. The plaintiff argued that this regulation constituted a violation of due process and an infringement on his right to control his own property. In his opinion, however, Lamar stressed the state's right to regulate occupations and control products "where from their nature they offer peculiar opportunities for imposition and fraud."

While Judge Lamar acknowledged the state's role in protecting persons and property, he refused to allow the courts to enforce any oral agreements which had been made "without consideration" when a binding written contract remained in force. Hence an employer, who had already agreed, in writing, to pay his employee a specific sum for a year's work, could not be legally bound by a subsequent oral promise to raise this figure if the worker faithfully fulfilled his obligations, (*Davis and Company* v. *Morgan,* 117 Georgia 504 [1903].)

Perhaps his most widely discussed decision came in the case of *Oliver* v. *Oliver,* 118 Georgia 362 (1903). A corporation director had secretly contracted to sell the firm's shares at $185. Without informing the stockholders of this transaction, he induced them to let him have their holdings for $110 per share. When the original owners discovered that they had been swindled, they sued for retribution. Lamar, writing the majority opinion for the Georgia Supreme Court, declared that a company director is a trustee for all the stockholders and that he is required to divulge all pertinent information to them. Since the shareowners had entrusted him with managerial responsibilities, his conduct was dishonest, and they were entitled to rescind the sale. The significance of the decision was that the court indicated it would not allow those entrusted with managerial responsibilities to benefit from information improperly withheld from the property owners.

Lamar performed his work on the court diligently, writing over 200 opinions during his two-year tenure, all of which are in *Georgia Reports,* volumes 117–122. Overwork, ill health, homesickness for Augusta, and possibly a desire for financial security, caused him to resign from his position on April 10, 1905 and resume private practice. This was done despite the fact that two years earlier a seat on the high bench of Georgia had supposedly been his "cherished ambition."

After leaving Georgia's Supreme Court, Lamar established a lucrative partnership with E. H. Callaway, formerly a judge of the superior court of the Augusta Circuit. Specializing in corporate law, they represented railroads as well as other corporations. The most famous case tried by the firm occurred when the state of Georgia attempted to collect back taxes from two state railroads. The Georgia Railroad and Banking Company and the Central of Georgia Railway each owned 15,000 shares in the Western Railway of Alabama, a "foreign corporation," exempt from state taxation under the laws of Georgia as understood during the nineteenth century. In 1901, however, the Attorney General ruled that income from "foreign corporations" was taxable. The Georgia Railroads disputed the ruling but the United States Supreme Court upheld the state. Shortly thereafter the Georgia comptroller assessed the railroads for twenty-two years of back taxes. The companies hired Joseph R. Lamar to represent them and he quickly obtained an injunction temporarily restraining the comptroller's order. Lamar's brief disputed the assessment because a hearing had been denied to the railroads before the edict had been issued. Stressing the due process clause of the Fourteenth Amendment, Lamar claimed that a hearing was mandatory before the comptroller's ruling could be effected. The case was then unsuccessfully appealed in Georgia but the United States Supreme Court upheld Lamar's logic and reversed the lower court ruling in *The Central of Georgia Railway Company* v. *Wright,* 207 U.S. 127 (1907). For the majority, Justice William Day wrote that an assessment of a tax is judicial in nature and that the taxpayer is entitled to a hearing before being deprived of his property. Lamar's associates agreed that Justice Day's decision rested on the specific arguments that the Georgia attorney had presented in his brief.

The Supreme Court decided the *Central of Georgia Railway* case in November, 1907. One year later President-elect William Howard Taft visited

Augusta, Georgia, in search of needed relaxation after his victorious campaign. During his stay Taft golfed frequently with Joseph R. Lamar. Although the two had not met previously, Taft found Lamar's personality and intellect particularly engaging. Upon entering the White House the new President did not forget his Georgia golfing companion. In 1910 Taft considered Lamar for an opening on the Commerce Court, but when he consulted Georgia's Senator Augustus O. Bacon, the legislator suggested that Lamar be nominated for the Supreme Court vacancy. Taft made additional inquiries and received glowing reports. "He is the best lawyer in Georgia," one correspondent wrote; another stated: "If I were called upon to construct a model for a judge, I would take Lamar as he is." With descriptions like these, Taft made the appointment.

Two days after the President nominated Edward D. White to assume the Chief Justiceship, he recommended Lamar to fill the chair that Associate Justice White would vacate. When informed of Taft's decision, Lamar expressed doubts about the Senate approving him. Only the third man ever tapped for the Supreme Court by a President of another party—Howell Jackson and Horace Lurton were the others—Lamar believed that as a southerner, a Democrat, and a relatively unknown figure outside of his state, he would have difficulty winning confirmation. His fears proved unfounded. On December 15, 1910, only three days after receiving the nomination, the Senate unanimously endorsed President Taft's choice. On January 3, 1911, Lamar became the fourth Georgian, and the only former member of the state's Supreme Court, accorded the honor of serving on the United States Supreme Court.

The distinguished Georgian, whose background and training made him receptive to gradual change in order to preserve society's essential foundations, joined the Court after the resounding political triumph of progressive candidates in the election of 1910. It is often said that the Supreme Court follows the election returns; this was certainly true during Lamar's years on the High Bench, 1911–1916. In this period the Justices sustained the federal Pure Food and Drug Act, (*Hipolite Egg Company* v. *United States,* 220 U.S. 45 [1911]), upheld the Mann Act which made it a federal offense to transport female minors across state lines for immoral purposes, (*Hoke* v. *United States,* 227 U.S. 308 [1913]), and sanctioned the Interstate Commerce Commission fixing intrastate railroad rates where the circumstances warranted it, (*The Shreveport Case, Houston, East & West Texas Ry. Co.* v. *United States,* 234 U.S. 342 [1914]). Furthermore, the Standard Oil Company was ordered to dissolve, (*United States* v. *Ohio Oil Co.,* 234 U.S. 548 [1914]), and the American Tobacco Company required to reorganize under Chief Justice Edward D. White's heralded "rule of reason," (*United States* v. *American Tobacco Co.,* 221 U.S. 106 [1911]). A majority of the brethren concurred in White's new dictum, and "reasonableness" became the rallying point for the Court. Whether it be due process, administrative discretion, or the extent of federal and state police powers, the Justices attempted to follow a "reasonable" policy. Their definition, of course, was merely a subjective interpretation arrived at by each man according to his own understanding of the motto.

There were relatively few diagreements among the members of the Court during Lamar's tenure. This can be attributed as much to President Taft as to the election returns. As President, Taft, extremely careful and quite concerned about his judicial appointments, virtually reconstituted the Court. He not only selected five new men but elevated Edward D. White to preside over all of them. In appointing new Justices, the President looked for sound lawyers, of moderately conservative or mildly progressive outlooks, and of high professional standing whose attitudes were similar to his own. Moreover, he sought vigorous men in their middle years who would carry their full load of the Court's work. In May, 1909, for example, he had lamented to his friend Horace Lurton, then still a circuit judge:

> *The condition of the Supreme Court is pitiable, and yet those old fools hold on with a tenacity that is most discouraging. Really the Chief Justice* [*Fuller*] *is almost senile; Harlan does no work; Brewer is so deaf that he cannot hear and has got beyond the point of the commonest accuracy in writing his opinions; Brewer and Harlan sleep almost through all the arguments. I don't know what can be done. It is most discouraging to the active men on the Bench.*

Taft did not hold tenaciously to all of these qualifications (Lurton, for example, was sixty-five at the time of his nomination), but the men that he selected (Lurton, Hughes, Willis Van Devanter, Lamar and Mahlon Pitney) were slightly left of center and generally in accord with the President's fundamental political and economic views. Since the holdover Judges (Harlan, Holmes, McKenna and Day) had been among the most liberal of those appointed by previous Presidents, the new Court assumed, to a considerable extent, a mildly progressive posture. Unlike the 1890's, there were no died-in-the-wool conservatives like Field and Peckham, nor did the Justices fear a radical take-over in society which would undermine American civilization. "Now the Court is working as a unit," *The Outlook* observed in July, 1914, "Its members seem to understand one another." The general consensus among the brethren precluded any expression of the negativism that had been exhibited in the *E. C. Knight* case, 156 U.S. 1 (1895), or the *Lochner* decision, 198 U.S. 45 (1905); there were, with perhaps one or two exceptions, no ringing dissents, no conflicts with the legislative or executive branches of the state or federal governments, and no strikingly significant constitutional interpretations propounded. Unlike Marshall and *McCulloch* v. *Maryland,* 4 Wheat. 316 (1819), Taney and *Dred Scott,* 19 How. 393 (1857), Warren and *Brown* v. *Board of Education,* 347 U.S. 483 (1954), the years 1911 through 1915—with the possible exception of White and the *Standard Oil* and *American Tobacco* cases—were singularly free of famous suits or markedly original enunciations of policy. In November, 1915, *The Nation* described the spirit of the Court as one of "mellow conservatism, informed with a full sympathy for rational progress."

Although it would be difficult to categorize the nature of the cases that came before the Court's purview during Lamar's tenure, the issues with which society seemed most concerned at the time did recur: antitrust suits, railroad regulation, the exercise of state and federal police powers, and the extent of administrative authority. Lamar's opinions do not lend themselves to neat classifications. The Georgian Justice, however, generally agreed with the conclusions of his colleagues. With regard to state economic regulations, for example, he voted with his fellow Justices in upholding the states' police powers on 150 occasions and opposed them only four times; when the Court ruled that the states had overstepped their bounds, Lamar agreed in seventy-one out of seventy-four cases. Mrs. Lamar observed afterwards that her husband was not a dissenting Judge, and the record of only eight written dissents in four years bears out this conclusion. It also underscores the strong similarity of viewpoints among the brethren during this period.

It is not surprising that foremost among Lamar's decisions are the opinions that he wrote giving wide latitude to members of the executive branch in their administrative decisions. His legal scholarship had impressed him with the importance of society's need for an intelligent administration of the laws, and his experiences as a reviser of Georgia's codes and a judge on its Supreme Court no doubt solidified these views. Finally, he had both absorbed and reflected the progressive concern with strong governmental management and efficient administration. Hence his rulings in *Degge* v. *Hitchcock,* 229 U.S. 162 (1913); *Interstate Commerce Commission* v. *Louisville and Nashville Railroad Company,* 227 U.S. 88 (1913); *United States* v. *Grimaud,* 220 U.S. 506 (1911); and *United States* v. *Midwest Oil Company,* 236 U.S. 459 (1915).

In *Degge* v. *Hitchcock,* a corporation which had been using the mails to engage in activities which the Postmaster General considered of dubious merit sued the Cabinet officer because he refused to allow delivery of their mail. When the case reached the Supreme Court, Lamar observed that this was the first time that a federal court had been asked to issue a writ of certiorari to review a ruling of a federal executive officer. Without commenting upon the nature of the firm's business, Lamar, for the Court, stated that a writ of certiorari could not be issued as such writs would make the executive departments completely dependent upon judicial review, a system which would "only lead to consequences of the most manifest inconvenience [and] would be an invasion of the Executive by the Judicial branch of the Government." In *Interstate Commerce Commission* v. *Louisville and Nashville Railroad,* Lamar wrote that an administrative ruling concerning a railroad rate could not be set aside by the Court because the Hepburn Act of 1906 had allowed the commission the authority to alter a rate which, after granting a proper hearing, it felt was not valid, "even if the finding was wholly without substantial evidence to support it." In reviewing the case, however, he noted that there was sufficient, albeit conflicting, evidence to sustain the commission's ruling. Parenthetically he also observed that an administrative decision without evidence was arbitrary, but this, he added, was not the question before the Court.

United States v. *Grimaud* and *United States* v. *Midwest Oil* are perhaps his two best known opinions with regard to administrative authority. In the former, the defense attorneys claimed that the powers delegated to the Secretary of Agriculture by Congress under the Forest Reserve Act of 1891 constituted an unconstitutional transfer of legislative authority, hence all administrative decisions made under this power must be void. The plaintiffs, however, disputed this claim. The government believed that the establishment of certain administrative procedures was perfectly coincident with the authority vested in the executive branch by Congress. Lamar upheld the constitutionality of the act in question. He wrote that Congress had the right to authorize administrators to carry out the details and management of a policy after it had indicated its intention. "In authorizing the Secretary of Agriculture to meet these local conditions," he stated, "Congress was merely conferring administrative functions upon an agent, and not delegating to him legislative power." The decision had marked and far reaching effects and proved a landmark in the development of administrative law. It stamped the Court's approval upon legislative delegation of administrative functions, thereby allowing Congress to state its objectives broadly while leaving details and minor policy determinations to administrative discretion. Finally this opinion helped to spawn numerous federal commissions and bureaus.

The other significant ruling which reinforced executive administrative powers came in *United States* v. *Midwest Oil Company*. In 1909 President Taft withdrew from public sale more than three million acres of valuable California and Wyoming land which were suspected of containing huge ore deposits. Six months later a corporation took over a tract of this acreage, drilled wells, and extracted oil from some of these fields. The federal government brought suit to recover the land but the federal district court in Wyoming upheld the company's rights, agreeing with the defendant that the President had exceeded his powers because no law had granted him authority to remove public lands from private access. Lamar, speaking for the Court, overruled the decision. The single controlling question, he declared, was whether the President had the right to withdraw acreage from public use in the absence of specific congressional authority. The Justice carefully reviewed the history of executive orders and demonstrated that on many previous occasions Presidents had withdrawn lands from private use. These orders were never counteracted by the courts or by Congress. In fact the legislators had "repeatedly acquiesced in the practice" and by 1910 there had been over 250 such executive orders. Lamar reasoned that these executive actions would not have continued had there been any substantial congressional opposition to the President exercising his discretion in this manner. His ruling is important because it sanctioned a material enlargement of federal executive power.

Lamar also showed considerable concern over what he interpreted as arbitrary statutes which impeded individuals or restricted their rights more severely than the needs of the community dictated. Mrs. Lamar has written, for example, that her husband "looked upon the law as a city of refuge for the friendless and the oppressed, and was always ready to invoke its aid for the weak and the defenseless against the powerful and the strong." There are a number of cases which came before the United States Supreme Court during Lamar's tenure which can be used to support his wife's contention: *Choate* v. *Trapp,* 224 U.S. 665 (1912); *Quong Wing* v. *Kirkendall,* 223 U.S. 59 (1912); *Smith* v. *Texas,* 233 U.S. 630 (1914); and *Diaz* v. *United States,* 223 U.S. 442 (1912).

In *Quong Wing* Lamar dissented from the majority which approved a Montana law taxing hand laundries operated by males. He opposed the conclusions of his fellow judges and objected to the law in question because he considered it a revenue measure making an arbitrary and discriminatory rather than an intelligent use of the state's police powers. The obvious intent of the Montana statute had been to discriminate against Chinese laundrymen who operated their own establishments, but since neither of the lawyers discussed this point in their briefs, the Court took no official cognizance of it. Justice Holmes, for the majority, made an oblique reference to this fact when he wrote, "Laws frequently are enforced which the Court recognizes as possibly or probably invalid if attacked by a different interest in a different way." Lamar, too, avoided the race issue in his dissent. He argued merely that the statute taxes some but not others engaged in the identical business. It discriminates according to sex and in reverse proportion of ability to pay because only the smaller shops and not the larger ones, which used steam, come under the purview of the law. He observed that "it does not graduate the license so that those doing a large volume of business pay more than those doing less. . . . A discrimination founded on the personal attributes of those engaged in the same occupation and not on the value or the amount of the business," Lamar finally concluded, "is arbitrary." And his conscience would not permit him to sanction such discriminatory legislation.

In *Choate* v. *Trapp,* Lamar showed his concern for a group of Indians whom the state of Oklahoma wanted to tax. The Choctaw and Chickasaw tribes had been given their lands, tax free, by the United States government. Part of the agreement stipulated that the land allotted to each member of the tribe could not be taxed "while title remains in the original allottee." Subsequently Congress amended the original treaty but did not specify whether the tax exemption should remain. Oklahoma argued that the provision allowing the land to remain tax free was not a contract but a gratuity which could be withdrawn at will. In his ruling, however, Justice Lamar noted that "doubtful expressions . . . are to be resolved in favor of a weak and defenseless people," and he disallowed the Oklahoma statute.

In another one of his rulings, Lamar's trenchant analysis exhibited a compassionate concern for an individual prohibited by law from employment which he was fully qualified to undertake. The state of Texas required freight train conductors to have had two years experience as brakemen. Smith, who had worked on the railroad for over twenty years in various capacities, including temporary assignments as brakeman, considered himself qualified to become a conductor, and the state of Texas did not dispute this. The Texas Attorney General argued that under its police powers the state had a right to stipulate the requisite skills and experience of men engaged in hazardous callings in order to prevent material injury to members of the public. The purpose of the statute, the Attorney General continued, was "to secure competent train operatives, and thus prevent delays and disasters to persons and property in transit. . . ." Lamar did not object to the state exercising its police powers in a just fashion but he did oppose "arbitrary tests by which competent persons would be excluded from lawful employment." Had the state provided an examination to test Smith's qualifications for the position that he sought, or had Texas provided some other means for the applicant to demonstrate his ability to hold the position in question, Lamar went on, he would have had no objection to the law. But the rigidity of the Texas statute which excluded all but experienced brakeman from the opportunity to exercise their skills did not secure the public safety but denied many the liberty of contract:

> *In so far as a man is deprived of the right to labor his liberty is restricted, his capacity to earn wages and acquire property is lessened, and he is denied the protection which the law affords those who are permitted to work. Liberty means more than freedom from servitude, and the constitutional guarantee is an assurance that the citizen shall be protected in the right to use his powers of mind and body in any lawful calling.*

The decision is significant because it once again demonstrated Lamar's impatience with what he interpreted as unreasonable legislation infringing on individual rights.

Lamar also expressed his concern about arbitrary denials of liberty as a dissenter in *Diaz* v. *United States.* The defendant, Gabriel Diaz, had been tried in the Philippines according to Spanish law, had been kept in jeopardy during repeated and lengthy suspensions, had not been able to confront witnesses, and had waived his presence in the courtroom during the legal proceedings. For the majority Justice Van Devanter ruled that in a non-capital case, if the accused voluntarily absents himself from the courtroom, he thereby waives his right to be present and leaves the Court free to proceed as it wishes. Lamar refused to go along with his colleagues on the grounds, among others, that if witnesses are examined, argument made, and verdict pronounced during the defendant's absence, due process of law, as required by the Fourteenth Amendment, had not been observed.

Lamar's dissenting opinion in Diaz was pounced upon two years later in the Leo Frank case when Frank's attorneys appealed to the Georgian member of the Court for a hearing. Counsel for Frank argued, among other things, that their client had not been in the courtroom when the jury pronounced him guilty of murdering a thirteen-year-old girl in Atlanta. Although his absence had not been mentioned in the first appeal to the Georgia Supreme Court, it was emphasized in subsequent attempts to win him a new trial. The Georgia Supreme Court had ruled, however, that this point should have been made in the first petition. Frank's attorneys then appealed to Justice Lamar for a writ of error, which he denied, and a few weeks later for a writ of *habeas corpus*—to free their client on the grounds that his trial had not been conducted in accord with the due process clause of the Fourteenth Amendment and hence the state held him in prison illegally. Lamar acceded to their request for a hearing; he thought that the entire Court should rule on whether a defendant in a state court could waive his constitutional right to be present at every stage of the trial. He also accepted the case for the Court because Frank's attorneys had not raised this issue in their first appeal in Georgia, and the Justice believed that the highest federal court should also rule on whether the failure to include a material point in the first appeal precludes counsel from injecting that question in future attempts to win a new trial. The Justices did hear the case, *Frank* v. *Mangum,* 237 U.S. 309 (1915), but by a vote of seven to two, Hughes and Holmes dissenting, they rejected the plaintiff's demand. That Lamar went along with a majority decision in which Justice Mahlon Pitney did not discuss Frank's guilt or innocence but merely upheld the views of the Georgia Supreme Court in regard to proper procedures having taken place seems puzzling in light of his previous concern about victims of injustice. Yet the fact that he was from Georgia and that he had served on its Supreme Court and knew its practices, may give a clue to his decision. A vote in favor of Frank would have been tantamount to a rejection of Georgia's criminal procedures as approved by its highest court. Considering his role in revising Georgia's law codes and his years on the state Supreme Court, not to mention his emotional ties to so many Georgians, this may have been very difficult for him to have done. Of course, Lamar might have sincerely believed that the Georgia court had acted with propriety and its judgment should be upheld, but in light of previous opinions his position is difficult to fathom.

The Georgian jurist's most famous decision, delivering the Court's verdict in *Gompers* v. *Bucks Stove and Range Company,* 221 U.S. 418 (1911), won few friends for him among the ranks of organized labor or civil libertarians. The Bucks Stove and Range Company, subject to an American Federation of Labor boycott, had obtained a court injunction restraining the union from carrying out its "conspiracy" to boycott. This pleased the labor organization because it had been looking for a test case challenging the constitutionality of boycotts. Samuel Gompers, American Federation of Labor president, contended that the injunction violated the First Amendment guarantee of free speech and free press. By the time the case reached the Supreme Court, however, the issues between the union and Bucks Stove had been settled and all that remained to be decided was whether Gompers should be cited for contempt because he had violated a lower court's cease and desist order. Lamar led a unanimous Court in deciding the issue on the technical ground that the order which Gompers had violated was civil in nature and that criminal contempt charges could not be upheld as the Bucks Stove Company had petitioned for relief, not punishment. More significantly, he said nothing about the right of free speech but he did uphold the legality of injunctions against boycotts. Under the Sherman Act, he wrote, the Court must extend its protective and restraining powers "to every device whereby property is irreparably damaged or commerce is illegally restrained. The law," he continued, *recognises the right of workingmen to unite and to invite others to join their ranks, thereby making available the strength, influence and power that come from such association. By virtue of this right, powerful labor unions have been organized.*

But the very fact that it is lawful to form these bodies, with multitudes of members, means that they have thereby acquired a vast power, in the presence of which the individual may be helpless. This power, when unlawfully used against one, cannot be met, except by his purchasing peace at the cost of submitting to terms which involve the sacrifice of rights protected by the Constitution; or by standing on such rights and appealing to the preventive powers of a court of equity. When such appeal is made it is the duty of government to protect the one against the many as well as the many against the one.

Lamar's ruling in this case reinforced the powers of industrialists in their dealings with their employees and also undermined one of labor's most potent devices against unyielding entrepreneurs.

Lamar's dissent in *German Alliance Insurance Company* v. *Lewis,* 233 U.S. 389 (1914), marked him as an economic conservative and a poor prognosticator. Justice Joseph McKenna, speaking for the Court, had upheld a Kansas statute regulating the rates of an insurance company on the grounds that the business of insurance was affected with a public interest justifying legislative concern. Although unable to give a precise definition as to which businesses were "affected with a public interest," McKenna explained that insurance had "a reach of influence and consequence beyond and different from that of the ordinary businesses of the commercial world," that it was a necessary commodity for other businesses and essentially different from most other businesses, and that it was a matter of serious public concern. Justice McKenna also acknowledged that "measures of government are determined by circumstances, by the presence or imminence of conditions, and of the legislative judgment of the means or the policy of removing them." He allowed, furthermore, that "what makes for the general welfare is . . . a matter of legislative judgment and a judicial review of such judgment is limited." The sweeping scope and essential vagueness of the majority ruling drew a sharp retort from Lamar's pen. In a ringing dissent, in which Chief Justice White and Associate Justice Van Devanter concurred (Horace Lurton had not participated in the decision), Lamar argued that if the power of regulation is "as extensive as is now, for the first time, decided, then the citizen holds his property and his individual right of contract and of labor under legislative favor rather than under constitutional guaranty." He thought that the majority's ruling pointed "inevitably to the conclusion that the price of every article sold and the price of every service offered can be regulated by statute." He then explained that the majority allowed Kansas to regulate the insurance industry on the grounds that it conducted a sizeable volume of business. Using the value of the property and the number of persons employed as a basis, the Georgian Justice continued, that considering

the aggregate number of persons engaged in agriculture and the public's absolute dependence upon that pursuit, it would follow that, farming being affected with a broad and definite public interest, the price of wheat and corn; cotton and wools; beef, pork, mutton and poultry; fruit and vegetables, could be fixed. Or if we take the aggregate of those who labor and consider the public's absolute dependence upon labor, it would inevitably follow that it, too, was affected with a broad and definite public interest and that wages in the United States of America in this Twentieth Century could be fixed by law, just as in England between the 14th and 18th centuries. And inasmuch as the prices of agricultural products are dependent on the price of land and labor, and as the price of labor is closely related to the cost of rent and food and clothes and the comforts of life, there would be the power to take the further step and regulate the cost of everything which enters into the cost of living. . . . There seems no escape from the conclusion that the asserted power to fix the price to be paid by one private person to another private person . . . will destroy the right of private property and break down the barriers which the Constitution has thrown around the citizen to protect him in his right of property. . . .

The vehemence with which Lamar disagreed in this case demonstrated how much difficulty he had in adjusting his values to the rational needs of a complex industrial society.

Regardless of how historians may rate Lamar, contemporaries thought highly of him. Many ranked him with Justice Charles Evans Hughes for the clearness and soundness of his decisions and he was generally considered one of the stronger members of the Court. (This evaluation may not have been wrong. After all, he did serve with Justices Lurton, Pitney, McReynolds and Van Devanter.) In 1911 Yale University awarded him a Doctor of Laws degree, two years later the Georgia Society of New York honored him as one of the greatest lawyers ever produced by the South, and in 1914, President Wilson selected him to head a three man American delegation to negotiate an end to the diplomatic crisis with Mexico.

When the Supreme Court began its October term in 1915, illness prevented Lamar from taking his place alongside his colleagues. In September he had had a paralytic stroke and recovery came slowly. In December, however, a severe cold led to inflamed lungs and his heart finally succumbed on January 2, 1916, a little more than two months after he had celebrated his fifty-eighth birthday. Former President William Howard Taft mourned, "for the Country and the Supreme Court the loss of a great Judge who united with his eminent ability and learning the fine edge of high character, judicial quality and purity of purpose."

Chroniclers of the past, however, have not dealt with the Justice in the same vein as Taft did. John Frank, in his book *Marble Palace: The Supreme Court in American Life,* listed Lamar among a group of "notable ciphers" and added that he was a man "who is remembered, if at all, only by his grandchildren." The reason for this evaluation is not difficult to explain. A contemporary's praiseworthy account of the Georgian Justice is especially revealing:

Imagine a scholarly jurist, combining something of the captivating modesty of William Dean Howells with the judicial acumen of Alton B. Parker, the purity in private life of William McKinley, and the integrity of Grover Cleveland, and

> *you have data concerning the personal equation of Joseph Rucker Lamar . . . which even the halting voice of dazzled envy would scarce gainsay.*

Parker's acumen, McKinley's purity, and Cleveland's integrity no longer fire American imaginations. Men of their stripe, moreover, are now regarded as symbols of mediocrity, hollow heroes of an age which failed to realize that an industrial nation demands a more enlightened and active government than contemporary conservatism allowed.

Like Cleveland and Parker, Lamar too, with minor exceptions, held steadfast to established principles. He believed in the sanctity of private contracts, the limited role of the government in the economy, and the hallowed activities of the private entrepreneur. His rulings in *United States* v. *Grimaud* and *United States* v. *Midwest Oil* demonstrated a keen understanding of executive administrative needs, and his dissents in *Quong Wing* and *Diaz* indicated a vigorous opposition to arbitrary laws and judicial procedures. Nevertheless his opinions in *Gompers* v. *Bucks Stove* and *German Alliance* v. *Lewis* showed how he stood on the major issues of the day. Both of these cases dealt with broadly significant areas—the right of labor unions to boycott and the right of a state to regulate a business "affected with a public interest." In each one Lamar expressed himself in favor of traditional but outworn philosophies. Unlike Marshall, Taney, Holmes, Brandeis, and Stone, the Georgian jurist did not bring new insights to contemporary problems; most of his opinions merely indicated that he accepted the predominant conservative ideas of his era. And while contemporaries tend to value the conformist and the exponent of the conventional ideology, the historian lionizes the maverick and the original thinker. Had Lamar spent all of his years in Georgia, he would have been secure in his local reputation for legal accomplishments. But accession to the United States Supreme Court dictated a different evaluation. In his broader and more significant judicial sphere his achievements were limited and his influence minimal.

The final irony came after death. President Wilson replaced the cautious, temperate, and conservative Georgian with one of the Progressive Era's most fiery, dynamic, and controversial figures, Louis D. Brandeis. Unlike his predecessor, Brandeis was to become one of the foremost Associate Justices in the Court's history. And the fight over his confirmation quickly overshadowed the memory of the man he was designated to replace.

SELECTED BIBLIOGRAPHY

There are no first-rate studies of Joseph Lamar. Sketches of his life and work appear in William J. Northen, *Men of Mark in Georgia,* IV (Atlanta, 1908) and Clarinda Pendleton Lamar, *The Life of Joseph Rucker Lamar* (New York, 1926). Biographical eulogies appeared in 241 U.S. and 146 Georgia 841. *Gompers* v. *Bucks Stove and Range Company* is discussed in Bernard Mandel, *Samuel Gompers* (Yellow Springs, 1963) while

United States v. *Midwest Oil* is covered in William E. Colby, "The New Land Policy," 3 *California Law Review* 269 (1915).

Daniel S. McHargue's "President Taft's Appointments to The Supreme Court," 12 *Journal of Politics* 478 (1950), examines the background of the judicial selections. Harding Coolidge Noblitt, *The Supreme Court and the Progressive Era—1902–1921,* unpublished doctoral dissertation (University of Chicago, 1955), analyzes the Justices' performances and voting records for the period stated while *The Nation* (November 11, 1915) and 27 *World's Work* 629 (1914) deals with the Court for the years of Lamar's tenure. Also of some value is Emlin McClain, "Decisions of the Supreme Court of the United States on Constitutional Questions, 1911–1914," 9 *American Political Science Review* 36 (1915); and Judge Samuel Hale Sibley, *Georgia's Contribution to Law—The Lamars* (New York, 1948).

Many of Lamar's articles may be found in various *Reports* of the Georgia Bar Association, 1893–1913.

Joseph Rucker Lamar

REPRESENTATIVE OPINIONS

GOMPERS v. BUCKS STOVE AND RANGE CO., 211 U.S. 418 (1911)

The significance of Lamar's decision in *Gompers* v. *Bucks Stove and Range Co.* lay less in the final adjudication—that Gompers had been incorrectly cited for criminal contempt—than in what it revealed about the Supreme Court's attitude toward labor conflicts. Gompers had hoped that the case would determine whether the First Amendment's guarantees of free speech and press sanctioned boycotts. But when Justice Lamar ignored this and ruled that "it is the duty of government to protect the one [the employer] against the many [the union] as well as the many against the one," it clearly indicated that the Supreme Court allied itself behind the employer in his altercations with representatives of labor.

MR. JUSTICE LAMAR, after making the foregoing statement, delivered the opinion of the court.

The defendants, Samuel Gompers, John Mitchell and Frank Morrison, were found guilty of contempt of court in making certain publications prohibited by an injunction from the Supreme Court of the District of Columbia. They were sentenced to imprisonment for twelve, nine and six months respectively, and this proceeding is prosecuted to reverse that judgment.

The order alleged to have been violated was granted in the equity suit of the *"Bucks Stove & Range Company* v. *The American Federation of Labor and others,"* in which the court issued an injunction restraining all the defendants from boycotting the complainant, or from publishing or otherwise making any statement that the Bucks Stove & Range Company was, or had been, on the "Unfair" or "We don't patronize" lists. Some months later the complainant filed a petition in the cause, alleging that the three defendants above-named, parties to the original cause, in contempt of court and in violation of its order, had disobeyed the injunction by publishing statements which either directly or indirectly called attention to the fact that the Bucks Stove & Range Company was on the "Unfair" list, and that they had thereby continued the boycott which had been enjoined.

The defendants filed separate answers under oath, and, each denied: (1) That they had been in contempt or disregard of the court's orders: (2) That the statements complained of constituted any violation of the order; and, on the argument, (3) contended that if the publication should be construed to amount to a violation of the injunction they could not be punished therefor, because the court must not only possess jurisdiction of the parties and the subject-matter, but must have authority to render the particular judgment. Insisting, therefore, that the court could not abridge the liberty of speech or freedom of the press, the defendants claim that the injunction as a whole was a nullity, and that no contempt proceeding could be maintained for any disobedience of any of its provisions, general or special.

If this last proposition were sound it would be unnecessary to go further into an examination of the case or to determine whether the defendants had in fact disobeyed the prohibitions contained in the injunction. *Ex parte Rowland,* 104 U.S. 612. But we will not enter upon a discussion of the constitutional question raised, for the general provisions of the injunction did not, in terms, restrain any form of publication. The defendants' attack on this part of the injunction raises no question as to an abridgment of free speech, but involves the power of a court of equity to enjoin the defendants from continuing a boycott which, by words and signals, printed or spoken, caused or threatened irreparable damage.

Courts differ as to what constitutes a boycott that may be enjoined. All hold that there must be a conspiracy causing irreparable damage to the business or property of the complainant. Some hold that a boycott against the complainant, by a combination of persons not immediately connected with him in business, can be restrained. Others hold that the secondary boycott can be enjoined, where the conspiracy extends not only to injuring the complainant, but secondarily coerces or attempts to coerce his customers to refrain from dealing with him by threats that unless they do they themselves will be boycotted. Others hold that no boycott can be enjoined unless there are acts of physical violence, or intimidation caused by threats of physical violence.

But whatever the requirement of the particular jurisdiction, as to the conditions on which the injunction against a boycott may issue; when these facts exist, the strong current of authority is that the publication and use of letters, circulars and printed matter may constitute a means whereby a boycott is unlawfully continued, and their use for such purpose may amount to a violation of the order of injunction. *Reynolds* v. *Davis,* 198 Massachusetts, 300; *Sherry* v. *Perkins,* 147 Massachusetts, 212; *Codman* v. *Crocker,* 203 Massachusetts, 150; *Brown* v. *Jacobs,* 115 Georgia, 452, 431; *Gray* v. *Council,* 91 Minnesota, 171; *Lohse Co.* v. *Fuelle,* 215 Missouri, 421, 472; *Thomas* v. *Railroad Co.,* 62 Fed. Rep. 803, 821; *Continental Co.* v. *Board of Underwriters,* 67 Fed. Rep. 310; *Beck* v. *Teamsters' Union,* 118 Michigan, 527; *Pratt Food Co.* v. *Bird,* 148 Michigan, 632; *Barr* v. *Essex,* 53 N.J. Eq. 102. See also *Ludwig* v. *Western Union Telegraph Co.,* 216 U.S. 156; *Bitterman* v. *L. & N. R. R.,* 207 U.S. 206; *Board of Trade* v. *Christie,* 198 U.S. 236; *Scully* v. *Bird,* 209 U.S. 489.

While the bill in this case alleged that complainant's interstate business was restrained, no relief was asked under the provisions of the Sherman anti-trust act. But if the contention be sound that no court under any circumstances can enjoin a boycott if spoken words or printed matter were used as one of the instrumentalities by which it was made effective, then it could not do so, even if interstate commerce was restrained by means of a blacklist, boycott or printed device to accomplish its purpose. And this, too, notwithstanding § 4 (act of July 2, 1890, c. 647, 26 Stat. 209) of that act provides, that where such commerce is unlawfully restrained it shall be the duty of the Attorney General to institute proceedings in equity to prevent and enjoin violations of the statute.

In *Loewe* v. *Lawlor,* 208 U.S. 274, the statute was held to apply to any unlawful combination resulting in restraint of interstate commerce. In that case the damages sued for were occasioned by acts which, among other things, did include the circulation of advertisements. But the principle announced by the court was general. It covered any illegal means by which interstate commerce is restrained, whether by unlawful combinations of capital, or unlawful combinations of labor; and we think also whether the restraint be occasioned by unlawful contracts, trusts, pooling arrangements, blacklists, boycotts, coercion, threats, intimidation, and whether these be made effective, in whole or in part, by acts, words or printed matter.

The court's protective and restraining powers extend to every device whereby property is irreparably damaged or commerce is illegally restrained. To hold that the restraint of trade under the Sherman anti-trust act, or on general principles of law, could be enjoined, but that the means through which the restraint was accomplished could not be enjoined would be to render the law impotent.

Society itself is an organization and does not object to organizations for social, religious, business and all legal purposes. The law, therefore, recognizes the right of workingmen to unite and to invite others to join their ranks, thereby making available the strength, influence and power that come from such association. By virtue of this right, powerful labor unions have been organized.

But the very fact that it is lawful to form these bodies, with multitudes of members, means that they have thereby acquired a vast power, in the presence of which the individual may be helpless. This power, when unlawfully used against one, cannot be met, except by his purchasing peace at the cost of submitting to terms which involve the sacrifice of rights protected by the Constitution; or by standing on such rights and appealing to the preventive powers of a court of equity. When such appeal is made it is the duty of government to protect the one against the many as well as the many against the one.

In the case of an unlawful conspiracy, the agreement to act in concert when the signal is published, gives the words "Unfair," "We don't patronize," or similar expressions, a force not inhering in the words themselves, and therefore exceeding any possible right of speech which a single individual might have. Under such circumstances they become what have been called "verbal acts," and as much subject to injunction as the use of any other force whereby property is unlawfully damaged. When the facts in such cases warrant it, a court having jurisdiction of the parties and subject-matter has power to grant an injunction.

Passing then to the consideration of the question as to whether the defendants disobeyed the injunction and were therefore guilty of contempt, we are met with the objection that for want of a bill of exceptions we must treat the decree as conclusive as to the fact of disobedience, and can only examine the petition and the finding to determine whether one charges and the other finds acts which constitute a contempt of court. This view was adopted by the majority of the Court of Appeals, which treated this as a criminal proceeding, refused to examine the testimony and affirmed the judgment in analogy to the rule that on a general verdict of guilty upon an indictment containing several counts, some of which were bad, the conviction would not be reversed if there was one good count warranting the judgment.

That rule originated in cases where the finding of guilt was by the jury while the sentence was by the judge. In such cases the presumption is that the judge ignored the finding of the jury on the bad counts and sentenced only on those which were sufficient to sustain the conviction.

But there is no room for such presumption here. The trial judge made no general finding that the defendants were guilty. But in one decree he adjudged that each defendant was respectively guilty of the nine independent acts set out in separate paragraphs of the petition. Having found that each was guilty of these separate acts he consolidated the sentence without indicating how much of the punishment was imposed for the disobedience in any particular instance. We cannot suppose that he found the defendants guilty of an act charged unless he considered that it amounted to a violation of the injunction. Nor can we suppose that having found them guilty of these nine specific acts he did not impose some punishment for each. Instead, therefore, of affirming the judgment if there is one good count, it should be reversed if it should appear that the defendants have been sentenced on any count which, in law or in fact, did not constitute a disobedience of the injunction.

But in making such investigation it is again insisted that this is a proceeding at law for criminal contempt, where the findings of fact by the trial judge must be treated as conclusive, and that our investigation must be limited solely to the question whether, as a matter of law, the acts of alleged disobedience set out in the finding constitute contempt of court.

This contention, on the part of the Bucks Stove & Range Company, prevents a consideration of the case on its merits, and makes it necessary to enter into a discussion of questions more or less technical, as to whether this was a proceeding in equity or at law. Where results so controlling depend upon proper classification, it becomes necessary carefully to consider whether this was a case at law for criminal contempt where the evidence could not be examined for want of a bill of exceptions; or a case in equity for civil contempt, where the whole record may be examined on appeal and a proper decree entered.

Contempts are neither wholly civil nor altogether criminal. And "it may not always be easy to classify a particular act as belonging to either one of these two classes. It may partake of the characteristics of both." *Bessette* v. *Conkey,* 194 U.S. 329. But in either event, and whether the proceedings be civil or criminal, there must be an allegation that in contempt of court the defendant has disobeyed the order, and a prayer that he be attached and punished therefor. It is not the fact of punishment but rather its character and purpose that often serve to distinguish between the two classes of cases. If it is for civil contempt the punishment is remedial, and for the benefit of the complainant. But if it is for criminal contempt the sentence is punitive, to vindicate the authority of the court. It is true that punishment by imprisonment may be remedial, as well as punitive, and many civil contempt proceedings have resulted not only in the imposition of a fine, payable to the complainant, but also in committing the defendant to prison. But imprisonment for civil contempt is ordered where the defendant has refused to do an affirmative act required by the provisions of an order which, either in form or substance, was mandatory in its character. Imprisonment in such cases is not inflicted as a punishment, but is intended to be remedial by coercing the defendant to do what he had refused to do. The decree in such cases is that the defendant stand committed unless and until he performs the affirmative act required by the court's order.

For example: If a defendant should refuse to pay alimony, or to surrender property ordered to be turned over to a receiver, or to make a conveyance required by a decree for specific performance, he could be committed until he complied with the order. Unless these were special elements of contumacy, the refusal to pay or to comply with the order is treated as being rather in resistance to the opposite party than in contempt of the court. The order for imprisonment in this class of cases, therefore, is not to vindicate the authority of the law, but is remedial and is intended to coerce the defendant to do the thing required by the order for the benefit of the complainant. If imprisoned, as aptly said in *In re Nevitt,* 117 Fed. Rep. 451, "he carries the keys of his prison in his own pocket." He can end the sentence and discharge himself at any moment by doing what he had previously refused to do.

On the other hand, if the defendant does that which he has been commanded not to do, the disobedience is a thing accomplished. Imprisonment cannot undo or remedy what has been done nor afford any compensation for the pecuniary injury caused by the disobedience. If the sentence is limited to imprisonment for a definite period, the defendant is furnished no key, and he cannot shorten the term by promising not to repeat the offense. Such imprisonment operates, not as a remedy coercive in its nature, but solely as punishment for the completed act of disobedience.

It is true that either form of imprisonment has also an incidental effect. For if the case is civil and the punishment is purely remedial, there is also a vindication of the court's authority. On the other hand, if the proceeding is for criminal contempt and the imprisonment is solely punitive, to vindicate the authority of the law, the complainant may also derive some incidental benefit from the fact that such punishment tends to prevent a repetition of the disobedience. But such indirect consequences will not change imprisonment which is merely coercive and remedial, into that which is solely punitive in character, or *vice versa.*

The fact that the purpose of the punishment could be examined with a view to determining whether it was civil or criminal, is recognized in *Doyle* v. *London Guarantee Co.,* 204 U.S. 599, 605, 607, where it was said that "While it is true that the fine imposed is not made payable to the opposite party, compliance with the order relieves from payment, and in that event there is no final judgment of either fine or imprisonment. . . . The proceeding is against a party, the compliance with the order avoids the punishment and there is nothing in the nature of a criminal suit or judgment imposed for public purposes upon a defendant in a criminal proceeding." *Bessette* v. *Conkey,* 194 U.S. 328; *In re Nevitt,* 117 Fed. Rep. 448; *Howard* v. *Durand,* 36 Georgia, 359; *Phillips* v. *Welch,* 11 Nevada, 187.

The distinction between refusing to do an act commanded,—remedied by imprisonment until the party performs the required act; and doing an act forbidden,—punished by imprisonment for a definite term; is sound in principle, and generally, if not universally, affords a test by which to determine the character of the punishment.

In this case the alleged contempt did

not consist in the defendant's refusing to do any affirmative act required, but rather in doing that which had been prohibited. The only possible remedial relief for such disobedience would have been to impose a fine for the use of complainant, measured in some degree by the pecuniary injury caused by the act of disobedience. Rapalje on Contempt, §§ 131–134; *Wells* v. *Oregon Co.,* 19 Fed. Rep. 20; *In re North Bloomfield Co.,* 27 Fed. Rep. 795; *Sabin* v. *Fogarty,* 70 Fed. Rep. 483.

But when the court found that the defendants had done what the injunction prohibited, and thereupon sentenced them to jail for fixed terms of six, nine and twelve months, no relief whatever was granted to the complainant, and the Bucks Stove & Range Company took nothing by that decree.

If then, as the Court of Appeals correctly held, the sentence was wholly punitive, it could have been properly imposed only in a proceeding instituted and tried as for criminal contempt. The question as to the character of such proceedings has generally been raised, in the appellate court, to determine whether the case could be reviewed by writ of error or on appeal. *Bessette* v. *Conkey,* 194 U.S. 324. But it may involve much more than mere matters of practice. For, notwithstanding the many elements of similarity in procedure and in punishment, there are some differences between the two classes of proceedings which involve substantial rights and constitutional privileges. Without deciding what may be the rule in civil contempt, it is certain that in proceedings for criminal contempt the defendant is presumed to be innocent, he must be proved to be guilty beyond a reasonable doubt, and cannot be compelled to testify against himself. *Boyd* v. *United States,* 116 U.S. 616; *United States* v. *Jose,* 63 Fed. Rep. 951; *State* v. *Davis,* 50 W. Va. 100; *King* v. *Ohio Ry.,* 7 Biss. 529; *Sabin* v. *Fogarty,* 70 Fed. Rep. 482, 483; *Drakeford* v. *Adams,* 98 Georgia, 724.

There is another important difference. Proceedings for civil contempt are between the original parties and are instituted and tried as a part of the main cause. But on the other hand, proceedings at law for criminal contempt are between the public and the defendant, and are not a part of the original cause. The Court of Appeals recognizing this difference held that this was not a part of the equity cause of the *Bucks Stove & Range Company* v. *The American Federation of Labor et al.,* and said that: "The order finding the defendants guilty of contempt was not an interlocutory order in the injunction proceedings. It was in a separate action, one personal to the defendants, with the defendants on one side and the court vindicating its authority on the other."

In this view we cannot concur. We find nothing in the record indicating that this was a proceeding with the court, or, more properly, the Government, on one side and the defendants on the other. On the contrary, the contempt proceedings were instituted, entitled, tried, and up to the moment of sentence treated as a part of the original cause in equity. The Bucks Stove & Range Company was not only the nominal, but the actual party on the one side, with the defendants on the other. The Bucks Stove Company acted throughout as complainant in charge of the litigation. As such and through its counsel, acting in its name, it made consents, waivers and stipulations only proper on the theory that it was proceeding in its own right in an equity cause, and not as a representative of the United States, prosecuting a case of criminal contempt. It appears here also as the sole party in opposition to the defendants; and its counsel, in its name, have filed briefs and made arguments in this court in favoring affirmance of the judgment of the court below.

But, as the Court of Appeals distinctly held that this was not a part of the equity cause it will be proper to set out in some detail the facts on this subject as they appear in the record.

In the first place the petition was not entitled "United States *v.* Samuel Gompers, *et al.*" or "*In re* Samuel Gompers, *et al.,*" as would have been proper, and according to some decisions necessary, if the proceedings had been at law for criminal contempt. This is not a mere matter of form, for manifestly every citizen, however unlearned in the law, by a mere inspection of the papers in contempt proceedings ought to be able to see whether it was instituted for private litigation or for public prosecution, whether it sought to benefit the complainant or vindicate the court's authority. He should not be left in doubt as to whether relief or punishment was the object in view. He is not only entitled to be informed of the nature of the charge against him, but to know that it is a charge and not a suit. *United States* v. *Cruikshank,* 92 U.S. 542, 559.

Inasmuch, therefore, as proceedings for civil contempt are a part of the original cause, the weight of authority is to the effect that they should be entitled therein. But the practice has hitherto been so unsettled in this respect that we do not now treat it as controlling, but only as a fact to be considered along with others as was done in *Worden* v. *Searls,* 121 U.S. 25, in determining a similar question. Thus considering it we find that the petition instituting the contempt proceeding was entitled in the main cause *"Bucks Stove & Range Company, plaintiff,* v. *The American Federation of Labor, et al., defendants, No. 27, 305, Equity,"* and that the answers of the defendants, every report by the examiner in chancery, every deposition, motion and stipulation, every order—including the final decree and the amended decree, were all uniformly entitled in the equity cause. Not only the pleadings in the original cause but all the testimony, oral and written, was, by reference in the petition, made a part of the contempt proceedings. The trial judge quoted largely from this oral testimony thus introduced in bulk, and the severity and character of the sentence indicate that he was largely influenced by this evidence which disclosed the great damage done to the complainant's business by the boycott before the injunction issued.

It is argued the defendants' answers concluded with a statement that as questions of criminal and quasi-criminal intent were involved, a jury was better qualified to pass on the issues than a judge, and in the event he should be of opinion that the charges had not been sworn away, they moved that issues of fact should be framed and submitted to a jury. Such a motion was not inconsistent with the theory that this was a proceeding for civil contempt in equity, but was in strict accord with the practice under which questions of fact may be referred by the chancellor to a jury for determination.

In proceedings for civil contempt the complainant, if successful, is entitled to costs. Rapalje on Contempt, § 132. And evidently on the theory that this was a civil proceeding and to be governed by the rules applicable to an equity cause, the Bucks Stove & Range Company moved the court to amend the decree so as to award to it "its costs." After argument by solicitors for both parties, the motion was granted, and the court adjudged that the complainant do recover against the defendants its costs in said contempt proceeding. This ruling was no doubt correct as this was a civil case, but could not have been granted in a proceeding for criminal contempt, where costs are not usually imposed in addition to the imprisonment. Where they are awarded they go to the Government, for the use of its officers, as held by Justice Miller, on circuit. *Durant* v. *Washington County,* 4 Woolw. 297.

In another most important particular the parties clearly indicated that they regarded this as a civil proceeding. The complainant made each of the defendants a witness for the company, and, as such, each was required to testify against himself—a thing that most likely would not have been done, or suffered, if either party had regarded this as a proceeding at law for criminal contempt—because the provision of the Constitution that "no person shall be compelled in any criminal case to be a witness against himself" is applicable, not only to crimes, but also to quasi-criminal and penal proceedings. *Boyd* v. *United States,* 116 U.S. 616.

Both on account of the distinct ruling to the contrary by the Court of Appeals, and the importance of the results flowing from a proper classification, we have with some detail discussed the facts appearing in the record, showing that both parties treated this as a proceeding which was a part of the original equity cause. In case of doubt this might, of itself, justify a determination of the question in accordance with the mutual understanding of the parties, and the procedure adopted by them. But there is another and controlling fact, found in the brief but sufficient prayer with which the petition concludes. We have already shown that in both classes of cases there must be allegation and proof that the defendant was guilty of contempt, and a prayer that he be punished. The classification then depends upon the question as to whether the punishment is punitive, in vindication of the court's authority, or whether it is remedial by way of a coercive imprisonment, or a compensatory fine payable to the complainant. Bearing these distinctions in mind, the prayer of the petition is significant and determinative. After setting out in detail the acts of alleged disobedience, the petition closes with the following prayers: (1) "that the defendants show cause why they should not be adjudged in contempt of court and be punished for the same," and (2) "that petitioner may have such other and further relief as the nature of its case may require."

"Its case,"—not the Government's case. "That petitioner may have relief"—not that the court's authority may be vindicated. The

Bucks Stove & Range Company was not asserting the rights of the public, but seeking "such other and further relief as the nature of its case may require." If it had asked that the defendants be forced to pay a fine to the Government, or be punished by confinement in jail, there could have been no doubt that punishment pure and simple was sought.

On the other hand, if it had prayed that the court impose a fine payable to the Bucks Stove & Range Company, the language would have left no doubt that remedial punishment was sought. It is not different in principle, if, instead of praying specifically for a fine payable to itself, it asks generally for "such relief as the nature of its case may require." In either event such a prayer was appropriate to a civil proceeding, and under it the court could have granted that form of relief to which the petitioner was entitled. But as the act of disobedience consisted not in refusing to do what had been ordered, but in doing what had been prohibited by the injunction, there could be no coercive imprisonment, and therefore the only relief, if any, which "the nature of petitioners case" admitted, was the imposition of a fine payable to the Bucks Stove & Range Company.

There was therefore a departure—a variance between the procedure adopted and the punishment imposed, when, in answer to a prayer for remedial relief, in the equity cause, the court imposed a punitive sentence appropriate only to a proceeding at law for criminal contempt. The result was as fundamentally erroneous as if in an action of "A. *vs.* B. for assault and battery," the judgment entered had been that the defendant be confined in prison for twelve months.

If then this sentence for criminal contempt was erroneously entered in a proceeding which was a part of the equity cause, it would be necessary to set aside the order of imprisonment, examine the testimony and thereupon make such decree as was proper, according to the practice in equity causes on appeal. And, if upon the examination of the record it should appear that the defendants were in fact and in law guilty of the contempt charged, there could be no more important duty than to render such a decree as would serve to vindicate the jurisdiction and authority of courts to enforce orders and to punish acts of disobedience. For while it is sparingly to be used, yet the power of courts to punish for contempts is a necessary and integral part of the independence of the judiciary, and is absolutely essential to the performance of the duties imposed on them by law. Without it they are mere boards of arbitration whose judgments and decrees would be only advisory.

If a party can make himself a judge of the validity of orders which have been issued, and by his own act of disobedience set them aside, then are the courts impotent, and what the Constitution now fittingly calls the "judicial power of the United States" would be a mere mockery.

This power "has been uniformly held to be necessary to the protection of the court from insults and oppressions while in the ordinary exercise of its duties, and to enable it to enforce its judgments and orders necessary to the due administration of law and the protection of the rights of suitors." *Bessette* v. *Conkey,* 194 U.S. 324, 333.

There has been general recognition of the fact that the courts are clothed with this power and must be authorized to exercise it without referring the issues of fact or law to another tribunal or to a jury in the same tribunal. For if there was no such authority in the first instance there would be no power to enforce its orders if they were disregarded in such independent investigation. Without authority to act promptly and independently the courts could not administer public justice or enforce the rights of private litigants. *Bessette* v. *Conkey,* 194 U.S. 337.

Congress in recognition of the necessity of the case has also declared (Rev. Stat., § 725) that the courts of the United States "shall have power to punish by fine or imprisonment contempts of their authority . . ." including "disobedience . . . by any party to any lawful order . . . of the said courts." But the very amplitude of the power is a warning to use it with discretion, and a command never to exert it where it is not necessary or proper. For that reason we can proceed no further in this case because it is both unnecessary and improper to make any decree in this contempt proceeding.

For on the hearing of the appeal and cross appeal in the original cause in which the injunction was issued, it appeared from the statement of counsel in open court that there had been a complete settlement of all matters involved in the case of *Bucks Stove & Range Company* v. *The American Federation of Labor et al.* This court therefore declined to further consider the case, which had become moot, and these two appeals were dismissed. 219 U.S. 581. When the main case was settled, every proceeding which was dependent on it, or a part of it, was also necessarily settled—of course without prejudice to the power and right of the court to punish for contempt by proper proceedings. *Worden* v. *Searls,* 121 U.S. 27. If this had been a separate and independent proceeding at law for criminal contempt, to vindicate the authority of the court, with the public on one side and the defendants on the other, it could not, in any way, have been affected by any settlement which the parties to the equity cause made in their private litigation.

But, as we have shown, this was a proceeding in equity for civil contempt where the only remedial relief possible was a fine payable to the complainant. The company prayed "for such relief as the nature of its case may require," and when the main cause was terminated by a settlement of all differences between the parties, the complainant did not require and was not entitled to any compensation or relief of any other character. The present proceeding necessarily ended with the settlement of the main cause of which it is a part. *Bessette* v. *Conkey,* 194 U.S. 328, 333; *Worden* v. *Searls,* 121 U.S. 27; *State* v. *Nathans,* 49 S. Car. 207. The criminal sentences imposed in the civil case, therefore, should be set aside.

The judgment of the Court of Appeals is reversed, and the case remanded with directions to reverse the judgment of the Supreme Court of the District of Columbia and remand the case to that court with direction that the contempt proceedings instituted by the Bucks Stove & Range Company be dismissed, but without prejudice to the power and right of the Supreme Court of the District of Columbia to punish by a proper proceeding, contempt, if any, committed against it.

Reversed

Mahlon Pitney

☆ 1858–1924 ☆

APPOINTED BY

WILLIAM HOWARD TAFT

YEARS ON COURT

1912–1922

Mahlon Pitney

by

FRED L. ISRAEL

IN REVIEWING HIS political difficulties in September, 1910, President William Howard Taft commented with satisfaction: "I shall have the appointment of probably a majority of the Supreme Court before the end of my term, which, in view of the present agitation in respect to the Constitution, is very important." Few Presidents have had the opportunity of naming a majority of Justices to the Supreme Court and no one-term President before or since Taft had the responsibility of choosing five Associate Justices and a Chief Justice. Mahlon Pitney was President Taft's last Court appointee. And, during the acrimonious 1912 campaign, the President took consolation in thinking that if, by some unhappy chance, Theodore Roosevelt was the victor, the Court would act as the great bulwark against radical innovations. Among the chief duties of a Supreme Court Justice, Taft had written in 1910, was the preservation of "the fundamental structure of our government as our fathers gave it to us." Justice Mahlon Pitney adequately fulfilled Taft's expectations.

Mahlon Pitney, the second son of Henry Cooper Pitney and Sarah Louise Halstead, was born on his parents' farm near Morristown, New Jersey, on February 5, 1858. Descended from James Pitney who had emigrated from England in the early 1700's, Mahlon was named for his paternal great-grandfather who had fought in the Revolutionary War. Young Pitney attended private schools in Morristown and entered Princeton University with the 1875 freshman class. (Another first-year man was Thomas Woodrow Wilson with whom Pitney maintained a casual acquaintance through the years.) Receiving his baccalaureate degree in 1879, Pitney studied law under his father's guidance. Years later, when asked why he had chosen the legal profession, Pitney replied: "I could hardly have escaped it, for my father lived in his work and was always ready to talk

FRED L. ISRAEL, Associate Professor of History at the City College of New York, is the author of Nevada's Key Pittman.

law, day and night. . . . I found the work very dull at first, and Blackstone very dry reading. I learned my law by absorption. I read and studied, of course, but I got most of it from my father who was a walking encyclopedia of law."

After admission to the New Jersey bar, Pitney established his own office in Dover, a very prosperous little town, then a leading iron industry center. He practiced there from 1882 to 1889, being counsel, director, and officer in the Cranbury Iron Company. In 1889 he returned to Morristown and assumed charge of his father's law office because of the latter's appointment as a New Jersey Vice-Chancellor. Within three years Pitney had doubled the firm's clientele and established a wide reputation for himself as a reliable and conscientious lawyer.

In the summer of 1894, the Republican leaders of New Jersey's Fourth Congressional District, comprising Morris, Hunterdon, Warren, and Sussex Counties, chose Pitney as their nominee for the House of Representatives—and the following November Pitney defeated Democrat Johnston Cornish by a plurality of 1,407 votes. In 1896, Pitney was easily reelected. During this campaign, he took an uncompromising stand in favor of sound money as defined in the Republican party platform and won the added support of the "gold" Democrats. In his second term he participated more frequently in House debates, delivering speeches on the lack of prudence shown by the Committee on Appropriations in granting excess funds to various governmental departments and on the Alaskan boundary dispute. Pitney resigned from the House on January 5, 1899, two months before his term expired, to accept election to the New Jersey Senate.

At this time, both the New Jersey Republican and Democratic parties were dominated by strong political machines closely allied with railroad, public utility, banking, and other corporations interested in manipulating government. William J. Sewall was the Republican "czar" and those interested in nominations obligingly made pilgrimages to his headquarters in a Camden railroad office. Early in 1898, Pitney made the pilgrimage seeking the Republican gubernatorial nomination for the following year. Sewall advised Pitney to first enlarge his base in state politics—and so the Congressman sought election to the New Jersey Senate in November, 1898, and was assured by Sewall of the minority leadership after his victory. When the Republicans gained control of the state senate in 1900, Pitney became the senate president. During his two years in the New Jersey legislature, Pitney's most outstanding accomplishment was his exhaustive study of the proposed Morris Canal Abandonment plan and his disclosure to the senate that the plan would exclusively benefit the Lehigh Valley Railroad, the canal lessee. His speeches against the bill as well as his brilliant defense of local community interests further enhanced his reputation, making him a leading gubernatorial contender in the 1901 election.

However, Pitney's plans changed before the election. On February 5, 1901, Republican Governor Foster M. Voorhees named Pitney to the New Jersey Supreme Court. The senate confirmed almost immediately and the new justice took the oath on February 19 for a seven-year term. By accepting the appointment, Pitney made a major decision in choosing to leave politics for a judicial career, one which would span the next twenty-one years. He served as an associate justice of the New Jersey Supreme Court from February 19, 1901 to January 22, 1908, writing 167 opinions on a wide variety of legal problems, both civil and criminal. The Court of Errors and Appeals reversed him in only four instances. In January, 1908, William J. Magie retired from the chancellorship, and on January 22 Governor J. Franklin Fort appointed Pitney to this most important New Jersey judicial position which Pitney held until his elevation to the United States Supreme Court in 1912. As chancellor, he headed both the law and equity branches of the appellate court, presiding over both. In four years, he delivered forty-seven decisions on law and eleven on equity.

Undoubtedly Pitney's major decision as chancellor is *Jonas Glass Co.* v. *Glass Bottle Blowers Association,* 77 N.J. Eq. 219 (1908). The defendants were the association, its officers, and former company employees. In 1901, the association instituted a boycott of the company's products in an attempt to force a union contract. When a strike ensued, a lower court issued an injunction which the appellate court reviewed. The majority opinion, written by Pitney, declared:

> *It is clear beyond dispute that the complainant has suffered grievously in its property and business through acts of the defendants, whose continuance is thus prohibited. That the injury to the complaint is irreparable by action at law is likewise clear. The conduct of defendants in using coercion in some cases and persuasion in others in order to bring about breach of the contracts of personal service . . . was unlawful and actionable upon well settled principles. . . . The rights of enjoying and defending life and liberty, acquiring, possessing and protecting property, and pursuing and obtaining safety and happiness, are declared by our constitution to be inalienable.*

This opinion, which unions looked upon with disdain, accounted for the opposition by many progressive senators to Pitney's confirmation to the United States Supreme Court.

"In looking over my administration," wrote President Taft four days before the expiration of his term, "there is nothing I take more pride in than I do in my appointments on the Supreme Court, from the Chief Justice to the last appointee." On February 19, 1912, Taft nominated fifty-four-year-old Mahlon Pitney to the Supreme Court. The appointment came as a complete surprise to Pitney. He had met the President at a dinner in Newark on February 12 but the conversation centered on Francis J. Swayze, an associate justice of the New Jersey Supreme Court whom state politicians had endorsed for the federal bench. Apparently, Pitney's geniality so impressed the President that, when he returned to Washington, he read most of Pitney's important decisions. Taft later informed Pitney: "I did consider with a good deal of care the question of appointing another lawyer from New Jersey." On March 14, 1912, the Senate ratified Pitney's nomination but only after three hours of bitter debate, a debate in which many progressive Republicans defied their party leaders. The opposition, led by Senators Charles Culberson of Texas and Albert Cummins of Iowa, pointed to Pitney's anti-labor decisions, especially the *Jonas Glass Co.* case, and claimed that the chancellor seemed pledged to property rights rather than to human dignity. When the regular Republicans pressed for a vote, the President's choice was approved by a fifty to twenty-six vote.

Pitney journeyed to Washington in the middle of March, when he again met the President. On the eighteenth, at noon, he was sworn in to his new office. "Every step of Justice Pitney's elevation to the Supreme Court was marked with dignity and old time customs. Meeting with the other Justices in the robing room, the New Jersey chancellor took his statutory oath of office, administered by Chief Justice White." Then, "attired in a long somber robe of office, he joined the procession of Judges as they marched across the corridor to take up their duties of the day. Once the eight members of the Bench had taken their seats, Chief Justice White announced the appointment of Mr. Pitney. A word of official welcome was extended and the Chief Justice directed the clerk to administer a second oath. This time Justice Pitney took the 'Judicial Oath' on the same Bible Justices had used for a century. He was then conducted to his seat at the extreme left" and the business of the Court resumed (35 *New Jersey Law Journal* 98 [1912]). The new Associate Justice, the sixty-fifth in the Court's history, had now attained the pinnacle of his career. From Trenton, Pitney received a telegram from New Jersey governor Woodrow Wilson reading: "My warmest congratulations. A better choice could not have been made."

During Pitney's ten-year, nine-month, and twelve-day tenure as an Associate Justice, he rendered 268 opinions—244 majority; nineteen dissenting; and five concurring. Seldom absent from the Bench, he participated in all but nineteen of the 2,412 decisions handed down during his service (March 18, 1912 to December 31, 1922). It is in the area of labor decisions, though, that the Justice made his most significant contribution. In *Coppage* v. *Kansas,* 236 U.S. 1 (1915), the question presented to the Court was whether or not a Kansas statute outlawing "yellow-dog" contracts arbitrarily interfered with the freedom of contract. The plaintiff, a superintendent for the St. Louis and San Francisco Railway Company, had fired one Hedges because he refused to sign an agreement requiring him to resign from a Switchmen's Union. Thus the plaintiff had violated a Kansas law, similar to those passed by fourteen other states, which made it a misdemeanor to "coerce, require, demand, or influence" any person to enter into an agreement not "to join or become or remain" a member of any labor organization as a condition for securing or continuing in employment. Coppage was found guilty of violating the statute and the Kansas Supreme Court affirmed the judgment, 87 Kans. 752 (1912). In speaking for a six to three court, Pitney reversed the Kansas Supreme Court and voided the statute on the grounds that it violated the Fourteenth Amendment's due process clause and had unlawfully deprived the employer of his freedom to make a contract. For support, Pitney relied extensively on *Adair* v. *United States,* 208 U.S. 161 (1908), where the Court had annulled an 1888 congressional act prohibiting interstate carriers from discharging employees because of labor union membership. The states, reasoned the Justice, are also similarly enjoined because of the Fourteenth Amendment. In a strikingly hostile labor opinion, in keeping with his earlier pronouncements, Pitney concluded:

> *And does not the ordinary contract of employment include an insistence by the employer that the employee shall agree, as a condition of the employment, that he will not be idle and will not work for whom he pleases but will serve his present employer, and him only, so long as the relation between them shall continue? Can the right of making contracts be enjoyed at all, except by parties coming together in an agreement that requires each party to forego during the time and for the purpose covered by the agreement, any inconsistent exercise of his constitutional rights?*
>
> *. . . Included in the right of personal liberty and the right of private property—partaking of the nature of each—is the right to make contracts for the acquisition of property. Chief among such contracts is that of personal employment, by which labor and other services are exchanged for money or other forms of property. If this right be struck down or arbitrarily interfered with, there is a substantial impairment of liberty in the long established constitutional sense. The right is as essential to the laborer as to the capitalist, to the poor as to the rich; for the vast majority of persons have no other honest way to begin to acquire property, save by working for money.*

This interference with liberty is very serious, he continued, as it disturbs the balance of bargaining power which should exist between employer and employee, and thus is unsustainable as a legitimate exercise of the state police power. "In short, an interference with the normal exercise of personal liberty and property rights is the primary object of the statute, and not an incident to the advancement of the general welfare." Thus, in voiding the Kansas law, Pitney ruled that the employer remained free to discharge an employee for any reason, providing that he first announced under what conditions the discharge would take effect—"Granted the equal freedom of both parties to the contract of employment, has not each party the right to stipulate upon what terms only he will consent to the inception, or to the continuance, of that relationship?"

In a brilliant dissenting opinion, Justice Oliver Wendell Holmes disagreed entirely with Pitney's reasoning. The statute is constitutional, concluded Holmes, because it promotes the liberty and equality of the individual:

> *In present conditions a workman not unnaturally may believe that only by belonging to a union can he secure a contract that shall be fair to him. . . . If that belief, whether right or wrong, may be held by a reasonable man, it seems to me that it may be enforced by law in order to establish the equality of position between the parties in which liberty of contract begins. Whether in the long run it is wise for the workingmen to enact legislation of this sort is not my concern, but I am strongly of opinion that there is nothing in the Constitution of the United States to prevent it. . . .* Id. at 26–27.

Though Holmes thought that the Kansas law promoted liberty and equality, Pitney considered it an interference with both. The meaning of liberty and equality was the main point upon which the majority and minority—Holmes,

Hughes, and Day—disagreed. Justice Day, with Hughes concurring, explained: "I think that the act now under consideration, and kindred ones, are intended to promote the same liberty of action for the employee as the employer confessedly enjoys." The Kansas law was a step toward making them both equal in bargaining power. To these arguments, Pitney replied that while an individual has a legal right to join a union, he has no inherent right to do this and still remain in the pay of one who is unwilling to employ a union man.

Two years after the Coppage decision, Pitney gave business still firmer judicial protection against unions. Speaking for the Court in *Hitchman Coal and Coke Co.* v. *Mitchell,* 245 U.S. 229 (1917), he ruled that an injunction could be issued to prevent workers from organizing unions if they had previously agreed to refrain from such action. The superintendent at the Hitchman mine had extracted from each employee a written promise not to join the United Mine Workers of America while in Hitchman employ. Union organizers persisted in proselytizing the miners and made secret agreements arranging for them to join the union at a later date but to strike when called upon to do so. In 1907, the company obtained a temporary restraining order, citing the general equitable ground of preventing irreparable loss and injury, 172 Fed. 963 (N.D.W.Va., 1909). A federal district court later found the U.A.W. an unlawful organization under the Sherman Act and enjoined all organizing of the complainant's workers, 202 Fed. 512 (N.D.W.Va., 1912). On appeal, the circuit court reversed the judgment, 214 Fed. 685 (4th Cir. 1914). The Supreme Court, on December 10, 1917, in a six to three decision, reversed the circuit court. Pitney, without mentioning the Sherman Act specifically, based the majority decision on the U.A.W.'s unlawful acts in inducing a breach of contract. The company, he argued, is as free to make non-membership in a union a condition of employment as the miner is free to join the union. While the miners and other workingmen undoubtedly have the right to form unions and invite other workers to join, this right is not absolute but one which must be exercised with a reasonable regard for the conflicting rights of others. But in this instance the U.A.W.'s role in instigating a strike was totally unjustifiable because the U.A.W. was not the official agent of the employees and, furthermore, the strike actions of the U.A.W. were illegal as employees were being induced to leave their employ *en masse* in order to cripple the plaintiff's business. Pitney concluded that an injunction should be issued prohibiting union attempts to secure secret membership promises when these same workers had previously agreed to relinquish their employment in case they became union members. Again, Pitney did not deal with the obnoxious "yellow-dog" contracts or with the horrible and exploitative working conditions in the mine fields. He based his opinion on a purely conceptual threat of illegal coercion by the union, which the Supreme Court, he reasoned, must prevent.

As in the *Coppage* case, there was a ringing challenge from the dissenters—Brandeis, Holmes, and Clarke. Justice Brandeis, for example, stressed the social and legal rights of labor. Trade unions and collective bargaining were legal, he reasoned, and the organizational methods employed were also legal. What Pitney called illegal coercion, Brandeis described as actions necessary to compel the company to change its operational methods. Protesting Pitney's logic, Brandeis wrote:

> . . . *[C]oercion, in a legal sense, is not exerted when a union merely endeavors to induce employees to join a union with the intention thereafter to order a strike unless the employer consents to unionize his shop. . . . Indeed, the plaintiff's whole case is rested upon agreements secured under similar pressure of economic necessity or disadvantage. If it is coercion to threaten to strike unless plaintiff consents to a closed union shop, it is coercion also to threaten not to give one employment unless the applicant will consent to a closed nonunion shop* (*245 U.S. 229, 271.*)

Pitney wrote several other majority opinions in labor cases, opinions which expressed the same philosophical bias, e.g., *Eagle Glass and Manufacturing Co.* v. *Rowe,* 245 U.S. 275 (1917), and *Duplex Printing Co.* v. *Deering,* 254 U.S. 443 (1921). In fact, Justice Pitney's labor decisions were merely reiterations and amplifications of the position he enunciated in *Jonas Glass Co.* v. *Glass Bottle Blowers Association,* 77 N.J. Eq. 219 (1908), and in his other New Jersey labor opinions, e.g., *Brennan* v. *United Hatters,* 73 N.J.L. 729 (1906). In retrospect, Pitney's labor opinions are now of only historical and antiquarian interest. Those progressive senators who had opposed Pitney's confirmation in 1912 had correctly anticipated the Justice's attitude toward organized labor.

Pitney wrote the Court's opinion in two civil liberties cases—*Frank* v. *Mangum,* 237 U.S. 309 (1915), and *Pierce* v. *United States,* 252 U.S 239 (1920). His opinion in the *Frank* case is certainly one of his most important decisions, because it illustrates the barely developed state of due process as applied to individuals in state criminal trials. Between Pitney's 1915 opinion and 1968 there have been at least a dozen cases which have redefined the due process concept in state criminal trials, e.g., *Moore* v. *Dempsey,* 261 U.S. 86 (1923), *Shepherd* v. *The State of Florida,* 341 U.S. 50 (1951), *Rideau* v. *Louisiana,* 373 U.S. 723 (1963). The question presented in the *Frank* case was whether the federal courts could issue a writ of *habeas corpus* on the allegation of an unfair state criminal trial. The Georgia district court denied the writ and Pitney affirmed this decision—Holmes and Hughes dissented. Leo Frank, accused of murdering a young girl in Atlanta, contended that he had been deprived of due process because he had not been in the courtroom during his entire trial. The presiding judge, aware of public hostility toward Frank and fearing that Frank might be lynched, had requested that he remain away from the Court when the jury announced its decision. The judge gave the same advice to Frank's lawyers, which they heeded. In presenting the *Frank* case to the Supreme Court in 1915, Louis Marshall argued that due process requires the defendant to be present during the entire trial. Pitney ruled that, despite these extraneous occurrences, there was no reason to doubt that the Georgia court did "fairly and justly perform its duty." It was proper, therefore, considering the delicate question of federal-state relations raised by the petitioner, to accept the Georgia decision without going behind the Court record. Holmes and Hughes, in joint dissent, angrily retorted: "Mob law does not become due process of law by securing the assent of a terrorized jury. . . . When the decision of the question of fact is so interwoven with the decision of constitutional right that the one necessarily involves the other, the Federal Court must examine the facts. . . . This is not a matter for polite presumptions; we must look facts in the face." (*Frank* v. *Mangum, supra* at 347.) Holmes had the satisfaction of enunciating his minority opinion as spokesman for the Court majority eight years later in *Moore* v. *Dempsey, supra.*

In *Pierce* v. *United States, supra,* Pitney, speaking for the Court in a seven to two decision, sustained the conviction under the Espionage Act of 1917 of distributors of a pamphlet which allegedly contained false statements. The Court upheld the constitutionality and applicability of the act, with Brandeis and Holmes dissenting. Pierce and other Socialists had been convicted for alleged interference with the prosecution of the First World War by distributing a pamphlet which contained "highly colored and sensational" statements. Justice Pitney found no difficulty in locating the inflammatory sections and he concluded that the defendants knew they were false. He cited as erroneous statements:

> *Into your homes the recruiting officers are coming. They will take your sons of military age and impress them into the Army;*
>
> *And still the recruiting officers will come; seizing age after age, mounting up to the elder ones and taking the younger ones as they grow to soldier size;*
>
> *The Attorney General of the United States is so busy sending to prison men who do not stand up when the Star Spangled Banner is played, that he has no time to protect the food supply from gamblers.*
>
> *Our entry into it was determined by the certainty that if the Allies do not win, J. P. Morgan's loan to the Allies will be repudiated, and those American investors who bit on his promises would be hooked. Id. at 245–246*

Pitney concluded that:

> *Common knowledge . . . would have sufficed to show at least that the statements as to the causes that led to the entry of the United States . . . were grossly false; and such common knowledge went to prove also that defendants knew they were untrue. That they were false if taken in a literal sense hardly is disputed. . . . The jury was warranted in finding the statements false in fact, and known to be so by the defendants, or else distributed recklessly, without effort to ascertain the truth. Id. at 251*

Pitney's decisions in both the *Pierce* and *Frank* cases were consistent with his position in other civil liberties cases. He joined the majority in upholding conviction under the Espionage Act and related state statutes, e.g., *Debs* v. *United States,* 249 U.S. 211 (1919), *Abrams* v. *United States,* 250 U.S. 616 (1919), *Gilbert* v. *Minnesota,* 254 U.S. 325 (1920), *Schenck* v. *United States,* 249 U.S. 47 (1919). He dissented, though, in that rare instance when the Supreme Court upheld the accused—*Berger* v. *United States,* 255 U.S. 22 (1921). (See 40

Virginia Law Review 763 [1954].) Pitney's stress on individual freedom in his labor decisions somehow was not carried over to his civil liberty opinions.

In August, 1922, Pitney suffered a stroke which left him physically and mentally unable to continue his judicial responsibilities, and, on December 31, 1922, he officially resigned from the Court. He died at his Washington home on December 9, 1924, leaving his wife Florence T. Shelton of Morristown, New Jersey whom he had married in 1891, and their three children—Guy Shelton, born in 1893; Mahlon Jr., born in 1899; and Beatrice Louis, born in 1904. He was buried in Evergreen Cemetery, Morristown. Pitney was a devoted and conscientious lawyer. His meticulously researched opinions, although often repetitious and quite heavy in style, reveal a troubled man's attempt to deal with complex legal and social problems in what seemed to him a logical and consistent manner.

SELECTED BIBLIOGRAPHY

Alan Ryder Breed, *Mahlon Pitney,* unpublished Senior thesis (Princeton University, 1932) is excellent for the Justice's early life. Mr. Breed had the assistance of the Pitney family in the writing of his essay. See also: David M. Levitan, "Mahlon Pitney—Labor Judge," 40 *Virginia Law Review* 733 (1954); Thomas Reed Powell, "Collective Bargaining Before the Supreme Court," 33 *Political Science Quarterly* 396 (1918); "Mr. Justice Pitney," 24 *Green Bag* 211 (1912).

Mahlon Pitney

REPRESENTATIVE OPINIONS

FRANK v. MANGUM, 239 U.S. 309 (1915)

In a trial punctuated by cries of a lynch mob outside the courtroom, Leo Frank was found guilty by a Georgia court in 1913 of murdering a fourteen-year-old girl. On appeal to the Georgia Supreme Court, Frank's lawyers maintained that hostile public sentiments improperly influenced the trial court and jury. Furthermore, Frank's lawful rights were hampered because he was not permitted to be present when the verdict was rendered. The state courts held that the allegations of mob violence were not substantiated and Frank's absence at the reading of the verdict had been waived by failure to raise this point at the trial. Frank then applied to the United States District Court for release on *habeas corpus,* claiming a denial of due process of law and that, in addition, the Georgia Supreme Court's ruling on his enforced absence from the courtroom was inconsistent with previous decisions of the same court. Pitney, in writing the majority opinion, wrote that, despite these extraneous occurrences, there was no reason to doubt the Georgia court did "fairly and justly perform its duty."

His opinion, with Holmes and Hughes in dissent, stated that the Court could not go behind that judicial record as long as legal procedures had been observed. Pitney's narrow opinion of the due process concept in state criminal trials has since been redefined. But his opinion illustrates the Court's pedantic thinking in civil liberties cases. Although Governor John Slaton of Georgia eventually commuted Frank's death sentence to life imprisonment in 1915 because of the doubt surrounding the case, a lynch mob spirited Frank from a state prison and hanged him.

MR. JUSTICE PITNEY, after making the foregoing statement, delivered the opinion of the court.

The points raised by the appellant may be reduced to the following:

(1) It is contended that the disorder in and about the court-room during the trial and up to and at the reception of the verdict amounted to mob domination, that not only the jury but the presiding judge succumbed to it, and that this in effect wrought a dis-

solution of the court, so that the proceedings were *coram non judice*.

(2) That Frank's right to be present during the entire trial until and at the return of the verdict was an essential part of the right of trial by jury, which could not be waived either by himself or his counsel.

(3) That his presence was so essential to a proper hearing that the reception of the verdict in his absence, and in the absence of his counsel, without his consent or authority, was a departure from the due process of law guaranteed by the Fourteenth Amendment, sufficient to bring about a loss of jurisdiction of the trial court and to render the verdict and judgment absolute nullities.

(4) That the failure of Frank and his counsel, upon the first motion for a new trial, to allege as a ground of that motion the known fact of Frank's absence at the reception of the verdict, or to raise any jurisdictional question based upon it, did not deprive him of the right to afterwards attack the judgment as a nullity, as he did in the motion to set aside the verdict.

(5) And that the ground upon which the Supreme Court of Georgia rested its decision affirming the denial of the latter motion (83 S. E. Rep. 645),—viz., that the objection based upon Frank's absence when the verdict was rendered was available on the motion for new trial and under proper practice ought to have been then taken, and because not then taken could not be relied upon as a ground for setting aside the verdict as a nullity,—was itself in conflict with the Constitution of the United States because equivalent in effect to an *ex post facto* law, since, as is said, it departs from the practice settled by previous decisions of the same court.

In dealing with these contentions, we should have in mind the nature and extent of the duty that is imposed upon a Federal court on application for the writ of *habeas corpus* under § 753, Rev. Stat. Under the terms of that section, in order to entitle the present appellant to the relief sought, it must appear that he is held in custody in violation of the Constitution of the United States. *Rogers* v. *Peck*, 199 U.S. 425, 434. Moreover, if he is held in custody by reason of his conviction upon a criminal charge before a court having plenary jurisdiction over the subject-matter or offense, the place where it was committed, and the person of the prisoner, it results from the nature of the writ itself that he cannot have relief on *habeas corpus*. Mere errors in point of law, however serious, committed by a criminal court in the exercise of its jurisdiction over a case properly subject to its cognizance, cannot be reviewed by *habeas corpus*. That writ cannot be employed as a substitute for the writ of error. *Ex parte Parks*, 93 U.S. 18, 21; *Ex parte Siebold*, 100 U.S. 371, 375; *Ex parte Royall*, 117 U.S. 241, 250; *In re Frederich, Pet'r*, 149 U.S. 70, 75; *Baker* v. *Grice*, 169 U.S. 284, 290; *Tinsley* v. *Anderson*, 171 U.S. 101, 105; *Markuson* v. *Boucher*, 175 U.S. 184.

As to the "due process of law" that is required by the Fourteenth Amendment, it is perfectly well settled that a criminal prosecution in the courts of a State, based upon a law not in itself repugnant to the Federal Constitution, and conducted according to the settled course of judicial proceedings as established by the law of the State, so long as it includes notice, and a hearing, or an opportunity to be heard, before a court of competent jurisdiction, according to established modes of procedure, is "due process" in the constitutional sense. *Walker* v. *Sauvinet*, 92 U.S. 90, 93; *Hurtado* v. *California*, 110 U.S. 516, 535; *Andrews* v. *Swartz*, 156 U.S. 272, 276; *Bergemann* v. *Backer*, 157 U.S. 655, 659; *Rogers* v. *Peck*, 199 U.S. 425, 434; *Drury* v. *Lewis*, 200 U.S. 1, 7; *Felts* v. *Murphy*, 201 U.S. 123, 129; *Howard* v. *Kentucky*, 200 U.S. 164.

It is, therefore, conceded by counsel for appellant that in the present case we may not review irregularities or erroneous rulings upon the trial, however serious, and that the writ of *habeas corpus* will lie only in case the judgment under which the prisoner is detained is shown to be absolutely void for want of jurisdiction in the court that pronounced it, either because such jurisdiction was absent at the beginning or because it was lost in the course of the proceedings. And since no question is made respecting the original jurisdiction of the trial court, the contention is and must be that by the conditions that surrounded the trial, and the absence of defendant when the verdict was rendered, the court was deprived of jurisdiction to receive the verdict and pronounce the sentence.

But it would be clearly erroneous to confine the inquiry to the proceedings and judgment of the trial court. The laws of the State of Georgia (as will appear from decisions elsewhere cited), provide for an appeal in criminal cases to the Supreme Court of that State upon divers grounds, including such as those upon which it is here asserted that the trial court was lacking in jurisdiction. And while the Fourteenth Amendment does not require that a State shall provide for an appellate review in criminal cases (*McKane* v. *Durston,* 153 U.S. 684, 687; *Andrews* v. *Swartz,* 156 U.S. 272, 275; *Rogers* v. *Peck,* 199 U.S. 425, 435; *Reetz* v. *Michigan,* 188 U.S. 505, 508), it is perfectly obvious that where such an appeal is provided for, and the prisoner has had the benefit of it, the proceedings in the appellate tribunal are to be regarded as a part of the process of law under which he is held in custody by the State, and to be considered in determining any question of alleged deprivation of his life or liberty contrary to the Fourteenth Amendment.

In fact, such questions as are here presented under the due process clause of the Fourteenth Amendment, though sometimes discussed as if involving merely the jurisdiction of some court or other tribunal, in a larger and more accurate sense involve the power and authority of the State itself. The prohibition is addressed to the State; if it be violated, it makes no difference in a court of the United States by what agency of the State this is done; so, if a violation be threatened by one agency of the State but prevented by another agency of higher authority, there is no violation by the State. It is for the State to determine what courts or other tribunals shall be established for the trial of offenses against its criminal laws, and to define their several jurisdictions and authority as between themselves. And the question whether a State is depriving a prisoner of his liberty without due process of law, where the offense for which he is prosecuted is based upon a law that does no violence to the Federal Constitution, cannot ordinarily be determined, with fairness to the State, until the conclusion of the course of justice in its courts. *Virginia* v. *Rives,* 100 U.S. 313, 318; *Civil Rights Cases,* 109 U.S. 3, 11; *McKane* v. *Durston,* 153 U.S. 684, 687; *Dreyer* v. *Illinois,* 187 U.S. 71, 83–84; *Reetz* v. *Michigan,* 188 U.S. 505, 507; *Carter* v. *Caldwell,* 200 U.S. 293, 297; *Waters-Pierce Oil Co.* v. *Texas* (No. 1), 212 U.S. 86, 107; *In re Frederich, Petitioner,* 149 U.S. 70, 75; *Whitten* v. *Tomlinson,* 160 U.S. 231, 242; *Baker* v. *Grice,* 169 U.S. 284, 291; *Minnesota* v. *Brundage,* 180 U.S. 499, 503; *Urquhart* v. *Brown,* 205 U.S. 179, 182.

It is, indeed, settled by repeated decisions of this court that where it is made to appear to a court of the United States that an applicant for *habeas corpus* is in the custody of a state officer in the ordinary course of a criminal prosecution, under a law of the State not in itself repugnant to the Federal Constitution, the writ, in the absence of very special circumstances, ought not to be issued until the state prosecution has reached its conclusion, and not even then until the Federal questions arising upon the record have been brought before this court upon writ of error. *Ex parte Royall,* 117 U.S. 241, 251; *In re Frederich, Petitioner,* 149 U.S. 70, 77; *Whitten* v. *Tomlinson,* 160 U.S. 231, 242; *Baker* v. *Grice,* 169 U.S. 284, 291; *Tinsley* v. *Anderson,* 171 U.S. 101, 105; *Markuson* v. *Boucher,* 175 U.S. 184; *Urquhart* v. *Brown,* 205 U.S. 179. And see *Henry* v. *Henkel,* 235 U.S. 219, 228. Such cases as *In re Loney,* 134 U.S. 372, 376; and *In re Neagle,* 135 U.S. 1; are recognized as exceptional.

It follows as a logical consequence that where, as here, a criminal prosecution has proceeded through all the courts of the State, including the appellate as well as the trial court, the result of the appellate review cannot be ignored when afterwards the prisoner applies for his release on the ground of a deprivation of Federal rights sufficient to oust the State of its jurisdiction to proceed to judgment and execution against him. This is not a mere matter of comity, as seems to be supposed. The rule stands upon a much higher plane, for it arises out of the very nature and ground of the inquiry into the proceedings of the state tribunals, and touches closely upon the relations between the state and the Federal governments. As was declared by this court in *Ex parte Royall,* 117 U.S. 241, 252—applying in a *habeas corpus* case what was said in *Covell* v. *Heyman,* 111 U.S. 176, 182, a case of conflict of jurisdiction:—"The forebearance which courts of coördinate jurisdiction, administered under a single system, exercise towards each other, whereby conflicts are avoided, by avoiding interference with the process of each other, is a principle of comity, with perhaps no higher sanction than the utility which comes from concord; but between state courts and those of the United States it is something more. It is a principle of right and of law, and, therefore, of necessity." And see *In re Tyler, Petitioner,* 149 U.S. 164, 186.

It is objected by counsel for appellee that the alleged loss of jurisdiction cannot be shown by evidence outside of the record; that where a prisoner is held under a judgment of conviction passed by a court having jurisdiction of the subject-matter, and the indictment against him states the case and is based upon a valid existing law, *habeas corpus* is not an available remedy, save for want of jurisdiction appearing upon the face of the record of the court wherein he was convicted. The rule at the common law, and under the act 31 Car. II, c. 2, and other acts of Parliament prior to that of July 1, 1816 (56 Geo. III, c. 100, § 3), seems to have been that a showing in the return to a writ of *habeas corpus* that the prisoner was held under final process based upon a judgment or decree of a court of competent jurisdiction, closed the inquiry. So it was held, under the judiciary act of 1789 (ch. 20, § 14, 1 Stat. 73, 81), in *Ex parte Watkins,* 3 Pet. 193, 202. And the rule seems to have been the same under the act of March 2, 1833 (ch. 57, § 7, 4 Stat. 632, 634), and that of Aug. 29, 1842 (ch. 257, 5 Stat. 539). But when Congress, in the act of February 5, 1867 (ch. 28, 14 Stat. 385), extended the writ of *habeas corpus* to all cases of persons restrained of their liberty in violation of the Constitution or a law or treaty of the United States, procedural regulations were included, now found in Rev. Stat., § § 754–761. These require that the application for the writ shall be made by complaint in writing signed by the applicant and verified by his oath, setting forth the facts concerning his detention, in whose custody he is detained, and by virtue of what claim or authority, if known; require that the return shall certify the true cause of the detention; and provide that the prisoner may under oath deny any of the facts set forth in the return or allege other material facts, and that the court shall proceed in a summary way to determine the facts by hearing testimony and arguments, and thereupon dispose of the party as law and justice require. The effect is to substitute for the bare legal review that seems to have been the limit of judicial authority under the common-law practice, and under the act of 31 Car. II, c. 2, a more searching investigation, in which the applicant is put upon his oath to set forth the truth of the matter respecting the causes of his detention, and the court, upon determining the actual facts, is to "dispose of the party as law and justice require."

There being no doubt of the authority of the Congress to thus liberalize the common law procedure on *habeas corpus* in order to safeguard the liberty of all persons within the jurisdiction of the United States against infringement through any violation of the Constitution or a law or treaty established thereunder, it results that under the sections cited a prisoner in custody pursuant to the final judgment of a state court of criminal jurisdiction may have a judicial inquiry in a court of the United States into the very truth and substance of the causes of his detention, although it may become necessary to look behind and beyond the record of his conviction to a sufficient extent to test the jurisdiction of the state court to proceed to judgment against him. *Cuddy, Petitioner,* 131 U.S. 280, 283, 286; *In re Mayfield,* 141 U.S. 107, 116; *Whitten* v. *Tomlinson,* 160 U.S. 231, 242; *In re Watts and Sachs,* 190 U.S. 1, 35.

In the light, then, of these established rules and principles: that the due process of law guaranteed by the Fourteenth Amendment has regard to substance of right, and not to matters of form or procedure; that it is open to the courts of the United States upon an application for a writ of *habeas corpus* to look beyond forms and inquire into the very substance of the matter, to the extent of deciding whether the prisoner has been deprived of his liberty without due process of law, and for this purpose to inquire into jurisdictional facts, whether they appear upon the record or not; that an investigation into the case of a prisoner held in custody by a State on conviction of a criminal offense must take into consideration the entire course of proceedings in the courts of the State, and not merely a single step in those proceedings; and that it is incumbent upon the prisoner to set forth in his application a sworn statement of the facts concerning his detention and by virtue of what claim or authority he is detained; we proceed to consider the questions presented.

1. And first, the question of the disorder and hostile sentiment that are said to have influenced the trial court and jury to an extent amounting to mob domination.

The District Court having considered the case upon the face of the petition, we must do the same, treating it as if demurred to by the sheriff. There is no doubt of the jurisdiction to issue the writ of *habeas corpus*. The question is as to the propriety of issuing it in the present case. Under § 755, Rev. Stat., it was the duty of the court to refuse the writ if it appeared from the petition itself that appellant was not entitled to it. And see *Ex parte Watkins,* 3 Pet. 193, 201; *Ex parte Milligan,* 4 Wall. 2, 110; *Ex parte Terry,* 128 U.S. 289, 301.

Now the obligation resting upon us, as upon the District Court, to look through the form and into the very heart and substance of the matter, applies as well to the averments of the petition as to the proceedings which the petitioner attacks. We must regard not any single clause or paragraph, but the entire petition, and the exhibits that are made a part of it. Thus, the petition contains a narrative of disorder, hostile manifestations, and uproar, which, if it stood alone, and were to be taken as true, may be conceded to show an environment inconsistent with a fair trial and an impartial verdict. But to consider this as standing alone is to take a wholly superficial view. The narrative has no proper place in a petition addressed to a court of the United States except as it may tend to throw light upon the question whether the State of Georgia, having regard to the entire course of the proceedings, in the appellate as well as in the trial court, is depriving appellant of his liberty and intending to deprive him of his life without due process of law. Dealing with the narrative, then, in its essence, and in its relation to the context, it clearly appears to be only a reiteration of allegations that appellant had a right to submit, and did submit, first to the trial court, and afterwards to the Supreme Court of the State, as a ground for avoiding the consequences of the trial; that the allegations were considered by those courts, successively, at times and places and under circumstances wholly apart from the atmosphere of the trial, and free from any suggestion of mob domination, or the like; and that the facts were examined by those courts not only upon the affidavits and exhibits submitted in behalf of the prisoner which are embodied in his present petition as a part of his sworn account of the causes of his detention, but also upon rebutting affidavits submitted in behalf of the State and which, for reasons not explained, he has not included in the petition. As appears from the prefatory statement, the allegations of disorder were found by both of the state courts to be groundless except in a few particulars as to which the courts ruled that they were irregularities not harmful in fact to defendant and therefore insufficient in law to avoid the verdict. 141 Georgia, 243, 280. And it was because the defendant was concluded by that finding that the Supreme Court upon the subsequent motion to set aside the verdict declined to again consider those allegations. 83 S. E. Rep. 645, 655.

Whatever question is raised about the jurisdiction of the trial court, no doubt is suggested but that the Supreme Court had full jurisdiction to determine the matters of fact and the questions of law arising out of this alleged disorder; nor is there any reason to suppose that it did not fairly and justly perform its duty. It is not easy to see why appellant is not, upon general principles, bound by its decision. It is a fundamental principle of jurisprudence, arising from the very nature of courts of justice and the objects for which they are established, that a question of fact or of law distinctly put in issue and directly determined by a court of competent jurisdiction cannot afterwards be disputed between the same parties. *Southern Pacific Railroad* v. *United States,* 168 U.S. 1, 48. The principle is as applicable to the decisions of criminal courts as to those of civil jurisdiction. As to its application, in *habeas corpus* cases, with respect to decisions by such courts of the facts pertaining to the jurisdiction over the prisoner, see *Ex parte Terry,* 128 U.S. 289, 305, 310; *Ex parte Columbia George,* 144 Fed. Rep. 985, 986.

However, it is not necessary, for the purposes of the present case, to invoke the doctrine of *res adjudicata,* and, in view of the impropriety of limiting in the least degree the authority of the courts of the United States in investigating an alleged violation by a State of the due process of law guaranteed by the Fourteenth Amendment, we put out of view for the present the suggestion that even the questions of fact bearing upon the jurisdiction of the trial court could be conclusively determined against the prisoner by the decision of the state court of last resort.

But this does not mean that that decision may be ignored or disregarded. To do this, as we have already pointed out, would be not merely to disregard comity, but to ignore the essential question before us, which is not the guilt or innocence of the prisoner, or the truth of any particular fact asserted by him, but whether the State, taking into view the entire course of its procedure, has deprived him of due process of law. This familiar phrase does not mean that the operations of the state government shall be conducted without error or fault in any particular case, nor that the Federal courts may substitute their judgment for that of the state courts, or exercise any general review over their proceedings, but only that the fundamental rights of the prisoner shall not be taken from him arbitrarily or without the right to be heard according to the usual course of law in such cases.

We of course agree that if a trial is in fact dominated by a mob, so that the jury is intimidated and the trial judge yields, and so that there is an actual interference with the course of justice, there is, in that court, a departure from due process of law in the proper sense of that term. And if the State, supplying no corrective process, carries into execution a judgment of death or imprisonment based upon a verdict thus produced by mob domination, the State deprives the accused of his life or liberty without due process of law.

But the State may supply such corrective process as to it seems proper. Georgia has adopted the familiar procedure of a motion for a new trial followed by an appeal to its Supreme Court, not confined to the mere record of conviction but going at large, and upon evidence adduced outside of that record, into the question whether the processes of justice have been interfered with in the trial court. Repeated instances are reported of verdicts and judgments set aside and new trials granted for disorder or mob violence interfering with the prisoner's right to a fair trial. *Myers* v. *State,* 97 Georgia 76 (5), 99; *Collier* v. *State*, 115 Georgia, 803.

Such an appeal was accorded to the prisoner in the present case [*Frank* v. *State,* 141 Georgia, 243 (16), 280], in a manner and under circumstances already stated, and the Supreme Court, upon a full review, decided appellant's allegations of fact, so far as matters now material are concerned, to be unfounded. Owing to considerations already adverted to (arising not out of comity merely, but out of the very right of the matter to be decided, in view of the relations existing between the States and the Federal Government), we hold that such a determination of the facts as was thus made by the court of last resort of Georgia respecting the alleged interference with the trial through disorder and manifestations of hostile sentiment cannot in this collateral inquiry be treated as a nullity, but must be taken as setting forth the truth of the matter, certainly until some reasonable ground is shown for an inference that the court which rendered it either was wanting in jurisdiction, or at least erred in the exercise of its jurisdiction; and that the mere assertion by the prisoner that the facts of the matter are other than the state court upon full investigation determined them to be will not be deemed sufficient to raise an issue respecting the correctness of that determination; especially not, where the very evidence upon which the determination was rested is withheld by him who attacks the finding.

It is argued that if in fact there was disorder such as to cause a loss of jurisdiction in the trial court, jurisdiction could not be restored by any decision of the Supreme Court. This, we think, embodies more than one error of reasoning. It regards a part only of the judicial proceedings, instead of considering the entire process of law. It also begs the question of the existence of such disorder as to cause a loss of jurisdiction in the trial court; which should not be assumed, in the face of the decision of the reviewing court, without showing some adequate ground for disregarding that decision. And these errors grow out of the initial error of treating appellant's narrative of disorder as the whole matter, instead of reading it in connection with the context. The rule of law that in ordinary cases requires a prisoner to exhaust his remedies within the State before coming to the courts of the United States for redress would lose the greater part of its salutary force if the prisoner's mere allegations were to stand the same in law after as before the state courts had passed judgment upon them.

We are very far from intimating that manifestations of public sentiment, or any other form of disorder, calculated to influence court or jury, are matters to be lightly treated. The decisions of the Georgia courts in this and other cases show that such disorder is repressed, where practicable, by the direct intervention of the trial court and the officers under its command; and that other means familiar to the common-law practice, such as postponing the trial, changing the venue, and granting a new trial, are liberally resorted to in order to protect persons accused of crime in the right to a fair trial by an impartial jury. The argument for appellant amounts to saying that this is not enough; that by force of the "due process of law" provision of the Fourteenth Amendment, when the first attempt at a fair trial is rendered abortive through outside interference, the State, instead of allowing a new trial under better auspices, must abandon jurisdiction over the accused and refrain from further inquiry into the question of his guilt.

To establish this doctrine would, in a very practical sense, impair the power of the States to repress and punish crime; for it would render their courts powerless to act in opposition to lawless public sentiment. The argument is not only unsound in principle but is in conflict with the practice that prevails in all of the States, so far as we are aware. The cases cited do not sustain the contention that disorder or other lawless conduct calculated to overawe the jury or the trial judge can be treated as a dissolution of the court or as rendering the proceedings *coram non judice,* in any such sense as to bar further proceedings. In *Myers* v. *State,* 97 Georgia, 76, (5), 99; *Collier* v. *State,* 115 Georgia, 803; *Sanders* v. *State,* 85 Indiana, 318; S. C., 44 Am. Rep. 29; *Massey* v. *State,* 31 Tex. Cr. Rep. 371, 381; S. C., 20 S. W. Rep. 758; and *State* v. *Weldon,* 91 S. Car. 29, 38; *S. C.,* 39 L. R. A., N. S., 667, 669;—in all of which it was held that the prisoner's right to a fair trial had been interfered with by disorder or mob violence—it was not held that jurisdiction over the prisoner had been lost; on the contrary, in each instance a new trial was awarded as the appropriate remedy. So, in the cases where the trial judge abdicated his proper functions or absented himself during the trial (*Hayes* v. *State,* 58 Georgia, 36 (12), 49; *Blend* v. *People,* 41 N.Y. 604; *Shaw* v. *People,* 3 Hun, 272; aff'd 63 N.Y. 36; *Hinman* v. *People,* 13 Hun, 266; *McClure* v. *State,* 77 Indiana, 287; *O'Brien* v. *People,* 17 Colorado, 561; *Ellerbe* v. *State,* 75 Mississippi, 522; *S. C.,* 41 L. R. A. 569) the reviewing of the State in each instance simply set aside the verdict and awarded a new trial.

The Georgia courts, in the present case, proceeded upon the theory that Frank would have been entitled to this relief had his charges been true, and they refused a new trial only because they found his charges untrue save in a few minor particulars not amounting to more than irregularities, and not prejudicial to the accused. There was here no denial of due process of law.

2. We come, next, to consider the effect to be given to the fact, admitted for present purposes, that Frank was not present in the court-room when the verdict was rendered, his presence having been waived by his counsel, but without his knowledge or consent. No question is made but that at the common law and under the Georgia decisions it is the right of the prisoner to be present throughout the entire trial, from the commencement of the selection of the jury until the verdict is rendered and jury discharged. *Wade* v. *State,* 12 Georgia, 25, 29; *Martin* v. *State,* 51 Georgia, 567; *Nolan* v. *State,* 53 Georgia, 137; *S. C.,* 55 Georgia, 521; *Smith* v. *State,* 59 Georgia, 513; *Bonner* v. *State,* 67 Georgia, 510; *Barton* v. *State,* 67 Georgia, 653; *Cawthon* v. *State,* 119 Georgia, 395, 412; *Bagwell* v. *State,* 129 Georgia, 170; *Lyons* v. *State,* 7 Ga. App. 50. But the effect of these decisions is that the prisoner may personally waive the right to be present when the verdict is rendered, and perhaps may waive it by authorized act of his counsel; and that where, without his consent, the verdict is received in his absence, he may treat this as an error, and by timely motion demand a new trial, or (it seems) he may elect to treat the verdict as a nullity by moving in due season to set it aside as such. But we are unable to find that the courts of Georgia have in any case held that, by receiving a verdict in the absence of the prisoner and without his consent, the jurisdiction of the trial court was terminated. In the *Nolan Case, supra,* the verdict was set aside as void on the ground of the absence of the prisoner; but this was not held to deprive the trial court of its jurisdiction. On the contrary, the jurisdiction was treated as remaining, and that court proceeded to exercise it by arraigning the prisoner a second time upon the same indictment, when he pleaded specially, claiming his discharge because of former jeopardy; the trial court overruled this plea, the defendant excepted, and the jury found the defendant guilty; and, upon review, the Supreme Court reversed this judgment, not for the want of jurisdiction in the trial court, but for error committed in the exercise of jurisdiction. To the same effect is *Bagwell v. State, supra.*

In most of the other States, where error is committed by receiving a verdict of guilty during the involuntary absence of the accused, it is treated as merely requiring a new trial. In a few cases, the appellate court has ordered the defendant to be discharged, upon the ground that he had been once in jeopardy and a new trial would be futile.

However, the Georgia Supreme Court in the present case (83 S. E. Rep. 645) held, as pointed out in the prefatory statement, that because Frank, shortly after the verdict, was made fully aware of the facts, and he then made a motion for a new trial upon over 100 grounds, without including this as one, and had the motion heard by both the trial court and the Supreme Court, he could not, after this motion had been finally adjudicated against him, move to set aside the verdict as a nullity because of his absence when the verdict was rendered. There is nothing in the Fourteenth Amendment to prevent a State from adopting and enforcing so reasonable a regulation of procedure. *Dreyer* v. *Illinois,* 187 U.S. 71, 77—80.

It is insisted that the enforced absence of Frank at that time was not only a deprivation of trial by jury, but was equally a deprivation of due process of law within the meaning of the Amendment, in that it took from him at a critical stage of the proceeding the right or opportunity to be heard. But repeated decisions of this court have put it beyond the range of further debate that the "due process" clause of the Fourteenth Amendment has not the effect of imposing upon the States any particular form or mode of procedure, so long as the essential rights of notice and a hearing, or opportunity to be heard, before a competent tribunal are not interfered with. Indictment by grand jury is not essential to due process (*Hurtado* v. *California,* 110 U.S. 516, 532, 538; *Lem Woon* v. *Oregon,* 229 U.S. 586, 589, and cases cited). Trial by jury is not essential to it, either in civil cases (*Walker* v. *Sauvinet,* 92 U.S. 90), or in criminal (*Hallinger* v. *Davis,* 146 U.S. 314, 324; *Maxwell* v. *Dow,* 176 U.S. 581, 594, 602, 604).

It is argued that a State may not, while providing for trial by jury, permit the accused to waive the right to be heard in the mode characteristic of such trial, including the presence of the prisoner up to and at the time of the rendition of the verdict. But the cases cited do not support this contention. In *Hopt* v. *Utah,* 110 U.S. 574, 578 (principally relied upon), the court had under review a conviction in a territorial court after a trial subject to the local code of criminal procedure, which declared: If "the indictment is for a felony, the defendant *must be* personally present at the trial." The judgment was reversed because of the action of the trial court in permitting certain challenges to jurors, based upon the ground of bias, to be tried out of the presence of the court, the defendant, and his counsel. The ground of the decision of this court was the violation of the plain mandate of the local statute; and the power of the accused or his counsel to dispense with the requirement as to his personal presence was denied on the ground that his life could not be lawfully taken except in the mode prescribed by law. No other question was involved. See *Diaz* v. *United States,* 223 U.S. 442, 455, 458.

The distinction between what the common law requires with respect to trial by jury in criminal cases, and what the States may enact without contravening the "due process" clause of the Fourteenth Amendment, is very clearly evidenced by *Hallinger* v. *Davis,* 146 U.S. 314, and *Lewis* v. *United States,* 146 U.S. 370, which were under consideration by the court at the same time, both opinions being written by Mr. Justice Shiras. In the *Lewis Case,* which was a conviction of murder in a Circuit Court of the United States, the trial practice being regulated by the common law, it was held to be a leading principle, pervading the entire law of criminal procedure, that after indictment nothing should be done in the absence of the prisoner; that the making of challenges is an essential part of the trial, and it was one of the substantial rights of the prisoner to be brought face to face with the jurors at the time the challenges were made; and that in the absence of a statute, this right as it existed at common law must not be abridged. But in the *Hallinger Case,* where a State by legislative enactment had permitted one charged with a capital offense to waive a trial by jury and elect to be tried by the court, it was held that this method of procedure did not conflict with the Fourteenth Amendment. So in *Howard* v. *Kentucky,* 200 U.S. 164, 175—a case closely in point upon the question now presented—this court, finding that by the law of the State an occasional absence of the accused from the trial, from which no injury resulted to his substantial rights, was not deemed material error, held that the application of this rule of law did not amount to a denial of due process within the meaning of the Fourteenth Amendment.

In fact, this court has sustained the States in establishing a great variety of departures from the common law procedure respecting jury trials. Thus, in *Brown* v. *New Jersey,* 175 U.S. 172, 176; a statute providing for the trial of murder cases by struck jury was sustained, notwithstanding it did not provide for twenty peremptory challenges. *Simon* v. *Craft,* 182 U.S. 427, 435, while not a criminal case, involved the property of a person alleged to be of unsound mind, and it was held that an Alabama statute, under which the sheriff determined that Mrs. Simon's health and safety would be endangered by her presence at the trial of the question of her sanity, so that while served with notice she was detained in custody and not allowed to be present at the hearing of the inquisition, did not deprive her of property without due process of law. In *Felts* v. *Murphy,* 201 U.S. 123, 129, where the prisoner was convicted of the crime of murder and sentenced to imprisonment for life, although he did not hear a word of the evidence given upon the trial because of his almost total deafness, his inability to hear being such that it required a person to speak through an ear-trumpet close to his ear in order that such person should be heard by him, and the trial court having failed to see to it that the testimony in the case was repeated to him through his ear-trumpet, this court said that this was "at most an error, which did not take away from the court its jurisdiction over the subject-matter and over the person of the accused." In *Twining* v. *New Jersey,* 211 U.S. 78, 101, 111, it was held that the exemption of a prisoner from compulsory self-incrimination in the state courts was not included in the guaranty of due process of law contained in the Fourteenth Amendment. In *Jordan* v. *Massachusetts,* 225 U.S. 167, 177, where one of the jurors was subject to reasonable doubt as to his sanity, and the state court, pursuant to the local law of criminal procedure, determined upon a mere preponderance of the evidence that he was sane, the conviction was affirmed. In *Garland* v. *Washington,* 232 U.S. 642, 645, it was held that the want of a formal arraignment, treated by the State as depriving the accused of no substantial right and as having been waived and thereby lost, did not amount to depriving defendant of his liberty without due process of law.

Our conclusion upon this branch of the case is, that the practice established in the criminal courts of Georgia: that a defendant may waive his right to be present when the jury renders its verdict, and that such waiver may be given after as well as before the event, and is to be inferred from the making of a motion for new trial upon other grounds alone, when the facts respecting the reception of the verdict are within the prisoner's knowledge at the time of making that motion; is a regulation of criminal procedure that it is within the authority of the State to adopt. In adopting it, the State declares in effect, as it reasonably may declare, that the right of the accused to be present at the reception of the verdict is but an incident of the right of trial by jury; and since the State may, without infringing the Fourteenth Amendment, abolish trial by jury, it may limit the effect to be given to an error respecting one of the incidents of such trial. The presence of the prisoner when the verdict is rendered is not so essential a part of the hearing that a rule of practice permitting the accused to waive it and holding him bound by the waiver amounts to a deprivation of "due process of law."

3. The insistence that the decision of the Supreme Court of Georgia in affirming the denial of the motion to set aside the verdict (83 S. E. Rep. 645) on the ground that Frank's failure to raise the objection upon the motion for a new trial amounted to a waiver of it, was inconsistent with the previous practice as established in *Nolan* v. *State,* 53 Georgia, 137; *S. C.,* 55 Georgia, 521; and therefore amounted in effect to an *ex post facto* law in contravention of § 10 of Article I of the Federal Constitution, needs but a word. Assuming the inconsistency, it is sufficient to say that the constitutional prohibition: "No State shall . . . pass any bill of attainder, *ex post facto* law, or law impairing the obligation of contracts," as its terms indicate, is directed against legislative action only, and does not reach erroneous or inconsistent decisions by the courts. *Calder* v. *Bull,* 3 Dall. 386, 389; *Fletcher* v. *Peck,* 6 Cr. 87, 138; *Kring* v. *Missouri,* 107 U.S. 221, 227; *Thompson* v. *Utah,* 170 U.S. 343, 351; *Cross Lake Club* v. *Louisiana,* 224 U.S. 632, 638; *Ross* v. *Oregon,* 227 U.S. 150, 161.

4. To conclude: Taking appellant's petition as a whole, and not regarding any particular portion of it to the exclusion of the rest—dealing with its true and substantial meaning and not merely with its superficial import—it shows that Frank, having been formally accused of a grave crime, was placed on trial before a court of competent jurisdiction, with a jury lawfully constituted; he had a public trial, deliberately conducted, with the benefit of counsel for his defense; he was found guilty and sentenced pursuant to the laws of the State; twice he has moved the trial court to grant a new trial, and once to set aside the verdict as a nullity; three times he has been heard upon appeal before the court of last resort of that State, and in every instance the adverse action of the trial court has been affirmed; his allegations of hostile public sentiment and disorder in and about the court-room, improperly influencing the trial court and the jury against him, have been rejected because found untrue in point of fact upon evidence presumably justifying that finding, and which he has not produced in the present proceeding; his contention that his lawful rights were infringed because he was not permitted to be present when the jury rendered its verdict, has been set aside because it was waived by his failure to raise the objection in due season when fully cognizant of the facts. In all of these

proceedings the State, through its courts, has retained jurisdiction over him, has accorded to him the fullest right and opportunity to be heard according to the established modes of procedure, and now holds him in custody to pay the penalty of the crime of which he has been adjudged guilty. In our opinion, he is not shown to have been deprived of any right guaranteed to him by the Fourteenth Amendment or any other provision of the Constitution or laws of the United States; on the contrary, he has been convicted, and is now held in custody, under "due process of law" within the meaning of the Constitution.

The final order of the District Court, refusing the application for a writ of *habeas corpus*, is

Affirmed.

James C. McReynolds

☆ 1862–1946 ☆

APPOINTED BY

WOODROW WILSON

YEARS ON COURT

1914–1941

James C. McReynolds

by

DAVID BURNER

OF THE FOUR conservative Justices famous for their opposition to Franklin Roosevelt's New Deal, James Clark McReynolds was probably the most reactionary and easily the most tenacious. His was the single negative vote in the case that tested the constitutionality of the TVA. In his acid dissent from the decision upholding Roosevelt's devaluation of gold, he announced that the Constitution familiar to him was "gone." After 1933 he refused to attend White House receptions, and at one Gridiron dinner he remained seated, his back to the President, while the rest of the audience rose to greet the Chief Executive. During those years McReynolds became furious at friends and relatives who sought to borrow money from him on what he saw as the pretext that they could not find work. After Butler, Van Devanter, and Sutherland had retired from the Court, McReynolds stayed on until 1941 as the "lone dissenter."

McReynolds' southern upbringing may have helped to produce in him a racist streak. His court decisions reflect his segregationist thinking; and he even issued a lone dissent in the first Scottsboro case, which ordered new trials for seven Negroes who, his colleagues declared, had been denied their constitutional rights. See *Powell* v. *Alabama,* 287 U.S. 45 (1932). And when Brandeis and Cardozo were raised to the bench, McReynolds is said to have snubbed them for being Jewish. He also refused to sign the customary letters on the retirement of both Brandeis and Clarke, and for many years would not speak to Justice Clarke, whom he considered stupid.

In many other respects McReynolds' views were anachronistic. He hated tobacco and forbade smoking in his presence. It was said that he was responsible for the "No Smoking" signs in the new Supreme Court Building, which he

DAVID BURNER is Associate Professor of History at the State University of New York, Stony Brook. He is the author of The Politics of Provincialism: The Democratic Party in Transition, 1918–1932.

referred to as the Temple of Karnak. A bachelor himself, he regarded the use of red fingernail polish by women as vulgar; and he thought the wearing of wrist watches by men to be effeminate. When a woman lawyer appeared in the courtroom McReynolds would mutter: "I see the female is here again." Tall, broad-shouldered, and possessing immaculate habits of bachelorhood, he was formidable when angered and very often intolerably rude. Justice Stone once remarked to him of an attorney's brief: "That was the dullest argument I ever heard in my life," to which McReynolds snappishly replied: "The only duller thing I can think of is to hear you read one of your opinions." *Time* called him "Puritanical," "intolerably rude," "savagely sarcastic," "incredibly reactionary," and "anti-Semitic." To Harold Laski it seemed that "McReynolds and the theory of a beneficent deity are quite incompatible." Yet in his private life this crustiest of conservatives was declared to be "gracious and considerate." "Poor McReynolds," wrote Oliver Wendell Holmes in 1926, "is, I think, a man of feeling and of more secret kindliness than he would get the credit for." He adopted thirty-three child victims of the 1940 Nazi blitzkrieg and left his own money to charity.

Born in Elkton, Kentucky, on February 3, 1862, McReynolds grew up in an area impressed with lingering traces of the frontier. During his formative years he was influenced by the individualistic philosophy of that time and place, as well as by memories of rebellion and the doctrine of states' rights, for considerable Confederate sympathy had existed in his neighborhood. Indeed, the aristocratic pattern of ante-bellum southern life survived in the isolated town of Elkton, which practically bordered on Tennessee. His father, Dr. John McReynolds, dubbed the "pope" because of his assumption of his own infallibility, had a keen sense of family background and little concern for social responsibilities. He opposed public schools. Ellen Reeves, the boy's mother, brought him up according to a strict moral code and was herself a formidable woman. Once, during a train journey, she had taken a pistol away from a man who was terrorizing women and children. Both parents belonged to the fundamentalist Campbellite sect. The Scotch-Irish family line was traced back to Milesius, a Spanish king, through his fifth son, Ir. About the year 60 A.D., so the McReynolds family discovered, Fergus, King of Connaught, and his consort, Queen Maude, began the family holdings in the Irish county of Donegal.

After an uneventful early life on his family's plantation, where his principal interests were botany and ornithology, the young McReynolds made a distinguished record in the sciences at Vanderbilt University in Nashville. He also became interested in politics, was a prominent debater, and served as editor of the school paper. A rigorous schedule of study, sleep, and recreation enabled him to participate in these extracurricular activities. McReynolds neither drank, played sports, nor displayed adeptness at social graces. He was personally remembered by one acquaintance as "belligerent." After three years of study he was graduated in 1882 as valedictorian in a class of almost a hundred, receiving the Founder's Gold Medal and a Bachelor of Science degree. He remained at the university for another year to do postgraduate work in the sciences.

Leaving behind his scientific studies, he went to the University of Virginia in order to study law. While Woodrow Wilson, who had left the law school the year before, was bored by what he derided as the "noble study," McReynolds took to it completely. Later in his life, when he was convinced that higher learning in America was in a state of deplorable decadence, he nostalgically recalled examinations that began at nine in the morning and lasted until late at night. His favorite teacher at Virginia was Professor John B. Minor, a man of firm convictions and a strict moralist who regularly taught Sunday Bible classes. Minor viewed the Constitution as one of limitations and considered law itself as permanent, not changing; coercive, not simply advisory. Minor would say, in contradiction of the progressive educators, that he taught not students, not even law, but *the* law. This conviction of unchanging verity was conveyed to McReynolds, who graduated from the University of Virginia after fourteen months of study.

Except for a two-year stint in Washington shortly after law school as secretary to Senator Howell Jackson, a Tennessee Democrat, the young attorney practiced law in Nashville from 1884 to 1903. Those years were ones of economic expansion for the city, which became the largest manufacturing center in the state by 1900. McReynolds was thought by his Nashville colleagues to be a capable lawyer but not an outstanding success. He was well-read and always careful to marshall the relevant facts and precedents in the course of a trial; but he made an unimpressive advocate. He became known as a legal adviser to business corporations such as the Illinois Central Railroad, and in 1900 was appointed Professor of Commercial Law, Insurance, and Corporations at Vanderbilt. His teaching was highly technical rather than theoretical, and he maintained an air of unbending dignity. Along with the other faculty, he ignored the increasingly popular Langdell case system of instruction. In his hours of public service McReynolds joined in reform campaigns aimed at ridding the town of gambling and prostitution, and he managed to ban the *Police Gazette* from the newsstands.

In 1896, aghast at the economic and class ideas of William Jennings Bryan, McReynolds ran for Congress as a "Gold Democrat" with Republican support. He made the basic theme of his campaign the harmony of interests between capital and labor and between different sections of the country. In his eyes the perfidy of Bryan was matched by that of the party platform, which was "fraught with evil." The campaign was brief but well-financed. McReynolds' manner, however, remained too reserved and aristocratic to appeal widely to the electorate and he failed to defeat the incumbent candidate.

Through the efforts of Jacob Dickinson, a prominent Nashville lawyer who would become Secretary of War under President Taft, McReynolds assumed in 1903 the post of Assistant Attorney General under Philander Knox. The future Justice, acceptable to Theodore Roosevelt as a Gold Democrat, was in 1907 put in charge of prosecuting the tobacco trust; and ultimately his work led to a victory for the government. McReynolds seemed to consider enforcing the Sherman Act a moral obligation; monopoly he regarded as "essentially wicked." He quickly established a reputation as a trustbuster although he also worked on immigration cases and inheritance taxation. He resigned in 1909, but President Taft called him back to the capital to help in the final dissolution of the tobacco trust and the anthracite coal trust. In answer to the charge that he wanted to violate the property rights of James B. Duke and others, McReynolds replied in a manner typical of his moralist legalism: "Since when has property illegally and criminally acquired come to have any rights?" The American Tobacco Company was to McReynolds a gang of "commercial wolves and highwaymen." (Perhaps his aversion to smoking caused this outburst.) In January, 1912, he resigned after Attorney General George Wickersham compromised on the final settlement of the tobacco case. This act established the Tennessean's independence from the Republican administration. His friendship with Colonel Edward House, his support for Wilson during the 1912 campaign, and the restricted field of candidates for the position of Attorney General prompted President Wilson to appoint him to that office in 1913.

On first meeting McReynolds, Wilson liked him. But the cabinet officer's career was to be brief and disastrous. By his intemperate manner he quickly alienated Senator George Norris, who concluded that the Justice Department was going soft on the trusts. Then a number of other Senators became furious over an alleged system of spying on federal judges; the charge was apparently false, but McReynolds' handling of the matter revealed his bad temper. Another controversy, this time with Secretary of the Treasury William Gibbs McAdoo, centered around the erection of a new Department of Justice building. Finally, though he had been strictly enforcing the Mann Act, McReynolds attempted to postpone prosecution, for violation of the act, of the son-in-law of the new Commissioner of Immigration. The Attorney General's motives were above suspicion, but the affair took on the dimensions of scandal. A way was sought to remove the controversial McReynolds from the Cabinet. The vacancy caused by Justice Harold Lurton's death in 1912 had never been filled. Since Lurton had also come from Tennessee, considerations of geography and politics led Wilson to elevate McReynolds to the Supreme Court in 1914.

During his twenty-seven years of service on the Court, McReynolds prepared a scant 503 opinions for the majority. The preponderance of these dealt with relatively technical legal points, often of statutory interpretation or of the procedures and jurisdiction of federal courts. Such cases included complicated questions of admiralty and maritime jurisdiction, disputes of priority among creditors in bankruptcy proceedings, agreements with Indian tribes, the validity of patents and copyrights, the contractual liability of carriers under the Hepburn and Uniform Bill of Lading Acts, and the application of principles governing conflicts of laws. McReynolds' opinions reflect the directness, even the abruptness, of his personality. Pungent or sarcastic language appeared not infrequently in remarks aimed at his fellow Justices. Nothing delighted him more than an opportunity to personalize his attacks; he relished quoting Woodrow Wilson on the independence of the Judiciary in ruling against a law of 1919, signed by the President, taxing the salaries of judges, in *Evans* v. *Gore,* 253 U.S. 245 (1920). This decision was later overruled in *Graves* v. *New York,* 306 U.S. 466 (1929).

As a trustbuster, McReynolds had favored equality of opportunity and the restoration of competition, and as a member of the Court he continued to believe in the efficacy of the Sherman Anti-Trust Act. The economic world, he held, should be free from restraint, both from the government and stifling monopolies, so that it might enjoy the interplay of "natural forces." To some extent, however, McReynolds apparently believed that the Federal Trade Commission Act had tipped the scales in the direction of governmental power over business. His method of righting the balance was to assume for the courts, rather than for the commission, the right to decide what were the unfair methods of competition prohibited by the act in *Federal Trade Commission* v. *Gratz,* 253 U.S. 421 (1920). Ethical conduct recognized by the common law was the standard to be followed. McReynolds believed, moreover, that a producer remained free to trade on his own terms with whomever he wished. This caused him to rule for a unanimous Court that the Colgate Company could set the price of soap and refuse to supply a seller who cut the price in *Colgate* v. *United States,* 250 U.S. 300, 307 (1919). In *Maple Flooring Manufacturers Association* v. *United States,* 268 U.S. 563 (1929), he inveighed against trade associations: "Ordinary knowledge of human nature and of the impelling force of greed ought to permit no serious doubt concerning the ultimate outcome of the arrangement . . . pious protestations and smug preambles but intensify distrust when men are found busy with schemes to enrich themselves through circumventions."

The issue of trusts was one of several for which McReynolds showed both a liberal and a conservative side. He was, it seemed, a man of contradictions rather than of paradoxes. However seriously, for example, he took his opposition to "bigness," he opposed it more in government and labor than in corporations. And the streak of didacticism that runs through some of his opinions rendered during the thirties clashes with the character of impersonality that he would impart to the law.

His civil liberties opinions could also be contradictory. Sometimes he was strikingly libertarian. In a lone dissent in *Carroll* v. *United States,* 267 U.S. 132 (1925), he condemned unreasonable search and seizure. "The damnable character of the bootlegger's business," he wrote, "should not close our eyes to the mischief which will surely follow any attempt to destroy it by unwarranted means. . . . Whenever Congress had intended that searches be made upon mere suspicion it had taken pains to say so; but in the provisions of the Volstead Act no such intentions are manifested."

McReynolds was also alone in disagreeing with Chief Justice Taft's opinion in *Myers* v. *United States,* 272 U.S. 52 (1926), which upheld the President's right to dismiss a postmaster without the consent of Congress. The Tennessean feared that members of all administrative boards and commissions would hold their places "subject to the President's pleasure or caprice." Nine years later in *Humphrey's Executor* v. *United States,* 295 U.S. 602 (1935), McReynolds joined in reversing President Roosevelt's firing of a Federal Trade Commissioner and restricting his power to the removal of executive officers. McReynolds dissented from *Casey* v. *United States,* 276 U.S. 413 (1928), a case declaring valid the state's presumption that narcotics in a defendant's possession were bought in the locality. "And where will the next case take us?" the Justice characteristically asked.

Most impressive of all were McReynolds' decisions relating to the public schools. In three important cases the Justice ruled against popular majorities seeking to impose their programs on children and teachers. In *Farrington* v. *Tokushiga,* 273 U.S. 284 (1927), McReynolds struck down a far-reaching Hawaii statute that sought to discourage the teaching of Japanese. He wrote the majority decision in *Meyer* v. *Nebraska,* 262 U.S. 390 (1923), which invalidated the state law prohibiting the teaching of any foreign language before the ninth grade of high school; liberty, he proclaimed, "denoted not merely freedom from bodily restraint but also the right of the individual to contract, to engage in any of the common occupations of life, to acquire useful knowledge, to marry, to establish a home and bring up children, [and] to worship God according to dictates of his own conscience. . . ." Using historical contrast he remarked on the communistic life of Plato's commonwealth and set against it the American regard for freedom in education. Justice Taft dissented, arguing that the federal judiciary could not enforce free speech at the state level. Finally, McReynolds wrote the unanimous decision in *Pierce* v. *Society of Sisters,* 268 U.S. 510 (1925), which declared against the Oregon compulsory public education law. "We think it . . . plain," he wrote, "that the Act . . . unreasonably interferes with the liberty of parents and guardians to direct the upbringing and education of children under their control. . . . The fundamental theory of liberty upon which all governments in this union repose excludes any general power to standardize its children. . . . The child," he said, "is not the mere creature of the state." McReynolds particularly opposed the brandishing of executive power. For *Myers* v. *United States,* 272 U.S. 52 (1926), he wrote a seventy page dissent blasting President Wilson for removing a first-class postmaster without the advice and consent of Congress, which the law required. The Justice threw in everything from an account of the origin and development of the post office under Benjamin Franklin to a convincing analysis of Congress' historical assumption of power to prescribe conditions concerning the removal of inferior officers. McReynolds believed that the present theory that the President may flagrantly "override the will of Congress" conflicted with the history of the Constitution and the practice of Congress from the beginning.

But McReynolds could also dissent in decisions strengthening civil rights, especially when national self-interest was at stake. In *Berger* v. *United States,* 255 U.S. 22 (1921), he did not agree that Judge Kennesaw Mountain Landis' prejudice against the Socialist Victor Berger invalidated his conviction. Such prejudice was laudable since it was directed "towards certain malevolents from Germany, a country then engaged in hunnish warfare and notoriously encouraged by many of its natives who, unhappily, had obtained citizenship here. The words attributed to the judge . . . may be fairly construed as showing only deep detestation for all persons of German extraction who were at that time wickedly abusing privileges granted by our indulgent laws. . . . A public officer who entertained no aversion toward disloyal German immigrants during the late war was simply unfit for his place. And while 'an over-speaking judge is no well-tuned symbol' neither is an amorphous dummy unspotted by human emotions a becoming receptacle for judicial power." In *Stromberg* v. *California,* 283 U.S. 359 (1931), McReynolds, along with Butler, dissented from a decision freeing a Communist who required the daily salute of a red flag in a children's camp; some of the outrageous state sedition law was "certainly good," he said. Much earlier, in *Butler* v. *Perry,* 240 U.S. 328 (1916), McReynolds had decided that Florida did not violate the constitutional provision against involuntary servitude by requiring six days of road work annually from its adult male citizens.

One of the most significant developments on the bench between the wars was its increasing liberalism in Negro civil rights issues. But McReynolds, in contrast to his concern for the individual in many other cases, could not go along with the Court's new direction. Dissenting alone he indicated that possible race prejudice, "whatever that may be," on the part of a juror in a murder trial of a Negro could not justify a review of the case, *Aldridge* v. *United States,* 283 U.S. 308 (1931). "Unhappily," he wrote, "the enforcement of our criminal laws is dangerously ineffective; crimes of violence multiply; punishment walks lamely. Courts ought not to increase the difficulties by magnifying theoretical possibilities." He signaled in a dissent his accord with a Texas primary law that in effect denied the franchise to Negroes in *Nixon* v. *Condon,* 286 U.S. 73 (1932); McReynolds worried that social or business clubs, corporations, and religious groups would also be liable to state regulation. In the Scottsboro case of *Powell* v. *Alabama,* 287 U.S. 45 (1932), McReynolds, along with Butler, could not distinguish between the form and substance of due process in the perfunctory defense of seven Negroes accused of rape. He dissented from an order that the University of Missouri give admission to a Negro law student in *Missouri ex rel., Gaines* v. *Canada,* 305 U.S. 337 (1938); he questioned the applicant's sincerity, although he had not thought it necessary to do the same with respect to a washerwoman who had demanded to work for less than the minimum wage, (*Adkins* v. *Children's Hospital,* 261 U.S. 525 [1925]). He also wondered at overturning the settled policy of the institution; "the state should not be unduly hampered through theorization inadequately restrained by experience." McReynolds thought it adequate to offer an equivalent course of study at a Negro school.

The most dramatic years of McReynolds' service on the Court were certainly those of the New Deal. It was then that he became most famous for his opposition to reform measures and for his bitter harangues against what he thought of as the spirit of opportunism. Behind his opposition to the New Deal lay a virulent hatred for Roosevelt, whom he called "utterly incompetent," "a fool," "a bad misfit—a megalomaniac," "bad through and through." F.D.R.'s farm program, for instance, was "evidence of his mental infirmity and lack of stability." "They [the administration]," he wrote, "simply have no decent idea of our system. There is only one way of escape. Put Roosevelt and all his gang on the outside. To do this will require a real fight, but 'tis a fight for existence in a land of order." McReynolds expressed his opinions privately to friends, but he was careless in disguising his contempt for the President. In the Gold Clause cases he lashed out in dissent at Roosevelt calling him "Nero in his worst form."

McReynolds voted against more New Deal measures than any other Justice on the Court. Between 1933 and his resignation in 1941 he wrote 146 dissents, 119 of them in the years 1937 to 1941, after the Court had shifted to upholding New Deal measures. Even earlier, however, he had been the Court's staunchest defender of due process in protecting the rights of businessmen. He had voted with the majority in *Hammer* v. *Dagenhart,* 247 U.S. 251 (1918), nullifying the Child Labor Act, and in the similar case of *Bailey* v. *Drexel Furniture Co.,* 259 U.S. 20 (1922), the child labor tax case. He also concurred in *Adkins* v. *Children's Hospital,* 261 U.S. 525 (1923), which declared a minimum wage law unconstitutional. In various workmen's compensation cases, such as *Arizona Employers' Liability Cases,* 250 U.S. 400 (1919), McReynolds refused to consider employers financially responsible for an accident not growing out of their own negligence. "Until now," wrote McReynolds in the *Arizona* cases, "I had supposed that a man's liberty and property . . . were under the protection of our charter and not subordinate to whims or caprices or fanciful ideas. . . . The contrary doctrine is revolutionary and leads straight toward destruction." Harold Laski called the dissent "unbelievable."

McReynolds claimed that the rights of consumers, as well as those of businessmen, were close to his heart. In a dissent to *Nebbia* v. *New York,* 291 U.S. 502 (1934), he inveighed against fixing the price of milk as an infringement not only of the grocer's right to charge what the market will bear but of the liberty of twelve million consumers to buy a necessity of life in an open market. Furthermore, the troubles of the producers stemmed from "the human tendency to raise too many heifers" when prices were high. When the depression came, consumers reduced their purchases and farmers naturally suffered. But any legislative attempt to alleviate their plight was "futility" since it flew in the face of unyielding economic laws. After citing a selected list of precedents supporting this view, McReynolds also warned: "The adoption of any 'concept of jurisprudence' which permits facile disregard of the Constitution as long interpreted and respected will inevitably lead to its destruction." In the final analysis, however, it seems that McReynolds believed that the Court could determine if legislation was good or bad, and that the test of constitutionality was sometimes merely a means to this end. In his dissent to *Nebbia* McReynolds wrote:

"Plainly, I think, this Court must have regard to the wisdom of the enactment. At least, we must inquire concerning its purpose and decide whether the means proposed have reasonable relation to something within legislative power—whether the end is legitimate, and the means appropriate." But McReynolds' view lost out in *Nebbia.* He coupled Roberts' majority opinion with that of the Dred Scott case and told a friend that the two decisions meant the "end of the Constitution as you and I regard it. An alien influence has prevailed." His concept of the taxation power was narrow; in a dissent in *United States* v. *Doremus,* 249 U.S. 86 (1919), he declared it could not be used, for instance, to regulate traffic in narcotics. Again and again, as in the case of *Union Tank Line* v. *Wright,* 249 U.S. 275 (1919), McReynolds ruled that the state taxation was discriminatory or unfair. A dozen elegant dissents can be counted that place McReynolds foremost among those defending the rights of property and the rights of wealthy men.

Though he was not an absolute literalist, McReynolds obviously could not bring himself to view the Constitution as a flexible instrument capable of meeting the changing needs of the people—even though he was willing enough to approve much social legislation initiated on the state level. The fundamental law, he thought, must be understood as it was by the founding fathers in 1787. This point of view is shown most clearly in two important issues of the nineteen thirties.

The three Gold Clause cases of 1935 were perhaps a turning point in McReynolds' life: *Norman* v. *Baltimore and Ohio Railroad Company,* 294 U.S. 240; *Nortz* v. *United States,* 294 U.S. 317; *Perry* v. *United States,* 294 U.S. 330. They tested, in effect, the constitutionality of America's going off the gold standard. To McReynolds this was a scheme to cancel or repudiate government obligations and to draw gold into the Treasury in exchange for promises to pay. In confiscating private property and abrogating contracts, the Justice believed, Roosevelt had deprived men of due process and had failed to satisfy the "just compensation" clause of the Fifth Amendment. Worse still, this violation of contract would lead to even more disastrous results in the long run—to something approaching moral chaos. McReynolds' dissent is memorable not for its logic but for its emotion. In a stirring, almost wholly extemporaneous speech, moralistic in tone, sometimes biblical in content, and southern in accent, he lashed out at the New Deal and pronounced the Constitution "gone." "Shame and humiliation are upon us . . . anarchy and despotism are at the door," he thundered. "Moral and financial chaos may confidently be expected. . . . Here we have a monetary system the extent—I almost said wickedness—of which is almost beyond comprehension. No such power was ever granted by the framers of the Constitution. It was not there then. It was not there yesterday. It is not there today." His rugged looks, broad brow, piercing eyes, and eagle nose must have added immeasurably to the drama of the occasion. The speech was considered too drastic to be printed as read in the Court reports, but the spoken version was carried in the *Wall Street Journal* on February 23, 1935.

Perhaps it was in the case of *Ashwander* v. *Tennessee Valley Authority,* 297 U.S. 288 (1936), that McReynolds moved farthest from his fellow Justices. Here he was alone in dissent against an otherwise unanimous Court. The main point at issue was whether the purchase of power transmission lines was an attempt to widen the market for electrical power produced at Wilson Dam. McReynolds believed it was more than that: it was a major invasion of an area hitherto left to private enterprise. The constitutional provision permitting regulation of commerce did not extend to "developing, distributing, and selling electrical power." That this was the aim of the authority the record left no doubt. Its *Annual Report* said that the government wished to provide a "yardstick" to measure the rates charged by private companies and to reach "no less a goal than the electrification of America." "When," McReynolds quoted the report, "we carry this program into every town and city and village, and every farm throughout the country, we will have written the greatest chapter in the economic, political and social development of America." This, the Justice declared, made it obvious that the notion of a yardstick was a subterfuge under which the government would take over the electrical power industry.

What came after the Gold Clause and TVA cases was, for McReynolds, largely anticlimactic. He argued repeatedly against the government's efforts to help labor by regulating manufacturing not clearly affecting interstate commerce. In *National Labor Relations Board* v. *Friedman,* 301 U.S. 58 (1937), a case concerning a relatively small clothing company, McReynolds warned of government regulation in "almost every field of human industry." A later decision, *National Labor Relations Board* v. *Fainblatt,* 306 U.S. 601 (1939), similarly appalled him; he complained of bringing "within the ambit of federal control most if not all activities of the nation," subjecting "states to the will of Congress;" and permitting "disruption of our federated system." The next year, in *Thornhill* v. *Alabama,* 310 U.S. 88, McReynolds stood alone against a decision holding anti-picketing legislation invalid under the Fourteenth Amendment.

Speaking for himself and Butler he declared that certain provisions of the Social Security law were "repugnant to the Tenth Amendment." See *Helvering* v. *Davis,* 301 U.S. 619 (1937). Title IX of the act "exceeds the power granted to Congress," he wrote, and "unduly interferes with the orderly government of the State by her own people and otherwise offends the Federal Constitution." "We should keep in mind," he wrote in that dissent, "that we are living under a written Constitution. No volume of words and no citation of irrelevant statistics and no appeal to feeling of humanity can expand the powers granted by Congress. . . . This Government is a union of indestructible States. If the States are destroyed, then the Union is destroyed." McReynolds also continued to argue against the broad interpretation of interstate commerce. "Production is not commerce but a step in preparing for commerce," he wrote. He quoted approvingly from the *E. C. Knight* case, 156 U.S. 1 (1894): "Acknowledged evils, however grave and urgent they may appear to be, had better be borne, than the risk be run, in the effort to suppress them, of more serious consequences by resort to expedients of even doubtful constitutionality."

McReynolds retired in 1941 and spent his remaining years in Washington. He died on August 24, 1946, of heart failure induced by bronchial pneumonia. His will contained bequests totaling almost $100,000 to the Children's Hospital in Washington, the Salvation Army, Washington National City Christian Church, Vanderbilt University, the University of Virginia, and other educational and charitable institutions. Amounts of $10,000 or less went to friends, relatives, and servants. Instructions for burial in the Elkton Cemetery—"westward of the family monument, head near the center, feet away from it"—were as meticulous as his parceling out of study time had been in college days. He left behind a judicial record upholding state and local rule and restricting that of the national government to the Constitution's "enumerated" powers. McReynolds also delimited the power of taxation, opposed monopoly, worked to insure contractual rights and due process, inquired about the "wisdom" of legislation, and preferred amendment to liberal construction of the Constitution.

SELECTED BIBLIOGRAPHY

Three doctoral students at about the same time completed dissertations on McReynolds: Doris A. Blaisdell, "The Constitutional Law of Mr. Justice McReynolds," (University of Wisconsin, 1952); Stephen T. Early, "James Clark McReynolds and the Judicial Process," (University of Virginia, 1952); and J. B. McCraw, "James Clark McReynolds and the Supreme Court, 1914–1941," (University of Texas, 1951). See also S. Price Gilbert, *James Clark McReynolds, 1862–1946* (privately printed, 1946). The University of Virginia Library has a small collection of McReynolds Papers.

James C. McReynolds

REPRESENTATIVE OPINIONS

MEYER v. NEBRASKA, 262 U.S. 390 (1923)

Following an example set by the state of Ohio, the Nebraska legislature during World War One passed a law prohibiting the teaching of German in grades below senior high school. The majority of the Court, speaking through one of its less libertarian judges, James McReynolds, overruled the law. McReynolds called it an invasion of liberty and assumed for the Court the responsibility to inquire into any state restriction on free speech.

Mr. JUSTICE MCREYNOLDS delivered the opinion of the Court.

Plaintiff in error was tried and convicted in the District Court for Hamilton County, Nebraska, under an information which charged that on May 25, 1920, while an instructor in Zion Parochial School, he unlawfully taught the subject of reading in the German language to Raymond Parpart, a child of ten years, who had not attained and successfully passed the eighth grade. The information is based upon "An act relating to the teaching of foreign languages in the State of Nebraska," approved April 9, 1919, which follows [Laws 1919, c. 249.]:

"Section 1. No person, individually or as a teacher, shall, in any private, denominational, parochial or public school, teach any subject to any person in any language other than the English language.

"Sec. 2. Languages, other than the English language, may be taught as languages only after a pupil shall have attained and successfully passed the eighth grade as evidenced by a certificate of graduation issued by the county superintendent of the county in which the child resides.

"Sec. 3. Any person who violates any of the provisions of this act shall be deemed guilty of a misdemeanor and upon conviction, shall be subject to a fine of not less than twenty-five dollars ($25), nor more than one hundred dollars ($100) or be confined in the county jail for any period not exceeding thirty days for each offense.

"Sec. 4. Whereas, an emergency exists, this act shall be in force from and after its passage and approval."

The Supreme Court of the State affirmed the judgment of conviction. 107 Neb. 657. It declared the offense charged and established was "the direct and intentional teaching of the German language as a distinct subject to a child who had not passed the eighth grade," in the parochial school maintained by Zion Evangelical Lutheran Congregation, a collection of Biblical stories being used therefor. And it held that the statute forbidding this did not conflict with the Fourteenth Amendment, but was a valid exercise of the police power. The following excerpts from the opinion sufficiently indicate the reasons advanced to support the conclusion.

"The salutary purpose of the statute is clear. The legislature had seen the baneful effects of permitting foreigners, who had taken residence in this country, to rear and educate their children in the language of their native land. The result of that condition was found to be inimical to our own safety. To allow the children of foreigners, who had emigrated here, to be taught from early childhood the language of the country of their parents was to rear them with that language as their mother tongue. It was to educate them so that they must always think in that language, and, as a consequence, naturally inculcate in them the ideas and sentiments foreign to the best interests of this country. The statute, therefore, was intended not only to require that the education of all children be conducted in the English language, but that, until they had grown into that language and until it had become a part of them, they should not in the schools be taught any other language. The obvious purpose of this statute was that the English language should be and become the mother tongue of all children reared in this state. The enactment of such a statute comes reasonably within the police power of the state. *Pohl* v. *State,* 132 N. E. (Ohio) 20; *State* v. *Bartels,* 181 N. W. (Ia.) 508.

"It is suggested that the law is an unwarranted restriction, in that it applies to all citizens of the state and arbitrarily interferes with the rights of citizens who are not of foreign ancestry, and prevents them, without reason, from having their children taught foreign languages in school. That argument is not well taken, for it assumes that every citizen finds himself restrained by the statute. The hours which a child is able to devote to study in the confinement of school are limited. It must have ample time for exercise or play. Its daily capacity for learning is comparatively small. A selection of subjects for its education, therefore, from among the many that might be taught, is obviously necessary. The legislature no doubt had in mind the practical operation of the law. The law affects few citizens, except those of foreign lineage. Other citizens, in their selection of studies, except perhaps in rare instances, have never deemed it of importance to teach their children foreign languages before such children have reached the eighth grade. In the legislative mind, the salutary effect of the statute no doubt outweighed the restriction upon the citizens generally, which, it appears, was a restriction of no real consequence."

The problem for our determination is whether the statute as construed and applied unreasonably infringes the liberty guaranteed to the plaintiff in error by the Fourteenth Amendment. "No State shall . . . deprive any person of life, liberty, or property, without due process of law."

While this Court has not attempted to define with exactness the liberty thus guaranteed, the term has received much consideration and some of the included things have been definitely stated. Without doubt, it denotes not merely freedom from bodily restraint but also the right of the individual to contract, to engage in any of the common occupations of life, to acquire useful knowledge, to marry, establish a home and bring up children, to worship God according to the dictates of his own conscience, and generally to enjoy those privileges long recognized at common law as essential to the orderly pursuit of happiness by free men. *Slaughter-House Cases,* 16 Wall. 36; *Butchers' Union Co.* v. *Crescent City Co.,* 111 U.S. 746; *Yick Wo* v. *Hopkins,* 118 U.S. 356; *Minnesota* v. *Barber,* 136 U.S. 313; *Allgeyer* v. *Louisiana,* 165 U.S. 578; *Lochner* v. *New York,* 198 U.S. 45; *Twining* v. *New Jersey,* 211 U.S. 78; *Chicago, Burlington & Quincy R. R. Co.* v. *McGuire,* 219 U.S. 549; *Truax* v. *Raich,* 239 U.S. 33; *Adams* v. *Tanner,* 244 U.S. 590; *New York Life Ins. Co.* v. *Dodge,* 246 U.S. 357; *Truax* v. *Corrigan,* 257 U.S. 312; *Adkins* v. *Children's Hospital,* 261 U.S. 525; *Wyeth* v. *Cambridge Board of Health,* 200 Mass. 474. The established doctrine is that this liberty may not be interfered with, under the guise of protecting the public interest, by legislative action which is arbitrary or without reasonable relation to some purpose within the competency of the State to effect. Determination by the legislature of what constitutes proper exercise of police power is not final or conclusive but is subject to supervision by the courts. *Lawton* v. *Steele,* 152 U.S. 133, 137.

The American people have always regarded education and acquisition of knowledge as matters of supreme importance which should be diligently promoted. The Ordinance of 1787 declares, "Religion, morality, and knowledge being necessary to good government and the happiness of mankind, schools and the means of education shall forever be encouraged." Corresponding to the right of control, it is the natural duty of the parent to give his children education suitable to their station in life; and nearly all the States, including Nebraska, enforce this obligation by compulsory laws.

Practically, education of the young is only possible in schools conducted by especially qualified persons who devote themselves thereto. The calling always has been regarded as useful and honorable, essential, indeed, to the public welfare. Mere knowledge of the German language cannot reasonably be regarded as harmful. Heretofore it has been commonly looked upon as helpful and desirable. Plaintiff in error taught this language in school as part of his occupation. His right thus to teach and the right of parents to engage him so to instruct their children, we think, are within the liberty of the Amendment.

The challenged statute forbids the teaching in school of any subject except in English; also the teaching of any other language until the pupil has attained and successfully passed the eighth grade, which is not usually accomplished before the age of twelve. The Supreme Court of the State has held that "the so-called ancient or dead languages" are not "within the spirit or the purpose of the act." *Nebraska District of Evangelical Lutheran Synod* v. *McKelvie,* 187 N. W. 927. Latin, Greek, Hebrew are not proscribed; but German, French, Spanish, Italian and every other alien speech are within the ban. Evidently the legislature has attempted materially to interfere with the calling of modern language teachers, with the opportunities of pupils to acquire knowledge, and with the power of parents to control the education of their own.

It is said the purpose of the legislation was to promote civic development by inhibiting training and education of the immature in foreign tongues and ideals before they could learn English and acquire American ideals; and "that the English language should be and become the mother tongue of all children reared in this State." It is also affirmed that the foreign born population is very large, that certain communities commonly use foreign words, follow foreign leaders, move in a foreign atmosphere, and that the children are thereby hindered from becoming citizens of the most useful type and the public safety is imperiled.

That the State may do much, go very far, indeed, in order to improve the quality of its citizens, physically, mentally and morally, is clear; but the individual has certain fundamental rights which must be respected. The protection of the Constitution extends to all, to those who speak other languages as well as to those born with English on the tongue. Perhaps it would be highly advantageous if all had ready understanding of our ordinary speech, but this cannot be coerced by methods which conflict with the Constitution—a desirable end cannot be promoted by prohibited means.

For the welfare of his Ideal Commonwealth, Plato suggested a law which should provide: "That the wives of our guardians are to be common, and their children are to be common, and no parent is to know his own child, nor any child his parent. . . . The proper officers will take the offspring of the good parents to the pen or fold, and there they will deposit them with certain nurses who dwell in a separate quarter; but the offspring of the inferior, or of the better when they chance to be deformed, will be put away in some mysterious, unknown place, as they should be." In order to submerge the individual and develop ideal citizens, Sparta assembled the males at seven into barracks and intrusted their subsequent education and training to official guardians. Although such measures have been deliberately approved by men of great genius, their ideas touching the relation between individual and State were wholly different from those upon which our institutions rest; and it hardly will be affirmed that any legislature could impose such restrictions upon the people of a State without doing violence to both letter and spirit of the Constitution.

The desire of the legislature to foster a homogeneous people with American ideals prepared readily to understand current discussions of civic matters is easy to appreciate. Unfortunate experiences during the late war and aversion toward every characteristic of truculent adversaries were certainly enough to quicken that aspiration. But the means adopted, we think, exceed the limitations upon the power of the State and conflict with rights assured to plaintiff in error. The interference is plain enough and no adequate reason therefor in time of peace and domestic tranquility has been shown.

The power of the State to compel attendance at some school and to make reasonable regulations for all schools, including a requirement that they shall give instructions in English, is not questioned. Nor has challenge been made of the State's power to prescribe a curriculum for institutions which it supports. Those matters are not within the present controversy. Our concern is with the prohibition approved by the Supreme Court. *Adams* v. *Tanner, supra,* p. 594, pointed out that mere abuse incident to an occupation ordinarily useful is not enough to justify its abolition, although regulation may be entirely proper. No emergency has arisen which renders knowledge by a child of some language other than English so clearly harmful as to justify its inhibition with the consequent infringement of rights long freely enjoyed. We are constrained to conclude that the statute as applied is arbitrary and without reasonable relation to any end within the competency of the State.

As the statute undertakes to interfere only with teaching which involves a modern language, leaving complete freedom as to other matters, there seems no adequate foundation for the suggestion that the purpose was to protect the child's health by limiting his mental activities. It is well known that proficiency in a foreign language seldom comes to one not instructed at an early age, and experience shows that this is not injurious to the health, morals or understanding of the ordinary child.

The judgment of the court below must be reversed and the cause remanded for further proceedings not inconsistent with this opinion.

Reversed.

THE GOLD CLAUSE CASES: NORMAN v. BALTIMORE AND OHIO RAILROAD CO., 294 U.S. 240 (1935); NORTZ v. UNITED STATES, 294 U.S. 317 (1935); PERRY v. UNITED STATES, 294 U.S. 330 (1935)

On June 5, 1933, Congress by joint resolution abrogated the requirement in any private contract, no matter when entered into, and every gold certificate or government bond, that repayment of any debt must be in gold. Instead, Congress said, payment could be made in any legal tender of the United States. The move was part of a concerted effort to bolster the dollar, take America off the gold standard, and funnel all gold into the United States Treasury. Suit was commenced by creditors and holders of gold certificates and government bonds demanding payment in gold as required by the original contracts. Attorney General Homer Cummings estimated that an adverse decision by the Court, ordering the government or private citizens to pay in gold or its equivalent, would permit claims of $100 billion to be asserted primarily against the Treasury. Chief Justice Hughes found for the government, declaring no loss could be shown by the suitors in question, but not before he declared it had broken its sacred obligation to creditors. McReynolds dissented in words so intemperate they were not reprinted in the official reports. The *Wall Street Journal* did report his dissent in full on February 23, 1935, as follows:

Mr. Justice Van Devanter, Mr. Justice Sutherland, Mr. Justice Butler and I do not accept the conclusions announced by the court. The record reveals clear purpose to bring about confiscation of private rights and the repudiation of national obligations. To us these things are abhorrent and we cannot believe the wise men who framed the Constitution intended they should find shelter there. On the contrary, words that ought not to be mistaken strictly inhibit them.

We have written down our views; they will be open for your observation. I assume that those who wish to comprehend will read them. I shall not read in extenso. It may be well, however, in order that you may hear now what will result from the conclusions reached, that I rehearse the situation, not minimizing, not covering it in a thousand words—a plain, simple tale that you may understand readily.

It is impossible to estimate the result of what has been done this day. The Constitution as many of us have understood it, the Constitution that has meant so much, has gone. The guarantees which men and women heretofore have supposed protected them against arbitrary action have been swept away. The powers of Congress have been enlarged to such an extent that no man can foresee their limitations. We stand today stripped of the fundamental guarantees we heretofore supposed stood between us and arbitrary action.

That statement is made to you with deliberation. It is not overdrawn and in the days to come as you see the panorama unfold you will necessarily accept this truth.

Let us inquire into this particular situation. There are three classes of cases; one class involves private obligations; the other class embraces the solemn promise of the Government; the third class perhaps a still more solemn promise. In harmony with a policy which had been sanctioned for many, many, years, these private individuals entered into contracts which they expected would protect them against a fluctuating currency, a depressed currency, if you will. Depressed currencies are nothing new. They have been known for two thousand years. Nero undertook to exercise the power at Rome. Six centuries ago in France it was claimed as a prerogative of the sovereign. Now men who have entered into contracts which were perfectly legitimate, have undertaken to protect themselves against it, the lender against a depreciated currency, the borrower against an appreciated currency. And so on the strength of these obligations hundreds of millions of dollars were loaned and the great corporations of this country have been constructed, and your railroads, your canals, your buildings, almost all the great enterprises of this country have been built up. These bonds were sold to men and women and children throughout the world, and with them went the solemn promise that the takers would receive their money in the coin which they had furnished. Now, Congress can sweep this away with a word and declare it against public policy.

Your Government bonds: Congress in 1900 enacted a solemn statute declaring that the basic money value should be the Gold Dollar, with 25.8 grains of gold. It later directed that in every Government bond there should be inserted a contract to pay in gold, and millions, billions of dollars were issued with that solemn obligation in every one of them.

During the World War men stood on the street corners and proclaimed the advantage of these bonds. They said, "We are offering you the finest investment the world has ever known, the solemn promise of the United States to pay you in Gold Dollars. Your country is in danger; your freedom is at stake; we need your assistance, and we beseech you to buy in order that we may prevail against the enemy." Billions were issued on that statement.

Not only that, but on May 2nd, 1933, after the Government commandeered all gold, it issued and sold five hundred millions of bonds with this same solemn promise.

In 1900, the Government introduced the policy, which had been followed before, of receiving on deposit Gold Dollars, and issuing certificates. The man took [gold] to the Treasury of the United States and deposited [it] there, and received a certificate acknowledging the receipt of it and promising to return it upon demand. Hundreds of millions of those certificates were outstanding, everyone of them bearing the solemn assurance that upon demand the holder could get his gold.

That was the situation in April, 1933; but under threat of heavy penalties Congress declared that every dollar of gold, all gold within the United States should come into the Treasury, and directed the Treasurer to issue for that any form of money. Millions, hundreds of millions, came. We had gone off the Gold Standard, had refused to recognize our obligations. Our currency had depreciated and for every dollar of the bullion received we issued paper currency. But that was not enough. Notwithstanding on the 2nd of May, five hundred millions of gold bonds had been sold to the public, on the 12th Congress passed a resolution saying it is our duty to raise the price of agricultural commodities and to lower the value of securities. It declared that every dollar issued by the United States, whatever the form, should be equal to every other dollar, and gave the President the right to depreciate the gold content of the dollar fifty per cent. If the President, in that state of affairs, had reduced the dollar fifty per cent, the holders of gold securities would have been entitled, under the contract, to the value of the thing contracted for. That would not have served the purpose, apparently, and so it seemed necessary to pass an act which undertook, by direct action, to destroy every one of these contracts for the payment of gold.

Later the President did depreciate the dollar to about sixty cents. Then all the world was told that for these government obligations, these private obligations, you must take sixty per cent of what you contracted to receive.

It seems our duty to reveal to the bar, perhaps to the country, in all its nakedness, just what has been accomplished. That is the state to which our Government has come, and the state of affairs out of which these suits arise. It is not an agreeable situation, not a thing which I like to talk about, but there are some responsibilities which attach to a position upon this bench which one may not ignore.

A man with one of these private bonds demands payment. His debtor says, "I have no gold with which to pay you; I am prohibited by act of Congress from carrying out the contract; here is a paper dollar you must take, and you are at the end of your road." This Court has just held Congress may do that very thing.

The holder of a government bond, which promises to pay in gold, presents it, and the Treasurer says: "Here is a paper dollar which you must take for your contract with the Government; we are prohibited from paying out any gold, and, you are prohibited from accepting it." You insist, "But my contract said that I would be paid in gold or its equivalent." The Treasurer of a great nation replies, "Take this paper dollar." He comes to this court. In one breath it says Congress has no power to repudiate government obligations, that the Constitution gives the right to contract and bind the Government for payment of bonds in any coin, in any way it chooses.

In the next breath it says, "True it is, you have sixty cents on a promise to pay a dollar, but Congress, without authority to repudiate debts, has declared unlawful to accept what it agreed to pay. Since it is unlawful for you to accept what you contracted for, you are not damaged!"

That reply knows no logic. To reason like that is to give with one hand and take away with the other.

Now, the gold certificates. A man comes with a hundred thousand dollars of gold certificates; they recite upon their face that there has been deposited in the Treasury of the United States one hundred thousand gold dollars, "which we promise to pay upon presentation of this certificate." He presents that certificate; what is he told? For each dollar, "we offer you sixty cents; you must take it." "But," he says, "you have in the Treasury of the United States my gold, one hundred thousand dollars of it, which I placed with you upon the solemn promise to return upon demand." The Treasurer says, "Congress has made it unlawful for us to pay out gold; it has made it unlawful for you to receive or to have gold in your possession; therefore, you are not hurt. It is true I have not paid you the kind of money which you left with me, but I have handed you a promise to pay something in the indefinite future, and that is the full value now." To us, reasoning like that seems no reason at all. It is to state a conclusion without regard to facts.

We are told that all this is possible because under the provisions of the Constitution giving power to coin money and regulate its value, Congress may adopt any monetary system, put this system into effect, and sweep out everything that interferes with its consummation.

In discussion of this matter it is well to observe the point at issue. Mere generalities with a multitude of words give no help.

No one denies the power of Congress to adopt a monetary system, but it does not follow that because Congress may adopt some monetary system that it may adopt any system. It must adopt a reasonable and proper one to carry out the purpose for which the power was given.

What was that purpose? It was to fix standards, to permit Congress to provide a circulating medium. It was not intended to enable Congress, under the guise of law, to repudiate. It was intended to give Congress the power to meet its honest obligations. That was the effort in the Legal Tender cases. But here we have the monetary system—the intent, I almost said the wickedness, of which is almost beyond comprehension. What is this monetary system?

First, the President is granted power to depreciate the dollar to fifty cents. He fixed sixty cents. Next, destroy private obligations by "A Statute to Regulate the Currency of the United States." Not only destroy private obligations, but Governments' obligations as well. The language of the same section covers both.

Having put out five hundred mills. of Gold bonds in May, Congress, in June says these promises to pay in gold are illegal, contrary to public policy, although the policy has been strictly observed for many years and approved by all courts.

Having undertaken to destroy the gold clauses, the dollar is next depreciated to sixty cents. Prices of commodities will now be estimated in deflated dollars. Instead of a dollar, we have sixty cents. Mortgages upon railroads, mortgages upon buildings, bank deposits, insurance funds, everything that a thrifty man has accumulated is all subjected to this depreciation! What a state for free men.

We venture to say that no such power was ever granted by the framers of our Constitution. It was not there originally. It was not there yesterday. It is not properly there today. We are confronted with a dollar reduced to sixty cents, possibly to twenty cents tomorrow, ten cents the next day, and one cent the day following.

This is the thing which we abhor. We have tried to prevent its entrance into our system, in vain. We are told that the Government has made out of these transactions $2,800,000,000, and that that amount of gold now in the Treasury may be used to discharge public obligations. On the same basis, depreciate the dollar to five cents and gain enough for all government debts and most of the private ones. Horrible dishonesty!

We protest. That never was, it never ought to be law. Shame and humiliation are upon us.

Louis D. Brandeis

☆ 1856–1941 ☆

APPOINTED BY

WOODROW WILSON

YEARS ON COURT

1916–1939

Louis D. Brandeis

by

ALPHEUS THOMAS MASON

LOUIS D. BRANDEIS combined several careers. Trained as a lawyer, he was a publicist and reformer, a Zionist and Associate Justice of the United States Supreme Court. Famous for his sociological briefs and dissenting opinions, all heavily weighted with facts and statistics, he was a leading exponent of "the living law," and credited with bringing the methods of the laboratory into the courtroom.

The passion for freedom was in Brandeis' blood. Born of a family long eminent for liberal sympathies and of a race whose history bears tragic evidence of bitter struggle for social justice, Louis Brandeis inherited capacities and bents which set him apart. His parents, Adolf Brandeis and Frederika Dembitz, came to America from Bohemia along with the "Forty-eighters"—a group whose political genius was heightened by the turmoil of European revolution. Louis' parents passed on to him the restless spirit that made them rebels in Europe.

The Brandeis family settled in Louisville, Kentucky, where the future Supreme Court Justice was born November 13, 1856. His father prospered as a grain merchant, enabling Louis to spend his early years in an atmosphere of comfort and culture. The Brandeis home was a gathering place for persons of talent, especially musicians. His report cards as a student in the public schools of Louisville show that he set a pace that must have earned him many a nod of approval from his elders. At the age of sixteen, he went with his family to Europe where he entered the *Annen-realschule* in Dresden. For two years the rigid formalism and stiff, almost military, discipline of academic routine which made German pre-university education a model of efficiency, stifled his youthful spirit. But it was here, at the preparatory school level, that he experienced creative power; many years later he recalled that while preparing an essay on a

ALPHEUS THOMAS MASON, Professor Emeritus, Princeton University, now Doherty Professor of Law and Government, University of Virginia, is the author of Brandeis: A Free Man's Life; Harlan Fiske Stone: Pillar of the Law; *and* William Howard Taft, Chief Justice.

subject about which he had known nothing, it dawned on him that ideas could be evolved by reflecting on your material. This was a new discovery for him. Entering the Harvard Law School at eighteen, without the advantage of college, he completed the course in two years, making a record of excellence perhaps still unequalled. He stayed on another year for graduate work, and in 1878 began to practice law in St. Louis, Missouri. After eight months he returned to the congenial atmosphere of Boston where he formed a partnership with Samuel D. Warren, Jr., his friend and fellow student at the Harvard Law School.

The firm's practice, varied and lucrative, included corporation law. It was inevitable, however, that Brandeis' creative mind would explore the economic and social implications of litigation. He constantly seized opportunities to go more deeply into the issues than strictly legalistic and procedural aspects demanded. He believed, with C. R. Henderson, that "a lawyer who has not studied economics and sociology is very apt to become a public enemy." More and more, his law office became a laboratory for social and economic research.

Brandeis began his professional career just as the free enterprise system was beginning to crystallize into a structure of corporate and super-corporate monopoly. Labor awakened and organized; a variety of populist movements flourished. Because he was unable to conceive, as he said, "of anyone being really sensible who was not a reformer, as well as earnest and progressive," he campaigned for "good causes" regardless of their political orientation. No formal party organization could count on his undeviating loyalty. In 1904, he supported progressive Theodore Roosevelt for the presidency and, in 1908, voted for conservative William Howard Taft. In 1912, he campaigned for Wisconsin Senator Robert M. La Follette, later switching to Governor Woodrow Wilson of New Jersey, exponent of the New Freedom. A strong, though silent, supporter of Herbert Hoover in 1920, he privately deplored the Old Guard's choice of Warren G. Harding and Calvin Coolidge as "a sad story of American political irresponsibility."

Brandeis' approach and values are reflected in his address of 1905 before the Harvard Ethical Society:

> *The leading lawyers of the United States have been engaged mainly in supporting the claims of the corporations; often in endeavoring to evade or nullify the extremely crude laws by which legislators sought to regulate the power or curb the excesses of corporations. . . . Instead of holding a position of independence, between the wealthy and the people, prepared to curb the excesses of either, able lawyers have, to a large extent, allowed themselves to become adjuncts of great corporations and have neglected the obligation to use their powers for the protection of the people. . . .*
>
> *The next generation must witness a continuing and ever-increasing contest between those who have and those who have not. The industrial world is in a state of ferment. The ferment is in the main peaceful, and, to a considerable extent, silent; but there is felt today very widely the inconsistency in this condition of political democracy and industrial absolutism. The people are begin-*

ning to doubt whether in the long run democracy and absolutism can co-exist in the same community; beginning to doubt whether there is justification for the great inequalities in the distribution of wealth, for the rapid creation of fortunes, more mysterious than the deeds of Aladdin's lamp.

Amid transition marked by conflicting ideas and forces, Brandeis became an "adviser of men." Dubbed the People's Attorney, he worked, without fee, for a great variety of causes. He did so not solely to battle for "the people," nor to undermine time-honored institutions. Society needs protection against ignorant change as well as ignorant opposition to change. Human aspirations for freedom needed to be canalized along structural lines of law and order. In blazing his trail as attorney for the people, he tried to curb the "excesses of capital" and put "a brake on democracy."

Brandeis was aligned emotionally with the reformer, but unlike run-of-the-mill liberals, he was not content merely to expose and deplore. While muckrakers trumpeted generalities, vagaries and invective, he toiled over dry details, facts and figures, using his inventive genius to fashion a remedy. His "sliding scale" system for public utility rates gave Boston cheaper gas and sounder gas securities. For railway regulation he vitalized Frederick L. Taylor's principles of scientific management. Deploring bigness as a "curse," he punctured the American delusion that efficiency must result from "combining the combiners." For industrial disputes he proposed and applied the preferential union-shop. Nearly three-quarters of a century ago, he exposed the economic and social wastes of unemployment, and advocated scientific management and the annual wage as correctives.

In no field did Brandeis demonstrate more convincingly his mastery of facts and figures, his faith in man, and his unfaltering confidence in democracy than in his surgical exposure of commercial life insurance abuses. As a remedy he successfully advocated the sale of life insurance by savings banks. Savings Bank Life Insurance, now in force in Massachusetts, New York State, and Connecticut, diverts money from the great financial centers, furnishes cheaper insurance for those least able to pay, and provides a fuller life for humble managers of savings bank life insurance departments in local communities. Illustrated in Savings Bank Life Insurance is his conviction that: "The great developer is responsibility. Hence no remedy can be hopeful which does not devolve upon the workers' participation in, responsibility for, the conduct of the business. . . . This participation in, and eventual control of, industry is likewise an essential of obtaining justice in distributing the fruits of industry."

Unlike many reformers of his day, Brandeis did not sally forth to win betterment on a broad front. "Seek for betterment," he advised, "within the broad lines of existing institutions. Do so by attacking evil *in situ;* and proceed from the individual to the general." Without exception, his reformist crusades grew out of his law practice. So it was also with his Zionism. His ancestral background included no formal religious observance, no nationalist leanings, no racial-cultural interests such as a knowledge of Hebrew and the Talmud. Several members of the Brandeis family married Gentiles. His law practice and social life had never been identified with any one race, sect, or interest. His friends were indiscriminately Jews and Gentiles. He never attended synagogue services or other religious observances. "I saw that my parents were good Jews, and yet did not associate with Jews and were different from them, and so there developed in me more affection for our race as a whole than for individuals." The only throwback to tradition was Brandeis' uncle, Lewis Dembitz, who became an early American Zionist. Brandeis admired his uncle, and this affection may have planted seeds of sympathy for Zionism.

Brandeis' first contact with Jews as a group came in 1910 when he was called in to help settle the New York garment workers' strike. Brandeis, then fifty-four, met face to face the teeming immigrant masses from Eastern Europe. In these people he saw reflected the hopes and aspirations which he held out for all men, and became poignantly conscious of "his people" and of their plight. This experience confronted him with a challenge no self-respecting person, least of all a successful Jew, could shirk.

The stimulus which, in 1912, finally brought Brandeis into the Zionist movement came from an English Jew, Jacob De Haas (1872–1937), who had been associated with Theodor Herzl (1860–1904), the father of modern Zionism, in London. At Herzl's suggestion, De Haas had come to America; he settled in Boston and in 1902 became editor of the *Jewish Advocate*. Brandeis' first meeting with him was in the fall of 1910, when he solicited De Haas' support, along with other editors, for savings-bank life insurance. In December that year a reporter for a Jewish paper inquired: "Have you any interest, Mr. Brandeis, with those Jews who are working for the revival of a Jewish state in Palestine?" Brandeis replied: "I have a great deal of sympathy with the Zionists. The movement is an exceedingly deserving one. These so-called dreamers are entitled to the respect and appreciation of the entire Jewish people."

Although engrossed in other matters, he considered the movement urgent and joined the Federation of American Zionism. This affiliation, his first formal identification with the cause, was reported at the Cleveland Zionist convention of 1912. In 1912 and 1913 Brandeis appeared frequently on the speakers' platform, practically making cross-country tours on behalf of Zionism. During the summer of 1914, he studied the Jewish problem intensively. But before he could complete this research the outbreak of World War I changed the whole situation. Zionist headquarters being in Berlin, American adherents began to consider a transfer to New York. De Haas asked Brandeis' authority for proposing his name as the chairman or directing head of the committee which might take charge of practically the whole Zionist movement. This bold idea appealed to Brandeis. His acceptance marked assumption of a new and satisfying role: acknowledged leadership of the Zionist movement in the United States.

At a conference in New York on August 30, 1914, attended by one hundred and fifty participants, a Provisional Executive Committee for General

Zionist Affairs was established and Brandeis unanimously elected chairman. "I feel my disqualification for this task," Brandeis said in accepting leadership.

Throughout long years which represent my own life, I have been to a great extent separated from Jews. I am very ignorant in things Jewish. But recent experiences, public and professional, have taught me this: I find Jews possessed of those very qualities which we of the twentieth century seek to develop in our struggle for justice and democracy; a deep moral feeling which makes them capable of noble acts; a deep sense of the brotherhood of man; and a high intelligence, the fruit of three thousand years of civilization.

Differences among American and European Zionist leaders, especially Brandeis' distrust of Dr. Chaim Weizmann, and the counter charge that Brandeis was an "American first and foremost, and would not dream of applying the term 'Jew' to himself as a national designation," removed Brandeis from official responsibilities. But he remained firm in the Zionist faith, proving, as in no other cause, his ability to stand alone. His beloved brother Alfred and entire family took no part in the movement. In the Justice's own household, only his daughter Susan (Mrs. Jacob Gilbert) became an active Zionist. His wife Alice Goldmark, a second cousin whom he married March 23, 1891, and his daughter Elizabeth (Mrs. Paul Raushenbush) remained aloof. Yet Zionism, more than any other cause, fired Brandeis' imagination and captured his heart. Zionism gave him "understanding and happiness." During the years of Nazi barbarism it became a consuming passion. Long before 1948, when Israel became an independent state, Zionism was, for him, a beautiful reality.

By 1916 Brandeis, having locked horns with powerful economic interests, including transportation, banking and insurance, had become suspect as a dangerous radical. President Wilson's nomination of him, January 28, 1916, as Associate Justice of the Supreme Court shocked both Wall Street and Washington. Seven former presidents of the American Bar Association, including former President Taft, considered him "not a fit person" to sit on the high bench. After Senate Judiciary Committee hearings dragged on nearly five months (January to June, 1916) he was confirmed forty-nine to twenty-two. When it was all over, friends wanted to know his reaction. Troublesome to him were not, he commented, "the attacks of my opponents, however vicious and unfounded, but the silence or acquiescence of those who were not opposed to or were actually in sympathy with me."

Brandeis' judicial career spanned more than two decades (1916–1939). During most of this time the Supreme Court was dominated by Chief Justice William Howard Taft's conviction that "the Constitution was intended, its very purpose was to prevent experimentation with the fundamental rights of the individual"—primarily property and contract rights. The same majority which disallowed regulation of the economy sometimes sanctioned restraints on the mind. In both areas, Brandeis' approach differed significantly from that of the majority. When the issue was economic regulation, he favored legislative experimentation.

The cleavage is dramatically illustrated in *Truax* v. *Corrigan,* 257 U.S. 312

(1921), involving an Arizona statute which prohibited state courts from issuing injunctions in labor cases, except under specified circumstances. Restaurant owners in Bisbee, Arizona, had requested injunctive relief against boycott and picketing of their place of business by former employees. The Arizona court denied such relief, evoking from the plaintiffs the contention that the statute deprived them of their property without due process of law, and denied them equal protection of the laws, both in violation of the Fourteenth Amendment.

By a five to four margin, the Supreme Court sustained this view. Assigning the opinion to himself, Chief Justice Taft began by defining the plaintiffs' business as a property right, free access to it being "an incident to such a right." If defendants used illegal means to prevent customers from patronizing plaintiffs' business, the due process clause protected their property right. Said the Chief Justice:

> *A law which operates to make lawful such a wrong as is described in plaintiffs' complaint deprives the owner of the business and the premises of his property without due process, and can not be held valid under the Fourteenth Amendment.*

The majority also held that the statute withholding equitable relief of injunction, in labor disputes only, denied equal protection of the laws. Deploring the rationale underlying the Arizona statute, Taft wrote, "Classification like the one with which we are here dealing is said to be the development of the philosophic thought of the world and is opening the door to legalized experiment." When the state attempts to take away such fundamental rights the Chief Justice warned, "we may well subject such experiment to attentive judgment."

In sharp disagreement, Justice Brandeis insisted tnat property rights were not beyond legislative reach. "For cause, [they] may be interfered with and even destroyed." Involved in this case was not the simple issue of right and wrong, but a baffling conflict between competing rights. Rules governing the contest between property rights and other rights "necessarily change from time to time." As conditions change, "the rules evolved, being merely experiments in government, must be discarded when they prove to be failures." Admonishing the Court not "to close the door to experiment within the law," Brandeis reviewed in detail the basis of popular opposition to the use of injunctions in labor disputes, a device Taft as a Federal Circuit Court judge had played a significant role in initiating and developing. Brandeis suspected that

> *the real motive in seeking the injunction was not ordinarily to prevent property from being injured nor to protect the owner in its use, but to endow property with active, militant power which would make it dominant over men. In other words, that, under the guise of protecting property rights, the employer was seeking sovereign power.*

"The law of property," Brandeis concluded, "was not appropriate for dealing with the forces beneath social unrest." The "rights of property and liberty of the individual must be remolded from time to time to meet the changing needs of society."

Brandeis criticized the fashion then current among lawyers and judges of invoking conceptual absolutes, such as liberty of contract, to block legislative attempts to correct the abuses of industrialism. Whether a law regulating the economy is unreasonable or arbitrary could not be determined by examining legal precedents. Nor would the test of "common knowledge" or what a "reasonable man" considered necessary to promote the general welfare be a safe guide. "Time and change happeneth to them all."

When Brandeis spoke for the Court in cases involving social and economic regulation, as in upholding the right of a state to regulate the commissions paid fire insurance agents, his approach was conventional.

> *. . . The presumption of constitutionality must prevail in the absence of some factual foundation of record for overthrowing the statute. It does not appear upon the face of the statute, or from any facts of which the court must take judicial notice, that in New Jersey evils did not exist in the business of fire insurance for which this statutory provision was an appropriate remedy. The action of the legislature and of the highest court of the state indicates that such evils did exist. The record is barren of any allegation of fact tending to show unreasonableness.* O'Gorman and Young *v.* Hartford Fire Insurance Co., *282 U.S. 251, 257–8 (1931).*

Justice Brandeis believed that legislative action on controversial social and economic policy can be informed only with the help of accumulated empirical data, "only by a consideration of the contemporary conditions, social, industrial and political, of the community to be affected thereby. . . . Resort to such facts is necessary, among other things, in order to appreciate the evils sought to be remedied and the possible effects of the remedy proposed." And "since government is not an exact science, prevailing public opinion concerning the evil and the remedy is among the important facts deserving consideration." *Truax* v. *Corrigan, supra,* at 356–57.

In the expanding scope of regulation so characteristic of modern society, many agencies take part—the voluntary association, the administrative commission, the legislature, and the judiciary. Brandeis assigned courts a relatively narrow role, particularly in reviewing evidence in anti-trust and rate cases. Thus, in 1920, when the Justices affirmed the judgment of a circuit court, annulling an order of the Federal Trade Commission that the offending company desist from imposing upon purchasers the so-called "tying clause," he protested.

> *The proceeding is . . . a novelty. It is a new device in administrative machinery, introduced by Congress in the year 1914, in the hope thereby of remedying conditions in business which a great majority of the American people regarded as menacing the general welfare and which for more than a generation they had vainly attempted to remedy by the ordinary processes of law. . . .*
>
> *Instead of undertaking to define what practices should be deemed unfair, as had been done in earlier legislation, the act left the determination to the Commission. . . . Recognizing that the question whether a method of competitive practice was unfair would ordinarily depend upon special facts, Congress imposed upon the Commission the duty of finding the facts; and it declared that*

> *findings of fact so made (if duly supported by evidence) were to be taken as final.* Federal Trade Commission *v.* Gratz, *253 U.S. 421, at 432, 436–37 (1920).*

In a concurring opinion, sixteen years later, Brandeis protested against judicial review of evidence in a stock yards rate case, arguing that such action would redound to the disadvantage of both administrative bodies and the courts. "Responsibility is the great developer of men," he said, reiterating an old theme. "May it not tend to emasculate or demoralize the rate-making body if ultimate responsibility is transferred to others? To the capacity of men there is a limit. May it not impair the quality of the work of the courts if this heavy task of reviewing questions of fact is assumed?" *St. Joseph Stock Yards Co.* v. *United States,* 298 U.S. 38, 92 (1936).

Justice Brandeis usually insisted that the Court confine its functions and jurisdiction to tasks it could perform intelligently and effectively. Even if the Justices entertained doubt as to whether a particular remedy was the best; even if they had reason to believe that the measure might lead to other evils, the Court must not interfere provided the act was of a character that might conceivably "produce results sought to be obtained." Legislatures must be accorded wide latitude.

> *There must be power in the States and the Nation to remould, through experimentation, our economic practices and institutions to meet changing social and economic needs. . . . This Court has the power to prevent an experiment. We may strike down the statute which embodies it on the ground that, in our opinion, the measure is arbitrary, capricious or unreasonable. . . . But in the exercise of this high power, we must be ever on our guard, lest we erect our prejudices into legal principles. If we would guide by the light of reason, we must let our minds be bold.* New State Ice Co. *v.* Liebmann, *285 U.S. 262, 311 (1932).*

Some observers saw in certain of Brandeis' opinions an element of collectivism not far removed from alien doctrines; others were confused when he looked with favor on business arrangements regulating competition. His endorsement of the economic policy embodied in the Sherman Act never committed him to such strict interpretation as would prevent businessmen from rationalizing competition. "The Sherman Law," he asserted, "does not prohibit every lessening of competition; and it certainly does not command that competition shall be pursued blindly, that business rivals shall remain ignorant of trade facts, or be denied aid in weighing their significance." *American Column and Lumber Co.* v. *United States,* 257 U.S. 377, 415 (1921). Just as the trade union was a necessity in securing higher wages, shorter hours, and better working conditions, so the trade association was commendable in its field.

In the *American Lumber* case (1921), an association of some four hundred producers was responsible for about thirty per cent of the annual production of hardwood lumber in the country. A large majority of these firms agreed to send to their association's manager of statistics, information on sales, production, and stock at hand. When the manager advised the members to curtail production, prices rose considerably. The Court held that since "the united action of this large and influential membership of dealers contributed greatly to the extraordinary price increase," it contravened the anti-trust laws. Brandeis, however, saw in this open competition plan enormous possibilities for improving conditions in the industry. He also feared that judicial frustration of this association among producers might lead to consolidation and monopoly. It seemed that the Sherman Act (originally intended to secure free competition) had become an instrument by which to destroy the small competitor or force him into the arms of monopoly.

> *The co-operation which is incident to this plan* [*open competition*] *does not suppress competition. On the contrary, it tends to promote all in competition which is desirable. By substituting knowledge for ignorance, rumor, guess, and suspicion, it tends also to substitute research and reasoning for gambling and piracy, without closing the door to adventure, or lessening the value of prophetic wisdom. In making such knowledge available to the smallest concern it creates among producers equality of opportunity. In making it available to purchasers and the general public, it does all that can actually be done to protect the community from extortion. . . . The evidence in this case, far from establishing an illegal restraint of trade, presents, in my opinion, an instance of commendable effort by concerns engaged in chaotic industry, to make possible its intelligent conduct under competitive conditions.* Ibid., *at 418.*

Amid industrial giants, wielding power over small competitors, employees, and consumers, liberty became vacuous unless men were free in both industry and finance. Despite various legislative restrictions, business corporations, through size, competed with the state itself. That is why as a Supreme Court Justice, Brandeis consistently exhibited sympathy for organized labor. The trade union was not only essential to the workers' freedom, but also a bulwark against overweening industrial power. For the same reasons he favored cooperatives among farmers, consumers, and small businessmen and placed great stress on voluntary cooperation and self-help. All could join in bringing men closer to freedom's goal.

Although he spurned various forms of statism advanced under the guise of liberalism, he conceded that government may have to aid individual and group effort if the people are to be saved from enslavement "by the most amazing plutocracy that the world has ever seen." Government must intervene to reduce the size and curb the power of large business combinations and to maintain fair competition among small business units. Before 1916 he warned that "the displacement of the small independent businessman by the huge corporation with its myriad of employees, its absentee ownership, and its financier control, presents a grave danger to our democracy. The social loss is great, and there is no economic gain." ("Cutthroat Prices, the Competition that Kills," *Harper's Weekly,* Nov. 15, 1913.)

His preference for small cooperating business units as against the crushing power of combined capital was shown in the *Quaker City Cab* case. The Philadelphia Cab Corporation objected to a Pennsylvania statute that placed a relatively heavier tax burden on it than on competitors operating as individuals and partnerships. Speaking for the Court in a six to three decision, Justice Butler declared the statute unconstitutional under the equal protection clause. The difference between individuals and partnerships on the one hand, and corporations on the other, did not furnish such "a real and substantial difference" as to justify classification for tax purposes. Brandeis dissented:

> *In Pennsylvania the practice of imposing heavier burdens upon corporations dates from a time when there, as elsewhere in America, the fear of growing corporate power was common. The present heavier imposition may be a survival of an earlier effort to discourage the resort to that form of organization. The apprehension is now less common. But there are still intelligent, informed, just-minded, and civilized persons who believe that the rapidly growing aggregation of capital through corporations constitutes an insidious menace to the liberty of the citizen . . . that the evils incident to the accelerating absorption of business by corporations outweigh the benefits thereby secured; and that the process of absorption should be retarded. The Court may think such views unsound. But obviously the requirement that a classification must be reasonable does not imply that the policy embodied in the classification made by the legislature of a state shall seem to this Court a wise one.* Quaker City Cab Co. *v.* Pa., *277 U.S. 389, 410–11 (1928).*

The primacy of facts, of informed action is the hallmark of Brandeis' life and work. "Knowledge is essential to understanding, and understanding should precede judging." His famous briefs and dissenting opinions underscore his conviction that for wise action there must be "much and constant inquiry into the facts." But overwhelming factual demonstrations alone do not account for the intensity of Brandeis' reformist zeal. "Mr. Brandeis," a friend once asked, "how can you be so sure of your course of action?" "When you are fifty-one per cent sure," the Justice replied, "then go ahead."

In dissenting opinions, he amassed facts and statistics to buttress legislative reasonableness in enacting the ill-fated regulatory measure. As the Court's spokesman, he did not utilize facts to prove that the legislators had been, *in fact,* reasonable. Indeed, he opposed this procedure. When, for example, the Court amassed facts to prove that a Nebraska standard-weight bread law to protect buyers from short weight and honest bakers from unfair competition was unconstitutional, he protested:

> *Put at its highest, our function is to determine, in the light of all facts which may enrich our knowledge and enlarge our understanding, whether the measure, enacted in the exercise of an unquestioned police power and of a character inherently unobjectionable, transcends the bounds of reason. That is, whether the provision as applied is so clearly arbitrary or capricious that legislators acting reasonably could not have believed it to be necessary or appropriate for the public welfare.*
>
> *To decide, as a fact, that the prohibition of excess weights "is not necessary for the protection of the purchasers against imposition and fraud by short*

> *weights"; that it "is not calculated to effectuate that purpose"; and that it "subjects bakers and sellers of bread" to heavy burdens, is, in my opinion, an exercise of the powers of a super-legislature—not the performance of the constitutional function of judicial review.* Burns Baking Co. *v.* Bryan, *264 U.S. 504, 534 (1924)*.

Like his reactionary colleagues, Brandeis was inclined by the pressures of his nature to translate his own preferences into the Constitution. Confident of the soundness of his principles, he would try to convince by flooding an opponent with massive documentation. "I told him once," Justice Holmes declared, "that when he had strong economic . . . convictions, I thought that he sometimes became the advocate and ceased to be detached—but it isn't often." Justice Stone, though usually voting with Brandeis, would sometimes refuse to join his opinion. "I think," he explained, "you are too much an advocate of this particular legislation." Judge Learned Hand, a Brandeis admirer, believed that Justice Stone "was a much more detached nature than Brandeis—more 'judicial' and reliable. . . . However," Hand added, "Brandeis was a great innovator, most of the time in good causes."

In his memoirs, Dean Acheson, Brandeis' law clerk (1919–1921) and later Secretary of State, recalls Harvard Law Professor Manley Hudson holding forth in the 1920's on Brandeis as Scientist of the Law. Doubting the accuracy of Hudson's assumptions, Acheson arranged an interview. Professor Hudson's negative views on National Prohibition led him unwittingly to arouse the Justice. "Moral principles," the law professor declared, "were no more than generalizations from the mores or accepted notions of a particular time and place." Acheson reports what happened:

> *The eruption was even more spectacular than I had anticipated. The Justice wrapped the Mantle of Isaiah around himself, dropped his voice a full octave, jutted his eyebrows forward in a most menacing way, and began to prophesy. Morality was truth; and truth had been revealed to man in an unbroken, continuous, and consistent flow by the great prophets and poets of all time. He quoted Goethe in German and from Euripides via Gilbert Murray. On it went—an impressive, almost frightening, glimpse of an elemental force.* [Morning and Noon, *95–96 (Boston, 1965)*.]

Later on, Acheson asked Professor Hudson what he now thought about Brandeis, Scientist of the Law. "Monstrous! It's monstrous!" Hudson shouted. Here, Acheson reflected, was proof "that if some of his [Brandeis'] admirers knew him better they would like him less. . . . What was truly surprising," Acheson concludes, "was not that Brandeis had absolutist convictions on the nature of truth, but that he kept his beliefs and emotions so sternly, even rigidly, disciplined and controlled in the performance of his judicial duties."

Brandeis' judicial detachment rivaled that of Justice Holmes, with whom he often joined in dissent. Yet Brandeis embraced two strangely inconsistent criteria of right and wrong (facts and moral absolutes) for which Holmes expressed disrelish or vehemently repudiated. "I hate facts," Holmes declared. Natural law, he wrote, represents the philosopher's effort "to prove that truth is absolute. . . . a demand for the superlative," so strong in all men that "the poor devil who has no other way of reaching it attains it by getting drunk."

It was one thing for the legislature to limit hours of work, to expose employers to "coercive" unionist activities by limiting the use of injunctions or to interfere with individual liberty by abolishing the yellow-dog contract or to approve a relatively heavier tax for corporations than for partnership and individual enterprise; it was something else when government restricted man's freedom of thought, speech, and press. When government action curbed these liberties, Brandeis became a judicial activist.

In 1920 the Court invoked the Federal Espionage Act of 1917 against those publishing statements alleged to interfere with prosecution of the war. The defendants were convicted for publishing in German, articles contemptuous of our war activities, hinting that the war had resulted from machinations of the President. For Justice McKenna the case afforded the curious spectacle of enemies taking shelter under a "great ordinance of government and orderly liberty . . . to justify the activities of anarchy. . . ." *Schaefer* v. *United States,* 251 U.S. 466, 477 (1920). Justice Brandeis thought the case was not so simple. If, under legislation regulating the labor contract, freedom is the rule and regulation the exception, the same principles apply, at least equally, to limitations on speech and press.

The Federal Espionage Act was also used against socialists for distributing sample copies of a four-page leaflet entitled "The Price We Pay," written by Episcopal clergyman, Irwin St. John Tucker. To Justice Pitney the leaflet was a "highly colored and sensational document" intended "to hamper the government in the prosecution of the war." To Brandeis it was a more or less harmless discussion of the causes of war. Truth in the social sciences, he reasoned, no less than in the natural sciences, depends on freedom to think, write, and speak, and, above all, on the right to differ:

> *The fundamental right of free men to strive for better conditions through new legislation and new institutions will not be preserved, if efforts to secure it by argument to fellow citizens may be construed as criminal incitement to disobey the existing law—merely because the argument presented seems to those exercising judicial power to be unfair in its portrayal of existing evils, mistaken in its assumptions, unsound in reasoning, or intemperate in language. No objections more serious than these can, in my opinion, reasonably be made to the arguments presented in "The Price We Pay."* Pierce v. United States, *252 U.S. 239, 273 (1920).*

In 1927, Brandeis summarized in undying words the sanctity of the constitutional protection afforded freedom of press and speech, suggesting that such protection is deeply rooted in American fundamentals. Anita Whitney, a member of the Communist Labor party, convicted and sentenced under California's Criminal Syndicalism Act, appealed to the United States Supreme Court. Miss Whitney had not, as she might have done, raised the question whether there was in fact a "clear and present danger" manifest in her acts. She claimed only that the criminal syndicalism statute violated the Constitution. The Justices rejected her plea and confirmed the state court's sentence. Justice Brandeis, concurring in the result, declared:

> *Those who won our independence believed that the final end of the state was to make men free to develop their faculties; and that in its government the deliberative forces should prevail over the arbitrary. They valued liberty both as an end and as a means. They believed liberty to be the secret of happiness and courage to be the secret of liberty. They believed that freedom to think as you will and to speak as you think are means indispensable to the discovery and spread of political truth; that without free speech and assembly discussion would be futile; that with them, discussion affords ordinarily adequate protection against the dissemination of noxious doctrine; that the greatest menace to freedom is an inert people; that public discussion is a political duty; and that this should be a fundamental principle of the American government. They recognized the risks to which all human institutions are subject. But they knew that order cannot be secured merely through fear of punishment for its infraction; that it is hazardous to discourage thought, hope, and imagination; that fear breeds repression; that repression breeds hate; that hate menaces stable government; that the path of safety lies in the opportunity to discuss freely supposed grievances and proposed remedies; and that the fitting remedy for evil counsels is good ones. Believing in the power of reason as applied through public discussion, they eschewed silence coerced by law—the argument of force in its worst form. Recognizing the occasional tyrannies of governing majorities, they amended the Constitution so that free speech and assembly should be guaranteed.*
>
> *Fear of serious injury cannot alone justify suppression of free speech and assembly. Men feared witches and burned women. It is the function of speech to free men from the bondage of irrational fears. To justify suppression of free speech there must be reasonable ground to fear that serious evil will result if free speech is practiced. There must be reasonable ground to believe that the danger apprehended is imminent. There must be reasonable ground to believe that the evil to be prevented is a serious one. . . .*
>
> *Those who won our independence by revolution were not cowards. They did not fear political change. They did not exalt order at the cost of liberty. To courageous, self-reliant men, with confidence in the power of free and fearless reasoning applied through the processes of popular government, no danger flowing from speech can be deemed clear and present, unless the incidence of the evil apprehended is so imminent that it may befall before there is opportunity for full discussion. If there be time to expose through discussion the falsehood and fallacies, to avert the evil by the processes of education, the remedy to be applied is more speech, not enforced silence. Only an emergency can justify repression. Such must be the rule if authority is to be reconciled with freedom. Such, in my opinion, is the command of the Constitution.* Whitney *v.* California, *274 U.S. 357, 375–377 (1927)*.

More than once, Brandeis pointedly called attention to the zeal with which the Court, often against his protest, had invoked the Constitution to strike down legislation regulating property and contract:

. . . I have difficulty in believing that the liberty guaranteed by the Constitution, which has been held to protect against state denial the right of an employer to discriminate against a workman because he is a member of a trade union . . . the right of a businessman to conduct a private employment agency, . . . or to contract outside the state for insurance of his property . . . although the legislature deems it inimical to the public welfare, does not include liberty to teach, either in the privacy of the home or publicly, the doctrine of pacifism. . . . I cannot believe that the liberty guaranteed by the Fourteenth Amendment includes only liberty to acquire and to enjoy property. Gilbert *v.* Minnesota, *254 U.S. 325, 343 (1920).*

Brandeis was sensitive to the judicial subtlety, Professor Felix Frankfurter noted in 1938. Reflecting on the constitutional jurisprudence of the nineteen-twenties, Frankfurter remarked:

That a majority of the Court which frequently disallowed restraints on economic power should so consistently have sanctioned restraints of the mind is perhaps only a surface paradox. There is an underlying unity between fear of ample experimentation in economics and fear of expression of heretical ideas. [*F. Frankfurter,* Mr. Justice Holmes and the Supreme Court *62 (1938).*]

Brandeis stood firm for the ancient liberty comprised in freedom of belief, thought, and discussion. But when he came to consider certain prescriptions "by men of zeal, well-meaning but without understanding," such as the Volstead Act, he was less alert to the invasion of liberty. The support he had given pacifists, socialists, and other radicals banned by regulatory legislation was not forthcoming for those who violated the "experiment noble in motive." In 1923, at the request of President Wilson, he prepared a memorandum stating his views:

The Eighteenth Amendment made prohibition the law of the nation. The Volstead Act prescribed for the nation what liquor should be deemed intoxicating. The intention was that each government [federal and state] should perform that part of the task for which it is peculiarly fitted. . . . To relieve the states from the duty of performing [their tasks] violates our traditions; and threatens the best interests of our country. The strength of the nation and its capacity for achievement is, in large measure, due to the federal system with its distribution of powers and duties. . . . But the Eighteenth Amendment should remain unchanged. And the Volstead Act should remain unchanged.

The antithetical values Brandeis placed on the right to drink as against the right to privacy were shown when federal agents tapped the telephone wires of men suspected of conspiring to violate the Volstead Act. Chief Justice Taft, delivering the opinion, overruled the defendants' claim that the evidence obtained when government agents tapped their telephone wires violated either unreasonable searches and seizures or the constitutional protection against self-incrimination. No tapped wires entered their homes and offices, Taft reasoned, so there was neither search nor seizure.

For Justice Brandeis such a narrow construction degraded our great charter of freedom to the level of a municipal ordinance. Quoting Chief Justice Marshall's famous admonition—"We must never forget that it is a Constitution we are expounding"—he pointed out that just as the power of Congress had by judicial interpretation been kept abreast of scientific progress, and extended the Fundamental Law to objects of which the Founding Fathers never dreamed, so also must the judges in construing limitations on the powers of Congress be ever-mindful of changes wrought by discovery and invention.

> *Subtler and more far-reaching means of invading privacy have become available to the government. . . . The progress of science in furnishing the government with means of espionage is not likely to stop with wire-tapping. Ways may some day be developed by which the government, without removing papers from secret drawers, can reproduce them in court, and by which it will be enabled to expose to a jury the most intimate occurrences of the home. . . .*
>
> *Our government is the potent, the omnipresent teacher. For good or ill, it teaches the whole people by example. Crime is contagious. If the government becomes a lawbreaker, it breeds contempt for law; it invites every man to become a law unto himself; it invites anarchy. To declare that in the administration of the criminal law the end justifies the means—to declare that the government may commit crimes in order to secure the conviction of a private criminal —would bring terrible retribution. . . .*
>
> *The makers of our Constitution undertook to secure conditions favorable to the pursuit of happiness. They recognized the significance of man's spiritual nature, of his feelings and of his intellect. They knew that only a part of the pain, pleasure, and satisfactions of life are to be found in material things. They sought to protect Americans in their beliefs, their thoughts, their emotions, and their sensations. They conferred, as against the government, the right to be let alone—the most comprehensive of rights and the right most valued by civilized men. . . .*
>
> *Experience should teach us to be most on our guard to protect liberty when the government's purposes are beneficent. Men born to freedom are naturally alert to repel invasion of their liberty by evil-minded rulers. The greatest dangers to liberty lurk in insidious encroachment by men of zeal, well-meaning, but without understanding.* Olmstead v. United States, *277 U.S. 438 at 473–74, 485, 478–79 (1928)*.

Few men live to see their ideas become realities, their views accepted, their philosophy enacted into law. That reward came, in large measure, to Justice Brandeis. In old age (he died in his eighty-fifth year) his Lincolnesque facial features, bold and craggy, his deep-seated, brooding eyes, accented by bushy eyebrows and long, unruly hair, suggested a Hebrew prophet. Without jest, his law clerks of later years referred to him as Isaiah. In an affectionate note of June 18, 1940, President Roosevelt addressed him, "My dear Isaiah."

In the popular mind, Brandeis won fame as a dissenter. Statistically, this is erroneous. Four hundred and fifty-four of his five hundred and twenty-eight opinions were written for the Court. His dissenting opinions, of quality, not quantity, are significant because, in so many instances, he stated the law as it was yet to be. In dissent, he did not need to keep his views strictly in step with others. "I alone am responsible," he said. "I expose myself." He could, and did, keep on crusading. Never content to state objections solely in terms of constitutional issues, his footnotes referred to trade and professional journals, federal, state, and foreign government reports, magazine articles, ranging from *The Nation* to *Nation's Business,* sometimes evoking critical comment from certain of his colleagues.

His law clerks' work consisted in checking draft opinions against the pleadings and evidence. After an opinion had reached what seemed final revision (sometimes running to a score or more) he was likely to say to his law clerk, "The opinion is now convincing, but what can we do to make it more instructive?"—a hint that often led to more research and fuller documentation.

It is doubtful whether any Supreme Court Justice held that tribunal in higher regard. His reverence was almost mystic. What moved him was not so much the drama of the Court's past, nor the majesty of judicial office—much less architectural splendor. He preferred the modest quarters in the old basement Senate Chamber to the present magnificent temple, fearing that the Court's prestige might consist in marble and columns rather than in its wisdom and craftsmanship.

Brandeis' most significant quality was restless curiosity, thirst for knowledge. It was not learning for its own sake but knowledge to put to some use. When he began on a problem, he wanted to absorb it all, to explore all implications. He studied the past, not to adore, but for the light accumulated wisdom threw on the living present. If he showed unusual moral discernment, or demonstrated extraordinary understanding of hard problems; if in his own time, and in a variety of fields, he helped to vindicate his prophetic vision, the reason is that curiosity drove him to toil over every inch of the complex segments of modern life. Much of his own scope and power came from infinite capacity for taking pains.

His expert handling of widely dispersed and distorted facts is a matter of common knowledge. What is not so well known is his capacity for moral indignation. This was even stronger in him than his sense of compassion. As his mind became absorbed, it caught fire. He was moved by the wrongs of economic privilege, by human suffering and exploitation, but what moved him more was public apathy and moral obtuseness in face of recognized wrong. He was sorely grieved by the fate of persecuted peoples in Europe, but he felt much more deeply the slowness with which the nations of the world rose in protest. Moral inertness, like bigness, was a menace to freedom.

The defects of great men reclaim them to humanity. So it was with Brandeis. Inevitably there were the defects of his qualities. His talent for figures and for factual demonstration, combined with the rigidity of his moral imperatives, developed in him an imperious quality. In his Zionist activities, Harold Laski accused him of giving orders like "an omnipotent Sultan" and of treating "fellow Zionists who differ from him almost as criminals." His instinct for freedom, privacy, and independence sometimes made his stand less than clear and unequivocal, even in the eyes of close associates. In certain complicated situations of which he was the storm center, friends and critics alike could and did mistake his position. He had reserved for himself an area of freedom from specific commitment such as would leave him independent no matter what might later ensue.

It was fitting that Brandeis joined the Supreme Court at the height of his powers. Membership on the Court not only gave him a vote in the citadel of corporate-financial power, but also provided an effective forum in which to continue his search. He pinned high hopes on education and held the teaching profession in highest regard. Discovering that more than half of his former law clerks were teaching, he commented with satisfaction, "Now I have a majority."

On America's highest Court, as during his years as lawyer and publicist, Brandeis was a teacher, trying to demonstrate that man does have considerable control over his own destiny, maintaining to the end that, given knowledge, leadership, participation and persistence, men can lay foundations for a closer approach than was ever thought possible to the ideal of an enlarging liberty through a living law.

SELECTED BIBLIOGRAPHY

Brandeis' personal and public papers are deposited at the University of Louisville. His court papers are at the Harvard Law School. Brandeis' publications include: *Business—A Profession* (Boston, 1914); *Other People's Money and How the Bankers Use It* (New York, 1914); "The Right to Privacy," 4 *Harvard Law Review* 193 (1890); "The Living Law," 10 *Illinois Law Review* 461 (1916). Selected opinions, essays, and addresses are collected by: A. Lief, ed., *The Social and Economic Views of Mr. Justice Brandeis* (New York, 1930); O. K. Fraenkel, ed., *The Curse of Bigness* (New York, 1934); A. Lief, ed., *The Brandeis Guide to the Modern World* (Boston, 1941); S. Goldman, *Brandeis on Zionism* (Washington, D.C., 1942). The authorized biography is Alpheus Thomas Mason, *Brandeis: A Free Man's Life* (New York, 1946). Other useful sources include: Felix Frankfurter, ed., *Mr. Justice Brandeis* (New Haven, 1932); A. Lief, *Brandeis: The Personal History of An American Ideal* (New York, 1936); A. T. Mason, *Brandeis: Lawyer and Judge in the Modern State* (Princeton, 1933); A. T. Mason, *The Brandeis Way* (Princeton, 1938); J. De Haas, *Louis D. Brandeis, a Biographical Sketch, with Special Reference to His Contributions to Jewish and Zionist History* (New York, 1929); I. Dilliard, ed., *Mr. Justice Brandeis: Great American: Press Opinion and Public Appraisal* (St. Louis, 1941); A. M. Bickel, *The Unpublished Opinions of Mr. Justice Brandeis: The Supreme Court at Work* (Cambridge, 1957).

Louis D. Brandeis

REPRESENTATIVE OPINIONS

TRUAX v. CORRIGAN, 257 U.S. 312 (1921)

Truax, a restauranteur in Bisbee, Arizona, was picketed by Corrigan and others (cooks and waiters employed by Truax) who went on strike over conditions of work. The defendants, carrying banners, picketed the restaurant and advertised their strike. Truax filed for an injunction, and was refused under an Arizona statute forbidding the issuance of injunctions in labor disputes. The case focused upon whether Truax had been unconstitutionally denied equal protection of the laws and deprived of his property without due process of law. Chief Justice Taft, for the five to four majority, threw out the Arizona statute on both counts. "A law which operates to make lawful such a wrong as is described in plaintiffs' complaint [conspiratorial annoyance and obstruction] deprives the owner of the business and the premises of his property without due process and can not be held valid under the Fourteenth Amendment." The purpose of the Fourteenth Amendment's equal protection clause of the Constitution was "to secure equality of protection not only for all but against all similarly situated." Employers as a class were denied a legal remedy available to others. The dissenting Justices, led by Brandeis, argued that the realities of labor-management relations and the widespread abuses of injunctions in labor disputes, justified this classification.

MR. JUSTICE BRANDEIS, dissenting.

The first legislature of the State of Arizona adopted in 1913 a Civil Code. By Title 6, c. III, it sets forth conditions and circumstances under which the courts of the State may or may not grant injunctions. Paragraph 1464 contains, among other things a prohibition against interfering by injunction between employers and employees, in any case growing out of a dispute concerning terms or conditions of employment, unless interposition by injunction is necessary to protect property from injury through violence. Its main purpose was doubtless to prohibit the courts from enjoining peaceful picketing and the boycott. With the wisdom of the statute we have no concern. Whether Arizona in enacting this statute transgressed limitations imposed upon the power of the States by the Fourteenth Amendment is the question presented for decision.

The employer has, of course, a legal right to carry on his business for profit; and incidentally the subsidiary rights to secure and retain customers, to fix such prices for his product as he deems proper, and to buy merchandise and labor at such prices as he chooses to pay. This right to carry on business—be it called liberty or property—has value; and, he who interferes with the right without cause renders himself liable. But for cause the right may be interfered with and even be destroyed. Such cause exists when, in the pursuit of an equal right to further their several interests, his competitors make inroads upon his trade, or when suppliers of merchandise or of labor make inroads upon his profits. What methods and means are permissible in this struggle of contending forces is determined in part by decisions of the courts, in part by acts of the legislatures. The rules governing the contest necessarily change from time to time. For conditions change; and, furthermore, the rules evolved, being merely experiments in government, must be discarded when they prove to be failures.

Practically every change in the law governing the relation of employer and employee must abridge, in some respect, the liberty or property of one of the parties—if liberty and property be measured by the standard of the law theretofore prevailing. If such changes are made by acts of the legislature, we call the modification an exercise of the police power. And, although the change may involve interference with existing liberty or property of individuals, the statute will not be declared a violation of the due process clause, unless the court finds that the interference is arbitrary or unreasonable or that, considered as a means, the measure has no real or substantial relation of cause to a permissible end.[1] Nor will such changes in the law governing contests between employer and employee be held to be violative of the equal protection clause, merely because the liberty or property of individuals in other relations to each other (for instance, as competitors in trade or as vendor and purchaser) would not, under similar circumstances, be subject to like abridgement. Few laws are of universal application. It is of the nature of our law that it has dealt not with man in general, but with him in relationships. That a peculiar relationship of individuals may furnish legal basis for the classification which satisfies the requirement of the Fourteenth Amendment[2] is clear. That the relation of employer and employee affords a constitutional basis for legislation applicable only to persons standing in that relation has been repeatedly held by this court.[3] The questions

[1] Muller *v*. Oregon, *208 U.S. 412;* Dominion Hotel *v*. Arizona, *249 U.S. 265.*

[2] *"The rule, therefore, is not a substitute for municipal law; it only prescribes that that law have the attribute of equality of operation, and equality of operation does not mean indiscriminate operation on persons merely as such, but on persons according to their relations." Mr. Justice McKenna in* Magoun *v*. Illinois Trust & Savings Bank, *170 U.S. 283, 293.*

In Fidelity Mutual Life Association *v*. Mettler, *185 U.S. 308, and* Northwestern National Life Insurance Co. *v*. Riggs, *203 U.S. 243, the relation of insurer and insured was made the subject of regulation; in* Western Union Telegraph Co. *v*. Commercial Milling Co., *218 U.S. 406;* Seaboard Air Line Ry. *v*. Seegers, *207 U.S. 73;* Yazoo & Mississippi Valley R. R. Co. *v*. Jackson Vinegar Co., *226 U.S. 217, that of public utility and patron; in* Noble State Bank *v*. Haskell, *219 U.S. 104, that of banker and depositor; in* St. Louis & San Francisco Ry. Co. *v*. Mathews, *165 U.S. 1;* Missouri, Kansas & Texas Ry. Co. *v*. May, *194 U.S. 267; and* Minneapolis & St. Louis Ry. Co. *v*. Emmons, *149 U.S. 364, that of railway and adjoining landowner.*

[3] Holden *v*. Hardy, *169 U.S. 366;* St. Louis, Iron Mountain & St. Paul Ry. Co. *v*. Paul, *173 U.S. 404;* Tullis *v*. Lake Erie & Western R. R. Co., *175 U.S. 348;* Knoxville Iron Co. *v*. Harbison, *183 U.S. 13;* Atkin *v*. Kansas, *191 U.S. 207;* Great Southern Hotel Co. *v*. Jones, *193 U.S. 532;* Minnesota Iron Co. *v*. Kline, *199 U.S. 593;* Wilmington Star Mining Co. *v*. Fulton, *205 U.S. 60;* Muller *v*. Oregon, *208 U.S. 412;* McLean *v*. Arkansas, *211 U.S. 539;* Louisville & Nashville R. R. Co. *v*. Melton, *218 U.S. 36;* Mobile, Jackson & Kansas City R. R. Co. *v*. Turnipseed, *219 U.S. 35;* Chicago, Rock Island & Pacific Ry. Co. *v*. Arkansas, *219 U.S. 453;* Arizona Employers' Liability Cases, *250 U.S. 400. Compare* Second Employers' Liability Cases, *223 U.S. 1.*

submitted are whether this statutory prohibition of the remedy by injunction is in itself arbitrary and so unreasonable as to deprive the employer of liberty or property without due process of law;—and whether limitation of this prohibition to controversies involving employment denies him equal protection of the laws.

Whether a law enacted in the exercise of the police power is justly subject to the charge of being unreasonable or arbitrary, can ordinarily be determined only by a consideration of the contemporary conditions, social, industrial and political, of the community to be affected thereby. Resort to such facts is necessary, among other things, in order to appreciate the evils sought to be remedied and the possible effects of the remedy proposed. Nearly all legislation involves a weighing of public needs as against private desires; and likewise a weighing of relative social values. Since government is not an exact science, prevailing public opinion concerning the evils and the remedy is among the important facts deserving consideration; particularly, when the public conviction is both deep-seated and widespread and has been reached after deliberation.[4] What, at any particular time, is the paramount public need is, necessarily, largely a matter of judgment. Hence, in passing upon the validity of a law challenged as being unreasonable, aid may be derived from the experience of other countries and of the several States of our Union in which the common law and its conceptions of liberty and of property prevail. The history of the rules governing contests between employer and employed in the several English-speaking countries illustrates both the susceptibility of such rules to change and the variety of contemporary opinion as to what rules will best serve the public interest. The divergence of opinion in this difficult field of governmental action should admonish us not to declare a rule arbitrary and unreasonable merely because we are convinced that it is fraught with danger to the public weal, and thus to close the door to experiment within the law.

In England a workingman struggling to improve his condition, even when acting singly, was confronted until 1813 with laws limiting the amount of wages which he might demand.[5] Until 1824 he was punishable as a criminal if he combined with his fellow workmen to raise wages or shorten hours or to affect the business in any way, even if there was no resort to a strike.[6] Until 1871 members of a union who joined in persuading employees to leave work were liable criminally, although the employees were not under contract and the persuasion was both peaceful and unattended by picketing.[7] Until 1871 threatening a strike, whatever the cause, was also a criminal act.[8] Not until 1875 was the right of workers to combine in order to attain their ends conceded fully. In that year Parliament declared that workmen combining in furtherance of a trade dispute should not be indictable for criminal conspiracy unless the act if done by one person would be indictable as a crime.[9] After that statute a combination of workmen to effect the ordinary objects of a strike was no longer a criminal offense. But picketing, though peaceful, in aid of a strike, remained illegal;[10] and likewise the boycott.[11] Not until 1906 was the ban on

[4] Muller *v.* Oregon, *208 U.S. 412, 420.*

[5] *53 Geo. 3, c. 40. For the earlier law see, for instance, 23 Edw. 3, c. 1–8; 25 Edw. 3, c. 1–7, The Statutes of Laborers; 5 Eliz., c. 4; 1 Jac. 1, c. 6.*

[6] *5 Geo. 4, c. 95, (replaced by 6 Geo. 4, c. 129). For the earlier law see, for instance, 34 Edw. 3, c. 9;* The King *v.* Journeymen Tailors of Cambridge, *8 Modern, 10; Wright, The Law of Criminal Conspiracies.*

[7] *Criminal Law Amendment Act (1871), 34 & 35 Vic., c. 32, § 1, last paragraph. For the earlier law see* Regina *v.* Rowlands, *2 Den. 363.*

[8] *Criminal Law Amendment Act (1871), 34 & 35 Vic., c. 32, § 1, sub-sec. 2. For the earlier law see* Walsby *v.* Anley, *3 E. & E. 516;* Skinner *v.* Kitch, *10 Cox C. C. 493; L. R. 2 Q. B. 393 (1867).*

[9] *The Conspiracy and Protection of Property Act (1875), 38 & 39 Vic., c. 86, § 3. But see* Rigby *v.* Connol, *L. R. 14 Ch. D. 482, 491.*

[10] *38 & 39 Vic., c. 86, § 7;* Regina *v.* Bauld, *13 Cox C. C. 282;* Lyons *v.* Wilkins, [*1896*] *1 Ch. 811, 826, 831;* [*1899*] *1 Ch. 255;* Taff Val Ry. Co. *v.* Amalgamated Society of Railway Servants, [*1901*] *A. C. 426.*

[11] Temperton *v.* Russell [*1893*] *1 Q. B. 715;* Quinn *v.* Leathem, [*1901*] *A. C. 495. But compare with these cases* Boots *v.* Grundy, *82 L. T. R. 769;* Scottish Co-operative Society *v.* Glasgow Fleshers, *35 Scottish L. R. 645;* Bulcock *v.* St. Anne's Master Builders' Federation, *19 T. L. R. 27; a distinction between these and the two former is pointed*

peaceful picketing and the bringing of pressure upon an employer by means of a secondary strike or a boycott removed.[12] In 1906, also, the act of inducing workers to break their contract of employment (previously held an actionable wrong)[13] was expressly declared legal.[14] In England improvement of the condition of workingmen and their emancipation appear to have been deemed recently the paramount public need.

In the British Dominions the rules governing the struggle between employer and employed were likewise subjected to many modifications; but the trend of social experiment took a direction very different from that followed in the mother country. Instead of enabling the worker to pursue such methods as he might deem effective in the contest, statutes were enacted in some of the Dominions which forbade the boycott, peaceful picketing, and even the simple strike and the lockout;[15] use of the injunction to enforce compliance with these prohibitions was expressly sanctioned;[16] and violation

---

out in Quinn *v.* Leathem, supra, *p. 539. The Royal Commission on Trade Disputes and Trade Combinations, whose recommendations were the basis of the Trade Disputes Act, 1906, 6 Edw. 7, c. 47, recommended, Report, p. 16, "that an act should be passed for the following objects:—. . . (2) To declare strikes from whatever motive or for whatever purposes (including sympathetic or secondary strikes), apart from crime or breach of contract, legal . . . It is probable that § § 1 and 3 of the Act of 1906 make the secondary strike or boycott in the course of a trade dispute legal. But see note 14, par. 2.*

[12] *The Trade Disputes Act (1906), 6 Edw. 7, c. 47, § 2.*

[13] Read *v.* Friendly Society of Stonemasons, *[1902] 2 K. B. 88;* id., *732;* South Wales Miners' Federation *v.* Glamorgan Coal Co., *[1905] A. C. 239.*

[14] *6 Edw. 7, c. 47, § 3, "An act done by a person in contemplation or furtherance of a trade dispute shall not be actionable on the ground only that it induces some other person to break a contract of employment or that it is an interference with the trade, business, or employment of some other person, or with the right of some other person to dispose of his capital or his labour as he wills." But the employee who breaks his contract remains personally liable in damages.*

The law of England still prohibits certain practices which might prove effective in the struggle between employer and employee. Thus the Trade Disputes Act, supra, *does not sanction some threats or coercion,* Conway *v.* Wade, *[1909] A. C. 506, 511. It does not permit a strike to force the discharge of a member of the union who has not paid a fine,* Conway *v.* Wade, supra. *Nor does it permit inducing an employer's men to break their contracts in order to force him to join an employers' association, since this is not a trade dispute within the meaning of the act,* Larkin *v.* Long, *[1915] A. C. 814. The judges are by no means agreed as to what constitutes coercion. Compare:* Hodges *v.* Webb, *[1920] 2 Ch. 70;* Valentine *v.* Hyde, *[1919] 2 Ch. 129;* Pratt *v.* British Medical Association, *[1919] 1 K. B. 244; and* Davies *v.* Thomas, *[1920] 1 Ch. 217.*

[15] *Australia: Commonwealth Conciliation and Arbitration Act, 1904–15, § § 6–9; New South Wales, Industrial Arbitration Act, 1912–1918, § § 48D and 48E; compare Queensland, Industrial Arbitration Act, 1916, § 65. New Zealand: Industrial Conciliation and Arbitration Act, 1908, § 108; Industrial Conciliation and Arbitration Amendment Act, 1908, Part I.*

[16] *The Industrial Disputes Act of New South Wales, 1908, § 60, made strikes and lockouts illegal and the Industrial Arbitration Act, 1912, which replaced it, continued their outlawry, § § 44–48, and expressly provided that they might be enjoined by the Court of Industrial Arbitration; but by the Act of 1918, § 15, § § 45 to 48 inclusive of the earlier act, dealing with strikes, were amended:*

"45. The following strikes and no others shall be illegal:—

"(a) Any strike by employees of the crown, etc.

"(b) Any strike by the employees in an industry the conditions of which are for the time being wholly or partially regulated by an award or by an industrial agreement: etc.

"(c) Any strike which has been commenced prior to the expiry of fourteen clear days' notice in writing of intention to commence the same or of the existence of such conditions as would be likely to lead to the same given the Minister, etc.

"46. In the event of an illegal strike occurring in any industry, the court may order any trade union, whose executive or members are taking part in or aiding or abetting

of the statute was also made punishable by criminal proceedings.[17] These prohibitions were the concomitants of prescribed industrial arbitration through administrative tribunals by which the right of both employer and employee to liberty and property were seriously abridged in the public interest. Australia[18] and New Zealand[19] made compulsory both arbitration and compliance with the award.[20] Canada limited the compulsion to a postponement of the right to strike until the dispute should have been officially investigated and reported upon.[21] In these Dominions the uninterrupted pursuit of industry and the prevention of the arbitrary use of power appear to be deemed the paramount public needs.

In the United States the rules of the common law governing the struggle between employer and employee have likewise been subjected to modifications. These have been made mainly through judicial decisions. The legal right of workingmen to combine and to strike in order to secure for themselves higher wages, shorter hours and better working conditions received early general recognition.[22] But there developed great diversity of opinion as to the means by which,[23] and also as to the person through whom,[24] and upon whom[25] pressure might permis-

---

the strike, to pay a penalty not exceeding five hundred pounds."

The Commonwealth Conciliation and Arbitration Act, 1904, § 38 (e), provides that the Court of Arbitration and Conciliation shall have power "to enjoin any organization or person from committing or continuing any contravention of this Act."

[17] *See note 15,* supra.

[18] *The Commonwealth Conciliation and Arbitration Act, 1904–1915, § § 19–31. (Printed as Appendix A to Commonwealth Acts 1914–1915.) See Henry B. Higgins, "A New Province for Law and Order," 29 Harv. Law Rev. 13; 32 Harv. Law Rev. 189; 34 Harv. Law Rev. 105.*

[19] *Industrial Conciliation and Arbitration Act, 1908,* supra, *§ § 53–104, as amended by Acts 1908, No. 239, Part II; Acts 1911, No. 33; Acts 1913, No. 7.*

[20] *Compare Kansas act creating a court of industrial relations, Laws 1920, c. 29.* State v. Howat, *107 Kan. 423;* State v. Howat, *109 Kan. 376;* Court of Industrial Relations v. Charles Wolff Packing Co., *109 Kan. 629.*

[21] *Industrial Disputes Investigation Act, 1907, 6–7 Edw. 7, c. 20, § § 56, 57.* Rex v. McGuire, *16 O. L. R. 522. 9–10 Edw. 7, c. 29. 8–9 Geo. 5, c. 27. 10–11 Geo. 5, c. 29.*

Picketing is illegal. Criminal Code, Canada, § 501; Krug Furniture Co. v. Union of Woodworkers, *5 O. L. R. 463;* Cotter v. Osborne, *18 Man. 471;* Vulcan Iron Works v. Winnipeg Lodge, *21 Man. 473;* Le Roi Mining Co. v. Rossland Miners Union, *8 B. C. 370. But see Rev. Stats., B. C., c. 228.*

[22] Commonwealth v. Hunt, *4 Met. 111; for earlier common law and statutory provisions see* Carew v. Rutherford, *106 Mass. 1, 14; 1 Weeden, Economic and Social History of New England, pp. 173, 334. Freud, Police Power, § 331; Commons, History of Labor in the United States, vol. 1, c. 5.*

[23] *For the boycott see note 28,* infra, *p. 364; and for peaceful picketing, note 29,* infra, *p. 365.*

In some jurisdictions the strike was considered an unlawful means of procuring the unionization of the shop,—see Plant v. Woods, *176 Mass. 492;* Pickett v. Walsh, *192 Mass. 572, 585;* Lucke v. Clothing Cutters' Assembly, *77 Md. 396;* Erdman v. Mitchell, *207 Pa. St. 79; Freund, Police Power, § 331;—while in others it was regarded as permissible,*—National Protective Association v. Cumming, *170 N.Y. 315;* Kemp v. Division No. 241, *255 Ill. 213;* Grant Construction Co. v. St. Paul Building Trades Council, *136 Minn. 167;* State v. Van Pelt, *136 N. Car. 633;* Jetton-Dekle Lumber Co. v. Mather, *53 Fla. 969;* Cohn & Roth Electric Co. v. Bricklayers Union, *92 Conn. 161.*

[24] *In some jurisdictions the officers of the national union, not being employees, are regarded as outsiders with no justification for their acts,*—Booth v. Burgess, *72 N.J. Eq. 181;* Jonas Class Co. v. Glass Bottle Blowers' Association, *72 N.J. Eq. 653; 77 N.J. Eq. 219. In other jurisdictions it is held that they are furthering a legitimate interest,—see* Allen v. Flood, *[1898] A. C. 1;* Jose v. Metallic Roofing Co., *[1908] A. C. 514, reversing 14 O. L. R. 156;* Gill Engraving Co. v. Doerr, *214 Fed. 111;* Lindsay & Co. v. Montana Federation of Labor, *37 Mont. 264. See* American Steel Foundries v. Tri-City Central Trades Council, ante, *184.*

[25] *In some jurisdictions the courts seek to localize the conflict by making it illegal to bring in any party beyond those between whom the original dispute arose,*—Burnham v. Dowd, *217 Mass. 351;* Booth v. Burgess, *72 N.J. Eq. 181;* Purvis v. United Brother-

sibly be exerted in order to induce the employer to yield to the demands of the workingmen. Courts were required, in the absence of legislation, to determine what the public welfare demanded;—whether it would not be best subserved by leaving the contestants free to resort to any means not involving a breach of the peace or injury to tangible property; whether it was consistent with the public interest that the contestants should be permitted to invoke the aid of others not directly interested in the matter in controversy; and to what extent incidental injury to persons not parties to the controversy should be held justifiable.

The earliest reported American decision on peaceful picketing appears to have been rendered in 1888[26]; the earliest on boycotting in 1886.[27] By no great majority the prevailing judicial opinion in America declares the boycott as commonly practiced an illegal means[28] (see *Duplex Printing Press*

hood, *214 Pa. St. 348;—in other jurisdictions it is considered that anyone having business relations with either party which bear on the matter in controversy has violated his neutrality and is subject to reprisal from the union which is carrying on the struggle,—* Bossert *v.* Dhuy, *221 N.Y. 342;* Master Builders' Association *v.* Domascio, *16 Colo. App. 25;* Pierce *v.* Stablemen's Union, *156 Cal. 70, 76;* Cohn & Roth Electric Co. *v.* Bricklayers Union, *92 Conn. 161;* Gill Engraving Co. *v.* Doerr, *214 Fed. 111;* Grant Construction Co. *v.* St. Paul Building Trades Council, *136 Minn. 167. See 31 Harv. Law Rev. 482, and* Auburn Draying Co. *v.* Wardell, *227 N.Y. 1 for limitations.*

*Again, in some States it is unlawful to resort to the method of notifying persons that a strike will occur if a non-union employer or his product is employed,—*Booth *v.* Burgess, *72 N.J. Eq. 181;* Gray *v.* Building Trades Council, *91 Minn. 171;—while in other States it is lawful,—*Cohn & Roth Electric Co. *v.* Bricklayers Union, *92 Conn. 161, 167;* Bossert *v.* Dhuy, *221 N.Y. 342.*

26 Sherry *v.* Perkins, *147 Mass. 212; but the doctrine was not established until eight years later,* Vegelahn *v.* Guntner, *167 Mass. 92.*

27 *The earliest reported cases seem to be* People *v.* Wilzig, *4 N.Y. Crim. 403; and* People *v.* Kostka, *4 N.Y. Crim. 429, both of which occurred in June, 1886; the leading case of* State *v.* Glidden, *55 Conn. 46, came the next year. Laidler, however, speaks of an unreported case in 1840; see Laidler, Boycotts and the Labor Struggle, p. 70; see also Commons, History of Labor in the United States, vol. 2, pp. 267, 317, 364.*

28 *Some of the difference of opinion results from a difference in definition. A boycott is sometimes defined so as to entail violence or malicious oppression,* State *v.* Glidden, *55 Conn. 46; while in other cases it is simply pressure exerted by abstention from business relations,* Mills *v.* United States Printing Co., *99 App. Div. 605, affd. 199 N.Y. 76. The terms primary and secondary as describing the boycott are also of uncertain content. Only a boycott that is free of violence or malevolence is anywhere held to be lawful. This peaceful boycott in support of a* bona fide *industrial conflict, however, is not everywhere held lawful, and its lawfulness often is held to depend on whether it is used against the industrial antagonist directly (primary boycott) or against an outsider because of his influence on or connection with the industrial antagonist (secondary boycott). Holding the boycott, primary and secondary, illegal:* Wilson *v.* Hey, *232 Ill. 389;* Beck *v.* Railway Teamsters' Union, *118 Mich. 497;* Gray *v.* Building Trades Council, *91 Minn. 171;* Booth *v.* Burgess, *72 N.J. Eq. 181;* Purvis *v.* United Brotherhood, *214 Pa. St. 348;* Patch Manufacturing Co. *v.* Protection Lodge, *77 Vt. 294;* State *v.* Glidden, *55 Conn. 46;* Crump *v.* Commonwealth, *84 Va. 927, 939;* Jensen *v.* Cooks', etc. Union, *39 Wash. 531;* Webb *v.* Cooks', etc. Union, *205 S. W. (Tex.) 465;* Seubert *v.* Reiff, *164 N.Y.S. 522;* American Federation of Labor *v.* Buck's Stove & Range Co., *33 App. D.C. 83;* Burnham *v.* Dowd, *217 Mass. 351;* My Maryland Lodge *v.* Adt. *100 Md. 238.*

Holding primary boycott legal: Foster *v.* Retail Clerks' Association, *78 N.Y.S. 860, 867;* Butterick Publishing Co. *v.* Typographical Union, *100 N.Y.S. 292;* Gill Engraving Co. *v.* Doerr, *214 Fed. 111;* Empire Theatre Co. *v.* Cloke, *53 Mont. 183;* Steffes *v.* Motion Picture Union, *136 Minn. 200;* Stoner *v.* Robert, *43 Wash. (D.C.) L. Rep. 437;* Guethler *v.* Altman, *26 Ind. App. 587;* Pierce *v.* Stablemen's Union, *156 Cal. 70;* Riggs *v.* Cincinnati Waiters, *5 Ohio Nisi Prius, 386;* McCormick *v.* Local Union, *13 Ohio Cir. Ct. (N.S.) 545;* Ex parte Sweitzer, *13 Okl. Cr. 154. See Laws of Utah, 1917, c. 68;* Root *v.* Anderson, *207 S. W. (Mo.) 255.*

Holding secondary boycott legal: Bossert *v.* Dhuy, *221 N.Y. 342–though compare* Auburn Draying Co. *v.* Wardell, *227*

Co. v. *Deering,* 254 U.S. 443), while it inclines towards the legality of peaceful picketing.[29] See *American Steel Foundries* v. *Tri-City Central Trades Council, ante,* 184. But in some of the States, notably New York, both peaceful picketing and the boycott are declared permissible.[30] Judges, being thus called upon to exercise a quasi-legislative function and weigh relative social values, naturally differed in their conclusions on such questions.[31]

In England, observance of the rules of the contest has been enforced by the courts almost wholly through the criminal law or through actions at law for compensation. An injunction was granted in a labor dispute as early as 1868.[32] But in England resort to the injunction has not been frequent and it has played no appreciable part there in the conflict between capital and labor. In America the injunction did not secure recognition as a possible remedy until 1888.[33] When a few years later its use became extensive and conspicuous, the controversy over the remedy overshadowed in bitterness the question of the relative substantive rights of the parties. In the storms of protest against this use many thoughtful lawyers joined.[34] The equitable remedy, although applied in accordance with established practice, involved incidents which, it was asserted, endangered the personal lib-

N.Y. 1; Stoner *v.* Robert, *43 Wash. (D.C.) L. Rep. 437;* Lindsay & Co. *v.* Montana Federation of Labor, *37 Mont. 264;* Pierce *v.* Stablemen's Union, *156 Cal. 70, 76;* Parkinson Co. *v.* Building Trades Council, *154 Cal. 581; see* Marx & Haas Jeans Clothing Co. *v.* Watson, *168 Mo. 133.*

29 *Holding picketing in itself illegal:*—Vegelahn *v.* Guntner, *167 Mass. 92;* Pierce *v.* Stablemen's Union, *156 Cal. 70;* Barnes & Co. *v.* Chicago Typographical Union, *232 Ill. 424;* Lyon & Healy *v.* Piano, etc. Workers' Union, *289 Ill. 176;* Beck *v.* Railway Teamsters' Union, *118 Mich. 497;* Clarage *v.* Luphringer, *202 Mich. 612;* Baldwin Lumber Co. *v.* Brotherhood of Teamsters, etc., *91 N.J. Eq. 240;* Baasch *v.* Cooks Union, *99 Wash. 378;* Webb *v.* Cooks', etc., Union, *205 S.W. (Tex.) 465; the Washington Act, 1915, c. 181, declaring picketing to be unlawful, was defeated on referendum in 1916;* Atchison, Topeka & Santa Fe Ry. Co. *v.* Gee, *139 Fed. 582.*

Stating that peaceful picketing is lawful:—Riggs *v.* Cincinnati Waiters, *5 Ohio Nisi Prius, 386;* McCormick *v.* Local Union, *13 Ohio Cir. Ct. (N.S.) 545;* Jones *v.* Van Winkle Machine Works, *131 Ga. 336, 340;* Karges Furniture Co. *v.* Amalgamated, etc., Union, *165 Ind. 421, 430, 431;* Everett Waddey Co. *v.* Richmond Typographical Union, *105 Va. 188, 197;* Steffes *v.* Motion Picture Union, *136 Minn. 200,—see also Laws 1917, c. 493;* Stoner *v.* Robert, *43 Wash. (D.C.) L. Rep. 437;* Empire Theatre Co. *v.* Cloke, *53 Mont. 183;* Mills *v.* United States Printing Co., *99 App. Div. 605, affd. 199 N.Y. 76;* Ex parte Sweitzer, *13 Okl. Cr. 154;* White Mountain Freezer Co. *v.* Murphy, *78 N.H.* 398; *see Utah, Laws of 1917, c. 68;* American Engineering Co. *v.* International Moulders Union, *25 Pa. Dist. 564;* Iron Molders' Union *v.* Allis-Chalmers Co., *166 Fed. 45;* St. Louis *v. Gloner, 210 Mo. 502.*

30 Mills *v.* United States Printing Co., *99 App. Div. 605, affd. 199 N.Y. 76; see also cases in note 29,* supra, *from Ohio, Minnesota, Montana, and Oklahoma.*

31 *Compare:*—Plant *v.* Woods, *176 Mass. 492, 502, last paragraph, with* Cohn & Roth Electric Co. *v.* Bricklayers Union, *92 Conn. 161, 167, and,* Bossert *v.* Dhuy, *221 N.Y. 342, 359. See Geldart, The Present Law of Trade Unions and Trade Disputes, p. 24; Hoxie, Trade Unionism in the United States, p. 231; "Strikes and Boycotts", 34 Harv. Law Rev. 880.*

32 Springhead Spinning Co. *v.* Riley, *L. R. 6 Eq. 551.*

33 *The earliest case of importance was* Sherry *v.* Perkins, *147 Mass. 212 (1888). But injunctions were granted four or five years earlier. Commons, History of Labor in the United States, vol. 2, p. 504.*

34 *"Government by Injunction" by W. H. Dunbar, 13 Law Quarterly Review, 347; "Government by Injunction," by Charles Noble Gregory, 11 Harv. Law Rev. 487; "Injunction and Organized Labor," by Charles C. Allen, 28 Am. Law Rev. 828; "The Modern Use of Injunctions," by F. J. Stimson, 10 Pol. Sci. Quarterly, 189; "Strikes and Courts of Equity," by William Draper Lewis, 46 Am. Law Reg. 1; "Government by Injunction," by Percy L. Edwards, 57 Albany Law Journal, 8; "The Abuses of Injunction," by Samuel Seabury, 29 Arena, 561; "Government by Injunction," by Cornelius H. Fauntleroy, 69 Cent. Law Journal, 129; "Government by Injunction," by Thomas F. Hargis, 4 Amer. Fed. 227. See Report of U.S. Industrial Commission (1901) vol. XVII, p. 611.*

erty of wage-earners. The acts enjoined were frequently, perhaps usually, acts which were already crimes at common law or had been made so by statutes. The issues in litigation arising out of trade disputes related largely to questions of fact. But in equity issues of fact as of law were tried by a single judge, sitting without a jury. Charges of violating an injunction were often heard on affidavits merely, without the opportunity of confronting or cross-examining witnesses.[35] Men found guilty of contempt were committed in the judge's discretion, without either a statutory limit upon the length of the imprisonment, or the opportunity of effective review on appeal, or the right to release on bail pending possible revisory proceedings.[36] The effect of the proceeding upon the individual was substantially the same as if he had been successfully prosecuted for a crime; but he was denied, in the course of the equity proceedings, those rights which by the Constitution are commonly secured to persons charged with a crime.

It was asserted that in these proceedings an alleged danger to property, always incidental and at times insignificant, was often laid hold of to enable the penalties of the criminal law to be enforced expeditiously without that protection to the liberty of the individual which the Bill of Rights was designed to afford; that through such proceedings a single judge often usurped the functions not only of the jury but of the police department; that, in prescribing the conditions under which strikes were permissible and how they might be carried out, he usurped also the powers of the legislature; and that incidentally he abridged the constitutional rights of individuals to free speech, to a free press and to peaceful assembly.

It was urged that the real motive in seeking the injunction was not ordinarily to prevent property from being injured nor to protect the owner in its use, but to endow property with active, militant power which would make it dominant over men. In other words, that, under the guise of protecting property rights, the employer was seeking sovereign power. And many disinterested men, solicitous only for the public welfare, believed that the law of property was not appropriate for dealing with the forces beneath social unrest; that in this vast struggle it was unwise to throw the power of the State on one side or the other according to principles deduced from that law; that the problem of the control and conduct of industry demanded a solution of its own; and that, pending the ascertainment of new principles to govern industry, it was wiser for the State not to interfere in industrial struggles by the issuance of an injunction.[37]

After the constitutionality and the propriety of the use of the injunction in labor disputes was established judicially, those who opposed the practice sought the aid of Congress and of state legislatures. The bills introduced varied in character and in scope. Many dealt merely with rights; and, of these, some declared, in effect, that no act done in furtherance of a labor dispute by a combination of workingmen should be held illegal, unless it would have been so if done by a single individual; while others purported to legalize specific practices, like boycotting or picketing. Other bills dealt

[35] *In* Long *v.* Bricklayers, etc. Union, *17 Pa. Dist. 984, the judge prefaced his opinion as follows, "Hardly anything of greater private or public gravity is ever presented to the court, and yet these matters are constantly receiving adjudication without a single witness brought before the judge. It is a bad practice. I confess my inability to determine with any satisfaction from an inspection of inanimate manuscript, questions of veracity. In disposing of the present rule, I am compelled to find, as best I may from perusing two hundred and thirty-five lifeless typewritten pages of conflicting evidence, the facts which must determine respondent's guilt or innocence on the quasi-criminal charge of contempt."*

[36] Hake *v.* People, *230 Ill. 174, 196, discretion of judge;* Tinsley *v.* Anderson, *171 U.S. 101, 107–108, unlimited commitment;* State *v.* Erickson, *66 Wash. 639, 641;* State *v.* Chouteau County Court, *51 Mont. 337, 342;* Scoric *v.* United States, *217 Fed. 871, scope of review;* People *v.* Tefft, *3 Cow. (N.Y.) 340,* Matter of Vanderbilt, *4 Johns. Ch. (N.Y.) 57, admission to bail within discretion of judge.*

[37] *See Final Report of the (U.S.) Industrial Commission (1902); Final Report of the (U.S.) Commission on Industrial Relations (1915), (Sen. Doc. 415, 64th Cong., 1st sess.), vol. 1, pp. 52–53, 90–92, vol. 11, testimony of Mr. Gilbert E. Roe, p. 10477; testimony of Mr. Arthur Woods, p. 10550; testimony of Dr. Frank Goodnow, p. 10599. American Federationist, vol. 7, p. 350; vol. 9, p. 685; vol. 15, p. 976.*

merely with the remedy; and of these, some undertook practically to abolish the use of the injunction in labor disputes, while some merely limited its use either by prohibiting its issue under certain conditions or by denying power to restrain certain acts. Some bills undertook to modify both rights and remedies.[38] These legislative proposals occupied the attention of Congress during every session but one in the twenty years between 1894 and 1914.[39] Reports recommending such legislation were repeatedly made by the Judiciary Committee of the House or that of the Senate; and at some sessions by both.[40] Prior to 1914, legislation of this character had at several sessions passed the House;[41] and in that year Congress passed and the President approved the Clayton Act, § 20 of which is substantially the same as Paragraph 1464 of the Arizona Civil Code. Act of October 15, 1914, c. 323, 38 Stat. 730, 738.

Such was the diversity of view concerning peaceful picketing and the boycott expressed in judicial decisions and legislation in English-speaking countries when in 1913 the new State of Arizona, in establishing its judicial system, limited the use of the injunction and when in 1918 its Supreme Court was called upon to declare for the first time the law of Arizona on these subjects. The case of *Truax* v. *Bisbee Local No. 380*, 19 Ariz. 379, presented facts identical with those of the case at bar.[42] In that case the Supreme Court made its decision on four controverted points of law. In the first place, it held that the officials of the union were not outsiders with no justification for their acts (19 Ariz. 379, 390).[43] In the second place, rejecting the view held by the federal courts and the majority of the state courts on the illegality of the boycott, it specifically accepted the law of New York, Montana and California, citing the decisions of those States (19 Ariz. 379, 388, 390).[44] In the third place, it rejected the law of New Jersey, Minnesota and Pennsylvania that it is

[38] *53rd Congress: S. 1563, S. 1898, S. 2253, H. R. 7362, H. R. 7363; 54th Congress: S. 237, S. 1750, S. 2984, H. R. 319; 56th Congress: S. 4233, H. R. 8917; 57th Congress: S. 1118, S. 4553, H. R. 9678, H. R. 11060; 58th Congress: H. R. 89, H. R. 1234, H. R. 4063, H. R. 6782, H. R. 8136, H. R. 18327; 59th Congress: S. 2829, H. R. 4445, H. R. 9328, H. R. 17976, H. R. 18171, H. R. 18446, H. R. 18752; 60th Congress: S. 4533, S. 4727, S. 5888, H. R. 69, H. R. 94, H. R. 17137, H. R. 21358, H. R. 21359, H. R. 21454, H. R. 21489, H. R. 21539, H. R. 21629, H. R. 21991, H. R. 22010, H. R. 22032, H. R. 22298, H. R. 26300, H. R. 24781, H. R. 36609; 61st Congress: S. 3291, S. 4481, H. R. 3058, H. R. 9766, H. R. 10890, H. R. 16026, H. R. 18410, H. R. 20486, H. R. 20680, H. R. 20827, H. R. 21334, H. R. 22566; 62nd Congress: S. 6266, H. R. 4015, H. R. 4651, H. R. 5328, H. R. 5606, H. R. 9435, H. R. 11032, H. R. 23189, H. R. 21486, H. R. 21595, H. R. 22208, H. R. 22349, H. R. 22354, H. R. 22355, H. R. 23635; 63rd Congress: S. 927, H. R. 1873, H. R. 4659, H. R. 5484, H. R. 15657 —which became the Clayton Act.*

[39] *See note 38,* supra. *Also 53rd Congress: resolutions to investigate the use of the injunction in certain cases, 26 Cong. Rec. 2466; 56th Congress: debate, 4 Cong. Rec. 2589; 60th Congress: hearings, Sen. Doc. 525; special message of the President, Sen. Doc. 213, 42 Cong. Rec. 1347; papers relating to injunctions in labor cases, Sen. Docs. 504 and 524; 61st Congress: debate, 45 Cong. Rec. 343; 62nd Congress: debate, 48 Cong. Rec. 6415–6470; hearings, Sen. Doc. 944; petitions, Sen. Doc. 440; hearings before the House Committee on the Judiciary, Jan. 11, 17–19, February 8, 14, 1912; hearings before a subcommittee of Senate Committee on the Judiciary, 62nd Congress, 2nd sess.; 63rd Congress, see debates on H. R. 15657 (the Clayton Act).*

[40] *54th Congress, House Report No. 2471; 56th Congress, House Report No. 1987, 2007; 57th Congress, Senate Report No. 1650, House Report No. 1522; 62nd Congress, House Report No. 612; 63rd Congress, Senate Report No. 698, House Report No. 627, Conference Report, Senate Document 585.*

[41] *In the 57th Congress, H. R. 11060 passed the House, 35 Cong. Rec. 4995. In the 62nd Congress, H. R. 23635 passed the House, 48 Cong. Rec. 6470, 6471.*

[42] *In this case the Supreme Court of Arizona said: "This action is founded upon the identical facts upon which the case of* Truax v. Bisbee Local No. 380, *19 Ariz. 379, was founded . . . The questions presented in this record were necessarily decided by this court in the former hearing of the matter."* Truax v. Corrigan, *20 Ariz. 7, 8.*

[43] *See note 24, p. 362,* supra.

[44] *See note 28, p. 364,* supra.

illegal to circularize an employer's customers, and again adopted the rule declared in the decisions of the courts of New York, Montana, California and Connecticut (19 Ariz. 379, 389).[45] In deciding these three points the Supreme Court of Arizona made a choice between well-established precedents laid down on either side by some of the strongest courts in the country. Can this court say that thereby it deprived the plaintiff of his property without due process of law?

The fourth question requiring decision was whether peaceful picketing should be deemed legal. Here, too, each of the opposing views had the support of decisions of strong courts.[46] If the Arizona court had decided that by the common law of the State the defendants might peacefully picket the plaintiffs, its decision, like those of the courts of Ohio, Minnesota, Montana, New York, Oklahoma and New Hampshire, would surely not have been open to objection under the Federal Constitution; for this court has recently held that peaceful picketing is not unlawful. *American Steel Foundries* v. *Tri-City Central Trades Council, supra.* The Supreme Court of Arizona found it unnecessary to determine what was the common law of the State on that subject, because it construed Paragraph 1464 of the Civil Code as declaring peaceful picketing to be legal. In the case at bar, commenting on the earlier case, the court said: "The statute adopts the view of a number of courts which have held 'picketing,' if peaceably carried on for a lawful purpose, to be no violation of any legal right of the party whose place of business is 'picketed,' and whether as a fact the picketing is carried on by peaceful means, as against the other view, taken by the federal courts and many of the state courts, that picketing is *per se* unlawful." Shortly before that decision the Criminal Court of Appeals of Oklahoma had placed a similar construction upon a statute of that State, declaring that "the doctrine [that picketing is not *per se* unlawful] represents the trend of legal thought of modern times, and is specifically reflected in the statute above construed." *Ex parte Sweitzer,* 13 Okl. Cr. 154, 160. See *St. Louis* v. *Gloner,* 210 Mo. 502. A State, which despite the Fourteenth Amendment possesses the power to impose on employers without fault unlimited liability for injuries suffered by employees,[47] and to limit the freedom of contract of some employers and not of others,[48] surely does not lack the power to select for its citizens that one of conflicting views on boycott by peaceful picketing which its legislature and highest court consider will best meet its conditions and secure the public welfare.

The Supreme Court of Arizona, having held as a rule of substantive law that the boycott as here practiced was legal at common law; and that the picketing was peaceful and, hence, legal under the statute (whether or not it was legal at common law), necessarily denied the injunction, since, in its opinion, the defendants had committed no legal wrong and were threatening none. But even if this court should hold that an employer has a constitutional right to be free from interference by such a boycott or that the picketing practiced was not in fact peaceful, it does not follow that Arizona would lack the power to refuse to protect that right by injunction. For it is clear that the refusal of an equitable remedy for a tort is not necessarily a denial of due process of law. And it seems to be equally clear that such refusal is not necessarily arbitrary and unreasonable when applied to incidents of the relation of employer and employee. The considerations which show that the refusal is not arbitrary or unreasonable show likewise that such refusal does not necessarily constitute a denial of equal protection of the laws merely because some, or even the same, property rights which are excluded by this statute from protection by injunction, receive such protection under other circumstances, or between persons standing in different relations. The acknowledged legislative discretion exerted in classification, so frequently applied in defining rights, extends equally to the grant of remedies.[49] It is for the legislature

[45] *See note 25, p. 362,* supra, *2nd paragraph; also* Lindsay & Co. *v.* Montana Federation of Labor, *37 Mont. 264;* Parkinson Co. *v.* Building Trades Council, *154 Cal. 581.*

[46] *See note 29, p. 365,* supra.

[47] Arizona Employers' Liability Cases, *250 U.S. 400.*

[48] Dominion Hotel *v.* Arizona, *249 U.S. 265.*

[49] *In* Gooch *v.* Stephenson, *1 Shepley (Me.) 371 (1836), the plaintiff attacked as unconstitutional a statute declaring that no action of trespass should be brought against an owner of cattle breaking through an insufficient fence. The court,* inter alia, *said:*

"It has been insisted that justice and the security of rights is best promoted by main-

to say—within the broad limits of the discretion which it possesses—whether or not the remedy for a wrong shall be both criminal and civil and whether or not it shall be both at law and in equity.

A State is free since the adoption of the Fourteenth Amendment, as it was before, not only to determine what system of law shall prevail in it, but, also, by what processes legal rights may be asserted, and in what courts they may be enforced. *Missouri* v. *Lewis,* 101 U.S. 22, 31; *Iowa Central Ry. Co.* v. *Iowa,* 160 U.S. 389. As a State may adopt or reject trial by jury, *Walker* v. *Sauvinet,* 92 U.S. 90; or adopting it may retain or discard its customary incidents, *Hayes* v. *Missouri,* 120 U.S. 68; *Brown* v. *New Jersey,* 175 U.S. 172; *Maxwell* v. *Dow,* 176 U.S. 581; as a State may grant or withhold review of a decision by appeal, *Reetz* v. *Michigan,* 188 U.S. 505; so it may determine for itself, from time to time, whether the protection which it affords to property rights through its courts shall be given by means of the preventive remedy or exclusively by an action at law for compensation.

Nor is a State obliged to protect all property rights by injunction merely because it protects some, even if the attending circumstances are in some respects similar. The restraining power of equity might conceivably be applied to every intended violation of a legal right. On grounds of expediency its application is commonly denied in cases where there is a remedy at law which is deemed legally adequate. But an injunction has been denied on grounds of expediency in many cases where the remedy at law is confessedly not adequate. This occurs whenever a dominant public interest is deemed to require that the preventive remedy, otherwise available for the protection of private rights, be refused and the injured party left to such remedy as courts of law may afford. Thus, courts ordinarily refuse, perhaps in the interest of free speech, to restrain actionable libels. *Boston Diatite Co.* v. *Florence Manufacturing Co.,* 114 Mass. 69; *Prudential Assurance Co.* v. *Knott,* L. R. 10 Ch. App. 142. In the interest of personal liberty they ordinarily refuse to enforce specifically, by mandatory injunction or otherwise, obligations involving personal service. *Arthur* v. *Oakes,* 63 Fed. 310, 318; *Davis* v. *Foreman,* [1894] 3 Ch. 654, 657; *Gossard* v. *Crosby,* 132 Ia. 155, 163, 164. In the desire to preserve the separation of governmental powers they have declined to protect by injunction mere political rights, *Giles* v. *Harris,* 189 U.S. 475; and have refused to interfere with the operations of the police department. *Davis* v. *American Society for the Prevention of Cruelty to Animals,* 75 N.Y. 362; *Delaney* v. *Flood,* 183 N.Y. 323; compare *Bisbee* v. *Arizona Insurance Agency,* 14 Ariz. 313. Instances are numerous where protection to property by way of injunction has been refused solely on the ground that serious public inconvenience would result from restraining the act complained of. Such, for example, was the case where a neighboring land owner sought to restrain a smelter from polluting the air, but that relief, if granted, would have necessitated shutting down the plant and this would have destroyed the business and impaired the means of livelihood of a large community.[50] There are also numerous instances where the circumstances would, according to general equity practice, have justified the issue of an injunction, but it was refused solely because the right sought to be enforced was created by statute, and the courts, applying a familiar rule, held that the remedy provided by the statute was exclusive.[51]

---

taining the remedy as it before existed; but that is an argument which addresses itself to the legislative power, and not to the judicial. . . . It was for the legislature to determine what protection should be thrown around this species of property; . . . and where he [the owner] might invoke the aid of courts of justice. They have no power to take away vested rights; but they may regulate their enjoyment."

In this case the public importance of good fences was held to justify the denial of an existing remedy for injuries to property or a curtailment of the right.

50 *See* McCarthy *v.* Bunker Hill & Sullivan Mining Co., *164 Fed. 927;* Bliss *v.* Anaconda Copper Mining Co., *167 Fed. 342; 186 Fed. 789;* Cameron Furnace Co. *v.* Pennsylvania Canal Co., *2 Pearson (Pa.) 208;* Johnson *v.* United Railways Co., *227 Mo. 423, 450;* Conger *v.* New York, W. S. & B. R. R. Co., *120 N.Y. 29;* Wilkins *v.* Diven, *106 Kan. 283;* Marconi Wireless Telegraph Co. *v.* Simon, *227 Fed. 906; 231 Fed. 1021.*

51 Dimmick *v.* Delaware, Lackawanna & Western R. R. Co., *180 Pa. St. 468;* Curran *v.* Delano, *235 Pa. St. 478;* Janney *v.* Buell, *55 Ala. 408; the mechanics' lien, for in-*

Such limitations upon the use of the injunction for the protection of private rights have ordinarily been imposed in the interest of the public by the court acting in the exercise of its broad discretion. But, in some instances, the denial of the preventive remedy because of a public interest deemed paramount, has been expressly commanded by statute. Thus, the courts of the United States have been prohibited from staying proceedings in any court of a State, Judicial Code, § 265; and also from enjoining the illegal assessment and collection of taxes. Revised Statutes, § 3224; *Snyder* v. *Marks,* 109 U.S. 189; *Dodge* v. *Osborn,* 240 U.S. 118. What Congress can do in curtailing the equity power of the federal courts, state legislatures may do in curtailing equity powers of the state courts; unless prevented by the constitution of the State. In other words States are free since the adoption of the Fourteenth Amendment as they were before, either to expand or to contract their equity jurisdiction. The denial of the more adequate equitable remedy for private wrongs is in essence an exercise of the police power, by which, in the interest of the public and in order to preserve the liberty and the property of the great majority of the citizens of a State, rights of property and the liberty of the individual must be remoulded, from time to time, to meet the changing needs of society.

For these reasons, as well as for others stated by Mr. Justice Holmes and Mr. Justice Pitney, [*ante,* 342, 344,] in which I concur, the judgment of the Supreme Court of Arizona should, in my opinion, be affirmed:—first, because in permitting damage to be inflicted by means of boycott and peaceful picketing Arizona did not deprive the plaintiffs of property without due process of law or deny them equal protection of the laws; and secondly, because, if Arizona was constitutionally prohibited from adopting this rule of substantive law, it was still free to restrict the extraordinary remedies of equity where it considered their exercise to be detrimental to the public welfare, since such restriction was not a denial to the employer either of due process of law or of equal protection of the laws.

---

stance, is not protected by equitable remedies but only by statutory provisions, Chandler *v.* Hanna, *73 Ala. 390;* Walker *v.* Daimwood, *80 Ala. 245; Phillips on Mechanics Liens, § § 307, 308.*

O'GORMAN AND YOUNG v. HARTFORD FIRE INSURANCE CO., 282 U.S. 251 (1931)

A New Jersey statute of 1928 regulated the commissions paid fire insurance agents. O'Gorman and Young brought suit to recover monies paid in excess of the rates established by the commission. Could the New Jersey statutes be sustained under the police power? For the Court Justice Brandeis held that the "business of insurance is so far affected with a public interest that the State may regulate the rates, and likewise the relations of those engaged in the business," and that the statute, "dealing with a subject clearly within the police power, can not be declared void upon the ground that the specific method of regulation prescribed is unreasonable"—in the absence of any factual foundation in the record to overcome the presumption of constitutionality. Justices Van Devanter, McReynolds, Sutherland, and Butler dissented, proclaiming the sanctity of the "general right to enter into contract," under the liberty clause of the Fourteenth Amendment, and maintaining that "the right to regulate a business does not necessarily imply power . . . to trespass on the duties of private management."

MR. JUSTICE BRANDEIS delivered the opinion of the Court.

These cases, which are here on appeals from the highest court of New Jersey, were argued together. They present the question whether the following statutory provision, effective March 29, 1928, is consistent with the due process clause of the Fourteenth Amendment:

"In order that rates of insurance against the hazards of fire shall be reasonable it shall be unlawful for any such insurer licensed in this State to . . . to allow . . . any commission . . . in excess of a reasonable amount to any person for acting as its agent in respect to any class of such insurance, nor . . . to allow . . . any commission . . . to any person for acting as its local agent in respect to any class of such insurance, in excess of that . . . allowed to any one of its local agents on such risks in this State." (New Jersey Laws 1928, c. 128, p. 258.)

In each case, O'Gorman and Young, Inc., a domestic corporation licensed as an insurance broker, sues a licensed foreign fire insurance company to recover a balance alleged to be due for services performed as local agent at Newark after the effective date of the statute. In the *Phoenix Assurance Company* case, the complaint is on a contract terminable at will, made prior to the enactment of the statute, by which the company agreed to pay to the agent twenty-five per cent. of the premiums. In the *Hartford Fire Insurance Company* case, the complaint is on a contract, made after the enactment of the statute, by which the defendant agreed to pay as compensation "what such services were reasonably worth"; and the complaint alleges that the services were reasonably worth twenty-five per cent. of the premiums. Each complaint alleges that the defendant has paid the plaintiff only twenty per cent. of the premiums. Each answer admits the facts alleged in the complaint. As a defense, it sets up the statute and the fact that the defendant had at the date of its enactment, and ever since has had, several persons acting as its local agents within the State to whom the compensation allowed in respect to the same class of business has been only twenty per cent. of the premiums.

Each case was heard upon a motion to strike out the answer and for judgment on the ground that the statute is void under the due process clause of the Fourteenth Amendment. In each case the trial court denied the motion and entered judgment against the plaintiff, the facts alleged in the answer being admitted. In an opinion discussing the question presented, that court said:

"Our statute provides that the rates for fire insurance 'shall be reasonable.' Since the commissions paid to local agents naturally enter into the cost of such insurance to the public, and therefore influence the rates which must be charged to the public for such insurance, it is within the police power of the state to require that the commissions must be reasonable, otherwise such large commissions might be allowed as to impair the financial stability of the insurance companies, and thus imperil their ability to meet their financial obligations to their policy holders.

"Since twenty per cent. is the amount of commissions paid to some of its local agents, the effect of this legislation is to determine that a commission in excess of that is unreasonable. The presumption is in favor of the reasonableness of the law until the contrary is made to appear.

"In the facts or argument, there is nothing to overcome that presumption. . . ." 105 N.J.L. 645.[1]

On that opinion the Court of Errors and Appeals affirmed the judgments of the trial court. 105 N.J.L. 642. We think it was right in so doing.

The business of insurance is so far affected with a public interest that the State may regulate the rates, *German Alliance Insurance Co.* v. *Lewis,* 233 U.S. 389; and

[1] *It is the settled practice in New Jersey that where the subject regulated is properly within the scope of the police power of the State, a charge of discrimination or lack of reasonable relation between the object of the act and the means employed, must be supported by facts in the record sufficient to overcome the general presumption of constitutionality.* Hopper *v.* Stack, *69 N.J.L. 562;* Meehan *v.* Board of Excise Commissioners, *75 N.J.L. 557, 562;* Commercial Trust Co. *v.* Hudson County Board, *86 N.J.L. 424, affirmed, 87 N.J.L. 179;* State *v.* Sutton, *83 N.J.L. 46, 49, affirmed, 87 N.J.L. 192, 193, affirmed, 244 U.S. 258;* Public Service Ry. Co. *v.* Public Utility Commissioners, *89 N.J.L. 24, 27, 28, affirmed, 254 U.S. 394; compare* Thorne *v.* Town of Kearny, *100 N.J.L. 228, affirmed sub. nom.* Thorne *v.* Casale, *101 N.J.L. 18.*

likewise the relations of those engaged in the business, *La Tourette* v. *McMaster*, 248 U.S. 465; *Stipcich* v. *Metropolitan Life Insurance Co.*, 277 U.S. 311, 320. Compare *McCarter* v. *Firemen's Insurance Co.*, 74 N. J. Eq. 372, 382. The agent's compensation, being a percentage of the premium, bears a direct relation to the rate charged the insured. The percentage commonly allowed is so large that it is a vital element in the rate structure and may seriously affect the adequacy of the rate. Excessive commissions may result in an unreasonably high rate level or in impairment of the financial stability of the insurer. It was stated at the bar that the commission on some classes of insurance is as high as thirty-five per cent. Moreover, lack of a uniform scale of commissions allowed local agents for the same service may encourage unfair discrimination among policy holders by facilitating the forbidden practice of rebating. In the field of life insurance, such evils led long ago to legislative limitation of agents' commissions.[2]

The statute here questioned deals with a subject clearly within the scope of the police power. We are asked to declare it void on the ground that the specific method of regulation prescribed is unreasonable and hence deprives the plaintiff of due process of law. As underlying questions of fact may condition the constitutionality of legislation of this character, the presumption of constitutionality must prevail in the absence of some factual foundation of record for overthrowing the statute.[3] It does not appear upon the face of the statute, or from any facts of which the court must take judicial notice, that in New Jersey evils did not exist in the business of fire insurance for which this statutory provision was an appropriate remedy. The action of the legislature and of the highest court of the State indicates that such evils did exist.[4] The record is barren of any allegation of fact tending to show unreasonableness.

Affirmed.

[2] *Laws of New York, 1906, c. 326, § 97, pp. 794–797; Insurance Law of New York (Baldwin), 1930 Edition, § 97, pp. 96–101. See Report of Joint (Armstrong) Insurance Investigating Committee, Feb. 22, 1906, pp. 399–417; Laws of New Jersey, 1927, c. 167, pp. 324, 325; 1928, c. 128, p. 257.*

[3] Close *v.* Glenwood Cemetery, *107 U.S. 466, 475;* Powell *v.* Pennsylvania, *127 U.S. 678, 685;* Lindsley *v.* Natural Carbonic Gas Co., *220 U.S. 61, 79, 83;* Chicago Dock Co. *v.* Fraley, *228 U.S. 680, 687;* Rast *v.* Van Deman & Lewis Co., *240 U.S. 342, 357;* Wampler *v.* Lecompte, ante, *p. 172. Compare* Minnesota Rate Cases, *230 U.S. 352,* 461; *Henry Wolf Biklé, "Judicial determination of facts affecting the constitutional validity of legislative action." 3 Harv. L. Rev. 6.*

[4] *Compare* Heath & Mulligan Mfg. Co. *v.* Worst, *207 U.S. 338, 355;* Welch *v.* Swasey, *214 U.S. 91, 108;* Laurel Hill Cemetery *v.* San Francisco, 216 *U.S. 358, 365;* Adams *v.* Milwaukee, *228 U.S. 572, 583;* Barrett *v.* Indiana, *229 U.S. 26, 29;* Patsone *v.* Pennsylvania, *232 U.S. 138, 144;* Price *v.* Illinois, *238 U.S. 446, 452;* Bunting *v.* Oregon, *243 U.S. 426, 438;* Dominion Hotel *v.* Arizona, *249 U.S. 265, 268. The alleged existence of such evils throughout the United States led recently to an enquiry by the National Convention of Insurance Commissioners. See report of proceedings at annual meeting Sept. 9, 1930. The United States Daily, Supplement Sept. 23, 1930.*

John H. Clarke

☆ 1857–1945 ☆

APPOINTED BY

WOODROW WILSON

YEARS ON COURT

1916–1922

John H. Clarke

by

DAVID BURNER

JOHN HESSIN CLARKE is the only Justice in the annals of the Supreme Court to leave the bench while in good physical health in order to devote himself to an idealistic crusade. The idea of public service was always important to Clarke, who typifies one of the varied strains to be found in the Progressive Era.

Born on September 18, 1857, in New Lisbon, Ohio—the birthplace of Mark Hanna—John Clarke was of Protestant Irish ancestry on both sides. His father had emigrated from Ireland in 1830 and settled in New Lisbon. There he established a thriving law practice and became active in liberal Democratic politics. A founder of the first Protestant Episcopal parish in New Lisbon and judge of the County Court of Common Pleas, the elder Clarke occupied a position of high standing in the small town that was also the county seat. At an early age John knew his own career would have to embody the social responsibility his father's career exemplified.

The young Clarke went from New Lisbon high school to Western Reserve College, then a small school in Hudson, Ohio. Western Reserve's curriculum was at that time thoroughly traditional, and three years of classical literature sharpened Clarke's command of spoken and written English. Classroom debate quickened his public sense; once he argued for "Civil Liberty as Productive of Intellectual Excellence." He took pleasure in the writings of Walter Bagehot, but the stuffy religious tracts in the curriculum bored him and he was never formally religious. He was graduated Phi Beta Kappa in 1877. The next year he studied law under his father's guidance and in the fall of 1878 he passed the bar examination *cum laude;* two years later he received a Master of Arts from Western Reserve.

DAVID BURNER is Associate Professor of History at the State University of New York, Stony Brook. He is the author of The Politics of Provincialism: The Democratic Party in Transition, 1918–1932.

He settled down in New Lisbon to practice law with his father and John McVicker, but the economic growth of the town had slackened and in 1880 Clarke moved to Youngstown, where he opened a law office and also purchased a half interest in the Youngstown *Vindicator*. The paper, originally established as an organ of the local Democratic party, eventually guaranteed Clarke a lifetime of financial independence. Under his guidance, the *Vindicator* rose to prominence as a leading progressive newspaper. Journalism was a means to public service, and writing a labor of love; and the temper of Clarke's civic mind is exactly represented in his call for national civil service reform and for free local public libraries. The *Vindicator* was the only major paper in Ohio to support Senator George Pendleton's 1883 civil service bill. The newspaper business led Clarke, like so many prominent Ohioans of his time, into politics. A member of a Youngstown literary society, he won statewide fame in the late 1880's for his public lectures on Shakespeare and on James Russell Lowell. The family tradition of public service was ever at work within him and he became a leading Ohio Democrat. But another activity was at once complement and competitor to Clarke's public career; he was increasingly in demand as a legal adviser to corporations.

In Youngstown, Clarke represented the Pennsylvania and Erie Railroads. Law firms as far away as Chicago heard of Clarke's legal talents and offered him lucrative positions. He finally left Youngstown in 1897 to join the Cleveland firm of Williamson and Cushing; here he became a trial lawyer and general counsel of the Nickel Plate Railroad. Yet he insisted that he was a lawyer to corporations and not a corporation lawyer, and he retained a concern for the workingman. As an insider, he saw the way in which some companies, especially the railroads, cheated the public. His business and political life seemed at times to run at cross purposes; he urged a maximum limit to railroad fares, and he spoke for antitrust and anti-rebate legislation.

Although Clarke had an active interest in politics, he seems to have formed a slight aversion to public affairs. He once stated that "my own sense of security has been ministered by the fact that I have never been ambitious in the usual sense of the word. Such honors as I have held have come to me unsought. I did not go after them." In 1892 he was offered, by acclamation, the congressional nomination from the eighteenth district of Ohio, but declined it. In 1893, he was second in balloting for governor at the Cincinnati convention of the state Democratic party, although he had refused to allow the use of his name. Clarke's first important political venture came at the state Democratic convention in Columbus during September, 1894. He took it upon himself to oppose the incumbent Democratic senator, Calvin S. Brice, who had betrayed the party's pledge for tariff reduction. Clarke pressed for a resolution in favor of the direct election of senators—a reprimand to Brice, who had been chosen by a legislative caucus. Clarke orated eloquently in support of the measure: "What one of you looks to the Senate of the United States as a depository of the best intelligence, statesmanship or patriotism of the country?" he asked. "When a senator is to be elected, the question is no longer what are his talents, what service has he done the state, but what is he worth in dollars." Although the resolutions committee defeated his proposal, the convention itself adopted it in modified form.

In the spring of 1896 Clarke threw the weight of the Youngstown *Vindicator* against the anti-Catholic American Protective Association, which had made some headway toward capturing the local Republican organization. Here Clarke's victory was complete, for the city chose the paper's candidate for mayor. Later that same year, Clarke again became engaged in politics, this time in a more conservative stance.

Clarke was a Gold Bug. Although he owned stock in a silver mine, he remained enough of a nineteenth-century liberal to believe that the federal government should not tinker with the nation's currency. In 1896, Clarke served as a delegate to the Democratic National Convention in Chicago. He disagreed with his party colleagues on the silver question, and later in the same year accepted the chairmanship of the Ohio State Democratic Sound Money Convention. He was also a delegate at large from Ohio to the national convention of the Gold Democrats at Indianapolis. Clarke's opposition to Bryan may have had its larger reason in the fastidious and rational character of Clarke's reformism. Perhaps it was merely a distrust of radicalism or a fear of embracing panaceas in the midst of a depression; but his uneasiness in the company of Bryan may have had its deeper roots in a brand of class prejudice that resisted giving power to the masses. Free silver symbolized Populism, and Populism implied demagoguery, exemplified in the oratory of Jerry Simpson and Ben Tillman and akin to the industrial anarchy of the Homestead strike. The experience of bolting his party in 1896 left its mark on Clarke; realizing his impetuousness and dogmatism, he never again deserted the Democrats. Learning from his 1896 experience, he persuaded his Democratic friend Newton D. Baker not to denounce Franklin Roosevelt forty years later.

Clarke usually supported the work of Cleveland's reform mayor Tom L. Johnson, and it was during these early years of the twentieth century that he and Newton Baker became intimate friends. But Clarke also clashed openly with Johnson over stiff taxation of railroad property along Cleveland's lake front, which Clarke opposed. Clarke eventually shied away from the argument, which the courts finally decided in favor of the city. In another instance, Clarke again sided with the corporations. One June morning in 1892 young Annie Kistler and her father approached a train crossing in their horsedrawn buggy. An oncoming locomotive sounded its whistle, which apparently caused the horse to bolt across the tracks. The father was killed and the daughter, seriously injured, sued the railroad. Clarke, as attorney, insisted that the economic benefit of fast railroads was important enough to resist giving the right of way to buggies. The Court, adopting Clarke's argument, held the Kistlers negligent, since no state law regulated the speed of trains.

In *Vindicator* editorials Clarke had proposed impartial mediation between labor and capital. He blamed capital more than labor for the strikes of the

1890's, but he thought that all disputes should be submitted to compulsory arbitration. By about 1907 Clarke began to limit his work for the railroads, work in which he had favored property over personal rights and to which he had made essentially conservative contributions.

Clarke, the Progressive Era Democrat, supported reforms he would have opposed two decades earlier. Perhaps the better economic times had eased his fear of change. In any case he now advocated an increased national power to regulate diverse areas of economic and social life. In international affairs he opposed imperialism and joined Bryan in demanding Philippine independence.

In 1903 Clarke placed Tom Johnson in nomination for governor of Ohio and was himself nominated for the United States Senate. Clarke's opponent was Mark Hanna, a lawyer and spokesman for the corporations. Clarke now advocated direct election of senators, home-rule for cities, municipally-owned street railways, equalization of taxes, and publicity of campaign expenditures. He was the first candidate for an important office in Ohio to publish voluntarily a statement of his campaign expenses. Even had senators been directly elected by the people, Clarke would not have been a strong candidate; despite his skill as a public speaker, his silver hair and courtly manners, he lacked the common touch even more than Hanna, whom the heavily Republican legislature chose. One month after the election Hanna died, and in the voting to fill his unexpired term Clarke was defeated by Charles W. F. Dick, in an almost identical tally.

As the years passed, Clarke continued an uneasy relationship to the progressive Tom Johnson. A railway attorney from Cincinnati, Judson Harmon, met Clarke's approval in his successful race to be governor of Ohio but not Johnson's. In 1910 the Johnson circle chose Atlee Pomerene as Senate nominee, and Clarke remained in obscurity. Yet on balance his progressivism had not waned but had enlarged. In 1911 Clarke endorsed most of the liberal proposals of the day and particularly pressed for woman suffrage and mandatory civil service. He was chairman of the Ohio Short Ballot Association. In 1914 Clarke again tried for the Senate in what was to be the first direct election of an Ohio senator. This time, however, he dropped out early in the race in face of the candidacy of Timothy Hogan, a charming Irish courthouse politician.

In 1914 President Wilson appointed Clarke to the Federal District Court of the Northern District of Ohio, almost certainly at the recommendation of Newton D. Baker. A senatorial inquiry subjected Clarke's record to intense scrutiny. As opposition to his appointment developed among conservatives who distrusted his progressive views, more advanced liberals looked askance at his legal work which they thought would prejudice him in favor of corporations. In his new office—where, in keeping with his character, he expedited court business and insisted on punctuality—he was criticized for being impatient and abrupt, for expressing personal views in instructing the jury, and for favoring the defense. He was highly unpopular with the bar. Certainly his social views affected his decisions. Once he countermanded an order from the receiver of a railroad closing some of the company's shops, saying the decision was "neither a wise one, economically considered, nor was it a just one from a social point of view." Though Clarke frequently lectured attorneys on moral questions involved in the case at hand, he had a firm grasp of legal procedure and none of his cases was reversed for error in ruling on the admission of evidence. Of 652 cases tried before him only eleven were appealed, and of these only five were reversed.

Clarke's most distinctive innovation as federal judge was in the method of naturalizing aliens. On the last Friday of each month he held a reception in his courtroom to welcome applicants for citizenship. Orchestral music, patriotic songs, and an address by a prominent Clevelander comprised the hour-long ceremony. At the close, certificates of naturalization were presented; the audience pledged allegiance to the flag and sang "America." The receptions became so popular that they had to be closed to the general public.

In the spring of 1916 Charles Evans Hughes resigned from the Supreme Court to run for the presidency on the Republican ticket. For the vacated post Wilson considered Attorney General Tom Gregory and, according to one report, even Warren G. Harding; but he wanted a dependable progressive who was antitrust, and he settled upon Clarke.

But what kind of progressive had Clarke become by the time of his elevation in 1916? Because of his association with Tom Johnson, his contest against Mark Hanna, and the proximity of his appointment to that of Louis D. Brandeis, the new appointee had something of the reputation of a radical. He was not. He had always drawn the line at such things as the recall of judges, the single tax, and prohibition. A member of the Union Club of Cleveland, Clarke liked to shock the stand-pat Republicans with his unconventional views; yet he felt at home with such people and was decidedly uncomfortable in the presence of such men as Debs or Bryan. At the same time, he had moved fairly far to the left within the limits of a sound progressivism, and was prepared to back up a broad extension of state and national power. In his years on the Supreme Court he would enter a dissent supporting a child labor law, in *Hammer* v. *Dagenhart,* 247 U.S. 251 (1918), approve a prohibitory federal tax on narcotics, *United States* v. *Doremus,* 249 U.S. 86 (1919), uphold the constitutionality of the federal inheritance tax, in *New York Trust Co.* v. *Fisner,* 256 U.S. 345 (1921), and support an extension of the federal income tax to include stock dividends and capital gains, in *Peabody* v. *Eisner,* 247 U.S. 347 (1918); *Eisner* v. *Macomber,* 252 U.S. 189, 220 (1920); and *Merchants' Loan & Trust Co.* v. *Smietanka,* 255 U.S. 509 (1921).

Clarke attempted to bring to the Court the theory of sociological jurisprudence, though in his mind that doctrine was vague; he would incorporate into the process of decision the kind of facts that had gained their symbolic triumph in the Brandeis brief, but he remained uncertain in defining their relevance. Clarke was not quite so concerned as Brandeis with factual data, but neither was he preoccupied with precedents. His fellow judges seemed generally unimpressed by his approach. Chief Justice Taft complained that Clarke was prone to decide some cases by the parties rather than the issues. Holmes later wrote to Harold Laski: "I didn't admire Clarke's rhetoric, but he believed it—which is something and I shall miss his affectionate companionship." Laski said of Clarke: "A nice fellow, I thought, who worked hard; but an obstinate and pedestrian mind." Clarke seemed often to use a standard of some natural or higher law which in the end meant his own personal ideas of what was right, particularly his sympathy for the poor and his antagonism toward big business. In matters of procedure, Clarke on the Court again used his influence in the interest of efficiency. He asked that cases of minor significance not be brought to the Court at all, and he persuaded his brother Justices to limit oral argument to one hour wherever possible. Always an enemy of excessive verbiage, he began one opinion: "Accepting the risk of obscuring the obvious by discussing it. . . ."

Shortly after his appointment to the Court, Clarke handed down an opinion in a group of cases involving attempts to defraud the United States by stuffing ballot boxes and by bribing voters, *United States* v. *Gradwell, United States* v. *O'Toole, etc.,* 243 U.S. 476 (1917). Clarke decided it was historically the government's policy to leave the regulation of elections entirely to the states. In a straightforward and convincing statement, he alluded to the correspondence of James Madison and to the *Federalist* No. 59, written by Alexander Hamilton. *United States* v. *Gradwell, et al.* contrasted sharply with what some of his colleagues regarded as Clarke's eccentric thinking. The Justice sometimes assumed a unique position, particularly in cases involving persons injured by "instrumentalities of big business." Most famous was his ringing dissent in *United Zinc Company* v. *Britt,* 258 U.S. 268 (1922). The company had demolished one of its buildings, leaving water to accumulate in the basement. The water looked clear but was actually poisoned by sulphuric acid. Britt's family had camped nearby, and two of his children died after swimming in the "pool." Speaking for the majority, Holmes ruled that landowners have no general duty to keep their land free of danger. Clarke accused Holmes of using "hard" doctrine which made "trespassers of little children." Holmes, in turn, scored the dissent as sentimental, rhetorical, and "rather wild." Clarke's feeling against big business is also seen in *Edgar A. Levy Leasing Company* v. *Siegal,* 258 U.S. 242 (1922), which tested the constitutionality of the 1920 Emergency Housing Law of New York State. Clarke affirmed the statute for the Court, employing the doctrine of business affected with a public interest.

In 1921 Clarke wrote the opinion in the Hardwood Lumber case, *American Column and Lumber Co.* v. *United States,* 257 U.S. 377, which concerned the open competition plan of various trade associations. The Justice Department challenged the dealers' program for the exchange of information upon future price trends and similar matters within the industry. Clarke examined the actual effects of the arrangement to see whether it determined and limited prices, concluded that it did, and upheld its invalidation. Justice Holmes wrote a lofty dissent, holding that what the companies did was protected by the First Amendment. As a result of the decision, Secretary of Commerce Herbert Hoover called a trade association meeting in April, 1922, to discuss the role of the association.

Clarke made another contribution to antitrust law in the Reading Railroad case, *United States* v. *Reading Railroad Co.,* 253 U.S. 26 (1920). He had dissented in *United States* v. *United Shoe Machinery Company,* 247 U.S. 32 (1918)—"It is impossible for me to agree that this securely entrenched monopoly is an innocent result of normal business development"—and in *United States* v. *United States Steel Corporation,* 251 U.S. 417 (1920), in each instance declaring that the companies had purchased other businesses in order to eliminate competition. Now, in the Reading case, Clarke's dissents became the majority view. He summarized the history of the anthracite coal industry, touching on the geology of the region, to demonstrate that though the Reading Company controlled only one-third of the industry it monopolized the Schuykill field and had such power as to be "a menace to . . . interstate commerce within the meaning of the Anti-Trust Act. . . ." The holding company was ordered dissolved. In the same year, in *United States* v. *Lehigh Valley Railroad,* 254 U.S. 255, Clarke reaffirmed the antitrust sentiments for a now unanimous Court. The Reading and Lehigh cases, both of which looked back to the Northern Securities and Union Pacific cases, was used in the New Deal as a precedent for antitrust decisions.

Clarke's decisions showed a particular generosity toward labor. Invariably he exempted labor unions from prosecution under the antitrust laws; see, for instance, *United Mine Workers* v. *Coronado Coal Co.,* 259 U.S. 344 (1922). He upheld (often in dissent) labor's right to strike, to picket, and to conduct secondary boycotts in *Duplex Printing Co.* v. *Deering,* 254 U.S. 443, 479 (1921); *American Steel Foundries* v. *Tur-City Central Trades Council,* 257 U.S. 184, 213 (1921); and *Hitchman Coal & Coke Co.* v. *Mitchell,* 245 U.S. 229, 274 (1917). He voted to sustain Oregon's minimum wage act and its ten-hour law for all factory hands, in *Bunting* v. *Oregon,* 243 U.S. 246 (1917). He voted with the majority in *Stafford* v. *Wallace,* 258 U.S. 495 (1922) to sustain a law regulating meat packers and stockyards which benefited labor. He upheld the constitutionality of the Adamson Act, which provided an eight-hour day for railroad workers, in *Wilson* v. *New,* 243 U.S. 332 (1917).

In the area of civil liberties Clarke's record is mixed. The importance he attached to due process in the immigration field is illustrated in a case in which an American-born Chinese had been refused readmission to the United States. "It is better," wrote Clarke, "that many Chinese immigrants be improperly admitted than one natural-born citizen of the United States should be permanently excluded from this country," (*Kwock Jan Fat* v. *White,* 253 U.S. 454, 464 [1920].) In another decision concerning unreasonable search, *Gouled* v. *United States,* 255 U.S. 298 (1921), Clarke joined in the opinion that "only contraband, stolen goods or articles used in connection with the crime," but not corroborating evidence, could be seized. He warned that the Fourth and Fifth Amendments should be liberally construed to prevent "stealthy encroachment upon or 'gradual depreciation' of the rights secured by them, through imperceptible practice of courts or through well-intentioned mistakenly over-zealous executive officers."

In cases of greater significance, involving the First Amendment, Clarke took a less liberal position. *Abrams* v. *United States,* 250 U.S. 616 (1919), tested the provisions of the amended Espionage Act of 1918. The six defendants, all Russian-born aliens, believed in some form of anarchy or socialism. They had printed about fifteen thousand leaflets, some in English and some in Yiddish, condemning Wilson for sending American troops to Siberia, urging the workers not to purchase war bonds, and calling for a general strike—especially within the war industry. Some of the messages were simply tossed out of office windows. The case was argued at the height of the Red Scare, October, 1919, and the Court seemed quick to decide against the agitators. Clarke argued that the pamphlet was "not an attempt to bring about a change of administration by candid discussion," but was designed to defeat our entire war effort. The leaflets, moreover, were distributed in a great manufacturing and maritime center, New York City, where weapons were being made and shipped overseas. Justice Holmes, speaking for himself and Brandeis, ridiculed Clarke for taking seriously "the surreptitious publishing of a silly leaflet by an unknown man." But a few months before, Clarke had spoken to friends of the murderous Reds. The *Abrams* decision radically extended the restrictions on civil liberties permitted in the *Schenck* case, for no longer was it necessary to show that the defendant was guilty of direct interference with the war effort.

In *Milwaukee Social Democratic Publishing Co.* v. *Burleson,* 255 U.S. 407 (1921), Clarke again rejected a liberal interpretation of the First Amendment. This was the decision that upheld Postmaster General Burleson in his denial of mailing privileges to the socialist Milwaukee *Leader*. Clarke emphasized that the second-class permit was a privilege, not a right. He suggested further that the inspectors might legitimately assume future guilt, since they could not cope with approving each issue in advance. But in *Schaeffer* v. *United States,* 251 U.S. 466 (1920), Clarke dissented from a decision upholding the suppression of pacifist or pro-German sentiment. He spoke of "errors of Law which would not have been committed but for the stress of strain . . . prevailing in the early months of the late deplorable war."

On September 1, 1922, Clarke surprised the whole country, including President Harding, by resigning from the Court. Newspapers assumed that Clarke had political ambitions; the Associated Press noted: "The strategy of the next Presidential campaign suggests a candidate from Ohio." Clarke himself said, "Politics has no place in my scheme"; he offered as his main reason the death of his two sisters, and let it be known that he wanted to work for America's entrance into the League of Nations. "I would die happier," he wrote, "if I should do all that is possible to promote the entrance of our government into the League of Nations than if I had continued to devote my time to determining whether a drunken Indian had been deprived of his land before he died or whether the digging of a ditch was constitutional or not."

Clarke apparently underestimated his importance on the Court as much as he overestimated the political chances of the League. Liberals thought he had betrayed them. The *New York Globe* wrote: "The public really has a grievance in Justice Clarke's resignation. He occupied a strategic place. He is a liberal among conservatives, and he was needed." Surprisingly enough, Woodrow Wilson himself—the embodiment of the League—strongly opposed Clarke's resignation. "I am only sorry, deeply sorry," the ex-President wrote. "Like thousands of other liberals throughout the country, I have been counting on the influence of you and Justice Brandeis to restrain the Court in some measure from the extreme reactionary course which it seems inclined to follow." Clarke replied that the work was dull, the cases unimportant, and that he and Brandeis "were agreeing less and less" on just what was "liberal."

There were other reasons. Justice McReynolds, who as Wilson's Attorney General had apparently advised the President to choose Clarke as a district court judge, made life miserable for Clarke after he had sided frequently with Brandeis. Even Justice Taft thought Clarke had certain tendencies that limited his usefulness on the bench; he acted, said Taft, as though each case were something to vote on as he would vote in Congress. Clarke even decided certain cases in advance, Holmes complained to Taft. The clash of personalities on the Court, the influence of the physical disintegration of Chief Justice White, who like Clarke suffered from bad hearing and hypochondria centering on the heart, Clarke's personal tragedies, his non-judicial temperament, and a genuine desire to work for the League—all of these contributed to his decision to resign.

As early as 1918, in an address to the American Bar Association, Clarke had appealed for a League. In 1920 the Youngstown *Vindicator,* in which Clarke retained an interest, spoke for James Cox and the League. Clarke's friend Newton Baker spurred the Justice's interest. Under Clarke's leadership, the League of Nations Non-Partisan Committee opened a campaign in 1922 to obtain the signatures of one hundred prominent Americans on a pro-League document. In 1923 the committee merged with the American Association for International Cooperation, an organization promoting disarmament, to form the League of Nations Non-Partisan Association of the United States. Clarke became its first president, and for almost the rest of his public life this association was to command his energies. He made numerous speeches throughout the country to almost any group he could include in his itinerary, urging American participation in the League of Nations. He did so against the advice of his physicians, who felt that active campaigning would damage his already affected heart. He was an effective orator, but his florid speeches contained many sentimentalities that would offend the modern temper. In 1924 Clarke delivered the Colver lectures at Brown University, published the following year as *America and World Peace*. As an appeal for American entry into the League and a warning of future war, the book was short on facts and shallow in argumentation. "It is written from deeply sincere, religious, and moral convictions," remarked one reviewer. "Indeed Judge Clarke has written with that power and charm that is only achieved where a public man of political wisdom and high probity writes from the heart." Vincent Sheean, however, thought that "Justice Clarke's panegyric on the League of Nations is greatly like other panegyrics except that it had less argumentative power and more bad grammar than most."

Clarke soon realized he had been optimistic in his hopes for American entry into the League. Although his group scored initial success in collecting pro-League signatures and sponsored many speaking engagements, it soon ran into financial trouble. Clarke gave much of his own money and several years of effort to the cause, but showed slight political acumen. When the Republican National Chairman asked who was putting up the money for Clarke's organization, the Ohioan protested that his budget was modest and his support slight. By 1927 Clarke finally understood that the election of 1920 had meant a conclusive rejection of the League. Clarke retired from active service in behalf of the world organization and moved to San Diego, where he spent the rest of his life.

At the age of seventy-nine he showed himself still to be a faithful Democrat when he publicly expressed his confidence in the New Deal—"In 1932 our people were filled with despair. Today [in 1936] they are full of confidence and hope." Clarke's favorable response to the New Deal was in contrast to the savage private denunciations on the part of his old friend, Newton D. Baker. Clarke's attitude was hardheaded and realistic. He considered only the NIRA to be unwise, but believed that it too was conceived in good faith for a useful purpose. He favored direct federal aid of various kinds because it "saved the needy from starving and perhaps revolt." In response to John W. Davis' invitation to join a committee contesting the constitutionality of Roosevelt measures, Clarke replied that he was not conscious that his constitutional rights were being invaded. On March 22, 1937, at the age of eighty, Clarke delivered a fifteen-minute talk over a nationwide radio hookup, supporting President Roosevelt's plan to enlarge the Supreme Court. He called his speech "The Naked Question of the Constitutionality of the Court Proposal." "Naked" referred to a purely legalistic, non-political consideration of constitutionality. Noting that the Court had been expanded or reduced in size several times in the past, he concluded that "such an act would plainly be within the powers granted to the Congress and therefore clearly constitutional."

In the late thirties Clarke became a strong advocate of preparedness and applauded Roosevelt's "quarantine" speech of October, 1937. The former Justice supported Roosevelt's third term in 1940, but after the war was under way he doubted the wisdom of calling for unconditional surrender. Clarke died still a bachelor on March 22, 1945, not long before the San Francisco Conference which created the United Nations. He left $100,000 to the free libraries of Youngstown, the income from which was to be used solely for the purchase of books, and over $1.5 million to Adelbert College, the liberal arts school that he feared was being overshadowed by the growing Western Reserve University.

SELECTED BIBLIOGRAPHY

John Clarke is fortunate in his biographers. Hoyt L. Warner's *Life of Mr. Justice Clarke* (Cleveland, 1959) is a lucid summary. Harry Zilber's unpublished Master's essay, "Mr. Justice Clarke," (University of Wisconsin, 1949), is worth consulting. Two strong articles that analyze Clarke's career are David M. Levitan, "The Jurisprudence of Mr. Justice Clarke," 7 *Miami Law Quarterly* 44 (December, 1952) and Carl Wittke, "Mr. Justice Clarke in Retirement," 1 *Western Reserve Law Rev.* 28 (June, 1949). Three manuscript boxes of Clarke Papers are to be found at the Western Reserve University Library in Cleveland, but they contain mostly letters written to Clarke by friends.

John H. Clarke

REPRESENTATIVE OPINIONS

ABRAMS v. UNITED STATES, 250 U.S. 616 (1919)

During the Red Scare, Justice Clarke upheld the conviction of six agitators found guilty under the Espionage Act of 1918 for distributing a pamphlet entitled "Revolutionists Revolt for Action." The wording of the decision seemed hurried to some observers and to others it revealed a chauvinistic bias. Justice Holmes, speaking also for Justice Brandeis, ridiculed Clarke for taking seriously "the surreptitious publishing of a silly leaflet by an unknown man." Clarke's argument speaks for itself.

MR. JUSTICE CLARKE delivered the opinion of the court.

On a single indictment, containing four counts, the five plaintiffs in error, hereinafter designated the defendants, were convicted of conspiring to violate provisions of the Espionage Act of Congress (§ 3, Title I, of Act approved June 15, 1917, as amended May 16, 1918, 40 Stat. 553).

Each of the first three counts charged the defendants with conspiring, when the United States was at war with the Imperial Government of Germany, to unlawfully utter, print, write and publish: In the first count, "disloyal, scurrilous and abusive language about the form of Government of the United States;" in the second count, language "intended to bring the form of Government of the United States into contempt, scorn, contumely and disrepute;" and in the third count, language "intended to incite, provoke and encourage resistance to the United States in said war." The charge in the fourth count was that the defendants conspired "when the United States was at war with the Imperial German Government, . . . unlawfully and wilfully, by utterance, writing, printing and publication, to urge, incite and advocate curtailment of production of things and products, to wit, ordnance and ammunition, necessary and essential to the prosecution of the war." The offenses were charged in the language of the act of Congress.

It was charged in each count of the indictment that it was a part of the conspiracy that the defendants would attempt to accomplish their unlawful purpose by printing, writing and distributing in the City of New York many copies of a leaflet or circular, printed in the English language, and of another printed in the Yiddish language, copies of which, properly identified, were attached to the indictment.

All of the five defendants were born in Russia. They were intelligent, had considerable schooling, and at the time they were arrested they had lived in the United States terms varying from five to ten years, but none of them had applied for naturalization. Four of them testified as witnesses in their own behalf and of these, three frankly avowed that they were "rebels," "revolutionists," "anarchists," that they did not believe in government in any form, and they declared that they had no interest whatever in the Government of the United States. The fourth defendant testified that he was a "socialist" and believed in "a proper kind of government, not capitalistic," but in his classification the Government of the United States was "capitalistic."

It was admitted on the trial that the defendants had united to print and distribute the described circulars and that five thousand of them had been printed and distributed about the 22d of August, 1918. The group had a meeting place in New York City, in rooms rented by defendant Abrams, under an assumed name, and there the subject of printing the circulars was discussed about two weeks before the defendants were arrested. The defendant Abrams, although not a printer, on July 27, 1918, purchased the printing outfit with which the circulars were printed and installed it in a basement room where the work was done at night. The circulars were distributed some by throwing them from a window of a building where one of the defendants was employed and others secretly, in New York City.

The defendants pleaded "not guilty," and the case of the Government consisted in showing the facts we have stated, and in introducing in evidence copies of the two printed circulars attached to the indictment, a sheet entitled "Revolutionists Unite for Action," written by the defendant Lipman, and found on him when he was arrested, and another paper, found at the headquarters of the group, and for which Abrams assumed responsibility.

Thus the conspiracy and the doing of the overt acts charged were largely admitted and were fully established.

On the record thus described it is argued, somewhat faintly, that the acts charged against the defendants were not unlawful because within the protection of that freedom of speech and of the press which is guaranteed by the First Amendment to the Constitution of the United States, and that the entire Espionage Act is unconstitutional because in conflict with that Amendment.

This contention is sufficiently discussed and is definitely negatived in *Schenck* v. *United States* and *Baer* v. *United States,* 249 U.S. 47; and in *Frohwerk* v. *United States,* 249 U.S. 204.

The claim chiefly elaborated upon by the defendants in the oral argument and in their brief is that there is no substantial evidence in the record to support the judgment upon the verdict of guilty and that the motion of the defendants for an instructed verdict in their favor was erroneously denied. A question of law is thus presented, which calls for an examination of the record, not for the purpose of weighing conflicting testimony, but only to determine whether there was some evidence, competent and substantial, before the jury, fairly tending to sustain the verdict. *Troxell* v. *Delaware, Lackawanna & Western R. R. Co.,* 227 U.S. 434, 442; *Lancaster* v. *Collins,* 115 U.S. 222, 225; *Chicago & Northwestern Ry. Co.* v. *Ohle,* 117 U.S. 123, 129. We shall not need to consider the sufficiency, under the rule just stated, of the evidence introduced as to all of the counts of the indictment, for, since the sentence imposed did not exceed that which might lawfully have been imposed under any single count, the judgment upon the verdict of the jury must be affirmed if the evidence is sufficient to sustain any one of the counts. *Evans* v. *United States,* 153 U.S. 608; *Claassen* v. *United States,* 142 U.S. 140; *Debs* v. *United States,* 249 U.S. 211, 216.

The first of the two articles attached to the indictment is conspicuously headed, "The Hypocrisy of the United States and Her Allies." After denouncing President Wilson as a hypocrite and a coward because troops were sent into Russia, it proceeds to assail our Government in general, saying:

"His [the President's] shameful, cowardly silence about the intervention in Russia reveals the hypocrisy of the plutocratic gang in Washington and vicinity."

It continues:

"He [the President] is too much of a coward to come out openly and say: 'We capitalistic nations cannot afford to have a proletarian republic in Russia.' "

Among the capitalistic nations Abrams testified the United States was included.

Growing more inflammatory as it proceeds, the circular culminates in:

"The Russian Revolution cries: Workers of the World! Awake! Rise! Put down your enemy and mine!

"Yes! friends, there is only one enemy of the workers of the world and that is CAPITALISM."

This is clearly an appeal to the "workers" of this country to arise and put down by force the Government of the United States which they characterize as their "hypocritical," "cowardly" and "capitalistic" enemy.

It concludes:

"Awake! Awake, you Workers of the World!

"REVOLUTIONISTS."

The second of the articles was printed in the Yiddish language and in the translation is headed, "Workers—Wake up." After referring to "his Majesty, Mr. Wilson, and the rest of the gang; dogs of all colors!", it continues:

"Workers, Russian emigrants, you who had the least belief in the honesty of *our* Government," which defendants admitted referred to the United States Government, "must now throw away all confidence, must spit in the face the false, hypocritic, military propaganda which has fooled you so relentlessly, calling forth your sympathy, your help, to the prosecution of the war."

The purpose of this obviously was to persuade the persons to whom it was addressed to turn a deaf ear to patriotic appeals in behalf of the Government of the United States, and to cease to render it assistance in the prosecution of the war.

It goes on:

"With the money which you have loaned, or are going to loan them, they will make bullets not only for the Germans, but also for the Workers Soviets of Russia. *Workers in the ammunition factories, you are producing bullets, bayonets, cannon, to murder not only the Germans, but also your dearest, best, who are in Russia and are fighting for freedom.*"

It will not do to say, as is now argued, that the only intent of these defendants was to prevent injury to the Russian cause. Men must be held to have intended, and to be accountable for, the effects which their acts were likely to produce. Even if their primary purpose and intent was to aid the cause of the Russian Revolution, the plan of action which they adopted necessarily involved, before it could be realized, defeat of the war program of the United States, for the obvious effect of this appeal, if it should become effective, as they hoped it might, would be to persuade persons of character such as those whom they regarded themselves as addressing, not to aid government loans and not to work in ammunition factories, where their work would produce "bullets, bayonets, cannon" and other munitions of war, the use of which would cause the "murder" of Germans and Russians.

Again, the spirit becomes more bitter as it proceeds to declare that—

"America and her Allies have betrayed (the Workers). Their robberish aims are clear to all men. The destruction of the Russian Revolution, that is the politics of the march to Russia.

"Workers, our reply to the barbaric intervention has to be a general strike! An open challenge only will let the Government know that not only the Russian Worker fights for freedom, but also *here in America lives the spirit of Revolution.*"

This is not an attempt to bring about a change of administration by candid discussion, for no matter what may have incited the outbreak on the part of the defendant anarchists, the manifest purpose of such a publication was to create an attempt to defeat the war plans of the Government of the United States, by bringing upon the country the paralysis of a general strike, thereby arresting the production of all munitions and other things essential to the conduct of the war.

This purpose is emphasized in the next paragraph, which reads:

"Do not let the Government scare you with their wild punishment in prisons, hanging and shooting. We must not and will not betray the splendid fighters of Russia. *Workers, up to fight.*"

After more of the same kind, the circular concludes:

"Woe unto those who will be in the way of progress. Let solidarity live!"

It is signed, "The Rebels."

That the interpretation we have put upon these articles, circulated in the greatest port of our land, from which great numbers of soldiers were at the time taking ship daily, and in which great quantities of war supplies of every kind were at the time being manufactured for transportation overseas, is not only the fair interpretation of them, but that it is the meaning which their authors consciously intended should be conveyed by them to others is further shown by the additional writings found in the meeting place of the defendant group and on the person of one of them. One of these circulars is headed: "Revolutionists! Unite for Action!"

After denouncing the President as "Our Kaiser" and the hypocrisy of the United States and her Allies, this article concludes:

"Socialists, Anarchists, Industrial Workers of the World, Socialists, Labor party men and other revolutionary organizations *Unite for action* and let us save the Workers' Republic of Russia!

"Know you lovers of freedom that in order to save the Russian revolution, we must keep the armies of the allied countries busy at home."

Thus was again avowed the purpose to throw the country into a state of revolution if possible and to thereby frustrate the military program of the Government.

The remaining article, after denouncing the President for what is characterized as hostility to the Russian revolution, continues:

"We, the toilers of America, who believe in real liberty, shall *pledge ourselves,* in case the United States will participate in that bloody conspiracy against Russia, *to create so great a disturbance that the autocrats of America shall be compelled to keep their armies at home, and not be able to spare any for Russia."*

It concludes with this definite threat of armed rebellion:

"If they will use arms against the Russian people to enforce their standard of order, *so will we use arms,* and they shall never see the ruin of the Russian Revolution."

These excerpts sufficiently show, that while the immediate occasion for this particular outbreak of lawlessness, on the part of the defendant alien anarchists, may have been resentment caused by our Government sending troops into Russia as a strategic operation against the Germans on the eastern battle front, yet the plain purpose of their propaganda was to excite, at the supreme crisis of the war, disaffection, sedition, riots, and, as they hoped, revolution, in this country for the purpose of embarrassing and if possible defeating the military plans of the Government in Europe. A technical distinction may perhaps be taken between disloyal and abusive language applied to the *form* of our government or language intended to bring the *form* of our government into contempt and disrepute, and language of like character and intended to produce like results directed against the President and Congress, the agencies through which that form of government must function in time of war. But it is not necessary to a decision of this case to consider whether such distinction is vital or merely formal, for the language of these circulars was obviously intended to provoke and to encourage resistance to the United States in the war, as the third count runs, and, the defendants, in terms, plainly urged and advocated a resort to a general strike of workers in ammunition factories for the purpose of curtailing the production of ordnance and munitions necessary and essential to the prosecution of the war as is charged in the fourth count. Thus it is clear not only that some evidence but that much persuasive evidence was before the jury tending to prove that the defendants were guilty as charged in both the third and fourth counts of the indictment and under the long established rule of law hereinbefore stated the judgment of the District Court must be.

AMERICAN COLUMN AND LUMBER COMPANY v. UNITED STATES, 257 U.S. 391 (1921)

In this antitrust case Clarke upheld a decision against an "open competition" plan of various trade associations to exchange data on sales, prices and production and other matters essential to their industries' well being. Clarke concluded that the arrangement contributed to the fixing of prices in the industry. His decision helped to strengthen the antitrust laws particularly against trade associations.

MR. JUSTICE CLARKE delivered the opinion of the court.

The unincorporated "American Hardwood Manufacturers' Association" was formed in December, 1918, by the consolidation of two similar associations, from one of which it took over a department of activity designated the "Open Competition Plan," and hereinafter referred to as the "Plan."

Participation in the "Plan" was optional

with the members of the Association, but, at the time this suit was commenced, of its 400 members, 365, operating 465 mills, were members of the "Plan." The importance and strength of the Association are shown by the admission in the joint answer that while the defendants operated only five per cent. of the number of mills engaged in hardwood manufacture in the country, they produced one-third of the total production of the United States. The places of business of the corporations and partnerships, members of the "Plan," were located in many States from New York to Texas, but chiefly in the hardwood producing territory of the Southwest. The defendants are the members of the "Plan," their personal representatives, and F. R. Gadd, its "Manager of Statistics."

The bill alleged, in substance, that the "Plan" constituted a combination and conspiracy to restrain interstate commerce in hardwood lumber by restricting competition and maintaining and increasing prices, in violation of the Anti-Trust Act of 1890, c. 647, 26 Stat. 209.

The answer denied that the "Plan" had any such purpose and effect as charged, and averred that it promoted competition, especially among its own members.

A temporary injunction, granted by the District Court, restricting the activities of the "Plan" in specified respects, by consent of the parties was made permanent and a direct appeal brings the case here for review.

The activities which we shall see were comprehended within the "Open Competition Plan," (which is sometimes called "The New Competition,") have come to be widely adopted in our country, and, as this is the first time their legality has been before this court for decision, some detail of statement with respect to them is necessary.

There is very little dispute as to the facts. The testimony of the Government consists of various documents and excerpts from others, obtained from the files of the "Plan," and the testimony of the defendants consists of like documents and excerpts from other documents, also from the same files, supplemented by affidavits of a number of persons, members and non-members, chiefly to the point that the confessedly great increases of prices during 1919 were due to natural trade and weather conditions and not to the influence of the "Plan."

The record shows that the "Plan" was evolved by a committee, which, in recommending its adoption, said:

"The purpose of this plan is to disseminate among members accurate knowledge of production and market conditions so that each member may gauge the market intelligently instead of guessing at it; to make competition open and above board instead of secret and concealed; to substitute, in estimating market conditions, frank and full statements of our competitors for the frequently misleading and colored statements of the buyer."

After stating that the purpose was not to restrict competition or to control prices but to "furnish information to enable each member to intelligently make prices and to intelligently govern his production," the committee continues:

"The chief concern of the buyer, as we all know, is to see that the price he pays is no higher than that of his competitors, against whom he must sell his product in the market. The chief concern of the seller is to get as much as anybody else for his lumber; in other words to get what is termed the top of the market for the quality he offers. By making prices known to each other they will gradually tend toward a standard *in harmony with market conditions,* a situation advantageous to both buyer and seller."

Not long after the consolidation, a further explanation of the objects and purposes of the "Plan" was made in an appeal to members to join it, in which it is said:

"The theoretical proposition at the basis of the Open Competition plan is that,

"Knowledge regarding prices actually made is all that is necessary to keep prices at reasonably stable and normal levels.

"The Open Competition plan is a central clearing house for information on prices, trade statistics and practices. By keeping all members fully and quickly informed of what the others have done, the work of the plan results in *a certain uniformity of trade practice.* There is no agreement to follow the practice of others, *although members do naturally follow their most intelligent competitors,* if they know what these competitors have been actually doing.

"The monthly meetings held in various sections of the country each month have improved *the human relations* existing between the members before the organization of this plan."

And in another later, and somewhat similar, appeal sent to all the members, this is found:

"Competition, blind, vicious, unreasoning, may stimulate trade to abnormal activity but such condition is no more sound than that mediæval spirit some still cling to of taking a club and going out and knocking the other fellow and taking away his bone.

"The keynote to modern business success is mutual confidence and co-operation. *Co-operative Competition, not Cut-throat Competition.* Co-operation is a matter of business because it pays, because it enables you to get the best price for your product, because you come into closer *personal contact with the market.*

"Co-operation will only replace *undesirable competition* as you develop a co-operative spirit. For the first time in the history of the industry, the hardwood manufacturers are organized into one compact, comprehensive body, equipped to serve the whole trade in a thorough and efficient manner. . . . More members mean more power to do more good for the industry. With co-operation of this kind we will very soon have enlisted in our efforts practically every producing interest, *and you know what that means.*"

Thus, the "Plan" proposed a system of coöperation among the members, consisting of the interchange of reports of, sales, prices, production and practices, and in meetings of the members for discussion, for the avowed purpose of substituting "Co-operative Competition" for "Cut-throat Competition," of keeping "prices at reasonably stable and normal levels," and of improving the "human relations" among the members. But the purpose to agree upon prices or production was always disclaimed.

Coming now to the fully worked out paper plan as adopted.

It required each member to make six reports to the Secretary, viz.:

1. A *daily* report of all sales actually made, with the name and address of the purchaser, the kind, grade and quality of lumber sold and all special agreements of every kind, verbal or written with respect thereto. "These reports are to be exact copies of orders taken."

2. A *daily* shipping report, with exact copies of the invoices, all special agreements as to terms, grade, etc. The classification shall be the same as with sales.

3. A *monthly* production report, showing the production of the member reporting during the previous month, with the grades and thickness classified as prescribed in the "Plan."

4. A *monthly* stock report by each member, showing the stock on hand on the first day of the month, sold and unsold, green and dry, with the total of each kind, grade and thickness.

5. Price-lists. Members must file at the beginning of each month price-lists showing prices f. o. b. shipping point, which shall be stated. New prices must be filed with the association as soon as made.

6. Inspection reports. These reports are to be made to the association by a service of its own, established for the purpose of checking up grades of the various members and the "Plan" provides for a chief inspector and sufficient assistants to inspect the stocks of all members from time to time.

The declared purpose of the inspection service is not to change any member's grading except with his consent, but to furnish each member a basis on which he can compare his prices with those of other members, thereby making all members' reports more intelligible and accurate.

All of these reports by members are subject to complete audit by representatives of the association. Any member who fails to report *shall not receive the reports* of the secretary, and failure to report for twelve days in six months shall cause the member failing to be dropped from membership.

Plainly it would be very difficult to devise a more minute disclosure of everything connected with one's business than is here provided for by this "Plan" and very certainly only the most attractive prospect could induce any man to make it to his rivals and competitors.

But, since such voluminous disclosures to the secretary would be valueless unless communicated to the members in a condensed and interpreted form, provision is made for this, as follows:

The secretary is required to send to each member:

1. A *monthly* summary showing the production of each member for the previous month, "subdivided as to grade, kind, thickness," etc.

2. A *weekly* report, not later than Saturday, of all sales, to and including the preceding Tuesday, giving each sale and the price, and the name of the purchaser.

3. On Tuesday of each week the secretary must send to each member a report of each shipment by each member, complete up to the evening of the preceding Thursday.

4. He must send a *monthly* report, showing the individual stock on hand of each member and a summary of all stocks,

green and dry, sold and unsold. This report is very aptly referred to by the managing statistician as a monthly inventory of the stock of each member.

5. Not later than the 10th of each month the secretary shall send a summary of the price-lists furnished by members, showing the prices asked by each, and any changes made therein must be immediately transmitted to all the members.

6. A market report letter shall be sent to each member of the association (whether participating in the "Plan" or not) pointing "out changes in conditions both in the producing and consuming sections, giving a comparison of production and sales and in general an analysis of the market conditions."

7. Meetings shall be held once a month at Cincinnati "or at points to be agreed upon by the members." "It is intended that the regular meetings shall afford opportunity for the discussion of all subjects of interest to the members."

"The 'Plan' also requires the selection of a man to take charge of the gathering and dissemination of data, with necessary assistants," and the defendant F. R. Gadd was selected and given the title of "Manager of Statistics."

This extensive interchange of reports, supplemented as it was by monthly meetings at which an opportunity was afforded for discussion "of all subjects of interest to the members," very certainly constituted an organization through which agreements, actual or implied, could readily be arrived at and maintained, if the members desired to make them.

Such, in outline, was the paper plan adopted by the association, but elaborate though it was, in practice three important additions were made to it.

First of all, the southwestern territory for meeting purposes was divided into four districts, and instead of the monthly meeting provided for in the "Plan," "in order that members could more conveniently attend," the record shows that forty-nine of these meetings were held between January 31, 1919, and February 19, 1920,—approximately one for each week, in some part of the territory.

Second. Before each of these meetings a questionnaire was sent out to the members, and from the replies received, supplementing the other reports, the statistician compiled an estimate of the condition of the market, actual and prospective, which was distributed to the members attending each meeting, and was mailed to those not present. There were eleven questions on this list of which the most important were:

"4th. What was your total production of hardwoods during the last month? What do you estimate your production will probably be for the next two months?"

"10th. Do you expect to shut down within the next few months on account of shortage of logs or for any other reason? If so, please state how long mill will be idle?"

"11th. What is your view of market conditions for the next few months? What is the general outlook for business? State all reasons for your conclusions."

The "Plan" on paper provided only for reports of past transactions and much is made of this in the record and in argument—that reporting to one another past transactions cannot fix prices for the future. But each of these three questions plainly invited an estimate and discussion of future market conditions by each member, and a coördination of them by an expert analyst could readily evolve an attractive basis for coöperative, even if unexpressed, "harmony" with respect to future prices.

Third. The "Plan" provided for a monthly "market report letter" to go to all members of the association. In practice this market report letter was prepared by F. R. Gadd, Manager of Statistics, but his review of the market and forecast for the future were contained, almost from the beginning, not only in these market letters but also in the weekly sales reports, so that they were sent out to all of the members nineteen times between February 1 and December 6, 1919, and they were discussed at all but one or two of the forty-nine meetings which were held. All the activities of the "Plan" plainly culminated in the counsels contained in these letters and reports.

This elaborate plan for the interchange of reports does not simply supply to each member the amount of stock held, the sales made and the prices received, by every other member of the group, thereby furnishing the data for judging the market, on the basis of supply and demand and current prices. It goes much farther. It not only furnishes such information, with respect to stock, sales and prices, but also reports, giving the views of each member as to "market conditions for the next few months"; what the production of each will be for the next "two months"; frequent analyses of the reports by an expert, with, we shall see, significant suggestions as to both future prices and production; and opportunities for future meetings for the interchange ot views, which the record shows were very important. It is plain that the only element lacking in this scheme to make it a familiar type of the competition suppressing organization is a definite agreement as to production and prices. But this is supplied: by the disposition of men "to follow their most intelligent competitors," especially when powerful; by the inherent disposition to make all the money possible, joined with the steady cultivation of the value of "harmony" of action; and by the system of reports, which makes the discovery of price reductions inevitable and immediate. The sanctions of the plan obviously are, financial interest, intimate personal contact, and business honor, all operating under the restraint of exposure of what would be deemed bad faith and of trade punishment by powerful rivals.

The principles of law by which we must judge of the legality of the scheme of doing business thus provided for, as it was worked out in practice, are clearly settled by the Anti-Trust statute and the decisions of this court interpreting it.

The applicable provision of the act (c. 647, 26 Stat. 209) reads:

"Sec. 1. Every contract, combination in the form of trust or otherwise, or conspiracy, in restraint of trade or commerce among the several States . . . is hereby declared to be illegal."

Obviously the organization of the defendants constitutes a combination and confessedly they are engaged in a large way in the transportation and sale of lumber in interstate commerce so that there remains for decision only the question whether the system of doing business adopted resulted in that direct and undue restraint of interstate commerce which is condemned by this Anti-Trust statute.

It has been repeatedly held by this court that the purpose of the statute is to maintain free competition in interstate commerce and that any concerted action by any combination of men or corporations to cause, or which in fact does cause, direct and undue restraint of competition in such commerce falls within the condemnation of the act and is unlawful.

In *Northern Securities Co.* v. *United States,* 193 U.S. 197, 337, it is declared that:

"In all the prior cases in this court the Anti-Trust Act has been construed as forbidding any combination which by its necessary operation destroys or restricts free competition among those engaged in interstate commerce; in other words, that to destroy or restrict free competition in interstate commerce was to restrain such commerce."

In *United States* v. *Union Pacific R. R. Co.,* 226 U.S. 61, 87, decided in 1912, long prior to the forming of their combination by the defendants, the law was condensed into this expression:

"To preserve from undue restraint the free action of competition in interstate commerce was the purpose which controlled Congress in enacting this statute, and the courts should construe the law with a view to effecting the object of its enactment."

And in *Eastern States Retail Lumber Dealers' Association* v. *United States,* 234 U.S. 600, 609, it was said:

"It [the Sherman Act] broadly condemns all combinations and conspiracies which restrain the free and natural flow of trade in the channels of interstate commerce."

And again, on p. 613:

"The argument that the course pursued is necessary to the protection of the retail trade and promotive of the public welfare in providing retail facilities is answered by the fact that Congress, with the right to control the field of interstate commerce, has so legislated as to prevent resort to practices which unduly restrain competition or unduly obstruct the free flow of such commerce, and private choice of means must yield to the national authority thus exerted."

With this rule of law and the details of the "Plan" in mind, we come to consider what the record shows as to the purpose of this combination and as to its effect upon interstate commerce.

We have seen that the "Plan" provided for the selection of a man to have charge of the gathering and dissemination of the data, which were to be contained in the various reports, and that the defendant F. R. Gadd was selected for this purpose, with the title of "Manager of Statistics." Mr. Gadd was a man of large experience in the lumber business, competent and aggressive, and the record makes it clear that he was in complete and responsible charge of all the activities of this "Open Competition Plan." He compiled the summaries of daily, weekly and monthly reports, and wrote the monthly market letter and the market comment in the weekly sales reports, which were distributed to the members. Some disposition appears in the argument, but not in the evidence, to suggest that Gadd exceeded his authority at times, but no objection appears to have been taken to any of his conduct, and the "Secretary-Manager" says in his affidavit that his office adjoins that of Gadd and that "he [Gadd] and the affiant have frequent conferences and discussions relating to their work, and that the affiant is familiar with the activities and methods of the Open Competition Plan."

It is plain that as the "Plan" was the "clearing house" of the members, "for information on prices, trade statistics, and practices," so Gadd was the "clearing house" of the "Plan," and that what he said and did, acquiesced in by the members, as it was, must be accepted as the authoritative expression of the combination.

The record shows that the lumber market was inactive in the months of January and February and the first part of March of 1919. It grew better late in March and progressively stronger until in July, when it became very active, with prices high, and so continued until the end of the year we are considering.

In the first quarter of the year the problem was to maintain the war prices then prevailing rather than to advance them, and although the minutes of the various meetings were kept in barest outline, we find that beginning within a month of the consolidation of the two associations, the members of the "Plan" began actively to coöperate, through the meetings, to suppress competition by restricting production. This is very clearly shown by the excerpts following from the minutes of meetings and from the market letters and sales reports distributed at them.

Thus, at the meeting held at Cincinnati, on January 21, 1919, in the discussion of business conditions, the chairman said:

"If there is *no increase in production,* particularly in oak, there is going to be good business." *"No man is safe in increasing his production.* If he does, he will be in bad shape, as the demand won't come."

Again, at the meeting held on May 9th, at Memphis, in the discussion of market conditions, appears this paragraph:

"Reference was made to members who contemplate running day and night, and it was stated that the lumber industry had seen these unusual market conditions before and that we ought to be very sure that the market is capable of taking care of night and day lumber."

This warning of May 9th against producing too much lumber was followed, on May 17th, by a sales report sent out by the Manager of Statistics to all members, which was headed, "Stop, Look and Listen." After saying that the hardwood market had assumed a decidedly better tone, with a tendency in quotations upward, with the demand on the increase and with stocks below normal, the writer continues:

"The lumbermen have gone through several lean years, but we are confronted with the possibility of killing the goose that laid the golden egg. *Overproduction will spell disaster,* as it should always be borne in mind that the maximum productive capacity of the sawmills of the country is much in excess of any demand the country has ever known."

He then quotes from an editorial in the Southern Lumberman, in which, among other things, it is said:

"The danger which we see lurking in the future for the lumber industry is overproduction. When the demand for lumber is keen and the prices are good, it is necessarily a strong temptation to the sawmill men to put on a night shift at the mill and an extra logging crew in the woods, and keep turning out lumber twenty-four hours out of the day. The desire to cash in while the cashing is good is natural and easy to understand; but every sawmill man who contemplates putting on a night shift should stop long enough to reflect on the past history of the lumber business. If he does indulge in such reflection, the chances are he will reconsider any ideas he may have had along that line. *Overproduction* has always been the curse of the lumber industry in America. It has caused more trouble and hardship than any other one factor. It would be criminal folly, therefore, for the lumber manufacturers to indulge themselves in any such form of commercial suicide."

Adding that the lumbermen have within their grasp an era of prosperity for some time to come, the writer continues:

"They can either reach forward to seize their opportunity, or *they can cast it aside by the policy of overproduction.* Which shall it be? It is up to the sawmill men themselves to decide."

The managing statistician of the association significantly adds: *"Are we guilty? If so, the warning is timely."*

Again, a week later, at a meeting at Shreveport, Louisiana, in the discussion of market conditions, one of the members declared: that in his opinion it was *"suicidal to run mills night and day;* that the pine mills had done it, but he hoped they [we] would profit by their past experience and not do it this year."

Much more of like purport appears in the minutes of the meetings throughout the year, but this is sufficient to convincingly show that one of the prime purposes of the meetings, held in every part of the lumber district, and of the various reports, was to induce members to cooperate in restricting production, thereby keeping the supply low and the prices high, and that whenever there was any suggestion of running the mills to an extent which would bring up the supply to a point which might affect prices, the advice against operations which might lead to such result was put in the strongest possible terms. The coöperation is palpable and avowed, its purpose is clear, and we shall see that it was completely realized.

Next, the record shows clearly that the members of the combination were not satisfied to secure, each for himself, the price which might be obtainable even as the result of coöperative restriction of production, but that throughout the year they assiduously cultivated, through the letters of Gadd, speaking for them all, and through the discussions at the meetings, the general conviction that higher and higher prices were obtainable and a disposition on the part of all to demand them. The intention to create such a common purpose is too clear to be doubted, evidenced as it is by the following excerpts from much of like character in the testimony:

As thus, in the stock report of March 8, 1919, after pointing out that the stock at the mills was only about three-fourths normal and that the production in the Memphis group of manufacturers was only fifty-six per cent. of normal, the letter of the Manager of Statistics continues:

"There has of course been a long drawn out and desperate effort to break the hardwood market by a withdrawal of demand; but be it said to the eternal credit of the hardwood producers that *they have maintained a stout heart and stiff backbone;* with the result that there has been exhibited a strength in the market which has been little short of remarkable in the face of the light demand, and the vigorous efforts which have been steadily made *to hammer down prices. . . .*

"With this information before him it is difficult to see how any intelligent hardwood manufacturer can entertain any hesitation as to *the proper course for him to pursue* in selling his lumber."

And it may be added that it is not difficult to see what this "proper course to pursue" was intended to be.

Again, three weeks later, in the market letter of March 29th, after stating that stocks had further decreased from the previous month, with a production not to exceed fifty per cent. of normal, the Manager of Statistics of the "Plan" adds:

"Naturally the situation ought to have an important bearing on the plans of every hardwood lumberman. If the facts were better understood *offers of business now at shaded prices would get scant consideration* and there would not only be *no good reason to cut prices,* but there would be every reason why they should be held at reasonable profit-making levels. . . . All conditions indicate a firm market for the balance of the year, with prices moving upward."

Another month later, in the market letter of April 26th, this influential agent of the association, after pointing out that stocks were less than seventy-five per cent. of normal, that production was about sixty per cent. of normal, and that the demand was far in excess of the supply, adds:

"If ever there was a time when rich rewards awaited the producer of hardwood lumber, now is that time. *There are glorious opportunities ahead. . . .* Supply and demand must necessarily govern prices. The demand is with us, the supply inadequate, therefore, *values must increase, as our competition in hardwoods is only among ourselves."*

Again, in another month, May 24th, in his market letter, the Manager of Statistics, after stating that production during the month of April was sixty-five per cent. of normal and that a careful estimate indicated that there would be no material increase in May and June, says:

"If anyone tells you that lumber prices are coming down, call their attention to the following: *Curtailed production of mills;* stocks at mill points are below normal; . . . *necessity* on the part of lumber operators *of maintaining a price level that will enable them to make a reasonable profit."*

And he concludes with:

"The tendency of the market is upward and will undoubtedly continue to advance as long as sales and production bear their present relation to each other."

Again on September 20th, in his market letter, he says:

"It has been rumored that a certain class of buyers, believing that the price of lumber was too high and that the temporary inactivity in the export market offered the opportune moment, have agreed to confine purchases to actual immediate requirements during the next sixty days. This is not going to worry the manufacturers very much; in fact, it will give them a much needed breathing spell and an opportunity to accumulate a supply of dry stocks which, in our opinion, is the same as gold dollars in the bank.

* * *

"Those who have been looking for lower prices overlook the very important factors: that production continues below normal . . . that unsold stocks at mills are 70 per cent. below normal; . . . that the export demand has just started, . . ."

And he concludes:

"With these conditions prevailing, there is *nothing in the situation that should encourage anyone to hope for a drop in quotations."*

To this we must add that constantly throughout the minutes of the various meetings there is shown discussion of the stock and production reports in which the shortage of supply was continually emphasized, with the implication, not disguised, that higher prices must result. Men in general are so easily persuaded to do that which will obviously prove profitable that this reiterated opinion from the analyst of their association, with all obtainable data before him, that higher prices were justified and could easily be obtained, must, inevitably have resulted, as it did result, in concert of action in demanding them.

But not only does the record thus show a persistent purpose to encourage members to unite in pressing for higher and higher prices, without regard to cost, but there are many admissions by members, not only that this was the purpose of the "Plan," but that it was fully realized.

Within four months of the consolidation, on April 23, 1919, the Manager of Statistics wrote to members asking each to write him "his experience with the Plan" and any incidents showing benefits derived from it.

The replies to this letter are significant confessions. One writes:

"All those who have access to your reports bring their prices to the top."

Another:

"There seems to be a friendly rivalry among members to see who can get the best prices, whereas, under the old plan it was cut throat competition."

Another:

"It has kept us in touch closely with the market and in many instances has made us one or more dollars per thousand feet on lumber that we have sold and we believe that the plan is going to be very successful in carrying out the purposes for which it is intended."

Another:

"The very first report which we received under this plan enabled us to increase our price $6 per thousand on a special item in oak. We had just taken a small order at what we thought was a satisfactory price, but discovered immediately that others were getting more money and since that time we have booked orders for a number of these special items at an increase of $6 per thousand."

Another:

"Since we have become members, we have been selling our lumber at several dollars per M more than formerly and we are perfectly satisfied with the plan."

And another:

"We have always left these meetings feeling that we did not get enough money for our lumber and that we ought to try to do better."

There was one discordant reply, saying:

"The Open Competition Plan has been absolutely accurate but instead of apparently stabilizing the market, it has caused a run-away market."—This on May 29th, within six months of the forming of the combination.

These quotations are sufficient to show beyond discussion that the purpose of the organization and especially of the frequent meetings was to bring about a concerted effort to raise prices regardless of cost or merit, and so was unlawful, and that the members were soon entirely satisfied that the "Plan" was "carrying out the purpose for which it was intended."

As to the price conditions during the year. Without going into detail the record shows that the prices of the grades of hardwood in most general use were increased to an unprecedented extent during the year. Thus, the increases in prices of varieties of oak, range from 33.3% to 296% during the year; of gum, 60% to 343%, and of ash, from 55% to 181%. While it is true that 1919 was a year of high and increasing prices generally and that wet weather may have restricted production to some extent, we cannot but agree with the members of the "Plan" themselves, as we have quoted them, and with the District Court in the conclusion that the united action of this large and influential membership of dealers contributed greatly to this extraordinary price increase.

Such close coöperation, between many persons, firms, and corporations controlling a large volume of interstate commerce, as is provided for in this "Plan," is plainly in theory, as it proved to be in fact, inconsistent with that free and unrestricted trade which the statute contemplates shall be maintained; and that the persons conducting the association fully realized this is apparent from their protesting so often as they did, in many of their confidential communications appearing in this record, that their purposes were not unlawful, that they sought only to supplant cut-throat competition with what in their own judgment would be "fair and reasonable competition," and to obtain, not make, fair prices, and by their repeated insistence that the Sherman Law "designed to prevent the restraint of trade is itself one of the greatest restrainers of trade, and should be repealed."

To call the activities of the defendants, as they are proved in this record, an "Open Competition Plan" of action is plainly a misleading misnomer.

Genuine competitors do not make daily, weekly and monthly reports of the minutest details of their business to their rivals, as the defendants did; they do not contract, as was done here, to submit their books to the discretionary audit and their stocks to the discretionary inspection of their rivals for the purpose of successfully competing with them; and they do not submit the details of their business to the analysis of an expert, jointly employed, and obtain from him a "harmonized" estimate of the market as it is and as, in his specially and confidentially informed judgment, it promises to be. This is not the conduct of competitors but is so clearly that of men united in an agreement, express or implied, to act together and pursue a common purpose under a common guide that, if it did not stand confessed a combination to restrict production and increase prices in interstate commerce and as, therefore, a direct restraint upon that commerce, as we have seen that it is, that conclusion must inevitably have been inferred from the facts which were proved. To pronounce such abnormal conduct on the part of 365 natural competitors, controlling one-third of the trade of the country in an article of prime necessity, a "new form of competition" and not an old form of combination in restraint of trade, as it so plainly is, would be for this court to confess itself blinded by words and forms to realities which men in general very plainly see and understand and condemn, as an old evil in a new dress and with a new name.

The "Plan" is, essentially, simply an expansion of the gentlemen's agreement of former days, skilfully devised to evade the law. To call it open competition because the meetings were nominally open to the public, or because some voluminous reports were transmitted to the Department of Justice, or because no specific agreement to restrict trade or fix prices is proved, cannot conceal the fact that the fundamental purpose of the "Plan" was to procure "harmonious" individual action among a large number of naturally competing dealers with respect to the volume of production and prices, without having any specific agreement with respect to them, and to rely for maintenance of concerted action in both respects, not upon fines and forfeitures as in earlier days, but upon what experience has shown to be the more potent and dependable restraints, of business honor and social penalties,—cautiously reinforced by many and elaborate reports, which would promptly expose to his associates any disposition in any member to deviate from the tacit understanding that all were to act together under the subtle direction of a single interpreter of their common purposes, as evidenced in the minute reports of what they had done and in their expressed purposes as to what they intended to do.

In the presence of this record it is futile to argue that the purpose of the "Plan" was simply to furnish those engaged in this industry, with widely scattered units, the equivalent of such information as is contained in the newspaper and government publications with respect to the market for commodities sold on boards of trade or stock exchanges. One distinguishing and sufficient difference is that the published reports go to both seller and buyer, but these reports go to the seller only; and another is that there is no skilled interpreter of the published reports, such as we have in this case, to insistently recommend harmony of action likely to prove profitable in proportion as it is unitedly pursued.

Convinced, as we are, that the purpose and effect of the activities of the "Open Competition Plan," here under discussion, were to restrict competition and thereby restrain interstate commerce in the manufacture and sale of hardwood lumber by concerted action in curtailing production and in increasing prices, we agree with the District Court that it constituted a combination and conspiracy in restraint of interstate commerce within the meaning of the Anti-Trust Act of 1890 (26 Stat. 209) and the decree of that court must be

Affirmed.

William Howard Taft

☆ 1857–1930 ☆

APPOINTED BY

WARREN G. HARDING

YEARS ON COURT

1921–1930

William Howard Taft

by

ALPHEUS THOMAS MASON

WILLIAM HOWARD TAFT appeared to be almost the stereotype of a Chief Justice. Large of frame and good-natured, weighing well over three hundred pounds with more than a little bay window, he filled out the popular image of the venerable patriarch dispensing unadulterated justice. His customary geniality aroused a pervasively good nature towards him. Taft was known as the politest man alive. "I heard that recently he arose in a streetcar," Justice Brewer reported, "and gave his seat to three women."

Taft's life is amazing both for length of public service (1881 to 1930) and for the variety of his activities: prosecuting attorney in his home state of Ohio, Superior Court judge in Cincinnati, Solicitor General of the United States, Federal Circuit Court judge, Governor General of the Philippines, Cabinet member, President of the United States, professor of law, and Chief Justice of the United States.

Someone has said life begins at forty. For Taft it really began at sixty-four when, on June 30, 1921, he became the tenth Chief Justice of the United States. Unhappy and ineffective as Chief Executive, lifelong aspirant to the Chief Justiceship, Taft is the only man in American history to occupy both offices.

Taft had a reformist zeal in bringing about improvements in judicial organization and procedure. But he was no social reformer, his enduring aim being to safeguard private property. Courts were America's primary reliance for preserving this bulwark of civilization. "The greatest advantage of our plan of government over every other, is the character of the judicial power vested in the Supreme Court." European statesmen and historians, Taft noted, rightly looked upon it "as the chief instrument in the maintenance of that self-restraint which the people of the United States have placed upon themselves and which has

ALPHEUS THOMAS MASON, Professor Emeritus, Princeton University, now Doherty Professor of Law and Government, University of Virginia, is the author of Brandeis: A Free Man's Life; Harlan Fiske Stone: Pillar of the Law; *and* William Howard Taft, Chief Justice.

made this Government the admiration of intelligent critics the world over." At the storm center of politics for nearly half a century, he tried to dam the surging tide of progressivism. As Chief Justice between 1921 and 1930, he stood at the crossroads of the dying old and the emerging new.

Taft was a thoroughgoing Social Darwinist, stubborn defender of the *status quo,* apologist for economic privilege, inveterate critic of social democracy—the gigantic symbol of standpattism. *Avoirdupois* alone made him the cartoonist's model of the bloated capitalist. Yet a remodeled federal judicial organization stands as his major achievement. In pursuit of this goal, he demonstrated singleness of purpose, a fertile imagination, and extraordinary dynamism. These two drives, one reactionary and obstructive, the other liberating and forward-looking, run simultaneously throughout his career.

Taft reached maturity and began his professional career in the last quarter of the nineteenth century—a time of economic transformation and incipient popular revolt. American industry had come of age and organized as the National Association of Manufacturers. Industrial trusts were rapidly replacing competing concerns; fabulous fortunes were being amassed; in lawmaking bodies economic interests rather than people had become the constituencies. Meanwhile, currents of popular revolt were beginning to run swiftly. These years witnessed Greenbackers, Grangers, Populists, Knights of Labor, Anarchists, and the largest Socialist vote ever cast in a presidential election. Organized labor expressed its resentment against corporate power in a wave of strikes and boycotts. Haymarket, Homestead, Pullman, and Coxey's Army blackened the headlines. When the courts intervened, usually on the side of property, protesting labor leaders promptly coined the derogatory rubric, "government by injunction."

Rarely had the country been more conscious of the Supreme Court. The Judiciary was rapidly becoming a crucial factor in the march of social democracy. Winning favor, and finally dominance, were the activists views of Supreme Court Justice David J. Brewer. "The many," he complained, "attempted to transfer to themselves through political power the wealth they lacked the ability or patience to earn in the ordinary pursuit of their business." This "movement of coercion," conspicuous in legislative halls and in the ranks of organized labor, ran counter to free government's primary concern—private property. What more logical agency "to lift the restraining hand than the courts of the land"? Brewer was convinced that "the salvation of the nation, the permanence of government of and by the people rests upon the independence and vigor of the judiciary." The "great body of judges," Justice Brewer declared, "will find no difficulty in determining what is right and wrong between employer and employees, . . . As for speed, is there any thing quicker than a writ of injunction?"

Taft shared Brewer's interventionist convictions, spelling them out in a notable address of 1894, delivered to the graduating class of the University of Michigan Law School. (Taft, "The Right of Private Property," 3 *Michigan Law Journal* 215 [1894].) Private property had led to the accumulation of capital, resulting in lower production costs, greater comforts, and higher income for all.

The Constitution made ours "a conservative government, . . . strongly buttressed by written law, against the attacks of anarchy, socialism and communism." "Princely profits" were but just rewards to "men of judgment, courage and executive ability . . . for the general good they have done." Taft believed that judicial reform could reduce the threat to private property by removing a justifiable source of popular unrest. By revising outmoded judicial organization and procedure, the legal profession might counteract the disruptive influence of wild-eyed reformers. This, indeed, was the link which bound together judicial reform and judicial defense of property.

An outspoken critic of schemes for social uplift, he thought of courts as a brake on democracy. That brake could be most effectively applied from the center chair of the U.S. Supreme Court. As realization of his lifelong ambition came closer, the major planks in his platform emerged with stark clarity: streamline judicial administration; use the strong arm of the judiciary to resist the attacks of unrestrained popular power.

The goal—Chief Justice of the United States—was realized in 1921, on the eve of the "fabulous twenties," a period of economic expansion, political corruption, and high finance. Taft's spirit of resistance to the social service state lived on into the New Deal years. In the early 1930's, it shackled the power to govern amid a national crisis that shook the foundations of our economic and political structure.

William Howard Taft was born in Cincinnati, Ohio, on September 15, 1857, the product of a drab line of moderately prosperous New England Yankees. The Chief Justice's father, Alphonso Taft, was a successful Ohio lawyer who served in President Grant's Cabinet. Alphonso had also yearned for high judicial office. "To be Chief Justice," Taft's father had written in 1864, "is more than to be President." Young Taft compiled an admirable record at Cincinnati's Woodward High School, graduated from Yale in 1878, entered Cincinnati Law School, and was admitted to the Ohio Bar in 1880. William Graham Sumner, professor of political and social science at Yale, was an abiding influence. Taft took to heart Sumner's famous advice to Yale seniors: "Don't be a damn fool." A generation later, the standpat principles he learned at Yale in the 1870's were still considered sound.

In 1886 Taft took a step that was to have untold consequences in his rise to political prominence: he married Helen Herron. In 1906, when a Supreme Court appointment was rumored for his father, a friend of the Taft family asked seventeen-year-old Robert (later U.S. Senator and "Mr. Republican") whether the War Secretary would go on the Court. "Nope," the youth answered, "Ma wants him to wait and be President."

Judging was Taft's natural bent. "The law" was in his blood; judges were the embodiment of his ideals. "I love judges, and I love courts," he said. "They are my ideals, that typify on earth what we shall meet hereafter in heaven under a just God." Yet his judicial career began almost by accident. Unexpectedly, in

1887 Judson Harmon resigned as judge on the Superior Court of Ohio. Prominent Cincinnati lawyers were considered, but on the recommendation of Judge Judson Harmon, Governor Joseph Benson Foraker appointed the twenty-nine-year-old Assistant County Solicitor, William Howard Taft.

It was the first step up the coveted judicial ladder. As early as 1889, at the age of thirty-two, he had pulled every available wire leading to President Benjamin Harrison and the place then vacant on the U.S. Supreme Court. Instead of a Court appointment, the President offered him the post of Solicitor General. Taft's acceptance proved important for his entire political and judicial career. The office required thorough grounding in constitutional law and procedure; it brought him into close contact with Republican bigwigs, including Theodore Roosevelt. In Washington he soon acquired "a pretty good knowledge of the persons who run things." Taft's performance in the Solicitor General's office, though effective, was undistinguished. Despite presentations marked chiefly by their soporific effect, he lost only two of the eighteen cases he argued.

The shift from judging to highfalutin' Washington politics, though flattering, had been motivated by his wife's promptings, rather than his own ambitions. "Politics," he declared, "when I am in it makes me sick." He had accepted the office of Solicitor General only after regretful glances at his beloved bench. Mrs. Taft, on the other hand, welcomed the move as an opportunity for her husband to get out of the "judicial groove." After a scant two years, he resigned, against his wife's strong misgivings, to accept President Harrison's appointment as U.S. Circuit judge, Sixth Judicial Circuit. In 1892, at thirty-four, he was again doing congenial work—hearing motions, writing opinions, and, within a few months, serving as presiding judge in open court at civil and criminal trials. Nor were all his time and energies given to judging. In 1896 he became dean and professor of property at the Cincinnati Law School, lecturing two hours a week. Meanwhile, he had begun to give serious consideration to ways of making the federal judiciary function more efficiently.

Politics soon beckoned again. President McKinley, in January of 1900, asked Taft to head a commission to establish civil rule in the Philippines. To Mrs. Taft the possibilities seemed boundless. Her husband was less certain. Mrs. Taft remembers resignation from the circuit court bench as "the hardest thing he ever did." Perhaps McKinley's implied promise of later judicial promotion eased the way.

In the Philippines, Taft found himself gripped by responsibilities that fully challenged him. Not even President Roosevelt's offer of a place on the Supreme Court (in partial payment of a political debt going back to T.R.'s appointment as Secretary of the Navy) could lure him away. It was not until February, 1904 that Taft could be persuaded to relinquish his post. A short six months after rejection of a Supreme Court appointment, the President practically ordered him to report to Washington to succeed the distinguished Elihu Root as Secretary of War. Soon he was deep in the affairs of his own department, and representing the President in various affairs of state. Purely political assignments were not beyond his ken. He was a vigorous participant in the President's winning presidential campaign of 1904, stimulating a *New York Sun* editorial that singled out the obese Ohioan as "the energy and force of the whole administration."

Taft's extraordinary political success was not solely the decree of fate. For both him and his wife, the stakes were high. Mrs. Taft kept her political eye on the White House; her husband's was fixed on the Chief Justiceship. Serious talk of Taft as presidential timber had begun while he was in the Philippines. As early as July, 1901, President Roosevelt had dangled both these prizes before him. "If I had the naming either of President or Chief Justice," T.R. had affirmed, "I should feel in honor bound to name you." By 1908, the President had apparently decided to lead the GOP to victory by selecting his peripatetic Cabinet officer as his successor. Taft yielded, but not without strong doubts. He never ceased "to regard a Supreme Court appointment as vastly more desirable than the Presidency." Besides his distaste for politics, he regarded himself as "unavailable." To be known as the inventor of "government by injunction," he commented wryly, "is not a valuable asset" for a presidential candidate.

A quirk of fate and conflicting personal ambitions were among the factors that made William Howard Taft President of the United States. In 1906, perhaps looking forward to the center chair, he was preoccupied with the War Department, the Panama Canal and Philippine politics and administration. He did not want appointment as Justice Henry Billings Brown's successor. And Mrs. Taft was, of course, adamant. For the time being she opposed any Supreme Court appointment, whether as Associate or as Chief Justice. The White House was her goal.

It may be that Chief Justice Melville W. Fuller's unbudging refusal to surrender the Chief Justiceship, in the face of concerted effort to persuade him to quit, kept Taft free to run for the Presidency in 1908. "If the Chief Justice would only retire," Taft moaned, "how simple everything would become." The wheel of fortune, aided by Mrs. Taft, dictated the higher prize. The newly elected Chief Executive was uncomfortable, his ambition still unsatisfied. "I pinch myself every little while to make myself realize that it is all true," he confided to a friend. "If I were now presiding in the Supreme Court of the United States as chief justice, I should feel entirely at home, but . . . I feel just like a fish out of water." In March, 1909, Chief Justice Fuller, frail and aging, had administered the oath to Taft. Still in office, Fuller died the next year.

"It seems strange," President Taft remarked sadly while the matter of Chief Justice Fuller's successor was pending, "that the one place in the government which I would have liked to fill myself I am forced to give to another."

The choice finally lay between Associate Justices Charles Evans Hughes and Edward Douglass White. In press speculations, Hughes' name figured prominently as the most likely choice. A few weeks earlier, Taft had told Archie Butt: "If I ever have the chance, I shall offer to him [Hughes] the Chief Justiceship." When that chance came, the President was troubled by indecision. Few Presidents have the opportunity of naming a Chief Justice. In the exercise of that mixed pleasure, William Howard Taft overlooked no contingency that might improve his own chances of winning the office. White was twelve years older than Taft, and seventeen years older than Hughes. To be the first man in American history to fill the two most exalted posts in the land must have been a glowing prospect. The selection of Hughes would almost certainly have precluded any possibility of realizing this distinction; the elevation of White would not.

Speculation can be more charitable. Taft had a profound distaste for bigotry. A midwestern Unitarian Republican, he selected Justice White, a southern Catholic Democrat, the first Associate Justice ever to win promotion. The chagrin Taft felt in appointing White to the position he cherished may have been mollified by this blow against sectional, partisan, and sectarian bigotry.

In March, 1913, Taft at sixty-three was out of office for the first time in his political life. Yale promptly solved his problem, welcoming him back to campus as Professor of Constitutional Law. President Woodrow Wilson was hardly settled in office before he began hearing what a wonderful thing it would be for the country if the Democratic incumbent, rising above partisan politics, would satisfy Mr. Taft's lifelong ambition. Had not President Taft himself set the example of highmindedness in 1910, when he selected White, a southern Democrat, Chief Justice. Taft, believing that President Wilson "could not recognize a generous impulse if he met it on the street," knew he must be patient.

With the smashing Republican victory of 1920, prospects brightened and the former President again advertised his availability. While field workers kept in close touch with President-elect Harding and his advisers, Taft himself was busy. Shortly after Harding's election, the unblushing aspirant, armed with helpful suggestions concerning appointments, made the pilgrimage to Marion, Ohio. Taft was "non-plussed," "nearly struck dumb," when the President-elect broached a Supreme Court appointment. Of course, the former President was available, but he made it clear that, having appointed three of the present bench and three others, and having vigorously opposed Brandeis' appointment in 1916, he would accept only the Chief Justiceship.

Taft then turned his attention to the enfeebled man whom he hoped to replace. To ascertain the likelihood of an early vacancy, Taft decided to find out more precisely the state of White's health. A visit with the Chief Justice in mid-March, 1921, proved discouraging. Though White referred to his illness, he said nothing about retiring. On May 18 the clouds parted; the Chief Justice's physician, Dr. J. J. Richardson, informed Taft that "the end is only a question of hours." White died the next day.

By June, 1921, Taft's tireless drive finally began to pay off. On the twenty-ninth, he heard the welcome news that "Mr. Harding is beginning to inform people that he intends soon to announce your appointment." The next day Taft was named Chief Justice. The nomination was promptly confirmed, with only four dissenting votes—those of Senators William E. Borah, Hiram Johnson, Robert M. La Follette, and Tom Watson. William Howard Taft was at long last entering the temple. The goal had been reached only after more than thirty years of dreaming, pining, skillful planning—and a dash of luck.

The office of the Chief Justice carries scant inherent powers. The Chief Justice manages the docket, presents the cases in conference, and guides the discussion. When in the majority, he assigns the writing of opinions. Whatever influence he exerts in the exercise of these prerogatives rests less on formal authority than on elusive personal characteristics. Taft annexed another power no previous Chief Justice had exercised—that of reformer, using devices that flew in the face of the proprieties.

By the second decade of the twentieth century, the federal courts were in dire need of modernization. Decentralized and encumbered by a staggering variety of outmoded procedures, including automatic appeals to the Supreme Court, the federal judicial system had become characterized by clogged dockets and delayed judgments. The first year in office, Taft launched his campaign for reform, making appeals in speeches across the continent, presenting his case in legal periodicals and in testimony before the House and Senate Judiciary Committees. Motivating these intense and far-flung activities was his determination to achieve efficiency and "teamwork" in the entire federal judiciary. The act of September 14, 1922 marks a new chapter in the administration of the federal judicial system. Previous legislation had been *ad hoc* and temporary, difficulties growing out of an ever increasing docket were met by increasing the number of judges or districts, or lengthening the term. Without disturbing the autonomy of district judges, the 1922 act enabled judges from various parts of the country to meet and work out means of eliminating defects in the administration of justice. Above all, it embodied the "executive principle," and enhanced the power and prestige of the Chief Justice. Taft then turned to the problem of congestion in the Supreme Court's docket.

"We made our preparation with care," he later gloated, "and it proved to be easier than we supposed." The Judges Bill of 1925, giving the Supreme Court greater control over its docket, went through with only token opposition. Two major aspects of the Chief Justice's three-pronged program had now been enacted into law. The judicial millennium had not, however, been achieved. The rules-of-procedure revision Taft long advocated never became a reality during his lifetime. Suspicious of judicial aggrandizement, the lawmakers were stubbornly opposed. The Chief Justice's impassioned plea that the grant of authority he desired was "not a delegation of great power to the Supreme Court" was to no avail. It was a cruel fate. On no other reform had Taft worked so long or so persistently. In 1934 Congress authorized some of the changes Taft had long advocated.

Despite this failure, Chief Justice Taft's place in history as a judicial reformer is firmly established. Bringing to the Chief Justiceship an almost majestic conception of its prerogatives, duties, and responsibilities, he seized the initiative and achieved substantial results. As judicial architect, Taft ranks second only to Oliver Ellsworth, who originally devised the judicial system.

Piercing the legislative barrier is not easy for a Chief Justice, even for one like Taft, uninhibited by the traditional proprieties. In overcoming his theoretical isolation from partisan politics, he utilized and exploited an intricate web of personal relations. By 1926 Taft's influence with legislators seemed presumptuous. Following the annual judicial conference, the Chief Justice, presenting his recommendations to Congress, "simply called the Chairman and the ranking member of each Judiciary Committee in to ask them to take up the subject and see if there could not be some plan devised."

To enlist support for his reform program, the Chief Justice occasionally communicated directly with newspaper editors. In 1926, agitated by the increasing audacity of mobsters and the feeble reaction of law-enforcement agencies, Chief Justice Taft granted an interview to Oliver P. Newman of *Collier's* magazine. Later Taft wondered about the propriety of his action. "I shrink from the publicity that you are giving to the article," the Chief wrote the editor. "It is not of sufficient importance, and I can not help doubting the propriety of my having given you the interview." Such misgivings did not curb his activities. In 1928, he enlisted press support against Senator George Norris' campaign to withdraw from the federal courts jurisdiction of diversity-of-citizenship cases. Much alarmed, the Chief Justice notified Casper Yost, editor of the St. Louis *Globe-Democrat,* of approval in Congress of "the most radical bill that has been introduced in either House. . . ." The next year he talked freely to Basil Manly of the Washington *Star,* attacking lax law enforcement. That such statements threw the spotlight on state and federal agents and judges did not matter. Nor was he deterred by the implication that he was passing judgment on the policies of relatively autonomous state government organizations and on those guiding federal executive departments.

Among the stabilizing forces in the United States, none was so powerful, so disposed to uphold the federal courts, or so receptive to appeals from their distinguished former president, as the American Bar Association. A faithful attendant at its annual meetings, the Chief Justice was not content merely to put in an appearance. An activist, he spared no effort to enlist the association's support.

The most striking example of Taft's effectiveness as a lobbyist was the campaign he waged for a new Supreme Court building. Though he had long favored a new building, Taft gave little serious attention to it until 1925, when a Senate bill authorized expenditures of fifty million dollars for new public buildings. This proposal met defeat in the Senate. However, since the Senate appropriations bill conflicted with the House version, it went to conference. There Taft's lobbying was more successful and the conference report called upon the Secretary of the Treasury to acquire a site for the Supreme Court. At the cornerstone ceremony, October, 1932, Chief Justice Hughes declared: "For this enterprise now progressing to completion, we are indebted to the late Chief Justice William Howard Taft more than any one else. This building is the result of his intelligent persistence."

Because of wide interests, ranging from the appointment of district judges to protection of the smallest entrepreneur, Chief Justice Taft found it advantageous to establish cordial relations with the President and various members of his official family. He often dealt directly with Presidents Harding, Coolidge, and Hoover. Though the Chief Justiceship did not encompass formal policy making, Taft's invaluable experience as a former President not unnaturally made him feel that any White House incumbent would welcome his help. Warren G. Harding clearly needed it, as he himself frankly confessed. Not one to ignore obvious receptiveness to advice, the Chief Justice sought to enlist White House influence on his program of judicial reform.

Calvin Coolidge's first full year in office was 1924. Taft's attempts to influence "silent Cal" brought varying results. When the Chief Justice hastened to the White House to ask for suppression of the Caraway bill, designed to restrict the role of federal judges in charging juries, Coolidge proved receptive. Less successful were Taft's efforts to put Coolidge behind the movement for higher judicial salaries. Despite Taft's lurid description of the dire financial plight of inferior federal judges, the frugal Vermonter refused to lend a hand. The apprehensive Chief Justice actively campaigned for presidential vetoes of the Bursum veteran's bonus bill, the proposed salary increase for post office employees, and the McNary-Haugen farm subsidy bill. The Chief Justice urged reduction of the military budget and became involved in the appointment of high ranking officials to the Philippines.

In his inaugural address President Hoover, touching on a theme close to Taft's heart, blasted "disregard and disobedience of law," and called for "reform, reorganization, and strengthening of our whole judicial and enforcement system. . . ." At a mid-March, 1929 luncheon with the Chief Justice, the President deplored the difficulty of finding the kind of men he intended to put on his proposed Commission on Law Observance and Enforcement. Though strongly sympathetic, Taft stopped short of acquiescence in Hoover's desire to raid the Court for qualified personnel, reacting icily to the President's suggestion that a Justice might temporarily withdraw to serve on the commission. Any Justice joining such a body, Taft insisted, must resign. He favored the appointment of Brandeis or Van Devanter, both entitled to retire. To the Chief's astonishment, the President favored neither. He wanted former Attorney General Harlan Fiske Stone. The most recent appointee, Stone was nowhere near retirement age, nor was he willing to retire. In Taft's mind, moreover, he was not qualified. The Court stood solidly behind Taft and Stone in their resolution not to be budged, and Hoover finally appointed George W. Wickersham chairman of the Crime Commission.

After this trying struggle with Hoover, Taft realized the insurmountable difficulty of dealing with the President on a personal basis. In the spring and summer of 1929, Taft brooded over Hoover's "radical" tendencies. "I think that Hoover is a new man and thinks that everything ought to be new." The Chief Justice's worst fear was that the President would use the first opportunity to fill the Court with "some rather extreme destroyers of the Constitution." Formerly he had turned to the White House when political storms threatened. Never before had impending disaster been more obvious, nor had his power to affect its onrush ever been so weak. Once he had found President Coolidge receptive to his advice. Now, a dying man, he poured out his recommendations to Colonel Isaac Ullman, corset manufacturer and Republican boss of New Haven: "The only real hope we have is the 'Do Nothing' policy . . . for with the 'Do Nothing' policy the insurgents can literally do nothing. . . ."

Taft's political activities spread beyond domestic politics. In the summer of 1922, he had plunged into the economic-political tangle that was Europe. More closely allied to his role as judicial leader were Taft's earnest efforts on behalf of America's participation in the Permanent Court of International Justice. Though remaining tactfully silent once the issue of the Permanent Court became embroiled in partisan politics, Taft went on a confidential mission, approved by Secretary of State Hughes, to "see if the League of Nations could not so modify the statute establishing the Court as the United States might become a participant in respect to the Court, without assuming any of the obligations of the League."

Probably no man ever had as much influence on the choice of judicial personnel as William Howard Taft. On the Circuit Court he had demonstrated unflagging interest in the selection of judges, strongly endorsing those he supported and outspokenly opposing those he considered disqualified. From his first month in the White House he gave close attention to judicial personnel. In four years, he appointed six members, including a Chief Justice, to the high bench. The Chief Justiceship placed him in a position to propound, and perhaps enforce, a political philosophy long in the making. This could be achieved only with a Court made up of judges whose minds went along with his own. As Chief Executive he had used his appointing power with notable success, only to have his effort neutralized by President Wilson. In 1921 the Supreme Court was not, the Chief Justice said, "in a strong position." Republican victory opened a "possibility of a great opportunity for Harding to make the Court staunch and strong." The Chief Justice let President Harding know promptly that he would be available as presidential advisor. While appointments were pending, Taft bombarded the President with suggestions and recommendations. He was not notably successful in winning his first choices, but in certain instances he used his influence to defeat selection of an "off-horse," such as the eminent Chief Judge Benjamin N. Cardozo of New York, who might "herd with Holmes and Brandeis."

Prior to Taft, the Court's titular head had rarely participated in such matters. Taft took a totally different view. His concern for lower federal court personnel was but another aspect of his abiding determination to unite and organize the judiciary of the country, not excluding state courts of last resort, into a harmonious system. Judges loyal to Taft—"team workers"—were necessary for carrying out Supreme Court decisions. After conferring with federal judges and members of various bar associations, he freely transmitted recommendations to the Attorney General and the President.

To win Taft's certification, judicial aspirants had to meet certain requirements. Foremost among these was approved ideological orientation. Principle, not party, was his test. Above all, it was necessary to have colleagues, with views corresponding to his own, who would join him in repelling assaults on the Constitution. John W. Davis, Democratic candidate for the Presidency in 1924, was at the top of his preferred list. Constitutional conservatism of the Chief Justice's brand was the only safeguard against "radicals," "progressives," "bolshevists," and "socialists." Regardless of party, all were considered subversive, and must be blocked at all cost. Overpowering concern for judicial personnel was a logical outcome of Taft's political philosophy: belief in the moral basis of a good society, in the natural existence of classes, and in the differentiation of functions among the classes.

Taft came to the bench determined to make promptness "a model for the courts of the country." To accelerate the Court's business, Taft suggested that the recess be shortened. To Taft's dismay his colleagues, some "lazy," others "old," demurred. The Chief Justice was often faced with "a cabal in the Court to try to influence me to reduce work." Yet, his success was remarkable. At the end of the 1922 term the Court broke all records in the number of cases disposed of. The period between the filing of a suit and the hearing of it had been reduced by three months. Taft sought to speed up the disposition of cases not only by appeals to his colleagues, but also by revising the Court's rules. Under pressure from Taft, the Court adopted the rule of putting cases out for hearing just as soon as they were ready.

Chief Justice Taft was a zealous economizer. Early in his tenure he cracked down on counsel who were slow to make an additional deposit to cover estimated costs in cases subject to dismissal. He also led a successful effort to cut printing costs.

Taft brought to the Court a clear image of the Chief Justiceship—the office and its powers. Motivating his tenure was a passion for "teamwork"; it alone could give "weight and solidarity" to judicial decisions. "Massing the Court" was a consuming ambition. To this end, he persuaded by example, frowned on dissents, exploited personal courtesy and charm, maximized the assignment and reassignment powers, relied on the expertise of his associates.

Taft had long harbored a grudge against Brandeis for his participation in the Ballinger scandal of 1910. On the Court, the hatchet was apparently buried. Bubbling with enthusiasm, Taft reported that "Brandeis and I are on most excellent terms and have some sympathetic views. . . ." One of the reasons Justice Clarke gave former President Wilson for resigning from the Court was that he and Brandeis "were agreeing less and less frequently in the decision of cases involving liberal principles."

Taft persuaded by example as well as by precept. During the early part of his tenure especially, he displayed rare open-mindedness. A striking example is

Sonneborn v. *Cureton,* 262 U.S. 506 (1923). Brandeis, joined by Clarke and Pitney, had dissented from a cursory opinion by Justice McReynolds. After reargument, Taft reassigned the opinion to himself. Again there were exchanges with Brandeis, leading to a unanimous opinion delivered by the Chief Justice. Proud of his accomplishment, Brandeis commented: "That's my opinion. Taft wrote it on the basis of a memo in which I analyzed all the cases." For a while, with Taft in the center chair, it seemed that the bitter divisions which had characterized the White Court had been forever banished.

Happy working relations were not accidental. Taft went to great pains to establish *esprit de corps*. Seemingly trivial personal considerations—the sending of salmon to Justice Van Devanter, the customary ride he gave Holmes and Brandeis after the Saturday conference, the Christmas card that always went out to Justice McKenna—all such personal attention to highly dissimilar human beings contributed immeasurably to judicial teamwork.

The Chief Justice's ability to gauge and utilize the capacities of his colleagues is reflected in the assignment of opinions. Apart from his "radical" views, Holmes was a source of much satisfaction, especially because of the rapidity with which the eighty-odd-year-old judge turned out opinions. Though Justice Sutherland was considered a "very strong man," Taft had to drive him unmercifully to get his opinions out. Though the "strongest man on the Court," Van Devanter was "opinion-shy," and a perfectionist, "never content to let an opinion go until he has polished it and worked on it until it is a gem." The extra load usually fell on Taft himself. The Chief Justice's capacity for bearing more than his share reenforced the magnetism of his personality.

Taft used his assignment power to promote unanimous or near-unanimous opinions. If the judge to whom the opinion had been initially assigned failed to enlist the largest possible support, Taft reassigned it. Reassignment did not correspond to a game of chance; it was but another means of developing teamwork. Toward the end, the Chief Justice's drive to "mass the Court" faltered. Impaired health of some of his associates and his own declining physical strength constantly threw monkey wrenches in his path. Personal idiosyncrasies also contributed to the growing disharmony, the break finally taking the form of bitter dissents. During Taft's last years at the helm these came fast and furious.

Joseph McKenna, seventy-eight years old and failing, was Taft's first serious problem. "In case after case he will write an opinion," the Chief Justice reported, "and bring it into conference and it will meet objection because he has missed a point in one case, or, as in one instance, he wrote an opinion deciding the case one way when there had been a unanimous vote the other, including his own." In the spring of 1924 the Chief Justice made an unsuccessful attempt to persuade McKenna to retire. Taft pushed on. The Associates finally authorized the Chief Justice to confer with McKenna, and the Associate Justice reluctantly agreed that the Court's opinion must control.

Another major obstacle to judicial teamwork was Justice James C. Mc-

Reynolds. Strongly anti-Semitic, McReynolds refused to sit with Brandeis for a Court photograph. McReynolds' meanness emerged in all its dinginess when he declined to sign the joint letter sent Justice Clarke on his resignation.

Brandeis presented a somewhat different problem. His appointment to the Court had been for the ex-President "one of the deepest wounds that I have ever had as an American and as a lover of the Constitution and a believer in progressive conservatism." Surface friendliness and a remarkable degree of give and take on both sides obscured Taft's deep-seated distrust. The Chief Justice feared that Brandeis' diabolical influence engulfed Holmes, giving him "two votes instead of one."

After 1927, the loss of Van Devanter as effective conference leader, combined with Taft's own failing health, made the Chief Justice increasingly despondent. "Three of the nine," he complained, "are pretty radical, and occasionally they get some of the other brethren, which is disquieting." As his customary sense of balance and fair play declined, Taft became ever more impatient with differences, more rigid in his determination to have everyone endorse the opinion on his side.

As President, Taft possessed extensive power. But since he did not know, as T.R. said, the "joys of leadership," the experience had been frustrating. As Chief Justice, he wielded the kind of authority he thoroughly enjoyed, "power without worry," moving him to endow the office with executive prerogatives he had abjured as President.

Shortly after Taft's appointment, an editorial in *The New Republic* seriously questioned his qualifications. The editorial's main trust was the contention that Taft's craving for the Chief Justiceship was stimulated by his recognition of the Court as the molder of social and economic policy. Taking a realistic stance, *The New Republic* affirmed that judges were not "merely passive interpreters of ready-made law; they adjust conflicting interests, and by so doing enforce, consciously or unconsciously, varying conceptions of public policy." On the vital public issues of the day, *The New Republic* had no doubt where the new Chief Justice would stand.

Taft's first major opinion, in *Truax* v. *Corrigan,* 257 U.S. 312 (1921) did not come as a surprise. Involved was the constitutionality of an Arizona statute, barring state courts from issuing injunctions in labor cases, except under special circumstances. Restaurant owners of Bisbee, Arizona, had resorted to the injunctive remedy against boycott and picketing of their place of business by ex-employees. The Arizona court's denial of equitable relief evoked from the plaintiffs in error the contention that the statute, as interpreted by the state supreme court, deprived them of property without due process of law and denied them equal protection of the laws contrary to the Fourteenth Amendment. A majority of five sustained this view.

The facts raised an issue with which the Chief Justice had been closely identified since his early years of judging in Ohio and in the Sixth Circuit. A strong exponent of the injunctive process in labor disputes, he seized this opportunity to pit the Fourteenth Amendment against state legislation favorable to labor. Taft began by defining plaintiffs' business as a property right; free access to it was "incident to such right." "A law which operates to make lawful such a wrong as is described in plaintiffs' complaint deprives the owner of the business and the premises of his property without due process, and can not be held valid under the Fourteenth Amendment."

Defendants had argued that the property right was not absolute, that "while the right to conduct a lawful business is property," no person had "a vested right" against state regulation in the public interest of the conditions surrounding that business. "It is true," the Chief Justice admitted, "that no one has a vested right in any particular rule of the common law." It was "also true" that "the legislative power of a State can only be exerted in subordination to the fundamental principles of right and justice which the guaranty of due process in the Fourteenth Amendment is intended to preserve, and that a purely arbitrary and capricious exercise of that power whereby a wrongful and highly injurious invasion of property rights, as here, is practically sanctioned and the owner stripped of all real remedy, is wholly at variance with those principles."

Taft confined his ruling to the particular means the defendants employed. "The real question here is, were the means used illegal?" States could and did differ on the legality of "peaceful" means, but this was not "the mere case of a peaceful secondary boycott." No statute could constitutionally legalize the methods used. Their illegality was "without doubt and fundamental." There is a minimum of protection to which property owners are entitled and of which they may not be deprived.

> *To give operation to such a statute whereby serious losses inflicted by such unlawful means are in effect made remediless, is, we think, to disregard fundamental rights of liberty and property and to deprive the person suffering the loss of due process of law.*

Taft's opinion had assumed that the Arizona court's construction of the statute in question operated to grant the defendants immunity from both civil and criminal action. Suppose, however, the highest court of Arizona had meant to withhold from plaintiffs only the equitable relief of injunction. Would this construction imply a denial of the equal protection of the laws?

Taft's reply was no less unequivocal than his answer to the due-process issue: "If this is not a denial of the equal protection of the laws, then it is hard to conceive what would be." Here was "a direct invasion" of property right, "unlawful when committed by any one, and remediable because of its otherwise irreparable character by equitable process"—*except* "when committed by ex-employees of the injured person." The Chief Justice deplored the rationale behind such legislation: "When fundamental rights are thus attempted to be taken away, we may well subject the experiment to attentive judgment. . . . The Constitution was intended, its very purpose was, to *prevent* experimentation with the fundamental rights of the individual."

Taft's first major opinion seemed to confirm his critic's worst fears. Taking a predictable position, the Chief Justice had strongly endorsed private property rights at the expense of social experimentation. Implicit in this landmark decision was a cleavage not easily fitted into the usual liberal-conservative dichotomy. The real breach concerned the Court's role: what was the proper scope of judicial review? In the *Truax* case, the Chief Justice's activist position seemed clear. His next major opinion in *Stafford* v. *Wallace,* 258 U.S. 495 (1922), however, not only upheld broad federal power under the commerce clause, but announced that Congress had a wide area of discretion, effectively free from judicial second-guessing.

At issue was the Packers and Stockyards Act of 1921, which sought to regulate the business of the packers done in interstate commerce. The object was to secure free and untrammeled flow of livestock from the ranges and farms of the West and Southwest through the various stockyards and ultimately in the form of meat products to consumers throughout the country. The "chief evil" Congress sought to regulate was the monopoly of the packers, "enabling them unduly and arbitrarily to lower prices to the shipper who sells, and unduly and arbitrarily to increase the price to the consumer who buys."

Taft's opinion evinced marked sensitivity to the factual situation. The stockyards were obviously "not a place of rest or final destination." Indeed, they were but "a throat through which the current flows, and the transactions which occur therein are only incident to this current from the West to the East, and from one State to another." Clearly the stockyards and the sales were "necessary factors in the middle of this great current of commerce." Congress, therefore, had treated the various stockyards as "great national public utilities," subject to national regulation.

"The only question," Taft declared, was "whether the business done in the stockyards between the receipt of the livestock in the yards and the shipments of them therefrom is a part of interstate commerce, or is so associated with it as to bring it within the power of national regulation." The controlling precedent was *Swift* v. *United States,* 196 U.S. 375 (1905) in which Justice Holmes' comprehensive decision, Taft declared, "leaves to us in this case little but the obvious application of the principles there declared." In language of an enlightened Progressive, Taft held that application of the commerce clause in *Swift* was "the result of the natural development of interstate commerce under modern conditions."

> *It was the inevitable recognition of the great central fact that such streams of commerce from one part of the country to another which are ever flowing are in their very essence the commerce among the states and with foreign nations which historically it was one of the chief purposes of the Constitution to bring under national protection and control. This court [in* Swift*] declined to defeat this purpose in respect of such a stream and take it out of complete national regulation by a nice and technical inquiry into the non-interstate character of some of its necessary incidents and facilities when considered alone and without reference to their association with the movement of which they were an essential but subordinate part.*

Echoing the nationalistic jurisprudence of Chief Justice Marshall, Taft wrote: "Whatever amounts to more or less constant practice, and threatens to obstruct or unduly to burden the freedom of interstate commerce, is within the regulatory power of Congress to consider and decide the fact of danger and meet it. This Court," the Chief Justice declared emphatically, "will certainly not substitute its judgment for that of Congress in such a matter unless the relation of the subject to interstate commerce and its effect upon it are clearly non-existent."

By 1926 the breach within the Court could no longer be hidden. That year witnessed one of the most significant decisions in American constitutional history—the six to three ruling in *Myers* v. *United States,* 272 U.S. 52 (1926) upholding the President's authority to remove a postmaster without the consent of the Senate. "I never wrote an opinion that I felt to be so important in its effect," Taft said after the decision came down. The previous year he had upheld the President's power to pardon a criminal contemnor. Writing for a unanimous Court in *Ex parte Grossman,* 267 U.S. 87 (1925), the former President, obviously influenced by his White House experience, had rejected the contention that sustaining such executive authority would necessarily weaken the power and dignity of the judiciary. He now seized the opportunity further to aggrandize the President's power, but not without aggravating the deep split in his own Court.

Taft might have adopted the so-called middle ground proposed by Solicitor General Beck in his brief for the government. This position would have permitted Congress to "guide and direct the discretion of the President by such statutory qualifications as are properly inherent in the nature of an office, but without disturbing the power of removal as the Constitution vested it" in the President. The Chief Justice might have restricted his holding to the facts at bar, that is, to purely executive offices. Instead, he chose to exalt the President's office and power by extending to him unlimited power to remove any executive officer, in high level or "inferior" posts. Taft did not live to see the Court limit his doctrine in the 1935 case of *Humphrey's Executor* v. *United States,* 295 U.S. 602 (1935).

"I would rather have been Marshall than any other American," President Taft mused. "Marshall is certainly the greatest jurist America has ever produced. . . . He made this country." Taft sometimes emulated—or appeared to emulate—his idol. His opinion in *Stafford* seemed to place him squarely in the Marshall tradition.

Though Taft's views of national power under the commerce clause are reminiscent of John Marshall, his ideas on the federal taxing power would have made the Great Nationalist turn over in his grave. In *Bailey* v. *Drexel Furniture Co.,* 259 U.S. 20 (1922), Taft, with only the dissenting vote of Justice Clarke, used the Tenth Amendment as an independent limitation on national taxing power and declared invalid the child labor tax of 1919. Marshall, in interpreting national power, never referred to the Tenth Amendment as a restriction. He considered it a truism, a constitutional tranquilizer, restating the content of the supremacy clause.

For Marshall the primary restraints on the national government were political. Though paying lip service to this view in *Stafford,* Taft sometimes converted the auxiliary judicial control into a primary check. Under him the "Guardian Kings" became a bulwark against the "overwhelming mass of ill-digested legislation poured out by the lawmakers." Not always sensitive to the danger of substituting judicial supremacy for judicial review, claiming always that he was moved by nothing but the *law,* Taft attempted to identfy judicial gloss with the Constitution itself. The Supreme Court became "a sacred priesthood immune from profane criticism." It seems never to have occurred to Taft that his presumably objective rule for protecting the people from themselves often coincided with subjective desire. An absolutist at heart, "the law" was his instrument of power. For a while, when dissents were few, the voice of the Chief Justice was the law. Finally, with the defection of the once loyal Stone to the Holmes-Brandeis bloc, Taft ironically became the prisoner of the same force—popular power—that wreaked havoc on his Presidency.

Under Chief Justice Taft's leadership, a firmly united judicial majority envisioned itself in the van of national progress. The *laissez-faire* dogma, glorified in the writings of Herbert Spencer and William Graham Sumner, was the principle avenue to wealth and social happiness. Responsibility for upholding time-tested values and for safeguarding society from the consequences of unwise legislative meddling rested primarily on the courts. In 1930, Professor Felix Frankfurter deplored what Dean Roscoe Pound called the "carnival of unconstitutionality":

> *Since 1920, the Court has invalidated more legislation than in fifty years preceding. Views that were antiquated twenty-five years ago have been resurrected in decisions nullifying minimum wage laws for women in industry, a standard weight bread law to protect buyers from short weight and honest bakers from unfair competition, a law fixing the resale price of theatre tickets by scalpers in New York, laws controlling exploitation of the unemployed by employment agencies and many tax laws. . . . Merely as a matter of arithmetic, this is an impressive mortality rate. But a numerical tally of the cases does not tell the tale. In the first place, all laws are not of the same importance. Secondly, a single decision may decide the fate of a great body of legislation. . . . Moreover, the discouragement of legislative effort through a particular adverse decision and the general weakening of the sense of legislative responsibility are destructive influences not measurable by statistics.*

Taft's triumphant march continued to the end, but the future was clouded with uncertainty. By 1930, the world he had known and the people on whom he had come to rely were in eclipse. As the economy slid rapidly toward the abyss, governmental intervention was openly advocated as an appropriate and essential remedy. A dying man, he became obsessed with the necessity of maintaining the Court's conservative composition. Taft resigned on February 3, 1930, and was undoubtedly cheered when Hoover passed over Stone (who had "definitely ranged himself with Brandeis and with Holmes"), and elevated Charles Evans Hughes to the Chief Justiceship. A little over a month later, March 8, 1930, before having to endure the New Deal, the "Big Chief" died.

William Howard Taft ranks higher in the roster of our Chief Justices than is generally supposed. His first three years were extraordinarily successful. The Chief Justice confessed his inadequacy with technical matters of procedure and jurisdiction, and leaned heavily on Justice Willis Van Devanter. Keeping the Court "consistent with itself" is, however, but a single aspect of the job of guiding and directing. Taft had remarkable success in the Chief Justice's role of Court moderator. He had a gift for "welding them together and making them harmonious."

None of Taft's predecessors, with the possible exception of Chief Justice Marshall, entertained such an expansive view of the Chief Justiceship or made such effective use of it on so many different fronts. Taft was an excellent administrator and unmatched as a judicial architect. On his own initiative, the tenth Chief Justice pressed for revisions in the judicial system. To win enactment, he stalked the halls of Congress, enlisted the support of newspapers, bar associations, and others.

Taft's Chief Justiceship might have been constructive, but for his haunting fear of progressivism and progressives. Had he maintained the powerful position he assumed in his commerce cases and minimum wage dissent, *Adkins* v. *Children's Hospital,* 261 U.S. 525 (1923), he might have, with the backing of Holmes, Brandeis, Stone, and possibly Sanford, swung the Court along the line the great triumvirate was so eloquently staking out. Lacking in William Howard Taft was the quality Woodrow Wilson suggested as an essential requirement of statesmanship—"a large vision of things to come."

SELECTED BIBLIOGRAPHY

Taft's voluminous papers are in the Manuscripts Division, Library of Congress. His own writings include: *Four Aspects of Civic Duty* (New York, 1906); *Popular Government: Its Essence, Its Permanence, and Its Perils* (New Haven, 1913); *The Anti-Trust Act and the Supreme Court* (New York, 1914); *Our Chief Magistrate and His Powers* (New York, 1916); *Liberty Under Law* (New Haven, 1922); *A Collection of Addresses Delivered on Various Occasions* (New York, 1908); "The Right of Private Property," 3 *Michigan Law Journal,* 215 (1894); "Criticisms of the Federal Judiciary," 24 *American Law Review* 641 (1895); "Delays and Defects in the Enforcement of Law in This Country," 70 *Albany Law Journal* 300 (1908); "The Jurisdiction of the Supreme Court under the Act of February 13, 1925," 35 *Yale Law Journal* 1 (1925). The most authoritative biographical writings are: H. F. Pringle, *The Life and Times of William Howard Taft* (New York, 1939) and Alpheus Thomas Mason, *William Howard Taft: Chief Justice* (New York, 1964). Other helpful references are: Mrs. W. H. Taft, *Recollections of Full Years* (New York, 1914); F. McHale, *President and Chief Justice: The Life and Public Services of William Howard Taft* (Philadelphia, 1931);

A. T. Mason, *The Supreme Court From Taft to Warren* (Baton Rouge, 1968); ——, "The Labor Decisions of Chief Justice Taft," 78 *University of Pennsylvania Law Review,* 585 (1930); W. F. Murphy, "Chief Justice Taft and the Lower Court Bureaucracy," 24 *Journal of Politics,* 461 (1962); ——, "In His Own Image: Mr. Justice Taft and Supreme Court Appointments," *Supreme Court Review,* 159 (1961).

William Howard Taft

REPRESENTATIVE OPINIONS

BAILEY v. DREXEL FURNITURE CO., 259 U.S. 20 (1922)

The Revenue Act of 1919 imposed a tax on mine and quarry employers of children under sixteen, and mill and factory owners who employed children under fourteen, or who permitted children between fourteen and sixteen to work more than an eight-hour day and a six-day week. A 10% tax was levied on net profits. The Drexel Furniture Company, which had employed a boy under fourteen, paid the tax under protest and then sued to recover. The question was whether the regulation could be sustained under the federal taxing power. Speaking through Chief Justice Taft, the Court condemned the act as a "penalty," not a true tax. In regulating a course of conduct, the act invaded the reserved powers of the states under the Tenth Amendment. Only Justice Clarke dissented.

MR. CHIEF JUSTICE TAFT delivered the opinion of the court.

This case presents the question of the constitutional validity of the Child Labor Tax Law. The plaintiff below, the Drexel Furniture Company, is engaged in the manufacture of furniture in the Western District of North Carolina. On September 20, 1921, it received a notice from Bailey, United States Collector of Internal Revenue for the District, that it had been assessed $6,312.79 for having during the taxable year 1919 employed and permitted to work in its factory a boy under fourteen years of age, thus incurring the tax of ten per cent. on its net profits for that year. The Company paid the tax under protest, and after rejection of its claim for a refund, brought this suit. On demurrer to an amended complaint, judgment was entered for the Company against the Collector for the full amount with interest. The writ of error is prosecuted by the Collector direct from the District Court under § 238 of the Judicial Code.

The Child Labor Tax Law is Title XII of an act entitled "An Act To provide revenue, and for other purposes," approved February 24, 1919, c. 18, 40 Stat. 1057, 1138. The heading of the title is "Tax on Employment of Child Labor." It begins with § 1200 and includes eight sections. Section 1200 is as follows:

"SEC. 1200. That every person (other than a bona fide boys' or girls' canning club recognized by the Agricultural Department of a State and of the United States) operating (a) any mine or quarry situated in the United States in which children under the age of sixteen years have been employed or permitted to work during any portion of the taxable year; or (b) any mill, cannery, workshop, factory, or manufacturing establishment situated in the United States in which children under the age of fourteen years have been employed or permitted to work, or children between the ages of fourteen and sixteen have been employed or permitted to work more than eight hours in any day or more than six days in any week, or after the hour of seven o'clock post meridian, or before the hour of six o'clock ante meridian, during any portion of the taxable year, shall pay for each taxable year, in addition to all other taxes imposed by law, an excise tax equivalent to 10 per centum of the entire net profits received or accrued for such year from the sale or disposition of the product of such mine, quarry, mill, cannery, workshop, factory, or manufacturing establishment."

Section 1203 relieves from liability to the tax any one who employs a child, believing him to be of proper age, relying on a certificate to this effect issued by persons prescribed by a Board consisting of the Secretary of the Treasury, the Commissioner of Internal Revenue and the Secretary of Labor, or issued by state authorities. The section also provides in paragraph (b) that "the tax imposed by this title shall not be imposed in the case of any person who proves to the satisfaction of the Secretary that the only employment or permission to work which but for this section would subject him to the tax, has been of a child employed or permitted to work under a mistake of fact as to the age of such child, and without intention to evade the tax."

Section 1206 gives authority to the Commissioner of Internal Revenue, or any other person authorized by him, "to enter and inspect at any time any mine, quarry, mill, cannery, workshop, factory, or manufacturing establishment." The Secretary of Labor, or any person whom he authorizes, is given like authority in order to comply with a request of the Commissioner to make such inspection and report the same. Any person who refuses entry or obstructs inspection is made subject to fine or imprisonment or both.

The law is attacked on the ground that it is a regulation of the employment of child labor in the States—an exclusively state function under the Federal Constitution and within the reservations of the Tenth Amendment. It is defended on the ground that it is a mere excise tax levied by the Congress of the United States under its broad power of taxation conferred by § 8, Article I, of the Federal Constitution. We must construe the law and interpret the intent and meaning of Congress from the language of the act. The words are to be given their ordinary meaning unless the context shows that they are differently used. Does this law impose a tax with only that incidental restraint and regulation which a tax must inevitably involve? Or does it regulate by the use of the so-called tax as a penalty? If a tax, it is clearly an excise. If it were an excise on a commodity or other thing of value we might not be permitted under previous decisions of this court to infer solely from its heavy burden that the act intends a prohibition instead of a tax. But this act is more. It provides a heavy exaction for a departure from a detailed and specified course of conduct in business. That course of business is that employers shall employ in mines and quarries, children of an age greater than sixteen years; in mills and factories, children of an age greater than fourteen years, and shall prevent children of less than sixteen years in mills and factories from working more than eight hours a day or six days in the week. If an employer departs from this prescribed course of business, he is to pay to the Government one-tenth of his entire net income in the business for a full year. The amount is not to be proportioned in any degree to the extent or frequency of the departures, but is to be paid by the employer in full measure whether he employs five hundred children for a year, or employs only one for a day. Moreover, if he does not know the child is within the named age limit, he is not to pay; that is to say, it is only where he knowingly departs from the prescribed course that payment is to be exacted. Scienter is associated with penalties not with taxes. The employer's factory is to be subject to inspection at any time not only by the taxing officers of the Treasury, the Department normally charged with the collection of taxes, but also by the Secretary of Labor and his subordinates whose normal function is the advancement and protection of the welfare of the workers. In the light of these features of the act, a court must be blind not to see that the so-called tax is imposed to stop the employment of children within the age limits prescribed. Its prohibitory and regulatory effect and purpose are palpable. All others can see and understand this. How can we properly shut our minds to it?

It is the high duty and function of this court in cases regularly brought to its bar to decline to recognize or enforce seeming laws of Congress, dealing with subjects not entrusted to Congress but left or committed by the supreme law of the land to the control of the States. We can not avoid the duty even though it require us to refuse to give effect to legislation designed to promote the highest good. The good sought in unconstitutional legislation is an insidious feature because it leads citizens and legislators of good purpose to promote it without thought of the serious breach it will make in the ark of our covenant or the harm which will come from breaking down recognized standards. In the maintenance of local self government, on the one hand, and the national power, on the other, our country has been able to endure and prosper for near a century and a half.

Out of a proper respect for the acts of a coördinate branch of the Government, this court has gone far to sustain taxing acts as such, even though there has been ground for suspecting from the weight of the tax it was intended to destroy its subject. But, in the act before us, the presumption of validity cannot prevail, because the proof of the contrary is found on the very face of its provisions. Grant the validity of this law, and all that Congress would need to do, hereafter, in seeking to take over to its control any one of the great number of subjects of public interest, jurisdiction of which the States have never parted with, and which are reserved to them by the Tenth Amendment, would be to enact a detailed measure of complete regulation of the subject and enforce it by a so-called tax upon departures from it. To give such magic to the word "tax" would be to break down all constitutional limitation of the powers of Congress and completely wipe out the sovereignty of the States.

The difference between a tax and a penalty is sometimes difficult to define and yet the consequences of the distinction in the required method of their collection often are important. Where the sovereign enacting the law has power to impose both tax and penalty the difference between revenue production and mere regulation may be immaterial, but not so when one sovereign can impose a tax only, and the power of regulation rests in another. Taxes are occasionally imposed in the discretion of the legislature on proper subjects with the primary motive of obtaining revenue from them and with the incidental motive of discouraging them by making their continuance onerous. They do not lose their character as taxes because of the incidental motive. But there comes a time in the extension of the penalizing features of the so-called tax when it loses its character as such and becomes a mere penalty with the characteristics of regulation and punishment. Such is the case in the law before us. Although Congress does not invalidate the contract of employment or expressly declare that the employment within the mentioned ages is illegal, it does exhibit its intent practically to achieve the latter result by adopting the criteria of wrongdoing and imposing its principal consequence on those who transgress its standard.

The case before us can not be distinguished from that of *Hammer* v. *Dagenhart,* 247 U.S. 251. Congress there enacted a law to prohibit transportation in interstate commerce of goods made at a factory in which there was employment of children within the same ages and for the same number of hours a day and days in a week as are penalized by the act in this case. This court held the law in that case to be void. It said:

"In our view the necessary effect of this act is, by means of a prohibition against the movement in interstate commerce of ordinary commercial commodities, to regulate the hours of labor of children in factories and mines within the States, a purely state authority."

In the case at the bar, Congress in the name of a tax which on the face of the act is a penalty seeks to do the same thing, and the effort must be equally futile.

The analogy of the *Dagenhart Case* is clear. The congressional power over interstate commerce is, within its proper scope, just as complete and unlimited as the congressional power to tax, and the legislative motive in its exercise is just as free from judicial suspicion and inquiry. Yet when Congress threatened to stop interstate commerce in ordinary and necessary commodities, unobjectionable as subjects of transportation, and to deny the same to the people of a State in order to coerce them into compliance with Congress's regulation of state concerns, the court said this was not in fact regulation of interstate commerce, but rather that of State concerns and was invalid. So here the so-called tax is a penalty to coerce people of a State to act as Congress wishes them to act in respect of a matter completely the business of the state government under the Federal Constitution. This case requires as did the *Dagenhart Case* the application of the principle announced by Chief Justice Marshall in *McCulloch* v. *Maryland,* 4 Wheat. 316, 423, in a much quoted passage:

"Should Congress, in the execution of its powers, adopt measures which are prohibited by the Constitution; or should Congress, under the pretext of executing its powers, pass laws for the accomplishment of objects not intrusted to the government; it would become the painful duty of this tribunal, should a case requiring such a decision come before it, to say, that such an act was not the law of the land."

But it is pressed upon us that this court has gone so far in sustaining taxing measures the effect or tendency of which was to accomplish purposes not directly within congressional power that we are bound by authority to maintain this law.

The first of these is *Veazie Bank* v. *Fenno,* 8 Wall. 533. In that case, the validity of a law which increased a tax on the circulating notes of persons and state banks from one per centum to ten per centum was in question. The main question was whether this was a direct tax to be apportioned among the several States "according to their respective numbers." This was answered in the negative. The second objection was stated by the court:

"It is insisted, however, that the tax in the case before us is excessive, and so excessive as to indicate a purpose on the part of Congress to destroy the franchise of the bank, and is, therefore, beyond the constitutional power of Congress."

To this the court answered (p. 548):

"The first answer to this is that the judicial cannot prescribe to the legislative departments of the government limitations upon the exercise of its acknowledged powers. The power to tax may be exercised oppressively upon persons, but the responsibility of the legislature is not to the courts, but to the people by whom its members are elected. So if a particular tax bears heavily upon a corporation, or a class of corporations, it cannot, for that reason only, be pronounced contrary to the Constitution."

It will be observed that the sole objection to the tax there was its excessive character. Nothing else appeared on the face of the act. It was an increase of a tax admittedly legal to a higher rate and that was all. There were no elaborate specifications on the face of the act, as here, indicating the purpose to regulate matters of state concern and jurisdiction through an exaction so applied as to give it the qualities of a penalty for violation of law rather than a tax.

It should be noted, too, that the court, speaking of the extent of the taxing power, used these cautionary words (p. 541):

"There are, indeed, certain virtual limitations, arising from the principles of the Constitution itself. It would undoubtedly be an abuse of the power if so exercised as to impair the separate existence and independent self-government of the States, or if exercised for ends inconsistent with the limited grants of power in the Constitution."

But more than this, what was charged to be the object of the excessive tax was within the congressional authority, as appears from the second answer which the court gave to the objection. After having pointed out the legitimate means taken by Congress to secure a national medium or currency, the court said (p. 549):

"Having thus, in the exercise of undisputed constitutional powers, undertaken to provide a currency for the whole country, it cannot be questioned that Congress may, constitutionally, secure the benefit of it to the people by appropriate legislation. To this end, Congress has denied the quality of legal tender to foreign coins, and has provided by law against the imposition of counterfeit and base coin on the community. To the same end, Congress may restrain, by suitable enactments, the circulation as money of any notes not issued under its own authority. Without this power, indeed, its attempts to secure a sound and uniform currency for the country must be futile."

The next case is that of *McCray* v. *United States,* 195 U.S. 27. That, like the *Veazie Bank Case,* was the increase of an excise tax upon a subject properly taxable in which the taxpayers claimed that the tax had become invalid because the increase was excessive. It was a tax on oleomargarine, a substitute for butter. The tax on the white oleomargarine was one-quarter of a cent a pound, and on the yellow oleomargarine was first two cents and was then by the act in question increased to ten cents per pound. This court held that the discretion of Congress in the exercise of its constitutional powers to levy excise taxes could not be controlled or limited by the courts because the latter might deem the incidence of the tax oppressive or even destructive. It was the same principle as that applied in the *Veazie Bank Case*. This was that Congress in selecting its subjects for taxation might impose the burden where and as it would and that a motive disclosed in its selection to discourage sale or manufacture of an article by a higher tax than on some other did not invalidate the tax. In neither of these cases did the law objected to show on its face as does the law before us the detailed specifications of a regulation of a state concern and business with a heavy exaction to promote the efficacy of such regulation.

The third case is that of *Flint* v. *Stone Tracy Co.*, 220 U.S. 107. It involved the validity of an excise tax levied on the doing of business by all corporations, joint stock companies, associations organized for profit having a capital stock represented by shares, and insurance companies, and measured the excise by the net income of the corporations. There was not in that case the slightest doubt that the tax was a tax, and a tax for revenue, but it was attacked on the ground that such a tax could be made excessive and thus used by Congress to destroy the existence of state corporations. To this, this court gave the same answer as in the *Veazie Bank* and *McCray Cases*. It is not so strong an authority for the Government's contention as they are.

The fourth case is *United States* v. *Doremus*, 249 U.S. 86. That involved the validity of the Narcotic Drug Act, 38 Stat. 785, which imposed a special tax on the manufacture, importation and sale or gift of opium or coca leaves or their compounds or derivatives. It required every person subject to the special tax to register with the Collector of Internal Revenue his name and place of business and forbade him to sell except upon the written order of the person to whom the sale was made on a form prescribed by the Commissioner of Internal Revenue. The vendor was required to keep the order for two years, and the purchaser to keep a duplicate for the same time and both were to be subject to official inspection. Similar requirements were made as to sales upon prescriptions of a physician and as to the dispensing of such drugs directly to a patient by a physician. The validity of a special tax in the nature of an excise tax on the manufacture, importation and sale of such drugs was, of course, unquestioned. The provisions for subjecting the sale and distribution of the drugs to official supervision and inspection were held to have a reasonable relation to the enforcement of the tax and were therefore held valid.

The court said that the act could not be declared invalid just because another motive than taxation, not shown on the face of the act, might have contributed to its passage. This case does not militate against the conclusion we have reached in respect of the law now before us. The court, there, made manifest its view that the provisions of the so-called taxing act must be naturally and reasonably adapted to the collection of the tax and not solely to the achievement of some other purpose plainly within state power.

For the reasons given, we must hold the Child Labor Tax Law invalid and the judgment of the District Court is

Affirmed.

ADKINS v. CHILDREN'S HOSPITAL, 261 U.S. 1 (1936)

In 1918 Congress sought to protect the standard of living of women and minor workers in the District of Columbia by authorizing a board of three members, representing employers, employees and the public, to set minimum wages. A hospital and a woman hotel worker obtained an injunction against the enforcement of the act. The court, through Justice Sutherland, confronted with a mass of sociological data in support of the act, brushed aside all such extra-legal matter as "interesting, but only mildly persuasive." "Freedom of contract is the general rule," Sutherland maintained, "and restraint the exception." In the eyes of the conservative majority, the wage and price features of a contract enjoyed special constitutional sanctity. The Constitution, however, says nothing of freedom of contract, nor of the general rule or exceptions to it. "Contract is not specifically mentioned in the text that we have to construe," Holmes said in dissent, "and contract is no more exempt from law than other acts." Chief Justice Taft, joined by Justice Sanford, disapproved of Sutherland's disinterment of the discredited Lochner precedent. "It is not the function of this court," the Chief Justice said, "to hold congressional acts invalid simply because they are passed to carry out economic views which the court believes to be unwise or unsound."

MR. CHIEF JUSTICE TAFT, dissenting.

I regret much to differ from the Court in these cases.

The boundary of the police power beyond which its exercise becomes an invasion of the guaranty of liberty under the Fifth and Fourteenth Amendments to the Constitution is not easy to mark. Our Court has been laboriously engaged in pricking out a line in successive cases. We must be careful, it seems to me, to follow that line as well as we can and not to depart from it by suggesting a distinction that is formal rather than real.

Legislatures in limiting freedom of contract between employee and employer by a minimum wage proceed on the assumption that employees, in the class receiving least pay, are not upon a full level of equality of choice with their employer and in their necessitous circumstances are prone to accept pretty much anything that is offered. They are peculiarly subject to the overreaching of the harsh and greedy employer. The evils of the sweating system and of the long hours and low wages which are characteristic of it are well known. Now, I agree that it is a disputable question in the field of political economy how far a statutory requirement of maximum hours or minimum wages may be a useful remedy for these evils, and whether it may not make the case of the oppressed employee worse than it was before. But it is not the function of this Court to hold congressional acts invalid simply because they are passed to carry out economic views which the Court believes to be unwise or unsound.

Legislatures which adopt a requirement of maximum hours or minimum wages may be presumed to believe that when sweating employers are prevented from paying unduly low wages by positive law they will continue their business, abating that part of their profits, which were wrung from the necessities of their employees, and will concede the better terms required by the law; and that while in individual cases hardship may result, the restriction will enure to the benefit of the general class of employees in whose interest the law is passed and so to that of the community at large.

The right of the legislature under the Fifth and Fourteenth Amendments to limit the hours of employment on the score of the health of the employee, it seems to me, has been firmly established. As to that, one would think, the line had been pricked out so that it has become a well formulated rule. In *Holden* v. *Hardy,* 169 U.S. 366, it was applied to miners and rested on the unfavorable environment of employment in mining and smelting. In *Lochner* v. *New York,* 198 U.S. 45, it was held that restricting those employed in bakeries to ten hours a day was an arbitrary and invalid interference with the liberty of contract secured by the Fourteenth Amendment. Then followed a number of cases beginning with *Muller* v. *Oregon,* 208 U.S. 412, sustaining the validity of a limit on maximum hours of labor for women to which I shall hereafter allude, and following these cases came *Bunting* v. *Oregon,* 243 U.S. 426. In that case, this Court sustained a law limiting the hours of labor of any person, whether man or woman, working in any mill, factory or manufacturing establishment to ten hours a day with a proviso as to further hours to which I shall hereafter advert. The law covered the whole field of industrial employment and certainly covered the case of persons employed in bakeries. Yet the opinion in the *Bunting Case* does not mention the *Lochner Case.* No one can suggest any constitutional distinction between employment in a bakery and one in any other kind of a manufacturing establishment which should make a limit of hours in the one invalid, and the same limit in the other permissible. It is impossible for me to reconcile the *Bunting Case* and the *Lochner Case* and I have always supposed that the *Lochner Case* was thus overruled *sub silentio.* Yet the opinion of the Court herein in support of its conclusion quotes from the opinion in the *Lochner Case* as one which has been sometimes distinguished but never overruled. Certainly there was no attempt to distinguish it in the *Bunting Case.*

However, the opinion herein does not overrule the *Bunting Case* in express terms, and therefore I assume that the conclusion in this case rests on the distinction between a minimum of wages and a maximum of hours in the limiting of liberty to contract. I regret to be at variance with the Court as to the substance of this distinction. In absolute freedom of contract the one term is as important as the other, for both enter equally into the consideration given and received, a restriction as to one is not any greater in essence than the other, and is of the same kind. One is the multiplier and the other the multiplicand.

If it be said that long hours of labor have a more direct effect upon the health of the employee than the low wage, there is very respectable authority from close observers, disclosed in the record and in the literature on the subject quoted at length in the briefs, that they are equally harmful in this regard. Congress took this view and we can not say it was not warranted in so doing.

With deference to the very able opinion of the Court and my brethren who concur in it, it appears to me to exaggerate the importance of the wage term of the contract of employment as more inviolate than its other terms. Its conclusion seems influenced by the fear that the concession of the power to impose a minimum wage must carry with it a concession of the power to fix a maximum wage. This, I submit, is a *non sequitur.* A line of distinction like the one under discussion in this case is, as the opinion elsewhere admits, a matter of degree and practical experience and not of pure logic. Certainly the wide difference between prescribing a minimum wage and a maximum wage could as a matter of degree and experience be easily affirmed.

Moreover, there are decisions by this Court which have sustained legislative limitations in respect to the wage term in contracts of employment. In *McLean* v. *Arkansas,* 211 U.S. 539, it was held within legislative power to make it unlawful to estimate the graduated pay of miners by weight after screening the coal. In *Knoxville Iron Co.* v. *Harbison,* 183 U.S. 13, it was held that store orders issued for wages must be redeemable in cash. In *Patterson* v. *Bark Eudora,* 190 U.S. 169, a law forbidding the payment of wages in advance was held valid. A like case is *Strathearn S. S. Co.* v. *Dillon,* 252 U.S. 348. While these did not impose a minimum on wages, they did take away from the employee the freedom to agree as to how they should be fixed, in what medium they should be paid, and when they should be paid, all features that might affect the amount or the mode of enjoyment of them. The first two really rested on the advantage the employer had in dealing with the employee. The third was deemed a proper curtailment of a sailor's right of contract in his own interest because of his proneness to squander his wages in port before sailing. In *Bunting* v. *Oregon, supra,* employees in a mill, factory or manufacturing establishment were required if they worked over ten hours a day to accept for the three additional hours permitted not less than fifty per cent. more than their usual wage. This was sustained as a mild penalty imposed on the employer to enforce the limitation as to hours; but it necessarily curtailed the employee's freedom to contract to work for the wages he saw fit to accept during those three hours. I do not feel, therefore, that either on the basis of reason, experience or authority, the boundary of the police power should be drawn to include maximum hours and exclude a minimum wage.

Without, however, expressing an opinion that a minimum wage limitation can be enacted for adult men, it is enough to say that the case before us involves only the application of the minimum wage to women. If I am right in thinking that the legislature can find as much support in experience for the view that a sweating wage has as great and as direct a tendency to bring about an injury to the health and morals of workers, as for the view that long hours injure their health, then I respectfully submit that *Muller* v. *Oregon,* 208 U.S. 412, controls this case. The law which was there sustained forbade the employment of any female in any mechanical establishment or factory or laundry for more than ten hours. This covered a pretty wide field in women's work and it would not seem that any sound distinction between that case and this can be built up on the fact that the law before us applies to all occupations of women with power in the board to make certain exceptions. Mr. Justice Brewer, who spoke for the Court in *Muller* v. *Oregon,* based its conclusion on the natural limit to women's physical strength and the likelihood that long hours would therefore injure her health, and we have had since a series of cases which may be said to have established a rule of decision. *Riley* v. *Massachusetts,* 232 U.S. 671; *Miller* v. *Wilson,* 236 U.S. 373; *Bosley* v. *McLaughlin,* 236 U.S. 385. The cases covered restrictions in wide and varying fields of employment and in the later cases it will be found that the objection to the particular law was based not on the ground that it had general application but because it left out some employments.

I am not sure from a reading of the opinion whether the Court thinks the authority of *Muller* v. *Oregon* is shaken by the adoption of the Nineteenth Amendment. The Nineteenth Amendment did not change the physical strength or limitations of women upon which the decision in *Muller* v. *Oregon* rests. The Amendment did give women political power and makes more certain that legislative provisions for their protection will be in accord with their interests as they see them. But I don't think we are warranted in varying constitutional construction based on physical differences between men and women, because of the Amendment.

But for my inability to agree with some general observations in the forcible opinion of MR. JUSTICE HOLMES who follows me, I should be silent and merely record my concurrence in what he says. It is perhaps wiser for me, however, in a case of this importance, separately to give my reasons for dissenting.

George Sutherland

☆ 1862–1942 ☆

APPOINTED BY

WARREN G. HARDING

YEARS ON COURT

1922–1938

George Sutherland

by

DAVID BURNER

GEORGE SUTHERLAND was the intellectual spokesman for the four reactionary Supreme Court Justices who opposed the New Deal. His decisions were tightly reasoned and systematic; his thinking, though it proceeded from narrow assumptions, could be subtle and complex.

The framework of his mind was determined by his early life and education in the West. Born in Buckinghamshire, England, on March 25, 1862, he was brought to Utah Territory in 1864 by his Scottish father, George Alexander Sutherland, and his English mother, Frances Slater. The 5,000-mile journey was a result of his father's conversion to the Church of Jesus Christ of Latter-day Saints, which may have defrayed the family's traveling expenses. Soon after arriving in Utah, however, Alexander Sutherland left the Mormon Church and moved his family to Montana, where he prospected for minerals. He finally returned in 1869 to Mormon country, first to Silver City and later to Provo; he continued to move restlessly from one job to another, serving as a postman and as a justice of the peace, and many years later he entered a brief law partnership with his son.

In the frontier of George Sutherland's youth individualistic vocations such as mining predominated. In elementary school Sutherland was exposed to the individualistic ideals of McGuffey's Readers, which inculcated diligence and promised material reward. "Nobody worried about child labor," the Justice was to remember years later. At the age of twelve the young Sutherland was himself forced out of school, owing to the improvidence of his father, and successively he held jobs as clothing store clerk, Wells Fargo agent, and mining recorder. It is a reflection of his early adherence to the principles of industry and frugality

DAVID BURNER is Associate Professor of History at the State University of New York, Stony Brook. He is the author of The Politics of Provincialism: The Democratic Party in Transition, 1918–1932.

that Sutherland at the age of sixteen had saved enough money to enter Brigham Young Academy in Provo. Destined to become today's Brigham Young University, this Mormon institution was ruled by a German convert, Karl Maeser; *School and Fireside,* published by Maeser in 1898, contains the Horatio Alger philosophy drilled into the minds of students at Brigham Young. Sutherland later acknowledged a large debt to his schoolmaster.

Maeser's favorite writer was Herbert Spencer, whose ideas about limited government were imparted to the young scholar. By the time he left Brigham Young in 1881, Sutherland had maintained his father's resistance to Mormonism but had developed a fundamentalist frame of mind. Out of it was to grow a rigid but deeply felt regard for the individual, for his civil as well as his property rights. But the doctrines of Spencer blocked any strong sympathy for those individuals not rugged enough to meet the tests of the American frontier.

The example of Mormonism in these first decades of Sutherland's life may have reinforced the philosophical individualism he was imbibing. While close in their communal associations, the followers of Brigham Young resisted the encroachments of government. They built their own schools. They owned modest farms in the manner of Jeffersonian freeholders; some of their cooperative ventures were such desolating failures that their faith in individuality was rekindled. In the 1930's the Mormon Church refused to permit its flock to accept government relief payments, a gesture Sutherland applauded.

After a year spent as agent for the contractors building the Rio Grande Western Railroad, Sutherland traveled to Ann Arbor, Michigan, to enroll in the University of Michigan's young and distinguished law school. Dean Thomas McIntyre Cooley, a specialist in constitutional law, encountered a receptive student in Sutherland, whom Maeser had already taught that the Constitution was "divinely inspired." The title of Cooley's most influential book, published in 1868, was *Treatise on the Constitutional Limitations Which Rest upon the Legislative Power of the States of the American Union.* In the preface he defined the state as a voluntary association of individuals for their own advantage and stated his "sympathy with the restraints which the caution of the fathers had imposed upon the exercise of the powers of government." For Cooley the Constitution was one of "efficient restraints" upon Congress. The police power, he believed, was restricted to the protection of health and morals, and the interstate commerce power was limited to the means of conveyance and not to its objects. As Supreme Court Justice, Sutherland would remember his professor's injunction that laws regulating prices and wages were "innovations on common right and usurpations of authority" not within the reach of the police power.

Sutherland spent less than a year at Michigan and did not earn a degree. In 1883 he married Rosamund Lee, a union that was to last nearly sixty years and produce two daughters, as well as a son who died in childhood. After his marriage Sutherland returned to Utah and was admitted to the state bar. He practiced law with Samuel Thurman, a future Chief Justice of the Utah Supreme Court, and William H. King, who was to become prominent in state politics. The young lawyer evidently became involved in some local crusades against drinking, but while he was an opponent of polygamy, he managed through legal maneuvers to hamper federal prosecution of that fruitful pursuit. In 1893 Sutherland moved to Salt Lake City, where he became a member of a prominent law firm, and the following year he helped to organize the Utah State Bar Association. In 1899 he was admitted to the bar of the United States Supreme Court.

When in 1896 Utah was admitted to the Union, Sutherland won election as a Republican to the new state legislature. He had supported William Jennings Bryan in that year's presidential campaign, but only because of Utah's vital economic stake in the free coinage of silver. In the state senate Sutherland led in the passage of a bill providing an eight-hour day in Utah's mine and smelting industries—a measure later upheld by a conservative Supreme Court as a valid use of the police power. His support of this labor legislation enhanced his chances for national office. Sutherland also was advantageously placed to gain from the religious split in the new state. As a non-Mormon he would easily win the votes of those who opposed the church; on the other hand, he had attended Mormon schools, could claim Mormon friends, and never had opposed the church with any great fervor. In 1900 he was elected to the United States Congress by a slight margin.

As Utah's only representative in the House, Sutherland was sensitive to the state's indigenous economic needs. He catered to local beet growers by denouncing President Theodore Roosevelt's sugar reciprocity agreement with Cuba. Despite his expressed belief in *laissez faire,* Sutherland repeatedly denounced free trade. After one term in Congress Sutherland returned to Utah to work for the state senate nomination to the United States Senate. Successful once again, in 1905 he returned to Washington where he proceeded to cast ballots for a large number of reform bills. Following his constituents' wishes, he voted for the Pure Food and Drug Act, the Postal Savings Act, the Hepburn Act, and a number of similar measures. When the New Deal Congress logically extended the government's reach into contiguous areas, Sutherland as a judge was then to decide that they threatened private property. As chairman of a committee investigating the question of compensation for workers injured in interstate commerce, Sutherland formulated and fought for a strong bill. Feeling compelled to set forth detailed defenses of the measure on constitutional grounds, he said that the police power "may be put forth in aid of what is sanctioned by usage, or held by the prevailing morality of strong preponderant opinion to be greatly and immediately necessary to the public welfare." He also declared that "an act of Congress is valid not only where it operates directly to carry into effect any of the specifically enumerated powers, but also where it can be seen in any degree, or under any circumstances, to promote the efficiency of such power." In 1913, arguing for his compensation program, Sutherland wrote of a growing feeling that "individualistic theory had been pushed too far with too much stress upon . . . logic . . . and too little regard for . . . the humanitarian point of view." Such words could easily have been spoken by Franklin Roosevelt two decades later. It must be added that in this period Sutherland's pronouncements on constitutional law were contradictory; they were to be resolved firmly in the course of his Associate Justiceship. One achievement of his Senate years is particularly noteworthy: an extensive revision and codification of federal criminal statutes which became law in 1910.

Property rights, by and large, were not at issue in the programs of the first administration of Theodore Roosevelt. Where the measures in Congress did not obtrude on these rights, Sutherland was free to express his humanitarian sentiments; he spoke and acted in behalf of reform. But when Taft and particularly Wilson occupied the White House, Sutherland's conservatism broadened and thrust out in many directions. In 1911 he opposed statehood for Arizona and New Mexico on grounds that their constitutions provided for the initiative, referendum, and recall. Especially dangerous in his thinking was the recall of judges, which Roosevelt had advocated in the Progressive party campaign in 1912: "If [their] decisions are wrong," he wrote, "the remedy is to appeal to the high court—not to the people." During Wilson's first term Sutherland condemned the Federal Reserve Act, the Federal Trade Commission, the Clayton Anti-Trust Act, and the constitutional amendment providing for an income tax. He also worked to block the appointment to the Supreme Court of Louis D. Brandeis.

In 1916 Sutherland was unable to win renomination to the Senate in a contest in which the electorate was no longer the state senate but the people themselves. He had always believed that the legislator's duty was to his own conscience and intelligence, not, as he had written years before, to the "stiff-necked and unappreciative public." He also criticized the notion that "there is some mysterious virtue in mere numbers. . . . There could be no greater delusion than to suppose that by putting a ballot into the hands of a voter you thereby put wisdom into his head." Sutherland blamed his defeat on isolationist sentiment abroad in the West, but intertwined in that sentiment was a decided approval of domestic reform.

Between 1917 and 1922 Sutherland practiced law in Washington, D.C. Indicative of his thinking at this time was an address on "Private Rights and Government Control" which he gave upon his election as president of the American Bar Association in 1917. Like Elihu Root whom he succeeded in office, Sutherland used the platform to attack Wilsonian reform. He saw the business community as "beset and bedeviled with vexatious statutes, prying commissions, and government intermeddling of all sorts." He lamented at one point: "We are creating an army of official agents, governmental bureaus and all sorts of commissions to pry into our affairs, smell out our shortcomings and tell us what we may and what we may not do." In 1918 Sutherland delivered a series of lectures at Columbia University, published the following year as *Constitutional Power and World Affairs*. The tone of his speeches was internationalist and he favored American membership on the World Court, but he opposed American entry into the League of Nations as an infringement on national sovereignty.

As a private citizen in Washington, Sutherland maintained friendly relations with his former colleagues, among them Warren G. Harding. When Harding received the Republican nomination for President in 1920, Sutherland helped convince the nominee to conduct a front-porch campaign. The journalist Mark Sullivan described the Utahan as Harding's most trusted campaign adviser "in the field of thought and policy." In that same year Sutherland expressed a theory of constitutional interpretation that would soon guide him on the Court, one that, as he wrote, considered "certain fundamental social and economic laws . . . beyond the right of official control." Quoting Cooley he later said the duty of a judge was to "declare the law as written." In interpreting the constitution we should, as nearly as possible, "place ourselves in the condition of those who framed and adopted it. . . . The whole aim of construction, as applied to a provision of the constitution, is to discover the meaning, to ascertain and give effect to the intent of its framers." In 1921 Sutherland served as chairman of the Advisory Committee to the Washington Armaments Conference; later that year and in the next he represented the United States in arbitration proceedings before the Hague tribunal. When Justice John H. Clarke unexpectedly quit the Supreme Court in 1922, Harding, on September 5, 1922, appointed Sutherland to the vacancy.

Sutherland joined the Court as it was about to pass on a number of important cases, and throughout his tenure he encountered serious questions of constitutional law. He dealt particularly with those concerning the necessary and proper clause of Article I, Section 8, and the due process and equal protection clauses of the Fifth and Fourteenth Amendments. After but one term on the Court, in recognition perhaps of his intellectual ability, Sutherland was asked to write a decision in what was to be one of the most important judicial matters of the decade: *Adkins* v. *Children's Hospital,* 261 U.S. 525 (1923).

The opinion usually cited under that title covered two cases concerning a congressional minimum wage law for women and children in the District of Columbia. In the first case the hospital argued that its employees were content to work for less than the minimum wage and should be protected by the due process clause. In the second case an elevator operator, Willie Lyons, insisted that she had been deprived of her job because the hospital could not afford to retain her at the higher rate of pay stipulated by the district wage board. She had been receiving $35 a month and two meals a day. To Sutherland, who spoke for a six-member majority, it did not matter how contrived the appeals were. They symbolized a situation wherein individuals, both employees and employers, were denied liberty of contract. "To sustain the individual freedom of action contemplated by the Constitution, is," he said, "not to strike down the common good but to exalt it; for surely the good of society as a whole cannot be better served than by the preservation against arbitrary restraints of the liberties of its constituent members." Whatever immediate social advantage might accrue from the law would be of little consequence if moral values, such as those embodied in the Constitution, were sacrificed. It was an "extraneous circumstance" that the employee might need "to get a prescribed sum of money to insure her subsistency, health, and morals." Of the considerable social and economic data on working conditions presented for the Court's perusal, Sutherland observed they were "all proper enough for consideration of the lawmaking bodies, since their tendency is to establish the desirability or undesirability of the legislation; but they reflect no legitimate light upon the question of its validity. . . ."

To support the doctrine of freedom of contract Sutherland seized upon the *Lochner* case of 1905, and argued that women could not be given protection denied to male workers. Since the time of *Lochner,* he argued, the Nineteenth Amendment had bestowed equality on the sexes so that only relevant physical differences justified restrictive legislation. Sutherland went far beyond this line of reasoning, however, and attempted to define liberty of contract as a natural right, albeit one that is not absolute. Prices and wages, unlike working conditions or hours of labor, constituted the "heart of the contract" and had been made inviolate under the Fifth Amendment. The clear implication of Sutherland's decision was that since regulation of minimum wages for women was unconstitutional, no wages could be regulated at all.

Yet Sutherland—who was no Neanderthal, and whose reasoning was careful—qualified what he had said: "There is, of course, no such thing as absolute freedom of contract. It is subject to a great variety of restraints. But freedom of contract is, nevertheless, the general rule and restraint the exception; and the exercise of legislative authority to abridge it can be justified only on the existence of exceptional circumstances. . . . The liberty of the individual must frequently yield to the common good, and the line beyond which the power of interference may not be pressed is neither definite nor unalterable but may be made to move, within limits not well defined, with changing need and circumstance." In dissent Chief Justice Taft lashed out at the special consideration the decision seemed to give to employers and condemned as formalistic and spurious the distinction made between regulation of hours and regulation of wages. Justice Holmes thought the decision "windy and poor," half of it never coming near the point at all. Nevertheless, after 1923 Sutherland's decision effectively forestalled federal and state legislatures from improving the lot of workers by the imposition of a minimum wage.

After *Adkins,* Sutherland became the leading spokesman for the conservative Justices. His expository style was the most trenchant and, unlike Justices McReynolds and Butler, he possessed a temperate and optimistic personality. Justice Stone found him "a man of character and ability, an altogether pleasant associate." During his sixteen years on the Court Sutherland wrote 295 majority opinions and only twenty-four dissents. He constantly reiterated the themes of limited government, dual federalism, and the separation of powers.

Sutherland also had in him a strain of constitutional realism, which showed itself immediately following the Adkins decision in the companion cases of *Massachusetts* v. *Mellon* and *Frothingham* v. *Mellon,* 262 U.S. 447 (1923). In the first, Massachusetts sought to enjoin a federal grant to the state under the

Maternity Act of 1921; in the second a taxpayer desired the same ends. In both cases the Court refused to exercise control of federal spending and thereby weakened its anti–New Deal arguments of the nineteen thirties. Sutherland refused to consider the state's plea since no concrete invasion of rights had been shown. The taxpayer also must prove special injury before he could bring suit. His interest, shared with millions of others, was not sufficient to warrant the Court's attention. In *Euclid* v. *Ambler Co.,* 272 U.S. 365 (1926), he recognized the basic constitutionality of zoning ordinances—which he, unlike the other conservatives, saw as inherently more protective than destructive of property rights.

In many cases Sutherland opposed government regulation of business. *Tyson Bros.* v. *Banton,* 273 U.S. 416 (1927), held unconstitutional a New York statute prohibiting brokers of theater tickets from reselling seats for more than fifty cents over the box office price. Because the ticket broker is "a mere appendage of the theatre," the legislature has no greater power over the broker's business than it has over that to which it is an appendage. Sutherland argued that public opinion decided whether businesses could be restricted, yet he went on to declare void the will of the people as represented in the state legislature. The case reduced the number of businesses "affected with a public interest." Explicit in Sutherland's decision was the fear that such a law would afford an entry to the actual fixing of prices. "Such subversions," he wrote, "are not only illegitimate but are fraught with the danger that, having begun on the ground of necessity, they will continue on the score of expediency, and finally, as a mere matter of course." He recommended that the danger of extortion be met instead by statutes aimed at collusion. *Ribnik* v. *McBride,* 277 U.S. 350 (1928), extended this point of view still further by forbidding a state to fix the fee charged by an employment agency—and through implication by any broker. Again Sutherland recommended some other kind of regulation to correct any abuses, but to this Justice Stone in his dissent replied: "If the business is subject to regulation, as seems to be admitted, the regulation which is appropriate and effective is some curtailment of the exorbitant fees charged. . . ." Sutherland dissented from the decision in *Nebbia* v. *New York,* 291 U.S. 502 (1934), in which Justice Roberts broadened the limitation upon the doctrine of business affected with a public interest. Sutherland was outraged at the conviction of Nebbia for selling milk at less than nine cents a quart and joined in Justice McReynolds' protest at "facile disregard of the Constitution as long interpreted and respected."

A number of Sutherland's decisions were particularly solicitous of the rights of the isolated individual. In *Liggett Co.* v. *Baldridge,* 278 U.S. 105 (1928), he wrote the decision declaring unconstitutional a Pennsylvania law requiring drugstore owners to be registered pharmacists. His dissent in *Lambert* v. *Yellowley,* 272 U.S. 581 (1926), denounced another trespass on individual rights. In this case Congress had provided that no more than a pint of liquor could be prescribed by a doctor for a single patient over a ten-day period. Sutherland believed that the therapeutic problem was not one even for the Supreme Court to decide; in any case the Eighteenth Amendment provided for congressional control only of beverages. For the majority Justice Brandeis said tersely: "Where the means adopted by Congress in exerting its express power are calculated to effect its purpose, it is not admissible for the judiciary to inquire into the degree of necessity." Sutherland's opinion in *Berger* v. *United States,* 295 U.S. 78 (1935), upheld the need of a fair trial against the deceit of a government prosecutor who misstated facts and bullied opposing witnesses: "The man strikes hard blows," observed the Justice, but "he is not at liberty to strike foul ones."

But when historical precedent or patriotism was a weighty consideration the Justice could rule in the government's favor. In the interesting case of *United States* v. *Dickey et al.,* 268 U.S. 378 (1925), he upheld the government's right to allow the publication of tax returns since the practice had been longstanding. In *Moore* v. *Dempsey,* 261 U.S. 86 (1923), he voted in dissent to affirm a murder conviction secured in a highly prejudiced atmosphere. He would not uphold free speech in the Gitlow or Near cases, *Gitlow* v. *New York,* 268 U.S. 652 (1925), *Near* v. *Minnesota,* 283 U.S. 697 (1931). In *United States* v. *MacIntosh,* 283 U.S. 605 (1931), he ruled that one who conscientiously objects to bear arms in defense of his country cannot be given citizenship. It was in this case that Sutherland issued his famous pronouncement regarding acts of the government in wartime; it is a sweeping dismissal of all the individual and corporate rights he upheld throughout his career: "To the end that war may not result in defeat, freedom of speech may, by act of Congress, be curtailed or denied so that the morale of the people and the spirit of the Army may not be broken by seditious utterances; freedom of the press curtailed to preserve our military plans and movements from the knowledge of the enemy; deserters and spies put to death without indictment or trial by jury; ships and supplies requisitioned; property of alien enemies, theretofore under the protection of the Constitution, seized without process and converted to the public use without compensation and without due process of law in the ordinary sense of that term; prices of food and other necessities of life fixed or regulated; railways taken over and operated by the government; and other drastic powers, wholly inadmissible in time of peace, exercised to meet the emergencies of war." During World War II the Court went even further than Sutherland in upholding the government's economic restrictions; but it went less far in dismissing the protection of civil liberties.

Powell v. *Alabama,* 287 U.S. 45 (1932)—the first "Scottsboro" case—sustained the right of an accused to counsel in a criminal proceeding in a state court. Sutherland, who was widely applauded for this influential decision, approached the problem sociologically, insisting that "compelling circumstances" dictated a new trial. The nine Negro defendants were "young, ignorant, illiterate, surrounded by hostile sentiment, hauled back and forth under guard of soldiers, charged with an atrocious crime regarded with especial horror in the community where they were to be tried." Buttressing his opinion by a historical survey of due process, tracing it to Magna Carta—the "law of the land" that hears before it condemns—Sutherland asked "What does a hearing include?" and answered

"The right to counsel." He climaxed his historical survey by demonstrating that in the Scottsboro affair the rights guaranteed by the Sixth Amendment had been infringed. "To decide otherwise," he wrote, "would simply be to ignore actualities." The realism of that statement sometimes evaded Sutherland in later years.

Until about 1930 Sutherland's views had been substantially those of a majority of the Court, but in that year the Court lost two fairly consistent conservatives—Chief Justice Taft by retirement and Justice Sanford by death; and of greater import for the future, the depression was under way. As the economy plunged, the question of Supreme Court interference in legislative policy developed renewed immediacy. Sutherland became one of President Roosevelt's more perceptive critics, though not a splenetic one.

Home Building and Loan Association v. *Blaisdell,* 290 U.S. 398 (1934), decided that Minnesota could, in the emergency of the thirties, postpone the due dates of mortgage payments. The obligation of contract was supposedly not thereby infringed; the law simply modified its terms of fulfillment. Justice Holmes argued that the law did not impair the integrity of the debt; it was, moreover, valid only in times of emergency and its tenure was to be decided by the judiciary, not the legislature. Sutherland dissented with some telling arguments. He surveyed judicial decisions on the contract clause to show that the "supposed necessities of the hour" did not infringe the constitutional principle of liberty of contract. The fundamentals of government, he argued quoting Cooley, were beyond the "varying moods of public opinion." Indeed, the contract clause must be regarded as inelastic *"especially* in time of financial distress," for that is when it comes into jeopardy. Conditions of financial distress had in fact made the clause necessary in the first place. He did believe that war constituted an emergency justifying modification of contracts, but depression was to be surmounted by "self-denial and painful effort." As in the *Adkins* case, Sutherland paid scant heed to the social conditions that precipitated the law.

In several important cases Sutherland managed to persuade Justices Roberts or Holmes to join in invalidating New Deal legislation. In *Carter* v. *Carter Coal Co.,* 298 U.S. 238 (1936), he wrote the decision nullifying the labor and pricing provisions of the Bituminous Coal or "Guffey" Act of 1935. The law was an attempt to bring order out of one of the most chaotic of American industries, and one in which misery had deeply infected the workers' lives. A national commission had been empowered to set both maximum and minimum prices and to collect a fifteen per cent sales tax from the mine operators, most of which would be returned to those who cooperated with the government. Sutherland dismissed at the outset "beneficent aims" that "can never serve in lieu of constitutional power." The "so-called excise tax" he exposed as a penalty forcing compliance with the law. He attacked the wage regulation provision as affecting mining interests local in origin and therefore not within congressional power under the commerce clause. Price fixing fell with the rest of the act. Justice Hughes, in dissent, objected to Sutherland's cavalier disregard of the congressional declaration of separability. The labor provisions were invalid, Hughes believed, but the price fixing was not.

Other important opinions either curtailed or questioned executive power, depending on Sutherland's ability to persuade a Court moderate to adopt his point of view. In *Humphrey's Executor* v. *United States,* 295 U.S. 602 (1935), unusual for its unanimous verdict, Sutherland spoke for the Court in defense of the separation of powers; he denied the President's right to remove a member of an independent administrative agency. The case was held to be unlike an earlier one, *Myers* v. *United States,* 272 U.S. 52 (1926), in which the President's right to remove a postmaster had been affirmed. Speaking for six Justices in 1936, Sutherland excoriated the SEC for compelling a Wall Street promoter to produce his books and papers; it was yet another "unreasonable and arbitrary" instance of the New Deal's diminution of liberty, *Jones* v. *Securities and Exchange Commission,* 298 U.S. 1. In *Grosjean* v. *American Press Co.,* 297 U.S. 233 (1935), Sutherland held for the Court that a state license tax on newspapers was a prior restraint upon the press. In *Associated Press* v. *National Labor Relations Board,* 301 U.S. 103 (1937), Sutherland, in dissent, argued forcefully that presidential control of the employment and discharge of editorial writers interfered with freedom of the press. The Justice also agreed in finding unconstitutional the outlawing of the gold clause, the NRA, the AAA, the National Labor Relations and Social Security Acts.

Sutherland was, of course, relieved that Roosevelt's plan to enlarge the Court failed to secure congressional approval. But he seems not to have hated Roosevelt in the way that, for instance, Justice McReynolds did. In one of his last cases, *United States* v. *Curtiss-Wright Export Corporation,* 299 U.S. 304 (1936), he succeeded in convincing his colleagues that the powers of the President and Congress in foreign affairs were not limited by other than the express provisions of the Constitution. This decision, along with that in *United States* v. *Belmont,* 301 U.S. 324 (1937), greatly extended the President's power to conclude executive agreements. Years later Senator John Bricker, with the help of the American Bar Association, tried in vain to amend the Constitution to curtail the kind of power Justice Sutherland had granted.

Sutherland retired from the Court early in January, 1938 and died on July 18, 1942 at the age of seventy-six. In the years after his retirement Sutherland's majority opinions were repudiated in record-breaking numbers. With the rise of a liberal judiciary went the decline not only of Sutherland's prestige but also of American conservative thought in this century. Not all of his decisions were overturned; many remain that extended civil liberties, distributed power among the three divisions of the national government or gave them additional powers. In these respects Sutherland usually had differed from the reactionary trio of McReynolds, Butler, and Van Devanter. Harlan Fiske Stone delivered a respectful eulogy for Sutherland on behalf of the Court. The Chief Justice said he could not now depreciate Sutherland's views on the dangers inherent in "encroachments of government on the freedom of the individual." Stone mourned the passing of "a man of stalwart independence, and of the purest character, who, without a trace of intellectual arrogance, and always with respectful toleration for the views of colleagues who differed with him, fought stoutly for the constitutional guaranties of the liberty of the individual." Sutherland left behind him one of the few coherent defenses of very conservative social values; though inconsistent on many points, it deserves respect and periodic reexamination.

SELECTED BIBLIOGRAPHY

Three secondary works treat George Sutherland: Joel Paschal's *Mr. Justice Sutherland* (Princeton, 1951), which is a fine book; a doctoral dissertation by Jay Benson Saks, "Mr. Justice Sutherland," (The Johns Hopkins University, 1940); and an unpublished Master's essay by James Banner, "Mr. Justice Sutherland and the Social Welfare" (Columbia University, 1961). A good-sized collection of Sutherland Papers is housed at the Library of Congress.

George Sutherland

REPRESENTATIVE OPINIONS

ADKINS v. CHILDREN'S HOSPITAL, 261 U.S. 539 (1923)

This famous conservative decision takes the measure of the Taft Court during the 1920's (although Taft himself dissented). Speaking for a six member majority, Justice Sutherland declared unconstitutional a minimum wage law for women and children passed by Congress for the District of Columbia. The law, according to Sutherland, denied liberty of contract both to the employer and the employed who in this case earned thirty-five dollars a month and two free meals a day. Sutherland thought unusual circumstances might sometimes warrant restricting liberty of contract, but sex was not among them.

MR. JUSTICE SUTHERLAND delivered the opinion of the Court.

The question presented for determination by these appeals is the constitutionality of the Act of September 19, 1918, providing for the fixing of minimum wages for women and children in the District of Columbia. 40 Stat. 960, c. 174.

The act provides for a board of three members, to be constituted, as far as practicable, so as to be equally representative of employers, employees and the public. The board is authorized to have public hearings, at which persons interested in the matter being investigated may appear and testify, to administer oaths, issue subpoenas requiring the attendance of witnesses and production of books, etc., and to make rules and regulations for carrying the act into effect.

By § 8 the board is authorized—

"(1), To investigate and ascertain the wages of women and minors in the different occupations in which they are employed in the District of Columbia; (2), to examine, through any member or authorized representative, any book, pay roll or other record of any employer of women or minors that in any way appertains to or has a bearing upon the question of wages of any such women or minors; and (3), to require from such employer full and true statements of the wages paid to all women and minors in his employment."

And by § 9, "to ascertain and declare, in the manner hereinafter provided, the following things: (a), Standards of minimum wages for women in any occupation within the District of Columbia, and what wages are inadequate to supply the necessary cost of living to any such women workers to maintain them in good health and to protect their morals; and (b), standards of minimum wages for minors in any occupation within the District of Columbia, and what wages are unreasonably low for any such minor workers."

The act then provides (§ 10) that if the board, after investigation, is of opinion that any substantial number of women workers in any occupation are receiving wages inadequate to supply them with the necessary cost of living, maintain them in health and protect their morals, a conference may be called to consider and inquire into and report on the subject investigated, the conference to be equally representative of employers and employees in such occupation and of the public, and to include one or more members of the board.

The conference is required to make and transmit to the board a report including, among other things, "recommendations as to standards of minimum wages for women workers in the occupation under inquiry and as to what wages are inadequate to supply the necessary cost of living to women workers in such occupation and to maintain them in health and to protect their morals." § 11.

The board is authorized (§ 12) to consider and review these recommendations and to approve or disapprove any or all of them. If it approve any recommendations it must give public notice of its intention and hold a public hearing at which the persons interested will be heard. After such hearing, the board is authorized to make such order as to it may appear necessary to carry into effect the recommendations, and to require all employers in the occupation affected to comply therewith. It is made unlawful for any such employer to violate in this regard any provision of the order or to employ any woman worker at lower wages than are thereby permitted.

There is a provision (§ 13) under which the board may issue a special license to a woman whose earning capacity "has been impaired by age or otherwise," authorizing her employment at less than the minimum wages fixed under the act.

All questions of fact (§ 17) are to be determined by the board, from whose decision there is no appeal; but an appeal is allowed on questions of law.

Any violation of the act (§ 18) by an employer or his agent or by corporate agents is declared to be a misdemeanor, punishable by fine and imprisonment.

Finally, after some further provisions not necessary to be stated, it is declared (§ 23) that the purposes of the act are "to protect the women and minors of the District from conditions detrimental to their health and morals, resulting from wages which are inadequate to maintain decent standards of living; and the Act in each of its provisions and in its entirety shall be interpreted to effectuate these purposes."

The appellee in the first case is a corporation maintaining a hospital for children in the District. It employs a large number of women in various capacities, with whom it had agreed upon rates of wages and compensation satisfactory to such employees, but which in some instances were less than the minimum wage fixed by an order of the board made in pursuance of the act. The women with whom appellee had so contracted were all of full age and under no legal disability. The instant suit was brought by the appellee in the Supreme Court of the District to restrain the board from enforcing or attempting to enforce its order on the ground that the same was in contravention of the Constitution, and particularly the due process clause of the Fifth Amendment.

In the second case the appellee, a woman twenty-one years of age, was employed by the Congress Hall Hotel Company as an elevator operator, at a salary of $35 per month and two meals a day. She alleges that the work was light and healthful, the hours short, with surroundings clean and moral, and that she was anxious to continue it for the compensation she was receiving and that she did not earn more. Her services were satisfactory to the Hotel Company and it would have been glad to retain her but was obliged to dispense with her services by reason of the order of the board and on account of the penalties prescribed by the act. The wages received by this appellee were the best she was able to obtain for any work she was capable of performing and the enforcement of the order, she alleges, deprived her of such employment and wages. She further averred that she could not secure any other position at which she could make a living, with as good physical and moral surroundings, and earn as good wages, and that she was desirous of continuing and would continue the employment but for the order of the board. An injunction was prayed as in the other case.

The Supreme Court of the District denied the injunction and dismissed the bill in each case. Upon appeal the Court of Appeals by a majority first affirmed and subsequently, on a rehearing, reversed the trial court. Upon the first argument a justice of the District Supreme Court was called in to take the place of one of the Appellate Court justices, who was ill. Application for rehearing was made and, by the court as thus constituted, was denied. Subsequently, and during the term, a rehearing was granted by an order concurred in by two of the Appellate Court justices, one being the justice whose place on the prior occasion had been filled by the Supreme Court member. Upon the rehearing thus granted, the Court of Appeals, rejecting the first opinion, held the act in question to be unconstitutional and reversed the decrees of the trial court. Thereupon the cases were remanded, and the trial court entered decrees in pursuance of the mandate, declaring the act in question to be unconstitutional and granting permanent injunctions. Appeals to the Court of Appeals followed and the decrees of the trial court were affirmed. It is from these final decrees that the cases come here.

Upon this state of facts the jurisdiction of the lower court to grant a rehearing, after first denying it, is challenged. We do not deem it necessary to consider the matter farther than to say that we are here dealing with the second appeals, while the proceedings complained of occurred upon the first appeals. That the lower court could properly entertain the second appeals and decide the cases does not admit of doubt; and this the appellants virtually conceded by having themselves invoked the jurisdiction. See *Rooker* v. *Fidelity Trust Co., ante,* 114.

We come then, at once, to the substantive question involved.

The judicial duty of passing upon the constitutionality of an act of Congress is one of great gravity and delicacy. The statute here in question has successfully borne the scrutiny of the legislative branch of the government, which, by enacting it, has affirmed its validity; and that determination must be given great weight. This Court, by an unbroken line of decisions from Chief Justice Marshall to the present day, has steadily adhered to the rule that every possible presumption is in favor of the validity of an act of Congress until overcome beyond rational doubt. But if by clear and indubitable demonstration a statute be opposed to the Constitution we have no choice but to say so. The Constitution, by its own terms, is the supreme law of the land, emanating from the people, the repository of ultimate sovereignty under our form of government. A congressional statute, on the other hand, is the act of an agency of this sovereign authority and if it conflict with the Constitution must fall; for that which is not supreme must yield to that which is. To hold it invalid (if it be invalid) is a plain exercise of the judicial power—that power vested in courts to enable them to administer justice according to law. From the authority to ascertain and determine the law in a given case, there necessarily results, in case of conflict, the duty to declare and enforce the rule of the supreme law and reject that of an inferior act of legislation which, transcending the Constitution, is of no effect and binding on no one. This is not the exercise of a substantive power to review and nullify acts of Congress, for no such substantive power exists. It is simply a necessary concomitant of the power to hear and dispose of a case or controversy properly before the court, to the determination of which must be brought the test and measure of the law.

The statute now under consideration is attacked upon the ground that it authorizes an unconstitutional interference with the freedom of contract included within the guaranties of the due process clause of the Fifth Amendment. That the right to contract about one's affairs is a part of the liberty of the individual protected by this clause, is settled by the decisions of this Court and is no longer open to question. *Allgeyer* v. *Louisiana,* 165 U.S. 578, 591; *New York Life Insurance Co.* v. *Dodge,* 246 U.S. 357, 373–374; *Coppage* v. *Kansas,* 236 U.S. 1, 10, 14; *Adair* v. *United States,* 208 U.S. 161; *Lochner* v. *New York,* 198 U.S. 45; *Butchers' Union Co.* v. *Crescent City Co.,* 111 U.S. 746; *Muller* v. *Oregon,* 208 U.S. 412, 421. Within this liberty are contracts of employment of labor. In making such contracts, generally speaking, the parties have an equal right to obtain from each other the best terms they can as the result of private bargaining.

In *Adair* v. *United States, supra,* Mr. Justice Harlan (pp. 174, 175), speaking for the Court, said:

"The right of a person to sell his labor upon such terms as he deems proper is, in its essence, the same as the right of the purchaser of labor to prescribe the conditions upon which he will accept such labor from the person offering to sell. . . . In all such particulars the employer and employé have equality of right, and any legislation that disturbs that equality is an arbitrary interference with the liberty of contract which no government can legally justify in a free land."

In *Coppage* v. *Kansas, supra* (p. 14), this Court, speaking through Mr. Justice Pitney, said:

"Included in the right of personal liberty and the right of private property—partaking of the nature of each—is the right to make contracts for the acquisition of property. Chief among such contracts is that of personal employment, by which labor and other services are exchanged for money or other forms of property. If this right be struck down or arbitrarily interfered with, there is a substantial impairment of liberty in the long-established constitutional sense. The right is as essential to the laborer as to the capitalist, to the poor as to the rich; for the vast majority of persons have no other honest way to begin to acquire property, save by working for money.

"An interference with this liberty so serious as that now under consideration, and so disturbing of equality of right, must be deemed to be arbitrary, unless it be supportable as a reasonable exercise of the police power of the State."

There is, of course, no such thing as absolute freedom of contract. It is subject to a great variety of restraints. But freedom of contract is, nevertheless, the general rule and restraint the exception; and the exercise of legislative authority to abridge it can be justified only by the existence of exceptional circumstances. Whether these circumstances exist in the present case constitutes the question to be answered. It will be helpful to this end to review some of the decisions where the interference has been upheld and consider the grounds upon which they rest.

(1) *Those dealing with statutes fixing rates and charges to be exacted by businesses impressed with a public interest.* There are many cases, but it is sufficient to cite *Munn* v. *Illinois,* 94 U.S. 113. The power here rests upon the ground that where property is devoted to a public use the owner thereby, in effect, grants to the public an interest in the use which may be controlled by the public for the common good to the extent of the interest thus created. It is upon this theory that these statutes have been upheld and, it may be noted in passing, so upheld even in respect of their incidental and injurious or destructive effect upon preëxisting contracts. See *Louisville & Nashville R. R. Co.* v. *Mottley,* 219 U.S. 467. In the case at bar the statute does not depend upon the existence of a public interest in any business to be affected, and this class of cases may be laid aside as inapplicable.

(2) *Statutes relating to contracts for the performance of public work. Atkin* v. *Kansas,* 191 U.S. 207; *Heim* v. *McCall,* 239 U.S. 175; *Ellis* v. *United States,* 206 U.S. 246. These cases sustain such statutes as depending, not upon the right to condition private contracts, but upon the right of the government to prescribe the conditions upon which it will permit work of a public character to be done for it, or, in the case of a State, for its municipalities. We may, therefore, in like manner, dismiss these decisions from consideration as inapplicable.

(3) *Statutes prescribing the character, methods and time for payment of wages.* Under this head may be included *McLean* v. *Arkansas,* 211 U.S. 539, sustaining a state statute requiring coal to be measured for payment of miners' wages before screening; *Knoxville Iron Co.* v. *Harbison,* 183 U.S. 13, sustaining a Tennessee statute requiring the redemption in cash of store orders issued in payment of wages; *Erie R. R. Co.* v. *Williams,* 233 U.S. 685, upholding a statute regulating the time within which wages shall be paid to employees in certain specified industries; and other cases sustaining statutes of like import and effect. In none of the statutes thus sustained, was the liberty of employer or employee to fix the amount of wages the one was willing to pay and the other willing to receive interfered with. Their tendency and purpose was to prevent unfair and perhaps fraudulent methods in the payment of wages and in no sense can they be said to be, or to furnish a precedent for, wage-fixing statutes.

(4) *Statutes fixing hours of labor.* It is upon this class that the greatest emphasis is laid in argument and therefore, and because such cases approach most nearly the line of principle applicable to the statute here involved, we shall consider them more at length. In some instances the statute limited the hours of labor for men in certain occupations and in others it was confined in its application to women. No statute has thus far been brought to the attention of this Court which by its terms, applied to all occupations. In *Holden* v. *Hardy,* 169 U.S. 366, the Court considered an act of the Utah legislature, restricting the hours of labor in mines and smelters. This statute was

sustained as a legitimate exercise of the police power, on the ground that the legislature had determined that these particular employments, when too long pursued, were injurious to the health of the employees, and that, as there were reasonable grounds for supporting this determination on the part of the legislature, its decision in that respect was beyond the reviewing power of the federal courts.

That this constituted the basis of the decision is emphasized by the subsequent decision in *Lochner* v. *New York,* 198 U.S. 45, reviewing a state statute which restricted the employment of all persons in bakeries to ten hours in any one day. The Court referred to *Holden* v. *Hardy, supra,* and, declaring it to be inapplicable, held the statute unconstitutional as an unreasonable, unnecessary and arbitrary interference with the liberty of contract and therefore void under the Constitution.

Mr. Justice Peckham, speaking for the Court (p. 56), said:

"It must, of course, be conceded that there is a limit to the valid exercise of the police power by the State. There is no dispute concerning this general proposition. Otherwise the Fourteenth Amendment would have no efficacy and the legislatures of the States would have unbounded power, and it would be enough to say that any piece of legislation was enacted to conserve the morals, the health or the safety of the people; such legislation would be valid, no matter how absolutely without foundation the claim might be. The claim of the police power would be a mere pretext—become another and delusive name for the supreme sovereignty of the State to be exercised free from constitutional restraint."

And again (pp. 57–58):

"It is a question of which of two powers or rights shall prevail—the power of the State to legislate or the right of the individual to liberty of person and freedom of contract. The mere assertion that the subject relates though but in a remote degree to the public health does not necesarily render the enactment valid. The act must have a more direct relation, as a means to an end, and the end itself must be appropriate and legitimate, before an act can be held to be valid which interferes with the general right of an individual to be free in his person and in his power to contract in relation to his own labor."

Coming then directly to the statute (p. 58), the Court said:

"We think the limit of the police power has been reached and passed in this case. There is, in our judgment, no reasonable foundation for holding this to be necessary or appropriate as a health law to safeguard the public health or the health of the individuals who are following the trade of a baker. If this statute be valid, and if, therefore, a proper case is made out in which to deny the right of an individual, *sui juris,* as employer or employé, to make contracts for the labor of the latter under the protection of the provisions of the Federal Constitution, there would seem to be no length to which legislation of this nature might not go."

And, after pointing out the unreasonable range to which the principle of the statute might be extended, the Court said (p. 60):

"It is also urged, pursuing the same line of argument, that it is to the interest of the State that its population should be strong and robust, and therefore any legislation which may be said to tend to make people healthy must be valid as health laws, enacted under the police power. If this be a valid argument and a justification for this kind of legislation, it follows that the protection of the Federal Constitution from undue interference with liberty of person and freedom of contract is visionary, wherever the law is sought to be justified as a valid exercise of the police power. Scarcely any law but might find shelter under such assumptions, and conduct, properly so called, as well as contract, would come under the restrictive sway of the legislature."

And further (p. 61):

"Statutes of the nature of that under review, limiting the hours in which grown and intelligent men may labor to earn their living, are mere meddlesome interferences with the rights of the individual, and they are not saved from condemnation by the claim that they are passed in the exercise of the police power and upon the subject of the health of the individual whose rights are interfered with, unless there be some fair ground, reasonable in and of itself, to say that there is material danger to the public health or to the health of the employés, if the hours of labor are not curtailed."

Subsequent cases in this Court have been distinguished from that decision, but the principles therein stated have never been disapproved.

In *Bunting* v. *Oregon,* 243 U.S. 426, a state statute forbidding the employment of any person in any mill, factory or manufacturing establishment more than ten hours in any one day, and providing payment for overtime not exceeding three hours in any one day at the rate of time and a half of the regular wage, was sustained on the ground that, since the state legislature and State Supreme Court had found such a law necessary for the preservation of the health of employees in these industries, this Court would accept their judgment, in the absence of facts to support the contrary conclusion. The law was attacked on the ground that it constituted an attempt to fix wages, but that contention was rejected and the law sustained as a reasonable regulation of hours of service.

Wilson v. *New,* 243 U.S. 332, involved the validity of the so-called Adamson Law, which established an eight-hour day for employees of interstate carriers for which it fixed a scale of minimum wages with proportionate increases for overtime, to be enforced, however, only for a limited period. The act was sustained primarily upon the ground that it was a regulation of a business charged with a public interest. The Court, speaking through the Chief Justice, pointed out that regarding "the private right and private interest as contradistinguished from the public interest the power exists between the parties, the employers and employees, to agree as to a standard of wages free from legislative interference" but that this did not affect the power to deal with the matter with a view to protect the public right, and then said (p. 353):

"And this emphasizes that there is no question here of purely private right since the law is concerned only with those who are engaged in a business charged with a public interest where the subject dealt with as to all the parties is one involved in that business and which we have seen comes under the control of the right to regulate to the extent that the power to do so is appropriate or relevant to the business regulated."

Moreover, in sustaining the wage feature, of the law, emphasis was put upon the fact (p. 345) that it was in this respect temporary "leaving the employers and employees free as to the subject of wages to govern their relations by their own agreements after the specified time." The act was not only temporary in this respect, but it was passed to meet a sudden and great emergency. This feature of the law was sustained principally because the parties, for the time being, could not or would not agree. Here they are forbidden to agree.

The same principle was applied in the *Rent Cases* (*Block* v. *Hirsh,* 256 U.S. 135, and *Marcus Brown Holding Co.* v. *Feldman,* 256 U.S. 170), where this Court sustained the legislative power to fix rents as between landlord and tenant upon the ground that the operation of the statutes was temporary to tide over an emergency and that the circumstances were such as to clothe "the letting of buildings . . . with a public interest so great as to justify regulation by law." The Court said (p. 157):

"The regulation is put and justified only as a temporary measure [citing *Wilson* v. *New, supra*]. A limit in time, to tide over a passing trouble, well may justify a law that could not be upheld as a permanent change."

In a subsequent case, *Pennsylvania Coal Co.* v. *Mahon,* 260 U.S. 393, 416, this Court, after saying "We are in danger of forgetting that a strong public desire to improve the public condition is not enough to warrant achieving the desire by a shorter cut than the constitutional way of paying for the change," pointed out that the *Rent Cases* dealt with laws intended to meet a temporary emergency and "went to the verge of the law."

In addition to the cases cited above, there are the decisions of this Court dealing with laws especially relating to hours of labor for women: *Muller* v. *Oregon,* 208 U.S. 412; *Riley* v. *Massachusetts,* 232 U.S. 671; *Miller* v. *Wilson,* 236 U.S. 373; *Bosley* v. *McLaughlin,* 236 U.S. 385.

In the *Muller Case* the validity of an Oregon statute, forbidding the employment of any female in certain industries more than ten hours during any one day was upheld. The decision proceeded upon the theory that the difference between the sexes may justify a different rule respecting hours of labor in the case of women than in the case of men. It is pointed out that these consist in differences of physical structure, especially in respect of the maternal functions, and also in the fact that historically woman has always been dependent upon man, who has established his control by superior physical strength. The cases of *Riley, Miller* and *Bosley* follow in this respect the *Muller Case.* But the ancient inequality of the sexes, otherwise than physical, as suggested in the *Muller Case* (p. 421) has continued "with diminishing intensity." In view of the great—not to say revolutionary—changes which have taken place since that utterance, in the contractual, political and civil status of women, culminating in the Nineteenth Amendment, it is not unreasonable to say that these differences have now come almost, if not quite, to the vanishing point. In this aspect of the matter, while the physical differences must be recognized in appropriate cases, and legislation fixing hours or conditions of work may properly take them into account, we cannot accept the doctrine that women of mature age, *sui juris,* require or may be subjected to restrictions upon their liberty of contract which could not lawfully be imposed in the case of men under similar circumstances. To do so would be to ignore all the implications to be drawn from the present day trend of legislation, as well as that of common thought and usage, by which woman is accorded emancipation from the old doctrine that she must be given special protection or be subjected to special restraint in her contractual and civil relationships. In passing, it may be noted that the instant statute applies in the case of a woman employer contracting with a woman employee as it does when the former is a man.

The essential characteristics of the statute now under consideration, which differentiate it from the laws fixing hours of labor, will be made to appear as we proceed. It is sufficient now to point out that the latter as well as the statutes mentioned under paragraph (3), deal with incidents of the employment having no necessary effect upon the heart of the contract, that is, the amount of wages to be paid and received. A law forbidding work to continue beyond a given number of hours leaves the parties free to contract about wages and thereby equalize whatever additional burdens may be imposed upon the employer as a result of the restrictions as to hours, by an adjustment in respect of the amount of wages. Enough has been said to show that the authority to fix hours of labor cannot be exercised except in respect of those occupations where work of long continued duration is detrimental to health. This Court has been careful in every case where the question has been raised, to place its decision upon this limited authority of the legislature to regulate hours of labor and to disclaim any purpose to uphold the legislation as fixing wages, thus recognizing an essential difference between the two. It seems plain that these decisions afford no real support for any form of law establishing minimum wages.

If now, in the light furnished by the foregoing exceptions to the general rule forbidding legislative interference with freedom of contract, we examine and analyze the statute in question, we shall see that it differs from them in every material respect. It is not a law dealing with any business charged with a public interest or with public work, or to meet and tide over a temporary emergency. It has nothing to do with the character, methods or periods of wage payments. It does not prescribe hours of labor or conditions under which labor is to be done. It is not for the protection of persons under legal disability or for the prevention of fraud. It is simply and exclusively a price-fixing law, confined to adult women (for we are not now considering the provisions relating to minors), who are legally as capable of contracting for themselves as men. It forbids two parties having lawful capacity—under penalties as to the employer—to freely contract with one another in respect of the price for which one shall render service to the other in a purely private employment where both are willing, perhaps anxious, to agree, even though the consequence may be to oblige one to surrender a desirable engagement and the other to dispense with the services of a desirable employee.[1] The price fixed by the board need have no relation to the capacity or earning power of the employee, the number of hours which may happen to constitute the day's work, the character of the place where the work is to be done, or the circumstances or surroundings of the employment; and, while it has no other basis to support its validity than the assumed necessities of the employee, it takes no account of any independent resources she may have. It is based wholly on the opinions of the members of the board and their advisers—perhaps an average of their opinions, if they do not precisely agree—as to what will be necessary to provide a living for a woman, keep her in health and preserve her morals. It applies to any and every occupation in the District, without regard to its nature or the character of the work.

The standard furnished by the statute for the guidance of the board is so vague as to be impossible of practical application

[1] *This is the exact situation in the Lyons case, as is shown by the statement in the first part of this opinion.*

with any reasonable degree of accuracy. What is sufficient to supply the necessary cost of living for a woman worker and maintain her in good health and protect her morals is obviously not a precise or unvarying sum—not even approximately so. The amount will depend upon a variety of circumstances: the individual temperament, habits of thrift, care, ability to buy necessaries intelligently, and whether the woman live alone or with her family. To those who practice economy, a given sum will afford comfort, while to those of contrary habit the same sum will be wholly inadequate. The coöperative economies of the family group are not taken into account though they constitute an important consideration in estimating the cost of living, for it is obvious that the individual expense will be less in the case of a member of a family than in the case of one living alone. The relation between earnings and morals is not capable of standardization. It cannot be shown that well paid women safeguard their morals more carefully than those who are poorly paid. Morality rests upon other considerations than wages; and there is, certainly, no such prevalent connection between the two as to justify a broad attempt to adjust the latter with reference to the former. As a means of safeguarding morals the attempted classification, in our opinion, is without reasonable basis. No distinction can be made between women who work for others and those who do not; nor is there ground for distinction between women and men, for, certainly, if women require a minimum wage to preserve their morals men require it to preserve their honesty. For these reasons, and others which might be stated, the inquiry in respect of the necessary cost of living and of the income necessary to preserve health and morals, presents an individual and not a composite question, and must be answered for each individual considered by herself and not by a general formula prescribed by a statutory bureau.

This uncertainty of the statutory standard is demonstrated by a consideration of certain orders of the board already made. These orders fix the sum to be paid to a woman employed in a place where food is served or in a mercantile establishment, at $16.50 per week; in a printing establishment, at $15.50 per week; and in a laundry, at $15 per week, with a provision reducing this to $9 in the case of a beginner. If a woman employed to serve food requires a minimum of $16.50 per week, it is hard to understand how the same woman working in a printing establishment or in a laundry is to get on with an income lessened by from $1 to $7.50 per week. The board probably found it impossible to follow the indefinite standard of the statute, and brought other and different factors into the problem; and this goes far in the direction of demonstrating the fatal uncertainty of the act, an infirmity which, in our opinion, plainly exists.

The law takes account of the necessities of only one party to the contract. It ignores the necessities of the employer by compelling him to pay not less than a certain sum, not only whether the employee is capable of earning it, but irrespective of the ability of his business to sustain the burden, generously leaving him, of course, the privilege of abandoning his business as an alternative for going on at a loss. Within the limits of the minimum sum, he is precluded, under penalty of fine and imprisonment, from adjusting compensation to the differing merits of his employees. It compels him to pay at least the sum fixed in any event, because the employee needs it, but requires no service of equivalent value from the employee. It therefore undertakes to solve but one-half of the problem. The other half is the establishment of a corresponding standard of efficiency, and this forms no part of the policy of the legislation, although in practice the former half without the latter must lead to ultimate failure, in accordance with the inexorable law that no one can continue indefinitely to take out more than he puts in without ultimately exhausting the supply. The law is not confined to the great and powerful employers but embraces those whose bargaining power may be as weak as that of the employee. It takes no account of periods of stress and business depression, of crippling losses, which may leave the employer himself without adequate means of livelihood. To the extent that the sum fixed exceeds the fair value of the services rendered, it amounts to a compulsory exaction from the employer for the support of a partially indigent person, for whose condition there rests upon him no peculiar responsibility, and therefore, in effect, arbitrarily shifts to his shoulders a burden which, if it belongs to anybody, belongs to society as a whole.

The feature of this statute which, perhaps more than any other, puts upon it the stamp of invalidity is that it exacts from the employer an arbitrary payment for a purpose and upon a basis having no causal connection with his business, or the contract or the work the employee engages to do. The declared basis, as already pointed out, is not the value of the service rendered, but the extraneous circumstance that the employee needs to get a prescribed sum of money to insure her subsistence, health and morals. The ethical right of every worker, man or woman, to a living wage may be conceded. One of the declared and important purposes of trade organizations is to secure it. And with that principle and with every legitimate effort to realize it in fact, no one can quarrel; but the fallacy of the proposed method of attaining it is that it assumes that every employer is bound at all events to furnish it. The moral requirement implicit in every contract of employment, viz., that the amount to be paid and the service to be rendered shall bear to each other some relation of just equivalence, is completely ignored. The necessities of the employee are alone considered and these arise outside of the employment, are the same when there is no employment, and as great in one occupation as in another. Certainly the employer by paying a fair equivalent for the service rendered, though not sufficient to support the employee, has neither caused nor contributed to her poverty. On the contrary, to the extent of what he pays he has relieved it. In principle, there can be no difference between the case of selling labor and the case of selling goods. If one goes to the butcher, the baker or grocer to buy food, he is morally entitled to obtain the worth of his money but he is not entitled to more. If what he gets is worth what he pays he is not justified in demanding more simply because he needs more; and the shopkeeper, having dealt fairly and honestly in that transaction, is not concerned in any peculiar sense with the question of his customer's necessities. Should a statute undertake to vest in a commission power to determine the quantity of food necessary for individual support and require the shopkeeper, if he sell to the individual at all, to furnish that quantity at not more than a fixed maximum, it would undoubtedly fall before the constitutional test. The fallacy of any argument in support of the validity of such a statute would be quickly exposed. The argument in support of that now being considered is equally fallacious, though the weakness of it may not be so plain. A statute requiring an employer to pay in money, to pay at prescribed and regular intervals, to pay the value of the services rendered, even to pay with fair relation to the extent of the benefit obtained from the service, would be understandable. But a statute which prescribes payment without regard to any of these things and solely with relation to circumstances apart from the contract of employment, the business affected by it and the work done under it, is so clearly the product of a naked, arbitrary exercise of power that it cannot be allowed to stand under the Constitution of the United States.

We are asked, upon the one hand, to consider the fact that several States have adopted similar statutes, and we are invited, upon the other hand, to give weight to the fact that three times as many States, presumably as well informed and as anxious to promote the health and morals of their people, have refrained from enacting such legislation. We have also been furnished with a large number of printed opinions approving the policy of the minimum wage, and our own reading has disclosed a large number to the contrary. These are all proper enough for the consideration of the lawmaking bodies, since their tendency is to establish the desirability or undesirability of the legislation; but they reflect no legitimate light upon the question of its validity, and that is what we are called upon to decide. The elucidation of that question cannot be aided by counting heads.

It is said that great benefits have resulted from the operation of such statutes, not alone in the District of Columbia but in the several States, where they have been in force. A mass of reports, opinions of special observers and students of the subject, and the like, has been brought before us in support of this statement, all of which we have found interesting but only mildly persuasive. That the earnings of women now are greater than they were formerly and that conditions affecting women have become better in other respects may be conceded, but convincing indications of the logical relation of these desirable changes to the law in question are significantly lacking. They may be, and quite probably are, due to other causes. We cannot close our eyes to the notorious fact that earnings everywhere in all occupations have greatly increased—not alone in States where the minimum wage law obtains but in the country generally—quite as much or more among men as among women and in occupations outside the reach of the law as in those governed by it. No real test of the economic value of the law can be had during periods of maximum employment, when general causes keep wages up to or above the minimum; that will come in periods of depression and struggle for employment when the efficient will be employed at the minimum rate while the less capable may not be employed at all.

Finally, it may be said that if, in the interest of the public welfare, the police power may be invoked to justify the fixing of a minimum wage, it may, when the public welfare is thought to require it, be invoked to justify a maximum wage. The power to fix high wages connotes, by like course of reasoning, the power to fix low wages. If, in the face of the guaranties of the Fifth Amendment, this form of legislation shall be legally justified, the field for the operation of the police power will have been widened to a great and dangerous degree. If, for example, in the opinion of future lawmakers, wages in the building trades shall become so high as to preclude people of ordinary means from building and owning homes, an authority which sustains the minimum wage will be invoked to support a maximum wage for building laborers and artisans, and the same argument which has been here urged to strip the employer of his constitutional liberty of contract in one direction will be utilized to strip the employee of his constitutional liberty of contract in the opposite direction. A wrong decision does not end with itself: it is a precedent, and, with the swing of sentiment, its bad influence may run from one extremity of the arc to the other.

It has been said that legislation of the kind now under review is required in the interest of social justice, for whose ends freedom of contract may lawfully be subjected to restraint. The liberty of the individual to do as he pleases, even in innocent matters, is not absolute. It must frequently yield to the common good, and the line beyond which the power of interference may not be pressed is neither definite nor unalterable but may be made to move, within limits not well defined, with changing need and circumstance. Any attempt to fix a rigid boundary would be unwise as well as futile. But, nevertheless, there are limits to the power, and when these have been passed, it becomes the plain duty of the courts in the proper exercise of their authority to so declare. To sustain the individual freedom of action contemplated by the Constitution, is not to strike down the common good but to exalt it; for surely the good of society as a whole cannot be better served than by the preservation against arbitrary restraint of the liberties of its constituent members.

It follows from what has been said that the act in question passes the limit prescribed by the Constitution, and, accordingly, the decrees of the court below are

Affirmed.

CARTER v. CARTER COAL, 298 U.S. 278 (1936)

This decision nullified the labor and pricing provisions of the Guffey Coal Act of 1935, which had established a national commission empowered to set prices and wages and to collect a fifteen per cent tax from mine owners. Most of the tax would be returned to those owners who complied with the Bituminous Coal Code set by the commission. Sutherland denounced the tax as a penalty forcing compliance with the law. The wage regulation, declared Sutherland, affected interests local in origin and therefore not within congressional power. Price fixing fell with the rest of the act.

MR. JUSTICE SUTHERLAND delivered the opinion of the Court.

The purposes of the "Bituminous Coal Conservation Act of 1935," involved in these suits, as declared by the title, are to stabilize the bituminous coal-mining industry and promote its interstate commerce; to provide for cooperative marketing of bituminous coal; to levy a tax on such coal and provide for a drawback under certain conditions; to declare the production, distribution, and use of such coal to be affected with a national public interest; to conserve the national resources of such coal; to provide for the general welfare, and for other purposes. C. 824, 49 Stat. 991. The constitutional validity of the act is challenged in each of the suits.

Nos. 636 and 651 are cross-writs of

certiorari in a stockholder's suit, brought in the Supreme Court of the District of Columbia by Carter against the Carter Coal Company and some of its officers, Guy T. Helvering (Commissioner of Internal Revenue of the United States), and certain other officers of the United States, to enjoin the coal company and its officers named from filing an acceptance of the code provided for in said act, from paying any tax imposed upon the coal company under the authority of the act, and from complying with its provisions or the provisions of the code. The bill sought to enjoin the Commissioner of Internal Revenue and the other federal officials named from proceeding under the act in particulars specified, the details of which it is unnecessary to state.

No. 649 is a suit brought in a federal district court in Kentucky by petitioners against respondent collector of internal revenue for the district of Kentucky, to enjoin him from collecting or attempting to collect the taxes sought to be imposed upon them by the act, on the ground of its unconstitutionality.

No. 650 is a stockholder's suit brought in the same court against the coal company and some of its officers, to secure a mandatory injunction against their refusal to accept and operate under the provisions of the Bituminous Coal Code prepared in pursuance of the act.

By the terms of the act, every producer of bituminous coal within the United States is brought within its provisions.

Section 1 is a detailed assertion of circumstances thought to justify the act. It declares that the mining and distribution of bituminous coal throughout the United States by the producer are affected with a national public interest; and that the service of such coal in relation to industrial activities, transportation facilities, health and comfort of the people, conservation by controlled production and economical mining and marketing, maintenance of just and rational relations between the public, owners, producers and employees, the right of the public to constant and adequate supplies of coal at reasonable prices, and the general welfare of the nation, require that the bituminous coal industry should be regulated as the act provides.

Section 1, among other things, further declares that the production and distribution by producers of such coal bear upon and directly affect interstate commerce, and render regulation of production and distribution imperative for the protection of such commerce; that certain features connected with the production, distribution, and marketing have led to waste of the national coal resources, disorganization of interstate commerce in such coal, and burdening and obstructing interstate commerce therein; that practices prevailing in the production of such coal directly affect interstate commerce and require regulation for the protection of that commerce; and that the right of mine workers to organize and collectively bargain for wages, hours of labor, and conditions of employment should be guaranteed in order to prevent constant wage cutting and disparate labor costs detrimental to fair interstate competition, and in order to avoid obstructions to interstate commerce that recur in industrial disputes over labor relations at the mines. These declarations constitute not enactments of law, but legislative averments by way of inducement to the enactment which follows.

The substantive legislation begins with § 2, which establishes in the Department of the Interior a National Bituminous Coal Commission, to be appointed and constituted as the section then specifically provides. Upon this commission is conferred the power to hear evidence and find facts upon which its orders and actions may be predicated.

Section 3 provides:

"There is hereby imposed upon the sale or other disposal of all bituminous coal produced within the United States an excise tax of 15 per centum on the sale price at the mine, or in the case of captive coal the fair market value of such coal at the mine, such tax, subject to the later provisions of this section, to be payable to the United States by the producers of such coal, and to be payable monthly for each calendar month, on or before the first business day of the second succeeding month, and under such regulations, and in such manner, as shall be prescribed by the Commissioner of Internal Revenue: *Provided,* That in the case of captive coal produced as aforesaid, the Commissioner of Internal Revenue shall fix a price therefor at the current market price for the comparable kind, quality, and size of coals in the locality where the same is produced: *Provided further,* That any such coal producer who has filed with the National Bituminous Coal Commission his acceptance of the code provided for in section 4 of this Act, and who acts in compliance with the provisions of such code, shall be entitled to a drawback in the form of a credit upon the amount of such tax payable hereunder, equivalent to 90 per centum of the amount of such tax, to be allowed and deducted therefrom at the time settlement therefor is required, in such manner as shall be prescribed by the Commissioner of Internal Revenue. Such right or benefit of drawback shall apply to all coal sold or disposed of from and after the day of the producer's filing with the Commission his acceptance of said code in such form of agreement as the Commission may prescribe. No producer shall by reason of his acceptance of the code provided for in section 4 or of the drawback of taxes provided in section 3 of this Act be held to be precluded or estopped from contesting the constitutionality of any provision of said code, or its validity as applicable to such producer."

Section 4 provides that the commission shall formulate the elaborate provisions contained therein into a working agreement to be known as the Bituminous Coal Code. These provisions require the organization of twenty-three coal districts, each with a district board the membership of which is to be determined in a manner pointed out by the act. Minimum prices for coal are to be established by each of these boards, which is authorized to make such classification of coals and price variation as to mines and consuming market areas as it may deem proper. "In order to sustain the stabilization of wages, working conditions, and maximum hours of labor, said prices shall be established so as to yield a return per net ton for each district in a minimum price area, as such districts are identified and such area is defined in the subjoined table designated 'Minimum-price area table,' equal as nearly as may be to the weighted average of the total costs, per net ton, determined as hereinafter provided, of the tonnage of such minimum price area. The computation of the total costs shall include the cost of labor, supplies, power, taxes, insurance, workmen's compensation, royalties, depreciation, and depletion (as determined by the Bureau of Internal Revenue in the computation of the Federal income tax) and all other direct expenses of production, coal operators' association dues, district board assessments for Board operating expenses only levied under the code, and reasonable costs of selling and the cost of administration." The district board must determine and adjust the total cost of the ascertainable tonnage produced in the district so as to give effect to any changes in wage rates, hours of employment, or other factors substantially affecting costs, which may have been established since January 1st, 1934.

Without repeating the long and involved provisions with regard to the fixing of minimum prices, it is enough to say that the act confers the power to fix the minimum price of coal at each and every coal mine in the United States, with such price variations as the board may deem necessary and proper. There is also a provision authorizing the commission, when deemed necessary in the public interest, to establish maximum prices in order to protect the consumer against unreasonably high prices.

All sales and contracts for the sale of coal are subject to the code prices provided for and in effect when such sales and contracts are made. Various unfair methods of competition are defined and forbidden.

The labor provisions of the code, found in Part III of the same section, require that in order to effectuate the purposes of the act the district boards and code members shall accept specified conditions contained in the code, among which are the following:

Employees to be given the right to organize and bargain collectively, through representatives of their own choosing, free from interference, restraint, or coercion of employers or their agents in respect of their concerted activities.

Such employees to have the right of peaceable assemblage for the discussion of the principles of collective bargaining and to select their own check-weighman to inspect the weighting or measuring of coal.

A labor board is created, consisting of three members, to be appointed by the President and assigned to the Department of Labor. Upon this board is conferred authority to adjudicate disputes arising under the provisions just stated, and to determine whether or not an organization of employees had been promoted, or is controlled or dominated by an employer in its organization, management, policy, or election of representatives. The board "may order a code member to meet the representatives of its employees for the purpose of collective bargaining."

Subdivision (g) of Part III provides:

"Whenever the maximum daily and weekly hours of labor are agreed upon in any contract or contracts negotiated between the producers of more than two-thirds the annual national tonnage production for the preceding calendar year and the representatives of more than one-half of the mine workers employed, such maximum hours of labor shall be accepted by all the code members. The wage agreement or agreements negotiated by collective bargaining in any district or group of two or more districts, between representatives of producers of more than two-thirds of the annual tonnage production of such district or each of such districts in a contracting group during the preceding calendar year, and representatives of the majority of the mine workers therein, shall be filed with the Labor Board and shall be accepted as the minimum wages for the various classifications of labor by the code members operating in such district or group of districts."

The bill of complaint in Nos. 636 and 651 was filed in the Supreme Court of the District of Columbia on August 31, 1935, the day after the Coal Conservation Act came into effect. That court, among other things, found that the suit was brought in good faith; that if Carter Coal Company should join the code it would be compelled to cancel existing contracts and pay its proportionate share of administering the code; that the production of bituminous coal is a local activity carried on within state borders; that coal is the nation's greatest and primary source of energy, vital to the public welfare, of the utmost importance to the industrial and economic life of the nation and the health and comfort of its inhabitants; and that its distribution in interstate commerce should be regular, continuous, and free of interruptions, obstructions, burdens, and restraints.

Other findings are to the effect that such coal is generally sold f. o. b. mine, and the predominant portion of it shipped outside the state in which it is produced; that the distribution and marketing is predominantly interstate in character, and that the intrastate distribution and sale are so connected that interstate regulation cannot be accomplished effectively unless transactions of intrastate distribution and sale be regulated.

The court further found the existence of a condition of unrestrained and destructive competition in the system of distribution and marketing such coal, and of destructive price-cutting, burdening and restraining interstate commerce and dislocating and diverting its normal flow.

The court concluded as a matter of law that the bringing of the suit was not premature; that the plaintiff was without legal remedy, and rightly invoked relief in equity; that the labor provisions of the act and code were unconstitutional for reasons stated, but the price-fixing provisions were valid and constitutional; that the labor provisions are separable; and, since the provisions with respect to price-fixing and unfair competition are valid, the taxing provisions of the act could stand. Therefore, except for granting a permanent injunction against collection of the "taxes" accrued during the suit (*Ex parte Young,* 209 U.S. 123, 147–148), the court denied the relief sought, and dismissed the bill.

Appeals were taken to the United States Court of Appeals for the District of Columbia by the parties; but pending hearing and submission in that court, petitions for writs of certiorari were presented asking us to review the decree of the Supreme Court of the District without awaiting such hearing and submission. Because of the importance of the question and the advantage of a speedy final determination thereof, the writs were granted.

The remaining two suits (Nos. 649 and 650), involving the same questions, were brought in the federal District Court for the Western District of Kentucky. That court held the act valid and constitutional in its entirety and entered a decree accordingly. 12 F. Supp. 570. Appeals were taken to the Circuit Court of Appeals for the Sixth Circuit; but, as in the Carter case and for the same reasons, this court granted writs of certiorari in advance of hearing and submission.

The questions involved will be considered under the following heads:

1. The right of stockholders to maintain suits of this character.

2. Whether the suits were prematurely brought.

3. Whether the exaction of 15 *per centum* on the sale price of coal at the mine is a tax or a penalty.

4. The purposes of the act as set forth in § 1, and the authority vested in Congress by the Constitution to effectuate them.

5. Whether the labor provisions of the act can be upheld as an exercise of the power to regulate interstate commerce.

6. Whether subdivision (g) of Part III of the Code, is an unlawful delegation of power.

7. The constitutionality of the price-fixing provisions, and the question of severability—that is to say, whether if either the

group of labor provisions or the group of price-fixing provisions be found constitutionally invalid, the other can stand as separable.

First. In the Carter case (Nos. 636 and 651) the stockholder who brought the suit had formally demanded of the board of directors that the company should not join the code, should refuse to pay the tax fixed by the act, and should bring appropriate judicial proceedings to prevent an unconstitutional and improper diversion of the assets of the company and to have determined the liability of the company under the act. The board considered the demand, determined that, while it believed the act to be unconstitutional and economically unsound and that it would adversely affect the business of the company if accepted, nevertheless it should accept the code provided for by the act because the penalty in the form of a 15% tax on its gross sales would be seriously injurious and might result in bankruptcy. This action of the board was approved by a majority of the shareholders at a special meeting called for the purpose of considering it.

In the Tway Company cases, the company itself brought suit to enjoin the enforcement of the act (No. 649); and a stockholder brought suit to compel the company to accept the code and operate under its provisions (No. 650).

Without repeating the long averments of the several bills, we are of opinion that the suits were properly brought and were maintainable in a court of equity. The right of stockholders to bring such suits under the circumstances disclosed is settled by the recent decision of this court in *Ashwander* v. *Tennessee Valley Authority,* 297 U.S. 288, and requires no further discussion.

Second. That the suits were not prematurely brought also is clear. Section 2 of the act is mandatory in its requirement that the commission be appointed by the President. The provisions of § 4 that the code be formulated and promulgated are equally mandatory. The so-called tax of 15% is definitely imposed, and its exaction certain to ensue.

In *Pennsylvania* v. *West Virginia,* 262 U.S. 553, 592–595, suits were brought by Pennsylvania and Ohio against West Virginia to enjoin the defendant state from enforcing an act of her legislature upon the ground that it would injuriously affect or cut off the supply of natural gas produced in her territory and carried by pipe lines into the territory of the plaintiff states and there sold and used. These suits were brought a few days after the West Virginia act became effective. No order had yet been made under it by the Public Service Commission, nor had it been tested in actual practice. But it appeared that the act was certain to operate as the complainant states apprehended it would. This court held that the suit was not premature. "One does not have to await the consummation of threatened injury to obtain preventive relief. If the injury is certainly impending that is enough."

Pierce v. *Society of Sisters,* 268 U.S. 510, 535–536, involved the constitutional validity of the Oregon Compulsory Education Act, which required every parent or other person having control of a child between the ages of eight and sixteen years to send him to the public school of the district where he resides. Suit was brought to enjoin the operation of the act by corporations owning and conducting private schools, on the ground that their business and property were threatened with destruction through the unconstitutional compulsion exercised by the act upon parents and guardians. The suits were held to be not premature, although the effective date of the act had not yet arrived. We said—"The injury to appellees was present and very real, not a mere possibility in the remote future. If no relief had been possible prior to the effective date of the Act, the injury would have become irreparable. Prevention of impending injury by unlawful action is a well recognized function of courts of equity."

See, also, *Terrace* v. *Thompson,* 263 U.S. 197, 215–216; *Swift & Co.* v. *United States,* 276 U.S. 311, 326; *Euclid* v. *Ambler Realty Co.,* 272 U.S. 365, 386; *City Bank Co.* v. *Schnader,* 291 U.S. 24, 34.

Third. The so-called excise tax of 15 *per centum* on the sale price of coal at the mine, or, in the case of captive coal the fair market value, with its drawback allowance of 13½%, is clearly not a tax but a penalty. The exaction applies to all bituminous coal produced, whether it be sold, transported or consumed in interstate commerce, or transactions in respect of it be confined wholly to the limits of the state. It also applies to "captive coal"—that is to say, coal produced for the sole use of the producer.

It is very clear that the "excise tax" is not imposed for revenue but exacted as a penalty to compel compliance with the regulatory provisions of the act. The whole purpose of the exaction is to coerce what is called an agreement—which, of course, it is not, for it lacks the essential element of consent. One who does a thing in order to avoid a monetary penalty does not agree; he yields to compulsion precisely the same as though he did so to avoid a term in jail.

The exaction here is a penalty and not a tax within the test laid down by this court in numerous cases. *Child Labor Tax Case,* 259 U.S. 20, 37–39; *United States* v. *La Franca,* 282 U.S. 568, 572; *United States* v. *Constantine,* 296 U.S. 287, 293 *et seq.; United States* v. *Butler,* 297 U.S. 1, 70. While the lawmaker is entirely free to ignore the ordinary meanings of words and make definitions of his own, *Karnuth* v. *United States,* 279 U.S. 231, 242; *Tyler* v. *United States,* 281 U.S. 497, 502, that device may not be employed so as to change the nature of the acts or things to which the words are applied. But it is not necessary to pursue the matter further. That the "tax" is in fact a penalty is not seriously in dispute. The position of the Government, as we understand it, is that the validity of the exaction does not rest upon the taxing power but upon the power of Congress to regulate interstate commerce; and that if the act in respect of the labor and price-fixing provisions be not upheld, the "tax" must fall with them. With that position we agree and confine our consideration accordingly.

Fourth. Certain recitals contained in the act plainly suggest that its makers were of opinion that its constitutionality could be sustained under some general federal power, thought to exist, apart from the specific grants of the Constitution. The fallacy of that view will be apparent when we recall fundamental principles which, although hitherto often expressed in varying forms of words, will bear repetition whenever their accuracy seems to be challenged. The recitals to which we refer are contained in § 1 (which is simply a preamble to the act), and, among others, are to the effect that the distribution of bituminous coal is of national interest, affecting the health and comfort of the people and the general welfare of the nation; that this circumstance, together with the necessity of maintaining just and rational relations between the public, owners, producers, and employees, and the right of the public to constant and adequate supplies at reasonable prices, require regulation of the industry as the act provides. These affirmations—and the further ones that the production and distribution of such coal "directly affect interstate commerce," because of which and of the waste of the national coal resources and other circumstances, the regulation is necessary for the protection of such commerce—do not constitute an exertion of the *will* of Congress which is legislation, but a recital of considerations which in the *opinion* of that body existed and justified the expression of its will in the present act. Nevertheless, this preamble may not be disregarded. On the contrary it is important, because it makes clear, except for the pure assumption that the conditions described "directly" affect interstate commerce, that the powers which Congress undertook to exercise are not specific but of the most general character—namely, to protect the general public interest and the health and comfort of the people, to conserve privately-owned coal, maintain just relations between producers and employees and others, and promote the general welfare, by controlling nation-wide production and distribution of coal. These, it may be conceded, are objects of great worth; but are they ends, the attainment of which has been committed by the Constitution to the federal government? This is a vital question; for nothing is more certain than that beneficent aims, however great or well directed, can never serve in lieu of constitutional power.

The ruling and firmly established principle is that the powers which the general government may exercise are only those specifically enumerated in the Constitution, and such implied powers as are necessary and proper to carry into effect the enumerated powers. Whether the end sought to be attained by an act of Congress is legitimate is wholly a matter of constitutional power and not at all of legislative discretion. Legislative congressional discretion begins with the choice of means and ends with the adoption of methods and details to carry the delegated powers into effect. The distinction between these two things—power and discretion—is not only very plain but very important. For while the powers are rigidly limited to the enumerations of the Constitution, the means which may be employed to carry the powers into effect are not restricted, save that they must be appropriate, plainly adapted to the end, and not prohibited by, but consistent with, the letter and spirit of the Constitution. *McCulloch* v. *Maryland,* 4 Wheat. 316, 421. Thus, it may be said that to a constitutional end many ways are open; but to an end not within the terms of the Constitution, all ways are closed.

The proposition, often advanced and as often discredited, that the power of the federal government inherently extends to purposes affecting the nation as a whole with which the states severally cannot deal or cannot adequately deal, and the related notion that Congress, entirely apart from those powers delegated by the Constitution, may enact laws to promote the general welfare, have never been accepted but always definitely rejected by this court. Mr. Justice Story, as early as 1816, laid down the cardinal rule, which has ever since been followed—that the general government "can claim no powers which are not granted to it by the Constitution, and the powers actually granted, must be such as are expressly given, or given by necessary implication." *Martin* v. *Hunter's Lessee,* 1 Wheat. 304, 326. In the Framers Convention, the proposal to confer a general power akin to that just discussed was included in Mr. Randolph's resolutions, the sixth of which, among other things, declared that the National Legislature ought to enjoy the legislative rights vested in Congress by the Confederation, and "moreover to legislate in all cases to which the separate States are incompetent, or in which the harmony of the United States may be interrupted by the exercise of individual Legislation." The convention, however, declined to confer upon Congress power in such general terms; instead of which it carefully limited the powers which it thought wise to entrust to Congress by specifying them, thereby denying all others not granted expressly or by necessary implication. It made no grant of authority to Congress to legislate substantively for the general welfare, *United States* v. *Butler, supra,* p. 64; and no such authority exists, save as the general welfare may be promoted by the exercise of the powers which are granted. Compare *Jacobson* v. *Massachusetts,* 197 U.S. 11, 22.

There are many subjects in respect of which the several states have not legislated in harmony with one another, and in which their varying laws and the failure of some of them to act at all have resulted in injurious confusion and embarrassment. See *Addyston Pipe & Steel Co.* v. *United States,* 175 U.S. 211, 232–233. The state laws with respect to marriage and divorce present a case in point; and the great necessity of national legislation on that subject has been from time to time vigorously urged. Other pertinent examples are laws with respect to negotiable instruments, desertion and nonsupport, certain phases of state taxation, and others which we do not pause to mention. In many of these fields of legislation, the necessity of bringing the applicable rules of law into general harmonious relation has been so great that a Commission on Uniform State Laws, composed of commissioners from every state in the Union, has for many years been industriously and successfully working to that end by preparing and securing the passage by the several states of uniform laws. If there be an easier and constitutional way to these desirable results through congressional action, it thus far has escaped discovery.

Replying directly to the suggestion advanced by counsel in *Kansas* v. *Colorado,* 206 U.S. 46, 89–90, to the effect that necessary powers national in their scope must be found vested in Congress, though not expressly granted or essentially implied, this court said:

"But the proposition that there are legislative powers affecting the Nation as a whole which belong to, although not expressed in the grant of powers, is in direct conflict with the doctrine that this is a government of enumerated powers. That this is such a government clearly appears from the Constitution, independently of the Amendments, for otherwise there would be an instrument granting certain specified things made operative to grant other and distinct things. This natural construction of the original body of the Constitution is made absolutely certain by the Tenth Amendment. This amendment, which was seemingly adopted with prescience of just such contention as the present, disclosed the widespread fear that the National Government might, under the pressure of a supposed general welfare, attempt to exercise powers which had not been granted. With equal determination the framers intended that no such assumption should ever find justification in the organic act, and that if in the future further powers seemed necessary they should be granted by the people in the manner they had provided for amending that act."

The general rule with regard to the respective powers of the national and the state governments under the Constitution, is not in doubt. The states were before the Constitution; and, consequently, their legislative powers antedated the Constitution. Those who framed and those who adopted that instrument meant to carve from the general mass of legislative powers, then possessed by the states, only such portions as it was thought wise to confer upon the federal government; and in order that there should be no uncertainty in respect of what was taken and what was left, the national powers of legislation were not aggregated but enumerated—with the result that what was not embraced by the enumeration remained vested in the states without change or impairment. Thus, "when it was found necessary to establish a national government for national purposes," this court said in *Munn* v. *Illinois,* 94 U.S. 113, 124, "a part of the powers of the States and of the people of the States was granted to the United States and the people of the United States. This grant operated as a further limitation upon the powers of the States, so that now the governments of the States possess all the powers of the Parliament of England, except such as have been delegated to the United States or reserved by the people." While the states are not sovereign in the true sense of that term, but only *quasi*-sovereign, yet in respect of all powers reserved to them they are supreme—"as independent of the general government as that government within its sphere is independent of the States." *Collector* v. *Day,* 11 Wall. 113, 124. And since every addition to the national legislative power to some extent detracts from or invades the power of the states, it is of vital moment that, in order to preserve the fixed balance intended by the Constitution, the powers of the general government be not so extended as to embrace any not within the express terms of the several grants or the implications necessarily to be drawn therefrom. It is no longer open to question that the general government, unlike the states, *Hammer* v. *Dagenhart,* 247 U.S. 251, 275, possesses no *inherent* power in respect of the internal affairs of the states; and emphatically not with regard to legislation. The question in respect of the inherent power of that government as to the external affairs of the nation and in the field of international law is a wholly different matter which it is not necessary now to consider. See, however, *Jones* v. *United States,* 137 U.S. 202, 212; *Nishimura Ekiu* v. *United States,* 142 U.S. 651, 659; *Fong Yue Ting* v. *United States,* 149 U.S. 698, 705 *et seq.; Burnet* v. *Brooks,* 288 U.S. 378, 396.

The determination of the Framers Convention and the ratifying conventions to preserve complete and unimpaired state self-government in all matters not committed to the general government is one of the plainest facts which emerge from the history of their deliberations. And adherence to that determination is incumbent equally upon the federal government and the states. State powers can neither be appropriated on the one hand nor abdicated on the other. As this court said in *Texas* v. *White,* 7 Wall. 700, 725—"the preservation of the States, and the maintenance of their governments, are as much within the design and care of the Constitution as the preservation of the Union and the maintenance of the National Government. The Constitution, in all its provisions, looks to an indestructible Union composed of indestructible States." Every journey to a forbidden end begins with the first step; and the danger of such a step by the federal government in the direction of taking over the powers of the states is that the end of the journey may find the states so despoiled of their powers, or—what may amount to the same thing—so relieved of the responsibilities which possession of the powers necessarily enjoins, as to reduce them to little more than geographical subdivisions of the national domain. It is safe to say that if, when the Constitution was under consideration, it had been thought that any such danger lurked behind its plain words, it would never have been ratified.

And the Constitution itself is in every real sense a law—the lawmakers being the people themselves, in whom under our system all political power and sovereignty primarily resides, and through whom such power and sovereignty primarily speaks. It is by that law, and not otherwise, that the legislative, executive, and judicial agencies which it created exercise such political authority as they have been permitted to possess. The Constitution speaks for itself in terms so plain that to misunderstand their import is not rationally possible. "We the people of the United States," it says, "do ordain and establish this Constitution . . ." Ordain and establish! These are definite words of enactment, and without more would stamp what follows with the dignity and character of law. The framers of the Constitution, however, were not content to let the matter rest here, but provided explicitly—"This Constitution, and the Laws of the United States which shall be made in Pursuance thereof; . . . shall be the supreme Law of the Land; . . ." The supremacy of the Constitution as law is thus declared without qualification. That supremacy is absolute; the supremacy of a statute enacted by Congress is not absolute but conditioned upon its being made in pursuance of the Constitution. And a judicial tribunal, clothed by that instrument with complete judicial power, and, therefore, by the very nature of the power, required to ascertain and apply the law to the facts in every case or proceeding properly brought for adjudication, must apply the supreme law and reject the inferior statute whenever the two conflict. In the discharge of that duty, the opinion of the lawmakers that a statute passed by them is valid must be given great weight, *Adkins* v. *Children's Hospital,* 261 U.S. 525, 544; but their opinion, or the court's opinion, that the statute will prove greatly or generally beneficial is wholly irrelevant to the inquiry. *Schechter* v. *United States,* 295 U.S. 495, 549–550.

We have set forth, perhaps at unnecessary length, the foregoing principles, because it seemed necessary to do so in order to demonstrate that the general purposes which the act recites, and which, therefore, unless the recitals be disregarded, Congress undertook to achieve, are beyond the power of Congress except so far, and only so far, as they may be realized by an exercise of some specific power granted by the Constitution. Proceeding by a process of elimination, which it is not necessary to follow in detail, we shall find no grant of power which authorizes Congress to legislate in respect of these general purposes unless it be found in the commerce clause—and this we now consider.

Fifth. Since the validity of the act depends upon whether it is a regulation of interstate commerce, the nature and extent of the power conferred upon Congress by the commerce clause becomes the determinative question in this branch of the case. The commerce clause vests in Congress the power—"To regulate Commerce with foreign Nations, and among the several States, and with the Indian Tribes." The function to be exercised is that of regulation. The thing to be regulated is the commerce described. In exercising the authority conferred by this clause of the Constitution, Congress is powerless to regulate anything which is not commerce, as it is powerless to do anything about commerce which is not regulation. We first inquire, then—What is commerce? The term, as this court many times has said, is one of extensive import. No all-embracing definition has ever been formulated. The question is to be approached both affirmatively and negatively—that is to say, from the points of view as to what it includes and what it excludes.

In *Gibbons* v. *Ogden,* 9 Wheat. 1, 189–190, Chief Justice Marshall said:

"Commerce, undoubtedly, is traffic, but it is something more: it is intercourse. It describes the commercial intercourse between nations, and parts of nations, in all its branches, and is regulated by prescribing rules for carrying on that intercourse. . . ."

As used in the Constitution, the word "commerce" is the equivalent of the phrase "intercourse for the purposes of trade," and includes transportation, purchase, sale, and exchange of commodities between the citizens of the different states. And the power to regulate commerce embraces the instruments by which commerce is carried on. *Welton* v. *Missouri,* 91 U.S. 275, 280; *Addyston Pipe & Steel Co.* v. *United States,* 175 U.S. 211, 241; *Hopkins* v. *United States,* 171 U.S. 578, 597. In *Adair* v. *United States,* 208 U.S. 161, 177, the phrase "Commerce among the several States" was defined as comprehending "traffic, intercourse, trade, navigation, communication, the transit of persons and the transmission of messages by telegraph—indeed, every species of commercial intercourse among the several States." In *Veazie* v. *Moor,* 14 How. 568, 573–574, this court, after saying that the phrase could never be applied to transactions wholly internal, significantly added: "Nor can it be properly concluded, that, because the products of domestic enterprise in agriculture or manufactures, or in the arts, may ultimately become the subjects of foreign commerce, that the control of the means or the encouragements by which enterprise is fostered and protected, is legitimately within the import of the phrase *foreign commerce,* or fairly implied in any investiture of the power to regulate such commerce. A pretension as far reaching as this, would extend to contracts between citizen and citizen of the same State, would control the pursuits of the planter, the grazier, the manufacturer, the mechanic, the immense operations of the collieries and mines and furnaces of the country; for there is not one of these avocations, the results of which may not become the subjects of foreign commerce, and be borne either by turnpikes, canals, or railroads, from point to point within the several States, towards an ultimate destination, like the one above mentioned. . . ."

The distinction between manufacture and commerce was discussed in *Kidd* v. *Pearson,* 128 U.S. 1, 20, 21, 22; and it was said:

"No distinction is more popular to the common mind, or more clearly expressed in economic and political literature, than that between manufacture and commerce. Manufacture is transformation—the fashioning of raw materials into a change of form for use. The functions of commerce are different. . . . If it be held that the term includes the regulation of all such manufactures as are intended to be the subject of commercial transactions in the future, it is impossible to deny that it would also include all productive industries that contemplate the same thing. The result would be that Congress would be invested, to the exclusion of the States, with the power to regulate, not only manufactures, but also agriculture, horticulture, stock raising, domestic fisheries, mining —in short, every branch of human industry. For is there one of them that does not contemplate, more or less clearly, an interstate or foreign market? Does not the wheat grower of the Northwest and the cotton planter of the South plant, cultivate, and harvest his crop with an eye on the prices at Liverpool, New York, and Chicago? The power being vested in Congress and denied to the States, it would follow as an inevitable result that the duty would devolve on Congress to regulate all of these delicate, multiform and vital interests—interests which in their nature are and must be local in all the details of their successful management."

And then, as though foreseeing the present controversy, the opinion proceeds:

"Any movement toward the establishment of rules of production in this vast country, with its many different climates and opportunities, could only be at the sacrifice of the peculiar advantages of a large part of the localities in it, if not of every one of them. On the other hand, any movement toward the local, detailed and incongruous legislation required by such interpretation would be about the widest possible departure from the declared object of the clause in question. Nor this alone. Even in the exercise of the power contended for, Congress would be confined to the regulation, not of certain branches of industry, however numerous, but to those instances in each and every branch where the producer contemplated an interstate market. . . . A situation more paralyzing to the state governments, and more provocative of conflicts between the general government and the States, and less likely to have been what the framers of the Constitution intended, it would be difficult to imagine."

Chief Justice Fuller, speaking for this court in *United States* v. *E. C. Knight Co.,* 156 U.S. 1, 12, 13, said:

"Doubtless the power to control the manufacture of a given thing involves in a certain sense the control of its disposition, but this is a secondary and not the primary sense; and although the exercise of that power may result in bringing the operation of commerce into play, it does not control it, and affects it only incidentally and indirectly. Commerce succeeds to manufacture, and is not a part of it. . . .

"It is vital that the independence of the commercial power and of the police power, and the delimitation between them, however sometimes perplexing, should always be recognized and observed, for while the one furnishes the strongest bond of union, the other is essential to the preservation of the autonomy of the States as required by our dual form of government; and acknowledged evils, however grave and urgent they may appear to be, had better be borne, than the risk be run, in the effort to suppress them, of more serious consequences by resort to expedients of even doubtful constitutionality.

". . . The regulation of commerce applies to the subjects of commerce and not to matters of internal police. Contracts to buy, sell, or exchange goods to be transported among the several States, the transportation and its instrumentalities, and articles bought, sold, or exchanged for the purposes of such transit among the States, or put in the way of transit, may be regulated, but this is because they form part of interstate trade or commerce. The fact that an article is manufactured for export to another State does not of itself make it an article of interstate commerce, and the intent of the manufacturer does not determine the time when the article or product passes from the control of the State and belongs to commerce. . . ."

That commodities produced or manufactured within a state are intended to be sold or transported outside the state does not render their production or manufacture subject to federal regulation under the commerce clause. As this court said in *Coe* v. *Errol,* 116 U.S. 517, 526, "Though intended for exportation, they may never be exported; the owner has a perfect right to change his mind; and until actually put in motion, for some place out of the State, or committed to the custody of a carrier for transportation to such place, why may they not be regarded as still remaining a part of the general mass of property in the State?" It is true that this was said in respect of a challenged power of the state to impose a tax; but the query is equally pertinent where the question, as here, is with regard to the power of regulation. The case was relied upon in *Kidd* v. *Pearson, supra,* p. 26. "The application of the principles above announced," it was there said, "to the case under consideration leads to a conclusion against the contention of the plaintiff in error. The police power of a State is as broad and plenary as its taxing power; and property within the State is subject to the operations of the former so long as it is within the regulating restrictions of the latter."

In *Heisler* v. *Thomas Colliery Co.,* 260 U.S. 245, 259–260, we held that the possibility, or even certainty of exportation of a product or article from a state did not determine it to be in interstate commerce before the commencement of its movement from the state. To hold otherwise "would nationalize all industries, it would nationalize and withdraw from state jurisdiction and deliver to federal commercial control the fruits of California and the South, the wheat of the West and its meats, the cotton of the South, the shoes of Massachusetts and the woolen industries of other States, at the very inception of their production or growth, that is, the fruits unpicked, the cotton and wheat ungathered, hides and flesh of cattle yet 'on the hoof,' wool yet unshorn, and coal yet unmined, because they are in varying percentages destined for and surely to be exported to States other than those of their production."

In *Oliver Iron Co.* v. *Lord,* 262 U.S. 172, 178, we said on the authority of numerous cited cases: "Mining is not interstate commerce, but, like manufacturing, is a local business subject to local regulation and taxation. . . . Its character in this regard is intrinsic, is not affected by the intended use or disposal of the product, is not controlled by contractual engagements, and persists even though the business be conducted in close connection with interstate commerce."

The same rule applies to the production of oil. "Such production is essentially a mining operation and therefore is not a part of interstate commerce even though the product obtained is intended to be and in fact is immediately shipped in such commerce." *Champlin Rfg. Co.* v. *Corporation Commission,* 286 U.S. 210, 235. One who produces or manufactures a commodity, subsequently sold and shipped by him in interstate commerce, whether such sale and shipment were originally intended or not, has engaged in two distinct and separate activities. So far as he produces or manufactures a commodity, his business is purely local. So far as he sells and ships, or contracts to sell and ship, the commodity to customers in another state, he engages in interstate commerce. In respect of the former, he is subject only to regulation by the state; in respect of the latter, to regulation only by the federal government. *Utah Power & L. Co.* v. *Pfost,* 286 U.S. 165, 182. Production is not commerce; but a step in preparation for commerce. *Chassaniol* v. *Greenwood,* 291 U.S. 584, 587.

We have seen that the word "commerce" is the equivalent of the phrase "intercourse for the purposes of trade." Plainly, the incidents leading up to and culminating in the mining of coal do not constitute such intercourse. The employment of men, the fixing of their wages, hours of labor and working conditions, the bargaining in respect of these things—whether carried on separately or collectively—each and all constitute intercourse for the purposes of production, not of trade. The latter is a thing apart from the relation of employer and employee, which in all producing occupations is purely local in character. Extraction of coal from the mine is the aim and the completed result of local activities. Commerce in the coal mined is not brought into being by force of these activities, but by negotiations, agreements, and circumstances entirely apart from production. Mining brings the subject matter of commerce into existence. Commerce disposes of it.

A consideration of the foregoing, and of many cases which might be added to those already cited, renders inescapable the conclusion that the effect of the labor provisions of the act, including those in respect of minimum wages, wage agreements, collective bargaining, and the Labor Board and its powers, primarily falls upon production and not upon commerce; and confirms the further resulting conclusion that production is a purely local activity. It follows that none of these essential antecedents of production constitutes a transaction in or forms any part of interstate commerce. *Schechter Corp.* v. *United States, supra,* p. 542 *et seq.* Everything which moves in interstate commerce has had a local origin. Without local production somewhere, interstate commerce, as now carried on, would practically disappear. Nevertheless, the local character of mining, of manufacturing and of crop growing is a fact, and remains a fact, whatever may be done with the products.

Certain decisions of this court, superficially considered, seem to lend support to the defense of the act now under review. But upon examination, they will be seen to be inapposite. Thus, *Coronado Coal Co.* v. *United Mine Workers,* 268 U.S. 295, 310, and kindred cases, involved conspiracies to restrain interstate commerce in violation of the Anti-trust laws. The acts of the persons involved were local in character, but the intent was to restrain interstate commerce, and the means employed were calculated to carry that intent into effect. Interstate commerce was the direct object of attack; and the restraint of such commerce was the necessary consequence of the acts and the immediate end in view. *Bedford Stone Co.* v. *Stone Cutters Assn.,* 274 U.S. 37, 46. The applicable law was concerned not with the character of the acts or of the means employed, which might be in and of themselves purely local, but with the intent and direct operation of those acts and means upon interstate commerce. "The mere reduction in the supply of an article," this court said in the *Coronado Co.* case, *supra,* p. 310, "to be shipped in interstate commerce by the illegal or tortious prevention of its manufacture or production is ordinarily an indirect and remote obstruction to that commerce. But when the intent of those unlawfully preventing the manufacture or production is shown to be to restrain or control the supply entering and moving in interstate commerce, or the price of it in interstate markets, their action is a direct violation of the Anti-Trust Act."

Another group of cases, of which *Swift & Co.* v. *United States,* 196 U.S. 375, is an example, rest upon the circumstance that the acts in question constituted direct interferences with the "flow" of commerce among the states. In the *Swift* case, livestock was consigned and delivered to stockyards—not as a place of final destination, but, as the court said in *Stafford* v. *Wallace,* 258 U.S. 495, 516, "a throat through which the current flows." The sales which ensued merely changed the private interest in the subject of the current without interfering with its continuity. *Industrial Assn.* v. *United States,* 268 U.S. 64, 79. It was nowhere suggested in these cases that the interstate commerce power extended to the growth or production of the things which, after production, entered the flow. If the court had held that the raising of the cattle, which were involved in the *Swift* case, including the wages paid to and working conditions of the herders and others employed in the business, could be regulated by Congress, that decision and decisions holding similarly would be in point; for it is that situation, and not the one with which the court actually dealt, which here concerns us.

The distinction suggested is illustrated by the decision in *Arkadelphia Milling Co.* v. *St. Louis S. W. Ry. Co.,* 249 U.S. 134, 150–152. That case dealt with orders of a state commission fixing railroad rates. One of the questions considered was whether certain shipments of rough material from the forest to mills in the same state for manufacture, followed by the forwarding of the finished product to points outside the state, was a continuous movement in interstate commerce. It appeared that when the rough material reached the mills it was manufactured into various articles which were stacked or placed in kilns to dry, the processes occupying several months. Markets for the manufactured articles were almost entirely in other states or in foreign countries. About 95% of the finished articles was made for outbound shipment. When the rough material was shipped to the mills, it was expected by the mills that this percentage of the finished articles would be so sold and shipped outside the state. And all of them knew and intended that this 95% of the finished product would be so sold and shipped. This court held that the state order did not interfere with interstate commerce, and that the *Swift* case was not in point; as it is not in point here.

The restricted field covered by the *Swift* and kindred cases is illustrated by the *Schechter* case, *supra,* p. 543. There the commodity in question, although shipped from another state, had come to rest in the state of its destination, and, as the court pointed out, was no longer in a current or flow of interstate commerce. The *Swift* doctrine was rejected as inapposite. In the *Schechter* case the flow had ceased. Here it had not begun. The difference is not one of substance. The applicable principle is the same.

But § 1 (the preamble) of the act now under review declares that all production and distribution of bituminous coal "bear upon and directly affect its interstate commerce"; and that regulation thereof is imperative for the production of such commerce. The contention of the government is that the labor provisions of the act may be sustained in that view.

That the production of every commodity intended for interstate sale and transportation has some effect upon interstate commerce may be, if it has not already been, freely granted; and we are brought to the final and decisive inquiry, whether here that effect is direct, as the "preamble" recites, or indirect. The distinction is not formal, but substantial in the highest degree, as we pointed out in the *Schechter* case, *supra,* p. 546, *et seq.* "If the commerce clause were construed," we there said, "to reach all enterprises and transactions which could be said to have an indirect effect upon interstate commerce, the federal authority would embrace practically all the activities of the people and the authority of the State over its domestic concerns would exist only by sufferance of the federal government. Indeed, on such a theory, even the development of the State's commercial facilities would be subject to federal control." It was also pointed out, p. 548, that "the distinction between direct and indirect effects of intrastate transactions upon interstate commerce must be recognized as a fundamental one, essential to the maintenance of our constitutional system."

Whether the effect of a given activity or condition is direct or indirect is not always easy to determine. The word "direct" implies that the activity or condition invoked or blamed shall operate proximately —not mediately, remotely, or collaterally— to produce the effect. It connotes the absence of an efficient intervening agency or condition. And the extent of the effect bears no logical relation to its character. The distinction between a direct and an indirect effect turns, not upon the magnitude of either the cause or the effect, but entirely upon the manner in which the effect has been brought about. If the production by one man of a single ton of coal intended for interstate sale and shipment, and actually so sold and shipped, affects interstate commerce indirectly, the effect does not become direct by multiplying the tonnage, or increasing the number of men employed, or adding to the expense or complexities of the business, or by all combined. It is quite true that rules of law are sometimes qualified by considerations of degree, as the government argues. But the matter of degree has no bearing upon the question here, since that question is not—What is the *extent* of the local activity or condition, or the *extent* of the effect produced upon interstate commerce? but—What is the *relation* between the activity or condition and the effect?

Much stress is put upon the evils which come from the struggle between employers and employees over the matter of wages, working conditions, the right of collective bargaining, etc., and the resulting strikes, curtailment and irregularity of production and effect on prices; and it is insisted that interstate commerce is *greatly* affected thereby. But, in addition to what has just been said, the conclusive answer is that the evils are all local evils over which the federal government has no legislative control. The relation of employer and employee is a local relation. At common law, it is one of the domestic relations. The wages are paid for the doing of local work. Working conditions are obviously local conditions. The employees are not engaged in or about commerce, but exclusively in producing a commodity. And the controversies and evils, which it is the object of the act to regulate and minimize, are local controversies and evils affecting local work undertaken to accomplish that local result. Such effect as they may have upon commerce, however extensive it may be, is secondary and indirect. An increase in the greatness of the effect adds to its importance. It does not alter its character.

The government's contentions in defense of the labor provisions are really disposed of adversely by our decision in the *Schechter* case, *supra.* The only perceptible difference between that case and this is that in the *Schechter* case the federal power was asserted with respect to commodities which had come to rest after their interstate transportation; while here, the case deals with commodities at rest before interstate commerce has begun. That difference is without significance. The federal regulatory power ceases when interstate commercial intercourse ends; and, correlatively, the power does not attach until interstate commercial intercourse begins. There is no basis in law or reason for applying different rules to the two situations. No such distinction can be found in anything said in the *Schechter* case. On the contrary, the situations were recognized as akin. In the opinion, at page 546, after calling attention to the fact that if the commerce clause could be construed to reach transactions having an indirect effect upon interstate commerce the federal authority would embrace practically all the activities of the people, and the authority of the state over its domestic concerns would exist only by sufferance of the federal government, we said: "Indeed, on such a theory, even the development of the State's commercial facilities would be subject to federal control." And again, after pointing out that hours and wages have no direct relation to interstate commerce and that if the federal government had power to determine the wages and hours of employees in the internal commerce of a state because of their relation to cost and prices and their indirect effect upon interstate commerce, we said, p. 549: "All the processes of production and distribution that enter into cost could likewise be controlled. If the cost of doing an intrastate business is in itself the permitted object of federal control, the extent of the regulation of cost would be a question of discretion and not of power." A reading of the entire opinion makes clear, what we now declare, that the want of power on the part of the federal government is the same whether the wages, hours of service, and working conditions, and the bargaining about them, are related to production before interstate commerce has begun, or to sale and distribution after it has ended.

Sixth. That the act, whatever it may be in form, in fact is compulsory clearly appears. We have already discussed § 3, which imposes the excise tax as a penalty to compel "acceptance" of the code. Section 14 provides that the United States shall purchase no bituminous coal produced at any mine where the producer has not complied with the provisions of the code; and that each contract made by the United States shall contain a provision that the contractor will buy no bituminous coal to use on, or in the carrying out of, such contract unless the producer be a member of the code, as certified by the coal commission. In the light of these provisions we come to a consideration of subdivision (g) of Part III of § 4, dealing with "Labor Relations."

That subdivision delegates the power to fix maximum hours of labor to a part of the producers and the miners—namely, "the producers of more than two-thirds of the annual national tonnage production for the preceding calendar year" and "more than one-half of the mine workers employed"; and to producers of more than two-thirds of the district annual tonnage during the preceding calendar year and a majority of the miners, there is delegated the power to fix minimum wages for the district or group of districts. The effect, in respect of wages and hours, is to subject the dissentient minority, either of producers or miners or both, to the will of the stated majority, since, by refusing to submit, the minority at once incurs the hazard of enforcement of the drastic compulsory provisions of the act to which we have referred. To "accept," in these circumstances, is not to exercise a choice, but to surrender to force.

The power conferred upon the majority is, in effect, the power to regulate the affairs of an unwilling minority. This is legislative delegation in its most obnoxious form; for it is not even delegation to an official or an official body, presumptively disinterested, but to private persons whose interests may be and often are adverse to the interests of others in the same business. The record shows that the conditions of competition differ among the various localities. In some, coal dealers compete among themselves. In other localities, they also compete with the mechanical production of electrical energy and of natural gas. Some coal producers favor the code; others oppose it; and the record clearly indicates that this diversity of view arises from their conflicting and even antagonistic interests. The difference between producing coal and regulating its production is, of course, fundamental. The former is a private activity; the latter is necessarily a governmental function, since, in the very nature of things, one person may not be entrusted with the power to regulate the business of another, and especially of a competitor. And a statute which attempts to confer such power undertakes an intolerable and unconstitutional interference with personal liberty and private property. The delegation is so clearly arbitrary, and so clearly a denial of rights safeguarded by the due process clause of the Fifth Amendment, that it is unnecessary to do more than refer to decisions of this court which foreclose the question. *Schechter Corp.* v. *United States,* 295 U.S. at p. 537; *Eubank* v. *Richmond,* 226 U.S. 137, 143; *Seattle Trust Co.* v. *Roberge,* 278 U.S. 116, 121–122.

Seventh. Finally, we are brought to the price-fixing provisions of the code. The necessity of considering the question of their constitutionality will depend upon whether they are separable from the labor provisions so that they can stand independently. Section 15 of the act provides:

"If any provision of this Act, or the application thereof to any person or circumstances, is held invalid, the remainder of the Act and the application of such provisions to other persons or circumstances shall not be affected thereby."

In the absence of such a provision, the presumption is that the legislature intends an act to be effective as an entirety—that is to say, the rule is against the mutilation of a statute; and if any provision be unconstitutional, the presumption is that the remaining provisions fall with it. The effect of the statute is to reverse this presumption in favor of inseparability and create the opposite one of separability. Under the nonstatutory rule, the burden is upon the supporter of the legislation to show the separability of the provisions involved. Under the statutory rule, the burden is shifted to the assailant to show their inseparability. But under either rule, the determination, in the end, is reached by applying the same test—namely, What was the intent of the lawmakers?

Under the statutory rule, the presumption must be overcome by considerations which establish "the clear probability that the invalid part being eliminated the legislature would not have been satisfied with what remains," *Williams* v. *Standard Oil Co.,* 278 U.S. 235, 241 *et seq.;* or, as stated in *Utah Power & L. Co.* v. *Pfost,* 286 U.S. 165, 184–185, "the clear probability that the legislature would not have been satisfied with the statute unless it had included the invalid part." Whether the provisions of a statute are so interwoven that one being held invalid the others must fall, presents a question of statutory construction and of legislative intent, to the determination of which the statutory provision becomes an aid. "But it is an aid merely; not an inexorable command." *Dorchy* v. *Kansas,* 264 U.S. 286, 290. The presumption in favor of separability does not authorize the court to give the statute "an effect altogether different from that sought by the measure viewed as a whole." *Railroad Retirement Board* v. *Alton R. Co.,* 295 U.S. 330, 362.

The statutory aid to construction in no way alters the rule that in order to hold one part of a statute unconstitutional and uphold another part as separable, they must not be mutually dependent upon one another. Perhaps a fair approach to a solution of the problem is to suppose that while the bill was pending in Congress a motion to strike out the labor provisions had prevailed, and to inquire whether, in that event, the statute should be so construed as to justify the conclusion that Congress, notwithstanding, probably would not have passed the price-fixing provisions of the code.

Section 3 of the act, which provides that no producer shall, by accepting the code or the drawback of taxes, be estopped from contesting the constitutionality of any provision of the code, is thought to aid the separability clause. But the effect of that provision is simply to permit the producer to challenge any provision of the code despite his acceptance of the code or the drawback. It seems not to have anything to do with the question of separability.

With the foregoing principles in mind, let us examine the act itself. The title of the act and the preamble demonstrate, as we have already seen, that Congress desired to accomplish certain general purposes therein recited. To that end it created a commission, with mandatory directions to formulate into a working agreement the provisions set forth in § 4 of the act. That being done, the result is a code. Producers accepting and operating under the code are to be known as code members; and § 4 specifically requires that, in order to carry out the policy of the act, "the code shall contain the following conditions, provisions, and obligations . . ." which are then set forth. No power is vested in the commission, in formulating the code, to omit any of these conditions, provisions, or obligations. The mandate to include them embraces all of them. Following the requirement just quoted, and, significantly, *in the same section* (*International Textbook Co.* v. *Pigg,* 217 U.S. 91, 112–113) under appropriate headings, the price-fixing and labor-regulating provisions are set out in great detail. These provisions, plainly meant to operate together and not separately, constitute the means designated to bring about the stabilization of bituminous-coal production, and thereby to regulate or affect interstate commerce in such coal. The first clause of the title is: "To stabilize the bituminous coal-mining industry and promote its interstate commerce."

Thus, the primary contemplation of the act is stabilization of the industry through the regulation of labor *and* the regulation of prices; for, since both were adopted, we must conclude that both were thought essential. The regulations of labor on the one hand and prices on the other furnish mutual aid and support; and their associated force—not one or the other but both combined—

was deemed by Congress to be necessary to achieve the end sought. The statutory mandate for a code upheld by two legs at once suggests the improbability that Congress would have assented to a code supported by only one.

This seems plain enough; for Congress must have been conscious of the fact that elimination of the labor provisions from the act would seriously impair, if not destroy, the force and usefulness of the price provisions. The interdependence of wages and prices is manifest. Approximately two-thirds of the cost of producing a ton of coal is represented by wages. Fair prices necessarily depend upon the cost of production; and since wages constitute so large a proportion of the cost, prices cannot be fixed with any proper relation to cost without taking into consideration this major element. If one of them becomes uncertain, uncertainty with respect to the other necessarily ensues.

So much is recognized by the code itself. The introductory clause of Part III declares that the conditions respecting labor relations are "To effectuate the purposes of this Act." And subdivision (a) of Part II, quoted in the forepart of this opinion, reads in part: "In order to sustain the stabilization of wages, working conditions, and maximum hours of labor, said prices shall be established so as to yield a return per net ton for each district in a minimum price area, . . . equal as nearly as may be to the weighted average of the total costs, per net ton . . ." Thus wages, hours of labor, and working conditions are to be so adjusted as to effectuate the purposes of the act; and prices are to be so regulated as to *stabilize* wages, working conditions, and hours of labor which have been or are to be fixed under the labor provisions. The two are so woven together as to render the probability plain enough that uniform prices, in the opinion of Congress, could not be fairly fixed or effectively regulated, without also regulating these elements of labor which enter so largely into the cost of production.

These two sets of requirements are not like a collection of bricks, some of which may be taken away without disturbing the others, but rather are like the interwoven threads constituting the warp and woof of a fabric, one set of which cannot be removed without fatal consequences to the whole. Paraphrasing the words of this court in *Butts* v. *Merchants Transportation Co.,* 230 U.S. 126, 133, we inquire—What authority has this court, by construction, to convert the manifest purpose of Congress to regulate production by the mutual operation and interaction of fixed wages and fixed prices into a purpose to regulate the subject by the operation of the latter alone? Are we at liberty to say from the fact that Congress has adopted an entire integrated system that it probably would have enacted a doubtfully effective fraction of the system? The words of the concurring opinion in the *Schechter* case, 295 U.S. at pages 554–555, are pertinent in reply. "To take from this code the provisions as to wages and the hours of labor is to destroy it altogether. . . . Wages and the hours of labor are essential features of the plan, its very bone and sinew. There is no opportunity in such circumstances for the severance of the infected parts in the hope of saving the remainder." The conclusion is unavoidable that the price-fixing provisions of the code are so related to and dependent upon the labor provisions as conditions, considerations or compensations, as to make it clearly probable that the latter being held bad, the former would not have been passed. The fall of the latter, therefore, carries down with it the former. *International Textbook Co.* v. *Pigg, supra,* p. 113; *Warren* v. *Charlestown,* 2 Gray [Mass.] 84, 98–99.

The price-fixing provisions of the code are thus disposed of without coming to the question of their constitutionality; but neither this disposition of the matter, nor anything we have said, is to be taken as indicating that the court is of opinion that these provisions, if separately enacted, could be sustained.

If there be in the act provisions, other than those we have considered, that may stand independently, the question of their validity is left for future determination when, if ever, that question shall be presented for consideration.

The decrees in Nos. 636, 649, and 650 must be reversed and the causes remanded for further consideration in conformity with this opinion. The decree in No. 651 will be affirmed.

POWELL v. ALABAMA, 287 U.S. 45 (1932)

Sutherland's opinion in the Powell case has earned him a justifiable place in the front ranks of civil libertarian judges. His decision incorporating the right to counsel as part of the due process clause of the Fourteenth Amendment will be remembered long after his antagonism to the New Deal is of interest only to historians. The Court overturned the convictions of the "Scottsboro boys," eight Negroes sentenced to death for rape, on the ground they had been denied their right to counsel since they had not been given reasonable time to secure a lawyer to defend them.

MR. JUSTICE SUTHERLAND delivered the opinion of the Court.

These cases were argued together and submitted for decision as one case.

The petitioners, hereinafter referred to as defendants, are negroes charged with the crime of rape, committed upon the persons of two white girls. The crime is said to have been committed on March 25, 1931. The indictment was returned in a state court of first instance on March 31, and the record recites that on the same day the defendants were arraigned and entered pleas of not guilty. There is a further recital to the effect that upon the arraignment they were represented by counsel. But no counsel had been employed, and aside from a statement made by the trial judge several days later during a colloquy immediately preceding the trial, the record does not disclose when, or under what circumstances, an appointment of counsel was made, or who was appointed. During the colloquy referred to, the trial judge, in response to a question, said that he had appointed all the members of the bar for the purpose of arraigning the defendants and then of course anticipated that the members of the bar would continue to help the defendants if no counsel appeared. Upon the argument here both sides accepted that as a correct statement of the facts concerning the matter.

There was a severance upon the request of the state, and the defendants were tried in three several groups, as indicated above. As each of the three cases was called for trial, each defendant was arraigned, and, having the indictment read to him, entered a plea of not guilty. Whether the original arraignment and pleas were regarded as ineffective is not shown. Each of the three trials was completed within a single day. Under the Alabama statute the punishment for rape is to be fixed by the jury, and in its discretion may be from ten years imprisonment to death. The juries found defendants guilty and imposed the death penalty upon all. The trial court overruled motions for new trials and sentenced the defendants in accordance with the verdicts. The judgments were affirmed by the state supreme court. Chief Justice Anderson thought the defendants had not been accorded a fair trial and strongly dissented. 224 Ala. 524; *id.* 531; *id.* 540; 141 So. 215, 195, 201.

In this court the judgments are assailed upon the grounds that the defendants, and each of them, were denied due process of law and the equal protection of the laws, in contravention of the Fourteenth Amendment, specifically as follows: (1) they were not given a fair, impartial and deliberate trial; (2) they were denied the right of counsel, with the accustomed incidents of consultation and opportunity of preparation for trial; and (3) they were tried before juries from which qualified members of their own race were systematically excluded. These questions were properly raised and saved in the courts below.

The only one of the assignments which we shall consider is the second, in respect of the denial of counsel; and it becomes unnecessary to discuss the facts of the case or the circumstances surrounding the prosecution except in so far as they reflect light upon that question.

The record shows that on the day when the offense is said to have been committed, these defendants, together with a number of other negroes, were upon a freight train on its way through Alabama. On the same train were seven white boys and the two white girls. A fight took place between the negroes and the white boys, in the course of which the white boys, with the exception of one named Gilley, were thrown off the train. A message was sent ahead, reporting the fight and asking that every negro be gotten off the train. The participants in the fight, and the two girls, were in an open gondola car. The two girls testified that each of them was assaulted by six different negroes in turn, and they identified the seven defendants as having been among the number. None of the white boys was called to testify, with the exception of Gilley, who was called in rebuttal.

Before the train reached Scottsboro, Alabama, a sheriff's posse seized the defendants and two other negroes. Both girls and the negroes then were taken to Scottsboro, the county seat. Word of their coming and of the alleged assault had preceded them, and they were met at Scottsboro by a large crowd. It does not sufficiently appear that the defendants were seriously threatened with, or that they were actually in danger of, mob violence; but it does appear that the attitude of the community was one of great hostility. The sheriff thought it necessary to call for the militia to assist in safeguarding the prisoners. Chief Justice Anderson pointed out in his opinion that every step taken from the arrest and arraignment to the sentence was accompanied by the military. Soldiers took the defendants to Gadsden for safekeeping, brought them back to Scottsboro for arraignment, returned them to Gadsden for safekeeping while awaiting trial, escorted them to Scottsboro for trial a few days later, and guarded the court house and grounds at every stage of the proceedings. It is perfectly apparent that the proceedings, from beginning to end, took place in an atmosphere of tense, hostile and excited public sentiment. During the entire time, the defendants were closely confined or were under military guard. The record does not disclose their ages, except that one of them was nineteen; but the record clearly indicates that most, if not all, of them were youthful, and they are constantly referred to as "the boys." They were ignorant and illiterate. All of them were residents of other states, where alone members of their families or friends resided.

However guilty defendants, upon due inquiry, might prove to have been, they were, until convicted, presumed to be innocent. It was the duty of the court having their cases in charge to see that they were denied no necessary incident of a fair trial. With any error of the state court involving alleged contravention of the state statutes or constitution we, of course, have nothing to do. The sole inquiry which we are permitted to make is whether the federal Constitution was contravened (*Rogers* v. *Peck,* 199 U.S. 425, 434; *Hebert* v. *Louisiana,* 272 U.S. 312, 316); and as to that, we confine ourselves, as already suggested, to the inquiry whether the defendants were in substance denied the right of counsel, and if so, whether such denial infringes the due process clause of the Fourteenth Amendment.

First. The record shows that immediately upon the return of the indictment defendants were arraigned and pleaded not guilty. Apparently they were not asked whether they had, or were able to employ, counsel, or wished to have counsel appointed; or whether they had friends or relatives who might assist in that regard if communicated with. That it would not have been an idle ceremony to have given the defendants reasonable opportunity to communicate with their families and endeavor to obtain counsel is demonstrated by the fact that, very soon after conviction, able counsel appeared in their behalf. This was pointed out by Chief Justice Anderson in the course of his dissenting opinion. "They were nonresidents," he said, "and had little time or opportunity to get in touch with their families and friends who were scattered throughout two other states, and time has demonstrated that they could or would have been represented by able counsel had a better opportunity been given by a reasonable delay in the trial of the cases, judging from the number and activity of counsel that appeared immediately or shortly after their conviction." 224 Ala., at pp. 554–555; 141 So. 201.

It is hardly necessary to say that, the right to counsel being conceded, a defendant should be afforded a fair opportunity to secure counsel of his own choice. Not only was that not done here, but such designation of counsel as was attempted was either so indefinite or so close upon the trial as to amount to a denial of effective and substantial aid in that regard. This will be amply demonstrated by a brief review of the record.

April 6, six days after indictment, the trials began. When the first case was called, the court inquired whether the parties were ready for trial. The state's attorney replied that he was ready to proceed. No one answered for the defendants or appeared to represent or defend them. Mr. Roddy, a Tennessee lawyer not a member of the local bar, addressed the court, saying that he had not been employed, but that people who were interested had spoken to him about the case. He was asked by the court whether he intended to appear for the defendants, and answered that he would like to appear along with counsel that the court might appoint. The record then proceeds:

"The Court: If you appear for these defendants, then I will not appoint counsel; if local counsel are willing to appear and assist you under the circumstances all right, but I will not appoint them.

"Mr. Roddy: Your Honor has appointed counsel, is that correct?

"The Court: I appointed all the members of the bar for the purpose of arraigning the defendants and then of course I anticipated them to continue to help them if no counsel appears.

"Mr. Roddy: Then I don't appear then as counsel but I do want to stay in and not be ruled out in this case.

"The Court: Of course I would not do that—

"Mr. Roddy: I just appear here through the courtesy of Your Honor.

"The Court: Of course I give you that right; . . ."

And then, apparently addressing all the lawyers present, the court inquired:

". . . well are you all willing to assist?

"Mr. Moody: Your Honor appointed us all and we have been proceeding along every line we know about it under Your Honor's appointment.

"The Court: The only thing I am trying to do is, if counsel appears for these defendants I don't want to impose on you all, but if you feel like counsel from Chattanooga—

"Mr. Moody: I see his situation of course and I have not run out of anything yet. Of course, if Your Honor purposes to appoint us, Mr. Parks, I am willing to go on with it. Most of the bar have been down and conferred with these defendants in this case; they did not know what else to do.

"The Court: The thing, I did not want to impose on the members of the bar if counsel unqualifiedly appears; if you all feel like Mr. Roddy is only interested in a limited way to assist, then I don't care to appoint—

"Mr. Parks: Your Honor, I don't feel like you ought to impose on any member of the local bar if the defendants are represented by counsel.

"The Court: That is what I was trying to ascertain, Mr. Parks.

"Mr. Parks: Of course if they have counsel, I don't see the necessity of the Court appointing anybody; if they haven't counsel, of course I think it is up to the Court to appoint counsel to represent them.

"The Court: I think you are right about it Mr. Parks and that is the reason I was trying to get an expression from Mr. Roddy.

"Mr. Roddy: I think Mr. Parks is entirely right about it, if I was paid down here and employed, it would be a different thing, but I have not prepared this case for trial and have only been called into it by people who are interested in these boys from Chattanooga. Now, they have not given me an opportunity to prepare the case and I am not familiar with the procedure in Alabama, but I merely came down here as a friend of the people who are interested and not as paid counsel, and certainly I haven't any money to pay them and nobody I am interested in had me to come down here has put up any fund of money to come down here and pay counsel. If they should do it I would be glad to turn it over—a counsel but I am merely here at the solicitation of people who have become interested in this case without any payment of fee and without any preparation for trial and I think the boys would be better off if I step entirely out of the case according to my way of looking at it and according to my lack of preparation of it and not being familiar with the procedure in Alabama, . . ."

Mr. Roddy later observed:

"If there is anything I can do to be of help to them, I will be glad to do it; I am interested to that extent.

"The Court: Well gentlemen, if Mr. Roddy only appears as assistant that way, I think it is proper that I appoint members of this bar to represent them, I expect that is right. If Mr. Roddy will appear, I wouldn't of course, I would not appoint anybody. I don't see, Mr. Roddy, how I can make a qualified appointment or a limited appointment. Of course, I don't mean to cut off your assistance in any way—Well gentlemen, I think you understand it.

"Mr. Moody: I am willing to go ahead and help Mr. Roddy in anything I can do about it, under the circumstances.

"The Court: All right, all the lawyers that will; of course I would not require a lawyer to appear if—

"Mr. Moody: I am willing to do that for him as a member of the bar; I will go ahead and help do anything I can do.

"The Court: All right."

And in this casual fashion the matter of counsel in a capital case was disposed of.

It thus will be seen that until the very morning of the trial no lawyer had been named or definitely designated to represent the defendants. Prior to that time, the trial judge had "appointed all the members of the bar" for the limited "purpose of arraigning the defendants." Whether they would represent the defendants thereafter if no counsel appeared in their behalf, was a matter of speculation only, or, as the judge indicated, of mere anticipation on the part of the court. Such a designation, even if made for all purposes, would, in our opinion, have fallen far short of meeting, in any proper sense, a requirement for the appointment of counsel. How many lawyers were members of the bar does not appear; but, in the very nature of things, whether many or few, they would not, thus collectively named, have been given that clear appreciation of responsibility or impressed with that individual sense of duty which should and naturally would accompany the appointment of a selected member of the bar, specifically named and assigned.

That this action of the trial judge in respect of appointment of counsel was little more than an expansive gesture, imposing no substantial or definite obligation upon any one, is borne out by the fact that prior to the calling of the case for trial on April 6, a leading member of the local bar accepted employment on the side of the prosecution and actively participated in the trial. It is true that he said that before doing so he had understood Mr. Roddy would be employed as counsel for the defendants. This the lawyer in question, of his own accord, frankly stated to the court; and no doubt he acted with the utmost good faith. Probably other members of the bar had a like understanding. In any event, the circumstance lends emphasis to the conclusion that during perhaps the most critical period of the proceedings against these defendants, that is to say, from the time of their arraignment until the beginning of their trial, when consultation, thoroughgoing investigation and preparation were vitally important, the defendants did not have the aid of counsel in any real sense, although they were as much entitled to such aid during that period as at the trial itself. *People ex rel. Burgess* v. *Risley,* 66 How. Pr. (N.Y.) 67; *Batchelor* v. *State,* 189 Ind. 69, 76; 125 N. E. 773.

Nor do we think the situation was helped by what occurred on the morning of the trial. At that time, as appears from the colloquy printed above, Mr. Roddy stated to the court that he did not appear as counsel, but that he would like to appear along with counsel that the court might appoint; that he had not been given an opportunity to prepare the case; that he was not familiar with the procedure in Alabama, but merely came down as a friend of the people who were interested; that he thought the boys would be better off if he should step entirely out of the case. Mr. Moody, a member of the local bar, expressed a willingness to help Mr. Roddy in anything he could do under the circumstances. To this the court responded, "All right, all the lawyers that will; of course I would not require a lawyer to appear if—." And Mr. Moody continued, "I am willing to do that for him as a member of the bar; I will go ahead and help do any thing I can do." With this dubious understanding, the trials immediately proceeded. The defendants, young, ignorant, illiterate, surrounded by hostile sentiment, haled back and forth under guard of soldiers, charged with an atrocious crime regarded with especial horror in the community where they were to be tried, were thus put in peril of their lives within a few moments after counsel for the first time charged with any degree of responsibility began to represent them.

It is not enough to assume that counsel thus precipitated into the case though there was no defense, and exercised their best judgment in proceeding to trial without preparation. Neither they nor the court could say what a prompt and thoroughgoing investigation might disclose as to the facts. No attempt was made to investigate. No opportunity to do so was given. Defendants were immediately hurried to trial. Chief Justice Anderson, after disclaiming any intention to criticize harshly counsel who attempted to represent defendants at the trials, said: ". . . the record indicates that the appearance was rather *pro forma* than zealous and active . . ." Under the circumstances disclosed, we hold that defendants were not accorded the right of counsel in any substantial sense. To decide otherwise, would simply be to ignore actualities. This conclusion finds ample support in the reasoning of an overwhelming array of state decisions, among which we cite the following: *Shep-*

pard v. *State,* 165 Ga. 460, 464; 141 S. E. 196; *Reliford* v. *State,* 140 Ga. 777; 79 S. E. 1128; *McArver* v. *State,* 114 Ga. 514; 40 S. E. 779; *Sanchez* v. *State,* 199 Ind. 235, 246; 157 N. E. 1; *Batchelor* v. *State,* 189 Ind. 69, 76; 125 N. E. 773; *Mitchell* v. *Commonwealth,* 225 Ky. 83; 7 S. W. (2d) 823; *Jackson* v. *Commonwealth,* 215 Ky. 800; 287 S. W. 17; *State* v. *Collins,* 104 La. 629; 29 So. 180; *State* v. *Pool,* 50 La. Ann. 449; 23 So. 503; *People ex rel. Burgess* v. *Risley,* 66 How. Pr. (N.Y.) 67; *State ex rel. Tucker* v. *Davis,* 9 Okla. Cr. 94; 130 Pac. 962; *Commonwealth* v. *O'Keefe,* 298 Pa. 169; 148 Atl. 73; *Shaffer* v. *Territory,* 14 Ariz. 329, 333; 127 Pac. 746.

It is true that great and inexcusable delay in the enforcement of our criminal law is one of the grave evils of our time. Continuances are frequently granted for unnecessarily long periods of time, and delays incident to the disposition of motions for new trial and hearings upon appeal have come in many cases to be a distinct reproach to the administration of justice. The prompt disposition of criminal cases is to be commended and encouraged. But in reaching that result a defendant, charged with a serious crime, must not be stripped of his right to have sufficient time to advise with counsel and prepare his defense. To do that is not to proceed promptly in the calm spirit of regulated justice but to go forward with the haste of the mob.

As the court said in *Commonwealth* v. *O'Keefe,* 298 Pa. 169, 173; 148 Atl. 73:

"It is vain to give the accused a day in court, with no opportunity to prepare for it, or to guarantee him counsel without giving the latter any opportunity to acquaint himself with the facts or law of the case.

* * *

"A prompt and vigorous administration of the criminal law is commendable and we have no desire to clog the wheels of justice. What we here decide is that to force a defendant, charged with a serious misdemeanor, to trial within five hours of his arrest, is not due process of law, regardless of the merits of the case."

Compare *Reliford* v. *State,* 140 Ga. 777, 778; 79 S. E. 1128.

Second. The Constitution of Alabama provides that in all criminal prosecutions the accused shall enjoy the right to have the assistance of counsel; and a state statute requires the court in a capital case, where the defendant is unable to employ counsel, to appoint counsel for him. The state supreme court held that these provisions had not been infringed, and with that holding we are powerless to interfere. The question, however, which it is our duty, and within our power, to decide, is whether the denial of the assistance of counsel contravenes the due process clause of the Fourteenth Amendment to the federal Constitution.

If recognition of the right of a defendant charged with a felony to have the aid of counsel depended upon the existence of a similar right at common law as it existed in England when our Constitution was adopted, there would be great difficulty in maintaining it as necessary to due process. Originally, in England, a person charged with treason or felony was denied the aid of counsel, except in respect of legal questions which the accused himself might suggest. At the same time parties in civil cases and persons accused of misdemeanors were entitled to the full assistance of counsel. After the revolution of 1688, the rule was abolished as to treason, but was otherwise steadily adhered to until 1836, when by act of Parliament the full right was granted in respect of felonies generally. 1 Cooley's Const. Lim., 8th ed., 698, *et seq.,* and notes.

An affirmation of the right to the aid of counsel in petty offenses, and its denial in the case of crimes of the gravest character, where such aid is most needed, is so outrageous and so obviously a perversion of all sense of proportion that the rule was constantly, vigorously and sometimes passionately assailed by English statesmen and lawyers. As early as 1758, Blackstone, although recognizing that the rule was settled at common law, denounced it as not in keeping with the rest of the humane treatment of prisoners by the English law. "For upon what face of reason," he says, "can that assistance be denied to save the life of a man, which yet is allowed him in prosecutions for every petty trespass?" 4 Blackstone 355. One of the grounds upon which Lord Coke defended the rule was that in felonies the court itself was counsel for the prisoner. 1 Cooley's Const. Lim., *supra.* But how can a judge, whose functions are purely judicial, effectively discharge the obligations of counsel for the accused? He can and should see to it that in the proceedings before the court the accused shall be dealt with justly and fairly. He cannot investigate the facts, advise and direct the defense, or participate in those necessary conferences between counsel and accused which sometimes partake of the inviolable character of the confessional.

The rule was rejected by the colonies. Before the adoption of the federal Constitution, the Constitution of Maryland had declared "That, in all criminal prosecutions, every man hath a right . . . to be allowed counsel; . . ." (Art. XIX, Constitution of 1776). The Constitution of Massachusetts, adopted in 1780 (Part the First, Art. XII), the Constitution of New Hampshire, adopted in 1784 (Part I, Art. XV), the Constitution of New York of 1777 (Art. XXXIV), and the Constitution of Pennsylvania of 1776 (Art. IX), had also declared to the same effect. And in the case of Pennsylvania, as early as 1701, the Penn Charter (Art. V) declared that "all Criminals shall have the same Privileges of Witnesses and Council as their Prosecutors"; and there was also a provision in the Pennsylvania statute of May 31, 1718 (Dallas, Laws of Pennsylvania, 1700–1781, Vol. 1, p. 134), that in capital cases learned counsel should be assigned to the prisoners.

In Delaware, the Constitution of 1776 (Art. 25), adopted the common law of England, but expressly excepted such parts as were repugnant to the rights and privileges contained in the Declaration of Rights; and the Declaration of Rights, which was adopted on September 11, 1776, provided (Art. 14), "That in all Prosecutions for criminal Offences, every Man hath a Right . . . to be allowed Counsel, . . ." In addition, Penn's Charter, already referred to, was applicable in Delaware. The original Constitution of New Jersey of 1776 (Art. XVI) contained a provision like that of the Penn Charter, to the effect that all criminals should be admitted to the same privileges of counsel as their prosecutors. The original Constitution of North Carolina (1776) did not contain the guarantee, but c. 115, § 85, Sess. Laws, N. Car., 1777 (N. Car. Rev. Laws, 1715–1796, Vol. 1, 316), provided ". . . That every person accused of any crime or misdemeanor whatsoever, shall be entitled to council in all matters which may be necessary for his defence, as well to facts as to law; . . ." Similarly, in South Carolina the original Constitution of 1776 did not contain the provision as to counsel, but it was provided as early as 1731 (Act of August 20, 1731, § XLIII, Grimke, S. Car. Pub. Laws, 1682–1790, p. 130) that every person charged with treason, murder, felony, or other capital offense, should be admitted to make full defense by counsel learned in the law. In Virginia there was no constitutional provision on the subject, but as early as August, 1734 (c. VII, § III, Laws of Va., 8th Geo. II, Hening's Stat. at Large, Vol. 4, p. 404), there was an act declaring that in all trials for capital offenses the prisoner, upon his petition to the court, should be allowed counsel.

The original Constitution of Connecticut (Art. I, § 9) contained a provision that "In all criminal prosecutions, the accused shall have the right to be heard by himself and by counsel"; but this constitution was not adopted until 1818. However, it appears that the English common law rule had been rejected in practice long prior to 1796. See Zephaniah Swift's "A System of the Laws of the State of Connecticut," printed at Windham by John Byrne, 1795–1796, Vol. II, Bk. 5, "Of Crimes and Punishments," c. XXIV, "Of Trials," pp. 398–399.*

* *This ancient work, consisting of six books, has long been out of print. A copy of it is preserved in the locked files of the Library of Congress. The following extract from the pages cited is both interesting and instructive:*

"The attorney for the state then proceeds to lay before the jury, all the evidence against the prisoner, without any remarks or arguments. The prisoner by himself or counsel, is then allowed to produce witnesses to counteract and obviate the testimony against him; and to exculpate himself with the same freedom as in civil cases. We have never admitted that cruel and illiberal principle of the common law of England that when a man is on trial for his life, he shall be refused counsel, and denied those means of defence, which are allowed, when the most trifling pittance of property is in question. The flimsy pretence, that the court are to be counsel for the prisoner will only heighten our indignation at the practice: for it is apparent to the least consideration, that a court can never furnish a person accused of a crime with the advice, and assistance necessary to make his defence. This doctrine might with propriety have been advanced, at the time when by the common law of England, no witnesses could be adduced on the part of the prisoner, to manifest his innocence, for he could then make no preparation for his defense. One cannot read without horror and astonishment, the abominable maxims of law, which deprived persons accused, and on trial for crimes, of the assistance of counsel, except as to points of law, and the advantage of

The original Constitution of Georgia (1777) did not contain a guarantee in respect of counsel, but the Constitution of 1798 (Art. III, § 8) provided that ". . . no person shall be debarred from advocating or defending his cause before any court or tribunal, either by himself or counsel, or both." What the practice was prior to 1798 we are unable to discover. The first constitution adopted by Rhode Island was in 1842, and this constitution contained the usual guarantee in respect of the assistance of counsel in criminal prosecutions. As early as 1798 it was provided by statute, in the very language of the Sixth Amendment to the Federal Constitution, that "In all criminal prosecutions, the accused shall enjoy the right . . . to have the assistance of counsel for his defence; . . ." An Act Declaratory of certain Rights of the People of this State, § 6, Rev. Pub. Laws, Rhode Island and Providence Plantations, 1798. Furthermore, while the statute itself is not available, it is recorded as a matter of history that in 1668 or 1669 the colonial assembly enacted that any person who was indicted might employ an attorney to plead in his behalf. 1 Arnold, History of Rhode Island, 336.

It thus appears that in at least twelve of the thirteen colonies the rule of the English common law, in the respect now under consideration, had been definitely rejected and the right to counsel fully recognized in all criminal prosecutions, save that in one or two instances the right was limited to capital offenses or to the more serious crimes; and this court seems to have been of the opinion that this was true in all the colonies. In *Holden* v. *Hardy,* 169 U.S. 366 ,386, Mr. Justice Brown, writing for the court, said:

"The earlier practice of the common law, which denied the benefit of witnesses to a person accused of felony, had been abolished by statute, though so far as it deprived him of the assistance of counsel and compulsory process for the attendance of his witnesses, it had not been changed in England. But to the credit of her American colonies, let it be said that so oppressive a doctrine had never obtained a foothold there."

One test which has been applied to determine whether due process of law has been accorded in given instances is to ascertain what were the settled usages and modes of proceeding under the common and statute law of England before the Declaration of Independence, subject, however, to the qualification that they be shown not to have been unsuited to the civil and political conditions of our ancestors by having been followed in this country after it became a nation. *Lowe* v. *Kansas,* 163 U.S. 81, 85. Compare *Murray's Lessee* v. *Hoboken Land & Improvement Co.,* 18 How. 272, 276–277; *Twining* v. *New Jersey,* 211 U.S. 78, 100–101. Plainly, as appears from the foregoing, this test, as thus qualified, has not been met in the present case.

We do not overlook the case of *Hurtado* v. *California,* 110 U.S. 516, where this court determined that due process of law does not require an indictment by a grand jury as a prerequisite to prosecution by a state for murder. In support of that conclusion the court (pp. 534–535) referred to

---

witnesses to exculpate themselves from the charge. It seems by the ancient practice, that whenever a person was accused of a crime, every expedient was adopted to convict him and every privilege denied him, to prove his innocence. In England, however, as the law now stands, prisoners are allowed the full advantage of witnesses, but excepting in a few cases, the common law is enforced, in denying them counsel, except as to points of law.

"Our ancestors, when they first enacted their laws respecting crimes, influenced by the illiberal principles which they had imbibed in their native country, denied counsel to prisoners to plead for them to anything but points of law. It is manifest that there is as much necessity for counsel to investigate matters of fact, as points of law, if truth is to be discovered.

"The legislature has become so thoroughly convinced of the impropriety and injustice of shackling and restricting a prisoner with respect to his defence, that they have abolished all those odious laws, and every person when he is accused of a crime, is entitled to every possible privilege in making his defence, and manifesting his innocence, by the instrumentality of counsel, and the testimony of witnesses."

The early statutes of Connecticut, upon examination, do not seem to be as clear as this last paragraph would indicate; but Mr. Swift, writing in 1796, was in a better position to know how the statutes had been interpreted and applied in actual practice than the reader of today; and we see no reason to reject his statement.

the fact that the Fifth Amendment, in addition to containing the due process of law clause, provides in explicit terms that "No person shall be held to answer for a capital, or otherwise infamous crime, unless on a presentment or indictment of a grand jury . . . ," and said that since no part of this important amendment could be regarded as superfluous, the obvious inference is that in the sense of the Constitution due process of law was not intended to include, *ex vi termini,* the institution and procedure of a grand jury in any case; and that the same phrase, employed in the Fourteenth Amendment to restrain the action of the states, was to be interpreted as having been used in the same sense and with no greater extent; and that if it had been the purpose of that Amendment to perpetuate the institution of the grand jury in the states, it would have embodied, as did the Fifth Amendment, an express declaration to that effect.

The Sixth Amendment, in terms, provides that in all criminal prosecutions the accused shall enjoy the right "to have the assistance of counsel for his defense." In the face of the reasoning of the *Hurtado* case, if it stood alone, it would be difficult to justify the conclusion that the right to counsel, being thus specifically granted by the Sixth Amendment, was also within the intendment of the due process of law clause. But the *Hurtado* case does not stand alone. In the later case of *Chicago, Burlington & Quincy R. Co.* v. *Chicago,* 166 U.S. 226, 241, this court held that a judgment of a state court, even though authorized by statute, by which private property was taken for public use without just compensation, was in violation of the due process of law required by the Fourteenth Amendment, notwithstanding that the Fifth Amendment explicitly declares that private property shall not be taken for public use without just compensation. This holding was followed in *Norwood* v. *Baker,* 172 U.S. 269, 277; *Smyth* v. *Ames,* 169 U.S. 466, 524; and *San Diego Land Co.* v. *National City,* 174 U.S. 739, 754.

Likewise, this court has considered that freedom of speech and of the press are rights protected by the due process clause of the Fourteenth Amendment, although in the First Amendment, Congress is prohibited in specific terms from abridging the right. *Gitlow* v. *New York,* 268 U.S. 652, 666; *Stromberg* v. *California,* 283 U.S. 359, 368; *Near* v. *Minnesota,* 283 U.S. 697, 707.

These later cases establish that notwithstanding the sweeping character of the language in the *Hurtado* case, the rule laid down is not without exceptions. The rule is an aid to construction, and in some instances may be conclusive; but it must yield to more compelling considerations whenever such considerations exist. The fact that the right involved is of such a character that it cannot be denied without violating those "fundamental principles of liberty and justice which lie at the base of all our civil and political institutions" (*Hebert* v. *Louisiana,* 272 U.S. 312, 316), is obviously one of those compelling considerations which must prevail in determining whether it is embraced within the due process clause of the Fourteenth Amendment, although it be specifically dealt with in another part of the federal Constitution. Evidently this court, in the later cases enumerated, regarded the rights there under consideration as of this fundamental character. That some such distinction must be observed is foreshadowed in *Twining* v. *New Jersey,* 211 U.S. 78, 99, where Mr. Justice Moody, speaking for the court, said that ". . . it is possible that some of the personal rights safeguarded by the first eight Amendments against National action may also be safeguarded against state action, because a denial of them would be a denial of due process of law. *Chicago, Burlington & Quincy R. Co.* v. *Chicago,* 166 U.S. 226. If this is so, it is not because those rights are enumerated in the first eight Amendments, but because they are of such a nature that they are included in the conception of due process of law." While the question has never been categorically determined by this court, a consideration of the nature of the right and a review of the expressions of this and other courts, makes it clear that the right to the aid of counsel is of this fundamental character.

It never has been doubted by this court, or any other so far as we know, that notice and hearing are preliminary steps essential to the passing of an enforceable judgment, and that they, together with a legally competent tribunal having jurisdiction of the case, constitute basic elements of the constitutional requirement of due process of law. The words of Webster, so often quoted, that by "the law of the land" is intended "a law which hears before it condemns," have been repeated in varying forms of expression in a multitude of decisions. In *Holden* v. *Hardy,* 169 U.S. 366, 389, the necessity of due notice and an opportunity of being heard is described as among the "immutable principles of justice which inhere in the very idea of free government which no member of the Union may disregard." And Mr. Justice Field, in an earlier case, *Galpin* v. *Page,* 18 Wall. 350, 368–369, said that the rule that no one shall be personally bound until he has had his day in court was as old as the law, and it meant that he must be cited to appear and afforded an opportunity to be heard. "Judgment without such citation and opportunity wants all the attributes of a judicial determination; it is judicial usurpation and oppression, and can never be upheld where justice is justly administered." Citations to the same effect might be indefinitely multiplied, but there is no occasion for doing so.

What, then, does a hearing include? Historically and in practice, in our own country at least, it has always included the right to the aid of counsel when desired and provided by the party asserting the right. The right to be heard would be, in many cases, of little avail if it did not comprehend the right to be heard by counsel. Even the intelligent and educated layman has small and sometimes no skill in the science of law. If charged with crime, he is incapable, generally, of determining for himself whether the indictment is good or bad. He is unfamiliar with the rules of evidence. Left without the aid of counsel he may be put on trial without a proper charge, and convicted upon incompetent evidence, or evidence irrelevant to the issue or otherwise inadmissible. He lacks both the skill and knowledge adequately to prepare his defense, even though he have a perfect one. He requires the guiding hand of counsel at every step in the proceedings against him. Without it, though he be not guilty, he faces the danger of conviction because he does not know how to establish his innocence. If that be true of men of intelligence, how much more true is it of the ignorant and illiterate, or those of feeble intellect. If in any case, civil or criminal, a state or federal court were arbitrarily to refuse to hear a party by counsel, employed by and appearing for him, it reasonably may not be doubted that such a refusal would be a denial of a hearing, and, therefore, of due process in the constitutional sense.

The decisions all point to that conclusion. In *Cooke* v. *United States,* 267 U.S. 517, 537, it was held that where a contempt was not in open court, due process of law required charges and a reasonable opportunity to defend or explain. The court added, "We think this includes the assistance of counsel, if requested, . . ." In numerous other cases the court, in determining that due process was accorded, has frequently stressed the fact that the defendant had the aid of counsel. See, for example, *Felts* v. *Murphy,* 201 U.S. 123, 129; *Frank* v. *Mangum,* 237 U.S. 309, 344; *Kelley* v. *Oregon,* 273 U.S. 589, 591. In *Ex parte Hidekuni Iwata,* 219 Fed. 610, 611, the federal district judge enumerated among the elements necessary to due process of law in a deportation case the opportunity at some stage of the hearing to secure and have the advice and assistance of counsel. In *Ex parte Chin Loy You,* 223 Fed. 833, also a deportation case, the district judge held that under the particular circumstances of the case the prisoner, having seasonably made demand, was entitled to confer with and have the aid of counsel. Pointing to the fact that the right to counsel as secured by the Sixth Amendment relates only to criminal prosecutions, the judge said, ". . . but it is equally true that that provision was inserted in the Constitution because the assistance of counsel was recognized as essential to any fair trial of a case against a prisoner." In *Ex parte Riggins,* 134 Fed. 404, 418, a case involving the due process clause of the Fourteenth Amendment, the court said, by way of illustration, that if the state should deprive a person of the benefit of counsel, it would not be due process of law. Judge Cooley refers to the right of a person accused of crime to have counsel as perhaps his most important privilege, and after discussing the development of the English law upon that subject, says: "With us it is a universal principle of constitutional law, that the prisoner shall be allowed a defense by counsel." I Cooley's Const. Lim., 8th ed., 700. The same author, as appears from a chapter which he added to his edition of Story on the Constitution, regarded the right of the accused to the presence, advice and assistance of counsel as necessarily included in due process of law. 2 Story on the Constitution, 4th ed., § 1949, p. 668. The state decisions which refer to the matter invariably recognize the right to the aid of counsel as fundamental in character. E. g., *People* v. *Napthaly,* 105 Cal. 641, 644; 39 Pac. 29; *Cutts* v. *State,* 54 Fla. 21, 23; 45 So. 491; *Martin* v. *State,* 51 Ga. 567, 568; *Sheppard* v. *State,* 165 Ga. 460, 464; 141 S.E. 196;

State v. *Moore,* 61 Kan. 732, 734; 60 Pac. 748; *State* v. *Ferris,* 16 La. Ann. 424; *State* v. *Simpson,* 38 La. Ann. 23, 24; *State* v. *Briggs,* 58 W. Va. 291, 292; 52 S. E. 218.

In the light of the facts outlined in the forepart of this opinion—the ignorance and illiteracy of the defendants, their youth, the circumstances of public hostility, the imprisonment and the close surveillance of the defendants by the military forces, the fact that their friends and families were all in other states and communication with them necessarily difficult, and above all that they stood in deadly peril of their lives—we think the failure of the trial court to give them reasonable time and opportunity to secure counsel was a clear denial of due process.

But passing that, and assuming their inability, even if opportunity had been given, to employ counsel, as the trial court evidently did assume, we are of opinion that, under the circumstances just stated, the necessity of counsel was so vital and imperative that the failure of the trial court to make an effective appointment of counsel was likewise a denial of due process within the meaning of the Fourteenth Amendment. Whether this would be so in other criminal prosecutions, or under other circumstances, we need not determine. All that it is necessary now to decide, as we do decide, is that in a capital case, where the defendant is unable to employ counsel, and is incapable adequately of making his own defense because of ignorance, feeble mindedness, illiteracy, or the like, it is the duty of the court, whether requested or not, to assign counsel for him as a necessary requisite of due process of law; and that duty is not discharged by an assignment at such a time or under such circumstances as to preclude the giving of effective aid in the preparation and trial of the case. To hold otherwise would be to ignore the fundamental postulate, already adverted to, "that there are certain immutable principles of justice which inhere in the very idea of free government which no member of the Union may disregard." *Holden* v. *Hardy, supra.* In a case such as this, whatever may be the rule in other cases, the right to have counsel appointed, when necessary, is a logical corollary from the constitutional right to be heard by counsel. Compare *Carpenter & Sprague* v. *Dane County,* 9 Wis. 274; *Dane County* v. *Smith,* 13 Wis. 585, 586. *Hendryx* v. *State,* 130 Ind. 265, 268–269; 29 N. E. 1131; *Cutts* v. *State,* 54 Fla. 21, 23; 45 So. 491; *People* v. *Goldenson,* 76 Cal. 328, 344; 19 Pac. 161; *Delk* v. *State,* 99 Ga. 667, 669–670; 26 S. E. 752.

In *Hendryx* v. *State, supra,* there was no statute authorizing the assignment of an attorney to defend an indigent person accused of crime, but the court held that such an assignment was necessary to accomplish the ends of public justice, and that the court possessed the inherent power to make it. "Where a prisoner," the court said (p. 269), "without legal knowledge, is confined in jail, absent from his friends, without the aid of legal advice or the means of investigating the charge against him, it is impossible to conceive of a fair trial where he is compelled to conduct his cause in court, without the aid of counsel. . . . Such a trial is not far removed from an *ex parte* proceeding."

Let us suppose the extreme case of a prisoner charged with a capital offense, who is deaf and dumb, illiterate and feeble minded, unable to employ counsel, with the whole power of the state arrayed against him, prosecuted by counsel for the state without assignment of counsel for his defense, tried, convicted and sentenced to death. Such a result, which if carried into execution, would be little short of judicial murder, it cannot be doubted would be a gross violation of the guarantee of due process of law; and we venture to think that no appellate court, state or federal, would hesitate so to decide. See *Stephenson* v. *State,* 4 Ohio App. 128; *Williams* v. *State,* 163 Ark. 623, 628; 260 S. W. 721; *Grogan* v. *Commonwealth,* 222 Ky. 484, 485; 1 S. W. (2d) 779; *Mullen* v. *State,* 28 Okla. Cr. 218, 230; 230 Pac. 285; *Williams* v. *Commonwealth,* (Ky.), 110 S. W. 339, 340. The duty of the trial court to appoint counsel under such circumstances is clear, as it is clear under circumstances such as are disclosed by the record here; and its power to do so, even in the absence of a statute, can not be questioned. Attorneys are officers of the court, and are bound to render service when required by such an appointment. See Cooley, Const. Lim., *supra,* 700 and note.

The United States by statute and every state in the Union by express provision of law, or by the determination of its courts, make it the duty of the trial judge, where the accused is unable to employ counsel, to appoint counsel for him. In most states the rule applies broadly to all criminal prosecutions, in others it is limited to the more serious crimes, and in a very limited number, to capital cases. A rule adopted with such unanimous accord reflects, if it does not establish, the inherent right to have counsel appointed, at least in cases like the present, and lends convincing support to the conclusion we have reached as to the fundamental nature of that right.

The judgments must be reversed and the causes remanded for further proceedings not inconsistent with this opinion.

Pierce Butler

☆ 1866–1939 ☆

APPOINTED BY

WARREN G. HARDING

YEARS ON COURT

1922–1939

Pierce Butler

by

DAVID BURNER

BORN ON SAINT PATRICK'S DAY, March 17, 1866, Pierce Butler was the son of Patrick and Mary Gaffney Butler, who had come to Minnesota from County Wicklow, Ireland, after the potato famine of the 1840's. The Butlers had settled on a farm in Pine Bend, where they raised eight children, of whom Pierce was the sixth. Pierce's father, though a graduate of a great Protestant institution in Trinity College, Dublin, was a stern Irish Catholic. His son rode each day on horseback to a small country school a few miles from Northfield. At the age of fifteen Pierce himself was teaching school; already more than six feet tall and an accomplished wrestler, Butler once physically disciplined a young student, threw a pail of water on the bloody nose of his chastened rebel, and proceeded with class.

In 1883, after some study in a preparatory school associated with Carleton College in Northfield, Butler enrolled at Carleton and worked in a neighboring dairy to pay his expenses. At college he took courses from Professor John Bates Clark, who had written articles promoting an orthodox view of marginal utility economics. Butler read such *laissez faire* texts as Cooley's *Constitutional Limitations* and Amasa Walker's *Briefer Political Economy,* imbibing a philosophy that must have seemed consistent with his experience of life on the frontier. In 1887 he received both a Bachelor of Science and a Bachelor of Arts degree from Carleton. The graduation speech of this staunch Roman Catholic was on the greatness of his church and its good influence in the world. Undiscouraged by a failing grade in constitutional law, Butler moved to St. Paul, read law for a year in the firm of Pinch and Twohy, and was admitted to the Minnesota bar in 1888, at the age of twenty-two. He practiced law briefly with Stan Donnelly, son of the

DAVID BURNER is Associate Professor of History at the State University of New York, Stony Brook. He is the author of The Politics of Provincialism: The Democratic Party in Transition, 1918–1932.

Populist Ignatius Donnelly. In 1891 he married Annie Cronin of St. Paul, and, like Butler's parents, they had eight children.

Pierce Butler next worked as assistant and then as state's attorney for Ramsey County, which included St. Paul. He earned the distinction of securing the highest number of criminal convictions for any occupant of that office. He even prosecuted an Irish saloonkeeper at the behest of the local W.C.T.U. In 1893, he formed the practice of How, Butler, and Mitchell and during the next thirty years he became an increasingly prominent railroad lawyer, representing particularly the Chicago, St. Paul, Minneapolis, and Omaha Railway and the interests of James J. Hill. The railroads lay at the economic heart of the West, and ambitious young attorneys, like Butler and his future Supreme Court colleague Willis Van Devanter, looked to them for advancement. In due course Butler became perhaps the foremost railroad lawyer of the Northwest, although he also worked for public utility companies and occasionally represented less privileged groups. In 1908, the Minnesota State Bar Association elected him its president.

Butler's professional career brought him to the attention of George Wickersham, President Taft's Attorney General, who made a practice of engaging conservative lawyers to prosecute antitrust cases. Upon receiving such an appointment Butler took his government cases seriously. In *United States* v. *Swift Co.,* 186 Fed. 1002 (N.D. Ill. 1911), he succeeded in obtaining a district court indictment, under the Sherman Act, charging a conspiracy to fix the selling price of dressed meat and the purchase price of livestock. The circuit court of appeals, however, finally ruled in favor of the packers. In a case concerning the selling of adulterated flour in violation of the Pure Food and Drug Act, *United States* v. *625 Sacks of Flour,* he won an important jury trial for the government, District Court, W.D. Missouri, July 6, 1910. But again a circuit court of appeals decided to reverse the earlier decision. Commenting on one of Butler's briefs that it presented the government's side "as well as it could be," the Attorney General later commended the Minnesotan for his work and called him the "foremost lawyer in his part of the country." The charge by Butler's critics that he was halfhearted in conducting the government's case is unfair. A few years later he worked for the Canadian government and saved it huge sums of money in valuation proceedings against some of the western railroads. And on the Supreme Court Butler concurred in decisions requiring a full crew on trains and in other "antirailroad" opinions.

Still, Butler's early career put him on the side of the railroad companies, and in saving their money he excelled. Though in court he could be bullying, insulting, and in every way offensive, he was notably successful in convincing the I.C.C. to raise the legal value of railroad properties in order that the lines could charge higher rates. He won fame for his defense of the railroads in the Minnesota rate cases, *Chicago, Milwaukee and St. Paul Railway Company* v. *Minnesota,* 134 U.S. 418 (1890). From 1913 to 1918 he was a leading member of the railroad's committee of counsel in valuation cases stemming from the Federal

Railroad Valuation Act of 1913. When he was appointed to the Supreme Court in 1923 he was senior member of Butler, Mitchell and Doherty, one of Minnesota's richest corporate law firms.

Throughout his life Butler took a special interest in higher education, being especially vigilant against academic liberals. He blamed college professors for contributing to the postwar unrest through "false teaching in the field of politics and social science." Speaking before the American Bar Association in 1923, he condemned professors who regarded religion as a hindrance to social progress. Between 1907 and 1924 he had held the office of Regent of the University of Minnesota. Beginning in 1931 he became a member of the Board of Trustees of the Catholic University of America. During his years on the Court he received honorary degrees from Carleton, Amherst, and Boston Colleges and from Catholic University. His membership on the Minnesota Board of Regents was to play an important part in the fight that developed when President Harding nominated him to the Court in 1922.

The reasons for Butler's appointment to the Court—his favor in the eyes of Chief Justice Taft, who campaigned actively on his behalf, his geographical and religious qualifications—make a fascinating study that may be found in David Danielski's *A Supreme Court Justice Is Appointed* (New York, 1964). Senators George Norris of Nebraska, Robert La Follette of Wisconsin, and Senator-elect Henrik Shipstead of Minnesota opposed his confirmation. Warning against the appointment of another reactionary to the courts, Shipstead declared: "The appointment of Judge Gary of the United States Steel Corporation would not in my opinion be more unfitting or improper than the appointment of Mr. Butler." Samuel Gompers agreed that Butler was an impossible reactionary, and the socialist City Council of Milwaukee declared that it would be a crime if Butler's nomination were approved by the Senate. Much of the animus against Butler was because, as a corporation lawyer, he was presumed to be biased. But opponents of the appointment, in an attempt to prove it unfit, made much of his part in the firing of several University of Minnesota professors during and after the war.

John H. Gray, head of the Economics Department at Minnesota, had taken a year's leave of absence to work as an adviser to the I.C.C.; as part of his job he opposed Butler in the matter of high railroad valuations. On his return to the university the trustees asked Gray to resign, and when he refused, economic and other sanctions were used to force him to leave. William A. Schaper, a political scientist with fifteen years' service at Minnesota, argued for municipal ownership of the street railways, which Butler happened to represent. After a cross-examination at the university by Butler, Schaper was dismissed without notice for alleged pro-German sentiment. (One of Butler's daughters had died in the line of duty as a Red Cross nurse.) In 1938 the university, admitting its error, paid Schaper $5,000, his 1917–18 salary, and made him professor *emeritus*. Stanley Rypins, a professor of English and former Rhodes scholar who had belonged to the radical Committee of Forty-Eight, was denied a renewal of his contract. Finally, Gerhard Ditrichson, a chemistry professor, was also discharged as pro-

German. The president of the university privately referred to Butler as a "huge bully." Albert Rankin, a member of the faculty committee on academic freedom, later said that he had learned "from reliable sources that it was the habit of Pierce Butler to issue orders to the university president directing him to dismiss, or fail to recommend, such persons as had fallen under Mr. Butler's displeasure because of their political or economic views."

A subcommittee of the Senate, consisting of Senators Nelson, Cummins, and Thomas J. Walsh, heard the allegations against Butler and yet unanimously recommended his appointment, for the committee members could not see that Butler was any more responsible for character assassination in the university cases than were the other trustees who had supported him. Some liberal senators who might have criticized Butler demurred on the grounds that the Ku Klux Klan was berating him on account of his religion. Butler was confirmed on January 2, 1923, by a vote of sixty-one to eight.

Butler's critics feared that his career as railroad attorney would cause the Court to pay special heed to his views on railroad valuation cases then before it. The Justice was careful not to sit in such cases as he or his firm had handled, but he did deliver influential opinions on related subjects such as railroad rates.

In *Smyth* v. *Ames,* 169 U.S. 466 (1898), the state of Nebraska had argued that the present cost of reproducing railroad property was to be a determining factor in arriving at fair rates; the railroads had declared that the original cost should dictate minimum rates. At that time the Court took a middle ground and ruled that both considerations should be taken into account in the determination of property values. But in the mildly inflationary years of the early twentieth century, railroads switched their position and adopted the now more advantageous cost of reproduction standard. In the Minnesota rate cases and later before the I.C.C., Butler forcefully put the case for this means of valuation; and as a member of the highest court he continued to press for a sympathetic interpretation of railroad cost.

Butler did not participate in *St. Louis and O'Fallon Railroad Co.* v. *United States,* 279 U.S. 461 (1929), but his views as shown in related cases were given careful consideration by the Court. His approach was revealed in cases concerning utilities, particularly in *Bluefield Water Works* v. *Public Service Commission,* 261 U.S. 679 (1923) and *McCardle* v. *Indianapolis Water Co.,* 272 U.S. 400 (1926). The *O'Fallon* case tested the section of the Transportation Act of 1920 used for determining the value of railroad property. The law required the I.C.C. to "give due consideration to all the elements of value recognized by the law of the land for rate-making purposes." The determination of rates, Butler would insist, must take into account the outstanding part the railroads had played in the creation of national wealth. The evaluators must begin by assuming the railroads do not exist and then proceed to reproduce the plant as it now is. While the value of the property itself can be computed as of the time the roads were constructed, all other assets are to be measured at the time of valuation. The commission should also consider the cost of coordinating present property into a smoothly functioning unit. Butler believed that "the weight to be given cost figures and other items or classes of evidence is to be determined in the light of the facts of the case in hand." Indeed, in his interpretation of *Smyth* v. *Ames,* he seemed to believe that railroads should be evaluated on either original cost or cost of reproduction, whichever happened to be higher at the time of valuation. Justice McReynolds, speaking for a five-man majority in the *O'Fallon* case, embraced Butler's views and rejected the I.C.C.'s valuation methods, requiring that it consider reproduction costs.

Butler's decisions throughout his years on the Court reveal an almost unrelenting conservatism. That strain in his thinking appeared in his dissent to *Euclid* v. *Ambler,* 272 U.S. 365 (1926), which upheld the constitutionality of zoning laws. Unlike his colleague George Sutherland, Butler, in dissent, argued for the freedom of expanding business rather than for protection of the homeowner. Just before, in *Weaver* v. *Palmer Bros. Co.,* 270 U.S. 402 (1924), Butler had set aside a Pennsylvania statute forbidding the use of "shoddy" in bedding as "purely arbitrary." The legislators had believed the unsterilized material likely to spread disease. In *DiSanto* v. *Pennsylvania,* 273 U.S. 34 (1927), Butler drew a distinction between state laws that impose only an "indirect burden" on interstate commerce, and those which impose a "direct burden" and are therefore unconstitutional. DiSanto, engaged in selling steamship tickets to foreign countries, was required by Pennsylvania to pay a fifty dollar license fee. The Court simply declared that the statute was null because it imposed a "direct burden" on foreign commerce. Justice Stone, in dissent, complained that the Court gave no reason for its classification; Butler ignored the purpose of the law, which was to protect illiterates from fraud.

He contributed to defining the phrase "business affected with a public interest" by consistently voting to narrow the classification. In *Coolidge* v. *Long,* 282 U.S. 582 (1930), Butler, spokesman for a majority of five, held that a state inheritance tax could not affect a trust deed made before the tax was enacted; it impaired the obligation of contract and violated the due process clause of the Fourteenth Amendment. He voted against state and federal taxes wherever conceivable grounds could be found. His emotions were evident in such vigorous anti-taxation opinions as *Miller* v. *Standard Nut Margarine Company,* 284 U.S. 489 (1932). Occasionally Butler's feelings spilled over into personal relations with other Justices. Once, after persuading all but Justice Holmes of the rightness of his thinking in a certain case, he stared at him and said with gravity: "I am glad we have finally arrived at a just decision." "Hell is paved with *just* decisions," Holmes replied.

A handful of decisions on civil liberties show that Butler was not totally insensitive to the conservative libertarian tradition. Opposed to national prohibition, he several times castigated federal agents for searches and seizures in violation of the Fourth Amendment. See for example *United States* v. *Lefkowitz,* 285 U.S. 452 (1932), and *Go-Bart Importing Co.* v. *United States,* 282 U.S. 344 (1931). In *Olmstead* v. *United States,* 277 U.S. 438 (1928), he sharply dissented from a majority opinion sanctioning wiretapping by prohibition agents. Butler believed that during the transmission of any message the exclusive use of the wire belongs to the persons served by it. Here Butler was in the unusual company of Justices Brandeis, Stone, and Holmes, each of whom wrote separate dissents. Butler also insisted on a jury trial in a case for which the majority ruled that the offense was too slight to warrant one, *District of Columbia* v. *Clawans,* 300 U.S. 617 (1937). Justice Hughes observed that Butler was a stickler for the rights of criminals.

One additional case found Butler perhaps accidentally in the libertarian camp. His was the lone dissent without opinion in *Buck* v. *Bell,* 274 U.S. 200 (1927), which upheld a Virginia law of 1924 providing for the sterilization of mental defectives in state institutions. Currie Buck was an institutionalized feeble-minded person on whom the state act required that a salpingectomy be performed. Butler's dissent against eight unanimous Justices was no doubt dictated by his Roman Catholic religion, but it is heartening to have even an unwritten disagreement with Justice Holmes's insensitive words: "We have seen more than once that the public welfare may call upon the best citizens for their lives. It would be strange if it could not call upon those who already sap the strength of the State for these lesser sacrifices . . . in order to prevent our being swamped with incompetence. It is better for all the world, if instead of waiting to execute degenerate offspring for crime, or to let them starve for their imbecility, society can prevent those who are manifestly unfit from continuing their kind. The principle that sustains compulsory vaccination is broad enough to cover cutting the Fallopian tubes. . . . Three generations of imbeciles are enough."

But when patriotic sentiment clashed with individualism, Butler could be counted on to denounce the eccentricity of the defendant. In two cases upholding the denial of citizenship, Butler was probably correct in his literal adherence to the law; but he managed to wave the flag and cast aspersions on the individuals concerned. In *United States* v. *Schwimmer,* 279 U.S. 644 (1929), he held Rosika Schwimmer, almost sixty, to be a potential menace because her refusal to take up arms showed she might "be opposed to the use of military force as contemplated by our Constitution and laws." Butler's opinion in *United States* v. *MacIntosh,* 283 U.S. 605 (1931), was equally severe with a Yale theologian who declared he would refuse to fight in a war he thought morally unjustified.

The hardness of Butler's position was perhaps best illustrated in *Kessler* v. *Strecker,* 307 U.S. 22 (1939). Called into question here was a federal law of 1918 that was being used to deport aliens who had been Communists. Strecker had joined the party but never paid dues and was no longer a member. Butler and McReynolds were alone in upholding the action of the government; the Constitution was satisfied, the two Justices held, so long as the deportee had become a party member after his entry into the United States.

Other cases also found Butler giving scant protection to individuals whose views he deplored. Along with McReynolds, Butler, rejecting the majority opinion in *Stromberg* v. *California,* 283 U.S. 359 (1931), held lawful the conviction of a young woman found guilty of displaying a red flag in public. In *Near* v. *Minnesota,* 283 U.S. 697 (1931), Butler dissented from the reversal of a law silencing a weekly newspaper severely critical of Minneapolis officials. The six-year-old statute, which newspapers were pleased to call the Minnesota "press gag" law, had been introduced originally by a legislator seeking to silence an editor critical of him. It was first used in 1927 by County Attorney Floyd B. Olsen to abate a nuisance named the *Saturday Press.* The *Press* was lurid enough—it preached anti-Semitism—but it also charged that a gangster was in control of bootlegging, gambling, and racketeering in Minneapolis and that the chief of police took graft. After an attempt to "bump off" one of the publishers, who was shot, presumably by gangsters, after the first issuance of the paper, the *Press* demanded a general investigation by a special grand jury and a special prosecutor. Colonel Robert McCormick, who retained counsel to assist the defendants, termed the statute tyrannical, despotic, oppressive, and un-American. Along with three other Justices for whom he wrote his dissent, Butler believed the *Press* threatened the peace and order of the state and therefore deserved no constitutional protection. In *Herndon* v. *Lowry,* 301 U.S. 444 (1938), Butler dissented from a decision finding a Negro Communist unfairly convicted of inciting insurrection. In *Hague* v. *Committee of Industrial Organizations,* 307 U.S. 496 (1939), Butler, unlike his colleagues, failed to see anything wrong with a municipal ordinance of Mayor Frank Hague that effectively prohibited labor meetings in public parks.

In a number of outstanding cases involving racial issues, Butler was not among the liberals. In the Scottsboro case of *Powell* v. *Alabama,* 287 U.S. 45 (1932), Butler could not see the rampant prejudice, which effectively denied due process, that caused seven Justices to give the accused Negroes a new trial. Nor would he concede the Court's right to strike down an all-white Texas primary law; in Butler's mind a political party was a private organization, *Nixon* v. *Condon,* 286 U.S. 73 (1932). In *Breedlove* v. *Suttles,* 302 U.S. 277 (1937), Butler held that a poll tax did not violate the Fourteenth Amendment. With McReynolds, Butler dissented in *Missouri ex rel. Gaines* v. *Canada,* 305 U.S. 337 (1938). Missouri had denied Gaines, a Negro, entrance to a law school; Butler thought Missouri should continue to handle the "delicate" issue as it had in the past. Once again over the objection of McReynolds and Butler, the Court in *Lane* v. *Wilson,* 307 U.S. 268 (1939), struck down an Oklahoma law providing that, except for those who appeared during a brief registration period, only voters registered in 1914 could henceforth exercise the franchise. Even more striking was Butler's record in upholding California and Washington laws that curtailed the ownership and acquisition of property by alien Japanese. Butler wrote four decisions in 1923 concerning the legislation. *Porterfield* v. *Webb,* 263 U.S. 225, and *Terrace* v. *Thompson,* 263 U.S. 197, acquiesced in measures preventing Japanese subjects from leasing agricultural land. *Frick* v. *Webb,* 263 U.S. 326, upheld their exclusion from stockholding in a corporation authorized to hold such land and *Webb* v. *O'brien,* 263 U.S. 313, confirmed their exclusion from cropping contracts for cultivating it. In 1925, in *Toyota* v. *United States,* 268 U.S. 402, Butler was faced with the petition of a Japanese immigrant who wished to become an American citizen. Following views expressed earlier by Justice Sutherland, Butler replied in the negative, upholding the established policy of Congress to deny citizenship in such cases.

On the question of minimum wages for women, Butler had his say for the Court in *Morehead* v. *New York ex rel. Tipaldo,* 298 U.S. 587 (1936). Under review in this case was *Adkins* v. *Children's Hospital,* 261 U.S. 525 (1923), which struck down a minimum wage law for women in Washington, D.C. That opinion, written by Justice Sutherland, was kept in mind by Felix Frankfurter as he helped in the drafting of a New York minimum wage law of 1933. The new law widened the "health standard" argument for a minimum wage and included also a wage "reasonably commensurate with the value of the service." Other provisions called for a commission to decide what constituted a minimum wage. The Court, however, held in *Tipaldo* that the New York law was indistinguishable from the District of Columbia act. Although in economic practice the two statutes did operate approximately the same, the decision surprised many New Dealers whose patience with the Court reached an end. The Butler decision and others like it they viewed as an anomaly in the history of the Court which time and again had set limits to freedom of contract. Butler's words certainly quickened their efforts to adopt some expedient that would prevent judicial nullification of congressional legislation. The Court, it seemed to Roosevelt and his supporters, had stymied the democratic process.

Butler simply insisted that, except under exceptional conditions, employer and employee must be free to obtain from each other the best possible terms of employment. "The state," Butler wrote, "is without power by any form of legislation to prohibit, change or nullify contracts between employers and adult women workers as to the amount paid. Any measure that deprives employers and adult women of freedom to agree upon wages, leaving employers and men free to do so, is necessarily arbitrary (a violation of due process)." The language was sweeping, and the law reviews filled with articles condemning the Court for overstepping itself.

During the New Deal Butler wrote few opinions, but he often dissented, particularly after *Morehead.* One of his last decisions, however, found him speaking in behalf of civil liberties. *Lanzetta* v. *New Jersey,* 306 U.S. 451 (1939), concerned a state law prohibiting membership in a "gang" by people of known criminal backgrounds. The expression "known to be a member" of a "gang" Justice Butler thought ridiculously vague. Due process, he pointed out, was not served by legal restrictions too indefinite to inform possible violators of conduct considered unlawful.

When Butler died on November 16, 1939, he was still a member of the Court; Roosevelt replaced him with his liberal Attorney General, Frank Murphy of Michigan. Butler was among the most rigid of the Justices who rejected New

Deal legislation. His philosophy was that of *laissez faire,* and he expressed it in its simplest forms. He was concerned for the rights of the criminal; he had no feeling for the rights of the radical dissenter. Nor will the reading of his opinions yield an easy understanding of the ambiguities in his thought.

SELECTED BIBLIOGRAPHY

A published Ph.D. dissertation on Butler is Francis Joseph Brown's *The Social and Economic Philosophy of Pierce Butler* (Washington, D.C., 1945). David J. Danielski has made a careful study of the circumstances surrounding Butler's appointment to the Court in *A Supreme Court Justice is Appointed* (New York, 1964). See also Richard J. Purcell, "Mr. Justice Pierce Butler," 42 *Catholic Educational Review,* 193 (April 1944).

Pierce Butler

REPRESENTATIVE OPINIONS

MOREHEAD v. NEW YORK EX REL. TIPALDO, 298 U.S. 602 (1936)

Morehead was the last important case in the 1930's in which conservative opinion held sway. Speaking through Justice Butler, five judges agreed that employer and employee, except under unusual conditions, should be free to obtain from one another the best possible terms of employment, and thus a New York State minimum wage law was unconstitutional. After many Court decisions nullifying federal laws as invasions of the reserved powers of the state, the *Morehead* decision, denying the states any power to deal with the problems of the depression, created a no-man's land where no governmental activity was to be allowed. It was the last straw for President Roosevelt, who immediately attacked the "horse and buggy" thinking of the Court. The language of the opinion was sweeping; it seemed to carry the Court back to the last century.

MR. JUSTICE BUTLER delivered the opinion of the Court.

This is a habeas corpus case originating in the supreme Court of New York. Relator was indicted in the county court of Kings county and sent to jail to await trial upon the charge that as manager of a laundry he failed to obey the mandatory order of the state industrial commissioner prescribing minimum wages for women employees.

The relator's petition for the writ avers that the statute, c. 584 of the Laws of 1933 (Cons. Law, c. 31, art. 19) under which the commissioner made the order, insofar as it purports to authorize him to fix women's wages, is repugnant to the due process clause, Art. I, § 6, of the constitution of the State and the due process clause of the Fourteenth Amendment to the Constitution of the United States. The application for the writ is grounded upon the claim that the state statute is substantially identical with the minimum wage law enacted by Congress for the District of Columbia, 40 Stat. 960, which in 1923 was condemned by this court as repugnant to the due process clause of the Fifth Amendment. *Adkins* v. *Children's Hospital*, 261 U.S. 525.

The warden's return, without disclosing

the commissioner's order, the prescribed wages, the findings essential to his jurisdiction to establish them, things done in pursuance of the Act, or the allegations of the indictment, merely shows that under an order of the county court he was detaining relator for trial. The case was submitted on petition and return. The court dismissed the writ. 156 Misc. 522; 282 N.Y.S. 576. Relator took the case to the Court of Appeals. It held the Act repugnant to the due process clauses of the state and federal constitutions. 270 N.Y. 233; 200 N.E. 799. The remittitur directed that the order appealed from be reversed, the writ sustained and the prisoner discharged; it certified that the federal constitutional question was presented and necessarily passed on. The supreme court entered judgment as directed. We granted a writ of certiorari.

The Act extends to women and minors in any "occupation" which "shall mean an industry, trade or business or branch thereof or class of work therein in which women or minors are gainfully employed, but shall not include domestic service in the home of the employer or labor on a farm." § 551 (6). It is not an emergency law. It does not regulate hours or any conditions affecting safety or protection of employees. It relates only to wages of adult women and minors. As the record is barren of details in respect of investigation, findings, amounts being paid women workers in laundries or elsewhere prior to the order, or of things done to ascertain the minimum prescribed, we must take it as granted that, if the State is permitted as against employers and their women employees to establish and enforce minimum wages, that power has been validly exerted. It is to be assumed that the rates have been fairly made in accordance with the procedure prescribed by the Act and in full compliance with the defined standards. If, consistently with the due process clause, the State may not enter upon regulation of the sort undertaken by the challenged enactment, then plainly it cannot by diligence to insure the establishment of just minima create power to enter that field. Cf. *St. Joseph Stock Yards Co.* v. *United States, ante,* p. 38; *Baltimore & Ohio R. Co.* v. *United States, ante,* p. 349.

The *Adkins* case, unless distinguishable, requires affirmance of the judgment below. The petition for the writ sought review upon the ground that this case is distinguishable from that one. No application has been made for reconsideration of the constitutional question there decided.[1] The validity of the principles upon which that decision rests is not challenged. This court confines itself to the ground upon which the writ was asked or granted. *Alice State Bank* v. *Houston Pasture Co.,* 247 U.S. 240, 242. *Clark* v. *Williard,* 294 U.S. 211, 216. Here the review granted was no broader than that sought by the petitioner *Johnson* v. *Manhattan Ry. Co.,* 289 U.S. 479, 494. He is not entitled and does not ask to be heard upon the question whether the *Adkins* case should be overruled. He maintains that it may be distinguished on the ground that the statutes are vitally dissimilar.

The District of Columbia Act provided for a board to ascertain and declare "standards of minimum wages" for women in any occupation and what wages were "inadequate to supply the necessary cost of living to any such women workers to maintain them in good health and to protect their morals." § 9. Violations were punishable by fine and imprisonment. § 18. The declared purposes were to protect women from conditions detrimental to their health and morals, resulting from wages inadequate to maintain decent standards of living. § 23.

The New York Act declares it to be against public policy for any employer to employ any woman at an oppressive and unreasonable wage (§ 552) defined as one which is "both less than the fair and reasonable value of the services rendered and less than sufficient to meet the minimum cost of living necessary for health." § 551 (7). "A fair wage" is one "fairly and reasonably commensurate with the value of the service or class of service rendered." § 551 (8). If the commissioner is of opinion that any substantial number of women in any occupation are receiving oppressive and unreasonable wages he shall appoint a wage board to report upon the establishment of minimum fair wage rates. § 554. After investigation, the board shall submit a report including its

[1] *Briefs of* amici curiae *in support of the application were filed by the City of New York and the State of Illinois. Briefs on the merits supporting the New York Act, were filed by the State of Ohio, and by the States of Connecticut, Illinois, Massachusetts, New Hampshire, New Jersey and Rhode Island. Briefs for affirmance were filed by the New York State Hotel Association, National Woman's Party, National Association of Women Lawyers, et al.*

recommendations as to minimum fair wage standards. § 555.

And for administrative guidance, the Act declares: "In establishing a minimum fair wage for any service or class of service under this article the commissioner and the wage board without being bound by any technical rules of evidence or procedure (1) may take into account all relevant circumstances affecting the value of the service or class of service rendered, and (2) may be guided by like considerations as would guide a court in a suit for the reasonable value of services rendered where services are rendered at the request of an employer without contract as to the amount of the wage to be paid, and (3) may consider the wages paid in the state for work of like or comparable character by employers who voluntarily maintain minimum fair wage standards." § 551 (8).

If the commissioner accepts the report, he shall publish it and a public hearing must be held. § 556. If after the hearing he approves the report, he "shall make a directory order which shall define minimum fair wage rates." § 557. Upon hearing and finding of disobedience the commissioner may publish the name of an employer as having failed to observe the directory order. § 559. If, after a directory order has been in effect for nine months, the commissioner is of opinion that persistent non-observance is a threat to the maintenance of the prescribed standards, he may after hearing make the order mandatory. § 560. Violation of a mandatory order is a misdemeanor punishable by fine, imprisonment or both. §565 (2).

Thus it appears: The minimum wage provided for in the District Act was one not less than adequate "to supply the necessary cost of living to any such women workers to maintain them in good health and to protect their morals." The New York Act defines an oppressive and unreasonable wage as containing two elements. The one first mentioned is: "less than the fair and reasonable value of the services rendered." The other is: "less than sufficient to meet the minimum cost of living necessary for health." The basis last mentioned is not to be distinguished from the living wage defined in the District act. The exertion of the granted power to prescribe minimum wages is by the State act conditioned upon a finding by the commissioner or other administrative agency that a substantial number of women in any occupation are receiving wages that are oppressive and unreasonable, i.e., less than value of the service and less than a living wage. That finding is essential to jurisdiction of the commissioner. In the state court there was controversy between the parties as to whether the "minimum fair wage rates" are required to be established solely upon value of service or upon that value and the living wage. Against the contention of the attorney general, the Court of Appeals held that the minimum wage must be based on both elements.

Speaking through its chief judge, that court said: "We find no material difference between the act of Congress and this act of the New York State Legislature. The act of Congress, it is said, was to protect women from conditions resulting from wages which were inadequate to maintain decent standards of living." The opinion then quotes from the brief of the attorney general: " 'The purpose of the statute in the *Adkins* case was to guarantee a wage based solely upon the necessities of the workers. The statute did not provide for the wages to have any relationship to earning power; was applicable to all vocations and not to the character of the work . . . As contrasted with this statute, the New York Minimum Wage Law provides a definite standard for wages paid. It provides that the worker is to be paid at least the value of the services rendered.' " The opinion continues: "This is a difference in phraseology and not in principle. The New York act, as above stated, prohibits an oppressive and unreasonable wage, which means *both* less than the fair and reasonable value of the services rendered *and* less than sufficient to meet the minimum cost of living necessary for health. The act of Congress had one standard, the living wage; this State act has added another, reasonable value. The minimum wage must include both. What was vague before has not been made any clearer. One of the elements, therefore, in fixing the fair wage is the very matter which was the basis of the congressional act. Forcing the payment of wages at a reasonable value does not make inapplicable the principle and ruling of the *Adkins* case. The distinctions between this case and the *Adkins* case are differences in details, methods and time; the exercise of legislative power to fix wages in any employment is the same."

The petitioner does not suggest and reasonably it cannot be thought that, so far as concerns repugnancy to the due process clause, there is any difference between the minimum wage law for the District of Columbia and the clause of the New York Act, "less than sufficient to meet the minimum cost of living necessary for health." Petitioner does not claim that element was validated by including with it the other ingredient, "less than the fair and reasonable value of the services rendered."

His brief repeats the state court's declaration: " 'The act of Congress had one standard, the living wage; this State act has added another, reasonable value. *The minimum wage must include both.* What was vague before has not been made any clearer. *One of the elements, therefore, in fixing the fair wage is the very matter which was the basis of the congressional act.*' " Then he says: "The italicized lines carry the Court's misconception of the statute. It is a basic misconception. From it flows the erroneous conclusion of the Court of Appeals that there exists no material difference between the two statutes. . . . Those two factors *do not* enter into the determination of the minimum *'fair wage'* as in the statute defined, nor as determined in this case. The only basis for evaluating and arriving at the 'fair minimum wage' is the fair value of the services rendered."

There is no blinking the fact that the state court construed the prescribed standard to include cost of living or that petitioner here refuses to accept that construction. Petitioner's contention that the Court of Appeals misconstrued the Act cannot be entertained. This court is without power to put a different construction upon the state enactment from that adopted by the highest court of the State. We are not at liberty to consider petitioner's argument based on the construction repudiated by that court. The meaning of the statute as fixed by its decision must be accepted here as if the meaning had been specifically expressed in the enactment. *Knights of Pythias* v. *Meyer,* 265 U.S. 30, 32. Exclusive authority to enact carries with it final authority to say what the measure means. *Jones* v. *Prairie Oil Co.,* 273 U.S. 195, 200. The standard of "minimum fair wage rates" for women workers to be prescribed must be considered as if both elements—value of service and living wage—were embodied in the statutory definition itself. *International Harvester Co.* v. *Kentucky,* 234 U.S. 216, 220. As our construction of an Act of Congress must be deemed by state courts to be the law of the United States, so this New York Act as construed by her court of last resort, must here be taken to express the intention and purpose of her lawmakers. *Green* v. *Neal's Lessee,* 6 Pet. 291, 295–298.

The state court rightly held that the *Adkins* case controls this one and requires that relator be discharged upon the ground that the legislation under which he was indicted and imprisoned is repugnant to the due process clause of the Fourteenth Amendment.

The general statement in the New York Act of the fields of labor it includes, taken in connection with the work not covered, indicates legislative intention to reach nearly all private employers of women. The Act does not extend to men. It does extend to boys and girls under the age of 21 years but there is here involved no question as to its validity in respect of wages to be prescribed for them. Relator's petition for the writ shows that the charge against him is that as manager of a laundry he "disobeyed a mandatory order prescribing certain minimum wages for certain adult women employees of the said laundry." The rights of no other class of workers are here involved.

Upon the face of the act the question arises whether the State may impose upon the employers state-made minimum wage rates for all competent experienced women workers whom they may have in their service. That question involves another one. It is: Whether the State has power similarly to subject to state-made wages all adult women employed in trade, industry or business, other than house and farm work. These were the questions decided in the *Adkins* case. So far at least as concerns the validity of the enactment under consideration, the restraint imposed by the due process clause of the Fourteenth Amendment upon legislative power of the State is the same as that imposed by the corresponding provision of the Fifth Amendment upon the legislative power of the United States.

This court's opinion shows (pp. 545, 546): The right to make contracts about one's affairs is a part of the liberty protected by the due process clause. Within this liberty are provisions of contracts between employer and employee fixing the wages to be paid. In making contracts of employment, generally speaking, the parties have equal right to obtain from each other the best terms they can by private bargaining. Legislative abridgement of that freedom can only be justified by the existence of exceptional circumstances. Freedom of contract is the general rule and restraint the exception. This court has found not repugnant to the due process clause statutes fixing rates and charges to be exacted by businesses impressed with a public interest, relating to contracts for the performance of public work, prescribing the character, methods and time of payment of wages, fixing hours of labor. Physical differences between men and women must be recognized in proper cases and legislation fixing hours or conditions of work may properly take them into account, but (p. 553) "we cannot accept the doctrine that women of mature age, *sui juris,* require or may be subjected to restrictions upon their liberty of contract which could not lawfully be imposed in the case of men under similar circumstances. To do so would be to ignore all the implications to be drawn from the present day trend of legislation, as well as that of common thought and usage, by which woman is accorded emancipation from the old doctrine that she must be given special protection or be subjected to special restraint in her contractual and civil relationships. . . . [p. 554] Enough has been said to show that the authority to fix hours of labor cannot be exercised except in respect of those occupations where work of long continued duration is detrimental to health. This Court has been careful in every case where the question has been raised, to place its decision upon this limited authority of the legislature to regulate hours of labor and to disclaim any purpose to uphold the legislation as fixing wages, thus recognizing an essential difference between the two. It seems plain that these decisions afford no real support for any form of law establishing minimum wages."

The decision and the reasoning upon which it rests clearly show that the State is without power by any form of legislation to prohibit, change or nullify contracts between employers and adult women workers as to the amount of wages to be paid.

Then, the opinion emphasizes objections specifically applicable to the requirement that the minimum wages to be prescribed under the District Act shall be adequate "to supply the necessary cost of living to any such women workers to maintain them in good health and to protect their morals." Some of them were: The price fixed by the board need have no relation to earning powers, hours or place or character of work; it is based wholly on opinion of the board as to what amount will be necessary to comply with the standard; it applies to every occupation without regard to the kind of work; the standard is so vague as to be impossible of practical application; the Act takes account of the necessities of only the employee; to the extent that the sum fixed exceeds fair value of service rendered, it amounts to a compulsory exaction for the support of a partially indigent person for whose condition there rests upon the employer no peculiar responsibility; the statute exacts from the employer an arbitrary payment for a purpose and upon a basis having no causal connection with his business or the contract or the work the employee engages to do; the declared basis is not the value of the service rendered but the extraneous circumstance that the employee needs to get a prescribed sum of money to insure her subsistence, health and morals. The court said (p. 558): "The ethical right of every worker, man or woman, to a living wage may be conceded. . . . The fallacy of the proposed method of attaining it is that it assumes that every employer is bound at all events to furnish it. The moral requirement, implicit in every contract of employment, viz., that the amount to be paid and the service to be rendered shall bear to each other some relation of just equivalence, is completely ignored. The necessities of the employee are alone considered and these arise outside of the employment and are as great in one occupation as in another."

Illustrating particular constitutional difficulties encountered by the enactment then before us, the opinion proceeds (p. 559): "Should a statute undertake to vest in a commission power to determine the quantity of food necessary for individual support and require the shopkeeper, if he sell to the individual at all, to furnish that quantity at not more than a fixed maximum, it would undoubtedly fall before the constitutional test. The fallacy of any argument in support of the validity of such a statute would be quickly exposed. The argument in support of that now being considered is equally fallacious, though the weakness of it may not be so plain. A statute requiring an employer to pay in money, to pay at prescribed and regular intervals, to pay the value of the services rendered, even to pay with fair relation to the extent of the benefit obtained from the service, would be understandable. But a statute which prescribes payment without regard to any of these things, and solely with relation to circumstances apart from the contract of employment, the business affected by it and the work done under it, is so clearly the product of a naked, arbitrary exercise of power that it cannot be allowed to stand under the Constitution of the United States."

Petitioner does not attempt to support the Act as construed by the state court. His claim is that it is to be tested here as if it did not include the cost of living and as if value of service were the sole standard. Plainly that position is untenable. If the State has power to single out for regulation the amount of wages to be paid women, the value of their services would be a material consideration. But that fact has no relevancy upon the question whether the State has any such power. And utterly without significance upon the question of power is the suggestion that the New York prescribed standard includes value of service with cost of living whereas the District of Columbia standard was based upon the latter alone. As shown above, the dominant issue in the *Adkins* case was whether Congress had power to establish minimum wages for adult women workers in the District of Columbia. The opinion directly answers in the negative. The ruling that defects in the prescribed standard stamped that Act as arbitrary and invalid was an additional ground of subordinate consequence.

The dissenting opinion of Mr. Chief Justice Taft (in which Mr. Justice Sanford concurred) assumes (p. 564) "that the conclusion in this [*Adkins*] case rests on the distinction between a minimum of wages and a maximum of hours." That is the only point he discussed; he did not refer to the validity of the standard prescribed by the Act. The dissenting opinion of Mr. Justice Holmes begins (p. 567): "The question in this case is the broad one, Whether Congress can establish minimum rates of wages for women in the District of Columbia with due provision for special circumstances, or whether we must say that Congress has no power to meddle with the matter at all." And, after assuming that women would not be employed at the wages fixed unless they were earned or unless the employer could pay them, the opinion says (p. 570): "But the ground on which the law is held to fail is fundamental and therefore it is unnecessary to consider matters of detail." If the decision of the court turned upon the question of the validity of the particular standard, that question could not have been ignored by the justices who were in favor of upholding the Act. Clearly they understood—and rightly—that, by the opinion of the court, it was held that Congress was without power to deal with the subject at all.

To distinguish this from the *Adkins* case, petitioner refers to changes in conditions that have come since that decision, cites great increase during recent years in the number of women wage earners and invokes the first section of the Act, called "Factual background."

The Act is not to meet an emergency; it discloses a permanent policy; the increasing number of women workers suggests that more and more they are getting and holding jobs that otherwise would belong to men. The "Factual background" must be read in the light of the circumstances attending its enactment. The New York legislature passed two minimum wage measures and contemporaneously submitted them to the governor. One was approved; it is the Act now before us. The other was vetoed and did not become law. They contained the same definitions of oppressive wage and fair wage and in general provided the same machinery and procedure culminating in fixing minimum wages by directory orders. The one vetoed was for an emergency; it extended to men as well as to women employees; it did not provide for the enforcement of wages by mandatory orders.

It is significant that their "factual backgrounds" are much alike. They are indicated in the margin.[2] These legislative declara-

[2] *Omitting the words in brackets, the following is the factual background in the first section of the Act before us. Adding the words in brackets and omitting those in italics, there is indicated the background in the bill that was not approved.*

"The employment of [*men and*] *women and minors in trade and industry in the state of New York at wages unreasonably low and not fairly commensurate with the value of the services rendered is a matter of grave and vital public concern. Many* [*men and*] *women and minors employed for gain in the state of New York are not as a class upon a level of equality in bargaining with their employers in regard to minimum fair wage standards, and 'freedom of contract' as applied to their relations with their employers is illusory. Since a very large percentage of such workers are obliged from their week to week wages to support themselves and others who are dependent upon them in whole or in part they are, by reason of their necessitous circumstances, forced to accept whatever wages*

tions, in form of findings or recitals of fact, serve well to illustrate why any measure that deprives employers and adult women of freedom to agree upon wages, leaving employers and men employees free so to do, is necessarily arbitrary. Much, if not all, that in them is said in justification of the regulations that the Act imposes in respect of women's wages applies with equal force in support of the same regulation of men's wages. While men are left free to fix their wages by agreement with employers, it would be fanciful to suppose that the regulation of women's wages would be useful to prevent or lessen the evils listed in the first section of the Act. Men in need of work are as likely as women to accept the low wages offered by unscrupulous employers. Men in greater number than women support themselves and dependents and because of need will work for whatever wages they can get and that without regard to the value of the service and even though the pay is less than minima prescribed in accordance with this Act. It is plain that, under circumstances such as those portrayed in the "Factual background," prescribing of minimum wages for women alone would unreasonably restrain them in competition with men and tend arbitrarily to deprive them of employment and a fair chance to find work.

This court, on the authority of the *Adkins* case and with the acquiescence of all the justices who dissented from the decision,[3] held repugnant to the due process clause of the Fourteenth Amendment statutes of Arizona and Arkansas,[4] respectively, fixing minimum wages for women. *Murphy* v. *Sardell,* 269 U.S. 530. *Donham* v. *West-Nelson Mfg. Co.,* 273 U.S. 657. We have adhered to the principle there applied and cited it as a guide in other cases. *Meyer* v. *Nebraska,* 262 U.S. 390, 399. *Wolff Packing Co.* v. *Industrial Court,* 262 U.S. 522, 534. *Ribnik* v. *McBride,* 277 U.S. 350, 356. See *Near* v. *Minnesota,* 283 U.S. 697, 707–708. States having similar enactments have construed it to prevent the fixing of wages for adult women. *Topeka Laundry Co.* v. *Court of Industrial Relations,* 119 Kan. 12;

---

are offered to them. Judged by any reasonable standard, wages are in many cases fixed by chance and caprice and the wages accepted are often found to bear no relation to the fair value of the service rendered. Women and minors employed for gain are peculiarly subject to the overreaching of inefficient, harsh or ignorant employers and under unregulated competition where no adequate machinery exists for the effective regulation and maintenance of minimum fair wage standards, [*and*] *the standards such as exist tend to be set by the least conscionable employers. In the absence of any effective minimum fair wage rates* for women and minors, *the constant lowering of wages by unscrupulous employers constitutes a serious form of unfair competition against other employers, reduces the purchasing power of* the workers [*a large proportion of the population of the state*] *and threatens the stability of industry. The evils of oppressive, unreasonable and unfair wages* as they affect women and minors employed in the state of New York *are such as to render imperative the exercise of the police power of the state for the protection of industry and of the* [*men and*] *women and minors employed therein and of the public interest of the community at large in their health and well-being and in the prevention of the deterioration of the race.* In the considered judgment of the legislature this article is constitutional."

[3] *Mr. Justice Brandeis took no part in the consideration of the* Adkins *case. He noted dissent without more in the Arizona case and Arkansas case.*

[4] *The Arizona Act declared: "No person . . . shall employ any female in any store, office, shop, restaurant, dining room, hotel, rooming house, laundry or manufacturing establishment at a weekly wage of less than Sixteen Dollars ($16.00) per week; a lesser amount being hereby declared inadequate to supply the necessary cost of living to any such female, to maintain her health, and to provide her with the common necessaries of life." Laws of Arizona, 1923, c. 3, § 1.*

The Arkansas Act declared: "It shall be unlawful for any employer . . . to pay any female worker in any establishment or occupation less than the wage specified in this section, to-wit, except as hereinafter provided: "All female workers who have had six months' practicable experience in any line of industry or labor shall be paid not less than one dollar and twenty-five cents per day. The minimum wage for inexperienced female workers who have not had six months experience in any line of industry or labor shall be paid not less than one dollar per day." § 7108, Crawford & Moses Digest.

237 Pac. 1041. *Stevenson* v. *St. Clair,* 161 Minn. 444; 201 N.W. 629. See *Folding Furniture Works* v. *Industrial Commission,* 300 Fed. 991. *People* v. *Successors of Laurnaga & Co.,* 32 P.R. 766.

The New York court's decision conforms to ours in the *Adkins* case, and the later rulings that we have made on the authority of that case. That decision was deliberately made upon careful consideration of the oral arguments and briefs of the respective parties and also of briefs submitted on behalf of States and others as amici curiae. In the Arizona case the attorney general sought to distinguish the District of Columbia Act from the legislation then before us and insisted that the latter was a valid exertion of the police power of the State. Counsel for the California commission submitted a brief amicus curiae in which he elaborately argued that our decision in the *Adkins* case was erroneous and ought to be overruled. In the Arkansas case the state officers, appellants there, by painstaking and thorough brief presented arguments in favor of the same contention. But this court, after thoughtful attention to all that was suggested against that decision, adhered to it as sound. And in each case, being clearly of opinion that no discussion was required to show that, having regard to the principles applied in the *Adkins* case, the state legislation fixing wages for women was repugnant to the due process clause of the Fourteenth Amendment, we so held and upon the authority of that case affirmed per curiam the decree enjoining its enforcement. It is equally plain that the judgment in the case now before us must also be

Affirmed.

Edward Terry Sanford

☆ 1865–1930 ☆

APPOINTED BY

WARREN G. HARDING

YEARS ON COURT

1923–1930

Edward Terry Sanford

by

DAVID BURNER

BORN IN KNOXVILLE, Tennessee, on July 23, 1865 Edward Terry Sanford grew up in an area of the state deeply divided over the Civil War. His father, a Connecticut Yankee of colonial stock, had come to Tennessee in 1852; Edward J. Sanford rose from destitution to become a millionaire in the lumber and construction business. An important Republican, he served for a time as party leader in the state and founded a daily newspaper. Sanford's mother, Emma Chavannes, a cultured Swiss, carefully directed her son's education in the local private schools. The combination of southern preparatory schooling and northern family background—a combination intensified by the crosscurrents of war's bitter aftermath—started Edward Terry Sanford on a cosmopolitan path. Two B.A.'s, one from the University of Tennessee and one from Harvard, a Ph.D. from Tennessee, an LL.B. and M.A. *magna cum laude* from Harvard Law School, and a postgraduate year in France and Germany studying languages and foreign economy insured that Sanford would never be a Tennessee provincial. At Harvard College he was Class Day orator; in professional school he was editor of the *Harvard Law Review,* a member of the Pow Wow law club, and president of Consolidated Signet.

Sanford had interrupted his Harvard law studies to pass the bar exam in Tennessee in 1888. In 1890 he returned from Europe to Knoxville, where he was to practice law for many years. He specialized in civil law, particularly chancery and appellate practice. His cautious disposition caused him to avoid juries and criminal law. Sanford married a local girl, Lutie Woodruff, and the couple had two daughters. A good speaker endowed with a pleasing personality, Sanford had little trouble in establishing himself as a prominent figure in his part of the state. In these years he demonstrated an interest in education that he

DAVID BURNER is Associate Professor of History at the State University of New York, Stony Brook. He is the author of The Politics of Provincialism: The Democratic Party in Transition, 1918–1932.

would maintain throughout his career: he was a trustee for the University of Tennessee from 1897 to 1923, and for George Peabody College for Teachers from 1909 until his death in 1930; in later years he would serve as president of the Harvard Alumni Association and receive honorary degrees from Harvard and the University of Cincinnati. He lectured in the University of Tennessee law division from 1898 to 1907.

Sanford moved to Washington in 1906 to work as a special assistant to the Attorney General to prosecute the fertilizer trust. As a Republican, he was a successful candidate for an Assistant Attorney General's position that became vacant under President Theodore Roosevelt in 1907. After serving efficiently in this office for seventeen months, Sanford was appointed federal district judge for an area comprising eastern and middle Tennessee; and though opportunities to make more money in a different capacity were always at hand, he held that position from 1908 until he was appointed to the Supreme Court in 1923.

Throughout his tenure as district judge, Sanford always paid great attention to legal detail. His decisions were often lenient, always sympathetic, and devoid of excessive pride; he would on occasion even reverse his own decisions. His opinions on equity and bankruptcy cases were among his best. He remained an exemplar of public service: he served on the board of governors of the Kentucky General Hospital, the University of Tennessee, the East Tennessee Institute, and the George Peabody College for Teachers. He was vice president of the American Bar Association and the Tennessee Historical Society, president of the Alumni Association of the University of Tennessee, and held dozens of like positions in educational, professional, and charitable institutions. In 1920 he wrote to his class secretary at Harvard: "My dockets are now crowded, and my work very heavy and done under constant pressure, but, with a bit of vacation now and then and a little golf [he owned some two hundred golf clubs] . . . , have kept in excellent health and continue to find enduring satisfaction and contentment in my work." His secretary, a Mr. Dove, gave this portrait: "He was a man of highly nervous temperament, and the moment he started dictating he arose to his feet and started walking around the office, always smoking. He smoked cigars of a small size that could be consumed during a five or ten minute recess at court, but during the latter part of his tenure as a district judge, he got to smoking my cigarettes, which he always borrowed by the fives and tens and would light one from another." In the years after the war he worked for the League of Nations, and his internationalism was one of the qualities that made him attractive to his friends Chief Justice Taft and Attorney General Daugherty when Justice Pitney's retirement in 1922 left a vacancy on the Supreme Court.

The Pitney vacancy was the fourth in two years. Political promises for a Court appointment had been exhausted. Since President Harding had received many southern votes, a southern Republican would be a reasonable choice. Sanford's most important champion was the Attorney General, assisted by the Chief Justice, who argued to the President that the federal courts were a good training ground for work on the highest tribunal. Support for Sanford came from many other sources: labor leaders, businessmen, the Republican governor of Tennessee, and the state Democratic legislature. Sanford had perhaps been aiming for the Senate, but he landed in the Supreme Court. Nominated on January 24, 1923, he was to serve seven years and deliver the Court's opinion in 130 cases.

Sanford's more important cases concerned government and business. His decisions were judicious, and he sustained a balance between the claims of government and those of enterprise. When the Public Utilities Commission of Tennessee asked the Cumberland Telephone and Telegraph Company to make an appraisal of its properties for rate-making purposes, the company sought an injunction, alleging "confiscation without due process of law." Sanford presented a closely reasoned answer upholding the right of the state to make such a request. But he sided with the Coca-Cola Company when the government, arguing that Coke contained "deleterious" drugs, seized "certain cases, kegs, and barrels of the soft-drink syrup."

Bankruptcy cases were Sanford's forte. In the curious case of *Taylor* v. *Voss,* 271 U.S. 176 (1926), Sanford's statement for the Court insisted that the bankruptcy of a deceased husband meant he had suffered a "civil death," and therefore under an Indiana law his widow might take a certain part of his realty free from creditors' claims. Sanford made a careful contribution in the bankruptcy cases of *Meek* v. *Centre County Banking Company,* 268 U.S. 426 (1925), and *Harrison* v. *Chamberlain,* 271 U.S. 191 (1926). In the latter case he decided that a bankrupt's wife need not surrender her money, even though it had been earned by her husband.

On the Supreme Court Sanford's most important decisions came in the area of civil liberties. *Gitlow* v. *New York,* 268 U.S. 652 (1925), concerned the power of state governments to regulate freedom of speech and of the press. In accepting the case the Court contended that the word "liberty" in the due process clause of the Fourteenth Amendment included freedom of speech and of the press. Sanford's words were to be of great significance: "We may and do assume that freedom of speech and of the press is one of the fundamental personal rights and liberties protected by the Due Process Clause." But the Justices, speaking through Sanford, upheld the conviction of the Communist Benjamin Gitlow under a New York criminal anarchy statute for publishing a pamphlet called *The Left Wing Manifesto.* The state law defined criminal anarchy as the advocacy, by written or spoken word, of the overthrow of organized government by force or other illegal means. The *Manifesto* urged violence as a means to destroy organized parliamentary government. It was argued for the defendant that, while he had advocated the forcible overthrow of the government, no actual evil flowed from his advocacy.

The Court upheld Gitlow's conviction as no impairment of free speech, though emphasizing that the Fourteenth Amendment did protect liberties of this kind. The opinion was in harmony with the postwar decisions upholding the conviction of Socialists and others who had opposed the war, even though they posed no clear and present danger. Justice Sanford declared that Gitlow had used "the language of direct incitement," not of "philosophical abstraction" in calling the proletariat to the final struggle, and that "free speech did not confer an absolute right to speak or publish, without responsibility, whatever one may choose." No evidence had been presented by the government of any evil resulting from the circulation of the pamphlet. But the state had every right to extinguish the spark without waiting for the flames; it "was sufficient," wrote Sanford, "if such revolutionary acts were advocated in general terms; and it was not essential that their immediate execution should have been advocated." The Justice warned: "A single revolutionary spark may kindle a fire that, smoldering for a time, may burst into a sweeping and destructive conflagration." Nor could the state be expected to cope with the precise effects of each such utterance; it cannot reasonably be asked to weigh the danger from every such remark in the nice balance of a jeweler's scale. The decision revived the "bad tendency" or presumptive intent doctrine for determining actions dangerous to public safety.

In a dissent, Justice Holmes argued that the "redundant discourse before us" had not a chance of starting a "present conflagration." Urging that the Court return to the clear and present danger yardstick of *Schenck* v. *United States,* 249 U.S. 47 (1919), Holmes observed that "every idea is an incitement." "If in the long run," he wrote, "the beliefs expressed in proletarian dictatorship are destined to be accepted by the dominant forces of the community, the only meaning of free speech is that they should be given their chance. . . ." No doubt Holmes realized, however, that the Gitlow case could also be used as a precedent for the extension of liberties. Charles Warren, writing in 1926, was apprehensive that "if the doctrine of the Gitlow case is to be carried to its logical . . . conclusion, every one of the rights contained in the Bill of Rights ought to be and must be included within the definition of 'liberty,' and must be held to be guaranteed by the Fourteenth Amendment against deprivation by a state 'without due process of law.' "

Whitney v. *California,* 274 U.S. 357 (1927), dealt with the criminal syndicalism law of California, which imposed heavy fines and imprisonment merely for joining an organization that favored violence in a political cause or industrial dispute. Miss Charlotte Whitney, the niece of Justice Stephen Field, insisted that although she had helped form the Communist Labor Party of California in 1919, it was not with the intent of shaping an "instrument of terrorism or violence." The use of force was not mentioned in the Communist program. The law itself was challenged on the ground that the statute was vague and that free speech and assembly were unduly infringed. Again Sanford, employing the concept of bad tendency, upheld the state law; he viewed with alarm "united and joint action" which "involves . . . greater danger to the public peace and security than the isolated utterance and act of individuals. All threats to the American form of government, no matter how remote, must be withstood." In a concurring opinion Justice Brandeis held that the statute should be qualified by requiring that a serious, immediate menace be proved. Such grounds, he admitted, might apply in the present case, but generally speaking "only an emergency can justify repression. Such must be the rule if authority is to be reconciled with freedom." Implicitly the Court declared that the Constitution knew no "right of revolution" than by way of the ballot, and Miss Whitney was guilty because of her association with those who preached syndicalism. Perhaps the real significance of the *Whitney* case, however, was its taking for granted what was carefully stated in *Gitlow* v. *New York:* that the Constitutional protection of free speech applied to the states as well as to the federal government. In a concurring opinion Justice Brandeis reminded Sanford that "the right of free speech, the right to teach, and the right of assembly are protected by the due process clause of the Fourteenth Amendment from invasion by the states."

Two similar cases reveal that Sanford was apparently not emotionally committed to denying rights to radicals. *Fiske* v. *Kansas,* 274 U.S. 380 (1927), marked the first successful defense invoking the Fourteenth Amendment to guarantee the federal right of free speech against state statutes. Sanford reversed a criminal anarchy conviction because the organization to which the defendant belonged, the Industrial Workers of the World, "was not shown to have advocated unlawful measures." The Justice went further, however, in his justification for the decision. He argued that the Kansas Act was unconstitutional because "the Act as applied was an arbitrary and unreasonable exercise of the police power of the state, unwarrantably infringing the liberty of the defendant in violation of the due process clause of the Fourteenth Amendment."

The Court had upheld California law in *Whitney* as within the police power of the state to punish acts which endangered the public peace and security. Such considerations did not apply in the *Fiske* case, because there was no evidence that the defendant or his organization advocated the use of crime, sabotage or unlawful violence to overthrow the present industrial system. Two years later Sanford concurred with Justice Holmes in a dissent in *United States* v. *Schwimmer,* 279 U.S. 649, 655 (1929). Rosika Schwimmer was a pacifist of Hungarian birth who had persuaded Henry Ford to sail his peace ship to Europe in 1915. Sanford argued that her refusal to bear arms in defense of the country should not be grounds for withholding American citizenship. What if citizenship were denied to those who would not obey the Eighteenth Amendment, he asked.

Sanford made clear his antitrust views in several cases. In *Cement Manufacturers Protective Association* v. *United States,* 268 U.S. 588 (1925), and *Maple Flooring Manufacturers Association* v. *United States,* 268 U.S. 563 (1929), the government had attempted to prosecute trade associations as combinations in restraint of trade; the majority of the Court rebuffed the Department of Justice, but Sanford, along with Taft and McReynolds, dissented. In the *Maple Flooring* case Sanford asked: "Why all this detailed interchange of information between competitors if not intended to restrain competition? For much of it I can see no other purpose." Sanford was often to be found on the side of the public interest. In *Tyson* v. *Banton,* 273 U.S. 418 (1927), he wrote a short dissent supporting the state's rights to regulate theatre ticket brokers: "The business of the . . . brokers, who stand in 'the very gateway' between the theatres and the public, depriving the public of access to the theatres for the purchase of desirable seats at the regular prices, . . . has become clothed with a public interest and is subject to regulation by the Legislature." That theatres themselves may or may not be so clothed is beside the point. The statute was not aimed at theatre owners but at ticket agencies. The Court, according to Sanford, also failed to have the customary strong presumptions in favor of the validity of the enactment assailed and of the familiarity of the legislature with matters of local concern. Curiously, one year later, he joined the majority of the Court in striking down a New Jersey law regulating employment agency fees although the claim for state regulation was at least as strong as in the *Tyson* case, *Ribnik* v. *McBride,* 277 U.S. 350 (1928).

In *Liberty Warehouse* v. *Grannis,* 273 U.S. 70 (1927), Sanford dealt with a jurisdictional dispute concerning declaratory judgments. Unlike an ordinary civil action, declaratory action seeks to remove uncertainty in disputes concerning existing rights and is preventive rather than curative in nature. The Liberty Warehouse case arose from a Kentucky statute imposing regulations on tobacco warehousing. The vagueness of the law prompted warehousemen, worried they would be forced into bankruptcy without a clear knowledge of their rights and duties under the statute, to bring action in federal district court against the commonwealth attorney. The attorney demurred on grounds of want of federal jurisdiction. When the lower court sustained the demurrer, the plaintiffs appealed to the Supreme Court. In speaking for the Court, Sanford severely limited the scope and usefulness of declaratory actions. Narrowly interpreting Article III of the Constitution, Sanford held that federal jurisdiction extended only to clearly defined "cases and controversies." The Court was not empowered to determine "abstract questions or issues framed for the purpose of invoking the advice of the Court without real parties or a real issue." Sanford did not, however, discuss the nature of declaratory action and emphasized instead the constitutional question involved. As a result, it appeared a federal court could not render a declaratory judgment, except in special circumstances, although Sanford's vague and confused opinion suggested the case was not ripe for declarative relief rather than a total want of power in any case. *Liberty Warehouse Co.* v. *Grannis,* 273 U.S. 70 (1927). Shortly after the opinion, however, Congress passed the Declaratory Judgments Act, which served to alter Sanford's decision.

One of the last cases for which Sanford wrote the decision was the "Pocket Veto" case of 1929: *The Okanogan, Methow, San Poelis, Nespelem, Colville, and Lake Indian Tribes . . .* v. *the United States,* 279 U.S. 655. This concerned an act passed by Congress and sent to President Coolidge on June 24, 1926. The legislation provided for Indian tribes in the state of Washington to present land claims in certain federal courts. The first session of the Sixty-ninth Congress adjourned *sine die* on July 3 and Coolidge had neither signed nor returned the bill. Arguing that the bill had become a law owing to the President's neglect, the Okanogan and other Indian tribes filed a petition in the Court of

Claims under the terms of the bill. The Judiciary Committee of the House of Representatives issued a report supporting the Indians' claim. The United States demurred to the petition, and the Court sustained the demurrer and dismissed the petition. Sanford ruled that Coolidge's inaction, under the circumstances, rendered the bill inoperative under clause 7 of Article I of the Constitution. The ten days referred to there meant calendar not legislative days, and adjournment did not mean only the final adjournment of Congress. So the clause had been construed over many years of governmental practice, and with Sanford historical precedent always carried great weight.

On March 8, 1930, Sanford died suddenly at the age of sixty-four. But the recently retired Chief Justice Taft died a few hours later, and Sanford's passing attracted little attention. Sanford had voted with Taft so consistently that it was fitting irony for the two to die on the same day.

SELECTED BIBLIOGRAPHY

Almost nothing has been published on Justice Sanford. A few biographical facts may be gleaned from brief sketches that appeared in the law journals at the time of his appointment. Seventy-five pieces make up the Sanford Collection at the University of Tennessee library in Knoxville.

Edward Terry Sanford

REPRESENTATIVE OPINIONS

GITLOW v. NEW YORK, 268 U.S. 652 (1925)

Gitlow dealt with the power of state governments to regulate freedom of speech and of the press. Speaking through Sanford, the Court upheld the conviction for criminal anarchy of Benjamin Gitlow, who had distributed a pamphlet calling for overthrow of the government. But at the same time, as grounds for accepting the case, the Court contended that the word "liberty" in the due process clause of the Fourteenth Amendment included freedom of speech and of the press. The Court, in other words, had positively assumed the right to declare unconstitutional state regulation of these freedoms.

MR. JUSTICE SANFORD delivered the opinion of the Court.

Benjamin Gitlow was indicted in the Supreme Court of New York, with three others, for the statutory crime of criminal anarchy. New York Penal Laws, §§ 160, 161.[1] He was separately tried, convicted, and sentenced to imprisonment. The judgment was affirmed by the Appellate Division and by the Court of Appeals. 195 App. Div. 773; 234 N.Y. 132 and 539. The case is here on writ of error to the Supreme Court, to which the record was remitted. 260 U.S. 703.

The contention here is that the statute, by its terms and as applied in this case, is repugnant to the due process clause of the Fourteenth Amendment. Its material provisions are:

"§ 160. *Criminal anarchy defined.* Criminal anarchy is the doctrine that organized government should be overthrown by force or violence, or by assassination of the executive head or of any of the executive officials of government, or by any unlawful means. The *advocacy* of such doctrine either by word of mouth or writing is a felony.

"§ 161. *Advocacy of criminal anarchy.* Any person who:

"1. By word of mouth or writing advocates, advises or teaches the duty, necessity or propriety of overthrowing or overturning organized government by force or violence, or by assassination of the executive head or of any of the executive officials of government, or by any unlawful means; or,

"2. Prints, publishes, edits, issues or

[1] *Laws of 1909, ch. 88; Consol. Laws, 1909, ch. 40. This statute was originally enacted in 1902. Laws of 1902, ch. 371.*

knowingly circulates, sells, distributes or publicly displays any book, paper, document, or written or printed matter in any form, containing or advocating, advising or teaching the doctrine that organized government should be overthrown by force, violence or any unlawful means . . . ,

"Is guilty of a felony and punishable" by imprisonment or fine, or both.

The indictment was in two counts. The first charged that the defendant had advocated, advised and taught the duty, necessity and propriety of overthrowing and overturning organized government by force, violence and unlawful means, by certain writings therein set forth entitled "The Left Wing Manifesto"; the second that he had printed, published and knowingly circulated and distributed a certain paper called "The Revolutionary Age," containing the writings set forth in the first count advocating, advising and teaching the doctrine that organized government should be overthrown by force, violence and unlawful means.

The following facts were established on the trial by undisputed evidence and admissions: The defendant is a member of the Left Wing Section of the Socialist Party, a dissenting branch or faction of that party formed in opposition to its dominant policy of "moderate Socialism." Membership in both is open to aliens as well as citizens. The Left Wing Section was organized nationally at a conference in New York City in June, 1919, attended by ninety delegates from twenty different States. The conference elected a National Council, of which the defendant was a member, and left to it the adoption of a "Manifesto." This was published in The Revolutionary Age, the official organ of the Left Wing. The defendant was on the board of managers of the paper and was its business manager. He arranged for the printing of the paper and took to the printer the manuscript of the first issue which contained the Left Wing Manifesto, and also a Communist Program and a Program of the Left Wing that had been adopted by the conference. Sixteen thousand copies were printed, which were delivered at the premises in New York City used as the office of the Revolutionary Age and the headquarters of the Left Wing, and occupied by the defendant and other officials. These copies were paid for by the defendant, as business manager of the paper. Employees at this office wrapped and mailed out copies of the paper under the defendant's direction; and copies were sold from this office. It was admitted that the defendant signed a card subscribing to the Manifesto and Program of the Left Wing, which all applicants were required to sign before being admitted to membership; that he went to different parts of the State to speak to branches of the Socialist Party about the principles of the Left Wing and advocated their adoption; and that he was responsible for the Manifesto as it appeared, that "he knew of the publication, in a general way and he knew of its publication afterwards, and is responsible for its circulation."

There was no evidence of any effect resulting from the publication and circulation of the Manifesto.

No witnesses were offered in behalf of the defendant.

Extracts from the Manifesto are set forth in the margin.[2] Coupled with a review

[2] *Italics are given as in the original, but the paragraphing is omitted.*

"The Left Wing Manifesto"

"Issued on Authority of the Conference by the National Council of the Left Wing.

"The world is in crisis. Capitalism, the prevailing system of society, is in process of disintegration and collapse. . . . Humanity can be saved from its last excesses only by the Communist Revolution. There can now be only the Socialism which is one in temper and purpose with the proletarian revolutionary struggle. . . . The class struggle is the heart of Socialism. Without strict conformity to the class struggle, in its revolutionary implications, Socialism becomes either sheer Utopianism, or a method of reaction. . . . The dominant Socialism united with the capitalist governments to prevent a revolution. The Russian revolution was the first act of the proletariat against the war and Imperialism. . . . [The] proletariat, urging on the poorer peasantry, conquered power. It accomplished a proletarian revolution by means of the Bolshevik policy of 'all power to the Soviets,'—organizing the new transitional state of proletarian dictatorship. . . . Moderate Socialism affirms that the bourgeois, democratic parliamentary state is the necessary basis for the introduction of Socialism. . . . Revolutionary Socialism, on the contrary, insists that the democratic parliamentary state can never be the basis for the introduction of Socialism; that it is necessary to destroy the parlimentary state, and construct a new state of the organized producers, which will

of the rise of Socialism, it condemned the dominant "moderate Socialism" for its recognition of the necessity of the democratic parliamentary state; repudiated its policy of introducing Socialism by legislative measures; and advocated, in plain and unequivocal language, the necessity of accomplishing the "Communist Revolution" by a militant

---

deprive the bourgeoisie of political power, and function as a revolutionary dictatorship of the proletariat. . . . Revolutionary Socialism alone is capable of mobilizing the proletariat for Socialism, for the conquest of the power of the state, by means of revolutionary mass action and proletarian dictatorship. . . . Imperialism is dominant in the United States, which is now a world power. . . . The war has aggrandized American Capitalism, instead of weakening it as in Europe. . . . These conditions modify our immediate task, but do not alter its general character; this is not the moment of revolution, but it is the moment of revolutionary struggle. . . . Strikes are developing which verge on revolutionary action, and in which the suggestion of proletarian dictatorship is apparent, the striker-workers trying to usurp functions of municipal government, as in Seattle and Winnipeg. The mass struggle of the proletariat is coming into being. . . . These strikes will constitute the determining feature of proletarian action in the days to come. Revolutionary Socialism must use these mass industrial revolts to broaden the strike, to make it general and militant; use the strike for political objectives, and, finally, develop the mass political strike against Capitalism and the state. Revolutionary Socialism must base itself on the mass struggles of the proletariat, engage directly in these struggles while emphasizing the revolutionary purposes of Socialism and the proletarian movement. The mass strikes of the American proletariat provide the material basis out of which to develop the concepts and action of revolutionary Socialism. . . . Our task . . . is to articulate and organize the mass of the unorganized industrial proletariat, which constitutes the basis for a militant Socialism. The struggle for the revolutionary industrial unionism of the proletariat becomes an indispensable phase of revolutionary Socialism, on the basis of which to broaden and deepen the action of the militant proletariat, developing reserves for the ultimate conquest of power. . . . Revolutionary Socialism adheres to the class struggle because through the class struggle alone—the mass struggle—can the industrial proletariat secure immediate concessions and finally conquer power by organizing the industrial government of the working class. The class struggle is a political struggle . . . in the sense that its objective is political—the overthrow of the political organization upon which capitalistic exploitation depends, and the introduction of a new social system. The direct objective is the conquest by the proletariat of the power of the state. Revolutionary Socialism does not propose to 'capture' the bourgeois parliamentary state, but to conquer and destroy it. Revolutionary Socialism, accordingly, repudiates the policy of introducing Socialism by means of legislative measures on the basis of the bourgeois state. . . . It proposes to conquer by means of political action . . . in the revolutionary Marxism sense, which does not simply mean parliamentarism, but the class action *of the proletariat* in any form *having as its objective the conquest of the power of the state. . . . Parliamentary action which emphasizes the implacable character of the class struggle is an indispensable means of agitation. . . . But parliamentarism cannot conquer the power of the state for the proletariat. . . . It is accomplished, not by the legislative representatives of the proletariat, but by* the mass power of the proletariat in action. *The supreme power of the proletariat inheres in the* political mass strike, *in using the industrial mass power of the proletariat for political objectives. Revolutionary Socialism, accordingly, recognizes that the supreme form of proletarian political action is* the political mass strike. . . . *The power of the proletariat lies fundamentally in its control of the industrial process. The mobilization of this control in action against the bourgeois state and Capitalism means the end of Capitalism, the initial form of the revolutionary mass action that will conquer the power of the state. . . . The revolution starts with strikes of protest, developing into mass political strikes and then into revolutionary mass action for the conquest of the power of the state. Mass action becomes political in purpose while extra-parliamentary in form; it is equally a process of revolution and the revolution itself in operation. The final objective of mass action is the conquest of the power of the state, the annihilation of the bourgeois parliamentary state and the intro-*

and "revolutionary Socialism," based on "the class struggle" and mobilizing the "power of the proletariat in action," through mass industrial revolts developing into mass political strikes and "revolutionary mass action," for the purpose of conquering and destroying the parliamentary state and establishing in its place, through a "revolutionary dictatorship of the proletariat," the system of Communist Socialism. The then recent strikes in Seattle and Winnipeg[3] were cited as instances of a development already verging on revolutionary action and suggestive of proletarian dictatorship, in which the strike-workers were "trying to usurp the functions of municipal government"; and revolutionary Socialism, it was urged, must use these mass industrial revolts to broaden the strike, make it general and militant, and develop it into mass political strikes and revolutionary mass action for the annihilation of the parliamentary state.

At the outset of the trial the defendant's counsel objected to the introduction of any evidence under the indictment on the grounds that, as a matter of law, the Manifesto "is not in contravention of the statute," and that "the statute is in contravention of" the due process clause of the Fourteenth Amendment. This objection was denied. They also moved, at the close of the evidence, to dismiss the indictment and direct an acquittal "on the grounds stated in the first objection to evidence," and again on the grounds that "the indictment does not charge an offense" and the evidence "does not show an offense." These motions were also denied.

The court, among other things, charged the jury, in substance, that they must determine what was the intent, purpose and fair meaning of the Manifesto; that its words must be taken in their ordinary meaning, as they would be understood by people whom it might reach; that a mere statement or

---

duction of the transition proletarian state, functioning as a revolutionary dictatorship of the proletariat. . . . The bourgeois parliamentary state is the organ of the bourgeoisie for the coercion of the proletariat. The revolutionary proletariat must, accordingly, destroy this state. . . . It is therefore necessary that the proletariat organize its own state for the coercion and suppression of the bourgeoisie. . . . *Proletarian dictatorship is a recognition of the necessity for a revolutionary state to coerce and suppress the bourgeoisie; it is equally a recognition of the fact that, in the Communist reconstruction of society, the proletariat as a class alone counts. . . . The old machinery of the state cannot be used by the revolutionary proletariat. It must be destroyed. The proletariat creates a new state, based directly upon the industrially organized producers, upon the industrial unions or Soviets, or a combination of both. It is this state alone, functioning as a dictatorship of the proletariat, that can realize Socialism. . . . While the dictatorship of the proletariat performs its negative task of crushing the old order, it performs the positive task of constructing the new. Together with the government of the proletarian dictatorship, there is developed a new 'government,' which is no longer government in the old sense, since it concerns itself with the management of production and not with the government of persons. Out of workers' control of industry, introduced by the proletarian dictatorship, there develops the complete structure of Communist Socialism, —industrial self-government of the communistically organized producers. When this structure is completed, which implies the complete expropriation of the bourgeoisie economically and politically, the dictatorship of the proletariat ends, in its place coming the full and free social and individual autonomy of the Communist order. . . . It is not a problem of immediate revolution. It is a problem of the immediate revolutionary struggle. The revolutionary epoch of the final struggle against Capitalism may last for years and tens of years; but the Communist International offers a policy and program immediate and ultimate in scope, that provides for the immediate class struggle against Capitalism, in its revolutionary implications, and for the final act of the conquest of power. The old order is in decay. Civilization is in collapse. The proletarian revolution and the Communist reconstruction of society*—the struggle for these—*is now indispensable. This is the message of the Communist International to the workers of the world. The Communist International calls the proletariat of the world to the final struggle!"*

3 *There was testimony at the trial that "there was an extended strike at Winnipeg commencing May 15, 1919, during which the production and supply of necessities, transportation, postal and telegraphic communication and fire and sanitary protection were suspended or seriously curtailed."*

analysis of social and economic facts and historical incidents, in the nature of an essay, accompanied by prophecy as to the future course of events, but with no teaching, advice or advocacy of action, would not constitute the advocacy, advice or teaching of a doctrine for the overthrow of government within the meaning of the statute; that a mere statement that unlawful acts might accomplish such a purpose would be insufficient, unless there was a teaching, advising and advocacy of employing such unlawful acts for the purpose of overthrowing government; and that if the jury had a reasonable doubt that the Manifesto did teach, advocate or advise the duty, necessity or propriety of using unlawful means for the overthrowing of organized government, the defendant was entitled to an acquittal.

The defendant's counsel submitted two requests to charge which embodied in substance the statement that to constitute criminal anarchy within the meaning of the statute it was necessary that the language used or published should advocate, teach or advise the duty, necessity or propriety of doing "some definite or immediate act or acts" of force, violence or unlawfulness directed toward the overthrowing of organized government. These were denied further than had been charged. Two other requests to charge embodied in substance the statement that to constitute guilt the language used or published must be "reasonably and ordinarily calculated to incite certain persons" to acts of force, violence or unlawfulness, with the object of overthrowing organized government. These were also denied.

The Appellate Division, after setting forth extracts from the Manifesto and referring to the Left Wing and Communist Programs published in the same issue of the Revolutionary Age, said:[4] "It is perfectly plain that the plan and purpose advocated . . . contemplate the overthrow and destruction of the governments of the United States and of all the States, not by the free action of the majority of the people through the ballot box in electing representatives to authorize a change of government by amending or changing the Constitution, . . . but by immediately organizing the industrial proletariat into militant Socialist unions and at the earliest opportunity through mass strike and force and violence, if necessary, compelling the government to cease to function, and then through a proletarian dictatorship, taking charge of and appropriating all property and administering it and governing through such dictatorship until such time as the proletariat is permitted to administer and govern it. . . . The articles in question are not a discussion of ideas and theories. They advocate a doctrine deliberately determined upon and planned for militantly disseminating a propaganda advocating that it is the duty and necessity of the proletariat engaged in industrial pursuits to organize to such an extent that, by massed strike, the wheels of government may ultimately be stopped and the government overthrown . . ."

The Court of Appeals held that the Manifesto "advocated the overthrow of this government by violence, or by unlawful means."[5] In one of the opinions representing the views of a majority of the court,[6] it was said: "It will be seen . . . that this defendant through the manifesto . . . advocated the destruction of the state and the establishment of the dictatorship of the proletariat. . . . To advocate . . . the commission of this conspiracy or action by mass strike whereby government is crippled, the administration of justice paralyzed, and the health, morals and welfare of a community endangered, and this for the purpose of bringing about a revolution in the state, is to advocate the overthrow of organized government by unlawful means." In the other[7] it was said: "As we read this manifesto . . . we feel entirely clear that the jury were justified in rejecting the view that it was a mere academic and harmless discussion of the advantages of communism and advanced socialism" and "in regarding it as a justification and advocacy of action by one class which would destroy the rights of all other classes and overthrow the state itself by use of revolutionary mass strikes. It is true that there is no advocacy in specific terms of the

[4] *195 App. Div. 773, 782, 790.*

[5] *Five judges, constituting the majority of the court, agreed in this view. 234 N.Y. 132, 138. And the two judges, constituting the minority—who dissented solely on a question as to the construction of the statute which is not here involved—said in reference to the Manifesto: "Revolution for the purpose of overthrowing the present form and the established political system of the United States government by direct means rather than by constitutional means is therein clearly advocated and defended . . ." p. 154.*

[6] *Pages 141, 142.*

[7] *Pages 149, 150.*

use of . . . force or violence. There was no need to be. Some things are so commonly incident to others that they do not need to be mentioned when the underlying purpose is described."

And both the Appellate Division and the Court of Appeals held the statute constitutional.

The specification of the errors relied on relates solely to the specific rulings of the trial court in the matters hereinbefore set out.[8] The correctness of the verdict is not questioned, as the case was submitted to the jury. The sole contention here is, essentially, that as there was no evidence of any concrete result flowing from the publication of the Manifesto or of circumstances showing the likelihood of such result, the statute as construed and applied by the trial court penalizes the mere utterance, as such, of "doctrine" having no quality of incitement, without regard either to the circumstances of its utterance or to the likelihood of unlawful sequences; and that, as the exercise of the right of free expression with relation to government is only punishable "in circumstances involving likelihood of substantive evil," the statute contravenes the due process clause of the Fourteenth Amendment. The argument in support of this contention rests primarily upon the following propositions: 1st, That the "liberty" protected by the Fourteenth Amendment includes the liberty of speech and of the press; and 2nd, That while liberty of expression "is not absolute," it may be restrained "only in circumstances where its exercise bears a causal relation with some substantive evil, consummated, attempted or likely," and as the statute "takes no account of circumstances," it unduly restrains this liberty and is therefore unconstitutional.

The precise question presented, and the only question which we can consider under this writ of error, then is, whether the statute, as construed and applied in this case by the state courts, deprived the defendant of his liberty of expression in violation of the due process clause of the Fourteenth Amendment.

The statute does not penalize the utterance or publication of abstract "doctrine" or academic discussion having no quality of incitement to any concrete action. It is not aimed against mere historical or philosophical essays. It does not restrain the advocacy of changes in the form of government by constitutional and lawful means. What it prohibits is language advocating, advising or teaching the overthrow of organized government by unlawful means. These words imply urging to action. Advocacy is defined in the Century Dictionary as: "1. The act of pleading for, supporting, or recommending; active espousal." It is not the abstract "doctrine" of overthrowing organized government by unlawful means which is denounced by the statute, but the advocacy of action for the accomplishment of that purpose. It was so construed and applied by the trial judge, who specifically charged the jury that: "A mere grouping of historical events and a prophetic deduction from them would neither constitute advocacy, advice or teaching of a doctrine for the overthrow of government by force, violence or unlawful means. [And] if it were a mere essay on the subject, as suggested by counsel, based upon deductions from alleged historical events, with no teaching, advice or advocacy of action, it would not constitute a violation of the statute. . . ."

The Manifesto, plainly, is neither the statement of abstract doctrine nor, as suggested by counsel, mere prediction that industrial disturbances and revolutionary mass strikes will result spontaneously in an inevitable process of evolution in the economic system. It advocates and urges in fervent language mass action which shall progressively foment industrial disturbances and through political mass strikes and revolutionary mass action overthrow and destroy organized parliamentary government. It concludes with a call to action in these words: "The proletariat revolution and the Communist reconstruction of society—*the struggle for these*—is now indispensable. . . . The Communist International calls the proletariat of the world to the final struggle!" This is not the expression of philosophical abstraction, the mere prediction of future events; it is the language of direct incitement.

The means advocated for bringing about the destruction of organized parliamentary government, namely, mass industrial revolts usurping the functions of municipal government, political mass strikes directed against the parliamentary state, and revolutionary mass action for its final destruction, necessarily imply the use of force and violence, and in their essential nature are inherently unlawful in a constitutional government of law and order. That the jury

[8] *Exceptions to all of these rulings had been duly taken.*

were warranted in finding that the Manifesto advocated not merely the abstract doctrine of overthrowing organized government by force, violence and unlawful means, but action to that end, is clear.

For present purposes we may and do assume that freedom of speech and of the press—which are protected by the First Amendment from abridgment by Congress—are among the fundamental personal rights and "liberties" protected by the due process clause of the Fourteenth Amendment from impairment by the States. We do not regard the incidental statement in *Prudential Ins. Co.* v. *Cheek,* 259 U.S. 530, 543, that the Fourteenth Amendment imposes no restrictions on the States concerning freedom of speech, as determinative of this question.[9]

It is a fundamental principle, long established, that the freedom of speech and of the press which is secured by the Constitution, does not confer an absolute right to speak or publish, without responsibility, whatever one may choose, or an unrestricted and unbridled license that gives immunity for every possible use of language and prevents the punishment of those who abuse this freedom. 2 Story on the Constitution, 5th ed., § 1580, p. 634; *Robertson* v. *Baldwin,* 165 U.S. 275, 281; *Patterson* v. *Colorado,* 205 U.S. 454, 462; *Fox* v. *Washington,* 236 U.S. 273, 276; *Schenck* v. *United States,* 249 U.S. 47, 52; *Frohwerk* v. *United States,* 249 U.S. 204, 206; *Debs* v. *United States,* 249 U.S. 211, 213; *Schaefer* v. *United States,* 251 U.S. 466, 474; *Gilbert* v. *Minnesota,* 254 U.S. 325, 332; *Warren* v. *United States,* (C. C. A.) 183 Fed. 718, 721. Reasonably limited, it was said by Story in the passage cited, this freedom is an inestimable privilege in a free government; without such limitation, it might become the scourge of the republic.

That a State in the exercise of its police power may punish those who abuse this freedom by utterances inimical to the public welfare, tending to corrupt public morals, incite to crime, or disturb the public peace, is not open to question. *Robertson* v. *Baldwin, supra,* p. 281; *Patterson* v. *Colorado, supra,* p. 462; *Fox* v. *Washington, supra,* p. 277; *Gilbert* v. *Minnesota, supra,* p. 339; *People* v. *Most,* 171 N.Y. 423, 431; *State* v. *Holm,* 139 Minn. 267, 275; *State* v. *Hennessy,* 114 Wash. 351, 359; *State* v. *Boyd,* 86 N. J. L. 75, 79; *State* v. *McKee,* 73 Conn. 18, 27. Thus it was held by this Court in the *Fox Case,* that a State may punish publications advocating and encouraging a breach of its criminal laws; and, in the *Gilbert Case,* that a State may punish utterances teaching or advocating that its citizens should not assist the United States in prosecuting or carrying on war with its public enemies.

And, for yet more imperative reasons, a State may punish utterances endangering the foundations of organized government and threatening its overthrow by unlawful means. These imperil its own existence as a constitutional State. Freedom of speech and press, said Story (*supra*) does not protect disturbances to the public peace or the attempt to subvert the government. It does not protect publications or teachings which tend to subvert or imperil the government or to impede or hinder it in the performance of its governmental duties. *State* v. *Holm, supra,* p. 275. It does not protect publications prompting the overthrow of government by force; the punishment of those who publish articles which tend to destroy organized society being essential to the security of freedom and the stability of the State. *People* v. *Most, supra,* pp. 431, 432. And a State may penalize utterances which openly advocate the overthrow of the representative and constitutional form of government of the United States and the several States, by violence or other unlawful means. *People* v. *Lloyd,* 304 Ill. 23, 34. See also, *State* v. *Tachin,* 92 N. J. L. 269, 274; and *People* v. *Steelik,* 187 Cal. 361, 375. In short this freedom does not deprive a State of the primary and essential right of self preservation; which, so long as human governments endure, they cannot be denied. *Turner* v. *Williams,* 194 U.S. 279, 294. In *Toledo Newspaper Co.* v. *United States,* 247 U.S. 402, 419, it was said: "The safeguarding and fructification of free and constitutional institutions is the very basis and mainstay upon which the freedom of the press rests, and that freedom, therefore, does not and cannot be held to include the right virtually to destroy such institutions."

By enacting the present statute the

[9] *Compare* Patterson *v.* Colorado, *205 U.S. 454, 462;* Twining *v.* New Jersey, *211 U.S. 78, 108;* Coppage *v.* Kansas, *236 U.S. 1, 17;* Fox *v.* Washington, *236 U.S. 273, 276;* Schaefer *v.* United States, *251 U.S. 466, 474;* Gilbert *v.* Minnesota, *254 U.S. 325, 338;* Meyer *v.* Nebraska, *262 U.S. 390, 399; 2 Story On the Constitution, 5th Ed., § 1950, p. 698.*

State has determined, through its legislative body, that utterances advocating the overthrow of organized government by force, violence and unlawful means, are so inimical to the general welfare and involve such danger of substantive evil that they may be penalized in the exercise of its police power. That determination must be given great weight. Every presumption is to be indulged in favor of the validity of the statute. *Mugler* v. *Kansas,* 123 U.S. 623, 661. And the case is to be considered "in the light of the principle that the State is primarily the judge of regulations required in the interest of public safety and welfare;" and that its police "statutes may only be declared unconstitutional where they are arbitrary or unreasonable attempts to exercise authority vested in the State in the public interest." *Great Northern Ry.* v. *Clara City,* 246 U.S. 434, 439. That utterances inciting to the overthrow of organized government by unlawful means, present a sufficient danger of substantive evil to bring their punishment within the range of legislative discretion, is clear. Such utterances, by their very nature, involve danger to the public peace and to the security of the State. They threaten breaches of the peace and ultimate revolution. And the immediate danger is none the less real and substantial, because the effect of a given utterance cannot be accurately foreseen. The State cannot reasonably be required to measure the danger from every such utterance in the nice balance of a jeweler's scale. A single revolutionary spark may kindle a fire that, smouldering for a time, may burst into a sweeping and destructive conflagration. It cannot be said that the State is acting arbitrarily or unreasonably when in the exercise of its judgment as to the measures necessary to protect the public peace and safety, it seeks to extinguish the spark without waiting until it has enkindled the flame or blazed into the conflagration. It cannot reasonably be required to defer the adoption of measures for its own peace and safety until the revolutionary utterances lead to actual disturbances of the public peace or imminent and immediate danger of its own destruction; but it may, in the exercise of its judgment, suppress the threatened danger in its incipiency. In *People* v. *Lloyd, supra,* p. 35, it was aptly said: "Manifestly, the legislature has authority to forbid the advocacy of a doctrine designed and intended to overthrow the government without waiting until there is a present and imminent danger of the success of the plan advocated. If the State were compelled to wait until the apprehended danger became certain, then its right to protect itself would come into being simultaneously with the overthrow of the government, when there would be neither prosecuting officers nor courts for the enforcement of the law."

We cannot hold that the present statute is an arbitrary or unreasonable exercise of the police power of the State unwarrantably infringing the freedom of speech or press; and we must and do sustain its constitutionality.

This being so it may be applied to every utterance—not too trivial to be beneath the notice of the law—which is of such a character and used with such intent and purpose as to bring it within the prohibition of the statute. This principle is illustrated in *Fox* v. *Washington, supra,* p. 277; *Abrams* v. *United States,* 250 U.S. 616, 624; *Schaefer* v. *United States, supra,* pp. 479, 480; *Pierce* v. *United States,* 252 U.S. 239, 250, 251;[10] and *Gilbert* v. *Minnesota, supra,* p. 333. In other words, when the legislative body has determined generally, in the constitutional exercise of its discretion, that utterances of a certain kind involve such danger of substantive evil that they may be punished, the question whether any specific utterance coming within the prohibited class is likely, in and of itself, to bring about the substantive evil, is not open to consideration. It is sufficient that the statute itself be constitutional and that the use of the language comes within its prohibition.

It is clear that the question in such cases is entirely different from that involved in those cases where the statute merely prohibits certain acts involving the danger of substantive evil, without any reference to language itself, and it is sought to apply its provisions to language used by the defendant for the purpose of bringing about the prohibited results. There, if it be contended that the statute cannot be applied to the language

[10] *This reference is to so much of the decision as relates to the conviction under the third count. In considering the effect of the decisions under the Espionage Act of 1917 and the amendment of 1918, the distinction must be kept in mind between indictments under those provisions which specifically punish certain utterances, and those which merely punish specified acts in general terms, without specific reference to the use of language.*

used by the defendant because of its protection by the freedom of speech or press, it must necessarily be found, as an original question, without any previous determination by the legislative body, whether the specific language used involved such likelihood of bringing about the substantive evil as to deprive it of the constitutional protection. In such cases it has been held that the general provisions of the statute may be constitutionally applied to the specific utterance of the defendant if its natural tendency and probable effect was to bring about the substantive evil which the legislative body might prevent. *Schenck* v. *United States, supra,* p. 51; *Debs* v. *United States, supra,* pp. 215, 216. And the general statement in the *Schenck Case* (p. 52) that the "question in every case is whether the words are used in such circumstances and are of such a nature as to create a clear and present danger that they will bring about the substantive evils,"—upon which great reliance is placed in the defendant's argument—was manifestly intended, as shown by the context, to apply only in cases of this class, and has no application to those like the present, where the legislative body itself has previously determined the danger of substantive evil arising from utterances of a specified character.

The defendant's brief does not separately discuss any of the rulings of the trial court. It is only necessary to say that, applying the general rules already stated, we find that none of them involved any invasion of the constitutional rights of the defendant. It was not necessary, within the meaning of the statute, that the defendant should have advocated "some definite or immediate act or acts" of force, violence or unlawfulness. It was sufficient if such acts were advocated in general terms; and it was not essential that their immediate execution should have been advocated. Nor was it necessary that the language should have been "reasonably and ordinarily calculated to incite certain persons" to acts of force, violence or unlawfulness. The advocacy need not be addressed to specific persons. Thus, the publication and circulation of a newspaper article may be an encouragement or endeavor to persuade to murder, although not addressed to any person in particular. *Queen* v. *Most,* L. R., 7 Q. B. D. 244.

We need not enter upon a consideration of the English common law rule of seditious libel or the Federal Sedition Act of 1798, to which reference is made in the defendant's brief. These are so unlike the present statute, that we think the decisions under them cast no helpful light upon the questions here.

And finding, for the reasons stated, that the statute is not in itself unconstitutional, and that it has not been applied in the present case in derogation of any constitutional right, the judgment of the Court of Appeals is

Affirmed.

Harlan Fiske Stone

☆ 1872–1946 ☆

APPOINTED BY CALVIN COOLIDGE

ASSOCIATE JUSTICE: 1925–1941

APPOINTED BY FRANKLIN D. ROOSEVELT

CHIEF JUSTICE: 1941–1946

Harlan Fiske Stone

by

ALPHEUS THOMAS MASON

HARLAN FISKE STONE, son of a New Hampshire farmer, often said that he attained high judicial position not by definitely planning it but "as the dog went to Dover, leg by leg." He had no set goal. In 1941, the Chief Justice recalled:

> *I was twenty-one in October, 1893. As near as I can remember I was then just setting out in the third year of my college course and beginning to look forward to securing something to do after graduation which would enable me to earn enough to go on to law school. I was also realizing that in those days college and law school education did not grow on every bush for students in my position in life, and I was doing the best I could to get the full advantage of my college courses in the belief that diligence and loyalty to my immediate job would best serve to fit me for some useful achievement in the years ahead.*
>
> *I cannot say I had any thought of being a member of the Supreme Court or any other court, for I believed then, as I do now, that the best insurance of a happy life and reasonable success in it is devotion to one's immediate job and happiness in doing it.*

For twenty-five years (1899–1923) Stone divided his time between law teaching and law practice in New York City. After thirteen years as dean of the Columbia Law School (1910–1923), President Coolidge appointed him, in 1924, Attorney General of the United States. Less than a year later he became an Associate Justice of the Supreme Court. In 1941 President Roosevelt, ignoring partisan politics, appointed him Chief Justice of the United States. Senior Associate at the time of his promotion to the center chair, Stone thus became the only man in American history to occupy consecutively every seat on the supreme bench.

Stone had judicial temperament to a degree that attracted his teachers in

ALPHEUS THOMAS MASON, Professor Emeritus, Princeton University, now Doherty Professor of Law and Government, University of Virginia, is the author of Brandeis: A Free Man's Life; Harlan Fiske Stone: Pillar of the Law; *and* William Howard Taft, Chief Justice.

precollege years. As an Amherst College undergraduate, he wrote his first judicial opinion, which overruled a faculty decision to dismiss a fellow undergraduate without the approval of the student senate which the faculty had joined in establishing. Fellow students at Columbia Law School predicted he would in time sit on the Supreme Court. When these predictions came true Stone, unlike his admiring friends, was content with his lot. For nearly two decades correspondents and politicians prodded him to get into line for the Presidency. Later on, devoted friends urged him to resign from the Court in order to take a cabinet post they thought of as a stepping-stone to the White House. Though flattered by these promptings the Justice showed no interest in a political promotion.

The judicial role was highly congenial to Stone's cast of mind. For him there was nothing more binding and satisfying than service as a judge. It just seemed "to exclude everything else." His method was to proceed slowly, deliberately, and to render judgment only after full inquiry and careful weighing of evidence. This was his way whether the issue fell within the formal context of a law case or required informal judgments on personal and public affairs. Popular passion for causes and scapegoats did not engulf him. When, in 1924, the press shouted loudly that Harry M. Daugherty, his predecessor in the Department of Justice, had left him "a legacy of chaos," Stone denied it. He did not minimize Daugherty's deficiencies, but such unqualified indictment was unjust to the faithful veterans in the Attorney General's office.

Though something of a giant physically and varsity football player in college, he was not a natural athlete, being more at home with a pitchfork or fishing rod. A science major, he was imbued with the scientific method. But the most enduring influence was a course in philosophy under Charles Edward Garman. Of Garman's impact, Stone wrote: "The student's critical faculties were stimulated; he was required *to weigh evidence,* to draw his conclusions and defend them. This method was the ultimate secret of Garman's profound influence on his students. For the first time in their daily lives, they were made to realize that they possessed a thinking apparatus of their own, and that only by use of it could they become masters of their own moral and intellectual destiny."

Experience gained at the Columbia Law School contributed directly to his preparation for the supreme Bench. His lifework of teaching and judging was completely integrated. At the university he had time and opportunity for study and reflection, time to develop ideas as to the nature of law and the function of courts. The methods learned from Professor Garman and the teaching technique employed in his own chemistry laboratory as a Newburyport High School teacher (1894–95) were carried over into his work on the Supreme Court.

Stone's part-time law practice, though helpful, was not closely related to issues of the kind that absorbed him as a Supreme Court Justice. Constitutional law had not been his field of special interest either in teaching or in practice. Before putting on judicial robes he had argued only one case, *Ownbey* v. *Morgan,* 256 U.S. 94 (1921), before the high court. In 1920, as counsel for J. P.

Morgan, he presented oral argument in defense of a judgment obtained under a Delaware statute which had been on the books since early colonial days and with origins going back to the ancient custom of London. In this case he adumbrated what was to become the major theme in his constitutional jurisprudence—judicial self-restraint. The correction of outmoded processes ought to be left, he contended, to legislatures rather than assumed by courts.

This principle of judicial self-restraint he had invoked earlier in a verbal tussle with sociologist and reformer Edward Devine. In 1912, Devine, an editor of *The Survey,* was casting about for causes to explain the waning respect for law. The editor cited as the most important single factor judicial obtuseness to the modern shift from sterile legalism to the urgent demand for social justice. Though Stone did not oppose social justice as a crusader's warcry, he took strong exception to Devine's contention that a statute's economic and social *desirability* was conclusive in determining its constitutionality.

Stone's ideas, incorporated in a series of lectures at Columbia University (*Law and Its Administration,* 1915), have been regarded as conservative, even reactionary. But when, as a Supreme Court Justice, he was equally harsh in his attack on the antithetical idea—that judicial *distrust* of social legislation was enough to condemn it—he was hailed as a liberal. The stand he took as a Supreme Court Justice is entirely consistent with his opposition to Devine's indiscriminate clamor for social justice.

It seems ironical that Stone, a solid, peace-loving man, should have been in the cross fires of controversy throughout his judicial career. On Taft's Court, also during a good part of Chief Justice Hughes's regime, he differed from colleagues on the Right who interposed their own social and economic predilections under the guise of interpreting the Constitution. During his own Chief Justiceship, Stone was at odds with colleagues on the left who were equally set on using their judicial office to further some political preference.

Stone's moderate approach is revealed in his consideration of governmental immunities from taxation—a vexing problem throughout the Chief Justiceships of Taft and Hughes. Rejecting the facile reciprocal immunities doctrine, established in *McCulloch* v. *Maryland* and *Collector* v. *Day,* he held that the federal system does not establish a "total want" of power in one government to tax the instrumentalities of the other. There is "no formula by which that line (which separates those activities having some relation to government from those which are immune) may be plotted in advance. . . . Neither government may destroy the other nor curtail in any substantial manner the exercise of its power." For him the extent and locus of the tax burden are the important considerations. No formula, no facile "black and white" distinction sufficed to resolve the issue. These views are elaborated in *Helvering* v. *Gerhardt,* 304 U.S. 405 (1938) and *Graves* v. *New York ex rel. O'Keefe,* 306 U.S. 466 (1939). Similarly in cases dealing with state regulation of economic affairs and state taxation affecting interstate and foreign commerce, no question-begging formulae as to "business affected with a public interest" or as to direct and indirect effects, was considered adequate. Here, as in the intergovernmental immunities tax cases, he insisted that the legislation be subjected to factual analysis.

Though an habitual Republican, Stone knew that increased use of government power is a necessary concomitant of twentieth century conditions. "Law functions best only when it is fitted to the life of a people," he said. This conviction usually aligned him with Holmes and Brandeis. Uniting the triumvirate was their conviction that a Justice's personal predilections must not thwart the realization of social democracy.

Stone's constitutional jurisprudence, long in the making, crystallized during 1936, the heyday of the Court's resistance to F. D. Roosevelt's sponsorship of government control and regulation. In the leading case of *United States* v. *Butler,* 297 U.S. 1 (1936), the Court voted six to three to outlaw the Agricultural Adjustment Act. Justice Roberts, the majority's spokesman, and Justice Stone, dissenting, were about equally skeptical of the AAA in terms of policy. Their differences concerned the scope of national power and the Court's role in the American system of government. Stone thought that the majority (which in this case included Chief Justice Hughes) had come to believe that any legislation the majority considered "undesirable" was necessarily unconstitutional. The Court had come, as Stone said, to think of itself as "the only agency of government that must be assumed to have capacity to govern."

Justice Roberts raised the forbidding spectacle of "legislative power without restriction or limitation." The majority was haunted by the possibility that Congress might become "a parliament of the whole people, subject to no restrictions save such as are self-imposed." But, Justice Stone countered, consider the status of our own power. The Executive and Congress are restrained by "the ballot box and the processes of democratic government," and "subject to judicial restraint; the only check upon our own exercise of power is our own sense of self-restraint." Precisely because it is unfettered, Stone reasoned, judicial power should be exercised more circumspectly. Roberts' suggestion that congressional action, unless "curtailed by judicial fiat," might be abused was dismissed as hardly rising to "the dignity of argument."

"Such suppositions," Stone declared, "are addressed to the mind accustomed to believe that it is the business of courts to sit in judgment on the wisdom of legislative action. . . . Congress and the courts both unhappily may falter or be mistaken in the performance of their constitutional duty. But interpretation of our great charter of government which proceeds on any assumption that the responsibility for the preservation of our institutions is the exclusive concern of any one of the three branches of government, or that it alone can save them from destruction, is far more likely, in the long run, 'to obliterate the constituent members' of 'an indestructible union of indestructible states' than the frank recognition that language, even of a Constitution, may mean what it says. . . ."

This was not the first (or last) time a dissenter expressly accused the Court of "torturing" the Constitution under the guise of interpreting it. But no other

Justice had used such strong language in condemning the practice. Privately, apropos the AAA decision, Justice Stone observed:

> *We see it frequently enough in the common untrained mind, which is accustomed to think that legislation which it regards as bad or unwise must necessarily be unconstitutional. Where there is a choice of interpretations of a constitutional provision, such a habit of thought is very likely to make a choice of the interpretation which would lessen the possibility of enacting a bad law. The difficulty with this method is that lessening the power to enact bad laws likewise lessens the power to enact good ones, and the judgment of what is bad or good, which is essentially a legislative function, is likely to be affected by the passions and prejudices of the moment. Such an approach to constitutional construction tends to increase the dead areas in the Constitution, the lacunae in which no power exists, neither state nor national, to deal with the problems of government.*

A few months later Stone reaffirmed his indictment, dissenting in the second minimum wage case, *Morehead* v. *New York ex rel. Tipaldo,* 298 U.S. 587, 636 (1936):

> *It is not for the court to resolve doubts whether the remedy by wage regulation is as efficacious as many believe, or is better than some other, or is better even than the blind operation of uncontrolled economic forces. The legislature must be free to choose unless government is to be rendered impotent. The Fourteenth Amendment has no more embedded in the Constitution our preference for some particular set of economic beliefs, than it has adopted, in the name of liberty, the system of theology which we may happen to approve.*

This frontal attack on judicial usurpation by one of the Court's most highly respected members aroused his conservative colleagues. Justice Sutherland, champion of the majority, deplored Stone's telltale revelations and criticized his advocacy of judicial self-restraint as "ill-considered and mischievous." Though the Court's own decisions had wiped out the distinction which judges were accustomed to make between judgment and will, Justice Sutherland boldly reiterated it. " 'Courts . . . declare the law as written,' " he asserted, citing the weighty authority of Thomas M. Cooley.

"The check upon the judge," Sutherland explained, "is that imposed by his oath of office, by the Constitution and by his own conscientious and informed convictions; and since he has the duty to make up his own mind and adjudge accordingly, it is hard to see how there could be any other restraint. . . . If the Constitution . . . stands in the way of desirable legislation, the blame must rest upon that instrument and not upon the Court for enforcing it according to its terms. The meaning of the Constitution does not change with the ebb and flow of events."

In his war on the recalcitrant four (Butler, McReynolds, Sutherland, and Van Devanter, sometimes joined after 1930 by Hughes and Roberts) Stone was frequently allied with Holmes and Brandeis. But they were not always in complete agreement. Though the divergence is less than that separating Stone from his right- and left-wing colleagues, the Illustrious Three were not entirely one as to the nature of the judicial function or how it should be exercised. Holmes, Brandeis, and Stone were all the stronger as a team for differences between them of background, philosophy, and technique. They might indeed be thought of as typifying the American dream of unity in diversity. Each brought a unique contribution to their joint attack on government by judiciary; each pursued a distinct course in driving the assault forward.

Chief among points of agreement was their recognition of the need for a living law, especially their understanding that judicial decisions based on rigid formulae were, as Holmes said, "a slumber, that prolonged means death." All three were acutely aware that the judiciary was most often wounded "in the house of its own guardians." The essence of their creed was judicial self-restraint, recognized as a desirable, rather than a realizable goal.

The bonds uniting them strengthened as the majority's doctrinaire approach became increasingly out of tune with the tenor of the times. Yet differences were evidenced by the fact that they often filed separate opinions in support of the same decision. In dissent Holmes, addicted to generalization and a gifted essayist, tended to avoid the tough issues and failed to meet the majority on its own ground. "This is a pretty good opinion on the point he decides," Stone remarked on one occasion, "but the old man leaves out all the troublesome facts and ignores all the tough points that worried the lower courts." "I wish," he once said in grudging admiration, "I could make my cases sound as easy as Holmes makes his."

Stone's divergence from Brandeis is likewise most vividly portrayed in dissent. When the Court struck down legislation Brandeis favored in terms of policy, the erstwhile People's Attorney did not hesitate to utilize the Court as a forum to persuade others of its wisdom. "I told him [Brandeis] long ago," Holmes commented in 1930, "that he really was an advocate rather than a judge. He is affected by his interest in a cause, and if he feels it he is not detached." Stone took specific exception to Brandeis' judicial activism. In reply on March 1, 1933 to a note in which his colleague invited concurrence with his Florida chain store dissent, *Liggett* v. *Lee,* 288 U.S. 517, 541 (1933), Stone said:

> *Your opinion is a very interesting and powerful document. But . . . it goes further than I am inclined to go, because I do not think it necessary to go that far in order to deal with this case. . . . I think you are too much an advocate of this particular legislation. I have little enthusiasm for it, although I think it constitutional. In any case I think our dissents are more effective if we take the attitude that we are concerned with power and not with the merits of its exercise. . . . Inquiry must be made whether the condition imposed is unconstitutional, and requires examination of the question whether it* [the statute] *is unduly discriminatory, because its method of graduation is unreasonable. My preference is to deal with the latter question as the more immediate, and as requiring no departure from the method of treatment employed in earlier cases.*

The popular notion, vigorously advanced in certain quarters, that Holmes and Brandeis were the "pacemakers" and Stone a sort of judicial "me-too," is not borne out by the record.

"When the time comes," Professor Karl Llewellyn wrote Justice Stone on May 18, 1936, apropos the Cardozo-Stone dissent in the Guffey Coal case, *Carter* v. *Carter Coal Co.,* 298 U.S. 238 (1936), "and the attitude you express becomes the majority attitude, the case should be clear, with the first victory, that (1) a whole new line of doctrine, and perhaps even (2) a whole new body of recorded precedent comes into alternative being together."

Without minimizing the great contributions of Holmes and Brandeis, it is fair to conclude that in a logical, as well as a chronological sense, Stone was the one who, in both the old and the new Court, carried the Holmes-Brandeis tradition to fulfillment. Perforce it fell to him, as his former law clerk Herbert Wechsler says, "to carry through the victory and consolidate the gain."

Stone built by precept and example an impressive catechism for judges. He took seriously the "aphorisms of his trade." This meant thorough probing of ambiguous statutes for the intent of the legislator; it meant according legislation he distrusted the full benefit of the "presumption of constitutionality." Nothing delighted Stone more than to take a morass of conflicting decisions, sort them all out, and then restate the rule with reasons having solid substance. His skillful trimming, elaborating, and blending of the Brandeis and Holmes approach makes him one of the creative judges of our time.

Chief Justice Taft paid high tribute to his pioneering even as he warned of the danger implicit in the former law teacher's methods. Said Taft, "He is quite disposed to be discursive and to write opinions as if he were writing an editorial or a comment for a legal journal, covering as much as he can upon a general subject and thus expressing opinions that have not been thought out by the whole Court. He is a learned lawyer in many ways but his judgments I do not altogether consider safe, and the ease with which he expresses himself and his interest in the whole branch of the law in which he is called upon to give an opinion on a single principle makes the rest of the Court impatient and doubtful. . . . Without impeaching at all his good faith in matters of that sort, we find we have to watch closely the language he uses."

"He was," Judge Learned Hand commented in 1951, "a thorough craftsman as a judge. He steered a course at times very difficult and he had the right—absolutely right—measure of the Court's limitation on constitutional questions, which appears in danger of being lost again."

Among other results of the 1937 judicial revolution, following President Roosevelt's Court-packing effort, was the abandonment of judicial guardianship of property as *the* preferred freedom. Soon thereafter the judiciary began propounding another category of preferred freedoms. Having adopted self-restraint as to regulatory commercial legislation, would the same narrow concept of judicial power apply to enactments allegedly infringing freedom of speech, thought, and religion?

For certain judges the Bill of Rights, especially those enumerated in the First Amendment, constitutes the basis of all our civil and political institutions. Their protection by the judiciary is considered an essential aspect of "free government." Other Justices are disinclined to accord a preferred position to any particular category of rights. Viewing Stone's dissent in *United States* v. *Butler, supra,* as "a lodestar for due regard between legislative and judicial powers," Justice Frankfurter interpreted the 1937 judicial about-face as signifying well-nigh complete withdrawal of the Court from the governing process. At first glance, it does seem paradoxical that Justice Stone, who led the campaign for judicial self-restraint in cases involving government regulation of economic affairs, should have articulated the so-called preferred freedoms doctrine.

The notion of a preferred position for civil liberties is implicit in the free speech opinions of Holmes and Brandeis. In the *Abrams* case, 250 U.S. 616 (1919), Holmes declared that "the theory of our Constitution" is that the ultimate good is better reached through "free trade in ideas." In the *Pierce* case, 252 U.S. 239 (1920), Brandeis spoke of a fundamental right in free men to strive for improved conditions through "new legislation and new institutions." The consequences of the doctrine were never spelled out, nor the full implications faced by either Justice.

Chief Justice Hughes saw much of the Holmes-Brandeis minority opinions on civil liberties become the majority view. Beginning with *Near* v. *Minnesota,* 283 U.S. 697 (1931), legislation affecting free speech and press was, in fact, no longer presumed constitutional. Hughes never formulated this approach in a doctrinal way, nor attempted to state his views definitively, as Brandeis had done in the Whitney case, 274 U.S. 357 (1927). It was not until 1938 that the rationale of preferred freedoms was formulated.

In the otherwise obscure case of *United States* v. *Carolene Products Co.,* 304 U.S. 144 (1938), Stone suggested in the body of the opinion that he would not go so far as to say that no economic legislation would ever violate constitutional restraints, but he did indicate that in this area the Court's role would be strictly confined. As to commercial regulations, in other words, the rule henceforth was judicial *laissez faire.* Attached to this proposition is the famous footnote suggesting special judicial responsibility in the orbit of civil rights. Stone's language is suggestive and tentative:

> *There may be narrower scope for operation of the presumption of constitutionality when legislation appears on its face to be within a specific prohibition of the Constitution, such as those of the first ten amendments, which are deemed equally specific when held to be embraced within the Fourteenth. . . .*
>
> *It is unnecessary to consider now whether legislation which restricts those political processes which can ordinarily be expected to bring about repeal of undesirable legislation, is to be subjected to more exacting judicial scrutiny under the general prohibitions of the Fourteenth Amendment than are most other types of legislation. . . .*
>
> *Nor need we enquire whether similar considerations enter into review of statutes directed at particular religions, . . . or national, . . . or racial minori-*

> *ties, . . . whether prejudice against discrete and insular minorities may be a special condition, which tends seriously to* curtail the operation of those political processes *ordinarily to be relied upon to protect minorities and which may call for a correspondingly more searching judicial inquiry.*

Less than two years after these words were written Hitler unleashed the Nazi forces. With Europe aflame in World War II, the judicial stage was set for a significant debate on the Court's role as guardian of First Amendment freedoms. In the grip of fear as to national security, men have ever seemed ready, as de Tocqueville reminds us, "to fling away their freedom at the first disturbance . . . before they discover how freedom itself serves to promote it." In 1940, the Court voted eight to one to uphold Pennsylvania's compulsory flag salute as applied to Jehovah's Witnesses, *Minersville School District* v. *Gobitis,* 310 U.S. 586 (1940). In justifying his stand the Court's spokesman, Justice Frankfurter, explained that "time and circumstances are surely not irrelevant considerations in resolving the conflicts that we do have to resolve in this particular case. . . . [I]t is relevant to make the adjustment that we have to make within the framework of present circumstances and those that are clearly ahead of us."

For Frankfurter "the ultimate foundation of a free society is the binding tie of cohesive sentiment. . . . Except where the transgression of constitutional liberty is too plain for argument, personal freedom is best maintained—so long as the remedial channels of the democratic process remain open and unobstructed—when it is ingrained in a people's habits and not enforced against popular policy by the coercion of adjudicated law." "The precise issue . . . for us to decide," Frankfurter wrote for the majority,

> *is whether the legislatures of the various states and the authorities in a thousand counties and school districts of this country are barred from determining the appropriateness of various means to evoke that unifying sentiment without which there can ultimately be no liberties, civil or religious. To stigmatize legislative judgment in providing for this universal gesture of respect for the symbol of our national life in the setting of the common school as a lawless inroad on that freedom of conscience which the Constitution protects, would amount to no less than the pronouncement of pedagogical and psychological dogma in a field where Courts possess no marked and certainly no controlling competence. . . .*
>
> *So to hold would in effect make us the school board for the country. That authority has not been given to this Court, nor should we assume it.*

"Judicial review," Frankfurter concluded, "itself a limitation on *popular government,* is a fundamental part of our constitutional scheme. But to the legislature no less than to courts is committed the guardianship of deeply cherished liberties. . . . Where all the effective means of inducing political changes are left free from interference, education in the abandonment of foolish legislation is itself a training in liberty."

In taking this line, the Court's spokesman assumed he was following Stone's rule of judicial self-restraint. In a five-page letter to Stone, Frankfurter spelled out his thought:

> *All my bias and pre-disposition are in favor of giving the fullest elbow room to every variety of religious, political, and economic view. . . . [But] I want to avoid the mistake comparable to that made by those whom* we *criticized when dealing with the control of property. . . . My intention . . . was to use this opinion as a vehicle for preaching the true democratic faith of not relying on the Court for the impossible task of assuring a vigorous, mature, self-protecting and tolerant democracy by bringing the responsibility for a combination of firmness and toleration directly home where it belongs—to the people and their representatives themselves. [Reprinted in Alpheus Mason,* Security Through Freedom, *217–20.*]

"We are not," Frankfurter emphasized, "the primary resolver of the clash. What weighs strongly on me in this case is my anxiety that, while we lean in the direction of the libertarian aspect, we do not exercise our judicial power unduly, and as though we ourselves were legislators by holding with too tight a rein the organs of popular government."

Stone dissented—alone. Any "vulgar intrusion" of the legislators into the domain of conscience, he countered, imposes on the Court a larger responsibility than in passing on statutes which regulate property. Jehovah's Witnesses constituted an unpopular minority subject to prejudice. Corrective political processes could not be effectively invoked in their behalf. If the Justices stood aloof, as the majority decreed, numerically inconsequential groups might become helpless victims of overpowering legislative majorities.

"I am truly sorry not to go along with you," Stone wrote Frankfurter. "The case is one of the relative weight of imponderables and I cannot overcome the feeling that the Constitution tips the scales in favor of religion."

Nor was the majority opinion consistent, as Justice Frankfurter supposed, with what Justice Stone had said in his AAA dissent. With specific reference to Frankfurter's assumption that he was following his colleague's own prescriptions, Stone observed:

> *I am not persuaded that we should refrain from passing upon the legislative judgment as long as the remedial channels of the democratic process remain open and unobstructed. This seems to me no less than the surrender of the constitutional protection of the liberty of small minorities to the popular will.*

As for Justice Frankfurter's notion that liberty is best maintained when instilled in the habits of the people and left to the "forum of public opinion," Stone commented:

> *The Constitution expresses more than the conviction of the people that democratic processes must be preserved at all costs. It is also an expression of faith and a command that freedom of mind and spirit must be preserved, which government must obey, if it is to adhere to that justice and moderation without which no* free government *can exist.*

Underlying the cleavage between Stone and Frankfurter are basic differences as to the meaning and requirements of the American system of government. Justice Frankfurter thought of judicial review as limiting *popular government.* Justice Stone considered judicial review as one of the auxiliaries of *free government.* The founding fathers insisted that the dependence of government on the people must not be carried to the point where individual rights are left unprotected. "A dependence on the people," Madison commented in *Federalist* No. 51, "is, no doubt, the primary control on the government, but experience has taught mankind the necessity of auxiliary precautions." Unless the Court invokes its authority against the majority to preserve the freedoms essential to the functioning of the political process, "no free government can exist." In piloting the bill of rights through the first Congress, Madison explained:

> *The prescriptions in favor of liberty ought to be levelled against that quarter where the greatest danger lies, namely, that which possesses the highest prerogative of power. But this is not found in either the Executive or Legislative departments of Government, but in the body of the people, operating by the majority against the minority. . . . If they* [*the bill of rights*] *are incorporated into the Constitution, independent tribunals of justice will consider themselves in a peculiar manner the guardians of those rights; they will be an impenetrable bulwark against every assumption of power in the Legislative or Executive; they will be naturally led to resist every incroachment upon rights, expressly stipulated for in the Constitution by the declaration of rights.* [Annals of Congress, *1st Cong., 1st Sess. (1789), 454–55, 457.*]

Judicial review is not at war with the principles of "free government"; it is, on the contrary, essential to its implementation.

With the triumph of judicial self-restraint in 1937, government won power to advance the cause of economic security. In the altered context of 1940, might not the Court be expected to safeguard national security by upholding the First Amendment freedoms? Stone believed that the legislature was free to regulate but not repress. To achieve this balance a positive duty of infinite complexity rests squarely on the judiciary. He put it this way:

> *Where there are competing demands of the interests of government and of liberty under the Constitution, and where the performance of governmental functions is brought into conflict with specific constitutional restrictions there must, when that is possible, be reasonable accommodation between them so as to preserve the essentials of both, and . . . it is the function of this Court to determine whether such accommodation is reasonably possible.* Minersville School District *v.* Gobitis, *supra, at 603.*

The presumption of constitutionality—a practical rule of government holding that the people and their representatives should be allowed to correct their own mistakes wherever possible—does not apply in a situation where, for one reason or another, the legislature cannot effectively correct its mistakes. The Court cannot, under the preferred freedoms doctrine, avoid responsibility for the result. It must be alert to legislative intrusions that prevent effective functioning of the political processes; it must extend its benefits to the novel, the unpopular, the unorthodox. "If only popular causes are entitled to enjoy the benefit of constitutional guaranties," Stone observed, "they serve no purpose and could as well not have been written." By standing aloof, as in the flag salute case, the

Court in effect sanctioned the authoritarian policy of coercion in the delicate realm of civil rights.

"The greater the importance of safeguarding the community from incitements to the overthrow of our institutions by force and violence," Chief Justice Hughes declared in 1937, "the more imperative is the need to preserve inviolate the constitutional rights of free speech, free press and free assembly in order to maintain the opportunity for free political discussion, to the end that government may be responsive to the will of the people, and that changes, if desired, may be obtained by peaceful means. Therein lies the security of the Republic, the very foundation of constitutional government." *De Jonge* v. *Oregon,* 299 U.S. 353, 365 (1937).

Stone won this battle. By 1943 three of the Justices (Hugo Black, W. O. Douglas, and Frank Murphy) who had joined the majority upholding the compulsory flag salute against solemnly avowed religious conviction, changed their minds; two new appointees (Jackson and Wiley Rutledge) agreed with Stone's dissent, thus transforming what was formerly a vote of eight to one in favor of the compulsory flag salute into a vote of six to three against it. *West Virginia State Board of Education* v. *Barnette,* 319 U.S. 624 (1943).

Stone has been described as "one of the great architects of civil liberties," as "a substantial but not a groundbreaking adherent to the rights of man." (J. P. Frank, "Harlan Fiske Stone: An Estimate," 9 *Stanford Law Review* 621, 624 [1957].) In 1919 he wrote a fresh and perceptive essay ("The Conscientious Objector," *Columbia University Quarterly,* [October 1919]) on the ages-old problem of conscientious objectors and thus laid the foundation for his opinion in the first flag salute case. He was often, but not invariably, joined with Holmes and Brandeis in defense of individual freedom. On the delicate problem of whether pacifists must take an oath to bear arms as a condition of naturalization, he wavered. In certain of the most hotly contested cases during his Chief Justiceship, including *Bridges* v. *California,* 314 U.S. 252 (1941), *Schneiderman* v. *United States,* 320 U.S. 118 (1943) and *In re Yamashita,* 327 U.S. 1 (1946), he was on the side of restriction. In full flower Stone refused to endorse the "preferred freedom" doctrine itself.

Stone's conception of this doctrine in the *Carolene Products* footnote had been phrased tentatively. He merely raised the question whether, in the case of legislation touching rights protected by the First Amendment, there may be "narrower scope for the operation of the presumption of constitutionality" and whether such legislation might not be "subjected to more exacting judicial scrutiny." He first used the expression in *Jones* v. *Opelika.* "The Constitution, by virtue of the First and Fourteenth Amendments, has put those freedoms [speech and religion] in a preferred position. Their commands are not restricted to cases where the protected privilege is sought out for attack. They extend at least to every form of taxation which, because it is a condition of the exercise of the privilege, is capable of being used to control or suppress it." 316 U.S. 584, 608 (1942). The Court presumed unconstitutionality in this case because the statute was void "on its face." Four years later, when the preferred freedoms doctrine was carried to the point where invalidity was presumed against all legislation relating to First Amendment freedom, Stone dissented.

The case, *Thomas* v. *Collins,* 323 U.S. 515 (1945), involved a Texas law requiring union organizers to register and obtain an organizer's card from the Texas secretary of state. The Texas statute, a regulation on the border between free speech and economic endeavor, was held invalid as extending into the domain of freedom of speech, where infringement of individual rights is contingent upon a clear and present danger. This case, Justice Rutledge observed in the opinion for the Court, requires a line to be drawn between individual freedom and state power. "Choice in that border, now as always delicate, is perhaps more so where the usual presumption supporting legislation is balanced by the preferred place given in our scheme to the great, the indispensable democratic freedoms secured by the First Amendment. . . . That priority gives these liberties a sanctity and sanction not permitting dubious intrusions. And it is the character of the right, not of the limitation, which determines what standard governs the choice."

The fact that the act was, on the face of it, an economic regulation did not protect the law. The right infringed was one of personal liberty. Rutledge went so far as to suggest that "as a matter of principle a requirement of registration of labor organizers would seem generally incompatible with an exercise of . . . free speech and assembly," and cited Stone's Carolene Products footnote as authority. Yet Stone himself, joined by Roberts, Stanley Reed, and Frankfurter, dissented. For them, this was an economic regulation and therefore not within the scope of the preferred freedoms doctrine. Speaking for the minority Justice Roberts used language reminiscent of Stone's own AAA dissent: "We may deem the statutory provision under review unnecessary or unwise, but it is not our function as judges to read our views of policy into a Constitutional guarantee, in order to overthrow a state policy we do not personally approve, by denominating that policy a violation of free speech."

The next year, 1946, when the Court, speaking through Justice Black in *Marsh* v. *Alabama,* 326 U.S. 501 (1946), upheld the right to distribute religious literature in a company town, Stone joined Justice Burton in a vigorous dissent by Justice Reed. Evidently the doctrine of preferred freedoms, as Stone understood it, had been transformed, carried too far.

By 1950, with the change of judicial personnel (particularly the passing of Justices Murphy and Rutledge) and intensification of the Cold War, the "preferred freedoms" doctrine fell into a sort of constitutional limbo. Justice Frankfurter attacked the doctrine fiercely in *Kovacs* v. *Cooper,* 336 U.S. 77 (1949). *Dennis* v. *United States,* 341 U.S. 494 (1951) dealt the doctrine (at least as interpreted by Justice Rutledge and his supporters) a serious blow. Yet even after the Dennis case some substance of the doctrine remained. Dissenting in *Dennis,* Justice Black expressed the hope "that in calmer times, when present pressures, passions and fears subside, this or some later Court will restore the

First Amendment liberties to the high preferred place where they belong in a free society." Black's forecast has since been realized.

Stone's guiding rule was judicial self-restraint, not judicial self-abnegation. Except for the short period between 1937 and 1941, he was destined to invoke this principle against the dominant tides of his time. Before 1937 he criticized right-wing colleagues who equated what they considered economically undesirable legislation with invalidity. After the Court was reconstructed in 1941 he was at loggerheads with judges, especially those on the extreme left, equally intent, he thought, on reading their preferences into the Constitution.

As leader of the Roosevelt Court, the Chief Justice met new antagonists on all sides. His convictions about the Constitution and judging induced him to call a halt somewhat in advance of a tenuous, unstable majority of his colleagues. Examples of this divergence are numerous. In the familiar field of intergovernmental tax immunities, he would not sanction Justice Frankfurter's formula forbidding merely discriminatory federal taxation—that is, except where the tax hits the "state as a state." Preferring now, as in the past, "to deal with the matter empirically," Stone refused to go along. Reiterating the stand he had taken on the Taft Court, the Chief Justice said:

> *The problem is not one to be solved by a formula, but we may look to the structure of the Constitution as our guide to decision. "In a broad sense, the taxing power of either government, even when exercised in a manner admittedly necessary and proper, unavoidably has some effect upon the other. The burden of federal taxation necessarily sets an economic limit to the practical operation of the taxing power of the states, and vice versa. . . .*
>
> *"But neither government may destroy the other nor curtail in any substantial manner the exercise of its powers. Hence the limitation upon the taxing power of each, so far as it affects the other, must receive a practical construction which permits both to function with the minimum of interference each with the other; and that limitation cannot be so varied or extended as seriously to impair either the taxing power of the government imposing the tax . . . or the appropriate exercise of the functions of the government affected by it."* New York *v.* United States, *326 U.S. 571, 589–90 (1945)*.

Stone also called a halt when his colleagues carried "to absurd lengths the deference which courts must pay to the rulings of administrative agencies." "It is just ridiculous," he exploded on one occasion, "to say that the money collectors in the Treasury Department know better than we or the federal courts what Congress intended to do by the legislation here involved." Far more than his colleagues he was inclined to scrutinize National Labor Relations Board rulings. In advising Justice Jackson to include in an opinion the exact wording of a modified board order, he warned: "Otherwise interpretation of what you have said will become a subject of debate and the National Labor Relations Board, with its usual tendencies, will reframe the order to suit its own purposes."

During the early years of labor's march to power Stone was able to move forthrightly because he felt that both Constitution and legislation clearly sustained the workingman's claim. But when the cases became more subtle, and the

National Labor Relations Board reached out for authority not plainly written into the statute, the Chief Justice retreated from the thesis he had advanced in his Harvard Tercentenary address of 1936 as to the judge's responsibility for rounding out statutory law. Stone, *The Common Law in the United States,* 50 Harvard Law Review 4 (1936). Repeated conflicts with Black and Douglas, whom he felt were prone to resolve all doubts in labor's favor, alienated him, and led him to believe that he was again, as in 1928 and 1936, confronted with judges too anxious to write their predilections into law. Though he left the qualification of labor's great gains largely to others, the record discloses diminishing sympathy with the majority views.

The last day the Chief Justice sat on the bench, his famous dictum "Courts are not the only agency of government that must be presumed to have capacity to govern" resounded as a grim valedictory.

Under the naturalization act of 1948, the oath of citizenship requires the applicant "to support and defend the Constitution." Should this provision be interpreted so as to bar anyone who refuses the oath to bear arms? In three previous cases the Court had turned down pacifists' pleas for citizenship on just this ground. In two of them Stone himself had dissented. Should the Court or Congress correct this judicial "error" in the construction of the naturalization laws? A majority claimed this authority for the Court. Stone dissented.

"With three other Justices of the Court," he observed, "I dissented in the Macintosh and Bland cases, for reasons which the Court now adopts as grounds for overruling them." A majority had then rejected his arguments. Now, he said, "the question, which for me is decisive in the present case, is whether Congress had likewise rejected that construction by its subsequent legislative action." The record clearly indicated to him a negative answer. Therefore, he concluded:

> *It is the responsibility of Congress, in reenacting a statute, to make known its purpose in a controversial matter of interpretation of its former language . . . it is not lightly to be implied that Congress has failed to perform it and has delegated to this Court the responsibility of giving new content to language deliberately readopted after this Court has construed it. For us to make such an assumption is to discourage, if not to deny, legislative responsibility.* Girouard v. United States, *328 U.S. 61, 76 (1946).*

Stone was creative, John P. Frank has written, "within the boundaries of the known." Any marked departure from existing principles left him "a little hurt, a little bewildered and sometimes even a little angry." When, in 1945, he found himself pitted against judicial activists on the Left, he dolefully reminisced:

> *My more conservative brethren in the old days enacted their own economic prejudice into law. What they did placed in jeopardy a great and useful institution of government. The pendulum has now swung to the other extreme, and history is repeating itself. The Court is now in as much danger of becoming a legislative Constitution-making body, enacting into law its own predilections, as it was then. The only difference is that now the interpretations of statutes whether "over-conservative" or "over-liberal" can be corrected by Congress.*

Stone's conception of judicial conduct was almost monastic. He strove against almost insuperable odds to keep the Court within what he considered appropriate bounds. A judge should limit himself precisely to the issue at hand. Contradictory precedents should usually be specifically overruled. The Court ought, he said, to "correct its own errors, even if I helped in making them." Each case should be dealt with in the light of precedent, facts, legislative intent, and the judge's own reason and values. Stone's judicial technique, in essence, stressed complexity. To oversimplify was convenient for the pedagogue, but disastrous for the judge. In constitutional law the "perpetual question" is where to draw the line between a variety of competing interests—between individual liberty and government action for the larger public good, between state policy designed to promote local interests and the larger welfare which the Constitution commits to the federal government. The judge must make an appraisal of the past and of the present. He must open his eyes to all the conditions and circumstances. His own idea of reasonableness will inevitably enter into the calculation. He would do well to set all this against "a considered judgment of what the community may regard as within the limits of the reasonable." In a process so intricate, the judge who rests on formula risks disaster. Life does not conform to legal categories or even to judicial decisions of the Supreme Court. The "sober second thought of the community," Stone said, "is the firm base on which all law must ultimately rest."

Stone urged restraint, not because he believed a judge's preference should not enter law, but precisely because it inevitably did. The sharp barbs of his thought were intended for the flesh of judges, both Right and Left, who, without taking the trouble to weigh social values, *prematurely* enforced private convictions as law. Awareness of the subjective element in judging must end in curbing it. He strove not to eliminate subjectivity, but to tame it. Recognition of self was to him the first step toward judicial self-control.

The overall appraisal of one privileged to observe Justice Stone in action is that he was "a careful and wise judge, who after two industrious decades has left the mark of his wisdom on almost every type of case which comes before the Supreme Court." As Chief Justice, Stone was less impressive. For a great variety of reasons he experienced difficulty in "massing" the Court. In 1929, when it was rumored that President Hoover might elevate Stone as Taft's successor, the Chief Justice had opposed it, saying that the Associate Justice was "not a great leader and would have a great deal of trouble in massing the Court." The bench Stone headed was the most frequently divided, the most openly quarrelsome in history. If success be measured by the Chief's ability to maintain the *appearance* of harmony, he certainly was a failure. There can be little doubt that his solid convictions handicapped him. He refused to use the high-pressure tactics of Chief Justice Taft and Chief Justice Hughes. Nor would he resort to ingenious reasoning, good fellowship, the caucus, or other familiar political devices useful in keeping the Court united; much less would he try to create that impression. Believing profoundly in freedom of expression for others no less than for himself, he was slow to cut off debate. He never surrendered his conviction that the Court's function was not simply to decide cases, but, through the clash of ideas, to find solutions that were considerate of the past, adequate for the present, and no obstacle to the future.

Stone had an abiding faith in "free government" and in judicial review as an essential adjunct to its operation. He believed that radical change is neither necessary nor generally desirable. Drastic change could be avoided, he believed, "if fear of legislative action, which Courts distrust or think unwise, is not overemphasized in interpreting the document." A free society needs continuity, "not of rules but of aims and ideals which will enable government in all the various crises of human affairs, to continue to function and to perform its appointed task within the bounds of reasonableness."

SELECTED BIBLIOGRAPHY

Stone's papers are on deposit at the Library of Congress. His writings include: *Law and Its Administration* (New York, 1915); "The Common Law in the United States," 50 *Harvard Law Review* 4 (1936); "Fifty Years Work of the Supreme Court," 14 *American Bar Association Journal* 428 (1928); "Obedience to Law and Social Change," 5 *New Hampshire Bar Association Proceedings* 3 (1925); "Some Aspects of the Problem of Law Simplification," 23 *Columbia Law Review* 319 (1923); "The Public Influence of the Bar," 48 *Harvard Law Review* 1 (1934). The authorized biography is Alpheus Thomas Mason, *Harlan Fiske Stone: Pillar of the Law* (New York, 1956). More specialized aspects of Stone's thought and work are discussed in S. J. Konefsky, *Chief Justice Stone and the Supreme Court* (New York, 1945); J. P. Frank, "Harlan Fiske Stone: An Estimate," 9 *Stanford Law Review* 621 (1957); N. T. Dowling, "Mr. Justice Stone and the Constitution," 36 *Columbia Law Review* 351 (1936); Learned Hand, "Chief Justice Stone's Conception of the Judicial Function," 46 *Columbia Law Review* 696 (1946); Herbert Weschsler, "Stone and the Constitution," 46 *Columbia Law Review* 793 (1946); W. O. Douglas, "Chief Justice Stone," 46 *Columbia Law Review* 764 (1946); N. T. Dowling, "The Methods of Mr. Justice Stone in Constitutional Cases," 41 *Columbia Law Review* 1160 (1941).

Harlan Fiske Stone

REPRESENTATIVE OPINIONS

UNITED STATES v. DARBY LUMBER CO., 312 U.S. 1 (1940)

The New Deal's Fair Labor Standards Act of 1938 provided for the fixing of minimum wages and maximum hours for employees in industries whose products were shipped in interstate commerce. A Georgia manufacturer challenged the act as unauthorized under the commerce clause. Speaking for a unanimous Court, Justice Stone harkened back to Chief Justice Marshall. The power of Congress under the commerce clause was the power to "prescribe the rule by which commerce is governed." Like Marshall also, Stone stressed judicial humility. "The motive and purpose of a regulation of interstate commerce are matters for the legislative judgment upon the exercise of which the Constitution places no restriction and over which the courts are given no control." In expressly overruling *Hammer* v. *Dagenhart,* 247 U.S. 251, the Court enthroned Justice Holmes' classic dissent of 1918.

MR. JUSTICE STONE delivered the opinion of the Court.

The two principal questions raised by the record in this case are, *first,* whether Congress has constitutional power to prohibit the shipment in interstate commerce of lumber manufactured by employees whose wages are less than a prescribed minimum or whose weekly hours of labor at that wage are greater than a prescribed maximum, and, *second,* whether it has power to prohibit the employment of workmen in the production of goods "for interstate commerce" at other than prescribed wages and hours. A subsidiary question is whether in connection with such prohibitions Congress can require the employer subject to them to keep records showing the hours worked each day and week by each of his employees including those engaged "in the production and manufacture of goods to-wit, lumber, for 'interstate commerce.'"

Appellee demurred to an indictment found in the district court for southern Georgia charging him with violation of § 15 (a) (1) (2) and (5) of the Fair Labor Standards Act of 1938; 52 Stat. 1060, 29 U. S. C. § 201, *et seq.* The district court sustained the demurrer and quashed the indictment and the case comes here on direct appeal under § 238 of the Judicial Code as amended, 28 U. S. C. § 345, and § 682, Title 18 U. S. C., 34 Stat. 1246, which authorizes an appeal to this Court when the judgment sustaining the demurrer "is based upon the invalidity or construction of the statute upon which the indictment is founded."

The Fair Labor Standards Act set up a comprehensive legislative scheme for preventing the shipment in interstate commerce of certain products and commodities produced in the United States under labor conditions as respects wages and hours which fail to conform to standards set up by the Act. Its purpose, as we judicially know from the declaration of policy in § 2 (a) of the Act,[1] and the reports of Congressional committees proposing the legislation, S. Rept. No. 884, 75th Cong. 1st Sess.; H. Rept. No. 1452, 75th Cong. 1st Sess.; H. Rept. No. 2182, 75th Cong. 3d Sess., Conference Report, H. Rept. No. 2738, 75th Cong. 3d Sess., is to exclude from interstate commerce goods produced for the commerce and to prevent their production for interstate commerce, under conditions detrimental to the maintenance of the minimum standards of living necessary for health and general well-being; and to prevent the use of interstate commerce as the means of competition in the distribution of goods so produced, and as the means of spreading and perpetuating such substandard labor conditions among the workers of the several states. The Act also sets up an administrative procedure whereby those standards may from time to time be modified generally as to industries subject to the Act or within an industry in accordance with specified standards, by an administrator acting in collaboration with "Industry Committees" appointed by him.

Section 15 of the statute prohibits certain specified acts and § 16 (a) punishes willful violation of it by a fine of not more than $10,000 and punishes each conviction after the first by imprisonment of not more than six months or by the specified fine or both. Section 15 (1) makes unlawful the shipment in interstate commerce of any goods "in the production of which any employee was employed in violation of section 6 or section 7," which provide, among other things, that during the first year of operation of the Act a minimum wage of 25 cents per hour shall be paid to employees "engaged in [interstate] commerce or the production of goods for [interstate] commerce," § 6, and that the maximum hours of employment for employees "engaged in commerce or the production of goods for commerce" without increased compensation for overtime, shall be forty-four hours a week. § 7.

Section 15 (a) (2) makes it unlawful to violate the provisions of §§ 6 and 7 including the minimum wage and maximum hour requirements just mentioned for employees engaged in production of goods for commerce. Section 15 (a) (5) makes it unlawful for an employer subject to the Act to violate § 11 (c) which requires him to keep such records of the persons employed by him and of their wages and hours of employment as the administrator shall prescribe by regulation or order.

The indictment charges that appellee is engaged, in the State of Georgia, in the business of acquiring raw materials, which he manufactures into finished lumber with the intent, when manufactured, to ship it in interstate commerce to customers outside the state, and that he does in fact so ship a large part of the lumber so produced. There are numerous counts charging appellee with the shipment in interstate commerce from Georgia to points outside the state of lumber in the production of which, for interstate commerce, appellee has employed workmen at less than the prescribed minimum wage or more than the prescribed maximum hours without payment to them of any wage for overtime. Other counts charge the employment by appellee of workmen in the production of lumber for interstate commerce at wages at less than 25 cents an hour or for more than the maximum hours per week

[1] *Sec. 2. (a) The Congress hereby finds that the existence, in industries engaged in commerce or in the production of goods for commerce, of labor conditions detrimental to the maintenance of the minimum standard of living necessary for health, efficiency, and general well-being of workers (1) causes commerce and the channels and instrumentalities of commerce to be used to spread and perpetuate such labor conditions among the workers of the several States; (2) burdens commerce and the free flow of goods in commerce; (3) constitutes an unfair method of competition in commerce; (4) leads to labor disputes burdening and obstructing commerce and the free flow of goods in commerce; and (5) interferes with the orderly and fair marketing of goods in commerce.*

Section 3 (b) defines "commerce" as "trade, commerce, transportation, transmission, or communication among the several States or from any State to any place outside thereof."

without payment to them of the prescribed overtime wage. Still another count charges appellee with failure to keep records showing the hours worked each day a week by each of his employees as required by § 11 (c) and the regulation of the administrator, Title 29, Ch. 5, Code of Federal Regulations, Part 516, and also that appellee unlawfully failed to keep such records of employees engaged "in the production and manufacture of goods, to-wit lumber, for interstate commerce."

The demurrer, so far as now relevant to the appeal, challenged the validity of the Fair Labor Standards Act under the Commerce Clause and the Fifth and Tenth Amendments. The district court quashed the indictment in its entirety upon the broad grounds that the Act, which it interpreted as a regulation of manufacture within the states, is unconstitutional. It declared that manufacture is not interstate commerce and that the regulation by the Fair Labor Standards Act of wages and hours of employment of those engaged in the manufacture of goods which it is intended at the time of production "may or will be" after production "sold in interstate commerce in part or in whole" is not within the congressional power to regulate interstate commerce.

The effect of the court's decision and judgment is thus to deny the power of Congress to prohibit shipment in interstate commerce of lumber produced for interstate commerce under the proscribed substandard labor conditions of wages and hours, its power to penalize the employer for his failure to conform to the wage and hour provisions in the case of employees engaged in the production of lumber which he intends thereafter to ship in interstate commerce in part or in whole according to the normal course of his business and its power to compel him to keep records of hours of employment as required by the statute and the regulations of the administrator.

The case comes here on assignments by the Government that the district court erred insofar as it held that Congress was without constitutional power to penalize the acts set forth in the indictment, and appellee seeks to sustain the decision below on the grounds that the prohibition by Congress of those Acts is unauthorized by the Commerce Clause and is prohibited by the Fifth Amendment. The appeal statute limits our jurisdiction on this appeal to a review of the determination of the district court so far only as it is based on the validity or construction of the statute. *United States* v. *Borden Co.,* 308 U.S. 188, 193–195, and cases cited. Hence we accept the district court's interpretation of the indictment and confine our decision to the validity and construction of the statute.

The prohibition of shipment of the proscribed goods in interstate commerce. Section 15 (a) (1) prohibits, and the indictment charges, the shipment in interstate commerce, of goods produced for interstate commerce by employees whose wages and hours of employment do not conform to the requirements of the Act. Since this section is not violated unless the commodity shipped has been produced under labor conditions prohibited by § 6 and § 7, the only question arising under the commerce clause with respect to such shipments is whether Congress has the constitutional power to prohibit them.

While manufacture is not of itself interstate commerce, the shipment of manufactured goods interstate is such commerce and the prohibition of such shipment by Congress is indubitably a regulation of the commerce. The power to regulate commerce is the power "to prescribe the rule by which commerce is governed." *Gibbons* v. *Ogden,* 9 Wheat. 1, 196. It extends not only to those regulations which aid, foster and protect the commerce, but embraces those which prohibit it. *Reid* v. *Colorado,* 187 U.S. 137; *Lottery Case,* 188 U.S. 321; *United States* v. *Delaware & Hudson Co.,* 213 U.S. 366; *Hoke* v. *United States,* 227 U.S. 308; *Clark Distilling Co.* v. *Western Maryland Ry. Co.,* 242 U.S. 311; *United States* v. *Hill,* 248 U.S. 420; *McCormick & Co.* v. *Brown,* 286 U.S. 131. It is conceded that the power of Congress to prohibit transportation in interstate commerce includes noxious articles, *Lottery Case, supra; Hipolite Egg Co.* v. *United States,* 220 U.S. 45; cf. *Hoke* v. *United States, supra;* stolen articles, *Brooks* v. *United States,* 267 U.S. 432; kidnapped persons, *Gooch* v. *United States,* 297 U.S. 124, and articles such as intoxicating liquor or convict made goods, traffic in which is forbidden or restricted by the laws of the state of destination. *Kentucky Whip & Collar Co.* v. *Illinois Central R. Co.,* 299 U.S. 334.

But it is said that the present prohibition falls within the scope of none of these categories; that while the prohibition is nominally a regulation of the commerce its motive or purpose is regulation of wages and hours of persons engaged in manufacture, the control of which has been reserved to the states and upon which Georgia and some of the states of destination have placed no restriction; that the effect of the present statute is not to exclude the proscribed articles from interstate commerce in aid of state regulation as in *Kentucky Whip & Collar Co.* v. *Illinois Central R. Co., supra,* but instead, under the guise of a regulation of interstate commerce, it undertakes to regulate wages and hours within the state contrary to the policy of the state which has elected to leave them unregulated.

The power of Congress over interstate commerce "is complete in itself, may be exercised to its utmost extent, and acknowledges no limitations other than are prescribed in the Constitution." *Gibbons* v. *Ogden, supra,* 196. That power can neither be enlarged nor diminished by the exercise or non-exercise of state power. *Kentucky Whip & Collar Co.* v. *Illinois Central R. Co., supra.* Congress, following its own conception of public policy concerning the restrictions which may appropriately be imposed on interstate commerce, is free to exclude from the commerce articles whose use in the states for which they are destined it may conceive to be injurious to the public health, morals or welfare, even though the state has not sought to regulate their use. *Reid* v. *Colorado, supra; Lottery Case, supra; Hipolite Egg Co.* v. *United States, supra; Hoke* v. *United States, supra.*

Such regulation is not a forbidden invasion of state power merely because either its motive or its consequence is to restrict the use of articles of commerce within the states of destination; and is not prohibited unless by other Constitutional provisions. It is no objection to the assertion of the power to regulate interstate commerce that its exercise is attended by the same incidents which attend the exercise of the police power of the states. *Seven Cases* v. *United States,* 239 U.S. 510, 514; *Hamilton* v. *Kentucky Distilleries & Warehouse Co.,* 251 U.S. 146, 156; *United States* v. *Carolene Products Co.,* 304 U.S. 144, 147; *United States* v. *Appalachian Electric Power Co.,* 311 U.S. 377.

The motive and purpose of the present regulation are plainly to make effective the Congressional conception of public policy that interstate commerce should not be made the instrument of competition in the distribution of goods produced under substandard labor conditions, which competition is injurious to the commerce and to the states from and to which the commerce flows. The motive and purpose of a regulation of interstate commerce are matters for the legislative judgment upon the exercise of which the Constitution places no restriction and over which the courts are given no control. *McCray* v. *United States,* 195 U.S. 27; *Sonzinsky* v. *United States,* 300 U.S. 506, 513 and cases cited. "The judicial cannot prescribe to the legislative department of the government limitations upon the exercise of its acknowledged power." *Veazie Bank* v. *Fenno,* 8 Wall. 533. Whatever their motive and purpose, regulations of commerce which do not infringe some constitutional prohibition are within the plenary power conferred on Congress by the Commerce Clause. Subject only to that limitation, presently to be considered, we conclude that the prohibition of the shipment interstate of goods produced under the forbidden substandard labor conditions is within the constitutional authority of Congress.

In the more than a century which has elapsed since the decision of *Gibbons* v. *Ogden,* these principles of constitutional interpretation have been so long and repeatedly recognized by this Court as applicable to the Commerce Clause, that there would be little occasion for repeating them now were it not for the decision of this Court twenty-two years ago in *Hammer* v. *Dagenhart,* 247 U.S. 251. In that case it was held by a bare majority of the Court over the powerful and now classic dissent of Mr. Justice Holmes setting forth the fundamental issues involved, that Congress was without power to exclude the products of child labor from interstate commerce. The reasoning and conclusion of the Court's opinion there cannot be reconciled with the conclusion which we have reached, that the power of Congress under the Commerce Clause is plenary to exclude any article from interstate commerce subject only to the specific prohibitions of the Constitution.

Hammer v. *Dagenhart* has not been followed. The distinction on which the decision was rested that Congressional power to prohibit interstate commerce is limited to articles which in themselves have some harmful or deleterious property—a distinction which was novel when made and unsupported by any provision of the Constitution—has long since been abandoned. *Brooks* v. *United States, supra; Kentucky Whip & Collar Co.* v. *Illinois Central R. Co., supra; Electric Bond & Share Co.* v. *Securities & Exchange Comm'n,* 303 U.S. 419; *Mulford* v. *Smith,* 307 U.S. 38. The thesis of the opinion that the motive of the prohibition or its effect to control in some measure the use or production within the states of the article thus excluded from the commerce can operate to deprive the regulation of its constitutional authority has long since ceased to have force. *Reid* v. *Colorado, supra; Lottery Case, supra; Hipolite Egg Co.* v. *United States, supra; Seven Cases* v. *United States, supra,* 514; *Hamilton* v. *Kentucky Distilleries & Warehouse Co., supra,* 156; *United States* v. *Carolene Products Co., supra,* 174. And finally we have declared "The authority of the federal government over interstate commerce does not differ in extent or character from that retained by the states over intrastate commerce." *United States* v. *Rock Royal Co-operative,* 307 U.S. 533, 569.

The conclusion is inescapable that *Hammer* v. *Dagenhart,* was a departure from the principles which have prevailed in the interpretation of the Commerce Clause both before and since the decision and that such vitality, as a precedent, as it then had has long since been exhausted. It should be and now is overruled.

Validity of the wage and hour requirements. Section 15 (a) (2) and §§ 6 and 7 require employers to conform to the wage and hour provisions with respect to all employees engaged in the production of goods for interstate commerce. As appellee's employees are not alleged to be "engaged in interstate commerce" the validity of the prohibition turns on the question whether the employment, under other than the prescribed labor standards, of employees engaged in the production of goods for interstate commerce is so related to the commerce and so affects it as to be within the reach of the power of Congress to regulate it.

To answer this question we must at the outset determine whether the particular acts charged in the counts which are laid under § 15 (a) (2) as they were construed below, constitute "production for commerce" within the meaning of the statute. As the Government seeks to apply the statute in the indictment, and as the court below construed the phrase "produced for interstate commerce," it embraces at least the case where an employer engaged, as is appellee, in the manufacture and shipment of goods in filling orders of extrastate customers, manufactures his product with the intent or expectation that according to the normal course of his business all or some part of it will be selected for shipment to those customers.

Without attempting to define the precise limits of the phrase, we think the acts alleged in the indictment are within the sweep of the statute. The obvious purpose of the Act was not only to prevent the interstate transportation of the proscribed product, but to stop the initial step toward transportation, production with the purpose of so transporting it. Congress was not unaware that most manufacturing businesses shipping their product in interstate commerce make it in their shops without reference to its ultimate destination and then after manufacture select some of it for shipment interstate and some intrastate according to the daily demands of their business, and that it would be practically impossible, without disrupting manufacturing businesses, to restrict the prohibited kind of production to the particular pieces of lumber, cloth, furniture or the like which later move in interstate rather than intrastate commerce. Cf. *United States* v. *New York Central R. Co.,* 272 U.S. 457, 464.

The recognized need of drafting a workable statute and the well known circumstances in which it was to be applied are persuasive of the conclusion, which the legislative history supports, S. Rept. No. 884, 75th Cong. 1st Sess., pp. 7 and 8; H. Rept. No. 2738, 75th Cong. 3d Sess., p. 17, that the "production for commerce" intended includes at least production of goods, which, at the time of production, the employer, according to the normal course of his business, intends or expects to move in interstate commerce although, through the exigencies of the business, all of the goods may not thereafter actually enter interstate commerce.[2]

There remains the question whether such restriction on the production of goods for commerce is a permissible exercise of the commerce power. The power of Congress over interstate commerce is not confined to the regulation of commerce among the states. It extends to those activities intrastate which so affect interstate commerce or the exercise of the power of Congress over it as to make regulation of them appropriate means to the attainment of a legitimate end, the exercise of the granted power of Congress to regulate interstate commerce. See *McCulloch* v. *Maryland,* 4 Wheat. 316, 421. Cf. *United States* v. *Ferger,* 250 U.S. 199.

While this Court has many times found

[2] *Cf. Administrator's Opinion, Interpretative Bulletin No. 5, 1940 Wage and Hour Manual, p. 131* et seq.

state regulation of interstate commerce, when uniformity of its regulation is of national concern, to be incompatible with the Commerce Clause even though Congress has not legislated on the subject, the Court has never implied such restraint on state control over matters intrastate not deemed to be regulations of interstate commerce or its instrumentalities even though they affect the commerce. *Minnesota Rate Cases,* 230 U.S. 352, 398 *et seq.,* and case cited; 410 *et seq.,* and cases cited. In the absence of Congressional legislation on the subject state laws which are not regulations of the commerce itself or its instrumentalities are not forbidden even though they affect interstate commerce. *Kidd* v. *Pearson,* 128 U.S. 1; *Bacon* v. *Illinois,* 227 U.S. 504; *Heisler* v. *Thomas Colliery Co.,* 260 U.S. 245; *Oliver Iron Co.* v. *Lord,* 262 U.S. 172.

But it does not follow that Congress may not by appropriate legislation regulate intrastate activities where they have a substantial effect on interstate commerce. See *Santa Cruz Fruit Packing Co.* v. *National Labor Relations Board,* 303 U.S. 453, 466. A recent example is the National Labor Relations Act for the regulation of employer and employee relations in industries in which strikes, induced by unfair labor practices named in the Act, tend to disturb or obstruct interstate commerce. See *National Labor Relations Board* v. *Jones & Laughlin Steel Corp.,* 301 U.S. 1, 38, 40; *National Labor Relations Board* v. *Fainblatt,* 306 U.S. 601, 604, and cases cited. But long before the adoption of the National Labor Relations Act this Court had many times held that the power of Congress to regulate interstate commerce extends to the regulation through legislative action of activities intrastate which have a substantial effect on the commerce or the exercise of the Congressional power over it.[3]

In such legislation Congress has sometimes left it to the courts to determine whether the intrastate activities have the prohibited effect on the commerce, as in the Sherman Act. It has sometimes left it to an administrative board or agency to determine whether the activities sought to be regulated or prohibited have such effect, as in the case of the Interstate Commerce Act, and the National Labor Relations Act, or whether they come within the statutory definition of the prohibited Act, as in the Federal Trade Commission Act. And sometimes Congress itself has said that a particular activity affects the commerce, as it did in the present Act, the Safety Appliance Act and the Railway Labor Act. In passing on the validity of legislation of the class last mentioned the only function of courts is to determine whether the particular activity regulated or prohibited is within the reach of the federal power. See *United States* v. *Ferger, supra; Virginian Ry. Co.* v. *Federation,* 300 U.S. 515, 553.

Congress, having by the present Act adopted the policy of excluding from interstate commerce all goods produced for the commerce which do not conform to the specified labor standards, it may choose the means reasonably adapted to the attainment of the permitted end, even though they involve control of intrastate activities. Such legislation has often been sustained with respect to powers, other than the commerce power granted to the national government, when the means chosen, although not themselves within the granted power, were nevertheless deemed appropriate aids to the accomplishment of some purpose within an admitted power of the national government. See *Jacob Ruppert, Inc.* v. *Caffey,* 251 U.S. 264; *Everard's Breweries* v. *Day,* 265 U.S. 545, 560; *Westfall* v. *United States,* 274 U.S.

[3] *It may prohibit wholly intrastate activities which, if permitted, would result in restraint of interstate commerce.* Coronado Coal Co. *v.* United Mine Workers, *268 U.S. 295, 310;* Local 167 *v.* United States, *291 U.S. 293, 297. It may regulate the activities of a local grain exchange shown to have an injurious effect on interstate commerce.* Chicago Board of Trade *v.* Olsen, *262 U.S. 1. It may regulate intrastate rates of interstate carriers where the effect of the rates is to burden interstate commerce.* Houston, E. & W. Texas Ry. Co. *v.* United States, *234 U.S. 342;* Railroad Commission of Wisconsin *v.* Chicago, B. & Q. R. Co., *257 U.S. 563;* United States *v.* Louisiana, *290 U.S. 70, 74;* Florida *v.* United States, *292 U.S. 1. It may compel the adoption of safety appliances on rolling stock moving intrastate because of the relation to and effect of such appliances upon interstate traffic moving over the same railroad.* Southern Ry. Co. *v.* United States, *222 U.S. 20. It may prescribe maximum hours for employees engaged in intrastate activity connected with the movement of any train, such as train dispatchers and telegraphers.* Baltimore & Ohio R. Co. *v.* Interstate Commerce Comm'n, *221 U.S. 612, 619.*

256, 259. As to state power under the Fourteenth Amendment, compare *Otis* v. *Parker,* 187 U.S. 606, 609; *St. John* v. *New York,* 201 U.S. 633; *Purity Extract & Tonic Co.* v. *Lynch,* 226 U.S. 192, 201–202. A familiar like exercise of power is the regulation of intrastate transactions which are so commingled with or related to interstate commerce that all must be regulated if the interstate commerce is to be effectively controlled. *Shreveport Case,* 234 U.S. 342; *Railroad Commission of Wisconsin* v. *Chicago, B. & Q. R. Co.,* 257 U.S. 563; *United States* v. *New York Central R. Co., supra,* 464; *Currin* v. *Wallace,* 306 U.S. 1; *Mulford* v. *Smith, supra.* Similarly Congress may require inspection and preventive treatment of all cattle in a disease infected area in order to prevent shipment in interstate commerce of some of the cattle without the treatment. *Thornton* v. *United States,* 271 U.S. 414. It may prohibit the removal, at destination, of labels required by the Pure Food & Drugs Act to be affixed to articles transported in interstate commerce. *McDermott* v. *Wisconsin,* 228 U.S. 115. And we have recently held that Congress in the exercise of its power to require inspection and grading of tobacco shipped in interstate commerce may compel such inspection and grading of all tobacco sold at local auction rooms from which a substantial part but not all of the tobacco sold is shipped in interstate commerce. *Currin* v. *Wallace, supra,* 11, and see to the like effect *United States* v. *Rock Royal Co-op., supra,* 568, note 37.

We think also that § 15 (a) (2), now under consideration, is sustainable independently of § 15 (a) (1), which prohibits shipment or transportation of the proscribed goods. As we have said the evils aimed at by the Act are the spread of substandard labor conditions through the use of the facilities of interstate commerce for competition by the goods so produced with those produced under the prescribed or better labor conditions; and the consequent dislocation of the commerce itself caused by the impairment or destruction of local businesses by competition made effective through interstate commerce. The Act is thus directed at the suppression of a method or kind of competition in interstate commerce which it has in effect condemned as "unfair," as the Clayton Act has condemned other "unfair methods of competition" made effective through interstate commerce. See *Van Camp & Sons Co.* v. *American Can Co.,* 278 U.S. 245; *Federal Trade Comm'n* v. *Keppel & Bro.,* 291 U.S. 304.

The Sherman Act and the National Labor Relations Act are familiar examples of the exertion of the commerce power to prohibit or control activities wholly intrastate because of their effect on interstate commerce. See as to the Sherman Act, *Northern Securities Co.* v. *United States,* 193 U.S. 197; *Swift & Co.* v. *United States,* 196 U.S. 375; *United States* v. *Patten,* 226 U.S. 525; *United Mine Workers* v. *Coronado Coal Co.,* 259 U.S. 344; *Local No. 167* v. *United States,* 291 U.S. 293; *Stevens Co.* v. *Foster & Kleiser Co.,* 311 U.S. 255. As to the National Labor Relations Act, see *National Labor Relations Board* v. *Fainblatt, supra,* and cases cited.

The means adopted by § 15 (a) (2) for the protection of interstate commerce by the suppression of the production of the condemned goods for interstate commerce is so related to the commerce and so affects it as to be within the reach of the commerce power. See *Currin* v. *Wallace, supra,* 11. Congress, to attain its objective in the suppression of nationwide competition in interstate commerce by goods produced under substandard labor conditions, has made no distinction as to the volume or amount of shipments in the commerce or of production for commerce by any particular shipper or producer. It recognized that in present day industry, competition by a small part may affect the whole and that the total effect of the competition of many small producers may be great. See H. Rept. No. 2182, 75th Cong. 1st Sess., p. 7. The legislation aimed at a whole embraces all its parts. Cf. *National Labor Relations Board* v. *Fainblatt, supra,* 606.

So far as *Carter* v. *Carter Coal Co.,* 298 U.S. 238, is inconsistent with this conclusion, its doctrine is limited in principle by the decisions under the Sherman Act and the National Labor Relations Act, which we have cited and which we follow. See also *Sunshine Anthracite Coal Co.* v. *Adkins,* 310 U.S. 381; *Currin* v. *Wallace, supra; Mulford* v. *Smith, supra; United States* v. *Rock Royal Co-op., supra; Clover Fork Coal Co.* v. *National Labor Relations Board,* 97 F. 2d 331; *National Labor Relations Board* v. *Crowe Coal Co.,* 104 F. 2d 633; *National Labor Relations Board* v. *Good Coal Co.,* 110 F. 2d 501.

Our conclusion is unaffected by the Tenth Amendment which provides: "The powers not delegated to the United States by the Constitution, nor prohibited by it to the States, are reserved to the States respectively, or to the people." The amendment states but a truism that all is retained which has not been surrendered. There is nothing in the history of its adoption to suggest that it was more than declaratory of the relationship between the national and state governments as it had been established by the Constitution before the amendment or that its purpose was other than to allay fears that the new national government might seek to exercise powers not granted, and that the states might not be able to exercise fully their reserved powers. See e.g., II Elliot's Debates, 123, 131; III *id.* 450, 464, 600; IV *id.* 140, 149; I Annals of Congress, 432, 761, 767–768; Story, Commentaries on the Constitution, §§ 1907–1908.

From the beginning and for many years the amendment has been construed as not depriving the national government of authority to resort to all means for the exercise of a granted power which are appropriate and plainly adapted to the permitted end. *Martin* v. *Hunter's Lessee,* 1 Wheat. 304, 324, 325; *McCulloch* v. *Maryland, supra,* 405, 406; *Gordon* v. *United States,* 117 U.S. 697, 705; *Lottery Case, supra; Northern Securities Co.* v. *United States, supra,* 344–345; *Everard's Breweries* v. *Day, supra,* 558; *United States* v. *Sprague,* 282 U.S. 716, 733; see *United States* v. *The Brigantine William,* 28 Fed. Cas. No. 16,700, p. 622. Whatever doubts may have arisen of the soundness of that conclusion, they have been put at rest by the decisions under the Sherman Act and the National Labor Relations Act which we have cited. See also, *Ashwander* v. *Tennessee Valley Authority,* 297 U.S. 288, 330–331; *Wright* v. *Union Central Ins. Co.,* 304 U.S. 502, 516.

Validity of the requirement of records of wages and hours. § 15 (a) (5) and § 11 (c). These requirements are incidental to those for the prescribed wages and hours, and hence validity of the former turns on validity of the latter. Since, as we have held, Congress may require production for interstate commerce to conform to those conditions, it may require the employer, as a means of enforcing the valid law, to keep a record showing whether he has in fact complied with it. The requirement for records even of the intrastate transaction is an appropriate means to the legitimate end. See *Baltimore & Ohio R. Co.* v. *Interstate Commerce Comm'n,* 221 U.S. 612; *Interstate Commerce Comm'n* v. *Goodrich Transit Co.,* 224 U.S. 194; *Chicago Board of Trade* v. *Olsen,* 262 U.S. 1, 42.

Validity of the wage and hour provisions under the Fifth Amendment. Both provisions are minimum wage requirements compelling the payment of a minimum standard wage with a prescribed increased wage for overtime of "not less than one and one-half times the regular rate" at which the worker is employed. Since our decision in *West Coast Hotel Co.* v. *Parrish,* 300 U.S. 379, it is no longer open to question that the fixing of a minimum wage is within the legislative power and that the bare fact of its exercise is not a denial of due process under the Fifth more than under the Fourteenth Amendment. Nor is it any longer open to question that it is within the legislative power to fix maximum hours. *Holden* v. *Hardy,* 169 U.S. 366; *Muller* v. *Oregon,* 208 U.S. 412; *Bunting* v. *Oregon,* 243 U.S. 426; *Baltimore & Ohio R. Co.* v. *Interstate Commerce Comm'n, supra.* Similarly the statute is not objectionable because applied alike to both men and women. Cf. *Bunting* v. *Oregon,* 243 U.S. 426.

The Act is sufficiently definite to meet constitutional demands. One who employs persons, without conforming to the prescribed wage and hour conditions, to work on goods which he ships or expects to ship across state lines, is warned that he may be subject to the criminal penalties of the Act. No more is required. *Nash* v. *United States,* 229 U.S. 373, 377.

We have considered, but find it unnecessary to discuss other contentions.

UNITED STATES v. BUTLER, 297 U.S. 1 (1936)

The Agricultural Adjustment Act (AAA) of 1933 levied processing and floor taxes on processors to pay for crop reduction benefits on cotton. Justice Roberts, for the Court, held that this was not a tax, but a payment of benefits to farmers to induce (or coerce) them into curtailing production. The tax thus became an invalid invasion of the reserved domain of the states. "From the accepted doctrine that the United States is a government of delegated powers," Roberts reasoned, "it follows that those not expressly granted, or reasonably to be implied from such as are conferred, are reserved to the states or to the people. To forestall any suggestion to the contrary, the *Tenth Amendment* was adopted." Justice Stone, joined by Brandeis and Cardozo, dissented, using the occasion to propound the nature and scope of judicial power. While the Executive and Congress are restrained by "the ballot box and the processes of democratic government [and] subject to judicial restraint, the only check upon our own exercise of power is our own sense of self-restraint."

MR. JUSTICE STONE, dissenting.

I think the judgment should be reversed.

The present stress of widely held and strongly expressed differences of opinion of the wisdom of the Agricultural Adjustment Act makes it important, in the interest of clear thinking and sound result, to emphasize at the outset certain propositions which should have controlling influence in determining the validity of the Act. They are:

1. The power of courts to declare a statute unconstitutional is subject to two guiding principles of decision which ought never to be absent from judicial consciousness. One is that courts are concerned only with the power to enact statutes, not with their wisdom. The other is that while unconstitutional exercise of power by the executive and legislative branches of the government is subject to judicial restraint, the only check upon our own exercise of power is our own sense of self-restraint. For the removal of unwise laws from the statute books appeal lies not to the courts but to the ballot and to the processes of democratic government.

2. The constitutional power of Congress to levy an excise tax upon the processing of agricultural products is not questioned. The present levy is held invalid, not for any want of power in Congress to lay such a tax to defray public expenditures, including those for the general welfare, but because the use to which its proceeds are put is disapproved.

3. As the present depressed state of agriculture is nation wide in its extent and effects, there is no basis for saying that the expenditure of public money in aid of farmers is not within the specifically granted power of Congress to levy taxes to "provide for the . . . general welfare." The opinion of the Court does not declare otherwise.

4. No question of a variable tax fixed from time to time by fiat of the Secretary of Agriculture, or of unauthorized delegation of legislative power, is now presented. The schedule of rates imposed by the Secretary in accordance with the original command of Congress has since been specifically adopted and confirmed by Act of Congress, which has declared that it shall be the lawful tax. Act of August 24, 1935, 49 Stat. 750. That is the tax which the government now seeks to collect. Any defects there may have been in the manner of laying the tax by the Secretary have now been removed by the exercise of the power of Congress to pass a curative statute validating an intended, though defective, tax. *United States* v. *Heinszen & Co.*, 206 U.S. 370; *Graham & Foster* v. *Goodcell*, 282 U.S. 409; cf. *Milliken* v. *United States*, 283 U.S. 15. The Agricultural Adjustment Act as thus amended declares that none of its provisions shall fail because others are pronounced invalid.

It is with these preliminary and hardly controverted matters in mind that we should direct our attention to the pivot on which the decision of the Court is made to turn. It is that a levy unquestionably within the taxing power of Congress may be treated as invalid because it is a step in a plan to regulate agricultural production and is thus a forbidden infringement of state power. The levy is not any the less an exercise of taxing power because it is intended to defray an expenditure for the general welfare rather than for some other support of government. Nor is the levy and collection of the tax pointed to as effecting the regulation. While all federal taxes inevitably have some influence on the internal economy of the states, it is not contended that the levy of a processing tax upon manufacturers using agricultural products as raw material has any perceptible regulatory effect upon either their production or manufacture. The tax is unlike the penalties which were held invalid in the *Child Labor Tax Case,* 259 U.S. 20, in *Hill* v. *Wallace,* 259 U.S. 44, in *Linder* v. *United States,* 268 U.S. 5, 17, and in *United States* v. *Constantine,* 296 U.S. 287, because they were themselves the instruments of regulation by virtue of their coercive effect on matters left to the control of the states. Here regulation, if any there be, is accomplished not by the tax but by the method by which its proceeds are expended, and would equally be accomplished by any like use of public funds, regardless of their source.

The method may be simply stated. Out of the available fund payments are made to such farmers as are willing to curtail their productive acreage, who in fact do so and who in advance have filed their written undertaking to do so with the Secretary of Agriculture. In saying that this method of spending public moneys is an invasion of the reserved powers of the states, the Court does not assert that the expenditure of public funds to promote the general welfare is not a substantive power specifically delegated to the national government, as Hamilton and Story pronounced it to be. It does not deny that the expenditure of funds for the benefit of farmers and in aid of a program of curtailment of production of agricultural products, and thus of a supposedly better ordered national economy, is within the specifically granted power. But it is declared that state power is nevertheless infringed by the expenditure of the proceeds of the tax to compensate farmers for the curtailment of their cotton acreage. Although the farmer is placed under no legal compulsion to reduce acreage, it is said that the mere offer of compensation for so doing is a species of economic coercion which operates with the same legal force and effect as though the curtailment were made mandatory by Act of Congress. In any event it is insisted that even though not coercive the expenditure of public funds to induce the recipients to curtail production is itself an infringement of state power, since the federal government cannot invade the domain of the states by the "purchase" of performance of acts which it has no power to compel.

Of the assertion that the payments to farmers are coercive, it is enough to say that no such contention is pressed by the taxpayer, and no such consequences were to be anticipated or appear to have resulted from the administration of the Act. The suggestion of coercion finds no support in the record or in any data showing the actual operation of the Act. Threat of loss, not hope of gain, is the essence of economic coercion. Members of a long depressed industry have undoubtedly been tempted to curtail acreage by the hope of resulting better prices and by the proffered opportunity to obtain needed ready money. But there is nothing to indicate that those who accepted benefits were impelled by fear of lower prices if they did not accept, or that at any stage in the operation of the plan a farmer could say whether, apart from the certainty of cash payments at specified times, the advantage would lie with curtailment of production plus compensation, rather than with the same or increased acreage plus the expected rise in prices which actually occurred. Although the Agricultural Adjustment Act was put into operation in June, 1933, the official reports of the Department of Agriculture show that 6,343,000 acres of productive cotton land, 14% of the total, did not participate in the plan in 1934, and 2,790,000 acres, 6% of the total, did not participate in 1935. Of the total number of farms growing cotton, estimated at 1,500,000, 33% in 1934 and 13% in 1935 did not participate.

It is significant that in the congressional hearings on the bill that became the Bankhead Act, 48 Stat. 598, as amended by Act of June 20, 1934, 48 Stat. 1184, which imposes a tax of 50% on all cotton produced in excess of limits prescribed by the Secretary of Agriculture, there was abundant testimony that the restriction of cotton production attempted by the Agricultural Adjustment Act could not be secured without the coercive provisions of the Bankhead Act. See Hearing before Committee on Agriculture, U.S Senate, on S. 1974, 73rd Cong., 2nd Sess.; Hearing before Committee on Agriculture, U.S. House of Representatives, on H. R. 8402, 73rd Cong., 2nd Sess. The Senate and House Committees so reported, Senate Report No. 283, 73rd Cong., 2nd Sess., p. 3; House Reports No. 867, 73rd Cong., 2nd Sess., p. 3. The Report of the Department of Agriculture on the administration of the Agricultural Adjustment Act (February 15, 1934 to December 31, 1934), p. 50, points out that the Bankhead Act was passed in response to a strong sentiment in favor of mandatory production control "that would prevent noncooperating farmers from increasing their own plantings in order to capitalize upon the price advances that had resulted from the reductions made by contract signers."[1] The presumption of constitutionality of a statute is not to be overturned by an assertion of its coercive effect which rests on nothing more substantial than groundless speculation.

It is upon the contention that state power is infringed by purchased regulation of agricultural production that chief reliance is placed. It is insisted that, while the Constitution gives to Congress, in specific and unambiguous terms, the power to tax and spend, the power is subject to limitations which do not find their origin in any express provision of the Constitution and to which other expressly delegated powers are not subject.

The Constitution requires that public funds shall be spent for a defined purpose, the promotion of the general welfare. Their expenditure usually involves payment on terms which will insure use by the selected recipients within the limits of the constitutional purpose. Expenditures would fail of their purpose and thus lose their constitutional sanction if the terms of payment were not such that by their influence on the action of the recipients the permitted end would be attained. The power of Congress to spend is inseparable from persuasion to action over which Congress has no legislative control. Congress may not command that the science of agriculture be taught in state universities. But if it would aid the teaching of that science by grants to state institutions, it is appropriate, if not necessary, that the grant be on the condition, incorporated in the Morrill Act, 12 Stat. 503, 26 Stat. 417, that it be used for the intended purpose. Similarly it would seem to be compliance with the Constitution, not violation of it, for the government to take and the university to give a contract that the grant would be so used. It makes no difference that there is a promise to do an act which the condition is calculated to induce. Condition and promise are alike valid since both are in furtherance of the national purpose for which the money is appropriated.

These effects upon individual action, which are but incidents of the authorized expenditure of government money, are pronounced to be themselves a limitation upon the granted power, and so the time-honored principle of constitutional interpretation that the granted power includes all those which are incident to it is reversed. "Let the end be legitimate," said the great Chief Justice, "let it be within the scope of the Constitution, and all means which are appropriate, which are plainly adapted to that end, which are not prohibited, but consist with the letter and spirit of the Constitution, are constitutional." *McCulloch* v. *Maryland,* 4 Wheat. 316, 421. This cardinal guide to constitutional exposition must now be re-phrased so far as the spending power of the federal government is concerned. Let the expenditure be to promote the general welfare, still, if it is needful in order to insure its use for the intended purpose to influence any action which Congress cannot command because within the sphere of state government, the expenditure is unconstitutional. And taxes otherwise lawfully levied are likewise unconstitutional if they are appropriated to the expenditure whose incident is condemned.

Congress through the Interstate Commerce Commission has set aside intrastate railroad rates. It has made and destroyed intrastate industries by raising or lowering tariffs. These results are said to be permissible because they are incidents of the commerce power and the power to levy duties on imports. See *Minnesota Rate Cases,* 230 U.S. 352; *Shreveport Case,* 234 U.S. 342; *Board of Trustees of the University of Illinois* v. *United States,* 289 U.S. 48. The only conclusion to be drawn is that results become lawful when they are incidents of those powers but unlawful when incident to the similarly granted power to tax and spend.

Such a limitation is contradictory and destructive of the power to appropriate for the public welfare, and is incapable of practical application. The spending power of Congress is in addition to the legislative power and not subordinate to it. This independent grant of the power of the purse, and its very nature, involving in its exercise the duty to insure expenditure within the granted power, presuppose freedom of selection among divers ends and aims, and the capacity to impose such conditions as will render the choice effective. It is a contradiction in terms to say that there is power to spend for the national welfare, while reject-

[1] *Whether coercion was the sole or the dominant purpose of the Bankhead Act, or whether the act was designed also for revenue or other legitimate ends, there is no occasion to consider now.*

ing any power to impose conditions reasonably adapted to the attainment of the end which alone would justify the expenditure.

The limitation now sanctioned must lead to absurd consequences. The government may give seeds to farmers, but may not condition the gift upon their being planted in places where they are most needed or even planted at all. The government may give money to the unemployed, but may not ask that those who get it shall give labor in return, or even use it to support their families. It may give money to sufferers from earthquake, fire, tornado, pestilence or flood, but may not impose conditions—health precautions designed to prevent the spread of disease, or induce the movement of population to safer or more sanitary areas. All that, because it is purchased regulation infringing state powers, must be left for the states, who are unable or unwilling to supply the necessary relief. The government may spend its money for vocational rehabilitation, 48 Stat. 389, but it may not, with the consent of all concerned, supervise the process which it undertakes to aid. It may spend its money for the suppression of the boll weevil, but may not compensate the farmers for suspending the growth of cotton in the infected areas. It may aid state reforestation and forest fire prevention agencies, 43 Stat. 653, but may not be permitted to supervise their conduct. It may support rural schools, 39 Stat. 929, 45 Stat. 1151, 48 Stat. 792, but may not condition its grant by the requirement that certain standards be maintained. It may appropriate moneys to be expended by the Reconstruction Finance Corporation "to aid in financing agriculture, commerce and industry," and to facilitate "the exportation of agricultural and other products." Do all its activities collapse because, in order to effect the permissible purpose, in myriad ways the money is paid out upon terms and conditions which influence action of the recipients within the states, which Congress cannot command? The answer would seem plain. If the expenditure is for a national public purpose, that purpose will not be thwarted because payment is on condition which will advance that purpose. The action which Congress induces by payments of money to promote the general welfare, but which it does not command or coerce, is but an incident to a specifically granted power, but a permissible means to a legitimate end. If appropriation in aid of a program of curtailment of agricultural production is constitutional, and it is not denied that it is, payment to farmers on condition that they reduce their crop acreage is constitutional. It is not any the less so because the farmer at his own option promises to fulfill the condition.

That the governmental power of the purse is a great one is not now for the first time announced. Every student of the history of government and economics is aware of its magnitude and of its existence in every civilized government. Both were well understood by the framers of the Constitution when they sanctioned the grant of the spending power to the federal government, and both were recognized by Hamilton and Story, whose views of the spending power as standing on a parity with the other powers specifically granted, have hitherto been generally accepted.

The suggestion that it must now be curtailed by judicial fiat because it may be abused by unwise use hardly rises to the dignity of argument. So may judicial power be abused. "The power to tax is the power to destroy," but we do not, for that reason, doubt its existence, or hold that its efficacy is to be restricted by its incidental or collateral effects upon the states. See *Veazie Bank* v. *Fenno,* 8 Wall. 533; *McCray* v. *United States,* 195 U.S. 27; compare *Magnano Co.* v. *Hamilton,* 292 U.S. 40. The power to tax and spend is not without constitutional restraints. One restriction is that the purpose must be truly national. Another is that it may not be used to coerce action left to state control. Another is the conscience and patriotism of Congress and the Executive. "It must be remembered that legislators are the ultimate guardians of the liberties and welfare of the people in quite as great a degree as the courts." Justice Holmes, in *Missouri, Kansas & Texas Ry. Co.* v. *May,* 194 U.S. 267, 270.

A tortured construction of the Constitution is not to be justified by recourse to extreme examples of reckless congressional spending which might occur if courts could not prevent—expenditures which, even if they could be thought to effect any national purpose, would be possible only by action of a legislature lost to all sense of public responsibility. Such suppositions are addressed to the mind accustomed to believe that it is the business of courts to sit in judgment on the wisdom of legislative action. Courts are not the only agency of government that must be assumed to have capacity to govern. Congress and the courts both unhappily may falter or be mistaken in the performance of their constitutional duty. But interpretation of our great charter of government which proceeds on any assumption that the responsibility for the preservation of our institutions is the exclusive concern of any one of the three branches of government, or that it alone can save them from destruction is far more likely, in the long run, "to obliterate the constituent members" of "an indestructible union of indestructible states" than the frank recognition that language, even of a constitution, may mean what it says: that the power to tax and spend includes the power to relieve a nationwide economic maladjustment by conditional gifts of money.

Owen J. Roberts

☆ 1875–1955 ☆

APPOINTED BY

HERBERT HOOVER

YEARS ON COURT

1930–1945

Owen J. Roberts

by

DAVID BURNER

SUPREME COURT JUSTICE Owen Roberts liked to boast that he was "virtually an immigrant." Roberts' grandfather had in fact come in 1808 from Wales to southeastern Pennsylvania, where he set up a prosperous grist mill and soon married a Pennsylvania Dutch girl, Sarah Heebner, of the Schwenkfelder faith. Josephus Roberts, Owen's father, was born in 1837 on the Perkiomen Pike, near Collegeville; Sarah chose the name Josephus because "it had a Biblical sound." Emma Laferty, mother of the Justice, was of Scotch-Irish descent. Her son was born May 2, 1875, in Germantown, now a suburb of Philadelphia.

At an early age Owen, who had no brothers and only one sister, found great pleasure in reading. He was not timid or passive, however; always large for his age, he was almost too assertive of principle in quarrels with other boys, and his classmates left unquestioned his preference for reading to playing football or baseball on the school teams. Owen's serious strain was apparently welcomed by his parents, who sent him to the Germantown Academy where he excelled as a member of the debating team.

Roberts entered the University of Pennsylvania in 1891, along with 126 other freshmen. Under the vigorous leadership of Provost William Pepper, the school was then transforming itself into a modern university. The young student took advantage of many opportunities on the growing campus. He worked on the college yearbook and in the Young Men's Christian Association. Again he joined the debating society. His list of extracurricular activities in the yearbook was longer than that of any other student save one. Yet he applied himself to academic work with such seriousness that he was elected to Phi Beta Kappa. His graduation essay, "The Agamemnon Myth as Treated by the Attic Dramatists,"

DAVID BURNER is Associate Professor of History at the State University of New York, Stony Brook. He is the author of The Politics of Provincialism: The Democratic Party in Transition, 1918–1932.

reveals a fascination for Greek and Latin that almost drew him from the study of law. In 1895, at the age of twenty, he graduated with honors.

The next autumn he entered the venerable University of Pennsylvania Law School, which had been founded in 1790 when the nation's capital was in Philadelphia—George Washington himself had attended lectures given there by Supreme Court Justice James Wilson. In Roberts' own days as a student, the law school was temporarily housed in the public buildings of Independence Square. The faculty included a number of noted scholars. Constitutional law—of special interest to him—was taught by C. Stuart Patterson, who was also general solicitor of the Pennsylvania Railroad. In his professional education Roberts continued to achieve academic success. In his second and third years he won the Faculty Prize for the best-written examination in the University. Associate editor of the *American Law Register* in 1897 and 1898, he was graduated *cum laude* in 1898 after winning honors in each of his three years. His spectacular record earned him a position as fellow in the university from 1898 to 1900. Although he never became a full-time faculty member, he rose in rank until he was appointed professor in 1907. He continued to lecture, despite his active trial practice, until his resignation in 1919.

During these years in Philadelphia, Roberts worked first in the firm of White and White and later in that of Roberts, Montgomery, and McKeehan. He also served in the office of the district attorney of Philadelphia County. In 1903 he was elected vice-president and the next year president of the Law Academy of Philadelphia. In 1906 he acquired further distinction in his election as secretary of the Law Association of Philadelphia. During the ensuing years his practice grew in size and scope. He was lawyer to several corporations, but he never served any one long enough to earn the title "corporation lawyer." In 1918 he worked briefly as special deputy attorney general on local cases arising under the Espionage Act.

By 1924 the press estimated that the offices of Roberts and Montgomery (McKeehan had been made a federal district judge the year before) grossed an annual income of about $150,000. In that same year came a great opportunity that meant, however, a considerable financial sacrifice. In February, President Coolidge, at the suggestion of Senator George Wharton Pepper of Pennsylvania and Harlan Fiske Stone of the Columbia Law School, nominated Roberts as one of two lawyers who would prosecute parties involved in the oil scandals of the Harding administration. Some resistance to Roberts' nomination developed in the Senate after Atlee Pomerene, a former Democratic senator from Ohio, had been approved as the first prosecutor. Thomas Walsh, chairman of the investigating committee that exposed the oil scandals, read into the *Congressional Record* a speech delivered by Roberts on February 16, 1923, to the trust company division of the American Bankers Association. The lawyer, said Walsh, had attempted to justify the high salaries paid to oil company officials and had attacked as propaganda the Senate subcommittee investigations into the oil industry. Roberts denied having made the slur on Walsh's work or even the defense of the executives' salaries, but he had complained about the encroachment of government in American life to an appreciative audience who had applauded his diatribe. In behalf of Roberts, Senator Pepper pointed out that he was not a professional defender of the corporate interests. On the contrary, he had recently won a verdict of $55,000 in a personal injury case against the Reading Railroad Company. The tally on approval of Roberts was sixty-eight to eight, a slightly better margin than that by which Pomerene had been approved.

The two lawyers set to work with much ingenuity and persistence; Roberts announced: "We will make haste, but we will make haste slowly." The statement was accurate; the prosecution lasted for six years. In an impressive display of shrewd detective work, Roberts and his agents discovered $200,000 in Liberty Bonds that Harry Sinclair had paid to Secretary of the Interior Albert Fall. The Teapot Dome and Elk Hill leases were successfully cancelled through suits initiated by the government in consultation with the lawyers, but in the matter of criminal prosecution they were less successful: Fall, convicted in 1929 of having accepted a bribe, served a scant year in jail and paid a fine; Sinclair was sentenced to jail for six months. It was clearly Roberts, rather than Pomerene, who had taken the leadership in prosecuting the evildoers. On hearing a reference to the Philadelphia attorney as one of the government's prosecutors, Sinclair reputedly replied: "Hell, that's all of them." Roberts collected his modest fee of $10,000 and in November, 1928, again devoted his full time to private practice.

In May of 1930 the Senate failed to confirm the Supreme Court appointment of a North Carolina judge, John J. Parker, who had upheld the yellow dog contract in a Fourth Circuit Court decision and had made a slighting reference about Negro participation in politics. As a candidate who would not stir factional feeling in the Senate, Roberts—a lifelong Republican and an investigator of the Harding scandals—appeared promising, and despite the Philadelphian's alleged statement that "Prohibition has no place in the Constitution," the President nominated him. The American Federation of Labor, which later criticized Roberts acidly, favored his nomination because he had charged some client labor leaders nominal fees. Senate liberals overlooked his connections with the Bell Telephone and Equitable Life Assurance companies, accepting him for his diligence in prosecuting the oil gang. On June 2, 1930, the Senate confirmed the appointment without any negative votes. In taking the Court appointment Roberts again sacrificed a lucrative practice, this time for an annual salary of $20,000.

Roberts' main contribution to the Court was in questions of civil liberties and business regulation. At the time Justice Roberts ascended the bench, the Fourteenth Amendment was undergoing expansion in the categories of freedom of speech and of the press. Before his first term was over, the Court declared invalid the California "red flag" law, *Stromberg* v. *California,* 283 U.S. 359 (1931)—the state had prosecuted Stromberg for requiring some children at camp to salute the Hammer and Sickle—and the Minnesota "press gag" law, *Near* v. *Minnesota,* 283 U.S. 697 (1931), as a "public nuisance." In both instances Roberts sided with the liberal majority to provide a five-to-four vote. In a third case decided the same year, Roberts voted with the conservatives, Sutherland, Van Devanter, McReynolds, and Butler, in another decision of five to four; here the federal government won the right to deny citizenship to a professor in the Yale Divinity School who qualified his oath of allegiance by reserving the right to bear arms only if he thought a war justified, *United States* v. *Macintosh,* 283 U.S. 605 (1931). These early cases, in which he moved freely between opposing judicial camps, showed that Roberts, above all, was his own man. By the end of 1931 he and the new Chief Justice, Charles Evans Hughes, could be characterized only as "unreliable members of the so-called liberal majority." Critics accused Roberts of "vacillation."

In subsequent cases for which Roberts wrote the majority opinion, the Court expanded the protection of the Fourth Amendment against unlawful searches and seizures (*Grau* v. *United States,* 287 U.S. 124 [1932]); declared against government interference with interstate, and later intrastate, communications—specifically wiretapping, though dictaphone recordings made in the speaker's presence were exempted (*Weiss* v. *United States,* 308 U.S. 321 [1939], *Goldman* v. *United States,* 316 U.S. 129 [1942]); contemptuously dismissed city ordinances restricting freedom of the press and distribution of circulars and pamphlets (but not advertising matter) (*Schneider* v. *State,* 308 U.S. 147 [1939]); protected the Jehovah's Witnesses' right to solicit funds and play phonograph records in the public streets (*Cantwell* v. *Connecticut,* 310 U.S. 296 [1940]); and argued that although unlawful coercion and abuse do not in themselves cause a case to be dismissed, in general due process is denied if rules are ignored even though no substantive injury results. Roberts also wrote a dissent in which he insisted that when the jury visits the scene of a crime the defendant and his counsel must be permitted to be present (*Snyder* v. *Massachusetts,* 291 U.S. 97, 123 [1934]).

Roberts spoke for a unanimous Court in *Grovey* v. *Townsend,* 295 U.S. 45 (1935), which held that Negroes could be excluded from voting in Democratic party primaries. Proceeding on largely technical grounds, Roberts argued that the action of the Democrats was not state action and therefore not a violation of the Fourteenth Amendment. The Justice viewed the case as rather perfunctory particularly since the Democrats paid for holding the primaries. The Court ignored the realities of the situation, which effectively disfranchised the Negro. *Grovey* was overturned in *Smith* v. *Allwright,* 321 U.S. 649 (1944). Roberts, dissenting in the later case, objected to the twenty or more reversals of the Court's opinions during the preceding seven years. The changes of mind, he wrote, "bring adjudications of this tribunal into the same class as a restricted railroad ticket, good for the day and train only."

In his most famous civil liberties decision, *Herndon* v. *Lowry,* 301 U.S. 242 (1937), Roberts wrote the five to four majority opinion setting aside the conviction of a Negro organizer for the Communist party. In a Georgia court Angelo Herndon had been found guilty of inciting insurrection by urging others to resist state authority. When arrested he had in his possession Communist pamphlets he planned to distribute at public meetings; although he had already enrolled a few members for the party, he had not given out any literature. Herndon could have been condemned to death under state law, but the jury was satisfied with sentencing him to eighteen to twenty years.

Roberts declared that two questions were before the Court: whether the state law under which Herndon was convicted violated freedom of speech and assembly guaranteed under the Fourteenth Amendment, and whether the state provided a clear standard of guilt. Roberts believed that Georgia law denied due process because it lacked certainty and so was not valid as a criminal statute.

More important, Roberts introduced the first sharp distinction in cases of freedom of speech between the "clear and present danger" test of Justice Holmes and the "bad tendency" test of Justice Sanford. Roberts maintained that the "clear and present danger" yardstick applies in instances, such as the *Herndon* case, where "criminal *acts* are forbidden and language is being punished on the theory that it constitutes such *acts*." The "bad tendency" standard, on the other hand, prevails where the law itself "forbids *language* and holds that under the police power *language* may be forbidden which *tends* to produce evils which the state may validly forbid." The distinction was a move in the direction of greater civil liberties, since the most punitive forms of legislation in the field have to do with acts rather than language. In the same case Roberts drew a clear line beyond which freedom of speech could not be infringed: "The power of a state to abridge freedom of speech and assembly is the exception rather than the rule and the penalizing even of utterances of a defined character must find its justification in a reasonable apprehension of danger to organized government. The judgment of the legislature is not unfettered. The limitation upon individual liberty must have appropriate relation to the safety of the state. Legislation which goes beyond this need violates the principle of the Constitution."

In 1939 Roberts wrote another important decision, upholding by five to two the right of the Committee for Industrial Organization to hold outdoor meetings in Jersey City without permits from the police and to distribute printed matter, *Hague* v. *Committee for Industrial Organization,* 307 U.S. 496 (1939). The municipal ordinances, Roberts argued, violated the privileges and immunities clause of the Fourteenth Amendment. He wrote: "Wherever the title of streets and parks may rest, they have immemorially been held in trust for the use of the public. . . . Such use . . . has, from ancient times, been a part of the privileges, immunities, rights, and liberties of citizens. The privilege of a citizen of the United States to use the streets and parks for communication of views on national questions may be regulated in the interest of all; it is not absolute, but relative. . . . But it must not, in the guise of regulation, be abridged or denied."

Roberts expanded the working definition of religious liberty in *Cantwell* v. *Connecticut,* 310 U.S. 296 (1940). Here was declared null a Connecticut law requiring licensing of any who collected for any religious or charitable cause.

Roberts denounced the statute for its implied power permitting the licensing official to pass upon the religious nature of any organization, in this case Jehovah's Witnesses. He conceived of religious freedom as so fundamental that it should not be outweighed unless a "clear and present danger" makes it necessary to do so. *Cantwell* contains the first explicit ruling that religious freedom is also a liberty protected from state interference by the Fourteenth Amendment. The state was required to draft a new law aimed specifically at fraudulent solicitation.

But if *Hague* and *Cantwell* advanced civil liberties, *Betts* v. *Brady,* 316 U.S. 455 (1942), set them back. Betts was indicted for robbery; his request that counsel be appointed for him was denied as contrary to local practice except in murder and rape cases. He pleaded not guilty, conducted his own defense, and after conviction eventually appealed to the Supreme Court. Speaking for six Justices, Roberts stated that to require counsel in all local cases fails to distinguish between charges of varying magnitude, or courts of varying jurisdiction. Where the issue is plain, the accused of average intelligence, the crime not capital, and counsel's appointment not required by state law, then the guarantee of the Sixth Amendment is not included in the due process clause of the Fourteenth. The case retarded the trend, since *Powell* v. *Alabama,* 287 U.S. 45 (1932), toward making the right of an accused to counsel one of the guarantees of the Fourteenth Amendment. In *Gideon* v. *Wainwright,* 372 U.S. 335 (1963), the *Betts* decision was overruled.

In the regulation of business Roberts was responsible for virtually discarding Justice McReynolds' narrow interpretation of an old doctrine, "business affected with a public interest," made famous by Chief Justice Waite in *Munn* v. *Illinois,* 94 U.S. 113 (1877). The important decision here is *Nebbia* v. *New York,* 291 U.S. 502 (1934), decided five to four with Roberts speaking for the majority. Leo Nebbia, a Rochester grocer, sold milk at a price below that set by the New York State Milk Control Board, for a temporary but unspecified period during the emergency of the depression; Roberts declared that the Constitution did not prohibit the state from empowering the board to fix the price of milk, especially if falling prices might adversely affect the supply. The Pitcher Committee of the legislature had recently concluded that many dairy farmers, who were receiving returns well below the cost of production, were forced into bankruptcy. He wrote: "The Constitution does not secure to any one liberty to conduct his business in such fashion as to inflict injury upon the public at large, or upon any substantial group of people. . . . Neither property rights nor contracts are absolute. . . . Equally fundamental with the private right is that of the public to regulate it in the common interest." "It is clear," he said, "that there is no closed class or category of businesses affected with a public interest, and the function of the courts . . . is to determine in each case whether circumstances vindicate the challenged regulation. . . ." Whether the regulation of a business is reasonable or not depends on the relevant facts about that business; and for many years the milk industry had been a subject of government regulation. "Affected with a public interest" simply means that "an industry, for adequate reason, is subject to control for the public good." And so, despite some formalistic distinctions, the Court overturned its former rulings in *Tyson* v. *Banton,* 273 U.S. 416 (1927), *Ribnik* v. *McBride,* 277 U.S. 350 (1928), and *Williams* v. *Standard Oil Co.,* 278 U.S. 235 (1929).

Roberts' decisions relating to New Deal legislation are restricted almost entirely to one subject, that of agriculture, and most notably the famous case of *United States* v. *Butler,* 297 U.S. 1 (1936). He wrote only one earlier opinion directly pertaining to the Roosevelt legislation, *Railroad Retirement Board* v. *Alton Railway Co.,* 295 U.S. 330 (1935), invalidating, by a vote of five to four, the Railway Retirement Act of 1934. Roberts for the majority argued that the act in some respects violated the due process clause of the Fifth Amendment. In forcing the companies to grant benefits to former employees, for example, it required them to pay funds to those who for some lawful reason might have been dismissed. The act also had other retroactive features, required contributions in some cases by one firm to the employees of another, and was arbitrary in many ways. The legislation, moreover, was not a regulation of interstate commerce; no relation existed between the pensioning system and the efficiency or safety of the railroads, Roberts contended. He effectively rejected all conceivable laws requiring participation in pension laws. Justice Stone observed that the decision "puts us back at least thirty years." It was "the worst performance of the Court in my time."

Perhaps the most famous decision declaring invalid a New Deal law is that in the *Butler* case. The vote was six to three, and Roberts wrote the majority opinion declaring the first Agricultural Adjustment Act unconstitutional. The purpose of the act was to restore the farmers' purchasing power to the levels of 1909 to 1914; during the depression of the 1930's, so the authors of the AAA declared, the plight of agriculture constituted an evil affecting the general welfare. The method was highly controversial. It required that farmers reduce the acreage of agricultural products in order to eradicate the surplus and thereby raise prices. In exchange for letting the land lie fallow, the farmers were compensated through the Department of Agriculture from funds raised by a processing tax on those who prepared the product for sale. The plan had been in operation for about three years, and farmers' incomes had been rising, before a test case appeared in the name of William M. Butler, a receiver for Hoosac Mills, who refused to pay the tax. George Wharton Pepper, Roberts' old mentor, was acting as counsel for Butler.

Justice Roberts declared against the AAA for several reasons. The processing tax was not really a tax at all, he argued, for it did not support the government; the money was in fact taken from one group of people and given to another, the Department of Agriculture acting as intermediary. The word "tax," Roberts said, "has never been thought to connote the expropriation of money from one group for the benefit of another." The power to tax for the general welfare carries with it a responsibility to spend for a like purpose. The Justice did not actually hold that the act was not national in purpose, though he did say that regulation of agriculture was not a national power. The law was also an invasion of those powers reserved to the states by the Tenth Amendment. Here Roberts argued vigorously the moribund doctrine of "dual federalism," and denied the right of Congress to pass laws lying within the reserved powers of the states. He contended that in its coercive character the AAA was a violation of the Tenth Amendment. The benefits awarded by the government were so generous that the farmer had no practical choice and was thereby forced to participate in the program. Roberts paraded imaginary horribles in the manner of McReynolds: "If the Act before us is a proper exercise of the federal taxing power, evidently the regulation of all industry throughout the United States may be accomplished by similar exercise of the same power. This country would be converted into a central government exercising uncontrolled police power in every state of the union, superseding all local control or regulation of the affairs or concerns of the states."

The reasoning of the decision was at times ingenious, but more often it was tortured. In suggesting that powers not expressly delegated to either the state or the national government were to be exercised only by the state, Roberts was neglecting the range of implied powers. Justice Stone wrote a forceful dissent, clear and artful in contrast to Roberts'. The former Columbia Law School Dean criticized Roberts for judging the wisdom of the statute; Stone urged "frank recognition that language, even of a constitution, may mean what it says: that the power to tax and spend includes the power to relieve a nation-wide economic maladjustment by conditional gifts of money." Law school journals also ridiculed Roberts' loose thinking. Henry M. Hoyt, Jr., a pseudonymous contributor to the *Harvard Law Review,* wrote that the protective tariff could be declared unconstitutional on the same grounds on which the processing tax was rejected. In contrast, the Court's conservatives cheered Roberts' decision. Both the wholesale destruction of agricultural products, including the slaughter of little pigs, and the effort to hamper the law of supply and demand were anathema to them. Justice Stone later remarked that "the whole history of the case was characterized by inadequate discussions and great haste in the production and circulation of opinions."

Congress based the second AAA on the commerce power, and Roberts wrote the decision, *Mulford* v. *Smith,* 307 U.S. 38 (1939), that upheld the act, seven to two. It was constitutional, he ruled, to regulate foreign and interstate commerce in certain goods to provide an "orderly, adequate and balanced flow of such commodities." The government could therefore legally establish marketing quotas and store reserves to maintain parity income. Robert H. Jackson, later a Justice himself, wrote of Roberts' agricultural decisions: "The regulation of marketing was all that the latter act attempted, and while regulation of marketing undoubtedly would have the effect of regulating production, nothing in the Constitution requires Congress to avoid such efforts. . . . The two opinions by Mr. Justice Roberts are not logically inconsistent. . . . I would agree, however, that the latter opinion indicates a broader and more tolerant approach to the constitutional problem than did his first opinion."

Roberts' remaining conservative colleagues still believed he had made an about-face on the subject of crop control, but the Justice was fiercely independent and not often inconsistent in his views. He wrote opinions for both the conservatives and liberals. He had joined four liberals to uphold the Minnesota mortgage moratorium and the gold clause cases; he had voted with the four conservatives against the AAA and, although he was a friend of Secretary of Labor Perkins, against the Federal Railroad Retirement Act.

In the later part of the New Deal Roberts markedly shifted his position, henceforth favoring virtually all of President Roosevelt's legislative program. The "famous switch" of Justice Roberts seems to have taken place between *Morehead* v. *New York ex rel. Tipaldo,* 298 U.S. 587, decided on June 1, 1936, and *West Coast Hotel Company* v. *Parrish,* 300 U.S. 379, reported on March 27, 1937. *Morehead* rejected and *Parrish* affirmed state minimum wage legislation. The dates are suggestive. A landslide election victory for the President had intervened in November, 1936. Serious labor unrest impended, taking its most revolutionary form in the sit-down strikes of 1937. Finally, it was well known by the end of 1936 that Roosevelt was considering several methods of executive assault on the Court, including the addition of liberal Justices to the bench. Roberts, already of two minds on the New Deal, was undoubtedly sensitive to these events in the nation at large. There were suggestions that the Court had better accommodate itself to public opinion if it wished to survive intact. We know Roberts heard that suggestion countless times.

Felix Frankfurter and others have defended Roberts against the charge that a mercurial Justice had switched in time to save nine. A memorandum prepared by Roberts himself, which Frankfurter used for an article in defense of his brother Justice that appeared in the *University of Pennsylvania Law Review* for 1955, explained the discrepancy between Roberts' *Morehead* and *Parrish* votes as resting on a technicality. His position in the earlier case, Roberts insisted, had been a response to the argument of New York State that its minimum wage law was consistent with the conservative decision of *Adkins* v. *Children's Hospital,* 261 U.S. 525 (1923). Roberts had disagreed, his memo recollected; but the Justice remembered having been quite prepared to overrule *Adkins* outright, and regretted having acted on his objection to the reasoning of New York rather than on his more general view of the matter. Particularly his silent acquiescence in Butler's decision, which cited *Adkins* explicitly, seems strange in view of the growing public concern over the Court.

In October of 1936, a minimum wage law challenged by the West Coast Hotel Company came before the Court. This time Roberts voted to consider the case against the wishes of the four conservatives, but he did not give his reasons. Late in December a vote was taken with Roberts going on record in affirmation of the law; but again fate intervened to keep the Court silent. Justice Stone had fallen ill, and *Parrish* was postponed until after his convalescence and recovery months later.

During this period, the Roberts memorandum insisted, the Justice had been indicating his own desire for a repudiation of *Adkins*. He claimed to have spoken, in March, 1936, against granting New York's petition for *certiorari* unless the Court was prepared to re-examine and overrule the 1923 decision; and he recalled saying in conference sometime later that he "did not propose to review and re-examine the *Adkins* case until a case should come to the Court requiring that this should be done." But he also recounts some consternation among the conservatives when he voted in October for notation of probable jurisdiction in *Parrish:* "I heard one of the brethren ask another, 'What is the matter with Roberts?' " Surely the Four Horsemen, unless their surprise was feigned, would have been wary of Roberts on this matter had he earlier in the year dropped the hints he remembered. Roberts' whole explanation seems unlikely. Possibly he did engage in independent thinking on *Adkins* that happened to move with the trend of events at large. But the historian has learned to be wary of public men who seek in retrospect to set the record right.

In *Chamberlain* v. *Andrews,* 299 U.S. 515 (1936), which included a series of similar cases voted upon that fall, Roberts was arguing to sustain such legislation. But Roberts' very last years on the Court reveal a growing conservatism. He was especially disturbed by what he saw as piecemeal repudiation of precedent. In *Machnich* v. *Southern Steamship Company,* 321 U.S. 96 (1944), a relatively insignificant case in itself, Roberts took the opportunity to pour out his indignation against the recent trend: "The law," he complained, "becomes not a chart to govern conduct but a game of chance; instead of settling rights and liabilities it unsettles them." Criticizing Chief Justice Stone, who had written the majority opinion, Roberts warned that "the more deplorable consequence will inevitably be that the administration of justice will fall into disrepute. Respect for tribunals must fall when the bar and the public come to understand that nothing that has been said in prior adjudications has force in a current controversy." Sarcastically, Roberts recommended that the Justices make public announcement, for the sake of clarity in the lower courts, "that they will change their votes on the same question when another case comes before the Court." Justice Frankfurter supported Roberts' dissent.

Roberts' nonpartisan position as a Republican on the Roosevelt Court caused the President to appoint him to duties beyond his normal work. In 1942 he prepared a report that exonerated F.D.R. of any wrongdoing in the events leading up to Pearl Harbor. Justice Stone commended Roberts' work: "It is altogether a thorough document, ably dealing with one of the most unhappy episodes. I am glad to see that it is being well received as a difficult task, adequately performed." In 1943 Roberts headed the Commission for the Protection and Salvage of Artistic and Historic Monuments in Europe, which cataloged and traced the art objects stolen or destroyed by the Germans. The point was to prepare a bill to present after the war's end and to insure the return of the art objects that would survive. The depredations of war troubled Roberts. C. Herman Pritchett lists him as upholding "wartime freedom" in each of seven representative cases, though generally his concern for civil liberties was not marked.

When Roberts quit the Court in 1945, he was, save for Justice Stone, the last to leave of the Nine Old Men of the thirties. During the last session of the

Court he had written twenty-one majority opinions and an unparalleled fifty-three vigorous dissents. *Time* hailed him as the "chief defender of precedent and legal stability." Roberts now was an archaic fixture on a Court which had moved beyond his mechanistic interpretations; no one again would propound, as he did in the *Butler* case, that the Court had "only one duty—to lay the article of the Constitution which is invoked beside the statute which is challenged and to decide whether the latter squares with the former." A shoddy quarrel over a letter of farewell marred his departure and revealed an ungenerous streak in several of the Justices, especially Hugo Black and even Chief Justice Stone himself, who rated Roberts high in ability. Finally, no letter was sent at all. Roberts' own opinion of his work was modest enough: "I have no illusions about my judicial career," he wrote. "But one can only do what one can. Who am I to revile the good God that he did not make me a Marshall, a Taney, a Bradley, a Holmes, a Brandeis, or a Cardozo." Yet if Roberts did not make one of the major figures in Supreme Court history, his career brought its own special strengths to American constitutional interpretation. His independent spirit, which held him aloof from total surrender to either the "liberal" or the "conservative" position, is itself a signal fact about him.

After his retirement from the Court, Roberts remained active in public life. From 1945 to 1948 he served as dean of the University of Pennsylvania Law School. In 1951 Harvard University Press published Roberts' Oliver Wendell Holmes lectures under the title *The Court and the Constitution.* Roberts in this book analyzed three areas in which jurisdictional conflicts between state and national laws have had to be resolved, those of taxation, economic regulation, and due process. Roberts concluded that "progressively, the Supreme Court has limited and surrendered the role the Constitution was intended to confer on it." The Justice thought it perhaps inevitable and even perhaps beneficial that the sharp division of powers intended had become blurred. In 1953 he was named chairman of the Fund for the Advancement of Education. Most of his energies in these years were devoted to the cause of world federalism, although he avoided formal ties with the organizations devoted to this end. He was now too old to work effectively in such a crusade. Roberts' death came on May 17, 1955, at the age of eighty.

SELECTED BIBLIOGRAPHY

Two unpublished doctoral dissertations treat Justice Roberts: William Oscar Trapp, "The Constitutional Doctrines of Owen J. Roberts" (Cornell University, 1943) and Ronald F. Howell, "Conservative Influences on Constitutional Development, 1923–1937" (The Johns Hopkins University, 1952). See also the unpublished master's essay by Paul E. Nelson, "The Constitutional Theory of Mr. Justice Roberts" (University of Chicago, 1960).

Owen J. Roberts

REPRESENTATIVE OPINIONS

HERNDON v. LOWRY, 301 U.S. 243 (1937)

This five to four opinion set aside the conviction of Angelo Herndon, a Negro organizer for the Communist party who had been found guilty of inciting insurrection by trying to enlist Negroes in that organization. The Georgia courts sentenced him to eighteen years in prison. Roberts' distinction in this case between the "clear and present danger" and "bad tendency" tests for freedom of speech considerably advanced civil liberties.

MR. JUSTICE ROBERTS delivered the opinion of the Court.

The appellant claims his conviction in a state court deprived him of his liberty contrary to the guarantees of the Fourteenth Amendment. He assigns as error the action of the Supreme Court of Georgia in overruling his claim and refusing him a discharge upon *habeas corpus*. The petition for the writ, presented to the Superior Court of Fulton County, asserted the appellant was unlawfully detained by the appellee as sheriff under the supposed authority of a judgment pronouncing him guilty of attempting to incite insurrection, as defined in § 56 of the Penal Code, and sentencing him to imprisonment for not less than eighteen nor more than twenty years. Attached were copies of the judgment and the indictment and a statement of the evidence upon which the verdict and judgment were founded. The petition alleged the judgment and sentence were void and appellant's detention illegal because the statute under which he was convicted denies and illegally restrains his freedom of speech and of assembly and is too vague and indefinite to provide a sufficiently ascertainable standard of guilt, and further alleged that there had been no adjudication by any court of the constitutional validity of the statute as applied to appellant's conduct. A writ issued. The appellee answered, demurred specially to, and moved to strike, so much of the petition as incorporated the evidence taken at the trial. At the hearing the statement of the evidence was identified and was conceded by the appellee to be full and accurate. The court denied the motion to strike, overruled the special demurrer and an objection to the admission of the trial record, decided that the statute, as construed and applied in the trial of the appellant, did not infringe his liberty of speech and of assembly but ran afoul of the Fourteenth Amendment because too vague and indefinite to provide a sufficiently ascertainable standard of guilt, and ordered the prisoner's discharge from custody. The appellee took the case to the Supreme Court of Georgia, assigning as error the ruling upon his demurrer, motion, and objection, and the decision against the validity of the statute. The appellant, in accordance with the state practice, also appealed, assigning as error the decision with respect to his right of free speech and of assembly. The two appeals were separately docketed but considered in a single opinion which reversed the judgment on the appellee's appeal and affirmed on that of the appellant,[1] concluding: "Under the pleadings and the evidence, which embraced the record on the trial that resulted in the conviction, the court erred, in the *habeas corpus* proceeding, in refusing to remand the prisoner to the custody of the officers."

The federal questions presented, and the manner in which they arise, appear from the record of appellant's trial and conviction embodied in the petition, and from the opinions of the State Supreme Court in the criminal proceeding.

At the July Term 1932 of the Superior Court of Fulton County an indictment was returned charging against the appellant an attempt to induce others to join in combined resistance to the lawful authority of the state with intent to deny, to defeat, and to overthrow such authority by open force, violent means, and unlawful acts; alleging that insurrection was intended to be manifested and accomplished by unlawful and violent acts. The indictment specified that the attempt was made by calling and attending public assemblies and by making speeches for the purpose of organizing and establishing groups and combinations of white and colored persons under the name of the Communist Party of Atlanta for the purpose of uniting, combining, and conspiring to incite riots and to embarrass and impede the orderly processes of the courts and offering combined resistance to, and, by force and violence, overthrowing and defeating the authority of the state; that by speech and persuasion, the appellant solicited and attempted to solicit persons to join, confederate with, and become members of the Communist Party and the Young Communist League and introduced into the state and circulated, aided and assisted in introducing and circulating booklets, papers, and other writings with the same intent and purpose. The charge was founded on § 56 of the Penal Code, one of four related sections. Section 55 defines insurrection, § 56 defines an attempt to incite insurrection, § 57 prescribes the death penalty for conviction of the offenses described in the two preceding sections unless the jury shall recommend mercy, and § 58 penalizes, by imprisonment, the introduction and circulation of printed matter for the purpose of inciting insurrection, riot, conspiracy, etc. The sections are copied in the margin.[2]

The appellant was brought to trial and convicted. He appealed on the ground that, under the statute as construed by the trial court in its instructions to the jury, there was no evidence to sustain a verdict of guilty. The Supreme Court affirmed the judgment upon a broader and different construction of the Act.[3] The appellant moved for a rehearing, contending, *inter alia,* that, as so construed, the statute violated the Fourteenth Amendment. The court refused to pass upon the constitutional questions thus raised, elaborated and explained its construction of the statute in its original

[1] *182 Ga. 582; 186 S.E. 429.*

[2] *"55. Insurrection shall consist in any combined resistance to the lawful authority of the State, with intent to the denial thereof, when the same is manifested or intended to be manifested by acts of violence.*

"56. Any attempt, by persuasion or otherwise, to induce others to join in any combined resistance to the lawful authority of the State shall constitute an attempt to incite insurrection.

"57. Any person convicted of the offense of insurrection, or an attempt to incite insurrection, shall be punished with death; or, if the jury recommend to mercy, confinement in the penitentiary for not less than five nor more than 20 years.

"58. If any person shall bring, introduce, print, or circulate, or cause to be introduced, circulated, or printed, or aid or assist, or be in any manner instrumental in bringing, introducing, circulating, or printing within this State any paper, pamphlet, circular, or any writing, for the purpose of inciting insurrection, riot, conspiracy, or resistance against the lawful authority of the State, or against the lives of the inhabitants thereof, or any part of them, he shall be punished by confinement in the penitentiary for not less than five nor longer than 20 years." (*Georgia Code, 1933, § § 26–901 to 26–904, inclusive.*)

[3] Herndon *v.* State, *178 Ga. 832; 174 S.E. 597.*

opinion, and denied a rehearing.[4] The appellant perfected an appeal to this court claiming that he had timely raised the federal questions and we, therefore, had jurisdiction to decide them. We held we were without jurisdiction.[5] Upon his commitment to serve his sentence he sought the writ of *habeas corpus.*

In the present proceeding the Superior Court and Supreme Court of Georgia have considered and disposed of the contentions based upon the Federal Constitution. The scope of a *habeas corpus* proceeding in the circumstances disclosed is a state and not a federal question and since the state courts treated the proceeding as properly raising issues of federal constitutional right, we have jurisdiction and all such issues are open here. We must, then, inquire whether the statute as applied in the trial denied appellant rights safeguarded by the Fourteenth Amendment.

The evidence on which the judgment rests consists of appellant's admissions and certain documents found in his possession. The appellant told the state's officers that some time prior to his arrest he joined the Communist Party in Kentucky and later came to Atlanta as a paid organizer for the party, his duties being to call meetings, to educate and disseminate information respecting the party, to distribute literature, to secure members, and to work up an organization of the party in Atlanta; and that he had held or attended three meetings called by him. He made no further admission as to what he did as an organizer, or what he said or did at the meetings. When arrested he carried a box containing documents. After he was arrested he conducted the officers to his room where additional documents and bundles of newspapers and periodicals were found, which he stated were sent him from the headquarters of the Communist Party in New York. He gave the names of persons who were members of the organization in Atlanta, and stated he had only five or six actual members at the time of his apprehension. The stubs of membership books found in the box indicated he had enrolled more members than he stated. There was no evidence that he had distributed any of the material carried on his person and found in his room, or had taken any of it to meetings, save two circulars or appeals respecting county relief which are confessedly innocuous.

The newspapers, pamphlets, periodicals, and other documents found in his room were, so he stated, intended for distribution at his meetings. These the appellee concedes were not introduced in evidence. Certain documents in his possession when he was arrested were placed in evidence. They fall into five classes: first, receipt books showing receipts of small sums of money, pads containing certificates of contributions to the Communist Party's Presidential Election Campaign Fund, receipts for rent of a post office box, and Communist Party membership books; secondly, printed matter consisting of magazines, pamphlets, and copies of the "Daily Worker," styled the "Central Organ of the Communist Party," and the "Southern Worker," also, apparently, an official newspaper of the party; thirdly, two books, one "Life and Struggles of Negro Toilers," by George Padmore, and the other "Communism and Christianism Analyzed and Contrasted from the Marxian and Darwinian Points of View," by Rt. Rev. William Montgomery Brown, D.D.; fourthly, transcripts of minutes of meetings apparently held in Atlanta; fifthly, two circulars, one of which was prepared by the appellant and both of which had been circulated by him in Fulton County. All of these may be dismissed as irrelevant except those falling within the first and second groups. No inference can be drawn from the possession of the books mentioned, either that they embodied the doctrines of the Communist Party or that they represented views advocated by the appellant. The minutes of meetings contain nothing indicating the purposes of the organization or any intent to overthrow organized government; on the contrary, they indicate merely discussion of relief for the unemployed. The two circulars, admittedly distributed by the appellant, had nothing to do with the Communist Party, its aims or purposes, and were not appeals to join the party but were concerned with unemployment relief in the county and included appeals to the white and Negro unemployed to organize and represent the need for further county aid. They were characterized by the Supreme Court of Georgia as "more or less harmless."

The documents of the first class disclose the activity of the appellant as an organizer but, in this respect, add nothing to his admissions.

The matter appearing upon the mem-

[4] Herndon *v.* State, *179 Ga. 597; 176 S.E. 620.*

[5] Herndon *v.* Georgia, *295 U.S. 441.*

bership blanks is innocent upon its face however foolish and pernicious the aims it suggests. Under the heading "What is the Communist Party?" this appears:

"The Party is the vanguard of the working class and consists of the best, most class conscious, most active, the most courageous members of that class. It incorporates the whole body of experience of the proletarian struggle, basing itself upon the revolutionary theory of Marxism and representing the general and lasting interests of the whole of the working class, the Party personifies the unity of proletarian principles, of proletarian will and of proletarian revolutionary action.

"We are the Party of the working class. Consequently, nearly the whole of that class (in time of war and civil war, the whole of that class) should work under the guidance of our Party, should create the closest contacts with our Party."

This vague declaration falls short of an attempt to bring about insurrection either immediately or within a reasonable time but amounts merely to a statement of ultimate ideals. The blanks, however, indicate more specific aims for which members of the Communist Party are to vote. They are to vote Communist for

"1. Unemployment and Social Insurance at the expense of the State and employers.

"2. Against Hoover's wage-cutting policy.

"3. Emergency relief for the poor farmers without restrictions by the government and banks; exemption of poor farmers from taxes and from forced collection of rents or debts.

"4. Equal rights for the Negroes and self-determination for the Black Belt.

"5. Against capitalistic terror: against all forms of suppression of the political rights of the workers.

"6. Against imperialist war; for the defense of the Chinese people and of the Soviet Union."

None of these aims is criminal upon its face. As to one, the 4th, the claim is that criminality may be found because of extrinsic facts. Those facts consist of possession by appellant of booklets and other literature of the second class illustrating the party doctrines. The State contends these show that the purposes of the Communist Party were forcible subversion of the lawful authority of Georgia. They contain, *inter alia,* statements to the effect that the party bases itself upon the revolutionary theory of Marxism, opposes "bosses' wars," approves of the Soviet Union, and desires the "smashing" of the National Guard, then C. M. T. C., and the R. O. T. C. But the State especially relies upon a booklet entitled "The Communist Position on the Negro Question," on the cover of which appears a map of the United States having a dark belt across certain Southern states and the phrase "Self-Determination for the Black Belt." The booklet affirms that the source of the Communist slogan "Right of Self-Determination of the Negroes in the Black Belt" is a resolution of the Communist International on the Negro question in the United States adopted in 1930, which states that the Communist Party in the United States has been actively attempting to win increasing sympathy among the Negro population, that certain things have been advocated for the benefit of the Negroes in the Northern states, but that in the Southern portion of the United States the Communist slogan must be "The Right of Self-Determination of the Negroes in the Black Belt." The resolution defines the meaning of the slogan as:

"(a) Confiscation of the landed property of the white landowners and capitalists for the benefit of the Negro farmers. . . . Without this revolutionary measure, without the agrarian revolution, the right of self-determination of the Negro population would be only a Utopia or, at best, would remain only on paper without changing in any way the actual enslavement."

"(b) Establishment of the State Unity of the Black Belt . . . If the right of self-determination of the Negroes is to be put into force, it is necessary wherever possible to bring together into one governmental unit all districts of the South where the majority of the settled population consists of Negroes . . ."

"(c) Right of Self-Determination. This means complete and unlimited right of the Negro majority to exercise governmental authority in the entire territory of the Black Belt, as well as to decide upon the relations between their territory and other nations, particularly the United States . . . First of all, true right to self-determination means that the Negro majority and not the white minority in the entire territory of the administratively united Black Belt exercises the right of administering governmental, legislative, and judicial authority. At the present time all this power is concentrated in the hands of the white bourgeoisie and landlords. It is they who appoint all officials, it is they who dispose of public property, it is they who determine the taxes, it is they who govern and make the laws. Therefore, the overthrow of this class rule in the Black Belt is unconditionally necessary in the struggle for the Negroes' right to self-determination. This, however, means at the same time the overthrow of the yoke of American imperialism in the Black Belt on which the forces of the local white bourgeoisie depend. Only in this way, only if the Negro population of the Black Belt wins its freedom from American imperialism even to the point of deciding itself the relations between its country and other governments, especially the United States, will it win real and complete self-determination. One should demand from the beginning that no armed forces of American imperialism should remain on the territory of the Black Belt."

Further statements appearing in the pamphlet are:

"Even if the situation does not yet warrant the raising of the question of uprising, one should not limit oneself at present to propaganda for the demand, 'Right to Self-Determination,' but should organize mass actions, such as demonstrations, strikes, tax boycott movements, etc."

"One cannot deny that it is just possible for the Negro population of the Black Belt to win the right to self-determination during capitalism; but it is perfectly clear and indubitable that this is possible only through successful revolutionary struggle for power against the American bourgeoisie, through wresting the Negroes' right of self-determination from American imperialism. Thus, the slogan of right to self-determination is a real slogan of National Rebellion which, to be considered as such, need not be supplemented by proclaiming struggle for the complete separation of the Negro zone, at least not at present."

There is more of the same purport, particularly references to the "revolutionary trade unions in the South," "revolutionary struggle against the ruling white bourgeoisie," and "revolutionary program of the Communist Party."

There is no evidence the appellant distributed any writings or printed matter found in the box he carried when arrested, or any other advocating forcible subversion of governmental authority. There is no evidence the appellant advocated, by speech or written word, at meetings or elsewhere, any doctrine or action implying such forcible subversion. There is evidence tending to prove that the appellant held meetings for the purpose of recruiting members of the Communist Party and solicited contributions for the support of that party and there is proof of the doctrines which that party espouses. Appellant's intent to incite insurrection, if it is to be found, must rest upon his procuring members for the Communist Party and his possession of that party's literature when he was arrested.

Section 55 of the Georgia Penal Code defines insurrection as "combined resistance to the lawful authority of the State, with intent to the denial thereof, when the same is manifested or intended to be manifested by acts of violence."[6] The appellant was not indicted under this section. Section 58 denounces the introduction, printing, or circulation, or assisting to print or circulate any document "for the purpose of inciting insurrection." The appellant was not indicted under this section.

Section 56, under which the indictment is laid, makes no reference to force or violence except by the phrase "combined resistance to the lawful authority of the State." The Supreme Court evidently importing from the similar phraseology in § 55 the additional element contained in that section, namely, "manifested or intended to be manifested by acts of violence," has decided that intended resort to force is an essential element of the offense defined by § 56.

To ascertain how the Act is held to apply to the appellant's conduct we turn to the rulings of the state courts in his case. The trial court instructed the jury: "In order to convict the defendant, . . . it must appear clearly by the evidence that immediate serious violence against the State of Georgia was to be expected or advocated." The jury rendered a verdict of guilty. In the Supreme Court the appellant urged that the evidence was wholly insufficient to sustain the verdict under the law as thus construed. That court sustained the conviction by construing the statute thus:

"Force must have been contemplated, but, as said above, the statute does not include either its occurrence or its imminence as an ingredient of the particular offense charged. . . . Nor would it be necessary to guilt that the alleged offender should have intended that an insurrection should follow instantly or at any given time,

[6] *Note 2,* supra.

but it would be sufficient that he intended it to happen at any time, as a result of his influence, by those whom he sought to incite."[7]

Upon application for rehearing the court further elaborated its views as to the meaning of the statute:

"Force must have been contemplated, but the statute does not include either its occurrence or its imminence as an ingredient of the particular offense charged. Nor would it be necessary to guilt that the alleged offender should have intended that an insurrection should follow instantly or at any given time, but as to this element it would be sufficient if he intended that it should happen at any time within which he might reasonably expect his influence to continue to be directly operative in causing such action by those whom he sought to induce. . . ."[8]

The affirmance of conviction upon the trial record necessarily gives § 56 the construction that one who seeks members for or attempts to organize a local unit of a party which has the purposes and objects disclosed by the documents in evidence may be found guilty of an attempt to incite insurrection.

The questions are whether this construction and application of the statute deprives the accused of the right of freedom of speech and of assembly guaranteed by the Fourteenth Amendment, and whether the statute so construed and applied furnishes a reasonably definite and ascertainable standard of guilt.

The appellant, while admitting that the people may protect themselves against abuses of the freedom of speech safeguarded by the Fourteenth Amendment by prohibiting incitement to violence and crime, insists that legislative regulation may not go beyond measures forefending against "clear and present danger" of the use of force against the state. For this position he relies upon our decisions under the Federal Espionage Acts[9] and cognate state legislation. These made it criminal wilfully to cause or to attempt to cause, or incite or attempt to incite, insubordination, disloyalty, mutiny or refusal of duty in the military or naval forces of the United States or wilfully to obstruct or attempt to obstruct the recruiting or enlistment service of the United States or to conspire for these purposes. We sustained the power of the government or a state to protect the war operations of the United States by punishing intentional interference with them. We recognized, however, that words may be spoken or written for various purposes and that wilful and intentional interference with the described operations of the government might be inferred from the time, place, and circumstances of the act. "The question in every case is whether the words used are used in such circumstances and are of such a nature as to create a clear and present danger that they will bring about the substantive evils that Congress has a right to prevent. It is a question of proximity and degree."[10]

The legislation under review differs radically from the Espionage Acts in that it does not deal with a wilful attempt to obstruct a described and defined activity of the government.

The State, on the other hand, insists that our decisions uphold state statutes making criminal utterances which have a "dangerous tendency" towards the subversion of government. It relies particularly upon *Gitlow* v. *New York,* 268 U.S. 652. There, however, we dealt with a statute which, quite unlike § 56 of the Georgia Criminal Code, denounced as criminal certain acts carefully and adequately described. We said:

"And a State may penalize utterances which openly advocate the overthrow of the representative and constitutional form of government of the United States and the several States, by violence or other unlawful means." (p. 668.)

"By enacting the present statute the State has determined, through its legislative body, that utterances advocating the overthrow of organized government by force, violence and unlawful means, are so inimical to the general welfare and involve such danger of substantive evil that they may be penalized in the exercise of its police power. That determination must be given great weight. Every presumption is to be indulged

[7] *178 Ga. 855, 174 S.E. 597.*

[8] *179 Ga. 600, 176 S.E. 622.*

[9] *Act of June 15, 1917, c. 30, 40 Stat. 217, 219; amended by Act of May 16, 1918, c. 75, 40 Stat. 553.*

[10] *See* Schenck *v.* United States, *249 U.S. 47, 52;* Frohwerk *v.* United States, *249 U.S. 204;* Debs *v.* United States, *249 U.S. 211;* Abrams *v.* United States, *250 U.S. 616;* Schaefer *v.* United States, *251 U.S. 466;* Pierce *v.* United States, *252 U.S. 239;* O'Connell *v.* United States, *253 U.S. 142;* State *v.* Holm, *139 Minn. 267; 166 N.W. 181;* Gilbert *v.* Minnesota, *254 U.S. 325.*

in favor of the validity of the statute. *Mugler* v. *Kansas,* 123 U.S. 623, 661. And the case is to be considered 'in the light of the principle that the State is primarily the judge of regulations required in the interest of public safety and welfare;' and that its police 'statutes may only be declared unconstitutional where they are arbitrary or unreasonable attempts to exercise authority vested in the State in the public interest.' "
And it was in connection with the statute there involved that the court quoted language relied upon below and in argument here from *People* v. *Lloyd,* 304 Ill. 23; 136 N. E. 505, to the effect that a state is not compelled to delay adoption of such preventive measures until the apprehended danger becomes certain. Out of excess of caution the distinction was again clearly drawn between acts of the order of the Espionage Act and the New York act under review.

". . . when the legislative body has determined generally, in the constitutional exercise of its discretion, that utterances of a certain kind involve such danger of substantive evil that they may be punished, the question whether any specific utterance coming within the prohibited class is likely, in and of itself, to bring about the substantive evil, is not open to consideration. It is sufficient that the statute itself be constitutional and that the use of the language comes within its prohibition.

"It is clear that the question in such cases is entirely different from that involved in those cases where the statute merely prohibits certain acts involving the danger of substantive evil, without any reference to language itself, and it is sought to apply its provisions to language used by the defendant for the purpose of bringing about the prohibited results. There, if it be contended that the statute cannot be applied to the language used by the defendant because of its protection by the freedom of speech or press, it must necessarily be found, as an original question, without any previous determination by the legislative body, whether the specific language used involved such likelihood of bringing about the substantive evil as to deprive it of the constitutional protection."

It is evident that the decision sustaining the New York statute furnishes no warrant for the appellee's contention that under a law general in its description of the mischief to be remedied and equally general in respect of the intent of the actor, the standard of guilt may be made the "dangerous tendency" of his words.

The power of a state to abridge freedom of speech and of assembly is the exception rather than the rule and the penalizing even of utterances of a defined character must find its justification in a reasonable apprehension of danger to organized government. The judgment of the legislature is not unfettered. The limitation upon individual liberty must have appropriate relation to the safety of the state. Legislation which goes beyond this need violates the principle of the Constitution. If, therefore, a state statute penalize innocent participation in a meeting held with an innocent purpose merely because the meeting was held under the auspices of an organization membership in which, or the advocacy of whose principles, is also denounced as criminal, the law, so construed and applied, goes beyond the power to restrict abuses of freedom of speech and arbitrarily denies that freedom.[11] And, where a statute is so vague and uncertain as to make criminal an utterance or an act which may be innocently said or done with no intent to induce resort to violence or on the other hand may be said or done with a purpose violently to subvert government, a conviction under such a law cannot be sustained. Upon this view we held bad a statute of California providing that "Any person who displays a red flag, . . . in any public place or in any meeting place or public assembly, or from or on any house, building or window as a sign, symbol or emblem of opposition to organized government . . . is guilty of a felony."[12]

After pointing out that peaceful agitation for a change of our form of government is within the guaranteed liberty of speech, we said of the act in question: "A statute which upon its face, and as authoritatively construed, is so vague and indefinite as to permit the punishment of the fair use of this opportunity is repugnant to the guaranty of liberty contained in the Fourteenth Amendment."

1. The appellant had a constitutional right to address meetings and organize parties unless in so doing he violated some prohibition of a valid statute. The only prohibition he is said to have violated is that of § 56 forbidding incitement or attempted incitement to insurrection by violence. If the

[11] DeJonge *v*. Oregon, *299 U.S. 353.*
[12] Stromberg *v*. California, *283 U.S. 359.*

evidence fails to show that he did so incite, then, as applied to him, the statute unreasonably limits freedom of speech and freedom of assembly and violates the Fourteenth Amendment. We are of opinion that the requisite proof is lacking. From what has been said above with respect to the evidence offered at the trial it is apparent that the documents found upon the appellant's person were certainly, as to some of the aims stated therein, innocent and consistent with peaceful action for a change in the laws or the constitution. The proof wholly fails to show that the appellant had read these documents; that he had distributed any of them; that he believed and advocated any or all of the principles and aims set forth in them, or that those he had procured to become members of the party knew or approved of any of these documents.

Thus, the crucial question is not the formal interpretation of the statute by the Supreme Court of Georgia but the application given it. In its application the offense made criminal is that of soliciting members for a political party and conducting meetings of a local unit of that party when one of the doctrines of the party, established by reference to a document not shown to have been exhibited to anyone by the accused, may be said to be ultimate resort to violence at some indefinite future time against organized government. It is to be borne in mind that the legislature of Georgia has not made membership in the Communist Party unlawful by reason of its supposed dangerous tendency even in the remote future. The question is not whether Georgia might, in analogy to what other states have done, so declare.[13] The appellant induced others to become members of the Communist Party. Did he thus incite to insurrection by reason of the fact that they agreed to abide by the tenets of the party, some of them lawful, others, as may be assumed, unlawful, in the absence of proof that he brought the unlawful aims to their notice, that he approved them, or that the fantastic program they envisaged was conceived of by anyone as more than an ultimate ideal? Doubtless circumstantial evidence might affect the answer to the question if appellant had been shown to have said that the Black Belt should be organized at once as a separate state and that that objective was one of his principal aims. But here circumstantial evidence is all to the opposite effect. The only objectives appellant is proved to have urged are those having to do with unemployment and emergency relief which are void of criminality. His membership in the Communist Party and his solicitation of a few members wholly fails to establish an attempt to incite others to insurrection. Indeed, so far as appears, he had but a single copy of the booklet the State claims to be objectionable; that copy he retained. The same may be said with respect to the other books and pamphlets, some of them of more innocent purport. In these circumstances, to make membership in the party and solicitation of members for that party a criminal offense, punishable by death, in the discretion of a jury, is an unwarranted invasion of the right of freedom of speech.

2. The statute, as construed and applied in the appellant's trial, does not furnish a sufficiently ascertainable standard of guilt. The Act does not prohibit incitement to violent interference with any given activity or operation of the state. By force of it, as construed, the judge and jury trying an alleged offender cannot appraise the circumstances and character of the defendant's utterances or activities as begetting a clear and present danger of forcible obstruction of a particular state function. Nor is any specified conduct or utterance of the accused made an offense.

The test of guilt is thus formulated by the Supreme Court of the state. Forcible action must have been contemplated but it would be sufficient to sustain a conviction if the accused intended that an insurrection "should happen at any time within which he might reasonably expect his influence to continue to be directly operative in causing such action by those whom he sought to induce." If the jury conclude that the defendant should have contemplated that any act or utterance of his in opposition to the established order or advocating a change in that order, might, in the distant future, eventuate in a combination to offer forcible resistance to the State, or as the State says, if the jury believe he should have known that his words would have "a dangerous tendency" then he may be convicted. To be guilty under the law, as construed, a defendant need not advocate resort to force. He need not teach any particular doctrine to come within its purview. Indeed, he need

[13] *See the statutes drawn in question in* Gitlow *v.* New York, *268 U.S. 652, at 654, and in* Whitney *v.* California, *274 U.S. 357, 359.*

not be active in the formation of a combination or group if he agitate for a change in the frame of government, however peaceful his own intent. If, by the exercise of prophecy, he can forecast that, as a result of a chain of causation, following his proposed action a group may arise at some future date which will resort to force, he is bound to make the prophecy and abstain, under pain of punishment, possibly of execution. Every person who attacks existing conditions, who agitates for a change in the form of government, must take the risk that if a jury should be of opinion he ought to have foreseen that his utterances might contribute in any measure to some future forcible resistance to the existing government he may be convicted of the offense of inciting insurrection. Proof that the accused in fact believed that his effort would cause a violent assault upon the state would not be necessary to conviction. It would be sufficient if the jury thought he reasonably might foretell that those he persuaded to join the party might, at some time in the indefinite future, resort to forcible resistance of government. The question thus proposed to a jury involves pure speculation as to future trends of thought and action. Within what time might one reasonably expect that an attempted organization of the Communist Party in the United States would result in violent action by that party? If a jury returned a special verdict saying twenty years or even fifty years the verdict could not be shown to be wrong. The law, as thus construed, licenses the jury to create its own standard in each case. In this aspect what was said in *United States* v. *Cohen Grocery Co.*, 255 U.S. 81, is particularly apposite:

"Observe that the section forbids no specific or definite act. It confines the subject-matter of the investigation which it authorizes to no element essentially inhering in the transaction as to which it provides. It leaves open, therefore, the widest conceivable inquiry, the scope of which no one can foresee and the result of which no one can foreshadow or adequately guard against. In fact, we see no reason to doubt the soundness of the observation of the court below, in its opinion, to the effect that, to attempt to enforce the section would be the exact equivalent of an effort to carry out a statute which in terms merely penalized and punished all acts detrimental to the public interest when unjust and unreasonable in the estimation of the court and jury . . ."

The decisions relied on by the State held the Sherman Law furnished a reasonable standard of guilt because it made a standard long recognized by the common law the statutory test.[14]

The statute, as construed and applied, amounts merely to a dragnet which may enmesh anyone who agitates for a change of government if a jury can be persuaded that he ought to have foreseen his words would have some effect in the future conduct of others. No reasonably ascertainable standard of guilt is prescribed. So vague and indeterminate are the boundaries thus set to the freedom of speech and assembly that the law necessarily violates the guarantees of liberty embodied in the Fourteenth Amendment.

The judgment is reversed and the case is remanded for further proceedings not inconsistent with this opinion.

Reversed.

[14] Waters-Pierce Oil Co. *v.* Texas, *212 U.S. 86;* Nash *v.* United States, *229 U.S. 373.*

UNITED STATES v. BUTLER, 297 U.S. 53 (1936)

This six to three decision declared the first Agricultural Adjustment Act unconstitutional. The law sought to decrease agricultural production by paying farmers for letting acreage lie fallow and thus increasing farm prices. A tax on food processors paid for the benefits. Roberts believed the law misused the taxing power and invaded the legislative domain of the states. It was a conservative decision, neglecting the range of implied powers of the government. Critics suggested Roberts was actually judging the wisdom of the law, whose coercive nature troubled him indeed. The decision was one of the most serious blows to the New Deal and produced one of Harlan Fiske Stone's finest dissents.

MR. JUSTICE ROBERTS delivered the opinion of the Court.

In this case we must determine whether certain provisions of the Agricultural Adjustment Act, 1933,[1] conflict with the Federal Constitution.

Title I of the statute is captioned "Agricultural Adjustment." Section 1 recites that an economic emergency has arisen, due to disparity between the prices of agricultural and other commodities, with consequent destruction of farmers' purchasing power and breakdown in orderly exchange, which, in turn, have affected transactions in agricultural commodities with a national public interest and burdened and obstructed the normal currents of commerce, calling for the enactment of legislation.

Section 2 declares it to be the policy of Congress:

"To establish and maintain such balance between the production and consumption of agricultural commodities, and such marketing conditions therefor, as will reëstablish prices to farmers at a level that will give agricultural commodities[2] a purchasing power with respect to articles that farmers buy, equivalent to the purchasing power of agricultural commodities in the base period."

The base period, in the case of cotton, and all other commodities except tobacco, is designated as that between August, 1909, and July, 1914.

The further policies announced are an approach to the desired equality by gradual correction of present inequities "at as rapid a rate as is deemed feasible in view of the current consumptive demand in domestic and foreign markets," and the protection of consumers' interest by readjusting farm production at such level as will not increase the percentage of the consumers' retail expenditures for agricultural commodities or products derived therefrom, which is returned to the farmer, above the percentage returned to him in the base period.

Section 8 provides, amongst other things, that "In order to effectuate the declared policy," the Secretary of Agriculture shall have power

"(1) To provide for reduction in the acreage or reduction in the production for market, or both, of any basic agricultural commodity, through agreements with producers or by other voluntary methods, and to provide for rental or benefit payments in connection therewith or upon that part of the production of any basic agricultural commodity required for domestic consumption, in such amounts as the Secretary deems fair and reasonable, to be paid out of any moneys available for such payments. . . ."

"(2) To enter into marketing agreements with processors, associations of producers, and others engaged in the handling, in the current of interstate or foreign commerce of any agricultural commodity or product thereof, after due notice and opportunity for hearing to interested parties. . . ."

[1] *May 12, 1933, c. 25, 48 Stat. 31.*

[2] *Section 11 denominates wheat, cotton, field corn, hogs, rice, tobacco, and milk and its products, "basic agricultural commodities," to which the act is to apply. Others have been added by later legislation.*

"(3) To issue licenses permitting processors, associations of producers, and others to engage in the handling, in the current of interstate or foreign commerce, of any agricultural commodity or product thereof, or any competing commodity or product thereof."

It will be observed that the Secretary is not required, but is permitted, if, in his uncontrolled judgment, the policy of the act will so be promoted, to make agreements with individual farmers for a reduction of acreage or production upon such terms as he may think fair and reasonable.

Section 9 (a) enacts:

"To obtain revenue for extraordinary expenses incurred by reason of the national economic emergency, there shall be levied processing taxes as hereinafter provided. When the Secretary of Agriculture determines that rental or benefit payments are to be made with respect to any basic agricultural commodity, he shall proclaim such determination, and a processing tax shall be in effect with respect to such commodity from the beginning of the marketing year therefor next following the date of such proclamation. The processing tax shall be levied, assessed, and collected upon the first domestic processing of the commodity, whether of domestic production or imported, and shall be paid by the processor. . . ."

The Secretary may from time to time, if he finds it necessary for the effectuation of the policy of the act, readjust the amount of the exaction to meet the requirements of subsection (b). The tax is to terminate at the end of any marketing year if the rental or benefit payments are discontinued by the Secretary with the expiration of that year.

Section 9 (b) fixes the tax "at such rate as equals the difference between the current average farm price for the commodity and the fair exchange value," with power in the Secretary, after investigation, notice, and hearing, to readjust the tax so as to prevent the accumulation of surplus stocks and depression of farm prices.

Section 9 (c) directs that the fair exchange value of a commodity shall be such a price as will give that commodity the same purchasing power with respect to articles farmers buy as it had during the base period and that the fair exchange value and the current average farm price of a commodity shall be ascertained by the Secretary from available statistics in his department.

Section 12 (a) appropriates $100,000,000 "to be available to the Secretary of Agriculture for administrative expenses under this title and for rental and benefit payments . . ."; and § 12 (b) appropriates the proceeds derived from all taxes imposed under the act "to be available to the Secretary of Agriculture for expansion of markets and removal of surplus agricultural products . . . administrative expenses, rental and benefit payments, and refunds on taxes."

Section 15 (d) permits the Secretary, upon certain conditions, to impose compensating taxes on commodities in competition with those subject to the processing tax.

By § 16 a floor tax is imposed upon the sale or other disposition of any article processed wholly or in chief value from any commodity with respect to which a processing tax is to be levied in amount equivalent to that of the processing tax which would be payable with respect to the commodity from which the article is processed if the processing had occurred on the date when the processing tax becomes effective.

On July 14, 1933, the Secretary of Agriculture, with the approval of the President, proclaimed that he had determined rental and benefit payments should be made with respect to cotton; that the marketing year for that commodity was to begin August 1, 1933; and calculated and fixed the rates of processing and floor taxes on cotton in accordance with the terms of the act.

The United States presented a claim to the respondents as receivers of the Hoosac Mills Corporation for processing and floor taxes on cotton levied under §§ 9 and 16 of the act. The receivers recommended that the claim be disallowed. The District Court found the taxes valid and ordered them paid.[3] Upon appeal the Circuit Court of Appeals reversed the order.[4] The judgment under review was entered prior to the adoption of the amending act of August 24, 1935,[5] and we are therefore concerned only with the original act.

First. At the outset the United States contends that the respondents have no standing to question the validity of the tax. The position is that the act is merely a revenue measure levying an excise upon the activity of processing cotton,—a proper subject for the imposition of such a tax,—the proceeds of which go into the federal treasury and

[3] Franklin Process Co. *v.* Hoosac Mills Corp., *8 F. Supp. 552.*

[4] Butler *v.* United States, *78 F. (2d) 1.*

[5] *49 Stat. 750, c. 641.*

thus become available for appropriation for any purpose. It is said that what the respondents are endeavoring to do is to challenge the intended use of the money pursuant to Congressional appropriation when, by confession, that money will have become the property of the Government and the taxpayer will no longer have any interest in it. *Massachusetts* v. *Mellon,* 262 U.S. 447, is claimed to foreclose litigation by the respondents or other taxpayers, as such, looking to restraint of the expenditure of government funds. That case might be an authority in the petitioners' favor if we were here concerned merely with a suit by a taxpayer to restrain the expenditure of the public moneys. It was there held that a taxpayer of the United States may not question expenditures from its treasury on the ground that the alleged unlawful diversion will deplete the public funds and thus increase the burden of future taxation. Obviously the asserted interest of a taxpayer in the federal government's funds and the supposed increase of the future burden of taxation is minute and indeterminable. But here the respondents who are called upon to pay moneys as taxes, resist the exaction as a step in an unauthorized plan. This circumstance clearly distinguishes the case. The Government in substance and effect asks us to separate the Agricultural Adjustment Act into two statutes, the one levying an excise on processors of certain commodities, the other appropriating the public moneys independently of the first. Passing the novel suggestion that two statutes enacted as parts of a single scheme should be tested as if they were distinct and unrelated, we think the legislation now before us is not susceptible of such separation and treatment.

The tax can only be sustained by ignoring the avowed purpose and operation of the act, and holding it a measure merely laying an excise upon processors to raise revenue for the support of government. Beyond cavil the sole object of the legislation is to restore the purchasing power of agricultural products to a parity with that prevailing in an earlier day; to take money from the processor and bestow it upon farmers[6] who will reduce their acreage for the accomplishment of the proposed end, and, meanwhile to aid these farmers during the period required to bring the prices of their crops to the desired level.

The tax plays an indispensable part in the plan of regulation. As stated by the Agricultural Adjustment Administrator, it is "the heart of the law"; a means of "accomplishing one or both of two things intended to help farmers attain parity prices and purchasing power."[7] A tax automatically goes into effect for a commodity when the Secretary of Agriculture determines that rental or benefit payments are to be made for reduction of production of that commodity. The tax is to cease when rental or benefit payments cease. The rate is fixed with the purpose of bringing about crop-reduction and price-raising. It is to equal the difference between the "current average farm price" and "fair exchange value." It may be altered to such amount as will prevent accumulation of surplus stocks. If the Secretary finds the policy of the act will not be promoted by the levy of the tax for a given commodity, he may exempt it. (§ 11.) The whole revenue from the levy is appropriated in aid of crop control; none of it is made available for general governmental use. The entire agricultural adjustment program embodied in Title I of the act is to become inoperative when, in the judgment of the President, the national economic emergency ends; and as to any commodity he may terminate the provisions of the law, if he finds them no longer requisite to carrying out the declared policy with respect to such commodity. (§ 13.)

The statute not only avows an aim foreign to the procurement of revenue for the support of government, but by its operation shows the exaction laid upon processors to be the necessary means for the intended control of agricultural production.

In these aspects the tax, so-called, closely resembles that laid by the Act of August 3, 1882, entitled "An Act to Regulate Immigration," which came before this court in the *Head Money Cases,* 112 U.S. 580. The statute directed that there should

[6] *U.S. Department of Agriculture, Achieving A Balanced Agriculture, p. 38: "Farmers should not forget that all the processing tax money ends up in their own pockets. Even in those cases where they pay part of the tax, they get it all back. Every dollar collected in processing taxes goes to the farmer in benefit payments."*

U.S. Dept. of Agriculture, The Processing Tax, p. 1: "Proceeds of processing taxes are passed to farmers as benefit payments."

[7] *U.S. Department of Agriculture, Agricultural Adjustment, p. 9.*

be levied, collected and paid a duty of fifty cents for each alien passenger who should come by vessel from a foreign port to one in the United States. Payment was to be made to the collector of the port by the master, owner, consignee or agent of the ship; the money was to be paid into the Treasury, was to be called the immigrant fund, and to be used by the Secretary of the Treasury to defray the expense of regulating immigration, for the care of immigrants and relieving those in distress, and for the expenses of effectuating the act.

Various objections to the act were presented. In answering them the court said:

"But the true answer to all these objections is that the power exercised in this instance is not the taxing power. The burden imposed on the ship owner by this statute is the mere incident of the regulation of commerce—of that branch of foreign commerce which is involved in immigration. . . ."

"It is true not much is said about protecting the ship owner. But he is the man who reaps the profit from the transaction, . . . The sum demanded of him is not, therefore, strictly speaking, a tax or duty within the meaning of the Constitution. The money thus raised, though paid into the Treasury, is appropriated in advance to the uses of the statute, and does not go to the general support of the government."

While there the exaction was sustained as an appropriate element in a plan within the power of Congress "to regulate commerce with foreign nations," no question was made of the standing of the shipowner to raise the question of the validity of the scheme and consequently of the exaction which was an incident of it.

It is inaccurate and misleading to speak of the exaction from processors prescribed by the challenged act as a tax, or to say that as a tax it is subject to no infirmity. A tax, in the general understanding of the term, and as used in the Constitution, signifies an exaction for the support of the Government. The word has never been thought to connote the expropriation of money from one group for the benefit of another. We may concede that the latter sort of imposition is constitutional when imposed to effectuate regulation of a matter in which both groups are interested and in respect of which there is a power of legislative regulation. But manifestly no justification for it can be found unless as an integral part of such regulation. The exaction cannot be wrested out of its setting, denominated an excise for raising revenue and legalized by ignoring its purpose as a mere instrumentality for bringing about a desired end. To do this would be to shut our eyes to what all others than we can see and understand. *Child Labor Tax Case,* 259 U.S. 20, 37.

We conclude that the act is one regulating agricultural production; that the tax is a mere incident of such regulation and that the respondents have standing to challenge the legality of the exaction.

It does not follow that as the act is not an exertion of the taxing power and the exaction not a true tax, the statute is void or the exaction uncollectible. For, to paraphrase what was said in the *Head Money Cases* (*supra*), if this is an expedient regulation by Congress, of a subject within one of its granted powers, "and the end to be attained is one falling within that power, the act is not void, because, within a loose and more extended sense than was used in the Constitution," the exaction is called a tax.

Second. The Government asserts that even if the respondents may question the propriety of the appropriation embodied in the statute their attack must fail because Article I, § 8 of the Constitution authorizes the contemplated expenditure of the funds raised by the tax. This contention presents the great and the controlling question in the case.[8] We approach its decision with a sense of our grave responsibility to render judgment in accordance with the principles established for the governance of all three branches of the Government.

There should be no misunderstanding as to the function of this court in such a

[8] *Other questions were presented and argued by counsel, but we do not consider or decide them. The respondents insist that the act in numerous respects delegates legislative power to the executive contrary to the principles announced in* Panama Refining Co. *v.* Ryan, *293 U.S. 388, and* Schechter Corp. *v.* United States, *295 U.S. 495; that this unlawful delegation is not cured by the amending act of August 24, 1935; that the exaction is in violation of the due process clause of the Fifth Amendment since the legislation takes their property for a private use; that the floor tax is a direct tax and therefore void for lack of apportionment amongst the states, as required by Article I, § 9; and that the processing tax is wanting in uniformity and so violates Article I, § 8, clause one, of the Constitution.*

case. It is sometimes said that the court assumes a power to overrule or control the action of the people's representatives. This is a misconception. The Constitution is the supreme law of the land ordained and established by the people. All legislation must conform to the principles it lays down. When an act of Congress is appropriately challenged in the courts as not conforming to the constitutional mandate the judicial branch of the Government has only one duty,—to lay the article of the Constitution which is invoked beside the statute which is challenged and to decide whether the latter squares with the former. All the court does, or can do, is to announce its considered judgment upon the question. The only power it has, if such it may be called, is the power of judgment. This court neither approves nor condemns any legislative policy. Its delicate and difficult office is to ascertain and declare whether the legislation is in accordance with, or in contravention of, the provisions of the Constitution; and, having done that, its duty ends.[9]

The question is not what power the Federal Government ought to have but what powers in fact have been given by the people. It hardly seems necessary to reiterate that ours is a dual form of government; that in every state there are two governments,—the state and the United States. Each State has all governmental powers save such as the people, by their Constitution, have conferred upon the United States, denied to the States, or reserved to themselves. The federal union is a government of delegated powers. It has only such as are expressly conferred upon it and such as are reasonably to be implied from those granted. In this respect we differ radically from nations where all legislative power, without restriction or limitation, is vested in a parliament or other legislative body subject to no restrictions except the discretion of its members.

Article I, § 8, of the Constitution vests sundry powers in the Congress. But two of its clauses have any bearing upon the validity of the statute under review.

The third clause endows the Congress with power "to regulate Commerce . . . among the several States." Despite a reference in its first section to a burden upon, and an obstruction of the normal currents of commerce, the act under review does not purport to regulate transactions in interstate or foreign[10] commerce. Its stated purpose is the control of agricultural production, a purely local activity, in an effort to raise the prices paid the farmer. Indeed, the Government does not attempt to uphold the validity of the act on the basis of the commerce clause, which, for the purpose of the present case, may be put aside as irrelevant.

The clause thought to authorize the legislation,—the first,—confers upon the Congress power "to lay and collect Taxes, Duties, Imposts and Excises, to pay the Debts and provide for the common Defence and general Welfare of the United States. . . ." It is not contended that this provision grants power to regulate agricultural production upon the theory that such legislation would promote the general welfare. The Government concedes that the phrase "to provide for the general welfare" qualifies the power "to lay and collect taxes." The view that the clause grants power to provide for the general welfare, independently of the taxing power, has never been authoritatively accepted. Mr. Justice Story points out that if it were adopted "it is obvious that under color of the generality of the words, to 'provide for the common defence and general welfare,' the government of the United States is, in reality, a government of general and unlimited powers, notwithstanding the subsequent enumeration of specific powers."[11] The true construction undoubtedly is that the only thing granted is the power to tax for the purpose of providing funds for payment of the nation's debts and making provision for the general welfare.

Nevertheless the Government asserts that warrant is found in this clause for the adoption of the Agricultural Adjustment Act. The argument is that Congress may appropriate and authorize the spending of moneys for the "general welfare"; that the phrase should be liberally construed to cover anything conducive to national welfare; that decision as to what will promote such welfare rests with Congress alone, and the courts may not review its determination; and finally that the appropriation under

[9] *Compare* Adkins *v.* Children's Hospital, *261 U.S. 525, 544;* Massachusetts *v.* Mellon, *262 U.S. 447, 488.*

[10] *The enactment of protective tariff laws has its basis in the power to regulate foreign commerce. See* Board of Trustees of the University of Illinois *v.* United States, *289 U.S. 48, 58.*

[11] *Story, Commentaries on the Constitution of the United States, 5th ed., Vol. I, § 907.*

attack was in fact for the general welfare of the United States.

The Congress is expressly empowered to lay taxes to provide for the general welfare. Funds in the Treasury as a result of taxation may be expended only through appropriation. (Art. I, § 9, cl. 7.) They can never accomplish the objects for which they were collected unless the power to appropriate is as broad as the power to tax. The necessary implication from the terms of the grant is that the public funds may be appropriated "to provide for the general welfare of the United States." These words cannot be meaningless, else they would not have been used. The conclusion must be that they were intended to limit and define the granted power to raise and to expend money. How shall they be construed to effectuate the intent of the instrument?

Since the foundation of the Nation sharp differences of opinion have persisted as to the true interpretation of the phrase. Madison asserted it amounted to no more than a reference to the other powers enumerated in the subsequent clauses of the same section; that, as the United States is a government of limited and enumerated powers, the grant of power to tax and spend for the general national welfare must be confined to the enumerated legislative fields committed to the Congress. In this view the phrase is mere tautology, for taxation and appropriation are or may be necessary incidents of the exercise of any of the enumerated legislative powers. Hamilton, on the other hand, maintained the clause confers a power separate and distinct from those later enumerated, is not restricted in meaning by the grant of them, and Congress consequently has a substantive power to tax and to appropriate, limited only by the requirement that it shall be exercised to provide for the general welfare of the United States. Each contention has had the support of those whose views are entitled to weight. This court has noticed the question, but has never found it necessary to decide which is the true construction. Mr. Justice Story, in his Commentaries, espouses the Hamiltonian position.[12] We shall not review the writings of public men and commentators or discuss the legislative practice. Study of all these leads us to conclude that the reading advocated by Mr. Justice Story is the correct one. While, therefore, the power to tax is not unlimited, its confines are set in the clause which confers it, and not in those of § 8 which bestow and define the legislative powers of the Congress. It results that the power of Congress to authorize expenditure of public moneys for public purposes is not limited by the direct grants of legislative power found in the Constitution.

But the adoption of the broader construction leaves the power to spend subject to limitations.

As Story says:

"The Constitution was, from its very origin, contemplated to be the frame of a national government, of special and enumerated powers, and not of general and unlimited powers."[13]

Again he says:

"A power to lay taxes for the common defence and general welfare of the United States is not in common sense a general power. It is limited to those objects. It cannot constitutionally transcend them."[14]

That the qualifying phrase must be given effect all advocates of broad construction admit. Hamilton, in his well known Report on Manufactures, states that the purpose must be "general, and not local."[15] Monroe, an advocate of Hamilton's doctrine, wrote: "Have Congress a right to raise and appropriate the money to any and to every purpose according to their will and pleasure? They certainly have not."[16] Story says that if the tax be not proposed for the common defence or general welfare, but for other objects wholly extraneous, it would be wholly indefensible upon constitutional principles.[17] And he makes it clear that the powers of taxation and appropriation extend only to matters of national, as distinguished from local welfare.

As elsewhere throughout the Constitution the section in question lays down principles which control the use of the power, and does not attempt meticulous or detailed directions. Every presumption is to be indulged in favor of faithful compliance by Congress with the mandates of the fundamental law. Courts are reluctant to adjudge any statute in contravention of them. But, under our frame of government, no other place is provided where the citizen may be heard to urge that the law fails to conform

[12] Loc. cit. *Chapter XIV*, passim.

[13] Loc. cit. *§ 909.*

[14] Loc. cit. *§ 922.*

[15] *Works, Vol. III, p. 250.*

[16] *Richardson, Messages and Papers of the Presidents, Vol. II, p. 167.*

[17] Loc. cit. *p. 673.*

to the limits set upon the use of a granted power. When such a contention comes here we naturally require a showing that by no reasonable possibility can the challenged legislation fall within the wide range of discretion permitted to the Congress. How great is the extent of that range, when the subject is the promotion of the general welfare of the United States, we hardly need remark. But, despite the breadth of the legislative discretion, our duty to hear and to render judgment remains. If the statute plainly violates the stated principle of the Constitution we must so declare.

We are not now required to ascertain the scope of the phrase "general welfare of the United States" or to determine whether an appropriation in aid of agriculture falls within it. Wholly apart from that question, another principle embedded in our Constitution prohibits the enforcement of the Agricultural Adjustment Act. The act invades the reserved rights of the states. It is a statutory plan to regulate and control agricultural production, a matter beyond the powers delegated to the federal government. The tax, the appropriation of the funds raised, and the direction for their disbursement, are but parts of the plan. They are but means to an unconstitutional end.

From the accepted doctrine that the United States is a government of delegated powers, it follows that those not expressly granted, or reasonably to be implied from such as are conferred, are reserved to the states or to the people. To forestall any suggestion to the contrary, the Tenth Amendment was adopted.[18] The same proposition, otherwise stated, is that powers not granted are prohibited. None to regulate agricultural production is given, and therefore legislation by Congress for that purpose is forbidden.

It is an established principle that the attainment of a prohibited end may not be accomplished under the pretext of the exertion of powers which are granted.

"Should Congress, in the execution of its powers, adopt measures which are prohibited by the constitution; or should Congress, under the pretext of executing its powers, pass laws for the accomplishment of objects not intrusted to the government; it would become the painful duty of this tribunal, should a case requiring such a decision come before it, to say that such an act was not the law of the land." *McCulloch* v. *Maryland,* 4 Wheat. 316, 423.

"Congress cannot, under the pretext of executing delegated power, pass laws for the accomplishment of objects not entrusted to the Federal Government. And we accept as established doctrine that any provision of an act of Congress ostensibly enacted under power granted by the Constitution, not naturally and reasonably adapted to the effective exercise of such power but solely to the achievement of something plainly within power reserved to the States, is invalid and cannot be enforced." *Linder* v. *United States,* 268 U.S. 5, 17.

These principles are as applicable to the power to lay taxes as to any other federal power. Said the court, in *McCulloch* v. *Maryland, supra,* 421:

"Let the end be legitimate, let it be within the scope of the constitution, and all means which are appropriate, which are plainly adapted to that end, which are not prohibited, but consist with the letter and spirit of the constitution, are constitutional."

The power of taxation, which is expressly granted, may, of course, be adopted as a means to carry into operation another power also expressly granted. But resort to the taxing power to effectuate an end which is not legitimate, not within the scope of the Constitution, is obviously inadmissible.

"Congress is not empowered to tax for those purposes which are within the exclusive province of the States." *Gibbons* v. *Ogden,* 9 Wheat. 1, 199.

"There are, indeed, certain virtual limitations arising from the principles of the Constitution itself. It would undoubtedly be an abuse of the [taxing] power if so exercised as to impair the separate existence and independent self-government of the States or if exercised for ends inconsistent with the limited grants of power in the Constitution." *Veazie Bank* v. *Fenno,* 8 Wall. 533, 541.

In the *Child Labor Tax Case,* 259 U.S. 20, and in *Hill* v. *Wallace,* 259 U.S. 44, this court had before it statutes which purported to be taxing measures. But their purpose was found to be to regulate the conduct of manufacturing and trading, not in interstate commerce, but in the states,—matters not within any power conferred upon Congress by the Constitution—and the levy of the tax a means to force compliance. The court held this was not a constitutional use, but an

[18] *The Tenth Amendment declares: "The powers not delegated to the United States by the Constitution, nor prohibited by it to the States, are reserved to the States respectively or to the people."*

unconstitutional abuse of the power to tax. In *Linder* v. *United States, supra,* we held that the power to tax could not justify the regulation of the practice of a profession, under the pretext of raising revenue. In *United States* v. *Constantine,* 296 U.S. 287, we declared that Congress could not, in the guise of a tax, impose sanctions for violation of state law respecting the local sale of liquor. These decisions demonstrate that Congress could not, under the pretext of raising revenue, lay a tax on processors who refuse to pay a certain price for cotton, and exempt those who agree so to do, with the purpose of benefiting producers.

Third. If the taxing power may not be used as the instrument to enforce a regulation of matters of state concern with respect to which the Congress has no authority to interfere, may it, as in the present case, be employed to raise the money necessary to purchase a compliance which the Congress is powerless to command? The Government asserts that whatever might be said against the validity of the plan if compulsory, it is constitutionally sound because the end is accomplished by voluntary cooperation. There are two sufficient answers to the contention. The regulation is not in fact voluntary. The farmer, of course, may refuse to comply, but the price of such refusal is the loss of benefits. The amount offered is intended to be sufficient to exert pressure on him to agree to the proposed regulation.[19] The power to confer or withhold unlimited benefits is the power to coerce or destroy. If the cotton grower elects not to accept the benefits, he will receive less for his crops; those who receive payments will be able to undersell him. The result may well be financial ruin. The coercive purpose and intent of the statute is not obscured by the fact that it has not been perfectly successful. It is pointed out that, because there still remained a minority whom the rental and benefit payments were insufficient to induce to surrender their independence of action, the Congress has gone further and, in the Bankhead Cotton Act, used the taxing power in a more directly minatory fashion to compel submission. This progression only serves more fully to expose the coercive purpose of the so-called tax imposed by the present act. It is clear that the Department of Agriculture has properly described the plan as one to keep a non-coöperating minority in line. This is coercion by economic pressure. The asserted power of choice is illusory.

In *Frost Trucking Co.* v. *Railroad Comm'n,* 271 U.S. 583, a state act was considered which provided for supervision and regulation of transportation for hire by automobile on the public highways. Certificates of convenience and necessity were to be obtained by persons desiring to use the highways for this purpose. The regulatory commission required that a private contract carrier should secure such a certificate as a condition of its operation. The effect of the commission's action was to transmute the private carrier into a public carrier. In other words, the privilege of using the highways as a private carrier for compensation was conditioned upon his dedicating his property to the quasi-public use of public transportation. While holding that the private carrier was not obliged to submit himself to the condition, the commission denied him the privilege of using the highways if he did not do so. The argument was, as here, that the carrier had a free choice. This court said, in holding the act as construed unconstitutional:

"If so, constitutional guaranties, so carefully safeguarded against direct assault, are open to destruction by the indirect but no less effective process of requiring a surrender, which, though, in form voluntary, in fact lacks none of the elements of compulsion. Having regard to form alone, the act here is an offer to the private carrier of a privilege, which the state may grant or deny, upon a condition, which the carrier is free to accept or reject. In reality, the carrier is given no choice, except a choice between the rock and the whirlpool,—an option to forego a privilege which may be vital to his

[19] *U.S. Dept. of Agriculture, Agricultural Adjustment, p. 9. "Experience of cooperative associations and other groups has shown that without such Government support, the efforts of the farmers to band together to control the amount of their product sent to market are nearly always brought to nothing. Almost always, under such circumstances, there has been a noncooperating minority, which, refusing to go along with the rest, has stayed on the outside and tried to benefit from the sacrifices the majority has made. . . . It is to keep this noncooperating minority in line, or at least prevent it from doing harm to the majority, that the power of the Government has been marshaled behind the adjustment programs."*

livelihood or submit to a requirement which may constitute an intolerable burden."

But if the plan were one for purely voluntary co-operation it would stand no better so far as federal power is concerned. At best it is a scheme for purchasing with federal funds submission to federal regulation of a subject reserved to the states.

It is said that Congress has the undoubted right to appropriate money to executive officers for expenditure under contracts between the government and individuals; that much of the total expenditures is so made. But appropriations and expenditures under contracts for proper governmental purposes cannot justify contracts which are not within federal power. And contracts for the reduction of acreage and the control of production are outside the range of that power. An appropriation to be expended by the United States under contracts calling for violation of a state law clearly would offend the Constitution. Is a statute less objectionable which authorizes expenditure of federal moneys to induce action in a field in which the United States has no power to intermeddle? The Congress cannot invade state jurisdiction to compel individual action; no more can it purchase such action.

We are referred to numerous types of federal appropriation which have been made in the past, and it is asserted no question has been raised as to their validity. We need not stop to examine or consider them. As was said in *Massachusetts* v. *Mellon, supra.*

". . . as an examination of the acts of Congress will disclose, a large number of statutes appropriating or involving the expenditure of moneys for non-federal purposes have been enacted and carried into effect."

As the opinion points out, such expenditures have not been challenged because no remedy was open for testing their constitutionality in the courts.

We are not here concerned with a conditional appropriation of money, nor with a provision that if certain conditions are not complied with the appropriation shall no longer be available. By the Agricultural Adjustment Act the amount of the tax is appropriated to be expended only in payment under contracts whereby the parties bind themselves to regulation by the Federal Government. There is an obvious difference between a statute stating the conditions upon which moneys shall be expended and one effective only upon assumption of a contractual obligation to submit to a regulation which otherwise could not be enforced. Many examples pointing the distinction might be cited. We are referred to appropriations in aid of education, and it is said that no one has doubted the power of Congress to stipulate the sort of education for which money shall be expended. But an appropriation to an educational institution which by its terms is to become available only if the beneficiary enters into a contract to teach doctrines subversive of the Constitution is clearly bad. An affirmance of the authority of Congress so to condition the expenditure of an appropriation would tend to nullify all constitutional limitations upon legislative power.

But it is said that there is a wide difference in another respect, between compulsory regulation of the local affairs of a state's citizens and the mere making of a contract relating to their conduct; that, if any state objects, it may declare the contract void and thus prevent those under the state's jurisdiction from complying with its terms. The argument is plainly fallacious. The United States can make the contract only if the federal power to tax and to appropriate reaches the subject matter of the contract. If this does reach the subject matter, its exertion cannot be displaced by state action. To say otherwise is to deny the supremacy of the laws of the United States; to make them subordinate to those of a State. This would reverse the cardinal principle embodied in the Constitution and substitute one which declares that Congress may only effectively legislate as to matters within federal competence when the States do not dissent.

Congress has no power to enforce its commands on the farmer to the ends sought by the Agricultural Adjustment Act. It must follow that it may not indirectly accomplish those ends by taxing and spending to purchase compliance. The Constitution and the entire plan of our government negative any such use of the power to tax and to spend as the act undertakes to authorize. It does not help to declare that local conditions throughout the nation have created a situation of national concern; for this is but to say that whenever there is a widespread similarity of local conditions, Congress may ignore constitutional limitations upon its own powers and usurp those reserved to the states. If, in lieu of compulsory regulation of subjects within the states' reserved jurisdiction, which is prohibited, the Congress could invoke the taxing and spending power as a means to accomplish the same end, clause 1 of § 8 of Article I would become the instrument for total subversion of the governmental powers reserved to the individual states.

If the act before us is a proper exercise of the federal taxing power, evidently the regulation of all industry throughout the United States may be accomplished by similar exercises of the same power. It would be possible to exact money from one branch of an industry and pay it to another branch in every field of activity which lies within the province of the states. The mere threat of such a procedure might well induce the surrender of rights and the compliance with federal regulation as the price of continuance in business. A few instances will illustrate the thought.

Let us suppose Congress should determine that the farmer, the miner or some other producer of raw materials is receiving too much for his products, with consequent depression of the processing industry and idleness of its employees. Though, by confession, there is no power vested in Congress to compel by statute a lowering of the prices of the raw material, the same result might be accomplished, if the questioned act be valid, by taxing the producer upon his output and appropriating the proceeds to the processors, either with or without conditions imposed as the consideration for payment of the subsidy.

We have held in *Schechter Poultry Corp.* v. *United States,* 295 U.S. 495, that Congress has no power to regulate wages and hours of labor in a local business. If the petitioner is right, this very end may be accomplished by appropriating money to be paid to employers from the federal treasury under contracts whereby they agree to comply with certain standards fixed by federal law or by contract.

Should Congress ascertain that sugar refiners are not receiving a fair profit, and that this is detrimental to the entire industry, and in turn has its repercussions in trade and commerce generally, it might, in analogy to the present law, impose an excise of two cents a pound on every sale of the commodity and pass the funds collected to such refiners, and such only, as will agree to maintain a certain price.

Assume that too many shoes are being manufactured throughout the nation; that the market is saturated, the price depressed, the factories running half-time, the employees suffering. Upon the principle of the statute in question Congress might authorize the Secretary of Commerce to enter into contracts with shoe manufacturers providing that each shall reduce his output and that the United States will pay him a fixed sum proportioned to such reduction, the money to make the payments to be raised by a tax on all retail shoe dealers or their customers.

Suppose that there are too many garment workers in the large cities; that this results in dislocation of the economic balance. Upon the principle contended for an excise might be laid on the manufacture of all garments manufactured and the proceeds paid to those manufacturers who agree to remove their plants to cities having not more than a hundred thousand population. Thus, through the asserted power of taxation, the federal government, against the will of individual states, might completely redistribute the industrial population.

A possible result of sustaining the claimed federal power would be that every business group which thought itself underprivileged might demand that a tax be laid on its vendors or vendees, the proceeds to be appropriated to the redress of its deficiency of income.

These illustrations are given, not to suggest that any of the purposes mentioned are unworthy, but to demonstrate the scope of the principle for which the Government contends; to test the principle by its applications; to point out that, by the exercise of the asserted power, Congress would, in effect, under the pretext of exercising the taxing power, in reality accomplish prohibited ends. It cannot be said that they envisage improbable legislation. The supposed cases are no more improbable than would the present act have been deemed a few years ago.

Until recently no suggestion of the existence of any such power in the Federal Government has been advanced. The expressions of the framers of the Constitution, the decisions of this court interpreting that instrument, and the writings of great commentators will be searched in vain for any suggestion that there exists in the clause under discussion or elsewhere in the Constitution, the authority whereby every provision and every fair implication from that instrument may be subverted, the independence of the individual states obliterated, and the United States converted into a central government exercising uncontrolled police power in every state of the Union, superseding all local control or regulation of the affairs or concerns of the states.

Hamilton himself, the leading advocate of broad interpretation of the power to tax and to appropriate for the general welfare, never suggested that any power granted by the Constitution could be used for the destruction of local self-government in the states. Story countenances no such doctrine. It seems never to have occurred to them, or to those who have agreed with them, that the general welfare of the United States, (which has aptly been termed "an indestructible Union, composed of indestructible States,") might be served by obliterating the constituent members of the Union. But to this fatal conclusion the doctrine contended for would inevitably lead. And its sole premise is that, though the makers of the Constitution, in erecting the federal government, intended sedulously to limit and define its powers, so as to reserve to the states and the people sovereign power, to be wielded by the states and their citizens and not to be invaded by the United States, they nevertheless by a single clause gave power to the Congress to tear down the barriers, to invade the states' jurisdiction, and to become a parliament of the whole people, subject to no restrictions save such as are self-imposed. The argument when seen in its true character and in the light of its inevitable results must be rejected.

Since, as we have pointed out, there was no power in the Congress to impose the contested exaction, it could not lawfully ratify or confirm what an executive officer had done in that regard. Consequently the Act of 1935 does not affect the rights of the parties.

The judgment is

Affirmed.

Benjamin Cardozo

☆ 1870–1938 ☆

APPOINTED BY

HERBERT HOOVER

YEARS ON COURT

1932–1938

Benjamin Cardozo

by

ANDREW L. KAUFMAN

ON JANUARY 12, 1932, at the age of ninety, Oliver Wendell Holmes sent his resignation as Justice of the Supreme Court of the United States to President Herbert Hoover. There followed the usual speculation about a successor, but with a difference. Throughout the country leading newspapers, political leaders, spokesmen for the bar, deans and professors at law schools, publicly stated their conviction that Benjamin Nathan Cardozo, then Chief Judge of the New York Court of Appeals, would be the most worthy successor to Holmes. This near unanimity of opinion was not merely surprising. It was unparalleled in the history of Supreme Court appointments. President Hoover deliberated for a month. Then, despite the fact that there were two Justices from New York City, Hughes and Stone, and one Jew, Brandeis, already on the bench, Hoover nominated Cardozo.

At the time of his nomination, Cardozo had made significant contributions to the law of his state and of the nation. As Associate Judge of the New York Court of Appeals for thirteen years and Chief Judge for five years, Cardozo was the most distinguished judge of the most distinguished state court in the country. In addition, he had contributed a unique series of lectures entitled *The Nature of the Judicial Process,* and was active in several movements for law reform.

Except for his obvious talents, nothing in the first forty-three years of Cardozo's life hinted at the prominence he was to attain so rapidly thereafter. His whole life theretofore had been characterized by devotion to his family and to his work. He was born on May 24, 1870, into a family of Sephardic Jews, both branches of which had lived in this country since the middle of the eighteenth century and had contributed men and women of talent to the American scene—a courageous rabbi during the Revolutionary War, who was one of the first trustees of Columbia College; prominent businessmen; the author of the

ANDREW L. KAUFMAN, is a Professor at the Harvard Law School and is completing a biography of Justice Cardozo.

moving words inscribed on the base of the Statue of Liberty. Closer to home and of vital but indeterminable effect on Benjamin Cardozo's life was the career of his father—a judge first of the Court of Common Pleas and then of the Supreme Court of New York who became heavily involved in the judicial machinations of the Tweed Ring and resigned just in time to avoid impeachment.

Benjamin Cardozo's childhood was lived in the aftermath of these events. His schooling was home tutoring, one tutor being Horatio Alger; Columbia College, which he entered at the age of fifteen and finished at the top of his class; and Columbia Law School, leaving, as was not uncommon in those days, before his third year to enter practice with his older brother. Cardozo never married, and he lived with his older, unmarried sister Ellen until her death in 1929. They were extremely close, both intellectually and emotionally, and this relationship was the most important in their lives.

Cardozo became known at the bar early, and before long other lawyers were referring important cases, especially at the appellate level, to him. By the time he went on the bench, he had already presented some seventy-five cases in the New York Court of Appeals during his twenty-two years as a practicing attorney. Cardozo's career at the bar, however, unlike that of Brandeis, was not linked with vital litigation affecting the organization of society or with any important reform movements. His counsel was sought primarily in corporate and commercial litigation and in litigation involving the disposition of property. The common law and statutes dealing with common law subjects were his bailiwick.

As an advocate, Cardozo's manner must have been deceptive. Quiet, mild-mannered, an almost feminine softness, gentle, shy, courteous, courtly, lonely, ascetic, saintly—these are the descriptive words most often associated with what John Lord O'Brian has called "the strangely compelling power of that reticent, sensitive and almost mystical personality." 305 U.S. ix (1938) Such a personality is not usually associated with the successful courtroom lawyer. But his intellectual equipment conjoined with, or perhaps overcame, these personal qualities to produce a persuasive advocate.

There was also another, less well-known side to Cardozo's personality. Learned Hand has said: "Very few have ever known what went on behind those blue eyes." (Interview with author.) The calm, courteous exterior concealed a detached, observing outlook on life and on people. As life and people are not always kindly, so his view of them was not always kindly. Cardozo did not like to cause hurt, however, and he usually kept his views to himself. It required an extraordinary occasion or a close friend, of whom there were few, for him to speak his mind. More often, he erred on the side of extravagant praise, which he both gave to others and enjoyed himself.

This unusual combination of qualities combined to make a compelling figure, and despite the fact that Cardozo had taken very little part in the extracurricular life of the bar and none at all in politics, he was known to Charles C. Burlingham and other leading lawyers in New York City who put forth his name as a judicial candidate on the fusion ticket that wrested control of the city government from Tammany Hall in 1913. The story is told that Cardozo would not campaign for himself and that his campaign was run by others. Cardozo's letters reveal, however, that he kept abreast of events and he made several suggestions that dispel any aura of political naiveté. He won a narrow victory, and at the age of forty-three, he began his public career as a judge of the New York Supreme Court. After one month he was assigned by Governor Glynn to the Court of Appeals to help in clearing its calendar and he thereafter became a permanent member of that bench.

It is most difficult to summarize adequately in a few pages Cardozo's contributions to the law during his eighteen years on the Court of Appeals. Unlike Marshall, who laid the foundations of national power, unlike Story and Kent, who gave substance to the primitive state of the common law in the new United States, and unlike Holmes, who rethought basic principles of the common law and expressed dynamically basic principles of constitutional adjudication, Cardozo's contributions, though numerous and important, are more difficult to characterize. In a short essay one can only suggest briefly and without detailed examination some of the more important aspects.

We turn first to Cardozo's opinions. In a joint memorial issue to Justice Cardozo published shortly after his death on July 9, 1938, by the Harvard, Yale and Columbia Law Reviews, Professor Corbin set forth his analysis of Cardozo's contribution to the law of contracts:

> *It cannot be said that he made any extensive changes in the existing law of contracts. To state the facts of the cases, the decision, and the reasoning of his opinion will not show the overthrow of old doctrine or the establishment of new. Instead, it will show the application of existing doctrines with wisdom and discretion; an application that does not leave those doctrines wholly unaffected, but one that carries on their evolution as is reasonably required by the new facts before the court. When Cardozo is through, the law is not exactly as it was before; but there has been no sudden shift or revolutionary change. . . .* [*"Mr. Justice Cardozo and the Law of Contracts," 52* Harvard Law Review *408–09 (1939)*].

It is true that Cardozo was not a Lord Mansfield. The common law and commercial law in particular was in a more rudimentary and formative state in the eighteenth century and Mansfield had comparatively a free hand. By the twentieth century, the generalized rules in all branches of the common law had become fairly well settled and no court could have attempted a large-scale revision. While the usual case did involve no more than application of "existing doctrines," occasionally, in the application of existing doctrine to new instances, the general principle, in that subtle, evolutionary manner of the common law, would itself be transformed. Sometimes, it was a question of resisting such a transformation. Most often, however, it was a matter of assimilating a particular set of facts to one or another of two lines of precedents, neither of which directly controlled the case at hand. The Cardozo court did not, because it could not, uproot established doctrine on any large scale. The great legal problems in the complex industrial society of the twentieth century implicate a myriad competing economic, social, and political interests whose resolution is far beyond the power of a court in a particularized case or cases. Grandiose solutions are for the legislature.

Cardozo himself summarized the work of the Court of Appeals and its function as follows:

> *Of the cases that come before the court in which I sit, a majority, I think, could not, with semblance of reason, be decided in any way but one. . . . In another and considerable percentage, the rule of law is certain, and the application alone doubtful. . . . Finally there remains a percentage, not large indeed, and yet not so small as to be negligible, where a decision one way or the other, will count for the future . . . These are the cases where the creative element in the judicial process finds its opportunity and power. . . . In a sense it is true of many of them that they might be decided either way. By that I mean that reasons plausible and fairly persuasive might be found for one conclusion as for another. Here come into play . . . balancing of judgment . . . testing and sorting of considerations of analogy and logic and utility and fairness . . . Here it is that the judge assumes the function of a lawgiver. . . . I have grown to see that the process in its highest reaches is not discovery, but creation . . .*
> [The Nature of the Judicial Process *(1921), 164–66*]

This approach was by no means obvious in Cardozo's time; it is not universally accepted today. The notion that law is a "brooding omnipresence in the sky" (to borrow the expression of Justice Holmes, in *Southern Pacific Co.* v. *Jensen,* 244 U.S. 205, 222 [1917] where he rejected that concept) still has its adherents—in theory and even more in practical application.

What were some of these cases in which Cardozo wrote important opinions? A railroad guard jostled a passenger, who dropped his package under a moving train. It contained fireworks, and the resulting explosion caused some scales to fall, thus injuring Mrs. Palsgraf some distance away on the platform. Does the railroad have to pay for her injuries? See *Palsgraf* v. *Long Island R.R.,* 248 N.Y. 339, 162 N.E. 99 (1928).

Mr. Wagner's cousin was thrown from a street railway car, through the railway's negligence, while the car was passing over a trestle. The car was stopped and Mr. Wagner was injured when he slipped from the trestle while searching for his cousin. Should the railroad have to pay for his injury? See *Wagner* v. *International Railway,* 232 N.Y. 176, 133 N.E. 437 (1921).

Mary Johnston pledged $5000 to a college, payable after her death, the purposes of the gift to be restricted and the fund to bear her name. While alive she made, and the college accepted, a part payment, but she later revoked the balance of the pledge. Can the college nevertheless enforce it? See *Allegheny College* v. *National Chautauqua County Bank,* 246 N.Y. 369, 159 N.E. 173 (1927).

A telegraph company failed to send a coded radiogram and thereby caused great loss to the sender. Is it liable for the loss? Does it make any difference that the code was a standard code contained in a book in the telegraph office? Does it make any difference that even if decoded the meaning of the radiogram was obscure? Should a court be influenced by the fact that the telegraph company if held liable could be exposed to a very great judgment whereas it may have received only a few dollars? Should a court take account of the fact that the company could obtain insurance against that risk? And if it does, should it also consider that the undefined amount of the loss and the experience of insurance companies might lead to very high premiums, raising the cost of service to all? What about the availability of insurance to the sender? See *Kerr S.S. Co.* v. *Radio Corporation of America,* 245 N.Y. 284, 157 N.E. 140 (1927).

Questions of the extent of common law liability in tort and contract have traditionally been decided by the courts, and the legislature has up to now played a relatively small role in the evolution of the various doctrines. Yet as the above summary of issues indicates, the problems today can involve issues some of which are beyond the court's power to resolve effectively. Nonetheless, when the legislature has not dealt with the problem, the court must assess the factors it deems relevant and decide the case. Occasionally, however, the competing considerations may be so complex that the court will not reassess them, but will simply reiterate an old rule and state that any change must come from the legislature. Such a case was that involving the radiogram that was never sent, and a generous extract from Cardozo's opinion may give some small hint of how he approached the issues of a case.

Referring to the usual rule that the telegraph company is liable only if the general nature of the transaction is disclosed to it, he stated:

> *We are not unmindful of the force of the plaintiff's assault upon the rule . . . in its application to the relation between telegraph carrier and customer. The truth seems to be that neither the clerk who receives the message over the counter nor the operator who transmits it nor any other employee gives or is expected to give any thought to the sense of what he is receiving or transmitting. This imparts to the whole doctrine as to the need for notice an air of unreality. The doctrine, however, has prevailed for years so many that it is tantamount to a rule of property. The companies have regulated their rates upon the basis of its continuance. They have omitted precautions that they might have thought it necessary to adopt if the hazard of the business was to be indefinitely increased. Nor is the doctrine without other foundation in utility and justice. Much may be said in favor of the social policy of a rule whereby the companies have been relieved of liabilities that might otherwise be crushing. The sender can protect himself by insurance in one form or another if the risk of nondelivery or error appears to be too great. The total burden is not heavy since it is distributed among many, and can be proportioned in any instance to the loss likely to ensue. The company, if it takes out insurance for itself, can do no more than guess at the loss to be avoided. To pay for this unknown risk, it will be driven to increase the rates payable by all, though the increase is likely to result in the protection of a few. We are not concerned to balance the considerations of policy that give support to the existing rule against others that weigh against it.*

> *Enough for present purposes that there are weights in either scale. Telegraph companies in interstate and foreign commerce are subject to the power of Congress . . . If the rule of damages long recognized by State and Federal decision is to give way to another, the change should come through legislation.* [*245 N.Y., at 291–92, 157 N.E., at 142*]

This is not the place to assess the decision in this case. The considerations are many and varied, and the question of whether and when a question "should be left to the legislature" is one of the more difficult that a court must decide. This case, like the others mentioned above, is of the type in which, as Cardozo stated, reasonable men could reach different results. The distinction of Cardozo was that, in this case as in so many others, he perceived and expounded the principles that were contending for recognition, realizing, as he himself later stated, that there is "many a common law-suit, which can be lifted from meanness up to dignity if the great judge is by to see what is within." See "Mr. Justice Holmes," 44 *Harvard Law Review* 682, 685 (1931). Recognizing the issue, he did not reach a conclusion merely by stating it, or by the route of the familiar cliché. "The repetition of a catchword," as he put it, "can hold analysis in fetters for fifty years and more." (*Id.,* at 689) A typical Cardozo opinion would reveal the relevant facts, expose the crucial issues, marshal the arguments, examine the relevant precedents, often in a highly imaginative fashion, and logically and persuasively reach a result in an opinion that covered only that case. The adulation that followed Cardozo throughout his judicial career extended also to his highly distinctive style although occasionally it was subjected to criticism, especially after his death. See, *e.g.,* Jerome Frank, "The Speech of Judges," 29 *Virginia Law Review* 625 (1943). Cardozo's writing was marked by a combination of short, pithy sentences and occasional long, involuted sentences with elegant phraseology. His fondness for words and the nice sounding phrase sometimes led him into extraordinary flights of language that enunciated principles of excessive generality to decide a particular case. But usually he kept his style under such control that it accomplished the result of making his reasoning explicit.

Cardozo's approach to the process of decision was exemplified in his opinions, spelled out in his lectures printed under the title, *The Nature of the Judicial Process,* and further refined in two subsequent series of lectures printed as *The Growth of the Law* and *The Paradoxes of Legal Science.* In these lectures Cardozo, drawing on and adding to the prior work of Holmes, not only made the legal profession think and re-think the nature of a judge's function, but also explained his ideas in such fashion that laymen as well could understand them. Although perhaps somewhat marred by a tendency to indiscriminate and excessive quotation, these books were one of the first efforts by a judge to articulate his function, and still possess the same validity and vitality that they had when published in the 1920's.

One final word should be said about Cardozo and the Court of Appeals. This brief summary of Cardozo's labors during his New York judicial career does not give any hint of the influence that he had on his fellow judges. The

Court of Appeals in Cardozo's time was an unusual collection of good judges. Two of Cardozo's colleagues, William Andrews and Cuthbert Pound, would have distinguished any court in the country. Many of the others with whom he sat during his long tenure were more than ordinarily able. That Cardozo's influence could pervade such a court attests the combination of gentle persuasiveness and intellectual power that was his. Judge Irving Lehman, his colleague and perhaps his closest friend in his later years, may have understated the power of Cardozo's written words, but he gave an appreciation of the power of his spoken words when he said, "Those who sat with Judge Cardozo in the Court of Appeals will, I am sure, agree with me that Judge Cardozo made his greatest contribution to the development of the common law, not in his written words—though they will long be read—but in the words spoken in the conference room, heard by few and soon forgotten, yet forgotten only after they had clarified each problem and had served to guide a great court along the road to sound development of the common law. I cannot bring back the spoken word, but I can record here its enduring influence." "Judge Cardozo in the Court of Appeals," 52 *Harvard Law Review* 364, 371 (1939).

This was in brief the extraordinary man who, at the age of sixty-one, left the congenial surroundings of chief judge in Albany to "homesick exile," as he called it, as junior Justice in Washington. Gone was the easy companionship of the Court of Appeals. In its place was the more solitary work that characterized the Supreme Court in those days. Social intercourse, even with Justice Stone with whom he was closest on the Court, was infrequent. Intellectual exchange about the Court's work was limited largely to the Saturday conference and to discussions with his law clerks with whom he had a very friendly, if slightly formal, relationship. Only in the last years did he regularly meet with Justices Stone and Brandeis for thirty minutes to an hour on Friday nights before the Saturday conference of the Court, and this only as a defensive reflex to the regular caucuses of Justices McReynolds, Sutherland, Van Devanter, and Butler.

The change was not only one of scene. A new type of labor was also involved. Cardozo's preoccupation was now to be primarily the field of public law, statutory and constitutional, instead of the common law. His tenure on the Court was only five and one-half terms, normally insufficient for any Justice to make an imprint. But Cardozo was not any Justice and these were not normal times. For almost three decades Holmes, joined in 1916 by Brandeis and in 1925 by Stone, had conducted the fight against the restrictive constitutional principles that had held unconstitutional much legislation, primarily state legislation, designed to mitigate the rigors and sufferings created by the workings of nineteenth-century capitalism. Cardozo's appointment in 1932 was followed by Franklin Roosevelt's election, and attention shifted from sporadic state legislation to the comprehensive New Deal program that poured out of Congress. This new and intensified struggle, for struggle it was, was carried out in an atmosphere of intense public interest. It reached one climax in the Court-packing plan, and another climax and conclusion in the startling series of decisions by the Court in the 1936 term—all within Cardozo's brief period on the Court.

Mere presence on the Court at that time would give interest to Cardozo's work, but he also made a definite contribution to the Court despite the fact that as junior Justice the more important opinions were not often assigned to him. Holmes' successor had long been devoted to Holmes, whom he referred to as "The Master." In his writings before his appointment to the Supreme Court, Cardozo had deplored the restrictive decisions of the Supreme Court and had indicated his complete sympathy with Holmes' constitutional philosophy: " 'The movement from individualistic liberalism to unsystematic collectivism' [in England] had brought changes in the social order which carried with them the need of a new formulation of fundamental rights and duties. In our country, the need did not assert itself so soon. Courts still spoke in the phrases of a philosophy that had served its day. Gradually, however, though not without frequent protest and intermittent movements backward, a new conception of the significance of constitutional limitations in the domain of individual liberty, emerged to recognition and to dominance. . . ." (*The Nature of the Judicial Process,* 78)

Cardozo's optimism was somewhat premature, as his long series of dissents indicates, but he carried on the effort to establish that philosophy, mostly as dissenter in the important cases but eventually as one of the majority. Cardozo, like Holmes and Stone, believed that the legislature had broad power to experiment in dealing with the problems confronting society and that the courts should not be inquiring expressly or implicitly into the wisdom of particular legislation. "It is not the function of a court to make itself the arbiter between competing economic theories professed by honest men on grounds not wholly frivolous." See *Stewart Dry Goods Co.* v. *Lewis,* 294 U.S. 550, 566, 569 (1935). This was the philosophy with which Cardozo approached such economic legislation when attacked as unconstitutional under the Fourteenth Amendment or the due process clause of the Fifth Amendment. It was a judicial, not a political or economic philosophy. That is what set him apart from Justice Brandeis. Their judicial philosophy was similar, but Brandeis had a well developed social and economic philosophy that affected his approach to particular cases.

The difference in view may best be perceived in a case in which both dissented. *Liggett Co.* v. *Lee,* 288 U.S. 517 (1933) involved the validity of Florida's chain store legislation. The Florida statute set a different rate of taxation based on the number of Florida stores owned, either by an individual or a corporation, and then set a higher rate for all stores if the chain operated in more than one county. The majority of the Court declared the statute unconstitutional, holding that there was no reasonable basis for a classification based on whether the stores were located in one, or more than one, county.

Justice Brandeis' dissent first noted that there was nothing in the record to show that the tax might not be reasonable in view of the Florida conditions. He then proceeded to broader grounds. Noting that only corporations were plaintiffs, he considered the case as if the statute were directed only at corporations.

He saw no reason why the tax could not be regarded as a charge for doing business in the corporate form and that since operation in more than one county was a greater privilege than operation in a single county, a larger fee could be charged. Finally, he delivered what was in effect an economics treatise on the danger of the chain store, especially the giant chain store, and justified the tax as socially and economically desirable to preserve the competition of independent stores with chain stores or even to eliminate chain stores. (*Id.,* at 541 *et seq.*)

Cardozo did not join Brandeis' opinion, but prepared a dissent along more conventional lines. His initial draft relied heavily on the fact that the county was the historical unit of government in the South. Further research disclosed statistics indicating that chain stores were often classified as local, sectional and national, and that the transition from local to either sectional or national tended to come when the chain store crossed the county line. (I am indebted to Melvin H. Siegel, Esq., Cardozo's law clerk during the 1932 term, for this information.) With these two bulwarks, the case was decided. "The question is how it [a business] *does* develop in normal or average conditions, and the answer to that question is to be found in life and history. When the problem is thus approached, the movement from one county to another becomes in a very definite sense the crossing of a frontier, a change as marked as the difference between wholesale trade and retail. . . . So at least the legislature might not unreasonably believe, and act on that belief in the formulation of the law. . . ." (*Id.,* at 580, 583) And he continued, in lines reminiscent of Holmes's classic statement in *The Common Law,* "In discarding as arbitrary symbols the lines that it has chosen, there is danger of forgetting that in social and economic life the grooves of thought and action are not always those of logic, and that symbols may mean as much as conduct has put into them." (*Id.,* at 586; see *The Common Law,* 1)

Having formulated a rational basis for the Florida legislation, Cardozo's function as a judge was ended. He would certainly not follow the Brandeis course. Not that he did not recognize the purpose of the statute. Indeed, he found in it another basis on which the statute could be supported:

> *It will not do to shut one's eyes to the motive that has led so many legislatures to lay hold of this difference and turn it into a basis for a new system of taxation. The system has had its origin in the belief that the social utility or inutility of one group is less or greater than that of others, and that the choice of subjects to be taxed should be adjusted to social gains and losses. Courts would be lacking in candor if they were not to concede the presence of such a motive behind this chain store legislation. . . . The concept may be right or wrong. At least it corresponds to an intelligible belief, and one widely prevalent today among honest men and women. . . . With that our function ends.* [*288 U.S., at 585–86*]

This was a very different approach from the Brandeis opinion which set forth his personal, social and economic views approving the statute in a powerful opinion that Professor Freund has described as a "labor of love." (Freund, *The Supreme Court of the United States* 124 [1961].) It seems fairly certain that Cardozo did not have any such comparably developed social or economic philosophy. It is quite clear that he did not believe that a judicial opinion was the proper form for its exposition. His job was "judging" and only judging. Indeed he even, in uncharacteristic fashion, chided Justice Brandeis, albeit somewhat obliquely:

> *Holding these views, I find it unnecessary to consider whether the statute may be upheld for the additional reasons that have been stated by* Mr. Justice Brandeis *with such a wealth of learning. They present considerations that were not laid before us by counsel either in the briefs or in the oral argument, and a determination of their validity and weight may be reserved with propriety until the necessity emerges.* [*288 U.S., at 586*]

The same deference was due to the legislation that poured forth from Congress, and to a lesser extent from the state legislatures, to meet the vast economic dislocation caused by the great depression. That deference was not given by the Court majority, and the history of the Court in the early 1930's is a long series of cases holding such legislation invalid, generally on the basis of the commerce clause, the Tenth Amendment, the Fifth Amendment, or the Fourteenth Amendment, and generally also with Justices Cardozo, Brandeis, Stone, and occasionally Chief Justice Hughes, dissenting.

The questions arising under the commerce clause were quite different from those presented under the due process or equal protection clauses. From the time of the decision of the Marshall Court in *Gibbons* v. *Ogden,* 9 Wheat. 1 (1824), subsequent courts had struggled with a proper formulation of the extent of congressional power over intrastate transactions affecting the interstate problem sought to be regulated. When the issues were presented directly, the Supreme Court generally had interpreted broadly the reach of national power under the commerce clause. Its expositions of the governing principles, however, were not absolutely consistent. The Court on occasion had indicated that there was a substantial area of "intrastate" commerce that was beyond the reach of congressional power notwithstanding its effect on interstate commerce, and it had occasionally stated explicitly its fear that a very broad reading of the commerce clause would permit Congress to regulate the whole national economy. See *Kidd* v. *Pearson,* 128 U.S. 1, 21 (1888); *United States* v. *E. C. Knight Co.,* 156 U.S. 1, 13–16 (1895); and *Hammer* v. *Dagenhart,* 247 U.S. 251, 272–76 (1918).

Cardozo believed that there was a portion of intrastate commerce that was exclusively a matter of state concern. Thus, he concurred in the unanimous decision in *Schechter Poultry Corp.* v. *United States,* 295 U.S. 495, 551 (1935), holding the NRA's Live Poultry Code of Fair Competition unconstitutional as involving an excessive delegation of legislative power to the executive and, as applied to the particular wholesale poultry slaughterhouses that were defendants, an unconstitutional exercise of the commerce power. Previously, Cardozo had been the lone dissenter in the "hot oil" case, *Panama Refining Co.* v. *Ryan,* 293 U.S. 388, 433 (1935), where a separate section of the National Industrial Recovery Act had been held to involve an unconstitutional delegation of legislative power to the President. His contrary conclusion in *Schechter* gave him some difficulty, even in the opinion writing stage, which was unusual. His initial draft opinion decided only that the code went beyond the congressional grant of authority. He then sought to avoid the delegation question entirely, writing an opinion discussing solely the commerce clause issue. Finally, his concurring opinion, which was joined only by Justice Stone, discussed both issues, holding the statute as well as the code unconstitutional on both grounds—too much undefined power delegated to the President and over a field of commerce too remote from interstate activity.

The commerce clause issue did not involve similar difficulty for Cardozo, and his draft opinions reflect his general concurrence with the line of argument taken by Chief Justice Hughes for the Court. The Government had argued in support of the wage and hour regulations that substandard wages and excessive hours of work enabled slaughterhouse operators to cut costs and prices, and that this demoralized the price structure in the whole industry. Indeed, the Circuit Court of Appeals for the Second Circuit had noted that the New York poultry market dominated the industry and that the "farmer's price reflects the price current in the New York market, so that the demoralization of price structure in New York produces a similar situation, not only in other markets throughout the country, but also in all poultry farming areas." 76 F. 2d 617, 618–19 (2d Cir. 1935). For Cardozo, however, notwithstanding his general sympathy with an expansive interpretation of the commerce clause, the crucial item was the fear that if a line were not drawn in this case, it could not be drawn anywhere.

> *There is a view of causation that would obliterate the distinction between what is national and what is local in the activities of commerce. Motion at the outer rim is communicated perceptibly, though minutely, to recording instruments at the center. . . . The law is not indifferent to considerations of degree. Activities local in their immediacy do not become interstate and national because of distant repercussions. . . . To find immediacy or directness here is to find it almost everywhere. If centripetal forces are to be isolated to the exclusion of the forces that oppose and counteract them, there will be an end to our federal system.* [*295 U.S., 554*]

His position merely stated a conclusion, unaided but at the same time unembarrassed, by any attempt to formulate standards for decision. The following term, however, when the Court formulated a restrictive, mechanical test of national power under the commerce clause in *Carter* v. *Carter Coal Co.,* 298 U.S. 238 (1936), Cardozo indicated his disagreement. In striking down the labor provisions of the Guffey Coal Act fixing maximum hours and minimum wages in the bituminous coal mining industry, and also striking down the provisions for fixing the price of sales of coal because they were deemed inseparable, Justice Sutherland held that regulation of labor conditions in the coal mining industry had only an "indirect" effect on interstate commerce and was, therefore, not within the commerce clause:

> *The word "direct" implies that the activity or condition invoked or blamed shall operate proximately—not mediately, remotely, or collaterally—to produce the effect. It connotes the absence of an efficient intervening agency or condition.*

And the extent of the effect bears no logical relation to its character. The distinction between a direct and an indirect effect turns, not upon the magnitude of either the cause or the effect, but entirely upon the manner in which the effect has been brought about. . . . It is quite true that rules of law are sometimes qualified by considerations of degree. . . . But the matter of degree has no bearing upon the question here . . . [*298 U.S., at 307–08*]

Justice Cardozo, in a dissenting opinion joined by Justices Brandeis and Stone, did not meet the majority holding directly. He regarded the attack on the labor provisions as premature and would have upheld the price-fixing provisions on their own merits. Without referring explicitly to Justice Sutherland's statement of the test, he discussed the general principles that should govern the decision whether the price regulation might constitutionally extend to the intrastate sale. For him the test was not the manner but the magnitude of the effect upon interstate commerce and his opinion reflected the same distrust of labels that had characterized his opinions on different subject matter in the New York Court of Appeals:

Sometimes it is said that the relation must be "direct" to bring that power [*to regulate intrastate commerce*] *into play. In many circumstances such a description will be sufficiently precise to meet the needs of the occasion. But a great principle of constitutional law is not susceptible of comprehensive statement in an adjective. The underlying thought is merely this, that "the law is not indifferent to considerations of degree." . . . The relation may be tenuous or the opposite according to the facts. . . . Perhaps, if one group of adjectives is to be chosen in preference to another, "intimate" and "remote" will be found to be as good as any. At all events, "direct" and "indirect," even if accepted as sufficient, must not be read too narrowly. . . .* [*298 U.S. 238, 324, 327–28*]

After stating the test, however, Cardozo did not consider whether the price-fixing provisions, which applied to all bituminous coal mines in the country, were constitutional *in toto*. Later cases would test the applicability of the commerce clause to regulation of an entire industry by reviewing only the reasonableness of the congressional declaration of the substantiality of the effect of intrastate activity upon interstate commerce in the light of the legislative record on which the act was based. See *United States* v. *Darby,* 312 U.S. 100, 117–24 (1941); *Wickard* v. *Filburn,* 317 U.S. 111, 125–29 (1942). Cardozo proceeded more cautiously, examining for himself the specific facts justifying the application of the provisions to the Kentucky and West Virginia companies that were parties to the suits. First, he noted that none of them had more than 25% of their sales in intrastate commerce. Then, turning from this limited reason based on the activities of the particular companies to a more general ground based on the industry and the sales picture in Kentucky and West Virginia, he noted that there was evidence of substantial competition between intrastate sales and coal from other states sold in those states and that there was no evidence that "interstate sales will not be prejudically affected . . . if intrastate prices are maintained on a lower level." (298 U.S., at 329)

At the end of the term in which *Carter* was decided, Justice Stone wrote to a friend, "We finished the term of court yesterday, I think in many ways one of the most disastrous in its history." (Quoted in A. T. Mason, *Harlan Fiske Stone* 425 [1956].) Indeed, the public clamor against the Court equalled the rage of the Jeffersonians over many of the Marshall Court's decisions, that of the North over *Dred Scott,* 19 How. 393 (1857), and that of the South over the *Segregation Cases,* 347 U.S. 483 (1954). Then in quick succession came the overwhelming re-election of President Roosevelt in November, 1936, the Court-packing plan in February, 1937, and the beginning in April, 1937, of a whole series of decisions eventually undoing much of the constitutional law doctrine that had restricted the regulatory power of the national and state governments since the beginning of the century.

There has been a great deal of discussion about the "switch in time": whether there actually was a "switch" by Chief Justice Hughes and Justice Roberts, and what cases demonstrate it. Cardozo, however, believed that there was a change of views between the decision in *Carter* and the decision in *NLRB* v. *Jones & Laughlin Steel Corp.,* 301 U.S. 1 (1937), which upheld the provisions of the National Labor Relations Act by recognizing what had been denied in *Carter,* the power of Congress to provide for collective bargaining in national industries.* Having unsuccessfully attempted to distinguish the two cases to his own satisfaction, Cardozo was amazed at the vote in conference in *Jones & Laughlin,* which in effect although not explicitly overruled the *Carter* case.**

Aside from the commerce clause cases involving New Deal legislation, Cardozo wrote other important commerce clause opinions dealing with the extent to which that clause inhibits a state's power of regulation or taxation. He wrote an important opinion for the Court in *Baldwin* v. *Seelig,* 294 U.S. 511 (1935), dealing with the power of a state to prohibit sale of out-of-state products not produced in accordance with local standards—in that case, the minimum price to be paid by milk dealers to producers. *Henneford* v. *Silas*

* *Justice Roberts' vote in* West Coast Hotel Co. *v.* Parrish, *300 U.S. 379 (1937), upholding state minimum wage legislation, and overruling* Adkins *v.* Children's Hospital, *261 U.S. 525 (1923), and New York* ex rel. Morehead *v.* Tipaldo, *298 U.S. 587 (1936), has been explained. See Frankfurter, "Mr. Justice Roberts," 104* University of Pennsylvania Law Review *311 (1955), reprinted in Frankfurter, Of Law and Men (Elman ed., 1956) 204. His vote and that of Chief Justice Hughes in* Jones & Laughlin, *however, are certainly inconsistent with the positiions they adopted in* Carter *and inconsistent, also, to some extent, with* United States *v.* Butler, *297 U.S. 1 (1936), holding unconstitutional the processing tax provisions of the Agricultural Adjustment Act of 1933. (See Freund, "Charles Evans Hughes as Chief Jusice," 81* Harvard Law Review *4, 34–35 for a discussion of Hughes's position.) It is possible to regard* Carter *and not* Jones & Laughlin *as the aberration. Hughes had previously read the commerce clause as allowing wide scope to congressional power to regulate intrastate activities that substantially affected interstate commerce, at least in the field of transportation. See* The Shreveport Case, *234 U.S. 342 (1914). Justice Roberts' position in* Jones & Laughlin *does not find similar support in prior cases.* Cf. Railroad Retirement Board *v.* Alton R.R., *295 U.S. 330 (1935).*

** *The change in attitude on the part of the Court is also reflected in the fact that Cardozo wrote for the majority in the* Social Security cases, *301 U.S. 548 and 301 U.S. 619 (1937), upholding the constitutionality of the Social Security Act of 1935.*

Mason Co., 300 U.S. 577 (1937) was the first case in which the Court passed on the power of a state to equalize the economic burden of its local sales tax by imposing a general compensating use tax on goods purchased out of state and then used within the state. Some commentators have criticized an apparent inconsistency between permitting the state to protect its own industry from harm by equalizing the economic effects of its sales tax legislation with a tax aimed at out-of-state purchases brought into the state, and forbidding a state from protecting its own industry from harm by equalizing the economic effects of its minimum price legislation by imposing the same requirement on the out-of-state purchase brought into the state. See Note, 51 *Harvard Law Review* 130 (1937); see also E. J. Brown, "The Open Economy: Justice Frankfurter and the Position of the Judiciary," 67 *Yale Law Journal* 219, 233–35 (1957). The cases may be harmonized, however, if one regards the use tax in *Henneford* as merely preserving the prior status quo by taxing a local incident—use in the taxing state—whereas the price regulation in *Baldwin,* operating on an out-of-state incident—price paid in the producing state—eliminated the possibility that industry in the producing state could retain any present advantage, or take future advantage, of lower costs that might exist there. Cardozo adverted to this factual situation by referring to New York's efforts to guard her farmers "against competition with the cheaper prices of Vermont," *id.,* at 522, and by his reference to an attempt "to neutralize advantages belonging to the place of origin," *id.,* at 527, although it is unclear whether he was referring to economic advantages of Vermont milk before, and not after, the passage of the New York minimum price legislation. However, Cardozo subsequently regarded *Baldwin* as standing for the proposition that "[p]rices in interstate commerce may not be regulated by the states." (*Carter* v. *Carter Coal Co.,* 298 U.S., at 326) And still later, Cardozo in *Henneford* differentiated *Baldwin* solely on the ground that *Baldwin* involved an attempt by one state to project its legislation beyond its borders. See 300 U.S., at 585–86. These cases presented as great a challenge to the intellect as any Cardozo had faced in Albany. That he failed to articulate in a satisfactory manner the difference he instinctively seems to have felt between the situation in *Baldwin* and that in *Henneford* may indicate no more than that even a powerful mind needs more than sporadic exposure to the intricate problems of federalism.

The Cardozo years on the Court mark a growing interest of the Supreme Court in problems of "civil liberties." Questions relating to the Commerce Clause and economic regulation had been a preoccupation of the Supreme Court ever since *Gibbons* v. *Ogden* and *The Slaughter-House Cases,* 16 Wall. 36 (1873). The Supreme Court, however, had been concerned very little with questions of individual rights, and it was primarily the restrictive World War I and post–World War I legislation that had forced the Supreme Court to re-examine the extent of the limitations placed by the Bill of Rights and the due process clauses on the power of the national and state governments to enact such legislation. There were no well-developed constitutional principles to guide the Court in this sphere, and the cases came before the Court in the context of those well-developed constitutional principles that had developed in the conflict over economic regulatory legislation that was then at the forefront of the Court's attention. But the rhetoric of the regulatory cases did not always seem appropriate to the newer problems. The effort to adapt old principles or develop new ones is primarily the story of the post-1937 era, but the beginnings of the effort may be seen in the prior period. The opinions of Justices Holmes and Brandeis had marked the way for those seeking to apply different standards to legislation affecting personal rights from those that were being applied to legislation dealing primarily with economic questions. Cases like *Meyer* v. *Nebraska,* 262 U.S. 390 (1923) and *Pierce* v. *Society of Sisters,* 268 U.S. 510 (1925), however, indicated that there were crosscurrents that affected judges in unpredictable fashion.

For Cardozo, the problem was an especially difficult one. He was widely read in literature and philosophy and he was interested in the political developments of the day. Although he had initially been elected to the New York judiciary as an independent reform Democrat on the Fusion ticket and was friendly both to Franklin Roosevelt and his program, his temperament was not passionate. He had no such burning sense of the right as did Justice Brandeis. While he could occasionally feel a sense of outrage when something affected him personally, the problems of the world generally did not touch his emotions deeply, if at all. Nor had his practice or personal life brought him into much contact with those problems of society of which questions of civil rights are a reflection. The attitude he brought to these problems was largely philosophic. Civil rights issues had not often come before the New York Court of Appeals, but prior to his selection to the Supreme Court, Cardozo had made a general statement of his views in paying tribute to Justice Holmes:

> *No one has labored more incessantly to demonstrate the truth that rights are never absolute, though they are ever struggling and tending to declare themselves as such. . . . Only in one field is compromise to be excluded, or kept within the narrowest limits. There shall be no compromise of the freedom to think one's thoughts and speak them, except at those extreme borders where thought merges into action. There is to be no compromise here, for thought freely communicated, if I may borrow my own words, is the indispensable condition of intelligent experimentation, the one test of its validity. There is no freedom without choice, and there is no choice without knowledge—or none that is not illusory. Here are goods to be conserved, however great the seeming sacrifice. We may not squander the thought that will be the inheritance of the ages.* [*"Mr. Justice Holmes," 44 Harvard Law Review 682, 687–88 (1931)*]

Cardozo had several opportunities to test his views during his short term of service on the Court. *Palko* v. *Connecticut,* 302 U.S. 319 (1937) presented the Court with an important question of the extent to which the limitations of the Bill of Rights would be imposed upon the states. The Court held that the double jeopardy provisions of the Fifth Amendment were not binding on the states *in toto,* if at all, and that, therefore, Connecticut could constitutionally give the state, with permission of the presiding judge, a right of appeal on a question of law in a criminal case. From today's vantage point it is ironic that the sole Justice who would have held the statute unconstitutional was Justice Butler. It is even more ironic that the majority should have included Justice Black, then in his first term on the Court, who has long since repudiated his concurrence in *Palko*. Cardozo, writing the opinion of the Court, considered the general proposition of the applicability of the Bill of Rights to the states by virtue of the Fourteenth Amendment and wrote that only those provisions were applicable that were "of the very essence of a scheme of ordered liberty." (*Id.,* p. 325) Cardozo's formulation of the guiding principle is still accepted by a majority of the Court today, although its application has been greatly expanded to include many provisions that Cardozo would have excluded.

Unlike other issues that Cardozo had to decide as a member of the Supreme Court, Cardozo had had long experience with criminal law questions in the New York Court of Appeals. An examination of those cases indicates that he had given great weight to the interests of society in effective law enforcement. While he had examined each case on its individual merits, an impressive showing of prejudice had to be made out before he would consider that error in the trial should result in the reversal of a conviction. Cardozo also had written the opinion in the important case of *People* v. *Defore,* 242 N.Y. 13; 150 N.E. 585 (1926), holding that evidence obtained through an illegal search and seizure was, nevertheless, admissible in a criminal proceeding. However, when the New York Criminal Anarchy Act was applied to convict Benjamin Gitlow for his publication of the "Left Wing Manifesto," a pamphlet of a splinter group of the Socialist party, Cardozo joined Judge Pound's dissent, which argued that the utterance was not within the prohibitions of a statute that was aimed at anarchism and not communism, which is something quite different. See *People* v. *Gitlow,* 234 N.Y. 132, 154; 136 N.E. 317, 326 (1922), *aff'd* 268 U.S. 652 (1925).

It is not too surprising, therefore, that in *Snyder* v. *Massachusetts,* 291 U.S. 97 (1934), Cardozo wrote for a majority of five, with Justices Roberts, Brandeis, Sutherland and Butler dissenting, in upholding a state court murder conviction where only defendant's counsel, but not defendant, was permitted to be present when the jury was taken to view the scene of the crime. Although he had originally voted to reverse the conviction, and was assigned to write the opinion, Cardozo found that such a view just "wouldn't write." (I am indebted to Ambrose Doskow, Esq., Cardozo's law clerk in the 1933 term, for this information.) Relying heavily on the common law precedents that a "view" is something different from the "trial" itself, where defendant's presence was required, and finding no prejudice to the defendant, Cardozo concluded that the trial judge's action did not deny the defendant due process of law:

> *The law . . . is sedulous in maintaining for a defendant charged with crime whatever forms of procedure are of the essence of an opportunity to defend. Privileges so fundamental as to be inherent in every concept of a fair trial that could be acceptable to the thought of reasonable men will be kept inviolate and inviolable, however crushing may be the pressure of incriminating proof. But*

justice, though due to the accused, is due to the accuser also. The concept of fairness must not be strained till it is narrowed to a filament. We are to keep the balance true. [Id., *at 122*]

In *Palko,* Cardozo differentiated the Fifth Amendment's guarantee against double jeopardy, which he was not prepared to make applicable to the states, from other provisions of the Bill of Rights which he did regard as being "of the very essence of a scheme of ordered liberty."

> *We reach a different plane of social and moral values when we pass to the privileges and immunities that have been taken over from the earlier articles of the federal bill of rights and brought within the Fourteenth Amendment by a process of absorption. . . . If the Fourteenth Amendment has absorbed them, the process of absorption has had its source in the belief that neither liberty nor justice would exist if they were sacrificed. . . . This is true, for illustration, of freedom of thought, and speech. Of that freedom one may say that it is the matrix, the indispensable condition, of nearly every other form of freedom. . . .* [*302 U.S. 319, 326–27* (*1937*)]

He demonstrated his devotion to these ideas in several cases that came to the Court during his short tenure. He joined in, and made substantial literary contribution to, Justice Roberts' opinion for the bare majority of the Court that reversed the conviction of Angelo Herndon in the Georgia courts for attempted insurrection, holding that the application of the statute to the particular facts of that case was an unreasonable infringement of freedom of speech and assembly. *Herndon* v. *Lowry,* 301 U.S. 242 (1937) (I am indebted to Joseph L. Rauh, Jr., Cardozo's law clerk during the 1936 and 1937 terms for this information.) See also *De Jonge* v. *Oregon,* 299 U.S. 353 (1937). *Grosjean* v. *American Press Co.,* 297 U.S. 233 (1936) involved an attack on a Louisiana gross advertising receipts tax as being violative of the equal protection clause and of freedom of the press. Justice Sutherland at first wrote an opinion holding the statute unconstitutional on the first ground. Cardozo, with strong views about the power of the legislature to adopt reasonable classifications in exercise of its taxing power, could not agree. He wrote a concurring opinion, disagreeing on the equal protection point but, after reviewing the history of such legislation in this country and in England, he found the statute unconstitutional as a discriminatory tax abridging the freedom of the press, protected by the Fourteenth Amendment against state infringement. Justice Sutherland then rewrote his opinion, adopting the position and much of the thought of the Cardozo opinion. Cardozo withdrew his opinion, and Sutherland spoke for a unanimous Court without passing on the equal protection issue.

When the University of California, however, required all students to take military science courses and refused to exempt conscientious objectors, Cardozo voted to uphold the regulation, although in addition to concurring in the majority opinion, he wrote a separate opinion for himself and Justices Brandeis and Stone. *Hamilton* v. *Regents,* 293 U.S. 245, 265 (1934). The majority had placed its principal reliance on the voluntary nature of attendance at the University and the duty of citizens to serve in the military forces. Cardozo's concurrence did not proclaim the same status for the free exercise clause of the First Amendment that he had theretofore enunciated for freedom of speech and thought. Nevertheless, he indicated that he perceived a narrower ground for decision than the majority in that it was something even less than military service that was being required. "Instruction in military science, unaccompanied here by any pledge of military service, is not an interference by the state with the free exercise of religion when the liberties of the constitution are read in the light of a century and a half of history during days of peace and war." (*Id.,* at 266) Noting that the constitutions and laws of many states had contained exemptions for conscientious objectors from military service but only on the condition that a substitute or the money to hire one be supplied instead, he concluded that the study of military science without a pledge of service was a lesser affront to the conscientious objector than the furnishing of money or a substitute to wage war. In addition, the fact that only those attending the state university had to undergo the training was seen as supporting the result since it indicated that the requirement could be avoided by going elsewhere. No Justice was prepared to view the selectiveness of the required training as minimizing the state's need or as operating unconstitutionally in that only a particular class of citizens—those seeking to enter the state university—were being forced to give up their religious beliefs. It would take many years before the free exercise clause would be seen as presenting a constitutional obstacle to the placing of otherwise reasonable conditions on benefits granted by the state. See *Sherbert* v. *Verner,* 374 U.S. 398 (1963); *Torcaso* v. *Watkins,* 367 U.S. 488 (1961). Cf. *West Virginia State Bd. of Education* v. *Barnette,* 319 U.S. 624 (1943).

One cannot avoid the impression in reading Cardozo's opinion in *Hamilton* that he was carefully spelling out his reasons for upholding a regulation that he recognized might be "condemned by some as unwise or illiberal or unfair when there is violence to conscientious scruples, either religious or merely ethical." (*Id.,* at 266) But, if he was troubled about the wisdom of the policy, his sympathies did not shape his constitutional views, and he followed the quoted sentence by stating that "[m]ore must be shown to set the ordinance at naught." *Ibid.* There was a toughness to Cardozo the judge, and he consciously sought to put aside influences that he regarded as being outside the decision-making process. Thus, he could conclude his opinion by stating that "[o]ne who is a martyr to a principle—which may turn out in the end to be a delusion or an error—does not prove by his martyrdom that he has kept within the law." (*Id.,* at 268)

How does one assess Cardozo's performance on the Supreme Court, or rather that portion of the Court's work that we have discussed here? It must be done in the context of the problems of the 1930's and not of the 1960's. On the other hand, since "it is *a constitution* we are expounding,"* it is not unfair to assess generally the constitutional principles, the theory of constitutional adjudication that he enunciated.

* *Cardozo was fond of quoting these words from John Marshall's opinion in* McCulloch *v.* Maryland, *4 Wheat. 316, 407 (1819).*

The most important issues faced by the Court during Cardozo's tenure were the New Deal regulatory cases, which involved principally an interpretation of the extent of the taxing and commerce power of Congress and the deterrent effect of the due process clauses. Of growing but subordinate interest were the so-called civil liberties cases. Virtually all the leading legal commentators of the day and since have been in accord in the view that the pre-1937 Court interpreted the commerce and taxing power too narrowly and the due process clauses too broadly. On the other hand, with respect to the commerce clause, although Justices Cardozo, Brandeis, and Stone set forth a broader view that nevertheless left a certain area to state power, they never formulated successfully the limits on congressional power that they believed to exist. The result was that after 1937 case after case pushed congressional power further and further so that there is not any significant area of "intrastate" commerce today that seems beyond the potential reach of the congressional commerce power. Perhaps that was inevitable, but Cardozo did not seem to think so. His *Schechter* opinion, which he might have used to develop his theories, is in this respect a failure since, unusually for Cardozo, it deals in generalities only. While he was more specific in *Carter,* he did not explain why *Schechter* was different.

Likewise, as one reads the decisions of the Supreme Court today, the constitutional principles with regard to "substantive due process" enunciated by Holmes, Brandeis and Cardozo seem somewhat remote, at least in the "economic" sphere. This may be partly because the problems those principles were designed to meet are no longer problems today. But perhaps it may also be due to the very formulation of the test that they applied: except where speech and thought were involved, legislative action was to be upheld once shown to be not unreasonable or "not wholly frivolous."

The cases that Cardozo was dealing with did not seem to him and his dissenting colleagues to raise difficult questions of competing rights. Perhaps if the cases had, they would have stated differently the test to be applied. But they had before them the example of how a so-called right (for example, the "right" of a man to contract to work for as many hours and as little money as he wanted, no matter that this contract was imposed upon him because of a crushing disparity of economic bargaining power) could be erected into a constitutional principle to thwart minimum hour and minimum wage legislation. It was doubtless this example that led to the formulation of a doctrine that would minimize the Court's role except where thought and speech were involved. This differentiation between the nature of the "rights" involved led to the subsequent formulation by Chief Justice Stone of the theory of the "preferred position" of certain individual rights and the more extreme formulation of Justice Black of the "absoluteness" of the specific provisions of the Bill of Rights.

It certainly is possible to regard legislation involving a regulation of business as involving different considerations from legislation affecting civil liberties and to apply a different test to each. Yet a great deal of legislation has a way of defying neat categorization. Is restriction of picketing one or the other? How about "Sunday closing laws"? Or closed shop legislation? Or fair trade laws? Or a law collectivizing farms? Justice Frankfurter has said:

> *Yesterday the active area in this field was concerned with "property." Today it is "civil liberties." Tomorrow it may again be "property." Who can say that in a society with a mixed economy, like ours, these two areas are sharply separated, and that certain freedoms in relation to property may not again be deemed, as they were in the past, aspects of individual freedom?*
>
> * * *
>
> *. . . The Due Process Clauses extend to triune interests—life, liberty and property—and "property" cannot be deleted by judicial fiat rendering it nugatory regarding legislation touching property. Moreover, protection of property interests may, as already indicated, quite fairly be deemed, in appropriate circumstances, an aspect of liberty. Regulation of property may be struck down on assumptions or beliefs other than narrow economic views. . . . ["John Marshall and the Judicial Function," 69* Harvard Law Review *217, 230 (1955), reprinted in Frankfurter,* Of Law and Men, *3, 19–20 (1956)*]

To this it might be added that in the history of man's strivings, the "right" to eat and to make a living, an "economic" right, has probably agitated man at least as much as the right to speak his mind and practice his religion freely. Somehow some of the "simple" constitutional principles enunciated by Cardozo and his dissenting colleagues in the 1930's do not seem completely satisfactory when we apply them to some of the more subtle and complex problems that the Court had to deal with thereafter.

This discussion of one phase of the work of Cardozo and his dissenting colleagues should not obscure the proper estimate of their work. The principal task of judges is to decide the particular cases presented to them, not cases that may be presented in the future, although one may hope that present statements will not embarrass future decision. This task Cardozo and his colleagues accomplished for themselves and eventually for the Court in eloquent fashion. In the great constitutional struggle of the first part of the twentieth century, theirs was the voice of the present and of the future, and they finally prevailed. This essay has attempted to summarize Justice Cardozo's contributions to common law, to constitutional law, and to law itself. The contribution as we have seen was not his alone, and we have noted the special influence of Justice Holmes. The result of Cardozo's twenty-five years as judge and jurist was the education of judges, lawyers, and laymen to a modern concept of the function of the courts in our twentieth-century society.

SELECTED BIBLIOGRAPHY

Cardozo's opinions are contained in Volumes 210–258 of the New York Reports and Volumes 285–302 of the United States Reports. The major non-judicial writings are collected in Margaret Hall, ed., *Selected Writings of Benjamin Nathan Cardozo* (New York, 1947).

George S. Hellman, *Benjamin N. Cardozo* (New York, 1940) is a biography that deals mainly with Cardozo's personality and character. Beryl H. Levy, *Cardozo and Frontiers of Legal Thinking* (New York, 1938) contains a valuable selection of the more important opinions written by Cardozo and a commentary on his legal thought. An uncritical discussion of Cardozo opinions is contained in Joseph P. Pollard, *Mr. Justice Cardozo* (New York, 1935). An illuminating series of essays on Cardozo's contributions to law was published concurrently in 52 *Harvard Law Review* (1939), 39 *Columbia Law Review,* (1939), and 48 *Yale Law Journal* (1939).

Mr. Kaufman is currently preparing a full-length biography of Justice Cardozo.

Benjamin Cardozo

REPRESENTATIVE OPINIONS

PALKO v. CONNECTICUT, 302 U.S. 319 (1937)

A Connecticut statute permitted the state, with the permission of the presiding judge, to appeal questions of law in criminal cases. The state had successfully appealed a conviction of murder in the second degree for which a life sentence had been imposed. A retrial led to a conviction of murder in the first degree and a sentence of death. The statute was attacked as violating the double jeopardy provisions of the Fifth Amendment, which, it was argued, were applicable to the states by reason of the Fourteenth Amendment. Justice Cardozo, for the Court, upheld the constitutionality of the statute. Assuming that the Connecticut statute giving the state a right to a trial free from substantial legal error would constitute double jeopardy under the Fifth Amendment, he did not find that it subjected defendant to "a hardship so acute and shocking that our polity will not endure it." In what subsequently became an important statement of constitutional theory, he wrote that only those provisions of the Bill of Rights that are "implicit in the concept of ordered liberty" are applicable to the states. Justice Butler dissented without opinion.

MR. JUSTICE CARDOZO delivered the opinion of the Court.

A statute of Connecticut permitting appeals in criminal cases to be taken by the state is challenged by appellant as an infringement of the Fourteenth Amendment of the Constitution of the United States. Whether the challenge should be upheld is now to be determined.

Appellant was indicted in Fairfield County, Connecticut, for the crime of murder in the first degree. A jury found him guilty of murder in the second degree, and he was sentenced to confinement in the state prison for life. Thereafter the State of Connecticut, with the permission of the judge presiding at the trial, gave notice of appeal to the Supreme Court of Errors. This it did pursuant to an act adopted in 1886 which is printed in the margin.[1] Public Acts, 1886, p.

[1] "*Sec. 6494.* Appeals by the state in criminal cases. *Appeals from the rulings and decisions of the superior court or of any criminal court of common pleas, upon all questions of law arising on the trial of*

560; now § 6494 of the General Statutes. Upon such appeal, the Supreme Court of Errors reversed the judgment and ordered a new trial. *State* v. *Palko,* 121 Conn. 669; 186 Atl. 657. It found that there had been error of law to the prejudice of the state (1) in excluding testimony as to a confession by defendant; (2) in excluding testimony upon cross-examination of defendant to impeach his credibility, and (3) in the instructions to the jury as to the difference between first and second degree murder.

Pursuant to the mandate of the Supreme Court of Errors, defendant was brought to trial again. Before a jury was impaneled and also at later stages of the case he made the objection that the effect of the new trial was to place him twice in jeopardy for the same offense, and in so doing to violate the Fourteenth Amendment of the Constitution of the United States. Upon the overruling of the objection the trial proceeded. The jury returned a verdict of murder in the first degree, and the court sentenced the defendant to the punishment of death. The Supreme Court of Errors affirmed the judgment of conviction, 122 Conn. 529; 191 Atl. 320, adhering to a decision announced in 1894, *State* v. *Lee,* 65 Conn. 265; 30 Atl. 1110, which upheld the challenged statute. Cf. *State* v. *Muolo,* 118 Conn. 373; 172 Atl. 875. The case is here upon appeal. 28 U. S. C., § 344.

1. The execution of the sentence will not deprive appellant of his life without the process of law assured to him by the Fourteenth Amendment of the Federal Constitution.

The argument for appellant is that whatever is forbidden by the Fifth Amendment is forbidden by the Fourteenth also. The Fifth Amendment, which is not directed to the states, but solely to the federal government, creates immunity from double jeopardy. No person shall be "subject for the same offense to be twice put in jeopardy of life or limb." The Fourteenth Amendment ordains, "nor shall any State deprive any person of life, liberty, or property, without due process of law." To retry a defendant, though under one indictment and only one, subjects him, it is said, to double jeopardy in violation of the Fifth Amendment, if the prosecution is one on behalf of the United States. From this the consequence is said to follow that there is a denial of life or liberty without due process of law, if the prosecution is one on behalf of the People of a State. Thirty-five years ago a like argument was made to this court in *Dreyer* v. *Illinois,* 187 U.S. 71, 85, and was passed without consideration of its merits as unnecessary to a decision. The question is now here.

We do not find it profitable to mark the precise limits of the prohibition of double jeopardy in federal prosecutions. The subject was much considered in *Kepner* v. *United States,* 195 U.S. 100, decided in 1904 by a closely divided court. The view was there expressed for a majority of the court that the prohibition was not confined to jeopardy in a new and independent case. It forbade jeopardy in the same case if the new trial was at the instance of the government and not upon defendant's motion. Cf. *Trono* v. *United States,* 199 U.S. 521. All this may be assumed for the purpose of the case at hand, though the dissenting opinions (195 U.S. 100, 134, 137) show how much was to be said in favor of a different ruling. Right-minded men, as we learn from those opinions, could reasonably, even if mistakenly, believe that a second trial was lawful in prosecutions subject to the Fifth Amendment, if it was all in the same case. Even more plainly, right-minded men could reasonably believe that in espousing that conclusion they were not favoring a practice repugnant to the conscience of mankind. Is double jeopardy in such circumstances, if double jeopardy it must be called, a denial of due process forbidden to the states? The tyranny of labels, *Snyder* v. *Massachusetts,* 291 U.S. 97, 114, must not lead us to leap to a conclusion that a word which in one set of facts may stand for oppression or enormity is of like effect in every other.

We have said that in appellant's view the Fourteenth Amendment is to be taken as embodying the prohibitions of the Fifth. His thesis is even broader. Whatever would be a violation of the original bill of rights

---

criminal cases, may be taken by the state, with the permission of the presiding judge, to the supreme court of errors, in the same manner and to the same effect as if made by the accused."

A statute of Vermont (G. L. 2598) was given the same effect and upheld as constitutional in State *v.* Felch, *92 Vt. 477; 105 Atl. 23.*

Other statutes, conferring a right of appeal more or less limited in scope, are collected in the American Law Institute Code of Criminal Procedure, June 15, 1930, p. 1203.

(Amendments I to VIII) if done by the federal government is now equally unlawful by force of the Fourteenth Amendment if done by a state. There is no such general rule.

The Fifth Amendment provides, among other things, that no person shall be held to answer for a capital or otherwise infamous crime unless on presentment or indictment of a grand jury. This court has held that, in prosecutions by a state, presentment or indictment by a grand jury may give way to informations at the instance of a public officer. *Hurtado* v. *California,* 110 U.S. 516; *Gaines* v. *Washington,* 277 U.S. 81, 86. The Fifth Amendment provides also that no person shall be compelled in any criminal case to be a witness against himself. This court has said that, in prosecutions by a state, the exemption will fail if the state elects to end it. *Twining* v. *New Jersey,* 211 U.S. 78, 106, 111, 112. Cf. *Snyder* v. *Massachusetts, supra,* p. 105; *Brown* v. *Mississippi,* 297 U.S. 278, 285. The Sixth Amendment calls for a jury trial in criminal cases and the Seventh for a jury trial in civil cases at common law where the value in controversy shall exceed twenty dollars. This court has ruled that consistently with those amendments trial by jury may be modified by a state or abolished altogether. *Walker* v. *Sauivnet,* 92 U.S. 90; *Maxwell* v. *Dow,* 176 U.S. 581; *New York Central R. Co.* v. *White,* 243 U.S. 188, 208; *Wagner Electric Mfg. Co.* v. *Lyndon,* 262 U.S. 226, 232. As to the Fourth Amendment, one should refer to *Weeks* v. *United States,* 232 U.S. 383, 398, and as to other provisions of the Sixth, to *West* v. *Louisiana,* 194 U.S. 258.

On the other hand, the due process clause of the Fourteenth Amendment may make it unlawful for a state to abridge by its statutes the freedom of speech which the First Amendment safeguards against encroachment by the Congress, *De Jonge* v. *Oregon,* 299 U.S. 353, 364; *Herndon* v. *Lowry,* 301 U.S. 242, 259; or the like freedom of the press, *Grosjean* v. *American Press Co.,* 297 U.S. 233; *Near* v. *Minnesota ex rel. Olson,* 283 U.S. 697, 707; or the free exercise of religion, *Hamilton* v. *Regents,* 293 U.S. 245, 262; cf. *Grosjean* v. *American Press Co., supra; Pierce* v. *Society of Sisters,* 268 U.S. 510; or the right of peaceable assembly, without which speech would be unduly trammeled, *De Jonge* v. *Oregon, supra; Herndon* v. *Lowry, supra;* or the right of one accused of crime to the benefit of counsel, *Powell* v. *Alabama,* 287 U.S. 45. In these and other situations immunities that are valid as against the federal government by force of the specific pledges of particular amendments[2] have been found to be implicit in the concept of ordered liberty, and thus, through the Fourteenth Amendment, become valid as against the states.

The line of division may seem to be wavering and broken if there is a hasty catalogue of the cases on the one side and the other. Reflection and analysis will induce a different view. There emerges the perception of a rationalizing principle which gives to discrete instances a proper order and coherence. The right to trial by jury and the immunity from prosecution except as the result of an indictment may have value and importance. Even so, they are not of the very essence of a scheme of ordered liberty. To abolish them is not to violate a "principle of justice so rooted in the traditions and conscience of our people as to be ranked as fundamental." *Snyder* v. *Massachusetts, supra,* p. 105; *Brown* v. *Mississippi, supra,* p. 285; *Hebert* v. *Louisiana,* 272 U.S. 312, 316. Few would be so narrow or provincial as to maintain that a fair and enlightened system of justice would be impossible without them. What is true of jury trials and indictments is true also, as the cases show, of the immunity from compulsory self-incrimination. *Twining* v. *New Jersey, supra.* This too might be lost, and justice still be done. Indeed, today as in the past there are students of our penal system who look upon the immunity as a mischief rather than a benefit, and who would limit its scope, or destroy it altogether.[3] No doubt there would remain the

[2] *First Amendment: "Congress shall make no law respecting an establishment of religion, or prohibiting the free exercise thereof; or abridging the freedom of speech, or of the press; or the right of the people peaceably to assemble, and to petition the Government for a redress of grievances."*

Sixth Amendment: "In all criminal prosecutions, the accused shall enjoy the right . . . to have the assistance of counsel for his defence."

[3] *See, e.g. Bentham, Rationale of Judicial Evidence, Book IX, Pt. 4, c. III; Glueck, Crime and Justice, p. 94; cf. Wigmore, Evidence, vol. 4, § 2251.*

Compulsory self-incrimination is part of the established procedure in the law of Continental Europe. Wigmore, supra, *p. 824; Garner, Criminal Procedure in France, 25 Yale L. J. 255, 260; Sherman, Roman*

need to give protection against torture, physical or mental. *Brown* v. *Mississippi, supra.* Justice, however, would not perish if the accused were subject to a duty to respond to orderly inquiry. The exclusion of these immunities and privileges from the privileges and immunities protected against the action of the states has not been arbitrary or casual. It has been dictated by a study and appreciation of the meaning, the essential implications, of liberty itself.

We reach a different plane of social and moral values when we pass to the privileges and immunities that have been taken over from the earlier articles of the federal bill of rights and brought within the Fourteenth Amendment by a process of absorption. These in their origin were effective against the federal government alone. If the Fourteenth Amendment has absorbed them, the process of absorption has had its source in the belief that neither liberty nor justice would exist if they were sacrificed. *Twining* v. *New Jersey, supra,* p. 99.[4] This is true, for illustration, of freedom of thought, and speech. Of that freedom one may say that it is the matrix, the indispensable condition, of nearly every other form of freedom. With rare aberrations a pervasive recognition of that truth can be traced in our history, political and legal. So it has come about that the domain of liberty, withdrawn by the Fourteenth Amendment from encroachment by the states, has been enlarged by latter-day judgments to include liberty of the mind as well as liberty of action.[5] The extension became, indeed, a logical imperative when once it was recognized, as long ago it was, that liberty is something more than exemption from physical restraint, and that even in the field of substantive rights and duties the legislative judgment, if oppressive and arbitrary, may be overridden by the courts. Cf. *Near* v. *Minnesota ex rel. Olson, supra; De Jonge* v. *Oregon, supra.* Fundamental too in the concept of due process, and so in that of liberty, is the thought that condemnation shall be rendered only after trial. *Scott* v. *McNeal,* 154 U.S. 34; *Blackmer* v. *United States,* 284 U.S. 421. The hearing, moreover, must be a real one, not a sham or a pretense. *Moore* v. *Dempsey,* 261 U.S. 86; *Mooney* v. *Holohan,* 294 U.S. 103. For that reason, ignorant defendants in a capital case were held to have been condemned unlawfully when in truth, though not in form, they were refused the aid of counsel. *Powell* v. *Alabama, supra,* pp. 67, 68. The decision did not turn upon the fact that the benefit of counsel would have been guaranteed to the defendants by the provisions of the Sixth Amendment if they had been prosecuted in a federal court. The decision turned upon the fact that in the particular situation laid before us in the evidence the benefit of counsel was essential to the substance of a hearing.

Our survey of the cases serves, we think, to justify the statement that the dividing line between them, if not unfaltering throughout its course, has been true for the most part to a unifying principle. On which side of the line the case made out by the appellant has appropriate location must be the next inquiry and the final one. Is that kind of double jeopardy to which the statute has subjected him a hardship so acute and shocking that our polity will not endure it? Does it violate those "fundamental principles of liberty and justice which lie at the base of all our civil and political institutions"? *Hebert* v. *Louisiana, supra.* The answer surely must be "no." What the answer would have to be if the state were permitted after a trial free from error to try the accused over again or to bring another case against him, we have no occasion to consider. We deal with the statute before us and no other. The state is not attempting to wear the accused out by a multitude of cases with accumulated trials. It asks no more than this, that the case against him shall go on until there shall be a trial free from the corrosion of substantial legal error. *State* v. *Felch,* 92 Vt. 477; 105 Atl. 23; *State* v. *Lee,*

Law in the Modern World, vol. 2, pp. 493, 494; Strumberg, Guide to the Law and Legal Literature of France, p. 184. Double jeopardy too is not everywhere forbidden. Radin, Anglo American Legal History, p. 228.

4 ". . . *it is possible that some of the personal rights safeguarded by the first eight Amendments against National action may also be safeguarded against state action, because a denial of them would be a denial of due process of law.* Chicago, Burlington & Quincy Railroad *v.* Chicago, *166 U.S. 226. If this is so, it is not because those rights are enumerated in the first eight Amendments, but because they are of such a nature that they are included in the conception of due process of law."*

5 *The cases are brought together in Warren, The New Liberty under the 14th Amendment, 39* Harv. L. Rev. *431.*

supra. This is not cruelty at all, nor even vexation in any immoderate degree. If the trial had been infected with error adverse to the accused, there might have been review at his instance, and as often as necessary to purge the vicious taint. A reciprocal privilege, subject at all times to the discretion of the presiding judge, *State* v. *Carabetta,* 106 Conn. 114; 127 Atl. 394, has now been granted to the state. There is here no seismic innovation. The edifice of justice stands, its symmetry, to many, greater than before.

2. The conviction of appellant is not in derogation of any privileges or immunities that belong to him as a citizen of the United States.

There is argument in his behalf that the privileges and immunities clause of the Fourteenth Amendment as well as the due process clause has been flouted by the judgment.

Maxwell v. *Dow, supra,* p. 584, gives all the answer that is necessary.

The judgment is

Affirmed.

BALDWIN v. SEELIG, 294 U.S. 511 (1935)

In an effort to deal with chaotic conditions in the milk industry during the Depression, New York enacted legislation that fixed minimum prices to be paid by dealers to producers. The legislation also prohibited sale within New York of milk produced outside the state when the producer had been paid a lower price than he would have received for a like transaction within New York. The statute was challenged as a violation of the commerce clause and the due process clause by a New York dealer purchasing Vermont milk and selling it in New York both in original cans and rebottled. Justice Cardozo, for a unanimous court, held that the act could not be applied either to the milk in the original cans or to the rebottled milk. Insofar as it was sought to be sustained as a health measure, alternate methods directed specifically towards that end were available to New York. New York could not, however, protect the economic welfare of its farmers by subjecting Vermont milk to what was in effect a customs duty equal to the price differential. Moreover, the "original package doctrine" was not to be treated as an inflexible standard where transactions in interstate commerce were concerned. Where the purpose of the statute is "to neutralize advantages belonging to the place of origin," the form of the package is immaterial. This case and a subsequent case raising similar problems, *Henneford* v. *Silas Mason Co.,* 300 U.S. 577 (1937), have been discussed in the main essay on Justice Cardozo.

MR. JUSTICE CARDOZO delivered the opinion of the Court.

Whether and to what extent the New York Milk Control Act (N.Y. Laws of 1933, c. 158; Laws of 1934, c. 126) may be applied against a dealer who has acquired title to the milk as the result of a transaction in interstate commerce is the question here to be determined.

G. A. F. Seelig, Inc. (appellee in No. 604 and appellant in No. 605) is engaged in business as a milk dealer in the city of New York. It buys its milk, including cream, in Fair Haven, Vermont, from the Seelig Creamery Corporation, which in turn buys from the producers on the neighboring farms. The milk is transported to New York by rail in forty-quart cans, the daily shipment amounting to about 200 cans of milk and 20 cans of cream. Upon arrival in New York about 90% is sold to customers in the original cans, the buyers being chiefly hotels, restaurants and stores. About 10% is bottled in New York, and sold to customers in bottles. By concession, title passes from the

Seelig Creamery to G. A. F. Seelig, Inc. at Fair Haven, Vermont. For convenience the one company will be referred to as the Creamery and the other as Seelig.

The New York Milk Control Act with the aid of regulations made thereunder has set up a system of minimum prices to be paid by dealers to producers. The validity of that system in its application to producers doing business in New York State has support in our decisions. *Nebbia* v. *New York,* 291 U.S. 502; *Hegeman Farms Corp.* v. *Baldwin,* 293 U.S. 163. Cf. *Borden's Farm Products Co.* v. *Baldwin,* 293 U.S. 194. From the farms of New York the inhabitants of the so-called Metropolitan Milk District, comprising the City of New York and certain neighboring communities, derive about 70% of the milk requisite for their use. To keep the system unimpaired by competition from afar, the Act has a provision whereby the protective prices are extended to that part of the supply (about 30%) which comes from other states. The substance of the provision is that, so far as such a prohibition is permitted by the Constitution, there shall be no sale within the state of milk bought outside unless the price paid to the producers was one that would be lawful upon a like transaction within the state. The statute, so far as pertinent, is quoted in the margin together with supplementary regulations by the Board of Milk Control.[1]

Seelig buys its milk from the Creamery in Vermont at prices lower than the minimum payable to producers in New York. The Commissioner of Farms and Markets refuses to license the transaction of its business unless it signs an agreement to conform to the New York statute and regulations in the sale of the imported product.[2] This the applicant declines to do. Because of that refusal other public officers, parties to these appeals, announce a purpose to prosecute for trading without a license and to recover heavy penalties. This suit has been brought to restrain the enforcement of the Act in its application to the complainant, repugnancy being charged between its provisions when so applied and limitations imposed by the Constitution of the United States. United States Constitution, Art. I, § 8, clause 3; Fourteenth Amendment, § 1. A District Court of three judges, organized in accordance with § 266 of the Judicial Code (28 U. S. C. § 380), has granted a final decree

1 *Section 258 (m) (4), Article 21-a, New York Agriculture & Markets Law, L. 1934, c. 126, formerly § 312 (g), Article 25, L. 1933, c. 158: "It is the intent of the legislature that the instant, whenever that may be, that the handling within the State by a milk dealer of milk produced outside of the State becomes a subject of regulation by the State, in the exercise of its police powers, the restrictions set forth in this article respecting such milk so produced shall apply and the powers conferred by this article shall attach. After any such milk so produced shall have come to rest within the State, any sale, within the State by a licensed milk dealer or a milk dealer required by this article to be licensed, of any such milk purchased from the producer at a price lower than that required to be paid for milk produced within the State purchased under similar conditions, shall be unlawful."*

Order of New York Milk Control Board, July 1, 1933: "Any continuous and regular purchase or sale or delivery or receipt of milk passing to a milk dealer at any place and available for utilization as fluid milk and/or cream within New York State, followed by such utilization in one or more instances, where the price involved in such purchase or sale or delivery or receipt is less than the sum of the minimum price established to be paid to producers for such milk plus actual costs of transporting and handling and processing such milk to the place and to the condition involved in such purchase or sale or delivery or receipt, hereby is forbidden."

2 *The application blank contains the following questions which show the form of the required agreement: "Do you agree not to sell within New York State after it has come to rest within the State, milk or cream purchased from producers without the State at a price lower than that required to be paid producers for milk or cream produced within the State purchased under similar conditions?"*

"Do you agree that you will obtain for the Commissioner and supply to him, at such times and in such manner as he requires, concerning milk and cream produced without the State and in any way dealt in by you, data to whatever extent is necessary to ascertain or compute whether the producers were paid for such milk or cream a price not lower than that required to be paid producers for milk or cream produced within New York State and purchased under similar conditions?"

restraining the enforcement of the Act in so far as sales are made by the complainant while the milk is in the cans or other original packages in which it was brought into New York, but refusing an injunction as to milk taken out of the cans for bottling, and thereafter sold in bottles. See opinion on application for interlocutory injunction:—7 F. Supp. 776; and cf. 293 U.S. 522. The case is here on cross-appeals 280 U. S. C. § 380.

First. An injunction was properly granted restraining the enforcement of the Act in its application to sales in the original packages.

New York has no power to project its legislation into Vermont by regulating the price to be paid in that state for milk acquired there. So much is not disputed. New York is equally without power to prohibit the introduction within her territory of milk of wholesome quality acquired in Vermont, whether at high prices or at low ones. This again is not disputed. Accepting those postulates, New York asserts her power to outlaw milk so introduced by prohibiting its sale thereafter if the price that has been paid for it to the farmers of Vermont is less than would be owing in like circumstances to farmers in New York. The importer in that view may keep his milk or drink it, but sell it he may not.

Such a power, if exerted, will set a barrier to traffic between one state and another as effective as if customs duties, equal to the price differential, had been laid upon the thing transported. Imposts or duties upon commerce with other countries are placed by an express prohibition of the Constitution, beyond the power of a state, "except what may be absolutely necessary for executing its inspection laws." Constitution, Art. I, § 10, clause 2; *Woodruff* v. *Parham,* 8 Wall. 123. Imposts and duties upon interstate commerce are placed beyond the power of a state, without the mention of an exception, by the provision committing commerce of that order to the power of the Congress. Constitution, Art. I, § 8, clause 3. "It is the established doctrine of this court that a state may not, in any form or under any guise, directly burden the prosecution of interstate business." *International Textbook Co.* v. *Pigg,* 217 U.S. 91, 112; and see *Brennan* v. *Titusville,* 153 U.S. 289; *Brown* v. *Houston,* 114 U.S. 622; *Webber* v. *Virginia,* 103 U.S. 344, 351; *Kansas City Southern Ry. Co.* v. *Kaw Valley Drainage District,* 233 U.S. 75, 79. Nice distinctions have been made at times between direct and indirect burdens. They are irrelevant when the avowed purpose of the obstruction, as well as its necessary tendency, is to suppress or mitigate the consequences of competition between the states. Such an obstruction is direct by the very terms of the hypothesis. We are reminded in the opinion below that a chief occasion of the commerce clauses was "the mutual jealousies and aggressions of the States, taking form in customs barriers and other economic retaliation." Farrand, Records of the Federal Convention, vol. II, p. 308; vol. III, pp. 478, 547, 548; The Federalist, No. XLII; Curtis, History of the Constitution, vol. 1, p. 502; Story on the Constitution, § 259. If New York, in order to promote the economic welfare of her farmers, may guard them against competition with the cheaper prices of Vermont, the door has been opened to rivalries and reprisals that were meant to be averted by subjecting commerce between the states to the power of the nation.

The argument is pressed upon us, however, that the end to be served by the Milk Control Act is something more than the economic welfare of the farmers or of any other class or classes. The end to be served is the maintenance of a regular and adequate supply of pure and wholesome milk, the supply being put in jeopardy when the farmers of the state are unable to earn a living income. *Nebbia* v. *New York, supra.* Price security, we are told, is only a special form of sanitary security; the economic motive is secondary and subordinate; the state intervenes to make its inhabitants healthy, and not to make them rich. On that assumption we are asked to say that intervention will be upheld as a valid exercise by the state of its internal police power, though there is an incidental obstruction to commerce between one state and another. This would be to eat up the rule under the guise of an exception. Economic welfare is always related to health, for there can be no health if men are starving. Let such an exception be admitted, and all that a state will have to do in times of stress and strain is to say that its farmers and merchants and workmen must be protected against competition from without, lest they go upon the poor relief lists or perish altogether. To give entrance to that excuse would be to invite a speedy end of our national solidarity. The Constitution was framed under the dominion of a political philosophy less parochial in range. It was framed upon the theory that the peoples of the several states must sink or swim together, and that in the long run prosperity and salvation are in union and not division.

We have dwelt up to this point upon the argument of the state that economic security for farmers in the milk-shed may be a means of assuring to consumers a steady supply of a food of prime necessity. There is, however, another argument which seeks to establish a relation between the well-being of the producer and the quality of the product. We are told that farmers who are underpaid will be tempted to save the expense of sanitary precautions. This temptation will affect the farmers outside New York as well as those within it. For that reason the exclusion of milk paid for in Vermont below the New York minimum will tend, it is said, to impose a higher standard of quality and thereby promote health. We think the argument will not avail to justify impediments to commerce between the states. There is neither evidence nor presumption that the same minimum prices established by order of the Board for producers in New York are necessary also for producers in Vermont. But apart from such defects of proof, the evils springing from uncared for cattle must be remedied by measures of repression more direct and certain than the creation of a parity of prices between New York and other states. Appropriate certificates may be exacted from farmers in Vermont and elsewhere (*Mintz* v. *Baldwin,* 289 U.S. 346; *Reid* v. *Colorado,* 187 U.S. 137); milk may be excluded if necessary safeguards have been omitted; but commerce between the states is burdened unduly when one state regulates by indirection the prices to be paid to producers in another, in the faith that augmentation of prices will lift up the level of economic welfare, and that this will stimulate the observance of sanitary requirements in the preparation of the product. The next step would be to condition importation upon proof of a satisfactory wage scale in factory or shop, or even upon proof of the profits of the business. Whatever relation there may be between earnings and sanitation is too remote and indirect to justify obstructions to the normal flow of commerce in its movement between states. Cf. *Asbell* v. *Kansas,* 209 U.S. 251, 256; *Railroad Co.* v. *Husen,* 95 U.S. 465, 472. One state may not put pressure of that sort upon others to reform their economic standards. If farmers or manufacturers in Vermont are abandoning farms or factories, or are failing to maintain them properly, the legislature of Vermont and not that of New York must supply the fitting remedy.

Many cases from our reports are cited by counsel for the state. They do not touch the case at hand. The line of division between direct and indirect restraints of commerce involves in its marking a reference to considerations of degree. Even so, the borderland is wide between the restraints upheld as incidental and those attempted here. Subject to the paramount power of the Congress, a state may regulate the importation of unhealthy swine or cattle (*Asbell* v. *Kansas, supra; Mintz* v. *Baldwin, supra*) or decayed or noxious foods. *Crossman* v. *Lurman,* 192 U.S. 189; *Savage* v. *Jones,* 225 U.S. 501; *Price* v. *Illinois,* 238 U.S. 446. Things such as these are not proper subjects of commerce, and there is no unreasonable interference when they are inspected and excluded. So a state may protect its inhabitants against the fraudulent substitution, by deceptive coloring or otherwise, of one article for another. *Plumley* v. *Massachusetts,* 155 U.S. 461; *Hebe Co.* v. *Shaw,* 248 U.S. 297; *Hygrade Provision Co.* v. *Sherman,* 266 U.S. 497. It may give protection to travelers against the dangers of overcrowded highways (*Bradley* v. *Public Utilities Comm'n,* 289 U.S. 92) and protection to its residents against unnecessary noises. *Hennington* v. *Georgia,* 163 U.S. 229. Cf., however, *Missouri, K. & T. Ry. Co.* v. *Texas,* 245 U.S. 484, 488. At times there are border cases, such as *Silz* v. *Hesterberg,* 211 U.S. 31, where the decision in all likelihood was influenced, even if it is not wholly explained, by a recognition of the special and restricted nature of rights of property in game. Interference was there permitted with sale and importation, but interference for a close season and no longer, and in aid of a policy of conservation common to many states. Cf. *Geer* v. *Connecticut,* 161 U.S. 519; *Foster Packing Co.* v. *Haydel,* 278 U.S. 1, 11; *Silz* v. *Hesterberg,* 184 N.Y. 126, 131; 76 N.E. 1032. None of these statutes—inspection laws, game laws, laws intended to curb fraud or exterminate disease—approaches in drastic quality the statute here in controversy which would neutralize the economic consequences of free trade among the states.

Second. There was error in refusing an injunction to restrain the enforcement of the Act in its application to milk in bottles to be sold by the importer.

The test of the "orginal package," which came into our law with *Brown* v.

Maryland, 12 Wheat. 419, is not inflexible and final for the transactions of interstate commerce, whatever may be its validity for commerce with other countries. Cf. *Woodruff* v. *Parham, supra; Anglo-Chilean Nitrate Sales Corp.* v. *Alabama,* 288 U.S. 218, 226. There are purposes for which merchandise, transported from another state, will be treated as a part of the general mass of property at the state of destination though still in the original containers. This is so, for illustration, where merchandise so contained is subjected to a non-discriminatory property tax which it bears equally with other merchandise produced within the state. *Sonneborn Bros.* v. *Cureton,* 262 U.S. 506; *Texas Co.* v. *Brown,* 258 U.S. 466, 475; *American Steel & Wire Co.* v. *Speed,* 192 U.S. 500. There are other purposes for which the same merchandise will have the benefit of the protection appropriate to interstate commerce, though the original packages have been broken and the contents subdivided. "A state tax upon merchandise brought in from another State, or upon its sales, whether in original packages or not, after it has reached its destination and is in a state of rest, is lawful only when the tax is not discriminating in its incidence against the merchandise because of its origin in another State." *Sonneborn Bros.* v. *Cureton, supra,* at p. 516. Cf. *McDermott* v. *Wisconsin,* 228 U.S. 115, 133; *Bowman* v. *Chicago & N. W. Ry. Co.,* 125 U.S. 465, 491; *Brimmer* v. *Rebman,* 138 U.S. 78; *Savage* v. *Jones, supra,* at p. 525; *Western Union* v. *Foster,* 247 U.S. 105, 114; *Pacific Co.* v. *Johnson,* 285 U.S. 480, 493. In brief, the test of the original package is not an ultimate principle. It is an illustration of a principle. *Pennsylvania Gas Co.* v. *Public Service Comm'n,* 225 N.Y. 397, 403; 122 N. E. 260. It marks a convenient boundary and one sufficiently precise save in exceptional conditions. What is ultimate is the principle that one state in its dealings with another may not place itself in a position of economic isolation. Formulas and catchwords are subordinate to this overmastering requirement. Neither the power to tax nor the police power may be used by the state of destination with the aim and effect of establishing an economic barrier against competition with the products of another state or the labor of its residents. Restrictions so contrived are an unreasonable clog upon the mobility of commerce. They set up what is equivalent to a rampart of customs duties designed to neutralize advantages belonging to the place of origin. They are thus hostile in conception as well as burdensome in result. The form of the packages in such circumstances is immaterial, whether they are original or broken. The importer must be free from imports framed for the very purpose of suppressing competition from without and leading inescapably to the suppression so intended.

The statute here in controversy will not survive that test. A dealer in milk buys it in Vermont at prices there prevailing. He brings it to New York, and is told he may not sell it if he removes it from the can and pours it into bottles. He may not do this for the reason that milk in Vermont is cheaper than milk in New York at the regimented prices, and New York is moved by the desire to protect her inhabitants from the cut prices and other consequences of Vermont competition. To overcome that competition a common incident of ownership—the privilege of sale in convenient receptacles—is denied to one who has bought in interstate commerce. He may not sell on any terms to any one, whether the orders were given in advance or came to him thereafter. The decisions of this court as to the significance of the original package in interstate transactions were not meant to be a cover for retortion or suppression.

The distinction is clear between a statute so designed and statutes of the type considered in *Leisy* v. *Hardin,* 135 U.S. 100, to take one example out of many available. By the teaching of that decision intoxicating liquors are not subject to license or prohibition by the state of destination without congressional consent.[3] They become subject, however, to such laws when the packages are broken. There is little, if any, analogy between restrictions of that type and those in controversy here. In licensing or prohibiting the sale of intoxicating liquors a state does not attempt to neutralize economic advantages belonging to the place of origin. What it does is no more than to apply its domestic policy, rooted in its conceptions of morality and order, to property which for such a purpose may fairly be deemed to have passed out of commerce and to be commingled in an absorbing mass. So also the analogy is remote between restrictions like the present ones upon the sale of imported milk and restrictions affecting sales in unsanitary sweat-shops. It is one thing for a state to exact adherence by an importer to

[3] *The rule is different today under the Twenty-first Amendment. Art. XXI, § 2.*

fitting standards of sanitation before the products of the farm or factory may be sold in its markets. It is a very different thing to establish a wage scale or a scale of prices for use in other states, and to bar the sale of the products, whether in the original packages or in others, unless the scale has been observed.

The decree in No. 604 is affirmed, and that in No. 605 reversed, and the cause remanded for proceedings in accordance with this opinion.

Hugo L. Black

☆ 1886–   ☆

APPOINTED BY

FRANKLIN D. ROOSEVELT

YEARS ON COURT

1937–

Hugo L. Black

by

JOHN P. FRANK

TIME, APRIL, 1967; place, the White House; occasion, Justice Black's thirtieth year on the Supreme Court. President Johnson, who had arranged the affair, was suddenly gone to a funeral of the ex-Chancellor of Germany. Present to assist Mrs. Johnson were Vice President Humphrey and Mrs. Humphrey; the Supreme Court attended in force. The other guests were friends and relatives of the Justice, mostly his clerks for the thirty-year span and their wives.

The affair was simple enough. There was a receiving line, an exceptionally felicitous introduction by the Vice President, the opening of the special fund at the University of Alabama Law School in Black's honor, and a few words from the Justice. He appreciated those who were there and he reminisced about those who were not. He spoke of the respect he felt for the Justices with whom he had served. There were many to remember; Black had sat with a quarter of all the Justices since George Washington's time, and a third of all the Chiefs.

Only a handful of Justices had served longer than he. His health was good, and with the completion of cataract operations scheduled after a return from an impending trip to Europe, there was every prospect that he would continue as an effective member of the Court for longer than any of his predecessors. His record fully warranted the observation of Professor Paul Freund, dean of America's Supreme Court observers, that: "He is without doubt the most influential of the many strong figures who have sat during the thirty years that have passed in his Justiceship. He has exhibited to a singular degree an intense moral commitment, concentrated through the focus of an unwavering vision, and brought to bear with immense prowess. One thinks of Justice Brandeis' confident formula for achievement: brains, rectitude, singleness of purpose, and time."

JOHN P. FRANK, former Professor of Law at Yale University, practices law in Phoenix, Arizona. He is the author of The Warren Court; Mr. Justice Black, the Man and His Opinions; *and numerous other books relating to the Supreme Court and its history.*

There had been another trip to the White House thirty years earlier. That earlier evening had been August 11, 1937. Then the invitation had come from President Franklin D. Roosevelt. The subject of the visit was not altogether a surprise, for three days earlier Attorney General Homer Cummings had commissioned Black's close friend and later Court colleague, Senator Sherman Minton of Indiana, to find out whether Black would go to the Court if appointed. On August 10, Black told Minton that he would accept the appointment if it were offered, and the visit with the President followed. While Black was at the White House visiting with the President, Mrs. Black went to a movie, "The Good Earth," a story touching some part on a plague of locusts in China. As each locust flashed before her eyes, they seemed to be saying to her, "Will he ask him? Won't he ask him?"

The President did ask. Taking an appointment form from a desk drawer, he said, "Hugo, this is a form for the nomination of a Supreme Court Justice. May I fill in your name?" Black replied, "Mr. President, are you sure that I'll be more useful in the Court than in the Senate?" The President replied, "Hugo, I wish you were twins because Barkley says he needs you in the Senate; but I think you'll be more useful on the Court." On August 12, 1937, the President put his hardest-hitting New Dealer on the Supreme Court.

At the time of his appointment, Black, who had been born February 27, 1886, was fifty-one years old. He was the eighth and last child of the family of William Black, a storekeeper and farmer in Clay County, Alabama. His middle name, Lafayette, came from his father, and Hugo was an adaptation from the name Hugh, much used in the family. His mother, Martha Toland Black, had been reading Victor Hugo before the baby was born.

Black's life began in a farmhouse, a good old-fashioned log cabin covered over with clapboard and expanded with a kitchen structure and extra bedrooms as need arose. The privy was in the rear; Black did not get accustomed to inside plumbing until he was twenty years old. Soon after Black was born, the family moved to the town of Ashland, a town of 350 people, where William Black became co-owner of a store. The Ashland home was more comfortable—a five room house with a large garden which supplied much of the family's food. William Black prospered and the family lived comfortably.

Here Hugo learned the sports of youth in late nineteenth-century Alabama. Common games were pitching silver dollars or horseshoes. These were games of skill, not of gambling; Hugo never played cards, even for pleasure, until after he had left Ashland. Baseball, fishing, and croquet were other sports.

Here Hugo also learned to work. As a cotton picker he was never very good, but he did become a typesetter for a weekly newspaper for which he could earn as much as seventy-five cents in a day. The one really big financial success of his early life was at a Fourth of July picnic at which he made thirteen dollars selling soda pop.

Life in Ashland was play and work and schooling. There was a very limited school available, which had one teacher for the first four grades. Following grade school there was a kind of enlarged high school in the community called Ashland College, which was in fact so nearly a high school that credits from it were not accepted for transfer at the University of Alabama.

Beyond play and books, Black also learned from the social outlook of the community. It was this education which most integrates the Black of the 1890's with the Black of the New Deal senate days and the Black of the Supreme Court. Black spent his youth during the pinnacle of the Populist movement in Alabama and in the country. This great political movement with its egalitarian economics and its agrarian radicalism captured the National Democratic party in 1896 under William Jennings Bryan and put a strong stamp on rural politics in the South for years to come.

Black, as a youngster, was not a Populist. His father, a prosperous country storekeeper, was a conservative Democrat. If Black ever in his life voted for a Republican, there is no record of it; someone's recollection of his childish years attributes to him the phrase "I'm a Democat" before he could pronounce the word. His closest identification with the Populists formally was as a typesetter for the *People's Party Advocate.*

But the formal distinction obscures the real impact. The anti-monopoly and rate regulation philosophies of the Populists and most of the rest of their social outlook on government and business have been a part of Black at least from young manhood. In terms of most of his social values, Black was an incipient New Dealer before he ever left home.

When he was seventeen years of age, Black went to medical school. This was a minor incident in his life occasioned by the fact that a brother was a doctor and his mother had great respect for the profession; he stayed in medical school only a year and then applied for admission to the University of Alabama Law School. He bypassed the college courses at the university entirely, because his previous education did not qualify him for the sophomore class, and under the practice of that time he could go to law school more easily than he could go to college.

As a law student, Black was at least adequate; because of a total lack of background education he had a far heavier load to carry than many of his fellow students, and yet he graduated with honors. He impressed his fellow graduates of 1906 as one who would "Use the devil himself with courtesy," a reference to an exceptional grace of manner always noticed in him. Upon graduation he went back to Ashland to practice law and stayed there for a year until the store building in which his office was located burned. Then, in September, 1907, as an almost penniless young man, he set out for Birmingham to make his career.

Black rented a desk in an attorney's office in Birmingham for seven dollars a month and began to get acquainted in the town. He was active in three lodges, the Masons, the Knights of Pythias, and the Oddfellows and engaged in some church activity as well. He earned fifty dollars a month doing credit checks for an insurance company.

Then, early in his career came his first case. In keeping with the practice of the time, convicts were not kept in jail but were leased out to perform work. Black's client was a Negro convict who had been held fifteen days overtime almost as a slave. Black sued for damages, and won his first verdict, $137.50.

As his practice grew, Black was also given a part-time job as a police court judge for the city of Birmingham, hearing cases against persons charged with minor crimes. There were great numbers of cases—there might be a hundred on a Monday morning after a boisterous Birmingham weekend. Black exercised a commonsense justice and a temperate handling of the many Negro defendants. When one Negro was charged with carrying a concealed weapon, a gun too rusty to use, Black examined the gun and dismissed the case. On the other hand, when another struck his wife with a knife, Black fined him twenty-five dollars. Black's respect for Negro rights was noticed in the local press.

The most conspicuous quality of Black's judgeship was its speed of operation. In one day, 118 cases were disposed of in 150 minutes. Eighty were pleas of guilty, eight were discharged, fifteen were continued, and fifteen were tried and resulted in convictions. The only recognized alternative was to leave defendants who could not make bail in jail, and the better practice was thought to be to roll the cases out.

When Black gave up his police court judgeship in 1912, he had the respect of the local community. He was also beginning to develop a practice of his own. In 1914 he became prosecuting attorney for the county and served until he resigned to join the Army in 1917. As prosecutor, Black inherited a loaded criminal docket with over 3,000 pending criminal cases. As a result of his endless driving energy, he had the docket current by the time he left the job. In the course of this experience he tried more murder cases than he could ever remember.

There were spectacular episodes. One involved a murder case on which a jury divided, ten for conviction and two against. While a new trial was pending, the defendant exploded dynamite in the men's room of a train, killing not only himself but other passengers as well. But the most spectacular incident of Black's prosecuting experience, and the one which has had the greatest influence on subsequent constitutional law, was his experience with the Bessemer Police Department. Bessemer, a suburb of Birmingham, was running a torture chamber to get confessions from Negro defendants. Black took the matter to a grand jury, which reported the existence of the third degree "in a manner so cruel that it would bring discredit and shame upon the most uncivilized and barbarous community." In one case, four officers strapped a seventy-year-old Negro to a door and beat him almost to death. The beatings were conducted with belts, fists, sticks, chairs—as one of the officers testified, "anything we could get hold of." When the job was done, the prisoner "looked like he had been hammered up a bit; like some of the police had ahold of him."

The grand jury report in Birmingham in 1915 could well have been a United States Supreme Court opinion fifty years later. It said that a man did not lose "his right to be treated as a human being by reason of the fact that he is charged with—or an officer suspects that—he is guilty of a crime. Instead of being ready and waiting to strike a prisoner in his custody, an officer should protect him."

In 1917, Black resigned his office to go into the service. The *Birmingham Ledger* said, "Mr. Black has served Jefferson County well. He has kept the county jail empty, he has lopped the payroll of the county, and has called attention to slack methods in the county affairs."

Black's military experience was of no great importance to him and, except as it gave him political standing, did not much affect his later life. He never served outside the United States. As was typical of the 1917 army, he took the experience in high spirits. On one furlough he returned to Ashland for a visit and showed the family youngsters military calisthenics. He had the children loud with laughter as he squatted, stretched out his arms in both directions, and displayed great skill in performing the exercises which the children could not do without falling over. The exercises stuck in his memory, and over forty years later, in the course of a visit to a member of his company, both men, then elderly, repeated the exercises for the amusement of a new generation of children. Of course the military experience left some residue, but the main relics are a couple of excellent pictures showing Captain Black in the tight-collared dress jacket and pinch-topped, flat-brimmed hat of the World War I army.

By the end of 1918, Black was back in law practice in Birmingham. For the next several years, he concentrated on his law practice and on purely personal affairs. The most important of those personal affairs was his marriage to Josephine Foster in Birmingham in 1921. It was an extremely successful marriage, one which lasted for thirty years until Josephine's untimely death. The marriage, into a "good family," gave Black an improved social standing, which was of little consequence to him. But it also gave him a companion and skilled hostess who became the center of his life. This satisfied a basic need of Black's personality: home for him was never a place simply to change to dress clothes for the pleasures of the evening. In the terribly turbulent years ahead, Black truly needed a home and a family as a sanctuary, and this Josephine provided. There were three children, Hugo, Jr., who graduated from Yale Law School and practices in Florida; Sterling, who graduated from Columbia Law School and practices in New Mexico; and Josephine, who graduated from Swarthmore and married Mario Pesaresi, a New Jersey psychiatrist.

A letter written in 1924 by a visitor at the house gives an impression of the family life in those days. The young lady was a college sophomore visiting Birmingham for its social delights. She recalls there was much planning with the Blacks as to how to manage the family cars so that she would get to the proper places on time. Black inquired of her adventures and showed a proper interest in her appearance. He paid for a permanent wave as a gift to the visitor and Josephine made the hairstyling arrangements. What comes through is a clear picture of middle-class concerns and middle-class comforts.

But Black's law practice was not a middle-class practice. He was a liberal lawyer with some labor union business and was astonishingly successful as a personal injury lawyer. The eloquence which in later life was to make him one of the most effective public speakers in the United States was developed in countless jury cases. His extraordinary forcefulness of argument was expressly noted by the Alabama Supreme Court. Black's practice became enormous. Between 1919 and 1925 he had over a hundred cases in the appellate courts of Alabama alone, with over half of them in the injury field. His practice did not deal with the problems of corporations or substantial business affairs; corporate business was the most minor part of his work.

By 1925, Black felt that he had made enough money to run for the United States Senate. In the Alabama of that period, the Democratic nomination was the election, and there were four candidates other than Black. In 1923, Black joined the Birmingham chapter of the Ku Klux Klan and dropped out again in 1925, before he began his campaign. The Klan, in fact, supported one of his opponents, L. Breckenridge Musgrove.

Black was the youngest and the poorest of the major candidates, and less known than some. But he did have more energy than any of the others. He had the support of the Baptists, the Prohibitionists, and the progenitors of the Tennessee Valley Authority. Black ran as the poor man's candidate. ("I am not now, and have never been, a railroad, power company, or corporation lawyer.") He reached every part of the state, wore out two automobiles, made sixty speeches in one period of thirty days, and in the words of one newspaper, persuaded the voters that "he knows better how to sympathize with the common people." He won easily.

Upon Black's arrival in Washington in 1927, he made a decision typical of his approach to large problems. He undertook to prepare himself for his job. Realizing that he had very little education and very limited experience, the new senator resolved to speak on the Senate floor only on those rare occasions when he really had something to say, and to learn as much as he could. The Library of Congress was next door to the Capitol and it became his university; there are many tales of the books sent to him and the books he went to get. He read in depth in American and European history, and he set out then to read the classics, a program he still follows today. His Livy has very possibly become the most marked up in the nation's capital.

Among his fellow senators, Black began to make his friendships and form his alliances. After a year or two he was firmly tied in with the liberals. This included the progressive Republicans, such as Senators Norris of Nebraska and La Follette of Wisconsin, and the liberal Democrats such as Senator Tom Walsh of Montana.

As Black slowly began to take an active hand in Senate affairs, he emerged as a senator with national interests. Working with Senator Norris, he broadened his entire conception of what was to become of the Tennessee Valley Authority, supporting it as a great public power project as well as a source of fertilizer.

As early as 1929, in a Senate speech, he foreshadowed his Supreme Court position on freedom of speech by opposing customs controls over obscene or subversive publications. He declared himself as altogether opposed to censorship—the American citizen should be "persuaded in no way except by logic and reason."

Black's first term was his educational period. His contributions were essentially routine, but they satisfied his constituents; he was easily re-elected in 1932. This was the absolute depth of the depression, and President Roosevelt was elected at the same time. When Roosevelt came in and Black came back, his party was in power; and he was ready to begin the significant part of his Senate career.

The major Black activities of the second term were:

1. *The sponsorship of the statute which became the Fair Labor Standards Act.* This is the basic wage-hour legislation of the United States. Black's original proposal was for a thirty-hour week, and Black began pushing this proposal in 1933. Black's thirty-hour week bill passed the Senate on April 6, 1933, by a vote of fifty-three to thirty. The bill was then derailed for a time but in 1936, Black and Michigan delegate Frank Murphy were both on the Democratic platform committee. The two working together did much to obtain a platform commitment in favor of minimum wage, maximum hour, and child labor legislation. After the 1936 election, Black and Representative Connery of Massachusetts introduced a bill controlling both wages and hours and eliminating child labor.

"We have waited too long for it already," Black told his fellow senators. It was time for action:

> *The Democratic party has promised the country this kind of legislation. The President has pledged it. The mandate of the election has ordered it. And at long last the American people are going to have it!*

The wage-hour debate was the last great economic fight between the new South and the old South. Old line southerners bewailed the passing of the ten cent wage and the ten-hour day. As one of their spokesmen said, the object of the wage-hour bill was to "overcome the splendid gifts of God to the South." But so far as Black was concerned, any business which depended on child labor, relied on long hours or paid pennies for an hour's work, would have to go. "I do not believe our civilization requires any such sacrifice on the part of any large percentage of our people," he said.

The wage-hour act went through still further changes after Black left the Senate for the Supreme Court in August of 1937, but it became law in 1938.

2. *The investigation of Merchant Marine subsidies.* At the very beginning of the Roosevelt administration, Black was appointed chairman of an investigating committee to inquire into airmail and ocean mail contracts. A comprehensive account of his work is Nicholas Johnson, "Senator Black and the American Merchant Marine," 14 *U.C.L.A. Law Review* 399 (1967). The Black hearings revealed corporate officers of the shipping companies who did not know what companies they were connected with. It exposed a system of subsidy of the merchant marine which Black concluded was "a sad, miserable, and corrupting

failure." The investigations unearthed salaries from $100,000 to $1,000,000 a year, based largely on government subsidies, and discovered the transfer of millions of dollars of government property to private hands. The Merchant Marine Act of 1936 followed and Black's connection with it is summarized by Mr. Johnson:

> *Senator Black's principal contributions to the 1936 act and its early administration were the hearings and committee report. After the hearings came fifteen months of debate, and thirty-five drafts of proposed legislation. Black's role in the compromise represented by the final draft, or that of any other individual Senator, is lost in the documentary record. He stimulated the nation's conscience, creating demand for Congressional maritime reform.*

3. *The investigation of airline subsidies.* Airline subsidies also were administered through the Post Office Department and were investigated by Black's committee. His investigation showed that investments of a few hundred dollars had brought returns of millions. It revealed large-scale corruption, as well as large-scale violation of the laws relating to competitive bidding. The companies being investigated destroyed records, and the former Assistant Secretary of Commerce and a high official of one of the airlines both went to jail for contempt of the Senate. The investigation led to the cancellation of airmail contracts, a disastrous attempt of the army to fly the mail, and a new system of handling airmail contracts.

4. *The investigation of utility lobbies.* The 1920's and 1930's were the days of holding companies in American corporate life. Utilities were particularly susceptible to this form of business organization. A series of scattered operating utilities might themselves have their stock held by a holding company which did not operate but merely held the stock; and the stock in the holding company might be held by another holding company and so on to the top of a long ladder. This device permitted the corporation at the top to dominate many others. A small investment at the top could control vast sums of other people's money at the bottom.

A bill to abolish holding companies, known as the Wheeler-Rayburn death sentence act, was before the Congress in 1935. The utilities waged an immense campaign against it, and the response was a Black investigation of the lobbying against the Wheeler-Rayburn bill.

The investigation was a sensation. An effective ruse of the holding companies had been a wave of correspondence and telegrams purporting to come from the general public in opposition to the bill. Investigation showed that they were not really from the general public; they were from holding companies which had borrowed names of persons from telephone directories. For example, a single individual sent 1,300 telegrams. Of one group of 14,782 messages sent against the bill, 14,779 were paid for by the utilities.

The greatest sensation of all was the testimony of Howard Hopson, president of one of the holding companies. He admitted that he gained the right to dictate editorials in many papers in return for immense advertising payments. In the wake of the investigation, the Wheeler-Rayburn bill passed. While Black was certainly not solely responsible for the result, his investigation undoubtedly contributed mightily to it.

5. *The investigation of lobbying activities in general.* The utility lobby investigation broadened into a general investigation of lobbying activities in the United States. The investigation was timed to affect the 1936 election. The investigation proved conclusively that many seemingly independent organizations, which appeared to be local representatives of local points of view in various parts of the country, were in fact subsidized by a small group of major financiers. For illustration, what purported to be a farmers group was in fact financed by the DuPont Company, the Sun Oil Company, Swift & Company, and General Motors.

In the course of this hearing, Black subpoenaed the originals of telegrams from the Western Union Company. For this he was denounced more violently than at any time in his life except during the period of the Supreme Court appointment. For example, the Hearst Press, which he had shown to have received direct payments from Howard Hopson, now retaliated with cartoons showing Black as a skunk and a peeping Tom. The Black investigation discovered that over $1,000,000 had been contributed by approximately ten organizations or groups to finance false front organizations around the country.

The success of Black's investigations was due to his extraordinary lawyer's skill. His hard-working, detailed preparation, and his ability to get the evidence from witnesses by cross-examination, both resulted from his years as a trial lawyer. As a lawyer, Black was courteous, but it was the courtesy of a tough customer.

By the time of his appointment to the Court in 1937, Black had developed a fixed philosophy about many matters which he would face while on the Court. A few of these follow:

(a) *Substantive due process.*

Between the 1880's and the time of Black's appointment, the Supreme Court had developed a constitutional rule that allowed it to review the "reasonableness" of state and federal legislation. It made its own balance, weighing public interest against private property rights, and held many times that state regulations of health or labor conditions unduly infringed on the rights of private property. This concept was the Court's major weapon against social legislation.

At the time Black came to the Court, there were two clear philosophies of substantive due process. The conservative Justices wished to use the good old doctrine to control legislation. The liberals, like Holmes and Brandeis, believed that it should be used very rarely and that all deference should be paid to the decision of the legislatures. Black's position, hardened in the Senate by the debates of those years, was that substantive due process should be abolished altogether. He believed that the power of the Court to pass upon the reasonableness of legislation did not exist at all. In March of 1937, he told the Senate,

A bare majority of the members of the Supreme Court of the United States have been for a number of years assuming the right on their part to determine the reasonableness of state and federal laws. The Constitution never gave that majority any such power.

(b) *The commerce clause.*

Black developed his philosophy of the commerce power of the federal government in debate on such matters as his own bill for wage-hour and child labor control and the public utility holding company act. In one debate he told the Senate that, "The federal government has complete, unrestricted power to regulate interstate commerce . . . unless there is something in the Constitution itself which directly stands in the way of that regulation of interstate commerce." On another occasion he told his fellow senators that Congress could regulate anything which would burden or directly affect interstate commerce.

(c) *Antitrust.*

Black's anti-monopoly philosophy was fully developed in the Senate. He was wholly opposed to business ventures which made small local businessmen cogs in giant commercial machines. He warned the Senate in 1930 that the business chains then forming were steadily merging until finally "they continue the merging and are gradually getting into one center."

(d) *Civil liberties.*

Black had two other solid commitments when he became a Supreme Court Justice. One was a strong commitment to freedom of speech; his attitude on obscenity legislation has been quoted earlier. Another was a solid commitment to fair criminal procedures. His own role in attacking the confession abuses in the Birmingham area when he was prosecuting attorney has already been described. In the Senate he had made it clear that he would not vote to confirm a former prosecutor as a federal judge if he felt the prosecutor had abused fair procedures.

(e) *Personal injuries.*

Black had made clear on the Senate floor his belief, based on his own legal experience, that the law of personal injury cases was truly important, as important as any other part of the law of the United States. He had argued that injured employees whose cases came up in the federal courts should have as much of a right to get their problems to the United States Supreme Court as those with problems of larger and more general interest.

In short, when President Roosevelt appointed Hugo Black to the Supreme Court in August, 1937, Black had a wide-open record. He was a really well-known figure, a demonstrated and a complete New Deal liberal. The reaction around the country to his appointment, therefore, was largely determined by people's attitude toward his social outlook. To Black's fellow liberals in the Senate, the appointment was great. To former President Herbert Hoover, the choice meant that the Court was "one-ninth packed." The Chicago *Tribune* said the President's choice was "the worst he could find"; and the New York *Herald Tribune* said the nomination was "as menacing as it is unfit." On the other hand, the Louisville *Courier Journal* said, "Black will carry to the Supreme Court the liberalism for which the President has fought—all the liberalism which one man can carry." Senator George W. Norris, the senior liberal Senator of Nebraska, expressed his regret at the "bitter, unreasonable, and sometimes malicious attacks which are being made upon him." Norris added, "He is a worthy representative of the common people. He understands their hopes and ambitions, and their liberties in his hands will be safe."

Black was confirmed by a vote of sixty-three to sixteen. A few days later, he set out for Europe for a short vacation with Mrs. Black.

The big attack came after Black was already confirmed and gone. In September, 1937, the Pittsburgh *Post Gazette* ran a series of stories revealing that Black had been a member of the Ku Klux Klan, a matter well-known through front page newspaper stories in Alabama for many years. The stories were extended over six days and became a great issue in the current New York mayoralty campaign. The attacks on Black were violent and some of his former supporters changed ground. Senator Norris stood firmly with Black, saying, "Actually, Justice Black is being subjected to all this criticism because he is a liberal, because he wants to bring the Supreme Court closer to the people—not because he is a Klansman."

The European vacation was thoroughly ruined by persistent newspaper reporters, but Black declined to make any statements until he returned. On October 1, he made a national radio address saying simply that he had been a member of the Klan, that he had long since resigned, and that he had nothing further to do with it. Black was an immensely effective speaker—after President Roosevelt, perhaps the best in the country. The radio audience was tremendous. Public opinion polls showed a heavy tide of opinion moving in Black's favor after the speech and the matter dropped from public notice.

On October 4, 1937, Black began his active duties as Justice.

A description of Black's judicial work is a task which is simply colossal. His length of service is approximately three times the average of the other eight Justices with whom he sits, and he has regularly done his share of the work. For purposes of some classification, his work can be considered from three standpoints: his work in the field of civil liberties and civil rights; his work outside the field of civil liberties and civil rights; and his methods of workmanship. In terms of chronology, the work outside the field of civil liberties had its greatest weight in the beginning, though after thirty years Black is still very much an old New Dealer on the Court. In the latter period of his career, the public has been so preoccupied with Black's role in matters of fair trial and free speech as to overlook all else. ("He is our First Amendment fundamentalist," one writer said.) For organizational convenience, we may follow this chronological pattern, but always with the understanding that the strands overlay each other.

A. *Black's Opinions, Largely Apart from Civil Liberties and Civil Rights.*

1. *Substantive due process.*

Black attacked substantive due process, or the judicial power to declare either rates or legislation invalid. He contended that the "persons" covered by the due process clause meant only natural persons and did not cover corporations. Since it is usually corporations which seek the protection of the clause, this would practically do away with substantive due process. While Black offered this proposal in *Connecticut Gen. Life Ins. Co.* v. *Johnson,* 303 U.S. 77 (1938), he has never been able to obtain Court acceptance of this point of view.

As a second line, he attacked the standards applicable to judicial review of public utility rates, opening the war in what was the most colorful opinion of his first year on the Court, a lone dissent in *McCart* v. *Indianapolis Water Co.,* 302 U.S. 419, 423 (1938). The addition of Justices Douglas and Murphy lead to the virtually complete elimination of judicial review of rates, the high spot being Justice Douglas' opinion for the Court in *Federal Power Commission* v. *Hope Natural Gas Co.,* 320 U.S. 591 (1944).

The other line of attack was on the whole business of judicial review of the reasonableness of social legislation. Black's leading opinions are *Lincoln Fed. Labor Union* v. *Northwestern Iron & Metal Co.,* 335 U.S. 525 (1949) and *Ferguson* v. *Skrupa,* 372 U.S. 726 (1963). In the latter case Black for the Court said:

> *The doctrine that prevailed in* [*several cases*] *that due process authorizes courts to hold laws unconstitutional when they believe the Legislature has acted unwisely—has long since been discarded. We have returned to the original constitutional proposition that courts do not substitute their social and economic beliefs for the judgment of legislative bodies, who are elected to pass laws.* [at 730.]

Since the day Black joined the Court, no state economic regulation has been invalidated on the grounds of denial of substantive due process. This is a result which has been the work of others, of course, as well as of Black, and includes the work of Justice Douglas in particular. But for Black this has been a particularly fundamental article of judicial faith, and he has been deeply alarmed at any reappearance of the concept of substantive due process under any other form. In *Griswold* v. *Connecticut,* 381 U.S. 479 (1965), the Court invalidated the Connecticut birth control legislation. At least some of the Justices rested expressly on a substantive due process ground. Black, who felt that the Connecticut law was totally absurd, nonetheless strongly dissented from what he felt was a dangerous re-emergence of substantive due process.

2. *Commerce and economic regulation.*

Since the New Deal appointments, the Court has regularly taken the view that the commerce power is as broad as the economic needs of the nation, and Black has joined in those conclusions. His own principal commerce clause opinion is *United States* v. *South-Eastern Underwriters Ass'n.,* 322 U.S. 533 (1944), a decision extending the commerce power to the insurance industry. Modern commerce doctrine is very close to the views Black expressed as a senator, but his writing role in the Supreme Court on this subject has been limited.

While Black has expanded federal power under the commerce clause, he has also strongly upheld state power under the same clause. He believes that the states have full right to regulate commerce or tax it so long as they do not discriminate against it; in other words, equal, nondiscriminatory legislation which Congress has not forbidden should be valid even though interstate commerce may be affected. For an example, see his dissent in *Gwin, White & Prince, Inc.* v. *Henneford,* 305 U.S. 434 (1939); and on regulatory legislation, see *Southern Pacific Co.* v. *Arizona,* 325 U.S. 761 (1945).

3. *Exercises of federal power.*

Black has enforced the general federal regulatory laws, such as the Fair Labor Standards Act, the National Labor Relations Act, and the various antitrust acts, to the hilt. His labor cases are discussed by Dean Ivan C. Rutledge, "Justice Black and Labor Law," 14 *U.C.L.A. Law Review* 501 (1967) who reviews the many cases. As Dean Rutledge says, "[*W*]hen Mr. Justice Black writes about federal supremacy in labor regulation, he is usually writing for the Court." (at 511) Of leading importance was *NLRB* v. *Waterman Steamship Corp.,* 309 U.S. 206 (1940) in which Black for the Court made *very* clear to the lower courts in the southern states that they would simply have to enforce the National Labor Relations Act whether they liked it or not.

In the antitrust field, Black's impact has been enormous. W. Wallace Kirkpatrick, "The Development of Antitrust," in Stephen Strickland's *Hugo Black* (Bobbs Merrill, 1967) says:

> *Statistics and figures cannot tell the complete story of Justice Black's activity in this field, but they do give some indication both of his interest and of the opportunity he has had to make an impact on the law. Since his appointment thirty years ago, there have been something over 200 cases decided by the Court involving antitrust and related questions. Black has written opinions in almost fifty of these cases; of these, thirty opinions were written for a majority of the Court and less than half that number were dissents; the rest were concurring opinions. In these 200-odd cases, Black voted against the application of the antitrust laws only about twenty times.* [p. 199.]

Black's approach to the Sherman Act and its policy was set forth by him in *Northern Pacific Railway Co.* v. *United States,* 356 U.S. 1 (1958):

> *The Sherman Act was designed to be a comprehensive charter of economic liberty aimed at preserving free and unfettered competition as the rule of trade. It rests on the premise that the unrestrained interaction of competitive forces will yield the best allocation of our economic resources, the lowest prices, the highest quality and the greatest material progress, while at the same time providing an environment conducive to the preservation of our democratic political and social institutions. But even were that premise open to question, the policy unequivocally laid down by the Act is competition.* [p. 4.]

All of which is not to say that the government has been winning all its cases. Two major defeats for the government were *United States* v. *Bethlehem Steel Corp.,* 315 U.S. 289 (1942) and *Youngstown Sheet & Tube Co.* v. *Sawyer,* 343 U.S. 579 (1952). In the *Bethlehem* case, the issue was whether the government could recover for war profits made in World War I. After the fashion of such everlastingly dangling disputes, the matter did not come up for decision until after World War II was started. Black rejected the government's claim under existing law, making it very clear that Congress should enact some profit control legislation with teeth in it. Under the spur of the *Bethlehem Steel* opinion, Congress did adopt the Renegotiation Act to control the profits of World War II.

The *Youngstown Sheet & Tube* case was an even more dramatic conflict with the government. In this opinion the Court held invalid the action of President Truman in seizing the entire steel industry. In what may be eventually recognized as his most important opinion, Black held that the President, without the authority of an act of Congress to back him up, had no power to seize an industry regardless of the emergency. As Black, an old congressman, saw it, "The Founders of this Nation entrusted the lawmaking power to the Congress alone in both good and bad times."

4. *Personal injuries.*

Black told his fellow senators in 1937 that he regarded personal injury cases as an important part of the Supreme Court's work, just as it had once been an important part of his own practice. That point of view he has sold to his fellow Justices, and while personal injury matters are never at the heart of the Supreme Court's work, they have certainly occupied a new and significant place during Black's tenure. His opinions have vastly expanded the interpretation of the Jones Act, relating to injured seamen, and the statute relating to injured longshoremen. The cases are reviewed by Judge J. Skelly Wright, "Justice at the Dock: The Maritime Worker and Mr. Justice Black," in 14 *U.C.L.A. Law Review* 524 (1967). One of the greatest injustices confronting longshoremen was a dispute over whether their cases were properly brought under state workmen's compensation laws or under the federal statute; if a shoreline worker guessed wrong, he might end up with no recovery at all. This unhappy situation was largely ended by Black's opinion in *Davis* v. *Department of Labor,* 317 U.S. 249 (1942), which for practical purposes created an overlapping jurisdiction between the two. As a result, as Judge Wright has said, "Litigation over jurisdictional conflicts in maritime injury cases dropped off sharply."

Black has great faith that juries in personal injury cases will usually do the just thing. He has strongly upheld the full and complete enforcement of the Seventh Amendment to the Constitution, providing for jury trials in civil cases. There has been an endless controversy about the allocation of authority between the judge and the jury. Black has pushed the jury's province to its utmost, so that the Supreme Court has time after time reversed lower court judges who have set aside jury verdicts or precluded cases from going to juries at all. In this area, Black's efforts have, in a major way, changed the course of practice in the United States. For a leading exposition of his own view, though in this case a dissent, see *Galloway* v. *United States,* 319 U.S. 372 (1943).

5. *State and federal power.*

Countless cases in the Supreme Court turn on the nature of the federal system. The issue may be one of the relative powers of the federal and the state governments or the relation of some agency of one government to the functioning of another. Here Black has written often; two examples may serve as illustrations. In *Testa* v. *Katt,* 330 U.S. 386 (1947), the case involved the operation of the Price Control Act in World War II. That statute provided that if someone was overcharged, he might recover treble damages. It clearly contemplated that he might sue for his damages in either the federal or the state court. The courts of Rhode Island declined to enforce this law on the grounds that a state court was not required to enforce a federal law which applied a penalty. The Supreme Court of Rhode Island argued that under well-settled rules of law, it would not have to enforce a penalty law of another state or of a foreign country and therefore it did not have to do so for the United States. Justice Black's unanimous opinion said: "Such a broad assumption flies in the face of the fact that the States of the Union constitute a nation." There can be no difference of policy between a state and the federal government: "The policy of the Federal Act is the prevailing policy in every state."

As was discussed in connection with the commerce cases, Black strongly upholds the federal commerce power, but he also strongly upholds state powers. In *Testa* v. *Katt,* he said, "the states must accept and apply the federal policy once it is established by Congress"; but in *Burford* v. *Sun Oil Company,* 319 U.S. 315 (1943), he noted, citing an earlier case: "It is in the public interest that federal courts of equity should exercise their discretionary power with proper regard for the rightful independence of state governments in carrying out their domestic policy." (at 318) *Burford* was a suit brought in the federal court to declare invalid a Texas administrative agency order regulating oil well drilling. The issue before the Court was whether the federal courts could review the state administrative orders at all or whether such cases should be left to the state courts to decide, subject to a final review in the United States Supreme Court, if necessary. In *Burford,* the Court held that as a matter of its discretion it would leave these disputes to the state courts, which, the Court found, were "working partners" with the state administrative agency in the business of regulating the oil industry. There was no need for federal intrusion and the matter would be left to the state to handle in its own way in its own institutions.

B. *The Civil Liberties and Civil Rights Cases.*

Much has been written about Black and civil liberties. Three key sources are Stephen Strickland, ed., *Hugo Black* (Indianapolis, 1967); Irving Dilliard, ed., *One Man's Stand for Freedom* (New York, 1963); and essays by Harry Kalven, Jr., Charles E. Rice, Paul A. Freund, and Arthur E. Sutherland in the 14 *U.C.L.A. Law Review* 397 et seq. (1967). Black's work in this entire area is so enormous that it needs to be classified in some workable fashion, and we here follow the order of the constitutional provisions themselves.

1. *Speech and press.*

Black believes that the First Amendment gives an individual an absolute right to discuss all government affairs and to argue for desired changes in the existing order. This is a right which may be subject to some restrictions as to time and place, but to none as to content. He once said in informal discussion of the Holmes observation that one may not shout "fire" in a crowded theater, "That is a wonderful aphorism about shouting 'fire' in a crowded theater. But you do not have to shout 'fire' to get arrested. If a person creates a disorder in the theater, they would get him out of there not because of what he hollered but because he *hollered*." Black rejects the "clear and present danger" test developed by Holmes which holds that speech may be suppressed if there is some "clear and present danger" of some evil which the state has a right to prevent. Black believes the absoluteness of the right precludes any control of speech, disassociated from action, regardless of circumstances. Black believes that in moments of tension those who are deciding whether clear present dangers exist will be far too prone to find such dangers.

During the height of the so-called McCarthy era, in the 1950's, the Court in salient opinions did give very restrictive interpretations to the right of freedom of speech in cases involving persons charged with Communist associations. Black strongly dissented in *Dennis* v. *United States,* 341 U.S. 494 (1951) and *American Communications Assn.* v. *Dowds,* 339 U.S. 382 (1950). The Court later moved in Black's direction in a case requiring a high standard of specific intent for violation of the laws involved, *Yates* v. *United States,* 354 U.S. 298 (1957), though Black in an opinion of his own in *Yates* held out for an even more complete freedom.

Perhaps the best single expression in any one opinion of Black's view on the difficult issues of the 1950's is the dissent in *Barenblatt* v. *United States,* 360 U.S. 109 (1959). The majority held that a person should be convicted for refusing to answer questions from a congressional committee asking whether he had ever been a member of the Communist party. In Black's opinion such a committee process abridged freedom of speech, press, assembly and the right to petition by holding out to exposure, obloquy and public scorn those who exercise these rights. The majority had adopted a so-called balancing test holding that the public interests outweighed the interest of the individual in this situation. Black denied that there could be any such balancing. Reviewing the activities of the Communist party, Black said,

> *[W]e cannot outlaw it, as a group, without endangering the liberty of all of us. The reason is not hard to find, for mixed among those aims of Communism which are illegal are perfectly normal political and social goals. And muddled with its revolutionary tenets is a drive to achieve power through the ballot, if it can be done. These things necessarily make it a political party whatever other, illegal, aims it may have.* [p. 149.]

Black stressed that he did not question the patriotism and sincerity of the House Un-American Activities Committee; but he did contend that it was punishing individuals by substituting hearings for trials, and that this was not a function of the legislative branch of the government. He concluded a lengthy opinion by saying:

> *Ultimately all the questions in this case really boil down to one—whether we as a people will try fearfully and futilely to preserve democracy by adopting*

> *totalitarian methods, or whether in accordance with our traditions and our Constitution we will have the confidence and courage to be free.* [p. 162]

A somewhat simpler free speech case was *Talley* v. *California,* 362 U.S. 60 (1960), in which Black wrote for the majority. The opinion invalidated the provision of the Los Angeles Municipal Code which prohibited the distribution of anonymous handbills. Black's opinion held that anonymity was itself a protected aspect of free speech. He said:

> *Persecuted groups and sects from time to time throughout history have been able to criticize oppressive practices and laws either anonymously or not at all . . . Before the Revolutionary War colonial patriots frequently had to conceal their authorship or distribution of literature that easily could have brought down on them prosecutions by English-controlled courts. Along about that time the Letters of Junius were written and the identity of their author is unknown to this day. Even the Federalist Papers, written in favor of the adoption of our Constitution, were published under fictitious names. It is plain that anonymity has sometimes been assumed for the most constructive purposes.* [p. 64–65.]

Another Black free speech opinion of note was *Bridges* v. *California,* 314 U.S. 252 (1941), an opinion sharply confining the power of courts to restrict newspaper publications.

Black contends that any control of publications on the grounds of obscenity is barred by the First Amendment. Since he believes that the Fourteenth Amendment makes the First Amendment applicable to the states and cities, it follows that no law on this subject passed by any government is valid, regardless of the nature of the material being distributed. For an expression of views on this subject, see Black's opinion in *Ginzburg* v. *United States,* 383 U.S. 463 (1966).

2. *Freedom of religion.*

The freedom of religion portion of the First Amendment commands that the government both protect the free exercise of religion and avoid the establishment of religion. After his early acceptance of the validity of requirements that school children salute the flag over the objection that, in some cases, this denied their religious rights, Black later reversed himself and held to the contrary. In a concurring opinion in *Board of Education* v. *Barnette,* 319 U.S. 624 (1943), Justices Black and Douglas together said:

> [*W*]*e cannot say that a failure, because of religious scruples, to assume a particular physical position and to repeat the words of a patriotic formula creates a grave danger to the nation. Such a statutory exaction is a form of test oath, and the test oath has always been abhorrent in the United States.*

They continued,

> *Neither our domestic tranquility in peace nor our martial effort in war depend on compelling little children to participate in a ceremony which ends in nothing for them but a fear of spiritual condemnation.* [p. 644.]

The establishment of religion cases present an acute difficulty. These cases usually involve the extent to which tax funds can be used to aid religious groups or the extent to which public property, usually schools, can be used for some religious purpose. Here Black makes a sharp distinction between legislation which is essentially for social welfare and legislation which is primarily for purposes of religious promotion. In *Everson* v. *Board of Education,* 330 U.S. 1(1947), his majority opinion held that taxpayer's money could be used for transportation of children to parochial as well as to public schools. This he found to be general social welfare legislation. At the same time the *Everson* opinion laid down the basic rules which guided all subsequent decisions:

> *The "establishment of religion" clause of the First Amendment means at least this: Neither a state nor the Federal Government can set up a church. Neither can pass laws which aid one religion, aid all religions, or prefer one religion over another. Neither can force nor influence a person to go to or to remain away from church against his will or force him to profess a belief or disbelief in any religion. No person can be punished for entertaining or professing religious beliefs or disbeliefs, for church attendance or non-attendance. No tax in any amount, large or small, can be levied to support any religious activities or institutions, whatever they may be called, or whatever form they may adopt to teach or practice religion. Neither a state nor the Federal Government can, openly or secretly, participate in the affairs of any religious organizations or groups and* vice versa. *In the words of Jefferson, the clause against establishment of religion by law was intended to erect "a wall of separation between church and State."*

In *Engel* v. *Vitale,* 370 U.S. 421 (1962), Black, writing for the Court, held unconstitutional the New York State system of beginning each school day with a classroom prayer. The opinion extensively considered the history of the establishment clause. The Court said:

> *It is neither sacrilegious nor antireligious to say that each separate government in this country should stay out of the business of writing or sanctioning official prayers and leave that purely religious function to the people themselves and to those the people choose to look to for religious guidance.* [p. 435.]

Yet another salient religious freedom opinion was *Marsh* v. *Alabama,* 326 U.S. 501 (1946), upholding the right to distribute religious literature even in privately held company towns.

3. *The procedures of criminal law.*

A paradox of Black's philosophy of civil liberties has been that his views of most of the provisions of the Bill of Rights have been expansive of the liberties involved, but this has not been his attitude toward the Fourth Amendment requirements that searches and seizures be conducted reasonably and only on warrant. His most extensive recent opinion on this score was a dissent in *Berger* v. *State of New York,* 388 U.S. 41 (1967), a case in which the majority held invalid a conviction based on electronic eavesdropping. The notion that the Fourth Amendment is somehow a projection of a right of privacy is rejected by Black in an opinion which is the most comprehensive statement of his views on this subject.

Black's opposition to forced confessions was fully established when he was a county attorney in Birmingham, and it has been re-established over and over again on the Supreme Court. Perhaps the most eloquent expression of opposition to this kind of police practice is his opinion in *Chambers* v. *Florida,* 309 U.S. 227 (1940).

Two of his greatest triumphs have come in areas of criminal procedure. In *Adamson* v. *California,* 332 U.S. 46 (1947), a majority of the Court held that the states were not, like the federal government, bound by the rule against self-incrimination. Black's dissent for four Justices was strong. The *Adamson* rule was reversed in *Malloy* v. *Hogan,* 378 U.S. 1 (1964).

Black has consistently upheld the right to counsel for all persons accused of crime. In his leading opinion of *Johnson* v. *Zerbst,* 304 U.S. 458 (1938), the Court held that the right to counsel existed in all federal prosecutions. The question remained as to whether it also existed in all state prosecutions. In *Betts* v. *Brady,* 316 U.S. 455 (1942) the Court held that counsel was not required in state courts and that the states could convict persons of certain crimes even if they were unable to afford counsel. The dissent by Justices Black, Douglas, and Murphy was exceptionally effective and the country's reaction was overwhelmingly on the side of the dissenters. Twenty-one years later in *Gideon* v. *Wainright,* 372 U.S. 335 (1963), Justice Black wrote for a unanimous Court overruling *Betts* v. *Brady* and adopting the original dissenting position.

4. *Race relations.*

The two most important constitutional developments in post-World War II America have been the development of the law of race relations and the requirement that legislative bodies be fairly distributed in accordance with population. In each, Black has been deeply involved. In the race relations field, the mammoth development of the 1950's and 60's has been the legal (if not necessarily the factual) end of segregation in the United States. Black has consistently joined in the opinions of the Court to this end. In *Griffin* v. *County School Bd.,* 377 U.S. 218 (1964), he wrote the opinion of the Court holding illegal the action of a county school board which had closed its public schools to resist integration and thereafter contributed to the support of private segregated schools. The opinion held illegal "the perpetuation of racial segregation by closing public schools and operating only segregated schools supported directly or indirectly by state or county funds." The opinion also broke important new ground by holding that the trial court may close all the schools of the state of Virginia if the public schools were not reopened in the affected county. The opinion said:

> *The time for mere "deliberate speed" has run out, and that phrase can no longer justify denying these Prince Edward County school children their constitutional rights to an education equal to that afforded by the public schools in the other parts of Virginia.*

As the civil rights movement has developed, cases have turned on its organizational activities. In *Gibson* v. *Florida Legis. Comm.,* 372 U.S. 539 (1963), the Court held that a Florida legislative committe was not authorized to require the Miami branch of the National Association for the Advancement of Colored People to reveal its membership list. The opinion was reached by the

Court majority on narrower ground than Black wished for himself. In his view, given in a concurring opinion,

> *[T]he constitutional right of association includes the privilege of any person to associate with Communists or anti-Communists, Socialists or anti-Socialists, or, for that matter, with people of all kinds of beliefs, popular or unpopular.*

Hence, he said,

> *I would reverse here on the ground that there has been a direct abridgment of the right of association of the National Association for the Advancement of Colored People and its members.*

Civil rights demonstrations fall into a different category. A demonstration is a kind of speech, in its own way. Whether anything is said or not, it certainly communicates a message. But Black has been strongly of the view that this right, while it is to be fully and completely protected at all places proper for its exercise, does not extend either to private or to public property which is not intended for such purposes. He long ago took the view that even speech was not protected when it was involved in action which was illegal, holding that picketing which might otherwise be simple communication was illegal when it was being used to violate the states' antitrust laws in *Giboney* v. *Empire Storage Co.,* 336 U.S. 490 (1949). As he said in a passage quoted earlier here, one may not legally holler in a theater. In this spirit he dissented in *Brown* v. *Louisiana,* 383 U.S. 131 (1966), the so-called library sit-in case in an opinion for four Justices beginning,

> *I do not believe that any provision of the United States Constitution forbids any one of the fifty States of the Union, including Louisiana, to make it unlawful to stage "sit-ins" or "stand-ups" in their public libraries for the purpose of advertising objections to the state's public policies.*

While Black did not persuade a majority to his point of view in *Brown,* he did so in *Adderley* v. *Florida,* 385 U.S. 39 (1966), in which he wrote a five to four opinion for the majority. The opinion upheld a conviction under a Florida statute for trespass by student demonstrators who entered jail grounds to protest arrests and city segregation policies, who blocked traffic, and who did not disperse when told to do so. "The state, no less than a private owner of property, has power to preserve the property under its control for the use to which it is lawfully dedicated," the opinion said.

5. *Equal representation in congress and state legislatures.*

The shifting population of the United States has caused the relative populations of some legislative and congressional districts to expand and others to shrink. As a consequence in the years following World War II it was common in the United States for there to be great disproportion in legislative representation. One congressional district might have three or four times as many people as an adjacent congressional district in the same state. Districts in the state legislatures became so disproportionate that it was not unusual to find a hundred times as many people in one district as in another. The practical effect was that the voters in the less populated districts had one hundred times the effective voting power of those in the more populous districts. Generally speaking, this malapportionment aided rural rather than urban interests.

In the period immediately after World War II, the Supreme Court set itself against doing anything about this situation in *Colegrove* v. *Green,* 328 U.S. 549 (1946). Such matters were "political questions" with which the Court could not deal. Black strongly dissented in *Colegrove* v. *Green,* and with the passage of time his views were adopted by the majority. See *Baker* v. *Carr,* 369 U.S. 186 (1962), an opinion which began the complete redistricting of the United States. These principles were applied and extended both to Congress and to each branch of the state legislature in *Wesberry* v. *Sanders,* 376 U.S. 1 (1964) and *Reynolds* v. *Sims,* 377 U.S. 533 (1964). Black wrote the opinion in *Wesberry* v. *Sanders,* and had the pleasure of noting that nothing was left of the earlier decision in *Colegrove* v. *Green.* "The right to vote is too important in our free society to be stripped of judicial protection by such an interpretation," Black said.

6. *Other matters.*

Black's work in the field of civil liberties has been so diverse and far-ranging that one could start this discussion over again with a wholly separate list. But four other matters deserve special mention. In *Adamson* v. *California, supra,* the Court held over Black's dissent that the right against self-incrimination was not applicable to the states. This specific conclusion was later reversed, as the earlier discussion shows. But one issue in *Adamson* was broader than the precise question. Black's reason for contending that this particular civil liberty applied to the states as well as the federal government was that he thought the Fourteenth Amendment made all of the liberties of the Bill of Rights applicable to the states. On this larger issue he has by now for all practical purposes carried the day. The Court has never adopted a universal view that the entire Bill of Rights is fully applicable to the states, but it has made applicable substantially all of the provisions of the Bill of Rights, one at a time. The only provision of any continuing consequence not made specifically applicable to the states is the provision requiring a civil jury in all cases over twenty dollars in value. For almost all meaningful purposes, Black's dissent has become the law.

In *Duncan* v. *Kahanamoku,* 327 U.S. 304 (1946), Black wrote the leading opinion of this century on the limitations of martial law within American territory. The opinion invalidated martial law as it existed in Hawaii during World War II. In *United States* v. *Lovett,* 328 U.S. 303 (1946), his opinion held unconstitutional the effort of Congress to discharge employees in the executive department. This is the leading case both on bills of attainder and on the rights of persons being permanently excluded from public employment. In *Reid* v. *Covert,* 354 U.S. 1 (1957), Black wrote the principal opinion dealing with court martial jurisdiction over civilians at foreign posts in cases of capital offenses in time of peace. The opinion held it unconstitutional to apply the provisions of the Uniform Code of Military Justice to a wife accompanying the armed forces outside the continental United States.

C. *Black's Work and Methods.*

The astounding output described in the preceding outline is the product of indefatigable and concentrated hard work. Black is not divertible. The social attractions of the Capital have never held any interests for him. He travels a little, but not widely until most recent years; his second trip to Europe was made in 1967. His principal diversion has been tennis, and this as a break between working sessions.

On Black's eightieth birthday, his law clerks from 1937–1965 published a little booklet of recollections of their associations for his amusement and theirs. A composite picture can be put together from those impressions of the men who have observed him most closely.

A consistent theme is work ("hours on end were spent in the Supreme Court office"), and tennis. As one said, "I have known many who have earned the designation of 'hard worker,' but none who match the Judge."

Early in his Supreme Court service, Black moved to the home in Alexandria, Virginia, which he occupied throughout his service and built a tennis court there. "The Judge never succeeded in defeating his first law clerk on the tennis court in any single set. Oh, to be sure, an occasional game was dropped to him, and at the end of every losing set, while the clerk gasped, the Judge always inquired, 'Why don't we play just one more set? I believe I could beat you.'" Another clerk ten years later, himself a regional champion, said, "The Judge is the only man I have ever known who made me feel a coward when I wanted to quit playing tennis after four or five sets." These qualities mixed together: "What I remember most is energy—vast quantities of it, like eight sets of tennis, calisthenics, and three or four hours of work on an opinion, all in one day."

This was not ordinary work, it was quick work. The most salient single feature of Justice Black is his extraordinary drive to the heart of the thing; as has been repeatedly noted, his questions from the bench lay bare the case. One clerk said with descriptive accuracy, "He still thinks twice as fast as the people I've gotten used to in Washington."

He wanted his work done quickly and concisely: "I learned, too, the importance of making one word do the work of two; of relentless question of premises, and thorough research; of speed. To 'get something to the printer today' was important." The Judge puts the highest possible premium on brevity, and thoroughly revised his and his clerk's work to shorten it. As one said, "The revised edition will be twice as good and half as long." The economy of his analysis struck boys used to the diffuseness of the law school.

In his personal relations he was completely kind; another clerk said, "The paradox of Hugo Black is steel and softness, the sharp cutting edge balanced with kindliness." Yet his tough quality was noticed by all about him, "He never yielded, he never faltered, he never gave an inch in those vital matters about which he felt and still feels so deeply, and yet he managed to carry it all off with an admirable lack of edge and, on the whole, an amiability of temper." This same quality was mentioned by another clerk: He "never lost his temper or betrayed any animosity to those who attacked him unmercifully."

His relations with the clerks were those of a co-worker; he liked the company of his clerks and they had become among his best friends. Sometimes he invited them to lunch in his office with him, and other times he went to the general public cafeteria to join them. One of his pleasures was taking a simple dinner with the boys, or with any other friend. First and foremost, he liked steaks, and sometimes he and the boys would buy them together, with the Judge carefully examining T-bones, pin-bones, and porterhouses. Sometimes they went instead to a Chinese restaurant.

A prime function of a clerk was to listen, to help the Judge develop his ideas with questions and thoughts of his own; the clerk was a backboard for the Judge's thoughts as he shaped his opinions. "The legal questions were talked, or rather bounced, about." The conversation with the clerk went two ways. The Judge was a good listener and if the clerk earnestly wanted to develop an argument in full, he had a complete and attentive audience. As one said, "Nor can one forget his remarkable willingness to listen to the views, the doubts, of others, particularly inexperienced, sometimes overly assertive law clerks." He did not reject or ignore differences of opinion.

The clerks and the Judge worked over and debated the drafts of opinions, line for line, hour after hour, either at the Judge's desk in the Supreme Court building, or in his study at home. Much of the work was done at home in the study, with long hours of drafting and debate over points of law in a library lined with the learning of Greece and Rome. These sessions often ran until midnight, with words added, but more usually dropped. Language was always clarified so that some mysterious "they" whom the Justice had in mind could understand. The clerks had no real effect on the work; as one of them said, "Although he sometimes let me practice writing an opinion before I read his first draft, the finished product always strongly resembled his first draft and seldom had any resemblance to my effort." No one, after the incredulity at his success in the first year, ever seriously suggested that the Judge's opinions were anyone's but his own.

Black's years during the McCarthy period were, from every standpoint, difficult. Josephine Black died. The views to which the Judge was deeply committed were regularly rejected. The clerks of those years noticed especially his stick-to-it-iveness and his absence of hard feeling. After weary conference hours he would come back down the marble corridor to the office "having lost the day's battle, but managing a whistle nevertheless." As another said, "he could have despaired, but I don't think he knows how." All judicial life changed radically with the appointment of Chief Justice Warren, with whom Black instantly had the closest of personal and of intellectual relations.

His clerks noticed his talent for hitting for the main issue in the case and for really understanding the facts of the matter; he had a strong sense of the value of putting facts so that they compelled his answer to the case.

The Justice constantly recommended to the boys that they broaden their reading, particularly in the Greek classics. It was a good-natured relationship; one of the clerks recalls that "I will never forget waking up from an after lunch nap on the sofa in the clerk's office just in time to see the Judge tiptoeing in to close the connecting door to his chambers. As I looked up startled and embarrassed, the Judge said, 'Go right ahead, George. The only reason I am closing the door is that the Chief and I can't hear each other over your snoring.' "

After twenty years on the Court, he was still working long hours during the day, at night, and on weekends. He spent any spare time not involved directly in Court work in further reading, trying to add to his knowledge and broaden his outlook. He wanted his clerks to bring him original materials, even if they might be hard to read. In one instance a clerk for another Justice and I were calmly assigned the duty of reading everything that had ever been written in 2,500 years on the law of admiralty to see how it might relate to a particular point. Another clerk recollects that he was sent to get a copy of an original fifteenth-century publication before the Justice would satisfy himself.

The young men can remember the Justice standing around in his own kitchen in a pair of tennis shorts, frying a steak for whomever was in the house. A full day's work was always followed by a briefcase taken home for more in the evening. His happy whistling down the marble corridors as he carried his own briefcase was noticed from generation to generation.

Anyone so firm in his final conclusions and so quick of mind might be expected to leap to his results. In new areas, this was not at all true. The clerks remember the Justice laboriously making up his mind, and can recall instances on which he changed it because he was persuaded that his original position was wrong. This was a quality that has stayed with him; his mind did not grow more rigid with the years so that the 1960 clerk was particularly struck with Black's freshness of view.

The plunge to the heart of the matter meant to the human heart of it. The Judge was rarely charmed with legal technicalities; he always thought there was more to law than how the game was played. The single individuals who were his concern in his practice were his concern on the Court.

He never was ostentatious. "It always seemed to me that the picture of the senior Associate Justice of the United States Supreme Court crawling in and out of my little Volkswagen itself told a tale not without meaning," wrote one clerk.

The number of cases in which the Justice has participated runs into the thousands, and he remembers them as best he can. The clerks are called upon to find "a case from Missouri that Wiley Rutledge wrote around 1948 and that had something about" some point or another. The lawyer may look up the case of *Reid* v. *Covert,* cited earlier; but for the Justice the instruction to the clerk will be to find out whether "there is something about that in my murdering wives case."

The thoroughness, the kindliness, and the tennis are the repeated beat of the clerk's impressions. The clerk who began in 1937 told a tennis anecdote, and so did the clerks in the middle. The same thing was true of the clerks who began in 1965, when the Justice was almost eighty years old. One reported a five-set game followed by the most systematic collection of even the oldest balls. Another reported a patience in tennis instruction which was very like the patience in the work on the opinions or in the general guidance to read the Magna Carta, the Bill of Rights, Baker's *Livy,* and Tucker's *Blackstone.*

The Court years have been largely work, the person merged with the job. There was but one extraordinary incident. In 1946, Chief Justice Stone died. At the time, Justice Robert Jackson was on leave from the Court in Nuremberg, conducting by designation of President Truman the post-war trials of the Nazis accused of war crimes. What induced Jackson to undertake so non-judicial a duty is unknown. It infuriated Stone, who referred to it as Jackson's "high-grade lynching party in Nuremberg," and who was deeply disturbed by the burden the absence put on the Court.

Nonetheless, Jackson was doing President Truman's wish and he had solid reason to hope that he had earned the Chief Justiceship. Certainly he was considered, but Truman finally chose his Secretary of the Treasury, Fred Vinson. Black had in fact done nothing whatsoever to oppose Jackson, and had never discussed the matter with the President. Black had certainly not been for Jackson, and the President's knowledge of this was one reason for the Vinson choice. Black's own first choice was Justice Douglas or, if Douglas were undesirable, Justice Reed, an ideal center man warmly regarded by all.

While Black in fact was uninvolved, Jackson a half a world away had no knowledge of this; he was, according to his devoted biographer Eugene Gerhart, in *Robert H. Jackson* (1958) in consultation with no one at the time. A few days after the Vinson appointment, Jackson, then ignoring the President's request to keep silence, unleashed a ferocious attack on Black for having sat in a case argued by a former partner. The attack breached the most sacred of Court rules, purporting to repeat the discussion on the case in the confidential conference of the Court.

Black had in fact heard a case argued by his former partner; so had at one time or another Justices Field, Harlan, Blatchford, Butler, Holmes, Brandeis, Cardozo, and Stone. This has been the invariable Supreme Court practice on cases not in the partnership office when the Justice was appointed. Black made no public comment on the Jackson statement, which aroused immense public interest and led to vigorous attacks on both Justices. In time, the matter blew over. In private conversation, Black, like many Jackson friends, attributed the episode to the immense strain of the Nuremberg assignment. He was never heard, by persons intimately associated with him, to express any personal bitterness toward Jackson.

For the more than twenty years following, Black's public sensations were purely as his work made them. His personal life continued with a small group of family, a few friends, and the ever lengthening list of clerks. The best friends of recent years have been Tom Corcoran and Ben Cohen, of old New Deal days; and Judge J. Skelly Wright of Louisiana, a member of the District of Columbia Court of Appeals. In many of the pleasant moments of life involving public recognition, Black is very careful to see that Wright and his wife are with him. He also takes immense pleasure in his two sons and daughter and their families.

In 1951, Josephine Black died. The years following held terrible loneliness, and came during the McCarthy era when the Justice's judicial effectiveness was at its lowest. During this period, close friends feared that his useful public service was done.

And then came in 1957 an extraordinarily successful marriage to Elizabeth Seay DeMeritte, an Alabaman and a then still youthful grandmother. She was at the time Black's secretary, a post she probably held by virtue of the maneuvering of Black's children, who had matrimony in mind for their lonely father.

The result was miraculous. Black revived personally and his next ten years were his most effective period on the bench. The mood of depression disappeared, and soon he could be heard driving down the streets of a strange city with his wife, singing his old favorite "I am a Dirty Rebel" at the top of a not very melodious voice.

In 1967 came the first serious physical disability; a cataract operation on one eye was successful and a second was briefly postponed while he attended an international conference in Geneva. The second operation, in late summer 1967, went as well, and Black shows every prospect of setting an all-time Court service record.

His record is an extraordinary paradox; the kindly colossus and the toughest and most rigorously determined Justice on the bench.

SELECTED BIBLIOGRAPHY

The standard biography of Justice Black is John P. Frank, *Mr. Justice Black* (New York, 1949). Another biography is Charlotte Williams, *Hugo L. Black* (Baltimore, 1950). An important essay on Justice Black which gives his own thoughts on free speech is included in Edmond Cahn, ed., *The Great Rights* (New York, 1963). For a collection of opinions, see Irving Dilliard, ed., *One Man's Stand for Freedom* (New York, 1963). A concise biographical sketch with excellent pictures is contained in John P. Frank and Yousuf Karsh, *The Warren Court* (New York, 1964). For a short, comparative essay of Justices Black and Frankfurter, see Wallace Mendelson, *Justices Black and Frankfurter: Conflict in the Court* (Chicago, 1961). The most recent analysis of the work of Justice Black in many fields, is Stephen Strickland, ed., *Hugo Black* (Indianapolis, 1967).

There have been more than two dozen substantial articles on Justice Black; a few of them of general interest are: D. M. Berman, "Freedom and Mr. Justice Black: The Record after Twenty Years," 25 *University of Missouri Law Review* 155 (1960); Edmond Cahn, "Justice Black and First Amendment 'Absolutes'," 37 *New York University Law Review* 549 (1962); Irving Dilliard, "Hugo Black and the Importance of Freedom," 10 *American University Law Review* 1

(1961); H. Kalven, Jr., "Upon Rereading Mr. Justice Black on the First Amendment," 14 *University of California Law Review* 397 (1967); D. J. Meader, "Justice Black and His Law Clerks," 15 *Alabama Law Review,* 57 (1962); Charles Reich, "Mr. Justice Black," 76 *Harvard Law Review* 673 (1963). For a general symposium on Black, see 14 *U.C.L.A. Law Review* (1967).

Hugo L. Black

REPRESENTATIVE OPINIONS

YOUNGSTOWN SHEET & TUBE CO. v. SAWYER, 343 U.S. 579 (1952)

This is one of the classic confrontations in American history between the President and the Supreme Court. During the Korean War, a labor dispute in the steel industry was referred to the Federal Wage Stabilization Board. The efforts of the board were unsuccessful, and a nationwide strike was threatened. Thereupon the President directed the Secretary of Commerce to take over and operate the country's steel mills.

No statute authorized this taking. The action reflected the President's belief that it was necessary to keep the steel mills functioning to avoid a national catastrophe because of the demands for steel caused by the war. The case received emergency treatment by the courts, a federal district court in the District of Columbia on April 30, 1952, issuing an injunction against the Secretary of Commerce from continuing this seizure of the plants. The matter was instantly taken to the Court of Appeals, and the Supreme Court thereupon exercised its own special authority to move a case up from the Court of Appeals instantly, hearing argument itself on May 12, 1952. The case was decided on June 2.

The opinion of the Court holding the seizure illegal was delivered by Justice Black. Justices Frankfurter, Douglas, Jackson and Burton joined the Black opinion but also wrote separately. Justice Clark concurred in the result. Chief Justice Vinson, joined by Justices Reed and Minton, dissented.

MR. JUSTICE BLACK delivered the opinion of the Court.

We are asked to decide whether the President was acting within his constitutional power when he issued an order directing the Secretary of Commerce to take possession of and operate most of the Nation's steel mills. The mill owners argue that the President's order amounts to lawmaking, a legislative function which the Constituion has expressly confided to the Congress and not to the President. The Government's position is that the order was made on findings of the President that his action was necessary to avert a national catastrophe which would inevitably result from a stoppage of steel production, and that in meeting this grave emergency the President was acting within the aggregate of his constitutional powers as the Nation's Chief Executive and the Commander in Chief of the Armed Forces of the United States. The issue emerges here from the following series of events:

In the latter part of 1951, a dispute arose between the steel companies and their employees over terms and conditions that should be included in new collective bargaining agreements. Long-continued conferences failed to resolve the dispute. On December 18, 1951, the employees' representative, United Steelworkers of America, C.I.O., gave notice of an intention to strike when the existing bargaining agreements expired on December 31. The Federal Mediation and Conciliation Service then intervened in an effort to get labor and management to agree. This failing, the President on December 22, 1951, referred the dispute to the Federal Wage Stabilization Board[1] to investigate and make recommendations for fair and equitable terms of settlement. This Board's report resulted in no settlement. On April 4, 1952, the Union gave notice of a nation-wide strike called to begin at 12:01 A.M. April 9. The indispensability of steel as a component of substantially all weapons and other war materials led the President to believe that the proposed work stoppage would immediately jeopardize our national defense and that governmental seizure of the steel mills was necessary in order to assure the continued availability of steel. Reciting these considerations for his action, the President, a few hours before the strike was to begin, issued Executive Order 10340, a copy of which is attached as an appendix, post p. 1168. The order directed the Secretary of Commerce to take possession of most of the steel mills and keep them running. The Secretary immediately issued his own possessory orders, calling upon the presidents of the various seized companies to serve as operating managers for the United States. They were directed to carry on their activities in accordance with regulations and directions of the Secretary. The next morning the President sent a message to Congress reporting his action. Cong. Rec., April 9, 1952, p. 3962. Twelve days later he sent a second message. Cong. Rec., April 21, 1952, p. 4192. Congress has taken no action.

Obeying the Secretary's orders under protest, the companies brought proceedings against him in the District Court. Their complaints charged that the seizure was not authorized by an act of Congress or by any constitutional provisions. The District Court was asked to declare the orders of the President and the Secretary invalid and to issue preliminary and permanent injunctions restraining their enforcement. Opposing the motion for preliminary injunction, the United States asserted that a strike disrupting steel production for even a brief period would so endanger the well-being and safety of the Nation that the President had "inherent power" to do what he had done—power "supported by the Constitution, by historical precedent, and by court decisions." The Government also contended that in any event no preliminary injunction should be issued because the companies had made no showing that their available legal remedies were inadequate or that their injuries from seizure would be irreparable. Holding against the Government on all points, the District Court on April 30 issued a preliminary injunction restraining the Secretary from "continuing the seizure and possession of the plants . . . and from acting under the purported authority of Executive Order No. 10340." 103 F Supp 569. On the same day the Court of Appeals stayed the District Court's injunction. 90 App DC —, — F2d —. Deeming it best that the issues raised be promptly decided by this Court, we granted certiorari on May 3 and set the cause for argument on May 12. 343 U.S. 937, 96 L. ed. 1344, 72 S. Ct. 775.

Two crucial issues have developed: *First.* Should final determination of the constitutional validity of the President's order be made in this case which has proceeded no further than the preliminary injunction stage? *Second.* If so, is the seizure order within the constitutional power of the President?

I.

It is urged that there were nonconstitutional grounds upon which the District Court could have denied the preliminary injunction and thus have followed the custom-

[1] *This Board was established under Executive Order 10233, 16 Fed. Reg. 3503.*

ary judicial practice of declining to reach and decide constitutional questions until compelled to do so. On this basis it is argued that equity's extraordinary injunctive relief should have been denied because (a) seizure of the companies' properties did not inflict irreparable damages, and (b) there were available legal remedies adequate to afford compensation for any possible damages which they might suffer. While separately argued by the Government, these two contentions are here closely related, if not identical. Arguments as to both rest in large part on the Government's claim that should the seizure ultimately be held unlawful, the companies could recover full compensation in the Court of Claims for the unlawful taking. Prior cases in this Court have cast doubt on the right to recover in the Court of Claims on account of properties unlawfully taken by government officials for public use as these properties were alleged to have been. See e.g., *Hooe* v. *United States,* 218 U.S. 322, 335, 336, 54 L. ed. 1055, 1060, 31 S. Ct. 85; *United States* v. *North American Transp. & Trading Co.* 253 U.S. 330, 333, 64 L. ed. 935, 937, 40 S. Ct. 518. But see *Larson* v. *Domestic & Foreign Commerce Corp.* 337 U.S. 682, 701, 702, 93 L. ed. 1628, 1642, 69 S. Ct. 1457. Moreover, seizure and governmental operation of these going businesses were bound to result in many present and future damages of such nature as to be difficult, if not incapable, of measurement. Viewing the case this way, and in the light of the facts presented, the District Court saw no reason for delaying decision of the constitutional validity of the orders. We agree with the District Court and can see no reason why that question was not ripe for determination on the record presented. We shall therefore consider and determine that question now.

II.

The President's power, if any, to issue the order must stem either from an act of Congress or from the Constitution itself. There is no statute that expressly authorizes the President to take possession of property as he did here. Nor is there any act of Congress to which our attention has been directed from which such a power can fairly be implied. Indeed, we do not understand the Government to rely on statutory authorization for this seizure. There are two statutes which do authorize the President to take both personal and real property under certain conditions.[2] However, the Government admits that these conditions were not met and that the President's order was not rooted in either of the statutes. The Government refers to the seizure provisions of one of these statutes (§ 201 (b) of the Defense Production Act) as "much too cumbersome, involved, and time-consuming for the crisis which was at hand."

Moreover, the use of the seizure technique to solve labor disputes in order to prevent work stoppages was not only unauthorized by any congressional enactment; prior to this controversy, Congress had refused to adopt that method of settling labor disputes. When the Taft-Hartley Act was under consideration in 1947, Congress rejected an amendment which would have authorized such governmental seizures in cases of emergency.[3] Apparently it was thought that the technique of seizure, like that of compulsory arbitration, would interfere with the process of collective bargaining.[4] Consequently, the plan Congress adopted in that Act did not provide for seizure under any circumstances. Instead, the plan sought to bring about settlements by use of the customary devices of mediation, conciliation, investigation by boards of inquiry, and public reports. In some instances temporary injunctions were authorized to provide cooling-off periods. All this failing, unions were left free to strike after a secret vote by employees as to whether they wished to accept their employers' final settlement offer.[5]

It is clear that if the President had authority to issue the order he did, it must be found in some provision of the Constitution. And it is not claimed that express constitutional language grants this power to the President. The contention is that presidential power should be implied from the aggregate of his powers under the Constitution. Particular reliance is placed on provisions in

[2] *The Selective Service Act of 1948, 62 Stat 604, 625–627, 50 USC Appx. (Supp. IV) § 468; the Defense Production Act of 1950, Title II, 64 Stat. 798, as amended, 65 Stat 132.*

[3] *93 Cong. Rec. 3637–3645.*

[4] *93 Cong. Rec. 3835–3836.*

[5] *Labor Management Relations Act, 1947, 61 Stat 136, 152–156, 29 USC (Supp. IV) § § 141, 171–180.*

Article II which say that "The executive Power shall be vested in a President . . ."; that "he shall take Care that the Laws be faithfully executed"; and that he "shall be Commander in Chief of the Army and Navy of the United States."

The order cannot properly be sustained as an exercise of the President's military power as Commander in Chief of the Armed Forces. The Government attempts to do so by citing a number of cases upholding broad powers in military commanders engaged in day-to-day fighting in a theater of war. Such cases need not concern us here. Even though "theater of war" be an expanding concept, we cannot with faithfulness to our constitutional system hold that the Commander in Chief of the Armed Forces has the ultimate power as such to take possession of private property in order to keep labor disputes from stopping production. This is a job for the Nation's lawmakers, not for its military authorities.

Nor can the seizure order be sustained because of the several constitutional provisions that grant executive power to the President. In the framework of our Constitution, the President's power to see that the laws are faithfully executed refutes the idea that he is to be a lawmaker. The Constitution limits his functions in the lawmaking process to the recommending of laws he thinks wise and the vetoing of laws he thinks bad. And the Constitution is neither silent nor equivocal about who shall make laws which the President is to execute. The first section of the first article says that "All legislative Powers herein granted shall be vested in a Congress of the United States. . . ." After granting many powers to the Congress, Article I goes on to provide that Congress may "make all Laws which shall be necessary and proper for carrying into Execution the foregoing Powers, and all other Powers vested by this Constitution in the Government of the United States, or in any Department or Officer thereof."

The President's order does not direct that a congressional policy be executed in a manner prescribed by Congress—it directs that a presidential policy be executed in a manner prescribed by the President. The preamble of the order itself, like that of many statutes, sets out reasons why the President believes certain policies should be adopted, proclaims these policies as rules of conduct to be followed, and again, like a statute, authorizes a government official to promulgate additional rules and regulations consistent with the policy proclaimed and needed to carry that policy into execution. The power of Congress to adopt such public policies as those proclaimed by the order is beyond question. It can authorize the taking of private property for public use. It can make laws regulating the relationships between employers and employees, prescribing rules designed to settle labor disputes, and fixing wages and working conditions in certain fields of our economy. The Constitution does not subject this lawmaking power of Congress to presidential or military supervision or control.

It is said that other Presidents without congressional authority have taken possession of private business enterprises in order to settle labor disputes. But even if this be true, Congress has not thereby lost its exclusive constitutional authority to make laws necessary and proper to carry out the powers vested by the Constitution "in the Government of the United States, or any Department or Officer thereof."

The Founders of this Nation entrusted the lawmaking power to the Congress alone in both good and bad times. It would do no good to recall the historical events, the fears of power and the hopes for freedom that lay behind their choice. Such a review would but confirm our holding that this seizure order cannot stand.

The judgment of the District Court is

Affirmed.

GIDEON v. WAINRIGHT, 372 U.S. 335 (1963)

This case involved one of the longest battles in Justice Black's life. In 1942, with Black dissenting along with Justices Douglas and Murphy, the Supreme Court decided *Betts* v. *Brady,* 316 U.S. 455 (1942), a decision holding that an impoverished and ignorant Maryland farmhand was not entitled to appointed counsel when charged in a state criminal proceeding.

The *Betts* rule was subject to considerable erosion with the passage of time, and numerous qualifications were added to it. For twenty years, Justice Black held the view that it had been wrongly decided.

In *Gideon* v. *Wainright,* the question came back to the Supreme Court. The facts are sufficiently set out in the opinion. The Court, since *Gideon* was proceeding in the Supreme Court as a person unable to afford counsel, appointed Abe Fortas, then a practicing lawyer in Washington, D.C. and later a Justice of the Supreme Court, to represent the petitioner. In this opinion, the Court unanimously overruled *Betts* v. *Brady*. Justices Douglas, Clark, and Harlan each filed separate concurring opinions.

MR. JUSTICE BLACK delivered the opinion of the Court.

Petitioner was charged in a Florida state court with having broken and entered a poolroom with intent to commit a misdemeanor. This offense is a felony under Florida law. Appearing in court without funds and without a lawyer, petitioner asked the court to appoint counsel for him, whereupon the following colloquy took place:

> "The COURT: Mr. Gideon, I am sorry, but I cannot appoint Counsel to represent you in this case. Under the laws of the State of Florida, the only time the Court can appoint Counsel to represent a Defendant is when that person is charged with a capital offense. I am sorry, but I will have to deny your request to appoint Counsel to defend you in this case.
>
> "The DEFENDANT: The United States Supreme Court says I am entitled to be represented by Counsel."

Put to trial before a jury, Gideon conducted his defense about as well as could be expected from a layman. He made an opening statement to the jury, cross-examined the State's witnesses, presented witnesses in his own defense, declined to testify himself, and made a short argument "emphasizing his innocence to the charge contained in the Information filed in this case." The jury returned a verdict of guilty, and petitioner was sentenced to serve five years in the state prison. Later, petitioner filed in the Florida Supreme Court this habeas corpus petition attacking his conviction and sentence on the ground that the trial court's refusal to appoint counsel for him denied him rights "guaranteed by the Constitution and the Bill of Rights by the United States Government."[1] Treating the petition for habeas corpus as properly before it, the State Supreme Court, "upon consideration thereof" but without an opinion, denied all relief. Since 1942, when *Betts* v. *Brady,* 316 U.S. 455, was decided by a divided Court, the problem of a defendant's federal constitutional right to counsel in a state court has been a continuing source of controversy and litigation in both state and federal courts.[2] To give this problem another review here, we granted certiorari. 370 U.S. 908. Since Gideon was proceeding *in forma pauperis,* we appointed counsel to represent him and requested both sides to discuss in their briefs and oral arguments the following: "Should

[1] *Later in the petition for habeas corpus, signed and apparently prepared by petitioner himself, he stated, "I, Clarence Earl Gideon, claim that I was denied the rights of the 4th, 5th and 14th amendments of the Bill of Rights."*

[2] *Of the many such cases to reach this Court, recent examples are* Carnley *v.* Cochran, *369 U.S. 506 (1962)*; Hudson *v.* North Carolina, *363 U.S. 697 (1960)*; Moore *v.* Michigan, *355 U.S. 155 (1957). Illustrative cases in the state courts are* Artrip *v.* State, *136 So. 2d 574 (Ct. App. Ala. 1962)*; Shaffer *v.* Warden, *211 Md. 635, 126 A. 2d 573 (1956). For examples of commentary, see Allen, The Supreme Court, Federalism, and State Systems of Criminal Justice, 8 De Paul L. Rev. 213 (1959)*; *Kamisar, The Right to Counsel and the Fourteenth Amendment: A Dialogue on "The Most Pervasive Right" of an Accused, 30 U. of Chi. L. Rev. 1 (1962)*; *The Right to Counsel, 45 Minn. L. Rev. 693 (1961).*

this Court's holding in *Betts* v. *Brady,* 316 U.S. 455, be reconsidered?"

I.

The facts upon which Betts claimed that he had been unconstitutionally denied the right to have counsel appointed to assist him are strikingly like the facts upon which Gideon here bases his federal constitutional claim. Betts was indicted for robbery in a Maryland state court. On arraignment, he told the trial judge of his lack of funds to hire a lawyer and asked the court to appoint one for him. Betts was advised that it was not the practice in that county to appoint counsel for indigent defendants except in murder and rape cases. He then pleaded not guilty, had witnesses summoned, cross-examined the State's witnesses, examined his own, and chose not to testify himself. He was found guilty by the judge, sitting without a jury, and sentenced to eight years in prison. Like Gideon, Betts sought release by habeas corpus, alleging that he had been denied the right to assistance of counsel in violation of the Fourteenth Amendment. Betts was denied any relief, and on review this Court affirmed. It was held that a refusal to appoint counsel for an indigent defendant charged with a felony did not necessarily violate the Due Process Clause of the Fourteenth Amendment, which for reasons given the Court deemed to be the only applicable federal constitutional provision. The Court said:

> "Asserted denial [of due process] is to be tested by an appraisal of the totality of facts in a given case. That which may, in one setting, constitute a denial of fundamental fairness, shocking to the universal sense of justice, may, in other circumstances, and in the light of other considerations, fall short of such denial." 316 U.S., at 462.

Treating due process as "a concept less rigid and more fluid than those envisaged in other specific and particular provisions of the Bill of Rights," the Court held that refusal to appoint counsel under the particular facts and circumstances in the *Betts* case was not so "offensive to the common and fundamental ideas of fairness" as to amount to a denial of due process. Since the facts and circumstances of the two cases are so nearly indistinguishable, we think the *Betts* v. *Brady* holding if left standing would require us to reject Gideon's claim that the Constitution guarantees him the assistance of counsel. Upon full reconsideration we conclude that *Betts* v. *Brady* should be overruled.

II.

The Sixth Amendment provides, "In all criminal prosecutions, the accused shall enjoy the right . . . to have the Assistance of Counsel for his defence." We have construed this to mean that in federal courts counsel must be provided for defendants unable to employ counsel unless the right is competently and intelligently waived.[3] Betts argued that this right is extended to indigent defendants in state courts by the Fourteenth Amendment. In response the Court stated that, while the Sixth Amendment laid down "no rule for the conduct of the States, the question recurs whether the constraint laid by the Amendment upon the national courts expresses a rule so fundamental and essential to a fair trial, and so, to due process of law, that it is made obligatory upon the States by the Fourteenth Amendment." 316 U.S., at 465. In order to decide whether the Sixth Amendment's guarantee of counsel is of this fundamental nature, the Court in *Betts* set out and considered "[r]elevant data on the subject . . . afforded by constitutional and statutory provisions subsisting in the colonies and the States prior to the inclusion of the Bill of Rights in the national Constitution, and in the constitutional, legislative, and judicial history of the States to the present date." 316 U.S., at 465. On the basis of this historical data the Court concluded that "appointment of counsel is not a fundamental right, essential to a fair trial." 316 U.S., at 471. It was for this reason the *Betts* Court refused to accept the contention that the Sixth Amendment's guarantee of counsel for indigent federal defendants was extended to or, in the words of that Court, "made obligatory upon the States by the Fourteenth Amendment." Plainly, had the Court concluded that appointment of counsel for an indigent criminal defendant was "a fundamental right, essential to a fair trial," it would have held that the Fourteenth Amendment requires appointment of counsel in a state court, just as the Sixth Amendment requires in a federal court.

We think the Court in *Betts* had ample precedent for acknowledging that those guarantees of the Bill of Rights which are fundamental safeguards of liberty immune from federal abridgment are equally pro-

[3] Johnson *v.* Zerbst, *304 U.S. 458 (1938)*.

tected against state invasion by the Due Process Clause of the Fourteenth Amendment. This same principle was recognized, explained, and applied in *Powell* v. *Alabama,* 287 U.S. 45 (1932), a case upholding the right of counsel, where the Court held that despite sweeping language to the contrary in *Hurtado* v. *California,* 110 U.S. 516 (1884), the Fourteenth Amendment "embraced" those " 'fundamental principles of liberty and justice which lie at the base of all our civil and political institutions,' " even though they had been "specifically dealt with in another part of the federal Constitution." 287 U.S., at 67. In many cases other than *Powell* and *Betts,* this Court has looked to the fundamental nature of original Bill of Rights guarantees to decide whether the Fourteenth Amendment makes them obligatory on the States. Explicitly recognized to be of this "fundamental nature" and therefore made immune from state invasion by the Fourteenth, or some part of it, are the First Amendment's freedoms of speech, press, religion, assembly, association, and petition for redress of grievances.[4] For the same reason, though not always in precisely the same terminology, the Court has made obligatory on the States the Fifth Amendment's command that private property shall not be taken for public use without just compensation,[5] the Fourth Amendment's prohibition of unreasonable searches and seizures,[6] and the Eighth's ban on cruel and unusual punishment.[7] On the other hand, this Court in *Palko* v. *Connecticut,* 302 U.S. 319 (1937), refused to hold that the Fourteenth Amendment made the double jeopardy provision of the Fifth Amendment obligatory on the States. In so refusing, however, the Court, speaking through Mr. Justice Cardozo, was careful to emphasize that "immunities that are valid as against the federal government by force of the specific pledges of particular amendments have been found to be implicit in the concept of ordered liberty, and thus, through the Fourteenth Amendment, become valid as against the states" and that guarantees "in their origin . . . effective against the federal government alone" had by prior cases "been taken over from the earlier articles of the federal bill of rights and brought within the Fourteenth Amendment by a process of absorption." 302 U.S., at 324–325, 326.

We accept *Betts* v. *Brady*'s assumption, based as it was on our prior cases, that a provision of the Bill of Rights which is "fundamental and essential to a fair trial" is made obligatory upon the States by the Fourteenth Amendment. We think the Court in *Betts* was wrong, however, in concluding that the Sixth Amendment's guarantee of counsel is not one of these fundamental rights. Ten years before *Betts* v. *Brady,* this Court, after full consideration of all the historical data examined in *Betts,* had unequivocally declared that "the right to the aid of counsel is of this fundamental character." *Powell* v. *Alabama,* 287 U.S. 45, 68 (1932). While the Court at the close of its *Powell* opinion did by its language, as this Court frequently does, limit its holding to the particular facts and circumstances of that case, its conclusions about the fundamental nature of the right to counsel are unmistakable. Several years later, in 1936, the Court reemphasized what it had said about the fundamental nature of the right to counsel in this language:

> "We concluded that certain fundamental rights, safeguarded by the first eight amendments against federal action, were also safeguarded against state action by the due process of law clause of the Fourteenth Amendment, and among them the fundamental right of the accused to the aid of counsel in a criminal prosecution." *Grosjean* v. *American Press Co.,* 297 U.S. 233, 243–244 (1936).

[4] E.g., Gitlow *v.* New York, *268 U.S. 652, 666 (1925) (speech and press)*; Lovell *v.* City of Griffin, *303 U.S. 444, 450 (1938) (speech and press)*; Staub *v.* City of Baxley, *355 U.S. 313, 321 (1958) (speech)*; Grosjean *v.* American Press Co., *297 U.S. 233, 244 (1936) (press)*; Cantwell *v.* Connecticut, *310 U.S. 296, 303 (1940) (religion)*; De Jonge *v.* Oregon, *299 U.S. 353, 364 (1937) (assembly)*; Shelton *v.* Tucker, *364 U.S. 479, 486, 488 (1960) (association)*; Louisiana ex rel. Gremillion *v.* NAACP, *336 U.S. 293, 296 (1961) (association)*; Edwards *v.* South Carolina, *372 U.S. 229 (1963) (speech, assembly, petition for redress of grievances)*.

[5] E.g., Chicago, B & Q. R. Co. *v.* Chicago, *166 U.S. 226, 235–241 (1897)*; Smith *v.* Ames, *169 U.S. 466, 522–526 (1898)*.

[6] E.g., Wolf *v.* Colorado, *338 U.S. 25, 27–28 (1949)*; Elkins *v.* United States, *364 U.S. 206, 213 (1960)*; Mapp *v.* Ohio, *367 U.S. 643, 655, (1961)*.

[7] Robinson *v.* California, *370 U.S. 660, 666 (1962)*.

And again in 1938 this Court said:

"[The assistance of counsel] is one of the safeguards of the Sixth Amendment deemed necessary to insure fundamental human rights of life and liberty. . . . The Sixth Amendment stands as a constant admonition that if the constitutional safeguards it provides be lost, justice will not 'still be done.'" *Johnson* v. *Zerbst,* 304 U.S. 458, 462 (1938). To the same effect, see *Avery* v. *Alabama,* 308 U.S. 444 (1940), and *Smith* v. *O'Grady,* 312 U.S. 329 (1941).

In light of these and many other prior decisions of this Court, it is not surprising that the *Betts* Court, when faced with the contention that "one charged with crime, who is unable to obtain counsel, must be furnished counsel by the State," conceded that "[e]xpressions in the opinions of this court lend color to the argument. . . ." 316 U.S., at 462–463. The fact is that in deciding as it did—that "appointment of counsel is not a fundamental right, essential to a fair trial"—the Court in *Betts* v. *Brady* made an abrupt break with its own well-considered precedents. In returning to these old precedents, sounder we believe than the new, we but restore constitutional principles established to achieve a fair system of justice. Not only these precedents but also reason and reflection require us to recognize that in our adversary system of criminal justice, any person haled into court, who is too poor to hire a lawyer, cannot be assured a fair trial unless counsel is provided for him. This seems to us to be an obvious truth. Governments, both state and federal, quite properly spend vast sums of money to establish machinery to try defendants accused of crime. Lawyers to prosecute are everywhere deemed essential to protect the public's interest in an orderly society. Similarly, there are few defendants charged with crime, few indeed, who fail to hire the best lawyers they can get to prepare and present their defenses. That government hires lawyers to prosecute and defendants who have the money hire lawyers to defend are the strongest indications of the widespread belief that lawyers in criminal courts are necessities, not luxuries. The right of one charged with crime to counsel may not be deemed fundamental and essential to fair trials in some countries, but it is in ours. From the very beginning, our state and national constitutions and laws have laid great emphasis on procedural and substantive safeguards designed to assure fair trials before impartial tribunals in which every defendant stands equal before the law. This noble ideal cannot be realized if the poor man charged with crime has to face his accusers without a lawyer to assist him. A defendant's need for a lawyer is nowhere better stated than in the moving words of Mr. Justice Sutherland in *Powell* v. *Alabama:*

"The right to be heard would be, in many cases, of little avail if it did not comprehend the right to be heard by counsel. Even the intelligent and educated layman has small and sometimes no skill in the science of law. If charged with crime, he is incapable, generally, of determining for himself whether the indictment is good or bad. He is unfamiliar with the rules of evidence. Left without the aid of counsel he may be put on trial without a proper charge, and convicted upon incompetent evidence, or evidence irrelevant to the issue or otherwise inadmissible. He lacks both the skill and knowledge adequately to prepare his defense, even though he have a perfect one. He requires the guiding hand of counsel at every step in the proceedings against him. Without it, though he be not guilty, he faces the danger of conviction because he does not know how to establish his innocence." 287 U.S., at 68–69.

The Court in *Betts* v. *Brady* departed from the sound wisdom upon which the Court's holding in *Powell* v. *Alabama* rested. Florida, supported by two other States, has asked that *Betts* v. *Brady* be left intact. Twenty-two States, as friends of the Court, argue that *Betts* was "an anachronism when handed down" and that it should now be overruled. We agree.

The judgment is reversed and the cause is remanded to the Supreme Court of Florida for further action not inconsistent with this opinion.

Reversed.

BARENBLATT v. UNITED STATES, 360 U.S. 109 (1959)

Justice Harlan began the majority opinion in this case, from which the Black opinion is a dissent, with the observation that "once more the Court is required to resolve the conflicting constitutional claims of congressional power and of an individual's right to resist its exercise." This describes the problem. Barenblatt had been an instructor in psychology at Vassar College for several years preceding his appearance before a subcommittee of the House of Representatives Committee on Un-American Activities. He declined to answer a number of questions, the general thrust of which was to inquire whether he was a member of the Communist Party or had had associations in the past with various organizations or people. His refusal was on grounds of asserted want of jurisdiction in the committee and on a number of constitutional grounds, the first of which was his right of free speech under the First Amendment. He expressly disclaimed reliance on the privilege against self-incrimination of the Fifth Amendment.

The witness was held in contempt and was given a sentence of six months' imprisonment and a fine of $250. This conviction was affirmed by the Supreme Court. Justice Black, in an opinion joined by Chief Justice Warren and Justice Douglas, dissented, and Justice Brennan dissented separately.

MR. JUSTICE BLACK, with whom THE CHIEF JUSTICE and MR. JUSTICE DOUGLAS concur, dissenting.

On May 28, 1954, petitioner Lloyd Barenblatt, then 31 years old, and a teacher of psychology at Vassar College, was summoned to appear before a Subcommittee of the House Committee on Un-American Activities. After service of the summons, but before Barenblatt appeared on June 28, his four-year contract with Vassar expired and was not renewed. He, therefore, came to the Committee as a private citizen without a job. Earlier that day, the Committee's interest in Barenblatt had been aroused by the testimony of an ex-Communist named Crowley. When Crowley had first appeared before the Un-American Activities Committee he had steadfastly refused to admit or deny Communist affiliations or to identify others as Communists. After the House reported this refusal to the United States Attorney for prosecution, Crowley "voluntarily" returned and asked to testify. He was sworn in and interrogated, but not before he was made aware by various Committee members of Committee policy to "make an appropriate recommendation" to protect any witness who "fully cooperates with the committee." He then talked at length, identifying by name, address and occupation, whenever possible, people he claimed had been Communists. One of these was Barenblatt, who, according to Crowley, had been a Communist during 1947–1950 while a graduate student and teaching fellow at the University of Michigan. Though Crowley testified in great detail about the small group of Communists who had been at Michigan at that time and though the Committee was very satisfied with his testimony, it sought repetition of much of the information from Barenblatt. Barenblatt, however, refused to answer their questions and filed a long statement outlining his constitutional objections. He asserted that the Committee was violating the Constitution by abridging freedom of speech, thought, press, and association, and by conducting legislative trials of known or suspected Communists which trespassed on the exclusive power of the judiciary. He argued that however he answered questions relating to membership in the Communist Party his position in society and his ability to earn a living would be seriously jeopardized; that he would, in effect, be subjected to a bill of attainder despite the twice-expressed constitutional mandate against such legislative punishments.[1] This would occur, he pointed out, even if he did no more than invoke the protection of clearly applicable provisions of the Bill of Rights as a reason for refusing to answer.

He repeated these, and other objections, in the District Court as a reason for dismissing an indictment for contempt of Congress. His position, however, was rejected at the trial and in the Court of Appeals for the District of Columbia Circuit over the strong dissents of Chief Judge Edgerton and Judges Bazelon, Fahy and Washington. The Court today affirms, and thereby sanctions the use of the contempt power to enforce questioning by congressional committees in the realm of speech and association. I cannot agree with this disposition of the case for I believe that the resolution establishing the House Un-American Activities Committee and the questions that Committee asked Barenblatt violate the Constitution in several respects. (1) Rule XI creating the Committee authorizes such a sweeping, unlimited, all-inclusive and undiscriminating compulsory examination of witnesses in the field of speech, press, petition and assembly that it violates the procedural requirements of the Due Process Clause of the Fifth Amendment. (2) Compelling an answer to the questions asked Barenblatt abridges freedom of speech and association in contravention of the First Amendment. (3) The Committee proceedings were part of a legislative program to stigmatize and punish by public identification and exposure all witnesses considered by the Committee to be guilty of Communist affiliations, as well as all witnesses who refused to answer Committee questions on constitutional grounds; the Committee was thus improperly seeking to try, convict, and punish suspects, a task which the Constitution expressly denies to Congress and grants exclusively to the courts, to be exercised by them only after indictment and in full compliance with all the safeguards provided by the Bill of Rights.

[1] *Bills of attainder are among the few measures explicitly forbidden to both State and Federal Governments by the body of the Constitution itself. U.S. Const., Art. I, § 9, cl. 3, states "No Bill of Attainder or ex post facto Law shall be passed." U.S. Const., Art. I, § 10, cl. 1, reads in part "No State shall . . . pass any Bill of Attainder* [or] *ex post facto Law. . . ."*

I.

It goes without saying that a law to be valid must be clear enough to make its commands understandable. For obvious reasons, the standard of certainty required in criminal statutes is more exacting than in noncriminal statutes.[2] This is simply because it would be unthinkable to convict a man for violating a law he could not understand. This Court has recognized that the stricter standard is as much required in criminal contempt cases as in all other criminal cases,[3] and has emphasized that the "vice of vagueness" is especially pernicious where legislative power over an area involving speech, press, petition and assembly is involved.[4] In this area the statement that a statute is void if it "attempts to cover so much that it effectively covers nothing," see *Musser* v. *Utah,* 333 U.S. 95, 97, takes on double significance. For a statute broad enough to support infringement of speech, writings, thoughts and public assemblies, against the unequivocal command of the First Amendment necessarily leaves all persons to guess just what the law really means to cover, and fear of a wrong guess inevitably leads people to forego the very rights the Constitution sought to protect above all others.[5] Vagueness becomes even more intolerable in this area if one accepts, as the Court today does, a balancing test to decide if First Amendment rights shall be protected. It is difficult at best to make a man guess—at the penalty of imprisonment—whether a court will consider the State's need for certain information superior to society's interest in unfettered freedom. It is unconscionable to make him choose between the right to keep silent and the need to speak when the statute supposedly establishing the "state's interest" is too vague to give him guidance. Cf. *Scull* v. *Virginia,* 359 U.S. 344.

Measured by the foregoing standards,

[2] E.g., Lanzetta *v.* New Jersey, *306 U.S. 451;* Winters *v.* New York, *333 U.S. 507, 515;* Jordan *v.* De George, *341 U.S. 223, 230–231.*

[3] E.g., Watkins *v.* United States, *354 U.S. 178, 207–208;* Flaxer *v.* United States, *358 U.S. 147;* Scull *v.* Virginia, *359 U.S. 344.*

[4] *See,* e.g., Herndon *v.* Lowry, *301 U.S. 242;* Winters *v.* New York, *333 U.S. 507;* Watkins *v.* United States, *354 U.S. 178;* Scull *v.* Virginia, *359 U.S. 344.*

[5] Thornhill *v.* Alabama, *310 U.S. 88, 97–98. Cf.* Herndon *v.* Lowry, *301 U.S. 242.*

Rule XI cannot support any conviction for refusal to testify. In substance it authorizes the Committee to compel witnesses to give evidence about all "un-American propaganda," whether instigated in this country or abroad.[6] The word "propaganda" seems to mean anything that people say, write, think or associate together about. The term "un-American" is equally vague. As was said in *Watkins* v. *United States,* 354 U.S. 178, 202, "Who can define [its] meaning . . . ? What is that single, solitary 'principle of the form of government as guaranteed by our Constitution'?" I think it clear that the boundaries of the Committee are, to say the least, "nebulous." Indeed, "It would be difficult to imagine a less explicit authorizing resolution." *Ibid.*

The Court—while not denying the vagueness of Rule XI—nevertheless defends its application here because the questions asked concerned communism, a subject of investigation which had been reported to the House by the Committee on numerous occasions. If the issue were merely whether Congress intended to allow an investigation of communism, or even of communism in education, it may well be that we could hold the data cited by the Court sufficient to support a finding of intent. But that is expressly not the issue. On the Court's own test, the issue is whether Barenblatt can know with sufficient certainty, at the time of his interrogation, that there is so compelling a need for his replies that infringement of his rights of free association is justified. The record does not disclose where Barenblatt can find what that need is. There is certainly no clear congressional statement of it in Rule XI. Perhaps if Barenblatt had had time to read all the reports of the Committee to the House, and in addition had examined the appropriations made to the Committee he, like the Court, could have discerned an intent by Congress to allow an investigation of communism in education. Even so he would be hard put to decide what the need for this investigation is since Congress expressed it neither when it enacted Rule XI nor when it acquiesced in the Committee's assertions of power. Yet it is knowledge of this need—what is wanted from him and why it is wanted—that a witness must have if he is to be in a position to comply with the Court's rule that he balance individual rights against the requirements of the State. I cannot see how that knowledge can exist under Rule XI.

But even if Barenblatt could evaluate the importance to the Government of the information sought, Rule XI would still be too broad to support his conviction. For we are dealing here with governmental procedures which the Court itself admits reach to the very fringes of congressional power. In such cases more is required of legislatures than a vague delegation to be filled in later by mute acquiescence.[7] If Congress wants ideas investigated, if it even wants them investigated in the field of education, it must be prepared to say so expressly and unequivocally. And it is not enough that a court through exhaustive research can establish, even conclusively, that Congress wished to allow the investigation. I can find no such unequivocal statement here.

For all these reasons, I would hold that Rule XI is too broad to be meaningful and cannot support petitioner's conviction.[8]

[6] *Rule XI in relevant part reads, "The Committee on Un-American Activities, as a whole or by subcommittee, is authorized to make from time to time investigations of (1) the extent, character, and objects of un-American propaganda activities in the United States, (2) the diffusion within the United States of subversive and un-American propaganda that is instigated from foreign countries or of a domestic origin and attacks the principle of the form of government as guaranteed by our Constitution, and (3) all other questions in relation thereto that would aid Congress in any necessary remedial legislation." H. Res. 5, 83d Cong., 1st Sess., 99 Cong. Rec. 15, 18, 24. See also H. Res. 7, 86th Cong., 1st Sess., Cong. Rec., Jan. 7, 1959, p. 13.*

[7] *See,* e.g., Panama Refining Co. *v.* Ryan, *293 U.S. 388;* Schechter Poultry Corp. *v.* United States, *295; U.S. 495* id., *at 551 (concurring opinion)*; Berra *v.* United States, *351 U.S. 131, 135 (dissenting opinion)*; Watkins *v.* United States, *354 U.S. 178, 203–205;* Sweezy *v.* New Hampshire, *354 U.S. 234. Cf.* United States *v.* Rumely, *345 U.S. 41;* Kent *v.* Dulles, *357 U.S. 116. These cases show that when this Court considered that the legislative measures in-substantively, it required explicit delegations volved were of doubtful constitutionality of power.*

[8] *It is of course no answer to Barenblatt's claim that Rule XI is too vague, to say that if it had been too vague it would have been so held in* Watkins *v.* United States, *354 U.S. 178. It would be a strange rule, indeed,*

II.

The First Amendment says in no equivocal language that Congress shall pass no law abridging freedom of speech, press, assembly or petition.[9] The activities of this Committee, authorized by Congress, do precisely that, through exposure, obloquy and public scorn. See *Watkins* v. *United States,* 354 U.S. 178, 197–198. The Court does not really deny this fact but relies on a combination of three reasons for permitting the infringement: (A) The notion that despite the First Amendment's command Congress can abridge speech and association if this Court decides that the governmental interest in abridging speech is greater than an individual's interest in exercising that freedom, (B) the Government's right to "preserve itself," (C) the fact that the Committee is only after Communists or suspected Communists in this investigation.

(A) I do not agree that laws directly abridging First Amendment freedoms can be justified by a congressional or judicial balancing process. There are, of course, cases suggesting that a law which primarily regulates conduct but which might also indirectly affect speech can be upheld if the effect on speech is minor in relation to the need for control of the conduct. With these cases I agree. Typical of them are *Cantwell* v. *Connecticut,* 310 U.S. 296, and *Schneider* v. *Irvington,* 308 U.S. 147. Both of these involved the right of a city to control its streets. In *Cantwell,* a man had been convicted of breach of the peace for playing a phonograph on the street. He defended on the ground that he was disseminating religious views and could not, therefore, be stopped. We upheld his defense, but in so doing we pointed out that the city did have substantial power over conduct on the streets even where this power might to some extent affect speech. A State, we said, might "by general and non-discriminatory legislation regulate the times, the places, and the manner of soliciting upon its streets and holding meetings thereon." 310 U.S., at 304. But even such laws governing conduct, we emphasized, must be tested, though only by a balancing process, if they indirectly affect ideas. On one side of the balance, we pointed out, is the interest of the United States in seeing that its fundamental law protecting freedom of communication is not abridged; on the other the obvious interest of the State to regulate conduct within its boundaries. In *Cantwell* we held that the need to control the streets could not justify the restriction made on speech. We stressed the fact that where a man had a right to be on a street, "he had a right peacefully to impart his views to others." 310 U.S., at 308. Similar views were expressed in *Schneider,* which concerned ordinances prohibiting the distribution of handbills to prevent littering. We forbade application of such ordinances when they affected literature designed to spread ideas. There were other ways, we said, to protect the city from littering which would not sacrifice the right of the people to be informed. In so holding, we, of course, found it necessary to "weigh the circumstances." 308 U.S., at 161. But we did not in *Schneider,* any more than in *Cantwell,* even remotely suggest that a law directly aimed at curtailing speech and political persuasion could be saved through a balancing process. Neither these cases, nor any others, can be read as allowing legislative bodies to pass laws abridging freedom of speech, press and association merely because of hostility to views peacefully expressed in a place where the speaker had a right to be. Rule XI, on its face and as here applied, since it attempts inquiry into beliefs, not action—ideas and associations, not conduct—does just that.[10]

---

which would imply the invalidity of a broad ground of decision from the fact that this Court decided an earlier case on a narrower basis.

[9] *The First Amendment reads: "Congress shall make no law respecting an establishment of religion, or prohibiting the free exercise thereof; or abridging the freedom of speech, or of the press; or the right of the people peaceably to assemble, and to petition the Government for a redress of grievances." There can be no doubt that the same Amendment protects the right to keep silent. See* West Virginia Board of Education *v.* Barnette, *319 U.S. 624;* N.A.A.C.P. *v.* Alabama, *357 U.S. 449, 460–466;* Sweezy *v.* New Hampshire, *354 U.S. 234, 255 (concurring opinion)*; Watkins *v.* United States, *354 U.S. 178;* Scull *v.* Virginia, *359 U.S. 344. Cf.* United States *v.* Rumely, *345 U.S. 41.*

[10] *I do not understand the Court's opinion in* Watkins *v.* United States, *354 U.S. 178, 198, to approve the type of balancing process adopted in the Court's opinion here. We did discuss in that case "the weight to be ascribed to . . . the interest of the Congress in demanding disclosures from an un-*

To apply the Court's balancing test under such circumstances is to read the First Amendment to say "Congress shall pass no law abridging freedom of speech, press, assembly and petition, unless Congress and the Supreme Court reach the joint conclusion that on balance the interest of the Government in stifling these freedoms is greater than the interest of the people in having them exercised." This is closely akin to the notion that neither the First Amendment nor any other provision of the Bill of Rights should be enforced unless the Court believes it is *reasonable* to do so. Not only does this violate the genius of our *written* Constitution, but it runs expressly counter to the injunction to Court and Congress made by Madison when he introduced the Bill of Rights. "If they [the first ten amendments] are incorporated into the Constitution, independent tribunals of justice will consider themselves in a peculiar manner the guardians of those rights; they will be an impenetrable bulwark against *every* assumption of power in the Legislative or Executive; they will be naturally led to resist *every* encroachment upon rights expressly stipulated for in the Constitution by the declaration of rights."[11] Unless we return to this view of our judicial function, unless we once again accept the notion that the Bill of Rights means what it says and that this Court must enforce that meaning, I am of the opinion that our great charter of liberty will be more honored in the breach than in the observance.

But even assuming what I cannot assume, that some balancing is proper in this case, I feel that the Court after stating the test ignores it completely. At most it balances the right of the Government to preserve itself, against Barenblatt's right to refrain from revealing Communist affiliations. Such a balance, however, mistakes the factors to be weighed. In the first place, it completely leaves out the real interest in Barenblatt's silence, the interest of the people as a whole in being able to join organizations, advocate causes and make political "mistakes" without later being subjected to governmental penalties for having dared to think for themselves. It is this right, the right to err politically, which keeps us strong as a Nation. For no number of laws against communism can have as much effect as the personal conviction which comes from having heard its arguments and rejected them, or from having once accepted its tenets and later recognized their worthlessness. Instead, the obloquy which results from investigations such as this not only stifles "mistakes" but prevents all but the most courageous from hazarding any views which might at some later time become disfavored. This result, whose importance cannot be overestimated, is doubly crucial when it affects the universities, on which we must largely rely for the experimentation and development of new ideas essential to our country's welfare. It is these interests of society, rather than Barenblatt's own right to silence, which I think the Court should put on the balance against the demands of the Government, if any balancing process is to be tolerated. Instead they are not mentioned, while on the other side the demands of the Government are vastly overstated and called "self preservation." It is admitted that this Committee can only seek information for the purpose of suggesting laws, and that Congress' power to make laws in the realm of speech and association is quite limited, even on the Court's test. Its interest in making such laws in the field of education, primarily a state function, is clearly narrower still. Yet the Court styles this attenuated interest self-preservation and allows it to overcome the need our country has to let us all think, speak, and associate politically as we like and without fear of reprisal. Such a result reduces "balancing" to a mere play on words and is completely inconsistent with the rules this Court has previously given for applying a "balancing test," where it is proper: "[T]he courts should be *astute* to examine the *effect* of the challenged legislation. Mere *legislative preferences or beliefs* . . . may well support regulation directed at other personal activi-

---

willing witness." As I read, and still read, the Court's discussion of this problem in Watkins *it was referring to the problems raised by* Kilbourn *v.* Thompson, *103 U.S. 168, which held that legislative committees could not make roving inquiries into the private business affairs of witnesses. The Court, in* Kilbourn, *held that the courts must be careful to insure that, on balance, Congress did not unjustifiably encroach on an individual's private business affairs. Needless to say, an individual's right to silence in such matters is quite a different thing from the public's interest in freedom of speech and the test applicable to one has little, if anything, to do with the test applicable to the other.*

[11] *1 Annals of Cong. 439 (1789). (Italics supplied.)*

ties, but be insufficient to justify such as diminishes the exercise of rights so vital to the maintenance of democratic institutions." *Schneider* v. *Irvington,* 308 U.S. 147, 161. (Italics supplied.)

(B) Moreover, I cannot agree with the Court's notion that First Amendment freedoms must be abridged in order to "preserve" our country. That notion rests on the unarticulated premise that this Nation's security hangs upon its power to punish people because of what they think, speak or write about, or because of those with whom they associate for political purposes. The Government, in its brief, virtually admits this position when it speaks of the "communication of unlawful ideas." I challenge this premise, and deny that ideas can be proscribed under our Constitution. I agree that despotic governments cannot exist without stifling the voice of opposition to their oppressive practices. The First Amendment means to me, however, that the only constitutional way our Government can preserve itself is to leave its people the fullest possible freedom to praise, criticize or discuss, as they see fit, all governmental policies and to suggest, if they desire, that even its most fundamental postulates are bad and should be changed; "Therein lies the security of the Republic, the very foundation of constitutional government."[12] On that premise this land was created, and on that premise it has grown to greatness. Our Constitution assumes that the common sense of the people and their attachment to our country will enable them, after free discussion, to withstand ideas that are wrong. To say that our patriotism must be protected against false ideas by means other than these is, I think, to make a baseless charge. Unless we can rely on these qualities—if, in short, we begin to punish speech—we cannot honestly proclaim ourselves to be a free Nation and we have lost what the Founders of this land risked their lives and their sacred honor to defend.

(C) The Court implies, however, that the ordinary rules and requirements of the Constitution do not apply because the Committee is merely after Communists and they do not constitute a political party but only a criminal gang. "[T]he long and widely accepted view," the Court says, is "that the tenets of the Communist Party include the ultimate overthrow of the Government of the United States by force and violence."[13] This justifies the investigation undertaken. By accepting this charge and allowing it to support treatment of the Communist Party and its members which would violate the Constitution if applied to other groups, the Court, in effect, declares that Party outlawed. It has been only a few years since there was a practically unanimous feeling throughout the country and in our courts that this could not be done in our free land. Of course it has always been recognized that members of the Party who, either individually or in combination, commit acts in violation of valid laws can be prosecuted. But the Party as a whole and innocent members of it could not be attainted merely because it had some illegal aims and because some of its members were lawbreakers. Thus in *De Jonge* v. *Oregon,* 299 U.S. 353, 357 (1937), on stipulated facts that the Communist Party advocated criminal syndicalism—"crime, physical violence, sabotage or any unlawful acts or methods as a means of accomplishing or effecting industrial or political change or revolution"—a unanimous Court, speaking through Chief Justice Hughes, held that a Communist addressing a Communist rally could be found guilty of no offense so long as no violence or crime was urged at the meeting. The Court absolutely refused to concede that either De Jonge or the Communist Party forfeited the protections of the First and Fourteenth Amendments because one of the Party's

[12] *"The greater the importance of safeguarding the community from incitements to the overthrow of our institutions by force and violence, the more imperative is the need to preserve inviolate the constitutional rights of free speech, free press and free assembly in order to maintain the opportunity for free political discussion, to the end that government may be responsive to the will of the people and that changes, if desired, may be obtained by peaceful means. Therein lies the security of the Republic, the very foundation of constitutional government."* De Jonge *v.* Oregon, *299 U.S. 353, 365.*

[13] *Cf. statement of Sir Richard Nagle presenting a bill of attainder against between two and three thousand persons for political offenses, " 'Many of the persons here attainted,' said he, 'have been proved traitors by such evidence as satisfies us. As to the rest we have followed common fame.' " Cited in* Joint Anti-Fascist Committee *v.* McGrath, *341 U.S. 123, 142, 148 (concurring opinion).*

purposes was to effect a violent change of government. See also *Herndon* v. *Lowry*, 301 U.S. 242.

Later, in 1948, when various bills were proposed in the House and Senate to handicap or outlaw the Communist Party, leaders of the Bar who had been asked to give their views rose up to contest the constitutionality of the measures. The late Charles Evans Hughes, Jr., questioned the validity under both the First and Fifth Amendments of one of these bills, which in effect outlawed the Party. The late John W. Davis attacked it as lacking an ascertainable standard of guilt under many of this Court's cases.[14] And the Attorney General of the United States not only indicated that such a measure would be unconstitutional but declared it to be unwise even if valid. He buttressed his position by citing a statement by J. Edgar Hoover, Director of the Federal Bureau of Investigation, and the declaration of this Court in *West Virginia Board of Education* v. *Barnette*, 319 U.S. 624, 642, that:

> "If there is any fixed star in our constitutional constellation, it is that no official, high or petty, can prescribe what shall be orthodox in politics, nationalism, religion, or other matters of opinion or force citizens to confess by word or act their faith therein."[15]

Even the proponent of the bill disclaimed any aim to outlaw the Communist Party and pointed out the "disadvantages" of such a move by stating that "the Communist Party was illegal and outlawed in Russia when it took over control of the Soviet Union."[16] Again, when the Attorney General testified on a proposal to bar the Communist Party from the ballot he said, "an organized group, whether you call it political or not, could hardly be barred from the ballot without jeopardizing the constitutional guarantees of all other political groups and parties."[17]

All these statements indicate quite clearly that no matter how often or how quickly we repeat the claim that the Communist Party is not a political party, we cannot outlaw it, as a group, without endangering the liberty of all of us. The reason is not hard to find, for mixed among those aims of communism which are illegal are perfectly normal political and social goals. And muddled with its revolutionary tenets is a drive to achieve power through the ballot, if it can be done. These things necessarily make it a political party whatever other, illegal, aims it may have. Cf. *Gerende* v. *Board of Supervisors*, 341 U.S. 56. Significantly until recently the Communist Party was on the ballot in many States. When that was so, many Communists undoubtedly hoped to accomplish its lawful goals through support

---

[14] *See Hearings, Senate Committee on the Judiciary on H. R. 5852, 80th Cong., 2d Sess. 415–420, 420–422.*

[15] Id., *at 422–425. See also Hearings, Subcommittee on Legislation of the House Committee on Un-American Activities on H. R. 4422, H. R. 4581, 80th Cong., 2d Sess. 16–37.*

[16] *Hearings, Subcommittee on Legislation of the Committee on Un-American Activities on H. R. 4422, H. R. 4581, 80th Cong., 2d Sess. 13. This statement was relied on by the Honorable Thomas E. Dewey, then a candidate for the presidency of the United States, in a speech given in Portland, Oregon, in May, 1948. Mr. Dewey went on to say, in opposing outlawry of the Communist Party:*

"I am against it because it is a violation of the Constitution of the United States and of the Bill of Rights, and clearly so. I am against it because it is immoral and nothing but totalitarianism itself. I am against it because I know from a great many years' experience in the enforcement of the law that the proposal wouldn't work, and instead it would rapidly advance the cause of communism in the United States and all over the world.

. . . . .

"There is an American way to do this job, a perfectly simple American way . . . outlawing every conceivable act *of subversion against the United States. . . .*

. . . . .

"Now, times are too grave to try any expedients and fail. This expedient has failed, this expedient of outlawing has failed in Russia. It failed in Europe, it failed in Italy, it failed in Canada. . . .

"Let us not make such a terrific blunder in the United States. . . . Let us go forward as Free Americans. Let us have the courage to be free." XIV Vital Speeches of the Day, 486–487. (Italics supplied.)

[17] *Hearings, Subcommittee on Legislation of the Committee on Un-American Activities on H. R. 4422, H. R. 4581, 80th Cong., 2d Sess. 20. Compare statement of John Lilburne, "what is done unto any one, may be done unto every one." Note 39,* infra.

of Communist candidates. Even now some such may still remain.[18] To attribute to them, and to those who have left the Party, the taint of the group is to ignore both our traditions that guilt like belief is "personal and not a matter of mere association" and the obvious fact that "men adhering to a political party or other organization notoriously do not subscribe unqualifiedly to all of its platforms or asserted principles." *Schneiderman* v. *United States,* 320 U.S. 118, 136. See also *Dennis* v. *United States,* 341 U.S. 494, 579, 581 (dissenting opinions).

The fact is that once we allow any group which has some political aims or ideas to be driven from the ballot and from the battle for men's minds because some of its members are bad and some of its tenets are illegal, no group is safe. Today we deal with Communists or suspected Communists. In 1920, instead, the New York Assembly suspended duly elected legislators on the ground that, being Socialists, they were disloyal to the country's principles.[19] In the 1830's the Masons were hunted as outlaws and subversives, and abolitionists were considered revolutionaries of the most dangerous kind in both North and South.[20] Earlier still, at the time of the universally unlamented alien and sedition laws, Thomas Jefferson's party was attacked and its members were derisively called "Jacobins." Fisher Ames described the party as a "French faction" guilty of "subversion" and "officered, regimented and formed to subordination." Its members, he claimed, intended to "take arms against the laws as soon as they dare."[21] History should teach us then, that in times of high emotional excitement minority parties and groups which advocate extremely unpopular social or governmental innovations will always be typed as criminal gangs and attempts will always be made to drive them out.[22] It was knowledge of this fact, and of its great dangers, that caused the Founders of our land to enact the First Amendment as a guarantee that neither Congress nor the people would do anything to hinder or destroy the capacity of individuals and groups to seek converts and votes for any cause, however radical or unpalatable their principles might seem under the accepted notions of the time. Whatever the States were left free to do, the First Amendment sought to leave Congress devoid of any kind or quality of power to direct any type of national laws against the freedom of individuals to think what they please, advocate whatever policy they choose, and join with others to bring about the social, religious, political and governmental changes which seem best to them.[23] Today's holding, in my judgment, marks another major step in the progressively increasing retreat from the safeguards of the First Amendment.

It is, sadly, no answer to say that this Court will not allow the trend to overwhelm

18 *S. Doc. No. 97, 85th Cong., 2d Sess. 149, lists the States with laws relating to the Communist Party and the ballot. See also, Fund For The Republic, Digest of the Public Record of Communism in the United States, 324–343. For a discussion of state laws requiring a minimum percentage of the votes cast to remain on the ballot, see Note, 57 Yale L. J. 1276.*

19 *See O'Brian, Loyalty Tests and Guilt by Association, 61 Harv. L. Rev. 592, 593. Significantly the action of the New York Assembly was strongly condemned by Charles Evans Hughes, then a former Associate Justice of this Court, and later its Chief Justice.*

20 *See generally, McCarthy, The Antimasonic Party: A Study of Political Antimasonry in the United States, 1827–1840. H. R. Doc. No. 461, 57th Cong., 2d Sess. 365. Nye, William Lloyd Garrison, 88–105; Korngold, Two Friends of Man, 82–104. Cf. St. George Tucker, Appendix, I Blackstone (Tucker ed. 1803) 315, discussing English laws "for suppressing assemblies of free-masons" and pointing out that similar laws cannot be enacted under our Constitution.*

21 *Ames, Laocoon, printed in Works of Fisher Ames (1809 ed.), 94, 97, 101, 106. See also* American Communications Assn. *v.* Douds, *339 U.S. 382, 445 (dissenting opinion).*

22 *Cf. Mill, On Liberty (1885 ed.), 30 (criticizing laws restricting the right to advocate tyrannicide).*

23 *Cf. St. George Tucker, Appendix, 1 Blackstone Commentaries (Tucker ed. 1803) 299. "[T]he judicial courts of the respective states are open to all persons alike, for the redress of injuries of this nature [libel]; . . . But the genius of our government will not permit the federal legislature to interfere with the subject; and the federal courts, are, I presume, equally restrained by the principles of the constitution, and the amendments which have since been adopted."*

us; that today's holding will be strictly confined to "Communists," as the Court's language implies. This decision can no more be contained than could the holding in *American Communications Assn.* v. *Douds,* 339 U.S. 382. In that case the Court sustained as an exercise of the commerce power an Act which required labor union officials to take an oath that they were not members of the Communist Party. The Court rejected the idea that the *Douds* holding meant that the Party and all its members could be attainted because of their Communist beliefs. It went to great lengths to explain that the Act held valid "touches only a relative handful of persons, leaving the great majority of persons of the identified affiliations and beliefs completely free from restraint." "[W]hile this Court sits," the Court proclaimed, no wholesale proscription of Communists or their Party can occur. 339 U.S., at 404, 410. I dissented and said:

> "Under such circumstances, restrictions imposed on proscribed groups are seldom static, even though the rate of expansion may not move in geometric progression from discrimination to arm-band to ghetto and worse. Thus I cannot regard the Court's holding as one which merely bars Communists from holding union office and nothing more. For its reasoning would apply just as forcibly to statutes barring Communists and their respective sympathizers from election to political office, mere membership in unions, and in fact from getting or holding any job whereby they could earn a living." 339 U.S., at 449.

My prediction was all too accurate. Today, Communists or suspected Communists have been denied an opportunity to work as government employees, lawyers, doctors, teachers, pharmacists, veterinarians, subway conductors, industrial workers and in just about any other job. See *Speiser* v. *Randall,* 357 U.S. 513, 531 (concurring opinion). Cf. *Barsky* v. *Board of Regents,* 347 U.S. 442, 456, 467, 472 (dissenting opinions). In today's holding they are singled out and, as a class, are subjected to inquisitions which the Court suggests would be unconstitutional but for the fact of "Communism." Nevertheless, this Court still sits![24]

III.

Finally, I think Barenblatt's conviction violates the Constitution because the chief aim, purpose and practice of the House Un-American Activities Committee, as disclosed by its many reports, is to try witnesses and punish them because they are or have been Communists or because they refuse to admit or deny Communist affiliations. The punishment imposed is generally punishment by humiliation and public shame. There is nothing strange or novel about this kind of punishment. It is in fact one of the oldest forms of governmental punishment known to mankind; branding, the pillory, ostracism and subjection to public hatred being but a few examples of it.[25] Nor is there anything strange about a court's reviewing the power of a congressional committee to inflict punishment. In 1880 this Court nullified the action of the House of Representatives in sentencing a witness to jail for failing to answer questions of a congressional committee. *Kilbourn* v. *Thompson,* 103 U.S. 168. The Court held that the Committee in its investigation of the Jay Cooke bankruptcy was seeking to exercise judicial power, and this, it emphatically said, no committee could do. It seems to me that the proof that the Un-American Activities Committee is here undertaking a purely judicial function is overwhelming, far stronger, in fact, than it was in the Jay Cooke investigation which, moreover, concerned only business transactions, not freedom of association.

The Un-American Activities Committee was created in 1938. It immediately conceived of its function on a grand scale as

[24] *The record in this very case indicates how easily such restrictions spread. During the testimony of one witness an organization known as the Americans for Democratic Action was mentioned. Despite testimony that this organization did not admit Communists, one member of the Committee insisted that it was a Communist front because "it followed a party line, almost identical in many particulars with the Communist Party line." Presumably if this accusation were repeated frequently and loudly enough that organization, or any other, would also be called a "criminal gang." Cf.* Feiner *v.* New York, *340 U.S. 315, 321, 329 (dissenting opinions).*

[25] *See generally, XII Encyclopedia of the Social Sciences 714; Barnes, The Story of Punishment, 62–64; Lowie, Primitive Society, 398; Andrews, Old-Time Punishments (1890 ed.), 1–145, 164–187; IV Plutarch's Lives (Clough, New Nat. ed. 1914) 43–44.*

one of ferreting out "subversives" and especially of having them removed from government jobs.[26] It made many reports to the House urging removal of such employees.[27] Finally, at the instigation of the Committee, the House put a rider on an appropriation bill to bar three government workers from collecting their salaries.[28] The House action was based on Committee findings that each of the three employees was a member of, or associated with, organizations deemed undesirable and that the "views and philosophies" of these workers "as expressed in various statements and writings constitute subversive activity within the definition adopted by your committee, and that [they are], therefore, unfit for the present to continue in Government employment."[29] The Senate and the President agreed to the rider, though not without protest. We held that statute void as a bill of attainder in *United States* v. *Lovett,* 328 U.S. 303 (1946), stating that its "effect was to inflict punishment without the safeguards of a judicial trial" and that this "cannot be done either by a State or by the United States." 328 U.S., at 316–317.

Even after our *Lovett* holding, however, the Committee continued to view itself as the "only agency of government that has the power of exposure," and to work unceasingly and sincerely to identify and expose all suspected Communists and "subversives" in order to eliminate them from virtually all fields of employment.[30] How well it has succeeded in its declared program of "pitiless publicity and exposure" is a matter of

[26] *In its very first report it stated, "The committee has felt that it is its sworn duty and solemn obligation to the people of this country to focus the spotlight of publicity upon every individual and organization engaged in subversive activities regardless of politics or partisanship." It further claimed that, "While Congress does not have the power to deny to citizens the right to believe in, teach, or advocate, communism, fascism, and nazism, it does have the right to focus the spotlight of publicity upon their activities. . . ." H. R. Rep. No. 2, 76th Cong., 1st Sess. 9–10, 13. See also the statement of the Committee's first Chairman, "I am not in a position to say whether we can legislate effectively in reference to this matter, but I do know that exposure in a democracy of subversive activities is the most effective weapon that we have in our possession." 83 Cong. Rec. 7570 (1938).*

[27] *See,* e.g., *H. R. Rep. No. 2748, 77th Cong., 2d Sess. 5. "On September 6, 1941, the chairman of this committee wrote the President a letter, accompanied by 43 exhibits, detailing the Communist affiliation and background of the following officials . . . and suggested that they be dismissed from their positions." "On November 28, 1941 . . . the chairman called the attention of the members to the case of [the] principal economists in the Department of Agriculture"; "On January 15, 1942, the chairman of the committee . . . called attention to . . . one Malcolm Cowley. . . . Several weeks later Mr. Cowley resigned his position with the Federal Government"; "On March 28, 1942, the chairman wrote a letter to the . . . Chairman of the Board of Economic Welfare, and called attention to . . . eight of its employees and made particular reference to one Maurice Parmelee. . . . The following week, Mr. Parmelee was dismissed. . . ."* Id., *at 6. "In the Chairman's speech of September 24 [1942] he also presented to the House the names of 19 officials of the Government. . . . Yet, to the committee's knowledge, no action has been taken in the cases of the 19 officials."* Id., *at 8.*

[28] *Section 304 of the Urgent Deficiency Appropriation Act, 1943, 57 Stat. 431, 450. The history of this rider is detailed in* United States *v.* Lovett, *328 U.S. 303.*

[29] *See,* e.g., *H. R. Rep. No. 448, 78th Cong., 1st Sess. 6, 8. The Un-American Activities Committee did not actually undertake the trials of these government employees. That task fell to a special Subcommittee of the Committee on Appropriations which was created in response to a speech by the Chairman of the Un-American Activities Committee.* Id., *at 3.*

[30] *Virtually every report of the Committee emphasizes that its principal function is exposure and that once exposed subversives must be driven out. Space, however, prevents listing more than a random sampling of statements by the Committee. These are given in an Appendix to this opinion,* post, *p. 163. For other similar statements by the Committee and its members see,* e.g., *notes 26, 27,* supra; *31–37,* infra; Watkins *v.* United States, *354 U.S. 178;* United States *v.* Josephson, *165 F. 2d 82, 93 (dissenting opinion)*; Barsky *v.* United States, *83 U.S. App. D.C. 127, 138, 167 F. 2d 241, 252 (dissenting opinion)*.

public record. It is enough to cite the experience of a man who masqueraded as a Communist for the F.B.I. and who reported to this same Committee that since 1952 when his "membership" became known he has been unable to hold any job.[31] To accomplish this kind of result, the Committee has called witnesses who are suspected of Communist affiliation, has subjected them to severe questioning and has insisted that each tell the name of every person he has ever known at any time to have been a Communist, and, if possible, to give the addresses and occupations of the people named. These names are then indexed, published, and reported to Congress, and often to the press.[32] The same technique is employed to cripple the job opportunities of those who strongly criticize the Committee or take other actions it deems undesirable.[33] Thus, in 1949, the Committee reported that it had indexed and printed some 335,000 names of people who had signed "Communist" petitions of one kind or another.[34] All this the Committee did and does to punish by exposure the many phases of "un-American" activities that it reports cannot be reached by legislation, by administrative action, or by any other agency of Government, which, of course, includes the courts.

The same intent to expose and punish is manifest in the Committee's investigation which led to Barenblatt's conviction. The declared purpose of the investigation was to identify to the people of Michigan the individuals responsible for the, alleged, Communist success there.[35] The Committee

[31] *This evidence was given before the Committee on May 7, 1959, in Chicago, Ill. It has not yet been published.*

Even those the Committee does not wish to injure are often hurt by its tactics, so all-pervasive is the effect of its investigations.

"It has been brought to the attention of the committee that many persons so subpeonaed . . . have been subjected to ridicule and discrimination as a result of having received such subpoenas"; "The committee . . . has met with many obstacles and difficulties. Not the least of these has been the reluctance of former Communists to give testimony before the committee which might bring upon them public censure and economic retaliation"; "To deny to these cooperative *witnesses a full opportunity for social, economic, and political rehabilitation . . . will . . . render more difficult the obtaining of authentic . . . information." H. R. Rep. No. 2431 82d Cong., 2d Sess. 5. (Italics added.)*

"While the American people . . . were fortunate to have this testimony, some of the witnesses themselves were not. Instances have come to the Committee's attention where several of these witnesses have been forced from gainful employment after testifying. Some have been released from the employment which they competently held for years prior to their testimony." H. R. Rep. No. 2516, 82d Cong., 2d Sess. 3.

[32] *Descriptions of the size and availability of Committee's files as well as the efficiency of its cross-indexing system can be found in most of its reports. See,* e.g., *H. R. Rep. No. 2742, 79th Cong., 2d Sess. 16–17; H. R. Rep. No. 1950, 81st Cong., 2d Sess. 18–23; H. R. Rep. No. 2431, 82d Cong., 2d Sess. 24–28.*

[33] *It is impossible even to begin to catalogue people who have been stigmatized by the Committee for criticizing it. In 1942 the Committee reported "Henry Luce's Time Magazine has been drawn sucker-fashion into this movement to alter our form of government. . . ." H. R. Rep. No. 2277, 77th Cong., 2d Sess. 2. In 1946 Harold Laski and socialists generally were attacked for their "impertinence in suggesting that the United States should trade its system of free economy for some brand of Socialism." The Committee deemed it "imperative" that it ascertain the "methods used to enable Mr. Laski to broadcast to [a] rally." H. R. Rep. No. 2233, 79th Cong., 2d Sess. 46–47. In 1951 a full report was issued on a "communist lobby"—a committee formed to urge defeat of a communist control bill before Congress. Among the distinguished sponsors of the group listed by the Committee was the late Prof. Zechariah Chafee. The Committee, nevertheless, advised "the American public that individuals who knowingly and actively support such a propaganda outlet . . . are actually aiding and abetting the Communist program in the United States." H. R. Rep. No. 3248, 81st Cong., 2d Sess. 1, 11–12, 15. See also, Gellhorn, Report on a Report of the House Committee on Un-American Activities, 60 Harv. L. Rev. 1193.*

[34] *H. R. Rep. No. 1950, 81st Cong., 2d Sess. 19.*

[35] *"The 1954 hearings were set up by the committee in order to demonstrate to the people of Michigan the fields of concentration of the Communist Party in the Michigan area, and the identity of those individ-*

claimed that its investigation "uncovered" members of the Communist Party holding positions in the school systems in Michigan; that most of the teachers subpoenaed before the Committee refused to answer questions on the ground that to do so might result in self-incrimination, and that most of these teachers had lost their jobs. It then stated that "the Committee on Un-American Activities approves of this action. . . ."[36] Similarly, as a result of its Michigan investigation, the Committee called upon American labor unions to amend their constitutions, if necessary, in order to deny membership to any Communist Party member.[37] This would, of course, prevent many workers from getting or holding the only kind of jobs their particular skills qualified them for. The Court, today, barely mentions these statements, which, especially when read in the context of past reports by the Committee, show unmistakably what the Committee was doing. I cannot understand why these reports are deemed relevant to a determination of a congressional intent to investigate communism in education, but irrelevant to any finding of congressional intent to bring about exposure for its own sake or for the purposes of punishment.

I do not question the Committee's patriotism and sincerity in doing all this.[38] I merely feel that it cannot be done by Congress under our Constitution. For, even assuming that the Federal Government can compel witnesses to testify as to Communist affiliations in order to subject them to ridicule and social and economic retaliation, I cannot agree that this is a legislative function. Such publicity is clearly punishment, and the Constitution allows only one way in which people can be convicted and punished. As we said in *Lovett,* "Those who wrote our Constitution well knew the danger inherent in special legislative acts which take away the life, liberty or property of particular named persons because the legislature thinks them guilty of conduct which deserves punishment. *They intended to safeguard the people of this country from punishment without trial by duly constituted courts.*" 328 U.S., at 317. (Italics added.) Thus if communism is to be made a crime, and Communists are to be subjected to "pains and penalties," I would still hold this conviction bad, for the crime of communism, like all others, can be punished only by court and jury after a trial with all judicial safeguards.

It is no answer to all this to suggest that legislative committees should be allowed to punish if they grant the accused some rules of courtesy or allow him counsel. For the Constitution proscribes *all* bills of attainder by State or Nation, not merely those which lack counsel or courtesy. It does this because the Founders believed that punishment was too serious a matter to be entrusted to any group other than an independent judiciary and a jury of twelve men acting on previously passed, unambiguous laws, with all the procedural safeguards they put in the Constitution as essential to a fair trial—safeguards which included the right to counsel, compulsory process for witnesses, specific indictments, confrontation of accusers, as well as protection against self-incrimination, double jeopardy and cruel and unusual punishment—in short, due process of law. Cf. *Chambers* v. *Florida,* 309 U.S. 227. They believed this because not long before worthy men had been deprived of their liberties, and indeed their lives, through parliamentary trials without these safeguards. The memory of one of these, John Lilburne—banished and disgraced by a parliamentary committee on penalty of death if he returned to his country—was particularly vivid when our Constitution was written. His attack on trials by such committees and his warning that "what is done unto any one, may be done unto every one"[39]

uals responsible for its success." H. R. Rep. No. 57, 84th Cong., 1st Sess. 15.

[36] Id., *at 17.*

[37] "*[T]he Committee on Un-American Activities calls upon the American labor movement . . . to amend its constitutions where necessary in order to deny membership to a member of the Communist Party or any other group which dedicates itself to the destruction of America's way of life.*" Ibid.

[38] *Sincerity and patriotism do not, unfortunately, insure against unconstitutional acts. Indeed, some of the most lamentable and tragic deaths of history were instigated by able, patriotic and sincere men. See generally Mill, On Liberty (1885 ed.), 43–48.*

[39] *"For certainly it cannot be denied, but if he be really an offender, he is such by the breach for some law, made and published before the fact, and ought by due process of law, and verdict of 12 men, to be thereof convict, and found guilty of such crime; unto which the law also hath prescribed such a punishment agreeable to that our fundamental liberty; which enjoineth that no freeman of England should be adjudged of life, limb, liberty, or estate, but by*

were part of the history of the times which moved those who wrote our Constitution to determine that no such arbitrary punishments should ever occur here. It is the protection from arbitrary punishments through the right to a judicial trial with all these safeguards which over the years has distinguished America from lands where drumhead courts and other similar "tribunals" deprive the weak and the unorthodox of life, liberty and property without due process of law. It is this same right which is denied to Barenblatt, because the Court today fails to see what is here for all to see—that exposure and punishment is the aim of this Committee and the reason for its existence. To deny this is to ignore the Committee's own claims and the reports it has issued ever since it was established. I cannot believe that the nature of our judicial office requires us to be so blind, and must conclude that the Un-American Activities Committee's "identification" and "exposure" of Communists and suspected Communists, like the activities of the Committee in *Kilbourn* v. *Thompson,* amount to an encroachment on the judiciary which bodes ill for the liberties of the people of this land.

Ultimately all the questions in this case really boil down to one—whether we as a people will try fearfully and futilely to preserve democracy by adopting totalitarian methods, or whether in accordance with our traditions and our Constitution we will have the confidence and courage to be free.

I would reverse this conviction.

Juries; a freedom which parliaments in all ages contended to preserve from violation; as the birthright and chief inheritance of the people, as may appear most remarkably in the Petition of Right, which you have stiled that most excellent law.

"And therefore we trust upon second thoughts, being the parliament of England, you will be so far from bereaving us, who have never forfeited our right, of this our native right, and way of Trials by Juries, (for what is done unto any one, may be done unto every one), that you will preserve them entire to us, and to posterity, from the encroachments of any that would innovate upon them. . . .

"And it is believed, that . . . had [the cause] at any time either at first or last been admitted to a trial at law, and had passed any way by verdict of twelve sworn men: all the trouble and inconveniences arising thereupon had been prevented: the way of determination by major votes of committees, being neither so certain nor so satisfactory in any case as by way of Juries, the benefit of challenges and exceptions, and unanimous consent, being all essential privileges in the latter; whereas committees are tied to no such rules, but are at liberty to be present or absent at pleasure. Besides, Juries being birthright, and the other but new and temporary, men do not, nor, as we humbly conceive, ever will acquiesce in the one as in the other; from whence it is not altogether so much to be wondered at, if upon dissatisfactions, there have been such frequent printing of men's cases, and dealings of Committees, as there have been; and such harsh and inordinate heats and expressions between parties interested, such sudden and importunate appeals to your authority, being indeed all alike out of the true English road, and leading into nothing but trouble and perplexity, breeding hatred and enmities between worthy families, affronts and disgust between persons of the same public affection and interest, and to the rejoicing of none but public adversaries. All which, and many more inconveniences, can only be avoided, by referring all such cases to the usual Trials and final determinations of law." 5 Howell's State Trials 411–412, Statement of John Lilburne (1653).

APPENDIX TO OPINION OF MR. JUSTICE BLACK, DISSENTING.

Random Selection of Statements by the House Un-American Activities Committee on Exposure and Punishment of "Subversives."

"[T]o inform the American people of the activities of any such organizations . . . is the real purpose of the House Committee." "The purpose of this committee is the task of protecting our constitutional democracy by turning the light of pitiless publicity on [these] organizations." H. R. Rep. No. 1476, 76th Cong., 3d Sess. 1–2, 24.

"The very first exposure which our committee undertook in the summer of 1938 was that of the German-American Bund." "Other organizations . . . have been greatly crippled . . . as a result of our exposures. The American Youth Congress once enjoyed a very considerable prestige. . . . Today many of its distinguished former sponsors refuse to be found in its company. . . . We kept the spotlight of publicity focused upon the American Youth Congress, and today it is clear to all that, in spite of a degree of participation in its activities by many fine young people, it was never at its core anything less than a tool of Moscow." "This committee is the only agency of Government that has the power of exposure. . . . There are many phases of un-American activities that cannot be reached by legislation or administrative action. We believe that the committee has shown that fearless exposure . . . is the . . . answer." H. R. Rep. No. 1, 77th Cong., 1st Sess. 21–22, 24.

"Our investigation has shown that a steady barrage against Congress comes . . . from the New Republic, one of whose editors . . . was recently forced out of an $8,000 Government job by the exposure of his Communist activities." H. R. Rep. No. 2277, 77th Cong., 2d Sess. 3.

"[T]he House Committee on Un-American Activities is empowered to explore and expose activities by un-American individuals and organizations which, while sometimes being legal, are nonetheless inimical to our American concepts." The Committee recommends that Congress "discharge . . . any employee or official of the Federal Government whose loyalty to the United States is found to be in doubt." H. R. Rep. No. 2742, 79th Cong., 2d Sess. 16, 17.

"Index of Persons and Organizations." (Six pages of names follow.) H. R. Rep. No. 2233, 79th Cong., 2d Sess. III–VIII.

"Early in 1947 the committee adopted the following eight point program. . . .

"1. To expose and ferret out the Communists and Communist sympathizers in the Federal Government.

"2. To spotlight the spectacle of . . . Communists . . . in American labor.

"In a sense the storm of opposition to the activities of the committee is a tribute to its achievements in the field of exposure. . . ." Report of the Committee on Un-American Activities to the United States House of Representatives, 80th Cong., 2d Sess., Dec. 31, 1948, 2, 3 (Committee print).

"The committee would like to remind the Congress that its work is part of an 11-year continuity of effort that began . . . in August 1938. The committee would also like to recall that at no time in those 11 years has it ever wavered from a relentless pursuit and exposure." "In the course of its investigations . . . the committee has made available a large, completely indexed, and readily accessible reference collection of lists of signers of Communist Party election petitions." H. R. Rep. No. 1950, 81st Cong., 2d Sess. 15, 19.

"To conduct the exposé . . . it was necessary for the investigative staff to interview over 100 persons. . . .

"The same tedious investigation of details was necessary prior to the successful exposure . . . in the Territory of Hawaii." "As a result of the investigation and hearings held by the committee, Dolivet's contract with the United Nations has not been renewed, and it is the committee's understanding that he was removed from editorship of the United Nations World." H. R. Rep. No. 3249, 81st Cong., 2d Sess. 4, 5.

"During 1951 the committee's hearings disclosed the positive identification of more individuals . . . than during any preceding year." "If communism in Hollywood is now mythical, it is only because this committee conducted three investigations to bring it about. The industry itself certainly did not accomplish this." "The committee's investigation . . . was concerned almost entirely with the problem of exposure of the actual members of the Communist Party and did not deal, except in a few instances, with . . . fellow travelers." "On the question of fellow travelers, suffice it to say . . . 'The time has come now when even the fellow traveler must get out.' " "Dr. Struik was identified as a Communist teacher. . . . Nevertheless, he was permitted to teach . . . until this year." "With individuals like . . . Struik . . . teaching in our leading universities, your committee wonders who the Professor Struiks were . . . who led Alger Hiss along the road of communism." H. R. Rep. No. 2431, 82d Cong., 2d Sess. 6, 8–9, 16–17.

"In this annual report, the committee feels that the Congress and the American people will have a much clearer and fuller picture . . . by having set forth the names and, where possible, the positions occupied by individuals who have been identified as Communists, or former Communists, during the past year." "The committee considers the failure of certain trade-unionists to rid themselves of Communists to be a national disgrace." "The following persons were identified." (Approximately fifty pages of names follow.) H. R. Rep. No. 2516, 82d Cong., 2d Sess. 6–7, 12–27, 28–34, 36–40, 41–56, 58–67 (similar lists can be found in various other reports).

"The focal point of the investigation

into the general area of education was to the individual who had been identified." "The question has been asked as to what purpose is served by the disclosure of the names of individuals who may long ago have left the conspiracy." "The committee has no way of knowing the status of his membership at present until he is placed under oath and the information is sought to be elicited." H. R. Rep. No. 1192, 83d Cong., 2d Sess. 1, 7.

Stanley Reed

☆ 1884– ☆

APPOINTED BY

FRANKLIN D. ROOSEVELT

YEARS ON COURT

1938–1957

Stanley Reed

by

C. HERMAN PRITCHETT

STANLEY FORMAN REED was nominated as the sixty-ninth Associate Justice of the United States Supreme Court on January 15, 1938, at the age of fifty-three, the second of President Franklin D. Roosevelt's appointees to the Court. He took his seat as George Sutherland's successor less than one year after the famous Court-packing controversy had convulsed the political life of the nation, and less than nine months after the Court had signaled its capitulation to the New Deal by upholding the constitutionality of the National Labor Relations Act. He served on the Court for nineteen years, under four Chief Justices—Hughes, Stone, Vinson, and Warren. He wrote 339 opinions—231 for the Court, twenty concurrences, and eighty-eight dissents. He retired in 1957 at the age of seventy-two, when health considerations indicated the desirability of reducing his work load.

During all those years Reed exercised a moderating influence on the Court. He was a "center judge," occupying generally a middle position between the Court's conservative and liberal wings, between the apostles of judicial activism and self-restraint. He brought onto the Court an acceptance of the social and economic legislation of the modern welfare state; he had himself defended the key measures of the New Deal before the Court as Solicitor General. A southerner, he was a full participant in the Court's historic effort to free the Negro from almost a century of denial of constitutional rights. In the area of civil liberties, which got increasingly more attention the longer he stayed on the Court, Reed was less likely to favor the use of judicial power, and more inclined to support the government and public order against the claims of individual right and freedom.

Reed was born on December 31, 1884, in Minerva, Kentucky, a small town in Mason County of which Maysville is the county seat. He was the son of Dr.

C. HERMAN PRITCHETT, Professor of Political Science at the University of Chicago, is the author of Civil Liberties and the Vinson Court *and* The Roosevelt Court.

John A. and Frances Forman Reed. He graduated from Kentucky Wesleyan College in 1902, and went on to Yale University for another bachelor's degree, graduating in 1906 with a major in economics and history. He then entered the University of Virginia Law School, but shifted to Columbia University to complete his law degree. He married a hometown girl, Winifred Elgin, and as a combined honeymoon and graduate course, the Reeds went to Paris where he studied for a year at the Sorbonne, mostly in civil and international law.

Returning to Kentucky, Reed was admitted to the bar and entered the general practice of law in Maysville, a town of 6,500. He soon became active in Democratic politics. From 1912 to 1916 he was a member of the state General Assembly, where he introduced child labor and workmen's compensation legislation. In the Wilson campaign of 1916 he was president of the Kentucky Young Democrats. In 1918 he entered the army, serving as a first lieutenant.

Two of Reed's principal law clients were the Chesapeake & Ohio Railroad and the Burley Tobacco Growers' Cooperative Association. He helped organize the cooperative, which engaged in a program of market control through the group handling and selling of tobacco, and his service as general counsel of the organization provided the contact which eventually brought him to Washington. The Hoover administration, plagued by burdensome surpluses of farm commodities, set up the Federal Farm Board to buy American surpluses for resale on the world market. Even though he was a Democrat, Reed was appointed counsel for the board in 1929 on the recommendation of James C. Stone, who had been president of the tobacco cooperative.

In December, 1932, the Hoover administration moved Reed to the more important post of General Counsel in the Reconstruction Finance Corporation. This organization was President Hoover's principal instrument for combatting the depression through loans to banking, business, and agricultural enterprises which found themselves in financial difficulties. Reed was retained in this position when President Roosevelt took office.

Under the New Deal the RFC undertook a wider variety of functions. One new task was responsibility for the program of buying newly mined foreign and domestic gold, by which it was hoped to lower the value of the dollar on foreign exchanges and thus raise domestic commodity prices. The Treasury Department argued that there was no legal authority for such purchases, but Reed issued an opinion upholding the program.

Reduction of the gold content of the dollar was an even more important and controversial Roosevelt device to raise prices. To help meet the legal attack on the government's power to abrogate clauses in private contracts requiring payment in gold, Reed was appointed a special assistant to the Attorney General, and he argued the Gold Clause cases, 294 U.S. 240 (1935), before the Supreme Court.

After this success, Reed was nominated on March 18, 1935, to the post of Solicitor General, where he had the responsibility for all of the government's important litigation before the Supreme Court. Attorney General Homer Cummings suggested that Reed select as his first case to argue before the Court one which he was sure to win. Reed chose a case challenging the authority of President Roosevelt to remove a member of the Federal Trade Commission. The President's power to take such action was clearly supported by the opinion of Chief Justice Taft in *Myers* v. *United States,* 272 U.S. 52 (1926), but the Court surprisingly and unanimously ruled against Roosevelt in *Humphrey's Executor* v. *United States,* 295 U.S. 602 (1935).

There were other defeats in store for Reed. The National Industrial Recovery Act was declared unconstitutional, also unanimously, in *Schechter Poultry Corp.* v. *United States,* 295 U.S. 495 (1935), and the Agricultural Adjustment Act was invalidated by a vote of six to three in *United States* v. *Butler,* 297 U.S. 1 (1936). But Reed was successful in defense of the Tennessee Valley Authority Act in *Ashwander* v. *TVA,* 297 U.S. 288 (1936), and federal aid to public power projects was upheld in *Alabama Power Co.* v. *Ickes,* 302 U.S. 464 (1938). The Wagner Act was approved by a five to four margin in *National Labor Relations Board* v. *Jones & Laughlin Corp.,* 301 U.S. 1 (1937), though Reed did not have the major responsibility of arguing the latter case.

Reed's three years as Solicitor General covered what was undoubtedly the most exciting period in the history of that office, as he defended the constitutionality of the New Deal's experimental legislation before the "nine old men" on the Supreme Court against the most costly legal talent in the country. Following the *Butler* decision in January, 1936, President Roosevelt was convinced that some steps had to be taken to bring the Court out of its "horse and buggy" thinking. Attorney General Cummings proposed as one possibility the "Court-packing" plan, under which the President would be authorized to add one Justice to the Court for each Justice who reached the age of seventy but failed to retire, up to a total of fifteen. While Solicitor General Reed contributed at least one memorandum on the Court reorganization plan, he remained largely aloof from the vicious political battle which ultimately defeated it.

The Supreme Court, chastened by this harrowing experience, upheld the Wagner Act in April, 1937, and shortly thereafter Justice Willis Van Devanter, one of the Court's conservatives, announced his retirement. For this vacancy, his first to fill in more than four years as President, Roosevelt selected the liberal and controversial senator from Alabama, Hugo Black. In January, 1938, Justice George Sutherland announced his retirement, and Roosevelt's second appointment went to Reed, whose experience as Solicitor General and loyalty to the administration had made him an obvious choice. It was generally agreed that, by selecting Reed, President Roosevelt was seeking to mollify the critics of the Black appointment, for Reed, though a liberal Democrat, was known for his judicious character and the soundness of his legal training. The appointment was greeted with general approbation; prophetically, some commentators praised him for his liberalism and others for his conservatism.

Reed was confirmed by the Senate on January 25, 1938, and took his seat on the Court on January 31. He retired on February 25, 1957. Following his retirement, he accepted numerous assignments to hear cases in the Court of Claims and the Court of Appeals for the District of Columbia. By 1966 he had sat in thirty-five cases in the former court, and twenty-five in the latter. He was also appointed by the Supreme Court as special master in one original proceeding.

The only extra-judicial task which Reed undertook during his service on the Court was as Chairman of President Roosevelt's Committee on Civil Service Improvement, of which Justice Frankfurter was also a member. Following his retirement from the Court, Reed accepted President Eisenhower's appointment as chairman of the U.S. Civil Rights Commission which had been set up by the Civil Rights Act of 1957. However, because he was still subject to call for service as a federal judge, he soon withdrew from the post because he doubted the propriety of even a retired Supreme Court Justice undertaking a non-judicial task of this character.

During Justice Reed's long service on the Court, he had the opportunity to participate in many major fields of constitutional development. Of prime importance was his role in recognizing the legitimacy of the welfare state, big government, and its powers of commercial, financial, and social regulation. He had of course made a major contribution in this direction as Solicitor General, and the change in judicial attitudes was well under way before he joined the Court. But as a Justice he wrote major opinions continuing the trend, particularly in expanding federal regulatory power over agriculture and water control.

It was peculiarly appropriate that Reed should write the opinion in *United States* v. *Rock Royal Cooperative,* 307 U.S. 533 (1939), holding constitutional the Agricultural Marketing Act which undertook to maintain regulated marketing conditions for agricultural commodities in interstate commerce. On the Farm Board he had seen the consequences of an inept statute which sought to control farm prices without regulating production. Moreover, as Solicitor General he had argued and lost the *Butler* case, in which Justice Roberts had concluded for the majority that agricultural production was "a purely local activity." In *Rock Royal* the Court reversed this restrictive view, and held that the commingling of sales of milk destined partly for local use and partly for interstate use permitted the sweep of the commerce clause to cover the whole. Reed's opinion for the Court in *H. P. Hood & Sons* v. *United States,* 307 U.S. 588 (1939), was to a similar effect.

In *United States* v. *Appalachian Electric Power Co.,* 311 U.S. 377 (1940), Reed, who had argued the *Ashwander* case as Solicitor General, spoke for the Court in announcing a revised test of navigability which greatly increased federal authority over the nation's inland waterways and its control over the generation of hydroelectric power. Previously the rule had been that rivers were navigable in law when they were used, or susceptible of being used, in their ordinary condition as highways for commerce. Reed modified this test by holding that rivers must be considered navigable if by the expenditure of a not unreasonable sum of money they could be made navigable. Moreover, Reed's opinion made clear that the government's power over navigable waters was not restricted to promoting navigation, but included flood protection, watershed development, and recovery of the cost of improvements through generation of power.

Reed likewise supported the broad interpretation of the commerce power which Congress had asserted in adopting the National Labor Relations and Fair Labor Standards acts. In *United States* v. *Darby Lumber Co,* 312 U.S. 100 (1941), he voted with the Court to overrule *Hammer* v. *Dagenhart,* 247 U.S. 251 (1918), perhaps the most notorious of all the previous decisions limiting congressional power to act under the commerce clause.

Reed interpreted federal regulatory power over interstate transmission of electricity broadly in *Jersey Central Power & Light Co.* v. *Federal Power Commission,* 319 U.S. 61 (1943), but he was more reluctant to depart from the older due process precedents governing rate regulation. He sought to maintain the "fair value" rule of *Smyth* v. *Ames,* 169 U.S. 466 (1898), in his decision for the Court in *Driscoll* v. *Edison Light & Power Co.,* 307 U.S. 104 (1939), a view which Frankfurter criticized as giving new vitality to a "mischievous formula." Moreover, in *Federal Power Commission* v. *Panhandle Eastern Pipe Line Co.,* 337 U.S. 498 (1949), Reed wrote an opinion denying the commission jurisdiction over natural gas reserves owned by a pipeline company, an opinion which Black criticized as going "far toward scuttling the Natural Gas Act."

Reed's attitude toward the two political branches of the federal government was rather consistently deferential, motivated no doubt by a resolve not to repeat the errors of his predecessors who had tried to declare the New Deal unconstitutional. He avoided challenges to the exercise of executive power, the most dramatic of which during his tenure was President Truman's seizure of the steel mills in 1952 to guarantee the supply of munitions to American troops in Korea. The Court majority in *Youngstown Sheet & Tube Co.* v. *Sawyer,* 343 U.S. 579 (1952), held the President's action unauthorized, but Reed joined Vinson's dissent which charged the Court with adopting a "messenger boy" concept of the Presidency. Again, in *Ludecke* v. *Watkins,* 335 U.S. 160 (1948), Reed agreed with Frankfurter's refusal to review an executive order directing the deportation of an alien enemy after the war was over. When the Court, in *Peters* v. *Hobby,* 349 U.S. 331 (1955), challenged executive action in a federal employee loyalty case, Reed dissented on the ground that "a reasonable interpretation promptly adopted and long-continued by the President" should be respected by the courts.

Likewise, Reed's deference to Congress was manifested on numerous occasions. There were no serious challenges to the congressional power of investigation while he was on the Court, but there were some minor confrontations. When the Court undertook to enforce a quorum rule on committees in *Christoffel* v. *United States,* 338 U.S. 84 (1949), Reed dissented, as he also did in two 1955 cases—*Emspak* v. *United States,* 349 U.S. 190, and *Quinn* v. *United States,* 349 U.S. 155—where the Court majority upheld Fifth Amendment claimants before the House Un-American Activities Committee.

In *United States* v. *C.I.O.,* 335 U.S. 106 (1948), Reed recognized the

Court's obligation to construe congressional statutes so as to avoid the danger of unconstitutionality. Consequently he interpreted the Taft-Hartley ban on expenditures by labor unions in federal elections as not applying to the costs of political publications by unions, though the dissenters thought that by this interpretation Reed had rewritten and emasculated a "patently invalid" statute. Reed wrote a dissent, twice as long as Black's majority opinion, in *Toth* v. *Quarles,* 350 U.S. 11 (1955), protesting the Court's infringement on congressional power over army discipline.

In *United States* v. *Kahriger,* 345 U.S. 22 (1953), Reed supported a congressional statute levying a tax on the business of accepting wagers, against a charge that Congress was infringing on the police powers of the states. He agreed that Congress seemed more interested in suppressing wagering than in raising revenue by this measure, but he did not propose to question congressional motives. He concurred with Frankfurter's famous opinion in *Colegrove* v. *Green,* 328 U.S. 549 (1946), in which the Court was warned to stay out of the political thicket of legislative apportionment and leave the correction of malapportionment to Congress.

With his considerable experience in federal administrative agencies, Reed was by no means unfriendly to administrative law, as the *Rock Royal* decision demonstrated. In *Gray* v. *Powell,* 314 U.S. 402 (1941), he wrote a strong opinion upholding the power of an administrative agency to interpret its statutes. "Where as here a determination has been left to an administrative body, this delegation will be respected and the administrative conclusion left untouched." When the Court majority subjected proposed network broadcasting regulations of the Federal Communications Commission to judicial review in 1942, Reed joined Frankfurter's dissent. On the other hand, Reed did insist on broad judicial review of administrative action in *Switchmen's Union* v. *National Mediation Board,* 320 U.S. 297 (1943), and *Stark* v. *Wickard,* 321 U.S. 288 (1943). His opinion in the latter case Frankfurter criticized as based on the mistaken assumption that there is a common law of judicial review, and he could not reconcile this ruling with Reed's *Rock Royal* opinion.

Reed tended to take an extraordinarily favorable attitude toward organized labor. In *National Labor Relations Board* v. *Fansteel Metallurgical Corp.,* 306 U.S. 240 (1939), where striking workers had been discharged after a sit-down in the plant, Reed voted for their reinstatement. While he did not approve of the sit-down, he did not believe an employer had the power to bar employees from protection under the Labor Act. In *Bay Ridge Operating Co.* v. *Aaron,* 334 U.S. 446 (1948), he wrote an "overtime on overtime" opinion which was such a windfall for employees that Congress immediately amended the Fair Labor Standards Act to nullify the effects of the decision. In a series of decisions—*Apex Hosiery Co.* v. *Leader* 310 U.S. 469 (1940), *United States* v. *Hutcheson,* 312 U.S. 219 (1941), *Hunt* v. *Crumboch,* 325 U.S. 821 (1945)—he voted with the Court majority in refusing to use the Sherman Act against labor.

But Reed was no more enthusiastic about upholding convictions of business firms for violation of the antitrust laws. He tended to agree with Frankfurter in giving judicial precedents priority over enforcement of the Sherman Act. Noteworthy opinions written by Reed taking this position were *United States* v. *Line Material Co.,* 333 U.S. 287 (1948), *United States* v. *Columbia Steel Co.,* 334 U.S. 495 (1948), and *United States* v. *DuPont,* 351 U.S. 377 (1956).

No firm pattern emerges in Reed's adjudication of federal-state relations. In conflicts of jurisdiction between federal and state courts he rather consistently favored the powers of the federal judiciary, but in *Erie Railroad Co.* v. *Tompkins,* 304 U.S. 64 (1938), he concurred with the Court's reversal of a century of practice in a ruling that federal courts must enforce state law in diversity of citizenship cases. With characteristic caution, however, he would have achieved this result by statutory construction, avoiding the constitutional issue which Brandeis' opinion raised.

Reed limited state taxation as burdening interstate commerce in several significant opinions, such as *Best & Co.* v. *Maxwell,* 311 U.S. 454 (1940), and *Joseph* v. *Carter & Weekes Stevedoring Co.,* 330 U.S. 422 (1947). He joined the Court's opinion in *Southern Pacific Railroad* v. *Arizona,* 325 U.S. 761 (1945), holding that a state law limiting the length of trains was invalid as a burden on commerce. His opinion in *Cloverleaf Butter Co.* v. *Patterson,* 315 U.S. 148 (1942), was a rather striking denial of state regulatory power on the ground that federal regulation had occupied the field. But in *Thomas* v. *Collins,* 323 U.S. 516 (1945), he dissented from the Court's holding that the Wagner Act forbade Texas to license labor union organizers, and in *United States* v. *California,* 332 U.S. 19 (1947), his dissenting opinion upheld state ownership of the mineral resources under the coastal tidelands.

Reed's period on the Court covered the dawning of its determination to attack the scandal of Negro inequality. He was, of course, a member of the unanimous Court which in 1954 handed down the most portentous judicial ruling of the century, *Brown* v. *Board of Education,* 347 U.S. 483, declaring racial segregation in the public schools unconstitutional. But he had also been a consistent participant in earlier steps toward the constitutional goal of equal protection for the Negro. He wrote the opinion in *Morgan* v. *Virginia,* 328 U.S. 373 (1946), declaring unconstitutional racial segregation on motor carriers in interstate commerce, and in *Bob-Lo Excursion Co.* v. *Michigan,* 333 U.S. 28 (1948), he joined in enforcing a state anti-discrimination law even though foreign commerce was involved. He also wrote the opinion in *Railway Mail Association* v. *Corsi,* 326 U.S. 88 (1945), frustrating the attempt of a labor union to avoid complying with a state civil rights law. He joined the Court's opinions in *Missouri ex rel. Gaines* v. *Canada,* 305 U.S. 337 (1938), *McLaurin* v. *Oklahoma State Regents,* 339 U.S. 637 (1950), and *Sweatt* v. *Painter,* 339 U.S. 629 (1950), opening up graduate schools and law schools to Negroes. He wrote the opinion in *Smith* v. *Allwright,* 321 U.S. 649 (1944), declaring the southern institution of the "white primary" invalid. Incidentally, Chief Justice Stone had originally assigned the writing of the *Smith* opinion to Frankfurter, but

Jackson suggested that as a matter of tactics it would be preferable if the white primary was invalidated by a southerner, and so the case was reassigned to Reed.

It must be admitted, however, that Reed was not as much concerned with the discriminatory treatment of Japanese-Americans. He joined the decisions in *Hirabayashi* v. *United States,* 320 U.S. 81 (1943), and *Korematsu* v. *United States,* 323 U.S. 214 (1944), upholding the forced evacuation of Japanese-Americans from the West Coast at the beginning of World War II, and in *Takahashi* v. *Fish and Game Commission,* 334 U.S. 410 (1948), he dissented from the Court's invalidation of a California law denying aliens ineligible to citizenship the right to engage in commercial fishing.

Reed was a consistent supporter of the government in both hot and cold war prosecutions and in its general anti-subversion efforts. He voted to uphold treason convictions in *Cramer* v. *United States,* 325 U.S. 1 (1945), where he was in the minority, and in *Haupt* v. *United States,* 330 U.S. 631 (1947), where he was with the majority. In *Hartzel* v. *United States,* 322 U.S. 680 (1944), the defendant had written scurrilous pro-Nazi articles depicting American participation in the war as a betrayal of the country and had mailed them to army officers and draft registrants, but Murphy for the majority did not find the necessary specific intent to cause insubordination in the armed forces which the Espionage Act required. Reed wrote the dissent, contending that a jury could reasonably have concluded Hartzel's purpose was to undermine the will of soldiers to fight.

The two most important decisions affecting communists during Reed's tenure were *American Communications Association* v. *Douds,* 339 U.S. 382 (1950), and *Dennis* v. *United States,* 341 U.S. 494 (1951), in both of which he supported Chief Justice Vinson's majority view. *Douds* upheld the validity of the non-communist oath required of labor union officers by the Taft-Hartley Act. The *Dennis* case was the important Smith Act conviction of the leaders of the American Communist Party. In *Communist Party* v. *Subversive Activities Control Board,* 351 U.S. 115 (1956), the Court reversed a finding that the party was a "communist-action organization" because three of the government's witnesses had perjured themselves, but Reed joined in Clark's dissent contending that this was merely an excuse for delaying the decision on the status of the party. Reed agreed with the Court's refusal in *Dennis* v. *United States,* 339 U.S. 162 (1950), to invalidate the conviction of a communist because government employees served on the jury.

The Court majority ruled in *Pennsylvania* v. *Nelson,* 350 U.S. 497 (1956), that Congress in passing the Smith Act had preempted the field of protecting the United States against subversion, and consequently that a state sedition act was invalid. Reed wrote a dissent for three Justices, contending that the Court should not strike down state legislation on preemption grounds without a clear mandate from Congress, adding: "We are citizens of the United States and of the State wherein we reside and are dependent upon the strength of both to preserve our rights and liberties."

Reed wrote the opinion for the Court in *Carlson* v. *Landon,* 342 U.S. 524 (1952), where a five to four vote upheld a statute under which the Attorney General held in custody without bail all alien communists against whom deportation charges had been brought. He was with the majority in *Adler* v. *Board of Education,* 342 U.S. 485 (1952), which upheld a New York law requiring the removal of school teachers who belonged to organizations believing in the overthrow of the government by force and violence. He dissented, citing the *Adler* decision, in *Slochower* v. *Board of Higher Education,* 350 U.S. 551 (1956), where the Court by a five to four vote held it was a denial of due process to discharge a public employee because he had taken the Fifth Amendment before a Senate committee on questions covering his political associations.

Reed upheld the government in all the cases involving the loyalty-security program for federal employees. In *Joint Anti-Fascist Refugee Committee* v. *McGrath,* 341 U.S. 123 (1951), the majority ruled that the Attorney General's list of subversive organizations, which was set up to aid in making loyalty findings, had denied due process to the organizations included on it, but Reed wrote a dissent arguing that judicial relief was inappropriate because the listings had no legal effect, did not subject them to any punishment, nor deprive them of liberty of speech or other freedoms. When the Court reversed the discharge of federal employees who had been charged as security risks in *Peters* v. *Hobby,* 349 U.S. 331 (1956), and *Cole* v. *Young,* 351 U.S. 536 (1956), Reed dissented to both rulings.

Reed was not known for his devotion to civil liberties, but his degree of support for freedom of expression was rather surprising. On the Roosevelt Court attitudes tended to polarize around the opposing positions taken by Justices Black and Frankfurter. Black contended that freedom of expression enjoyed a preferred status among constitutional rights, and that judges had a special responsibility to guarantee its protection. Frankfurter, on the other hand, believed that the Court must treat all constitutional values equally and give due deference to the legislature's balancing of these rights in the practical adjustments it was called on to make.

Reed was on occasion to be found in either camp, illustrating the moderate role he played on the Court. He joined Black and Douglas in dissenting from Frankfurter's opinion upholding a "group libel" law in *Beauharnais* v. *Illinois,* 343 U.S. 250 (1952). Beauharnais had been convicted of violating this law by circulating on Chicago streets petitions to the city council containing defamatory and derogatory comments about Negroes. Reed contended that the statute was too vague and might permit "the punishment of incidents secured by the guarantee of free speech." Reed's vote made the Black-Douglas position prevail in the five to four decision of *Terminiello* v. *Chicago,* 337 U.S. 1 (1949), reversing the disorderly conduct conviction of an American fascist whose speech had provoked a riot. Reed agreed with Douglas that the ordinance under which the conviction had been secured was unconstitutional, because it made it a breach of the peace merely to "stir the public to anger" or "invite dispute."

Reed supported one of the distinctive doctrines of the Roosevelt Court, the denial to judges of the power to punish press criticism of judicial action as contempt of court. The leading case was *Bridges* v. *California,* 314 U.S. 252 (1941), where Black held for the five-judge majority that there must be a clear and present danger that such comments would obstruct justice before a contempt citation would be justified. In a subsequent case taking the same position, *Pennekamp* v. *Florida,* 328 U.S. 331 (1946), Reed wrote the opinion applying the *Bridges* rule and concluding that "the danger under this record to fair judicial administration has not the clearness and immediacy necessary to close the door of permissible public comment. When that door is closed, it closes all doors behind it."

Reed also found the Black-Douglas position on labor picketing more congenial than the Frankfurter view. *Thornhill* v. *Alabama,* 310 U.S. 88 (1940), was a unanimous opinion placing peaceful picketing under the protection of the free speech clause of the Constitution, but soon thereafter a split developed among the Justices concerning the extent of this protection. In *Milk Wagon Drivers Union* v. *Meadowmoor Dairies,* 312 U.S. 287 (1941), Frankfurter for the majority held that the *Thornhill* rule did not prevent a state court from enjoining all picketing in a labor dispute which had been so marred by past violence that the Court believed it was impossible for future picketing to be maintained on a peaceful basis. Reed dissented, saying that "the right to picket peacefully in industrial disputes is a recognized means for the marshaling of public opinion on the side of the worker."

The following year Reed joined Black, Douglas, and Murphy in protesting Frankfurter's opinion in *Carpenters and Joiners Union* v. *Ritter's Cafe,* 315 U.S. 722 (1942), which he contended had denied "orderly, regulated picketing" the protection of the Fourteenth Amendment. Reed dissented along with Minton in *International Brotherhood of Teamsters* v. *Hanke,* 339 U.S. 470 (1950), from a Frankfurter ruling which they contended was directed not at an abuse of picketing but at all picketing.

Reed was a vigorous opponent of censorship. He wrote the opinion in *Winters* v. *New York,* 333 U.S. 507 (1948), striking down a state law prohibiting the distribution of publications which featured stories of violent crime. In *Burstyn* v. *Wilson,* 343 U.S. 495 (1952), Reed concurred with Clark's opinion bringing motion pictures within the protection of the First Amendment and invalidating a New York censorship law on the ground that the statutory standards provided too vague a guide for the censors.

In two cases, *Kunz* v. *New York,* 340 U.S. 290 (1951), and *Niemotko* v. *Maryland,* 340 U.S. 268 (1951), Reed voted with the majority in holding unconstitutional licensing systems covering street preaching and meetings in a public park. In both situations the Court held that the public officials responsible for granting the permits were given too much discretion and were not controlled by adequate standards.

However, Reed upheld a licensing statute in *Poulos* v. *New Hampshire,* 345

U.S. 395 (1953), a case which demonstrates how his position on prior restraint differed from that of Black. This statute, he contended, did not permit officials to discriminate or use their discretion in granting licenses for speaking in public parks. Reed agreed that First Amendment rights had a preferred position, but that did not mean they were free from regulation. "Regulation and suppression are not the same, either in purpose or result, and courts of justice can tell the difference." Douglas and Black, dissenting, argued that a permit system, no matter how well administered, was incompatible with the Constitution.

Reed likewise disagreed with the absolutist position in several cases where prior restraint was imposed to protect rights of privacy. In *Martin* v. *Struthers,* 319 U.S. 141 (1943), Black struck down a city ordinance, intended to safeguard the daytime sleep of wartime night-shift workers, which made it unlawful to ring doorbells or knock on doors for the purpose of summoning the occupants to give them handbills or circulars. Reed would have upheld this "trivial town police regulation" which involved no censorship or suppression of ideas. He would defer to the judgment of the city council that this form of distribution of printed matter could be disturbing and irritating to householders.

Reed's position was later vindicated by the Court in *Breard* v. *Alexandria,* 341 U.S. 622 (1951), which upheld a city ordinance forbidding the visitation of private residences to solicit orders for the sale of goods without prior consent of the occupants; in the present case the law had been applied against solicitors for magazine subscriptions. Reed rejected the contention that this barrier was an interference with interstate commerce or free speech and press. These were commercial operations which a community might find to be a nuisance from which its residents should be protected.

The Hatch Act, forbidding political activity by federal civil servants, was upheld by a four to three vote in *United Public Workers* v. *Mitchell,* 330 U.S. 75 (1947). Reed wrote the majority opinion that this was not an unconstitutional invasion of the rights of free speech. "To declare that the present supposed evils of political activity are beyond the power of Congress to redress would leave the nation impotent to deal with what many sincere men believe is a material threat to the democratic system."

Reed had an important role in working out the Court's policy of permitting restrictions on the use of sound trucks. After dissenting in *Saia* v. *New York,* 334 U.S. 558 (1948), where Douglas for the majority invalidated a permit requirement covering the use of sound trucks, Reed wrote the Court's opinion in *Kovacs* v. *Cooper,* 336 U.S. 77 (1949), which substantially overruled *Saia* by upholding a city ordinance banning all sound amplifiers emitting loud and raucous noises from the city streets.

A final indication of where Reed drew the line on freedom of expression came in *Feiner* v. *New York,* 340 U.S. 315 (1951). A university student making a hot-headed speech on a street corner which had stirred up some opposition in the small crowd listening to him, was arrested by the police for disorderly conduct. Six Justices, including Reed, felt that they could not question the judgment of the police, which had been confirmed by the state courts, that there was likelihood of riot if the speaker continued.

The religion clauses of the First Amendment received their first serious consideration during Reed's period of service on the Court. The initial cases were brought principally by members of the Jehovah's Witnesses sect claiming denial of the free exercise of their religion. Reed was on the whole unsympathetic to their contentions. He was with the majority in *Minersville School District* v. *Gobitis,* 310 U.S. 586 (1940), in which the Court, with only Stone dissenting, ruled that a compulsory flag salute in the public schools was not a denial of religious freedom to children of Jehovah's Witnesses who believed the salute was forbidden by the Bible as bowing down to a graven image.

In *Jones* v. *Opelika,* 316 U.S. 584 (1942), Reed wrote the opinion for a five-judge majority upholding municipal license fees on transient merchants or book agents as applied to Jehovah's Witnesses engaged in the door-to-door peddling of religious tracts. When religious advocates resort to commercial methods to raise funds for religious propaganda, Reed said, it is natural and proper to subject them to the payment of a fee, "The First Amendment does not require a subsidy in the form of fiscal exemption."

Reed's disposition to deny exemption on religious grounds from the enforcement of non-discriminatory regulations or exactions was manifested in a number of subsequent decisions, often in dissent. The *Opelika* case itself was reversed in less than a year. A change in the Court's membership (Rutledge having replaced Byrnes) paved the way for an overturn of Reed's opinion in *Murdock* v. *Pennsylvania,* 319 U.S. 105 (1943), which held license fees on Jehovah's Witnesses' book sales invalid as a tax on the free exercise of religion. The new majority refused to regard the incidental collection of small sums for books and tracts as making this evangelism commercial, any more than passing the collection plate makes a church service commercial.

Reed's dissent in *Murdock* represented the first effort by any of the Justices to make a serious study of the intention of the framers of the First Amendment's religion provisions. He concluded that "the draftsmen of the amendments had in mind the practice of religion and the right to be heard, rather than the abridgement or interference with either by taxation in any form." He did not see how the Court could protect distribution of religious books from taxation without similarly protecting the distributors of all books and newspapers, for the Constitution protects both press and religion. When the Court repeated its *Murdock* holding in *Follett* v. *McCormick,* 321 U.S. 573 (1944), Reed concurred because this position was now "the law of the land," but he added that he still thought his *Opelika* decision was the correct one.

Reed again found it necessary to dissent when the Court reversed its *Gobitis* holding in the second flag salute case, *West Virginia State Board of Education* v. *Barnette,* 319 U.S. 624 (1943). The *Gobitis* decision had been little short of a disaster. It had helped to trigger nationwide persecution of Jehovah's Witnesses and its reasoning had been generally condemned by the press and legal commentators. In *Barnette* the Court reversed *Gobitis* by a vote of six to three, Jackson declaring that "compulsory unification of opinion achieves only the unanimity of the graveyard." Reed, however, maintained the position he had taken in *Gobitis* and, along with Roberts, joined Frankfurter's dissent.

In *Prince* v. *Massachusetts,* 321 U.S. 158 (1944), a member of the Witnesses had taken her nine-year-old niece along when she sold literature of the Witnesses on a Boston street corner at night, contrary to state law which forbade girls under eighteen to sell newspapers or other merchandise on the streets. Reed was part of the five-judge majority which held this statute to be a reasonable police regulation designed to protect the welfare of children, taking precedence over the competing claims of religious freedom.

Reed was not favorable to the position of conscientious objectors to war when their views involved them in conflict with general regulations. He wrote the opinion in *In re Summers,* 325 U.S. 561 (1945), where a conscientious objector had been refused admission to the bar in Illinois because the state constitution required military service of all able-bodied men. Reed denied that this action amounted to discrimination based on religious affiliation. He relied on two previous decisions upholding the right of Congress to bar from citizenship aliens who refused to pledge military service. One year later, when in *Girouard* v. *United States,* 328 U.S. 61 (1946), the Court overruled these two earlier decisions, Reed joined Stone and Frankfurter in dissent. They felt that Congress, not the Court, should change the law on this subject if it was to be changed.

Reed was perhaps the Court's most consistent advocate of a narrow interpretation of the establishment of religion clause. The Court's first such problem at the state level was *Everson* v. *Board of Education,* 330 U.S. 1 (1947), involving a New Jersey statute which authorized local school boards to reimburse parents for money expended to transport their children to public or Catholic schools. A taxpayer challenged the expenditure for Catholic school transportation as an establishment of religion. Reed joined Black in a five-judge majority opinion rejecting this contention and upholding the payments. Black agreed that the use of tax funds to support an institution which teaches the tenets of any church would be unconstitutional, but he regarded this program not as support of religion but as public welfare legislation like police or fire protection or the provision of sidewalks.

The next year in *McCollum* v. *Board of Education,* 333 U.S. 203 (1948), the Court found an educational practice which it could not approve. The public schools of Champaign, Illinois, operated a "released time" program of religious education under which pupils attended classes in Protestant, Catholic, or Jewish religious instruction during school hours and in the school building. The religious teachers were not paid by the schools, but were under the supervision of the school superintendents, and attendance was compulsory for participants in the program.

Reed was the sole member of the Court who saw no constitutional objection to this arrangement. To the rest of the Court it was clear that tax-supported school buildings were being used in disseminating religious doctrines, and the public school machinery was providing pupils for religious classes. Reed admitted that the establishment clause forbade aid to religion, but he did not interpret aid as covering "those incidental advantages that religious bodies, with other groups similarly situated, obtain as a by-product of organized society." He pointed to the fact that all churches receive aid from government in the form of tax exemption and numerous other advantages. The only aid which he understood the establishment clause to forbid was "purposeful assistance directly to the church itself or to some religious group or organization doing religious work of such a character that it may fairly be said to be performing ecclesiastical functions."

On general policy grounds, Reed noted that comparable programs of religious education in public schools were provided for in many states, and he felt that "this Court cannot be too cautious in upsetting practices embedded in our society by many years of experience." Perhaps the most quotable sentence in the dissent was aimed at Jefferson's warning of the necessity of maintaining a "wall of separation between church and state." Reed rejoined: "A rule of law should not be drawn from a figure of speech."

Reed's solitary dissent was destined to be vindicated. The *McCollum* decision was heavily criticized in church circles, and in fact was widely ignored as similar released time programs were continued in many cities. In 1952 the Court reconsidered the issue in *Zorach* v. *Clauson,* 343 U.S. 306 (1952), involving a New York program which differed from the one in Champaign only in that the religious classes were not held in the school buildings. Six Justices voted to uphold the New York program for reasons similar to those given in Reed's *McCollum* dissent. But Douglas, not Reed, was assigned to write the *Zorach* decision, and he endeavored to establish that *McCollum* was only being distinguished, not overruled. He also added a feature of questionable value. Where Reed's dissent had been strictly objective and had made no effort to justify practices of church-state cooperation, Douglas inserted in his opinion such value-laden observations as that Americans "are a religious people whose institutions presuppose a Supreme Being," and that acts of cooperation between church and state represent "the best of our traditions."

In *Kedroff* v. *St. Nicholas Cathedral of Russian Orthodox Church,* 344 U.S. 94 (1952), the New York legislature had sought to free the members of the Russian Orthodox Church in America from control by the Moscow church authorities by making them subject to an autonomous Russian Church in America. Applying general principles of religious liberty, Reed held for the Court that the New York law transferring control over church property from one group of persons to another was an inadmissible use of state power.

A final issue on which Reed took a significant position was the extent to which the standards for criminal prosecutions in the Fourth through the Eighth Amendments were to be enforced on the states. Reed's general view on criminal prosecutions was summed up in this comment from *McNabb* v. *United States,* 318 U.S. 332 (1943): "I am opposed to broadening the possibilities of defendants escaping punishment by these more rigorous technical requirements in the administration of justice." This was one area in which the Court during Reed's tenure largely resisted changes in the established constitutional doctrines, and Reed was one of the traditionalists. It was not until after his retirement that a startling overruling of precedents, which he would undoubtedly have disapproved, brought the state courts under the same constitutional obligations as the federal courts.

From the time of *Hurtado* v. *California,* 110 U.S. 516 (1884), the Court's consistent position had been that the Fourteenth Amendment did not automatically incorporate the Bill of Rights and make all its provisions applicable to the states. In the area of criminal justice the states were thus free to adopt practices contrary to those specified for federal courts. Justice Reed was the spokesman for this tradition in what was to be the last of its landmark decisions, *Adamson* v. *California,* 332 U.S. 46 (1947). For a five-judge majority he argued that the self-incrimination rule of the Fifth Amendment was not binding on the states, and consequently the failure of a defendant to take the stand to explain or deny evidence against him could be commented on by the trial judge and be considered by the court and jury.

Claims that confessions were involuntarily extracted from suspects were less likely to convince Reed than any other member of the Court. In the *McNabb* case a confession had been secured by federal agents who questioned two suspects about a murder for a period of two days. The Court held the confession invalid because the men had not been brought before a judicial officer for arraignment "without unnecessary delay" as required by statute. Reed was the sole member of the Court to dissent. He believed the only test for the admissibility of a confession was whether it was given voluntarily or not, and he opposed adding any more "technical" requirements. In *Gallegos* v. *Nebraska,* 342 U.S. 55 (1951), and *Brown* v. *Allen,* 344 U.S. 443 (1953), he wrote the opinions upholding confessions secured during suspiciously long periods between arrest and arraignment.

Reed did agree in *Ashcraft* v. *Tennessee,* 322 U.S. 143 (1944), that a confession secured after a 36-hour period of questioning of a suspect held incommunicado by the police was not voluntary. However, he took a harder line thereafter. Between 1945 and 1953, in six five to four decisions where the Court threw out confessions on the ground that they were obtained by mental coercion, Reed was always in the dissenting minority.

Reed was a member of the majority for Frankfurter's holding, in the important case of *Wolf* v. *Colorado,* 338 U.S. 25 (1949), that unreasonable searches and seizures are unconstitutional in the states, but that illegally seized evidence can still be used to convict in state courts. He continued to support this position in *Irvine* v. *California,* 347 U.S. 128 (1954), in which five Justices held evidence acceptable which had been secured by police breaking into a house, planting a microphone in the bedroom, and listening to all the conversations for a period of a month. Interestingly, Frankfurter was one of the four dissenters in *Irvine* and condemned this procedure as contrary to "elementary standards of justice."

Reed was part of the majority in *Betts* v. *Brady,* 316 U.S. 455 (1942), which held that in non-capital cases counsel need not be provided for a defendant if he was unable to secure legal assistance himself. In 1945 Reed wrote the opinion in *Louisiana ex rel. Francis* v. *Resweber,* 329 U.S. 459, holding that it would not be double jeopardy or cruel and unusual punishment to send to the electric chair for a second time a condemned prisoner after the chair had failed to work the first time. In *Stein* v. *New York,* 346 U.S. 156 (1953), he joined Jackson's ruling that, even though evidence not constitutionally admissible had been used in a trial, the defendant was not entitled to a new trial if the state could show that there was sufficient other evidence to justify the jury in finding guilt.

It is not easy to label Reed. He tended to be an economic liberal and a civil rights conservative. He believed in governmental power to regulate the economy and to protect labor's position, but not to the extent that Black did. He believed in judicial restraint and deference to legislatures, but not to the extent that Frankfurter did. He was more inclined than either to favor the government and public order against the claims of the individual in the various situations where such a confrontation was presented.

This characteristic was most clearly evident in Reed's reluctance to grant any new constitutional protections to defendants in criminal cases, and in rejecting the constitutional contentions of aliens and radicals. His overall record of support for civil liberties was one of the lowest on the Court. Between 1941 and 1946 on the Roosevelt Court, Reed was only slightly less liberal than the Court majority in economic controversies, but in personal liberty cases he was substantially less favorable than the majority. During the seven terms of the Vinson Court from 1946 to 1953, out of 113 non-unanimous civil liberties decisions, the Court decided thirty-five per cent favorably to the liberty claimed, but Reed voted favorably in only thirteen per cent.

An analysis of voting alignments in non-unanimous decisions shows that on the Roosevelt Court Reed was somewhat more likely to vote with Frankfurter than with Black, but his closest alignment was with Stone during the latter's last two years as Chief Justice. From 1946 to 1949 Reed was a rather consistent member of a three-judge bloc along with Vinson and Burton at the center of the Court, a grouping which Minton and Clark joined on their appointment to the Court in 1949. On the Warren Court Reed maintained his closest ties with Minton and Burton.

By way of summary, two major themes can be distinguished in Reed's decisions. One was a belief in government and organization. For Reed big government was not an evil, and organization was not to be feared. He had no romantic Jeffersonian notions about rugged individualism. Just as tobacco farmers had to organize in a cooperative to market their product, so citizens had to have a strong central government to deal with the depression. At a time when the American business and professional class still largely thought that the best government was the least government and regarded "that man in the White House" as a wild-eyed radical, it was most important that the case for equipping the government with adequate powers for economic control and social welfare should be stated by a man with the soberly conservative instincts of Stanley Reed. The problem created by his devotion to the public philosophy was that it tended to make him insensitive to the claims of aberrant individuals or groups, and this largely accounted for his general negativism on so many civil liberties issues.

The second thread running through Reed's decisions is that of judicial restraint. As a judge he did not think he should dictate to the President or Congress. He accepted the Holmes weak-judiciary–strong-legislature formula. Neither did he want to interfere with state or local autonomy, except in so far as it was necessary to safeguard federal powers of regulation and taxation. He would leave the states free to adopt their own versions of fair criminal procedures, and he would leave the localities free to decide how much religion they wanted in their schools. Here too the individual might suffer as a result. But Reed had no social philosophy to promote. He was a legal craftsman who believed in giving the political branches of government the power and the responsibility for governing.

SELECTED BIBLIOGRAPHY

The principal studies of Justice Reed are by F. William O'Brien, *Justice Reed and the First Amendment* (Washington, 1958); Mark J. Fitzgerald, *Justice Reed: A Study of a Center Judge*. Unpublished doctoral dissertation (University of Chicago, 1950); and Wesley McCune, *The Nine Young Men* (New York, 1947) chapter 6. Justice Reed's position on the Court in relation to his colleagues is examined in two books by C. Herman Pritchett, *The Roosevelt Court: A Study in Judicial Politics and Values, 1937–1947* (New York, 1948) and *Civil Liberties and the Vinson Court* (Chicago, 1954).

Stanley Reed

REPRESENTATIVE OPINIONS

UNITED STATES v. ROCK ROYAL COOPERATIVE, 307 U.S. 568 (1939)

The basic statute embodying the New Deal agricultural program, the Agricultural Adjustment Act of 1933, was held unconstitutional by the Supreme Court in *United States* v. *Butler,* 297 U.S. 1 (1936). Congress then reenacted the principal features of the 1933 act in a series of new laws. One of these, the Agricultural Marketing Agreement Act of 1937, provided for control of the marketing of certain commodities through marketing agreements and orders issued by the Secretary of Agriculture. The Secretary issued an order under this statute regulating the handling of milk in the New York metropolitan area, and *United States* v. *Rock Royal Cooperative* involved an action filed by the United States against a milk cooperative to enforce compliance with provisions of the order.

Mr. Justice Reed for the Court upheld the constitutionality of the act against contentions that the statute involved unconstitutional regulation and price fixing of local commerce or that it amounted to an unconstitutional delegation of legislative power. Justices Black and Douglas concurred in the opinion. Justices McReynolds, Butler, and Roberts dissented, while Chief Justice Hughes dissented in part. *H. P. Hood and Sons* v. *United States,* 307 U.S. 588 (1939), was a companion case.

MR. JUSTICE REED delivered the opinion of the Court:

* * *

II Constitutionality of the Act.

A. *Minimum Prices.* The Act authorizes and the Order undertakes the fixing of minimum prices for the purchase of milk "in the current of interstate or foreign commerce, or which directly burdens, obstructs, or affects, interstate or foreign commerce" in milk.[36] There is no challenge to the fact that the milk of all four defendants reaches

[36] *§ 8c (1).*

the marketing area through the channels of interstate commerce. Nor is any question raised as to the power of the Congress to regulate the distribution in the area of the wholly intrastate milk. It is recognized that the federal authority covers the sales of this milk, as its marketing is inextricably intermingled with and directly affects the marketing in the area of the milk which moves across state lines.[37]

The challenge is to the regulation "of the price to be paid upon the sale by a dairy farmer who delivers his milk to some country plant." It is urged that the sale, a local transaction, is fully completed before any interstate commerce begins and that the attempt to fix the price or other elements of that incident violates the Tenth Amendment. But where commodities are bought for use beyond state lines, the sale is a part of interstate commerce.[38] We have likewise held that where sales for interstate transportation were commingled with intrastate transactions, the existence of the local activity did not interfere with the federal power to regulate inspection of the whole.[39] Activities conducted within state lines do not by this fact alone escape the sweep of the Commerce Clause. Interstate commerce may be dependent upon them.[40] Power to establish quotas for interstate marketing gives power to name quotas for that which is to be left within the state of production.[41] Where local and foreign milk alike are drawn into a general plan for protecting the interstate commerce in the commodity from the interferences, burdens and obstructions, arising from excessive surplus and the social and sanitary evils of low values, the power of the Congress extends also to the local sales.

This power over commerce when it exists is complete and perfect.[42] It has been exercised to fix a wage scale for a limited period,[43] railroad tariffs[44] and fees and charges for live-stock exchanges.[45]

The authority of the Federal Government over interstate commerce does not differ in extent or character from that retained by the states over intrastate commerce. Since *Munn* v. *Illinois,* this Court has had occasion repeatedly to give consideration to the action of states in regulating prices.[46] Recently, upon a reëxamination of the grounds of state power over prices, that power was phrased by this Court to mean that "upon proper occasion and by appropriate measures the state may regulate a business in any of its aspects, including the prices to be charged for the products or commodities it sells."[47]

The power of a state to fix the price of milk has been adjudicated by this Court.[48] The people of great cities depend largely upon an adequate supply of pure fresh milk. So essential is it for health that the consumer has been willing to forego unrestricted competition from low cost territory to be assured of the producer's compliance with sanitary requirements, as enforced by the municipal health authorities. It belongs to that category of commodities that for

[37] Stafford *v.* Wallace, *258 U.S. 495;* Chicago Board of Trade *v.* Olsen, *262 U.S. 1;* Houston & Texas Ry. Co. *v.* United States, *234 U.S. 342, 351–2;* Minnesota Rate Cases, *230 U.S. 352, 399;* Labor Board Cases, *301 U.S. 1;* Currin *v.* Wallace, *306 U.S. 1;* Mulford *v.* Smith, ante, *p. 38;* National Labor Relations Board *v.* Fainblatt, *306 U.S. 601.*

[38] Dahnke-Walker Milling Co. *v.* Bondurant, *257 U.S. 282, 290, 291;* Lemke *v.* Farmers' Grain Co., *258 U.S. 50, 54; cf.* Foster-Fountain Packing Co. *v.* Haydel, *278 U.S. 1, 10.*

[39] Currin *v.* Wallace, *306 U.S. 1.*

[40] Consolidated Edison Co. *v.* National Labor Relations Board, *305 U.S. 197, 220.*

[41] Mulford *v.* Smith, supra, *note 37.*

[42] Gibbons *v.* Ogden, *9 Wheat. 1, 196;* Minnesota Rate Cases, *230 U.S. 352, 398.*

[43] Wilson *v.* New, *243 U.S. 332, 346.*

[44] *34 Stat. 589, 49 U.S.C. § 15 (1).*

[45] Tagg Bros. & Moorhead *v.* United States, *280 U.S. 420;* Stafford *v.* Wallace, *258 U.S. 495.*

[46] Munn *v.* Illinois, *94 U.S. 113;* Budd *v.* New York, *143 U.S. 517;* Brass *v.* North Dakota, *153 U.S. 391;* German Alliance Insurance Co. *v.* Lewis, *233 U.S. 389;* O'Gorman & Young *v.* Hartford Insurance Co., *282 U.S. 251;* Nebbia *v.* New York, *291 U.S. 502;* West Coast Hotel Co. *v.* Parrish, *300 U.S. 379;* Townsend *v.* Yeomans, *301 U.S. 441.*

Wolff Packing Co. *v.* Industrial Court, *262 U.S. 522;* Tyson & Bro. *v.* Banton, *273 U.S. 418;* Fairmont Creamery Co. *v.* Minnesota, *274 U.S. 1;* Ribnik *v.* McBride, *277 U.S. 350;* Williams *v.* Standard Oil Co., *278 U.S. 235.*

[47] Nebbia *v.* New York, *291 U.S. 502, 537.*

[48] Id.

many years has been subjected to the regulatory power of the state. A thorough exposition of the milk situation in the New York shed was made in the *Nebbia* case. There is nothing to add to what was there said, save to point out that since that decision, we have held that a state cannot prohibit the sale of imported milk where the extra-state purchase price was below the prescribed minimum[49] and that a Pennsylvania regulatory law, including minimum prices, applied in the absence of federal legislation to milk purchased in Pennsylvania for shipment into the New York marketing area.[50] In *Hegeman Farms Corp.* v. *Baldwin,*[51] this Court sustained again the New York Milk Control Statute against the complaint that the price limits were arbitrary. A variation in prices to be charged the consumer between dealers who had and dealers who had not well advertised trade names was upheld.[52] The power enjoyed by the states to regulate the prices for handling and selling commodities within their internal commerce[53] rests with the Congress in the commerce between the states.

B. *Equalization Pool.*—In order to equalize the prices received by producers, handlers are required to clear their purchases through the producer settlement fund. Payments into and withdrawals from this fund depend upon the "value" of the milk received which is fixed by the Order at different prices governed by the use made by the handler of the purchased milk and upon whether his obligations to producers are greater or less than the uniform price due the producers under the scheme. The result of the use of the device of an equalization pool is that each producer, dealing with a proprietary handler, gets a uniform or weighted average price for his milk, with differentials for quality, location or other usual market variations, irrespective of the manner of its use. The Act, § 8c (5) (B) (ii) and (C) and the Order, Articles IV, VI and VII, authorize such an adjustment.

The defendants' objection to the equalization pool, here considered, is not to the disbursements from the fund for expenses of standby or marketing services authorized by Article VII, §§ 5 and 6, concerning which we hold the handler has no standing to complain. It is to the alleged deprivation of liberty and property accomplished by the pooling requirement in taking away from the defendants their right to acquire milk from their patrons at the minimum class price, according to its use, and forcing the handlers to pay their surplus, over the uniform price, to the equalization pool instead of to their patrons. This argument assumes the validity of price regulation, as such, but denies the constitutionality of the pooling arrangement because handlers are not at liberty to pay the producer in accordance with the use of the producer's milk but must distribute the surplus to others whose milk was resold less advantageously. It is urged that to carry this principle of contribution to its logical conclusion would mean that the wages of the employed should be shared with the unemployed; the highly paid, with the underpaid; and the receipts of the able, the fortunate and the diligent, with the incompetent, the unlucky and the drone.

No such exaggerated equalization of wealth and opportunity is proposed. The pool is only a device reasonably adapted to allow regulation of the interstate market upon terms which minimize the results of the restrictions. It is ancillary to the price regulation designed, as is the price provision, to foster, protect and encourage interstate commerce by smoothing out the difficulties of the surplus and cut-throat competition which burdened this marketing. In *Mulford* v. *Smith,*[54] we made it clear that volume of commodity movement might be controlled or discouraged. As the Congress would have, clearly, the right to permit only limited amounts of milk to move in interstate commerce, we are of the opinion it might permit the movement on terms of pool settlement here provided.

Common funds for equalizing risks are not unknown and have not been considered violative of due process. The pooling principle was upheld in workmen's compensation,[55] bank deposit insurance,[56] and distri-

[49] Baldwin *v.* Seelig, *294 U.S. 511.*
[50] Milk Control Board *v.* Eisenberg Farm Products, *306 U.S. 346.*
[51] *293 U.S. 163.*
[52] Borden's Co. *v.* Ten Eyck, *297 U.S. 251.*
[53] Nebbia *v.* New York, *291 U.S. 502;* Townsend *v.* Yeomans, *301 U.S. 441.*
[54] Supra, *note 37.*
[55] Mountain Timber Co. *v.* Washington, *243 U.S. 219;* New York Central R. Co. *v.* White, *243 U.S. 188.*
[56] Noble State Bank *v.* Haskell, *219 U.S. 104;* Abie State Bank *v.* Bryan, *282 U.S. 765.*

bution of benefits in the Transportation Act.[57]

The defendants rely particularly upon *Thompson* v. *Consolidated Gas Utilities Corp.*,[58] and *Railroad Retirement Board* v. *Alton R. Co.*[59] In the *Thompson* case, the Texas Railroad Commission ordered proration of gas production in the Panhandle. It was assumed that proration to prevent waste and protect correlative rights in a pool was valid but it was held that the proration order in issue was for none of these purposes. It was for the "sole purpose . . . to compel those [with market outlets] . . . to purchase gas from potential producers" who have no market. This was not deemed to be reasonably related to the conservation of gas or the protection of correlative rights. In the *Retirement Board* case, the pooling principle was involved but was found to be invalid because the burdens on the roads were not equalized with the benefits. Entry on service was made at different age levels for different roads. Employees seventy or older were required to retire. Some roads had none. Solvent and insolvent roads were liable alike. All carriers were treated as a single employer. It was these provisions, deemed unequal, which led to the conclusion that the manner of pooling of funds denied due process. In this case, the pooling has differentials to cover the variations of quality and location.

C. *Delegation.*—There are three issues of delegation presented: (1) the delegation of authority to the Secretary of Agriculture to establish marketing areas; (2) the delegation of authority to producers to approve a marketing order without an agreement of handlers; and (3) the delegation of authority to coöperatives to cast the votes of producer patrons.

From the earliest days the Congress has been compelled to leave to the administrative officers of the government authority to determine facts which were to put legislation into effect and the details of regulations which would implement the more general enactments. It is well settled, therefore, that it is no argument against the constitutionality of an act to say that it delegates broad powers to executives to determine the details of any legislative scheme. This necessary authority has never been denied.[60] In dealing with legislation involving questions of economic adjustment, each enactment must be considered to determine whether it states the purpose which the Congress seeks to accomplish and the standards by which that purpose is to be worked out with sufficient exactness to enable those affected to understand these limits. Within these tests the Congress needs specify only so far as is reasonably practicable.[61] The present Act, we believe, satisfies these tests.

1. *Delegation to the Secretary of Agriculture.*—The purpose of the Act is "to establish and maintain such orderly marketing conditions for agricultural commodities in interstate commerce as will establish prices to farmers at a level that will give agricultural commodities a purchasing power with respect to articles that farmers buy, equivalent to the purchasing power of agricultural commodities in the base period." To accomplish this, the Secretary of Agriculture is directed to issue orders, whenever he has reason to believe the issuance of an order will tend to effectuate the declared policy of the act. Unlike the language of the National Industrial Recovery Act condemned in the *Schechter* case, page 538, the tests here to determine the purpose and the powers dependent upon that conclusion are defined. In the Recovery Act the Declaration of Policy was couched in most general terms.[62] In this Act it is to restore

57 New England Divisions Case, *261 U.S. 184;* Dayton Goose Creek Ry. *v.* United States, *263 U.S. 456.*

58 *300 U.S. 55, 77, 78.*

59 *295 U.S. 330, 355 et seq.*

60 Panama Refining Co. *v.* Ryan, *293 U.S. 388, 421;* Schechter Corp. *v.* United States, *295 U.S. 495, 529;* Currin *v.* Wallace, *306 U.S. 1.*

61 Buttfield *v.* Stranahan, *192 U.S. 470, 496;* United States *v.* Chemical Foundation, *272 U.S. 1, 12;* Monongahela Bridge Co. *v.* United States, *216 U.S. 177, 193;* United States *v.* Grimaud, *220 U.S. 506, 516;* Avent *v.* United States, *266 U.S. 127, 130.*

62 *"Section 1. A national emergency productive of widespread unemployment and disorganization of industry, which burdens interstate and foreign commerce, affects the public welfare, and undermines the standards of living of the American people, is hereby declared to exist. It is hereby declared to be the policy of Congress to remove obstructions to the free flow of interstate and foreign commerce which tend to diminish the amount thereof; and to provide for the general welfare by promoting the organization of industry for the purpose of*

parity prices, § 2. Under the Recovery Act, general welfare might be sought through codes of any industry, formulated to express standards of fair competition for the businesses covered. Here the terms of orders are limited to the specific provisions, minutely set out in § 8c (5) and (7). While considerable flexibility is provided by § 8c (7) (D), it gives opportunity only to include provisions auxiliary to those definitely specified.

The Secretary is not permitted freedom of choice as to the commodities which he may attempt to aid by an order. The Act, § 8c (2), limits him to milk, fresh fruits except apples, tobacco, fresh vegetables, soybeans and naval stores. The Act authorizes a marketing agreement and order to be issued for such production or marketing regions or areas as are practicable. A city milkshed seems homogeneous. This standard of practicality is a limit on the power to issue orders. It determines when an order may be promulgated.

It is further to be observed that the Order could not be and was not issued until after the hearing and findings as required by § 8c (4). Public hearings were held at Albany, Malone, Syracuse, Elmira, and New York from May 16 to June 7, 1938, with four days' recess. Nearly three thousand pages of testimony were introduced, eighty-eight documentary exhibits and some twenty briefs by interested parties were filed. On July 23, 1938, the Secretary, in the Federal Register, notified the public of his findings and the terms of the Order and again invited comment. Numerous parties again filed briefs. A right by statute is given handlers to object to the Secretary to any provision of an order as not "in accordance with law," with the privilege of appeal to the courts. § 8c (15) (A) and (B). Even though procedural safeguards cannot validate an unconstitutional delegation, they do furnish protection against an arbitrary use of properly delegated authority.[63]

A further provision of the Act is to be noted as it was employed as a standard to determine the minimum price. This is § 8c (18). Acting under this section, the Secretary fixed a fluctuating minimum price based upon wholesale butter prices in New York. While it is true that the determination of price under this section has a less definite standard than the parity tests of §§ 2 and 8e, we cannot say that it is beyond the power of the Congress to leave this determination to a designated administrator, with the standards named. The Secretary must have first determined the prices in accordance with § 2 and § 8e, that is, the prices that will give the commodity a purchasing power equivalent to that of the base period, considering the price and supply of feed and other pertinent economic conditions affecting the milk market in the area. If he finds the price so determined unreasonable, it is to be fixed at a level which will reflect such factors, provide adequate quantities of wholesome milk and be in the public interest. This price cannot be determined by mathematical formula but the standards give ample indications of the various factors to be considered by the Secretary.

2. *Delegation to Producers.*—Under § 8c (9) (B) of the Act it is provided that any order shall become effective notwithstanding the failure of 50 percent of the handlers to approve a similar agreement, if the Secretary of Agriculture with the approval of the President determines, among other things, that the issuance of the order is approved by two-thirds of the producers interested or by interested producers of two-thirds of the volume produced for the market of the specified production area. By subsection 19 it is provided that for the purpose of ascertaining whether the issuance of such order is approved "the Secretary may conduct a referendum among producers." The objection is made that this is an unlawful delegation to producers of the legislative power to put an order into effect in a market. In considering this question, we must assume that the Congress had the power to put this Order into effect without the approval of anyone. Whether producer approval by election is necessary or not, a question we reserve, a requirement of such

cooperative action among trade groups, to induce and maintain united action of labor and management under adequate governmental sanctions and supervision, to eliminate unfair competitive practices, to promote the fullest possible utilization of the present productive capacity of industries, to avoid undue restriction of production (except as may be temporarily required), to increase the consumption of industrial and agricultural products by increasing purchasing power, to reduce and relieve unemployment, to improve standards of labor, and otherwise to rehabilitate industry and to conserve natural resources." 48 Stat. 195.

[63] *Cf.* Schechter Corp. *v.* United States, *295 U.S. at 533.*

approval would not be an invalid delegation.[64]

3. *Authorization of Coöperatives to Cast the Votes of Producer Patrons.*—This objection, too, falls before the answering argument that inasmuch as Congress could place the Order in effect without any vote, it is permissible for it to provide for approval or disapproval in such way or manner as it may choose.

Coöperatives in the Equalization Fund.—The defendant, Central New York Coöperative Association, denies liability under Articles VI, VII and VIII of the Order on the ground that it is not liable to pay its net pool obligation into the administrative fund or to meet the expenses of administration. The asserted reason for its freedom from liability is that it is a coöperative composed of milk producers and distributes the milk of its members and others as agent.

The coöperative owns no farms. Its members are diary farmers. By their contract they agree "to deliver . . . all . . . milk produced . . . which said milk is to be marketed and distributed by the [coöperative] . . ." The latter "agrees to pay . . . for the milk . . . a price . . . based upon the amount received . . . less the expenses . . ." Nonmembers' milk is marketed under the same contract. The coöperative leases receiving and distributing facilities from a business corporation. The milk is received by the coöperative at receiving plants and shipped to the city depot. It distributes through other business corporations which are wholly-owned subsidiaries of the coöperative. These distributing subsidiaries use the leased physical facilities under verbal contracts with the coöperative. The coöperative receives the net amount from the sales and distributes to its patrons under license from the Director of the Division of Milk Control of New York permitting the marketing in the manner described.

Section 8c (5) (A) authorizes an order to classify milk and fix minimum prices which all handlers shall pay for milk purchased from producers. Section 8c (5) (C) authorizes the equalization pool and the handlers' payment to this settlement fund. It is urged that coöperatives which merely act as agents for their members are not included in handlers purchasing from producers. This is said to be definitely shown by the provisions of § 8c (5) (F) providing that nothing contained in the subsection shall be construed to prevent a Capper-Volstead coöperative from making distribution to its "producers in accordance with the contract." The Order defines a handler as including a coöperative association "with respect to any milk received from producers at any plant operated by such association or with respect to any milk which it causes to be delivered" to other handlers. Under the provisions of the Order, Article VII, § § 8 and 9, coöperative handlers as other handlers equalize their purchases by payment into the producer settlement fund, even though they are not required to pay the uniform price to their producers by reason of the exception of Article VII, § 1, and the provisions of § 8c (5) (F), as explained at page 561.

Coöperative contracts are of two general types, sale and agency.[65] The Central New York Coöperative operates under the agency type.

It is obvious that the use of the word "purchased" in the Act, § 8c (5) (A) and (C), would not exclude the "sale" type of coöperative. When § 8c (5) (F) was drawn, however, it was made to apply to both the "sale" and "agency" type without distinction. This would indicate there had been no intention to distinguish between the two types by (A) and (C). The section which authorizes all orders, § 8c (1), makes no distinction. The orders are to be applicable to "processors, associations of producers, and others engaged in the handling" of commodities. The reports on the bill show no effort to differentiate.[66] Neither do the debates in Congress. The statutory provisions for equalization of the burdens of surplus would be rendered nugatory by the exception of "agency" coöperatives. The administrative construction has been to include such organizations as handlers.[67] With this we agree. As here used the word "purchased" means "acquired for marketing." Subsection (A) cannot be construed as freeing agents, coöperative or proprietary, from the requirement to account at the minimum prices for milk handled.

As a corollary the contention is made also by Central Coöperative that no coöp-

[64] Currin *v.* Wallace, *306 U.S. 1, 15.*

[65] *Hanna, Law of Coöperative Marketing Associations, pp. 210, 256.*

[66] *House Report No. 1241, 74th Cong., 1st Sess.; Senate Report No. 1011, 74th Cong., 1st Sess.*

[67] Costanzo *v.* Tillinghast, *287 U.S. 341, 345;* United States *v.* Chicago North Shore R. Co., *288 U.S. 1, 13–14.*

erative may be required to pay its surplus receipts over uniform prices into the equalization fund. This, too, is based upon a construction of § 8c (5) (F) as permitting a coöperative to make settlement with its members in accordance with the terms of its own contract with them. If the coöperative members were freed of the burden of carrying their proportion of milk going to manufacturing use, the discrimination in their favor would be most strongly marked. Such a construction is not required. Coöperatives are covered by § 8c (1) and (5) (A) and (B), and by the provisions of the Order, except as to the payment of the uniform price. Any payments below the uniform price fall on their members. We are of the view that the administrative construction is correct and that the "net proceeds" of (F) refer to the result of the coöperative sales in the marketing area after complying with the equalization requirements.

The defendant, Central New York Coöperative Association, raises for itself a final point. In determining the net pool obligation of any handler for milk received from producers,[68] the handler is authorized to subtract pro rata out of each class from the milk involved in the pool "the quantity of milk received from the handler's own farm." We have determined that this coöperative, though marketing milk under an agency contract with its members, is a handler subject to the Act and Order. The coöperative argues that as its members, farmers, would not need to account to the pool for their personal sales to consumers, the coöperative, being utilized as an agent to market the farmers' milk, is under no obligation to contribute to equalization. As the coöperative does not have its own farm but is itself a handler under the Act, it must pay into the producer settlement fund.

Inasmuch as all the defendants in these appeals are handling milk in interstate commerce, the petition for the enforcement of Official Order No. 126, issued under c. 383 of the Laws of 1937 of the State of New York, concerning milk not covered by Order No. 27 of the Secretary of Agriculture, should be dismissed.

The order of the District Court in Nos. 771, 827 and 828 is reversed and the causes are remanded to that Court with instructions to enter an order specifically enforcing up to the time of suspension the provisions of Order No. 27, issued by the Secretary of Agriculture August 15, 1938, regulating the handling of milk in the New York marketing area, as to all the defendants and enjoining defendants, their officers, agents and servants, from further violation of the Order.

The order of the District Court in dismissing the petition of Holton V. Noyes, as Commissioner of Agriculture and Markets of the State of New York, is affirmed.

[68] *Article VI, § 1.*

McNABB v. UNITED STATES, 318 U.S. 347 (1943)

In the 1930's the Supreme Court began to develop a heightened concern for enforcing stricter procedural safeguards in criminal prosecutions. Outstanding illustrations were the two Scottsboro cases, *Powell* v. *Alabama,* 287 U.S. 45 (1932), guaranteeing right to counsel in capital cases, and *Norris* v. *Alabama,* 294 U.S. 587 (1935), invalidating convictions where there was racial discrimination in jury selection. Another important example was *Brown* v. *Mississippi,* 297 U.S. 278 (1936), voiding a conviction secured on the basis of a confession extorted by force.

McNabb v. *United States* presented the issue of the voluntary character of confessions used in securing convictions in federal court. Several Tennessee mountaineers suspected of the murder of a federal revenue agent had been held in custody by federal officers and questioned over a period of two days, without the aid of friends or benefit of counsel, until confessions were secured. The Supreme Court, through Mr. Justice Frankfurter, acting on the basis of its power to establish and maintain civilized standards of procedure and evidence in the federal courts, held that the failure of the arresting officers to take the suspects promptly before a committing officer for arraignment, as required by federal statute, rendered the subsequent confessions inadmissible as evidence. This holding made it unnecessary for the Court to consider whether the confessions were involuntary under the Fifth Amendment. Mr. Justice Rutledge did not participate in the decision. Mr. Justice Reed was the sole dissenter.

MR. JUSTICE REED, dissenting:

I find myself unable to agree with the opinion of the Court in this case. An officer of the United States was killed while in the performance of his duties. From the circumstances detailed in the Court's opinion, there was obvious reason to suspect that the petitioners here were implicated in firing the fatal shot from the dark. The arrests followed. As the guilty parties were known only to the McNabbs who took part in the assault at the burying ground, it was natural and proper that the officers would question them as to their actions.[1]

The cases just cited show that statements made while under interrogation may be used at a trial if it may fairly be said that the information was given voluntarily. A frank and free confession of crime by the culprit affords testimony of the highest credibility and of a character which may be verified easily. Equally frank responses to officers by innocent people arrested under misapprehension give the best basis for prompt discharge from custody. The realization of the convincing quality of a confession tempts officials to press suspects unduly for such statements. To guard accused persons against the danger of being forced to confess, the law admits confessions of guilt only when they are voluntarily made. While the connotation of voluntary is indefinite, it affords an understandable label under which can be readily classified the various acts of terrorism, promises, trickery and threats which have led this and other courts to refuse admission as evidence to confessions.[2]

[1] Hopt *v.* Utah, *110 U.S. 574, 584;* Sparf and Hansen *v.* United States, *156 U.S. 51, 55;* Pierce *v.* United States, *160 U.S. 355;* Wilson *v.* United States, *162 U.S. 613, 623; cf.* Bilokumsky *v.* Tod, *263 U.S. 149, 157.*

[2] *"In short, the true test of admissibility is that the confession is made freely, voluntarily and without compulsion or inducement of any sort."* Wilson *v.* United States, *162 U.S. 613, 623;* Lisenba *v.* California, *314 U.S. 219, 239.*

The cases cited in the Court's opinion show the broad coverage of this rule of law. Through it those coerced into confession have found a ready defense from injustice.

Were the Court today saying merely that in its judgment the confessions of the McNabbs were not voluntary, there would be no occasion for this single protest. A notation of dissent would suffice. The opinion, however, does more. Involuntary confessions are not constitutionally admissible because violative of the provision of self-incrimination in the Bill of Rights. Now the Court leaves undecided whether the present confessions are voluntary or involuntary and declares that the confessions must be excluded because in addition to questioning the petitioners, the arresting officers failed promptly to take them before a committing magistrate. The Court finds a basis for the declaration of this new rule of evidence in its supervisory authority over the administration of criminal justice. I question whether this offers to the trial courts and the peace officers a rule of admissibility as clear as the test of the voluntary character of the confession. I am opposed to broadening the possibilities of defendants escaping punishment by these more rigorous technical requirements in the administration of justice. If these confessions are otherwise voluntary, civilized standards, in my opinion, are not advanced by setting aside these judgments because of acts of omission which are not shown to have tended toward coercing the admissions.

Our police officers occasionally overstep legal bounds. This record does not show when the petitioners were taken before a committing magistrate. No point was made of the failure to commit by defendant or counsel. No opportunity was given to the officers to explain. Objection to the introduction of the confessions was made only on the ground that they were obtained through coercion. This was determined against the accused both by the court, when it appraised the fact as to the voluntary character of the confessions preliminarily to determining the legal question of their admissibility, and by the jury. The court saw and heard witnesses for the prosecution and the defense. The defendants did not take the stand before the jury. The uncontradicted evidence does not require a different conclusion. The officers of the Alcohol Tax Unit should not be disciplined by overturning this conviction.

Felix Frankfurter

☆ 1882–1965 ☆

APPOINTED BY

FRANKLIN D. ROOSEVELT

YEARS ON COURT

1939–1962

Felix Frankfurter

by

ALBERT M. SACKS

ON AUGUST 28, 1962, Mr. Justice Felix Frankfurter felt constrained to retire from the post he had held upon the Supreme Court for close to a quarter of a century. Physical disability, the tragic residue of a stroke, made it impossible for him to perform the role that his conception of the Court demanded. Shortly thereafter, in response to a collective letter of his colleagues, he stated for the last time in official setting his view of the Court's true role:

> *My years on the Court have only deepened my conviction that its existence and functioning according to its best historic traditions are indispensable for the well-being of the nation. The nature of the issues which are involved in the legal controversies that are inevitable under our constitutional system does not warrant the nation to expect identity of views among the members of the Court regarding such issues, nor even agreement on the routes of thought by which decisions are reached. The nation is merely warranted in expecting harmony of aims among those who have been called to the Court. This means pertinacious pursuit of the processes of Reason in the disposition of the controversies that come before the Court. This presupposes intellectual disinterestedness in the analysis of the factors involved in the issues that call for decision. This in turn requires rigorous self-scrutiny to discover, with a view to curbing, every influence that may deflect from such disinterestedness.* [*371 U.S. x.*]

For virtually his entire adult life, Felix Frankfurter was to the Supreme Court a student, a teacher, a critic—and a lover. The only other institution that commanded comparable involvement and affection from him was the Harvard Law School. As with lovers generally, he set the highest standards for the tribunal that he cherished. Whereas John Marshall had said, it is *a Constitution* that the Court expounds, Felix Frankfurter might have said, it is *a Court* that expounds that Constitution.

ALBERT M. SACKS is Associate Dean and Professor of Law at the Harvard Law School.

I

Felix Frankfurter was born in Vienna in 1882 and came to the United States when he was a boy of 12. He was educated at the City College of New York (1899–1902) and at the Harvard Law School (1903–1906). When in 1906 he became Assistant United States Attorney in the Southern District of New York he began a career of public service which was not to end until his death in 1965. Here he first combined the elements which were to remain intertwined in his life—the craft of the law, the purposive molding of government action, and the development of transforming friendships with men of public and private stature. Henry L. Stimson, the United States Attorney, was but the first of a distinguished line. "I don't see how a young fellow coming to the bar could possibly have had a more desirable, more deepening, and altogether more precious influence during his formative years." (*Reminisces,* 48.) He accompanied Mr. Stimson, as he always called him, to Washington as Assistant to the Secretary of War. One of his tasks was to represent the government before the Supreme Court in cases relating to the new insular possessions of the United States, Puerto Rico and the Philippines. He remained in government until called to the Faculty of the Harvard Law School in 1914. For a brief time in 1917–18 he returned to Washington as secretary and counsel to President Wilson's Mediation Commission on labor problems. It was this group which investigated the Tom Mooney case in San Francisco, and the famed Bisbee Deportations in which local law enforcement officers placed 1,100 striking miners in Arizona aboard a train and shipped them hundreds of miles away to New Mexico. In both cases Frankfurter condemned local authorities for their high-handed treatment of labor.

Felix Frankfurter was a classroom teacher for a quarter century, but he was an educator all of his life. Those who never met him and who seek clues to his charismatic impact on those around him are doomed to wonder. Dean Acheson, one of his closest friends, and a brilliant personality in his own right, has described Frankfurter thus:

> *It has been said of Leslie Stephen, by Maitland, I think, that those who did not know him would never understand the source and magnitude of his influence. For that reason he would be an enigma to future generations. Reading his written words would give a quite inadequate, often erroneous, impression of the man, and no sense at all of the effect on the hearer of the spoken word. This is preeminently true of Felix Frankfurter. One could read everything that he has written—a formidable task from several points of view—and still have little more than an inkling, if that, of why this man has evoked in so many such passionate devotion and exercised for half a century so profound an influence. I can think of no one in our time remotely comparable to him, though it would not surprise me if in another time Dr. Franklin might have had something of the same personal influence.*

In the same way, the words, especially the written words, of another cannot convey the reality of Felix Frankfurter. There is no substitute for the apprehension of the senses. One needs to see, to hear—particularly to hear his laugh, his general noisiness—to realize what an obstreperous person this man is, to have one's arm numbed by his vise-like grip just above one's elbow, to feel the intensity of his nervous energy. Above all one needs years of experience to know the depth of his concern about people. He lives in personal relationships as a fish lives in water. This is no secluded scholar immured in library or laboratory, absorbed in intellectual problems, but a man immersed in people. At a moment's notice he will concentrate his mind and heart on their interests, their joys, or their troubles.

Frankfurter saw his own legal education at Harvard as a joyous osmosis. The concern for excellence, the emphasis on craftsmanship, the ethical integrity of the lawyer, the de-emphasis of wealth and influence—these were not found in the books, but absorbed from the atmosphere. "There weren't any courses on ethics, but the place was permeated by ethical presuppositions and assumptions and standards." (*Reminisces,* 19.) And Frankfurter the teacher was true to the perceptions of the student.

He taught a course called Public Utilities and two seminars in Federal Jurisdiction and Administrative Law. In truth, they were all courses in the legal process as seen by Frankfurter. His students have reported the impact of a brilliant, roving, probing mind, one that leaped to intellectual confrontation. Whether he dealt with a case, a statute, or an executive decision, he placed it in the flow of the system, the interaction of law and people. His treatment was rarely orderly, but it enriched and excited his students. Professor Paul Freund has described the system as follows:

A case was explored as a process, through the record, the briefs, the counsel, the judges, the statute, its legislative background, indeed the geography of the area involved, preferably to be reported on by a student who came from that locality. The law of public utilities was learned almost by osmosis. As you breathed it in while absorbing the insights of lawyership.

Perhaps I can convey some sense of the man by an experience I had with him very early in my year as his law clerk. He asked me what I thought of a certain case before the Court, and I stated my conclusion, of which he obviously approved. In making my point, I questioned the soundness of a related case decided by the Court the year before, 5–4, in which the Justice had voted in the majority. He had an immediate and overwhelming reaction. I was wrong and he was going to prove it to me. Our exchange lasted over an hour, and the Justice brought to bear every pressure available to verbal man. Anger, scorn, sarcasm, humor buttressed straightforward argument. At times I was hit by the sledge, and at others cut by the rapier. He did not shrink from using the rank of his experience, his age, and his office, and yet as he was more and more drawn into the ecstasy of combat, he placed us—as I now realize—on an equal footing. I sought to hold my ground, and I emerged, I think, bloodied and bent but not bowed or broken. That night, I wondered whether our relationship for the year had been irremediably impaired. The following morning, the Justice bounced into his office, called me in, and made it clear by his manner that, far from leaving any scars, our exchange had drawn us closer together. A little later that day, I heard the Justice say to a spectator of part of yesterday's encounter, "Wasn't Al good? Good, wasn't he!"

He did not limit the educational process to the classroom. Frankfurter demonstrated to his students by his deeds, which impressed far more than words, that the teacher and scholar could care about the society around him, that he could relate law to life, and that he could have an impact. Frankfurter's service as advisor of those in public affairs was only generally known, but it was known. His concern for the integrity of the judicial process was indelibly demonstrated to his students by his participation in the Sacco-Vanzetti case, in which he wrote a famous article and book showing the many abuses in the original trial. His strong attacks on the "establishment" disturbed some, but his presentation convinced many on the issue of fair trial. In the long run people and especially students must have been proud. Here was more than precept; here was example.

His long teaching career was interrupted often by public service. He attended the Paris Peace Conference after World War I, representing Dr. Chaim Weizmann and the Zionists in negotiations with the Arabs. He participated in a number of important Supreme Court arguments, such as *Bunting* v. *Oregon,* 243 U.S. 426 (1917) (in which he supported the Oregon maximum hour law) and *Adkins* v. *Children's Hospital,* 261 U.S. 525 (1923) (he defended the District of Columbia's minimum wage law). One of the founders of the Civil Liberties Union, a legal adviser to the N.A.A.C.P., counsel to the National Consumers' League, Frankfurter followed in the tradition of Brandeis, a close friend, as a "people's counsel." With Nathan Greene he wrote a now famous book on the abuses of *The Labor Injunction* and during the 1920's he spoke out strongly against the Supreme Court's voiding of state legislation regulating business through an expanded reading of the due process clause and liberty of contract. By the early 1930's he had acquired a nationwide reputation as a liberal and thorough scholar and public servant. In recognition of his talents, Governor Richard Ely of Massachusetts nominated Frankfurter to a seat on the Massachusetts Supreme Judicial Court in 1932, but he declined, citing his strong interest in legal education.

A year later Frankfurter turned down President Franklin D. Roosevelt's offer to be Solicitor General of the United States. In a long interview Roosevelt told him that the position would be an important stepping stone to the Supreme Court, where he belonged. The president said it would be difficult to appoint him directly from the Harvard Law School, since he had never held judicial office, had not for long practiced law and added that "then there is the Sacco and Vanzetti case (again smiling) and (this time with a grave countenance) your race." But Frankfurter demurred, saying that the job would require too much time for him to advise Roosevelt on other matters. "I can do much more to be of use to you by staying in Cambridge than by becoming Solicitor General." (*Roosevelt and Frankfurter,* 112–13.)

Frankfurter proved to be right. In the early years of the New Deal, he advised the President on numerous executive appointments, on legislation (such as the Securities Act and the Holding Company Act), and on many Presidential speeches. Their correspondence, recently assembled and annotated by Max Freedman, shows the thousands of matters, large and small, that passed between the two men, from answering an insulting letter from A. Lawrence Lowell of Harvard concerning the Chief Executive's role at the 1936 Harvard tercentenary, to drafting the 1935 Gold Clause message to Congress. Frankfurter responded quickly and carefully to every request made by the President, who relied heavily on him for his advice and scholarship.

The relationship between these two unusual men will evoke varying interpretations by different readers of their correspondence. Frankfurter praised Roosevelt so lavishly and constantly that he might appear to be indulging in fawning. He would send a telegram to Roosevelt about "the candor, courage and conscience of your humane leadership so triumphantly again revealed tonight," or refer to an F.D.R. letter as "one of those bits of Presidential utterances—as rare as they are precious that will live forever in the amber of history." (*Roosevelt and Frankfurter,* 310, 315.) After one visit Frankfurter wrote: "It was a great joy to see you so fit—your energy of mind and spirit, and above all the serenity of your soul." (*Ibid.,* 607.)

But Frankfurter was not obsequious. He could be so effusive not only because he was naturally generous and unreserved in displaying strong emotions toward his friends, but because he saw Roosevelt as one of the greatest of this country's presidents. His first note to Roosevelt after his appointment to the Court stated:

> *Dear Frank:*
> *In the mysterious ways of Fate, the Dutchess County American and the Viennese American have for decades pursued the same directions of devotion to our beloved country, and now, on your blessed birthday I am given the gift of opportunity for service to the nation which in any circumstances would be owing, but which I would rather have had at your hands than at those of any other President barring Lincoln.* [Ibid., *485.*]

The President was, after all, the leader of the country he loved fervently and continuously. He wrote to Roosevelt: "not even you can quite feel what this country means to a man like me, who was brought here as an eager sensitive lad of twelve . . ." (*Ibid.,* 512.) To have an aristocrat of the nation as a personal friend who would also deliver the United States from economic disaster and war and give him the opportunity for service at the highest level made Frankfurter's cup run over, and provoked his ardent patriotism and personal loyalty.

II

It was inevitable that Professor Frankfurter, given his scholarly interests, his friendship with preeminent judges, such as Holmes and Brandeis, and his work with government officials, from Stimson and Wilson to Roosevelt, would focus on the constitutional role of the Supreme Court. He had developed a comprehensive view of that role before he went on the Court in 1939, succeeding Benjamin Cardozo. There are those who believe that the liberal professor gave way to the conservative judge, but a careful study of his work, professorial and judicial, shows an essential consistency of view.

Its function of constitutional review required that the Supreme Court decide issues drenched in political controversy. It could not avoid decisions having profound political consequences. This position of the Court was foreshadowed at least a century earlier in de Tocqueville's observations on the pervasiveness of law in American society. To Frankfurter, this role was historically justified, and in any case necessary and desirable. But unless properly exercised, the role could be dangerously abused, and in fact had been. The solution lay in understanding its true exercise, an understanding for which judges had prime responsibility.

For those who challenged the Court's reviewing role as a usurpation of power, Frankfurter had a short answer. In 1924, he referred to "all the loose talk of 'usurpation,'" and added: "Lack of historical scholarship, combined with fierce prepossessions, can alone account for the existence of this talk." But the review function had more than the initial legitimacy of eighteenth-century practice and concept behind it. It had been broadened and strengthened by the Supreme Court, as events disclosed by cases had shown this to be necessary. Frankfurter recognized that constitutional review was a response to the nation's experience and, properly exercised, it should be and was welcomed by the people and by the national political branches of government.

Most of all, as Frankfurter saw it, the Court was needed to umpire the federal system (in the apt phrase of Professor Paul Freund). Again and again, Frankfurter invoked the language of Holmes:

> *I do not think the United States would come to an end if we lost our power to declare an Act of Congress void. I do think the Union would be imperiled if we could not make that declaration as to the laws of the several States. For one in my place sees how often a local policy prevails with those who are not trained to national views and how often action is taken that embodies what the Commerce Clause was meant to end.* [*Oliver Wendell Holmes Speeches, 102*]

In assigning priority to the Court's safeguarding of our federalism, Frankfurter was not asserting this as its only power, as we shall see. His point, rather, was that both the scope and exercise of the Court's power should be governed by its character as a nonpolitical institution, acting as a check on political organs of government. Its legitimacy obviously did not reside in rapid responsiveness to popular opinion. If constitutional readings were clear and simple, so too would be the Court's job. But the genius of the Constitution lies in its grand, general language creating a foundation for social ordering. The judges can not simply draw out its meaning, as miners dig out coal; they must play a creative role. Policies and purposes are to be developed from the document, relating both to the problems of people and to the practicalities of government.

To be sure, the Court's policy judgments have to be translated into law—not simply fiat with the trappings of law. As Professor Henry Hart has written, the Court "is predestined in the long run . . . to be a voice of reason, charged with the creative function of discerning afresh and of articulating and developing impersonal and durable principles of constitutional law. . . ." This view is essential if we are to have an intelligible distinction between the political process and the judicial.

Yet, accepting all this, Justice Frankfurter remained troubled. Of course decision must be principled, but this approach merely sets a goal without revealing the pitfalls in the path. "The core of the difficulty is that there is hardly a question of any real difficulty before the Court that does not entail more than one so-called principle. Anybody can decide a question if only a single principle is in controversy." (*Of Law and Men,* 43.) Absolutes were categorically rejected. The use of reason and principle were only part of his answer.

What more could be expected of the Court? First, that it insist on "cases or controversies" (the bases of the judicial power conferred by the Constitution) that pose concrete, focused issues and demand adjudication. (I have not attempted in this presentation to delve into Justice Frankfurter's views in this area; the issues involved—such as political question, standing, and ripeness—are particularly technical and complex.)

Second, that the justices make every effort to distinguish between policies derived from shifting social and economic arrangements and principles based on more permanent foundations. Here Frankfurter placed his emphasis on the relative narrowness of language of certain clauses—such as the search and seizure clause—or the history that permeated a particular provision. But there was also a suggestion, as we shall see, that certain values might be identified as fundamental, though not without care.

Third, precedent had claims to respect beyond its mere persuasiveness. In discussing judges whom he greatly admired, Frankfurter added: "I venture to suggest that had they the minds of such originators [of transforming thought], the bench is not the place for its employment. Transforming thought implies too great a break with the past, implies too much discontinuity, to be imposed upon society by one who is entrusted with enforcing its law." (Sutherland ed., *Government under Law,* 9.)

Fourth and most important, the judges must guard against simply reading into the Constitution what they read out of it. Particularly in reviewing social and economic legislation, but not merely in that area, the judges are not to declare statutes invalid unless the legislative judgment fails to strike a reasonable balance. The judges' strong disagreement with the statute is not enough. Here, then, was the capstone of self-restraint.

External restraints may be imposed upon the Court by political processes, as Frankfurter fully appreciated. In his time, two efforts were undertaken by such means, one a good deal more serious than the other. Theodore Roosevelt in 1912 proposed the recall of certain judicial decisions by popular vote, and other political leaders proposed recall of judges. Frankfurter condemned these proposals as ill-conceived, insisting that the true solution lay in informing "the sympathies and the intelligence of our judges." (*Law and Politics,* 7.)

In 1936, Franklin D. Roosevelt proposed a plan to Congress to "pack" the Supreme Court through the addition of up to six justices. He acted in response to a series of Court decisions invalidating national and state social and economic legislation. Frankfurter regarded many of these decisions as flagrantly abusive exercises of the Court's power, yet he made no public statements on the President's plan. The correspondence between Frankfurter and Roosevelt is said by Max Freedman to show that Frankfurter privately supported the plan. In fact, the letters show that Frankfurter remained true to his position; he castigated the justices responsible for the line of decisions, he indicated a sympathetic understanding of the President's plight, and he even criticized (though privately) some of those who fought the President, but he never approved of court-packing. Frankfurter's reasons seem apparent. The Court's proper role was nonpolitical; only by departure from that role had it attracted political attack. Yet, if the attack were successful, the Court would not only be generally undermined but it would be even more identified with the politics of the day than before. In institutional terms, the remedy would reenforce the disease. It was vital to the Court and its contribution to our scheme of government, therefore, that it avoid external movements against it by exercising restraint internally. It was for these reasons among others that Frankfurter urged on the justices the virtues of detachment, disinterest, deliberation, and of reasoned restraint.

III

Faithfulness to his general views of the Court's proper role did not lead Justice Frankfurter to treat all constitutional values alike. Judicial restraint was not judicial paralysis. In the end, the judge must exercise judgment. I have chosen to treat of his views in a number of categories of cases, not exhaustively, but simply to illustrate the themes which he pursued—and at times had to reconcile when they came into conflict—and the way in which his more general philosophy influenced his work.

Social and Economic Regulation.—The emphasis on the Court's circumscribed role, previously described, had evolved in Professor Frankfurter's thinking in direct response to decisions of the Supreme Court invalidating social and economic legislation. In this area, the vague and amorphous restrictions of the due process clause had to be lifted, and rationally supportable legislation allowed to function. And so it was natural that the Justice was in accord with Court decisions upholding such New Deal legislation as the Fair Labor Standards Act. Ten years after going on the bench, in *Lincoln Federal Labor Union* v. *Northwestern Iron & Metal Co.,* 335 U.S. 525, 538 (1949), the Justice confronted a challenge to a different kind of socio-economic legislation: state "right to work" laws which made it unlawful to forbid employment to a person either because he belonged or did not belong to a union. He may have disapproved of the legislation, but the resolution of conflicting interests which it embodied must be upheld. "Unless we are to treat as unconstitutional what goes against the grain because it offends what we may strongly believe to be socially desirable, that resolution must be given respect." Frankfurter took the occasion to summarize the views developed over the past forty years:

> *Even where the social undesirability of a law may be convincingly urged, invalidation of the law by a court debilitates popular democratic government. Most laws dealing with economic and social problems are matters of trial and error. That which before trial appears to be demonstrably bad may belie prophecy in actual operation. It may not prove good, but it may prove innocuous. But even if a law is found wanting on trial, it is better that its defects should be demonstrated and removed than that the law should be aborted by judicial fiat. Such an assertion of judicial power deflects responsibility from those on whom in a democratic society it ultimately rests—the people. . . .*

Frankfurter then commented on the Court's role in the political process:

> *But there is reason for judicial restraint in matters of policy deeper than the value of experiment: it is founded on a recognition of the gulf of difference between sustaining and nullifying legislation. This difference is theoretical in that the function of legislating is for legislatures who have also taken oaths to support the Constitution, while the function of courts, when legislation is challenged, is merely to make sure that the legislature has exercised an allowable judgment, and not to exercise their own judgment, whether a policy is within or without "the vague contours" of due process. Theory is reinforced by the notorious fact that lawyers predominate in American legislatures. In practice also the difference is wide. In the day-to-day working of our democracy it is vital that the power of the non-democratic organ of our Government be exercised with rigorous self-restraint. Because the powers exercised by this Court are inherently oligarchic, Jefferson all of his life thought of the Court as "an irresponsible body" and "independent of the nation itself." The Court is not saved from being oligarchic because it professes to act in the service of humane ends. As history amply proves, the judiciary is prone to misconceive the public good by confounding private notions with constitutional requirements, and such misconceptions are not subject to legitimate displacement by the will of the people except at too slow a pace. Judges appointed for life whose decisions run counter to prevailing opinion cannot be voted out of office and supplanted by men of views more consonant with it. They are even farther removed from democratic pressures by the fact that their deliberations are in secret and*

> *remain beyond disclosure either by periodic reports or by such a modern device for securing responsibility to the electorate as the "press conference." But a democracy need not rely on the courts to save it from its own unwisdom. If it is alert—and without alertness by the people there can be no enduring democracy—unwise or unfair legislation can readily be removed from the statute books. It is by such vigilance over its representatives that democracy proves itself.*

With respect to judicial review, Frankfurter had the following observations.

> *Our right to pass on the validity of legislation is now too much part of our constitutional system to be brought into question. But the implications of that right and the conditions for its exercise must constantly be kept in mind and vigorously observed. Because the Court is without power to shape measures for dealing with the problems of society but has merely the power of negation over measures shaped by others, the indispensable judicial requisite is intellectual humility, and such humility presupposes complete disinterestedness. And so, in the end, it is right that the Court should be indifferent to public temper and popular wishes. Mr. Dooley's "th' Supreme Coort follows th' iliction returns" expressed the wit of cynicism, not the demand of principle. A court which yields to the popular will thereby license itself to practice despotism, for there can be no assurance that it will not on another occasion indulge its own will. Courts can fulfill their responsibility in a democratic society only to the extent that they succeed in shaping their judgments by rational standards, and rational standards are both impersonal and communicable. Matters of policy, however, are by definition matters which demand the resolution of conflicts of value, and the elements of conflicting values are largely imponderable. Assessment of their competing worth involves differences of feeling; it is also an exercise in prophecy. Obviously the proper forum for mediating a clash of feelings and rendering a prophetic judgment is the body chosen for those purposes by the people. Its functions can be assumed by this Court only in disregard of the historic limits of the Constitution.* [*335 U.S. 553–57.*]

Fair Procedure and Process.—Issues of fair procedure presented a very different problem for Justice Frankfurter—at least at the federal level. They usually arise out of relatively specific constitutional clauses whose language and history conveys a clear core meaning and suggests a more active judicial role. Not only are these issues peculiarly within the experience and understanding of judges, not only are procedural restrictions less likely to impair the essential power of political branches to govern even in the short run, but fair procedures will probably strengthen government in the ultimate sense:

> *Man being what he is cannot safely be trusted with complete immunity from outward responsibility in depriving others of their rights. At least such is the conviction underlying our Bill of Rights. That a conclusion satisfies one's private conscience does not attest its reliability. The validity and moral authority of a conclusion largely depend on the mode by which it was reached. Secrecy is not congenial to truth-seeking and self-righteousness gives too slender an assurance of rightness. No better instrument has been devised for arriving at truth than to give a person in jeopardy of serious loss notice of the case against him and opportunity to meet it. Nor has a better way been found for*

> *generating the feeling, so important to a popular government, that justice has been done.* [Joint Anti-Fascist Refugee Committee *v.* McGrath, *341 U.S. 123, 171–172 (1951)*.]

Procedure may be viewed more broadly, so that it encompasses the processes by which the police enforce the criminal laws. Here the integrity of the individual is at stake, his right to be "let alone." In dealing with confessions and searches and seizures, Justice Frankfurter subjected the police to rigorous scrutiny. To be sure, the policy-making hand of the Congress was not here challenged. Yet, the Justice insisted on safeguards to be vigorously implanted in the Constitution. When federal officers held a defendant fourteen hours without arraignment, Frankfurter held, as a matter of federal decisional law, apart from constitutional standards, the prosecution could not use any admissions obtained during that period (*McNabb* v. *United States,* 318 U.S. 332 [1943]). He noted:

> *Judicial supervision of the administration of criminal justice in the federal courts implies the duty of establishing and maintaining civilized standards of procedure and evidence.*

In dissenting from a judgment upholding a federal search of papers and effects without a warrant, he stated:

> *If I begin with some general observations, it is not because I am unmindful of Mr. Justice Holmes' caution that "General propositions do not decide concrete cases . . ." Whether they do or not often depends on the strength of the conviction with which such "general propositions" are held. A principle may be accepted "in principle," but the impact of an immediate situation may lead to deviation from the principle. Or, while accepted "in principle," a competing principle may seem more important. Both these considerations have doubtless influenced the application of the search and seizure provisions of the Bill of Rights. Thus, one's views regarding circumstances like those here presented ultimately turn on whether one gives that amendment a place second to none in the Bill of Rights, or considers it on the whole a kind of a nuisance, a serious impediment in the war against crime.*
>
> * * *
>
> *For me the background is respect for that provision of the Bill of Rights which is central to the enjoyment of the other guarantees of the Bill of Rights. How can there be freedom of thought or freedom of speech or freedom of religion, if the police can, without warrant, search your house and mine from garrett to cellar merely because they are executing a warrant of arrest? How can men feel free if all their papers can be searched, as an incident to the arrest of someone in the house, on the chance that something may turn up, or rather, be turned up? Yesterday the justifying document was an illicit ration book, tomorrow it may be some suspect piece of literature.* [Harris *v.* United States, *331 U.S. 145, 157, 163 (1947)*.]

When the states engaged in similar practices, the Justice applied a different standard. *Wolf* v. *Colorado,* 338 U.S. 25 (1949) He based this, in part, on the language of the Constitution which in textual and historical context he read as imposing those procedural safeguards that comport with "canons of decency and fairness." But beyond this he saw value in leaving states free to work out their own destiny through a process of trial and error. Centralization, at least by Court decision, might carry with it the deadening influence of uniform and remote criminal administration. And so, even though Justice Frankfurter had long deprecated the vague contours of the due process clause, he rejected the argument made by Justice Black in the *Adamson* case that the clause should incorporate the first eight amendments of the Bill of Rights and nothing else. And he continued to review state procedures by reference to broad standards. When a state obtained evidence by pumping it out of the defendant's stomach, he voted to exclude the evidence. "Due process of law . . . is not to be turned into a destructive dogma against the States in the administration of their systems of criminal justice. However, this Court too has its responsibilities." *Rochin* v. *California,* 342 U.S. 165, 168 (1952).

Speech and Religion.—Justice Frankfurter's positions in dealing with speech and religion are not easily reduced to formulas—for he characteristically resisted formulas.

In his pre-court days, the Justice had seen freedom of speech and press as specific clauses free of the dangers besetting substantive due process adjudication. But as concrete cases came before the Justice, he saw the characteristic problem before the Court as the need to resolve a conflict of values—free press against fair trial; free association against an industry free of political strikes; free speech against internal security. What weight should legislative judgment be given? The Justice would not treat these cases as though they were economic due process problems, but he categorically rejected the view that speech and press were absolutes to be protected against all conflicting interests. Nor would he embrace the general approach that treated speech and press as "preferred" freedoms, the restriction of which was even presumptively invalid unless justified. He insisted upon a case-by-case approach free of categorical prepossession and yet recognized speech as having special values in our system. In *Kovacs* v. *Cooper,* 336 U.S. 77 (1949), involving the regulation of sound trucks, he set forth his views on the "preferred position" of speech and press:

> *This is a phrase that has uncritically crept into some recent opinions of this Court. I deem it a mischievous phrase, if it carries the thought, which it may subtly imply, that any law touching communication is infected with presumptive invalidity. . . . I say the phrase is mischievous because it radiates a constitutional doctrine without avowing it. Clarity and candor in these matters, so as to avoid gliding unwittingly into error, make it appropriate to trace the history of the phrase 'preferred position.' . . .*

Frankfurter cited Oliver Wendall Holmes in defense of his position.

> *Behind the notion sought to be expressed by the formula as to 'the preferred position of freedom of speech' lies a relevant consideration in determining whether an enactment relating to the liberties protected by the Due Process Clause of the Fourteenth Amendment is violative of it. In law also, doctrine is illuminated by history. The ideas now governing the constitutional protection of freedom of speech derive essentially from the opinions of Mr. Justice Holmes.*

The philosophy of his opinions on that subject arose from a deep awareness of the extent to which sociological conclusions are conditioned by time and circumstance. Because of this awareness Mr. Justice Holmes seldom felt justified in opposing his own opinion to economic views which the legislature embodied in law. But since he also realized that the progress of civilization is to a considerable extent the displacement of error which once held sway as official truth by beliefs which in turn have yielded to other beliefs, for him the right to search for truth was of a different order than some transient economic dogma. And without freedom of expression, thought becomes checked and atrophied. Therefore, in considering what interests are so fundamental as to be enshrined in the Due Process Clause, those liberties of the individual which history has attested as the indispensable conditions of an open as against a closed society come to this Court with a momentum for respect lacking when appeal is made to liberties which derive merely from shifting economic arrangements. Accordingly, Mr. Justice Holmes was far more ready to find legislative invasion where free inquiry was involved than in the debatable area of economics. See my Mr. Justice Holmes and the Supreme Court, *58 et seq.*

The objection to summarizing this line of thought by the phrase 'the preferred position of freedom of speech' is that it expresses a complicated process of constitutional adjudication by a deceptive formula. . . . Such a formula makes for mechanical jurisprudence.

Relating these principles to the specific facts of the *Kovacs* case, Frankfurter wrote:

Only a disregard of vital differences between natural speech, even of the loudest spellbinders, and the noise of sound trucks would give sound trucks the constitutional rights accorded to the unaided human voice. Nor is it for this Court to devise the terms on which sound trucks should be allowed to operate, if at all. These are matters for the legislative judgment controlled by public opinion. So long as a legislature does not prescribe what ideas may be noisily expressed and what may not be, nor discriminate among those who would make inroads upon the public peace, it is not for us to supervise the limits the legislature may impose in safeguarding the steadily narrowing opportunities for serenity and reflection. Without such opportunities freedom of thought becomes a mocking phrase, and without freedom of thought there can be no free society.

The sensitivity to freedom of expression revealed here, though not unqualified, led Justice Frankfurter to hold unconstitutional a Michigan obscenity law which banned the distribution to all of any matter which was inappropriate for the young. "Surely, this is to burn the house to roast the pig." *Butler* v. *Michigan,* 352 U.S. 380, 383 (1957). It led him also, in *Sweezy* v. *New Hampshire,* 354 U.S. 234 (1957) to go beyond most of his brethren in protecting freedom of expression in a class room setting. The line he drew in two internal security cases is revealing. In *Dennis* v. *United States,* 341 U.S. 494 (1951) he voted to uphold criminal prosecution of Communist Party leaders under the Smith Act. The conflicting assessments of the danger to internal security were so varied and uncertain that, in this framework, the judge's role had to be limited. But in the *Sweezy* case, in dealing with academic freedom and the Progressive Party of Henry Wallace's time, he came to a confident contrary conclusion.

In dealing with religious establishment and freedom, Justice Frankfurter often found in the language of the Constitution and its history a warrant for imposing barriers on political action. Thus, he felt that public financing of transportation for parochial school children, holding religious classes after hours in public schools, and releasing children during school hours to attend religious exercises elsewhere were all banned by the First Amendment. In the flag-salute cases the Justice concluded that the state could require Jehovah's Witness children to salute the flag, on pain of expulsion from public school. He voted with the majority in *Minersville School District* v. *Gobitis,* 310 U.S. 586 (1940) and dissented when the Court reversed its position three years later to forbid compulsory flag-saluting in *West Virginia State Board of Education* v. *Barnette,* 319 U.S. 624 (1943). He began his famous dissent by noting:

> *One who belongs to the most vilified and persecuted minority in history is not likely to be insensible to the freedoms guaranteed by our Constitution . . . as judges we are neither Jew nor Gentile, neither Catholic nor agnostic . . . As a member of this Court I am not justified in writing my private notions of policy into the Constitution, no matter how deeply I may cherish them or how mischievous I may deem their disregard . . . I cannot bring my mind to believe that the "liberty" secured by the Due Process Clause gives this Court authority to deny to the State of West Virginia the attainment of that which we all recognize as a legitimate legislative end, namely, the promotion of good citizenship, by employment of the means here chosen . . . .*

This position suggests an uncritical transplanting of his views on the Court's role in the due process area. One can not be certain, but a reading of the Justice's opinions in later cases, particularly on Sunday laws near the end of his judicial career, suggests a changed point of view. See *McGowan* v. *Maryland,* 366 U.S. 420 (1961).

Interstate Commerce and the States.—Despite his pre-Court emphasis on the Court's role as arbiter of the federal system—and of the importance of judicial checks on state parochialism—Justice Frankfurter at first flirted with a contrary view. He thought that perhaps the states should be free to regulate and tax commerce, unless Congress acted to protect it. Perhaps the commerce clause should afford no more protection against the states than did the due process clause. In an early joint dissent, he agreed that "it becomes more and more important that potential conflicts between state and national powers should not be found where Congress has not found them, unless conflict is established by demonstrable concreteness." (*McCarroll* v. *Dixie Greyhound Lines, Inc.,* 309 U.S. 176, 183, 186 [1940]).

Within a few years, the Justice had abandoned this approach. Presumably he found that state legislatures and officials could not resist the temptation to favor local against national interests. It became obvious that Congress was unlikely either to redress isolated instances of local bias or to formulate general standards for the protection of commerce. And so he returned to the more traditional view, whereby state action was tested by whether or not it burdened commerce "unduly," a test that brought to bear the independent judgment of the Court. Justice Frankfurter fully appreciated the subtleties and intricacies of the task. As a Professor, he had written:

> *Practical necessities and shrewd judgments about practical matters decide the fate of state legislation when challenged by the power or the action of Congress. State necessities, the fitness of state relief as against nation-wide action, the limited manifestation of a given evil or the limited benefits of its correction, the actual interest of the whole country in a phenomenon especially virulent in a particular state, the advantage of local regulation balanced against the cost or inconvenience to interests outside the state—these and like questions are involved in the process by which the Supreme Court in concrete cases has held for or against state and national action in the interacting areas of state and national interests.* [*Frankfurter,* The Public and its Government, *74.*]

Judicial weighing of considerations of this kind had been opposed by Frankfurter in a due process context. But for commerce clause purposes he came to accept it, and for a variety of reasons. Here, the state political process was peculiarly untrustworthy. The judicial role had the force of precedent behind it—not only the Court's decisions going back to *Gibbons* v. *Ogden,* but the acquiescence of Congress over that time. Most important, the Court did not have the last word in commerce clause cases involving state action—as it in principle did in due process matters. Congress could broaden or narrow the state power by ordinary legislation. The judicial role should reflect these distinctions.

* * * * *

Throughout his long career on the bench, Justice Frankfurter often showed his professorial background. His points at oral arguments before the Court frequently had a classroom quality about them. Lawyers prepared specifically to meet his probing, often testy, questions, his excursions into legislative history, his inquiries about parallel situations in widely diverse areas. He did not suffer sloppiness in preparation or logic and showed no favorites. When John W. Davis, an old friend, one of the leaders of the American bar, and 1924 Presidential candidate argued the school segregation cases in 1952, the following exchange occurred:

Justice Frankfurter:	*Mr. Davis, do you think that 'equal' is a less fluid term than 'commerce between the states'?*
Mr. Davis:	*Less fluid?*
Justice Frankfurter:	*Yes.*
Mr. Davis:	*I have not compared the two on the point of fluidity.*
Justice Frankfurter:	*Suppose you do it now.*

Many of Justice Frankfurter's opinions reflected the scholar at work. He would prepare long and detailed appendices to show the history of a particular practice under constitutional attack. If the states or other jurisdictions had long followed a given practice, that was strongly persuasive that the practice did not violate due process, Frankfurter would reason. Thus in *Wolf* v. *Colorado,* 338 U.S. 25 (1949) he noted that thirty out of forty-eight states and ten British Commonwealth jurisdictions admitted evidence that was illegally seized. Thus the practice could not be such a "departure from basic standards" to justify voiding that procedure. In *Bartkus* v. *Illinois,* 359 U.S. 121 (1959) a similar approach upheld the right of a state to try a man after he had been acquitted of a federal crime based on the same facts.

The course of history weighed heavily with Justice Frankfurter. The Court should not inquire into malapportionment of legislative districts since, along with other reasons, "this Court has traditionally held aloof . . . from the determination of such issues," *Colegrove* v. *Green,* 328 U.S. 549, 556 (1946). When the Court struck down a New York statute as too indefinite in *Winters* v. *New York,* 333 U.S. 507 (1948) Frankfurter began his dissent by noting: "By today's decision the Court strikes down an enactment that has been part of the laws of New York for more than sixty years, and New York is but one of twenty states having such legislation." In *Bridges* v. *California,* 314 U.S. 252 (1941) he dissented when the Court reversed the contempt conviction of a California newspaper for its strong comment on a court decision. "Our whole history repels the view" that attempts to overawe a judge in a pending case cannot be punished.

IV

Throughout his judicial career, Frankfurter came to decisions which disappointed some, perhaps many, of his earlier liberal followers, and which were said to show that the young liberal had evolved into a conservative. This paper has referred to decisions of his which arrived at a "conservative" result, and has also mentioned some with a "liberal" outcome. Many others could be cited both ways. The point is, as I hope this paper shows, that for Justice Frankfurter the political orientation of the result did not pose the relevant questions for decision. Professor Louis Jaffe, writing as long ago as 1949, put the matter very well:

> *Mr. Justice Frankfurter has now sat for ten years on the Supreme Court, and comment on his record most often centers on the question whether he has "become a conservative."* [*By this test, Frankfurter could not be considered a liberal judge because he could not*] *be counted upon to deliver a judgment for the reason that it immediately implemented some accepted tenet of the liberal legislative program. But it is demonstrable, I believe, that Mr. Justice Frankfurter is in this sense no more a conservative than he is a liberal. It is of the very essence of his judicial philosophy that his role as a judge precludes him from having a program couched in these terms of choice.*

What is to be said, in summary and conclusion? This presentation has not fully revealed all there is of Felix Frankfurter, the man, the scholar, the government servant, and the judge. But a few conclusions may be ventured. He sought to promote both the integrity of the individual and of government. In the larger sense, he saw these not as incompatible but reenforcing, though the tasks of day-by-day accommodation were difficult and required meticulous attention to detail.

He saw government as a group of institutions and processes, each in its own way serving the purposes of the society. In monitoring this allocation of roles, the Court must be especially careful to respect the limitations of its own role. It is here that Justice Frankfurter touched a tender spot in the society's effort to govern itself. Perhaps the Justice was too optimistic about the capacities of his fellow man. Perhaps he overestimated the ability of men, even judges, to draw lines between principle and will, between power and wisdom, between reason and rationalization. Certainly, he did not minimize the difficulties, he only insisted that the effort be made because this was the Court's reason for being, as a constitutional tribunal.

Perhaps Justice Frankfurter failed to appreciate sufficiently the defects of the political process. His thought matured during an era when legislatures, by and large, were seeking to express the needs and wishes of great masses coping with the ills of industrial society, and courts often confused the familiarities of the past with immutable principle. Perhaps the lessons of this era were limited to its time or to a particular body of doctrine. As I have tried to show, Justice Frankfurter drew distinctions in the role of the Court. He did not mistake truism for truth. But perhaps the balance that he struck expressed an overidealistic assessment of what popular processes can achieve.

One can only admire the effort he made to live by his convictions. It was not easy for this passionate man—who displayed and evoked intense affection and loyalty in many as well as intense irritation in others—to function as a dispassionate, restrained judge. The issues of role and function that he insisted were primary will continue to confront the Supreme Court, and one may predict that his views will have their impact in the long run.

Felix Frankfurter pursued his calling with conviction and integrity. Ably and consistently, he performed his role as he saw it. What he said of Mr. Justice Holmes in 1938 expresses what he sought for himself:

> *His own constitutional outlook was, throughout a long life, free from fluctuations. This was so because it was born of a deeply rooted and coherent philosophy concerning the dynamic character of the American Constitution and of a judge's function in construing it. If he threw the weight of his authority on the side of social readjustments through legislation it was not because of any faith in panaceas in general or in measures of social amelioration in particular. . . . But his skepticism and even hostility, as a matter of private judgment, toward legislation which he was ready to sustain as a judge only serve to add cubits to his judicial stature. For he thereby transcended personal predilections and private notions of social policy and became truly the impersonal voice of the Constitution.* [*Frankfurter,* Law and Politics, *44–45.*]

SELECTED BIBLIOGRAPHY

Writings by Frankfurter: For the general reader, probably the most interesting works are *Felix Frankfurter Reminisces* (New York, 1960) a series of autobiographical monologues developed from taped interviews with Dr. Harlan B. Phillips, consisting of recollections of important or dramatic episodes in Frankfurter's life, plus comments on people, events, and life's affairs; and occasional papers and addresses collected in three volumes for different time periods: MacLeish and Prichard, eds., *Law and Politics* (New York, 1939) (1913–1938); Elman, ed., *Of Law and Men* (New York, 1956) (1939–1956); Kurland, ed., *Of Law and Life* (Cambridge, 1965) (1956–1963); and finally the correspondence between President Franklin D. Roosevelt and Frankfurter, which contains much more by and tells us much more about the latter than the former, Freedman, ed., *Roosevelt and Frankfurter* (Boston, 1968). On the scholarly side, there are a vast number of books and articles. Two larger works in book form are *The Business Of The Supreme Court* (New York, 1927) with James M. Landis, (court jurisdiction, seen historically and functionally), and *The Labor Injunction* (New York, 1930), with Nathan Greene, which explored abusive exercise of injunctive and contempt powers of courts in labor disputes and led to the enactment of the Norris-LaGuardia Act by Congress. Other books include *The Case of Sacco and Vanzetti* (Boston, 1927); *The Public and Its Government* (New Haven, 1930); *The Commerce Clause Under Marshall, Taney, and Waite* (Chapel Hill, 1937); and *Mr. Justice Holmes and The Supreme Court* (Cambridge, 1938).

Periodical articles appear mainly in the *Harvard Law Review,* at the rate of close to one a year, in volumes 29 to 52 inclusive (1916–1939) and deal with a variety of issues relating primarily to the Constitution and the Supreme Court. A few articles appear in other journals, notably including "Distribution Of Judicial Power Between The Courts of the United States and the Courts of the States," 13 *Cornell Law Quarterly* 499 (1928); (with Landis) "The Contract Clause of the Constitution: A Study in Interstate Adjustments," 34 *Yale Law Journal* 685 (1925). Two papers are especially noteworthy because they were delivered while Frankfurter was on the bench and reflect his judicial experience and outlook. "Some Reflections on the Reading of Statutes," 47 *Columbia Law Review* 527 (1947) (Cardozo Lecture); "John Marshall and the Judicial Function" in Sutherland, ed. *Government Under Law* (Cambridge, 1956) (Marshall Bicentennial Conference).

Writings about Frankfurter: No effort is made here to collect even a fair sample of all the writings. There is no single-author book, either biographical or evaluative, to which one could confidently refer a reader. For appraisal of the man and his work by a collection, written with a generally sympathetic outlook, see Mendelson, ed. *Felix Frankfurter: A Tribute* (New York, 1964), and Mendelson, ed. *Felix Frankfurter; The Judge* (New York, 1964); 67 *Yale Law Journal* 179–323 (1957) (issue marking Frankfurter's 75th birthday). An excellent commentary on the first ten years of the Justice's work on the bench, but applicable in many respects to his entire judicial career, is Jaffe, "The Judicial Universe Of Mr. Justice Frankfurter," 62 *Harvard Law Review* 357 (1949).

Felix Frankfurter

REPRESENTATIVE OPINIONS

DENNIS v. UNITED STATES, 341 U.S. 494 (1951)

Chief Justice Vinson wrote a four-man opinion upholding the conviction of the Communist Party leaders under the Smith Act. He relied primarily on the "clear and present danger" test of Justice Holmes, noting that the words "cannot mean that before the Government may act, it must wait until the *putsch* is about to be executed, the plans have been laid and the signal is awaited." Frankfurter concurred in affirming the conviction but felt obliged to offer his own reasons in support of the government, since he felt Holmes' phrase was being used too freely without an understanding of its purpose and meaning. His opinion analyzed the different areas in which speech had been restricted by the federal authorities and examined the rationale behind the Smith Act.

MR. JUSTICE FRANKFURTER, concurring in affirmance of the judgment.

The defendants were convicted under § 3 of the Smith Act for conspiring to violate § 2 of that Act, which makes it unlawful "to organize or help to organize any society, group, or assembly of persons who teach, advocate, or encourage the overthrow or destruction of any government in the United States by force or violence." Act of June 28, 1940, § 2 (a) (3), 54 Stat. 670, 671, 18 U.S.C. § 10, now 18 U.S.C. § 2385. The substance of the indictment is that the defendants between April 1, 1945, and July 20, 1948, agreed to bring about the dissolution of a body known as the Communist Political Association and to organize in its place the Communist Party of the United States; that the aim of the new party was "the overthrow and destruction of the Government of the United States by force and violence"; that the defendants were to assume leadership of the Party and to recruit members for it and that the Party was to publish books and conduct classes, teaching the duty and the necessity of forceful overthrow. The jury found all the defendants guilty. With one exception, each was sentenced to imprisonment for five years and to a fine of $10,000. The convictions were affirmed by the Court of Appeals for the Second Circuit. 183 F. 2d 201. We were asked to review this affirmance on all the grounds considered by the Court of Appeals. These included not only the scope of the freedom of speech guaranteed by the Constitution, but also serious questions regarding the legal composition of the jury and the fair conduct of the trial. We granted certiorari, strictly limited, however, to the contention that §§ 2 and 3 of the

Smith Act, inherently and as applied, violated the First and Fifth Amendments. 340 U.S. 863. No attempt was made to seek an enlargement of the range of questions thus defined, and these alone are now open for our consideration. All others are foreclosed by the decision of the Court of Appeals.

As thus limited, the controversy in this Court turns essentially on the instructions given to the jury for determining guilt or innocence. 9 F. R. D. 367. The first question is whether—wholly apart from constitutional matters—the judge's charge properly explained to the jury what it is that the Smith Act condemns. The conclusion that he did so requires no labored argument. On the basis of the instructions, the jury found, for the purpose of our review, that the advocacy which the defendants conspired to promote was to be a rule of action, by language reasonably calculated to incite persons to such action, and was intended to cause the overthrow of the Government by force and violence as soon as circumstances permit. This brings us to the ultimate issue. In enacting a statute which makes it a crime for the defendants to conspire to do what they have been found to have conspired to do, did Congress exceed its constitutional power?

Few questions of comparable import have come before this Court in recent years. The appellants maintain that they have a right to advocate a political theory, so long, at least, as their advocacy does not create an immediate danger of obvious magnitude to the very existence of our present scheme of society. On the other hand, the Government asserts the right to safeguard the security of the Nation by such a measure as the Smith Act. Our judgment is thus solicited on a conflict of interests of the utmost concern to the well-being of the country. This conflict of interests cannot be resolved by a dogmatic preference for one or the other, nor by a sonorous formula which is in fact only a euphemistic disguise for an unresolved conflict. If adjudication is to be a rational process, we cannot escape a candid examination of the conflicting claims with full recognition that both are supported by weighty title-deeds.

I.

There come occasions in law, as elsewhere, when the familiar needs to be recalled. Our whole history proves even more decisively than the course of decisions in this Court that the United States has the powers inseparable from a sovereign nation. "America has chosen to be, in many respects, and to many purposes, a nation; and for all these purposes, her government is complete; to all these objects, it is competent." Chief Justice Marshall in *Cohens* v. *Virginia,* 6 Wheat. 264, 414. The right of a government to maintain its existence—self-preservation—is the most pervasive aspect of sovereignty. "Security against foreign danger," wrote Madison, "is one of the primitive objects of civil society." The Federalist, No. 41. The constitutional power to act upon this basic principle has been recognized by this Court at different periods and under diverse circumstances. "To preserve its independence, and give security against foreign aggression and encroachment, is the highest duty of every nation, and to attain these ends nearly all other considerations are to be subordinated. It matters not in what form such aggression and encroachment come. . . . The government, possessing the powers which are to be exercised for protection and security, is clothed with authority to determine the occasion on which the powers shall be called forth. . . ." *Chinese Exclusion Case,* 130 U.S. 581, 606. See also *De Lima* v. *Bidwell,* 182 U.S. 1; *Mackenzie* v. *Hare,* 239 U.S. 299; *Missouri* v. *Holland,* 252 U.S. 416; *United States* v. *Curtiss-Wright Corp.,* 299 U.S. 304. The most tragic experience in our history is a poignant reminder that the Nation's continued existence may be threatened from within. To protect itself from such threats, the Federal Government "is invested with all those inherent and implied powers which, at the time of adopting the Constitution, were generally considered to belong to every government as such, and as being essential to the exercise of its functions." Mr. Justice Bradley, concurring in *Legal Tender Cases,* 12 Wall. 457, 554, 556; and see *In re Debs,* 158 U.S. 564, 582.

But even the all-embracing power and duty of self-preservation are not absolute. Like the war power, which is indeed an aspect of the power of self-preservation, it is subject to applicable constitutional limitations. See *Hamilton* v. *Kentucky Distilleries Co.,* 251 U.S. 146, 156. Our Constitution has no provision lifting restrictions upon governmental authority during periods of emergency, although the scope of a restriction may depend on the circumstances in which it is invoked.

The First Amendment is such a restriction. It exacts obedience even during periods of war; it is applicable when war clouds are not figments of the imagination no less than when they are. The First Amendment categorically demands that "Congress shall make no law respecting an establishment of religion, or prohibiting the free exercise thereof; or abridging the freedom of speech, or of the press; or the right of the people peaceably to assemble, and to petition the Government for a redress of grievances." The right of a man to think what he pleases, to write what he thinks, and to have his thoughts made available for others to hear or read has an engaging ring of universality. The Smith Act and this conviction under it no doubt restrict the exercise of free speech and assembly. Does that, without more, dispose of the matter?

Just as there are those who regard as invulnerable every measure for which the claim of national survival is invoked, there are those who find in the Constitution a wholly unfettered right of expression. Such literalness treats the words of the Constitution as though they were found on a piece of outworn parchment instead of being words that have called into being a nation with a past to be preserved for the future. The soil in which the Bill of Rights grew was not a soil of arid pedantry. The historic antecedents of the First Amendment preclude the notion that its purpose was to give unqualified immunity to every expression that touched on matters within the range of political interest. The Massachusetts Constitution of 1780 guaranteed free speech; yet there are records of at least three convictions for political libels obtained between 1799 and 1803.[1] The Pennsylvania Constitution of 1790 and the Delaware Constitution of 1792 expressly imposed liability for abuse of the right of free speech.[2] Madison's own State put on its books in 1792 a statute confining the abusive exercise of the right of utterance.[3] And it deserves to be noted that in writing to John Adams's wife, Jefferson did not rest his condemnation of the Sedition Act of 1798 on his belief in unrestrained utterance as to political matter. The First Amendment, he argued, reflected a limitation upon Federal power, leaving the right to enforce restrictions on speech to the States.[4]

[1] *Mass. Const., 1780, Part I, Art. XVI. See Duniway, Freedom of the Press in Massachusetts, 144–146.*

[2] *Pa. Const., 1790, Art. IX, § 7; Del. Const. 1792, Art. 1, § 5.*

[3] *The General Assembly of Virginia passed a statute on December 26, 1792, directed at establishment of "any government separate from, or independent of the government of* Virginia, *within the limits thereof, unless by act of the legislature of this commonwealth for that purpose first obtained." The statute provided that "EVERY person . . . who shall by writing or advised speaking, endeavour to instigate the people of this commonwealth to erect or establish such government without such assent as aforesaid, shall be adjudged guilty of a high crime and misdemeanor. . . ." Va. Code, 1803, c. CXXXVI.*

[4] *In a letter to Abigail Adams, dated September 11, 1804, Jefferson said with reference to the Sedition Act:*

"Nor does the opinion of the unconstitutionality and consequent nullity of that law remove all restraint from the overwhelming torrent of slander which is confounding all vice and virtue, all truth and falsehood in the US. The power to do that is fully possessed by the several state legislatures. It was reserved to them, and was denied to the general government, by the constitution according to our construction of it. While we deny that Congress have a right to controul the freedom of the press, we have ever asserted the right of the states, and their exclusive right, to do so."

The letter will be published in a forthcoming volume of The Papers of Thomas Jefferson (Boyd ed.), to which I am indebted for its reproduction here in its exact form.

The Sedition Act of July 14, 1798, was directed at two types of conduct. Section 1 made it a criminal offense to conspire "to impede the operation of any law of the United States," and to "counsel, advise or attempt to procure any insurrection, riot, unlawful assembly, or combination." Section 2 provided:

"That if any person shall write, print, utter or publish, or shall cause or procure to be written, printed, uttered or published, or shall knowingly and willingly assist or aid in writing, printing, uttering or publishing any false, scandalous and malicious writing or writings against the government of the United States, or either house of the Congress of the United States, or the President of the United States, with intent to de-

fame the said government, or either house of the said Congress, or the said President, or to bring them, or either of them, into contempt or disrepute; or to excite against them, or either or any of them, the hatred of the good people of the United States, or to stir up sedition within the United States, or to excite any unlawful combinations therein, for opposing or resisting any law of the United States, or any act of the President of the United States, done in pursuance of any such law, or of the powers in him vested by the constitution of the United States, or to resist, oppose, or defeat any such law or act, or to aid, encourage or abet any hostile designs of any foreign nation against the United States, their people or government, then such person, being thereof convicted before any court of the United States having jurisdiction thereof, shall be punished by a fine not exceeding two thousand dollars, and by imprisonment not exceeding two years." 1 Stat. 596–597.

No substantial objection was raised to § 1 of the Act. The argument against the validity of § 2 is stated most fully in the Virginia Report of 1799–1800. That Report, prepared for the House of Delegates by a committee of which Madison was chairman, attempted to establish that the power to regulate speech was not delegated to the Federal Government by the Constitution, and that the First Amendment had prohibited the National Government from exercising the power. In reply it was urged that power to restrict seditious writing was implicit in the acknowledged power of the Federal Government and prohibit seditious acts, and that the liberty of the press did not extend to the sort of speech restricted by the Act. See the Report of the Committee of the House of Representatives to which were referred memorials from the States, H. R. Rep. No. 110, 5th Cong., 3d Sess., published in American State Papers, Misc. Vol. 1, p. 181. For an extensive contemporary account of the controversy, see St. George Tucker's 1803 edition of Blackstone's Commentaries, Appendix to Vol. First, Part Second, Note G.

The language of the First Amendment is to be read not as barren words found in a dictionary but as symbols of historic experience illumined by the presuppositions of those who employed them. Not what words did Madison and Hamilton use, but what was it in their minds which they conveyed? Free speech is subject to prohibition of those abuses of expression which a civilized society may forbid. As in the case of every other provision of the Constitution that is not crystallized by the nature of its technical concepts, the fact that the First Amendment is not self-defining and self-enforcing neither impairs its usefulness nor compels its paralysis as a living instrument.

"The law is perfectly well settled," this Court said over fifty years ago, "that the first ten amendments to the Constitution, commonly known as the Bill of Rights, were not intended to lay down any novel principles of government, but simply to embody certain guaranties and immunities which we had inherited from our English ancestors, and which had from time immemorial been subject to certain well-recognized exceptions arising from the necessities of the case. In incorporating these principles into the fundamental law there was no intention of disregarding the exceptions, which continued to be recognized as if they had been formally expressed." *Robertson* v. *Baldwin,* 165 U.S. 275, 281. That this represents the authentic view of the Bill of Rights and the spirit in which it must be construed has been recognized again and again in cases that have come here within the last fifty years. See, *e.g., Gompers* v. *United States,* 233 U.S. 604, 610. Absolute rules would inevitably lead to absolute exceptions, and such exceptions would eventually corrode the rules.[5]

[5] *Professor Alexander Meiklejohn is a leading exponent of the absolutist interpretation of the First Amendment. Recognizing that certain forms of speech require regulation, he excludes those forms of expression entirely from the protection accorded by the Amendment. "The constitutional status of a merchant advertising his wares, of a paid lobbyist fighting for the advantage of his client, is utterly different from that of a citizen who is planning for the general welfare." Meiklejohn, Free Speech, 39. "The radio as it now operates among us is not free. Nor is it entitled to the protection of the First Amendment. It is not engaged in the task of enlarging and enriching human communication. It is engaged in making money."* Id. *at 104. Professor Meiklejohn even suggests that scholarship may now require such subvention and control that it no longer is entitled to protection by the First Amendment. See* id. *at 99–100. Professor Chafee in his review of the Meiklejohn book, 62 Harv. L. Rev. 891, has subjected this position to trenchant comment.*

The demands of free speech in a democratic society as well as the interest in national security are better served by candid and informed weighing of the competing interests, within the confines of the judicial process, than by announcing dogmas too inflexible for the non-Euclidian problems to be solved.

But how are competing interests to be assessed? Since they are not subject to quantitative ascertainment, the issue necessarily resolves itself into asking, who is to make the adjustment?—who is to balance the relevant factors and ascertain which interest is in the circumstances to prevail? Full responsibility for the choice cannot be given to the courts. Courts are not representative bodies. They are not designed to be a good reflex of a democratic society. Their judgment is best informed, and therefore most dependable, within narrow limits. Their essential quality is detachment, founded on independence. History teaches that the independence of the judiciary is jeopardized when courts become embroiled in the passions of the day and assume primary responsibility in choosing between competing political, economic and social pressures.

Primary responsibility for adjusting the interests which compete in the situation before us of necessity belongs to the Congress. The nature of the power to be exercised by this Court has been delineated in decisions not charged with the emotional appeal of situations such as that now before us. We are to set aside the judgment of those whose duty it is to legislate only if there is no reasonable basis for it. *Sinking-Fund Cases,* 99 U.S. 700, 718; *Mugler* v. *Kansas,* 123 U.S. 623, 660–661; *United States* v. *Carolene Products Co.,* 304 U.S. 144. We are to determine whether a statute is sufficiently definite to meet the constitutional requirements of due process, and whether it respects the safeguards against undue concentration of authority secured by separation of power. *United States* v. *Cohen Grocery Co.,* 255 U.S. 81. We must assure fairness of procedure, allowing full scope to governmental discretion but mindful of its impact on individuals in the context of the problem involved. *Joint Anti-Fascist Refugee Comm.* v. *McGrath,* 431 U.S. 123. And, of course, the proceedings in a particular case before us must have the warrant of substantial proof. Beyond these powers we must not go; we must scrupulously observe the narrow limits of judicial authority even though self-restraint is alone set over us. Above all we must remember that this Court's power of judicial review is not "an exercise of the powers of a super-legislature." Mr. Justice Brandeis and Mr. Justice Holmes, dissenting in *Burns Baking Co.* v. *Bryan,* 264 U.S. 504, 534.

A generation ago this distribution of responsibility would not have been questioned. See *Fox* v. *Washington,* 236 U.S. 273; *Meyer* v. *Nebraska,* 262 U.S. 390; *Bartels* v. *Iowa,* 262 U.S. 404; cf. *New York ex rel. Bryant* v. *Zimmerman,* 278 U.S. 63. But in recent decisions we have made explicit what has long been implicitly recognized. In reviewing statutes which restrict freedoms protected by the First Amendment, we have emphasized the close relation which those freedoms bear to maintenance of a free society. See *Kovacs* v. *Cooper,* 336 U.S. 77, 89, 95 (concurring). Some members of the Court—and at times a majority—have done more. They have suggested that our function in reviewing statutes restricting freedom of expression differs sharply from our normal duty in sitting in judgment on legislation. It has been said that such statutes "must be justified by clear public interest, threatened not doubtfully or remotely, but by clear and present danger. The rational connection between the remedy provided and the evil to be curbed, which in other contexts might support legislation against attack on due process grounds, will not suffice." *Thomas* v. *Collins,* 323 U.S. 516, 530. It has been suggested, with the casualness of a footnote, that such legislation is not presumptively valid, see *United States* v. *Carolene Products Co.,* 304 U.S. 144, 152, n. 4, and it has been weightily reiterated that freedom of speech has a "preferred position" among constitutional safeguards. *Kovacs* v. *Cooper,* 336 U.S. 77, 88.

The precise meaning intended to be conveyed by these phrases need not now be pursued. It is enough to note that they have recurred in the Court's opinions, and their cumulative force has, not without justification, engendered belief that there is a constitutional principle, expressed by those attractive but imprecise words, prohibiting restriction upon utterance unless it creates a situation of "imminent" peril against which legislation may guard.[6] It is on this

[6] *In* Hartzel *v.* United States, *322 U.S. 680, 687, the Court reversed a conviction for wilfully causing insubordination in the military forces on the ground that the intent required*

body of the Court's pronouncements that the defendants' argument here is based.

In all fairness, the argument cannot be met by reinterpreting the Court's frequent use of "clear" and "present" to mean an entertainable "probability." In giving this meaning to the phrase "clear and present danger," the Court of Appeals was fastidiously confining the rhetoric of opinions to the exact scope of what was decided by them. We have greater responsibility for having given constitutional support, over repeated protests, to uncritical libertarian generalities.

Nor is the argument of the defendants adequately met by citing isolated cases. Adjustment of clash of interests which are at once subtle and fundamental is not likely to reveal entire consistency in a series of instances presenting the clash. It is not too difficult to find what one seeks in the language of decisions reporting the effort to reconcile free speech with the interests with which it conflicts. The case for the defendants requires that their conviction be tested against the entire body of our relevant decisions. Since the significance of every expression of thought derives from the circumstances evoking it, results reached rather than language employed give the vital meaning. See *Cohens* v. *Virginia,* 6 Wheat. 264, 442; Wambaugh, The Study of Cases, 10.

There is an added reason why we must turn to the decisions. "Great cases," it is appropriate to remember, "like hard cases make bad law. For great cases are called great, not by reason of their real importance in shaping the law of the future, but because of some accident of immediate overwhelming interest which appeals to the feelings and distorts the judgment. These immediate interests exercise a kind of hydraulic pressure which makes what previously was clear seem doubtful, and before which even well settled principles of law will bend." Mr. Justice Holmes, dissenting in *Northern Securities Co.* v. *United States,* 193 U.S. 197, 400–401.

This is such a case. Unless we are to compromise judicial impartiality and subject these defendants to the risk of an *ad hoc* judgment influenced by the impregnating atmosphere of the times, the constitutionality of their conviction must be determined by principles established in cases decided in more tranquil periods. If those decisions are to be used as a guide and not as an argument, it is important to view them as a whole and to distrust the easy generalizations to which some of them lend themselves.

II.

We have recognized and resolved conflicts between speech and competing interests in six different types of cases.[7]

1. The cases involving a conflict between the interest in allowing free expression of ideas in public places and the interest in protection of the public peace and the primary uses of streets and parks, were too recently considered to be rehearsed here. *Niemotko* v. *Maryland,* 340 U.S. 268, 273. It suffices to recall that the result in each case was found to turn on the character of the interest with which the speech clashed, the method used to impose the restriction, and the nature and circumstances of the utterance prohibited. While the decisions

---

by the statute was not shown. It added that there was a second element necessary to conviction, "consisting of a clear and present danger that the activities in question will bring about the substantive evils which Congress has a right to prevent. Schenck *v.* United States, *249 U.S. 47. Both elements must be proved by the Government beyond a reasonable doubt."*

Other passages responsible for attributing to the Court the principle that imminence of the apprehended evil is necessary to conviction in free-speech cases are collected in an Appendix to this opinion, post, *p. 556.*

[7] *No useful purpose would be served by considering here decisions in which the Court treated the challenged regulation as though it imposed no real restraint on speech or on the press.* E.g., Associated Press *v.* Labor Board, *301 U.S. 103;* Valentine *v.* Chrestensen, *316 U.S. 52;* Railway Express Agency *v.* New York, *336 U.S. 106;* Lewis Publishing Co. *v.* Morgan, *229 U.S. 288. We recognized that restrictions on speech were involved in* United States ex rel. Milwaukee Publishing Co. *v.* Burleson, *255 U.S. 407, and* Gilbert *v.* Minnesota, *254 U.S. 325; but the decisions raised issues so different from those presented here that they too need not be considered in detail. Our decisions in* Stromberg *v.* California, *283 U.S. 359, and* Winters *v.* New York, *333 U.S. 507, turned on the indefiniteness of the statutes.*

recognized the importance of free speech and carefully scrutinized the justification for its regulation, they rejected the notion that vindication of the deep public interest in freedom of expression requires subordination of all conflicting values.

2. A critique of the cases testing restrictions on picketing is made more difficult by the inadequate recognition by the Court from the outset that the loyalties and responses evoked and exacted by picket lines differentiate this form of expression from other modes of communication. See *Thornhill* v. *Alabama,* 310 U.S. 88. But the crux of the decision in the *Thornhill* case was that a State could not constitutionally punish peaceful picketing when neither the aim of the picketing nor the manner in which it was carried out conflicted with a substantial interest. In subsequent decisions we sustained restrictions designed to prevent recurrence of violence, *Milk Wagon Drivers Union* v. *Meadowmoor Dairies,* 312 U.S. 287, or reasonably to limit the area of industrial strife, *Carpenters & Joiners Union* v. *Ritter's Cafe,* 315 U.S. 722; cf. *Bakery & Pastry Drivers Local* v. *Wohl,* 315 U.S. 769. We held that a State's policy against restraints of trade justified it in prohibiting picketing which violated that policy, *Giboney* v. *Empire Storage Co.,* 336 U.S. 490; we sustained restrictions designed to encourage self-employed persons, *International Brotherhood of Teamsters Union* v. *Hanke,* 339 U.S. 470; and to prevent racial discrimination, *Hughes* v. *Superior Court,* 339 U.S. 460. The Fourteenth Amendment bars a State from prohibiting picketing when there is no fair justification for the breadth of the restriction imposed. *American Federation of Labor* v. *Swing,* 312 U.S. 321; *Cafeteria Employees Union* v. *Angelos,* 320 U.S. 293. But it does not prevent a State from denying the means of communication that picketing affords in a fair balance between the interests of trade unionism and other interests of the community.

3. In three cases we have considered the scope and application of the power of the Government to exclude, deport, or denaturalize aliens because of their advocacy or their beliefs. In *United States ex rel. Turner* v. *Williams,* 194 U.S. 279, we held that the First Amendment did not disable Congress from directing the exclusion of an alien found in an administrative proceeding to be an anarchist. "[A]s long as human governments endure," we said, "they cannot be denied the power of self-preservation, as that question is presented here." 194 U.S. at 294. In *Schneiderman* v. *United States,* 320 U.S. 118, and *Bridges* v. *Wixon,* 326 U.S. 135, we did not consider the extent of the power of Congress. In each case, by a closely divided Court, we interpreted a statute authorizing denaturalization or deportation to impose on the Government the strictest standards of proof.

4. History regards "freedom of the press" as indispensable for a free society and for its government. We have, therefore, invalidated discriminatory taxation against the press and prior restraints on publication of defamatory matter. *Grosjean* v. *American Press Co.,* 297 U.S. 233; *Near* v. *Minnesota,* 283 U.S. 697.

We have also given clear indication of the importance we attach to dissemination of ideas in reviewing the attempts of States to reconcile freedom of the press with protection of the integrity of the judicial process. In *Pennekamp* v. *Florida,* 328 U.S. 331, the Court agreed that the Fourteenth Amendment barred a State from adjudging in contempt of court the publisher of critical and inaccurate comment about portions of a litigation that for all practical purposes were no longer pending. We likewise agreed, in a minor phase of our decision in *Bridges* v. *California,* 314 U.S. 252, that even when statements in the press relate to matters still pending before a court, convictions for their publication cannot be sustained if their utterance is too trivial to be deemed a substantial threat to the impartial administration of justice.

The Court has, however, sharply divided on what constitutes a sufficient interference with the course of justice. In the first decision, *Patterson* v. *Colorado,* 205 U.S. 454, the Court affirmed a judgment for contempt imposed by a State supreme court for publication of articles reflecting on the conduct of the court in cases still before it on motions for rehearing. In the *Bridges* case, however, a majority held that a State court could not protect itself from the implied threat of a powerful newspaper that failure of an elected judge to impose a severe sentence would be a "serious mistake." The same case also placed beyond a State's power to punish the publication of a telegram from the president of an important union who threatened a damaging strike in the event of an adverse decision. The majority in *Craig* v. *Harney,* 331 U.S. 367, 376, held that the Fourteenth Amendment protected "strong," "intemperate," "unfair" criticism of the way an elected lay judge was conducting a pending civil case. None of the cases establishes that the public interest in a free press must in all instances prevail over the public interest in dispassionate adjudication. But the *Bridges* and *Craig* decisions, if they survive, tend to require a showing that interference be so imminent and so demonstrable that the power theoretically possessed by the State is largely paralyzed.

5. Our decision in *American Communications Assn.* v. *Douds,* 339 U.S. 382, recognized that the exercise of political rights protected by the First Amendment was necessarily discouraged by the requirement of the Taft-Hartley Act that officers of unions employing the services of the National Labor Relations Board sign affidavits that they are not Communists. But we held that the statute was not for this reason presumptively invalid. The problem, we said, was "one of weighing the probable effects of the statute upon the free exercise of the right of speech and assembly against the congressional determination that political strikes are evils of conduct which cause substantial harm to interstate commerce and that Communists and others identified by § 9 (h) pose continuing threats to that public interest when in positions of union leadership." 339 U.S. at 400. On balance, we decided that the legislative judgment was a permissible one.[8]

6. Statutes prohibiting speech because of its tendency to lead to crime present a conflict of interests which bears directly on the problem now before us. The first case in which we consider this conflict was *Fox* v. *Washington, supra.* The statute there challenged had been interpreted to prohibit publication of matter "encouraging an actual breach of law." We held that the Fourteenth Amendment did not prohibit application of the statute to an article which we concluded incited a breach of laws against indecent exposure. We said that the statute "lays hold of encouragements that, apart from statute, if directed to a particular person's conduct, generally would make him who uttered them guilty of a misdemeanor if not an accomplice or a principal in the crime encouraged, and deals with the publication of them to a wider and less selected audience." 236 U.S. at 277–278. To be sure, the *Fox* case preceded the explicit absorption of the substance of the First Amendment in the Fourteenth. But subsequent decisions extended the *Fox* principle to free-speech situations. They are so important to the problem before us that we must consider them in detail.

(a) The first important application of the principle was made in six cases arising under the Espionage Act of 1917. That Act prohibits conspiracies and attempts to "obstruct the recruiting or enlistment service." In each of the first three cases, Mr. Justice Holmes wrote for a unanimous Court, affirming the convictions. The evidence in *Schenck* v. *United States,* 249 U.S. 47, showed that the defendant had conspired to circulate among men called for the draft 15,000 copies of a circular which asserted a "right" to oppose the draft. The defendant in *Frohwerk* v. *United States,* 249 U.S. 204, was shown to have conspired to publish in a newspaper twelve articles describing the sufferings of American troops and the futility of our war aims. The record was inadequate, and we said that it was therefore "impossible to say that it might not have been found that the circulation of the paper was in quarters where a little breath would be enough to kindle a flame and that the fact was known and relied upon by those who sent the paper out." 249 U.S. at 209. In *Debs* v. *United States,* 249 U.S. 211, the indictment charged that the defendant had delivered a public speech expounding socialism and praising Socialists who had been convicted of abetting violation of the draft laws.

The ground of decision in each case was the same. The First Amendment "cannot have been, and obviously was not, intended to give immunity for every possible use of language. *Robertson* v. *Baldwin,* 165 U.S. 275, 281." *Frohwerk* v. *United States, supra,* at 206. "The question in every case is whether the words used are used in such circumstances and are of such a nature as to create a clear and present danger that they will bring about the substantive evils

[8] *The Taft-Hartley Act also requires that an officer of a union using the services of the National Labor Relations Board take oath that he "does not believe in, and is not a member of or supports any organization that believes in or teaches, the overthrow of the United States Government by force or by any illegal or unconstitutional methods." The Court divided on the validity of this requirement. Test oaths raise such special problems that decisions on their validity are not directly helpful here. See* West Virginia Board of Education *v.* Barnette, *319 U.S. 624.*

that Congress has a right to prevent. It is a question of proximity and degree." *Schenck* v. *United States, supra,* at 52. When "the words used had as their natural tendency and reasonably probable effect to obstruct the recruiting service," and "the defendant had the specific intent to do so in his mind," conviction in wartime is not prohibited by the Constitution. *Debs* v. *United States, supra,* at 216.

In the three succeeding cases Holmes and Brandeis, JJ., dissented from judgments of the Court affirming convictions. The indictment in *Abrams* v. *United States,* 250 U.S. 616 was laid under an amendment to the Espionage Act which prohibited conspiracies to advocate curtailment of production to material necessary to prosecution of the war, with the intent thereby to hinder the United States in the prosecution of the war. It appeared that the defendants were anarchists who had printed circulars and distributed them in New York City. The leaflets repeated standard Marxist slogans, condemned American intervention in Russia, and called for a general strike in protest. In *Schaefer* v. *United States,* 251 U.S. 466, the editors of a German-language newspaper in Philadelphia were charged with obstructing the recruiting service with and wilfully publishing false reports with the intent to promote the success of the enemies of the United States. The evidence showed publication of articles which accused American troops of weakness and mendacity and in one instance misquoted or mistranslated two words of a Senator's speech. The indictment in *Pierce* v. *United States,* 252 U.S. 239, charged that the defendants had attempted to cause insubordination in the armed forces and had conveyed false reports with intent to interfere with military operations. Conviction was based on circulation of a pamphlet which belittled Allied war aims and criticized conscription in strong terms.

In each case both the majority and the dissenting opinions relied on *Schenck* v. *United States.* The Court divided on its view of the evidence. The majority held that the jury could infer the required intent and the probable effect of the articles from their content. Holmes and Brandeis, JJ., thought that only "expressions of opinion and exhortations," 250 U.S. at 631, were involved, that they were "puny anonymities," 250 U.S. at 629, "impotent to produce the evil against which the statute aimed," 251 U.S. 493, and that from them the specific intent required by the statute could not reasonably be inferred. The Court agreed that an incitement to disobey the draft statute could constitutionally be punished. It disagreed over the proof required to show such an incitement.

(b) In the eyes of a majority of the Court, *Gitlow* v. *New York,* 268 U.S. 652, presented a very different problem. There the defendant had been convicted under a New York statute nearly identical with the Smith Act now before us. The evidence showed that the defendant was an official of the Left Wing Section of the Socialist Party, and that he was responsible for publication of a Left Wing Manifesto. This document repudiated "moderate Socialism," and urged the necessity of a militant "revolutionary Socialism," based on class struggle and revolutionary mass action. No evidence of the effect of the Manifesto was introduced; but the jury were instructed that they could not convict unless they found that the document advocated employing unlawful acts for the purpose of overthrowing organized government.

The conviction was affirmed. The question, the Court held, was entirely different from that involved in *Schenck* v. *United States,* where the statute prohibited acts without reference to language. Here, where "the legislative body has determined generally, in the constitutional exercise of its discretion, that utterances of a certain kind involve such danger of substantive evil that they may be punished, the question whether any specific utterance coming within the prohibited class is likely, in and of itself, to bring about the substantive evil, is not open to consideration." 268 U.S. at 670. It is sufficient that the defendant's conduct falls within the statute, and that the statute is a reasonable exercise of legislative judgment.

This principle was also applied in *Whitney* v. *California,* 274 U.S. 357, to sustain a conviction under a State criminal syndicalism statute. That statute made it a felony to assist in organizing a group assembled to advocate the commission of crime, sabotage, or unlawful acts of violence as a means of effecting political or industrial change. The defendant was found to have assisted in organizing the Communist Labor Party of California, an organization found to have the specified character. It was held that the legislature was not unreasonable in believing organization of such a party "involves such danger to the public peace and the security of the State, that these acts should be penalized in the exercise of its police power." 274 U.S. at 371.

In neither of these cases did Mr. Justice Holmes and Mr. Justice Brandeis accept the reasoning of the Court. " 'The question,' " they said, quoting from *Schenck* v. *United States,* " 'in every case is whether the words used are used in such circumstances and are of such a nature as to create a clear and present danger that they will bring about the substantive evils that [the State] has a right to prevent.' " 268 U.S. at 672–673. Since the Manifesto circulated by Gitlow "had no chance of starting a present conflagration," 268 U.S. at 673, they dissented from the affirmance of his conviction. In *Whitney* v. *California,* they concurred in the result reached by the Court, but only because the record contained some evidence that organization of the Communist Labor Party might further a conspiracy to commit immediate serious crimes, and the credibility of the evidence was not put in issue by the defendant.[9]

(c) Subsequent decisions have added little to the principles established in these two groups of cases. In the only case arising under the Espionage Act decided by this Court during the last war, the substantiality of the evidence was the crucial issue. The defendant in *Hartzel* v. *United States,* 322 U.S. 680, was an educated man and a citizen, not actively affiliated with any political group. In 1942 he wrote three articles condemning our wartime allies and urging that the war be converted into a racial conflict. He mailed the tracts to 600 people, including high-ranking military officers. According to his testimony his intention was to "create sentiment against war amongst the white races." The majority of this Court held that a jury could not reasonably infer from these facts that the defendant had acted with a specific intent to cause insubordination or disloyalty in the armed forces.

Of greater importance is the fact that the issue of law which divided the Court in the *Gitlow* and *Whitney* cases has not again been clearly raised, although in four additional instances we have reviewed convictions under comparable statutes. *Fiske* v. *Kansas,* 274 U.S. 380, involved a criminal syndicalism statute similar to that before us in *Whitney* v. *California.* We reversed a conviction based on evidence that the defendant exhibited an innocuous preamble to the constitution of the Industrial Workers of the World in soliciting members for that organization. In *Herndon* v. *Lowry,* 301 U.S. 242, the defendant had solicited members for the Communist Party, but there was no proof that he had urged or even approved those of the Party's aims which were unlawful. We reversed a conviction obtained under a statute prohibiting an attempt to incite to insurrection by violence, on the ground that the Fourteenth Amendment prohibited conviction where on the evidence a jury could not reasonably infer that the defendant had violated the statute the State sought to apply.[10]

The other two decisions go no further than to hold that the statute as construed by the State courts exceeded the bounds of a legislative judgment founded in reason. The statute presented in *De Jonge* v. *Oregon,* 299 U.S. 353, had been construed to apply to any one who merely assisted in the conduct of a meeting held under the auspices of the Communist Party. In *Taylor* v. *Mississippi,* 319 U.S. 583, the statute prohibited dissemination of printed matter "designed and calculated to encourage violence, sabotage, or disloyalty to the government of the United States, or the state of Mississippi." We reversed a conviction for what we concluded was mere criticism and prophesy, without indicating whether we thought the statute could in any circumstances validly be applied. What the defendants communicated, we said, "is not claimed or shown to have been done with an evil or sinister purpose, to have advocated or incited subversive action against the nation or state, or to have threatened any clear and present danger to our institutions or our Government." 319 U.S. at 589–590.

I must leave to others the ungrateful task of trying to reconcile all these decisions. In some instances we have too readily permitted juries to infer deception from error, or intention from argumentative or critical statements. *Abrams* v. *United States, supra; Schaefer* v. *United States, supra; Pierce* v. *United States, supra; Gilbert* v. *Minnesota,*

[9] Burns *v.* United States, *274 U.S. 328, adds nothing to the decision in* Whitney *v.* California.

[10] *In* Herndon *v.* Georgia, *295 U.S. 441, the opinion of the Court was concerned solely with a question of procedure. Mr. Justice Brandeis, Mr. Justice Stone, and Mr. Justice Cardozo, however, thought that the problem of* Gitlow *v.* New York *was raised. See 295 U.S. at 446.*

254 U.S. 325. In other instances we weighted the interest in free speech so heavily that we permitted essential conflicting values to be destroyed. *Bridges* v. *California, supra; Craig* v. *Harney, supra.* Viewed as a whole, however, the decisions express an attitude toward the judicial function and a standard of values which for me are decisive of the case before us.

First.—Free-speech cases are not an exception to the principle that we are not legislators, that direct policy-making is not our province. How best to reconcile competing interests is the business of legislatures, and the balance they strike is a judgment not to be displaced by ours, but to be respected unless outside the pale of fair judgment.

On occasion we have strained to interpret legislation in order to limit its effect on interests protected by the First Amendment. *Schneiderman* v. *United States, supra; Bridges* v. *Wixon, supra.* In some instances we have denied to States the deference to which I think they are entitled. *Bridges* v. *California, supra; Craig* v. *Harney, supra.* Once in this recent course of decisions the Court refused to permit a jury to draw inferences which seemed to me to be obviously reasonable. *Hartzel* v. *United States, supra.*

But in no case has a majority of this Court held that a legislative judgment, even as to freedom of utterance, may be overturned merely because the Court would have made a different choice between the competing interests had the initial legislative judgment been for it to make. In the cases in which the opinions go farthest towards indicating a total rejection of respect for legislative determinations, the interests between which choice was actually made were such that decision might well have been expressed in the familiar terms of want of reason in the legislative judgment. In *Thomas* v. *Collins,* 323 U.S. 516, for example, decision could not unreasonably have been placed on the ground that no substantial interest justified a State in requiring an out-of-State labor leader to register before speaking in advocacy of the cause of trade unionism. In *Martin* v. *City of Struthers,* 319 U.S. 141, it was broadly held that a municipality was not justified in prohibiting knocking on doors and ringing doorbells for the purpose of delivering handbills. But since the good faith and reasonableness of the regulation were placed in doubt by the fact that the city did not think it necessary also to prohibit door-to-door commercial sales, decision could be sustained on narrower ground. And compare *Breard* v. *Alexandria, post,* p. 622, decided this day.

In other cases, moreover, we have given clear indication that even when free speech is involved we attach great significance to the determination of the legislature. *Gitlow* v. *New York, supra; Whitney* v. *California, supra; American Communications Assn.* v. *Douds, supra;* cf. *Bridges* v. *California,* 314 U.S. at 260. And see *Hughes* v. *Superior Court, supra; International Brotherhood of Teamsters Union* v. *Hanke, supra.*

In *Gitlow* v. *New York,* we put our respect for the legislative judgment in terms which, if they were accepted here, would make decision easy. For that case held that, when the legislature has determined that advocacy of forceful overthrow should be forbidden, a conviction may be sustained without a finding that in the particular case the advocacy had a close relation to a serious attempt at overthrow. We held that it was enough that the statute be a reasonable exercise of the legislative judgment, and that the defendant's conduct fall within the statute.

One of the judges below rested his affirmance on the *Gitlow* decision, and the defendants do not attempt to distinguish the case. They place their argument squarely on the ground that the case has been overruled by subsequent decisions. It has not been explicitly overruled. But it would be disingenuous to deny that the dissent in *Gitlow* has been treated with the respect usually accorded to a decision.

The result of the *Gitlow* decision was to send a left-wing Socialist to jail for publishing a Manifesto expressing Marxist exhortations. It requires excessive tolerance of the legislative judgment to suppose that the *Gitlow* publication in the circumstances could justify serious concern.

In contrast, there is ample justification for a legislative judgment that the conspiracy now before us is a substantial threat to national order and security. If the Smith Act is justified at all, it is justified precisely because it may serve to prohibit the type of conspiracy for which these defendants were convicted. The court below properly held that as a matter of separability the Smith Act may be limited to those situations to which it can constitutionally be applied. See 183 F. 2d at 214–215. Our decision today certainly does not mean that the Smith Act can constitutionally be applied to facts like those in *Gitlow* v. *New York.* While reliance may properly be placed on the attitude of judicial self-restraint which the *Gitlow* decision reflects, it is not necessary to depend on the facts or the full extent of the theory of that case in order to find that the judgment of Congress, as applied to the facts of the case now before us, is not in conflict with the First Amendment.

Second.—A survey of the relevant decisions indicates that the results which we have reached are on the whole those that would ensue from careful weighing of conflicting interests. The complex issues presented by regulation of speech in public places, by picketing, and by legislation prohibiting advocacy of crime have been resolved by scrutiny of many factors besides the imminence and gravity of the evil threatened. The matter has been well summarized by a reflective student of the Court's work. "The truth is that the clear-and-present-danger test is an oversimplified judgment unless it takes account also of a number of other factors: the relative seriousness of the danger in comparison with the value of the occasion for speech or political activity; the availability of more moderate controls than those which the state has imposed; and perhaps the specific intent with which the speech or activity is launched. No matter how rapidly we utter the phrase 'clear and present danger,' or how closely we hyphenate the words, they are not a substitute for the weighing of values. They tend to convey a delusion of certitude when what is most certain is the complexity of the strands in the web of freedoms which the judge must disentangle." Freund, On Understanding the Supreme Court, 27–28.

It is a familiar experience in the law that new situations do not fit neatly into legal conceptions that arose under different circumstances to satisfy different needs. So it was when the injunction was tortured into an instrument of oppression against labor in industrial conflicts. So it is with the attempt to use the direction of thought lying behind the criterion of "clear and present danger" wholly out of the context in which it originated, and to make of it an absolute dogma and definitive measuring rod for the power of Congress to deal with assaults against security through devices other than overt physical attempts.

Bearing in mind that Mr. Justice Holmes regarded questions under the First Amendment as questions of "proximity and degree," *Schenck* v. *United States,* 249 U.S. at 52, it would be a distortion, indeed a mockery, of his reasoning to compare the "puny anonymities," 250 U.S. at 629, to which he was addressing himself in the *Abrams* case in 1919 or the publication that was "futile and too remote from possible consequences," 268 U.S. at 673, in the *Gitlow* case in 1925 with the setting of events in this case in 1950.

"It does an ill-service to the author of the most quoted judicial phrases regarding freedom of speech, to make him the victim of a tendency which he fought all his life, whereby phrases are made to do service for critical analysis by being turned into dogma. 'It is one of the misfortunes of the law that ideas become encysted in phrases and thereafter for a long time cease to provoke further analysis.' Holmes, J., dissenting, in *Hyde* v. *United States,* 225 U.S. 347, 384, at 391." The phrase "clear and present danger," in its origin, "served to indicate the importance of freedom of speech to a free society but also to emphasize that its exercise must be compatible with the preservation of other freedoms essential to a democracy and guaranteed by our Constitution." *Pennekamp* v. *Florida,* 328 U.S. 331, 350, 352–353 (concurring). It were far better that the phrase be abandoned than that it be sounded once more to hide from the believers in an absolute right of free speech the plain fact that the interest in speech, profoundly important as it is, is no more conclusive in judicial review than other attributes of democracy or than a determination of the people's representatives that a measure is necessary to assure the safety of government itself.

Third.—Not every type of speech occupies the same position on the scale of values. There is no substantial public interest in permitting certain kinds of utterances: "the lewd and obscene, the profane, the libelous, and the insulting or 'fighting' words —those which by their very utterance inflict injury or tend to incite an immediate breach of the peace." *Chaplinsky* v. *New Hampshire* 315 U.S. 568, 572. We have frequently indicated that the interest in protecting speech depends on the circumstances of the occasion. See cases collected in *Niemotko* v. *Maryland,* 340 U.S. at 275–283. It is pertinent to the decision before us to consider where on the scale of values we have in the past placed the type of speech now claiming constitutional immunity.

The defendants have been convicted of conspiring to organize a party of persons who advocate the overthrow of the Government by force and violence. The jury has found that the object of the conspiracy is advocacy as "a rule or principle of action," "by language reasonably and ordinarily calculated to incite persons to such action," and with the intent to cause the overthrow "as speedily as circumstances would permit."

On any scale of values which we have hitherto recognized, speech of this sort ranks low.

Throughout our decisions there has recurred a distinction between the statement of an idea which may prompt its hearers to take unlawful action, and advocacy that such action be taken. The distinction has its root in the conception of the common law, supported by principles of morality, that a person who procures another to do an act is responsible for that act as though he had done it himself. This principle was extended in *Fox* v. *Washington, supra,* to words directed to the public generally which would constitute an incitement were they directed to an individual. It was adapted in *Schenck* v. *United States, supra,* into a rule of evidence designed to restrict application of the Espionage Act. It was relied on by the Court in *Gitlow* v. *New York, supra.* The distinction has been repeated in many of the decisions in which we have upheld the claims of speech. We frequently have distinguished protected forms of expression from statements which "incite to violence and crime and threaten the overthrow of organized government by unlawful means." *Stromberg* v. *California,* 283 U.S. at 369. See also *Near* v. *Minnesota,* 283 U.S. at 716; *De Jonge* v. *Oregon,* 299 U.S. at 365; *Cantwell* v. *Connecticut,* 310 U.S. 296, 308; *Taylor* v. *Mississippi,* 319 U.S. at 589.

It is true that there is no divining rod by which we may locate "advocacy." Exposition of ideas readily merges into advocacy. The same Justice who gave currency to application of the incitement doctrine in this field dissented four times from what he thought was its misapplication. As he said in the *Gitlow* dissent, "Every idea is an incitement." 268 U.S. at 673. Even though advocacy of overthrow deserves little protection, we should hesitate to prohibit it if we thereby inhibit the interchange of rational ideas so essential to representative government and free society.

But there is underlying validity in the distinction between advocacy and the interchange of ideas, and we do not discard a useful tool because it may be misused. That such a distinction could be used unreasonably by those in power against hostile or unorthodox views does not negate the fact that it may be used reasonably against an organization wielding the power of the centrally controlled international Communist movement. The object of the conspiracy before us is so clear that the chance of error in saying that the defendants conspired to advocate rather than to express ideas is slight. MR. JUSTICE DOUGLAS quite properly points out that the conspiracy before us is not a conspiracy to overthrow the Government. But it would be equally wrong to treat it as a seminar in political theory.

III.

These general considerations underlie decision of the case before us.

On the one hand is the interest in security. The Communist Party was not designed by these defendants as an ordinary political party. For the circumstances of its organization, its aims and methods, and the relation of the defendants to its organization and aims we are concluded by the jury's verdict. The jury found that the Party rejects the basic premise of our political system—that change is to be brought about by nonviolent constitutional process. The jury found that the Party advocates the theory that there is a duty and necessity to overthrow the Government by force and violence. It found that the Party entertains and promotes this view, not as a prophetic insight or as a bit of unworldly speculation, but as a program for winning adherents and as a policy to be translated into action.

In finding that the defendants violated the statute, we may not treat as established fact that the Communist Party in this country is of significant size, well-organized, well-disciplined, conditioned to embark on unlawful activity when given the command. But in determining whether application of the statute to the defendants is within the constitutional powers of Congress, we are not limited to the facts found by the jury. We must view such a question in the light of whatever is relevant to a legislative judgment. We may take judicial notice that the Communist doctrines which these defendants have conspired to advocate are in the ascendency in powerful nations who cannot be acquitted of unfriendliness to the institutions of this country. We may take account of evidence brought forward at this trial and elsewhere, much of which has long been common knowledge. In sum, it would amply justify a legislature in concluding that recruitment of additional members for the Party would create a substantial danger to national security.

In 1947, it has been reliably reported, at least 60,000 members were enrolled in the Party.[11] Evidence was introduced in this case that the membership was organized in small units, linked by an intricate chain of command, and protected by elaborate precautions designed to prevent disclosure of individual identity. There are no reliable data tracing acts of sabotage or espionage directly to these defendants. But a Canadian Royal Commission appointed in 1946 to investigate espionage reported that it was "overwhelmingly established" that "the Communist movement was the principal base within which the espionage network was recruited."[12] The most notorious spy in recent history was led into the service of the Soviet Union through Communist indoctrination.[13] Evidence supports the conclusion that members of the Party seek and occupy positions of importance in political and labor organizations.[14] Congress was not barred by the Constitution from believing that indifference to such experience would be an exercise not of freedom but of irresponsibility.

On the other hand is the interest in free speech. The right to exert all governmental powers in aid of maintaining our institutions and resisting their physical overthrow does not include intolerance of opinions and speech that cannot do harm although opposed and perhaps alien to dominant, traditional opinion. The treatment of its minorities, especially their legal position, is among the most searching tests of the level of civilization attained by a society. It is better for those who have almost unlimited power of government in their hands to err on the side of freedom. We have enjoyed so much freedom for so long that we are perhaps in danger of forgetting how much blood it cost to establish the Bill of Rights.

Of course no government can recognize a "right" of revolution, or a "right" to incite revolution if the incitement has no other purpose or effect. But speech is seldom restricted to a single purpose, and its effects may be manifold. A public interest is not wanting in granting freedom to speak their minds even to those who advocate the overthrow of the Government by force. For, as the evidence in this case abundantly illustrates, coupled with such advocacy is criticism of defects in our society. Criticism is the spur to reform; and Burke's admonition that a healthy society must reform in order to conserve has not lost its force. Astute observers have remarked that one of the characteristics of the American Republic is indifference to fundamental criticism. Bryce, The American Commonwealth, c. 84. It is a commonplace that there may be a grain of truth in the most uncouth doctrine, however false and repellent the balance may be. Suppressing advocates of overthrow inevitably will also silence critics who do not advocate overthrow but fear that their criticism may be so construed. No matter how clear we may be that the defendants

[11] *See the testimony of the Director of the Federal Bureau of Investigation. Hearings before the House Committee on Un-American Activities, on H.R. 1884 and H.R. 2122, 80th Cong., 1st Sess., Part 2, p. 37.*

[12] *Report of the Royal Commission to Investigate Communication of Secret and Confidential Information to Agents of a Foreign Power, June 27, 1946, p. 44. There appears to be little reliable evidence demonstrating directly that the Communist Party in this country has recruited persons willing to engage in espionage or other unlawful activity on behalf of the Soviet Union. The defection of a Soviet diplomatic employee, however, led to a careful investigation of an espionage network in Canada, and has disclosed the effectiveness of the Canadian Communist Party in conditioning its members to disclose to Soviet agents vital information of a secret character. According to the Report of the Royal Commission investigating the network, conspiratorial characteristics of the Party similar to those shown in the evidence now before us were instrumental in developing the necessary motivation to cooperate in the espionage. See pp. 43–83 of the Report.*

[13] *The Communist background of Dr. Klaus Fuchs was brought out in the proceedings against him. See* The [London] Times, *Mar. 2, 1950, p. 2, col. 6.*

[14] *See* American Communications Assn. *v.* Douds, *339 U.S. 382. Former Senator Robert M. La Follette, Jr., has reported his experience with infiltration of Communist sympathizers into congressional committee staffs. Collier's, Feb. 8, 1947, p. 22.*

now before us are preparing to overthrow our Government at the propitious moment, it is self-delusion to think that we can punish them for their advocacy without adding to the risks run by loyal citizens who honestly believe in some of the reforms these defendants advance. It is a sobering fact that in sustaining the convictions before us we can hardly escape restriction on the interchange of ideas.

We must not overlook the value of that interchange. Freedom of expression is the well-spring of our civilization—the civilization we seek to maintain and further by recognizing the right of Congress to put some limitation upon expression. Such are the paradoxes of life. For social development of trial and error, the fullest possible opportunity for the free play of the human mind is an indispensable prerequisite. The history of civilization is in considerable measure the displacement of error which once held sway as official truth by beliefs which in turn have yielded to other truths. Therefore the liberty of man to search for truth ought not to be fettered, no matter what orthodoxies he may challenge. Liberty of thought soon shrivels without freedom of expression. Nor can truth be pursued in an atmosphere hostile to the endeavor or under dangers which are hazarded only by heroes.

"The interest, which [the First Amendment] guards, and which gives it its importance, presupposes that there are no orthodoxies—religious, political, economic, or scientific—which are immune from debate and dispute. Back of that is the assumption —itself an orthodoxy, and the one permissible exception—that truth will be most likely to emerge, if no limitations are imposed upon utterances that can with any plausibility be regarded as efforts to present grounds for accepting or rejecting propositions whose truth the utterer asserts, or denies." *International Brotherhood of Electrical Workers* v. *Labor Board,* 181 F. 2d 34, 40. In the last analysis it is on the validity of this faith that our national security is staked.

It is not for us to decide how we would adjust the clash of interests which this case presents were the primary responsibility for reconciling it ours. Congress has determined that the danger created by advocacy of overthrow justifies the ensuing restriction on freedom of speech. The determination was made after due deliberation, and the seriousness of the congressional purpose is attested by the volume of legislation passed to effectuate the same ends.[15]

Can we then say that the judgement Congress exercised was denied it by the Constitution? Can we establish a constitutional doctrine which forbids the elected representatives of the people to make this choice? Can we hold that the First Amendment deprives Congress of what it deemed necessary for the Government's protection?

To make validity of legislation depend on judicial reading of events still in the womb of time—a forecast, that is, of the outcome of forces at best appreciated only with knowledge of the topmost secrets of nations—is to charge the judiciary with duties beyond its equipment. We do not expect courts to pronounce historic verdicts on bygone events. Even historians have conflicting views to this day on the origins and conduct of the French Revolution, or, for that matter, varying interpretations of "the glorious Revolution" of 1688. It is as absurd to be confident that we can measure the present clash of forces and their outcome as to ask us to read history still enveloped in clouds of controversy.

In the light of their experience, the Framers of the Constitution chose to keep

[15] *Immigration laws require, for instance, exclusion and deportation of aliens who advocate the overthrow of the Government by force and violence, and declare ineligible for naturalization aliens who are members of organizations so advocating. Act of Feb. 5, 1917, § 19, 39 Stat. 889, 8 U.S.C. § 155; Act of Oct. 16, 1918, 40 Stat. 1012, 8 U.S.C. § 137; Act of Oct. 14, 1940, § 305, 54 Stat. 1141, 8 U.S.C. § 705. The Hatch Act prohibits employment by any Government agency of members of organizations advocating overthrow of "our constitutional form of government." Act of Aug. 2, 1939, § 9A, 53 Stat. 1148, 5 U.S.C. (Supp. III) § 118j. The Voorhis Act of Oct. 17, 1940, was passed to require registration of organizations subject to foreign control which engage in political activity. 54 Stat. 1201, 18 U.S.C. § 2386. The Taft-Hartley Act contains a section designed to exclude Communists from positions of leadership in labor organizations. Act of June 23, 1947, § 9 (h), 61 Stat. 146, 29 U.S.C. (Supp. III) § 159 (h). And, most recently, the McCarran Act requires registration of "Communist-action" and "Communist-front" organizations. Act of Sept. 23, 1950, § 7, 64 Stat. 987, 993.*

the judiciary dissociated from direct participation in the legislative process. In asserting the power to pass on the constitutionality of legislation, Marshall and his Court expressed the purposes of the Founders. See Charles A. Beard, The Supreme Court and the Constitution. But the extent to which the exercise of this power would interpenetrate matters of policy could hardly have been foreseen by the most prescient. The distinction which the Founders drew between the Court's duty to pass on the power of Congress and its complementary duty not to enter directly the domain of policy is fundamental. But in its actual operation it is rather subtle, certainly to the common understanding. Our duty to abstain from confounding policy with constitutionality demands perceptive humility as well as self-restraint in not declaring unconstitutional what in a judge's private judgment is deemed unwise and even dangerous.

Even when moving strictly within the limits of constitutional adjudication, judges are concerned with issues that may be said to involve vital finalities. The too easy transition from disapproval of what is undesirable to condemnation as unconstitutional, has led some of the wisest judges to question the wisdom of our scheme in lodging such authority in courts. But it is relevant to remind that in sustaining the power of Congress in a case like this nothing irrevocable is done. The democratic process at all events is not impaired or restricted. Power and responsibility remain with the people and immediately with their representatives. All the Courts says is that Congress was not forbidden by the Constitution to pass this enactment and that a prosecution under it may be brought against a conspiracy such as the one before us.

IV.

The wisdom of the assumptions underlying the legislation and prosecution is another matter. In finding that Congress has acted within its power, a judge does not remotely imply that he favors the implications that lie beneath the legal issues. Considerations there enter which go beyond the criteria that are binding upon judges within the narrow confines of their legitimate authority. The legislation we are here considering is but a truncated aspect of a deeper issue. For me it has been most illuminatingly expressed by one in whom responsibility and experience have fructified native insight, the Director-General of the British Broadcasting Corporation:

> "We have to face up to the fact that there are powerful forces in the world today misusing the privileges of liberty in order to destroy her. The question must be asked, however, whether suppression of information or opinion is the true defense. We may have come a long way from Mill's famous dictum that:
>
> > " 'If all mankind minus one were of one opinion, and only one person were of the contrary opinion, mankind would be no more justified in silencing that one person, than he, if he had the power, would be justified in silencing mankind,'
>
> but Mill's reminders from history as to what has happened when suppression was most virulently exercised ought to warn us that no debate is ever permanently won by shutting one's ears or by even the most Draconian policy of silencing opponents. The *debate* must be won. And it must be won with full information. Where there are lies, they must be shown for what they are. Where there are errors, they must be refuted. It would be a major defeat if the enemies of democracy forced us to abandon our faith in the power of informed discussion and so brought us down to their own level. Mankind is so constituted, moreover, that if, where expression and discussion are concerned, the enemies of liberty are met with a denial of liberty, many men of goodwill will come to suspect there is something in the proscribed doctrine after all. Erroneous doctrines thrive on being expunged. They die if exposed." Sir William Haley, What Standards for Broadcasting? Measure, Vol. I, No. 3, Summer 1950, pp. 211–212.

In the context of this deeper struggle, another voice has indicated the limitations of what we decide today. No one is better equipped than George F. Kennan to speak on the meaning of the menace of Communism and the spirit in which we should meet it.

> "If our handling of the problem of Communist influence in our midst is not carefully moderated—if we permit it, that is, to become an emotional preoccupation and to blind us to the more important positive tasks before us—we can do a damage to our national purpose beyond comparison greater than anything that threatens us today from the Communist side. The American Communist party is

today, by and large, an external danger. It represents a tiny minority in our country; it has no real contact with the feelings of the mass of our people; and its position as the agency of a hostile foreign power is clearly recognized by the overwhelming mass of our citizens.

"But the subjective emotional stresses and temptations to which we are exposed in our attempt to deal with this domestic problem are not an external danger: they represent a danger within ourselves—a danger that something may occur in our own minds and souls which will make us no longer like the persons by whose efforts this republic was founded and held together, but rather like the representatives of that very power we are trying to combat: intolerant, secretive, suspicious, cruel, and terrified of internal dissension because we have lost our own belief in ourselves and in the power of our ideals. The worst thing that our Communists could do to us, and the thing we have most to fear from their activities, is that we should become like them.

"That our country is beset with external dangers I readily concede. But these dangers, at their worst, are ones of physical destruction, of the disruption of our world security, of expense and inconvenience and sacrifice. These are serious, and sometimes terrible things, but they are all things that we can take and still remain Americans.

"The internal danger is of a different order. America is not just territory and people. There is lots of territory elsewhere, and there are lots of people; but it does not add up to America. America is something in our minds and our habits of outlook which causes us to believe in certain things and to behave in certain ways, and by which, in its totality, we hold ourselves distinguished from others. If that once goes there will be no America to defend. And that can go too easily if we yield to the primitive human instinct to escape from our frustrations into the realms of mass emotion and hatred and to find scapegoats for our difficulties in individual fellow-citizens who are, or have at one time been, disoriented or confused." George F. Kennan, Where Do You Stand on Communism? New York Times Magazine, May 27, 1951, pp. 7, 53, 55.

Civil liberties draw at best only limited strength from legal guaranties. Preoccupation by our people with the constitutionality, instead of with the wisdom, of legislation or of executive action is preoccupation with a false value. Even those who would most freely use the judicial brake on the democratic process by invalidating legislation that goes deeply against their grain, acknowledge, at least by paying lip service, that constitutionality does not exact a sense of proportion or the sanity of humor or an absence of fear. Focusing attention on constitutionality tends to make constitutionality synonymous with wisdom. When legislation touches freedom of thought and freedom of speech, such a tendency is a formidable enemy of the free spirit. Much that should be rejected as illiberal, because repressive and envenoming, may well be not unconstitutional. The ultimate reliance for the deepest needs of civilization must be found outside their vindication in courts of law; apart from all else, judges, howsoever they may conscientiously seek to discipline themselves against it, unconsciously are too apt to be moved by the deep undercurrents of public feeling. A persistent, positive translation of the liberating faith into the feelings and thoughts and actions of men and women is the real protection against attempts to strait-jacket the human mind. Such temptations will have their way, if fear and hatred are not exorcized. The mark of a truly civilized man is confidence in the strength and security derived from the inquiring mind. We may be grateful for such honest comforts as it supports, but we must be unafraid of its incertitudes. Without open minds there can be no open society. And if society be not open the spirit of man is mutilated and becomes enslaved.

APPENDIX TO OPINION OF MR. JUSTICE FRANKFURTER.

Opinions responsible for the view that speech could not constitutionally be restricted unless there would result from it an imminent—*i.e.,* close at hand—substantive evil.

1. *Thornhill* v. *Alabama,* 310 U.S. 88, 104–105 (State statute prohibiting picketing held invalid): ". . . Every expression of opinion on matters that are important has the potentiality of inducing action in the interests of one rather than another group in society. But the group in power at any moment may not impose penal sanctions on peaceful and truthful discussion of matters of public interest merely on a showing that others may thereby be persuaded to take

action inconsistent with its interests. Abridgment of the liberty of such discussion can be justified only where the clear danger of substantive evils arises under circumstances affording no opportunity to test the merits of ideas by competition for acceptance in the market of public opinion. . . .

". . . [N]o clear and present danger of destruction of life or property, or invasion of the right of privacy, or breach of the peace can be thought to be inherent in the activities of every person who approaches the premises of an employer and publicizes the facts of a labor dispute involving the latter."

2. *Bridges* v. *California,* 314 U.S. 252, 262–263 (convictions for contempt of court reversed): ". . . [T]he 'clear and present danger' language of the *Schenck* case has afforded practical guidance in a great variety of cases in which the scope of constitutional protections of freedom of expression was in issue. It has been utilized by either a majority or minority of this Court in passing upon the constitutionality of convictions under espionage acts, *Schenck* v. *United States, supra* [249 U.S. 47]; *Abrams* v. *United States,* 250 U.S. 616; under a criminal syndicalism act, *Whitney* v. *California, supra* [274 U.S. 357]; under an 'anti-insurrection' act, *Herndon* v. *Lowry, supra* [301 U.S. 242]; and for breach of the peace at common law, *Cantwell* v. *Connecticut, supra* [310 U.S. 296]. And very recently we have also suggested that 'clear and present danger' is an appropriate guide in determining the constitutionality of restrictions upon expression where the substantive evil sought to be prevented by the restriction is 'destruction of life or property, or invasion of the right of privacy.' *Thornhill* v. *Alabama,* 310 U.S. 88, 105.

. . .

"What finally emerges from the 'clear and present danger' cases is a working principle that the substantive evil must be extremely serious and the degree of imminence extremely high before utterances can be punished. Those cases do not purport to mark the furthermost constitutional boundaries of protected expression, nor do we here. They do no more than recognize a minimum compulsion of the Bill of Rights. For the First Amendment does not speak equivocally. It prohibits any law 'abridging the freedom of speech, or of the press.' It must be taken as a command of the broadest scope that explicit language, read in the context of a liberty-loving society, will allow."

3. *West Virginia Board of Education* v. *Barnette,* 319 U.S. 624, 639 (flag-salute requirement for school children held invalid): "In weighing arguments of the parties it is important to distinguish between the due process clause of the Fourteenth Amendment as an instrument for transmitting the principles of the First Amendment and those cases in which it is applied for its own sake. The test of legislation which collides with the Fourteenth Amendment, because it also collides with the principles of the First, is much more definite than the test when only the Fourteenth is involved. Much of the vagueness of the due process clause disappears when the specific prohibitions of the First become its standard. The right of a State to regulate, for example, a public utility may well include, so far as the due process test is concerned, power to impose all of the restrictions which a legislature may have a 'rational basis' for adopting. But freedoms of speech and of press, of assembly, and of worship may not be infringed on such slender grounds. They are susceptible of restriction only to prevent grave and immediate danger to interests which the State may lawfully protect. It is important to note that while it is the Fourteenth Amendment which bears directly upon the State it is the more specific limiting principles of the First Amendment that finally govern this case."

4. *Thomas* v. *Collins,* 323 U.S. 516, 529–530 (State statute requiring registration of labor organizers held invalid as applied): "The case confronts us again with the duty our system places on this Court to say where the individual's freedom ends and the State's power begins. Choice on that border, now as always delicate, is perhaps more so where the usual presumption supporting legislation is balanced by the preferred place given in our scheme to the great, the indispensable democratic freedoms secured by the First Amendment. Cf. *Schneider* v. *State,* 308 U.S. 147; *Cantwell* v. *Connecticut,* 310 U.S. 296; *Prince* v. *Massachusetts,* 321 U.S. 158. That priority gives these liberties a sanctity and a sanction not permitting dubious intrusions. And it is the character of the right, not of the limitation, which determines what standard governs the choice. Compare *United States* v. *Carolene Products Co.,* 304 U.S. 144, 152–153.

"For these reasons any attempt to restrict those liberties must be justified by clear public interest, threatened not doubtfully or remotely, but by clear and present danger.

The rational connection between the remedy provided and the evil to be curbed, which in other contexts might support legislation against attack on due process grounds, will not suffice. These rights rest on firmer foundation. Accordingly, whatever occasion would restrain orderly discussion and persuasion, at appropriate time and place, must have clear support in public danger, actual or impending. Only the gravest abuses, endangering paramount interests, give occasion for permissible limitation."

5. *Craig* v. *Harney,* 331 U.S. 367, 376 (conviction for contempt of court reversed): "The fires which [the language] kindles must constitute an imminent, not merely a likely, threat to the administration of justice. The danger must not be remote or even probable; it must immediately imperil."

6. *Giboney* v. *Empire Storage Co.,* 336 U.S. 490, 503 (injunction against picketing upheld): ". . . There was clear danger, imminent and immediate, that unless restrained, appellants would succeed in making [the State's policy against restraints of trade] a dead letter insofar as purchases by nonunion men were concerned. . . ."

7. *Terminiello* v. *Chicago,* 337 U.S. 1, 4–5 (conviction for disorderly conduct reversed): "Speech is often provocative and challenging. It may strike at prejudices and preconceptions and have profound unsettling effects as it presses for acceptance of an idea. That is why freedom of speech, though not absolute, *Chaplinsky* v. *New Hampshire, supra,* [315 U.S. 568] 571–572, is nevertheless protected against censorship or punishment, unless shown likely to produce a clear and present danger of a serious substantive evil that rises far above public inconvenience, annoyance, or unrest. See *Bridges* v. *California,* 314 U.S. 252, 262; *Craig* v. *Harney,* 331 U.S. 367, 373. There is no room under our Constitution for a more restrictive view. For the alternative would lead to standardization of ideas either by legislatures, courts, or dominant political or community groups."

8. *American Communications Assn.* v. *Douds,* 339 U.S. 382, 396, 412 ("Non-Communist affidavit" provision of Taft-Hartley Act upheld): "Speech may be fought with speech. Falsehoods and fallacies must be exposed, not suppressed, unless there is not sufficient time to avert the evil consequences of noxious doctrine by argument and education. That is the command of the First Amendment." And again, "[The First] Amendment requires that one be permitted to believe what he will. It requires that one be permitted to advocate what he will unless there is a clear and present danger that a substantial public evil will result therefrom."

MR. JUSTICE JACKSON, concurring.

This prosecution is the latest of never-ending, because never successful, quests for some legal formula that will secure an existing order against revolutionary radicalism. It requires us to reappraise, in the light of our own times and conditions, constitutional doctrines devised under other circumstances to strike a balance between authority and liberty.

Activity here charged to be criminal is conspiracy—that defendants conspired to teach and advocate, and to organize the Communist Party to teach and advocate, overthrow and destruction of the Government by force and violence. There is no charge of actual violence or attempt at overthrow.[1]

The principal reliance of the defense in this Court is that the conviction cannot stand under the Constitution because the conspiracy of these defendants presents no "clear and present danger" of imminent or foreseeable overthrow.

[1] *The Government's own summary of its charge is: "The indictment charged that from April 1, 1945, to the date of the indictment petitioners unlawfully, wilfully, and knowingly conspired with each other and with other persons unknown to the grand jury (1) to organize as the Communist Party of the United States of America a society, group and assembly of persons who teach and advocate the overthrow and destruction of the Government of the United States by force and violence, and (2) knowingly and wilfully to advocate and teach the duty and necessity of overthrowing and destroying the Government of the United States by force and violence. The indictment alleged that Section 2 of the Smith Act proscribes these acts and that the conspiracy to take such action is a violation of Section 3 of the act (18 U.S.C. 10, 11 (1946 ed.))."*

SWEEZY v. NEW HAMPSHIRE, 354 U.S. 234 (1957)

Paul Sweezy, the noted economist, was called to appear before the New Hampshire Attorney General sitting as a one-man legislative committee to answer questions about possible subversive activities. He refused to respond to inquiries made about his connection with the Progressive Party or his knowledge of the political affiliations of certain acquaintances. After his conviction for contempt, the Supreme Court reversed. Frankfurter concurred in a short opinion which focused on the need for the widest scope to be given to academic freedom.

MR. JUSTICE FRANKFURTER, whom MR. JUSTICE HARLAN joins, concurring in the result.

For me this is a very different case from *Watkins* v. *United States, ante,* p. 178. This case comes to us solely through the limited power to review the action of the States conferred upon the Court by the Fourteenth Amendment. Petitioner claims that respect for liberties guaranteed by the Due Process Clause of that Amendment precludes the State of New Hampshire from compelling him to answer certain questions put to him by the investigating arm of its legislature. Ours is the narrowly circumscribed but exceedingly difficult task of making the final judicial accommodation between the competing weighty claims that underlie all such questions of due process.

In assessing the claim of the State of New Hampshire to the information denied it by petitioner, we cannot concern ourselves with the fact that New Hampshire chose to make its Attorney General in effect a standing committee of its legislature for the purpose of investigating the extent of "subversive" activities within its bounds. The case must be judged as though the whole body of the legislature had demanded the information of petitioner. It would make the deepest inroads upon our federal system for this Court now to hold that it can determine the appropriate distribution of powers and their delegation within the forty-eight States. As the earlier Mr. Justice Harlan said for a unanimous Court in *Dreyer* v. *Illinois,* 187 U.S. 71, 84:

> "Whether the legislative, executive and judicial powers of a State shall be kept altogether distinct and separate, or whether persons or collections of persons belonging to one department may, in respect to some matters, exert powers which, strictly speaking, pertain to another department of government, is for the determination of the State. And its determination one way or the other cannot be an element in the inquiry whether the due process of law prescribed by the Fourteenth Amendment has been respected by the State or its representatives when dealing with matters involving life or liberty."

Whether the state legislature should operate largely by committees, as does the Congress, or whether committees should be the exception, as is true of the House of Commons, whether the legislature should have two chambers or only one, as in Nebraska, whether the State's chief executive should have the pardoning power, whether the State's judicial branch must provide trial by jury, are all matters beyond the reviewing powers of this Court. Similarly, whether the Attorney General of New Hampshire acted within the scope of the authority given him by the state legislature is a matter for the decision of the courts of that State, as it is for the federal courts to determine whether an agency to which Congress has delegated power has acted within the confines of its mandate. See *United States* v. *Rumely,* 345 U.S. 41. Sanction of the delegation rests with the New Hampshire Supreme Court, and its validation in *Nelson* v. *Wyman,* 99 N.H. 33, 105 A. 2d 756, is binding here.

Pursuant to an investigation of subversive activities authorized by a joint resolution of both houses of the New Hampshire Legislature, the State Attorney General subpoenaed petitioner before him on January 8, 1954, for extensive questioning. Among the matters about which petitioner was questioned were: details of his career and personal life, whether he was then or ever had been a member of the Communist Party, whether he had ever attended its meetings, whether he had ever attended meetings that he knew were also attended by Party members, whether he knew any Communists in or out of the State, whether he knew named persons with alleged connections with organizations either on the United States Attorney General's list or cited by the Un-American Activities Committee of the United States House of Representatives or had ever attended meetings with them, whether he had ever taught or supported the overthrow of the State by force or violence or had ever known or assisted any persons or groups that had done so, whether he had ever been connected with organizations on the Attorney General's list, whether he had supported or written in behalf of a variety of allegedly subversive, named causes, conferences, periodicals, petitions, and attempts to raise funds for the legal defense of certain persons, whether he knew about the Progressive Party, what positions he had held in it, whether he had been a candidate for Presidential Elector for that Party, whether certain persons were in that Party, whether Communists had influenced or been members of the Progressive Party, whether he had sponsored activities in behalf of the candidacy of Henry A. Wallace, whether he advocated replacing the capitalist system with another economic system, whether his conception of socialism involved force and violence, whether by his writings and actions he had ever attempted to advance the Soviet Union's "propaganda line," whether he had ever attended meetings of the Liberal Club at the University of New Hampshire, whether the magazine of which he was co-editor was "a Communist-line publication," and whether he knew named persons.

Petitioner answered most of these questions, making it very plain that he had never been a Communist, never taught violent overthrow of the Government, never knowingly associated with Communists in the State, but was a socialist believer in peaceful change who had at one time belonged to certain organizations on the list of the United States Attorney General (which did not include the Progressive Party) or cited by the House Un-American Activities Committee. He declined to answer as irrelevant or violative of free speech guarantees certain questions about the Progressive Party and whether he knew particular persons. He stated repeatedly, however, that he had no knowledge of Communists or of Communist influence in the Progressive Party, and he testified that he had been a candidate for that Party, signing the required loyalty oath, and that he did not know whether an alleged Communist leader was active in the Progressive Party.

Despite the exhaustive scope of this inquiry, the Attorney General again subpoenaed petitioner to testify on June 3, 1954, and the interrogation was similarly sweeping. Petitioner again answered virtually all questions, including those concerning the relationship of named persons to the Communist Party or other causes deemed subversive under state laws, alleged Communist influence on all organizations with which he had been connected including the Progressive Party, and his own participation in organizations other than the Progressive Party and its antecedent, the Progressive Citizens of America. He refused, however, to answer certain questions regarding (1) a lecture given by him at the University of New Hampshire, (2) activities of himself and others in the Progressive political organizations, and (3) "opinions and beliefs," invoking the constitutional guarantees of free speech.

The Attorney General then petitioned the Superior Court to order petitioner to answer questions in these categories. The court ruled that petitioner had to answer those questions pertaining to the lectures and to the Progressive Party and its predecessor but not those otherwise pertaining to "opinions and beliefs." Upon petitioner's refusal to answer the questions sanctioned by the court, he was found in contempt of court and ordered committed to the county jail until purged of contempt.

The Supreme Court of New Hampshire affirmed the order of the Superior Court. It held that the questions at issue were relevant and that no constitutional provision permitted petitioner to frustrate the State's demands. 100 N.H. 103, 121 A 2d 783.

The questions that petitioner refused to answer regarding the university lecture, the third given by him in three years at the invitation of the faculty for humanities, were:

> "What was the subject of your lecture?"
>
> "Didn't you tell the class at the University of New Hampshire on Monday, March 22, 1954, that Socialism was inevitable in this country?"

"Did you advocate Marxism at that time?"

"Did you express the opinion, or did you make the statement at that time that Socialism was inevitable in America?"

"Did you in this last lecture on March 22 or in any of the former lectures espouse the theory of dialectical materialism?"

"I have in the file here a statement from a person who attended your class, and I will read it in part because I don't want you to think I am just fishing. 'His talk this time was on the inevitability of the Socialist program. It was a glossed-over interpretation of the materialist dialectic.' Now, again I ask you the original question."

In response to the first question of this series, petitioner had said at the hearing:

"I would like to say one thing in this connection, Mr. Wyman. I stated under oath at my last appearance that, and I now repeat it, that I do not advocate or in any way further the aim of overthrowing constitutional government by force and violence. I did not so advocate in the lecture I gave at the University of New Hampshire. In fact I have never at any time so advocated in a lecture anywhere. Aside from that I have nothing I want to say about the lecture in question."

The New Hampshire Supreme Court, although recognizing that such inquiries "undoubtedly interfered with the defendant's free exercise" of his constitutionally guaranteed right to lecture, justified the interference on the ground that it would occur "in the limited area in which the legislative committee may reasonably believe that the overthrow of existing government by force and violence is being or has been taught, advocated or planned, an area in which the interest of the State justifies this intrusion upon civil liberties." 100 N.H., at 113, 114, 121 A. 2d, at 792. According to the court, the facts that made reasonable the Committee's belief that petitioner had taught violent overthrow in his lecture were that he was a Socialist with a record of affiliation with groups cited by the Attorney General of the United States or the House Un-American Activities Committee and that he was co-editor of an article stating that, although the authors hated violence, it was less to be deplored when used by the Soviet Union than by capitalist countries.

When weighed against the grave harm resulting from governmental intrusion into the intellectual life of a university, such justification for compelling a witness to discuss the contents of his lecture appears grossly inadequate. Particularly is this so where the witness has sworn that neither in the lecture nor at any other time did he ever advocate overthrowing the Government by force and violence.

Progress in the natural sciences is not remotely confined to findings made in the laboratory. Insights into the mysteries of nature are born of hypothesis and speculation. The more so is this true in the pursuit of understanding in the groping endeavors of what are called the social sciences, the concern of which is man and society. The problems that are the respective preoccupations of anthropology, economics, law, psychology, sociology and related areas of scholarship are merely departmentalized dealing, by way of manageable division of analysis, with interpenetrating aspects of holistic perplexities. For society's good—if understanding be an essential need of society—inquiries into these problems, speculations about them, stimulation in others of reflection upon them, must be left as unfettered as possible. Political power must abstain from intrusion into this activity of freedom, pursued in the interest of wise government and the people's well-being, except for reasons that are exigent and obviously compelling.

These pages need not be burdened with proof, based on the testimony of a cloud of impressive witnesses, of the dependence of a free society on free universities. This means the exclusion of governmental intervention in the intellectual life of a university. It matters little whether such intervention occurs avowedly or through action that inevitably tends to check the ardor and fearlessness of scholars, qualities at once so fragile and so indispensable for fruitful academic labor. One need only refer to the address of T. H. Huxley at the opening of Johns Hopkins University, the Annual Reports of President A. Lawrence Lowell of Harvard, the Reports of the University Grants Committee in Great Britain, as illustrative items in a vast body of literature. Suffice it to quote the latest expression on this subject. It is also perhaps the most poignant because its plea on behalf of continuing the free spirit of the open universities of South Africa has gone unheeded.

"In a university knowledge is its own end, not merely a means to an end. A university ceases to be true to its own nature if it becomes the tool of Church or State or any sectional interest. A university is characterized by the spirit of free inquiry, its ideal being the ideal of Socrates—'to follow the argument where it leads.' This implies the right to examine, question, modify or reject traditional ideas and beliefs. Dogma and hypothesis are incompatible, and the concept of an immutable doctrine is repugnant to the spirit of a university. The concern of its scholars is not merely to add and revise facts in relation to an accepted framework, but to be ever examining and modifying the framework itself.

. . .

"Freedom to reason and freedom for disputation on the basis of observation and experiment are the necessary conditions for the advancement of scientific knowledge. A sense of freedom is also necessary for creative work in the arts which, equally with scientific research, is the concern of the university.

. . .

". . . It is the business of a university to provide that atmosphere which is most conducive to speculation, experiment and creation. It is an atmosphere in which there prevail 'the four essential freedoms' of a university—to determine for itself on academic grounds who may teach, what may be taught, how it shall be taught, and who may be admitted to study." The Open Universities in South Africa 10–12. (A statement of a conference of senior scholars from the University of Cape Town and the University of the Witwatersrand, including A. v. d. S. Centlivres and Richard Feetham, as Chancellors of the respective universities.[1])

I do not suggest that what New Hampshire has here sanctioned bears any resemblance to the policy against which this South African remonstrance was directed. I do say that in these matters of the spirit inroads on legitimacy must be resisted at their incipiency. This kind of evil grows by what it is allowed to feed on. The admonition of this Court in another context is applicable here. "It may be that it is the obnoxious thing in its mildest and least repulsive form; but illegitimate and unconstitutional practices get their first footing in that way, namely, by silent approaches and slight deviations from legal modes of procedure." *Boyd* v. *United States,* 116 U.S. 616, 635.

Petitioner stated, in response to questions at the hearing, that he did not know of any Communist interest in, connection with, influence over, activity in, or manipulation of the Progressive Party. He refused to answer, despite court order, the following questions on the ground that, by inquiring into the activities of a lawful political organization, they infringed upon the inviolability of the right to privacy in his political thoughts, actions and associations:

"Was she, Nancy Sweezy, your wife, active in the formation of the Progressive Citizens of America?"

"Was Nancy Sweezy then working with individuals who were then members of the Communist Party?"[2]

"Was Charles Beebe active in forming the Progressive Citizens of America?"

"Did he work with your present wife —Did Charles Beebe work with your present wife in 1947?"

"Did it [a meaning at the home of one Abraham Walenko] have anything to do with the Progressive Party?"

The Supreme Court of New Hampshire justified this intrusion upon his freedom on the same basis that it upheld questioning about the university lecture, namely, that the restriction was limited to situations where the Committee had reason to believe that violent overthrow of the Government was being advocated or planned. It ruled:

". . . That he [the Attorney General] did possess information which was sufficient to reasonably warrant inquiry concerning the Progressive Party is evident from his statement made during the hearings held before him that 'considerable sworn testi-

[1] *The Hon. A. v. d. S. Centlivres only recently retired as Chief Justice of South Africa, and the Hon. Richard Feetham is also an eminent, retired South African judge.*

[2] *Inclusion of this question among the unanswered questions appears to have been an oversight in view of the fact that petitioner attempted to answer it at the hearing by stating that he had never to his knowledge known members of the Communist Party in New Hampshire. In any event, petitioner's brief states that he is willing to repeat the answer to this question if the Attorney General so desires. This is consistent with his demonstrated willingness to answer all inquiries regarding the Communist Party, including its relation to the Progressive Party.*

mony has been given in this investigation to the effect that the Progressive Party in New Hampshire has been heavily infiltrated by members of the Communist Party and that the policies and purposes of the Progressive Party have been directly influenced by members of the Communist Party.' " 100 N.H., at 111, 121 A. 2d, at 790.

For a citizen to be made to forego even a part of so basic a liberty as his political autonomy, the subordinating interest of the State must be compelling. Inquiry pursued in safeguarding a State's security against threatened force and violence cannot be shut off by mere disclaimer, though of course a relevant claim may be made to the privilege against self-incrimination. (The New Hampshire Constitution guarantees this privilege.) But the inviolability of privacy belonging to a citizen's political loyalties has so overwhelming an importance to the well-being of our kind of society that it cannot be constitutionally encroached upon on the basis of so meagre a countervailing interest of the State as may be argumentatively found in the remote, shadowy threat to the security of New Hampshire allegedly presented in the origins and contributing elements of the Progressive Party and in petitioner's relations to these.

In the political realm, as in the academic, thought and action are presumptively immune from inquisition by political authority. It cannot require argument that inquiry would be barred to ascertain whether a citizen had voted for one or the other of the two major parties either in a state or national election. Until recently, no difference would have been entertained in regard to inquiries about a voter's affiliations with one of the various so-called third parties that have had their day, or longer, in our political history. This is so, even though adequate protection of secrecy by way of the Australian ballot did not come into use till 1888. The implications of the United States Constitution for national elections and "the concept of ordered liberty" implicit in the Due Process Clause of the Fourteenth Amendment as against the States, *Palko* v. *Connecticut,* 302 U.S. 319, 325, were not frozen as of 1789 or 1868, respectively. While the language of the Constitution does not change, the changing circumstances of a progressive society for which it was designed yield new and fuller import to its meaning. See *Hurtado* v. *California,* 110 U.S. 516, 528–529; *McCulloch* v. *Maryland,* 4 Wheat. 316. Whatever, on the basis of massive proof and in the light of history, of which this Court may well take judicial notice, be the justification for not regarding the Communist Party as a conventional political party, no such justification has been afforded in regard to the Progressive Party. A foundation in fact and reason would have to be established far weightier than the intimations that appear in the record to warrant such a view of the Progressive Party.[3] This precludes the questioning that petitioner resisted in regard to that Party.

To be sure, this is a conclusion based on a judicial judgment in balancing two contending principles—the right of a citizen to political privacy, as protected by the Fourteenth Amendment, and the right of the State to self-protection. And striking the balance implies the exercise of judgment. This is the inescapable judicial task in giving substantive content, legally enforced, to the Due Process Clause, and it is a task ultimately committed to this Court. It must not be an exercise of whim or will. It must be an overriding judgment founded on something much deeper and more justifiable than personal preference. As far as it lies within human limitations, it must be an impersonal judgment. It must rest on fundamental presuppositions rooted in history to which widespread acceptance may fairly be attributed. Such a judgment must be arrived at in a spirit of humility when it counters the judgment of the State's highest court. But, in the end, judgment cannot be escaped—the judgment of this Court. See concurring opinions in *Haley* v. *Ohio,* 332 U.S. 596, 601; *Louisiana ex rel. Francis* v. *Resweber,* 329 U.S. 459, 466, 470–471; *Malinski* v. *New York,* 324 U.S. 401, 412, 414–417.

And so I am compelled to conclude that the judgment of the New Hampshire court must be reversed.

[3] *The Progressive Party was on the ballot in forty-four States, including New Hampshire, in 1948, and in twenty-six States in 1952.*